2018
新疆生产建设兵团
统计年鉴

XINJIANG PRODUCTION & CONSTRUCTION CORPS
STATISTICAL YEARBOOK

U0921384

XINJIANG PRODUCTION & CONSTRUCTION CORPS

新疆生产建设兵团 2018 统计年鉴

STATISTICAL YEARBOOK

总第29期

No.29

© 中国统计出版社 2018
版权所有。未经许可，本书的任何部分不得以任何方式在世界任何地区以任何文字翻印、拷贝、仿制或转载。
© 2018 CHINA STATISTICS PRESS
All rights reserved. No part of the publication may be reproduced or transmitted in any form or by any means, electronic or mechanical, including photocopying, recording, or any information storage and retrieval system, without written permission from the publisher.

图书在版编目（CIP）数据

新疆生产建设兵团统计年鉴. 2018 ：汉英对照 / 新疆生产建设兵团统计局、国家统计局兵团调查总队编.
--北京 ：中国统计出版社, 2018.7
ISBN 978-7-5037-8533-7
Ⅰ. ①新… Ⅱ. ①新… Ⅲ. ①生产建设兵团
—统计资料—新疆—2018—年鉴—汉、英 Ⅳ. ①F324.1-66 ②F327.45-66
中国版本图书馆CIP数据核字(2018)第155063号

《新疆生产建设兵团统计年鉴2018》

作　　者　新疆生产建设兵团统计局 国家统计局兵团调查总队
责任编辑　钟　钰
责任校对　孔　晨
封面设计　康　燕
出版发行　中国统计出版社
地　　址　北京市丰台区西三环南路甲6号
邮　　编　100073
电　　话　邮购（010）63376909 书店（010）68783171
网　　址　http://www.zgtjcbs.com
印　　刷　新疆生产建设兵团印刷厂
经　　销　新华书店
开　　本　890mm×1240mm　1/16
字　　数　1000千字
印　　张　39.25　彩页1
版　　别　2018年7月第1版
版　　次　2018年7月第1次印刷
定　　价　360.00元　Price:360.00 (RMB)

本书附同版本CD-ROM一张，光盘内容以书面文字为准。
如有印装错误，本社发行部负责调换。

《新疆生产建设兵团统计年鉴2018》编辑委员会

名誉主任　彭家瑞

主　　任　李冀东

副 主 任　陈春雷　王新农　孙学光

委　　员　（以姓氏笔画为序）

王子彬　王文铎　邓志耕　王贵荣　王新农　王靖国　刘军国　刘亚康　孙学光　孙新民　孙新春　张东升　何　玮
李学辉　周新军　徐秀芝　秦　斌　黄　斌　雷　鸣　谢　强　黎兴平

《新疆生产建设兵团统计年鉴2018》编辑人员

主　　编　王新农　孙学光

副 主 编　张　鹏　傅茂淑　姜勤德

执行副主编　魏凤英

编　　辑　（以姓氏笔画为序）

于宏业　王希光　王　兵　邓金剑　邓　郭　王莉敏　王　瑶　王　磊　龙　华　冯　陆　龙海全　田晓辰　包桂芬
艾　雷　刘玉亮　闫海燕　吴己冬　陈　宁　杨永梅　张　建　李　威　杨荣方　张莉耘　陈雪梅　陈　喆　张富棠
杨鹏飞　孟颖颖　张　震　佟德福　郭建业　闻　亮　宫爱荣　秦子啸　热比古丽·马木提　倪全松　殷建涛　陶　涛
秦　浩　桂家新　郭　晶　高新康　曹　君　蒋　伟　景启利　董新杰　雷　蕾　魏　杰　蹇娅婷

编　　务　孔　晨

光盘开发　刘　俊　赵述军　孔　晨

英文翻译　王维基　孔　晨

英文校对　王维基　孔　晨

NAME LIST OF EDITORIAL BOARD

Honorary Director: Peng Jiarui

Director: Li Jidong

Vice- directors: Chen Chunlei　Wang Xinnong　Sun Xueguang

Members of Editorial Board: (Sequence is based on Chinese surname stroke)

Wang Zibin　Wang Wenduo　Deng Zhigeng　Wang Guirong　Wang Xinnong　Wang Jingguo
Liu Junguo　Liu Yanan　Sun Xueguang　Sun Xinmin　Sun Xinchun　Zhang Dongsheng
He Wei　Li Xuehui　Zho Xinjun　Xu Xiuzhi　Qin Bin　Huang Bin　Lei Ming
Xie Qiang　Li Xingping

NAME LIST OF EDITORIAL STAFF

Editor-in-chief: Wang Xinnong　Sun Xueguang

Deputy Editor-in-chief: Zhang Peng　Fu Maoshu　Jiang Qinde

Deputy Executive Editor-in-chief: Wei Fengying

Editors: (Sequence is based on Chinese surname stroke)

Yu Hongye　Wang Xiguang　Wang Bing　Deng Jinjian　Deng Guo　Wang Limin
Wang Yao　Wang Lei　Long Hua　Feng Lu　Long Haiquan　Tian Xiaochen
Bao Guifen　Ai Lei　Liu Yuliang　Yan Haiyan　Wu Jidong　Chen Ning　Yang Yongmei
Li Xuguang　Zhang Jian　Li Wei　Yang Rongfang　Zhang Liyun　Chen Xuemei
Chen Zhe　Zhang Futang　Yang Pengfei　Meng Yingying　Zhang zhen　Tong Defu
Guo Jianye Wei Liang　Gong Airong　Qin Zixiao　Rebiguli. Mamuti　Ni Quansong
Yin Jiantao　Tao Tao　Qin Hao　Gui Jiaxin　Guo Jing　Gao Xinkang　Cao Jun
Jiang Wei　Jing Qili　Dong Xinjie　Lei Lei　Wei Jie　Jian Yating

Editing Affair: Kong Chen

Developer of CD-ROM Software: Liu Jun　Li Lu　Kong Chen

English Translators: Wang Weiji　Kong Chen

English Proofreader: Wang Weiji　Kong Chen

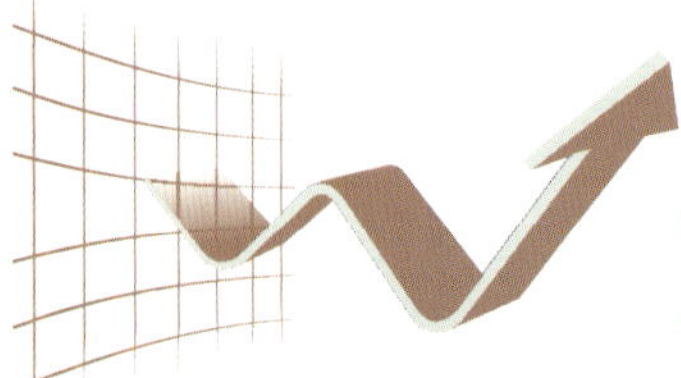

发展与成就 DEVELOPMENT AND ACHIEVEMENT

兵团生产总值及发展速度(亿元，%)
Total GDP and Growth Rate in XPCC (100 million yuan,%)

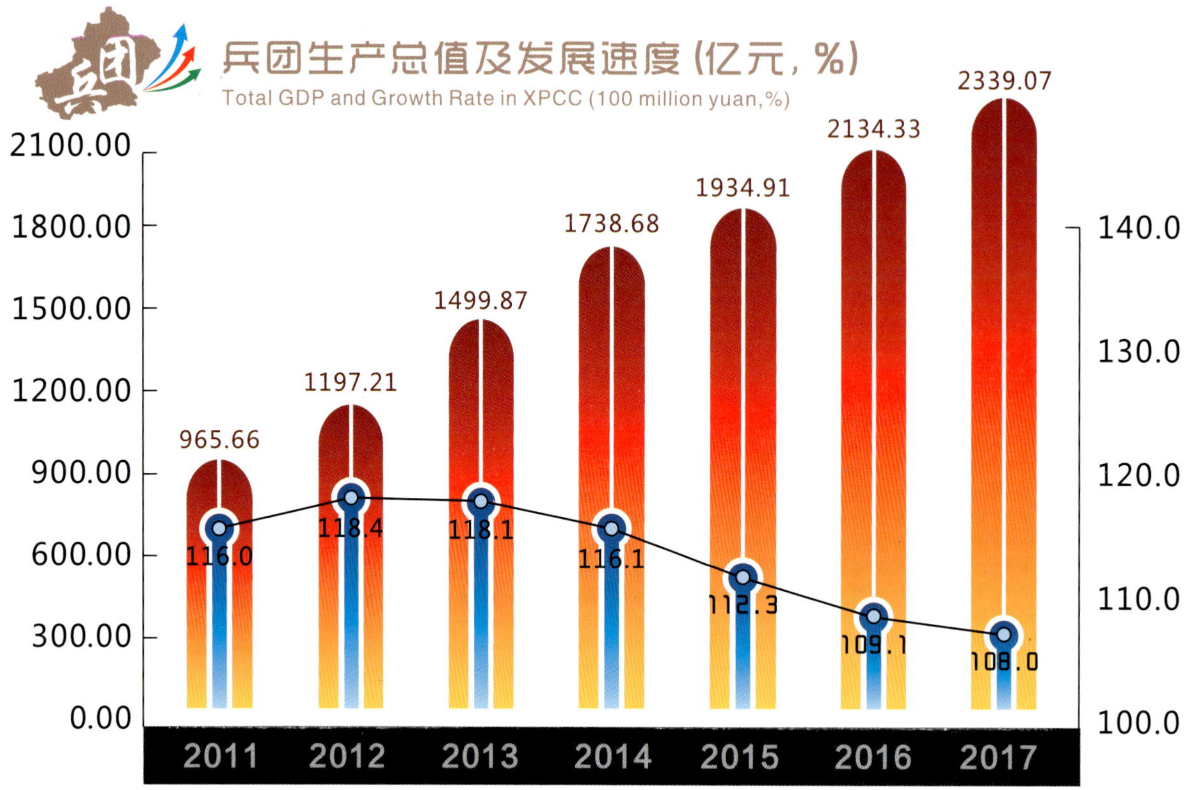

2017年兵团生产总值构成(%)
Composition of GDP in XPCC (%)

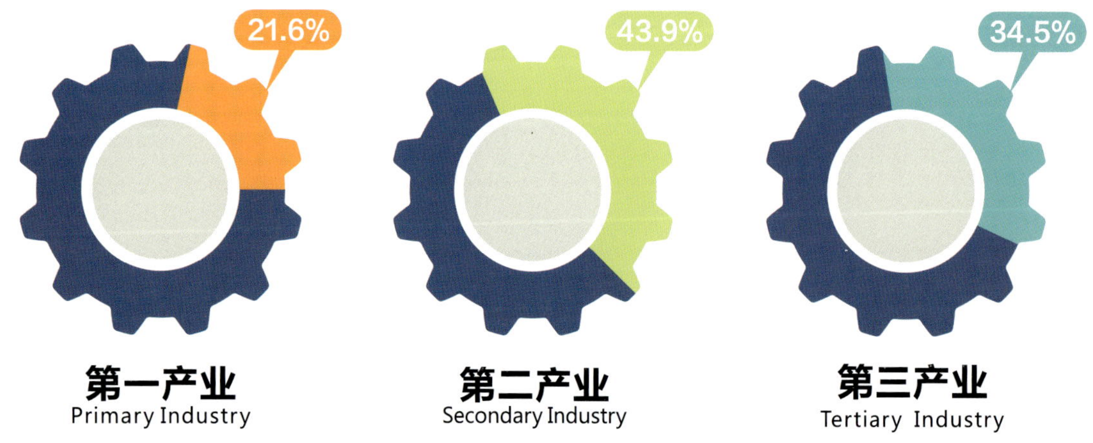

兵团人均生产总值（元）
Per Capita in XPCC (yuan)

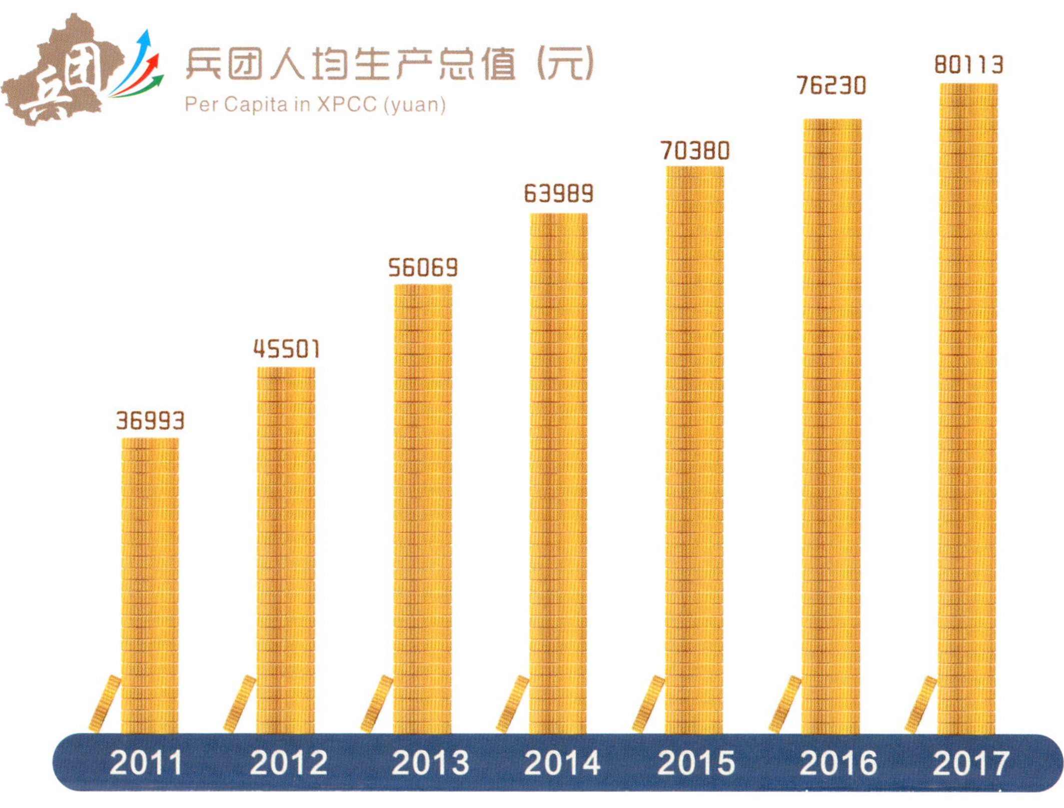

就业人员数（万人）
Number of Employed Persons (10000 persons)

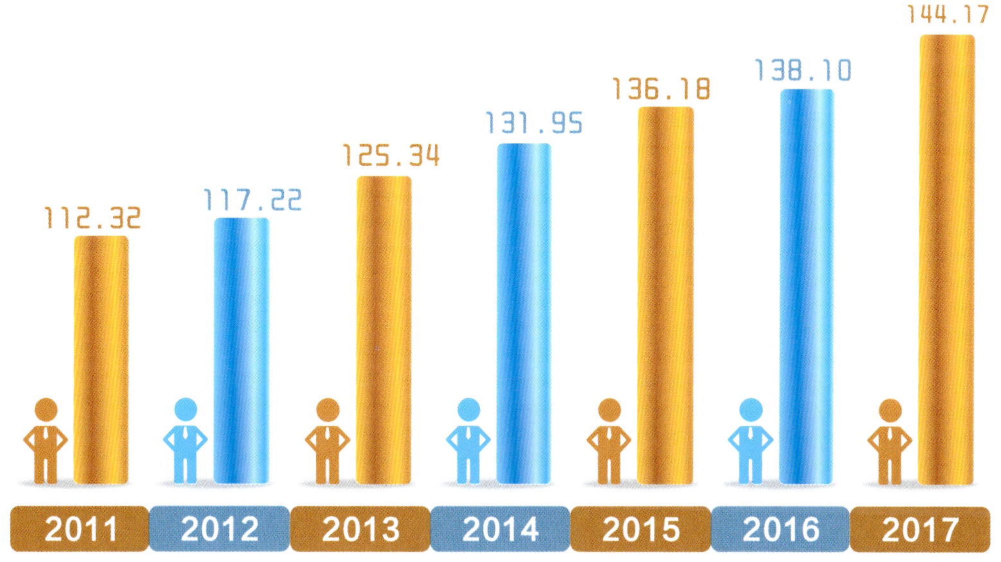

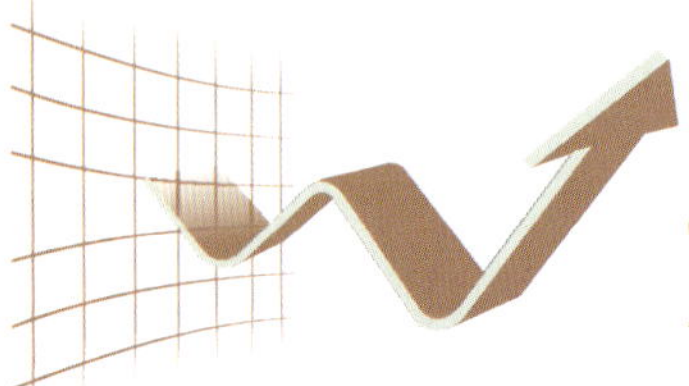

发展与成就 DEVELOPMENT AND ACHIEVEMENT

农林牧渔业总产值及发展速度（亿元，%）

Gross Output Value of Farming,Forest,Animal Husbandary and Fishery and Growth Rate (100 million yuan,%)

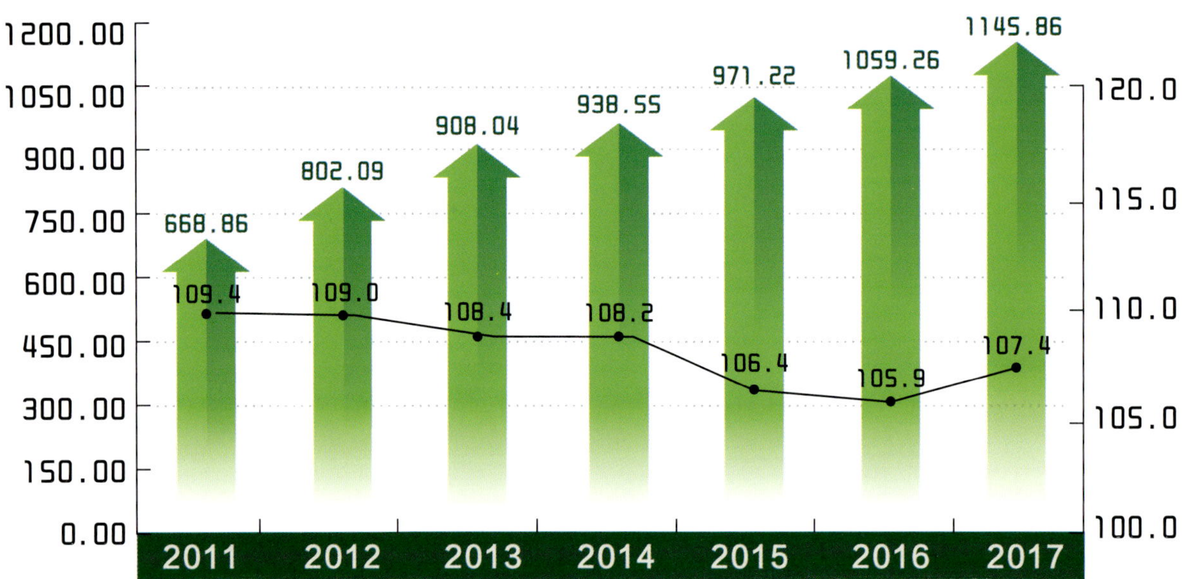

粮食、棉花产量（万吨）

Yield of Grain Corps and Cotton (10000 tons)

粮　食
Yield of Grain Corps

棉　花
Yield of Cotton

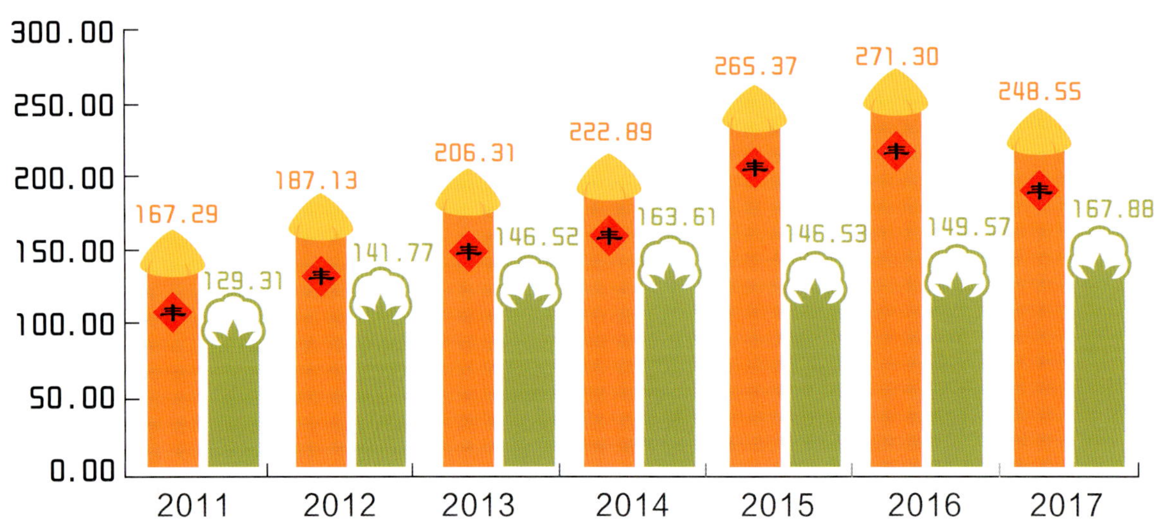

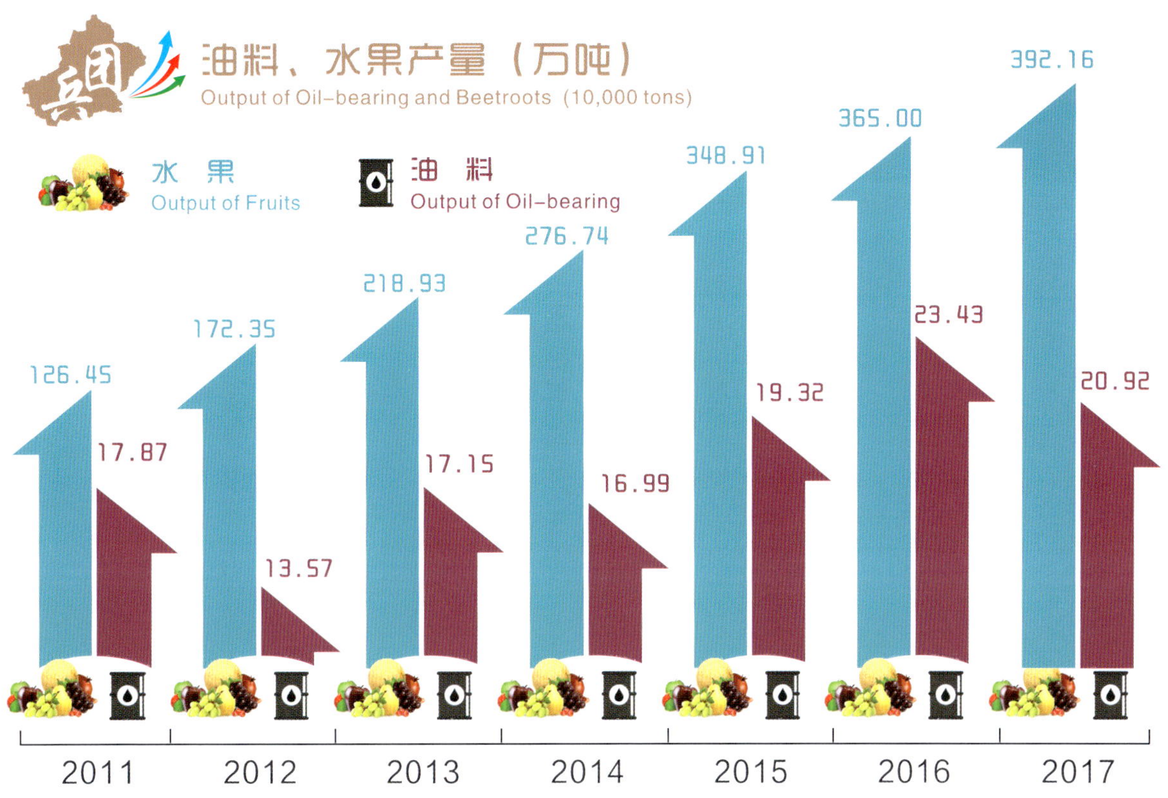
油料、水果产量（万吨）
Output of Oil-bearing and Beetroots (10,000 tons)
水 果
Output of Fruits
油 料
Output of Oil-bearing
126.45
17.87
172.35
13.57
218.93
17.15
276.74
16.99
348.91
19.32
365.00
23.43
392.16
20.92

2011
2012
2013
2014
2015
2016
2017

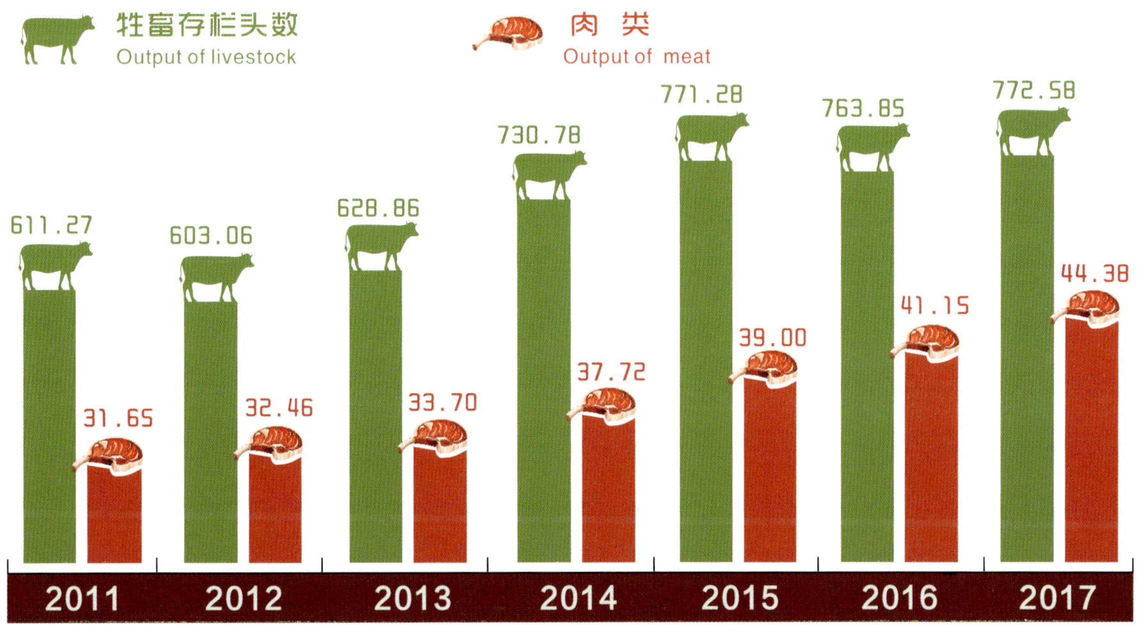
牲畜存栏头数（万头、万只），肉类产量（万吨）
Output of Livestock and Meat (10000 tons)
牲畜存栏头数
Output of livestock
肉 类
Output of meat
611.27
31.65
603.06
32.46
628.86
33.70
730.78
37.72
771.28
39.00
763.85
41.15
772.58
44.38
2011
2012
2013
2014
2015
2016
2017

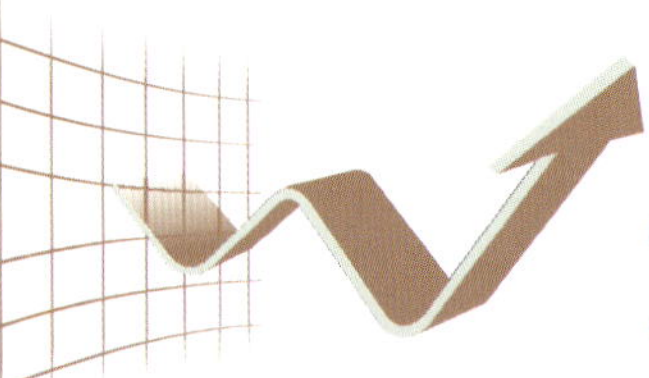

发展与成就 DEVELOPMENT AND ACHIEVEMENT

工业总产值及发展速度（亿元，%）
Gross Output Value of Industry and Growth Rate (100 million yuan,%)

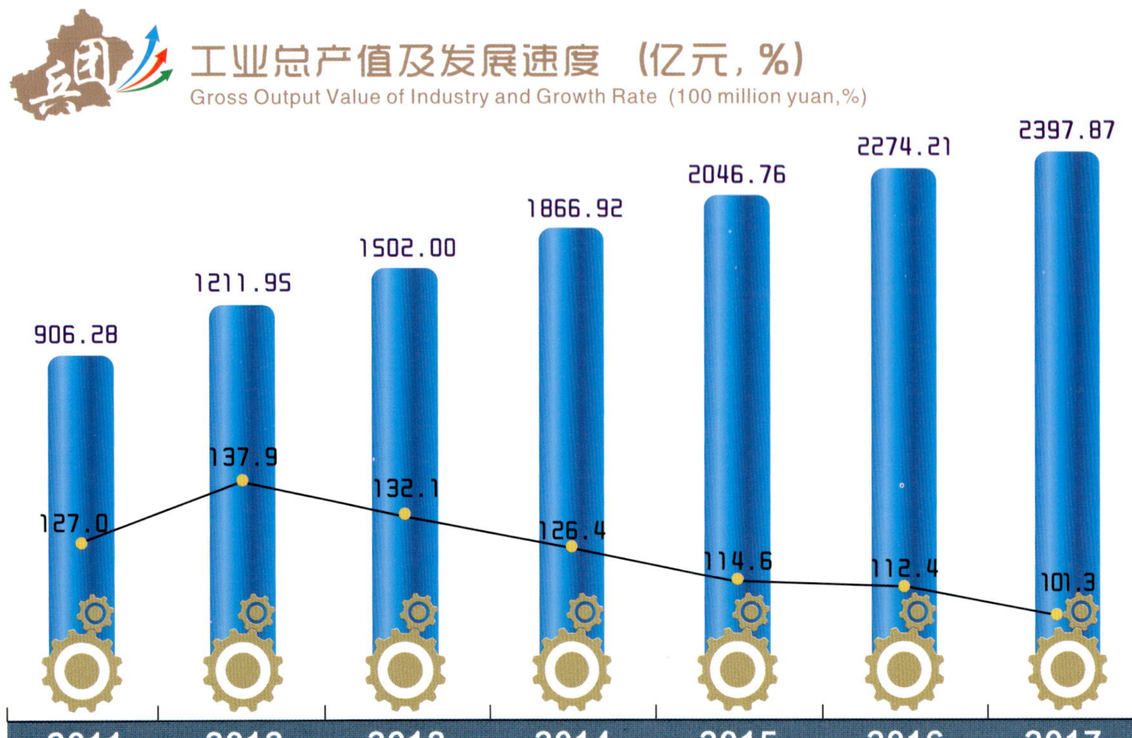

工业总产值构成（%）
Composition of Gross Output Value of Industry (%)

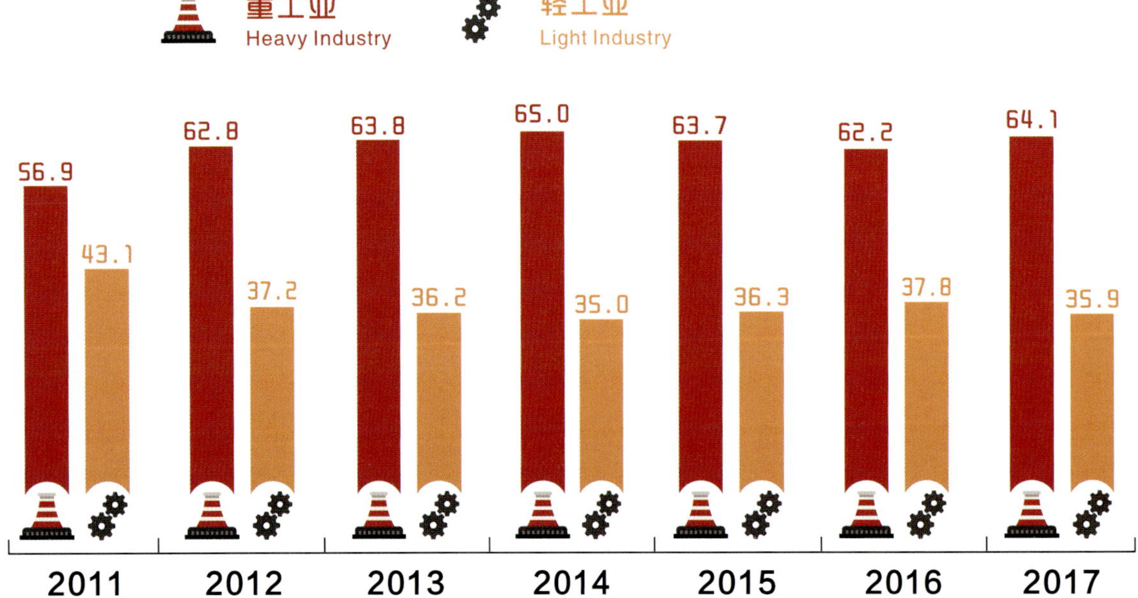

主要工业产品产量
Output of Main Industrial Products

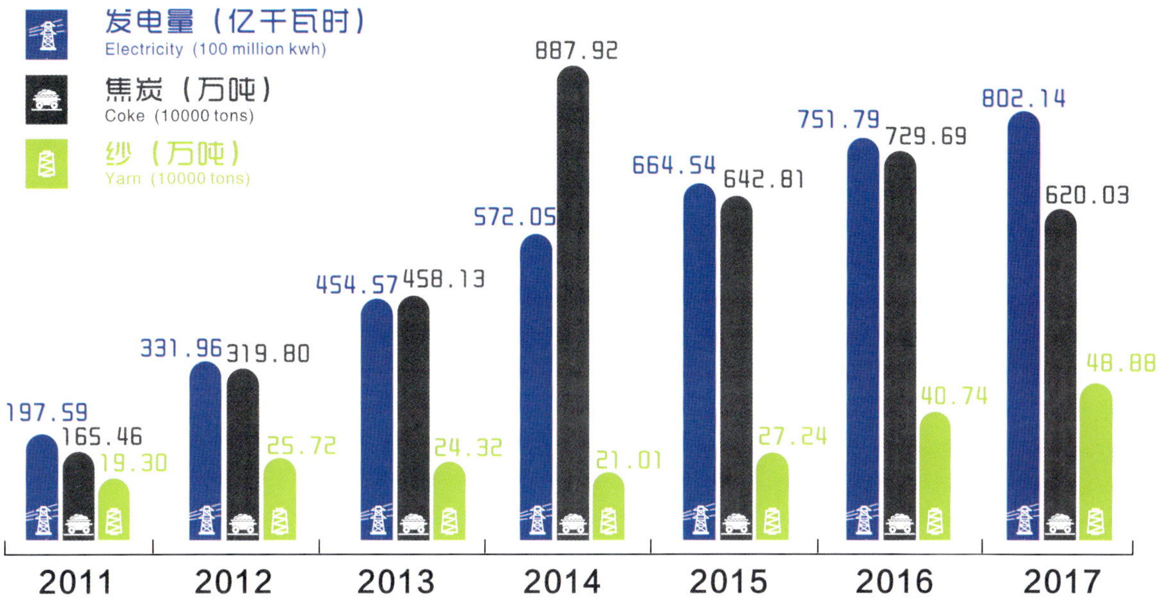
发电量（亿千瓦时）
Electricity (100 million kwh)
焦炭（万吨）
Coke (10000 tons)
纱（万吨）
Yarn (10000 tons)
197.59
165.46
19.30
331.96
319.80
25.72
454.57
458.13
24.32
572.05
887.92
21.01
664.54
642.81
27.24
751.79
729.69
40.74
802.14
620.03
48.88
2011
2012
2013
2014
2015
2016
2017

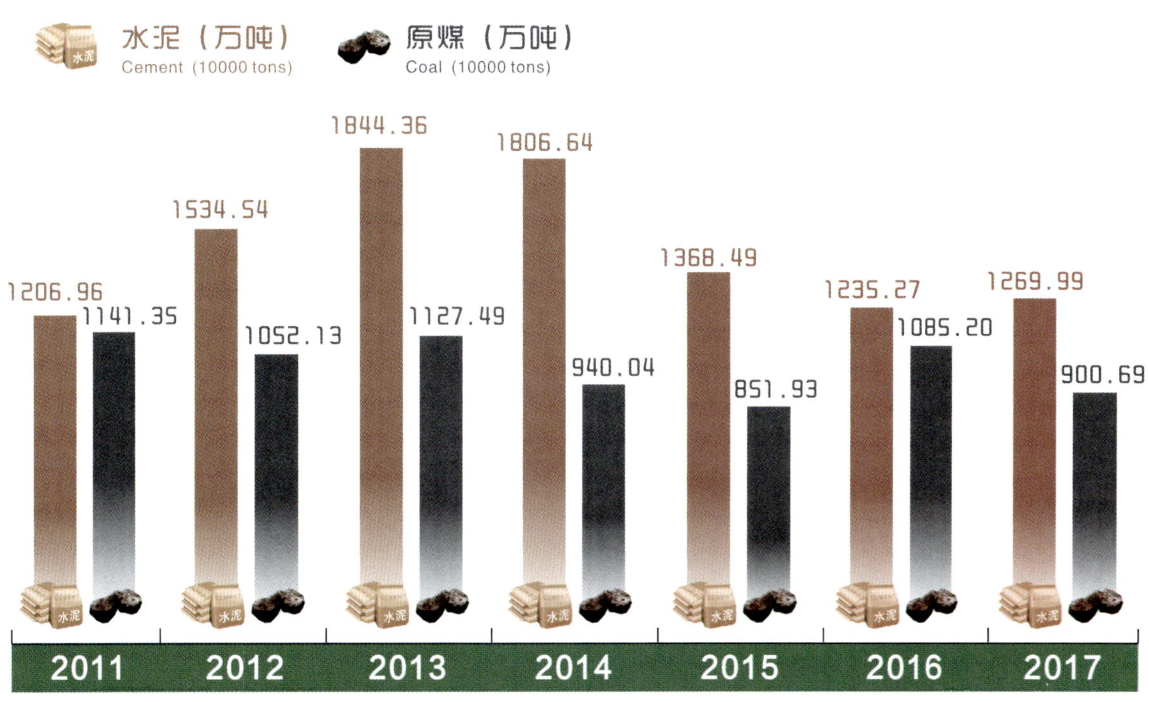
水泥（万吨）
Cement (10000 tons)
原煤（万吨）
Coal (10000 tons)
1206.96
1141.35
1534.54
1052.13
1844.36
1127.49
1806.64
940.04
1368.49
851.93
1235.27
1085.20
1269.99
900.69
2011
2012
2013
2014
2015
2016
2017

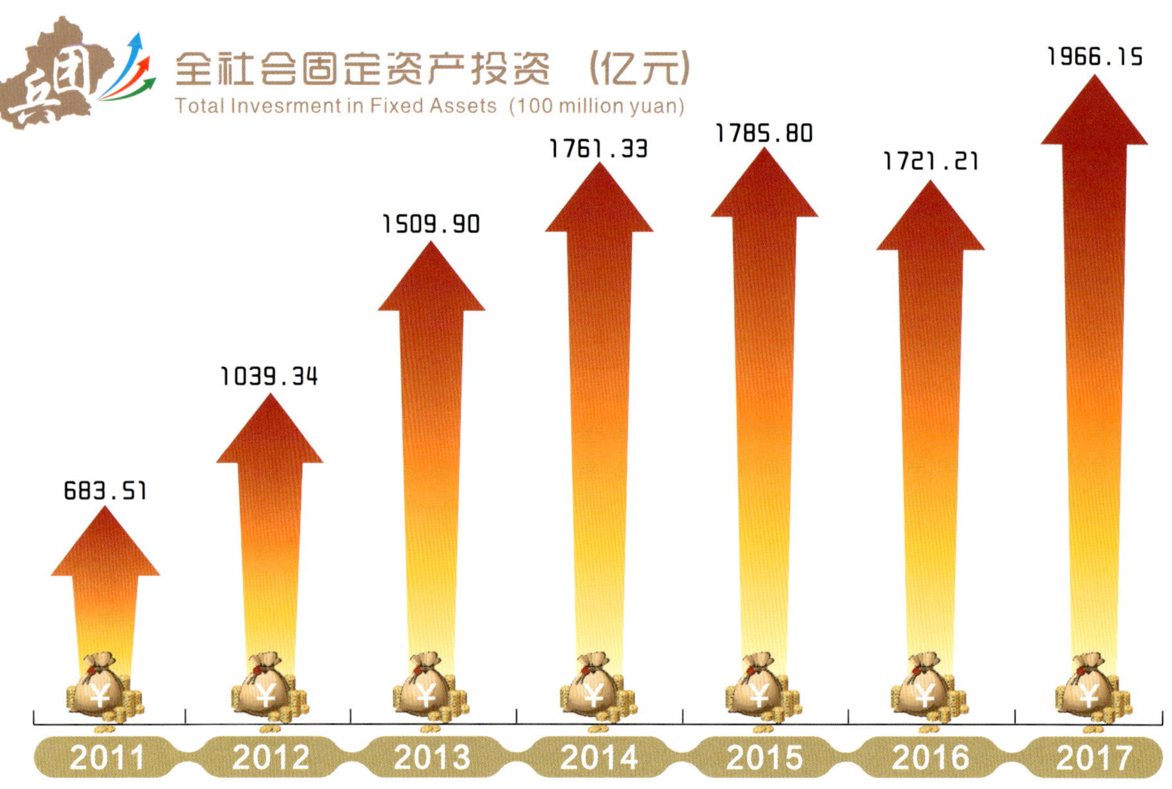

全社会固定资产投资（亿元）
Total Invesrment in Fixed Assets (100 million yuan)
683.51
1039.34
1509.90
1761.33
1785.80
1721.21
1966.15
2011
2012
2013
2014
2015
2016
2017

2017年全社会固定资产投资构成（%）
Composition of Investment in Fixed Assets (%)

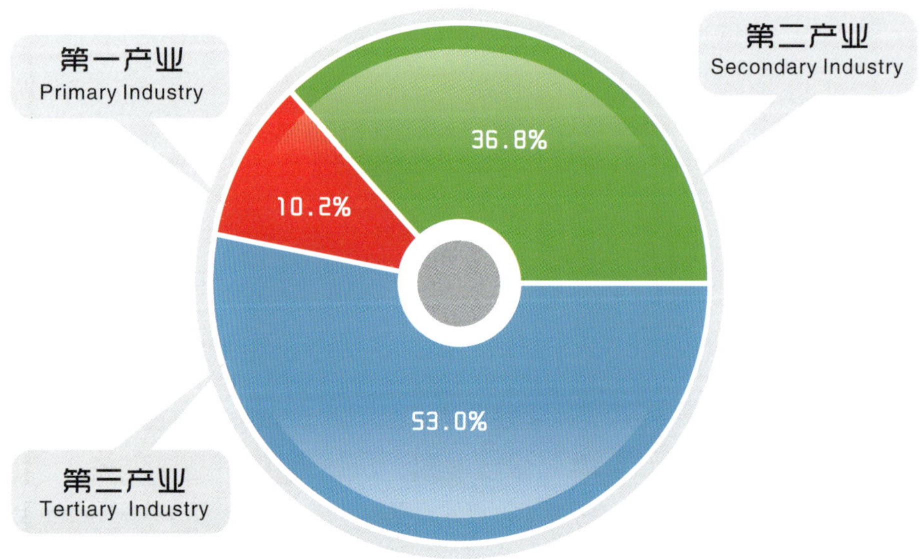

第一产业
Primary Industry
10.2%
第二产业
Secondary Industry
36.8%
第三产业
Tertiary Industry
53.0%

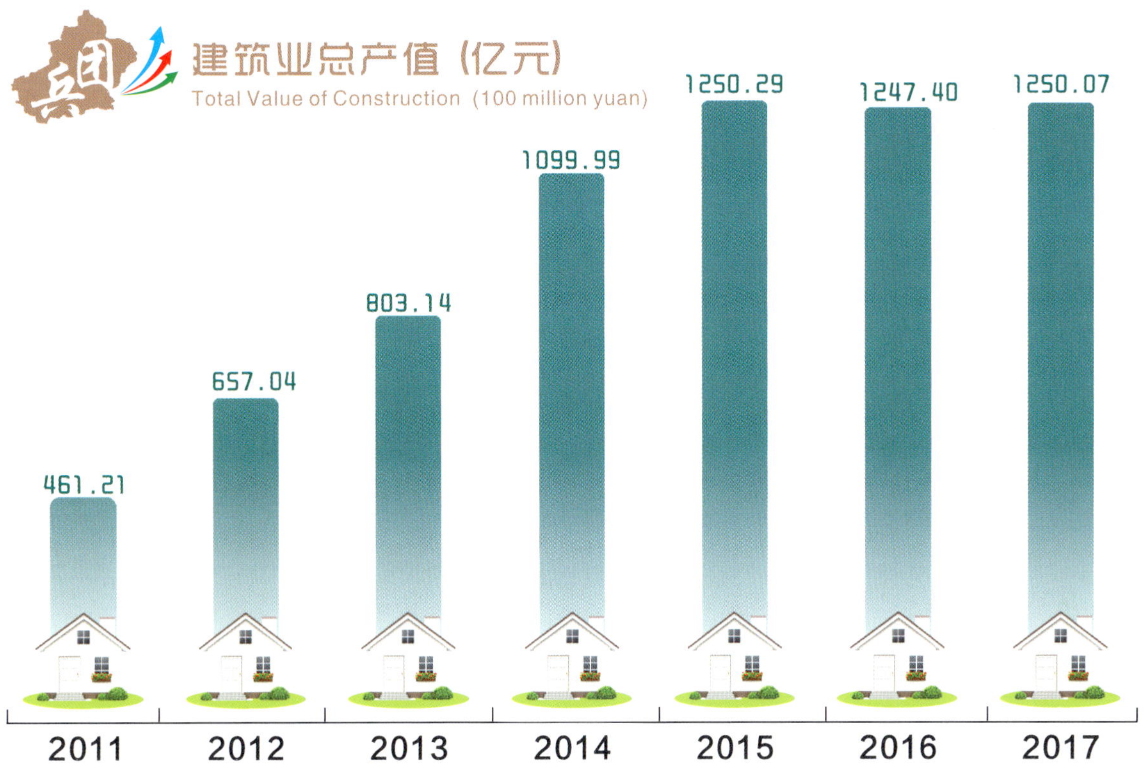
建筑业总产值（亿元）
Total Value of Construction (100 million yuan)
461.21
657.04
803.14
1099.99
1250.29
1247.40
1250.07
2011
2012
2013
2014
2015
2016
2017

建筑企业生产情况
Production of Construction Enterprises

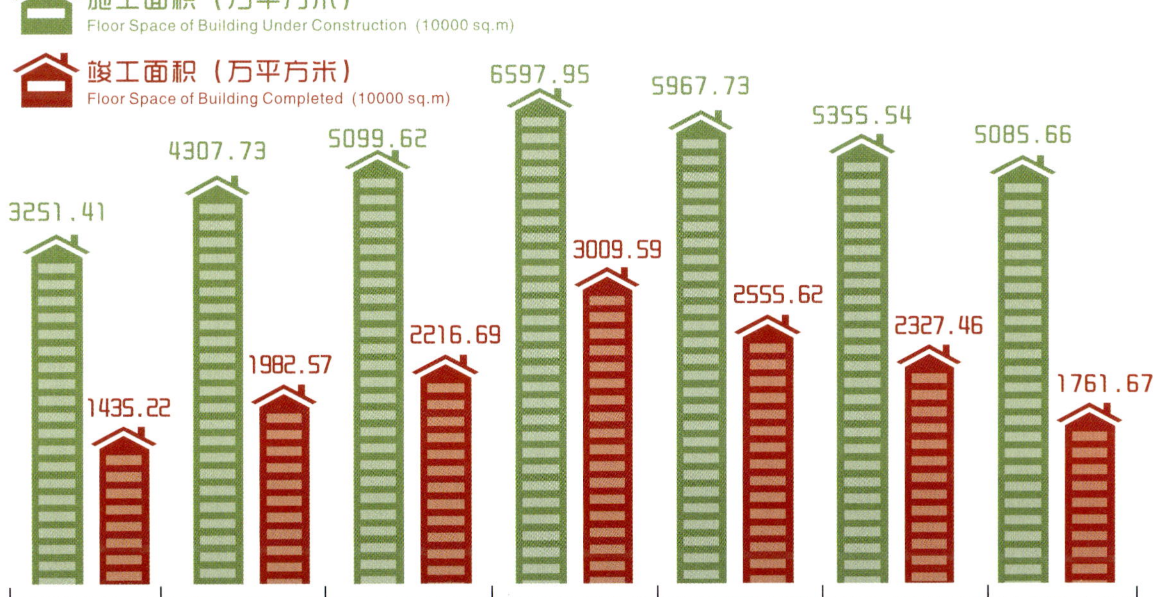
施工面积（万平方米）
Floor Space of Building Under Construction (10000 sq.m)
竣工面积（万平方米）
Floor Space of Building Completed (10000 sq.m)
3251.41
1435.22
4307.73
1982.57
5099.62
2216.69
6597.95
3009.59
5967.73
2555.62
5355.54
2327.46
5085.66
1761.67
2011
2012
2013
2014
2015
2016
2017

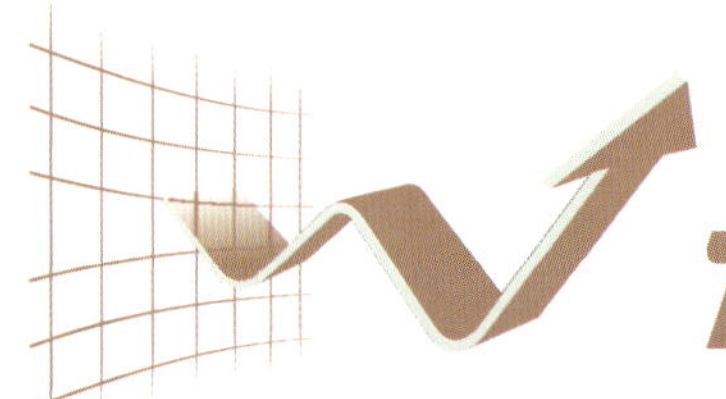

发展与成就 DEVELOPMENT AND ACHIEVEMENT

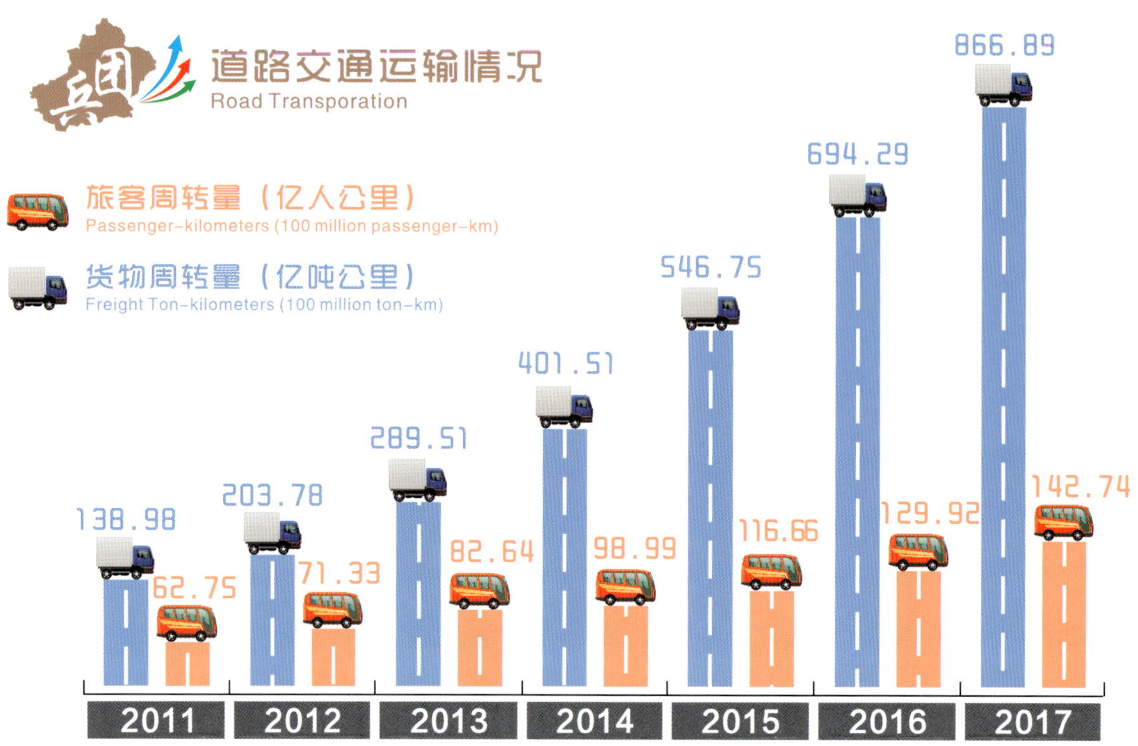

社会消费品零售总额（亿元）
Total Retail Sales of Consumer Goods (100 million yuan)

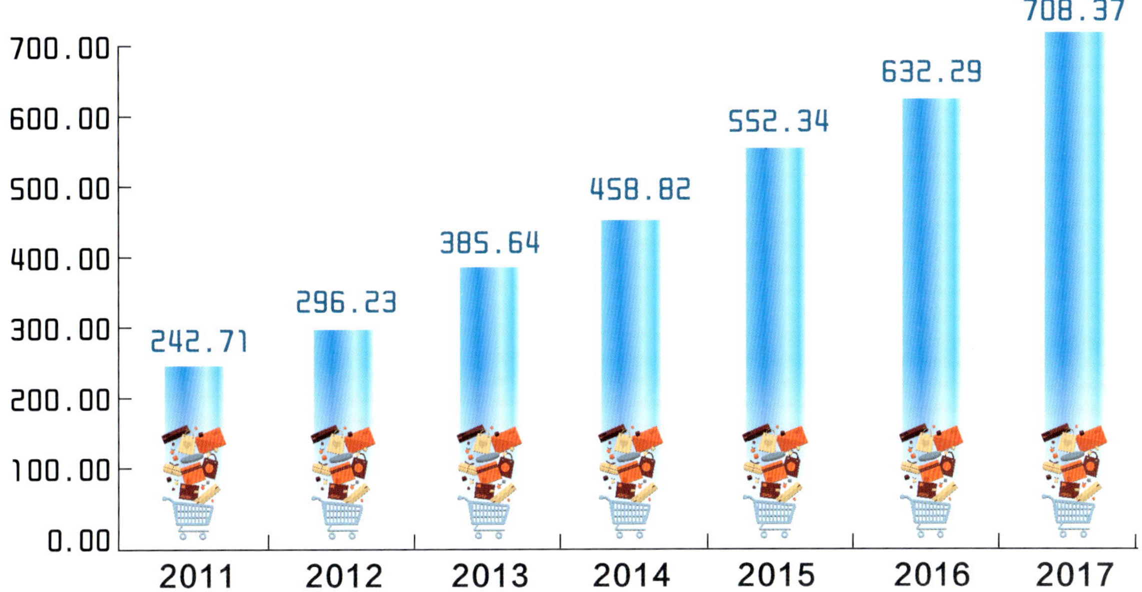

进出口情况(亿美元)
Imports and Exports(USD 100 million)

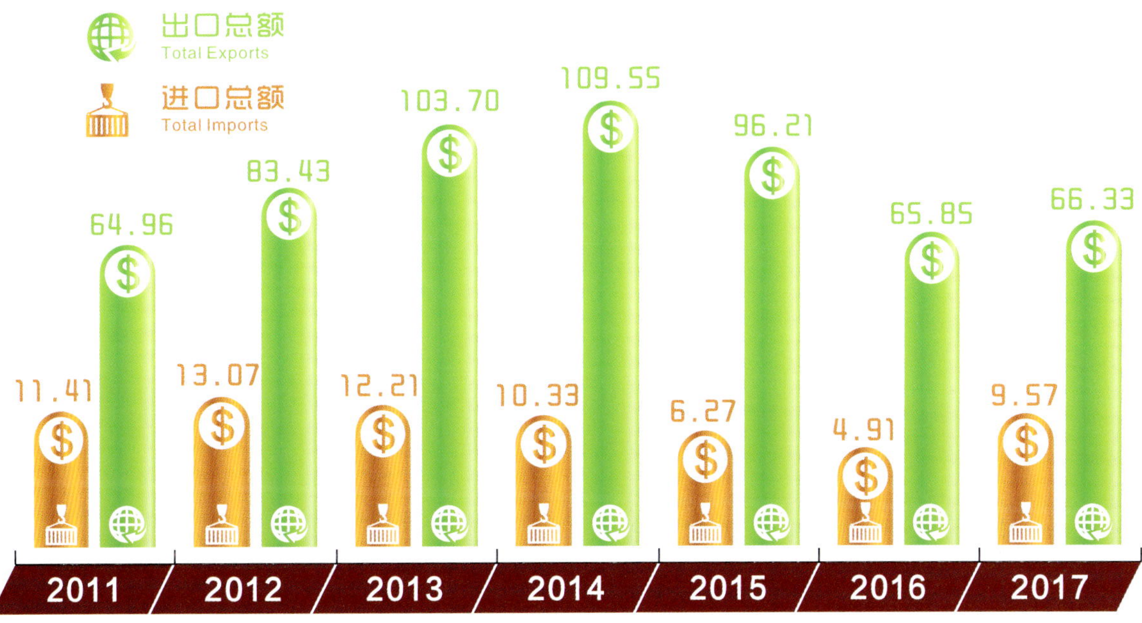

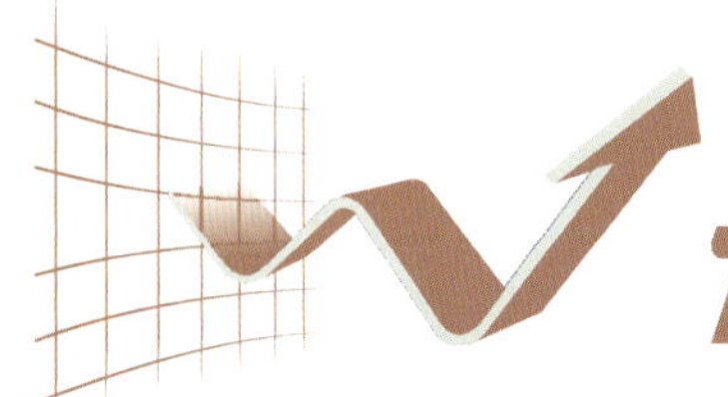

发展与成就 DEVELOPMENT AND ACHIEVEMENT

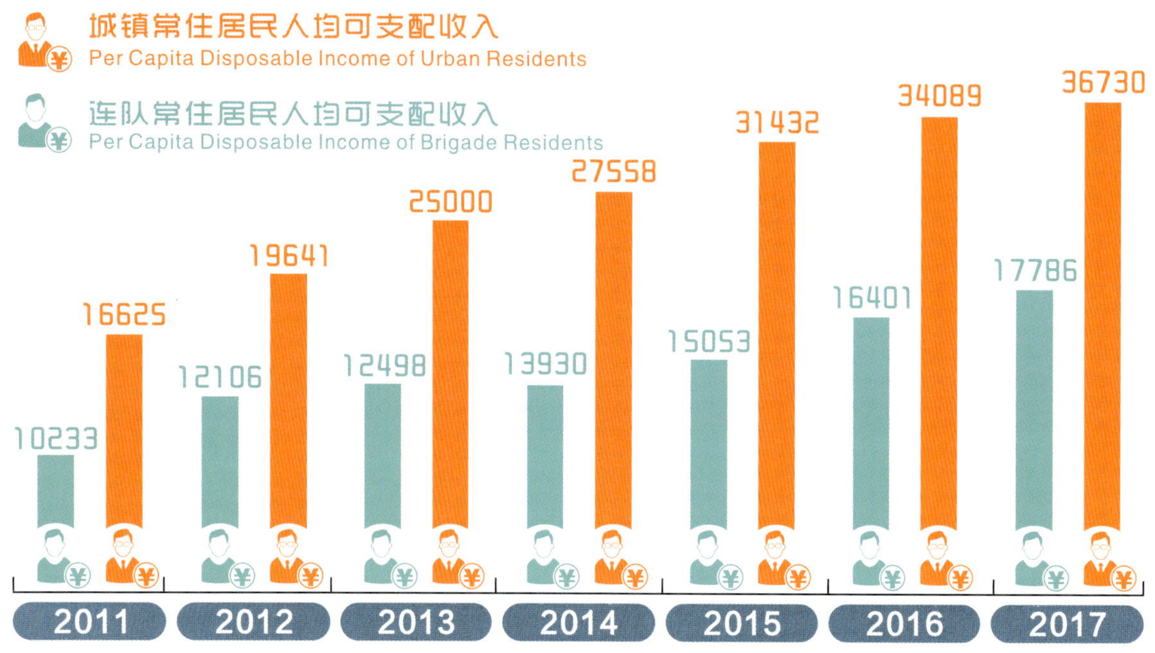

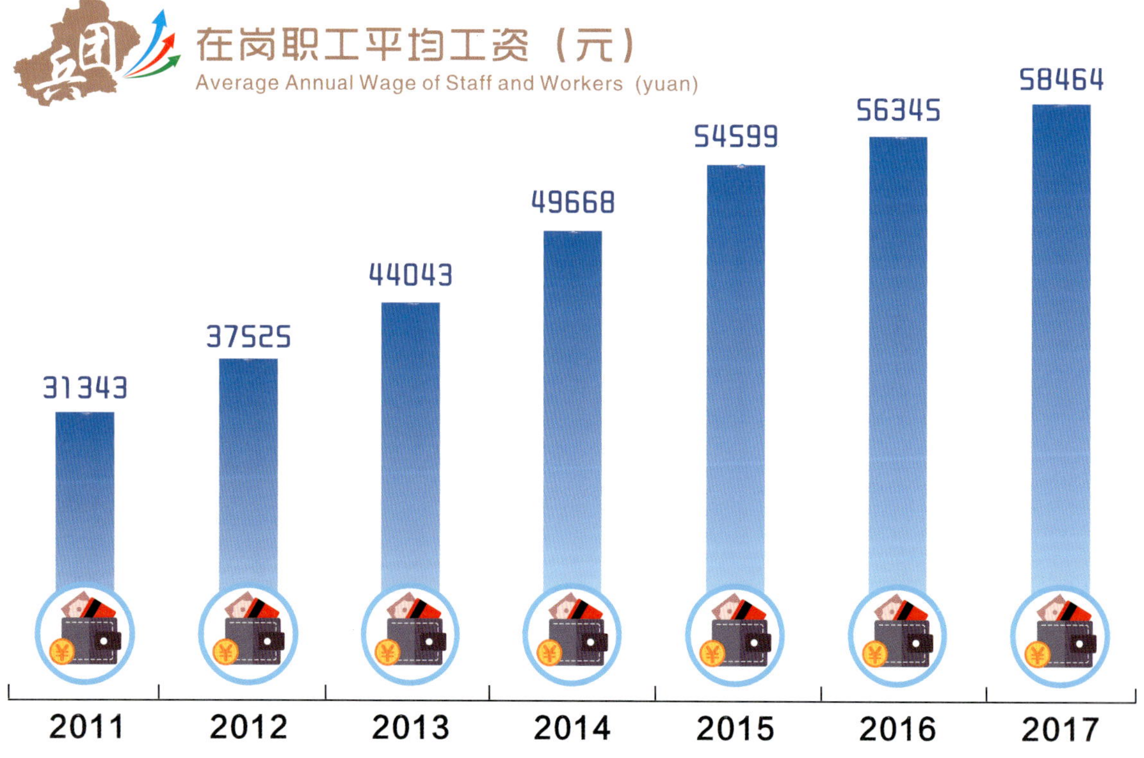

各级各类学校在校学生数（万人）
Number of Schools Enrollment by Level and Type of School (10000 persons)

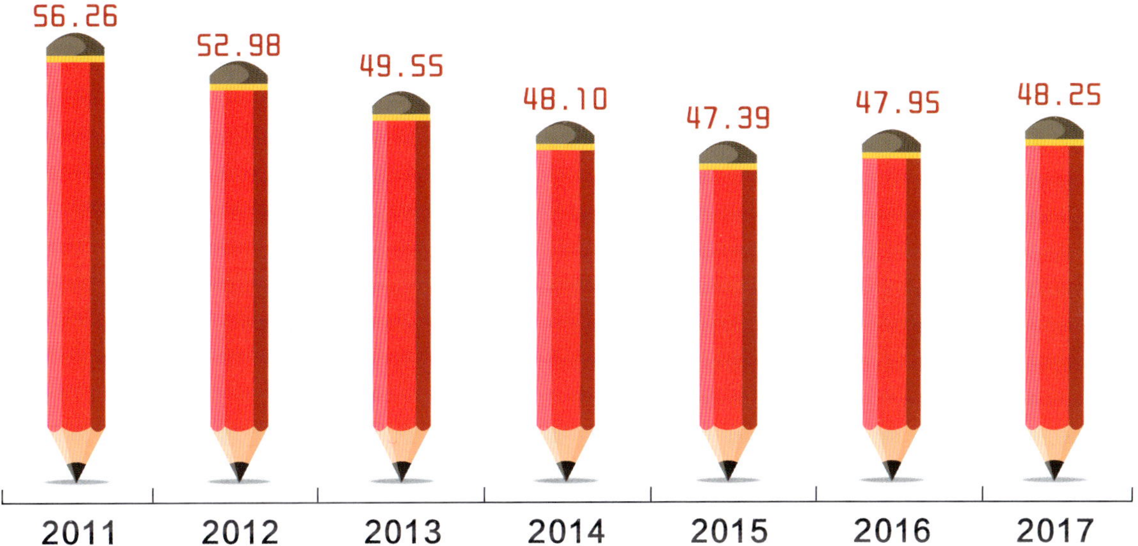

电视覆盖率
TV Coverage Rate

2017年：98.4%

广播覆盖率
Radio Broadcasting Coverage Rate

2017年：97.7%

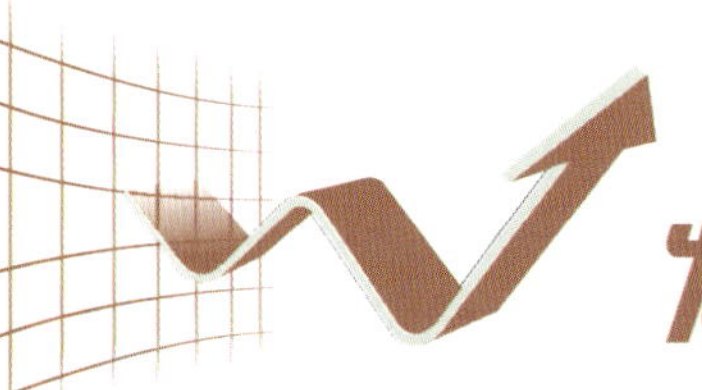

发展与成就 DEVELOPMENT AND ACHIEVEMENT

旅游业情况
Tourism

2017年旅游人数：
1896.12万人次
Number of Tourist (10000 persons)

2017年旅游收入：
101.80亿元
Income of Tourism (100 million yuan)

每万人医院床位数(张)
Number of Hospital Bads per 10000 persons (unit)

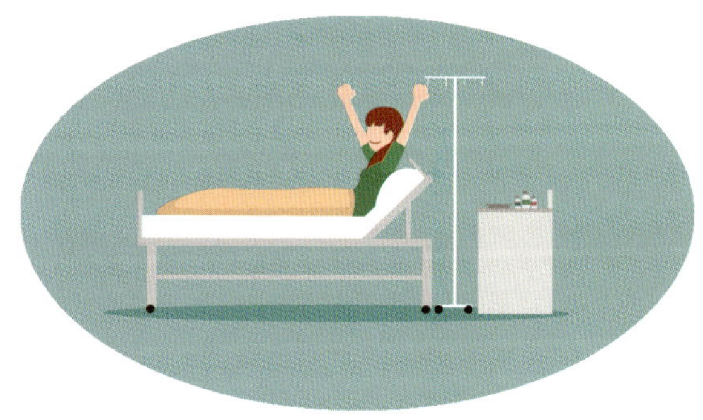

2017年：76.01张

2017年：91人

每万人拥有卫生技术人员数(人)
Number of Medical Technical Personel Per 10000 Persons (person)

编 者 说 明

一、《新疆生产建设兵团统计年鉴-2018》（以下简称《年鉴》），是一部全面反映新疆生产建设兵团国民经济和社会发展情况的综合性资料年刊，刊载兵团、各师（市）和团场（镇）2017年国民经济和社会发展各方面统计数据，沿天山北坡经济带自治区与兵团主要统计数据，新疆及分地（州、市）、全国及分省（区、市）主要统计数据，兵团、师、团场主要经济指标排序资料与各省（区、市）主要指标排序等资料。

二、全书内容分为特载和统计资料两部分，特载部分刊载了兵团2017年国民经济和社会发展统计公报；统计资料部分包括20篇数据资料：1.综合；2.国民经济核算；3.人口与就业；4.固定资产投资；5.资源与环境；6.财政和财务；7.价格指数；8.人民生活；9.农业；10.工业；11.建筑业；12.交通运输业；13.国内贸易；14.能源生产与消费；15.对外贸易、经济技术协作和规模以上服务业；16.金融业和上市公司；17.科技、教育、文化和卫生；18.公共管理、社会保障和其他；19.城市、乡（镇）和团场基本情况；20.各师、团场主要经济指标排序。另附各省（区、市）主要经济指标排序资料。各篇前为简要说明，对本篇章的主要内容、资料来源、统计范围、统计方法以及历史变动情况作简要概述。

三、《年鉴》中使用的度量衡单位均采用国际统一标准计量单位。

四、《年鉴》根据出版要求，标明的2018年为出版年份，正文为2017年度资料。

五、《年鉴》中符号含义说明：

“…”表示数据不足本指标最小单位数；

“空格”表示无指标数据；

“#”表示其中的主要项。

六、《年鉴》中大部分资料来自年度统计报表，部分来自抽样调查和有关业务部门。为便于读者使用，对某些指标在表下作了简要注释。凡之前发布的统计数字与本年鉴不一致的，以本《年鉴》为准。

七、在编辑过程中，得到了国家统计局、自治区统计局、国家统计局新疆调查总队和兵团机关有关部、委、办、局的大力支持与协助，在此表示衷心感谢！限于编辑水平，对于《年鉴》中存在的差错和缺点，敬请广大读者和各位统计同仁提出宝贵意见。

编　者

2018年7月

The Editors' Explanatory Notes

Ⅰ. Xinjiang Production & Construction Corps Statistical Yearbook-2018(Hereinafter referred to as Yearbook) is a comprehensive data annual, which covers entirely national economy and social development of XPCC. The yearbook reflects various aspects of main statistical data in 2017 at levels of XPCC , divisions (cities) and farms(towns); main indicators between Xinjiang and XPCC on the economic belt of the northern slope of the Tianshan Mountains and main indicators on Xinjiang and prefectures and cities, and data in to National Ranking data of main economic indicators on XPCC, divisions,brigades and provinces.

Ⅱ. The book contains two parts. Special Issue and data. Special Issue is published the Statistical Communique on National Econnmy and Social Development of XPCC in 2017.Data includes twenty parts, namely, 1. General Survey; 2. National Accounts; 3. Population and Employment; 4. Investment in Fixed Assets; 5. Natural Resources and Environment Protection; 6. Government Finance; 7. Price Indices; 8. People' s Livelihood 9. Agriculture; 10. Industry; 11. Construction; 12. Transportation; 13. Domestic Trade; 14. Energy production and consumption ; 15.Foreign Trade, Economic Cooperation, Tourism and Service above Designated Size ; 16.Financial Intermediation and Listed Company; 17.Science,Education, Culture and Public Health; 18.Public Management,Social Security and Other Data; 19.Basic Conditions of Cities, Townships(towns) and Farms; Ranking Data of Main Indicators by Province and City are attached in the appendix. In brief introduction at the beginning of each part, mainly coverage of this chapter, data sources, statistical coverage, statistical methods and historical changes are concerned.

Ⅲ. The units of measurement used in this book are internationally standard measurement units.

Ⅳ. According to publication request, the year marked in this book is 2018, but the year of data is 2017.

Ⅴ. Notations used in this book:

"..." indicates that the figure is not large enough to be measured with the smallest unit in the table;

"(Blank)" indicates that the data are not available;

"#" indicates the major items of the total.

Ⅵ. The major data sources of this yearbook are obtained from annual statistical reports, some from sample surveys and some from data provided by relative administrative departments. For the convenience of readers, brief notes concerning some indicators are placed at the lower part of relevant tables. In case of inconsistency of formerly issued some statistical data with this yearbook, this publication shall govern.

Ⅶ.In the course of compilation, the yearbook has received great support and assistance from National Bureau of Statistics, Xinjiang Bureau of Statistics,NBS Survey Office in Xinjiang and many units of XPCC . We would like to acknowledge them. Because of inadequate editing proficiency, readers and colleagues from statistical front are welcome to make precious opinions on mistakes and faults .

Editors
July 2018

目　　录
CONTENTS

特　载
Special Issue

一、综　合
Chapter 1 General Survey

二、国民经济核算

Chapter 2 National Accounts

三、人口与就业

Chapter 3 Population and Employment

四、固定资产投资

Chapter 4 Investment in Fixed Assets

五、资源与环境

Chapter 5 Natural Resource and Environment Protection

六、财政、财务

Chapter 6 Government Finance

七、价格指数

Chapter 7 Price Indices

八、人民生活

Chapter 8 People's Living Conditions

九、农业

Chapter 9 Agriculture

十、工业
Chapter 10 Industry

十一、建筑业

Chapter 11 Construction

十二、交通运输业
Chapter 12 Transportation Industry

十三、国内贸易

Chapter 13 Domestic Trade

十四、能源生产与消费

Chapter 14 Energy Production and Consumption

十五、对外贸易、经济技术协作、旅游业和规模以上服务业

Chapter 15 Foreign Trade, Economic and Technological Cooperation, Tourism and Service above Designated Size

十六、金融业和上市公司

Chapter 16 Financial Intermediation and Listed Company

十七、科技、教育、文化和卫生

Chapter 17 Science and Technology, Education, Culture and Public Health

十八、公共管理、社会保障和其他

Chapter 18 Public Mangement、Social Security and Others

十九、城市、乡(镇)和团场基本情况

Chapter 19 Basic Conditions of Cities、Townships(towns) and Farms

二十、各师、团场主要经济指标排序

Chapter 20 Ranking of Main Economic Indicators by Division and Farm

附录1　各省(区、市)主要经济指标排序

Appendix Ⅰ　Ranking of Main Economic Indicators by Province

附录 2　东、中、西部和东北地区主要经济指标

Appendix Ⅱ Main Economic Indicators of Eastern, Middle, Western and Northeastern Provinces

附录 3　新疆各地州市主要经济指标

Appendix Ⅲ Main Economic Indicators of XinJiang's Prefectures、Autonomous Prefectures and Cities

2018

BING TUAN

特　载

Special Issue

简要说明

一、本篇资料主要内容

本篇资料登载2017年新疆生产建设兵团国民经济和社会发展统计公报，反映2017年兵团经济和社会事业取得的成就。

二、本篇资料来源

本篇公报由兵团统计局国民经济综合统计处撰写，数据取自兵团统计局、国家统计局兵团调查总队各专业统计年报和兵团有关部门统计年报。

Brief Introduction

1. Main Contents

This chapter carries the Statistical Communique on National Economy and Social Development of Xinjiang Production and Construction Corps in 2017, reflecting achievements of economy and social undertakings of XPCC in 2017.

2. Sources of Data

This communique is compiled by the Comprehensive Office of Statistics Bureau of XPCC. Data in this communique are obtained from professional statistical annuals of the Statistics Bureau of XPCC, Survey Office of the National Bureau of Statistics of XPCC and statistical annuals of XPCC's relevant departments.

新疆生产建设兵团2017年国民经济和社会发展统计公报

新疆生产建设兵团统计局　国家统计局兵团调查总队

2018年3月26日

2017年，兵团各级各部门在以习近平同志为核心的党中央坚强领导和自治区党委统一领导下，不断增强政治意识、大局意识、核心意识、看齐意识，深入贯彻落实党的十八大和十八届三中、四中、五中、六中、七中全会精神，以习近平新时代中国特色社会主义思想和党的十九大精神为指导，按照兵团第七次党代会和兵团党委七届一次、二次全会部署，坚持稳中求进工作总基调，坚定不移贯彻新发展理念，以提高发展质量和效益为中心，统筹推进"五位一体"总体布局和协调推进"四个全面"战略布局，以供给侧结构性改革为主线，全力推进稳增长、促改革、调结构、惠民生、防风险各项工作，经济运行缓中趋稳、稳中有进、稳中向好，经济社会保持平稳健康发展。

一、综　合

全年兵团生产总值2339.07亿元，比上年增长8.0%。其中，第一产业增加值506.33亿元，增长7.6%；第二产业增加值1026.50亿元，增长4.6%；第三产业增加值806.24亿元，增长12.9%。三次产业增加值占生产总值比重分别为21.6%、43.9%、34.5%。三次产业对经济的贡献率分别为20.4%、26.9%和52.7%，分别拉动经济增长1.6、2.1和4.2个百分点。全年人均生产总值80117元，比上年增长3.5%。

兵团年末总人口300.53万人，比上年末增加17.12万人、增长6.0%。其中，男性156.76万人，女性143.77万人，总人口性别比（以女性为100，男性对女性的比例）为109.04。全年出生人口2.29万人，出生率为7.85‰；死亡人口1.59万人，死亡率为5.44‰；人口自然增长率为2.41‰。年末户籍人口237.86万人，比上年末增加9.63万人、增长4.2%。其中，城镇人口126.98万人，乡村（连队）人口110.87人。

年末从业人员144.17万人，比上年增长4.4%。年末非私营单位在岗职工74.32万人，比上年增长5.4%。全年城镇新增就业12.92万人，比上年增加2.56万人，其中援助就业困难人员就业1.56万人。城镇登记失业率控制在3%以内。全年完成各类职业技能培训13.03万人（次）。引进外国专家项目9项，引进专家158人（次）。出国（境）培训项目7项，培训各级各类人员103人（次）。

全年新疆居民消费价格比上年上涨2.2%，其中，食品烟酒价格上涨2.1%，居住价格上涨0.4%。农业生产资料价格上涨0.8%。固定资产投资价格上涨3.5%。

全年兵团工业生产者出厂价格比上年上涨8.3%。工业生产者购进价格上涨9.0%。兵团农产品生产者价格上涨0.8%。

表1　2017年新疆居民消费价格增减变动情况

指　　标	比上年增长(%)
居民消费价格总水平	2.2
城　市	2.4
农　村	1.8
食品烟酒	2.1
#粮　食	0.7
畜　肉	3.4
蛋　类	0.0
水产品	3.4
鲜　菜	−4.8
鲜　果	3.7
衣　着	1.3
居　住	0.4
生活用品及服务	1.5
交通和通信	0.8
教育文化和娱乐	2.7
医疗保健	9.6
其他用品和服务	1.0

供给侧结构性改革扎实推进。水泥、煤炭年度去产能任务圆满完成。年末商品房待售面积比上年末下降0.2%。年末规模以上工业企业资产负债率为65.3%，比上年末下降1.6个百分点。全年规模以上工业企业每百元主营业务收入中的成本为80.59元，比全国水平低4.67元；规模以上工业企业每百元主营业务收入中的三项费用比上年减少0.39元。全年农林牧渔业、道路运输业、生态保护和环境治理业等短板领域投资分别比上年增长12.3%、121.5%和53.2%。

新动能新产业新业态较快成长。工业战略性新兴产业增加值比上年增长29.4%，占规模以上工业增加值的比重为8.1%。高技术制造业增加值增长16.1%，占规模以上工业增加值的比重为3.7%。装备制造业增加值增长8.8%，占规模以上工业增加值的比重为2.2%。全年高技术产业投资53.28亿元，下降10.1%，占固定资产投资（不含农户）的比重为2.7%。全年限额以上企业商品零售中通过公共网络实现的商品零售额同比增长7倍。

发展质量效益改善。全年兵团一般公共预算收入129.60亿元，比上年增长21.7%，其中税收收入67.76亿元，比上年增加7.03亿元、增长11.6%。年末兵、师国资委监管企业合计资产总额4474.19亿元，比上年增长10.4%；所有者权益1079.90亿元，增长9.9%；全年实现营业收入1960.85亿元，增长12.3%；实现利润总额55.31亿元，增长132.2%。全年规模以上工业企业实现利润218.78亿元，比上年增长8.2%。分经济类型看，国有控股企业增长80.1%；股份制企业增长5.2%，外商及港澳台商投资企业增长148.9%；私营企业下降0.9%。分门类看，采矿业增长100.0%；制造业增长12.3%；电力、热力、燃气及水生产和供应业下降12.4%。全年全员劳动生产率为161324元/人，比上年提高4.9%。

二、农　　业

全年农作物播种面积1362.77千公顷(2044.15万亩)，比上年下降0.7%。其中，粮食面积284.24千公顷(426.36万亩)，下降14.3%；棉花面积686.93千公顷(1030.40万亩)，增长10.6%；油料面积56.82千公顷(85.24万亩)，下降11.8%；甜菜面积23.73千公顷(35.60万亩)，下降2.7%；蔬菜面积(含菜用瓜)87.42千公顷(131.13万亩)，下降2.9%。

农作物精量半精量播种面积955.6千公顷(1433.4万亩)，比上年增长6.0%。其中，棉花精量播种面积612.7千公顷(919.05万亩)，增长5.0%。

全年粮食产量248.55万吨，比上年下降8.4%；棉花产量167.88万吨，增长12.2%；油料产量20.92万吨，下降10.7%；甜菜产量198.46万吨，下降4.7%；蔬菜产量670.54万吨，下降0.7%，其中，工业用番茄342.85万吨，下降2.5%。

年末牲畜存栏772.58万头(只)，比上年增长1.1%。其中，牛50.77万头，增长6.7%；猪167.47万头，增长11.9%；羊548.49万只，下降2.3%。年内牲畜出栏882.71万头(只)，增长6.0%。全年肉类总产量44.38万吨，增长7.9%。羊毛产量1.99万吨，增长4.4%。禽蛋产量10.92万吨，增长15.9%。牛奶产量68.14万吨，增长8.3%。

全年水果产量392.16万吨，比上年增长7.4%。其中，红枣181.73万吨，增长8.6%；葡萄79.43万吨，下降0.9%；香梨40.63万吨，增长15.0%；苹果63.08万吨，增长14.1%。全年核桃产量2.81万吨，增长6.4%。

全年水产品产量5.39万吨，比上年增长4.7%。

年末有效灌溉面积1258.22千公顷(1887.33万亩)，比上年增长2.5%。其中，高新节水灌溉面积1041.99千公顷(1562.99万亩)，增长3.0%。

种植业耕种收综合机械化率94%，采棉机2221台，机采棉面积530千公顷(795万亩)，棉花机采率80.0%。畜牧业机械化水平68%。

全年新建及改扩建各类标准化规模养殖场112个，累计达标创建全国标准化示范场88个。畜禽良种推广覆盖率达到76.0%，养殖粪污资源化利用率达到69.0%。

年末国家级兵团级农业产业化龙头企业128家。其中，国家级15家，兵团级113家。销售收入超100亿元的企业2家，超30亿元的企业6家，超10亿元的7家。已建成2个全国农业产业化示范基地，4个全国现代农业示范区，23个国家级无公害农产品示范基地和国家级农业标准化示范团场，35个全国“一村一品”示范团场。

三、工业和建筑业

全年全部工业增加值725.98亿元，比上年增长6.4%。规模以上工业增加值增长6.7%。在规模以上工业中，分经济类型看，国有控股企业增长8.7%；股份制企业增长5.3%，外商及港澳台商投资企业增长34.1%；私营企业增长5.6%。分门类看，采矿业增长9.7%，制造业增长5.3%，电力、热力、燃气及水生产和供应业增长12.7%。分轻重工业看，轻工业增长4.5%，重工业增长8.0%。

全年规模以上工业中，煤炭开采和洗选业增加值比上年增长4.2%，农副食品加工业增长8.0%，食品制造业增长2.3%，酒饮料和精制茶制造业下降0.9%，纺织业增长9.4%，化学原料及化学制品制造业增长4.1%，非金属矿物制品业增长7.8%，黑色金属冶炼和压延加工业增长89.9%，有色金属冶炼及压延加工业增长2.8%，电力、热力生产和供应业增长12.8%。六大高耗能行业增加值比上年增长7.3%，占规模以上工业增加值的比重为58.3%。

表2　2017年主要工业产品产量及其增长速度

产品名称	计量单位	绝对数	比上年增长(%)
原　煤	万吨	900.69	−17.0
发电量	亿千瓦小时	798.10	6.2
#火　电	亿千瓦小时	722.24	3.8
水　电	亿千瓦小时	15.98	−5.8
太阳能	亿千瓦小时	35.99	198.4
精制食用植物油	万吨	71.67	−17.8
乳制品	万吨	24.08	20.8
番茄酱罐头	万吨	60.81	2.9
饮料酒	万千升	20.21	−8.6
软饮料	万吨	52.49	−39.8
纱	万吨	48.88	20.0
布	亿米	1.50	30.4
机制纸及纸板	万吨	7.32	−43.8
农用氮、磷、钾化学肥料(折纯)	万吨	49.51	−1.7
初级形态的塑料	万吨	135.21	−2.8
塑料制品	万吨	88.32	13.4
硅酸盐水泥熟料	万吨	836.45	2.7
水　泥	万吨	1 269.99	2.8
钢　材	万吨	155.90	94.2
原　铝	万吨	283.60	2.7

年末兵团规上工业发电装机容量1724万千瓦，比上年末增长10.5%。其中，火电装机容量1354万千瓦，增长7.0%；水电装机容量34万千瓦，下降5.3%；并网风电装机容量124万千瓦，增长66.6%；并网太阳能发电装机容量212万千瓦，增长15.1%。

年末兵团拥有各类园区32个，其中国家级4个，国家兵团分区2个，自治区级工业园区3个，兵团级工业园区23个。

全年全社会建筑业增加值300.73亿元，比上年增长0.6%。资质以上建筑业企业总产值1250.07亿元，比上年增长0.6%。具有资质等级的总承包和专业承包建筑企业实现利润18.79亿元，增长12.1%，其中国有控股企业12.27亿元，增长18.8%。各类建筑施工单位(含十一师海外项目)签订合同额1901.17亿元，比上年增长2.4%。全年房屋建筑施工面积5085.65万平方米，下降4.3%。

四、固定资产投资

全年固定资产投资(不含农户)1966.15亿元，比上年增长14.2%。分产业看，第一产业200.86亿元，增长12.3%；第二产业724.38亿元，增长11.7%；第三产业1040.91亿元，增长16.5%。固定资产投资三次产业构成为10.4∶37.7∶51.9。分区域看，南疆垦区投资565.56亿元，增长23.0%；北疆垦区投资1400.59亿元，增长11.0%。民间固定资产投资783.29亿元，增长21.1%，占固定资产投资(不含农户)的比重为39.8%。基础设施投资774.47亿元，增长13.3%，占固定资产投资(不含农户)的比重为39.4%。六大高耗能行业投资391.71亿元，下降1.2%，占固定资产投资(不含农户)的比重为19.9%。

表3　2017年固定资产投资(不含农户)及其增长速度

指　　标	绝对数(亿元)	比上年增长(%)
全社会固定资产投资	1 966.15	14.2
# 房地产开发投资	155.02	－15.6
按经济类型分		
国有经济	908.03	8.7
私营个体	541.12	39.2
其　他	517.00	4.1
按用途分		
第一产业	200.86	12.3
第二产业	724.38	11.7
第三产业	1 040.91	16.5

全年工业完成投资723.65亿元，比上年增长15.5%。其中，制造业完成投资518.00亿元，增长49.8%；电力、热力、燃气及水的生产和供应业完成投资199.38亿元，下降28.1%。全年交通运输、仓储和邮政业投资298.48亿元，比上年增长104.0%。

全年房地产开发投资155.02亿元，比上年下降15.6%。商品房销售面积333.44万平方米，下降9.4%。其中，住宅138.75万平方米，增长2.6%。年末商品房待售面积225.34万平方米，下降0.2%。商品房销售额148.76亿元，下降11.3%。

表4　2017年分行业固定资产投资(不含农户)及其增长速度

指　　标	绝对数(亿元)	比上年增长(%)
总　计	1 966.15	14.2
农、林、牧、渔业	200.86	12.3
采矿业	6.28	97.1
制造业	518.00	49.8
# 农副食品加工业	56.49	129.3
食品制造业	15.28	15.9
酒、饮料和精制茶制造业	10.30	37.7
纺织业	84.98	15.6
石油加工、炼焦及核燃料加工业	27.60	48.9
化学原料及化学制品制造业	117.80	33.9
非金属矿物制品业	59.48	197.7
黑色金属冶炼及压延加工业	12.45	2.5
有色金属冶炼及压延加工业	14.94	－24.7
电力、热力、燃气及水的生产和供应业	199.38	－28.1
建筑业	0.73	－96.7
批发和零售业	34.85	1.2
交通运输、仓储和邮政业	298.48	104.0
住宿和餐饮业	16.00	181.9
信息传输、软件和信息技术服务业	18.61	46.2
金融业	1.45	458.5
房地产业	244.40	－20.6
租赁和商务服务业	36.16	65.5
科学研究和技术服务	6.01	－59.6
水利、环境和公共设施管理业	258.01	4.3
居民服务、修理和其他服务业	6.07	130.5
教　育	31.82	10.1
卫生和社会工作	24.24	19.9
文化、体育和娱乐业	31.14	16.4
公共管理、社会保障和社会组织	33.66	41.2

全年实施棚户区改造4万户，续建保障房项目基本建成2万户，完成1500户贫困农户危房改造。

全年“十件实事”累计完成投资420.45亿元。其中，基本建设实事投资209.33亿元，财政补助实事投资211.13亿元。

固定资产投资建设资金来源总额1711.38亿元，比上年增长5.7%。其中，本年资金1647.72亿元，增长6.4%。本年资金来源中，国家预算内资金193.92亿元，下降25.4%；国内贷款126.94亿元，增长39.0%；自筹资金1132.61亿元，增长7.8%；其他资金192.98亿元，增长34.1%。

全年新增固定资产1614.11亿元，比上年增长33.4%。主要新增生产能力或效益：原煤开采151万吨，塑料树脂及共聚物0.10万吨，白酒0.80万吨，其他酒1.0万吨，棉纺锭94.34万锭，发电装机容量164.1万千瓦，输电线路521.95公里，城市自来水供水能力29.69万吨/日，城市污水处理能力6.78万吨/日，新建公路878.75公里，改(扩)建公路1055.1公里。

五、国内贸易

全年批发零售业实现商品销售总额3826.13亿元，比上年增长14.5%。

全年实现社会消费品零售总额708.37亿元，比上年增长12.0%。按销售单位所在地分，城镇消费品零售额630.08亿元，增长11.7%；乡村(连队)零售额78.29亿元，增长14.6%。按消费形态分，餐饮收入133.75亿元，增长22.7%；商品零售574.62亿元，增长9.8%。

在限额以上企业商品零售额中，粮油食品零售额比上年增长17.2%，饮料类增长7.1%，烟酒类增长6.1%，服装、鞋帽、针纺织品类增长5.8%，化妆品类增长3.7%，金银珠宝类下降13.1%，日用品类增长11.0%，家用电器和音像器材类增长19.0%，中西药品类增长14.8%，文化办公用品类增长1.7%，家具类增长7.8%，通讯器材类增长80.6%，建筑及装潢材料类增长19.9%，汽车类下降3.5%，石油及制品类增长10.0%。

六、对外经济

全年货物进出口总额75.90亿美元，比上年增长6.2%。其中，货物出口66.33亿美元，下降0.3%；货物进口9.57亿美元，增长94.4%。货物出口中，自产品出口7.80亿美元，增长20.0%。货物进出口差额(出口减进口)56.76亿美元。

全年实际利用外资4.1亿美元，比上年增长23.5%。新设外商投资企业24家，投资总额11亿美元，合同外资4亿美元。

全年完成非金融类对外直接投资8797万美元，比上年增长11.6%。完成对外承包工程营业额6.8亿美元，增长1.6%，对外承包工程项目累计派出各类劳务人员491人，减少196人。

表5　2017年货物进出口总额及其增长速度

指　　标	金额(亿美元)	比上年增长(%)
货物进出口总额	75.90	6.2
货物出口额	66.33	－0.3
其中：一般贸易	9.44	－37.4
边境小额贸易	54.79	13.3
货物进口额	9.57	94.4
其中：一般贸易	7.88	122.2
边境小额贸易	1.22	12.4
货物进出口差额(出口减进口)	56.76	—

全年实施招商引资项目3095个，到位资金1757.09亿元，比上年增长42.4%。其中，新建项目2284个，当年到位资金1098.09亿元；续建项目811个，当年到位资金659.00亿元。各类招商引资项目中，第一产业项目519个，到位资金117.75亿元，增长93.5%；第二产业项目1514个，到位资金971.33亿元，增长39.3%；第三产业项目1062个，到位资金668.01亿元，增长39.4%。与19个援疆省市产业合作项目609个，总投资2690.94亿元，当年到位资金691.91亿元，占全兵团到位资金的39.4%。

七、交通运输和旅游

全年道路运输货运量6.81亿吨，比上年增长17.0%。货物周转量866.89亿吨公里，增长24.9%。客运量2.50亿人，增长10.1%。旅客周转量142.74亿人公里，增长9.9%。

表8　2017年道路运输业营运情况

指　　标	计量单位	绝对数	比上年增长(%)
货运量	亿吨	6.81	17.0
# 个　体	亿吨	5.57	26.9
货运周转量	亿吨公里	866.89	24.9
# 个　体	亿吨公里	715.69	30.3
客运量	亿人	2.50	10.1
# 个　体	亿人	1.98	15.1
旅客周转量	亿人公里	142.74	9.9
# 个　体	亿人公里	113.71	19.8
营运收入	亿元	324.81	20.7
个体纯收入	亿元	109.44	18.5

年末民用汽车保有量30.96万辆，比上年末增长7.4%。其中，载客汽车21.91万辆，增长13.3%；载货汽车5.98万辆，降低4.6%；其他汽车3.06万辆，下降4.1%。民用轿车保有量18.11万辆，增长15.0%。

年末兵团公路通达里程34727公里。其中，一级72.5公里，二级3879.4公里，三级5278.2公里，四级12850公里。全年新改建二级以上公路447.8公里，改扩建通营、连公路437公里。

年末兵团航空企业管理局执管飞机42架。全年飞行总时间4334小时，起落7561架次。其中，用于农林牧业飞行2351小时，作业处理土地面积75千公顷(112.5万亩)；工业飞行739小时。

年末兵团城市区域光网覆盖率99.28%，城市家庭光网覆盖率99.4%，团场及连队光网覆盖率98%，光纤宽带用户占比95%，4G网络覆盖全部师团及65%的连队。

年末拥有旅游企业381家，其中旅行社141家，旅游星级饭店62家，国家等级景区55个，星级农家乐117家，旅游集团公司6家。全国优秀旅游城市1个，全国特色景观旅游名镇9个，兵团特色景观旅游名团(镇)37个，全国红色旅游经典景区3个，全国休闲农业与乡村旅游示范县3个，全国休闲农业与乡村旅游示范点8个，全国工农业旅游示范点12家，导游3670人。

全年旅游接待总人数1892万人次，比上年增长33%。旅游总收入101.8亿元，增长37.6%。其中，入境旅游人数20.9万人次、增长10%，国内旅游人数1871.1万人次、增长33%。国内旅游收入99.8亿元，增长37.4%；旅游外汇收入0.32亿美元，增长10.9%。带动直接就业人员5万人，增长11.1%，间接就业人员20万人，增长11.1%。

八、金　　融

全年驻疆各银行金融机构对兵团贷款余额2545.68亿，比上年增长22.3%。

农行兵团分行年末各项本外币存款余额1262.74亿元，比年初增长9.6%。其中，个人存款595.80亿元，增长2.9%；单位存款666.94亿元，增长16.4%。各项贷款年末余额658.16亿元，比年初增长19.8%。

全年兵团17家企业实现直接融资合计254.01亿元，其中，利用债券市场实现融资209.80亿元，上市公司利用资本市场实现融资44.21亿元。利用债券市场实现融资中，超短期融资券98亿元，短期融资券40亿元，中期票据30亿元，公司债33亿元，其它8.8亿元；上市公司利用资本市场实现融资中，通过定向增发融资26.72亿元，通过资产证券化融资7.49亿元，通过发行可转换债券融资10亿元。

九、人民生活和社会保障

全年兵团居民人均可支配收入29430元，比上年增长8.1%，扣除价格因素，实际增长5.8%。按常住地分，城镇居民人均可支配收入36730元，比上年增长7.7%，扣除价格因素，实际增长5.2%；连队居民人均可支配收入17786元，比上年增长8.4%，扣除价格因素，实际增长6.5%。

全年兵团居民人均消费支出18908元，比上年下降1.3%。按常住地分，城镇居民人均消费支出21827元，下降2.4%；连队居民人均消费支出14252元，增长0.9%。居民家庭恩格尔系数为27.3%，比全国水平低2.0个百分点，其中城镇为27.5%，连队为26.6%。

全年非私营单位在岗职工工资总额493.54亿元，比上年增长6.7%。非私营单位在岗职工平均工资58464元，比上年增加2119元，增长3.8%。

按照每人每年2300元(2010年不变价)的农村贫困标准计算，2017年，年末贫困人口2.19万人，比上年末减少2.96万人；贫困发生率1.2%，比上年下降1.6个百分点。全年有10个贫困团场摘帽，通过金融扶贫平台向建档立卡贫困户发放扶贫贷款10.21亿元。

年末参加基本养老保险人数185.1万人，比上年增加7.9万人，其中，参加城镇职工基本养老保险人数168.2万人，增加6.5万人；参加城乡居民基本养老保险人数16.9万人，增加1.4万人。参加基本医疗保险人数245万人，增加9.3万人，其中，参加职工基本医疗保险人数135.3万人，增加4.2万人；参加城镇居民基本医疗保险人数109.7万人，增加5.1万人。参加失业保险人数66.6万人，减少1.3万人。年末兵团领取失业保险金人数0.86万人。参加工伤保险人数80万人，增加5.4万人。参加生育保险人数的67.9万人，增加0.9万人。全年兵团发放低保资金3.43亿元，7.99万人享受最低生活保障；发放临时救助资金1.07亿元，17.8万人(次)得到临时救助；发放特困人员救助供养资金1316万元，1313名特困人员得到救助供养；发放医疗救助资金9851万元，12.9万人(次)得到医疗救助。全年国家抚恤、补助各类优抚对象2593人。

全年受理人事劳动争议案件913起，结案910起，结案率99.67%。受理劳动保障监察案件696件，结案682件，结案率97.99%；受理行政复议案件13件，结案13件，结案率100%。

十、教育、科学技术和文化体育

年末有各类学校601所，在校学生48.14万人，教职工

4.30万人。全年研究生招生0.16万人，在校研究生0.43万人，毕业生0.11万人。普通本专科招生1.34万人，在校生4.95万人，毕业生1.25万人。成人本专科招生0.79万人，在校生2.12万人，毕业生0.75万人。中等职业教育招生0.93万人，在校生2.72万人，毕业生0.85万人。普通高中招生1.83万人，在校生5.49万人，毕业生1.79万人。初中招生2.94万人，在校生8.4万人，毕业生2.78万人。小学招生2.75万人，在校生16.22万人，毕业生2.69万人。幼儿园招生3.53万人，在校生7.82万人，毕业生2.56万人。小学学龄儿童净入学率100%，初中适龄少年净入学率99.91%。九年义务教育巩固率98.42%，高中阶段毛入学率92.68%。兵团中小学及幼儿园有母语为非汉语的少数民族在校(园)学生接受国家通用语言文字教学覆盖率98.53%，其中，中小学覆盖率达到97.89%，学前教育覆盖率达到100%。主要劳动力人口(16—65岁)平均受教育年限11.47年。

年末兵团有科学研究与技术开发机构20个。全年争取各类国家科技计划项目批准立项133项，国拨经费到位资金0.81亿元。兵团本级科技计划项目立项196项，兵团本级财务科技拨款1.78亿元，比上年增长12.6%。

全年累计认定工程技术研究中心5个、1个科技企业孵化器(国家级)、3个产业技术创新战略联盟、5个高新技术企业(国家级)、14个创新型企业、21个众创空间(其中5个通过国家备案)、12个星创天地。累计支持建设6个重点领域创新团队、10个中青年科技创新领军人才。

表9　2017年各类学校基本情况

计量单位:所、人

指　标	学校数	在校生数	# 新招生	教职工数	# 专任教师	毕业生数
合　计	601	481 443	142 700	43 038	33 677	127 876
普通高等学校	6	53 758	15 014	4 627	3 295	13 662
成人高等学校	2	21 237	7 944	924	651	7 543
中等职业学校	20	27 169	9 312	1 472	1 029	8 476
普通中学	237	13 8890	47 631	29 231	13 274	45 689
普通小学	55	162 228	27 476		11 458	26 902
幼儿园	281	78 161	35 323	6 784	3 970	25 604

全年新增国家和地方联合工程研究实验室3个，自治区级企业技术中心6家，兵团工程研究中心(实验室)7家。截至年底，累计认定国家地方联合工程研究中心(实验室)19个，国家级企业技术中心5家，自治区级企业技术中心58家，兵团工程研究中心(实验室)18家。

全年专利申请量1757件、比上年增长4.4%；专利授权量982件，下降1.0%，其中发明专利173件，下降14.8%；每万人口发明专利拥有量2.48件，增长22.2%。

年末兵团累计有新疆名牌产品67个，新疆著名商标92件，中国驰名商标12件，“全国质量强市示范城市”1家。全年新批准国家级农业标准化示范区5个，累计国家级农业标准化示范区65个，国家级服务业标准化示范区5个。

年末兵团共有专业文艺团体9个，其中兵团直属4个、师市5个，从业人员600余人。各级拥有博物馆、纪念馆89座、图书馆4座(其中国家三级图书馆1座)和美术馆2座。已建成1个兵团文化中心、13个师市综合文化活动中心、190个团场综合文化活动中心和1230个连队综合文化活动室。年末广播节目综合人口覆盖率为98.7%，电视节目综合人口覆盖率为99.6%，有线电视入户率达到70%。全年出版各类报纸6867.32万份，各类期刊133.75万册，图书311种。

兵团参加第十三届全国运动会，获得2枚银牌，3个第五名，代表团获得“体育道德风尚奖”；参加第十三届全国学生运动会，获得1个第七名，代表团获得“体育道德风尚奖”；参加2017年世界青年射箭锦标赛，获得1枚射箭团体银牌和个人第六名的好成绩。兵团有33所学校被教育部命名为全国校园足球特色学校，第三师图木舒克市被命名为全国青少年校园足球试点县(区)。

十一、卫生和社会服务

年末有各类卫生机构1212个(含营利性卫生机构)，其中，医院211个，门诊部14个，社区卫生服务中心31个，社区卫生服务站86个，诊所、卫生所、医务室752个，疾病预防控制中心(防疫站)99个。各类卫生技术人员26610人，其中，执业医师和执业助理医师9717人，注册护士11847人。医疗卫生机构床位22183张。每千人执业(助理)医师3.24人，每千人注册护士3.95人，每千人拥有床位7.60张。传染病报告发病率(甲乙类传染病)298.47/10万，婴儿死亡率5.12‰。孕产妇死亡率14.02/10万。

年末有养老服务机构154个，床位数18810张，收养人数7986人。年末有城镇社区服务设施771个。

十二、资源、环境和安全生产

全年批准建设用地8.23千公顷(12.35万亩)，供应土地4.87千公顷(7.31万亩)，土地出让合同价款28.09亿元。

年末已建成水库141座，总库容33.65亿立方米。其中，大型水库11座，中型水库31座，小型水库99座。已建成水电站99座、泵站(含节水灌溉首部)3994座、水闸5739座、农村集中式供水工程1291处、机电井27147眼(均为浅层地下水机电井)。堤防建设长度2017.54千米，堤防保护人口138.94万人，保护耕地面积538.31千公顷(807.47万亩)。现有2000亩以上灌区110处，干、支、斗渠道总长度37195.02千米。现有入河湖排污口17个，废污水排放量8717.20万吨。

全年总灌溉面积1505.25千公顷(2257.88万亩)。其中，耕地灌溉面积1132.63千公顷(1698.95万亩)，林地灌溉面积173.05千公顷(259.58万亩)，园地灌溉面积180.97千公顷(271.46万亩)，牧草地灌溉面积18.60千公顷(27.90万亩)。

全年水利工程供水量129.56亿立方米，其中，向农业灌溉供水108.53亿立方米，向工业生产供水2.94亿立方米，向城镇生活供水1.83亿立方米，向乡村生活供水0.69亿立方米，向生态环境供水4.93亿立方米。

全年完成造林面积30.04千公顷(45.06万亩)，其中人工造林21.99千公顷(32.99万亩)。林业重点工程完成造林面积25.78千公顷(38.67万亩)。全年水土流失综合治理面积253.71千公顷(380.57万亩)，新增水土流失综合治理面积25.62千公顷(38.43万亩)。

全年规模以上工业企业综合能源消费量3358.70万吨标准煤，比上年增长6.6%。其中，原煤消费量5529.22万吨，增长4.0%；电力消费量742.51亿千瓦小时，增长5.8%。

全年化学需氧量排放量9.84万吨，比上年下降1.09%；氨氮排放量0.52万吨，下降0.55%；二氧化硫排放量10.24万吨，下降5.68%；氮氧化物排放量9.18万吨，下降5.13%。

年末兵团城镇自来水、燃气、集中供热(含燃气采暖)基本实现全覆盖，污水集中处理率达81.4%，生活垃圾集中处理率达85.2%(其中无害化处理率达55.2%)。

全年农作物受灾面积61.2千公顷(91.8万亩)，其中绝收11.6千公顷(17.4万亩)。全年因灾造成直接经济损失22.52亿元，其中，因洪涝灾害造成直接经济损失3.61亿元，因旱灾造成直接经济损失0.55亿元,因风雹灾害造成直接经济损失10.6亿元,因地震灾害造成7.25亿元。全年全疆共发生5.0级以上地震4次,对兵团造成较大影响的1次,造成直接经济损失10.8亿元。

全年兵团工矿商贸行业领域未发生较大以上生产安全死亡事故,发生一般生产安全死亡事故24起,死亡26人。亿元生产总值生产安全事故死亡人数0.011人。工矿商贸企业就业人员10万人生产安全事故死亡人数2.364人。煤矿百万吨死亡人数为0.111人。

注释:〔1〕本公报中数据均为初步统计数,最终数据以《2018年兵团统计年鉴》为准。部分数据因四舍五入原因,存在着与分项合计不等的情况。

〔2〕生产总值、各产业增加值和人均生产总值绝对数按现价计算,增长速度按不变价格计算。

〔3〕工业战略性新兴产业包括节能环保产业,新一代信息技术产业,生物产业,高端装备制造产业,新能源产业,新材料产业,新能源汽车产业等七大产业中的工业相关行业。

〔4〕高技术制造业包括医药制造业,航空、航天器及设备制造业,电子及通信设备制造业,计算机及办公设备制造业,医疗仪器设备及仪器仪表制造业,信息化学品制造业。

〔5〕装备制造业包括金属制品业,通用设备制造业,专用设备制造业,汽车制造业,铁路、船舶、航空航天和其他运输设备制造业,电气机械和器材制造业,计算机、通信和其他电子设备制造业,仪器仪表制造业。

〔6〕全员劳动生产率为生产总值(以2015年价格计算)与全部就业人员的比率。

〔7〕六大高耗能行业包括石油加工、炼焦和核燃料加工业,化学原料和化学制品制造业,非金属矿物制品业,黑色金属冶炼和压延加工业,有色金属冶炼和压延加工业,电力、热力生产和供应业。

〔8〕本公报中南疆垦区为第一、二、三、十四师,北疆垦区为第四、五、六、七、八、九、十、十一(建工师)、十二、十三师及兵团直属单位。

〔9〕基础设施投资是指建造或购置为社会生产和生活提供基础性、大众性服务的工程和设施的支出。公报中的基础设施投资包括电力、热力、燃气及水生产和供应业,交通运输、邮政业,电信、广播电视和卫星传输服务业,互联网和相关服务业,水利、环境和公共设施管理业投资。

〔10〕民间固定资产投资是指具有集体、私营、个人性质的内资企事业单位以及由其控股(包括绝对控股和相对控股)的企业单位建造或购置固定资产的投资。

〔11〕高技术产业投资包括医药制造、航空航天器及设备制造等六大类高技术制造业投资和信息服务、电子商务服务等九大类高技术服务业投资。

〔12〕房地产业投资除房地产开发投资外,还包括建设单位自建房屋以及物业管理、中介服务和其他房地产投资。

〔13〕贫困发生率是指贫困人口占团场总人口的比重。

资料来源:本公报中户籍人口数据来自兵团公安局;城镇新增就业、登记失业率、外国专家、社会保险、劳动保障监察数据来自兵团人力资源和社会保障局;新疆物价数据来自国家统计局新疆调查总队;财政数据来自兵团财政局;监管企业数据来自兵团国资委;低保补助、医疗救助、优抚、收养、灾害数据来自兵团民政局;农作物精量播种面积、测土配方施肥面积、机械化、良种推广、龙头企业、"三品一标"、农业示范区、造林数据来自兵团农业局(畜牧局、林业局);园区、电信数据来自兵团工业和信息化委员会;公路通达里程数据来自兵团交通运输局;棚户区住房改造、保障房、贫困农户危房改造、城镇水气热普及、污水处理率、生活垃圾集中处理率、地震数据来自兵团住房和城乡建设局;"十件实事"、工程研究中心、企业技术中心等数据来自兵团发展改革委;货物进出口、利用外资、对外承包工程、劳务合作、旅游数据来自兵团商务局(旅游局);招商引资、对口援疆数据来自兵团经协办(援疆办);飞机、飞行时间数据来自兵团航空企业管理局;金融信贷数据来自兵团金融办;农行存贷款数据来自农行兵团分行;扶贫开发数据来自兵团扶贫办;教育数据来自兵团教育局;科技、专利数据来自兵团科技局;名牌、商标、标准化数据来自兵团市场监督管理局;文化、广播、电视、出版和体育数据来自兵团文化体育新闻出版广电局;卫生数据来自兵团卫生计生委;国有建设用地、供应地、土地出让数据来自兵团国土资源局;水利设施、灌溉面积、供水量、水土流失数据来自兵团水利局;主要污染物排放数据来自兵团环境保护局;安全生产数据来自兵团安全生产监督管理局;其他数据均来自兵团统计局和国家统计局兵团调查总队。

Statistical Communiqué of Xinjiang Production & Construction Corps on the 2017 National Economic and Social Development

Statistics Bureau of Xinjiang Production & Construction Corps
The Survey Office of Xinjiang Production & Construction Corps of National Bureau of Statistics

March 26, 2018

In 2017, under strong leadership of the Central Committee of the Communist Party of China with Comrade Xi Jinping as the core and unified leadership of the Committee of the Xinjiang Uygur Autonomous Region of the CPC, all regions and department of Xinjiang Production & Construction Corps (Hereinafter shortened as XPCC) have steadily strengthened their consciousness of the need to maintain political integrity, think in big—picture terms, uphold the leadership core and keep in alignment, implemented the spirit of the 18th National Congress of the CPC and the third, forth, fifth, sixth and seventh plenary sessions of the 18th Central Committee of the CPC, studied and carried out the spirit of the 19th National Congress of the CPC and taken Xi Jinping Thought on Socialism with Chinese Characteristics for a New Era as the guideline. Following the arrangements of the Seventh Congress of XPCC of the CPC, the first and second plenary sessions of the Seventh Congress of XPCC of the CPC, all regions and departments have adhered to the general working guideline of making progress while maintaining stability, stuck to the new development philosophy, taken the improvement of the quality and efficacy of development as the core, promoted balanced economic, political, cultural, social and ecological progress, coordinated the implementation of the four—pronged comprehensive strategy, focused on the supply—side structural reform and coordinated the efforts in stabilizing growth, stimulating reform, adjusting structure, benefiting people's livelihood and fending off risks. As a result, the national economy has maintained the momentum of stable and sound development and exceeded the expectation and the economy and society are moving forward steadily and healthily.

Ⅰ. General Outlook

The gross domestic product (GDP) in 2017 was 233.907 billion yuan, up by 8.0 percent over the previous year. Of this total, the value added of the primary industry was 50.633 billion yuan, up by 7.6 percent, that of the secondary industry was 102.650 billion yuan, up by 4.6 percent, and that of the tertiary industry was 80.624 billion yuan, up by 12.9 percent. The value added of the primary industry accounted for 21.6 percent of the GDP, that of the secondary industry made up 43.9 percent, and that of the tertiary industry represented 34.5 percent. The contribution of the three industries to economy was 20.4 percent, 26.9 percent and 52.7 percent, driving economic growth by 1.6, 2.1 and 4.2 percent. The per capita GDP in 2017 was 80,117 yuan, up by 3.5 percent over the previous year.

By the end of 2017, the total number of the XPCC population reached 3.0053 million, an increase of 171.2 thousand over that at the end of 2016, up by 6.0 percent. Of this total, male population totaled 1.5676 million and female population numbered 1.4377 million. The sex ratio was 109.04(female=100). The year 2017 saw 22.9 thousand births, a crude birth rate of 7.85 per thousand, and 15.9 thousand deaths, or a crude death rate of 5.44 per thousand. The natural growth rate was 2.41 per thousand. The number of population with household registration was 2.3786 million, an increase of 96.3 thousand over that at the end of 2016, up by 4.2 percent. Of this total, urban permanent residents numbered 1.2698 million and rural residents totaled 1.1087 million.

At the end of 2017, the number of employed people in XPCC was 1.4417 million, up by 4.4 percent over the previous year and that of employed people on—the—job in non—private units was 743.2 thousand, up by 5.4 percent over the previous year. The newly increased employed people in urban areas numbered 129.2 thousand, 25.6 thousand more than last year. Of this total, the number of assistance employment with difficulty was 15.6 thousand persons. The registered urban unemployment rate was within 3.0 percent. 130.3 thousand persons (times) received various vocational training. 9 foreign expertise projects were carried out and 158 foreign experts were introduced. The number of the outbound training program was 7 and 103 various persons at different levels were trained.

The consumer prices in Xinjiang went up by 2.2 percent over the previous year. Of this total, the prices for food, tobacco and liquor increased by 2.1 percent. The prices for residential housing went up by 0.4 percent. The prices for means of agricultural production were up by 0.8 percent. The prices for investment in fixed assets increased by 3.5 percent.

The producer prices for manufactured goods increased by

8.3 over the previous year. The purchasing prices for manufactured goods went up by 9.0 percent. The producer prices for farm products increased by 0.8 percent.

Table 1: Changes of Consumer Prices in 2017

Unit: %

Item	Increase over 2016(%)
General level of consumer prices	2.2
Urban	2.4
Rural	1.8
Food, tobacco and liquor	2.1
Grain	0.7
Meats	3.4
Eggs	0.0
Aquatic products	3.4
Fresh vegetables	−4.8
Fresh fruits	3.7
Clothing	1.3
Residence	0.4
Household facilities, articles and services	1.5
Transportation and telecommunication	0.8
Education, culture and recreation	2.7
Health care and medical services	9.6
Miscellaneous goods and services	1.0

The supply—side structural reform was pushed forward solidly. The annual tasks of reducing cement and coal production capacity were accomplished. At the end of 2017, the floor space of commercial buildings for sale was down by 0.2 percent. The asset—liability ratio of the industrial enterprises above the designated size was 65.3 percent, 1.6 percentage point less than that at the end of 2016. In 2017, the cost for per—hundred—yuan turnover of principal activities of the industrial enterprises above the designated size was 80.59 yuan, 4.67 yuan less than that compared with the national level; the expense for per—hundred—yuan turnover of principal activities of the industrial enterprises above the designated size was 0.39 yuan less than last year. In 2017, the fixed assets investment in agriculture(farming, forestry, animal husbandry and fishery), ecological protection and treatment of environmental pollution went up by 12.3 percent, 121.5 percent and 53.2 percent compared with last year.

The growth of new driving forces, new industries and new forms of businesses accelerated. In 2017, the value added of the industrial strategic emerging industries above the designated size grew by 29.4 percent compared with last year, accounting for 8.1 percent of that of the industrial enterprises above the designated size. The value added of the high technology manufacturing industry was up by 16.1 percent over the previous year, accounting for 3.7 percent of that of the industrial enterprises above the designated size. The value added for manufacture of equipment was up by 8.8 percent, accounting for 2.2 percent of that of industrial enterprises above the designated size. In 2017, the investment in high technology industries reached 5.328 billion yuan, an decrease of 10.1 percent over last year, accounting for 2.7 percent of the investment in fixed assets (excluding by rural households). The online retail sales of commodities of enterprises above the designated size grew by 700 percent on year—year basis.

The quality and efficacy of development improved. The general public budget revenue reached 12.96 billion yuan in 2017, up by 21.7 percent over the previous year. Of this total, the taxes collected in 2017 reached 6.776 billion yuan, an increase of 703 million yuan or up by 11.6 percent. At the end of 2017, the total assets of enterprises supervised by State—owned Assets Supervision and Administration Commissions of XPCC and divisions were 447.419 billion yuan, an increase of 10.4 percent over the previous year. Owners' equity was 107.99 billion yuan, up by 9.9 percent. The operation revenue was 196.085 billion yuan, up by 12.3 percent. The total profit volume was 5.531 billion yuan, up by 132.2 percent. The profits made by the industrial enterprises above the designated size in 2017 were 21.878 billion yuan, an increase of 8.2 percent over the previous year. By ownership, the profits of state—holding enterprises were up by 80.1 percent; those of share—holding enterprises up by 5.2 percent; those of the enterprises by foreign investors and investors from Hong Kong, Macao and Taiwan up by 148.9 percent; and those of private enterprises down by 0.9 percent. In terms of different sectors, the profit of mining was up by 100 percent compared with last year; those of manufacturing up by 12.3 percent; those of the production and supply of electricity, heat power, gas and water down by 12.4 percent. The overall labor productivity was 161,324 yuan per person in 2017, an increase of 4.9 percent compared with that in 2016.

Ⅱ. Agriculture

In 2017, the sown area of crops was 1,362.77 thousand hectares (20.44151 million mu), down by 0.7 percent over the previous year. Of this total, the sown area of grain was 284.24 thousand hectares (4.2636 million mu), down by 14.3 percent; the sown area of cotton was 686.93 thousand hectares (10.304 million mu), up by 10.6 percent; the sown area of oil—bearing crops was 56.82 thousand hectares (0.8524 million mu), down by 11.8 percent; the sown area of beetroot crop was 23.73 thousand hectares (0.356 million mu), down by 2.7 percent; and the sown area of vegetables (including table gourds) was 87.42 thousand hectares (1.311 million mu), down by 2.9 percent.

The precision and semi—precision sown area of crops was 955.6 thousand hectares (14.334 million mu), up by 6.0 percent over the previous year. Of this total, the precision sown area of cotton was 612.7 thousand hectares (9.1905 million mu), up by 5.0 percent.

The total output of grain in 2017 was 2.4855 million tons, down by 8.4 percent over the previous year; that of cotton was 1.6788 million tons, up by 12.2 percent; that of oil—bearing crops was 209.2 thousand tons, down by 10.7 percent; that of beetroot was 1.9846 million tons, down by 4.7 percent; and that of vegetable was 6.7054 million tons, down by 0.7 percent, of which that of industrial tomato was 3.4285 million tons, down by 2.5 percent.

At the end of 2017, the number of livestock on hand was 7.7258 million heads, up by 1.1 percent over the previous year. Of this total, the number of cattle was 507.7 thousand heads, up by 6.7 percent; that of pig was 1.6747 million heads, up by 11.9 percent; that of sheep was 5.4849 million heads, down by 2.3 percent. The number of slaughtered livestock was 8.8271 million heads, up by 6.0 percent. The total output of meat in 2017 reached 443.8 thousand tons, up by 7.9 percent. The output of wool was 19.9 thousand tons, up by 4.4 percent. The output of eggs was 109.2 thousand tons, up by 15.9 percent. The production of milk was 681.4 thousand tons, up by 8.3 percent.

The total output of fruits in 2017 was 3.9216 million tons, up by 7.4 percent over the previous year. Of this total, the output of jujube was 1.8173 million tons, up by 8.6 percent; that of grape was 794.3 thousand tons, down by 0.9 percent; that of fragrant pear was 406.3 thousand tons, up by 15.0 percent; that of apple was 630.8 thousand tons, up by 14.1 percent; and that of walnut was 28.1 thousand tons, up by 6.4 percent.

The total output of aquatic products was 53.9 thousand tons, up by 4.7 percent over the previous year.

The effectively irrigated area was 1,258.22 thousand hectares (18.733 million mu), up by 2.5 percent over the previous year. Of this total, the area for high and new technology water—saving irrigation was 1,041.99 thousand hectares (15.6299 million mu), up by 3.0 percent.

The comprehensive mechanization rate in crop farming was 94 percent. There were 2,221 sets of cotton pickers. The area of cotton harvested by machines was 530 thousand hectares (7.95 million mu). The proportion of the cotton area harvested by machines was 80.0 percent. The mechanization level in animal husbandry was 68.0 percent.

The number of various standardization scale raising farms which were newly built, renovated and expanded was 112.The cumulative number of national standardization demonstration farms up to the national standard was 88. The extension coverage rate of improved livestock and poultry breeds reached 76.0 percent. The manure resource utilization rate in livestock raising was 69.0 percent.

At the end of 2017, the number of key leading enterprises of the agricultural industrialization was 128 at national and provincial levels, of which 15 were at the national level and 113 at the XPCC level. The number of enterprises with sales income of over 10 billion yuan was 2. The number of enterprises with sales income of over 3 billion yuan was 6. The number of enterprises with sales income of over 1 billion yuan was 7. There were 2 national agricultural industrialization demonstration bases, 4 national modern agricultural demonstration districts, 23 national pollution—free agricultural demonstration bases and agricultural standardization demonstration farms, and 35 national OTOP demonstration farms.

Ⅲ. Industry and Construction

In 2017, the total value added of the industrial sector was 72.598 billion yuan, up by 6.4 percent over the previous year. The value added of industrial enterprises above the designated size increased by 6.7 percent. Of the industrial enterprises above the designated size, in terms of ownership, the value added of the state—holding enterprises grew by 8.7 percent, that of the share—holding enterprises up by 5.3 percent, that of the enterprises by foreign investors and investors from Hong Kong, Macao and Taiwan up by 34.1 percent and that of private enterprises up by 5.6 percent. In terms of sectors, the value added of the mining industry increased by 9.7 percent, that of manufacturing up by 5.3 percent, that of the production and supply of electricity, heat power, gas and water up by 12.7 percent. Analyzed by light and heavy industries, the growth of the light industry was 4.5 percent and that of the heavy industry was 8.0 percent.

In 2017, of the industrial enterprises above the designated size, the value added for the mining and washing of coal industry was up by 4.2 percent over the previous year; for processing of food from agricultural products up by 8.0 percent; for food manufacturing up by 2.3 percent; for liquor, beverage and refined tea manufacturing down by 0.9 percent; for textile industry up by 9.4 percent; for manufacture of raw chemical materials and chemical products up by 4.1 percent; for manufacture of non—metallic mineral products up by 7.8 percent; for smelting and pressing of ferrous metals up by 89.9 percent; for smelting and pressing of non—ferrous metals up by 2.8 percent; and for production and supply of electric power and heat power up by 12.8 percent. The value added for the six major high energy consuming industries was up by 7.3 percent, accounting for 58.3 percent of that of industrial enterprises above the designated size.

Table 2: Output of Major Industrial Products and Their Growth Rates in 2017

Product	Unit	Output	Increase over 2016 (%)
Coal	10000 tons	900.69	—17.0
Electricity	100 million kilowatt—hours	798.10	6.2
of which: Thermal power	100 million kilowatt—hours	722.24	3.8
Hydropower	100 million kilowatt—hours	15.98	—5.8
Solar power	100 million kilowatt—hours	35.99	198.4
Refined edible plant oil	10000 tons	71.67	—17.8
Dairy product	10000 tons	24.08	20.8
Tomato paste	10000 tons	60.81	2.9
Beverage alcohol	10000 liters	20.21	—8.6
Soft beverage	10000 tons	52.49	—39.8
Yarn	10000 tons	48.88	20.0
Cloth	10000 meters	1.50	30.4
Machine—made paper and paper board	10000 tons	7.32	—43.8
NPK chemical fertilizer for agricultural use(100 percent equivalent)	10000 tons	49.51	—1.7
The primary forms of plastics	10000 tons	135.21	—2.8
Plastic product	10000 tons	88.32	13.4
Portland cement clinker	10000 tons	836.45	2.7
Cement	10000 tons	1 269.99	2.8
Steel material	10000 tons	155.90	94.2
Crude aluminum	10000 tons	283.60	2.7

By the end of 2017, the installed power generation capacity above the designated size was 17.24 million kilowatts, up by 10.5 percent over that at the end of 2016, among which the installed thermal power generation capacity was 13.54 million kilowatts, up by 7.0 percent; the installed hydropower generation capacity was 0.34 million kilowatts, down by 5.3 percent; The installed grid—connected wind power generation capacity was 1.24 million kilowatts, up by 66.6 percent and the installed grid—connected solar power generation capacity was 12.12 million kilowatts, an increase of 15.1 percent.

By the end of 2017, the number of various parks was 32, of which there were 4 at the national level, 2 national sub—parks, 3 industrial parks at the provincial level and 22 industrial parks at the level of XPCC.

In 2017, the value added of construction enterprises was 30.073 billion yuan, up by 0.6 percent over the previous year. The total output value of construction enterprises with qualification was 125.007 billion yuan, up by 0.6 percent over the previous year. The profits made by construction enterprises qualified for general contracts and specialized contracts reached 1.879 billion yuan, up by 12.1 percent, of which the profits made by state—holding enterprises were 1.227 billion yuan, up by 18.8 percent. The contract value of various construction enterprises (including overseas projects made by the Eleventh Division) was 190.117 billion yuan, up by 2.4 percent over the previous year. The floor space of buildings under construction was 50.8565 million square meters, down by 4.3 percent.

Ⅳ. Investment in Fixed Assets

The total investment in fixed assets (excluding by rural households) in 2017 was 196.615 billion yuan, up by 14.2 percent over the previous year. Of the total investment, the investment in the primary industry was 20.086 billion yuan, up by 12.3 percent; that in the secondary industry was 72.438 billion yuan, up by 11.7 percent; and that in the tertiary industry was 104.091 billion yuan, up by 16.5 percent. The proportion of the three industries was 10.4:37.7:51.9. By regions, the investment in southern XPCC was 56.556 billion yuan, up by 23.0 percent; and in northern XPCC 140.059 billion yuan, up by 11.0 percent. The private investment in fixed assets was 78.329 billion yuan, up 21.1 percent, accounting for 39.8 percent of the total investment in fixed assets (excluding by rural households). The investment in infrastructure was 77.447 billion yuan, up by 13.3 percent, accounting for 39.4 percent of the total investment in fixed assets (excluding by rural households). The investment in the six major high energy consuming industries was 39.171 billion yuan, down by 1.2 percent, accounting for 19.9 of the total investment in fixed assets (excluding by rural households).

Table 3: Fixed Assets Investment
(Excluding by Rural Households) and Its Growth Rates in 2017

Unit: 100 million yuan

Item	Value	Increase over 2016(%)
Investment in fixed assets	1966.15	14.2
Real estate investment	155.02	−15.6
Classified by ownership		
State—owned	908.03	8.7
Private—owned	541.12	39.2
Other	517.00	4.1
Classified by industry		
The primary industry	200.86	12.3
The secondary industry	724.38	11.7
The tertiary industry	1040.91	16.5

In 2017, the completed investment in industry was 72.365 billion yuan, up by 15.5 percent over the previous year. Of this total, the completed investment in manufacturing was 51.8 billion yuan, up by 49.8 percent; that in production and supply of electricity, heat power, gas and water was 19.938 billion yuan, down by 28.1 percent. The completed investment in transport, storage and post was 29.848 billion yuan, up by 104.0 percent over the previous.

In 2017, the investment in real estate development was 15.502 billion yuan, down by 15.6 percent over the previous year. The floor space of sales of commercial buildings was 3.3344 million square meters, down by 9.4 percent. Of this total, the floor space of residential buildings was 1.3875 million square meters, up by 2.6 percent; that of commercial buildings at the year—end for sale was 2.2534 million square meters, down by 0.2 percent. The sale value of commercial buildings was 14.876 billion yuan, down by 11.3 percent.

Table 4: Fixed Assets Investment
(Excluding by Rural Households) and Its Growth by Sector in 2017

Unit: 100 million yuan

Sector	Value	Increase over 2016 (%)
Total	1966.15	14.2
Agriculture, forestry, animal husbandry and fishery	200.86	12.3
Mining	6.28	97.1
Manufacturing	518.00	49.8
Processing of food from agricultural products	56.49	129.3
Manufacture of foods	15.28	15.9
Manufacture of alcohol, beverage and refined tea	10.30	37.7
Textile industry	84.98	15.6
Processing of petroleum, coking and nuclear fuel	27.60	48.9
Manufacture of raw chemical materials and chemical products	117.80	33.9
Manufacture of non—metallic mineral products	59.48	197.7
Smelting and pressing of ferrous metals	12.45	2.5
Smelting and pressing of non—ferrous metals	14.94	−24.7
Production and supply of electricity, gas and water	199.38	−28.1
Construction	0.73	−96.7
Wholesale and retail trade	34.85	1.2
Transport, storage and post	298.48	104.0
Lodging and catering services	16.00	181.9
Information transmission, computer services and software	18.61	46.2
Banking	1.45	458.5
Real estate	244.40	−20.6
Leasing and business services	36.16	65.5
Scientific research and technical service	6.01	−59.6
Water conservancy, environment and public facilities management	258.01	4.3
Services to households, maintenance and other services	6.07	130.5
Education	31.82	10.1
Health and social welfare	24.24	19.9
Culture, sports and entertainment	31.14	16.4
Public management, social security and social organization	33.66	41.2

In 2017, 40 thousand housing units were started to be built in rundown urban areas. The number of housing units rebuilt under the urban affordable housing projects was 20 thousand, and that of dilapidated houses of 1.5 thousand poverty—stricken households were rebuilt and renovated.

The completed investment in the Ten Benefit Things which were mainly people's livelihood building and condition improvement for production and service facilities was 42.045 billion yuan. Of this total, the investment in capital construction projects was 20.933 billion yuan and that in financial aid was 21.113 billion yuan.

The total construction fund of investment in fixed assets was 17.1138 billion yuan, up by 5.7 percent over the previous year. Of this total, the fund source in 2017 was 164.772 billion yuan, up by 6.4 percent. Among which, the internal budgetary fund from the State was 19.392 billion yuan, down by 25.4 percent; the domestic loan was 12.694 billion yuan, up by 39.0 percent; the self—raised fund was 113.261 billion yuan, up by 7.8 percent; and other fund was 19.298 billion yuan, up by 34.1 percent.

The newly increased fixed assets were 161.411 billion yuan, up by 33.4 percent over the previous year. Main newly increased production capacities and efficiency through fixed assets investment were: 1.51 million tons of raw coal yearly, one thousand tons of plastic resin and copolymer, 8 thousand tons of white spirit, 10 thousand tons of other liquor, 943.4 thousand spindles of cotton yarns, 1.641 million kilowatts of installed generating, 521.95 kilometers of electricity transmission line, 296.9 thousand tons of urban water supply daily, 67.8 thousand tons of urban sewage treatment daily, 878.75 kilometers of newly constructed highway, 1055.1 kilometers of renovated and expanded highway.

Ⅴ. Domestic Trade

In 2017, the total wholesale and retail sales of consumer goods reached 382.613 billion yuan, a growth of 14.5 percent over the previous year.

The total retail sales of consumer goods reached 70.837 billion yuan, a growth of 12.0 percent over the previous year. An analysis on different areas showed that the retail sales of consumer goods in urban areas stood at 63.008 billion yuan, up by 11.7 percent, and that in rural areas reached 7.829 billion yuan, up by 14.6 percent. Grouped by consumption patterns, the retail sales of catering industry was 13.375 billion yuan, up by 22.7 percent; and that of commodities was 57.462 billion yuan, up by 9.8 percent.

Of the total retail sales of commodities by enterprises above the designated size, the year—on—year growth of sales for grain, oil, food was up by 17.2 percent, for beverage up 7.1 percent, for tobacco and liquor up by 6.1 percent, for clothes, shoes, hats and textiles up by 5.8 percent, for cosmetics up by 3.7 percent, for gold, silver and jewelry down by 13.1 percent, for daily necessities up by 11.0 percent, for household appliances and audio—video equipments up by 19.0 percent, for traditional Chinese and western medicines up by 14.8 percent, for cultural and office appliances up by 1.7 percent, for furniture up by 7.8 percent, for telecommunication equipments up by 80.6 percent, for building and decoration materials up by 19.9 percent, for motor vehicles down by 3.5 percent, and for petroleum and petroleum products up by 10.0 percent,

Ⅵ. Foreign Economic Relations

The total value of imports and exports of goods in 2017 reached 7.59 billion US dollars, up by 6.2 percent over the previous year. Of this total, the value of goods exported was 6.633 billion US dollars, down by 0.3 percent; and the value of goods imported was 957 million US dollars, up by 94.4 percent. Of the value of goods exported, the value of products manufactured in XPCC was 780 million US dollars, up by 20.0 percent. The balance of imports and exports (exports minus imports) was 5.676 billion US dollars.

The foreign capital actually utilized for the year 2017 was 410 million US dollars, up by 23.5 percent over the previous year. The year 2017 witnessed the establishment of 24 enterprises with foreign investment. The total investment was 1.1 billion US dollars with a foreign contracted capital of 400 million US dollars.

In 2017, the overseas direct investment in non—financial sector was 87.97 million US dollars, up by 11.6 percent over the previous year. The accomplished business revenue through contracted overseas engineering projects and overseas labor contracts was 680 million US dollars, up by 1.6 percent over the previous year. The number of labor forces sent abroad through the overseas labor contracts was 491 persons, a decrease of 196 persons.

Table 5: Total Value of Import and Export of Goods and the Growth Rates in 2017

Item	Value (100 million US dollars)	Increase over 2016 (%)
Total value of import and export of goods	75.90	6.2
Exports	66.33	−0.3
Of which: General trade	9.44	−37.4
Small border trade	54.79	13.3
Imports	9.57	94.4
Of which: General trade	7.88	122.2
Small border trade	1.22	12.4
Trade surplus (exports minus imports)	56.76	—

3,095 projects were attracted. The paid—in capital was 175.709 billion yuan, up by 42.4 percent over the previous year. Of this total, the number of newly started projects was 2,284, with paid—in capital of 109.809 billion yuan; that of renewed projects was 811, with paid—in capital of 65.9 billion yuan. Among the various investment attraction projects, the number of projects of the primary industry was 519, with the paid—in capital of 11.775 billion yuan, up by 93.5 percent; that of the secondary industry was 1,514, with the paid—in capital of 97.133 billion yuan, up by 39.3 percent; that of the tertiary industry was 1,062, with the paid—in capital of 66.801 billion yuan, up by 39.4 percent.The number of industrial cooperation projects with 19 pair—assisting provinces and municipalities was 609, with a total investment capital of 269.094 billion yuan. The paid—in capital was 69.191 billion yuan, accounting for 39.4 percent of the total paid—in capital in XPCC.

Ⅶ. Transportation and Tourism

The freight traffic by highway reached 681 million tons, up by 17.0 percent over the previous year, and the freight flows were 86.689 billion ton—kilometers, up by 24.9 percent. The passenger traffic reached 250 million persons, up by 10.1 percent, and the passenger flows were 14.274 billion person—kilometers, up by 9.9 percent.

Table 6: Highway Transportation Operation in 2017

Item	Unit	Value	Increase over 2016 (%)
Freight Traffic	100 million tons	6.81	17.0
Individual	100 million tons	5.57	26.9
Freight flows	100 million ton—kms	866.89	24.9
Individual	100 million ton—kms	715.69	30.3
Passenger traffic	100 million persons	2.50	10.1
Individual	100 million persons	1.98	15.1
Passenger flows	100 million person—kms	142.74	9.9
Individual	100 million person—kms	113.71	19.8
Operation income	100 million yuan	324.81	20.7
Individual net income	100 million yuan	109.44	18.5

By the end of 2017, the total number of motor vehicles for civilian use reached 309.6 thousand, up by 7.4 percent over the previous year. Of this total, the number of passenger vehicles stood at 219.1 thousand, up by 13.3 percent; that of load—carrying vehicles was 59.8 thousand, down by 4.6 percent; and that of other vehicles was 30.6 thousand, down by 4.1 percent. The total number cars for civilian use totaled 181.1 thousand, up by 15.0 percent.

The highway mileage in XPCC reached 34,727 kilometers by the end of 2017. Of this total, the mileage at the first grade was 72.5 kilometers, that at the second grade was 3,879.4 kilometers, that at the third grade was 5,278.2 kilometers, and that at the fourth grade was 12,850 kilometers. The newly renovated highway mileage at the second grade or above stood at 447.8 kilometers and the renovated and expanded highway mileage access to towns and villages numbered 437 kilometers.

The number of airplanes reached 42 at the end of 2017. The flying time totaled 4,334 hours, with 7,561 sorties. Of this total, the flying time for agriculture, forestry and animal husbandry stood at 2,351 hours, with the operational land area of 75 thousand hectares(1.125 million mu), and that for industry numbered 739 hours.

By the end of 2017, the optical—fiber network coverage was 99.28 percent in urban areas of XPCC and the urban household optical network coverage rate was 99.4 percent. The optical—fiber network coverage rate was 98 percent in rural areas. The optical—fiber broadband users accounted for 95 percent. The 4G network covered all divisions and regiments, and 65 percent of companies..

The number of tourist enterprises reached 381 by the end of 2017, of which there were 141 travel agencies, 62 star—rated hotels, 55 tourist scenic spots at the national level, 117 star—rated farm stays, and 6 tourist corporations. There was one national excellent tourist city, 9 national famous tourist towns with characteristic landscapes, 37 famous tourist farms (towns) with characteristic landscapes at the XPCC level, 3 national red tourist classic scenic spots, 3 national tourist demonstration counties of leisure agriculture and village tourism, 8 national demonstration spots of leisure agriculture and village tourism, and 12 national tourist demonstration spots of industry and agriculture. Tourist guides numbered 3,670.

The year 2017 registered 18.92 million tourists, up by 33 percent over the previous year. The total revenue from tourism totaled 10.18 billion yuan, up by 37.6 percent. Among the total tourists, the number of inbound tourists totaled 209 thousand, an increase of 10 percent, that of domestic tourists was 18.711 million, up by 33 percent. The revenue from domestic tourism totaled 9.98 billion yuan, up 37.4 percent; earnings from international tourism topped 32 million US dollars, up by 10.9 percent. The number of directly employed people in tourism was 50 thousand, up by 11.1 percent and that indirectly employed people was 200 thousand, up by 11.1 percent.

Ⅷ. Financial Intermediation

In 2017, loans to XPCC from banking and financial institutions stationed in Xinjiang reached 254.568 billion yuan, an increase of 22.3 percent over the previous year.

Savings deposit in Renminbi and foreign currencies in all of terms of the Agricultural Bank of China of XPCC totaled 126.274 billion yuan at the end of 2017, up by 9.6 percent over the beginning of 2017. Of this total, individual savings deposit stood at 59.58 billion yuan, up by 2.9 percent and that of units reached 66.694 billion yuan, up by 16.4 percent. Loans in all terms by the end of 2017 reached 65.816 billion yuan, up by 19.8 percent over the beginning of 2017.

Funds raised directly in 2017 by 17 enterprises amounted to 25.401 billion yuan. Of this total, the capital raised through the bond market totaled 20.98 billion yuan and the listed companies financed 4.421 billion yuan through the capital market. Among financing through the bond market, the ultra short — term financing reached 9.8 billion yuan, the short—term financing stood at 4.0 billion yuan, the medium—term notes totaled 3.0 billion yuan, corporate bonds numbered 3.3 billion yuan, and other bonds topped 880 million yuan. Of funds raised by listed companies through the capital market, the financing through targeted placement raised 2.672 billion yuan, that through exchangeable asset — backed securities totaled 749 million yuan, and that through issuing convertible bonds reached 1.0 billion yuan.

Ⅸ. Living Conditions and Social Security

In 2017, the per capita disposable income of households in XPCC was 29,430 yuan, an increase of 8.1 percent over the previous year, or a real increase of 5.8 percent when price factors were deducted. In terms of permanent residence, the per capita net income of urban households was 36,730 yuan, up by 7.7 percent over the previous year, or a real growth of 5.2 percent when price factors were deducted. The per capita net income of rural households was 17,786 yuan, up by 8.4 percent over the previous year, or a real growth of 6.5 percent when price factors were deducted.

The per capita consumption expenditure was 18, 908 yuan, down by 1.3 percent over the previous year. In terms of permanent residence, the per capita consumption of urban households was 21,827 yuan, down by 2.4 percent over the previous year. The per capita consumption of rural households was 14,252 yuan, up by 0.9 percent over previous year. The Engel's Coefficient was 27.3 percent, 2.0 percentage point less than the national average, with that of urban and rural households standing at 27.5 percent and 26.6 percent respectively.

The total wages of workers on—the—job in non—private units were 49.354 billion yuan, up by 6.7 percent over the previous year. The annual per capita wage of workers on—the—job in non—private units was 58,4645 yuan, an increase of 2,119 yuan over the previous year, up by 3.8 percent.

According to the rural poverty line of annual per capita income of 2,300 yuan (at 2010 constant prices), the population in poverty in rural areas numbered 21.9 thousand by the end of 2017, 29.6 thousand less than that at the end of 2016. The incidence of poverty was 1.2 percent, 1.6 percentage points lower than that in last year. 10 poverty—stricken regiments shook off poverty. The poverty alleviation fund of 1.021 billion yuan was offered to poverty—stricken households in the registered file cards through the financial poverty alleviation platform.

By the end of 2017, a total of 1.851 million people participated in basic pension program, a year—on—year increase of 79 thousand, of whom, 1.682 million people participated in urban basic pension program for staff and workers, a year—on—year increase of 65 thousand, and 169 thousand people participated in basic pension program for urban and rural residents, a year—on—year increase of 14 thousand. A total of 2.45 million people participated in basic health insurance program, an increase of 93 thousand, of whom, 1.353 million people participated in basic health insurance program for staff and workers, a year—on—year increase of 42 thousand, and 1.097 million people participated in basic health insurance program for urban residents, a year—year increase of 51 thousand. A total of 0.666 million people participated in unemployment insurance programs, a year— year decrease of 13 thousand. The number of people receiving unemployment insurance payment stood at 8.6 thousand at the end of 2017. A total of 0.8 million people participated in work accident insurance, an increase of 54 thousand. A total of 0.679 million people participated in maternity insurance programs, an increase of 9 thousand. Minimum subsistence allowances totaled 343 million yuan. Minimum living allowances were granted to 79.9 thousand residents. The temporary relief and assistance fund of 107 million yuan was given out and 178 thousand person—times received the temporary relief and assistance. The relief and assistance fund of 13.16 million yuan for people living in extreme poverty was disbursed. 1,363 thousand people living in extreme poverty received relief and assistance. The funds for medical assistance amounted to 98.51 million yuan. The funds for medical assistance were granted to 129 thousand persons. National subsidies and allowances were provided to 2,593 entitled people.

913 cases of labor dispute were received by arbitration institutions at all levels and 910 cases were settled, with a settlement rate of 99.67 percent. 696 cases of labor security supervision were received and 682 cases were settled, with a settlement rate of 97.99 percent. 13 cases of administrative reconsideration were received and 13 cases were settled, with a settlement rate of 100 percent.

Ⅹ. Education, Science & Technology and Culture & Sports

By the end of 2017, there were 601 various schools. Enrollment of various schools was 481.4 thousand students with 43.0 thousand teaching staff and workers. The post—graduate education enrollment was 4.3 thousand students with 1.6 thousand new students and 1.1 thousand graduates. The general tertiary education enrollment was 49.5 thousand students with 13.4 thousand new students and 12.5 thousand graduates. Adult college education enrollment was 21.2 thousand thousand students with 7.9 thousand new students and 7.5 thousand graduates. Vocational secondary schools had 27.2 thousand enrolled students, including 9.3 thousand new entrants, and 8.5 thousand graduates. General senior secondary schools had 54.9 thousand enrolled students, including 18.3 thousand new entrants, and 17.9 thousand graduates. Students enrolled in junior secondary schools totaled 84.0 thousand, including 29.4 thousand new entrants, and 27.8 thousand graduates. The primary education enrollment was 162.2 thousand students with 2.75 thousand new entrants and 26.9 thousand graduates. Kindergartens accommodated 78.2 thousand children, including 35.3 thousand new entrants, and 25.6 thousand graduates. Net enrollment rate of primary school—age children was 100 percent and that of junior secondary school—age people reached 99.91 percent. The number of students graduating from compulsory education reached 98.42 percent of the total enrollment and the gross enrollment rate in senior high schools reached 92.68 percent. In primary and secondary schools and kindergartens where the native language of the ethnic minorities were not the Chinese language, the coverage rate of students who were taught in the national common language and characters reached 98.53 percent, that of primary and secondary schools was 97.89 percent, and that of preschool education was up to 100 percent. The average education duration of labor force (16—65 years old) was 11.47 years.

By the end of 2017, the number of scientific research and technological development bodies was 20. 133 projects of various national science and technology programs were approved and implemented, with a paid—in national fund of 81 million yuan. 196 projects of science and technology at the level of XPCC were arranged, with an appropriation of 178 million yuan, up by 12.6 percent over the previous year.

In 2017, there were 5 engineering technical research centers, one national science and technology business incubator, 3 industrial technology alliances, 5 national high—tech enterprises, 14 innovative enterprises, 21 mass innovation entrepreneurship spaces (including 5 which were reviewed and were registered by the Ministry of Science and Technology), 12 rural mass innovation and entrepreneurship spaces. 6 innovation teams in key fields and 10 young and middle—aged scientific and technological innovation leaders were supported.

In 2017, 3 national and local joint engineering research

laboratories, 6 enterprise technical centers at the provincial level and 7 engineering research centers (laboratories) at XPCC level were newly added. By the end of 2017, there were altogether 19 national and local joint engineering research centers (laboratories), 5 enterprise technical centers at the national level, and 58 enterprise technical centers at the provincial level, and 16 engineering research centers (laboratories) at XPCC level.

1,757 patent applications were accepted, up by 4.4 percent over the previous year, and a total of 982 patents were authorized, down by 1.0 percent, of which 173 were invention patents, down by 14.8 percent. The number of invention patents per 10,000 people was 2.48, up by 22.2 percent.

At the end of 2017, there were 67 famous brand products and 92 famous trademarks in Xinjiang, 12 well — known trademarks in China, and one Demonstration City of National Quality—Driven City. 5 national agricultural standardization demonstration zones were newly approved. There were 65 national agricultural standardization demonstration zones and 5 national service standardization demonstration zones in total.

Table 7: Basic statistics of Various Types of Schools in 2017

Unit: set, person

Item	School	Enrollment	New entrants	Teachers and staff	Full-time teachers	Graduates
Total	601	481 443	142 700	43 038	33 677	127 876
Regular institution of higher education	6	53 758	15 014	4 627	3 295	13 662
Adult institution of higher education	2	21 237	7 944	924	651	7 543
Secondary vocational school	20	27 169	9 312	1 472	1 029	8 476
General secondary school	237	138 890	47 631		13 274	45 689
General primary school	55	162 228	27 476	29 231	11 458	26 902
Kindergarten	281	78 161	35 323	6 784	3 970	25 604

At the end of 2017, there were 9 professional art—performing groups, including 4 directly under XPCC and 5 at the level of divisions or cities, with more than 600 employees. There were 89 museums and memorials, 4 libraries (including one at the third national class), and 2 art gallery. There was one XPCC' s culture center, 13 divisional integrated culture activity centers, 190 integrated culture activity centers at the regiment level, and 1,230 integrated culture rooms at the village level. Radio broadcasting and television broadcasting coverage rates were 98.7 percent and 99.6 percent respectively. Cable television coverage rate was 70 percent. 68.6732 million copies of various newspapers and 1.3375 million copies of various magazines were issued, and 311 kinds of books were published.

In 2017, XPCC participated in the Thirteenth National Games and won 2 silver medals and 3 fifth places. The delegation won the Sportsmanship Award. It won one seventh place and the Sportsmanship Award in the Thirteenth National Students Games. XPCC delegation attended the 2017 World Youth Archery Championship and won one team silver medal and one sixth place. 33 primary and secondary schools of XPCC were named the National Campus Football Specialist School by the Ministry of Education. Tumushuke city was named the National Juvenile Campus Football Pilot County (District)

Ⅺ. Public Health and Social Services

By the end of 2017, there were 1,212 various medical and health institutions (including profit — making institutions), including 211 hospitals, 14 outpatients, 31 community service centers, 86 community health service stations, 752 clinics, 99 centers (stations) for disease prevention and control. There were various 26,610 health workers, including 9,717 practicing doctors and assistant practicing doctors and 11,847 registered nurses. The medical and health institutions possessed 22,183 beds. The number of practicing doctors and assistant practicing doctors per one thousand people was 3.24, that of registered nurses per one thousand was 3.95, and that of beds per one thousand people was 7.24. Reported annual incidence of A or B infectious diseases were 298.47 per 100 thousand. Infant mortality rate was 5.12 per thousand and pregnant women death rate was 14.02 per 100 thousand.

By the end of 2017, there were altogether 154 elder—caring organizations, with 18,810 beds and 7,986 thousand persons adopted. The number of urban community service facilities reached 771.

Ⅻ. Resources, Environment and Work Safety

In 2017, 8.23thousand hectares (123.5 thousand mu) of land for construction use were approved and the land supply was 4.87 thousand hectares (73.1 thousand mu). The contract value of land transfer was 2.809 billion yuan.

By the end of 2017, there were 141 reservoirs, with a total capacity of 3.365 billion cubic meters. Of this total, there were 11 large reservoirs, 31 medium — sized reservoirs, and 99 small — sized reservoirs. There were 99 hydropower stations, 3,994 pump stations (including head controls of efficient irrigation), 5,739 sluices, 1,291 rural centralized water supply projects and 27,147 electrical wells (all shallow groundwater electromechanical wells). The length of the embankment construction totaled 2,017.54 kilometers, protecting 1.3894 million people and 538.31 thousand hectares (8.0747 million mu) of the cultivated land. There were 110 irrigation districts with over 2 thousand mu, with 37,195.02 kilometers of irrigation channel length. There were 17 sewage outlets to rivers and lakes, with the waste water discharge of 87.172 million tons.

The total irrigation area was 1,505.25 thousand hectares (22.5788 million mu), of which that for cultivated land was 1,132.63 thousand hectares (16.9895 million mu), for woodland 173.05 thousand hectares (2.5958 million mu), for horticulture 180.97 thousand hectares (2.7164 million mu), and for forage 18.60 thousand hectares (279 thousand mu).

The total water consumption reached 12.956 billion cubic meters. Of this total, water consumption for agricultural use was 10.853 billion cubic meters; for industrial use 294 million cubic meters; for urban living purposes 183 million cubic meters; for rural living purposes 69 million cubic meters; and for ecological water supplement 493 million cubic meters.

In 2017, a total of 30.04 thousand hectares (450.6 thousand mu) of forests were planted, of which 21.99 thousand hectares (329.9 thousand mu) were afforested by manpower. 25.78 thousand hectares (386.7 thousand mu) of forest were afforested through key projects of tree planting. A total of 253.71 thousand hectares (3.8057 million mu) of eroded land was controlled comprehensively. A total of 25.62 thousand hectares (384.3 thousand mu) of eroded land was put under treatment programs.

In 2017, the comprehensive energy consumption by industrial enterprises above the designated size amounted to 33.587 million tons of standard coal equivalent, up 6.6 percent over the previous year. Of this total, the consumption of coal totaled 55.2922 million tons, up 4.0 percent; and electric power 74.251 billion kilowatt—hours, up 5.8 percent.

The COD pollution emission was 98.4 thousand tons, down 1.09 percent over the previous year; ammonia nitrogen emission was 5.2 thousand tons, down 0.55 percent; sulfur dioxide emission was 102.4 thousand tons, down 5.68 percent; and nitrogen oxide emission was 91.8 thousand tons, down 5.13 percent.

At the end of 2017, the coverage rate of tap water, natural gas and central heating systems (including gas—fired system) was basically 100 percent in cities and towns. Sewage treatment rate was 81.4 percent. The centralized treatment rate of solid waste was 85.2 percent (of which harmless treatment rate was 55.2 percent).

In 2017, natural disasters hit 61.2 thousand hectares (918 thousand mu) of crops, of which 11.6 thousand hectares (174 thousand mu) of crops were demolished. Natural disasters caused a direct economic loss of 2.252 billion yuan. Of this total, flood and waterlog caused a direct economic loss of 361 million yuan, drought caused a direct economic loss of 55 million yuan, hailstorms made a total direct economic loss of 1.06 billion yuan, and earthquake caused a direct economic loss of 725 million yuan. Regions under jurisdiction of XPCC recorded 4 earthquakes with magnitude 5 and over, one of which caused a bigger impact, causing a direct economic loss of 1.08 billion yuan.

There were not bigger death accidents in industrial, mining and trade sectors, There were 24 work accidents, with 26 death tolls. The death toll from work accidents every 100 million yuan worth of GDP was 0.011 people. Work accidents in industrial, mining and trade enterprises caused 2.364 deaths out of every 100 thousand employees. The death toll for producing one million tons of coal in coal mines was 0.111 persons.

In case of any differences between English translation and the original Chinese text, the Chinese edition shall prevail.

Notes:

〔1〕All figures in this Communiqué are preliminary statistics. Data in the Statistic Book—2018 of XPCC shall be taken as final. Due to the rounding—off reasons, the subentries may not add up to the aggregate totals.

〔2〕Gross domestic product (GDP), value added and per capita GDP as quoted in this Communiqué are calculated at current prices whereas their growth rates are at constant prices.

〔3〕Industrial strategic emerging industries refer to the related industrial sectors of energy—saving and environmental protection, information technology of new generation, biotech, manufacture of high—end equipment, new energy, new materials, and new energy cars.

〔4〕High technology manufacturing industry includes manufacture of medicine, manufacture of aerospace vehicle and equipment, manufacture of electronic and communication equipment, manufacture of computers and office equipment, manufacture of medical equipment, manufacture of measuring instrument and equipment and manufacture of optical and photographic equipment.

〔5〕Manufacture of equipment includes manufacture of metal products, general purpose equipment, special purpose equipment, automobiles, railway, ship, aerospace and other transport equipment, electrical machinery and apparatus, computers, communication and other electric equipment and measuring instrument and machinery.

〔6〕The overall labor productivity refers to the ratio between the GDP (at 2015 constant price) and the total number of persons employed.

〔7〕The six major high energy consuming industries consist of processing of petroleum, coking and processing of nuclear fuel, manufacture of raw chemical materials and chemical products, manufacture of non—metallic mineral products, smelting and pressing of ferrous metals, smelting and pressing of non—ferrous metals and production and supply of electricity and heat power.

〔8〕The reclamation region in Southern Xinjiang includes Division No.1, Division No.2, Division No.3, and Division No.14; the reclamation region in Northern Xinjiang includes Division No.4, Division No.5 Division No.6, Division No.7, Division No.8, Division No.9, Division No.10 Division No.12 Division No.13, the Construction and Industry Division, and institutions under the direct jurisdiction of XPCC.

〔9〕Investment in infrastructure refers to the investment in the construction or purchase of fundamental, public—serving projects and facilities for the social production and people's life, including transportation, postal service, telecommunication, radio, TV and satellite transmission, internet and related services, management of water conservancy, environment and public facilities.

〔10〕Private investment in fixed assets refers to investment in the construction or purchase of fixed assets by domestic collective, private and individual—owned enterprises or organizations or their holding enterprises (with absolute holding and relative holding enterprises).

〔11〕Investment in high technology industries refers to investment in six high technology manufacturing industries, including the manufacture of medicine and manufacture of aerospace vehicle and equipment, and nine high technology service industries, including information service and e—commerce service.

〔12〕The investment in real estate includes the investment made in real estate development, construction of buildings for own use, property management, intermediary services and other real estate development.

〔13〕The incidence of poverty refers to the proportion of population to the total population on farms.

Data Sources:

In this Communiqué, data of population are from the Bureau of Public Security; data of newly increased em-

ployed people, unemployment rate through unemployment registration, foreign experts, social insurance, and social security inspection are from the Bureau of Human Resources and Social Security; data of consumer prices are from the Xinjiang Survey Office of the National Bureau of Statistics of China; financial data are from the Bureau of Finance; data of supervised enterprises are from the State — owned Assets Supervision and Administration Commission; data of minimum living allowances, medical aid, special care, adoption, and disasters are from the Bureau of Civil Affairs; data of crop precision sown area, soil formula fertilization area, agricultural mechanization, extension of improved crop varieties, leading enterprises, certification of organic agricultural products, pollution — free agricultural products, green food and geographical indications of agricultural products, agricultural demonstration districts, and afforestation are from the Bureau of Agriculture (Bureau of Animal husbandry, Bureau of Forestry); data of industrial parks and telecommunications are from the Commission of Industry and Information Technology; data of highway access mileage are from the Bureau of Transport; data of housing units rebuilt in rundown areas, affordable housing, dilapidated houses rebuilt for poverty — stricken households, urban tap water rate, emission of major pollutants, central heating system rate, gas use rate, sewage treatment rate, central treatment rate of solid waste, and earthquakes are from Bureau of Housing and Urban — Rural Development; data of the Ten benefit Things, engineering research centers and enterprise technical centers are from the Development and Reform Commission; data of imports and exports of goods, foreign capital utilization, overseas contracted projects, overseas labor contracts and tourism are from the Bureau of Commerce (Bureau of tourism); data of investment promotion and paired assistance projects are from the Economic Coordination Office (the Office of Paired Assistance to XPCC); data of airplanes and flying times are from the Civil Aviation Enterprise Administration of XPCC; Data of financial credit are from the Finance Office; data of savings deposits and loans are from the XPCC branch of the Bank of Agriculture; Data of poverty alleviation and development are from the Poverty Alleviation Office; data of education are from the Bureau of Education; data of science and technology, and patents are from the Bureau of Science & Technology; data of brand name, trademark and standardization are from the Market Supervision Administration; data of culture, radio broadcasting, TV, publication, and sports are from the Administration of Culture, Sports, Press, Publication, Radio, Film and Television; data of public health are from the Public Health and Family Planning Commission; data of state — owned land for construction use, land for supply and land transfer are from the Bureau of Land and Resources; data of water conservancy facilities, irrigation area, water supply and soil erosion are from the Bureau of Water Resources; data of main pollutant emission are from the Bureau of environmental protection; data of work safety are from the Administration of Work Safety; all the other data are from the Bureau of Statistics and the Survey Office of XPCC of National Bureau of Statistics.

2018

BING TUAN

第一篇

综　合

Chapter 1 General Survey

简要说明

一、本篇资料主要内容

本篇资料包括兵团各部门单位数，主要年份国民经济主要指标及发展速度、结构和效益情况，兵团各师主要指标资料，兵团主要指标占全国、全国农垦和新疆比重，南疆师国民经济主要指标，改革开放40年国民经济主要指标和托管团场（园区）国民经济主指标等内容。

二、本篇资料来源

主要年份国民经济主要指标、兵团各时期五年计划完成情况取自历年兵团统计资料，兵团资料来自本书各篇。各部门单位数由兵团统计局、国家统计局兵团调查总队和兵团有关部门根据年报资料汇总整理。

Brief Introduction

1. Main Contents

This chapter contains number of units in various sectors of XPCC, main indicators, growth rate, structure and efficiency of national economy in major years, data on important indicators in the major years of XPCC, data on divisions of XPCC, percentage of XPCC's main indicators to the whole country, the farmland reclamation system and Xinjiang, XPCC's population, Main national economic indications of XPCC's southern divisions, Main Indicators of National Economy in Reform and Opening Up 40 Years, The main indicators of the national economy of the Management group(Park).

2. Sources of Data

Data on main indicators on national economy in major years, and data on completion of Five-Year Plans in every period of XPCC are obtained from statistical data of XPCC over past years. Data of XPCC are from chapters of this book. Number of units in various sectors are compiled by the Statistics Bureau of XPCC and Survey Office of the National Bureau of Statistics of XPCC and XPCC's relevant departments according to data of statistical annuals. Natural resource, water conservancy, projects irrigation capacity and data including land, rivers and reservoirs are from statistical annuals of Land Resource Bureau and Water Conservancy Bureau of XPCC.

1—1 年末单位数

Number of Units at Year-end

计量单位：个 (unit)

指 标	Item	2017
师	Division	14
市	City	9
团 场	Farm and Ranch	178
镇	Towns	10
乡	country	1
村民委员会	Village Committees	24
工业单位	Industrial Units	6 577
# 法人单位	Corporative Units	3 549
资质以上建筑业单位	Qualification Construction Enterprises and Units	224
# 法人单位	Corporative Units	224
交通运输业单位	Transportation Enterprises and Units	85
# 法人单位	Corporative Units	85
批发和零售业、住宿和餐饮业单位	Wholesale and Retail Trade，Accommodation and Catering Services Industry Enterprises and Units	5 005
# 法人单位	Corporative Units	4 283
房地产开发经营业单位	Real Estate Development Trade and Units	316
# 法人单位	Corporative Units	316
科研机构	Scientific and Research Institution	18
学 校	School	
普通高等学校	Regular Institutions of Higher Education	6
成人高等学校	Adult Institutions of Higher Education	2
中等职业学校	Secondary Vocational Schools	30
# 技工学校	Technical Schools	10
普通中学	Regular Secondary Schools	237
小 学	Primary Schools	55
幼儿园	Kindergartens	281
文 化	Culture	
艺术表演团体	Art Performance Groups	7
兵团广播电视台	Broadcast and TV Stations of XPCC	1
师(市)广播电视台	Cabled TV Stations of Divisions(City)	13
团场广播电视播出机构	Cabled TV Institution of Farms	178
卫生机构	Health Institution	1 212
# 医 院	Hospitals	211
金融机构	Financial Insititution	10
勘察设计机构	Survey and Design Institution	19

1—2 各师单位数

Unit Numbers by Division

计量单位:个 (2017 年) (unit)

单位	Unit	团场 Farm and Ranch	# 农场 Farm	# 牧场 Ranch	# 团场中连队数 Brigade of Farm and Ranch	工业法人单位 Industrial Enterprises Units
总计	**Total**	**178**	**166**	**12**	**1 973**	**3 549**
一师	Division 1	16	16		243	533
二师	Division 2	19	19		177	249
三师	Division 3	18	16	2	181	182
四师	Division 4	21	19	2	196	293
五师	Division 5	11	11		124	139
六师	Division 6	19	18	1	194	337
七师	Division 7	10	10		168	246
八师	Division 8	18	17	1	331	695
九师	Division 9	11	10	1	95	80
十师	Division 10	11	10	1	91	187
十一师	Division 11					44
十二师	Division 12	8	6	2	49	169
十三师	Division 13	11	10	1	85	325
十四师	Division 14	5	4	1	39	57
兵团直属	Directly under XPCC					13

单位	Unit	资质以上建筑业法人单位 Qualification Construction Corporative Units	交通运输法人单位 Transpo -rtation Corporative Units	批发和零售、住宿和餐饮法人单位 Wholesale and Retail Trade, Accommodation and Catering Services Corporative Units	房地产开发法人单位 Real Estate Development Corporative Units
总计	**Total**	**224**	**85**	**4 283**	**316**
一师	Division 1	28	21	571	26
二师	Division 2	5	2	214	15
三师	Division 3	13	3	186	12
四师	Division 4	8	5	221	14
五师	Division 5	7	1	189	11
六师	Division 6	32	34	454	57
七师	Division 7	17	2	73	22
八师	Division 8	39	6	1 343	70
九师	Division 9	10	1	82	3
十师	Division 10	20	3	526	23
十一师	Division 11	31	2	54	4
十二师	Division 12	7	2	267	29
十三师	Division 13	6	2	25	27
十四师	Division 14	1	1	18	3
兵团直属	Directly under XPCC			60	

1—2 续表 Continued

单 位	Unit	科研机构 Scientific and Research Institution	普通高等学校 Institutions of Higher Eductation	普通中等专业学校 Secondary Vocational Schools	技工学校 Technical Schools	普通中学 Regular Secondary Schools
总 计	**Total**	**18**	**6**	**20**	**10**	**237**
一 师	Division 1	1		1	1	22
二 师	Division 2	1		1	1	25
三 师	Division 3	1		1		21
四 师	Division 4	1		1	1	23
五 师	Division 5	1		1	1	14
六 师	Division 6	1		1	1	25
七 师	Division 7	1		1	1	13
八 师	Division 8	3		2	1	34
九 师	Division 9	1		1		13
十 师	Division 10	1		1	1	12
十一师	Division 11	2		1	1	5
十二师	Division 12	1		1		9
十三师	Division 13	1		1		13
十四师	Division 14			1		5
兵团直属	Directly under XPCC	2	6	5	1	3

单 位	Unit	小学 Primary Schools	幼儿园 Kinder-gartens	卫生机构 Medical Institutions	# 医院 Hospital
总 计	**Total**	**55**	**281**	**1 212**	**211**
一 师	Division 1	4	25	102	21
二 师	Division 2		22	76	21
三 师	Division 3	14	36	45	15
四 师	Division 4	3	29	46	21
五 师	Division 5	2	12	64	13
六 师	Division 6	10	42	176	22
七 师	Division 7		12	115	14
八 师	Division 8	16	32	381	30
九 师	Division 9		12	40	13
十 师	Division 10		12	43	13
十一师	Division 11		1	14	2
十二师	Division 12	1	18	31	7
十三师	Division 13		13	66	14
十四师	Division 14	5	13	9	4
兵团直属	Directly under XPCC		2	4	1

1—3 主要年份国民经济主要指标

Main Indicators of National Economy in Major Years

指 标		Item		1990	1995	2000	2005
年末总人口	**(万人)**	**Total Population in the Year-end**	**(10 000 persons)**	**214.35**	**228.79**	**242.79**	**256.98**
# 团 场		Population of Farms		162.30	171.37	183.85	189.64
# 少数民族		Ethnic Minority		24.61	26.58	28.42	31.25
就业人员数	**(万人)**	**Employment**	**(10 000 persons)**	**106.30**	**106.55**	**92.58**	**98.81**
# 在岗职工人数		Staff and Workers		97.05	93.36	70.23	66.54
生产总值	**(亿元)**	**Gross Domestic Product**	**(100 million yuan)**	**45.69**	**121.60**	**176.41**	**331.12**
# 第一产业		Primary Industry		20.91	56.00	71.63	130.64
第二产业		Secondary Industry		14.69	31.87	48.53	83.35
第三产业		Tertiary Industry		10.09	33.73	56.25	117.13
# 工 业		Industry		11.51	23.89	32.16	56.50
建筑业		Construction		3.18	7.98	16.37	26.85
全社会固定资产投资	**(亿元)**	**Total Investment in Fixed Assets**	**(100 million yuan)**	**9.59**	**36.94**	**73.61**	**137.24**
# 国有单位		State-owned Units		8.85	30.72	65.49	102.51
# 第一产业		Primary Industry		2.37	5.94	17.84	29.13
第二产业		Secondary Industry		4.11	16.31	18.35	39.53
第三产业		Tertiary Industry		3.11	14.69	37.42	68.58
# 民间投资		Private					
# 工业投资		Industry					
新增固定资产		Newly Increased Fixed Assets		8.36	28.98	67.72	113.43
财 政	**(亿元)**	**Finance**	**(100 million yuan)**				
一般公共预算收入		General Public Budget Revenue					
一般公共预算支出		General Public Budget Expenditure					
物价指数(上年=100)		**Price Indices**	**(preceding year=100)**				
商品零售价格指数		General Retail Price Index		104.10	116.70	98.30	99.40
居民消费价格指数		General Consumer Price Index		105.00	119.70	99.40	100.70
农 业		**Agriculture**					
总播面积	(千公顷)	Total Sown Area	(1 000 hectares)	780.80	813.00	909.80	1 023.77
农林牧渔业总产值	(亿元)	Gross Output Value of Farming, Forestry, Animal Husbandry and Fishery	(100 million yuan)	38.32	105.55	141.43	264.56
主要农产品产量	(万吨)	Output of Major Farm Products	(10 000 tons)				
粮 食		Grain		157.18	145.77	118.71	118.12
棉 花		Cotton		19.48	38.19	69.39	106.85
油 料		Oil-bearing Crops		8.87	15.01	14.97	9.88
甜 菜		Beetroots		91.96	128.21	106.07	119.18
水 果		Fruits		8.42	15.79	28.46	45.90
肉 类		Meat		4.71	6.70	12.52	15.02
水产品		Aquatic Products		0.82	1.00	1.29	2.00
工 业		**Industry**					
工业总产值	(亿元)	Gross Industrial Output Value	(100 million yuan)	44.45	132.46	97.69	175.64
# 规模以上工业		Gross Industrial Output Value above Designated Siaze					116.37
主要工业产品产量		Output of Major Industrial Products					
布	(百万米)	Cloth	(100 million meter)	96.76	113.89	126.90	83.71
机制纸及纸板	(万吨)	Machine-Made Paper and Paperboards	(10 000 tons)	4.32	6.15	4.99	6.33
成品糖	(万吨)	Refined Sugar	(10 000 tons)	5.78	10.89	10.64	15.32
原 煤	(万吨)	Crude Coal	(10 000 tons)	343.09	304.56	335.92	367.86
发电量	(亿千瓦时)	Electricity	(100 million kwh)	7.04	11.64	17.87	36.09
水 泥	(万吨)	Cement	(10 000 tons)	78.80	113.37	169.00	293.64
建筑业		**Construction**					
建筑业总产值	(亿元)	Gross Construction Output Value	(100 million yuan)	9.64	29.20	58.28	100.24
房屋施工面积	(万平方米)	Floor Space of Buildings Under Construction	(10 000 sq.m)	289.00	453.88	703.50	900.52
房屋竣工面积	(万平方米)	Floor Space of Buildings Completed	(10 000 sq.m)	193.00	267.81	500.96	590.32

注:1.本表价值量指标按当年价格计算。因方法制度改革,两项收入自2013年起变更为城镇常住居民人均可支配收入和连队常住居民人均可支配收入。

1—3 续表 1 Continued

指 标	Item	2010	2015	2016	2017
年末总人口 （万人）	**Total Population in the Year-end (10 000 persons)**	**260.72**	**276.56**	**283.41**	**300.53**
# 团 场	Population of Farms	175.87	178.96	184.96	202.07
# 少数民族	Ethnic Minority	37.73	39.27	40.90	45.08
就业人员数 （万人）	**Employment (10 000 persons)**	**106.18**	**136.18**	**138.10**	**144.17**
# 在岗职工人数	Staff and Workers	67.75	71.69	70.53	74.32
生产总值 （亿元）	**Gross Domestic Product (100 million yuan)**	770.62	1 934.91	2 134.33	2 339.07
# 第一产业	Primary Industry	278.81	428.03	467.87	506.33
第二产业	Secondary Industry	262.27	883.88	965.58	1 026.50
第三产业	Tertiary Industry	229.54	623.00	700.88	806.24
# 工 业	Industry	186.29	583.39	665.79	725.98
建筑业	Construction	75.98	300.49	299.97	300.73
全社会固定资产投资 （亿元）	**Total Investment in Fixed Assets (100 million yuan)**	**448.27**	**1 785.80**	**1 721.21**	**1 966.15**
# 国有单位	State-owned Units	231.84	803.80	835.60	908.03
# 第一产业	Primary Industry	39.16	149.38	178.93	200.86
第二产业	Secondary Industry	230.47	780.14	648.60	724.38
第三产业	Tertiary Industry	178.64	856.28	893.68	1 040.91
# 民间投资	Private		779.30	646.84	783.29
# 工业投资	Industry		764.82	626.31	723.65
新增固定资产	Newly Increased Fixed Assets	331.76	1 463.91	1 265.71	1 614.11
财 政 （亿元）	**Finance (100 million yuan)**				
一般公共预算收入	General Public Budget Revenue	57.69	83.31	106.48	129.60
一般公共预算支出	General Public Budget Expenditure	343.03	1 048.45	935.01	880.37
物价指数(上年＝100)	**Price Indices (preceding year＝100)**				
商品零售价格指数	General Retail Price Index	104.6	99.6	100.5	100.5
居民消费价格指数	General Consumer Price Index	104.3	100.6	102.3	102.3
农 业	**Agriculture**				
总播面积 （千公顷）	Total Sown Area (1 000 hectares)	1 119.20	1 352.90	1 372.21	1 362.77
农林牧渔业总产值 （亿元）	Gross Output Value of Farming, Forestry, Animal Husbandry and Fishery (100 million yuan)	569.28	971.22	1 059.26	1 145.86
主要农产品产量 （万吨）	Output of Major Farm Products (10 000 tons)				
粮 食	Grain	213.64	265.37	271.30	248.55
棉 花	Cotton	115.01	146.53	149.57	167.88
油 料	Oil-bearing Crops	18.62	19.32	23.43	20.92
甜 菜	Beetroots	181.66	184.41	208.20	198.46
水 果	Fruits	122.54	348.91	365.00	392.16
肉 类	Meat	31.99	39.00	41.15	44.38
水产品	Aquatic Products	2.67	4.61	5.15	5.39
工 业	**Industry**				
工业总产值 （亿元）	Gross Industrial Output Value (100 million yuan)	656.59	2 046.76	2 274.21	2 397.87
# 规模以上工业	Gross Industrial Output Value above Designated Siaze	559.24	1 672.06	1 882.38	2 062.06
主要工业产品产量	Output of Major Industrial Products				
布 （百万米）	Cloth (100 million meter)	89.74	63.98	115.37	149.77
机制纸及纸板 （万吨）	Machine-Made Paper and Paperboards (10 000 tons)	12.70	11.39	13.03	7.32
成品糖 （万吨）	Refined Sugar (10 000 tons)	17.24	14.08	14.65	18.17
原 煤 （万吨）	Crude Coal (10 000 tons)	925.83	851.93	1 085.20	900.69
发电量 （亿千瓦时）	Electricity (100 million kwh)	134.87	664.54	751.79	802.14
水 泥 （万吨）	Cement (10 000 tons)	966.89	1 368.49	1 235.27	1 269.99
建筑业	**Construction**				
建筑业总产值 （亿元）	Gross Construction Output Value (100 million yuan)	298.47	1 250.29	1 247.40	1 250.07
房屋施工面积 （万平方米）	Floor Space of Buildings Under Construction (10 000 sq.m)	2 059.97	5 967.73	5 355.54	5 085.66
房屋竣工面积 （万平方米）	Floor Space of Buildings Completed (10 000 sq.m)	1 115.28	2 555.62	2 327.46	1 761.67

Note: 1.Data in value terms in this table are calculated at current prices. two income changes as Per Capita Disposable Income of Urban and Brigade Permanent Households because of the reform of method system since 2013 .

1—3 续表 2 Continued

指 标	Item	1990	1995	2000	2005
道路运输业	**Highways Transportation**				
货运量 (万吨)	Freight Traffic (10 000 tons)	2 007.00	2 853.60	4 636.80	6 552.00
客运量 (万人)	Passenger Traffic Volume (10 000 persons)	1 246.00	2 399.80	5 205.50	7 458.00
货物周转量 (亿吨公里)	Freight Ton-Kilometers (100 million ton-km)	18.66	27.24	31.28	44.33
旅客周转量 (亿人公里)	Passenger-Kilometers (100 million passenger-km)	9.53	14.85	23.71	33.54
国内贸易	**Domestic Trade**				
社会消费品零售总额 (亿元)	Total Retail Sales of Consumer Goods (100 million yuan)	19.70	35.71	54.00	93.38
商品销售总额 (亿元)	Total Sales Value (100 million yuan)	23.08	146.00	185.43	369.31
能源(规模以上工业企业)	**Energy (Industrial Enterprises above Designated Size)**				
综合能源消费量 (万吨标准煤)	Comsuption of Comprehensive Energy (10 000 ton standard coal)				275.65
对外经济贸易和旅游	**Foreign Trade and Tourism**				
进出口总额 (亿美元)	Total Exports and Imports (USD 100 million)	0.20	1.82	7.53	31.05
出口总额	Total Exports	0.13	0.80	4.50	18.92
进口总额	Total Imports	0.07	1.02	3.03	12.13
旅游人数 (万人)	Tourists (10 000 persons)	0.05	0.40	133.13	227.54
旅游总收入 (亿元)	Income of Tourism (100 million yuan)			4.19	5.87
金 融 (亿元)	**Finance (100 million yuan)**				
金融机构各项贷款	Loans of Financial Institutions				
兵团农行各项存款	Deposits of Agricultural Bank of XPCC		75.29	173.54	358.17
兵团农行各项贷款	Loans of Agricultural Bank of XPCC		59.47	117.69	170.90
教 育	**Education**				
专任教师数 (人)	Full-time Teachers (person)				
普通高等学校	Institution of Higher Education	1 140	1 256	1 198	2 341
中等职业学校	Specialized Secondary Schools	892	776	914	1 100
普通中学	Regular Secondary Schools	14 293	9 814	9 347	13 679
小 学	Primary Schools	12 374	11 673	13 992	15 097
在校学生数 (人)	Student Enrollment (person)				
普通高等学校	Institution of Higher Education	5 827	8 615	11 735	30 663
中等职业学校	Secondary Vocational Schools	15 346	21 267	13 528	20 412
普通中学	Regular Secondary Schools	200 822	107 491	129 812	206 440
小 学	Primary Schools	199 624	209 351	288 707	269 811
人民生活	**People's Livelihood**				
全体居民人均可支配收入 (元)	Per Capita Disposable Income of Households				
城镇常住居民人均可支配收入 (元)	Per Capita Annual Disposable Income of Urban Permanent Households (yuan)				8 353
城镇常住居民家庭恩格尔系数(%)	Engle Coefficient of Urban Permanent Households (%)				37.80
连队常住居民人均可支配收入(元)	Per Capita Annual Disposable Income of Brigade Permanent Households (yuan)				4 105
连队常住居民家庭恩格尔系数(%)	Engle Coefficient of Brigade Permanent Households (%)				33.00
工 资	**Wages**				
在岗职工工资总额 (亿元)	Total Wages of Staff and Workers (100 million yuan)	17.95	39.59	51.69	88.73
在岗职工平均工资 (元)	Average Wage of Staff and Workers (yuan)	1 877	4 183	6 763	12 136
卫 生	**Health Care**				
医院床位数 (万张)	Hospital Beds (10 000 units)	2.01	1.99	1.73	1.65
卫生技术人员数 (万人)	Medical Technical Personnel (10 000 persons)	2.28	2.38	2.27	2.06
# 医 生	Doctors	0.98	1.01	1.03	0.90

2.本表有关在岗职工的指标统计口径均为非私营单位。

1—3 续表 3 Continued

指　　标	Item	2010	2015	2016	2017
道路运输业	**Highways Transportation**				
货运量（万吨）	Freight Traffic (10 000 tons)	11 853	49 431	58 216	68 105
客运量（万人）	Passenger Traffic Volume (10 000 persons)	11 019	21 172	22 724	25 013
货物周转量（亿吨公里）	Freight Ton-Kilometers (100 million ton-km)	106.75	546.75	694.29	866.89
旅客周转量（亿人公里）	Passenger-Kilometers (100 million passenger-km)	66.60	116.66	129.92	142.74
国内贸易	**Domestic Trade**				
社会消费品零售总额（亿元）	Total Retail Sales of Consumer Goods (100 million yuan)	202.87	552.34	632.29	708.37
商品销售总额（亿元）	Total Sales Value (100 million yuan)	649.36	2 926.35	3 341.37	3 826.13
能源（规模以上工业企业）	**Energy (Industrial Enterprises above Designated Size)**				
综合能源消费量（万吨标准煤）	Comsuption of Comprehensive Energy (10 000 ton standard coal)	797.88	2 891.87	3 129.85	3 358.70
对外经济贸易和旅游	**Foreign Trade and Tourism**				
进出口总额（亿美元）	Total Exports and Imports (USD 100 million)	55.89	102.48	70.76	75.90
出口总额	Total Exports	49.80	96.21	65.85	66.33
进口总额	Total Imports	6.09	6.27	4.91	9.57
旅游人数（万人）	Tourists (10 000 persons)	401.00	1 054.22	1 422.40	1 896.12
旅游总收入（亿元）	Income of Tourism (100 million yuan)	16.90	52.80	74.00	101.80
金　融（亿元）	**Finance (100 million yuan)**				
金融机构各项贷款	Loans of Financial Institutions	875.46	2 030.00	2 100.00	2 545.68
兵团农行各项存款	Deposits of Agricultural Bank of XPCC	746.56	1 084.89	1 151.97	1 262.74
兵团农行各项贷款	Loans of Agricultural Bank of XPCC	232.29	516.37	549.45	658.16
教　育	**Education**				
专任教师数（人）	Full-time Teachers (person)				
普通高等学校	Institution of Higher Education	2 741	3 205	3 219	3 295
中等职业学校	Specialized Secondary Schools	1 305	1 197	1 107	1 722
普通中学	Regular Secondary Schools	14 541	13 833	13 846	13 274
小　学	Primary Schools	13 581	11 576	11 598	11 458
在校学生数（人）	Student Enrollment (person)				
普通高等学校	Institution of Higher Education	46 776	51 595	52 843	53 758
中等职业学校	Secondary Vocational Schools	35 798	29 515	30 276	28 183
普通中学	Regular Secondary Schools	190 362	141 730	138 672	138 890
小　学	Primary Schools	217 600	160 032	160 350	162 228
人民生活	**People's Livelihood**				
全体居民人均可支配收入（元）	Per Capita Disposable Income of Households (yuan)		25 287	27 215	29 430
城镇常住居民人均可支配收入（元）	Per Capita Annual Disposable Income of Urban Permanent Households (yuan)	14 559	31 432	34 089	36 730
城镇常住居民家庭恩格尔系数（%）	Engle Coefficient of Urban Permanent Households (%)	29.72	28.00	26.30	27.50
连队常住居民人均可支配收入（元）	Per Capita Annual Disposable Income of Brigade Permanent Households (yuan)	8 782	15 053	16 401	17 786
连队常住居民家庭恩格尔系数（%）	Engle Coefficient of Brigade Permanent Households (%)	30.30	27.60	26.40	26.60
工　资	**Wages**				
在岗职工工资总额（亿元）	Total Wages of Staff and Workers (100 million yuan)	198.34	467.80	462.55	493.54
在岗职工平均工资（元）	Average Wage of Staff and Workers (yuan)	26 741	54 599	56 345	58 464
卫　生	**Health Care**				
医院床位数（万张）	Hospital Beds (10 000 units)	1.82	2.12	2.14	2.22
卫生技术人员数（万人）	Medical Technical Personnel (10 000 persons)	2.06	2.59	2.59	2.66
# 医　生	Doctors	0.81	0.92	0.91	0.97

2.Statistical indicators of data on staff and workers on the job is non—private units.

1—4　主要年份国民经济和社会发展主要比例和效益指标

Indicators on National Economic and Social Development in Major Years

指　　标	Item	2005	2010	2015	2016	2017
人　口	**Population**					
出生率　(‰)	Birth Rate　(‰)	6.38	6.30	6.04	7.00	7.85
死亡率　(‰)	Death Rate　(‰)	4.65	4.08	4.84	4.70	5.44
自然增长率　(‰)	Natural Growth Rate　(‰)	1.73	2.22	1.20	2.30	2.42
就　业	**Employment**					
就业者负担人口	Dependency Ratio	2.60	2.42	2.03	2.05	2.08
三次产业从业者比例（以第一产业为 100）	Employment Ratio by Type of Industry (Employment in primary industry=100)					
第一产业	Primary Industry	100.0	100.0	100.0	100.0	100.0
第二产业	Secondary Industry	39.8	43.1	113.0	146.4	113.8
第三产业	Tertiary Industry	64.4	75.2	168.3	247.2	207.9
城镇登记失业率　(%)	Registered Unemployment Rate in Urban Areas　(%)	2.8	2.4	2.59	2.55	2.74
国民经济核算	**National Accounting**					
三次产业增加值比例（以第一产业为 100）	Ratio of Value-added by Type of Industry (Value-added in primary industry=100)					
第一产业	Primary Industry	100.0	100.0	100.0	100.0	100.0
第二产业	Secondary Industry	63.8	94.1	206.5	206.4	202.7
第三产业	Tertiary Industry	89.7	82.3	145.5	149.8	159.2
全社会劳动生产率　(元/人)	Overall Labor Productivity(in terms of value-added per employee)　(yuan/person)	33 719	73 483	144 326	155 630	154 475
第一产业	Primary Industry	26 760	57 484	115 718	146 916	167 256
第二产业	Secondary Industry	44 455	129 067	221 190	237 521	235 570
第三产业	Tertiary Industry	38 240	63 673	109 077	108 424	101 310
人均生产总值　(元)	Per Capita GDP　(yuan)	12 900	29 752	70 380	76 230	80 117
固定资产投资	**Investment in Fixed Assets**					
全社会固定资产投资相当于生产总值比例　(%)	Proportion of Investment in Fixed Assets to GDP　(%)	41.4	58.2	92.1	80.6	80.6
全社会房屋建筑面积竣工率　(%)	Rate of Total Floor Space of Buildings Completed in Constrcution　(%)	77.7	54.5	41.7	23.0	23.0
固定资产交付使用率　(%)	Rate of Fixed Assets Completed and Put Into Use　(%)	82.7	74.0	82.0	70.8	70.8
农　业	**Agriculture**					
人均耕地面积　(公顷)	Per Capita Cultivated Land　(hectare)	0.41	0.48	0.45	0.45	0.44
农牧团场从业者人均耕地面积　(公顷)	Cultivated Land Per Agricultural Laborer　(hectare)	1.53	1.80	1.31	1.46	1.43
每公顷耕地农业机械总动力　(千瓦)	Total Power of Agricultural Machinery per Hectare of Cultivated Land　(kw)	2.41	2.97	4.07	4.14	4.15
每公顷耕地用电量　(千瓦小时)	Electric Power Consumption per Hectare of Cultivated Land　(kwh)	1 522	2 259	2 707	2 870	2 937
每公顷耕地化肥施用量　(公斤)	Chemical Fertilizer Consumption per Hectare of Cultivated Land　(kg)	361	439	623	587	593
每公顷耕地生产的农业产值　(元)	Agricultural Output Value per Hectare of Cultivated Land　(yuan)	25 147	45 843	79 096	84 442	90 055
团场从业者人均农产品产量　(公斤)	Output of Farm Products per Agricultural Laborer　(kg)					
粮　食	Grain	1 695	3 118	3 216	3 163	2 797

注：本表工业企业经济效益 2006 年以后数据为规模以上口径。

1—4 续表 Continued

指 标	Item	2005	2010	2015	2016	2017
棉 花	Cotton	1 553	1 679	1 776	1 744	1 889
油 料	Oil-bearing Crops	144	272	234	273	235
甜 菜	Beetroots	1 732	2 651	2 235	2 427	2 233
肉 类	Meat	218	467	473	480	499
水产品	Aquatic Products	29	39	49	60	61
每公顷播种面积农产品产量 (公斤)	Output of Farm Crops per Hectare of Sown Area (kg)					
粮 食	Grain	6 146	7 504	8 229	8 179	8 744
棉 花	Cotton	1 939	2 310	2 328	2 409	2 444
油 料	Oil-bearing Crops	2 031	2 748	3 363	3 635	3 681
甜 菜	Beetroots	63 160	71 184	87 856	85 323	83 617
规模以上工业企业经济效益	**Economic Benefit of Industry above Designated Size**					
经济效益综合指数	Comprehensive Index of Industry Economic Benefit	98.16	195.73	272.07	308.55	324.29
总资产贡献率 (%)	Ratio of Total Assets to Industrial Output Value (%)	5.14	9.02	8.22	9.26	9.12
资产负债率 (%)	Assets-Liability Ratio (%)	69.11	64.02	68.33	66.88	65.70
成本费用利润率 (%)	Ratio of Profits to Industrial Cost (%)	2.20	10.86	8.80	12.06	11.80
流动资产周转次数 (次/年)	Number of Times of Annual Turnover Circulation Funds (times/year)	0.93	1.27	1.58	1.69	1.53
建筑业	**Construction**					
产值利税率(法人企业) (%)	Ratio of Per-tax Profits to Gross Output Value (corporative enterprise) (%)	3.9	4.9	3.7	4.6	4.9
全员劳动生产率(按总产值计算) (元/人)	Overall Labor Productivity (in terms of gross output value per employee) (yuan/person)	89 748	149 112	296 158	324 574	333 808
道路运输业	**Highways Transportation**					
客运量弹性系数	Elasticity of Passenger Traffic	0.95	0.85	0.93	0.80	1.26
货运量弹性系数	Elasticity of Freight Traffic	1.07	1.54	1.86	1.95	2.13
国内贸易	**Domestic Trade**					
人均社会消费品零售额 (元)	Per Capita Retail Sales of Consumer Goods (yuan)	3 638	7 884	20 091	22 310	24 262
对外经济贸易	**Foreign Trade**					
进出口总额相当于生产总值比例 (%)	Proportion of Total Imports & Exports to GDP (%)	75.8	49.1	32.9	22.0	21.9
财 政	**Finance**					
一般公共预算收入相当于兵团生产总值比例 (%)	Proportion of General Budgetary Revenue to GDP of XPCC (%)				5.0	5.5
一般公共预算支出相当于兵团生产总值比例 (%)	Proportion of General Expenditure Revenue to GDP of XPCC (%)				43.8	37.6
金融业	**Banking**					
金融机构贷款相当于兵团生产总值比例(%)	BankLoans as Percentage of CDP in XPCC (%)	51.6	113.6	95.1	98.4	108.8
教 育	**Education**					
学龄儿童入学率 (%)	Rate of School-age Children Enrollment (%)	99.0	99.9	99.9	99.9	100.0
小学升学率 (%)	Rate of Graduates of Primary Schools Entering Junior Secondary Schools (%)	100.0	105.8	103.1	104.3	109.1
初中入学率 (%)	Rate of Junior Secondary Schools Entering Senior Secondary Schools (%)	67.9	96.1	97.1	97.1	99.9
学校专任教师负担系数	Student-Full Time teachers Ratio					
高等学校	Colleges and Universities	14.8	17.1	17.9	18.0	18.6
中等学校	Secondary Schools	18.6	27.4	24.7	12.7	23.6
中学学校	Regular Secondary Schools	15.1	13.1	10.2	8.8	10.5
小学学校	Primary Schools	17.9	16.0	13.8	13.8	14.2
卫 生	**Health Care**					
每万人医院数 (个)	Numberof Hospitals per 10000 Persons (unit)	0.88	0.81	0.76	0.76	0.72
每万人医生数 (人)	Number of Doctors per 10000 Persons (unit)	35.11	31.32	33.17	32.93	33.28
每万人医院床位数 (张)	Number of Hospital Beds per 10000 Persons (unit)	64.81	70.70	76.53	77.34	76.01
医院病床使用率 (%)	Utilization Rate of Hospital Beds (%)	66.9	82.2	84.72	85.01	79.50

Note: Statistical scope of economic efficiency of industrial enterprises in this table refers to enterprises above designated size since 2006.

1—5 主要年份国民经济主要指标比例关系

Percentage of Main National Economic Indicators in Major Years

计量单位：%　　　　(%)

指　　标	Item	2005	2010	2015	2016	2017
就业人员数	**Employment**					
第一产业	Plimary Industry	49.0	45.8	26.2	20.3	23.7
第二产业	Secondary Industry	19.5	19.8	29.7	29.6	27.0
第三产业	Tertiary Industry	31.5	34.4	44.1	50.1	49.3
生产总值	**Gross Domestic Product**					
第一产业	Plimary Industry	39.4	36.2	22.1	21.9	21.6
第二产业	Secondary Industry	25.2	34.0	45.7	45.3	43.9
第三产业	Tertiary Industry	35.4	29.8	32.2	32.8	34.5
全社会固定资产投资	**Total Investment in Fixed Assets**					
第一产业	Plimary Industry	21.2	8.7	8.4	10.4	10.2
第二产业	Secondary Industry	28.8	51.4	43.7	37.7	36.8
第三产业	Tertiary Industry	50.0	39.9	47.9	51.9	53.0
国有单位固定资产投资中	Of Investment in Fixed Assets of State-owned Units					
# 能源工业	Energy Industry	11.4	6.2	7.8	6.4	8.7
运输邮政业	Transport and Post Services Industry	12.1	7.7	11.9	12.5	12.8
固定资产投资资金来源结构	**Structure of Fund Sources**					
国家预算内	State Budgetary Appropriation	19.6	12.7	14.6	16.7	11.8
国内贷款	Domestic Loans	12.6	17.9	9.7	5.9	7.7
债　券	Bonds				0.1	
利用外资	Foreign Investment	1.4	0.7	…	0.1	0.1
自筹和其他	Fundraising and Others Investment	66.4	68.7	75.7	77.2	80.4
农林牧渔业总产值	**Gross Output Value of Farming, Forestry, Animal Husbandry and Fishery**					
农　业	Farming	81.0	79.1	76.3	76.7	76.2
林　业	Forestry	1.2	1.0	1.6	1.7	1.8
牧　业	Animal Husbandry	9.7	13.5	14.9	14.5	14.8
渔　业	Fishery	0.5	0.5	0.8	0.8	0.8
农林牧渔服务业	Services	7.6	5.9	6.4	6.3	6.4
规上工业总产值	**Gross Output Value of Above Scale Industry**					
轻工业	Light Industry	54.5	51.4	36.8	37.8	37.4
重工业	Heavy Industry	45.5	48.6	63.2	62.2	62.6
社会消费品零售总额	**Total Retail Sales of Consumer Goods**					
商品零售	Wholesale and Retail Trade	78.2	84.6	83.2	82.8	81.1
餐饮收入	Accommodation and Catering Trade	13.3	15.4	16.8	17.2	18.9

注：本表价值量指标按当年价格计算。1950—2015年社会消费品零售总额执行按行业(批发和零售业、住宿和餐饮业)分组，从2016年起，执行按消费形态分组，取消行业分组。

Note: Data in value terms in this table are calculated at current prices. Total Retail Sales of Consumer Goods grouped by industries in 1950—2015, Grouped by Sector(Wholesale and Retail Trade、Accommodation and Catering Trade) is effective from 2016.

1—6 按登记注册类型分国民经济主要指标比例关系

Percentage of Major National Economic Indicators by Types of Registration

计量单位:% (%)

指 标	Item	2005	2010	2015	2016	2017
就业人员数	**Employment**					
国有企业	State-owned Enterprises	60.7	54.0	38.8	37.2	36.9
集体企业	Collective-owned Enterprises	0.1	…	…	…	…
股份制企业	Share Holding Enterprises	7.2	10.0	16.6	14.8	16.8
其他企业	Others	8.6	11.7	16.1	19.1	18.2
个 体	Individuals	23.4	24.3	28.5	28.9	28.1
全社会固定资产投资	**Investment in Fixed Assets**					
国有企业	State-owned Enterprises	74.7	51.7	45.0	48.5	48.5
集体企业	Collective-owned Enterprises	0.1	0.1	0.1	0.1	0.1
股份制企业	Share Holding Enterprises	16.8	30.2	30.5	46.9	56.1
其他企业	Others	1.4	16.3	24.1	4.1	4.7
个 体	Individuals	7.0	1.7	0.3	0.4	0.1
工业总产值	**Gross Industrial Output Value**					
国有企业	State-owned Enterprises	32.0	12.6	4.2	3.2	2.3
集体企业	Collective-owned Enterprises	0.5	…	…	…	…
股份制企业	Share Holding Enterprises	58.1	74.9	86.6	87.2	89.7
其他企业	Others	3.5	6.6	4.1	4.6	4.9
个 体	Individuals	5.9	5.9	5.1	4.9	3.1
建筑业总产值	**Total Value of Construction**					
国有企业	State-owned Enterprises	42.2	32.1	5.0	5.0	4.2
集体企业	Collective-owned Enterprises	0.1	…			
股份制企业	Share Holding Enterprises	52.8	60.2	95.0	95.0	
其他企业	Others	1.5	5.8			95.8
个 体	Individuals	0.2	1.9			
公路货运量	**Freight Traffic of Highways**					
国有企业	State-owned Enterprises	8.7	6.7	3.1		
集体企业	Collective-owned Enterprises					
股份制企业	Share Holding Enterprises	5.7	2.2	16.7	20.3	26.8
个 体	Individuals	85.6	91.1	77.9	79.7	73.2
社会消费品零售总额	**Total Retail Sales of Consumer Goods**					
国有企业	State-owned Enterprises	8.8	17.9	17.4	17.3	16.8
集体企业	Collective-owned Enterprises	1.7	…		…	…
股份制企业	Share Holding Enterprises	18.4	4.2	4.6	4.3	4.2
其他企业	Others	17.5	10.5	9.4	9.5	9.8
个 体	Individuals	53.6	67.4	68.6	68.9	69.2

注:本表价值量指标按当年价格计算。
Note: Data in value terms in this table are calculated at current prices.

1—7 主要时期国民经济主要指标平均增长速度

Average Growth Rates of Main National Economic Indicators in Major Periods

指　　标	Item	"九五"时期年均增长速度(%) Average Annual Growth Rate in Seventh Five-Year Plan Period	"十五"时期年均增长速度(%) Average Annual Growth Rate in Eighth Five-Year Plan Period	"十一五"时期年均增长速度(%) Average Annual Growth Rate in Ninth Five-Year Plan Period	"十二五"时期年均增长速度(%) Average Annual Growth Rate in Tenth Five-Year Plan Period	2017年比2016年增长(%) Increase Rate % in 2017 Against 2016
年末总人口	**Total Population in the Year-end**	**1.2**	**1.1**	**0.3**	**1.2**	**6.0**
在岗职工	**Staff and Workers on the Job**					
人　数	Numbers	−5.5	−1.1	−1.5	1.1	5.4
工资总额	Total Wages	5.5	11.4	17.5	18.7	6.7
平均工资	Average Wage	10.1	12.4	17.1	15.3	3.8
生产总值	**Gross Domestic Product**	**7.6**	**11.3**	**12.5**	**16.1**	**8.0**
# 第一产业	Primary Industry	7.3	9.7	9.3	7.6	7.6
第二产业	Secondary Industry	7.6	9.6	20.5	24.7	4.6
第三产业	Tertiary Industry	8.0	14.5	10.4	13.3	12.9
# 工　业	Iudustry	6.1	10.5	21.9	24.9	6.4
建筑业	Coustruction	12.0	7.6	17.3	24.2	0.6
人均生产总值	Per Capita GDP	6.0	10.0	12.9	14.7	3.5
全社会固定资产投资	**Total Investment in Fixed Assets**	**13.6**	**15.5**	**23.3**	**28.8**	**14.2**
第一产业	Primary Industry	35.6	16.0	7.5	31.6	12.3
第二产业	Secondary Industry	−9.7	16.6	40.5	21.9	11.7
第三产业	Tertiary Industry	20.5	14.8	16.2	37.1	16.5
农　业	**Agriculture**					
农林牧渔业总产值	Gross Output Value of Farming,Forestry, Animal Husbandry and Fishery	9.4	10.2	9.0	8.3	7.4
主要农产品产量	Output of Major Farm Products					
粮　食	Grain	−4.1	4.1	12.6	4.4	−8.4
棉　花	Cotton	12.7	7.3	1.5	5.0	12.2
油　料	Oil-bearing Crops	−0.1	−8.6	13.5	0.7	−10.7
甜　菜	Beetroots	−3.7	4.3	8.8	13.9	−4.7
水　果	Fruits	12.5	10.0	21.7	23.3	7.4
肉　类	Meat	13.3	12.8	16.3	4.0	7.9
水产品	Aquatic Products	5.2	9.2	5.9	10.5	4.7
工　业	**Industry**					
工业总产值	Gross Industrial Output Value	7.5	12.9	24.3	28.6	1.3
主要工业产品产量	Output of Major Industrial Products					
原　煤	Crude Coal	2.0	1.8	20.3	−1.6	−17.0
发电量	Electricity	9.0	15.1	30.2	37.6	6.7
成品糖	Refined Sugar	−0.5	7.6	2.4	−4.0	24.0
布	Cloth	2.2	−8.0	1.4	−6.5	29.8
机制纸及纸板	Machine-Made Paper and Paperboards	−4.1	4.9	14.9	−2.1	−43.8
水　泥	Cement	8.3	11.7	26.9	7.2	2.8
建筑业	**Construction**					
建筑业总产值	Gross Construction Output Value	14.8	11.5	24.4	38.6	0.6
房屋施工面积	Floor Space of Buildings Under Construction	9.2	5.1	18.0	30.2	−5.0
房屋竣工面积	Floor Space of Buildings Completed	13.3	3.3	13.6	27.1	−24.3
道路运输业	**Highways Transportation**					
旅客周转量	Passenger-Kilometers	9.8	7.2	14.7	18.8	9.9
货物周转量	Freight Ton-Kilometers	2.8	7.2	19.2	36.7	24.9
社会消费品零售总额	**Total Retail Sales of Consumer Goods**	**8.6**	**11.6**	**16.8**	**22.2**	**12.0**
进出口总额	**Total Exports and Imports**	**30.2**	**32.8**	**12.2**	**12.9**	**6.2**

注:本表有关在岗职工的指标统计口径均为非私营单位。

Note:Statistical indicators of data on staff and workers on the job is non—private units(the same as follows).

1—8 全国、全国农垦、新疆及兵团国民经济主要指标指数

Indices of Main National Economic Indicators by the Whole Country, State Farmland Reclamation System, Xinjiang and XPCC

(2017 年,上年=100)(2017, Preceding year=100)

指　　标	Item	全　国 the Whole Country	全国农垦 State Farmland Reclamation System	新　疆 Xinjiang	兵　团 XPCC
年末总人口	**Total Population in the Year-end**	**100.5**	**100.9**	**101.9**	**106.0**
就业人员数	**Employment**	**100.0**		**103.5**	**104.4**
生产总值	**Gross Domestic Product**	**106.9**	**107.1**	**107.6**	**108.0**
# 第一产业	Primary Industry	103.9	105.5	105.6	107.6
第二产业	Secondary Industry	106.1	106.6	105.9	104.6
第三产业	Tertiary Industry	108.0	109.0	109.8	112.9
# 工　业	Value-added in Industry		105.8	106.1	106.4
建筑业	Value-added in Construction			105.6	100.6
人均生产总值	Per Capita GDP	106.3	106.8	105.8	103.5
全社会固定资产投资	**Total Investment in Fixed Assets**	**107.0**	**108.5**	**120.0**	**114.2**
# 工业投资	Industrial Investment	102.1		86.9	115.5
# 民间投资	Private Investment	106.0		101.3	121.1
# 房地产开发投资	Real Estate Development Investment	107.0		112.4	84.4
财　政	**Finance**				
一般公共预算收入	General Public Budget Revenue	107.4		116.9	121.7
一般公共预算支出	General Public Budget Expenditure			112.1	94.2
农　业	**Agriculture**				
主要农产品产量	Output of Major Farm Products				
粮　食	Grain	100.3	100.9	95.7	91.6
棉　花	Cotton	103.5	111.1	108.7	112.2
油　料	Oil-bearing Crops	102.8	93.7	99.7	89.3
糖　料	Sugar	101.7	105.5	95.6	95.3
水　果	Fruits		108.9	96.0	107.4
肉　类	Meat	100.8	102.9	102.1	107.9
水产品	Aquatic Products	100.5	108.5		104.7
工　业	**Industry**				
主要工业产品产量	Output of Major Industrial Products				
原　煤	Crude Coal	103.3	124.3	110.6	83.0
发电量	Electricity	105.9	110.0	110.7	106.7
成品糖	Refined Sugar	101.9	107.9	120.9	124.0
纱	Yarn	108.5	115.7	136.8	120.0
布	Cloth	95.7	111.1	156.9	130.4
机制纸及纸板	Machine-Made Paper and Paperboards		98.9	100.0	56.2
水　泥	Cement	96.9	97.1	108.2	102.8
社会消费品零售总额	**Total Retail Sales of Consumer Goods**	**110.2**		**107.7**	**112.0**
进出口总额	**Total Exports and Imports**	**114.2**		**117.1**	**106.2**
出口总额	Total Exports	110.8	104.4	113.8	99.7
进口总额	Total Imports	118.7		142.6	194.4
人民生活	**People's Livelihood**				
城镇常住居民人均可支配收入	Per Capita Disposable Income of Urban Permanent Households	108.3		108.1	107.7
农村常住居民人均可支配收入	Per Capita Disposable Income of Rural Permanent Households	108.6		108.5	108.4

注:1.本表生产总值指标增长速度指标按可比价格计算。2.全国指标来源于中国统计摘要。

Note: 1.Growth rate of GDP in this table is calculated at comparable prices.

2.Data on the whole country are from the China statistical abstract.

1—9 兵团主要指标占全国、全国农垦及新疆的比重

Proportion of Main Economic Indicators of XPCC to the Whole Country, State Farmland Reclamation System and Xinjiang

(2017 年)

指 标	Item	全 国 the Whole Country	全国农垦 State Farmland Reclamation System	新 疆 Xinjiang	兵 团 XPCC
年末总人口 (万人)	**Total Population in the Year-end (10 000 persons)**	**139 008**	**1 455.21**	**2 444.67**	**300.53**
就业人员数 (万人)	**Employment (10 000 persons)**	**77 640**		**1 307.64**	**144.17**
生产总值 (亿元)	**Gross Domestic Product (100 million yuan)**	**827 122**	**7 913.62**	**10 920.09**	**2 339.07**
# 第一产业	Primary Industry	65 468	1 907.51	1 691.63	506.33
第二产业	Secondary Industry	334 623	3 570.30	4 291.95	1 026.50
第三产业	Tertiary Industry	427 032	2 435.81	4 936.51	806.24
# 工 业	Value-added in Industry	279 997		3 229.09	725.98
建筑业	Value-added in Construction	55 689		1 160.00	300.73
全社会固定资产投资 (亿元)	**Total Investment in Fixed Assets (100 million yuan)**	**641 238**	**5 231.08**	**11 795.64**	**1 966.15**
# 工业投资	Industrial Investment			3 195.06	723.65
# 民间投资	Private Investment	381 510		3 416.85	783.29
# 房地产开发投资	Investment for Real-estate Development	109 799		1 037.86	155.02
财 政 (亿元)	**Finance (100 million yuan)**				
一般公共预算收入	General Public Budget Revenue	172 567		1 466.52	129.60
一般公共预算支出	General Public Budget Expenditure			4 637.24	880.37
农 业	**Agriculture**				
主要农产品产量 (万吨)	Output of Major Farm Products (10 000 tons)	61 791	3 515.49	1 447.60	248.55
粮 食	Grain	549	208.58	456.60	167.88
棉 花	Cotton	3 732	76.57	71.20	20.92
油 料	Oil-bearing Crops	12 556	774.78	530.68	198.46
糖 料	Sugar		737.53		392.16
水 果	Fruits	8 431	258.20	153.73	44.38
肉 类	Meat	6 938	160.94		5.39
水产品	Aquatic Products				
工 业	**Industry**				
主要工业产品产量	Output of Major Industrial Products	86 810	643.00	276.41	149.77
布 (百万米)	Cloth (A million meter)	4 050	99.03	155.69	48.88
纱 (万吨)	Yarn (10 000 tons)		56.65	29.21	7.32
机制纸及纸板 (万吨)	Machine-Made Paper and Paperboards (10 000 tons)	1 471	272.27	53.12	18.17
成品糖 (万吨)	Refined Sugar (10 000 tons)	352 000	1 959.09	17 782.30	900.69
原 煤 (万吨)	Crude Coal (10 000 tons)	64 951	873.47	3 010.78	802.14
发电量 (亿千瓦时)	Electricity (100 million kwh)	234 000	1 958.32	4 581.04	1 269.99
水 泥 (万吨)	Cement (10 000 tons)	366 262		3 044.58	708.37
社会消费品零售总额 (亿元)	**Total Retail Sales of Consumer Goods (100 million yuan)**	**41 162**		**206.60**	**75.90**
进出口总额 (亿美元)	**Total Exports and Imports (USD 100 million)**	**22 708**	**694.58**	**177.29**	**66.33**
出口总额	Total Exports	18 455		29.31	9.57
进口总额	Total Imports				

注:本表价值量指标按当年价格计算。

1—9 续表 Continued

(2017 年)

指 标	Item	占全国比重(%) Ratio of XPCC to the Whole Country (%)	占全国农垦比重(%) Ratio of XPCC to State Farmland Reclamation System (%)	占新疆比重(%) Ratio of XPCC to Xinjiang (%)
年末总人口 (万人)	**Total Population in the Year-end (10 000 persons)**	**0.2**	**20.7**	**12.3**
就业人员数 (万人)	**Employment (10 000 persons)**	**0.2**		**11.0**
生产总值 (亿元)	**Gross Domestic Product (100 million yuan)**	**0.3**	**29.6**	**21.4**
# 第一产业	Primary Industry	0.8	26.5	29.9
第二产业	Secondary Industry	0.3	28.8	23.9
第三产业	Tertiary Industry	0.2	33.1	16.3
# 工 业	Value-added in Industry	0.3		22.5
建筑业	Value-added in Construction	0.5		25.9
全社会固定资产投资 (亿元)	**Total Investment in Fixed Assets (100 million yuan)**	**0.3**	**37.6**	**16.7**
# 工业投资	Industrial Investment			22.6
# 民间投资	Private Investment	0.2		22.9
# 房地产开发投资	Investment for Real-estate Development	0.1		14.9
财 政 (亿元)	**Finance (100 million yuan)**			
一般公共预算收入	General Public Budget Revenue	0.1		8.8
一般公共预算支出	General Public Budget Expenditure			19.0
农 业	**Agriculture**			
主要农产品产量 (万吨)	Output of Major Farm Products (10 000 tons)	0.4	7.1	17.2
粮 食	Grain	30.6	80.5	36.8
棉 花	Cotton	0.6	27.3	29.4
油 料	Oil-bearing Crops	1.6	25.6	37.4
糖 料	Sugar		53.2	
水 果	Fruits	0.5	17.2	28.9
肉 类	Meat	0.1	3.3	
水产品	Aquatic Products			
工 业	**Industry**			
主要工业产品产量	Output of Major Industrial Products	0.2	23.3	54.2
布 (百万米)	Cloth (A million meter)	1.2	49.4	31.4
纱 (万吨)	Yarn (10 000 tons)		12.9	25.1
机制纸及纸板 (万吨)	Machine-Made Paper and Paperboards (10 000 tons)	1.2	6.7	34.2
成品糖 (万吨)	Refined Sugar (10 000 tons)	0.3	46.0	5.1
原 煤 (万吨)	Crude Coal (10 000 tons)	1.2	91.8	26.6
发电量 (亿千瓦时)	Electricity (100 million kwh)	0.5	64.9	27.7
水 泥 (万吨)	Cement (10 000 tons)	0.2		23.3
社会消费品零售总额 (亿元)	**Total Retail Sales of Consumer Goods (100 million yuan)**	**0.2**		**36.7**
进出口总额 (亿美元)	**Total Exports and Imports (USD 100 million)**	**0.3**	**9.5**	**37.4**
出口总额	Total Exports	…		32.7
进口总额	Total Imports			

Note: Data in value terms in this table are calculated at current prices.

1—10 全国、全国农垦、新疆及兵团人均国民经济主要指标

Per Capital Main National Indicators of the Whole Country, State Farmland Reclamation System, Xinjiang and XPCC

(2017 年)

指 标	Item	全 国 the Whole Country	全国农垦 State Farmland Reclamation System	新 疆 Xinjiang	兵 团 XPCC
生产总值 (元)	**Gross Domestic Product (yuan)**	**59 660**	**56 208**	**45 099**	**80 113**
全社会固定资产投资(元)	**Total Investment in Fixed Assets (yuan)**	**46 252**	**36 353**	**98 376**	**67 341**
财 政	**Finance**				
一般公共预算收入 (元)	General Budgetary Revenue in Local Finance (yuan)	12 447		6 052	4 439
一般公共预算支出 (元)	General Budgetary Expenditure in Local Finance (yuan)			19 168	30 153
农 业	**Agriculture**				
主要农产品产量 (公斤)	Output of Major Farm Products (mg)				
粮 食	Grain	446	2 443	1 207	851
棉 花	Cotton	4	145	381	575
油 料	Oil-bearing Crops	27	53	59	72
糖 料	Sugar	91	538	443	680
水 果	Fruits		513		1 343
肉 类	Meat	61	179	128	152
水产品	Aquatic Products	50	112		18
工 业	**Industry**				
主要工业产品产量	Output of Major Industrial Products				
布 (米)	Cloth (meter)	63	45	23	51
纱 (公斤)	Yarn (kg)	29	69	130	167
机制纸及纸板 (公斤)	Machine-Made Paper and Paperboards (kg)		39	24	25
成品糖 (公斤)	Refined Sugar (kg)	11	189	44	62
原 煤 (公斤)	Crude Coal (kg)	2 539	1 361	14 830	3 085
发电量 (千瓦小时)	Electricity (kwh)	4 685	6 070	25 110	27 473
水 泥 (公斤)	Cement (kg)	1 688	1 361	3 821	4 350
社会消费品零售总额(元)	**Total Retail Sales of Consumer Goods (yuan)**	**26 418**		**25 392**	**24 262**
进出口总额 (美元)	**Total Exports and Imports (USD)**	**2 969**		**1 723**	**2 600**
出口总额	Total Exports	1 638	4 827	1 479	2 272
进口总额	Total Imports	1 331		244	328
人民生活	**People's Livelihood**				
城镇常住居民人均可支配收入 (元)	Per Capita Disposable Income of Urban Permanent Households (yuan)	36 396		28 463	36 730
农村常住居民人均可支配收入 (元)	Per Capita Disposable Income of Rural Permanent Households (yuan)	13 432		10 183	17 786
教 育 (人/万人)	**Education (person/10 000 persons)**				
在校学生数	Student Enrollment				
普通高等学校	Institution of Higher Education	218		306	184
普通中学	Regular Secondary Schools	492		1 225	476
小 学	Primary Schools	728		1 907	556
卫 生	**Health Care**				
卫生技术人员数 (人/万人)	Medical Technical Personnel (person/10 000 person)	64		123	91
# 医 生	Doctors	24		44	33
医院床位数 (张/万人)	Hospital Beds (unit/10 000 persons)	44		115	76

注：本表价值量指标按当年价格计算。

1—10 续表 Continued

(2017 年)

指　　标	Item	为全国的(%) Ratio of XPCC to the Whole Country (%)	为全国农垦的(%) Ratio of XPCC to State Farmland Reclamation System (%)	为新疆的(%) Ratio of XPCC to Xinjiang (%)
生产总值 (元)	**Gross Domestic Product (yuan)**	**134.3**	**142.5**	**177.6**
全社会固定资产投资(元)	**Total Investment in Fixed Assets (yuan)**	**145.6**	**185.2**	**68.5**
财　政	**Finance**			
一般公共预算收入 (元)	General Budgetary Revenue in Local Finance (yuan)	35.7		73.3
一般公共预算支出 (元)	General Budgetary Expenditure in Local Finance (yuan)			157.3
农　业	**Agriculture**			
主要农产品产量 (公斤)	Output of Major Farm Products (mg)			
粮　食	Grain	191.0	34.8	70.5
棉　花	Cotton	14 520.3	396.7	151.0
油　料	Oil-bearing Crops	266.2	134.7	120.7
糖　料	Sugar	750.5	126.2	153.6
水　果	Fruits		262.1	
肉　类	Meat	250.0	84.7	118.6
水产品	Aquatic Products	36.9	16.5	
工　业	**Industry**			
主要工业产品产量	Output of Major Industrial Products			
布 (米)	Cloth (meter)	81.9	114.8	222.5
纱 (公斤)	Yarn (kg)	573.1	243.3	128.9
机制纸及纸板 (公斤)	Machine-Made Paper and Paperboards (kg)		63.7	
成品糖 (公斤)	Refined Sugar (kg)	586.7	32.9	140.5
原　煤 (公斤)	Crude Coal (kg)	121.5	226.6	
发电量 (千瓦小时)	Electricity (kwh)	586.4	452.6	109.4
水　泥 (公斤)	Cement (kg)	257.7	319.6	113.8
社会消费品零售总额(元)	**Total Retail Sales of Consumer Goods (yuan)**	**91.8**		**95.6**
进出口总额 (美元)	**Total Exports and Imports (USD)**	**87.6**		**150.9**
出口总额	Total Exports	138.7	47.1	153.6
进口总额	Total Imports	24.6		134.1
人民生活	**People's Livelihood**			
城镇常住居民人均可支配收入 (元)	Per Capita Disposable Income of Urban Permanent Households (yuan)	100.9		129.0
农村常住居民人均可支配收入 (元)	Per Capita Disposable Income of Rural Permanent Households (yuan)	132.4		174.7
教　育 (人/万人)	**Education (person/10 000 persons)**			
在校学生数	Student Enrollment			
普通高等学校	Institution of Higher Education	84.6		60.1
普通中学	Regular Secondary Schools	96.8		38.8
小　学	Primary Schools	76.3		29.1
卫　生	**Health Care**			
卫生技术人员数 (人/万人)	Medical Technical Personnel (person/10 000 person)	141.8		74.3
#医　生	Doctors	137.5		75.7
医院床位数 (张/万人)	Hospital Beds (unit/10 000 persons)	173.1		66.1

Note: Data in value terms in this table are calculated at current prices.

1—11　国民经济主要指标分月变化情况

（2017年）

指　　标	Item	1月 1 Month	1—2月 1—2 Month
核　算	**Accounts**		
生产总值　（亿元）	**Gross Domestic Product　(100 million yuan)**		
# 第一产业	Primary Industry		
第二产业	Secondary Industry		
第三产业	Tertiary Industry		
# 工　业	Industry		
生产总值增长速度（%）（比上年同期）	Gross Domestic Product Annual Growth Rate（%）(Ratio Last Year Same Period)		
# 第一产业	Primary Industry		
第二产业	Secondary Industry		
第三产业	Tertiary Industry		
# 工　业	Industry		
规模以上工业	**Industry above Designated Size**		
增加值增长速度　（%）	Added Value Growth　（%）		7.3
# 轻工业	Light Industry		14.7
重工业	Heavy Industry		3.3
# 国有控股企业	State-owned Holding Enterprises		6.5
# 大中型企业	Large and Medium Scale Enterprises		2.7
主要工业产品产量	Output of Major Industrial Products		
纱　（万吨）	Yarn　(10 000 tons)		6.43
布　（亿米）	Cloth　(100 million m)		0.13
成品糖　（万吨）	Refined Suagar　(10 000 tons)		2.74
原　煤　（万吨）	Crude Coal　(10 000 tons)		79.45
发电量　（亿千瓦时）	Electrcity　(100 million kwh)		115.34
水　泥　（万吨）	Cement　(10 000 tons)		2.96
焦　炭　（万吨）	Coke　(10 000 tons)		108.68
番茄酱罐头　（万吨）	Canned Ketchup　(10 000 tons)		0.20
塑料树脂及共聚物　（万吨）	Plastics resin and　(10 000 tons)		22.10
规模以上工业企业财务指标	Financial Indicators of Industrial Enterprises above Designated Size		
产品销售收入　（亿元）	Sales Revenue　(10 000 yuan)		13.50
税金总额　（亿元）	Total Tax　(10 000 yuan)		201.80
利润总额　（亿元）	Total Profits　(10 000 yuan)		33.10
# 亏损企业亏损额　（亿元）	Total Loss of Lost Enterprises　(10 000 yuan)		−17.90
应收帐款净额　（亿元）	Net Accounts Receivable　(10 000 yuan)		19.60
产成品　（亿元）	Semi-finished Products　(10 000 yuan)		6.80
建筑业	**Construction**		
建筑业产值　（亿元）	Output Value of Contruction　(100 million yuan)		
建筑业产值增长速度（%）（比上年同期）	Output Value of Contruction Annual Growth Rate（%）(Ratio Last Year Same Period)		

Main Indicators on National Economy by Month

1—3月 1-3 Month	1—4月 1-4 Month	1—5月 1-5 Month	1—6月 1-6 Month	1—7月 1-7 Month	1—8月 1-8 Month	1—9月 1-9 Month	1—10月 1-10 Month	1—11月 1-11 Month	1—12月 1-12 Month
315.92			736.70			1 387.82			2 339.07
21.97			46.87			228.56			506.33
150.03			382.31			641.99			1 026.50
143.92			307.52			517.27			806.24
136.12			291.90			436.67			725.98
8.8			8.1			7.7			8.0
7.6			7.2			7.5			7.6
9.6			6.1			4.0			4.6
8.1			10.9			12.8			12.9
9.4			8.1						6.4
7.3	6.9	5.0	7.1	6.1	4.8	3.3	2.1	2.1	
13.3	9.8	7.3	7.6	5.0	3.7	−0.5	−1.7	−1.8	
4.0	5.4	3.8	6.7	6.5	5.3	4.8	4.0	4.2	
5.0	5.9	5.1	6.8	6.8	7.8	6.4	6.6	5.6	
2.2	1.8	0.2	2.3	3.9	3.3	2.4	2.3	2.0	
10.51	14.71	18.20	22.12	26.82	30.70	34.84	38.56	48.99	
0.28	0.38	0.44	0.50	0.58	0.68	0.82	0.98	1.17	
2.74	2.74	2.74	2.75	2.74	2.74	3.92	7.86	13.24	
122.95	209.14	277.25	353.50	436.43	530.97	612.04	684.00	778.19	
180.22	239.37	294.50	357.27	443.79	509.95	573.55	636.61	700.37	
52.73	151.09	297.07	466.18	600.37	742.67	904.90	1 061.47	1 429.72	
177.51	239.33	293.52	364.73	422.98	450.07	492.42	535.61	581.45	
0.31	0.49	0.66	0.78	1.06	20.19	42.99	46.16	46.51	
34.12	44.91	56.40	70.87	80.96	91.43	103.78	112.89	164.11	
15.50	11.70	10.30	11.10	11.70	15.40	11.60	10.90	9.70	
−56.70	−34.30	−28.10	−40.40	−9.50		21.00	22.80		
29.40	15.40	5.30	2.30	4.90	3.30	4.10	5.20	6.00	
−17.20	−9.80	−11.30	−4.60	−3.40	−7.00	−1.50	−3.10	−15.00	
12.30	14.00	16.20	11.70	−7.60	−19.80	−25.50	−21.10	−37.20	
14.50	18.00	25.70	18.30	14.00	12.80	13.60	17.30	10.00	
58.71			376.91			856.08			1 250.07
13.70			−1.90			2.50			0.6

1—11 续表

（2017 年）

指 标	Item	1月 1 Month	1—2月 1-2 Month
竣工产值 （亿元）	Output Value Completed (100 million yuan)		
房屋建筑施工面积 （万平方米）	Floor Space of Buildings under Construction (10 000 sq.m)		
# 新开工面积	Newly-opened Floor Space		
房屋建筑竣工面积 （万平方米）	Floor Space of Buildings Colmpleted (10 000 sq.m)		
道路运输业	**Highways Transportation**		
旅客周转量 （亿人公里）	Passenger-Kilometers (100 million passenger-km)		
货物周转量 （亿吨公里）	Freight Ton-Kilometers (100 million ton-km)		
国内贸易	**Domestic Trade**		
社会消费品零售总额 （亿元）	Total Retail Sales of Consumer Goods (100 million yuan)		
社会消费品零售总额增长速度 （%）（比上年同期）	Total Retail Sales of Consumer Goods Annual Growth Rate (%) (Ratio Last Year Same Period)		
商品销售总额 （亿元）	Total Sales of Goods (100 million yuan)		
对外经济贸易	**Foreign Tread**		
进出口总额 （亿美元）	Total Exports and Imports (USD 100 million)		
# 出口总额	Total Exports		
进出口总额增长速度 （%）（比上年同期）	Total Exports and Imports Annual Growth Rate (%) (Ratio Last Year Same Period)		
# 出口总额	Total Exports		
全社会固定资产投资总额（亿元）	**Total Investment in Fixed Assets (100 million yuan)**		**13.58**
# 国 有	State-owned		6.83
# 第一产业	Primary Industry		1.20
第二产业	Secondary Industry		9.16
第三产业	Tertiary Industry		3.22
# 工业投资	Industry		9.14
# 民间投资	Private		4.26
全社会固定资产投资增长速度 （%）（比上年同期）	Total Investment in Fixed Assets Annual Growth Rate (%) (Ratio Last Year Same Period)		97.9
# 国 有	State-owned		256.8
# 第一产业	Primary Industry		335.9
第二产业	Secondary Industry		45.5
第三产业	Tertiary Industry		1 015.1
# 工业投资	Industry		45.3
# 民间投资	Private		10.5
财 政 （亿元）	**Finance (100 million yuan)**		
一般公共预算收入	General Public Budget Income		
一般公共预算支出	General Public Budget Expenditure		
在岗职工	**Staff and Workers**		
在岗职工人数 （万人）	Staff and Workers on the Job (10 000 persons)		
在岗职工工资总额 （亿元）	Total Wages of Staff and Workers on the Job (100 million yuan)		

注：在岗职工人数和在岗职工工资总额的统计范围为规模以上工业法人企业、资质以上建筑业法人企业、规模以上服务业、限额以上批发和零售业法人企业非私营单位。

Continued

1—3月 1-3 Month	1—4月 1-4 Month	1—5月 1-5 Month	1—6月 1-6 Month	1—7月 1-7 Month	1—8月 1-8 Month	1—9月 1-9 Month	1—10月 1-10 Month	1—11月 1-11 Month	1—12月 1-12 Month
8.98			76.41			231.05			6 144.68
1 566.62			3 031.17			4 029.00			5 085.65
105.74			1 016.06			1 733.52			2 433.20
11.88			206.40			650.24			1 761.67
27.35			57.76			93.38			142.74
107.54			285.85			582.37			866.89
126.82			277.72			439.32			708.37
11.50			11.30			10.40			12.00
722.24			1 549.36			2 421.35			3 826.13
10.95			31.59			44.13			75.90
10.01			28.62			38.98			66.33
47.7			25.9			0.3			6.2
51.9			24.3			—4.8			—0.3
118.67	**293.44**	**500.80**	**766.75**	**969.47**	**1 213.77**	**1 509.63**	**1744.88**	**1 930.27**	**1 966.15**
79.09	182.95	304.69	459.46	572.57	715.53	898.44	1 044.98	1 154.8	908.03
13.22	38.36	61.25	89.63	109.95	134.36	158.13	179.93	195.99	200.86
55.37	116.30	186.69	282.48	356.60	448.79	568.78	643.21	713.57	724.38
50.08	138.78	252.87	394.63	502.91	630.62	782.72	921.74	1020.71	1 040.91
54.37	116.18	186.48	282.33	356.45	448.55	568.20	642.61	712.84	723.65
37.94	108.36	193.97	304.61	393.92	494.85	607.23	695.31	770.41	783.29
46.5	38.2	20.3	8.7	8.3	11.6	12.7	12.6	14.4	14.2
61.4	45.5	26.2	9.1	6.0	10.6	11.7	11.6	11.2	11.4
97.3	109.4	70.4	46.5	33.5	30.8	23.2	15.6	13.4	12.3
28.8	19.1	5.6	—4.4	—2.1	1.1	6.2	7.9	11.6	11.7
59.9	44.0	24.1	13.2	12.2	16.5	15.8	15.5	16.7	16.5
26.5	19.1	6.7	—3.8	—0.9	2.8	8.4	10.0	15.5	15.5
26.6	35.0	15.9	10.5	14.4	15.3	16.7	16.5	21.9	21.1
25.04	34.18	45.04	53.95	65.32	77.69	86.68	101.92	111.54	129.60
121.27	176.95	243.27	350.15	413.37	504.03	575.61	641.55	739.01	880.37
21.75			27.97			31.58			21.37
25.67			74.39			128.00			209.50

Note: The statistical scope of Staff and Workers on the Job and Total Wages of Staff and Workers on the Job refers to industrial corporative enterprises、construction corporative enterprises above qualification,service enterprises above designated size ,wholesale and retail corporative ,enterprises above designated size and non—private nuits.

1—12　各师主要国民经济指标

（2017 年）

指　　标	Item	一　师 Division 1	二　师 Division 2	三　师 Division 3	四　师 Division 4
人口与劳动力　（万人）	**Population and Labor force　(10 000 persons)**				
年末总人口	Year-end Population	35.80	21.48	25.37	24.52
就业人员数	Employment	18.16	9.64	11.61	11.00
# 在岗职工人数	Staff and Workers on the job	8.87	5.36	4.98	6.24
生产总值　（亿元）	**Gross Domestic Product　(10 000 yuan)**	**299.34**	**138.17**	**120.59**	**175.64**
# 第一产业	Primary Industry	121.03	40.90	41.93	42.23
第二产业	Secondary Industry	116.59	60.88	46.11	89.50
第三产业	Tertiary Industry	61.72	36.39	32.55	43.91
# 工　业	Industry	76.06	42.52	31.32	76.80
建筑业	Construction	40.57	18.36	14.79	12.70
生产总值构成　（%）	**Composition of GDP　(%)**				
# 第一产业	Primary Industry	40.4	29.6	34.8	24.0
第二产业	Secondary Industry	38.9	44.1	38.2	51.0
第三产业	Tertiary Industry	20.6	26.3	27.0	25.0
# 工　业	Industry	25.4	30.8	26.0	43.7
建筑业	Construction	13.6	13.3	12.3	7.2
全社会固定资产投资（亿元）	**Total Investment in Fixed Assets　(100 million yuan)**	**179.82**	**152.29**	**187.91**	**139.50**
# 房地产开发	Real Estate Development	4.89	2.78	0.36	9.64
财　政　（亿元）	**Finance　(100 million yuan)**				
一般公共预算收入	General Public Budget Income	8.54	3.49	4.14	4.24
一般公共预算支出	General Public Budget Expenditure	81.49	66.33	76.76	68.57
人民生活	**People's Livelihood**				
城镇常住居民人均可支配收入	Per Capita Disposable Income of Urban Permanent Households	36 485	36 671	36 412	36 048
连队常住居民人均可支配收入	Per Capita Disposable Income of Brigade Permanent Households	19 130	18 105	17 053	16 242
农　业	**Agriculture**				
总播种面积　（千公顷）	Total Sown Area　(1 000 hectares)	174.18	88.53	128.32	129.46
农林牧渔业总产值（亿元）	Gross Output Value of Farming, Forestry, Animal Husbandry and Fishery　(100 million yuan)	258.27	90.08	98.19	91.56
农　业	Farming	231.70	70.60	83.43	59.11
林　业	Forestry	2.73	0.77	0.91	1.19
牧　业	Animal Husbandry	14.07	13.34	8.04	25.46
渔　业	Fishery	0.99	1.00	0.25	1.69
服务业	Services	8.78	4.37	5.56	4.11
主要农产品产量　（万吨）	Output of Major Farm Products　(10 000 tons)				
粮　食	Grain	21.43	7.00	18.44	67.76
棉　花	Cotton	33.40	10.14	15.02	1.56
油　料	Oil-bearing Crops	0.21	0.18	0.69	8.20
甜　菜	Beetroots	0.44	14.40		46.43
水　果	Fruits	169.83	40.56	49.91	34.72
牲畜存栏头数（万头只）	Number of Livestock　(10 000 heads)	66.88	64.48	78.42	116.16
肉　类	Meat	3.33	4.25	2.36	5.75
工　业	**Industry**				
工业总产值　（亿元）	Gross Industrial Output Value　(10 000 million yuan)	274.28	162.62	129.24	184.88
# 国有控股企业	State-owned and State-holding Entenrprises	91.56	33.82	55.42	64.93
# 轻工业	Light Industry	181.83	104.00	76.23	89.48
重工业	Heavy Industry	89.33	54.13	51.16	87.79
主要工业产品产量（万吨）	Output of Major Industrial Products　(10 000 tons)				
纱	Yarn	11.69	6.77	4.85	
布　（万米）	Cloth　(10 000 meter)	3 165		6 284	
机制糖	Machine-made Sugar	4.61			4.73
原　煤	Crude Coal	101.23	211.21		54.53
发电量　（亿千瓦小时）	Electricity　(10 000 million kwh)	24.05	8.19	15.08	35.81
水　泥	Cement	399.29	39.50	31.21	179.88
能源（规模以上工业企业）	**Energy (Industrial Enterprises above Designated Size)**				
综合能源消费量（万吨标准煤）	Comsuption of Comprehensive Energy　(10 000 tons standard coal)	153.13	43.57	40.53	268.37
建筑业总产值　（亿元）	**Output Value of Construction　(100 million yuan)**	**180.31**	**81.60**	**65.73**	**52.03**
道路运输业	**Highways Transportation**				
客运量　（万人）	Passenger Traffic Volume　(10 000 persons)	2 927	1 805	894	1 968
货运量　（万吨）	Freight Traffic　(10 000 tons)	11 929	3 826	898	3 512
旅客周转量　（亿人公里）	Passenger-Kilometers　(100 million passenger-km)	24.34	7.56	6.25	12.63
货物周转量　（亿吨公里）	Freight Ton-Kilometers　(100 million ton-km)	139.67	22.16	10.73	52.87
贸易业	**Trade**				
社会消费品零售总额（亿元）	Total Retail Sales of Consumer Goods　(100 million yuan)	76.92	69.24	46.40	29.99
进出口总额　（万美元）	Total Exports and Imports　(USD 10 000)	1 123	8 088	75 532	248 555

注：本表在岗职工人数指标统计口径为非私营单位。

Main National Economic Indicators by Division

五 师 Division 5	六 师 Division 6	七 师 Division 7	八 师 Division 8	九 师 Division 9	十 师 Division 10	十一师 Division 11	十二师 Division 12	十三师 Division 13	十四师 Division 14
12.72	35.53	23.35	64.11	7.72	10.12	6.91	12.24	10.89	5.70
5.86	15.98	11.37	31.77	3.73	4.37	4.56	5.69	5.76	2.67
3.88	7.81	4.94	15.71	2.41	2.19	3.67	2.47	2.06	2.11
58.20	**271.58**	**161.07**	**505.35**	**36.09**	**73.16**	**103.99**	**180.68**	**116.33**	**19.54**
19.87	49.66	45.81	82.77	14.63	13.08	0.08	8.94	16.31	9.09
16.19	138.37	68.06	203.57	8.41	35.84	86.63	70.10	71.70	6.21
22.14	83.55	47.21	219.00	13.06	24.24	17.28	101.63	28.32	4.23
11.24	106.77	36.45	168.03	4.89	23.22	7.73	66.39	65.03	1.19
4.97	31.61	31.65	35.58	3.53	12.61	78.90	3.78	6.67	5.02
34.1	18.3	28.4	16.4	40.5	17.9	0.1	4.9	14.0	46.5
27.8	51.0	42.3	40.3	23.3	49.0	83.3	38.8	61.6	31.8
38.0	30.8	29.3	43.3	36.2	33.1	16.6	56.3	24.3	21.7
19.3	39.3	22.6	33.2	13.5	31.7	7.4	36.7	55.9	6.1
8.5	11.6	19.7	7.0	9.8	17.2	75.9	2.1	5.7	25.7
39.12	**195.58**	**173.05**	**346.99**	**31.36**	**105.51**	**42.29**	**146.07**	**178.69**	**45.52**
0.49	62.55	4.21	26.89	0.75	2.57	9.72	24.37	4.81	0.99
0.73	2.33	3.51	1.62	0.59	2.82	0.37	5.51	2.13	0.94
31.05	74.29	53.90	102.56	29.37	37.21	10.48	25.47	31.50	18.71
36 140	36 402	36 601	37 200	35 954	36 006	38 178	36 886	38 115	36 919
17 663	17 798	17 995	19 020	16 173	16 898		18 206	17 808	13 730
68.92	175.91	135.14	270.40	81.22	65.60	0.42	12.81	26.54	5.32
44.91	117.43	100.49	194.60	32.72	36.99	0.17	23.01	36.99	20.45
33.38	79.48	78.29	136.25	19.34	22.42	0.17	14.47	26.20	18.11
0.47	0.88	1.12	8.66	0.52	0.57		1.89	0.21	0.42
7.10	24.92	15.28	28.68	10.84	8.00		4.35	7.30	1.74
0.20	0.46	0.66	0.88	0.02	2.76		0.33	0.04	
3.76	11.69	5.14	20.13	2.00	3.24		1.97	3.24	0.18
13.41	44.68	11.73	15.16	31.06	11.04	0.09	2.11	3.78	0.86
10.79	20.15	21.99	50.28		0.55	0.06	0.02	3.93	
0.64	2.31	1.70	0.10	3.17	3.18	0.01	0.49	0.04	0.01
13.72	11.96	24.24	8.47	70.11	8.69				
10.38	5.87	12.81	23.19	0.75	0.63	0.01	7.37	15.54	20.60
33.01	85.09	57.31	89.77	87.84	37.22		9.92	30.68	15.80
1.89	7.65	3.24	7.99	2.72	1.77		0.94	2.00	0.48
36.34	421.07	126.69	626.96	18.22	60.03	28.08	52.46	218.62	6.58
10.69	28.01	47.41	263.77	8.38	10.29	19.21	33.51	19.59	2.93
12.44	72.46	40.42	121.82	10.65	25.44	0.07	36.81	21.11	2.50
21.15	344.25	77.74	497.51	6.25	27.69	28.01	13.53	187.84	3.45
0.56	2.67	5.66	15.45					1.19	0.03
		530	4 993					5	
		2.67		6.16					
	248.12	78.05	54.14		143.88		9.53		
14.57	225.93	24.82	406.30	1.56	7.25		2.79	34.89	0.91
20.00	99.32	91.98	302.25		7.31	56.85		42.41	
55.29	1340.61	168.14	2251.32	17.54	26.62	2.21	23.29	949.18	0.16
21.13	**131.69**	**131.89**	**146.42**	**14.69**	**53.67**	**302.87**	**16.07**	**29.63**	**22.33**
924	3 081	3 505	1 519	679	3 246	450	2 158	1 569	285
762	15 669	5 282	11 895	906	1 070	185	6 298	5 850	12
6.05	16.28	32.65	17.82	3.15	6.77	1.29	3.67	3.81	0.49
13.64	168.44	95.77	265.46	15.17	23.27	1.26	19.56	37.84	0.33
22.28	110.24	54.16	119.37	14.70	37.34	1.50	66.98	18.95	1.87
59 089	22 341	10 029	45 553	18 668	94 539	28 593	11 351	5 855	623

Note: Statistical indicators of data on staff and workers on the job is non-private anits.

1—13　南疆师主要国民经济指标

Main National Economic Indicators of XPCC's Southern Divisions

指　　标	Item	2016 绝对量 Absolute Value	比去年增长(%) Increase Rate Against Last Year(%)	占兵团比重(%) Ratio to XPCC(%)
人口与劳动力　(万人)	**Population and Labor Force　(10 000 persons)**			
年末总人口	Year-end Population	81.09	2.5	28.6
# 少数民族	Minority Population	21.10	4.1	51.6
# 团　场	Farm Population	60.80	5.1	32.9
就业人员数	Employment	38.37	2.8	27.8
# 非私营单位在岗职工人数	Staff and Workers in Non-private Units	19.10	0.5	27.1
生产总值　(亿元)	**Gross Domestic Product　(100 million yuan)**	**530.47**	**10.4**	**24.9**
# 第一产业	Primary Industry	197.81	7.0	42.3
第二产业	Secondary Industry	213.89	15.2	22.2
第三产业	Tertiary Industry	118.76	7.7	16.9
# 工　业	Industry	136.30	23.2	20.5
建筑业	Construction	77.63	3.2	25.9
生产总值构成　(%)	Composition of GDP　(%)	100.0		
# 第一产业	Primary Industry	37.3		
第二产业	Secondary Industry	40.3		
第三产业	Tertiary Industry	22.4		
# 工　业	Industry	25.7		
建筑业	Construction	14.6		
全社会固定资产投资(亿元)	**Total Investment in Fixed Assets　(100 million yuan)**	**459.82**	**−2.6**	**26.7**
# 房地产开发	Real Estate Development	11.63	−8.1	6.3
农　业	**Agriculture**			
总播种面积　(千公顷)	Total Sown Area　(1 000 hectares)	410.20	0.3	29.9
农林牧渔业总产值(亿元)	Gross Output Value of Farming, Forestry, Animal Husbandry and Fishery　(100 million yuan)	433.29	9.9	40.9
农　业	Farming	376.07	10.5	46.3
林　业	Forestry	4.90	31.0	26.3
牧　业	Animal Husbandry	33.27	2.6	21.7
渔　业	Fishery	2.06	9.6	24.6
服务业	Services	17.00	5.8	25.7
主要农产品产量　(万吨)	**Output of Major Farm Products　(10 000 tons)**			
粮　食	Grain	58.50	2.9	21.6
棉　花	Cotton	56.94	1.6	38.1
油　料	Oil-bearing Crops	1.75	21.4	7.5
甜　菜	Beetroots	28.30	98.0	13.6
水　果	Fruits	254.44	8.4	69.7
牲畜存栏头数　(万头只)	Number of Livestock　(10 000 heads)	232.94	3.3	30.5
肉　类	Meat	9.73	4.6	23.6
工　业	**Industry**			
工业总产值　(亿元)	Gross Industrial Output Value　(100 million yuan)	538.63	25.4	23.7
# 国有控股企业	State-owned and State-holding Entenrprises	165.05	14.3	24.9
主要工业产品产量　(万吨)	Output of Major Industrial Products　(10 000 tons)			
纱	Yarn	13.68	69.6	33.6
布　(万米)	Cloth　(10 000 meter)	3 830.98	64.5	33.2
机制糖	Machine-made Sugar	5.04	57.4	34.4
原　煤	Crude Coal	268.85	2.9	24.8
发电量　(亿千瓦小时)	Electricity　(10 000million kwh)	40.54	5.0	5.4
水　泥	Cement	463.55	−1.3	37.5
能源 (规模以上工业企业)	**Energy　(Industrial Enterprises above Designated Size)**			
综合能源消费量 (万吨标准煤)	Comsuption of Comprehensive Energy　(10 000 tons standard coal)	161.34	5.9	5.2
建筑业总产值　(亿元)	**Output Value of Construction(100 million yuan)**	345.02	3.0	27.7
道路运输业	**Highways Transportation**			
客运量　(万人)	Passenger Traffic Volume　(10 000 persons)	5 601	8.7	24.6
货运量　(万吨)	Freight Traffic(10 000 tons)	13 433	21.3	23.1
旅客周转量　(万人公里)	Passenger-Kilometers　(10 000 passenger-km)	351 001	14.2	27.0
货物周转量　(万吨公里)	Freight Ton-Kilometers　(10 000 ton-km)	1 418 831	31.0	20.4
贸易业	**Trade**			
社会消费品零售总额　(亿元)	Total Retail Sales of Consumer Goods　(100 million yuan)	171.10	17.1	27.1
进出口总额　(万美元)	Total Exports and Imports　(USD 10 000)	80 485	−3.0	11.4

注：南疆四师包括一师、二师、三师和十四师。

1—13 续表 Continued

指 标	Item	2017 绝对量 Absolute Value	比去年增长(%) Increase Rate Against Last Year(%)	占兵团比重(%) Ratio to XPCC(%)
人口与劳动力 (万人)	**Population and Labor Force (10 000 persons)**			
年末总人口	Year-end Population	88.35	9.0	29.4
# 少数民族	Minority Population	22.68	7.5	50.3
# 团 场	Farm Population	67.92	11.7	33.6
就业人员数	Employment	42.08	9.7	29.2
# 非私营单位在岗职工人数	Staff and Workers in Non-private Units	21.32		
生产总值 (亿元)	**Gross Domestic Product (100 million yuan)**	**577.63**	**11.6**	**28.7**
# 第一产业	Primary Industry	212.96	7.0	42.1
第二产业	Secondary Industry	229.78	7.4	22.4
第三产业	Tertiary Industry	134.89	11.4	16.7
# 工 业	Industry	151.08	10.8	20.8
建筑业	Construction	78.74	1.4	26.2
生产总值构成 (%)	Composition of GDP (%)	100.0		
# 第一产业	Primary Industry	36.9		
第二产业	Secondary Industry	39.8		
第三产业	Tertiary Industry	23.4		
# 工 业	Industry	26.2		
建筑业	Construction	13.6		
全社会固定资产投资(亿元)	**Total Investment in Fixed Assets (100 million yuan)**	**565.56**	**23.0**	**28.8**
# 房地产开发	Real Estate Development	9.01	—22.5	5.8
农 业	**Agriculture**			
总播种面积 (千公顷)	Total Sown Area (1 000 hectares)	396.35	—3.4	29.1
农林牧渔业总产值(亿元)	Gross Output Value of Farming, Forestry, Animal Husbandry and Fishery (100 million yuan)	466.99	7.1	40.8
农 业	Farming	403.83	6.9	46.3
林 业	Forestry	4.83	0.3	23.7
牧 业	Animal Husbandry	37.20	9.0	22.0
渔 业	Fishery	2.25	11.2	24.2
服务业	Services	18.88	8.0	25.5
主要农产品产量 (万吨)	**Output of Major Farm Products (10 000 tons)**			
粮 食	Grain	47.73	—18.4	19.2
棉 花	Cotton	58.55	2.8	34.9
油 料	Oil-bearing Crops	1.09	—37.8	5.2
甜 菜	Beetroots	14.85	—47.5	7.5
水 果	Fruits	280.90	10.4	71.6
牲畜存栏头数 (万头只)	Number of Livestock (10 000 heads)	225.58	—3.2	29.2
肉 类	Meat	10.42	7.1	23.5
工 业	**Industry**			
工业总产值 (亿元)	Gross Industrial Output Value (100 million yuan)	562.64	3.7	23.9
# 国有控股企业	State-owned and State-holding Entenrprises	183.74	10.6	25.2
主要工业产品产量 (万吨)	Output of Major Industrial Products (10 000 tons)			
纱	Yarn	23.35	70.7	47.8
布 (万米)	Cloth (10 000 meter)	9 449.40	146.7	63.1
机制糖	Machine-made Sugar	4.61	—8.6	25.4
原 煤	Crude Coal	312.44	16.2	34.7
发电量 (亿千瓦小时)	Electricity (10 000million kwh)	48.23	19.0	6.0
水 泥	Cement	470.00	1.4	37.0
能源 (规模以上工业企业)	**Energy (Industrial Enterprises above Designated Size)**			
综合能源消费量(万吨标准煤)	Comsuption of Comprehensive Energy (10 000 tons standard coal)	172.81	6.3	5.1
建筑业总产值 (亿元)	**Output Value of Construction(100 million yuan)**	**349.97**	**1.4**	**28.0**
道路运输业	**Highways Transportation**			
客运量 (万人)	Passenger Traffic Volume (10 000 persons)	5 911	5.5	23.6
货运量 (万吨)	Freight Traffic(10 000 tons)	16 665	24.1	24.5
旅客周转量 (万人公里)	Passenger-Kilometers (10 000 passenger-km)	386 266	10.0	27.1
货物周转量 (万吨公里)	Freight Ton-Kilometers (10 000 ton-km)	1 728 903	21.9	19.9
贸易业	**Trade**			
社会消费品零售总额 (亿元)	Total Retail Sales of Consumer Goods (100 million yuan)	194.42	13.6	27.4
进出口总额 (万美元)	Total Exports and Imports (USD 10 000)	85 366	6.1	11.2

Note: Southern Divisions are Division 1、Division 2、Division 3 and Division 14.

1—14 改革开放40年国民经济主要指标

Main Indicators of National Economy in Reform and Opening Up 40 Years

指 标	Item	1978	2017	1979—2017年均增长(%) 1979—2017 Annual Growth(%)
年末总人口 （万人）	**Total Population in the Year-end (10 000 persons)**	**211.98**	**300.53**	**0.9**
# 农牧团场	Population of Farms	186.30	202.07	0.2
# 少数民族	Ethnic Minority	21.33	45.08	1.9
就业人员数 （万人）	**Employment (10 000 persons)**	**91.85**	**144.17**	**1.2**
# 在岗职工人数	Staff and Workers	91.85	74.32	—0.5
生产总值 （亿元）	**Gross Domestic Product (100 million yuan)**	**7.40**	**2 339.07**	**10.7**
# 第一产业	Primary Industry	3.51	506.33	8.1
第二产业	Secondary Industry	2.28	1 026.50	12.4
第三产业	Tertiary Industry	1.61	806.24	12.4
# 工 业	Industry	1.95	725.98	9.8
建筑业	Construction	0.34	300.73	14.9
全社会固定资产投资 （亿元）	**Total Investment in Fixed Assets (100 million yuan)**	**1.46**	**1 966.15**	**20.6**
# 国有单位	State-owned Units	1.46	908.03	18.2
# 第一产业	Primary Industry	0.78	200.86	14.8
第二产业	Secondary Industry	0.35	724.38	22.7
第三产业	Tertiary Industry	0.33	1 040.91	23.3
新增固定资产	Newly Increased Fixed Assets	1.23	1 614.11	20.2
农 业	**Agriculture**			
总播面积 （千公顷）	Total Sown Area (1 000 hectares)	740.19	1 362.77	1.6
农林牧渔业总产值（亿元）	Gross Output Value of Farming, Forestry, Animal Husbandry and Fishery (100 million yuan)	6.23	1 145.86	14.3
主要农产品产量 （万吨）	Output of Major Farm Products (10 000 tons)			
粮 食	Grain	86.69	248.55	2.7
棉 花	Cotton	1.95	167.88	12.1
油 料	Oil-bearing Crops	2.29	20.92	5.8
甜 菜	Beet Roots	12.55	198.46	7.3
水 果	Fruits	2.57	392.16	13.8
肉 类	Meat	2.07	44.38	8.2
水产品	Aquatic Products	0.30	5.39	7.7
工 业	**Industry**			
工业总产值 （亿元）	Gross Industrial Output Value (100 million yuan)	5.45	2 397.87	15.0
主要工业产品产量	Output of Major Industrial Products			
布 （百万米）	Cloth (100 million meter)	42.37	149.77	3.3
机制纸及纸板 （万吨）	Machine-Made Paper and Paperboards (10 000 tons)	0.73	7.32	6.1

1—14 续表 Continued

指 标	Item	1978	2017	1979—2017年均增长(%) 1979—2017 Annual Growth(%)
成品糖 (万吨)	Refined Sugar (10 000 tons)	1.90	18.17	6.0
原 煤 (万吨)	Crude Coal (10 000 tons)	223.16	900.69	3.6
发电量 (亿千瓦时)	Electricity (100 million kwh)	2.54	798.10	15.9
水 泥 (万吨)	Cement (10 000 tons)	7.66	1 269.99	14.0
建筑业	**Construction**			
建筑业总产值 (亿元)	Gross Construction Output Value (100 million yuan)	0.96	1 250.07	20.2
房屋施工面积(万平方米)	Floor Space of Buildings Under Construction (10 000 sq.m)	123.16	5 085.65	10.0
房屋竣工面积(万平方米)	Floor Space of Buildings Completed (10 000 sq.m)	108.71	1 761.67	7.4
道路运输业	**Highways Transportation**			
货运量 (万吨)	Freight Traffic (10 000 tons)	393.72	68 105.00	14.1
客运量 (万人)	Passenger Traffic Volume (10 000 persons)	39.81	25 013.00	18.0
货物周转量 (亿吨公里)	Freight Ton-Kilometers (100 million ton-km)	5.01	866.89	14.1
旅客周转量 (亿人公里)	Passenger-Kilometers (100 million passenger-km)	0.63	142.74	14.9
国内贸易	**Domestic Trade**			
社会消费品零售总额 (亿元)	Total Retail Sales of Consumer Goods (100 million yuan)	5.71	708.37	13.2
教 育	**Education**			
学校数 (所)	Number of Schools (unit)			
普通高等学校	Regular Institutions of Higher Education	3	6	1.8
中等职业学校	Secondary Vocational Schools	5	30	4.7
普通中学	Regular Secondary Schools	672	237	−2.6
小 学	Primary Schools	2 055	55	−8.9
在校学生数 (人)	Student Enrollment (person)			
普通高等学校	Institution of Higher Education	1 920	53 758	8.9
中等职业学校	Specialized Secondary Schools	466	28 183	11.1
普通中学	Regular Secondary Schools	262 626	138 890	−1.6
小 学	Primary Schools	294 083	162 228	−1.5
工 资	**Wages**			
在岗职工工资总额(亿元)	Total Wages of Staff and Workers (100 million yuan)	5.78	493.54	12.1
在岗职工平均工资 (元)	Average Wage of Staff and Workers on the Job (yuan)	638	58 464	12.3
卫 生	**Health Care**			
医院床位数 (万张)	Hospital Beds (10 000 units)	1.68	2.22	0.7
卫生技术人员数 (万人)	Medical Technical Personnel (10 000 persons)	1.35	2.66	1.8
# 医 生	Doctors	0.38	0.97	2.4

1—15　代管团场(园区)国民经济主要指标

The Main Indicators of the National Economy of the Management Group (Park)

(2017 年)

指　　标	Item	一　团(七师代管) Farm 1 (7 Division)	五　团(十一师代管) Farm 5 (11 Division)	三十六团(四师代管) Farm 36 (4 Division)	五〇团(六师代管) Farm 50 (6 Division)	四十七团(十二师代管) Farm 47 (12 Division)	皮墨(北京)工业园区(八师代管) Pimo(Beijing) Park (8 Division)
年末总人口　(人)	**Population at the Year-end　(person)**	**23 685**	**21 153**	**8 136**	**23 597**	**5 874**	**1 039**
# 少数民族	Ethnic Minority	6 872	3 673	478	13 561	2 078	574
就业人员数　(人)	**Employment at the Year-end　(person)**	**9 979**	**9 651**	**4 139**	**8 472**	**2 898**	**1 039**
# 在岗职工	Staff and Workers	3 135	4 880	2 214	2 634	2 529	636
生产总值　(万元)	**Gross Domestic Product　(10 000 yuan)**	**206 222**	**162 699**	**59 320**	**76 752**	**14 612**	
第一产业	Primary Industry	83 712	68 667	29 891	38 350	10 406	
第二产业	Secondary Industry	89 359	70 543	15 902	18 416	333	
第三产业	Tertiary Industry	33 151	23 489	13 527	19 986	3 873	
# 工　业	Industry	77 683	28 752	15 902	18 416	333	
固定资产投资　(亿元)	**Total Investment in Fixed Assets (100 million yuan)**	**8.05**	**5.21**	**6.81**	**3.01**	**1.46**	**10.09**
农　业	**Agriculture**						
农业总产值　(亿元)	Gross Output Value of Farming, Forestry, Animal Husbandry and Fishery (100 million yuan)	17.83	16.73	5.13	9.04	2.65	
总播种面积　(千公顷)	Total Sown Area　(1 000 hectares)	12.78	8.04	0.90	14.26	0.97	
主要农产品产量　(万吨)	Output of Major Farm Products (10 000 tons)						
粮　食	Grain	2.14	1.17		1.75	0.26	
棉　花	Cotton	2.39	0.90		1.87		
油　料	Oil-bearing Crops		0.10			…	
甜　菜	Beet Roots		0.44				
水　果	Fruits	10.36	18.88	3.16	3.19	2.27	
牲畜年末头数　(万头/只)	Head Number of livestock at the end of Year (10 000 heads)	5.59	5.62	1.27	7.32	1.50	
肉类　(万吨)	Meat　(10 000 tons)	0.21	0.28	0.14	0.23	0.10	
工　业	**Industry**						
规上工业主营业务收入(万元)	Industry Main Business Income above Scale (10 000 yuan)	173 908	49 397	36 999	54 656		21 379
建筑业	**Construction**						
建筑业施工产值　(万元)	Gross Construction Output Value (100 million yuan)	51 893	185 736				
国内贸易	**Domestic Trade**						
社会消费品零售总额(万元)	Total Retail Sales of Consumer Goods (100 million yuan)	50 012	34 930	12 055	31 851	1 821	

2018

BING TUAN

第二篇

国民经济核算

Chapter 2 National Accounts

简要说明

一、本篇资料主要内容

本篇资料包括兵团生产总值及分产业情况等内容。

二、本篇资料来源

国民经济核算资料由兵团统计局国民经济核算设计管理处根据《兵团生产总值核算报表制度》收集、测算、整理提供。

Brief Introduction

1. Main contents

This chapter mainly contains data on gross domestic product and industries of XPCC.

2. Sources of Data

Relevant data on national accounts are collected, measured and calculated and compiled by the National Accounts Section of the Statistics Bureau of XPCC according to *the Reporting Form System on GDP of XPCC*.

2—1　生产总值(当年价)

Gross Domestic Product(Current Prices)

计量单位:万元　　　　(10 000 yuan)

单位 Unit	年份 Year	生产总值 Gross Domestic Product	第一产业 Primary Industry	第二产业 Secondary Industry	第三产业 Tertiary Industry
	1950	2 351	579	1 018	754
	1952	11 995	2 364	7 496	2 135
	1954	11 780	1 721	7 459	2 600
	1957	23 306	4 730	11 415	7 161
	1962	41 328	12 458	16 862	12 008
	1965	56 461	19 359	23 732	13 370
	1970	61 439	24 935	20 481	16 023
	1975	35 648	20 670	8 021	6 957
	1978	73 999	35 054	22 824	16 121
	1980	101 937	43 846	40 988	17 103
	1985	201 281	80 919	79 270	41 092
	1990	456 919	209 110	146 872	100 937
	1995	1 216 042	560 034	318 684	337 324
	2000	1 764 103	716 298	485 276	562 529
	2001	1 897 094	628 242	558 056	710 796
	2002	2 141 330	763 586	605 907	771 837
	2003	2 577 755	1 091 024	638 721	848 010
	2004	2 888 118	1 151 287	709 091	1 027 740
	2005	3 311 246	1 306 458	833 482	1 171 306
	2006	3 760 294	1 421 888	994 196	1 344 210
	2007	4 412 150	1 625 837	1 274 481	1 511 832
	2008	5 232 964	1 823 154	1 660 880	1 748 930
	2009	6 106 945	2 047 350	2 065 678	1 993 917
	2010	7 706 152	2 788 111	2 622 637	2 295 404
	2011	9 656 558	3 240 425	3 676 635	2 739 498
	2012	11 972 109	3 883 741	4 751 585	3 336 783
	2013	14 998 657	4 354 495	6 264 139	4 380 023
	2014	17 386 812	4 169 645	7 768 622	5 448 545
	2015	19 349 122	4 280 411	8 838 760	6 229 951
	2016	21 343 307	4 678 739	9 655 779	7 008 789
	2017	23 390 728	5 063 290	10 265 022	8 062 416
一　师	Division 1	2 993 351	1 210 313	1 165 850	617 188
二　师	Division 2	1 381 750	409 040	608 776	363 934
三　师	Division 3	1 205 862	419 303	461 050	325 509
四　师	Division 4	1 756 372	422 270	894 955	439 147
五　师	Division 5	581 968	198 722	161 886	221 360
六　师	Division 6	2 715 833	496 599	1 383 742	835 492
七　师	Division 7	1 610 672	458 066	680 553	472 053
八　师	Division 8	5 053 487	827 734	2 035 705	2 190 048
九　师	Division 9	360 950	146 257	84 141	130 552
十　师	Division 10	731 566	130 759	358 380	242 427
十一师	Division 11	1 039 890	784	866 272	172 834
十二师	Division 12	1 806 768	89 408	701 019	1 016 341
十三师	Division 13	1 163 283	163 097	717 006	283 180
十四师	Division 14	195 362	90 938	62 120	42 304
兵团直属	Directly under XPCC	793 614		83 567	710 047

注:本表按当年价格计算。2014 年按新产业划分标准农林牧渔服务业等划入第三产业。(下同)

2—1续表　Continued

计量单位:万元　　　　(10 000 yuan)

单　位 Unit	年　份 Year	#工　业 Industry	#建筑业 Construction	#批发和零售业 Wholesale and Retail Trade	#交通运输仓储和邮政业 Transport, Storage and Postal Services	人均生产总值(元) Per Capita GDP(yuan)
	1950		1 018	268	249	
	1952	1 415	6 081	667	645	439
	1954	2 359	5 100	738	741	723
	1957	5 862	5 553	1 883	1 948	764
	1962	13 575	3 287	3 290	2 761	478
	1965	18 073	5 659	3 770	3 516	465
	1970	17 481	3 000	4 839	4 679	330
	1975	6 627	1 394	2 358	2 052	177
	1978	19 459	3 365	5 666	4 508	374
	1980	32 433	8 555	5 832	5 165	464
	1985	57 977	21 293	14 343	9 501	900
	1990	115 096	31 776	27 614	17 594	2 134
	1995	238 917	79 767	97 204	37 523	5 390
	2000	321 603	163 673	145 006	66 867	7 276
	2001	364 601	193 455	180 913	91 208	7 773
	2002	398 492	207 415	176 029	93 276	8 644
	2003	409 605	229 116	176 541	101 599	10 222
	2004	455 845	253 246	185 673	101 724	11 313
	2005	564 964	268 518	196 842	115 084	12 900
	2006	693 498	300 698	235 352	134 448	14 605
	2007	910 969	363 512	277 496	157 708	17 088
	2008	1 201 483	459 397	331 738	174 244	20 291
	2009	1 486 955	578 723	375 456	195 454	23 734
	2010	1 862 830	759 807	394 095	229 614	29 752
	2011	2 542 782	1 133 853	483 672	310 292	36 993
	2012	3 277 020	1 474 565	587 945	392 728	45 501
	2013	4 266 072	1 998 067	1 080 262	478 473	56 069
	2014	5 192 189	2 576 433	1 344 182	583 799	63 989
	2015	5 833 857	3 004 903	1 577 871	718 912	70 380
	2016	6 657 925	2 999 747	1 758 369	866 126	76 230
	2017	7 259 772	3 007 251	2 019 781	1 047 460	80 113
一　师	Division 1	760 551	405 697	139 380	77 095	87 422
二　师	Division 2	425 168	183 608	108 469	36 858	66 965
三　师	Division 3	313 165	147 885	58 772	17 807	49 336
四　师	Division 4	767 992	126 963	116 945	64 270	73 353
五　师	Division 5	112 389	49 663	43 167	19 192	46 856
六　师	Division 6	1 067 688	316 054	193 533	174 285	77 334
七　师	Division 7	364 452	316 545	117 457	125 717	69 810
八　师	Division 8	1 680 265	355 806	317 104	408 305	80 859
九　师	Division 9	48 879	35 262	31 379	11 330	47 565
十　师	Division 10	232 249	126 131	70 716	36 751	74 938
十一师	Division 11	77 297	788 975	21 616	872	151 254
十二师	Division 12	663 881	37 765	628 203	35 357	159 324
十三师	Division 13	650 341	66 665	69 176	38 920	110 068
十四师	Division 14	11 888	50 232	4 352	701	36 155
兵团直属	Directly under XPCC	83 567		99 512	195 311	

Note: Data in value terms in this table are calculated at current prices. According to the new national classification standard of industries, farming, forestry, animal husbandry and fishery Services are divided into the tertiary industry (the same as follows).

2—2 生产总值构成(当年价)

Composition of Gross Domestic Product(Current Prices)

计量单位:% (生产总值=100,GDP=100) (%)

单 位 Unit	年 份 Year	第一产业 Primary Industry	第二产业 Secondary Industry	第三产业 Tertiary Industry	# 工 业 Industry	# 建筑业 Construction	# 批发和零售业 Wholesale and Retail Trade	# 交通运输仓储和邮政业 Transport, Storage and Postal Services
	1950	24.6	43.3	32.1		43.3	11.4	10.6
	1952	19.7	62.5	17.8	11.8	50.7	5.6	5.4
	1954	14.6	63.3	22.1	20.0	43.3	6.3	6.3
	1957	20.3	49.0	30.7	25.2	23.8	8.1	8.4
	1962	30.1	40.8	29.1	32.8	8.0	8.0	6.7
	1965	34.3	42.0	23.7	32.0	10.0	6.7	6.2
	1970	40.6	33.3	26.1	28.4	4.9	7.9	7.6
	1975	58.0	22.5	19.5	18.6	3.9	6.6	5.8
	1978	47.4	30.8	21.8	26.3	4.5	7.7	6.1
	1980	43.0	40.2	16.8	31.8	8.4	5.7	5.1
	1985	40.2	39.4	20.4	28.8	10.6	7.1	4.7
	1990	45.8	32.1	22.1	25.2	6.9	6.0	3.9
	1995	46.1	26.2	27.7	19.6	6.6	8.0	3.1
	2000	40.6	27.5	31.9	18.2	9.3	8.2	3.8
	2001	33.1	29.4	37.5	19.2	10.2	9.5	4.8
	2002	35.7	28.3	36.0	18.6	9.7	8.2	4.4
	2003	42.3	24.8	32.9	15.9	8.9	6.8	3.9
	2004	39.9	24.5	35.6	15.8	8.7	6.4	3.5
	2005	39.4	25.2	35.4	17.1	8.1	5.9	3.5
	2006	37.8	26.4	35.8	18.4	8.0	6.3	3.6
	2007	36.8	28.9	34.3	20.7	8.2	6.3	3.6
	2008	34.9	31.7	33.4	22.9	8.8	6.3	3.3
	2009	33.5	33.8	32.7	24.3	9.5	6.1	3.2
	2010	36.2	34.0	29.8	24.2	9.8	5.1	3.0
	2011	33.5	38.1	28.4	26.3	11.8	5.0	3.2
	2012	32.4	39.7	27.9	27.4	12.3	4.9	3.3
	2013	29.0	41.8	29.2	28.5	13.3	7.2	3.2
	2014	24.0	44.7	31.3	29.9	14.8	7.7	3.4
	2015	22.1	45.7	32.2	30.2	15.5	8.2	3.7
	2016	21.9	45.2	32.8	31.2	14.1	8.2	4.1
	2017	21.6	43.9	34.5	31.0	12.9	8.6	4.5
一 师 Division 1		40.4	38.9	20.6	25.4	13.6	4.7	2.6
二 师 Division 2		29.6	44.1	26.3	30.8	13.3	7.9	2.7
三 师 Division 3		34.8	38.2	27.0	26.0	12.3	4.9	1.5
四 师 Division 4		24.0	51.0	25.0	43.7	7.2	6.7	3.7
五 师 Division 5		34.1	27.8	38.0	19.3	8.5	7.4	3.3
六 师 Division 6		18.3	51.0	30.8	39.3	11.6	7.1	6.4
七 师 Division 7		28.4	42.3	29.3	22.6	19.7	7.3	7.8
八 师 Division 8		16.4	40.3	43.3	33.2	7.0	6.3	8.1
九 师 Division 9		40.5	23.3	36.2	13.5	9.8	8.7	3.1
十 师 Division 10		17.9	49.0	33.1	31.7	17.2	9.7	5.0
十一师 Division 11		0.1	83.3	16.6	7.4	75.9	2.1	0.1
十二师 Division 12		4.9	38.8	56.3	36.7	2.1	34.8	2.0
十三师 Division 13		14.0	61.6	24.3	55.9	5.7	5.9	3.3
十四师 Division 14		46.5	31.8	21.7	6.1	25.7	2.2	0.4
兵团直属 Directly under XPCC			10.5	89.5	10.5		12.5	

注:本表按当年价格计算。
Note:Data in value terms in this table are calculated at current prices.

2—3 生产总值(可比价)

Gross Domestic Product(Comparable Prices)

计量单位:万元 (10 000 yuan)

单位 Unit	年份 Year	生产总值 Gross Domestic Product	第一产业 Primary Industry	第二产业 Secondary Industry	第三产业 Tertiary Industry
	1950	4 696	1 461	2 158	1 077
	1952	22 761	6 237	14 127	2 397
	1954	22 198	4 620	14 544	3 034
	1957	44 008	12 661	21 899	9 448
	1962	74 219	28 961	26 901	18 357
	1965	114 099	52 144	42 467	19 488
	1970	131 391	66 654	40 203	24 534
	1975	76 948	50 342	15 472	11 134
	1978	148 812	75 506	45 958	27 348
	1980	185 848	79 728	77 801	28 319
	1985	319 193	127 351	132 879	58 963
	1990	468 049	213 569	153 543	100 937
	1995	670 018	293 976	192 461	183 581
	2000	964 777	417 586	277 391	269 800
	(2000)	1 764 103	716 298	485 276	562 529
	2001	1 871 389	680 008	522 488	668 893
	2002	2 129 251	790 975	575 511	762 765
	2003	2 405 517	953 114	613 211	839 192
	2004	2 705 844	1 048 284	668 224	989 336
	2005	3 012 939	1 137 769	766 482	1 108 688
	(2005)	3 311 246	1 306 458	833 482	1 171 306
	2006	3 687 941	1 415 562	967 167	1 305 212
	2007	4 136 450	1 523 206	1 176 357	1 436 887
	2008	4 652 765	1 661 328	1 395 790	1 595 647
	2009	5 287 837	1 776 928	1 748 858	1 762 051
	2010	6 025 403	1 986 104	2 119 104	1 920 195
	(2010)	7 706 152	2 788 111	2 622 637	2 295 404
	2011	8 912 072	2 971 350	3 423 826	2 516 896
	2012	10 556 306	3 239 768	4 433 840	2 882 698
	2013	12 470 683	3 499 765	5 604 441	3 366 477
	2014	14 484 296	3 559 950	6 845 831	4 078 515
	2015	16 268 323	3 805 123	7 904 693	4 558 507
	(2015)	19 349 122	4 280 411	8 838 760	6 229 951
	2016	21 100 478	4 535 128	9 736 431	6 828 919
	2017	22 767 404	4 877 946	10 177 327	7 712 131
一师	Division 1	2 949 732	1 161 667	1 179 777	608 288
二师	Division 2	1 366 788	399 403	611 703	355 682
三师	Division 3	1 176 351	404 483	463 893	307 975
四师	Division 4	1 729 098	409 807	912 024	407 267
五师	Division 5	567 780	187 583	165 477	214 720
六师	Division 6	2 668 386	490 879	1 366 051	811 456
七师	Division 7	1 581 829	435 157	683 228	463 444
八师	Division 8	4 795 381	780 166	1 952 271	2 062 944
九师	Division 9	355 483	146 530	83 086	125 867
十师	Division 10	714 881	125 946	357 381	231 554
十一师	Division 11	1 011 718	683	878 586	132 449
十二师	Division 12	1 786 651	89 186	701 695	995 770
十三师	Division 13	1 116 743	154 116	690 003	272 624
十四师	Division 14	204 481	92 340	71 375	40 766
兵团直属	Directly under XPCC	742 102		60 777	681 325

注:本表数据 2000 年(含 2000 年)以前按 1990 年可比价格计算,2000 年以后按 2000 年可比价计算,2005 年以后按 2005 年可比价计算,2010 年以后按 2010 年可比价计算,2015 年以后按 2015 年可比价计算。

2－3 续表 Continued

计量单位:万元 (10 000 yuan)

单位 Unit	年份 Year	# 工业 Industry	# 建筑业 Construction	# 批发和零售业 Wholesale and Retail Trade	# 交通运输仓储和邮政业 Transport, Storage and Postal Services	人均生产总值(元) Per Capita GDP(yuan)
	1950		2 158	436	219	
	1952	2 274	11 853	843	354	833
	1954	3 829	10 715	1 194	730	1 363
	1957	9 417	12 482	3 622	1 573	1 443
	1962	19 541	7 360	5 739	2 668	858
	1965	29 719	12 748	6 581	3 460	939
	1970	32 957	7 246	8 764	4 694	706
	1975	12 554	2 918	4 340	2 097	382
	1978	38 371	7 587	10 631	4 384	752
	1980	64 566	13 235	10 377	5 421	846
	1985	111 318	21 561	22 154	9 969	1 427
	1990	121 767	31 776	27 615	17 569	2 186
	1995	148 539	43 922	50 371	24 761	2 970
	2000	199 923	77 468	66 162	36 284	3 979
	(2000)	321 603	163 673	145 006	66 867	7 276
	2001	348 355	174 133	168 012	83 023	7 667
	2002	384 779	190 732	173 330	87 238	8 595
	2003	403 054	210 157	176 456	95 204	9 539
	2004	440 651	227 573	180 846	99 526	10 599
	2005	530 464	236 018	193 192	110 760	11 738
	(2005)	564 964	268 518	196 842	115 084	12 900
	2006	672 943	294 224	229 587	128 209	14 324
	2007	838 190	338 167	259 848	142 698	16 020
	2008	1 020 578	375 212	283 473	156 787	18 042
	2009	1 284 121	464 737	323 712	170 237	20 550
	2010	1 522 183	590 921	329 153	198 324	23 263
	(2010)	1 862 830	759 807	394 095	229 614	29 752
	2011	2 395 778	1 028 048	452 555	287 928	34 140
	2012	3 122 109	1 311 731	520 741	351 113	40 120
	2013	3 989 243	1 615 198	645 381	422 278	46 619
	2014	4 870 826	1 975 005	765 055	508 498	53 307
	2015	5 658 820	2 245 873	861 264	602 846	59 174
	(2015)	5 833 857	3 004 903	1 577 871	718 912	70 380
	2016	6 735 603	3 002 750	1 680 983	846 414	75 363
	2017	7 169 067	3 010 260	1 902 181	1 036 153	77 978
一 师	Division 1	774 079	406 103	139 130	77 680	86 148
二 师	Division 2	427 911	183 792	106 216	37 138	66 240
三 师	Division 3	315 860	148 033	58 529	17 944	48 128
四 师	Division 4	784 934	127 090	102 528	64 758	72 214
五 师	Division 5	115 936	49 712	42 421	18 861	45 714
六 师	Division 6	1 049 681	316 370	189 778	175 608	75 983
七 师	Division 7	366 813	316 862	115 981	126 671	68 560
八 师	Division 8	1 596 456	356 163	236 981	392 621	76 729
九 师	Division 9	47 790	35 296	30 266	11 416	46 844
十 师	Division 10	231 124	126 257	68 023	37 030	73 229
十一师	Division 11	88 822	789 764	21 337	879	147 157
十二师	Division 12	664 521	37 803	620 101	35 626	157 550
十三师	Division 13	623 270	66 733	68 356	39 214	105 665
十四师	Division 14	21 093	50 282	4 303	707	37 842
兵团直属	Directly under XPCC	60 777		98 231		182 633

Note: Figures in value terms in this table are calculated at 1990 comparable prices before 2000 and at 2000 comparable prices since 2000. Figures are calculated at 2005 comparable prices since 2005 , at 2010 comparable prices since 2010 and at 2015 comparable prices since 2015 .

2—4 生产总值指数(可比价)

Indices of Gross Domestic Product(Comparable Prices)

计量单位:% (上年=100,preceding year=100) (%)

单 位 Unit	年 份 Year	生产总值 Gross Domestic Product	第一产业 Primary Industry	第二产业 Secondary Industry	第三产业 Tertiary Industry
	1951	141.1	156.3	96.2	210.5
	1952	343.6	273.2	680.8	105.7
	1954	143.2	109.9	156.5	151.1
	1957	123.6	119.0	113.2	167.8
	1962	90.3	106.9	81.5	82.9
	1965	111.8	116.4	111.1	102.1
	1970	119.7	121.5	131.0	101.0
	1975	59.5	97.4	27.8	50.7
	1978	174.0	144.6	213.6	232.4
	1980	113.1	98.4	138.5	104.4
	1985	112.7	107.5	113.2	124.4
	1990	112.7	133.1	94.4	109.6
	1995	110.6	119.2	99.1	111.5
	2000	111.5	112.8	115.1	106.1
	2001	106.1	94.9	107.7	118.9
	2002	113.8	116.3	110.1	114.0
	2003	113.0	108.4	113.3	117.9
	2004	112.5	110.0	109.0	117.9
	2005	111.3	108.5	114.7	112.1
	2006	112.6	111.4	116.0	111.4
	2007	112.2	107.6	121.6	110.1
	2008	112.5	109.1	118.7	111.0
	2009	113.6	107.0	125.3	110.4
	2010	113.9	111.8	121.2	109.0
	2011	116.0	107.6	130.5	109.6
	2012	118.4	109.0	129.5	114.5
	2013	118.1	108.0	126.4	116.8
	2014	116.1	107.9	122.2	114.3
	2015	112.3	106.9	115.5	111.8
	2016	109.1	106.0	110.2	109.6
	2017	108.0	107.6	104.6	112.9
一 师	Division 1	106.7	105.9	105.6	110.5
二 师	Division 2	109.4	108.6	108.3	112.4
三 师	Division 3	110.2	108.0	110.7	112.5
四 师	Division 4	110.3	107.9	106.2	123.7
五 师	Division 5	96.5	109.6	81.7	100.1
六 师	Division 6	103.9	108.8	101.2	105.7
七 师	Division 7	108.2	107.4	106.2	112.2
八 师	Division 8	107.9	107.0	102.6	113.8
九 师	Division 9	110.7	107.1	119.0	109.9
十 师	Division 10	119.6	110.0	123.6	119.4
十一师	Division 11	103.6	91.5	100.2	134.6
十二师	Division 12	105.2	106.1	98.3	110.5
十三师	Division 13	111.8	110.1	114.2	107.0
十四师	Division 14	110.0	110.9	110.3	107.3
兵团直属	Directly under XPCC	108.2		119.3	123.8

注:本表数据2000年(含2000年)以前按1990年可比价格计算,2000年以后按2000年可比价计算,2005年以后按2005年可比价计算,2010年以后按2010年可比价计算,2015年以后按2015年可比价计算。

2—4 续表 Continued

计量单位:% (%)

单 位 Unit	年 份 Year	# 工 业 Industry	# 建筑业 Construction	# 批发和零售业 Wholesale and Retail Trade	# 交通运输仓储和邮政业 Transport, Storage and Postal Services	人均生产总值(元) Per Capita GDP(yuan)
	1951		96.2	211.0	212.3	
	1952		571.2	91.6	76.1	
	1954	139.8	163.5	165.8	294.4	186.2
	1957	132.3	102.2	186.2	150.4	102.3
	1962	77.0	96.5	95.2	91.9	83.1
	1965	114.3	104.4	95.7	97.5	96.7
	1970	126.2	158.7	102.3	106.9	111.4
	1975	25.7	43.6	55.9	52.0	65.4
	1978	250.2	122.7	221.5	212.3	158.3
	1980	148.2	105.0	102.0	106.9	111.0
	1985	118.1	93.2	137.8	113.5	113.5
	1990	92.3	103.5	117.7	105.4	113.1
	1995	96.9	107.3	107.9	108.2	108.4
	2000	118.7	106.8	109.2	103.9	111.0
	2001	108.3	106.4	115.9	124.2	105.4
	2002	110.5	109.5	103.2	105.1	112.1
	2003	115.2	110.2	121.5	109.1	111.0
	2004	109.3	108.3	102.5	104.5	111.1
	2005	120.4	103.7	106.8	111.3	110.8
	2006	119.1	109.6	116.6	111.4	112.2
	2007	124.6	114.8	113.2	111.3	111.8
	2008	121.8	111.0	109.1	109.9	112.6
	2009	125.8	123.9	111.2	108.5	113.9
	2010	118.5	128.4	101.7	116.5	113.9
	2011	128.6	135.3	114.8	125.4	115.1
	2012	130.3	127.6	115.1	121.9	117.5
	2013	127.8	123.1	123.9	120.3	116.2
	2014	122.1	122.3	118.5	120.4	114.3
	2015	116.2	113.7	112.6	118.6	111.0
	2016	115.5	99.9	106.5	117.7	107.1
	2017	106.4	100.6	113.2	122.4	103.5
一 师	Division 1	110.6	97.3	108.8	120.5	100.5
二 师	Division 2	107.6	110.0	115.4	126.0	103.3
三 师	Division 3	116.3	100.4	113.0	125.0	103.6
四 师	Division 4	107.3	100.0	115.3	112.1	106.6
五 师	Division 5	92.9	63.7	104.9	99.3	93.6
六 师	Division 6	99.6	107.3	110.5	120.5	102.1
七 师	Division 7	110.4	101.8	110.2	133.4	106.1
八 师	Division 8	103.7	98.2	118.2	125.9	104.1
九 师	Division 9	121.5	115.7	108.7	123.4	108.3
十 师	Division 10	112.1	152.4	123.6	127.3	112.0
十 一 师	Division 11	115.5	98.7	258.2	63.7	102.1
十 二 师	Division 12	99.6	80.4	110.1	97.9	94.6
十 三 师	Division 13	119.1	82.4	117.1	122.1	106.5
十 四 师	Division 14	107.6	111.5	98.0	113.6	102.1
兵团直属	Directly under XPCC	119.5		115.6		121.5

Note: Figures in value terms in this table are calculated at 1990 comparable prices before 2000 and at 2000 comparable prices since 2000. Figures are calculated at 2005 comparable prices since 2005 and at 2010 comparable prices since 2010 and at 2015 comparable prices since 2015.

2—5 三次产业和主要行业贡献率

Share of the Contributions of the Three Strata of Industry and Main Sectors to the Increase of the GDP

计量单位:% (%)

单位 Unit	年份 Year	生产总值 Gross Domestic Product	第一产业 Primary Industry	第二产业 Secondary Industry	第三产业 Tertiary Industry
	1990	100.0	100.6	−17.3	16.8
	1991	100.0	0.0	53.7	46.3
	1992	100.0	−14.9	36.5	78.4
	1993	100.0	−1.1	47.0	54.1
	1994	100.0	68.1	3.7	28.2
	1995	100.0	73.3	−2.7	29.4
	1996	100.0	−49.7	−67.2	216.9
	1997	100.0	74.6	17.1	8.3
	1998	100.0	51.1	20.7	28.1
	1999	100.0	5.3	57.1	37.6
	2000	100.0	47.7	36.7	15.6
	2001	100.0	−33.8	34.7	99.1
	2002	100.0	43.0	20.6	36.4
	2003	100.0	58.7	13.6	27.7
	2004	100.0	31.7	18.3	50.0
	2005	100.0	29.1	32.0	38.9
	2006	100.0	29.0	35.5	35.5
	2007	100.0	24.0	46.6	29.4
	2008	100.0	26.8	42.5	30.7
	2009	100.0	18.2	55.6	26.2
	2010	100.0	28.4	50.2	21.4
	2011	100.0	15.2	66.4	18.4
	2012	100.0	16.3	61.4	22.2
	2013	100.0	13.6	61.1	25.3
	2014	100.0	12.9	61.5	25.6
	2015	100.0	13.7	59.4	26.9
	2016	100.0	14.5	51.3	34.2
	2017	100.0	20.4	26.9	52.7
一 师	Division 1	100.0	34.8	33.9	31.2
二 师	Division 2	100.0	27.0	39.8	33.2
三 师	Division 3	100.0	27.4	41.1	31.4
四 师	Division 4	100.0	18.6	33.1	48.2
五 师	Division 5	100.0	−80.5	181.7	−1.2
六 师	Division 6	100.0	39.8	16.7	43.5
七 师	Division 7	100.0	24.8	33.3	41.9
八 师	Division 8	100.0	14.5	14.3	71.2
九 师	Division 9	100.0	28.4	38.5	33.1
十 师	Division 10	100.0	9.8	58.2	32.0
十一师	Division 11	100.0	−0.2	4.0	96.1
十二师	Division 12	100.0	5.9	−13.5	107.7
十三师	Division 13	100.0	12.0	72.8	15.2
十四师	Division 14	100.0	49.0	36.0	15.0
兵团直属	Directly under XPCC	100.0	0.0	7.0	93.0

注:本表按不变价格计算。贡献率指三次产业或主要行业增加值增量与生产总值增量之比。

2—5 续表 Continued

计量单位:% (%)

单 位 Unit	年 份 Year	# 工 业 Industry	# 建筑业 Construction	# 批发和零售业 Wholesale and Retail Trade	# 交通运输仓储和邮政业 Transport, Storage and Postal Services
	1990	−19.3	2.0	7.9	1.7
	1991	46.0	7.7	27.4	3.3
	1992	21.3	15.2	19.6	9.2
	1993	30.7	16.3	30.5	3.7
	1994	6.3	−2.6	−4.9	1.9
	1995	−7.4	4.7	5.7	2.9
	1996	−87.7	20.5	59.9	33.1
	1997	17.0	0.1	−9.9	1.2
	1998	5.5	15.2	8.8	5.1
	1999	30.0	27.1	4.2	3.5
	2000	31.7	5.0	5.6	1.4
	2001	24.9	9.7	21.4	15.1
	2002	14.1	6.4	2.1	1.6
	2003	6.6	7.0	1.1	2.9
	2004	12.5	5.8	1.5	1.4
	2005	29.2	2.7	4.0	3.7
	2006	28.7	6.8	8.7	3.5
	2007	36.8	9.8	6.7	3.2
	2008	35.3	7.2	4.6	2.7
	2009	41.5	14.1	6.3	2.1
	2010	32.3	17.9	0.7	3.8
	2011	44.2	22.2	4.8	4.8
	2012	44.2	17.3	4.1	3.8
	2013	45.3	15.9	6.5	3.7
	2014	43.7	17.8	5.9	4.3
	2015	44.2	15.2	5.4	5.3
	2016	51.5	−0.1	5.9	7.3
	2017	25.8	1.0	13.2	11.3
一 师	Division 1	40.1	−6.1	6.1	7.2
二 师	Division 2	25.6	14.2	12.1	6.5
三 师	Division 3	40.6	0.5	6.2	3.3
四 师	Division 4	33.1	0.0	8.4	4.3
五 师	Division 5	43.6	138.2	−9.6	0.7
六 师	Division 6	−4.7	21.4	18.0	29.9
七 师	Division 7	28.7	4.7	8.9	26.3
八 师	Division 8	16.1	−1.8	10.4	23.0
九 师	Division 9	24.6	13.9	7.0	6.3
十 师	Division 10	21.3	37.0	11.1	6.8
十一师	Division 11	33.6	−29.6	36.9	−1.4
十二师	Division 12	−3.0	−10.5	64.6	−0.9
十三师	Division 13	85.0	−12.2	8.5	6.0
十四师	Division 14	8.1	27.9	−0.5	0.5
兵团直属	Directly under XPCC	7.0	0.0	9.4	0.0

Note: Data in this table are calculated at constant prices. Share of the contributions of the three strata of industry or main sectors to the increase of the GDP refers to the proportion of the increment of the value-added of each industry to the increment of GDP.

2—6 三次产业和主要行业对生产总值增长的拉动百分点
Contribution of the Three Strata of Industry and Main Sectors to GDP Growth

单位 Unit	年份 Year	生产总值 Gross Domestic Product	第一产业 Primary Industry	第二产业 Secondary Industry	第三产业 Tertiary Industry
	1990	12.7	12.8	−2.2	2.1
	1991	6.8	0.0	3.7	3.1
	1992	4.8	−0.7	1.8	3.8
	1993	5.2	−0.1	2.4	2.8
	1994	9.9	6.7	0.4	2.8
	1995	10.6	7.8	−0.3	3.1
	1996	1.7	−0.8	−1.1	3.7
	1997	8.0	6.0	1.4	0.7
	1998	10.1	5.2	2.1	2.8
	1999	6.8	0.4	3.9	2.6
	2000	11.5	5.5	4.2	1.8
	2001	6.1	−2.1	2.1	6.0
	2002	13.8	5.9	2.8	5.0
	2003	13.0	7.6	1.8	3.6
	2004	12.5	4.0	2.3	6.2
	2005	11.3	3.3	3.6	4.4
	2006	12.6	3.6	4.5	4.5
	2007	12.2	2.9	5.7	3.6
	2008	12.5	3.3	5.3	3.8
	2009	13.6	2.5	7.6	3.6
	2010	13.9	4.0	7.0	3.0
	2011	16.0	2.4	10.7	2.9
	2012	18.4	3.0	11.3	4.1
	2013	18.1	2.5	11.1	4.6
	2014	16.1	2.1	10.0	4.0
	2015	12.3	1.7	7.3	3.3
	2016	9.1	1.3	4.7	3.1
	2017	8.0	1.6	2.1	4.2
一 师	Division 1	6.7	2.3	2.3	2.1
二 师	Division 2	9.4	2.5	3.7	3.1
三 师	Division 3	10.2	2.8	4.2	3.2
四 师	Division 4	10.3	1.9	3.4	5.0
五 师	Division 5	−3.5	2.8	−6.3	0.0
六 师	Division 6	3.9	1.5	0.7	1.7
七 师	Division 7	8.2	2.0	2.7	3.4
八 师	Division 8	7.9	1.2	1.1	5.6
九 师	Division 9	10.7	3.0	4.1	3.5
十 师	Division 10	19.6	1.9	11.4	6.3
十一师	Division 11	3.6	0.0	0.1	3.5
十二师	Division 12	5.2	0.3	−0.7	5.6
十三师	Division 13	11.8	1.4	8.6	1.8
十四师	Division 14	10.0	4.9	3.6	1.5
兵团直属	Directly under XPCC	23.4	0.0	1.6	21.8

注：本表按不变价格计算。拉动指生产总值增长速度与三次产业或主要行业贡献率之乘积。

2—6 续表 Continued

单 位 Unit	年 份 Year	# 工 业 Industry	# 建筑业 Construction	# 批发和零售业 Wholesale and Retail Trade	# 交通运输仓储和邮政业 Transport, Storage and Postal Services
	1990	—2.5	0.3	1.0	0.2
	1991	3.1	0.5	1.9	0.2
	1992	1.0	0.7	0.9	0.4
	1993	1.6	0.8	1.6	0.2
	1994	0.6	—0.3	—0.5	0.2
	1995	—0.8	0.5	0.6	0.3
	1996	—1.5	0.3	1.0	0.6
	1997	1.4	0.0	—0.8	0.1
	1998	0.6	1.5	0.9	0.5
	1999	2.0	1.8	0.3	0.2
	2000	3.6	0.6	0.6	0.2
	2001	1.5	0.6	1.3	0.9
	2002	1.9	0.9	0.3	0.2
	2003	0.9	0.9	0.1	0.4
	2004	1.6	0.7	0.2	0.2
	2005	3.3	0.3	0.5	0.4
	2006	3.6	0.9	1.1	0.4
	2007	4.5	1.2	0.8	0.4
	2008	4.4	0.9	0.6	0.3
	2009	5.7	1.9	0.9	0.3
	2010	4.5	2.5	0.1	0.5
	2011	7.1	3.6	0.8	0.8
	2012	8.1	3.2	0.8	0.7
	2013	8.2	2.9	1.2	0.7
	2014	7.1	2.9	1.0	0.7
	2015	5.4	1.9	0.7	0.7
	2016	4.7	0.0	0.5	0.7
	2017	2.1	0.1	1.0	0.9
一 师	Division 1	2.7	—0.4	0.4	0.5
二 师	Division 2	2.4	1.3	1.1	0.6
三 师	Division 3	4.1	0.1	0.6	0.3
四 师	Division 4	3.4	0.0	0.9	0.4
五 师	Division 5	—1.5	—4.8	0.3	0.0
六 师	Division 6	—0.2	0.8	0.7	1.2
七 师	Division 7	2.4	0.4	0.7	2.2
八 师	Division 8	1.3	—0.1	0.8	1.8
九 师	Division 9	2.6	1.5	0.8	0.7
十 师	Division 10	4.2	7.3	2.2	1.3
十 一 师	Division 11	1.2	—1.1	1.3	—0.1
十 二 师	Division 12	—0.2	—0.5	3.3	0.0
十 三 师	Division 13	10.0	—1.4	1.0	0.7
十 四 师	Division 14	0.8	2.8	0.0	0.0
兵团直属	Directly under XPCC	1.6	0.0	2.2	0.0

Note: Data in this table are calculated at constant prices. Contribution of the three strata of industry or main sectors to GDP growth refers to the growth rate of GDP multiplied by the contribution share of every industry.

2—7 按要素分列的分行业增加值

Value-added by Factor and Sector

计量单位：万元　　　　(2017 年)　　　　(10 000 yuan)

指　　标	Item	合计(按当年价计算) Total (Calculated at Current Prices)	劳动者报酬 Compensation of Laborers	生产税净额 Net Taxes on Production
生产总值	**Gross Domestic Product**	**23 390 728**	**12 300 298**	**1 913 779**
按产业分	**Grouped by Industries**			
第一产业	Primary Industry	5 063 290	3 701 825	−23 740
第二产业	Secondary Industry	10 265 022	4 222 122	1 288 621
第三产业	Tertiary Industry	8 062 416	4 376 351	648 898
按行业分	**Grouped by sectors**			
农、林、牧、渔业	Farming ,Forestry,Animal Husbandry and Fishery	5 385 098	3 916 727	−24 888
工　业	Industry	7 259 772	1 790 386	978 715
建筑业	Construction	3 007 251	2 432 540	310 028
批发和零售业	Wholesale and Retail Trade	2 019 781	788 552	306 350
交通运输、仓储和邮政业	Transport,Storage and Postal Services	1 047 460	455 834	103 398
住宿和餐饮业	Accommodation and Catering Services Industry	474 678	221 289	43 600
信息传输、软件和信息技术服务业	Information Deliver,Software and Information Technique Services Industry	110 175	27 934	2 764
金融业	Finance	717 755	309 654	34 655
房地产业	Real Estate Trade	528 858	121 038	99 532
租赁和商务服务业	Leasing and Business Service	273 807	108 538	30 838
科学研究和技术服务业	Scientific Research and Technical Service	175 667	111 909	9 820
水利、环境和公共设施管理业	Water Conservancy,Environment and Public Facilities Management	124 868	110 698	724
居民服务、修理和其他服务业	Resident,Repair and Other Services	233 305	145 531	11 065
教　育	Education	624 647	554 737	253
卫生和社会工作	Health Care and Social Security	475 719	382 007	271
文化、体育和娱乐业	Culture,Sports and Recreation	120 163	71 455	5 992
公共管理、社会保障和社会组织	Public Management and Social Organization	811 724	751 469	662

指　　标	Item	固定资产折旧 Depreciation of Fixed Assets	营业盈余 Operating Surplus	按 2015 年可比价计算 Calculated at Comparable Prices in 2015
生产总值	**Gross Domestic Product**	**3 008 989**	**6 167 662**	**22 767 404**
按产业分	**Grouped by Industries**			
第一产业	Primary Industry	408 901	976 304	4 877 946
第二产业	Secondary Industry	1 658 553	3 095 726	10 177 327
第三产业	Tertiary Industry	941 535	2 095 632	7 712 131
按行业分	**Grouped by sectors**			
农、林、牧、渔业	Farming ,Forestry,Animal Husbandry and Fishery	465 061	1 028 198	5 183 903
工　业	Industry	1 593 593	2 897 078	7 169 067
建筑业	Construction	65 133	199 550	3 010 260
批发和零售业	Wholesale and Retail Trade	141 039	783 840	1 902 181
交通运输、仓储和邮政业	Transport,Storage and Postal Services	213 630	274 598	1 036 153
住宿和餐饮业	Accommodation and Catering Services Industry	63 613	146 176	436 197
信息传输、软件和信息技术服务业	Information Deliver,Software and Information Technique Services Industry	30 659	48 818	107 057
金融业	Finance	34 092	339 354	692 453
房地产业	Real Estate Trade	168 427	139 861	529 994
租赁和商务服务业	Leasing and Business Service	25 424	109 007	249 281
科学研究和技术服务业	Scientific Research and Technical Service	10 349	43 589	156 237
水利、环境和公共设施管理业	Water Conservancy,Environment and Public Facilities Management	16 465	−3 019	120 055
居民服务、修理和其他服务业	Resident,Repair and Other Services	24 360	52 349	229 350
教　育	Education	42 259	27 398	602 644
卫生和社会工作	Health Care and Social Security	61 899	31 542	450 716
文化、体育和娱乐业	Culture,Sports and Recreation	10 488	32 228	112 365
公共管理、社会保障和社会组织	Public Management and Social Organization	42 498	17 095	779 491

2—8 各师按要素分生产总值

Gross Domestic Product by Factor and Division

计量单位:万元 (2017 年) (10 000 yuan)

单 位 Unit	合计(按当年价计算) Total (Calculated at Current Prices)	劳动者报酬 Compensation of Laborers	生产税净额 Net Taxes on Production	固定资产折旧 Depreciation of Fixed Assets	营业盈余 Operating Surplus	按 2015 年可比价计算 Calculated at Comparable Prices in 2015
总 计 Total	**23 390 728**	**12 300 298**	**1 913 779**	**3 008 989**	**6 167 662**	**22 767 404**
一 师 Division 1	2 993 351	1 794 170	115 495	325 595	758 091	2 949 732
二 师 Division 2	1 381 750	854 770	63 098	149 866	314 016	1 366 788
三 师 Division 3	1 205 862	742 007	56 507	135 895	271 453	1 176 351
四 师 Division 4	1 756 372	797 875	149 319	189 187	619 991	1 729 098
五 师 Division 5	581 968	417 000	24 154	81 658	59 156	567 780
六 师 Division 6	2 715 833	1 192 420	326 929	378 773	817 711	2 668 386
七 师 Division 7	1 610 672	949 516	100 935	195 917	364 304	1 581 829
八 师 Division 8	5 053 487	2 410 260	419 792	829 587	1 393 848	4 795 381
九 师 Division 9	360 950	272 882	16 148	43 065	28 855	355 483
十 师 Division 10	731 566	330 662	53 766	72 561	274 577	714 881
十 一 师 Division 11	1 039 890	822 095	115 536	43 768	58 491	1 011 718
十 二 师 Division 12	1 806 768	751 762	322 981	240 038	491 987	1 786 651
十 三 师 Division 13	1 163 283	433 603	65 710	237 872	426 098	1 116 743
十 四 师 Division 14	195 362	147 956	1 726	28 782	16 898	204 481
兵团直属 Directly under XPCC	793 614	383 320	81 683	56 425	272 186	742 102

2—9 各师生产总值要素构成

Composition of Key Factor of Gross Domestic Product by Division

(2017 年,生产总值=100,GDP=100)

单 位 Unit	劳动者报酬 Compensation of Laborers	生产税净额 Net Taxes on Production	固定资产折旧 Depreciation of Fixed Assets	营业盈余 Operating Surplus
总 计 Total	**52.6**	**8.2**	**12.9**	**26.4**
一 师 Division 1	59.9	3.9	10.9	25.3
二 师 Division 2	61.9	4.6	10.8	22.7
三 师 Division 3	61.5	4.7	11.3	22.5
四 师 Division 4	45.4	8.5	10.8	35.3
五 师 Division 5	71.7	4.2	14.0	10.2
六 师 Division 6	43.9	12.0	13.9	30.1
七 师 Division 7	59.0	6.3	12.2	22.6
八 师 Division 8	47.7	8.3	16.4	27.6
九 师 Division 9	75.6	4.5	11.9	8.0
十 师 Division 10	45.2	7.3	9.9	37.5
十 一 师 Division 11	79.1	11.1	4.2	5.6
十 二 师 Division 12	41.6	17.9	13.3	27.2
十 三 师 Division 13	37.3	5.6	20.4	36.6
十 四 师 Division 14	75.7	0.9	14.7	8.6
兵团直属 Directly under XPCC	48.3	10.3	7.1	34.3

注:本表按当年价格计算。
Note:Data in value terms in this table are calculated at current prices.

2—10 各师第一产业增加值

Value-added of Primary Industry by Division

计量单位:万元　　(2017 年)　　(10 000 yuan)

单　位	Unit	合计(按当年价计算) Total (Calculated at Current Prices)	劳动者报酬 Compensation of Laborers	生产税净额 Net Taxes on Production	固定资产折旧 Depreciation of Fixed Assets	营业盈余 Operating Surplus	按 2015 年可比价计算 Calculated at Comparable Prices in 2015
总　计	**Total**	**5 063 290**	**3 701 825**	**−23 740**	**408 901**	**976 304**	**4 877 946**
一　师	Division 1	1 210 313	927 210	2 504	83 834	196 765	1 161 667
二　师	Division 2	409 040	367 557	−13 578	26 760	28 301	399 403
三　师	Division 3	419 303	292 915	15	37 344	89 029	404 483
四　师	Division 4	422 270	304 504	329	19 729	97 708	409 807
五　师	Division 5	198 722	164 186	177	16 087	18 272	187 583
六　师	Division 6	496 599	311 219	121	42 750	142 509	490 879
七　师	Division 7	458 066	324 687	16	29 862	103 501	435 157
八　师	Division 8	827 734	573 948	−14 387	71 783	196 390	780 166
九　师	Division 9	146 257	133 012	5	9 344	3 896	146 530
十　师	Division 10	130 759	86 637		13 498	30 624	125 946
十一师	Division 11	784	495	−41	176	154	683
十二师	Division 12	89 408	65 000	145	8 703	15 560	89 186
十三师	Division 13	163 097	95 060	950	26 565	40 522	154 116
十四师	Division 14	90 938	55 395	4	22 466	13 073	92 340
兵团直属	Directly under XPCC						

2—11 各师第二产业增加值

Value-added of Secondary Industry by Division

计量单位:万元　　(2017 年)　　(10 000 yuan)

单　位	Unit	合计(按当年价计算) Total (Calculated at Current Prices)	劳动者报酬 Compensation of Laborers	生产税净额 Net Taxes on Production	固定资产折旧 Depreciation of Fixed Assets	营业盈余 Operating Surplus	按 2015 年可比价计算 Calculated at Comparable Prices in 2015
总　计	**Total**	**10 265 022**	**4 222 122**	**1 288 621**	**1 658 553**	**3 095 726**	**10 177 327**
一　师	Division 1	1 165 850	521 448	88 907	161 389	394 106	1 179 777
二　师	Division 2	608 776	293 112	60 370	58 668	196 626	611 703
三　师	Division 3	461 050	206 115	46 422	60 144	148 369	463 893
四　师	Division 4	894 955	286 191	121 505	110 296	376 963	912 024
五　师	Division 5	161 886	94 646	16 186	32 324	18 730	165 477
六　师	Division 6	1 383 742	414 213	272 479	230 464	466 586	1 366 051
七　师	Division 7	680 553	406 315	61 947	119 222	93 069	683 228
八　师	Division 8	2 035 705	488 632	299 296	447 560	800 217	1 952 271
九　师	Division 9	84 141	50 230	11 261	15 902	6 748	83 086
十　师	Division 10	358 380	144 519	36 156	34 927	142 778	357 381
十一师	Division 11	866 272	711 439	93 868	36 662	24 303	878 586
十二师	Division 12	701 019	335 733	125 900	159 062	80 324	701 695
十三师	Division 13	717 006	179 059	51 106	173 717	313 124	690 003
十四师	Division 14	62 120	53 386	1 093	4 123	3 518	71 375
兵团直属	Directly under XPCC	83 567	37 084	2 125	14 093	30 265	60 777

2—12 各师第三产业增加值

Value-added of Tertiary Industry by Division

计量单位:万元　　(2017 年)　　(10 000 yuan)

单　位　Unit	合计(按当年价计算) Total (Calculated at Current Prices)	劳动者报酬 Compensation of Laborers	生产税净额 Net Taxes on Production	固定资产折旧 Depreciation of Fixed Assets	营业盈余 Operating Surplus	按 2015 年可比价计算 Calculated at Comparable Prices in 2015
总　计　Total	**8 062 416**	**4 376 351**	**648 898**	**941 535**	**2 095 632**	**7 712 131**
一　师　Division 1	617 188	345 512	24 084	80 372	167 220	608 288
二　师　Division 2	363 934	194 101	16 306	64 438	89 089	355 682
三　师　Division 3	325 509	242 977	10 070	38 407	34 055	307 975
四　师　Division 4	439 147	207 180	27 485	59 162	145 320	407 267
五　师　Division 5	221 360	158 168	7 791	33 247	22 154	214 720
六　师　Division 6	835 492	466 988	54 329	105 559	208 616	811 456
七　师　Division 7	472 053	218 514	38 972	46 833	167 734	463 444
八　师　Division 8	2 190 048	1 347 680	134 883	310 244	397 241	2 062 944
九　师　Division 9	130 552	89 640	4 882	17 819	18 211	125 867
十　师　Division 10	242 427	99 506	17 610	24 136	101 175	231 554
十一师　Division 11	172 834	110 161	21 709	6 930	34 034	132 449
十二师　Division 12	1 016 341	351 029	196 936	72 273	396 103	995 770
十三师　Division 13	283 180	159 484	13 654	37 590	72 452	272 624
十四师　Division 14	42 304	39 175	629	2 193	307	40 766
兵团直属　Directly under XPCC	710 047	346 236	79 558	42 332	241 921	681 325

2—13 各师工业增加值

Value-added in Industry by Division

计量单位:万元　　(2017 年)　　(10 000 yuan)

单　位　Unit	合计(按当年价计算) Total (Calculated at Current Prices)	劳动者报酬 Compensation of Laborers	生产税净额 Net Taxes on Production	固定资产折旧 Depreciation of Fixed Assets	营业盈余 Operating Surplus	按 2015 年可比价计算 Calculated at Comparable Prices in 2015
总　计　Total	**7 259 772**	**1 790 386**	**978 715**	**1 593 593**	**2 897 078**	**7 169 067**
一　师　Division 1	760 551	213 098	44 083	143 617	359 753	774 079
二　师　Division 2	425 168	123 469	48 755	57 792	195 152	427 911
三　师　Division 3	313 165	79 694	37 988	59 175	136 308	315 860
四　师　Division 4	767 992	186 854	107 234	108 938	364 966	784 934
五　师　Division 5	112 389	59 665	9 887	29 855	12 982	115 936
六　师　Division 6	1 067 688	191 395	198 206	229 516	448 571	1 049 681
七　师　Division 7	364 452	145 572	36 665	109 088	73 127	366 813
八　师　Division 8	1 680 265	144 570	294 138	444 411	797 146	1 596 456
九　师　Division 9	48 879	28 694	4 051	14 373	1 761	47 790
十　师　Division 10	232 249	73 949	25 579	31 749	100 972	231 124
十一师　Division 11	77 297	50 406	5 025	15 856	6 010	88 822
十二师　Division 12	663 881	312 009	119 151	157 944	74 777	664 521
十三师　Division 13	650 341	138 244	45 390	173 167	293 540	623 270
十四师　Division 14	11 888	5 683	438	4 019	1 748	21 093
兵团直属　Directly under XPCC	83 567	37 084	2 125	14 093	30 265	60 777

2—14 各师建筑业增加值

Value-added in Construction by Division

计量单位:万元 (2017 年) (10 000 yuan)

单 位 Unit	合计(按当年价计算) Total (Calculated at Current Prices)	劳动者报酬 Compensation of Laborers	生产税净额 Net Taxes on Production	固定资产折旧 Depreciation of Fixed Assets	营业盈余 Operating Surplus	按 2015 年可比价计算 Calculated at Comparable Prices in 2015
总 计 Total	**3 007 251**	**2 432 540**	**310 028**	**65 133**	**199 550**	**3 010 260**
一 师 Division 1	405 697	308 531	44 827	17 772	34 567	406 103
二 师 Division 2	183 608	169 643	11 615	876	1 474	183 792
三 师 Division 3	147 885	126 421	8 434	969	12 061	148 033
四 师 Division 4	126 963	99 337	14 271	1 358	11 997	127 090
五 师 Division 5	49 663	35 122	6 299	2 489	5 753	49 712
六 师 Division 6	316 054	222 818	74 273	948	18 015	316 370
七 师 Division 7	316 545	260 854	25 288	10 205	20 198	316 862
八 师 Division 8	355 806	344 144	5 250	3 216	3 196	356 163
九 师 Division 9	35 262	21 536	7 210	1 529	4 987	35 296
十 师 Division 10	126 131	70 570	10 577	3 178	41 806	126 257
十一师 Division 11	788 975	661 033	88 843	20 806	18 293	789 764
十二师 Division 12	37 765	24 013	6 770	1 133	5 849	37 803
十三师 Division 13	66 665	40 815	5 716	550	19 584	66 733
十四师 Division 14	50 232	47 703	655	104	1 770	50 282
兵团直属 Directly under XPCC						

2—15 各师批发和零售业增加值

Value-added in Wholesale and Retail Trade by Division

计量单位:万元 (2017 年) (10 000 yuan)

单 位 Unit	合计(按当年价计算) Total (Calculated at Current Prices)	劳动者报酬 Compensation of Laborers	生产税净额 Net Taxes on Production	固定资产折旧 Depreciation of Fixed Assets	营业盈余 Operating Surplus	按 2015 年可比价计算 Calculated at Comparable Prices in 2015
总 计 Total	**2 019 781**	**788 552**	**306 350**	**141 039**	**783 840**	**1 902 181**
一 师 Division 1	139 380	41 022	9 108	8 869	80 381	139 130
二 师 Division 2	108 469	39 319	8 102	10 453	50 595	106 216
三 师 Division 3	58 772	35 279	2 619	4 848	16 026	58 529
四 师 Division 4	116 945	41 738	13 483	7 213	54 511	102 528
五 师 Division 5	43 167	34 388	1 325	7 993	—539	42 421
六 师 Division 6	193 533	99 444	9 079	17 416	67 594	189 778
七 师 Division 7	117 457	29 815	14 717	11 565	61 360	115 981
八 师 Division 8	317 104	206 383	42 324	22 181	46 216	236 981
九 师 Division 9	31 379	17 365	2 506	2 576	8 932	30 266
十 师 Division 10	70 716	22 488	7 149	4 413	36 666	68 023
十一师 Division 11	21 616	7 784	7 921	1 815	4 096	21 337
十二师 Division 12	628 203	155 106	135 684	28 959	308 454	620 101
十三师 Division 13	69 176	25 373	3 615	6 541	33 647	68 356
十四师 Division 14	4 352	3 508	410	38	396	4 303
兵团直属 Directly under XPCC	99 512	29 540	48 308	6 159	15 505	98 231

2—16 各师交通运输、仓储和邮政业增加值

Value-added in Transport, Storage and Post Services by Division

计量单位:万元 (2017 年) (10 000 yuan)

单位	Unit	合计(按当年价计算) Total (Calculated at Current Prices)	劳动者报酬 Compensation of Laborers	生产税净额 Net Taxes on Production	固定资产折旧 Depreciation of Fixed Assets	营业盈余 Operating Surplus	按 2015 年可比价计算 Calculated at Comparable Prices in 2015
总　计	**Total**	**1 047 460**	**455 834**	**103 398**	**213 630**	**274 598**	**1 036 153**
一　师	Division 1	77 095	27 069	5 994	3 120	40 912	77 680
二　师	Division 2	36 858	22 849	2 748	4 702	6 559	37 138
三　师	Division 3	17 807	12 999	2 502	1 867	439	17 944
四　师	Division 4	64 270	27 915	4 642	8 400	23 313	64 758
五　师	Division 5	19 192	9 215	1 795	3 060	5 122	18 861
六　师	Division 6	174 285	50 546	22 658	41 828	59 253	175 608
七　师	Division 7	125 717	35 509	14 741	13 115	62 352	126 671
八　师	Division 8	408 305	211 358	37 404	118 730	40 813	392 621
九　师	Division 9	11 330	4 380	684	2 836	3 430	11 416
十　师	Division 10	36 751	5 542	4 660	4 572	21 977	37 030
十一师	Division 11	872	415	−197	228	426	879
十二师	Division 12	35 357	25 553	2 266	6 501	1 037	35 626
十三师	Division 13	38 920	21 769	3 438	4 660	9 053	39 214
十四师	Division 14	701	715	63	11	−88	707
兵团直属	Directly under XPCC						

2—17 总产出

Total Output

计量单位:万元 (2017 年) (10 000 yuan)

指　标	Item	按当年价计算 Calculated at Current Prices 2016	2017	按 2015 年可比价计算 Calculated at Comparable Prices in 2015 2016	2017
总产出	**Total Output**	**66 610 666**	**73 488 581**	**66 017 633**	**71 797 225**
按产业分	**Grouped by Industries**				
第一产业	Primary Industry	10 094 471	10 782 130	9 723 459	10 357 086
第二产业	Secondary Industry	37 106 080	38 368 199	37 520 798	38 263 040
第三产业	Tertiary Industry	19 410 115	24 338 252	18 773 376	23 177 099
按行业分	**Grouped by sectors**				
农、林、牧、渔业	Farming, Forestry, Animal Husbandry and Fishery	10 767 503	11 527 734	10 385 721	11 070 565
工　业	Industry	24 651 717	25 874 783	25 056 140	25 823 735
建筑业	Construction	12 466 723	12 503 258	12 477 159	12 449 034
批发和零售业	Wholesale and Retail Trade	7 473 317	9 683 678	7 114 887	9 176 764
交通运输、仓储和邮政业	Transport, Storage and Postal Services	3 283 238	3 998 964	3 199 677	3 911 449
住宿和餐饮业	Accommodation and Catering Services Industry	1 855 070	2 210 336	1 808 547	2 052 317
信息传输、软件和信息技术服务业	Information Deliver, Software and Information Technique Services Industry	146 621	221 832	143 360	214 046
金融业	Finance	1 084 238	1 404 656	1 066 720	1 324 247
房地产业	Real Estate Trade	696 847	846 787	685 028	831 366
租赁和商务服务业	Leasing and Business Service	589 661	1 066 342	568 289	973 159
科学研究和技术服务业	Scientific Research and Technical Service	262 628	330 877	245 367	301 238
水利、环境和公共设施管理业	Water Conservancy, Environment and Public Facilities Management	174 541	214 345	168 378	202 299
居民服务、修理和其他服务业	Resident, Repair and Other Services	548 577	725 564	528 164	676 503
教　育	Education	768 271	767 332	757 572	746 407
卫生和社会工作	Health Care and Social Security	584 479	571 221	564 648	552 116
文化、体育和娱乐业	Culture, Sports and Recreation	275 266	389 199	280 612	379 262
公共管理、社会保障和社会组织	Public Management and Social Organization	981 969	1 151 673	967 364	1 112 718

2—18 各师按产业分总产出

Total Output by Branch of Industry and by Division

计量单位:万元　　(2017年)　　(10 000 yuan)

单　位	Unit	合　计 Total	第一产业 Primary Industry	第二产业 Secondary Industry	第三产业 Tertiary Industry
总　计	**Total**	**73 488 581**	**10 782 130**	**38 368 199**	**24 338 252**
一　师	Division 1	9 900 630	2 525 891	4 270 659	3 104 080
二　师	Division 2	4 256 121	851 138	2 431 612	973 371
三　师	Division 3	3 626 155	926 290	1 960 247	739 618
四　师	Division 4	4 703 008	875 203	2 510 710	1 317 095
五　师	Division 5	1 581 717	411 471	637 129	533 117
六　师	Division 6	9 483 058	1 057 411	5 709 698	2 715 949
七　师	Division 7	4 854 471	992 809	2 437 160	1 424 502
八　师	Division 8	15 491 160	1 748 486	7 791 361	5 951 313
九　师	Division 9	956 230	307 190	350 031	299 009
十　师	Division 10	3 759 500	337 479	1 140 693	2 281 328
十一师	Division 11	3 913 644	1 949	3 373 289	538 406
十二师	Division 12	4 822 760	206 692	2 495 651	2 120 417
十三师	Division 13	3 622 470	337 441	2 521 542	763 487
十四师	Division 14	562 961	202 680	290 102	70 179
兵团直属	Directly under XPCC	1 954 696		448 315	1 506 381

单　位	Unit	#工　业 Industry	#建筑业 Construction	#批发和零售业 Wholesale and Retail Trade	#交通运输仓储和邮政业 Transport, Storage and Postal Services	按2015年可比价计算 Calculated at Comparable Prices in 2015
总　计	**Total**	**25 874 783**	**12 503 258**	**9 683 678**	**3 998 964**	**71 797 225**
一　师	Division 1	2 387 922	1 883 985	1 809 987	450 156	9 506 103
二　师	Division 2	1 615 610	816 002	446 602	109 646	4 222 231
三　师	Division 3	1 302 980	657 267	207 858	50 628	4 039 652
四　师	Division 4	1 997 926	512 784	288 347	263 702	4 556 611
五　师	Division 5	426 578	211 333	206 194	44 290	1 559 554
六　师	Division 6	4 392 807	1 316 891	1 028 826	768 805	9 340 260
七　师	Division 7	1 170 671	1 269 111	669 296	327 255	4 838 062
八　师	Division 8	6 329 879	1 464 221	1 136 466	1 543 592	14 629 190
九　师	Division 9	203 108	146 923	77 764	44 332	941 007
十　师	Division 10	603 964	536 729	1 802 606	142 228	3 653 938
十一师	Division 11	365 923	3 007 366	24 188	13 994	3 864 578
十二师	Division 12	2 336 999	161 103	1 141 957	116 184	4 713 960
十三师	Division 13	2 225 251	296 291	322 387	121 012	3 487 061
十四师	Division 14	66 850	223 252	8 660	3 140	615 238
兵团直属	Directly under XPCC	448 315		512 540		1 829 780

2018 BING TUAN

第三篇 人口与就业

Chapter 3 Population and Employment

简要说明

一、本篇资料主要内容

本篇人口资料反映兵团2017年及历年人口基本情况，包括兵团各师及兵直单位主要人口数据。如：总人口、人口出生率、死亡率、自然增长率、分民族人口数、分师按性别、职业分组的年末人口数；各师人口变动情况、各师分民族人口数，按县市、按师分列的农牧团场户数及人口数，以及各师计划生育情况。

本篇就业资料反映兵团劳动经济方面的基本情况，包括各师及兵直单位主要劳动统计数据。如全社会就业人员数、在岗职工人数、在岗职工工资总额、平均工资等主要指标。

二、本篇资料统计范围

《兵团劳动和人口统计报表制度》调查范围为兵团范围内全部法人单位，包括国有单位、集体单位、其他各种经济类型单位。全社会就业人员统计范围单位就业人员、个体劳动者及有劳动能力并从事各项劳动的人员。

三、本篇资料来源

本篇人口资料由兵团统计局社会科技贸易统计处根据《兵团劳动和人口统计报表制度》收集、汇总、整理提供。计划生育情况由兵团人口和计划生育委员会汇总、整理提供。

就业及工资情况由兵团统计局社会科技贸易统计处根据《兵团劳动和人口统计报表制度》汇总整理。

四、本篇资料调查方法

就业和职工工资调查方法为全面调查。

Brief Introduction

1. Main Contents

The data on population show the basic conditions of population of XPCC in 2017 and over past years, including main population of divisions, and units directly under XPCC population, such as birth rate, death rate, natural growth rate, population by nationalities, year-end population on sex, occupation by Division, population changes by division and population on nationality by division, households and population on farm by county and city and division, and family planning by division.

Data on employment reflect the basic conditions of labor and Population of XPCC, including main labor statistical data of divisions, and units directly under XPCC, such as main indicators of staff and workets on the job.

2. Scope of Statistics

The Reporting Form System on Labor Wages covers whole corporate units in XPCC, including State-owned units, collective-owned units and units of other ownership .

Employment in the whole society covers number of employment, individual laborers and persons with labor capability and engaging in various labor .

3. Sources of Data

Data on population are prepared by the Society Science Trade Statistical Section of the Statistics Bureau of XPCC according to *the Reporting Form System on Labor and Population of XPCC*. Data on Family Planning are provided by Populatation and Family Planning Commission of XPCC.

Data on employment and wages are prepared by the Society, Science and Trade Statistical Section of Statistics Bureau of XPCC according to *the Reporting Form System on Labor and Population of XPCC.*

4. Methodology of Survey

It is a comprehensive survey .

3—1 年末人口数及构成

Population and Its Composition at Year-end

年 份 Year	年末人口数(人) Total Population atthe Year-end (person)	男 Male	女 Female	占总人口比重(%) Percentage to Total Population(%) 男 Male	女 Female	性别比(女=100) Sex Ratio (Female=100)
1952	273 279	206 666	66 613	75.6	24.4	310.2
1954	175 451	132 684	42 767	75.6	24.4	310.2
1957	311 470	231 874	79 596	74.4	25.6	291.3
1962	862 124	537 138	324 986	62.3	37.7	165.3
1965	1 293 151	741 413	551 738	57.3	42.7	134.4
1970	1 943 157	1 045 486	897 671	53.8	46.2	116.5
1975	1 771 097	921 502	849 595	52.0	48.0	108.5
1978	2 199 835	1 090 674	1 029 161	51.5	48.5	106.0
1980	2 200 755	1 127 050	1 073 705	51.2	48.8	105.0
1985	2 222 350	1 142 630	1 079 720	51.4	48.6	105.8
1990	2 143 528	1 110 475	1 033 053	51.8	48.2	107.5
1995	2 287 896	1 194 166	1 093 730	52.2	47.8	109.2
2000	2 427 920	1 272 719	1 155 201	52.4	47.6	110.2
2001	2 453 575	1 289 954	1 163 621	52.6	47.4	110.9
2002	2 501 189	1 311 750	1 189 439	52.4	47.6	110.3
2003	2 542 170	1 330 666	1 211 504	52.3	47.7	109.8
2004	2 563 837	1 341 213	1 222 624	52.3	47.7	109.7
2005	2 569 756	1 346 901	1 222 855	52.4	47.6	110.1
2006	2 579 435	1 352 541	1 226 894	52.4	47.6	110.2
2007	2 584 732	1 353 053	1 231 679	52.3	47.7	109.9
2008	2 573 077	1 344 445	1 228 632	52.3	47.7	109.4
2009	2 573 145	1 346 229	1 226 916	52.3	47.7	109.7
2010	2 607 184	1 376 580	1 230 604	52.8	47.2	111.9
2011	2 613 724	1 372 606	1 241 118	52.5	47.5	110.6
2012	2 648 636	1 390 548	1 258 088	52.5	47.5	110.5
2013	2 701 427	1 423 075	1 278 352	52.7	47.3	111.3
2014	2 732 868	1 434 671	1 298 197	52.5	47.5	110.5
2015	2 765 608	1 447 041	1 318 567	52.3	47.7	109.7
2016	2 834 099	1 483 094	1 351 005	52.3	47.7	109.8
2017	3 005 309	1 567 570	1 437 739	52.2	47.8	109.0

3—2 各师按性别、职业分的年末人口数

Population at the Year-end by Sex and Ocuppation and by Division

计量单位:人 (2017 年) (person)

单 位 Unit	年末人口数 Total Population at the year-end	男 Male	女 Female	按农业非农业人口分 by Agriculture and Non-Agriculture 农业人口 Agricultural Population	非农业人口 Non-Agricultural Population
总 计 Total	**3 005 309**	**1 567 570**	**1 437 739**	**1 093 711**	**1 911 598**
一 师 Division 1	357 961	186 100	171 861	137 453	220 508
二 师 Division 2	214 820	114 873	99 947	66 450	148 370
三 师 Division 3	253 704	134 161	119 543	147 282	106 422
四 师 Division 4	245 195	125 890	119 305	83 129	162 066
五 师 Division 5	127 214	65 253	61 961	67 298	59 916
六 师 Division 6	355 279	186 685	168 594	140 994	214 285
七 师 Division 7	233 479	125 132	108 347	74 496	158 983
八 师 Division 8	641 117	319 084	322 033	206 634	434 483
九 师 Division 9	77 243	40 161	37 082	29 999	47 244
十 师 Division 10	101 229	52 602	48 627	23 849	77 380
十一师 Division 11	69 107	44 121	24 986	23	69 084
十二师 Division 12	122 408	64 022	58 386	27 342	95 066
十三师 Division 13	108 879	56 875	52 004	46 623	62 256
十四师 Division 14	57 028	29 706	27 322	42 139	14 889
兵团直属 Directly under XPCC	40 646	22 905	17 741		40 646

3—3 人口出生率、死亡率、自然增长率
Birth Rate, Death Rate and Natural Growth Rate of Population

年份 Year	单位 Unit	出生数（人） Birth Population (person)	死亡数（人） Death Population (person)	出生率（‰） Birth Rate (‰)	死亡率（‰） Death Rate (‰)	自然增长率（‰） Natural Growth Rate(‰)
	1953	2 383	656	15.85	4.36	11.49
	1954	4 782	647	29.36	3.97	25.39
	1957	10 878	993	35.68	3.26	32.42
	1962	29 828	2 985	34.47	3.45	31.02
	1965	65 497	6 182	53.92	5.09	48.83
	1970	92 399	8 808	49.65	4.73	44.92
	1975	49 466	6 535	24.55	3.24	21.31
	1978	32 749	6 203	16.56	3.14	13.42
	1980	26 972	7 162	12.27	3.26	9.01
	1985	16 893	7 977	7.55	3.57	3.98
	1990	24 589	9 305	11.48	4.35	7.13
	1995	22 519	10 044	9.98	4.45	5.53
	1996	21 965	10 093	9.49	4.36	5.13
	1997	20 877	9 721	8.83	4.11	4.72
	1998	20 919	10 480	8.70	4.40	4.30
	1999	20 565	9 716	8.50	4.00	4.50
	2000	22 674	12 525	9.40	5.20	4.20
	2001	19 061	9 014	7.80	3.70	4.10
	2002	18 179	9 842	7.37	3.99	3.38
	2003	17 218	9 914	6.84	3.94	2.90
	2004	15 860	9 864	6.21	3.86	2.35
	2005	16 381	11 934	6.38	4.65	1.73
	2006	14 687	11 859	5.71	4.61	1.10
	2007	13 289	10 131	5.15	3.92	1.23
	2008	14 612	11 183	5.67	4.34	1.33
	2009	14 447	11 285	5.61	4.39	1.22
	2010	19 205	10 572	6.30	4.08	2.22
	2011	13 838	12 198	5.33	4.70	0.63
	2012	14 916	14 794	5.67	5.62	0.05
	2013	15 305	13 203	5.72	4.94	0.79
	2014	17 126	12 666	6.30	4.66	1.64
	2015	16 619	13 303	6.04	4.84	1.20
	2016	19 610	13 182	7.00	4.70	2.30
	2017	22 932	15 880	7.85	5.44	2.42
一　师	Division 1	3 469	1 869	10.13	5.46	4.67
二　师	Division 2	1 149	1 227	5.57	5.95	−0.38
三　师	Division 3	2 673	924	10.94	3.78	7.16
四　师	Division 4	1 339	1 253	5.59	5.23	0.36
五　师	Division 5	963	541	7.75	4.36	3.40
六　师	Division 6	2 420	1 889	6.89	5.38	1.51
七　师	Division 7	1 431	1 730	6.20	7.50	−1.30
八　师	Division 8	5 458	4 267	8.73	6.83	1.91
九　师	Division 9	432	559	5.69	7.37	−1.67
十　师	Division 10	461	307	4.72	3.14	1.58
十一师	Division 11	153	233	2.23	3.39	−1.16
十二师	Division 12	1 024	295	9.03	2.60	6.43
十三师	Division 13	1 165	437	11.02	4.13	6.89
十四师	Division 14	626	196	11.59	3.63	7.96
兵团直属	Directly under XPCC	169	153	4.16	3.77	0.39

3—4 分民族人口数

Population by Nationality

计量单位:人 (person)

年 份 Year	单 位 Unit	年末人口数 Total Population (year-end)	汉 族 Han	维吾尔族 Uygur	哈萨克族 Kazak	回 族 Hui	蒙古族 Mongolian	其他民族 Others
	1952	273 279						
	1954	175 451	169 076	3 017	1 072	2 054	35	197
	1957	311 470	295 759	6 132	4 525	4 429	125	500
	1962	862 124	820 887	12 649	9 840	15 793	1 047	1 908
	1965	1 293 151	1 229 105	19 652	16 884	22 011	2 407	3 092
	1970	1 943 157	1 833 174	43 527	23 512	32 062	3 303	7 579
	1975	1 771 097	1 624 096	67 479	20 545	33 828	3 011	22 138
	1978	2 119 835	1 906 546	115 325	29 439	50 723	2 591	15 211
	1980	2 200 755	1 985 191	124 422	31 199	52 645	4 485	2 813
	1985	2 222 350	1 993 968	128 577	33 885	53 423	5 047	7 450
	1990	2 143 528	1 897 473	138 856	35 921	55 521	5 812	9 945
	1991	2 168 428	1 918 075	141 251	36 299	56 518	5 785	10 500
	1992	2 181 926	1 927 650	143 365	36 858	56 953	5 901	11 199
	1993	2 197 596	1 938 805	145 307	37 439	57 433	6 123	12 489
	1994	2 223 957	1 963 330	146 008	37 863	57 569	6 284	12 903
	1995	2 287 896	2 022 108	148 692	38 792	58 152	6 361	13 791
	1996	2 343 308	2 076 765	148 510	38 710	58 897	6 150	14 276
	1997	2 383 983	2 114 412	150 875	39 208	58 824	6 193	14 471
	1998	2 407 148	2 132 512	153 918	40 141	59 266	6 130	15 181
	1999	2 420 902	2 142 989	155 866	40 305	59 846	6 100	15 796
	2000	2 427 920	2 143 676	157 511	40 713	62 175	5 941	17 904
	2001	2 453 575	2 166 942	158 605	41 090	62 934	5 992	18 012
	2002	2 501 189	2 204 494	164 962	42 702	64 705	6 172	18 154
	2003	2 542 170	2 243 096	165 713	42 317	64 985	6 313	19 746
	2004	2 563 837	2 256 983	174 198	42 359	65 645	6 425	18 227
	2005	2 569 756	2 257 260	178 730	43 102	65 234	6 498	18 932
	2006	2 579 435	2 264 260	181 859	43 169	65 458	6 465	18 224
	2007	2 584 732	2 266 091	183 462	43 775	66 345	6 452	18 607
	2008	2 573 077	2 247 742	188 953	44 437	66 673	6 473	18 799
	2009	2 573 145	2 242 176	191 675	45 629	68 232	6 467	18 966
	2010	2 607 184	2 229 849	212 254	49 508	79 931	6 393	29 249
	2011	2 613 724	2 252 225	210 286	47 422	76 517	6 274	21 000
	2012	2 648 636	2 280 712	212 984	48 688	79 093	6 525	20 634
	2013	2 701 427	2 325 962	218 539	49 267	78 826	6 753	22 080
	2014	2 732 868	2 347 559	223 732	50 915	79 495	7 017	24 150
	2015	2 765 608	2 372 888	230 254	51 777	79 250	7 278	24 161
	2016	2 834 099	2 425 053	241 477	52 361	81 244	7 477	26 487
	2017	3 005 309	2 554 554	265 743	56 755	88 798	7 936	31 523
一 师	Division 1	357 961	319 971	26 832	142	2 688	365	7 963
二 师	Division 2	214 820	204 941	4 903	20	1 455	884	2 617
三 师	Division 3	253 704	110 197	139 958	13	1 146	66	2 324
四 师	Division 4	245 195	190 245	13 977	26 336	9 873	2 434	2 330
五 师	Division 5	127 214	110 059	5 995	3 558	5 603	1 244	755
六 师	Division 6	355 279	315 117	9 458	7 704	19 143	748	3 109
七 师	Division 7	233 479	221 720	2 159	1 568	6 184	475	1 373
八 师	Division 8	641 117	606 630	6 480	3 705	16 062	871	7 369
九 师	Division 9	77 243	72 391	92	2 981	1 106	287	386
十 师	Division 10	101 229	98 339	142	735	1 408	119	486
十一师	Division 11	69 107	67 102	577	52	937	80	359
十二师	Division 12	122 408	92 537	4 970	3 683	19 854	196	1 168
十三师	Division 13	108 879	88 202	11 354	5 961	2 358	77	927
十四师	Division 14	57 028	21 565	35 194	3	185	7	74
兵团直属	Directly under XPCC	40 646	35 538	3 652	294	796	83	283

3—5 人口增减变动情况

Increase and Decrease of Population

计量单位:人 (2017 年) (person)

指标 Item	合计 Total	#团场 Farm	汉族 Han	维吾尔族 Uygur	哈萨克族 Kazak	回族 Hui	蒙古族 Mongolian	其他民族 Others
年初人口 Total Population(Year-beginning)	**2 834 099**	**1 849 566**	**2 425 053**	**241 477**	**52 361**	**81 244**	**7 477**	**26 487**
年内增加数 Added Population	**328 387**	**231 893**	**264 002**	**36 215**	**7 245**	**12 598**	**1 028**	**7 299**
迁入 Moveinto	305 455	215 536	246 295	33 060	6 617	11 597	950	6 936
出生 Birth	22 932	16 357	17 707	3 155	628	1 001	78	363
出生率(‰) Birth Rate(‰)	7.85	8.45	7.11	12.44	11.51	11.77	10.12	12.51
年内减少数 Decreased Population	**157 177**	**60 797**	**134 501**	**11 949**	**2 851**	**5 044**	**567**	**2 265**
迁出 Moveout	141 297	47 858	120 537	10 865	2 594	4 653	532	2 116
死亡 Death	15 880	12 939	13 964	1 084	257	391	35	149
死亡率(‰) Death Rate(‰)	5.44	6.69	5.61	4.27	4.71	4.60	4.54	5.14
年底人口数 Total Population(Year-end)	**3 005 309**	**2 020 662**	**2 554 554**	**265 743**	**56 755**	**88 798**	**7 936**	**31 523**
男 Male	1 567 570	1 042 523	1 331 965	140 451	29 229	45 284	4 084	16 557
女 Female	1 437 739	978 139	1 222 589	125 292	27 526	43 514	3 852	14 966
农业人口 Agricultural Population	1 093 711	1 064 162						
非农业人口 Non-agricultural Population	1 911 598	956 500						
自然增长率(‰) Natural Growth Rate(‰)	**2.41**	**1.76**	**1.50**	**8.17**	**6.80**	**7.17**	**5.58**	**7.38**
年底总户数(户) Total Household(Year-end)(household)	**1 130 434**	**726 936**						

注:本表团场数据包括一师阿拉尔农场和幸福城农场。
Note: Item of farm in this table includes Aral and Xinfu farms.

3—6 按县(区、市)分团场户数、人口数

Households and Population of Farms by Country (Area、City)

(2017 年)

地(州、市)、县(区、市)及团场名称	Names of Prefecture (Region、City), Country (Area、City) and Farm	户 数(户) Nember of Households (household)	人口数(人) Population (person)
总　计	**Total**	**726 936**	**2 020 662**
乌鲁木齐市	**Urumqi city**	**34 261**	**94 192**
沙依巴克区	Shayibak District	13 165	36 713
104 团	Farm 104	8 288	24 461
西山农场	Xishan Farm	4 877	12 252
头屯河区	Tou Tunhe District	21 096	57 479
三坪农场	Sanping Farm	9 224	22 662
五一农场	MayIst Farm	5 887	18 862
头屯河农场	TouTunhe Farm	5 985	15 955
克拉玛依市	**Karamay city**	**14 631**	**37 887**
129 团	Farm 136	7 191	18 039
136 团	Farm 136	4 072	11 119
137 团	Farm 137	3 368	8 729
石河子市	**Shi Hezi City**	**19 465**	**58 095**
152 团	Farm 152	2 232	6 397
石河子总场	General Shihezi Farm	17 233	51 698
吐鲁番市	**Turpan City**	**1 886**	**5 393**
高昌区	Gao chang Area	1 886	5 393
221 团	Farm 221	1 886	5 393
哈密市	**Hami [Kumul] City**	**34 320**	**89 589**
伊州区	Yi zhou Area	28 517	73 152
红星一场	Red Star No.1 Farm	3 728	9 875
红星二场	Red Star No.2 Farm	3 124	8 378
红星四场	Red Star No.4 Farm	2 768	8 732
黄田农场	Huangtian Farm	3 540	12 214
火箭农场	Huojian Farm	11 583	22 432
柳树泉农场	LiuShuquan Farm	3 774	11 521
巴里坤哈萨克自治县	Barkol Kazak Autonomous County	4 606	13 586
红山农场	Hongshan Farm	4 606	13 586
伊吾县	Yiwu [Araturuk] County	1 197	2 851
淖毛湖农场	Nao Maohu Farm	1 197	2 851
昌吉回族自治州	**Changji Hui Autonomous Prefecture**	**126 869**	**332 174**
五家渠市	Wujiaqu City	19 271	48 354
101 团	Farm 101	5 066	11 771
102 团	Farm 102	7 309	19 763
103 团	Farm 103	6 896	16 820
昌吉市	Changji City	9 407	25 910
共青团农场	Communist League Farm	3 629	10 886
军户农场	Junhu Farm	5 778	15 024
呼图壁县	Hutubi county	29 010	80 776
105 团	Farm 105	4 966	13 807
106 团	Farm 106	1 696	5 653
芳草湖农场	Fang Caohu Farm	22 348	61 316
玛纳斯县	Manas County	43 558	109 224
147 团	Farm 147	6 440	15 472
148 团	Farm 148	9 394	24 761
149 团	Farm 149	6 386	16 606
150 团	Farm 150	6 899	15 446
新湖农场	Xinhu Farm	14 439	36 939
奇台县	Qitai County	11 998	32 477
奇台农场	Qitai Farm	10 887	28 613
北塔山农场	Bei Tashan Ranch	1 111	3 864
阜康市	Fukang County	8 600	22 232
222 团	Farm 222	3 909	10 713
十蹾子农场	Tu Dunzi Farm	2 133	5 509
六运湖农场	Liu Yunhu Farm	2 558	6 010
吉木萨尔县	Jimsar County	5 025	13 201
红旗农场	Red Flag Farm	5 025	13 201
伊犁哈萨克自治州	**Ili Kazak Autonomous Prefecture**	**85 587**	**225 341**
奎屯市	Kuytun City	8 371	18 835
131 团	Farm 131	8 371	18 835
伊犁地区	Counties (Cities) Direct Under Ili Prefecture	77 216	206 506
可克达拉市	Kirk Dallas City	30 593	88 024
63 团	Farm 63	3 297	9 054
64 团	Farm 64	9 005	25 899
66 团	Farm 66	10 144	29 494
67 团	Farm 67	4 458	13 927
68 团	Farm 68	3 689	9 650
伊宁县	Yining [Gulja] County	4 815	11 796
70 团	Farm 70	4 815	11 796
察布察尔锡伯自治县	Qapqal Xibe Autonomous County	3 050	7 063
69 团	Farm 69	3 050	7 063
霍城县	Huocheng [Korgas] County	12 907	33 320
61 团	Farm 61	4 386	13 289
62 团	Farm 62	8 521	20 031

3-6 续表1 Continued

(2017年)

地(州、市)、县(区、市)及团场名称	Names of Prefecture (Region、City), Country (Area、City) and Farm	户数(户) Nember of Households (household)	人口数(人) Population (person)	地(州、市)、县(区、市)及团场名称	Names of Prefecture (Region、City), Country (Area、City) and Farm	户数(户) Nember of Households (household)	人口数(人) Population (person)
巩留县	Gongliu [Tokkuztara] County	3 074	7 561	133团	Farm 133	8 711	22 018
73团	Farm 73	3 074	7 561	134团	Farm 134	7 311	21 034
新源县	Xinyuan [Kunes] County	9 923	22 858	141团	Farm 141	4 489	10 765
71团	Farm 71	5 325	11 483	142团	Farm 142	10 166	25 333
72团	Farm 72	4 598	11 375	143团	Farm 143	13 523	34 088
昭苏县	Zhaosu [Mongolkure] County	8 958	25 394	144团	Farm 144	5 355	12 751
74团	Farm 74	1 428	3 678	托里县	Toli County	1 534	3 396
75团	Farm 75	1 235	3 231	170团	Farm 170	1 534	3 396
76团	Farm 76	3 816	10 874	裕民县	Yumin [Qagantokay] County	2 157	5 379
77团	Farm 77	2 479	7 611	161团	Farm 161	2 157	5 379
特克斯县	Tekes County	2 047	5 485	和布克赛尔蒙古自治县	Hoboksar Mongol Autonomous County	3 217	8 009
78团	Farm 78	2 047	5 485	184团	Farm 184	3 217	8 009
尼勒克县	Nilka County	1 849	5 005	**阿勒泰地区**	**Altay Administrative Offices**	**18 391**	**49 381**
79团	Farm 79	1 849	5 005	阿勒泰市	Altay City	3 752	10 683
塔城地区	**Tacheng [Tarbagatai] Administrative Offices**	**133 089**	**350 807**	181团	Farm 181	3 752	10 683
塔城市	Tacheng City	5 893	15 965	福海县	Fuhai [Burultokay] County	2 017	5 306
163团	Farm 163	3 481	9 984	182团	Farm 182	2 017	5 306
164团	Farm 164	2 412	5 981	北屯市	Beitun City	10 472	27 396
额敏县	Emin [Dorbiljin] County	11 803	32 724	183团	Farm 183	3 418	9 294
165团	Farm 165	1 751	5 490	187团	Farm 187	2 611	6 796
166团	Farm 166	2 513	8 150	188团	Farm 188	4 443	11 306
167团	Farm 167	2 112	5 708	哈巴河县	Habahe [Kaba] County	1 163	3 346
168团	Farm 168	4 036	9 745	185团	Farm 185	1 163	3 346
团结农场	Tuanjie Farm	1 391	3 631	吉木乃县	Jeminay County	987	2 650
乌苏市	Usu City	43 540	121 376	186团	Farm 186	987	2 650
123团	Farm 123	8 503	22 957	**博尔塔拉蒙古自治州**	**Bortala Mongol Autonomous Prefecture**	**36 729**	**98 631**
124团	Farm 124	6 017	17 029	双河市	Shuanghe city	25 230	66 226
125团	Farm 125	7 079	18 893	81团	Farm 81	3 894	11 188
126团	Farm 126	4 059	11 760	84团	Farm 84	3 378	7 815
127团	Farm 126	5 136	14 647	86团	Farm 86	8 888	22 315
128团	Farm 128	4 885	14 655	89团	Farm 89	5 906	16 446
130团	Farm 130	7 861	21 435	90团	Farm 90	3 164	8 462
沙湾县	Shawan County	64 945	163 958	精河县	Jinghe [Jing] County	8 508	25 170
121团	Farm 121	15 390	37 969	83团	Farm 83	7 140	21 294
				91团	Farm 91	1 368	3 876
				温泉县	Wenquan [Araxang] County	2 991	7 235
				87团	Farm 87	1 719	4 190

3—6 续表 2 Continued

(2017 年)

地(州、市)、县(区、市)及团场名称	Names of Prefecture (Region、City), Country (Area、City) and Farm	户 数(户) Nember of Households (household)	人口数(人) Population (person)
88 团	Farm 88	1 272	3 045
巴音郭楞蒙古自治州	**Bayangol Mongol Autonomous Prefecture**	**58 742**	**162 533**
铁门关市	Tiemenguan City	14 110	39 763
29 团	Farm 29	10 230	29 665
30 团	Farm 30	3 880	10 098
尉犁县	Yuli [Lopnur] County	13 111	37 339
31 团	Farm 31	3 735	10 082
33 团	Farm 33	4 832	14 198
34 团	Farm 34	4 544	13 059
若羌县	Ruoqiang [Qarkilik] County	3 016	8 136
36 团	Farm 36	3 016	8 136
且末县	Qiemd [Qarqan] County	2 667	9 742
37 团	Farm 37	866	2 954
38 团	Farm 38	1 801	6 788
焉耆回族自治县	Yanji Hui Autonomous County	4 023	10 788
27 团	Farm 27	4 023	10 788
和静县	Hejing County	14 958	38 224
21 团	Farm 21	4 230	10 572
22 团	Farm 22	7 507	19 066
223 团	Farm 223	3 221	8 586
和硕县	Hoxud County	5 020	13 327
24 团	Farm 24	5 020	13 327
博湖县	Bohu [Bagrax] County	1 837	5 214
25 团	Farm 25	1 837	5 214
阿克苏地区	**Aksu Administrative Offices**	**84 044**	**244 278**
阿拉尔市	Aralcity	81 518	238 005
1 团	Farm 1	6 820	23 685
2 团	Farm 2	5 511	15 731
3 团	Farm 3	6 132	16 300
5 团	Farm 5	7 894	21 153
6 团	Farm 6	4 184	11 790
7 团	Farm 7	5 971	14 728
8 团	Farm 8	4 200	11 640
10 团	Farm 10	6 700	19 579
11 团	Farm 11	3 626	13 215
12 团	Farm 12	7 272	21 860
13 团	Farm 13	7 658	24 036
14 团	Farm 14	4 320	12 014
16 团	Farm 16	6 026	16 360
幸福农场	Xinfu Farm	1 989	5 116
阿拉尔农场	Alaer Farm	3 215	10 798
乌什县	Wushi [Uxturpan] County	2 526	6 273
4 团	Farm 4	2 526	6 273
克孜勒苏柯尔克孜自治州	**Kizilsu Kirgiz Autonomous Prefecture**	**1 547**	**5 356**
阿图什市	Artux City	1 181	4 212
红旗农场	Red Flag Farm	1 181	4 212
乌恰县	Wuqia [Ulugqat] County	366	1 144
托云牧场	Tuoyun Ranch	366	1 144
喀什地区	**Kashgar [Kaxgar] Administrative Offices**	**62 180**	**213 725**
疏勒县	Shule County	4 589	10 708
41 团	Farm 41	4 589	10 708
英吉沙县	Yengisar County	550	1 730
东风农场	Dong Feng Farm	550	1 730
叶城县	Yecheng [Kagilik] County	372	1 303
叶城牧场	Yechen Ranch	372	1 303
麦盖提县	Makit County	10 432	29 462
45 团	Farm 45	9 212	25 999
46 团	Farm 46	1 220	3 463
岳普湖县	Yopurga County	1 265	4 275
42 团	Farm 42	1 265	4 275
伽师县	Jiashi[Payzawat] County	3 972	15 068
伽师总场	General Jiashi Farm	3 972	15 068
巴楚县	Bachu[Maralbexi] County	2 650	7 829
48 团	Farm 48	2 650	7 829
图木舒克市	Tumkuk City	37 921	142 012
44 团	Farm 44	7 371	27 714
49 团	Farm 49	4 323	16 442
50 团	Farm 50	6 671	23 597
51 团	Farm 51	13 421	50 122
53 团	Farm 53	6 135	24 137
莎车县	Shache County	429	1 338
54 团	Farm 54	429	1 338
和田地区	**Hotan Administrative Offices**	**15 195**	**53 280**
昆玉市	Kunyu City	15 195	53 280
47 团	Farm 47	2 094	5 874
224 团	Farm 224	4 121	14 349
225 团	Farm 225	11	14
皮山农场	Pishan Farm	8 160	30 189
一牧场	Ranch 1	809	2 854

3—7 各师分团场户数、人口数

Households and Population of Farms by Division

（2017 年）

师、团场名称	Names of Division and Farm	户数（户）Nember of Households (household)	人口数（人）Population (person)	团部人口数（人）Population of Farm (person)
总 计	**Total**	**726 936**	**2 020 662**	**1 581 510**
一 师	**Division 1**	**84 044**	**244 278**	**179 959**
1团(七师代管)	Farm 1(Division 7)	6 820	23 685	21 686
2 团	Farm 2	5 511	15 731	5 795
3 团	Farm 3	6 132	16 300	9 453
4 团	Farm 4	2 526	6 273	3 463
5团(十一师代管)	Farm 5(Division 11)	7 894	21 153	18 509
6 团	Farm 6	4 184	11 790	7 055
7 团	Farm 7	5 971	14 728	13 490
8 团	Farm 8	4 200	11 640	7 656
10 团	Farm 10	6 700	19 579	15 660
11 团	Farm 11	3 626	13 215	9 253
12 团	Farm 12	7 272	21 860	19 250
13 团	Farm 13	7 658	24 036	21 775
14 团	Farm 14	4 320	12 014	8 365
16 团	Farm 16	6 026	16 360	11 703
幸福农场	Xinfu Farm	1 989	5 116	1 156
阿拉尔农场	Alaer Farm	3 215	10 798	5 690
二 师	**Division 2**	**58 742**	**162 533**	**118 453**
21 团	Farm 21	4 230	10 572	9 113
22 团	Farm 22	7 507	19 066	9 943
24 团	Farm 24	5 020	13 327	10 830
25 团	Farm 25	1 837	5 214	3 937
27 团	Farm 27	4 023	10 788	8 239
29 团	Farm 29	10 230	29 665	15 551
30 团	Farm 30	3 880	10 098	8 584
31 团	Farm 31	3 735	10 082	8 267
33 团	Farm 33	4 832	14 198	9 721
34 团	Farm 34	4 544	13 059	12 210
36团(四师代管)	Farm 36(Division 4)	3 016	8 136	6 255
223 团	Farm 223	3 221	8 586	6 574
37 团	Farm 37	866	2 954	2 441
38 团	Farm 38	1 801	6 788	6 788
三 师	**Division 3**	**63 727**	**219 081**	**154 806**
41 团	Farm 41	4 589	10 708	10 356
42 团	Farm 42	1 265	4 275	3 762
44 团	Farm 44	7 371	27 714	16 523
45 团	Farm 45	9 212	25 999	13 162
46 团	Farm 46	1 220	3 463	2 910
48 团	Farm 48	2 650	7 829	6 523
49 团	Farm 49	4 323	16 442	14 723
50团(六师代管)	Farm 50(Division 6)	6 671	23 597	18 170
51 团	Farm 51	13 421	50 122	33 782
53 团	Farm 53	6 135	24 137	19 382
54 团	Farm 53	429	1 338	1 338
伽师总场	General Jiashi Farm	3 972	15 068	8 770
东风农场	Dong Feng Farm	550	1 730	1 730
红旗农场	Red Flag Farm	1 181	4 212	2 093
叶城二牧场	Yechen Ranch 2	372	1 303	885
托云牧场	Tuoyun Ranch	366	1 144	697
四 师	**Division 4**	**77 216**	**206 506**	**153 955**
61 团	Farm 61	4 386	13 289	11 694
62 团	Farm 62	8 521	20 031	19 238
63 团	Farm 63	3 297	9 054	6 760
64 团	Farm 64	9 005	25 899	18 155
66 团	Farm 66	10 144	29 494	14 342
67 团	Farm 67	4 458	13 927	12 175
68 团	Farm 68	3 689	9 650	7 033
69 团	Farm 69	3 050	7 063	5 650
70 团	Farm 70	4 815	11 796	7 847
71 团	Farm 71	5 325	11 483	9 601
72 团	Farm 72	4 598	11 375	7 988
73 团	Farm 73	3 074	7 561	6 915
74 团	Farm 74	1 428	3 678	2 781
75 团	Farm 75	1 235	3 231	2 784
76 团	Farm 76	3 816	10 874	7 723
77 团	Farm 77	2 479	7 611	5 776
78 团	Farm 78	2 047	5 485	4 283
79 团	Farm 79	1 849	5 005	3 210
五 师	**Division 5**	**36 729**	**98 631**	**79 771**
81 团	Farm 81	3 894	11 188	10 586
83 团	Farm 83	7 140	21 294	17 814
84 团	Farm 84	3 378	7 815	7 116
86 团	Farm 86	8 888	22 315	11 627
87 团	Farm 87	1 719	4 190	3 716
88 团	Farm 88	1 272	3 045	2 741
89 团	Farm 89	5 906	16 446	15 006
90 团	Farm 90	3 164	8 462	7 500
91 团	Farm 91	1 368	3 876	3 665
六 师	**Division 6**	**93 841**	**249 176**	**197 655**
101 团	Farm 101	5 066	11 771	11 362
102 团	Farm 102	7 309	19 763	15 738
103 团	Farm 103	6 896	16 820	13 217
105 团	Farm 105	4 966	13 807	10 374

3—7 续表 Continued

(2017 年)

师、团场名称	Names of Division and Farm	户数(户) Nember of Households (household)	人口数(人) Population (person)	团部人口数(人) Population of Farm (person)
106 团	Farm 106	1 696	5 653	5 346
芳草湖农场	Fang Caohu Farm	22 348	61 316	46 825
新湖农场	Xinhu Farm	14 439	36 939	32 928
军户农场	Junhu Farm	5 778	15 024	12 770
共青团农场	Communist League Farm	3 629	10 886	10 445
六运湖农场	Liu Yunhu Farm	2 558	6 010	5 667
土墩子农场	Tu Dunzi Farm	2 133	5 509	4 938
红旗农场	Red Flag Farm	5 025	13 201	12 045
奇台农场	Qitai Farm	10 887	28 613	14 910
北塔山牧场	Bei Tashan Ranch	1 111	3 864	1 090
七　师	**Division 7**	**62 470**	**166 979**	**149 999**
123 团	Farm 123	8 503	22 957	21 809
124 团	Farm 124	6 017	17 029	13 003
125 团	Farm 125	7 079	18 893	17 694
126 团	Farm 126	4 059	11 760	10 060
127 团	Farm 127	5 136	14 647	12 695
128 团	Farm 128	4 885	14 655	16 821
129 团	Farm 129	7 191	18 039	13 548
130 团	Farm 130	7 861	21 435	20 940
131 团	Farm 131	8 371	18 835	15 068
137 团	Farm 137	3 368	8 729	8 361
八　师	**Division 8**	**117 601**	**305 457**	**265 234**
121 团	Farm 121	15 390	37 969	21 049
133 团	Farm 133	8 711	22 018	14 195
134 团	Farm 134	7 311	21 034	12 761
136 团	Farm 136	4 072	11 119	11 075
141 团	Farm 141	4 489	10 765	11 735
142 团	Farm 142	10 166	25 333	25 163
143 团	Farm 143	13 523	34 088	27 931
144 团	Farm 144	5 355	12 751	12 004
石河子总场	General Shihezi Farm	17 233	51 698	51 631
147 团	Farm 147	6 440	15 472	15 355
148 团	Farm 148	9 394	24 761	24 265
149 团	Farm 149	6 386	16 606	16 440
150 团	Farm 150	6 899	15 446	15 291
152 团	Farm 152	2 232	6 397	6 339
九　师	**Division 9**	**21 387**	**57 464**	**41 929**
161 团	Farm 161	2 157	5 379	4 409
163 团	Farm 163	3 481	9 984	4 922
164 团	Farm 164	2 412	5 981	5 465
165 团	Farm 165	1 751	5 490	4 737
166 团	Farm 166	2 513	8 150	6 216
167 团	Farm 167	2 112	5 708	4 778
168 团	Farm 168	4 036	9 745	5 690
170 团	Farm 170	1 534	3 396	2 852
团结农场	Tuanjie Farm	1 391	3 631	2 860
十　师	**Division 10**	**21 608**	**57 390**	**44 095**
181 团	Farm 181	3 752	10 683	7 790
182 团	Farm 182	2 017	5 306	4 739
183 团	Farm 183	3 418	9 294	7 659
184 团	Farm 184	3 217	8 009	6 809
185 团	Farm 185	1 163	3 346	2 217
186 团	Farm 186	987	2 650	1 988
187 团	Farm 187	2 611	6 796	5 852
188 团	Farm 188	4 443	11 306	7 041
十二师	**Division 12**	**40 056**	**110 298**	**92 447**
104 团	Farm 104	8 288	24 461	18 857
三坪农场	Sanping Farm	9 224	22 662	14 500
五一农场	May1st Farm	5 887	18 862	18 656
头屯河农场	Tou Tunhe Farm	5 985	15 955	15 955
西山农牧场	Xishan Farm	4 877	12 252	10 495
221 团	Farm 221	1 886	5 393	4 365
222 团	Farm 222	3 909	10 713	9 619
十三师	**Division 13**	**34 320**	**89 589**	**74 125**
红星一场	Red Star No.1 Farm	3 728	9 875	9 875
红星二场	Red Star No.2 Farm	3 124	8 378	8 378
红星四场	Red Star No.4 Farm	2 768	8 732	4 910
黄田农场	Huangtian Farm	3 540	12 214	12 214
火箭农场	Huojian Farm	11 583	22 432	17 935
柳树泉农场	Liu Shuquan Farm	3 774	11 521	9 900
红山农场	Hongshan Farm	4 606	13 586	8 691
淖毛湖农场	Nao Maohu Farm	1 197	2 851	2 222
十四师	**Division 14**	**15 195**	**53 280**	**29 082**
皮山农场	Pishan Farm	8 160	30 189	19 050
47 团(十二师代管)	Farm 47(Division 12)	2 094	5 874	3 433
一牧场	Ranch 1	809	2 854	1 541
224 团	Farm 224	4 121	14 349	5 044
225 团	Farm 225	11	14	14

注:225 团 2017 年未正式移交。

Note:Farm 225 is not farmal handover in 2017.

3—8 各师计划生育情况

Family Planning by Division

（2017 年）

单　位	Unit	政策符合率(%) Match the Policy Rate (%)		综合避孕率(%) Synthesize Cotrolled Birth Rate(%)		领证率(%) Acceptance Rate (%)	
		汉　族 Han	少数民族 Minority Nationalities	汉　族 Han	少数民族 Minority Nationalities	汉　族 Han	少数民族 Minority Nationalities
总　计	**Total**	**99.76**	**94.36**	**89.31**	**89.14**	**44.61**	**38.92**
一　师	Division 1	99.96	99.65	85.59	86.53	30.98	46.49
二　师	Division 2	100.00	100.00	91.63	90.97	37.36	47.00
三　师	Division 3	97.60	88.32	87.53	86.71	18.27	23.29
四　师	Division 4	99.87	99.26	90.59	90.00	50.36	53.90
五　师	Division 5	100.00	100.00	90.07	87.66	45.53	53.58
六　师	Division 6	99.83	97.44	88.54	90.30	36.62	45.41
七　师	Division 7	99.82	100.00	89.46	93.84	39.98	64.89
八　师	Division 8	99.85	98.87	89.71	89.43	63.33	47.93
九　师	Division 9	100.00	100.00	88.53	89.38	68.63	56.75
十　师	Division 10	100.00	100.00	90.97	91.75	51.20	27.88
十一师	Division 11	100.00	100.00	73.28	79.41	68.71	43.14
十二师	Division 12	99.41	99.50	92.42	93.38	20.90	42.40
十三师	Division 13	99.86	100.00	94.25	94.94	41.95	67.05
十四师	Division 14	100.00	96.40	95.51	91.12	8.09	20.06
兵团直属	Directly under XPCC	100.00	100.00	90.71	84.17	69.09	31.17

单　位	Unit	已婚育龄妇女人数(人) Number of Women of Childbearing Age (person)		采取节育措施人数(人) Number of Women Adopting Birth Control (person)		领证人数(人) Number of Acceptance(person)	
		汉　族 Han	少数民族 Minority Nationalities	汉　族 Han	少数民族 Minority Nationalities	汉　族 Han	少数民族 Minority Nationalities
总　计	**Total**	**429 284**	**83 809**	**383 392**	**74 704**	**191 502**	**32 618**
一　师	Division 1	55 048	6 614	47 117	5 723	17 055	3 075
二　师	Division 2	34 319	2 515	31 447	2 288	12 821	1 182
三　师	Division 3	17 374	26 773	15 208	23 214	3 175	6 236
四　师	Division 4	31 792	11 007	28 800	9 906	16 009	5 933
五　师	Division 5	19 585	3 421	17 640	2 999	8 917	1 833
六　师	Division 6	57 109	6 536	50 562	5 902	20 915	2 968
七　师	Division 7	33 184	1 202	29 686	1 128	13 268	780
八　师	Division 8	100 937	6 576	90 550	5 881	63 921	3 152
九　师	Division 9	10 716	904	9 487	808	7 354	513
十　师	Division 10	18 193	800	16 551	734	9 315	223
十一师	Division 11	6 142	204	4 501	162	4 220	88
十二师	Division 12	19 057	5 375	17 612	5 019	3 983	2 279
十三师	Division 13	16 220	4 055	15 288	3 850	6 805	2 719
十四师	Division 14	4 745	7 227	4 532	6 585	384	1 450
兵团直属	Directly under XPCC	4 863	600	4 411	505	3 360	187

3—9 按三次产业分全社会就业人员数及构成

Number of Employed Persons and Composition of All Society by Type of Industry

年 份 Year	单 位 unit	就业人员数(人) Total Number of Employed Persons at the Year-end (person)	第一产业 Primary Industry	第二产业 Secondary Industry	第三产业 Tertiary Industry	构 成(%) Composition(%) 第一产业 Primary Industry	第二产业 Secondary Industry	第三产业 Tertiary Industry
1952		212 580	114 751	92 705	5 124	54.0	43.6	2.4
1954		133 283	58 732	68 888	5 663	44.1	51.7	4.2
1957		238 171	93 457	133 523	11 191	39.2	56.1	4.7
1962		497 967	316 169	139 003	42 795	63.5	27.9	8.6
1965		688 188	387 804	220 077	80 307	56.4	32.0	11.6
1970		908 867	536 889	272 912	99 066	59.1	30.0	10.9
1975		761 036	578 929	114 530	67 577	76.1	15.0	8.9
1978		918 448	638 736	186 453	93 259	69.5	20.3	10.2
1980		929 995	611 007	210 179	108 809	65.7	22.6	11.7
1985		1 034 301	581 277	293 741	159 283	56.2	28.4	15.4
1990		1 063 031	548 583	319 978	194 470	51.6	30.1	18.3
1995		1 065 463	502 644	315 050	247 769	47.2	29.6	23.2
2000		925 796	438 192	213 997	273 607	47.3	23.1	29.6
2001		933 073	438 757	212 441	281 875	47.0	22.8	30.2
2002		955 062	451 909	208 988	294 165	47.3	21.9	30.8
2003		975 457	493 197	192 899	289 361	50.6	19.8	29.6
2004		975 937	492 508	182 482	300 947	50.5	18.7	30.8
2005		988 064	483 903	192 495	311 666	49.0	19.5	31.5
2006		987 509	487 023	183 790	316 696	49.3	18.6	32.1
2007		995 146	489 686	190 711	314 749	49.2	19.2	31.6
2008		1 023 976	480 905	189 448	353 623	47.0	18.5	34.5
2009		1 035 654	483 710	196 577	355 367	46.7	19.0	34.3
2010		1 061 763	486 324	209 819	365 620	45.8	19.8	34.4
2011		1 123 192	493 494	248 003	381 695	43.9	22.1	34.0
2012		1 172 160	461 359	289 663	421 138	39.4	24.7	35.9
2013		1 253 353	425 320	337 808	490 225	33.9	27.0	39.1
2014		1 319 457	382 576	395 570	541 311	29.0	30.0	41.0
2015		1 361 802	357 190	403 580	601 032	26.2	29.7	44.1
2016		1 381 017	279 736	409 465	691 816	20.3	29.6	50.1
2017		1 441 651	341 859	388 987	710 805	23.7	27.0	49.3
一 师	Division 1	181 583	41 886	54 856	84 841	23.1	30.2	46.7
二 师	Division 2	96 408	25 500	20 488	50 420	26.5	21.3	52.3
三 师	Division 3	116 090	38 640	28 794	48 656	33.3	24.8	41.9
四 师	Division 4	110 015	35 670	25 452	48 893	32.4	23.1	44.4
五 师	Division 5	58 564	18 127	9 589	30 848	31.0	16.4	52.7
六 师	Division 6	159 840	37 897	35 976	85 967	23.7	22.5	53.8
七 师	Division 7	113 701	24 739	33 109	55 853	21.8	29.1	49.1
八 师	Division 8	317 652	54 609	95 314	167 729	17.2	30.0	52.8
九 师	Division 9	37 332	14 575	4 704	18 053	39.0	12.6	48.4
十 师	Division 10	43 665	11 452	10 228	21 985	26.2	23.4	50.3
十一师	Division 11	45 601	14	36 559	9 028	0.0	80.2	19.8
十二师	Division 12	56 947	9 531	11 154	36 262	16.7	19.6	63.7
十三师	Division 13	57 607	12 431	16 556	28 620	21.6	28.7	49.7
十四师	Division 14	26 726	15 719	2 867	8 140	58.8	10.7	30.5
兵团直属	Direct Under XPCC	19 920	1 069	3 341	15 510	5.4	16.8	77.9

注：此表是按从事职业划分三次产业。1952年—2015年第一产业包括农林牧渔服务业，第二产业包括开采辅助活动、金属制品机械设备修理业。2016年以后农林牧渔服务业、开采辅助活动、金属制品机械设备修理业归入第三产业(下同)。

Note: This table is divided into three industries according to the occupation. Primary Industry refers to agriculture、forestry、animal husbandry and fishery and services in support of these industries , Secondary Industry includes mining auxiliary activities、metal products machanical equipment repair industry in 1952—2015. Above industries belong to Tertiary Industry in 2016(the same below).

3—10 按从事职业分全社会就业人员数

计量单位：人 （2017年）

指 标	Item	就业人员数 Total Employed Persons at the Year-end
总 计	**Total**	**1 441 651**
按产业分	**Grouped by Industries**	
第一产业	Primary Industry	341 859
第二产业	Secondary Industry	388 987
第三产业	Tertiary Industry	710 805
按行业分	**Grouped by Sectors**	
农 业	Planting	267 574
林 业	Forestry	12 218
畜牧业	Animal Husbandry	60 433
渔 业	Fishery	1 634
农、林、牧、渔服务业	Farming ,Forestry,Animal Husbandry and Fishery Services	57 831
采矿业	Mining	11 113
制造业	Manufacturing	211 737
电力、热力、燃气及水生产和供应业	Production and Supply of Electric Power,Gas,Heat Power and Water	23 407
建筑业	Construciton	143 628
批发和零售业	Wholesale and Retail Trade	211 279
交通运输、仓储和邮政业	Transport,Storage,and Postal Service Industry	73 739
住宿和餐饮业	Accommodation and Catering Services Industry	75 484
信息传输、软件和信息技术服务业	Information Deliver,Software and Information Technique Services Industry	3 081
金融业	Finance	11 408
房地产业	Real Estate Trade	14 839
租赁和商务服务业	Leasing and Business Service	17 686
科学研究和技术服务业	Scientific Research and Technical Service	10 743
水利、环境和公共设施管理业	Water Conservancy,Environment and Public Facilities Management	15 057
居民服务、修理和其他服务业	Resident,Repair and Other Services	66 090
教 育	Education	45 740
卫生和社会工作	Health Care and Social Security	35 287
文化、体育和娱乐业	Culture,Sports and Entertainment	13 407
公共管理和社会组织	Public Management and Social Organization	58 236

Number of Employed Persons of All Society by Occupation

(person)

非私营单位就业人员 Employed Persons in Non-private Units	私营单位就业人员 Private Vnits	个体劳动者 Induvidual Labors	乡村及其他人员 Rural Labors and Others	年末就业人员数中：团场就业人员数 of Total：Employed Persons of Farms
789 194	**181 824**	**405 743**	**64 890**	**911 883**
274 399	2 611	22 321	42 528	329 410
231 295	106 501	33 900	17 291	166 651
283 500	72 712	349 522	5 071	415 822
232 502	1 613	3 214	30 245	261 008
10 591	47	989	591	11 804
30 715	880	17 147	11 691	55 126
591	71	971	1	1 472
44 121	946	10 948	1 816	56 791
6 628	3 118	1 152	215	5 650
98 664	75 228	22 742	15 103	109 491
20 115	3 063	229		6 952
105 956	25 467	10 232	1 973	45 169
20 671	40 000	150 269	339	116 787
6 279	3 256	64 056	148	54 787
3 027	2 320	70 055	82	51 015
1 415	778	888		855
9 432	1 820	156		284
6 426	7 456	957		5 995
10 150	5 266	2 270		3 233
9 528	1 146	69		1 563
12 886	1 934	157	80	8 437
20 890	3 314	39 743	2 143	50 037
43 693	1 072	874	101	25 353
32 410	821	1 987	69	14 880
4 377	2 182	6 557	291	6 371
58 127	26	81	2	18 823

3—11 各师按从事职业分全社会就业人员数

计量单位:人 (2017 年)

指　　标	Item	合　计 Total	一　师 Division 1
总　计	**Total**	**1 441 651**	**181 583**
按产业分	**Grouped by Industries**		
第一产业	Primary Industry	341 859	41 886
第二产业	Secondary Industry	388 987	54 856
第三产业	Tertiary Industry	710 805	84 841
按行业分	**Grouped by Sectors**		
农　业	Planting	267 574	37 725
林　业	Forestry	12 218	896
畜牧业	Animal Husbandry	60 433	3 030
渔　业	Fishery	1 634	235
农、林、牧、渔服务业	Farming ,Forestry,Animal Husbandry and Fishery Services	57 831	5 711
采矿业	Mining	11 113	501
制造业	Manufacturing	211 737	41 554
电力、热力、燃气及水生产和供应业	Production and Supply of Electric Power,Gas,Heat Power and Water	23 407	1 725
建筑业	Construciton	143 628	11 344
批发和零售业	Wholesale and Retail Trade	211 279	24 192
交通运输、仓储和邮政业	Transport,Storage,and Postal Service Industry	73 739	7 670
住宿和餐饮业	Accommodation and Catering Services Industry	75 484	9 764
信息传输、软件和信息技术服务业	Information Deliver,Software and Information Technique Services Industry	3 081	117
金融业	Finance	11 408	111
房地产业	Real Estate Trade	14 839	2 211
租赁和商务服务业	Leasing and Business Service	17 686	1 188
科学研究和技术服务业	Scientific Research and Technical Service	10 743	890
水利、环境和公共设施管理业	Water Conservancy,Environment and Public Facilities Management	15 057	2 301
居民服务、修理和其他服务业	Resident,Repair and Other Services	66 090	10 496
教　育	Education	45 740	5 818
卫生和社会工作	Health Care and Social Security	35 287	4 469
文化、体育和娱乐业	Culture,Sports and Entertainment	13 407	1 561
公共管理和社会组织	Public Management and Social Organization	58 236	8 074

Number of Employed Persons of All Society by Occupation and Division

(person)

二　师 Division 2	三　师 Division 3	四　师 Division 4	五　师 Division 5	六　师 Division 6	七　师 Division 7
96 408	**116 090**	**110 015**	**58 564**	**159 840**	**113 701**
25 500	38 640	35 670	18 127	37 897	24 739
20 488	28 794	25 452	9 589	35 976	33 109
50 420	48 656	48 893	30 848	85 967	55 853
18 709	29 583	28 466	16 198	25 131	20 906
3 673	1 700	367	876	347	660
3 014	7 325	6 439	971	12 303	3 059
104	32	398	82	116	114
6 553	3 722	6 679	3 395	12 804	2 937
1 741	317	772	116	1 109	922
15 178	12 940	18 106	4 851	22 687	15 987
1 431	1 650	2 047	1 605	2 281	1 928
2 138	13 887	4 527	3 079	9 899	14 576
16 011	14 378	9 185	8 480	22 004	16 610
4 513	3 040	6 232	2 316	11 909	11 461
4 735	6 057	5 787	5 714	8 471	6 262
172	26	365	32	475	109
178	10	169	107	576	257
328	518	181	428	3 477	560
457	280	696	245	1 624	869
563	346	1 010	396	669	741
470	984	1 952	145	1 916	1 118
5 367	5 575	6 878	3 411	5 267	5 032
3 053	4 268	3 580	2 449	4 887	2 346
3 405	2 177	2 691	1 607	3 582	2 629
873	928	749	286	1 664	1 434
3 742	6 347	2 739	1 775	6 642	3 184

3－11续表

计量单位:人 (2017年)

指　　标	Item	八　师 Division 8	九　师 Division 9
总　计	**Total**	**317 652**	**37 332**
按产业分	**Grouped by Industries**		
第一产业	Primary Industry	54 609	14 575
第二产业	Secondary Industry	95 314	4 704
第三产业	Tertiary Industry	167 729	18 053
按行业分	**Grouped by Sectors**		
农　业	Planting	40 253	10 499
林　业	Forestry	2 247	369
畜牧业	Animal Husbandry	11 808	3 700
渔　业	Fishery	301	7
农、林、牧、渔服务业	Farming ,Forestry,Animal Husbandry and Fishery Services	9 198	3 090
采矿业	Mining	395	38
制造业	Manufacturing	49 082	2 710
电力、热力、燃气及水生产和供应业	Production and Supply of Electric Power,Gas,Heat Power and Water	6 602	637
建筑业	Construciton	39 235	1 319
批发和零售业	Wholesale and Retail Trade	62 786	4 369
交通运输、仓储和邮政业	Transport,Storage,and Postal Service Industry	11 926	1 577
住宿和餐饮业	Accommodation and Catering Services Industry	15 590	2 120
信息传输、软件和信息技术服务业	Information Deliver,Software and Information Technique Services Industry	1 186	189
金融业	Finance	8 957	25
房地产业	Real Estate Trade	2 654	27
租赁和商务服务业	Leasing and Business Service	6 791	68
科学研究和技术服务业	Scientific Research and Technical Service	1 603	303
水利、环境和公共设施管理业	Water Conservancy,Environment and Public Facilities Management	4 038	338
居民服务、修理和其他服务业	Resident,Repair and Other Services	10 036	1 543
教　育	Education	11 026	1 210
卫生和社会工作	Health Care and Social Security	7 909	1 201
文化、体育和娱乐业	Culture,Sports and Entertainment	2 941	426
公共管理和社会组织	Public Management and Social Organization	11 088	1 567

Continued

(person)

十 师 Division 10	十一师 Division 11	十二师 Division 12	十三师 Division 13	十四师 Division 14	兵团直属 Direct Under XPCC
43 665	**45 601**	**56 947**	**57 607**	**26 726**	**19 920**
11 452	14	9 531	12 431	15 719	1 069
10 228	36 559	11 154	16 556	2 867	3 341
21 985	9 028	36 262	28 620	8 140	15 510
8 972	14	6 503	10 288	14 276	51
332		390	304	57	
2 008		2 551	1 821	1 386	1 018
140		87	18		
1 292		325	1 431	694	
916		600	3 217		469
6 454	2 634	5 221	9 453	2 325	2 555
931	5	493	1 629	145	298
1 927	33 920	4 840	2 521	397	19
6 195	2 015	12 029	6 941	1 347	4 737
2 344	248	3 875	5 519	585	524
2 197	344	3 478	3 418	878	669
111	59	65	124	4	47
228	84	262	144	29	271
511	1 196	1 427	325	140	856
806	709	2 159	553	262	979
179	2 395	29	477	35	1 107
571	155	249	737	50	33
1 828	211	7 293	2 478	649	26
1 612	949	787	1 414	934	1 407
1 366	263	493	1 639	356	1 500
415	16	447	789	132	746
2 330	384	3 344	2 367	2 045	2 608

3—12 按行业和登记注册类型分非私营单位就业人员数

计量单位:人 (2017 年)

指　　标	Item	非私营单位就业人员数 Employed Persons in Units	国有单位 State-owned Units
总　　计	**Total**	**789 194**	**536 777**
农、林、牧、渔业	Farming ,Forestry,Animal Husbandry and Fishery	391 347	387 348
采矿业	Mining	6 065	787
制造业	Manufacturing	87 731	1 939
电力、热力、燃气及水生产和供应业	Production and Supply of Electric Power,Gas,Heat Power and Water	17 508	2 344
建筑业	Construciton	97 116	7 993
批发和零售业	Wholesale and Retail Trade	19 206	3 384
交通运输、仓储和邮政业	Transport,Storage,and Postal Service Industry	4 784	1 615
住宿和餐饮业	Accommodation and Catering Services Industry	2 347	1 142
信息传输、软件和信息技术服务业	Information Deliver,Software and Information Technique Services Industry	1 469	153
金融业	Finance	9 435	1 369
房地产业	Real Estate Trade	8 716	1 454
租赁和商务服务业	Leasing and Business Service	12 429	3 919
科学研究、技术服务业	Scientific Research and Technical Service	9 395	4 842
水利、环境和公共设施管理业	Water Conservancy,Environment and Public Facilities Management	7 582	6 064
居民服务、修理和其他服务业	Resident,repair and Other Services	1 206	797
教　育	Education	43 581	43 214
卫生和社会工作	Health Care and Social Security	29 067	28 971
文化、体育和娱乐业	Culture,Sports and Entertainment	3 169	2 410
公共管理和社会组织	Public Management and Social Organization	37 041	37 032

注:本表按单位划分行业(下同)。

Number of Employed Persons in Non-private Units by Types of Registration and Sector

(person)

集体单位 Collective-owned Units	股份合作 Share Cooperative	联 营 Joint Owneship Units	有限责任公司 Limited Liability Corporations	股份有限公司 Share-holding Corporations Ltd	港澳台商投资 Units With Funds From Hong Kong, Macao&Twiwan	外商投资 Foreign Funded Units	其 他 Other
140	**306**	**24**	**200 486**	**40 765**	**626**	**3 497**	**6 573**
		18	1 867	39			2 075
			5 278				
39		1	71 762	8 911	450	2 439	2 190
			12 297	2 737		123	7
			68 132	20 991			
			12 138	1 019		533	2 132
			3 035	134			
			906	214		85	
			500	365	134	317	
101	280		2 139	5 546			
			7 117	103	42		
	22	5	8 013	460			10
			4 549				4
	4		1 472	42			
			395	14			
			162	190			15
							96
			724				35
							9

Note: This table is divided into sectors according to the unit (the same as follows).

3—13 非私营单位就业人员数和劳动报酬情况

计量单位:人、万元 (2017 年)

指 标	Item	单位数(个) Number of Units(unit)	单位就业人员数 Number of Employed Persons in Units
总 计	**Total**	**5 264**	**789 194**
按企业、事业、机关	**Grouped by Enterprises, Institutions and Agencies**		
# 企 业	Enterprises	3 172	667 461
事 业	Institutions	1 350	90 197
机 关	Agencies	717	31 219
按国民经济行业	**Grouped by Sector**		
农、林、牧、渔业	Farming ,Forestry,Animal Husbandry and Fishery	1 431	391 347
采矿业	Mining	29	6 065
制造业	Manufacturing	445	87 731
电力、热力、燃气及水生产和供应业	Production and Supply of Electric Power,Gas,Heat Power and Water	109	17 508
建筑业	Construciton	118	97 116
批发和零售业	Wholesale and Retail Trade	402	19 206
交通运输、仓储和邮政业	Transport,Storage,and Postal Service Industry	81	4 784
住宿和餐饮业	Accommodation and Catering Services Industry	36	2 347
信息传输、软件和信息技术服务业	Information Deliver,Software and Information Technique Services Industry	21	1 469
金融业	Finance	87	9 435
房地产业	Real Estate Trade	190	8 716
租赁和商务服务业	Leasing and Business Service	215	12 429
科学研究和技术服务业	Scientific Research and Technical Service	207	9 395
水利、环境和公共设施管理业	Water Conservancy,Environment and Public Facilities Management	79	7 582
居民服务、修理和其他服务业	Resident,repair and Other Services	32	1 206
教 育	Education	378	43 581
卫生和社会工作	Health Care and Social Security	282	29 067
文化、体育和娱乐业	Culture,Sports and Entertainment	74	3 169
公共管理、社会保障和社会组织	Public Management and Social Organization	1 048	37 041

Number of Employed Persons and Labour Remuneration in Non-private Units

(person,10 000 yuan)

# 女 性 Female	# 国有单位 State-owned Units	在岗职工 Fully Empolyed Staff and Workers	劳务派遣人员 Persons of Labor Sent	其他就业人员 Other Employed Persons	单位就业人员年平均人数 Average Annual Number of Persons Employed in Units	在岗职工平均人数 Average Annual Number of Staff and Workers	劳务派遣人员平均人数 Average Annual Number of Persons of Laber Sent
299 344	**231 069**	**743 173**	**31 399**	**14 622**	**917 763**	**844 172**	**57 817**
236 578	168 351	626 345	28 861	12 255	796 147	727 653	55 148
55 364	55 364	86 206	2 020	1 971	90 222	86 052	2 141
7 343	7 343	30 305	518	396	31 061	30 134	528
160 737	159 538	389 072	825	1 450	376 598	374 649	759
1 129	145	5 535	515	15	6 529	5 977	520
32 651	684	82 792	2 869	2 070	86 420	80 986	3 060
4 541	783	16 577	718	213	17 205	16 357	642
9 798	861	72 444	20 265	4 407	239 996	188 816	46 152
6 558	1 153	16 048	1 434	1 724	19 551	16 407	1 514
1 242	571	4 468	170	146	4 805	4 507	164
1 253	708	2 331		16	2 362	2 343	3
743	66	1 296	160	13	1 479	1 302	164
5 941	836	9 174	247	14	8 922	8 568	340
3 669	754	7 255	549	912	9 974	8 410	572
5 234	1 752	10 493	1 135	801	12 484	10 159	1 239
2 758	1 572	8 780	55	560	9 464	8 729	55
2 787	2 158	6 688	603	291	8 228	7 162	706
535	334	760	218	228	1 253	779	263
27 486	27 350	42 638	538	405	43 442	42 552	522
20 565	20 481	28 075	261	731	29 043	27 959	264
1 481	1 092	3 050	62	57	3 153	3 030	63
10 236	10 231	35 697	775	569	36 855	35 480	815

3—13 续表

计量单位:人、万元　　　　(2017 年)

指　　标	Item	其他就业人员平均人数 Average Annual Number of Persons Employed in Others	单位就业人员劳动报酬 Earnings of Employed Persons in Units
总　计	**Total**	**15 774**	**5 331 238**
按企业、事业、机关分	**Grouped by Enterprises, Institutions and Agencies**		
# 企　业	Enterprises	13 346	4 332 520
事　业	Institutions	2 029	705 289
机　关	Agencies	399	291 959
按国民经济行业分	**Grouped by Sector**		
农、林、牧、渔业	Farming ,Forestry,Animal Husbandry and Fishery	1 190	1 715 220
采矿业	Mining	32	34 463
制造业	Manufacturing	2 374	501 975
电力、热力、燃气及水生产和供应业	Production and Supply of Electric Power,Gas,Heat Power and Water	206	117 887
建筑业	Construciton	5 028	1 504 138
批发和零售业	Wholesale and Retail Trade	1 630	118 709
交通运输、仓储和邮政业	Transport,Storage,and Postal Service Industry	134	29 677
住宿和餐饮业	Accommodation and Catering Services Industry	16	12 867
信息传输、软件和信息技术服务业	Information Deliver,Software and Information Technique Services Industry	13	16 203
金融业	Finance	14	74 903
房地产业	Real Estate Trade	992	54 028
租赁和商务服务业	Leasing and Business Service	1 086	79 301
科学研究和技术服务业	Scientific Research and Technical Service	680	88 801
水利、环境和公共设施管理业	Water Conservancy,Environment and Public Facilities Management	360	47 716
居民服务、修理和其他服务业	Resident,repair and Other Services	211	5 185
教　育	Education	368	340 539
卫生和社会工作	Health Care and Social Security	820	235 131
文化、体育和娱乐业	Culture,Sports and Entertainment	60	23 682
公共管理、社会保障和社会组织	Public Management and Social Organization	560	330 814

Continued

(person,10 000 yuan)

# 国有单位 State-owned Units	在岗职工工资总额 Wages of Fully Employed Staff and Workers	劳务派遣人员工资总额 Wages of Persons of Laber Sent	其他就业人员劳动报酬 Earnings of Other Employed Persons in Units	单位就业人员平均工资(元) Average Money Wage of Employed Persons in Units (yuan)	在岗职工平均工资(元) Average Money Wage of Staff and Workers (yuan)	劳务派遣人员平均工资(元) Average Money Wage of Persons of Laber Sent (yuan)	其他就业人员平均工资(元) Average Money Wage of Other Employed Persons (yuan)
2 945 660	**4 935 377**	**321 533**	**74 328**	**58 089**	**58 464**	**55 612**	**47 120**
1 948 352	3 953 232	312 556	66 733	54 419	54 329	56 676	50 002
705 289	692 135	6 654	6 501	78 173	80 432	31 077	32 041
291 959	288 541	2 324	1 094	93 995	95 753	44 013	27 419
1 693 423	1 707 177	4 212	3 831	45 545	45 567	55 493	32 192
7 271	31 753	2 596	114	52 784	53 126	49 921	35 563
8 619	477 285	15 733	8 957	58 085	58 934	51 414	37 729
10 905	114 089	2 964	834	68 519	69 749	46 174	40 461
131 662	1 202 942	265 079	36 117	62 673	63 710	57 436	71 832
21 861	102 968	11 839	3 902	60 718	62 759	78 198	23 937
9 983	27 926	869	882	61 762	61 961	52 963	65 843
6 414	12 754	9	104	54 475	54 436	31 000	64 688
1 133	14 072	2 042	89	109 554	108 076	124 530	68 615
12 366	73 438	1 404	61	83 953	85 712	41 300	43 286
5 765	49 039	2 254	2 734	54 169	58 311	39 411	27 564
25 391	71 372	3 327	4 602	63 522	70 255	26 849	42 378
51 265	83 722	290	4 788	93 830	95 913	52 727	70 418
35 329	45 138	1 520	1 057	57 992	63 024	21 534	29 367
2 910	3 972	700	513	41 382	50 985	26 624	24 327
337 071	337 427	1 928	1 184	78 389	79 298	36 929	32 174
234 843	231 399	1 094	2 639	80 960	82 764	41 420	32 178
18 689	23 163	324	195	75 110	76 447	51 429	32 467
330 761	325 740	3 349	1 725	89 761	91 809	41 090	30 807

3—14 各师非私营单位就业人员数

Number of Employed Persons in Non-private Units by Division

计量单位：人　　　　(2017年)　　　　(person)

单　位	Unit	合计 Total	#企业 Enterprises	#事业 Institutions	#机关 Agencies& Organizations	农、林、牧、渔业 Farming, Forestry, Animal Husbandry and Fishery	采矿业 Mining	制造业 Manufacturing	电力、热力、燃气及水的生产和供应业 Production and Supply of Electric Power, Heat Power, Gas and Water
总　计	**Total**	**789 194**	**667 461**	**90 197**	**31 219**	**391 347**	**6 065**	**87 731**	**17 508**
一　师	Division 1	89 795	75 729	9 304	4 756	51 767	375	14 208	1 575
二　师	Division 2	55 504	47 408	6 141	1 955	36 748	1 287	2 174	1 030
三　师	Division 3	52 578	41 538	7 000	4 016	23 919		5 856	918
四　师	Division 4	62 892	54 681	6 972	1 239	40 048	290	6 434	1 794
五　师	Division 5	39 654	34 641	4 307	706	27 471	8	1 638	1 128
六　师	Division 6	80 881	68 019	9 312	3 289	39 662	1 020	14 945	1 785
七　师	Division 7	51 429	44 213	5 413	1 803	28 399	872	4 371	1 410
八　师	Division 8	178 389	150 291	21 687	6 411	65 179		28 112	6 265
九　师	Division 9	25 018	21 235	2 984	773	18 455		1 255	267
十　师	Division 10	23 839	18 886	3 645	1 308	14 476	892	813	701
十一师	Division 11	39 775	38 305	1 086	384	14	334	1 371	5
十二师	Division 12	28 321	25 764	1 891	666	12 040	538	2 218	122
十三师	Division 13	21 106	16 748	3 598	760	14 294	428	592	97
十四师	Division 14	21 444	19 260	1 701	483	17 806		823	113
兵团直属	Directlty under XPCC	18 569	10 743	5 156	2 670	1 069	21	2 921	298

单　位	Unit	建筑业 Construction	批发和零售业 Wholesale and Retail Trade	交通运输、仓储和邮政业 Transport, Storage and Postal Service	住宿和饮业 Accommodation and Catering Services Industry	信息传输、软件和信息技术服务业 Information Deliver, Software and Information Technique Services Industry	金融业 Finance	房地产业 Real Estate Trade	租赁和商务服务业 Leasing and Business Service
总　计	**Total**	**97 116**	**19 206**	**4 784**	**2 347**	**1 469**	**9 435**	**8 716**	**12 429**
一　师	Division 1	5 152	1 031	222	61		23	642	327
二　师	Division 2	681	3 315	236	228	4	52	684	185
三　师	Division 3	8 333	710	365	139	11	6	144	458
四　师	Division 4	3 337	811	431	487	5	149	45	550
五　师	Division 5	2 313	898	331	49		90	310	212
六　师	Division 6	3 566	1 630	729	236	240	484	1 176	1 289
七　师	Division 7	6 161	431	335	11		302	87	149
八　师	Division 8	33 805	1 212	1 027	790	976	7 378	704	3 688
九　师	Division 9	346	627	97	17	26	6	19	80
十　师	Division 10	975	162	139	75		151	103	191
十一师	Division 11	30 365	2 064	6	1		84	1 138	520
十二师	Division 12	1 275	2 148	196	44	65	282	2 661	3 566
十三师	Division 13	418	272	32		81	149	69	186
十四师	Division 14	370	33	39			8	43	73
兵团直属	Directlty under XPCC	19	3 862	599	209	61	271	891	955

3—14 续表 Continued

计量单位:人 (2017 年) (person)

单 位	Unit	科学研究和技术服务业 Scientific Research and Technical Service	水利、环境和公共设施管理业 Water Conservancy, Environment and Public Facilities Management	居民服务、修理和其他服务业 Resident, repair and Other Services	教 育 Education	卫生和社会工作 Health Care and Social Security	文化、体育和娱乐业 Culture, Sports and Recreation	公共管理、社会保障和社会组织 Public Management, Social Security and Social Organization
总 计	**Total**	**9 395**	**7 582**	**1 206**	**43 581**	**29 067**	**3 169**	**37 041**
一 师	Division 1	741	828		5 180	2 095	212	5 356
二 师	Division 2	589	259	134	2 933	2 696	58	2 211
三 师	Division 3	370	610	36	4 340	1 851	320	4 192
四 师	Division 4	623	188	249	3 230	2 568	113	1 540
五 师	Division 5	376	113		2 290	1 468	57	902
六 师	Division 6	463	885	71	4 571	3 130	557	4 442
七 师	Division 7	832	1 057	32	2 335	2 281	116	2 248
八 师	Division 8	959	2 536	92	10 293	6 775	588	8 010
九 师	Division 9	218	352	4	1 194	1 027	68	960
十 师	Division 10	240	234	108	1 605	1 296	122	1 556
十 一 师	Division 11	2 292	126	42	836	183	10	384
十 二 师	Division 12	165	193	296	1 089	443	127	853
十 三 师	Division 13	356	51	136	1 354	1 470	30	1 091
十 四 师	Division 14	78	117		924	284	45	688
兵团直属	Directly under XPCC	1 093	33	6	1 407	1 500	746	2 608

3—15 各师非私营单位女性就业人员数

Number of Femal Employed Persons in Non-private Units by Division

计量单位:人 (2017 年) (person)

单 位	Unit	合 计 Total	# 企 业 Enterprises	# 事 业 Institutions	# 机 关 Agencies & Organizations	农、林、牧、渔业 Farming, Forestry, Animal Husbandry and Fishery	采矿业 Mining	制造业 Manufacturing	电力、热力、燃气及水的生产和供应业 Production and Supply of Electric Power, Heat Power, Gas and Water
总 计	**Total**	**299 344**	**236 578**	**55 364**	**7 343**	**160 737**	**1 129**	**32 651**	**4 541**
一 师	Division 1	37 617	31 398	5 490	723	21 865	88	7 146	501
二 师	Division 2	24 030	19 729	3 912	389	16 141	191	980	185
三 师	Division 3	20 216	15 208	4 262	728	10 577		2 788	244
四 师	Division 4	24 462	19 893	4 241	328	15 915	44	1 959	362
五 师	Division 5	16 509	13 296	3 047	166	10 806	1	638	411
六 师	Division 6	30 498	23 714	6 059	692	15 667	169	3 967	408
七 师	Division 7	19 276	15 526	3 435	315	11 401	93	1 905	327
八 师	Division 8	63 157	48 536	12 645	1 976	26 263		10 222	1 610
九 师	Division 9	10 257	8 225	1 873	157	7 339		475	54
十 师	Division 10	9 778	7 117	2 265	396	5 905	189	226	222
十 一 师	Division 11	6 154	5 275	719	160	4	110	274	2
十 二 师	Division 12	11 182	9 570	1 272	340	4 576	139	759	38
十 三 师	Division 13	8 722	6 210	2 315	197	5 501	101	162	17
十 四 师	Division 14	9 708	8 655	975	78	8 275		216	27
兵团直属	Directly under XPCC	7 778	4 226	2 854	698	502	4	934	133

3—15 续表　Continued

计量单位：人　　　　(2017 年)　　　　(person)

单　位	Unit	建筑业 Construction	批发和零售业 Wholesale and Retail Trade	交通运输、仓储和邮政业 Transport, Storage and Postal Service	住宿和餐饮业 Accommodation and Catering Services Industry	信息传输、软件和信息技术服务业 Information Deliver, Software and Information Technique Services Industry	金融业 Finance	房地产业 Real Estate Trade	租赁和商务服务业 Leasing and Business Servic
总　计	**Total**	**9 798**	**6 558**	**1 242**	**1 253**	**743**	**5 941**	**3 669**	**5 234**
一　师	Division 1	896	307	67	47		12	231	118
二　师	Division 2	13	1 314	88	129		23	398	71
三　师	Division 3	775	234	89	92	3	3	28	129
四　师	Division 4	509	344	91	286	1	93	20	238
五　师	Division 5	613	377	59	29		52	152	98
六　师	Division 6	345	594	119	153	181	234	448	739
七　师	Division 7	931	109	90	6		130	17	44
八　师	Division 8	1 782	502	375	302	473	4 929	314	1 434
九　师	Division 9	70	152	30	13	14	1	8	38
十　师	Division 10	113	54	32	62		80	41	97
十一师	Division 11	3 333	193	3	1		35	512	206
十二师	Division 12	194	598	50	3	28	154	1 087	1 650
十三师	Division 13	121	76	12		18	74	38	76
十四师	Division 14	94	9	9			4	13	30
兵团直属	Directly under XPCC	9	1 695	128	130	25	117	362	266

单　位	Unit	科学研究和技术服务业 Scientific Research and Technical Service	水利、环境和公共设施管理业 Water Conservancy, Environment and Public Facilities Management	居民服务、修理和其他服务业 Resident, repair and Other Services	教　育 Education	卫生和社会工作 Health Care and Social Security	文化、体育和娱乐业 Culture, Sports and Recreation	公共管理、社会保障和社会组织 Public Management, Social Security and Social Organization
总　计	**Total**	**2 758**	**2 787**	**535**	**27 486**	**20 565**	**1 481**	**10 236**
一　师	Division 1	205	317		3 263	1 430	83	1 041
二　师	Division 2	141	71	53	1 762	1 919	25	526
三　师	Division 3	104	241	10	2 658	1 262	170	809
四　师	Division 4	156	46	135	1 943	1 780	54	486
五　师	Division 5	136	47		1 642	1 160	29	259
六　师	Division 6	157	484	20	2 963	2 281	264	1 305
七　师	Division 7	210	319	7	1 493	1 581	57	556
八　师	Division 8	353	881	22	6 063	4 741	260	2 631
九　师	Division 9	66	193	1	825	713	30	235
十　师	Division 10	63	56	32	1 090	951	61	504
十一师	Division 11	562	41	18	554	139	7	160
十二师	Division 12	70	63	177	765	310	68	453
十三师	Division 13	111	14	55	913	1 098	15	320
十四师	Division 14	35	11		628	176	19	162
兵团直属	Directly under XPCC	389	3	5	924	1 024	339	789

3—16 各师非私营单位就业人员劳动报酬

Labor Remuneration of Employed Persons in Non-private Units by Division

计量单位：万元　　　　(2017 年)　　　　(10 000 yuan)

单位	Unit	合计 Total	#企业 Enterprises	#事业 Institutions	#机关 Agencies & Organizations	农、林、牧、渔业 Farming, Forestry, Animal Husbandry and Fishery	采矿业 Mining	制造业 Manufacturing	电力、热力、燃气及水的生产和供应业 Production and Supply of Electric Power, Heat Power, Gas and Water
总　计	**Total**	**5 331 238**	**4 332 520**	**705 289**	**291 959**	**1 715 220**	**34 463**	**501 975**	**117 887**
一　师	Division 1	502 147	385 424	72 880	43 775	135 482	2 394	66 565	10 397
二　师	Division 2	336 940	274 000	42 674	20 266	150 236	8 051	11 924	5 838
三　师	Division 3	386 836	296 696	50 387	39 580	131 547		29 556	7 200
四　师	Division 4	378 803	319 243	48 224	11 336	178 616	1 718	36 712	10 875
五　师	Division 5	218 242	178 824	33 094	6 325	136 990	35	6 184	5 632
六　师	Division 6	457 806	358 320	71 276	27 058	172 941	6 307	97 088	13 334
七　师	Division 7	394 192	340 033	38 633	15 526	138 849	5 606	26 074	9 342
八　师	Division 8	1 196 983	955 031	186 146	55 806	373 608		164 877	45 795
九　师	Division 9	93 475	66 122	20 067	7 208	53 489		5 139	1 373
十　师	Division 10	107 270	76 631	23 351	7 288	45 962	4 736	4 312	4 002
十一师	Division 11	662 375	650 750	8 092	3 534	473	1 351	7 864	16
十二师	Division 12	191 881	169 786	13 634	8 462	54 302	2 105	12 300	789
十三师	Division 13	113 250	76 903	28 483	7 864	61 462	1 868	2 821	863
十四师	Division 14	112 025	94 129	11 501	6 395	72 142		2 469	1 017
兵团直属	Directly under XPCC	179 013	90 630	56 846	31 537	9 120	292	28 092	1 415

单位	Unit	建筑业 Construction	批发和零售业 Wholesale and Retail Trade	交通运输、仓储和邮政业 Transport, Storage and Postal Service	住宿和餐饮业 Accommodation and Catering Services Industry	信息传输、软件和信息技术服务业 Information Deliver, Software and Information Technique Services Industry	金融业 Finance	房地产业 Real Estate Trade	租赁和商务服务业 Leasing and Business Service
总　计	**Total**	**1 504 138**	**118 709**	**29 677**	**12 867**	**16 203**	**74 903**	**54 028**	**79 301**
一　师	Division 1	155 808	5 932	909	309		186	2 594	2 219
二　师	Division 2	64 666	19 123	1 375	1 007	37	349	2 730	1 095
三　师	Division 3	111 896	4 561	1 728	720	91	43	531	2 621
四　师	Division 4	70 918	5 176	2 769	3 001	36	1 797	246	3 390
五　师	Division 5	18 496	4 277	805	375		782	1 230	1 299
六　师	Division 6	25 583	10 173	4 455	974	3 728	4 056	7 359	6 501
七　师	Division 7	142 814	2 471	1 838	28		2 153	429	1 363
八　师	Division 8	254 936	9 652	8 060	4 464	10 710	51 431	4 982	18 956
九　师	Division 9	2 258	2 146	438	80	150	43	189	561
十　师	Division 10	11 174	772	845	362		1 271	389	1 264
十一师	Division 11	582 818	14 869	30	8		932	13 015	4 186
十二师	Division 12	43 048	11 799	1 218	311	414	1 992	15 478	22 641
十三师	Division 13	2 497	1 662	258		526	1 906	419	1 747
十四师	Division 14	17 141	219	283			82	169	780
兵团直属	Directly under XPCC	87	25 878	4 666	1 229	511	7 879	4 269	10 678

3—16 续表 Continued

计量单位:万元 (2017 年) (10 000 yuan)

单 位	Unit	科学研究和技术服务业 Scientific Research and Technical Service	水利、环境和公共设施管理业 Water Conservancy, Environment and Public Facilities Management	居民服务、修理和其他服务业 Resident, repair and Other Services	教 育 Education	卫生和社会工作 Health Care and Social Security	文化、体育和娱乐业 Culture, Sports and Recreation	公共管理、社会保障和社会组织 Public Management, Social Security and Social Organization
总 计	**Total**	**88 801**	**47 716**	**5 185**	**340 539**	**235 131**	**23 682**	**330 814**
一 师	Division 1	5 822	5 135		41 335	17 848	1 635	47 577
二 师	Division 2	6 322	2 218	488	22 666	16 574	500	21 743
三 师	Division 3	3 956	3 539	219	29 910	14 947	2 892	40 880
四 师	Division 4	6 007	940	640	22 844	18 412	833	13 874
五 师	Division 5	4 225	444		18 059	11 062	448	7 901
六 师	Division 6	3 216	3 245	389	34 780	26 377	3 465	33 838
七 师	Division 7	4 607	5 777	204	17 129	16 301	989	18 220
八 师	Division 8	7 468	14 299	510	93 058	63 388	3 931	66 859
九 师	Division 9	1 353	1 521	16	8 319	7 394	484	8 523
十 师	Division 10	1 690	1 314	409	10 476	8 825	646	8 822
十一师	Division 11	18 924	6 644	139	6 129	1 377	67	3 534
十二师	Division 12	1 207	1 107	1 693	7 866	2 888	830	9 894
十三师	Division 13	2 987	391	431	10 223	13 307	274	9 609
十四师	Division 14	599	988		5 827	1 880	342	8 089
兵团直属	Directly under XPCC	20 420	154	49	11 920	14 553	6 350	31 452

3—17 各师国有单位就业人员数

Number of Employed Persons in State-owned Unit by Division

计量单位:人 (2017 年) (person)

单 位	Unit	合 计 Total	#企 业 Enterprises	#事 业 Institutions	#机 关 Agencies& Organizations	农、林、牧、渔业 Farming, Forestry, Animal Husbandry and Fishery	采矿业 Mining	制造业 Manufacturing	电力、热力、燃气及水的生产和供应业 Production and Supply of Electric Power, Heat Power, Gas and Water
总 计	**Total**	**536 777**	**415 344**	**90 197**	**31 219**	**387 348**	**787**	**1 939**	**2 344**
一 师	Division 1	66 192	52 132	9 304	4 756	51 672		48	
二 师	Division 2	47 646	39 550	6 141	1 955	36 748	241		392
三 师	Division 3	36 130	25 114	7 000	4 016	23 798		546	
四 师	Division 4	49 921	41 710	6 972	1 239	40 048	52	23	23
五 师	Division 5	33 908	28 895	4 307	706	27 369		41	944
六 师	Division 6	51 950	39 332	9 312	3 289	37 832	99	104	418
七 师	Division 7	37 765	30 549	5 413	1 803	28 399	360	103	33
八 师	Division 8	96 183	68 085	21 687	6 411	65 072		371	
九 师	Division 9	22 144	18 387	2 984	773	18 006		107	94
十 师	Division 10	20 454	15 501	3 645	1 308	14 476			332
十一师	Division 11	8 539	7 069	1 086	384			7	
十二师	Division 12	17 542	14 985	1 891	666	11 828		448	
十三师	Division 13	19 103	14 745	3 598	760	14 294	35	23	
十四师	Division 14	20 011	17 827	1 701	483	17 806		14	
兵团直属	Directly under XPCC	9 289	1 463	5 156	2 670			104	108

3—17 续表 Continued

计量单位：人 (2017 年) (person)

单 位	Unit	建筑业 Construction	批发和零售业 Wholesale and Retail Trade	交通运输、仓储和邮政业 Transport, Storage and Postal Service	住宿和餐饮业 Accommodation and Catering Services Industry	信息传输、软件和信息技术服务业 Information Deliver, Software and Information Technique Services Industry	金融业 Finance	房地产业 Real Estate Trade	租赁和商务服务业 Leasing and Business Service
总 计	**Total**	**7 993**	**3 384**	**1 615**	**1 142**	**153**	**1 369**	**1 454**	**3 919**
一 师	Division 1			83	61		23	50	56
二 师	Division 2	86	860	53	228	4	39	224	156
三 师	Division 3		325	325	111	11	6		29
四 师	Division 4	461	347		487	5			123
五 师	Division 5		355	13				163	114
六 师	Division 6	52	126	48	7		85		433
七 师	Division 7	169	299	335					27
八 师	Division 8	37	71	619			1 172	60	213
九 师	Division 9	31	110	20		26			59
十 师	Division 10	157	117	10	75			33	93
十一师	Division 11	7 000						21	6
十二师	Division 12		74	11		46	13	614	1 904
十三师	Division 13		37	32			31		163
十四师	Division 14		7	6				43	25
兵团直属	Directly under XPCC		656	60	173	61		246	518

单 位	Unit	科学研究和技术服务业 Scientific Research and Technical Service	水利、环境和公共设施管理业 Water Conservancy, Environment and Public Facilities Management	居民服务、修理和其他服务业 Resident, repair and Other Services	教 育 Education	卫生和社会工作 Health Care and Social Security	文化、体育和娱乐业 Culture, Sports and Recreation	公共管理、社会保障和社会组织 Public Management, Social Security and Social Organization
总 计	**Total**	**4 842**	**6 064**	**797**	**43 214**	**28 971**	**2 410**	**37 032**
一 师	Division 1	709	688		5 180	2 089	177	5 356
二 师	Division 2	324	259	134	2 933	2 696	58	2 211
三 师	Division 3	90	432	36	4 325	1 851	62	4 183
四 师	Division 4	464	188	249	3 230	2 568	113	1 540
五 师	Division 5	164	28		2 290	1 468	57	902
六 师	Division 6	168	318	6	4 532	3 130	150	4 442
七 师	Division 7	167	890	32	2 335	2 281	87	2 248
八 师	Division 8	786	2 472	40	9 987	6 685	588	8 010
九 师	Division 9	86	352	4	1 194	1 027	68	960
十 师	Division 10	240	234	108	1 605	1 296	122	1 556
十一师	Division 11	50		42	836	183	10	384
十二师	Division 12	93	25	4	1 089	443	97	853
十三师	Division 13	356	51	136	1 354	1 470	30	1 091
十四师	Division 14	52	117		924	284	45	688
兵团直属	Directly under XPCC	1 093	10	6	1 400	1 500	746	2 608

3—18 各师国有单位就业人员劳动报酬

Labor Remuneration of Employed Persons in State-owned Units by Division

计量单位:万元　　(2017 年)　　(10 000 yuan)

单　位	Unit	合　计 Total	#企　业 Enterprises	#事　业 Institutions	#机　关 Agencies& Organizations	农、林、牧、渔业 Farming, Forestry, Animal Husbandry and Fishery	采矿业 Mining	制造业 Manufacturing	电力、热力、燃气及水的生产和供应业 Production and Supply of Electric Power, Heat Power, Gas and Water
总　计	**Total**	**2 945 660**	**1 948 352**	**705 289**	**291 959**	**1 693 423**	**7 271**	**8 619**	**10 905**
一　师	Division 1	254 797	138 143	72 880	43 775	134 984		186	
二　师	Division 2	231 980	169 039	42 674	20 266	150 236	3 055		1 214
三　师	Division 3	227 529	137 562	50 387	39 580	131 135		2 568	
四　师	Division 4	249 836	190 275	48 224	11 336	178 616	350	141	157
五　师	Division 5	182 619	143 201	33 094	6 325	136 598		154	3 936
六　师	Division 6	273 187	174 793	71 276	27 058	165 719	550	342	2 627
七　师	Division 7	206 031	151 873	38 633	15 526	138 849	3 138	758	183
八　师	Division 8	637 023	395 071	186 146	55 806	372 997		1 571	
九　师	Division 9	80 865	53 589	20 067	7 208	52 153		219	417
十　师	Division 10	84 547	53 908	23 351	7 288	45 962			1 842
十一师	Division 11	135 029	123 403	8 092	3 534			43	
十二师	Division 12	92 138	70 042	13 634	8 462	52 570		2 061	
十三师	Division 13	101 148	64 801	28 483	7 864	61 462	178	94	
十四师	Division 14	90 146	72 250	11 501	6 395	72 142		67	
兵团直属	Directly under XPCC	98 785	10 403	56 846	31 537			416	531

单　位	Unit	建筑业 Construction	批发和零售业 Wholesale and Retail Trade	交通运输、仓储和邮政业 Transport, Storage and Postal Service	住宿和餐饮业 Accommodation and Catering Services Industry	信息传输、软件和信息技术服务业 Information Deliver, Software and Information Technique Services Industry	金融业 Finance	房地产业 Real Estate Trade	租赁和商务服务业 Leasing and Business Service
总　计	**Total**	**131 662**	**21 861**	**9 983**	**6 414**	**1 133**	**12 366**	**5 765**	**25 391**
一　师	Division 1			341	309		186	152	387
二　师	Division 2	411	6 316	184	1 007	37	193	637	858
三　师	Division 3		1 698	1 510	592	91	43		186
四　师	Division 4	3 891	2 086		3 001	36			541
五　师	Division 5		1 621	87				660	719
六　师	Division 6	130	970	393	60		1 227		1 863
七　师	Division 7	948	1 814	1 838					123
八　师	Division 8	203	650	4 647			10 343	465	1 266
九　师	Division 9	76	361	110		150			464
十　师	Division 10	2 798	515	58	362			224	607
十一师	Division 11	123 206						60	15
十二师	Division 12		450	103		309	100	1 970	12 254
十三师	Division 13		138	258			274		1 523
十四师	Division 14		41	37				169	194
兵团直属	Directly under XPCC		5 203	417	1 084	511		1 428	4 390

3—18 续表 Continued

计量单位：万元　　(2017 年)　　(10 000 yuan)

单 位	Unit	科学研究和技术服务业 Scientific Research and Technical Service	水利、环境和公共设施管理业 Water Conservancy, Environment and Public Facilities Management	居民服务、修理和其他服务业 Resident, repair and Other Services	教 育 Education	卫生和社会工作 Health Care and Social Security	文化、体育和娱乐业 Culture, Sports and Recreation	公共管理、社会保障和社会组织 Public Management, Social Security and Social Organization
总 计	**Total**	**51 265**	**35 329**	**2 910**	**337 071**	**234 843**	**18 689**	**330 761**
一 师	Division 1	5 638	4 368		41 335	17 780	1 555	47 577
二 师	Division 2	3 644	2 218	488	22 666	16 574	500	21 743
三 师	Division 3	819	2 601	219	29 790	14 947	503	40 827
四 师	Division 4	3 475	940	640	22 844	18 412	833	13 874
五 师	Division 5	1 201	175		18 059	11 062	448	7 901
六 师	Division 6	1 389	1 828	28	34 619	26 377	1 229	33 838
七 师	Division 7	1 193	4 515	204	17 129	16 301	819	18 220
八 师	Division 8	6 573	14 197	253	89 901	63 168	3 931	66 859
九 师	Division 9	660	1 521	16	8 319	7 394	484	8 523
十 师	Division 10	1 690	1 314	409	10 476	8 825	646	8 822
十一师	Division 11	460		139	6 129	1 377	67	3 534
十二师	Division 12	745	183	36	7 866	2 888	710	9 894
十三师	Division 13	2 987	391	431	10 223	13 307	274	9 609
十四师	Division 14	372	988		5 827	1 880	342	8 089
兵团直属	Directly under XPCC	20 420	91	49	11 892	14 553	6 350	31 452

3—19 各师国有单位女性就业人员数

Number of Female Employed Persons in State-owned Units by Division

计量单位：人　　(2017 年)　　(person)

单 位	Unit	合 计 Total	#企 业 Enterprises	#事 业 Institutions	#机 关 Agencies & Organizations	农、林、牧、渔业 Farming, Forestry, Animal Husbandry and Fishery	采矿业 Mining	制造业 Manufacturing	电力、热力、燃气及水的生产和供应业 Production and Supply of Electric Power, Heat Power, Gas and Water
总 计	**Total**	**231 069**	**168 351**	**55 364**	**7 343**	**159 538**	**145**	**684**	**783**
一 师	Division 1	28 246	22 033	5 490	723	21 837		9	
二 师	Division 2	21 424	17 123	3 912	389	16 141	86		70
三 师	Division 3	15 954	10 964	4 262	728	10 556		154	
四 师	Division 4	21 004	16 435	4 241	328	15 915	2	4	6
五 师	Division 5	14 639	11 426	3 047	166	10 802		14	361
六 师	Division 6	22 647	15 885	6 059	692	15 243	29	37	148
七 师	Division 7	15 668	11 918	3 435	315	11 401	20	48	7
八 师	Division 8	42 296	27 675	12 645	1 976	26 253		171	
九 师	Division 9	9 347	7 317	1 873	157	7 180		42	25
十 师	Division 10	8 965	6 304	2 265	396	5 905			90
十一师	Division 11	1 688	809	719	160			2	
十二师	Division 12	7 562	5 950	1 272	340	4 529		155	
十三师	Division 13	8 148	5 636	2 315	197	5 501	8	4	
十四师	Division 14	9 335	8 282	975	78	8 275		5	
兵团直属	Directly under XPCC	4 146	594	2 854	698			39	76

3—19 续表 Continued

计量单位:人 (2017 年) (person)

单 位	Unit	建筑业 Construction	批发和零售业 Wholesale and Retail Trade	交通运输、仓储和邮政业 Transport, Storage and Postal Service	住宿和餐饮业 Accommodation and Catering Services Industry	信息传输、软件和信息技术服务业 Information Deliver, Software and Information Technique Services Industry	金融业 Finance	房地产业 Real Estate Trade	租赁和商务服务业 Leasing and Business Service
总 计	**Total**	**861**	**1 153**	**571**	**708**	**66**	**836**	**754**	**1 752**
一 师	Division 1			40	47		12	29	21
二 师	Division 2	13	311	10	129		16	143	55
三 师	Division 3		97	82	71	3	3		15
四 师	Division 4	8	159		286	1			60
五 师	Division 5		148	6				89	58
六 师	Division 6	3	32	9	5		33		298
七 师	Division 7	9	69	90					17
八 师	Division 8	7	43	292			746	33	68
九 师	Division 9	3	24	5		14			33
十 师	Division 10	40	36	6	62			15	54
十一师	Division 11	778						10	5
十二师	Division 12		25	1		23	8	304	884
十三师	Division 13		9	12			18		70
十四师	Division 14		2	2				13	16
兵团直属	Directly under XPCC		198	16	108	25		118	98

单 位	Unit	科学研究和技术服务业 Scientific Research and Technical Service	水利、环境和公共设施管理业 Water Conservancy, Environment and Public Facilities Management	居民服务、修理和其他服务业 Resident, repair and Other Services	教 育 Education	卫生和社会工作 Health Care and Social Security	文化、体育和娱乐业 Culture, Sports and Recreation	公共管理、社会保障和社会组织 Public Management, Social Security and Social Organization
总 计	**Total**	**1 572**	**2 158**	**334**	**27 350**	**20 481**	**1 092**	**10 231**
一 师	Division 1	194	265		3 263	1 424	64	1 041
二 师	Division 2	94	71	53	1 762	1 919	25	526
三 师	Division 3	31	182	10	2 645	1 262	39	804
四 师	Division 4	119	46	135	1 943	1 780	54	486
五 师	Division 5	61	10		1 642	1 160	29	259
六 师	Division 6	65	147	1	2 944	2 281	67	1 305
七 师	Division 7	57	278	7	1 493	1 581	35	556
八 师	Division 8	282	868	15	5 964	4 663	260	2 631
九 师	Division 9	24	193	1	825	713	30	235
十 师	Division 10	63	56	32	1 090	951	61	504
十一师	Division 11	15		18	554	139	7	160
十二师	Division 12	41	14	2	765	310	48	453
十三师	Division 13	111	14	55	913	1 098	15	320
十四师	Division 14	26	11		628	176	19	162
兵团直属	Direct Under XPCC	389	3	5	919	1 024	339	789

3—20 各师除国有、集体外其他非私营单位就业人员数

Number of Employed Persons in Other Units Except State-owned Units and Collective-owned Units by Division

计量单位：人 （2017 年） (person)

单位	Unit	合计 Total	农、林、牧、渔业 Farming, Forestry, Animal Husbandry and Fishery	采矿业 Mining	制造业 Manufacturing	电力、热力、燃气及水的生产和供应业 Production and Supply of Electric Power, Heat Power, Gas and Water	建筑业 Construction	批发和零售业 Wholesale and Retail Trade	交通运输、仓储和邮政业 Transport, Storage and Postal Service	住宿和餐饮业 Accommodation and Catering Services Industry	信息传输、软件和信息技术服务业 Information Deliver, Software and Information Technique Services Industry
总　计	**Total**	**252 277**	**3 999**	**5 278**	**85 753**	**15 164**	**89 123**	**15 822**	**3 169**	**1 205**	**1 316**
一　师	Division 1	23 603	95	375	14 160	1 575	5 152	1 031	139		
二　师	Division 2	7 858		1 046	2 174	638	595	2 455	183		
三　师	Division 3	16 448	121		5 310	918	8 333	385	40	28	
四　师	Division 4	12 971		238	6 411	1 771	2 876	464	431		
五　师	Division 5	5 746	102	8	1 597	184	2 313	543	318	49	
六　师	Division 6	28 931	1 830	921	14 841	1 367	3 514	1 504	681	229	240
七　师	Division 7	13 664		512	4 268	1 377	5 992	132		11	
八　师	Division 8	82 167	107		27 702	6 265	33 768	1 141	408	790	976
九　师	Division 9	2 874	449		1 148	173	315	517	77	17	
十　师	Division 10	3 284		892	813	369	818	45	129		
十一师	Division 11	31 236	14	334	1 364	5	23 365	2 064	6	1	
十二师	Division 12	10 779	212	538	1 770	122	1 275	2 074	185	44	19
十三师	Division 13	2 003		393	569	97	418	235			81
十四师	Division 14	1 433			809	113	370	26	33		
兵团直属	Directly under XPCC	9 280	1 069	21	2 817	190	19	3 206	539	36	

单位	Unit	金融业 Finance	房地产业 Real Estate Trade	租赁和商务服务业 Leasing and Business Service	科学研究和技术服务业 Scientific Research and Technical Service	水利、环境和公共设施管理业 Water Conservancy, Environment and Public Facilities Management	居民服务、修理和其他服务业 Resident, repair and Other Services	教育 Education	卫生和社会工作 Health Care and Social Security	文化、体育和娱乐业 Culture, Sports and Recreation	公共管理、社会保障和社会组织 Public Management, Social Security and Social Organization
总　计	**Total**	**7 965**	**7 262**	**8 510**	**4 553**	**1 518**	**409**	**367**	**96**	**759**	**9**
一　师	Division 1		592	271	32	140			6	35	
二　师	Division 2	13	460	29	265						
三　师	Division 3		144	429	280	178		15		258	9
四　师	Division 4	149	45	427	159						
五　师	Division 5	90	147	98	212	85					
六　师	Division 6	399	1 176	856	295	567	65	39		407	
七　师	Division 7	302	87	122	665	167				29	
八　师	Division 8	6 206	644	3 475	173	64	52	306	90		
九　师	Division 9	6	19	21	132						
十　师	Division 10	50	70	98							
十一师	Division 11	84	1 117	514	2 242	126					
十二师	Division 12	269	2 047	1 662	72	168	292			30	
十三师	Division 13	118	69	23							
十四师	Division 14	8		48	26						
兵团直属	Directly under XPCC	271	645	437		23		7			

3—21 非私营单位在岗职工数构成及个体劳动者

Composition of Staff and Workers on the Job and Individual Labors in Non-private Units

年份 单位 Year Unit	职工人数（人） Number of Staff and Workers (person)				构成(%)(职工人数=100) Composition(%)			个体、私营劳动者（人） Self-employed Individuals (person)
		国有单位 State-owned Units	集体单位 Collective-owned Units	其他单位 Other Units	国有单位 State-owned Units	集体单位 Collective-owned Units	其他单位 Other Units	
1952	175 179	175 179			100.0			
1954	105 546	105 546			100.0			
1957	178 667	178 667			100.0			
1962	460 194	460 194			100.0			
1965	666 805	666 805			100.0			
1970	908 867	876 202	32 665		96.4	3.6		
1975	761 036	730 073	30 963		95.9	4.1		
1978	918 448	878 770	39 678		95.7	4.3		
1980	929 995	897 509	32 486		96.5	3.5		
1985	948 322	899 776	48 546		94.9	5.1		36 441
1990	970 507	935 170	35 337		96.4	3.6		34 688
1995	933 595	917 670	13 834	2 091	98.3	1.5	0.2	63 521
2000	702 257	683 518	5 962	12 777	97.3	0.8	1.9	121 965
2001	687 903	640 236	5 024	42 643	93.1	0.7	6.2	148 013
2002	691 027	629 468	3 916	57 643	91.1	0.6	8.3	168 816
2003	684 073	616 485	3 081	64 507	90.1	0.5	9.4	192 840
2004	669 986	604 264	2 878	62 844	90.2	0.4	9.4	215 344
2005	665 360	593 653	869	70 838	89.2	0.1	10.6	231 580
2006	662 285	586 691	567	75 027	88.6	0.1	11.3	238 058
2007	660 630	579 189	92	81 349	87.7		12.3	243 150
2008	673 220	584 917	225	88 078	86.9		13.1	262 118
2009	671 985	568 433	214	103 338	84.6		15.4	269 223
2010	677 570	568 885	278	108 407	84.0		16.0	293 940
2011	681 585	569 084	261	112 240	83.5		16.5	319 652
2012	687 887	549 365	299	138 223	79.9		20.1	362 974
2013	711 135	544 199	336	166 600	76.5		23.5	419 565
2014	716 373	524 453	150	191 770	76.5		23.5	487 891
2015	716 893	519 220	171	197 502	72.4		27.6	537 511
2016	705 325	503 351	125	201 849	71.4		28.6	572 472
2017	743 173	528 254	140	214 779	71.1		28.9	587 567
一师 Division 1	88 699	65 843		22 856	74.2		25.8	82 393
二师 Division 2	53 585	46 753		6 832	87.3		12.7	40 684
三师 Division 3	49 826	36 130		13 696	72.5		27.5	36 693
四师 Division 4	62 422	49 558		12 864	79.4		20.6	45 460
五师 Division 5	38 780	33 878		4 902	87.4		12.6	18 910
六师 Division 6	78 123	51 222		26 901	65.6		34.4	71 655
七师 Division 7	49 409	37 721		11 688	76.3		23.7	59 898
八师 Division 8	157 069	95 142	39	61 888	60.6		39.4	127 419
九师 Division 9	24 058	21 488		2 570	89.3		10.7	11 424
十师 Division 10	21 936	19 227	101	2 608	87.7		12.3	19 826
十一师 Division 11	36 661	7 939		28 722	21.7		78.3	5 826
十二师 Division 12	24 655	16 025		8 630	65.0		35.0	28 609
十三师 Division 13	20 605	18 628		1 977	90.4		9.6	33 094
十四师 Division 14	21 092	20 006		1 086	94.9		5.1	4 325
兵团直属 Directly Under XPCC	16 253	8 694		7 559	53.5		46.5	1 351

注：1998年及以后年份职工数据为非私营单位在岗职工数据（下同）。

Note: data since 1998 refer to data of non-private units staff and workers on the job (the same follows)。

3－22 各师非私营单位在岗职工数

Number of Staff and Workers on the Job in Non-private Units by Division

计量单位：人　　　　(2017 年)　　　　(person)

单位	Unit	合计 Total	#企业 Enterprises	#事业 Institutions	#机关 Agencies& Organizations	农、林、牧、渔业 Farming, Forestry, Animal Husbandry and Fishery	采矿业 Mining	制造业 Manufacturing	电力、热力、燃气及水的生产和供应业 Production and Supply of Electric Power, Heat Power, Gas and Water
总　计	**Total**	**743 173**	**626 345**	**86 206**	**30 305**	**389 072**	**5 535**	**82 792**	**16 577**
一　师	Division 1	88 699	74 982	9 074	4 637	51 767	375	13 776	1 571
二　师	Division 2	53 585	45 930	5 805	1 850	36 359	772	2 005	1 005
三　师	Division 3	49 826	38 786	7 000	4 016	23 919		5 853	918
四　师	Division 4	62 422	54 569	6 656	1 197	40 048	290	6 432	1 759
五　师	Division 5	38 780	33 794	4 283	703	27 471	8	1 636	1 107
六　师	Division 6	78 123	65 953	8 743	3 166	39 658	1 020	14 219	1 691
七　师	Division 7	49 409	42 207	5 400	1 802	28 399	872	4 340	1 410
八　师	Division 8	157 069	129 860	20 871	6 338	65 162		26 471	5 654
九　师	Division 9	24 058	20 879	2 421	732	18 454		971	257
十　师	Division 10	21 936	17 452	3 346	1 138	13 945	887	709	622
十一师	Division 11	36 661	35 280	1 028	353	13	334	1 314	3
十二师	Division 12	24 655	22 238	1 751	666	11 425	531	1 737	111
十三师	Division 13	20 605	16 591	3 273	741	14 173	425	585	82
十四师	Division 14	21 092	18 913	1 696	483	17 806		480	113
兵团直属	Directly under XPCC	16 253	8 911	4 859	2 483	473	21	2 264	274

单位	Unit	建筑业 Construction	批发和零售业 Wholesale and Retail Trade	交通运输、仓储和邮政业 Transport, Storage and Postal Service	住宿和餐饮业 Accommodation and Catering Services Industry	信息传输、软件和信息技术服务业 Information Deliver, Software and Information Technique Services Industry	金融业 Finance	房地产业 Real Estate Trade	租赁和商务服务业 Leasing and Business Service
总　计	**Total**	**72 444**	**16 048**	**4 468**	**2 331**	**1 296**	**9 174**	**7 255**	**10 493**
一　师	Division 1	5 102	881	222	61		23	543	316
二　师	Division 2	681	3 007	236	228	4	52	663	175
三　师	Division 3	5 682	667	365	139	11	6	93	454
四　师	Division 4	3 337	798	398	484	5	134	44	503
五　师	Division 5	1 539	884	327	49		90	288	211
六　师	Division 6	2 650	1 432	713	236	225	460	1 094	1 288
七　师	Division 7	4 261	417	335	11		302	49	149
八　师	Division 8	17 497	1 036	879	778	833	7 225	452	2 690
九　师	Division 9	315	621	81	16	26	6	14	78
十　师	Division 10	393	136	121	75		147	52	166
十一师	Division 11	29 638	505	6	1		79	950	420
十二师	Division 12	545	1 795	158	44	65	228	2 195	2 863
十三师	Division 13	418	272	32		79	149	69	183
十四师	Division 14	367	33	38			8	43	73
兵团直属	Directly under XPCC	19	3 564	557	209	48	265	706	924

3—22 续表 Continued

计量单位:人 (2017 年) (person)

单位 Unit		科学研究和技术服务业 Scientific Research and Technical Service	水利、环境和公共设施管理业 Water Conservancy, Environment and Public Facilities Management	居民服务、修理和其他服务业 Resident, repair and Other Services	教育 Education	卫生和社会工作 Health Care and Social Security	文化、体育和娱乐业 Culture, Sports and Recreation	公共管理、社会保障和社会组织 Public Management, Social Security and Social Organization
总计	**Total**	**8 780**	**6 688**	**760**	**42 638**	**28 075**	**3 050**	**35 697**
一师	Division 1	674	827		5 059	2 095	204	5 203
二师	Division 2	557	259	91	2 853	2 509	34	2 095
三师	Division 3	370	610	36	4 340	1 851	320	4 192
四师	Division 4	611	185	89	3 200	2 516	96	1 493
五师	Division 5	363	113		2 284	1 456	57	897
六师	Division 6	458	885	71	4 359	3 043	542	4 079
七师	Division 7	831	1 034	32	2 335	2 270	115	2 247
八师	Division 8	955	1 890	92	10 212	6 725	588	7 930
九师	Division 9	207	142	1	1 110	786	58	915
十师	Division 10	205	234	68	1 539	1 185	105	1 347
十一师	Division 11	1 932	121	15	825	142	10	353
十二师	Division 12	163	189	238	1 002	406	107	853
十三师	Division 13	331	51	21	1 293	1 409	30	1 003
十四师	Division 14	78	117		924	281	45	686
兵团直属	Directly under XPCC	1 045	31	6	1 303	1 401	739	2 404

3—23 各师国有单位在岗职工数

Number of Staff and Workers in State-owned Units by Division

计量单位:人 (2017 年) (person)

单位 Unit		合计 Total	#企业 Enterprises	#事业 Institutions	#机关 Agencies & Organizations	农、林、牧、渔业 Farming, Forestry, Animal Husbandry and Fishery	采矿业 Mining	制造业 Manufacturing	电力、热力、燃气及水的生产和供应业 Production and Supply of Electric Power, Heat Power, Gas and Water
总计	**Total**	**528 254**	**411 726**	**86 206**	**30 305**	**385 682**	**784**	**1 766**	**2 251**
一师	Division 1	65 843	52 132	9 074	4 637	51 672		48	
二师	Division 2	46 753	39 098	5 805	1 850	36 359	241		371
三师	Division 3	36 130	25 114	7 000	4 016	23 798		546	
四师	Division 4	49 558	41 705	6 656	1 197	40 048	52	23	23
五师	Division 5	33 878	28 892	4 283	703	27 369		41	944
六师	Division 6	51 222	39 296	8 743	3 166	37 828	99	104	400
七师	Division 7	37 721	30 519	5 400	1 802	28 399	360	92	33
八师	Division 8	95 142	67 933	20 871	6 338	65 055		371	
九师	Division 9	21 488	18 335	2 421	732	18 006		59	94
十师	Division 10	19 227	14 743	3 346	1 138	13 945			278
十一师	Division 11	7 939	6 558	1 028	353			7	
十二师	Division 12	16 025	13 608	1 751	666	11 224		337	
十三师	Division 13	18 628	14 614	3 273	741	14 173	32	23	
十四师	Division 14	20 006	17 827	1 696	483	17 806		14	
兵团直属	Directly under XPCC	8 694	1 352	4 859	2 483			101	108

3—23 续表 Continued

计量单位:人 (2017 年) (person)

单位 Unit	建筑业 Construction	批发和零售业 Wholesale and Retail Trade	交通运输、仓储和邮政业 Transport, Storage and Postal Service	住宿和餐饮业 Accommodation and Catering Services Industry	信息传输、软件和信息技术服务业 Information Deliver, Software and Information Technique Services Industry	金融业 Finance	房地产业 Real Estate Trade	租赁和商务服务业 Leasing and Business Service
总 计 Total	**7 405**	**3 306**	**1 458**	**1 139**	**140**	**1 343**	**1 179**	**3 360**
一 师 Division 1			83	61		23	50	56
二 师 Division 2	86	860	53	228	4	39	224	147
三 师 Division 3		325	325	111	11	6		29
四 师 Division 4	461	347		484	5			76
五 师 Division 5		355	9				161	113
六 师 Division 6	52	124	33	7		78		433
七 师 Division 7	169	299	335					27
八 师 Division 8	31	71	491			1 153	48	213
九 师 Division 9	28	110	14		26			57
十 师 Division 10	46	94	6	75			29	71
十一师 Division 11	6 532						11	
十二师 Division 12		74	11		46	13	407	1 455
十三师 Division 13		37	32			31		162
十四师 Division 14		7	6				43	25
兵团直属 Directly under XPCC		603	60	173	48		206	496

单位 Unit	科学研究和技术服务业 Scientific Research and Technical Service	水利、环境和公共设施管理业 Water Conservancy, Environment and Public Facilities Management	居民服务、修理和其他服务业 Resident, repair and Other Services	教育 Education	卫生和社会工作 Health Care and Social Security	文化、体育和娱乐业 Culture, Sports and Recreation	公共管理、社会保障和社会组织 Public Management, Social Security and Social Organization
总 计 Total	**4 620**	**5 183**	**409**	**42 271**	**27 979**	**2 291**	**35 688**
一 师 Division 1	643	687		5 059	2 089	169	5 203
二 师 Division 2	300	259	91	2 853	2 509	34	2 095
三 师 Division 3	90	432	36	4 325	1 851	62	4 183
四 师 Division 4	460	185	89	3 200	2 516	96	1 493
五 师 Division 5	164	28		2 284	1 456	57	897
六 师 Division 6	163	318	6	4 320	3 043	135	4 079
七 师 Division 7	166	871	32	2 335	2 270	86	2 247
八 师 Division 8	784	1 826	40	9 906	6 635	588	7 930
九 师 Division 9	82	142	1	1 110	786	58	915
十 师 Division 10	205	234	68	1 539	1 185	105	1 347
十一师 Division 11	44		15	825	142	10	353
十二师 Division 12	91	25	4	1 002	406	77	853
十三师 Division 13	331	51	21	1 293	1 409	30	1 003
十四师 Division 14	52	117		924	281	45	686
兵团直属 Directly under XPCC	1 045	8	6	1 296	1 401	739	2 404

3－24 历年非私营单位在岗职工工资总额及构成

Total Wages of Staff and Workers on the Job and Composition in Non-privats Units over the Years

年 份 Year	在岗职工工资总额（万元） Total Wages (10 000 yuan)				构成(%)(工资总额=100) Composition in Percentage		
		# 国有单位 State-owned Units	# 集体单位 Collective-owned Units	# 其他单位 Other Units	# 国有单位 State-owned Units	# 集体单位 Collective-owned Units	# 其他单位 Other Units
1956	11 388	11 388			100.0		
1957	14 308	14 308			100.0		
1962	27 256	27 256			100.0		
1965	37 931	37 931			100.0		
1970	48 178	46 933	1 245		97.4	2.6	
1975	43 450	42 173	1 277		97.1	2.9	
1978	57 800	56 003	1 797		96.9	3.1	
1980	76 082	74 178	1 904		97.5	2.5	
1985	100 652	96 846	3 806		96.2	3.8	
1990	179 535	175 000	4 535		97.5	2.5	
1995	395 901	389 608	5 330	963	98.4	1.3	0.2
2000	516 897	500 038	4 390	12 469	96.7	0.8	2.4
2001	525 694	479 079	3 583	43 032	91.1	0.7	8.2
2002	594 249	524 738	3 026	66 485	88.3	0.5	11.2
2003	788 776	702 984	2 673	83 119	89.1	0.3	10.5
2004	830 326	728 785	3 439	98 102	87.8	0.4	11.8
2005	887 344	772 908	861	113 575	87.1	0.1	12.8
2006	998 870	866 335	677	131 858	86.7	0.1	13.2
2007	1 169 377	994 314	85	174 978	85.0		15.0
2008	1 386 606	1 158 836	844	226 926	83.6	0.1	16.3
2009	1 574 974	1 272 612	1 186	301 176	80.8	0.1	19.1
2010	1 983 365	1 562 590	1 500	419 275	78.8	0.1	21.1
2011	2 301 737	1 786 260	2 062	513 415	77.6	0.1	22.3
2012	2 866 979	2 037 789	2 945	826 245	71.1	0.1	28.8
2013	3 583 507	2 292 775	3 797	1 286 935	64.0	0.1	35.9
2014	4 145 392	2 432 569	1 482	1 711 341	58.7	…	41.3
2015	4 677 965	2 761 135	1 940	1 914 891	59.0	…	40.9
2016	4 625 477	2 731 712	1 024	1 892 741	59.1	…	40.9
2017	4 935 377	2 897 020	996	2 037 361	58.7	…	41.3

注：1998年及以后年份工资总额为非私营单位在岗职工工资总额。

Note: Data on total wages since 1998 refer to wages of fully employed staff and workers in non-private units.

3－25 各师非私营单位在岗职工工资总额

Total Wages of Staff and Workers on the Job in Non-private Units by Division

计量单位:万元 (2017 年) (10 000 yuan)

单位	Unit	合计 Total	#企业 Enterprises	#事业 Institutions	#机关 Agencies& Organizations	农、林、牧、渔业 Farming, Forestry, Animal Husbandry and Fishery	采矿业 Mining	制造业 Manufacturing	电力、热力、燃气及水的生产和供应业 Production and Supply of Electric Power, Heat Power, Gas and Water
总计	**Total**	**4 935 377**	**3 953 232**	**692 135**	**288 541**	**1 707 177**	**31 753**	**477 285**	**114 089**
一师	Division 1	498 480	382 759	72 276	43 378	135 482	2 354	65 085	10 385
二师	Division 2	328 582	267 556	41 354	19 672	148 452	5 489	11 099	5 775
三师	Division 3	360 247	270 107	50 387	39 580	131 547		29 532	7 200
四师	Division 4	377 542	318 915	47 411	11 216	178 616	1 718	36 706	10 715
五师	Division 5	216 195	176 873	33 012	6 311	136 990	35	6 176	5 527
六师	Division 6	442 980	345 798	69 366	26 665	172 930	6 295	91 634	12 914
七师	Division 7	378 627	324 558	38 547	15 522	138 849	5 606	25 892	9 319
八师	Division 8	986 115	747 009	183 655	55 451	373 567		156 060	43 214
九师	Division 9	90 398	64 676	18 536	7 108	53 476		4 558	1 362
十师	Division 10	100 162	71 025	22 260	6 877	44 891	4 721	3 983	3 731
十一师	Division 11	627 149	615 819	7 872	3 458	472	1 340	7 533	11
十二师	Division 12	139 401	117 801	13 139	8 462	52 303	2 052	9 570	768
十三师	Division 13	111 463	76 277	27 380	7 806	61 073	1 853	2 778	762
十四师	Division 14	111 429	93 548	11 486	6 395	72 142		1 905	1 017
兵团直属	Directly under XPCC	166 606	80 511	55 454	30 641	6 386	292	24 775	1 389

单位	Unit	建筑业 Construction	批发和零售业 Wholesale and Retail Trade	交通运输、仓储和邮政业 Transport, Storage and Postal Service	住宿和餐饮业 Accommodation and Catering Services Industry	信息传输、软件和信息技术服务业 Information Deliver, Software and Information Technique Services Industry	金融业 Finance	房地产业 Real Estate Trade	租赁和商务服务业 Leasing and Business Service
总计	**Total**	**1 202 942**	**102 968**	**27 926**	**12 754**	**14 072**	**73 438**	**49 039**	**71 372**
一师	Division 1	155 490	5 645	909	309		186	2 288	2 187
二师	Division 2	64 666	18 132	1 375	1 007	37	349	2 628	1 064
三师	Division 3	85 603	4 437	1 728	720	91	43	412	2 593
四师	Division 4	70 918	5 149	2 713	2 992	36	1 761	242	3 288
五师	Division 5	16 808	4 233	791	375		782	1 165	1 296
六师	Division 6	20 751	9 036	4 395	965	3 603	3 781	7 166	6 471
七师	Division 7	127 848	2 441	1 838	28		2 153	302	1 301
八师	Division 8	66 492	8 711	7 228	4 372	8 844	50 572	4 165	16 131
九师	Division 9	1 590	2 105	403	77	150	43	110	557
十师	Division 10	7 724	711	771	362		1 253	275	1 207
十一师	Division 11	562 577	5 563	30	8		897	12 388	3 760
十二师	Division 12	2 767	10 191	1 027	311	414	1 806	13 446	20 293
十三师	Division 13	2 497	1 662	258		514	1 906	419	1 727
十四师	Division 14	17 125	219	282			82	169	780
兵团直属	Directly under XPCC	87	24 732	4 177	1 229	383	7 823	3 867	8 718

3—25 续表 Continued

计量单位:万元 (2017年) (10 000 yuan)

单位	Unit	科学研究和技术服务业 Scientific Research and Technical Service	水利、环境和公共设施管理业 Water Conservancy, Environment and Public Facilities Management	居民服务、修理和其他服务业 Resident, repair and Other Services	教育 Education	卫生和社会工作 Health Care and Social Security	文化、体育和娱乐业 Culture, Sports and Recreation	公共管理、社会保障和社会组织 Public Management, Social Security and Social Organization
总计	**Total**	**83 722**	**45 138**	**3 972**	**337 427**	**231 399**	**23 163**	**325 740**
一师	Division 1	5 677	4 953		40 981	17 848	1 612	47 089
二师	Division 2	6 125	2 218	439	22 348	15 903	380	21 096
三师	Division 3	3 956	3 539	219	29 910	14 947	2 892	40 880
四师	Division 4	5 971	933	318	22 773	18 162	795	13 737
五师	Division 5	4 185	444		18 041	11 018	448	7 881
六师	Division 6	3 199	3 245	389	34 221	25 976	3 392	32 621
七师	Division 7	4 601	5 691	204	17 129	16 223	987	18 217
八师	Division 8	7 457	12 622	510	92 725	63 238	3 931	66 278
九师	Division 9	1 309	989	7	8 098	6 705	449	8 410
十师	Division 10	1 475	1 287	347	10 359	8 170	609	8 286
十一师	Division 11	15 025	6 612	90	6 079	1 239	67	3 458
十二师	Division 12	1 199	1 080	1 281	7 556	2 783	663	9 894
十三师	Division 13	2 861	391	119	9 913	13 116	274	9 341
十四师	Division 14	599	988		5 827	1 870	342	8 083
兵团直属	Directly under XPCC	20 087	147	49	11 469	14 202	6 325	30 469

3—26 各师国有单位在岗职工工资总额

Total Wages of Staff and Workers on the Job in State-owned Units by Division

计量单位:万元 (2017年) (10 000 yuan)

单位	Unit	合计 Total	#企业 Enterprises	#事业 Institutions	#机关 Agencies & Organizations	农、林、牧、渔业 Farming, Forestry, Animal Husbandry and Fishery	采矿业 Mining	制造业 Manufacturing	电力、热力、燃气及水的生产和供应业 Production and Supply of Electric Power, Heat Power, Gas and Water
总计	**Total**	**2 897 020**	**1 916 285**	**692 135**	**288 541**	**1 688 150**	**7 256**	**7 648**	**10 631**
一师	Division 1	253 796	138 143	72 276	43 378	134 984		186	
二师	Division 2	228 195	167 169	41 354	19 672	148 452	3 055		1 172
三师	Division 3	227 529	137 562	50 387	39 580	131 135		2 568	
四师	Division 4	248 889	190 263	47 411	11 216	178 616	350	141	157
五师	Division 5	182 515	143 193	33 012	6 311	136 598		154	3 936
六师	Division 6	270 726	174 636	69 366	26 665	165 707	550	342	2 572
七师	Division 7	205 790	151 721	38 547	15 522	138 849	3 138	678	183
八师	Division 8	633 360	394 254	183 655	55 451	372 956		1 571	
九师	Division 9	79 110	53 466	18 536	7 108	52 153		100	417
十师	Division 10	78 933	49 796	22 260	6 877	44 891			1 664
十一师	Division 11	115 820	104 489	7 872	3 458			43	
十二师	Division 12	86 554	64 954	13 139	8 462	50 593		1 298	
十三师	Division 13	99 533	64 347	27 380	7 806	61 073	163	94	
十四师	Division 14	90 130	72 250	11 486	6 395	72 142		67	
兵团直属	Directly under XPCC	96 138	10 043	55 454	30 641			406	531

3—26 续表 Continued

计量单位:万元 (2017 年) (10 000 yuan)

单 位 Unit	建筑业 Construction	批发和零售业 Wholesale and Retail Trade	交通运输、仓储和邮政业 Transport, Storage and Postal Service	住宿和餐饮业 Accommodation and Catering Services Industry	信息传输、软件和信息技术服务业 Information Deliver, Software and Information Technique Services Industry	金融业 Finance	房地产业 Real Estate Trade	租赁和商务服务业 Leasing and Business Service
总 计 Total	**110 239**	**21 621**	**9 152**	**6 405**	**1 006**	**12 239**	**4 968**	**23 428**
一 师 Division 1			341	309		186	152	387
二 师 Division 2	411	6 316	184	1 007	37	193	637	828
三 师 Division 3		1 698	1 510	592	91	43		186
四 师 Division 4	3 891	2 086		2 992	36			439
五 师 Division 5		1 621	73				656	716
六 师 Division 6	130	946	339	60		1 178		1 863
七 师 Division 7	948	1 814	1 838					123
八 师 Division 8	195	650	3 910			10 265	412	1 266
九 师 Division 9	73	361	94		150			461
十 师 Division 10	216	460	49	362			202	556
十 一 师 Division 11	104 376						39	
十 二 师 Division 12		450	103		309	100	1 419	10 552
十 三 师 Division 13		138	258			274		1 520
十 四 师 Division 14		41	37				169	194
兵团直属 Directly under XPCC		5 041	417	1 084	383		1 284	4 336

单 位 Unit	科学研究和技术服务业 Scientific Research and Technical Service	水利、环境和公共设施管理业 Water Conservancy, Environment and Public Facilities Management	居民服务、修理和其他服务业 Resident, repair and Other Services	教 育 Education	卫生和社会工作 Health Care and Social Security	文化、体育和娱乐业 Culture, Sports and Recreation	公共管理、社会保障和社会组织 Public Management, Social Security and Social Organization
总 计 Total	**50 239**	**33 004**	**2 108**	**333 960**	**231 111**	**18 170**	**325 687**
一 师 Division 1	5 504	4 365		40 981	17 780	1 532	47 089
二 师 Division 2	3 519	2 218	439	22 348	15 903	380	21 096
三 师 Division 3	819	2 601	219	29 790	14 947	503	40 827
四 师 Division 4	3 465	933	318	22 773	18 162	795	13 737
五 师 Division 5	1 201	175		18 041	11 018	448	7 881
六 师 Division 6	1 372	1 828	28	34 059	25 976	1 156	32 621
七 师 Division 7	1 187	4 443	204	17 129	16 223	817	18 217
八 师 Division 8	6 569	12 521	253	89 567	63 018	3 931	66 278
九 师 Division 9	644	989	7	8 098	6 705	449	8 410
十 师 Division 10	1 475	1 287	347	10 359	8 170	609	8 286
十 一 师 Division 11	429		90	6 079	1 239	67	3 458
十 二 师 Division 12	737	183	36	7 556	2 783	543	9 894
十 三 师 Division 13	2 861	391	119	9 913	13 116	274	9 341
十 四 师 Division 14	372	988		5 827	1 870	342	8 083
兵团直属 Directly under XPCC	20 087	83	49	11 441	14 202	6 325	30 469

3－27 历年非私营单位在岗职工年平均工资及指数

Average Annual Wage and Indices of Staff and Workers on Job in Non-private Units over the Years

年 份 Year	平均工资(元) Average Annual Wage(yuan)				指数(上年=100) Indices(preceding year=100)			
	在岗职工 Staff and Workers on Job	国有单位 State-owned Units	集体单位 Collective-owned Units	其他单位 Other Units	在岗职工 Staff and Workers on Job	国有单位 State-owned Units	集体单位 Collective-owned Units	其他单位 Other Units
1956	852	852			100.0	100.0		
1957	827	827			97.1	97.1		
1962	580	580			100.7	100.7		
1965	608	608			103.4	103.4		
1970	534	540	381		104.9	104.4	104.4	
1975	578	584	412		78.3	78.4	78.5	
1978	638	643	453		111.5	110.9	110.8	
1980	821	831	586		116.5	116.2	116.3	
1985	1 053	1 067	789		111.3	111.1	115.2	
1990	1 877	1 901	1 267		116.4	116.8	101.4	
1995	4 183	4 187	3 770	5 045	133.1	133.3	114.9	
2000	6 763	6 715	6 386	9 784	124.0	118.4	117.4	133.9
2001	6 970	6 797	6 423		103.1	101.2	100.6	
2002	8 094	7 869	7 237		116.1	115.8	112.7	
2003	10 781	10 660	7 767		133.2	135.5	107.3	
2004	11 332	11 140	10 193		105.1	104.5	131.2	
2005	12 136	11 925	9 373	13 833	107.1	107.0	92.0	106.0
2006	13 909	13 679	9 709	15 668	114.6	114.7	103.6	113.3
2007	16 272	15 987	9 517	18 119	117.0	116.9	98.0	115.6
2008	18 772	18 421	37 323	20 754	115.4	115.2	392.2	114.5
2009	21 876	21 393	56 218	24 044	116.5	116.1	150.6	115.9
2010	26 741	26 189	55 563	28 961	122.2	122.4	98.8	120.5
2011	31 343	30 330	86 272	35 362	117.2	115.8	155.3	122.1
2012	37 525	35 668	103 721	42 943	119.7	117.6	120.2	121.4
2013	44 043	42 131	119 776	50 038	117.4	118.1	115.5	116.5
2014	49 668	46 397	99 497	55 173	112.8	110.1	83.1	110.3
2015	54 599	51 652	117 552	59 459	109.9	111.3	118.1	107.8
2016	56 345	53 197	83 471	61 596	103.2	103.0	71.0	103.6
2017	58 464	55 227	73 763	62 393	103.8	103.8	88.4	101.3

注：1998 年及以后年份为非私营单位在岗职工平均工资。
Note：data in this table are average annual wage of staff and workers on the job in non-private units since 1998。

3—28 各师非私营单位在岗职工平均工资

Average Annual Wage of Staff and Workers on the Job in Non-private Units by Division

计量单位:元 (2017 年) (yuan)

单 位	Unit	合 计 Total	# 企 业 Enterprises	# 事 业 Institutions	# 机 关 Agencies& Organizations	农、林、牧、渔业 Farming, Forestry, Animal Husbandry and Fishery	采矿业 Mining	制造业 Manufacturing	电力、热力、燃气及水的生产和供应业 Production and Supply of Electric Power, Heat Power, Gas and Water
总 计	**Total**	**58 464**	**54 329**	**80 432**	**95 753**	**45 567**	**53 126**	**58 934**	**69 749**
一 师	Division 1	52 236	46 755	79 572	96 955	32 851	69 442	49 091	67 655
二 师	Division 2	54 555	50 868	71 585	106 104	43 765	50 261	52 929	56 896
三 师	Division 3	64 368	59 903	74 012	97 873	56 543		55 097	78 943
四 师	Division 4	54 665	52 168	70 922	89 868	44 836	63 633	60 560	60 676
五 师	Division 5	52 298	48 685	76 861	88 382	49 715	43 250	36 140	50 799
六 师	Division 6	56 570	52 273	79 303	85 054	43 857	60 527	65 290	75 123
七 师	Division 7	59 734	57 733	71 822	86 139	48 734	64 963	57 069	67 579
八 师	Division 8	63 346	58 210	87 488	87 338	56 552		60 584	78 643
九 师	Division 9	38 194	31 600	76 186	96 449	29 645		46 601	53 211
十 师	Division 10	44 634	39 014	69 131	67 687	31 858	51 258	57 969	59 989
十 一 师	Division 11	66 457	66 248	76 061	91 487	58 988	41 991	55 801	37 333
十 二 师	Division 12	56 265	52 696	74 778	127 435	45 736	32 563	52 932	67 333
十 三 师	Division 13	54 208	46 114	83 348	106 064	42 934	42 797	45 163	92 939
十 四 师	Division 14	49 290	45 794	67 922	131 047	43 941		41 592	91 631
兵团直属	Directly under XPCC	101 862	89 616	113 706	122 809	113 433	47 065	108 950	53 423

单 位	Unit	建筑业 Construction	批发和零售业 Wholesale and Retail Trade	交通运输、仓储和邮政业 Transport, Storage and Postal Service	住宿和餐饮业 Accommodation and Catering Services Industry	信息传输、软件和信息技术服务业 Information Delivery, Software and Information Technique Services Industry	金融业 Finance	房地产业 Real Estate Trade	租赁和商务服务业 Leasing and Business Service
总 计	**Total**	**63 710**	**62 759**	**61 961**	**54 436**	**108 076**	**85 712**	**58 311**	**70 255**
一 师	Division 1	67 379	58 136	37 730	50 639		80 913	45 477	73 154
二 师	Division 2	71 258	54 847	58 021	43 584	92 000	67 135	40 992	62 571
三 师	Division 3	64 777	67 742	47 746	51 820	82 727	72 333	43 787	64 493
四 师	Division 4	67 476	64 523	67 656	61 812	71 800	155 796	55 068	65 117
五 师	Division 5	42 189	46 520	33 927	47 468		86 900	41 470	61 422
六 师	Division 6	60 763	62 752	66 396	42 307	152 648	89 808	50 110	55 403
七 师	Division 7	71 608	60 126	43 854	25 091		71 525	60 320	57 813
八 师	Division 8	40 254	86 414	75 847	57 678	106 938	75 684	92 139	60 848
九 师	Division 9	50 320	33 849	48 518	45 176	57 769	71 667	78 357	77 389
十 师	Division 10	78 494	51 144	62 715	48 240		85 259	52 885	73 145
十 一 师	Division 11	65 693	98 286	49 667	84 000		104 349	66 927	88 475
十 二 师	Division 12	51 042	54 819	63 789	70 750	66 710	79 211	61 116	75 466
十 三 师	Division 13	66 061	97 216	78 273		61 964	127 946	61 544	96 464
十 四 师	Division 14	52 020	66 455	74 158			102 000	44 421	105 432
兵团直属	Directly under XPCC	45 526	70 202	75 267	57 167	79 875	305 590	55 887	94 345

3－28 续表 Continued

计量单位：元 (2017 年) (yuan)

单 位	Unit	科学研究和技术服务业 Scientific Research and Technical Service	水利、环境和公共设施管理业 Water Conservancy, Environment and Public Facilities Management	居民服务、修理和其他服务业 Resident, repair and Other Services	教 育 Education	卫生和社会工作 Health Care and Social Security	文化、体育和娱乐业 Culture, Sports and Recreation	公共管理、社会保障和社会组织 Public Management, Social Security and Social Organization
总 计	**Total**	**95 913**	**63 024**	**50 985**	**79 298**	**82 764**	**76 447**	**91 809**
一 师	Division 1	83 357	61 375		81 183	84 029	80 995	93 785
二 师	Division 2	107 270	84 981	48 231	78 387	63 920	111 765	100 794
三 师	Division 3	108 370	58 588	60 722	71 130	83 504	88 699	96 871
四 师	Division 4	97 557	51 811	37 376	70 178	72 331	82 833	89 144
五 师	Division 5	115 597	39 310		78 815	75 722	78 579	86 133
六 师	Division 6	73 698	53 023	55 529	78 561	85 363	62 117	81 105
七 师	Division 7	54 903	54 356	63 719	73 736	72 164	85 817	81 071
八 师	Division 8	78 001	63 782	55 380	90 728	93 354	70 571	83 536
九 师	Division 9	62 033	69 613	73 000	72 957	84 232	77 414	91 318
十 师	Division 10	71 583	54 783	52 591	66 919	77 149	64 105	67 585
十一师	Division 11	80 606	82 337	56 500	73 235	86 035	67 000	91 487
十二师	Division 12	68 902	58 690	48 711	75 407	67 539	56 624	116 264
十三师	Division 13	85 904	76 608	56 857	76 137	92 954	91 167	93 594
十四师	Division 14	77 766	87 425		62 651	66 319	79 535	116 803
兵团直属	Directly under XPCC	192 219	47 419	81 833	88 700	99 871	84 667	125 854

3－29 各师国有单位在岗职工平均工资

Average Annual Wage of Staff and Workers on the Job in State-owned Units by Division

计量单位：元 (2017 年) (yuan)

单 位	Unit	合 计 Total	#企 业 Enterprises	#事 业 Institutions	#机 关 Agencies& Organizations	农、林、牧、渔业 Farming, Forestry, Animal Husbandry and Fishery	采矿业 Mining	制造业 Manufacturing	电力、热力、燃气及水的生产和供应业 Production and Supply of Electric Power, Heat Power, Gas and Water
总 计	**Total**	**53 197**	**44 372**	**79 795**	**95 376**	**42 625**	**71 397**	**50 156**	**46 414**
一 师	Division 1	43 501	25 912	77 560	106 430	25 410		36 256	
二 师	Division 2	50 600	42 957	76 720	111 513	41 645	70 472	63 333	65 812
三 师	Division 3	60 309	52 558	72 351	83 446	52 239		60 199	
四 师	Division 4	47 098	42 072	69 210	96 428	40 844	66 385	53 739	57 962
五 师	Division 5	50 168	46 452	69 974	82 284	46 866		32 805	36 164
六 师	Division 6	50 595	42 431	78 769	80 083	41 719	41 841	26 746	58 371
七 师	Division 7	52 351	46 578	71 214	91 541	45 967	79 019	72 086	51 543
八 师	Division 8	65 302	56 289	88 250	92 196	55 670		46 552	
九 师	Division 9	33 955	26 084	72 660	96 686	25 732		19 510	29 583
十 师	Division 10	37 507	29 410	64 972	69 251	26 216			49 817
十一师	Division 11	59 877	58 988	68 143	85 256			61 500	
十二师	Division 12	54 018	47 163	84 658	119 079	46 979		41 885	
十三师	Division 13	52 350	43 023	84 067	97 052	41 920	110 233	47 381	
十四师	Division 14	44 149	39 293	66 221	133 098	39 274		61 400	
兵团直属	Directly under XPCC	107 262	77 313	113 422	111 443			72 515	65 000

3—29 续表 Continued

计量单位:元 (2017 年) (yuan)

单 位	Unit	建筑业 Construction	批发和零售业 Wholesale and Retail Trade	交通运输、仓储和邮政业 Transport, Storage and Postal Service	住宿和餐饮业 Accommodation and Catering Services Industry	信息传输、软件和信息技术服务业 Information Deliver, Software and Information Technique Services Industry	金融业 Finance	房地产业 Real Estate Trade	租赁和商务服务业 Leasing and Business Service
总 计	**Total**	**58 775**	**67 082**	**58 348**	**51 633**	**62 044**	**85 040**	**37 245**	**64 063**
一 师	Division 1			38 462	48 619		80 913	25 063	73 339
二 师	Division 2	31 662	33 034	49 387	43 131	92 500	46 462	21 529	118 787
三 师	Division 3		59 032	56 580	52 225	77 818	70 333		58 552
四 师	Division 4	61 967	72 517		59 731	69 600			62 845
五 师	Division 5	36 000	51 681	61 143				37 469	55 289
六 师	Division 6	32 288	75 354	56 924	83 571	46 927	128 910		39 798
七 师	Division 7	65 341	47 470	30 806					48 348
八 师	Division 8	49 590	108 575	71 136	45 241	60 797	82 761	70 326	46 934
九 师	Division 9	46 000	37 879	64 647		53 957			77 685
十 师	Division 10	69 781	44 446	77 333	38 943			63 893	78 507
十一师	Division 11	58 953	87 982					23 600	25 857
十二师	Division 12	41 111	59 500	66 917		62 659	68 714	35 784	53 622
十三师	Division 13		85 182	93 294			92 500		99 368
十四师	Division 14		51 833	106 500				44 344	102 741
兵团直属	Directly under XPCC		83 783	38 304	53 353	80 698		54 325	81 715

单 位	Unit	科学研究和技术服务业 Scientific Research and Technical Service	水利、环境和公共设施管理业 Water Conservancy, Environment and Public Facilities Management	居民服务、修理和其他服务业 Resident, repair and Other Services	教 育 Education	卫生和社会工作 Health Care and Social Security	文化、体育和娱乐业 Culture, Sports and Recreation	公共管理、社会保障和社会组织 Public Management, Social Security and Social Organization
总 计	**Total**	**102 289**	**59 733**	**50 701**	**78 640**	**82 121**	**81 168**	**92 517**
一 师	Division 1	80 488	53 420		79 948	82 988	74 469	101 827
二 师	Division 2	109 595	72 839		85 163	66 186	135 912	107 123
三 师	Division 3	82 667	58 411	71 000	72 234	75 699	70 097	83 059
四 师	Division 4	74 100	51 355	42 273	69 233	71 442	60 462	91 997
五 师	Division 5	71 538	69 647		68 909	72 262	76 745	80 552
六 师	Division 6	78 551	76 709	42 000	80 238	81 909	93 092	76 408
七 师	Division 7	65 488	47 881	43 167	72 346	71 756	92 033	86 764
八 师	Division 8	82 366	62 850	64 425	86 356	99 300	78 654	90 536
九 师	Division 9	78 904	68 731	87 000	70 191	77 631	78 052	92 317
十 师	Division 10	69 903	53 805	50 140	61 069	74 540	55 663	68 248
十一师	Division 11	88 421		80 000	66 554	71 494	61 900	85 256
十二师	Division 12	89 145	82 467	42 406	83 778	71 430	68 769	111 021
十三师	Division 13	82 684	107 224	57 762	80 857	86 667	81 774	91 209
十四师	Division 14	37 932	70 510		63 673	69 444	73 133	117 833
兵团直属	Directly under XPCC	179 104	98 750	95 000	105 969	94 735	88 449	114 316

3—30 各师私营单位就业人员及个体劳动者人数

Private Enterprises Employed Persons Individual Labors by Division

计量单位:人 (2017 年) (person)

单 位 Unit	年末人数 Population (Year end)	第一产业 Primary Industry	第二产业 Secondary Industry	第三产业 Tertiary Industry	# 农、林、牧、渔业 Farming, Forestry, Animal Husbandry and Fishery	# 工 业 Industry	# 批发和零售业 Wholesale and Retail Trade	# 交通运输、仓储和邮政业 Transport, Storage and Postal Service	# 住宿和餐饮业 Accommodation and Catering Services Industry
总 计 Total	**587 567**	**24 932**	**140 401**	**422 234**	**36 826**	**106 362**	**190 269**	**67 312**	**72 375**
一 师 Division 1	82 393	1 989	26 621	53 783	3 009	21 014	22 768	7 283	9 583
二 师 Division 2	40 684	1 556	12 990	26 138	2 423	11 665	12 452	4 052	4 308
三 师 Division 3	36 693		10 520	26 173	205	6 189	13 488	2 751	5 886
四 师 Division 4	45 460	3 539	13 065	28 856	6 766	11 999	7 979	5 788	5 153
五 师 Division 5	18 910	76	2 651	16 183	123	2 410	6 560	1 757	5 534
六 师 Division 6	71 655	5 115	14 018	52 522	9 142	8 031	19 838	10 980	8 162
七 师 Division 7	59 898	2 193	17 130	40 575	3 002	9 018	15 965	10 983	6 228
八 师 Division 8	127 419	5 789	14 226	107 404	6 722	12 430	60 988	10 658	15 059
九 师 Division 9	11 424	7	2 355	9 062	400	1 443	3 593	1 447	2 040
十 师 Division 10	19 826	1 415	5 681	12 730	1 664	4 805	5 972	1 723	2 082
十 一 师 Division 11	5 826		3 096	2 730		1 121	1 675	215	343
十 二 师 Division 12	28 609	2 639	3 433	22 537	2 679	2 639	10 284	3 639	3 308
十 三 师 Division 13	33 094	570	13 642	18 882	647	12 652	6 520	5 479	3 379
十 四 师 Division 14	4 325	44	973	3 308	44	566	1 312	557	878
兵团直属 Directly Under XPCC	1 351			1 351		380	875		432

3—31 私营单位就业人员和工资

Employed Persons and Wages in Private Enterprises

(2017 年)

指 标	Item	单位数(个) Number of Units(unit)	单位就业人员 Number of Employed Persons in Units: 年末人数(人) Persons in Year-end (person)	平均人数(人) Average Annual Number of Persoms (person)	工资总额(万元) Wages (10 000 yuan)	平均工资(元) Average Annual Wage (yuan)
总 计	**Total**	**6 199**	**181 824**	**213 074**	**1 081 180**	**50 742**
农、林、牧、渔业	Farming ,Forestry, Animal Husbandry and Fishery	202	3 487	3 546	14 093	39 745
采矿业	Mining	65	3 305	3 162	11 943	37 771
制造业	Manufacturing	1 842	88 367	94 853	472 138	49 776
电力、热力、燃气及水生产和供应业	Production and Supply of Electric Power, Heat Power, Gas and Water	116	3 383	3 221	17 549	54 484
建筑业	Construciton	231	34 483	60 321	357 441	59 257
批发和零售业	Wholesale and Retail Trade	1 880	18 157	17 020	69 950	41 099
交通运输、仓储和邮政业	Transport, Storage, and Postal Service Industry	189	4 691	4 842	24 504	50 607
住宿和餐饮业	Accommodation and Catering Services Industry	85	2 644	2 560	10 567	41 278
信息传输、软件和信息技术服务业	Information Deliver, Software and Information Technique Services Industry	72	847	696	3 645	52 367
金融业	Finance	75	332	325	1 515	46 619
房地产业	Real Estate Trade	372	9 178	8 883	39 698	44 690
租赁和商务服务业	Leasing and Business Service	416	4 747	4 990	19 984	40 047
科学研究和技术服务业	Scientific Research and Technical Service	111	1 490	1 848	11 115	60 149
水利、环境和公共设施管理业	Water Conservancy, Environment and Public Facilities Management	67	2 294	2 367	10 099	42 666
居民服务、修理和其他服务业	Resident, repair and Other Services	124	1 535	1 564	6 162	39 399
教 育	Education	55	736	782	2 668	34 116
卫生和社会工作	Health Care and Social Security	28	884	873	3 430	39 284
文化、体育和娱乐业	Culture, Sports and Entertainment	269	1 264	1 221	4 679	38 319
公共管理、社会保障和社会组织	Public Management and Social Organization					

2018

BING TUAN

第四篇

固定资产投资

Chapter 4 Investment in Fixed Assets

简要说明

一、本篇资料主要内容

本篇资料反映一定时期兵团全社会固定资产投资规模、速度和结构，固定资产投资资金来源和固定资产投资效果等情况。主要指标有固定资产投资按经济类型、产业分组；主要年份房屋建筑施工面积、竣工面积；固定资产投资及新增固定资产按行业分组。

二、本篇资料统计范围

固定资产投资统计范围为城乡建设投资、房地产开发投资、其他固定资产投资、城镇集体固定资产投资、农村集体固定资产投资、私人、私营固定资产投资。

三、本篇资料来源

本篇资料由兵团统计局工业投资统计处根据《兵团固定资产投资统计报表制度》搜集、汇总、整理、提供。

四、本篇资料调查方法

调查方法为全面调查。统计数据资料起点为500万元及以上的固定资产投资项目。

Brief Introduction

1. Main Contents

Data in this chapter reflect the size, growth, structure, source of fund and results of the investment in fixed assets of the whole society of XPCC during a given period of time. Main indicators cover investment in fixed assets grouped by economic status, industry; floor space of buildings under construction and completed in major years, newly increased investment in fixed assets by sector.

2. Scope of Statistics

Statistics on investment in fixed assets cover investment in capital construction projects in urban and rural areas, real estate development, other investment in fixed assets, urban collective-owned investment in fixed assets, rural collective-owned investment in fixed assets and private investment in fixed assets.

3. Sources of Data

Data in this chapter are collected, prepared and provided by Industry Assets Statistical Section of Statistics Bureau of XPCC according to *the Statistical Reporting Form System of Investment in Fixed Assets of XPCC*.

4. Methodology of Survey

Survey method of investment in fixed assets statistics is complete statistical. The cut-off point of statistical data in this chapter is projects of investment in fixed assets with above 5 million yuan.

4—1 按三次产业分全社会固定资产投资及构成

Total Investment in Fixed Assets and Its Composition by the Three Industries

年 份 Year	单 位 Unit	投资总额（万元） Total (10 000 yuan)	第一产业 Primary Industry	第二产业 Secondary Industry	第三产业 Tertiary Industry	构成(%) Composition(%) 第一产业 Primary Industry	第二产业 Secondary Industry	第三产业 Tertiary Industry
	1950	2 434	1 850		584	76.0		24.0
	1952	11 311	3 996	4 495	2 820	35.3	39.8	24.9
	1954	4 924	1 753	1 880	1 291	35.6	38.2	26.2
	1957	12 227	7 129	574	4 524	58.3	4.7	37.0
	1962	10 636	5 908	2 187	2 541	55.5	20.6	23.9
	1965	12 471	5 567	3 451	3 453	44.6	27.7	27.7
	1970	13 907	4 177	6 509	3 221	30.0	46.8	23.2
	1975	6 258	3 882	570	1 806	62.0	9.1	28.9
	1978	14 575	7 787	3 463	3 325	53.4	23.8	22.8
	1980	35 225	17 613	5 424	12 188	50.0	15.4	34.6
	1985	55 895	11 008	20 707	24 180	19.7	37.0	43.3
	1990	95 876	23 696	41 055	31 125	24.7	42.8	32.5
	1995	369 435	59 381	163 096	146 958	16.1	44.1	39.8
	2000	736 077	178 403	183 486	374 188	24.3	24.9	50.8
	2001	874 698	242 417	157 184	475 097	27.7	18.0	54.3
	2002	1 046 123	254 546	264 479	527 098	24.3	25.3	50.4
	2003	1 212 157	316 902	314 953	580 302	26.1	26.0	47.9
	2004	1 289 870	318 885	357 342	613 643	24.7	27.7	47.6
	2005	1 372 367	291 324	395 231	685 812	21.2	28.8	50.0
	2006	1 530 067	352 619	485 149	692 299	23.1	31.7	45.2
	2007	1 896 156	370 202	815 803	710 151	19.5	43.0	37.5
	2008	2 359 518	341 029	1 052 493	965 996	14.5	44.6	40.9
	2009	3 184 664	363 353	1 481 274	1 340 037	11.4	46.5	42.1
	2010	4 482 739	391 574	2 304 709	1 786 456	8.7	51.4	39.9
	2011	6 835 110	501 787	3 654 880	2 678 443	7.3	53.5	39.2
	2012	10 393 354	621 691	5 004 192	4 767 471	6.0	48.1	45.9
	2013	15 098 995	867 565	6 878 798	7 352 632	5.7	45.6	48.7
	2014	17 613 292	1 239 348	7 882 070	8 491 874	7.0	44.8	48.2
	2015	17 858 038	1 493 817	7 801 418	8 562 803	8.4	43.7	47.9
	2016	17 212 068	1 789 322	6 485 950	8 936 796	10.4	37.7	51.9
	2017	19 661 510	2 008 598	7 243 815	10 409 097	10.2	36.8	53.0
一 师	Division 1	1 798 228	263 377	998 707	536 144	14.7	55.5	29.8
二 师	Division 2	1 522 935	199 918	534 567	788 450	13.1	35.1	51.8
三 师	Division 3	1 879 144	213 166	486 089	1 179 889	11.3	25.9	62.8
四 师	Division 4	1 395 015	122 203	314 964	957 848	8.7	22.6	68.7
五 师	Division 5	391 201	111 797	65 915	213 489	28.6	16.8	54.6
六 师	Division 6	1 955 767	170 198	694 829	1 090 740	8.7	35.5	55.8
七 师	Division 7	1 730 478	89 934	919 159	721 385	5.2	53.1	41.7
八 师	Division 8	3 469 925	504 535	1 581 539	1 383 851	14.5	45.6	39.9
九 师	Division 9	313 615	48 036	85 055	180 524	15.3	27.1	57.6
十 师	Division 10	1 055 089	105 533	152 924	796 632	10.0	14.5	75.5
十一师	Division 11	422 886		39 709	383 177		9.4	90.6
十二师	Division 12	1 460 737	41 069	281 050	1 138 618	2.8	19.2	78.0
十三师	Division 13	1 786 855	85 643	979 900	721 312	4.8	54.8	40.4
十四师	Division 14	455 248	50 017	100 259	304 972	11.0	22.0	67.0
兵团直属	Directly under XPCC	24 387	3 172	9 149	12 066	13.0	37.5	49.5

4—2 按登记注册类型分全社会固定资产投资

Total Investment in Fixed Assets and Its Composition by Status of Registration

计量单位：万元 (10 000 yuan)

年份 Year	单位 unit	合计 Total	国有 State-owned	集体 Collective	私营个体 Private Individual	其他 Other
1950		2 434	2 434			
1952		11 311	11 311			
1954		4 924	4 924			
1957		12 227	12 227			
1962		10 636	10 636			
1965		12 471	12 471			
1970		13 907	13 907			
1975		6 258	6 258			
1978		14 575	14 575			
1980		35 225	35 225			
1985		55 895	49 707	1 045	5 143	
1990		95 876	88 549	103	7 224	
1995		369 435	307 170	26 884	18 055	17 326
2000		736 077	654 858	815	25 620	54 784
2001		874 698	732 942	750	30 810	110 196
2002		1 046 123	823 534	165	61 997	160 427
2003		1 212 157	946 698	555	67 102	197 802
2004		1 289 870	886 215	1 249	90 751	311 655
2005		1 372 367	1 025 106	640	96 195	250 426
2006		1 530 067	1 082 649	338	119 611	327 469
2007		1 896 156	1 461 604	2 764	139 507	292 281
2008		2 359 518	1 573 090	1 295	210 846	574 287
2009		3 184 664	2 041 739	4 381	283 537	855 007
2010		4 482 739	2 318 366	5 190	746 337	1 412 846
2011		6 835 110	2 956 473	2 220	1 074 161	2 802 256
2012		10 393 354	4 608 623	33 116	1 498 523	4 253 092
2013		15 098 995	6 564 700	13 363	2 818 982	5 701 950
2014		17 613 292	7 053 067	10 273	4 710 623	5 839 329
2015		17 858 038	8 038 033	20 815	4 663 252	5 135 938
2016		17 212 068	8 356 008	14 561	3 888 383	4 953 116
2017		19 661 510	9 080 284	18 193	5 411 182	5 151 851
一师	Division 1	1 798 228	542 472		665 192	590 564
二师	Division 2	1 522 935	812 981	500	526 738	182 716
三师	Division 3	1 879 144	1 321 978		281 510	275 656
四师	Division 4	1 395 015	859 518		363 234	172 263
五师	Division 5	391 201	205 872	9 300	79 501	96 528
六师	Division 6	1 955 767	560 124		672 780	722 863
七师	Division 7	1 730 478	796 312		775 580	158 586
八师	Division 8	3 469 925	1 139 235	7 485	672 620	1 650 585
九师	Division 9	313 615	203 233		58 880	51 502
十师	Division 10	1 055 089	810 433	908	200 051	43 697
十一师	Division 11	422 886	82 193		23 839	316 854
十二师	Division 12	1 460 737	748 721		385 854	326 162
十三师	Division 13	1 786 855	640 563		628 659	517 633
十四师	Division 14	455 248	356 649		76 744	21 855
兵团直属	Directly under XPCC	24 387				24 387

4—3 主要年份全社会固定资产投资

Total Investment in Fixed Assets in Major Years

指　标	Item	2000	2005	2010	2015	2016	2017
投资总额　　（万元）	**Total Investment　　(10 000 yuan)**	**736 077**	**1 372 367**	**4 482 739**	**17 858 038**	**17 212 068**	**19 661 510**
按构成分	Grouped by Purpose of Funds						
建筑工程	Construction	478 559	807 589	2 562 841	11 576 675	11 840 009	13 816 071
安装工程	Installation	45 119	73 180	240 155	1 270 442	1 314 993	1 450 119
设备工器具购置	Purchase of Equipment and Instrucments	167 744	393 636	1 406 475	4 423 876	3 443 599	3 495 012
其他费用	Others	44 655	97 962	273 268	587 045	613 467	900 308
按三次产业分	Grouped by the Three Industries						
第一产业	Primary Industry	178 403	291 324	391 574	1 493 817	1 789 322	2 008 598
第二产业	Secondary Industry	183 486	395 231	2 304 709	7 801 418	6 485 950	7 243 815
第三产业	Tertiary Industry	374 188	685 812	1 786 456	8 562 803	8 936 796	10 409 097
投资总额构成　　（%）	**Composition of Total Investment　　(%)**						
按构成分	Grouped by Purpose of Funds						
建筑工程	Construction	65.0	58.9	57.2	64.8	68.8	70.2
安装工程	Installation	6.1	5.3	5.3	7.1	7.6	7.4
设备工器具购置	Purchase of Equipment and Instrucments	22.8	28.7	31.4	24.8	20.0	17.8
其他费用	Others	6.1	7.1	6.1	3.3	3.6	4.6
按三次产业分	Grouped by the Three Industries						
第一产业	Primary Industry	24.2	21.2	8.7	8.4	10.4	10.2
第二产业	Secondary Industry	24.9	28.8	51.4	43.7	37.7	36.8
第三产业	Tertiary Industry	50.9	50.0	39.9	47.9	51.9	53.0
固定资产投资资金来源（万元）	**Grouped by Source of Funds　(10 000 yuan)**	**735 029**	**1 363 818**	**4 508 010**	**16 215 624**	**15 583 751**	**16 477 159**
国家预算内资金	State Budgetary Appropriation	108 567	267 787	572 337	2 366 567	2 604 983	1 939 222
国内贷款	Domestic Loans	138 289	171 798	807 025	1 567 855	919 725	1 269 419
债　券	Bonds					14 900	
利用外资	Foreign Investment	716	19 198	30 037	3 000	12 972	12 674
自筹资金	Fund Raising	294 522	682 183	2 328 397	10 479 906	10 465 018	11 326 090
其他资金	Others	192 935	222 852	770 214	1 798 296	1 566 153	1 929 754
固定资产投资资金来源构成（%）	**Composition of Source of Funds　(%)**						
国家预算内资金	State Budgetary Appropriation	14.8	19.6	12.7	14.6	16.7	11.8
国内贷款	Domestic Loans	18.8	12.6	17.9	9.7	5.9	7.7
债　券	Bonds					0.1	
利用外资	Foreign Investment	0.1	1.4	0.7		0.1	0.1
自筹资金	Fund Raising	40.1	50.0	51.6	64.6	67.2	68.7
其他资金	Others	26.2	16.4	17.1	11.1	10.0	11.7
房屋建筑面积　（万平方米）	**Floor Space of Buildings　(10 000 sq.m)**						
施工面积	Floor Space under Construction	568	685	1 630	6 578	4 169	3 660
#住　宅	Residential Buildings	378	389	1 019	2 789	2 035	1 526
竣工面积	Floor Space Completed	497	532	888	2 745	960	940
#住　宅	Residential Buildings	367	349	632	1108	452	364

4—4 全社会固定资产投资及构成

Total Investment in Fixed Assets and Its Composition

(2017 年)

指　标	Item	合　计 Total	按登记注册类型分 Grouped by Registration Status 国　有 State-owned	集　体 Collective	私营个体 Private Individual	其　他 Other	# 房地产开发 Real Estate Development
投资总额　(万元)	**Total Investment　(10 000 yuan)**	**19 661 510**	**9 080 284**	**18 193**	**5 411 182**	**5 151 851**	**1 550 184**
按建设性质分	Grouped by Type of Construction						
# 新　建	New Construction	16 901 809	7 514 143	16 888	4 294 359	3 526 235	1 550 184
扩　建	Expansion	953 248	498 435		263 363	191 450	
改　建	Reconstruction	1 556 371	814 006	1 305	77 918	663 142	
按构成分	Grouped by Purpose of Funds						
建筑工程	Construction	13 816 071	7 677 679	13 803	3 572 966	2 551 623	1 200 102
安装工程	Installation	1 450 119	523 623	790	448 170	477 536	154 428
设备工器具购置	Purchase of Equipment and Instrucments	3 495 012	653 059	2 620	1 175 090	1 664 243	52 459
其他费用	Others	900 308	225 923	980	214 956	458 449	143 195
按三次产业分	Grouped by the Three Industries						
第一产业	Primary Industry	2 008 598	1 139 804	12 500	493 934	362 360	
第二产业	Secondary Industry	7 243 815	1 180 008	1 305	3 099 545	2 962 957	
第三产业	Tertiary Industry	10 409 097	6 760 472	4 388	1 817 703	1 826 534	1 550 184
投资总额构成 (%)	**Composition of Total Investment (%)**						
按建设性质分	Grouped by Type of Construction						
# 新　建	New Construction	86.0	82.8	92.8	79.4	68.4	100.0
扩　建	Expansion	4.8	5.5		4.9	3.7	
改　建	Reconstruction	7.9	9.0	7.2	1.4	12.9	
按构成分	Grouped by Purpose of Funds						
建筑工程	Construction	70.2	84.5	75.9	66.0	49.5	77.4
安装工程	Installation	7.4	5.8	4.3	8.3	9.3	10.0
设备工器具购置	Purchase of Equipment and Instrucments	17.8	7.2	14.4	21.7	32.3	3.4
其他费用	Others	4.6	2.5	5.4	4.0	8.9	9.2
按三次产业分	Grouped by the Three Industries						
第一产业	Primary Industry	10.2	12.5	68.7	9.1	7.0	
第二产业	Secondary Industry	36.9	13.0	7.2	57.3	57.5	
第三产业	Tertiary Industry	52.9	74.5	24.1	33.6	35.5	100.0
固定资产投资资金来源　(万元)	**Grouped by Source of Funds (10 000 yuan)**	**16 477 159**	**6 892 961**	**16 791**	**4 578 740**	**4 988 667**	**1 756 208**
国家预算内资金	State Budgetary Appropriation	1 939 222	1 797 458		5 596	136 168	
国内贷款	Domestic Loans	1 269 419	383 673		184 737	701 009	93 620
债　券	Bonds						
利用外资	Foreign Investment	12 674	3 180			9 494	
自筹资金	und Raising	11 326 090	4 018 741	13 378	3 673 210	3 620 761	849 866
其他资金	Others	1 929 754	689 909	3 413	715 197	521 235	812 722
固定资产投资资金来源构成 (%)	**Composition of Source of Funds (%)**						
国家预算内资金	State Budgetary Appropriation	11.8	26.1		0.1	2.7	
国内贷款	Domestic Loans	7.7	5.6		4.1	14.1	5.3
债　券	Bonds						
利用外资	Foreign Investment	0.1	…			0.2	
自筹资金	Fund Raising	68.7	58.3	79.7	80.2	72.6	48.4
其他资金	Others	11.7	10.0	20.3	15.6	10.4	46.3

注:按登记注册类型分中"新建"不含房地产开发投资。

Note: The new construction grouped by registration status does not include investment in real estate development.

4—5 按建设性质分全社会固定资产投资

Total Investment in Fixed Assets by Type of Construction

计量单位:万元 (2017 年) (10 000 yuan)

指标	Item	投资总额 Total	# 新建 New Construction	# 扩建 Expansion	# 改建 Reconst -ruction	# 单纯生活设施 Pure Life -Facilities	# 单纯购置 Purely Purchase
总计	**Total**	**19 661 510**	**16 901 809**	**953 248**	**1 556 371**	**146 751**	**39 936**
农、林、牧、渔业	Farming Forestry Animal Husbandry and Fishery	2 008 598	1 743 804	87 677	163 556	3 443	2 593
采矿业	Mining	62 781	32 345	12 001	17 892		543
制造业	Manufacturing	5 179 964	4 543 550	244 034	327 280		17 400
电力、热力、燃气及水生产和供应业	Production and Supply of Electric Power Gas Heat Power and Water	1 993 761	1 471 202	93 136	428 155	1 268	
建筑业	Construction	7 309	7 309				
批发和零售业	Wholesale and Retail Trade	348 473	329 432	10 136	8 905		
交通运输、仓储和邮政业	Transport Storage and Postal Service	2 984 824	2 525 255	179 288	263 886	4 715	11 680
住宿和餐饮业	Accommodation and Catering Services Industry	160 047	149 871	2 676	7 500		
信息传输、软件和信息技术服务业	Information Deliver Software and Information Technique Services Industry	186 104	174 109	10 500	1 495		
金融业	Finance	14 498	14 498				
房地产业	Real Estate Trade	2 443 989	2 206 755	6 617	102 001	128 616	
租赁和商务服务业	Leasing and Business Service	361 649	357 813	1 320	2 516		
科学研究和技术服务业	Scientific Research and Technical Service	60 137	60 137				
水利、环境和公共设施管理业	Water Conservancy Environment and Public Facilities Management	2 580 050	2 152 872	209 451	207 438	8 429	
居民服务、修理和其他服务业	Resident Repair and Other Services	60 660	56 780		2 600	280	1 000
教育	Education	318 235	302 184	5 112	4 719		6 220
卫生和社会工作	Health Care and Social Security	242 382	227 178	8 559	6 645		
文化、体育和娱乐业	Culture Sports and Entertainment	311 437	302 028	1 772	7 037		
公共管理、社会保障和社会组织	Public Management, Social Security and Social Organization	336 612	244 687	80 969	4 746		500

4—6 各师按建设性质分全社会固定资产投资

Total Investment in Fixed Assets by Type of Construction and by Division

计量单位:万元 (2017 年) (10 000 yuan)

单位	Unit	投资总额 Total	# 新建 New Construction	# 扩建 Expansion	# 改建 Reconstruction	# 单纯生活设施 Pure Life Facilities	# 单纯购置 Purely Purchase
总计	**Total**	**19 661 510**	**16 901 809**	**953 248**	**1 556 371**	**146 751**	**39 936**
一师	Division 1	1 798 228	1 556 901	108 680	120 790	857	
二师	Division 2	1 522 935	1 366 028	53 766	102 598		543
三师	Division 3	1 879 144	1 642 192	150 167	77 487	3 078	6 220
四师	Division 4	1 395 015	1 209 026	53 788	129 467	2 734	
五师	Division 5	391 201	321 991	43 232	20 097	921	3 100
六师	Division 6	1 955 767	1 633 080	57 821	260 841		
七师	Division 7	1 730 478	1 494 528	77 912	147 529	10 509	
八师	Division 8	3 469 925	2 693 783	141 400	584 313	6 629	
九师	Division 9	313 615	230 273	55 114	26 635		1 593
十师	Division 10	1 055 089	920 471	87 707	23 901	6 000	16 800
十一师	Division 11	422 886	276 453	84 067	2 280	60 086	
十二师	Division 12	1 460 737	1 448 169	200	12 368		
十三师	Division 13	1 786 855	1 725 219	29 546	11 539	18 051	
十四师	Division 14	455 248	371 183	9 848	36 331	37 886	
兵团直属	Directly under XPCC	24 387	12 512		195		11 680

4—7　各师按构成分全社会固定资产投资

Total Investment in Fixed Assets by Composition and by Division

计量单位:万元　　(2017 年)　　(10 000 yuan)

单　位	Unit	合　计 Total	建筑工程 Construction Works	安装工程 Works of Installation	设备工具器具购置 Purchase of Equip-ment and Devices	其他费用 Other Expenses
总　计	**Total**	**19 661 510**	**13 816 071**	**1 450 119**	**3 495 012**	**900 308**
一　师	Division 1	1 798 228	1 112 159	160 112	484 169	41 788
二　师	Division 2	1 522 935	1 248 678	47 066	216 179	11 012
三　师	Division 3	1 879 144	1 366 696	130 411	310 086	71 951
四　师	Division 4	1 395 015	1 192 255	52 346	130 368	20 046
五　师	Division 5	391 201	345 135	10 297	31 882	3 887
六　师	Division 6	1 955 767	1 505 455	122 519	286 718	41 075
七　师	Division 7	1 730 478	1 186 110	165 771	337 041	41 556
八　师	Division 8	3 469 925	1 682 772	398 088	992 323	396 742
九　师	Division 9	313 615	278 612	328	30 404	4 271
十　师	Division 10	1 055 089	830 324	113 654	64 771	46 340
十一师	Division 11	422 886	283 839	25 677	15 288	98 082
十二师	Division 12	1 460 737	1 251 197	75 504	65 996	68 040
十三师	Division 13	1 786 855	1 139 416	122 144	479 334	45 961
十四师	Division 14	455 248	386 565	24 790	36 505	7 388
兵团直属	Directly under XPCC	24 387	6 858	1 412	13 948	2 169

4—8　按行业分全社会固定资产投资

Total Investment in Fixed Assets by Sector

计量单位:万元　　(2017 年)　　(10 000 yuan)

指　标	Item	合　计 Total	按登记注册类型分 Grouped by Registration Status			
			国　有 State-owned	集　体 Collective	私营个体 Private Individual	其　他 Other
总　计	**Total**	**19 661 510**	**9 080 284**	**18 193**	**5 411 182**	**5 151 851**
农、林、牧、渔业	Farming, Forestry, Animal Husbandary and Fishery	2 008 598	1 139 804	12 500	493 934	362 360
采矿业	Mining	62 781	24 021		26 524	12 236
制造业	Manufacturing	5 179 964	338 494	1 305	2 793 829	2 046 336
电力、热力、燃气及水生产和供应业	Production and Supply of Electric Power Gas Heat Power and Water	1 993 761	814 293		277 702	901 766
建筑业	Construction	7 309	3 200		1 490	2 619
批发和零售业	Wholesale and Retail Trade	348 473	75 297		195 233	77 943
交通运输、仓储和邮政业	Transport Storage and Postal Service	2 984 824	2 311 905		315 400	357 519
住宿和餐饮业	Accommodation and Catering Services Industry	160 047	25 689		81 768	52 590
信息传输、软件和信息技术服务业	Information Deliver Software and Information Technique Services Industry	186 104	58 337		84 493	43 274
金融业	Finance	14 498		4 388		10 110
房地产业	Real Estate Trade	2 443 989	803 780		820 884	819 325
租赁和商务服务业	Leasing and Business Service	361 649	278 675		73 199	9 775
科学研究和技术服务业	Scientific Research and Technical Service	60 137	25 873		31 160	3 104
水利、环境和公共设施管理业	Water Conservancy Environment and Public Facilities Management	2 580 050	2 224 868		105 742	249 440
居民服务、修理和其他服务业	Resident Repair and Other Services	60 660	26 453		29 857	4 350
教　育	Education	318 235	292 988		13 510	11 737
卫生和社会工作	Health Care and Social Security	242 382	180 096		12 131	50 155
文化、体育和娱乐业	Culture Sports and Entertainment	311 437	139 514		54 326	117 597
公共管理、社会保障和社会组织	Public Management, Social Security and Social Organization	336 612	316 997			19 615

4—9 各师按行业分全社会固定资产投资

Total Investment in Fixed Assets by Sector and Division

计量单位:万元 (2017 年) (10 000 yuan)

单 位	Unit	投资总额 Total	农、林、牧、渔业 Farming Forestry Animal Husbandary	采矿业 Mining	制造业 Manufac-turing	电力、热力、燃气及水生产和供应业 Production and Supply of Electric Power,Gas, heat Power and Water	建筑业 Constru-ction	批发零售业 Wholesale and Retail Trade	交通运输、仓储和邮政业 Transport, Storage and Postal Service	住宿和餐饮业 Accommo-dation and Catering Services Industry	信息传输、软件和信息技术服务业 Information Deliver, Software and Information Technique Services industry
总 计	**Total**	**19 661 510**	**2 008 598**	**62 781**	**5 179 964**	**1 993 761**	**7 309**	**348 473**	**2 984 824**	**160 047**	**186 104**
一 师	Division 1	1 798 228	263 377	1 000	948 156	47 061	2 490	25 039	159 418	15 047	
二 师	Division 2	1 522 935	199 918	23 541	427 026	84 000		50 017	186 805	14 156	20 635
三 师	Division 3	1 879 144	213 166		378 581	104 889	2 619	24 060	480 779	10 595	14 463
四 师	Division 4	1 395 015	122 203	7 685	234 727	72 552		13 589	432 782	36 652	40 454
五 师	Division 5	391 201	111 797	400	41 624	23 891		18 930	40 389	1 970	3 000
六 师	Division 6	1 955 767	170 198	11 956	491 321	189 352	2 200	11 616	125 848	8 270	1 495
七 师	Division 7	1 730 478	89 934	1 122	699 965	218 072		22 159	99 718	8 000	13 955
八 师	Division 8	3 469 925	504 535	11 979	950 300	619 260		96 686	156 781	42 644	36 800
九 师	Division 9	313 615	48 036	4 418	42 265	38 372		7 517	80 852	850	
十 师	Division 10	1 055 089	105 533	680	108 644	43 600		8 020	379 723	3 600	21 248
十一师	Division 11	422 886			38 759	950		2 615	214 941		
十二师	Division 12	1 460 737	41 069		250 623	30 427		50 368	265 695		34 054
十三师	Division 13	1 786 855	85 643		487 287	492 613		13 686	261 862	13 800	
十四师	Division 14	455 248	50 017		80 363	19 896		4 171	87 165	4 463	
兵团直属	Directly under XPCC	24 387	3 172		323	8 826			12 066		

单 位	Unit	金融业 Finance	房地产业 Real Estate Trade	租赁和商务服务业 Leasing and Business Service	科学研究和技术服务业 Scientific Research and Tech-nical Service	水利、环境和公共设施管理业 Water Con-servancy, Enviro nment and Public Facilities Management	居民服务、修理和其他服务业 Resident repair and Other Services	教育 Education	卫生和社会工作 Health Care and Social Security	文化、体育和娱乐业 Culture, Sports and Recreation	公共管理、社会保障和社会组织 Public Man-agerment, Social Security and Social Organ-ization
总 计	**Total**	**14 498**	**2 443 989**	**361 649**	**60 137**	**2 580 050**	**60 660**	**318 235**	**242 382**	**311 437**	**336 612**
一 师	Division 1		82 474	6 759	8 093	143 205	7 765	36 512	18 372	12 272	21 188
二 师	Division 2	500	111 994	560	858	291 026	6 602	10 899	18 601	31 292	44 505
三 师	Division 3		48 494	19 165	13 839	333 469	595	63 165	12 295	42 480	116 490
四 师	Division 4		116 164	33 513	10 015	195 628	3 863	33 570	24 048	10 466	7 104
五 师	Division 5		27 323	4 403		74 145		2 000	8 456	11 547	21 326
六 师	Division 6		632 449	557	3 800	199 143	5 505	32 077	15 384	37 397	17 199
七 师	Division 7		148 990	6 205	3 500	376 886	6 600	11 489	12 723	8 710	2 450
八 师	Division 8	13 090	404 330	40 331	7 043	398 786	6 051	47 296	44 391	52 701	36 921
九 师	Division 9		15 374		850	64 179		1 618	1 521	900	6 863
十 师	Division 10	908	67 751	3 958	2 000	247 192	21 339	9 062	6 144	7 115	18 572
十一师	Division 11		157 316	2 096		3 321		678	2 210		
十二师	Division 12		379 566	221 386	8 020	101 108	1 740	61 393	3 340	7 478	4 470
十三师	Division 13		159 479	18 480	2 119	95 008		1 500	68 337	86 691	350
十四师	Division 14		92 285	4 236		56 954	600	6 976	6 560	2 388	39 174
兵团直属	Directly under XPCC										

4—10 各师按登记注册类型分第一产业全社会固定资产投资

Total Investment in Fixed Assets of Primary Industry by Registration and Division

计量单位:万元 (2017 年) (10 000 yuan)

单 位	Unit	合 计 Total	国 有 State-owned	集体经济 Collective	私营个体 Private Individual	其 他 Other
总 计	**Total**	**2 008 598**	**1 139 804**	**12 500**	**493 934**	**362 360**
一 师	Division 1	263 377	128 707		97 053	37 617
二 师	Division 2	199 918	119 647		60 831	19 440
三 师	Division 3	213 166	150 367		61 397	1 402
四 师	Division 4	122 203	47 642		32 000	42 561
五 师	Division 5	111 797	52 009	9 300	36 280	14 208
六 师	Division 6	170 198	33 758		61 021	75 419
七 师	Division 7	89 934	50 784		26 910	12 240
八 师	Division 8	504 535	358 033	3 200	32 630	110 672
九 师	Division 9	48 036	30 453		15 583	2 000
十 师	Division 10	105 533	71 288		21 405	12 840
十一师	Division 11					
十二师	Division 12	41 069	27 593		4 776	8 700
十三师	Division 13	85 643	19 506		44 048	22 089
十四师	Division 14	50 017	50 017			
兵团直属	Directly under XPCC	3 172				3 172

4—11 各师按登记注册类型分第二产业全社会固定资产投资

Total Investment in Fixed Assets of Secondry Industry and by Registration and Division

计量单位:万元 (2017 年) (10 000 yuan)

单 位	Unit	合 计 Total	国 有 State-owned	集 体 Collective	私营个体 Private Individual	其 他 Other
总 计	**Total**	**7 243 815**	**1 180 008**	**1 305**	**3 099 545**	**2 962 957**
一 师	Division 1	998 707	26 903		459 183	512 621
二 师	Division 2	534 567	98 733		344 597	91 237
三 师	Division 3	486 089	92 936		175 799	217 354
四 师	Division 4	314 964	45 635		163 982	105 347
五 师	Division 5	65 915	16 430		31 975	17 510
六 师	Division 6	694 829	139 260		242 782	312 787
七 师	Division 7	919 159	153 161		624 552	141 446
八 师	Division 8	1 581 539	179 755	1 305	312 763	1 087 716
九 师	Division 9	85 055	16 437		28 866	39 752
十 师	Division 10	152 924	49 172		82 305	21 447
十一师	Division 11	39 709	14 520		23 839	1 350
十二师	Division 12	281 050	100 462		116 756	63 832
十三师	Division 13	979 900	222 024		438 322	319 554
十四师	Division 14	100 259	24 580		53 824	21 855
兵团直属	Directly under XPCC	9 149				9 149

4－12 各师按登记注册类型分第三产业全社会固定资产投资

Total Investment in Fixed Assets of Tertiary by Registration Status

计量单位:万元 （2017 年） (10 000 yuan)

单位	Unit	合计 Total	国有 State-owned	集体经济 Collective	私营个体 Private Individual	其他 Other
总计	**Total**	**10 409 097**	**6 760 472**	**4 388**	**1 817 703**	**1 826 534**
一师	Division 1	536 144	386 862		108 956	40 326
二师	Division 2	788 450	594 601	500	121 310	72 039
三师	Division 3	1 179 889	1 078 675		44 314	56 900
四师	Division 4	957 848	766 241		167 252	24 355
五师	Division 5	213 489	137 433		11 246	64 810
六师	Division 6	1 090 740	387 106		368 977	334 657
七师	Division 7	721 385	592 367		124 118	4 900
八师	Division 8	1 383 851	601 447	2 980	327 227	452 197
九师	Division 9	180 524	156 343		14 431	9 750
十师	Division 10	796 632	689 973	908	96 341	9 410
十一师	Division 11	383 177	67 673			315 504
十二师	Division 12	1 138 618	620 666		264 322	253 630
十三师	Division 13	721 312	399 033		146 289	175 990
十四师	Division 14	304 972	282 052		22 920	
兵团直属	Directly under XPCC	12 066				12 066

4－13 主要年份各师全社会工业固定资产投资

Total Investment in Industrial Fixed Assets by Division in Major Years

计量单位:万元 （2017 年） (10 000 yuan)

单位	Unit	2011	2012	2013	2014	2015	2016	2017
总计	**Total**	**3 636 697**	**4 987 426**	**6 855 572**	**7 858 319**	**7 673 375**	**6 263 068**	**7 236 506**
一师	Division 1	439 009	517 768	584 780	605 476	634 066	545 030	996 217
二师	Division 2	50 147	175 199	407 451	635 949	556 663	342 259	534 567
三师	Division 3	84 157	101 696	339 213	397 800	495 180	478 690	483 470
四师	Division 4	213 818	321 698	363 012	479 981	481 933	296 090	314 964
五师	Division 5	56 455	108 957	177 809	302 478	214 069	82 680	65 915
六师	Division 6	967 844	1 249 297	1 748 825	1 105 817	727 609	570 408	692 629
七师	Division 7	195 828	501 404	540 142	767 905	755 164	843 786	919 159
八师	Division 8	1 360 573	1 562 336	1 886 193	2 200 061	1 801 387	1 447 260	1 581 539
九师	Division 9	39 383	29 415	71 234	123 509	133 840	35 091	85 055
十师	Division 10	37 669	44 579	77 824	109 062	228 934	156 068	152 924
十一师	Division 11	6 385	28 993	19 282	58 073	46 103	19 866	39 709
十二师	Division 12	109 101	127 532	233 652	243 459	335 879	342 188	281 050
十三师	Division 13	45 712	188 482	371 338	806 140	1 127 764	1 005 680	979 900
十四师	Division 14	5 001	8 343	12 469	21 208	110 060	82 041	100 259
兵团直属	Directly under XPCC	24 645	21 727	22 348	1 401	24 724	15 931	9 149

4—14 按行业分全社会固定资产投资资金来源

Funds Source of Total Investment in Fixed Assets by Sector

计量单位:万元 (2017 年) (10 000 yuan)

指 标	Item	资金来源合计 Total of Capital Sources	国家预算内资金 State Budgetary Appropriation	国内贷款 Domestic Loans	债券 Bonds	利用外资 Foreign Investment	自筹资金 Fund Raising	其他资金 Others
总 计	Total	**16 477 159**	**1 939 222**	**1 269 419**		**12 674**	**11 326 090**	**1 929 754**
农、林、牧、渔业	Farming Forestry Animal Husbandry and Fishery	1 764 064	308 386	45 196		2 180	1 276 382	131 920
采矿业	Mining	62 830	5 161				50 724	6 945
制造业	Manufacturing	4 149 818	33 327	269 402		730	3 643 497	202 862
电力、热力、燃气及水生产和供应业	Production and Supply of Electric Power Gas Heat Power and Water	1 732 257	150 059	402 821			1 038 453	140 924
建筑业	Construction	7 309	1 000				6 309	
批发和零售业	Wholesale and Retail Trade	306 209	4 800	19 678		6 900	232 827	42 004
交通运输、仓储和邮政业	Transport Storage and Postal Service	2 250 550	549 894	288 842			1 222 032	189 782
住宿和餐饮业	Accommodation and Catering Services Industry	160 606		4 100			148 354	8 152
信息传输、软件和信息技术服务业	Information Deliver Software and Information Technique Services Industry	161 617	10 245	3 000			135 301	13 071
金融业	Finance	14 198					13 290	908
房地产业	Real Estate Trade	2 511 835	75 054	136 251		1 864	1 464 723	833 943
租赁和商务服务业	Leasing and Business Service	335 051	53 823				240 753	40 475
科学研究和技术服务业	Scientific Research and Technical Service	41 735	4 084	300			31 962	5 389
水利、环境和公共设施管理业	Water Conservancy Environment and Public Facilities Management	1 982 144	429 978	81 259		1 000	1 213 757	256 150
居民服务、修理和其他服务业	Resident Repair and Other Services	51 421	5 152				42 869	3 400
教 育	Education	274 824	126 303	2 140			133 672	12 709
卫生和社会工作	Health Care and Social Security	222 006	32 566	15 600			151 031	22 809
文化、体育和娱乐业	Culture Sports and Entertainment	276 181	64 854	230			193 986	17 111
公共管理、社会保障和社会组织	Public Management, Social Security and Social Organization	172 504	84 536	600			86 168	1 200

4—15 各师全社会固定资产投资资金来源

Funds Source of Total Investment in Fixed Assets by Division

计量单位:万元 (2017 年) (10 000 yuan)

单 位	Unit	资金来源合计 Total of Capital Sources	国家预算内资金 State Budgetary Appropriation	国内贷款 Domestic Loans	债券 Bonds	利用外资 Foreign Investment	自筹资金 Fund Raising	其他资金 Others
总 计	**Total**	**16 477 159**	**1 939 222**	**1 269 419**		**12 674**	**11 326 090**	**1 929 754**
一 师	Division 1	1 540 771	199 225	166 710			1 024 223	150 613
二 师	Division 2	996 362	138 428	89 087		8 764	698 944	61 139
三 师	Division 3	759 445	318 258	18 805			395 365	27 017
四 师	Division 4	1 365 962	103 354	6 655			1 210 532	45 421
五 师	Division 5	365 421	83 306	8 057		1 600	220 637	51 821
六 师	Division 6	2 036 323	172 207	9 920			1 406 561	447 635
七 师	Division 7	945 969	59 381	87 445		1 580	541 489	256 074
八 师	Division 8	3 302 307	151 429	424 424			2 443 328	283 126
九 师	Division 9	267 848	99 685	16 763			63 656	87 744
十 师	Division 10	652 065	44 832	13 631			392 945	200 657
十一师	Division 11	541 994	3 728	193 631		730	206 654	137 251
十二师	Division 12	1 493 721	250 861	49 045			1 093 451	100 364
十三师	Division 13	1 843 369	185 106	183 246			1 406 408	68 609
十四师	Division 14	344 265	117 271	2 000			212 711	12 283
兵团直属	Directly under XPCC	21 337	12 151				9 186	

4—16 按行业分全社会新增固定资产

Total Newly Increased Fixed Assets by Sector

计量单位:万元 (2017 年) (10 000 yuan)

指 标	Item	新增固定资产 Newly Increased Fixed Assets	国 有 State-owned	集 体 Collective	私营个体 Private and Individuals	其 他 Other
总 计	**Total**	**16 141 062**	**7 257 541**	**26 889**	**5 519 568**	**3 337 064**
农、林、牧、渔业	Farming Forestry Animal Husbandry and Fishery	1 821 734	1 116 922	12 800	398 765	293 247
采矿业	Mining	41 392	6 186		25 906	9 300
制造业	Manufacturing	3 990 480	154 101	1 325	2 679 801	1 155 253
电力、热力、燃气及水生产和供应业	Production and Supply of Electric Power Gas Heat Power and Water	3 216 588	960 968		1 470 220	785 400
建筑业	Construction	3 169	1 000		1 500	669
批发和零售业	Wholesale and Retail Trade	332 556	64 822		206 508	61 226
交通运输、仓储和邮政业	Transport Storage and Postal Service	1 341 988	988 079		235 939	117 970
住宿和餐饮业	Accommodation and Catering Services Industry	97 798	24 371		44 337	29 090
信息传输、软件和信息技术服务业	Information Deliver Software and Information Technique Services Industry	59 761	9 863		46 898	3 000
金融业	Finance	12 764		12 764		
房地产业	Real Estate Trade	1 443 621	742 447		237 672	463 502
租赁和商务服务业	Leasing and Business Service	146 973	111 605		33 668	1 700
科学研究和技术服务业	Scientific Research and Technical Service	81 818	14 592		5 800	61 426
水利、环境和公共设施管理业	Water Conservancy Environment and Public Facilities Management	2 601 408	2 323 435		86 716	191 257
居民服务、修理和其他服务业	Resident Repair and Other Services	55 761	26 054		25 357	4 350
教 育	Education	230 524	212 919		6 310	11 295
卫生和社会工作	Health Care and Social Security	263 799	206 499		1 800	55 500
文化、体育和娱乐业	Culture Sports and Entertainment	231 941	137 636		12 371	81 934
公共管理、社会保障和社会组织	Public Management, Social Security and Social Organization	166 987	156 042			10 945

4—17 各师按三次产业分全社会新增固定资产

Total Newly Increased Fixed Assets by the Three Industries and Division

(2017 年)

单 位	Unit	新增固定资产(万元) Newly Increased Fixed Assets (10 000 yuan)	第一产业 Primary Industry	第二产业 Secondary Industry	第三产业 Tertiary Indusry
总 计	**Total**	**16 141 062**	**1 821 734**	**7 251 629**	**7 067 699**
一 师	Division 1	929 531	253 980	326 109	349 442
二 师	Division 2	2 048 077	205 686	727 654	1 114 737
三 师	Division 3	2 075 354	230 145	717 980	1 127 229
四 师	Division 4	867 522	99 584	289 219	478 719
五 师	Division 5	281 256	103 934	63 631	113 691
六 师	Division 6	1 119 801	111 615	446 483	561 703
七 师	Division 7	1 171 106	67 579	539 991	563 536
八 师	Division 8	5 160 227	481 008	3 490 506	1 188 713
九 师	Division 9	299 515	49 280	132 643	117 592
十 师	Division 10	477 592	95 778	90 716	291 098
十 一 师	Division 11	10 008		1 400	8 608
十 二 师	Division 12	468 108	27 918	82 143	358 047
十 三 师	Division 13	895 879	46 522	311 393	537 964
十 四 师	Division 14	333 542	48 636	28 286	256 620
兵团直属	Directly under XPCC	3 544	69	3 475	

4—18 各师按登记注册类型分全社会新增固定资产

Total Newly Increased Fixed Assets by Registration Status and Division

(2017 年)

单　位	Unit	新增固定资产（万元） Newly Increased Fixed Assets (10 000 yuan)	国　有 State-owned	集　体 Collective	私营个体 Private Individual Economy	其　他 Others
总　计	**Total**	**16 141 062**	**7 257 541**	**26 889**	**5 519 568**	**3 337 064**
一　师	Division 1	929 531	386 008		410 687	132 836
二　师	Division 2	2 048 077	1 284 966	500	444 521	318 090
三　师	Division 3	2 075 354	1 610 491		283 057	181 806
四　师	Division 4	867 522	486 377		289 622	91 523
五　师	Division 5	281 256	149 661	9 600	82 311	39 684
六　师	Division 6	1 119 801	272 143		227 770	619 888
七　师	Division 7	1 171 106	644 734		474 896	51 476
八　师	Division 8	5 160 227	951 264	15 881	2 779 577	1 413 505
九　师	Division 9	299 515	133 417		43 016	123 082
十　师	Division 10	477 592	306 198	908	146 821	23 665
十一师	Division 11	10 008	10 008			
十二师	Division 12	468 108	307 904		25 355	134 849
十三师	Division 13	895 879	409 789		287 974	198 116
十四师	Division 14	333 542	304 581		23 961	5 000
兵团直属	Directly under XPCC	3 544				3 544

4—19 全社会固定资产投资新增生产能力(或效益)

Newly Increased Production Capacity or Efficiency of Total Investment in Fixed Assets

(2017 年)

能力(或效益)名称		Item		合　计 Total
新建公路	（公里）	Length of New Highways	(km)	878.75
改建公路	（公里）	Length of Reconstructed Highways	(km)	1055.1
发电机组容量	（万千瓦）	Capacity of Generation Setes	(10 000 kwh)	164.1
水力发电		Water Power Generate Electricity		
火力发电		Firepower Generate Electricity		140.9
风力发电		Wind Power		10.8
太阳能发电		Slar Energy Generate Electricity		12.4
输电线路	（公里）	Transmission Line	(km)	521.95
# 11 万伏及以上的		110 000 V and Above it		521.95
焦　炭	（万吨/年）	Coke	(10 000 tons/year)	
棉纺绽	（锭）	Cotton Hasp	(ingot)	94.34
白　酒	（万吨/年）	White spirit	(10 000 tons/year)	0.8
其他酒	（万吨/年）	Other Wine	(10 000 tons/year)	1
塑料树脂及共聚物	（万吨/年）	Plastics Resin	(10 000 tons/year)	0.1
城市自来水供水能力	（万吨/日）	Tap Water Supply Capacity	(10 000 tons/day)	29.69
城市污水处理能力	（万吨/日）	Waste Water Treatment Capacity	(10 000 tons/day)	6.78

4—20 房地产开发投资

Investment in Real Estate Development

指　标	Item	2016	2017
房地产开发投资　(万元)	**Investment for Real-estate Development (10 000 yuan)**	**1 836 429**	**1 550 184**
按构成分	Grouped by Field of Investment		
建筑工程	Construction Works	1 465 415	1 200 102
安装工程	Works of Installation	153 652	154 428
设备工器具购置	Purchase of Equipment and Devices	38 381	52 459
其他费用	Other Expenses	178 981	143 195
按工程用途分	Grouped by Purpose of Works		
住　宅	Flat	1 013 812	776 525
办公楼	Office Building	69 761	69 621
商业营业用房	Houses for Business Use	640 727	564 288
其　他	Others	112 129	139 750
新增固定资产　(万元)	**Newly Increased Fixed Assets (10 000 yuan)**	**667 758**	**856 136**
本年购置土地面积　(万平方米)	**Land Area Purchased for the Current Year (10 000 sq.m)**	**181.03**	**63.38**
商品房屋施工面积　(万平方米)	**Floor Space of Consturction for Commercial Houses (10 000 sq.m)**	**2 123.46**	**2 125.03**
住　宅	Flat	1 322.95	1 301.59
办公楼	Office Building	37.93	35.56
商业营业用房	Houses for Business Use	599.67	620.12
其　他	Others	162.90	167.76
商品房屋竣工面积　(万平方米)	**Completed Area of Commercial Houses (10 000 sq.m)**	**260.27**	**272.67**
住　宅	Flat	168.42	181.35
办公楼	Office Building	4.71	11.96
商业营业用房	Houses for Business Use	67.67	65.22
其　他	Others	19.47	14.14
商品房屋销售建筑面积(万平方米)	**Floor Space of Sales and Construction for Commercial Houses (10 000 sq.m)**	367.87	333.44
住　宅	Flat	279.67	260.66
办公楼	Office Building	1.65	0.51
商业营业用房	Houses for Business Use	83.63	70.31
其　他	Others	2.92	1.96
竣工房屋造价　(元/平方米)	**Price of Completed Houses (yuan/sq.m)**	**2 283**	**2 687**
商品房屋销售额　(万元)	**Sales Sum of Commercial Houses (10 000 yuan)**	**1 676 739**	**1 487 584**
# 住　宅	Flat	1 071 522	1 026 593

4—21 各师房地产开发投资

(2017 年)

指　　标	Item	合　计 Total	一　师 Division 1	二　师 Division 2	三　师 Division 3	四　师 Division 4
房地产开发投资　(万元)	**Investment for Real-estate Development (10 000 yuan)**	**1 550 184**	**48 868**	**27 772**	**3 575**	**96 410**
按构成分	Grouped by Field of Investment					
建筑工程	Construction Works	1 200 102	34 278	26 752	3 200	80 457
安装工程	Works of Installation	154 428	8 682	1 020	130	5 685
设备工器具购置	Purchase of Equipment and Devices	52 459	2 586		45	
其他费用	Other Expenses	143 195	3 322		200	10 268
按工程用途分	Grouped by Purpose of Works					
住　宅	Flat	776 525	26 595	13 789	400	60 968
办公楼	Office Building	69 621	2 112	3 320		84
商业营业用房	Houses for Business Use	564 288	19 435	5 963	3 075	27 662
其　他	Others	139 750	726	4 700	100	7 696
新增固定资产　(万元)	**Newly Increased Fixed Assets (10 000 yuan)**	**856 136**	**33 673**	**41 400**	**6 090**	**44 739**
本年购置土地面积　(万平方米)	**Land Area Purchased for the Current Year (10 000 sq.m)**	**63.38**	**19.66**		**0.11**	**13.40**
商品房屋施工面积　(万平方米)	**Floor Space of Construction for Commercial Housee (10 000 sq.m)**	**2 125.03**	**80.82**	**74.17**	**24.41**	**72.54**
住　宅	Flat	1 301.59	49.51	52.01	11.99	54.94
办公楼	Office Building	35.56	2.51	2.31		0.07
商业营业用房	Houses for Business Use	620.12	27.27	8.41	12.24	17.13
其　他	Others	167.76	1.54	11.43	0.18	0.40
商品房屋竣工面积　(万平方米)	**Cmpleted Area of Commercial Houses (10 000 sq.m)**	**272.67**	**14.69**	**15.34**	**4.71**	**13.39**
住　宅	Flat	181.35	11.29	11.06	2.26	10.35
办公楼	Office Building	11.96		2.09		0.07
商业营业用房	Houses for Business Use	65.22	2.36	2.18	2.45	2.95
其　他	Others	14.14	1.04		0.01	0.03
商品房屋销售建筑面积 (万平方米)	**Floor Space of Sales and Construction for Commercial Houses (10 000 sq.m)**	**333.44**	**24.36**	**14.05**	**1.08**	**10.20**
住　宅	Flat	260.66	21.35	9.10	0.55	7.62
办公楼	Office Building	0.51		0.08		
商业营业用房	Houses for Business Use	70.31	2.78	4.87	0.53	2.59
其　他	Others	1.96	0.23			
竣工房屋造价　(元/平方米)	**Price of Completed Houses (yuan/sq.m)**	**2 687**	**1 755**	**2 698**	**1 277**	**2 259**
商品房屋销售额　(万元)	**Sales Sum of Commercial Houses (10 000 yuan)**	**1 487 584**	**75 147**	**59 561**	**2 998**	**34 866**
# 住　宅	Flat	1 026 593	61 351	28 693	1 347	18 695

Investment in Real Estate Development by Division

五 师 Division 5	六 师 Division 6	七 师 Division 7	八 师 Division 8	九 师 Division 9	十 师 Division 10	十一师 Division 11	十二师 Division 12	十三师 Division 13	十四师 Division 14	兵团直属 Directly under XPCC
4 936	**625 516**	**42 057**	**268 888**	**7 500**	**25 675**	**97 230**	**243 717**	**48 130**	**9 910**	
3 936	477 514	40 857	218 627	7 500	23 347	66 323	162 544	44 857	9 910	
945	70 899		9 664		1 990	19 327	34 714	1 372		
55	45 351		2 623				1 769	30		
	31 752	1 200	37 974		338	11 580	44 690	1 871		
1 276	184 626	13 546	174 992	7 500	13 060	68 821	176 197	27 980	6 775	
	44 469		3 082		765	10 267	4 682	840		
3 558	335 441	27 051	71 706		11 700	7 227	30 930	17 952	2 588	
102	60 980	1 460	19 108		150	10 915	31 908	1 358	547	
9 070	**393 851**		**127 364**		**1 745**	**14 297**	**128 312**	**55 595**		
	4.58	**1.61**	**19.75**					**4.27**		
52.04	**593.37**	**104.82**	**519.13**	**3.65**	**65.72**	**85.77**	**322.37**	**107.88**	**13.10**	**5.24**
20.43	308.21	90.70	340.88	3.65	29.10	57.68	228.53	45.62	8.34	
	11.89		6.38		1.24	3.94	2.41	1.73		3.07
30.61	244.62	11.63	104.26		33.12	7.69	61.79	56.62	3.40	1.34
1.00	28.65	2.49	67.62		2.26	16.47	29.63	3.90	1.36	0.84
4.33	**113.06**		**34.37**		**0.70**	**4.78**	**53.77**	**13.54**		
0.98	66.09		26.23		0.70	0.45	47.02	4.91		
	9.76						0.04			
3.29	33.65		4.85			4.33	1.73	7.43		
0.06	3.56		3.28				4.98	1.19		
3.17	**97.20**	**28.76**	**43.89**	**3.41**	**4.64**	**16.09**	**72.03**	**11.75**	**2.69**	**0.12**
1.94	60.96	24.63	38.61	2.34	1.71	13.71	65.31	10.04	2.69	0.12
						0.43				
1.22	36.23	4.13	4.85	1.07	2.70	0.92	6.72	1.71		
0.01	0.01		0.44		0.23	1.03				
2 074	**3 053**		**3 131**		**2 501**	**2 990**	**2 237**	**2 311**		
9 830	**503 049**	**125 177**	**201 518**	**13 909**	**16 721**	**113 870**	**276 674**	**43 017**	**10 265**	**982**
4 422	258 367	105 949	170 664	7 495	4 091	102 893	221 294	30 085	10 265	982

4—22 各师房地产开发投资新增固定资产

Newly Increased Fixed Assets of Investment in Real Estate Development by Division

计量单位:万元 (2017年) (10 000 yuan)

单位	Unit	新增固定资产 Newly Incresased Fixed Assets	国有 State-owned	集体 Collective	私营个体 Private and individuals	其他 Other
总计	**Total**	**856 136**	**25 038**		**226 272**	**604 826**
一师	Division 1	33 673			32 273	1 400
二师	Division 2	41 400			18 000	23 400
三师	Division 3	6 090			5 790	300
四师	Division 4	44 739	10 741		33 998	
五师	Division 5	9 070				9 070
六师	Division 6	393 851			47 372	346 479
七师	Division 7					
八师	Division 8	127 364			29 587	97 777
九师	Division 9					
十师	Division 10	1 745				1 745
十一师	Division 11	14 297	14 297			
十二师	Division 12	128 312			7 202	121 110
十三师	Division 13	55 595			52 050	3 545
十四师	Division 14					
兵团直属	Directly under XPCC					

4—23 按行业分全社会施工和竣工房屋建筑面积

Floor Space of Buildings Under Construction and Completed by Sector

(2017年)

指标	Item	施工房屋面积合计(平方米) Floor Space Under Construction (sq.m)	#本年新开工 Started in this Year	竣工房屋面积(平方米) Floor Space Completed (sq.m)
总计	**Total**	**36 599 217**	**24 786 891**	**9 400 251**
农、林、牧、渔业	Farming Forestry Animal Husbandry and Fishery	2 465 896	2 465 896	736 524
采矿业	Mining	3 550	3 550	950
制造业	Manufacturing	4 119 077	4 119 077	2 483 587
电力、热力、燃气及水生产和供应业	Production and Supply of Electric Power Gas Heat Power and Water	423 553	423 553	114 338
建筑业	Construction	10 839	10 839	
批发和零售业	Wholesale and Retail Trade	665 656	665 656	319 684
交通运输、仓储和邮政业	Transport Storage and Postal Service	639 007	639 007	218 172
住宿和餐饮业	Accommodation and Catering Services Industry	362 841	362 841	137 631
信息传输、软件和信息技术服务业	Information Deliver Software and Information Technique Services Industry	17 351	17 351	2 800
金融业	Finance	72 415	72 415	32 810
房地产业	Real Estate Trade	22 357 402	10 580 701	4 272 923
租赁和商务服务业	Leasing and Business Service	167 641	167 641	37 319
科学研究和技术服务业	Scientific Research and Technical Service	83 154	83 154	31 800
水利、环境和公共设施管理业	Water Conservancy Environment and Public Facilities Management	722 238	722 238	118 334
居民服务、修理和其他服务业	Resident Repair and Other Services	78 162	78 162	39 200
教育	Education	2 173 345	2 173 345	241 830
卫生和社会工作	Health Care and Social Security	948 013	948 013	383 175
文化、体育和娱乐业	Culture Sports and Entertainment	707 277	707 277	171 438
公共管理、社会保障和社会组织	Public Management, Social Security and Social Organization	581 800	546 175	57 736

4—24　各师全社会施工和竣工房屋建筑面积

Floor Space of Buildings Under Construction and Completed by Division

(2017 年)

单　位	Unit	施工房屋面积合计（平方米） Floor Space Under Construction (sq.m)	# 本年新开工 Started in this Year	竣工房屋面积（平方米） Floor Space Completed (sq.m)
总　计	**Total**	**36 599 217**	**24 786 891**	**9 400 251**
一　师	Division 1	3 226 153	2 741 421	2 227 468
二　师	Division 2	1 466 749	1 306 562	174 308
三　师	Division 3	2 025 236	1 983 206	1 045 340
四　师	Division 4	2 110 181	1 570 993	719 535
五　师	Division 5	299 869	226 007	124 789
六　师	Division 6	4 423 191	1 305 459	574 422
七　师	Division 7	2 831 196	2 801 531	111 214
八　师	Division 8	8 373 289	5 446 991	1 860 024
九　师	Division 9	322 307	285 849	152 677
十　师	Division 10	706 355	232 117	51 904
十一师	Division 11	1 833 978	1 082 067	
十二师	Division 12	4 339 463	2 172 242	434 259
十三师	Division 13	3 059 097	2 181 293	1 307 065
十四师	Division 14	1 582 153	1 451 153	617 246
兵团直属	Directly under XPCC			

4—25　各师全社会住宅建设投资及竣工面积

Total Investment in Housing Construction and Floor Space of Housing Buildings Completed by Division

(2017 年)

单　位	Unit	住宅投资（万元） Housing Construction Investment (10 000 yuan)	# 国　有 State-owned	# 私营个体 Private-and individuals	竣工面积（平方米） Completed Floor Space (sq.m)	# 国　有 State-owned	# 私营个体 Private-and individuals
总　计	**Total**	**1 260 544**	**479 396**	**310 037**	**3 639 119**	**2 339 880**	**365 801**
一　师	Division 1	47 746	17 843	26 888	176 261	52 982	123 079
二　师	Division 2	35 566	19 300	238	45 520	45 520	
三　师	Division 3	25 315	24 606	400	777 458	753 447	
四　师	Division 4	67 934	48 104	18 380	100 424	47 825	52 599
五　师	Division 5	5 626	4 350		12 400	2 600	
六　师	Division 6	189 826	5 200	27 860	225 023	4 839	100 558
七　师	Division 7	102 756	89 210	13 546	23 780	23 780	
八　师	Division 8	281 949	63 667	87 089	657 547	324 612	328
九　师	Division 9	23 372	6 054	9 318	36 050	6 500	7 250
十　师	Division 10	45 347	28 347	11 740	18 438	11 000	
十一师	Division 11	74 841	33 818				
十二师	Division 12	186 711	514	82 031	353 473		39 235
十三师	Division 13	83 540	55 143	25 772	714 399	568 429	42 752
十四师	Division 14	90 015	83 240	6 775	498 346	498 346	
兵团直属	Directly under XPCC						

4—26 按三次产业分国有单位固定资产投资及构成

Investment in Fixed Assets of State-owned Units and Its Composition by the Three Industries

年份 Year	单位 Unit	投资总额（万元） Total (10 000yuan)	第一产业 Primary Industry	第二产业 Secondary Industry	第三产业 Tertiary Industry	构成(%) Composition(%) 第一产业 Primary Industry	第二产业 Secondary Industry	第三产业 Tertiary Industry
	1950	2 434	1 850		584	76.0		24.0
	1952	11 311	3 996	4 495	2 820	35.3	39.8	24.9
	1954	4 924	1 753	1 880	1 291	35.6	38.2	26.2
	1957	12 227	7 129	574	4 524	58.3	4.7	37.0
	1962	10 636	5 908	2 187	2 541	55.5	20.6	23.9
	1965	12 471	5 567	3 451	3 453	44.6	27.7	27.7
	1970	13 907	4 177	6 509	3 221	30.0	46.8	23.2
	1975	6 258	3 882	570	1 806	62.0	9.1	28.9
	1978	14 575	7 787	3 463	3 325	53.4	23.8	22.8
	1980	35 225	17 613	5 424	12 188	50.0	15.4	34.6
	1985	49 707	8 268	20 236	21 203	16.6	40.7	42.7
	1990	88 549	22 061	40 952	25 536	24.9	46.2	28.9
	1995	307 170	40 081	125 398	141 691	13.1	40.8	46.1
	2000	654 858	151 904	150 739	352 215	23.2	23.0	53.8
	2001	732 942	193 836	124 480	414 626	26.4	17.0	56.6
	2002	823 534	216 017	158 589	448 928	26.2	19.3	54.5
	2003	946 698	275 194	180 012	491 492	29.1	19.0	51.9
	2004	886 215	286 248	131 962	468 005	32.3	14.9	52.8
	2005	1 025 106	230 603	206 062	588 441	22.5	20.1	57.4
	2006	1 082 649	300 356	208 762	573 531	27.7	19.3	53.0
	2007	1 461 604	300 603	579 909	581 092	20.6	39.7	39.7
	2008	1 573 090	273 011	570 208	729 871	17.4	36.2	46.4
	2009	2 041 739	275 959	745 922	1 019 858	13.5	36.5	50.0
	2010	2 318 366	293 007	663 057	1 362 302	12.6	28.6	58.8
	2011	2 956 473	378 399	531 459	2 046 615	12.8	18.0	69.2
	2012	4 608 623	466 748	852 947	3 288 928	10.1	18.5	71.4
	2013	6 564 700	686 623	1 238 418	4 639 659	10.4	18.9	70.7
	2014	7 053 067	821 638	1 156 773	5 074 656	11.6	16.4	72.0
	2015	8 038 033	1 154 432	1 611 395	5 272 206	14.4	20.0	65.6
	2016	8 356 008	1 368 483	1 465 101	5 522 424	16.4	17.5	66.1
	2017	9 080 284	1 139 804	1 180 008	6 760 472	12.6	13.0	74.5
一　师	Division 1	542 472	128 707	26 903	386 862	23.7	5.0	71.3
二　师	Division 2	812 981	119 647	98 733	594 601	14.7	12.1	73.1
三　师	Division 3	1 321 978	150 367	92 936	1 078 675	11.4	7.0	81.6
四　师	Division 4	859 518	47 642	45 635	766 241	5.5	5.3	89.1
五　师	Division 5	205 872	52 009	16 430	137 433	25.3	8.0	66.8
六　师	Division 6	560 124	33 758	139 260	387 106	6.0	24.9	69.1
七　师	Division 7	796 312	50 784	153 161	592 367	6.4	19.2	74.4
八　师	Division 8	1 139 235	358 033	179 755	601 447	31.4	15.8	52.8
九　师	Division 9	203 233	30 453	16 437	156 343	15.0	8.1	76.9
十　师	Division 10	810 433	71 288	49 172	689 973	8.8	6.1	85.1
十一师	Division 11	82 193		14 520	67 673		17.7	82.3
十二师	Division 12	748 721	27 593	100 462	620 666	3.7	13.4	82.9
十三师	Division 13	640 563	19 506	222 024	399 033	3.0	34.7	62.3
十四师	Division 14	356 649	50 017	24 580	282 052	14.0	6.9	79.1
兵团直属	Directly under XPCC							

4—27 各师按构成分国有单位固定资产投资

Investment in Fixed Assets of State-owned Units by Composition and by Division

计量单位:万元 (2017 年) (10 000 yuan)

单 位	Unit	投资总额 Total	建筑工程 Construction Works	安装工程 Works of Installation	设备工具器具购置 Purchase of Equip-ment and Devices	其他费用 Other Expenses
总 计	**Total**	**9 080 284**	**7 677 679**	**523 623**	**653 059**	**225 923**
一 师	Division 1	542 472	475 792	29 281	27 381	10 018
二 师	Division 2	812 981	748 138	26 536	33 057	5 250
三 师	Division 3	1 321 978	1 105 900	90 818	107 435	17 825
四 师	Division 4	859 518	806 634	19 169	20 346	13 369
五 师	Division 5	205 872	189 358	3 665	11 962	887
六 师	Division 6	560 124	510 929	11 071	37 678	446
七 师	Division 7	796 312	665 021	52 863	69 314	9 114
八 师	Division 8	1 139 235	756 886	104 822	174 644	102 883
九 师	Division 9	203 233	192 218	128	6 616	4 271
十 师	Division 10	810 433	677 184	76 870	11 798	44 581
十一师	Division 11	82 193	58 602	17 706	1 787	4 098
十二师	Division 12	748 721	696 198	29 185	19 559	3 779
十三师	Division 13	640 563	474 337	41 553	116 694	7 979
十四师	Division 14	356 649	320 482	19 956	14 788	1 423
兵团直属	Directly under XPCC					

4—28 各师按建设性质分国有单位固定资产投资

Investment in Fixed Assets of State-owned Units by Type of Construction and by Division

计量单位:万元 (2017 年) (10 000 yuan)

单 位	Unit	投资总额 Total	#新 建 New Construction	#扩 建 Expansion	#改 建 Reconstruction	#单纯生活设施 Pure Life Facilities	#单纯购置 Purely Purchase
总 计	**Total**	**9 080 284**	**7 661 740**	**498 435**	**814 006**	**89 188**	**6 720**
一 师	Division 1	542 472	465 808	14 619	60 188	857	
二 师	Division 2	812 981	754 751	14 950	43 280		
三 师	Division 3	1 321 978	1 106 451	148 515	57 714	3 078	6 220
四 师	Division 4	859 518	722 855	24 303	109 626	2 734	
五 师	Division 5	205 872	162 358	21 336	18 897	921	500
六 师	Division 6	560 124	299 382	47 821	208 896		
七 师	Division 7	796 312	625 034	26 740	134 029	10 509	
八 师	Division 8	1 139 235	985 913	59 602	88 191	4 929	
九 师	Division 9	203 233	124 183	52 415	26 635		
十 师	Division 10	810 433	712 882	67 440	23 901	6 000	
十一师	Division 11	82 193	75 690		2 280	4 223	
十二师	Division 12	748 721	745 192	200	3 329		
十三师	Division 13	640 563	608 657	10 646	709	18 051	
十四师	Division 14	356 649	272 584	9 848	36 331	37 886	
兵团直属	Directly under XPCC						

4—29 各师国有单位固定资产投资资金来源

Funds Source of Investment in State-owned Units Fixed Assets by Division

计量单位:万元　　(2017 年)　　(10 000 yuan)

单　位	Unit	资金来源合计 Total of Capital Sources	国家预算内资金 State Budgetary Appropriation	国内贷款 Domestic Loans	债券 Bonds	利用外资 Foreign Investment	自筹资金 Fund Raising	其他资金 Others
总　计	**Total**	**6 892 961**	**1 797 458**	**383 673**		**3 180**	**4 018 741**	**689 909**
一　师	Division 1	399 648	181 951	3 727			203 656	10 314
二　师	Division 2	435 654	130 707	3 000			281 631	20 316
三　师	Division 3	511 720	309 208	3 190			188 659	10 663
四　师	Division 4	829 911	100 986	4 455			685 101	39 369
五　师	Division 5	183 749	55 046	4 557		1 600	117 600	4 946
六　师	Division 6	560 842	172 207	6 670			319 298	62 667
七　师	Division 7	529 518	57 581	66 425		1 580	188 082	215 850
八　师	Division 8	1 075 536	121 089	133 861			737 346	83 240
九　师	Division 9	157 423	97 439	9 563			42 734	7 687
十　师	Division 10	431 951	44 832	9 851			200 990	176 278
十一师	Division 11	91 841	3 728	3 631			59 054	25 428
十二师	Division 12	754 930	249 744	9 575			488 004	7 607
十三师	Division 13	652 243	155 669	123 168			355 305	18 101
十四师	Division 14	277 995	117 271	2 000			151 281	7 443
兵团直属	Directly under XPCC							

4—30 各师国有单位施工和竣工房屋建筑面积

Floor Space of Buildings Under Construction and Completed in State-owned Units by Division

(2017 年)

单　位	Unit	施工房屋面积合计(平方米) Floor Space Under Construction (sq.m)	#本年新开工 Started in this Year	竣工房屋面积(平方米) Floor Space Completed (sq.m)
总　计	**Total**	**11 371 427**	**10 538 565**	**4 006 894**
一　师	Division 1	382 170	382 170	186 602
二　师	Division 2	687 379	647 396	77 913
三　师	Division 3	1 896 835	1 896 835	994 295
四　师	Division 4	1 184 009	850 785	310 043
五　师	Division 5	287 275	170 875	58 946
六　师	Division 6	51 190	51 190	7 997
七　师	Division 7	1 110 008	1 110 008	63 491
八　师	Division 8	2 184 922	2 113 980	871 885
九　师	Division 9	129 245	129 245	62 133
十　师	Division 10	193 441	193 441	41 676
十一师	Division 11	284 601	12 288	47 818
十二师	Division 12	794 645	794 645	18 000
十三师	Division 13	791 251	791 251	665 436
十四师	Division 14	1 394 456	1 394 456	600 659
兵团直属	Directly under XPCC			

2018

BING TUAN

第五篇

资源与环境

Chapter 5 Natural Resources and Environment Protection

简要说明

一、本篇资料主要内容

本篇主要反映兵团自然资源、自然状况及环境保护事业发展情况等资料。主要内容包括自然资源和水库、水利工程情况、水环境、大气环境、固体废物、工业废气及污染物排放、生态环境、环境污染治理投资及全疆16个主要城市平均气温、降水量、日照时数等内容。

二、本篇资料来源

本篇资料分别由国土资源局、水利局、环境保护局提供，平均气温、降水量、日照时数由新疆维吾尔自治区统计局提供。

Brief Introduction

1. Main Contents

Data in this chapter mainly reflects the natural resources,natural conditions and the development of environmental protection. The matin contents include natural resources and reservoirs, water conservancy projects, water environment, atmospheric environment, solid waste, emission of industrial waste gas and pollution, ecological atmospheric environment, environmental pollution control investment and the average temperature, precipitation, sunshine hours in the 16 major cities of Xinjiang.

2. Sources of Data

The data are provided by the Bureau of Land and Resources,the Water Conservancy Bureau and the Environmental Protection Bureau respectively. The temperature,precipitation and sunshine hours are provided by the the Xinjiang Bureau of statistics.

5－1 自然资源

Resources

指 标		Item		2017
土地资源	**（千公顷）**	**Land Resources**	**(1 000 hectares)**	
土地总面积		Total Areas of Land		7 000.82
农用地		Land for Agriculture		4 328.42
耕地面积		Area of Cultivated Land		1 272.40
园地面积		Garden Area		151.06
林地面积		Woodland Area		908.01
牧草地面积		Pastureland Area		1 719.32
其他农用地		Other Land for Agriculture		277.63
建设用地		Land for Construction		287.48
居民点及工矿用地面积		Area for Residence and Factory		160.10
交通运输用地		Area for Transportation and Conveyance		16.04
水利设施用地		Area for Water Conservancy		111.34
未利用地		Land yet to be Unused		2 384.92
气 候		**Climate**		
年平均气温	（摄氏度）	Annual Average Temperature	(℃)	10.6
北 疆		North Xinjiang		8.5
南 疆		Sourth Xinjiang		12.8
东 疆		East Xinjiang		14.9
年平均降水量	（毫米）	Annual Average Precipitation	(mm)	163.3
北 疆		North Xinjiang		222.9
南 疆		Sourth Xinjiang		113.3
东 疆		East Xinjiang		19.8
年平均日照时数	（小时）	Average Sunshine Hours	(hour)	2 704.3
北 疆		North Xinjiang		2 553.6
南 疆		Sourth Xinjiang		2 794.5
东 疆		East Xinjiang		3 156.7
林木资源		**Forest Resources**		
森林资源面积	（万公顷）	Forest Resources Area	(10 000 hectares)	135.66
森林覆盖率	（%）	Forest－Coverage Rate	(%)	19.23
水利资源		**Water Resources**		
引用水	（亿立方米）	Volume of Water Resources	(100 million cu.m)	123.09
地表水资源(引用量)		Surface Water Volume		103.79
地下水资源		Ground Water Volume		19.29
水库:总座数	（座）	Reservoir:Number of Total	(unit)	140
库容量	（亿立方米）	Reservoir Capacity	(10 million cu.m)	33.62
大型水库:水库座数		Large－scale Reservoir :Number		11
库容量		Reservoir Capacity		18.52
中型水库:水库座数		Medium－scale Reservoir:Number		31.00
库容量		Reservoir Capacity		12.16
小型水库:水库座数		Small－scale Reservoir:Number		98
库容量		Reservoir Capacity		2.94

注:本表土地资源数据为 2016 年数据,来源于兵团国土资源局。
Note:Data of land resources in 2016 come from the Land and Resources Bureau of XPCC.

5－2 各师水库基本情况

Statistics on Reservoir by Division

单位	Unit	2016 水库座数(座) Number (unit)	2016 库容量(万立方米) Reservoir Capacity (10 000 cu.m)	2017 水库座数(座) Number(unit)	2017 库容量(万立方米) Reservoir Capacity (10 000 cu.m)
总计	**Total**	**141**	**336 830**	**140**	**336 219**
一师	Division 1	6	52 700	6	52 700
二师	Division 2	3	16 310	3	16 310
三师	Division 3	5	83 000	5	83 000
四师	Division 4	27	6 887	27	6 887
五师	Division 5	5	2 907	5	2 907
六师	Division 6	25	25 121	25	25 121
七师	Division 7	16	36 721	16	36 721
八师	Division 8	16	72 640	16	72 640
九师	Division 9	7	6 745	7	6 745
十师	Division 10	16	24 272	15	23 661
十二师	Division 12	7	6 830	7	6 830
十三师	Division 13	4	983	4	983
十四师	Division 14	4	1 714	4	1 714

5－3 历年水利工程及灌溉能力

Water Conservancy Project and Irrigation Capacity

年份 Year	水库 Reservoir 座数(座) Number (unit)	水库 Reservoir 库容(万立方米) Reservoir Capacity (10 000 cu.m)	场外引水干渠 Trunk Canal 条数(条) Number (unit)	场外引水干渠 Trunk Canal 引水能力(立方/秒) Water Supply Capacity (cu.m/second)	年实际引水量(亿立方米) Amount of Water Supply (100 million cu.m)	实际灌溉面积(千公顷) Actually Irrigated Area (1 000 hectares)
1978	68	218 974	214	2 447	69.18	725.00
1980	79	226 476	221	2 961	80.02	724.70
1985	91	265 968			89.47	725.30
1990	93	275 365			92.95	814.10
1991	93	276 067			89.93	834.00
1992	93	276 567			88.51	836.90
1993	93	276 567			87.53	840.00
1994	94	279 513			91.90	843.00
1995	101	280 935			96.60	847.40
1996	101	288 575			97.25	869.70
1997	104	291 926			113.39	880.30
1998	105	296 316			114.97	928.70
1999	105	296 316			116.51	962.00
2000	105	299 709			117.93	982.70
2001	108	303 553			120.30	1 072.30
2002	109	304 723			116.08	1 119.03
2003	113	314 692			123.63	1 151.64
2004	114	315 135			120.60	1 128.90
2005	114	316 250			123.89	1 164.48
2006	125	324 487			125.55	1 256.09
2007	125	327 346			123.84	1 222.30
2008	125	327 346			124.82	1 297.76
2009	125	327 838			116.43	1 326.50
2010	125	327 839			125.95	1 332.06
2011	125	327 183			126.78	1 341.23
2012	125	327 169			131.36	1 361.43
2013	135	335 849			123.22	1 411.11
2014	135	335 849			121.76	1 522.88
2015	141	335 374			126.02	1 522.24
2016	141	336 830			130.15	1 527.48
2017	140	336 219			123.09	1 506.24

注：1.年实际引水量指：蓄水、引水、机电井、机电站及水轮泵、其他工程供水合计。2.实际灌溉面积指：农田、园林、草场及其他面积合计。
Note：1.In the table amount of water supply refers to aggregate water—stored，water—supplyed，electromechanical well，electromechanical station，pump and other engineering water supply 2.In the table actuallly irrigated area refers to aggregate farmland，orchard，grass field and other area.

5—4 水利基本情况

Basic Statistics on Water Conservancy

指　　标		Item		2016	2017
总灌溉面积	**(千公顷)**	**Total Irrigated Area**	**(1 000 hectares)**	**1 527.48**	**1 506.24**
耕地灌溉面积		Effective Irrigated Area		1 145.17	1 134.38
林地灌溉面积		Irrigated Woodland Area		175.67	170.49
园地灌溉面积		Irrigated Orchard Area		188.95	182.37
牧草地灌溉面积		Irrigated Pasture Area		17.69	19.00
其他灌溉面积		Other Irrigated Area			
节水灌溉面积	**(千公顷)**	**Water-Saving Irrigated Area**	**(1 000 hectares)**	**1 285.83**	**1 291.55**
# 喷灌面积		Sprinkling irrigated Area		10.12	9.33
微灌面积		Micro-Irrigation Area		1 232.31	1 240.99
低压管灌面积		Low Tension Pipe-Irrigation Area		0.52	0.22
渠道防渗面积		Canal Anti-Seepage Area		42.88	41.01
实际耕地灌溉面积	**(千公顷)**	**Effective Real Irrigated Area**	**(1 000 hectares)**	**1 128.24**	**1 116.27**
农村集中式供水人口	**(万人)**	**Rural Concentrate of Water Supply People**	**(10 000 persons)**	**278.94**	**331.04**
渠　道		**Canal Length**			
2000亩以上灌区渠道长度	(公里)	Canal Length of Irrigated Area above 2000 mu	(kilometer)	38 234.53	39 161.92
# 衬砌防渗渠道长度		Lining Seepage Control Canal Length		24 683	25 454
堤　防		**Dike**			
堤防总长度	(公里)	Total Length of Dikes	(kilometer)	2006	2018
保护人口	(万人)	Protected Population	(10 000 persons)	138.44	138.94
保护耕地	(千公顷)	Cultivated Area Protected by Dikes	(1 000 hectares)	537.94	538.31
水电站		**Hydropower station**			
水电站数量	(座)	Number of Hydropower Station	(set)	100	100
水闸数量	(座)	Number of Sluice	(set)	5 714	5 739
# 河湖引水闸数量		Number of Sluice of River and Lake		286	276
水库引水闸数量		Number of Sluice of Reservoir		116	120
机电井		**Electromechanical Well**			
机电井数量	(眼)	Number of Electromechanical Wells	(set)	27 594	27 146
城乡供水		**Urban and Rural Water Supply**			
城乡集中式供水工程处数	(处)	Urban and Rural Concentrate Water Supply Engineering	(set)	1 158	1 174
# 城镇自来水厂		Waterworks of Town		47	53
农村集中式供水工程		Farm Concentrate Water Supply Engineering		1 111	1 121
农村分散式供水工程处数	(处)	Farm Disperse Water Supply Engineering	(set)	3 926	2 473
水土流失综合治理面积	**(千公顷)**	**Water Loss and Soil Erosion Comprehensive Management Area**	**(1 000 hectares)**	**228.12**	**253.74**
水利总投入		**Total Investment in Water Conservancy**			
本年水利资金总投入	(万元)	Total Water Conservancy Fund Input in the Year	(10 000 yuan)	604 534	553 795

5—5 主要城市平均气温

Monthly Average Temperature of Major Cities

计量单位:摄氏度　　(2017年)　　(℃)

城　市	City	一　月 Jan.	二　月 Feb.	三　月 Mar.	四　月 Apr.	五月 May	六月 June
乌鲁木齐市	Urumqi City	−11.3	−8.0	−2.8	11.1	18.7	23.1
克拉玛依市	Karamay City	−15.9	−10.4	−1.8	14.2	21.7	26.5
石河子市	Shi Hezi City	−15.2	−10.7	−2.1	13.3	20.4	24.3
阜康市	Fukang City	−16.2	−11.2	−2.8	12.9	20.2	25.4
米东区	Midong Area	−13.5	−8.5	−2.0	13.3	21.1	25.8
伊宁市	Yining [Gulja] City	−6.6	−2.8	4.7	12.1	20.1	23.2
塔城市	Tacheng [Qoqek] City	−9.0	−4.6	0.1	11.5	18.4	22.7
阿勒泰市	Altay City	−15.2	−10.9	−7.4	9.8	16.9	22.0
博乐市	Bole City	−14.9	−10.0	−1.7	12.2	19.2	23.6
库尔勒市	Korla City	−6.8	0.4	7.9	15.7	22.5	25.8
阿克苏市	Aksu City	−6.2	1.3	8.7	15.8	22.2	23.8
阿图什市	Artux City	−5.5	2.1	9.5	16.6	23.7	26.1
喀什市	Kashgar [Kaxgar] City	−7.7	1.5	7.8	15.5	22.0	24.6
和田市	Hotan City	−3.5	3.1	10.4	17.2	23.6	25.6
高昌区	Gaochang Area	−4.0	4.7	12.7	21.5	29.1	34.5
伊州区	Yizhou Area	−8.8	−0.5	7.2	16.2	22.4	27.3

城　市	City	七月 July	八月 Aug.	九月 Sept.	十月 Oct.	十一月 Nov.	十二月 Dec.	全年平均 Annual Average
乌鲁木齐市	Urumqi City	26.7	22.2	17.1	7.5	1.6	−6.9	8.3
克拉玛依市	Karamay City	29.5	25.6	18.9	9.1	2.1	−8.0	9.3
石河子市	Shi Hezi City	26.9	23.1	17.6	7.0	2.3	−6.6	8.4
阜康市	Fukang City	28.3	24.0	17.8	7.3	0.8	−7.9	8.2
米东区	Midong Area	28.9	24.7	19.2	8.4	2.1	−6.4	9.4
伊宁市	Yining [Gulja] City	26.5	22.4	18.5	9.3	4.1	−3.4	10.7
塔城市	Tacheng [Qoqek] City	24.9	21.6	15.9	7.5	2.1	−4.7	8.9
阿勒泰市	Altay City	23.1	19.3	12.8	6.5	−3.7	−10.7	5.2
博乐市	Bole City	26.0	22.3	16.7	6.8	0.9	−8.1	7.8
库尔勒市	Korla City	27.1	23.7	19.9	10.4	1.9	−4.8	12.0
阿克苏市	Aksu City	25.6	22.3	20.4	11.9	4.0	−3.6	12.2
阿图什市	Artux City	26.2	23.7	21.9	13.7	5.9	−1.8	13.5
喀什市	Kashgar [Kaxgar] City	24.9	22.5	20.7	13.1	5.4	−3.2	12.3
和田市	Hotan City	25.3	24.0	22.2	14.3	6.9	−1.0	14.0
高昌区	Gaochang Area	37.3	33.1	27.6	15.8	6.5	−3.4	18.0
伊州区	Yizhou Area	29.3	25.6	19.0	9.2	1.1	−7.1	11.7

5－6 主要城市降水量

Monthly Precipitation of Major Cities

计量单位:毫米 （2017 年） （Milli meter）

城 市	City	一 月 Jan.	二 月 Feb.	三 月 Mar.	四 月 Apr.	五月 May	六月 June
乌鲁木齐市	Urumqi City	4.7	32.4	7.6	62.2	38.6	40.7
克拉玛依市	Karamay City	1.7	2.1	1.0	11.2	12.8	16.8
石河子市	Shi Hezi City	1.7	16.3	0.6	30.8	36.7	34.6
阜康市	Fukang City	2.2	17.8	6.4	32.3	31.8	41.2
米东区	Midong Area	2.6	24.8	7.8	35.8	24.6	26.6
伊宁市	Yining [Gulja] City	13.8	30.1	8.4	82.4	22.1	18.0
塔城市	Tacheng [Qoqek] City	14.7	17.2	3.9	37.3	30.0	29.5
阿勒泰市	Altay City	7.0	14.0	1.6	5.4	22.5	77.8
博乐市	Bole City	2.6	5.2	1.6	34.4	58.9	33.3
库尔勒市	Korla City	0.1	13.9		8.6	8.2	36.3
阿克苏市	Aksu City	1.4	1.1		18.5	0.1	12.0
阿图什市	Artux City	12.9	19.6	3.2	18.8	5.8	10.1
喀什市	Kashgar [Kaxgar] City	12.2	15.5	18.5	16.5		7.0
和田市	Hotan City	2.5	10.8	2.7	22.1	8.6	6.3
高昌区	Gaochang Area				3.4		2.9
伊州区	Yizhou Area	0.2	2.5		2.7	5.9	0.5

城 市	City	七月 July	八月 Aug.	九月 Sept.	十月 Oct.	十一月 Nov.	十二月 Dec.	全年平均 Annual Average
乌鲁木齐市	Urumqi City	3.7	22.0	8.0	20.0	40.0	29.8	309.7
克拉玛依市	Karamay City	10.7	6.8	8.7	0.3	3.4	3.7	79.2
石河子市	Shi Hezi City	3.9	19.7	1.6	11.4	22.0	11.9	191.2
阜康市	Fukang City	3.2	14.5	3.7	8.7	25.9	10.2	197.9
米东区	Midong Area	3.2	19.3	4.1	12.2	30.6	14.4	206.0
伊宁市	Yining [Gulja] City	5.4	11.5	21.3	15.6	34.7	23.9	287.2
塔城市	Tacheng [Qoqek] City	12.6	6.7	38.5	35.5	17.3	23.4	266.6
阿勒泰市	Altay City	13.8	14.5	43.8	13.4	9.6	5.6	229.0
博乐市	Bole City	16.7	22.7	29.1	3.0	22.6	9.6	239.7
库尔勒市	Korla City	7.8	9.4	0.5				84.8
阿克苏市	Aksu City	18.8	17.5		0.2		0.7	70.3
阿图什市	Artux City	39.1	69.3	4.0	4.9		4.0	191.7
喀什市	Kashgar [Kaxgar] City	28.1	26.2	4.8	3.6		4.3	136.7
和田市	Hotan City	14.7	11.7		1.8		2.0	83.2
高昌区	Gaochang Area		1.1				0.3	7.7
伊州区	Yizhou Area	2.1	16.2	1.4	0.1	0.3		31.9

5—7 主要城市日照时数
Monthly Sunshine Hours of Major Cities

计量单位:毫米 (2017年) (Milli meter)

城　市	City	一月 Jan.	二月 Feb.	三月 Mar.	四月 Apr.	五月 May	六月 June
乌鲁木齐市	Urumqi City	129.6	160.5	132.2	205.8	325.9	295.2
克拉玛依市	Karamay City	90.7	120.4	96.8	233.4	331.5	289.1
石河子市	Shi Hezi City	54.3	97.4	95.4	208.2	335.6	295.5
阜康市	Fukang City	23.3	70.4	124.7	200.0	307.8	263.4
米东区	Midong Area	20.1	93.3	114.0	206.6	312.3	278.0
伊宁市	Yining [Gulja] City	164.0	153.0	197.1	201.4	340.2	305.4
塔城市	Tacheng [Qoqek] City	163.6	150.6	211.7	251.1	332.1	300.1
阿勒泰市	Altay City	162.3	166.7	227.4	268.1	340.4	318.2
博乐市	Bole City	124.1	125.0	94.6	192.0	315.8	280.8
库尔勒市	Korla City	186.0	198.4	253.2	262.8	355.2	297.4
阿克苏市	Aksu City	177.6	152.0	259.6	235.2	351.1	301.4
阿图什市	Artux City	113.9	88.7	109.9	196.3	308.7	292.0
喀什市	Kashgar [Kaxgar] City	170.0	142.3	180.3	233.7	341.3	327.3
和田市	Hotan City	141.6	135.8	190.9	221.2	316.4	273.4
高昌区	Gaochang Area	141.6	190.0	259.3	259.7	350.7	312.7
伊州区	Yizhou Area	167.9	210.7	308.3	295.7	360.2	313.9

城　市	City	七月 July	八月 Aug.	九月 Sept.	十月 Oct.	十一月 Nov.	十二月 Dec.	全年平均 Annual Average
乌鲁木齐市	Urumqi City	350.4	318.7	281.5	232.4	152.3	83.4	2 667.9
克拉玛依市	Karamay City	347.3	297.4	251.1	188.2	106.1	91.5	2 443.5
石河子市	Shi Hezi City	351.8	324.7	287.6	214.4	104.0	30.4	2 399.3
阜康市	Fukang City	336.1	300.1	270.6	213.6	134.0	17.3	2 261.3
米东区	Midong Area	328.6	305.6	258.9	191.1	95.5	21.6	2 225.6
伊宁市	Yining [Gulja] City	370.2	318.1	301.2	242.0	159.8	89.8	2 842.2
塔城市	Tacheng [Qoqek] City	371.6	326.0	265.1	207.7	156.7	121.8	2 858.1
阿勒泰市	Altay City	383.8	311.6	254.4	205.7	173.8	158.1	2 970.5
博乐市	Bole City	333.6	292.2	268.0	156.9	62.1	69.2	2 314.3
库尔勒市	Korla City	310.1	274.1	302.2	265.8	255.4	174.3	3 134.9
阿克苏市	Aksu City	304.3	285.6	289.5	240.8	249.7	172.2	3 019.0
阿图什市	Artux City	276.2	264.8	211.8	157.1	175.7	107.6	2 302.7
喀什市	Kashgar [Kaxgar] City	297.0	288.8	289.2	221.3	236.0	142.3	2 869.5
和田市	Hotan City	198.8	221.6	256.1	274.2	251.3	165.1	2 646.4
高昌区	Gaochang Area	327.6	301.8	309.0	256.1	214.2	137.7	3 060.4
伊州区	Yizhou Area	321.6	317.2	322.0	237.4	206.0	192.1	3 253.0

5—8 环境保护基本情况

Basic Statisitcs onf environmental protection

指 标	Item	2016	2017
水环境	**Water Environment**		
废水排放总量 (万吨)	Waste Water Discharged (10 000 tons)	18 986.58	21 969.90
# 工业废水排放量	Industrial wastewater discharged	9 808.17	5 986.47
城镇生活废水排放量	Urban Living Wastewater Discharged	9 177.70	15 982.70
集中式治理设施废水排放量	Centralized Treatment for Wastewater Facilities	0.71	0.73
化学需氧量排放量 (万吨)	COD Emission (10 000 tons)	8.81	8.26
# 工业化学需氧量排放量	Industrial COD Emission	1.61	0.82
城镇生活化学需氧量排放量	Urban Living COD Emission	1.33	3.76
农业化学需氧量排放量	Agricultural COD Emission	5.86	3.68
集中式治理设施化学需氧量排放量(吨)	Centralized chemical facility (COD) emissions (ton)	38.00	38.00
氨氮排放量 (万吨)	Ammonia Nitrogen Discharged (10 000 tons)	0.40	0.58
# 工业氨氮排放量	Industrial Ammonia Nitrogen Discharged	0.09	0.05
城镇生活氨氮排放量	Urban Living Ammonia Nitrogen Discharged	0.23	0.48
农业氨氮排放量	Agricultural ammonia nitrogen emissions	0.09	0.05
集中式治理设施氨氮排放量(吨)	Amount of Centralized Treatment for Ammonia Nitrogen Facilities (tons)	2.00	3.00
大气环境	**Atmospheric Environment**		
工业废气排放量 (亿标立方米)	Industrial Exhaust Emission (100 million cu.m)	6 626.95	
二氧化硫排放量 (万吨)	Sulfur Dioxide Emission (10 000 tons)	9.70	7.70
# 工业二氧化硫排放量	Industrial Sulfur Dioxide Emission	9.27	6.76
城镇生活二氧化硫排放量	Urban Living Sulfur Dioxide Emission	0.43	0.94
氮氧化物排放量 (万吨)	Nitrogen Oxide Emission (10 000 tons)	9.44	6.10
# 工业氮氧化物排放量	Industrial Nitrogen Oxide Emission	8.54	5.97
城镇生活氮氧化物排放量	Urban Living Nitrogen Oxide Emission	0.07	0.13
机动车氮氧化物排放量	Motor Vehicles Nitrogen Oxide Emission	0.82	
烟(粉)尘排放量 (万吨)	Volume of Soot Emission (10 000 tons)	5.29	5.06
# 工业烟(粉)尘排放量	Volume of Industrial Soot Emission	4.88	4.74
城镇生活烟(粉)尘排放量	Urban Living Soot Emission	0.30	0.32
机动车烟(粉)尘排放量(总颗粒物排放量)	Soot Emission by Motor Vehicle	0.11	
固体废物 (万吨)	**Solid Waste (10 000 tons)**		
一般工业固体废物产生量	Common Industrial Solid Wastes Produced	1 014.92	982.70
一般工业固体废物综合利用量	Common Industrial Solid Wastes Comprehensive Utilization	849.47	790.40
一般工业固体废物处置量	Common Industrial Solid Wastes Disposed	121.10	72.38
一般工业固体废物储存量	Stock of Common Industrial Solid Wastes	83.37	133.76
一般工业固体废物倾倒丢弃量	Common Industrial Solid Wastes Discharged	4.19	2.48
危险废物产生量	Hazardous waste Produced	151.03	28.05
环境污染治理投资	**Investment in Treatment of Environmental Pollution**		
环境保护验收项目总投资 (亿元)	Total Investment in Pollution Treatment (100 million yuan)	456.13	409.25
环境污染治理投资总额相当于兵团生产总值比例 (%)	Investment in Treatment Out of Percent of XPCC GDP (%)	21.40	17.50
城镇环境基础设施建设投资额	Investment in Urban Environmental Infrastructure Construction	5.03	1.13
工业污染治理项目年完成投资总额	Investment Completed in Treatment Projects of Industrial Pollution	10.66	13.75
当年完成环保验收项目环保投资总额	Total environmental protection investment completed in the year	17.77	19.25
当年施工工业污染治理项目数 (个)	Number of Projects in Industrial Pollution Treatment under Construction of the Year (unit)	18.00	54
当年竣工工业污染治理项目数 (个)	Number of Projects Completed in Industrial Pollution Treatment of the Year (unit)	12.00	29

5—9 按行业重点调查工业企业废气及污染物排放情况

Emission and Treatment of Waste Water and Pollution in Industrial Enterprises by Sector

(2017 年)

指　　标	Item	废气排放量（亿立方米） Exhaust Emission (100 million cu.m)	二氧化硫排放量（吨） Sulfur Dioxide Emission (ton)	氮氧化物排放量（吨） Nitrogen Oxide Emission (ton)	烟(粉)尘排放量（吨） Soot Emission (ton)
总　　计	**Total**	**238 143.04**	**50 739.17**	**45 502.99**	**42 296.85**
钢铁行业	Iron and Steel Industry	110.49	1 207.10	1 251.03	2 844.11
有色金属矿采选业	Mining and Mining of Non—ferrous Metals	0.09	2.47	2.50	5.85
农副产品加工业	Agricultural and Sideline Products Processing Industry	21.41	1 478.34	623.72	598.89
造纸及纸制品业	Papermaking and Paper Industry	1.61	104.19	45.49	55.59
石油加工、炼焦及核燃料加工业	Petroleum Processing, Coking and Nuclear Fuel Processing Industry	67.31	1 568.89	713.15	1 142.93
化学原料及化学制品制造业	Chemical Raw materials and Chemical Products Manufacturing Industry	232.21	818.96	953.72	1 635.01
非金属矿物制品业	Nonmetallic mineral products industry	1 457.77	2 158.41	9 478.34	5 179.04
黑色金属冶炼及压延加工业	Ferrous Metal Smelting and Calendering Industry	110.49	1 207.10	1 251.03	2 844.11
有色金属冶炼及压延加工业	Nonferrous Metal Smelting and Calendering Processing Industry	3 630.10	20 052.62	4 922.83	6 200.28
电力、热力的生产和供应业	Production and Supply of Electricity and Heat	232 510.91	22 085.69	26 241.86	21 757.29
其他行业	Others	0.64	55.40	19.32	33.75

5—10 按行业重点调查工业企业废水及污染物排放情况

Emission and Treatment of Waste Water and Pollutant in Industrial Enterprises by Sector

(2017 年)

指　　标	Item	工业废水排放量（万吨） Volume of Waste Water Industial Discharged (10 000 ton)	工业废水中化学需氧量排放量(吨) COD Discharge from Industral Waste Water (ton)	工业废水中氨氮排放量(吨) Ammonia Nitrogen Discharge from Industrial Waste Water(ton)
总　　计	**Total**	**5 187.60**	**7 237.31**	**470.62**
农副食品加工业	Processing of Food from Agricultural Products	590.53	2 196.71	59.50
食品制造业	Food manufacturing	1 694.75	1 746.46	102.79
酒、饮料和精制茶制造业	Manufacture of Liguor,Beverages and Pefined Tea	470.70	466.86	37.49
纺织业	Manufacture of Textle	758.03	1 349.63	78.68
造纸及纸制品业	Paper and Paper Products Manufacturing	40.36	40.87	1.42
石油加工、炼焦及核燃料加工业	Oil Processing,Coking and Nuclear Fuel Processing	76.93	56.16	11.05
化学原料及化学制品制造业	Raw Chemical Material and Chemical Products	838.23	488.80	111.21
化学纤维制造业	Chemical Fiber Manufacturing	350.58	727.23	50.45
黑色金属冶炼及压延加工业	Smelting and Pressing of Ferrous Metals			
电力、热力的生产和供应业	Electricity and Thermal Production and Supply	367.49	164.59	18.03
其他行业	Others			

5－11 按行业重点调查工业企业固体废物产生量及处理利用情况

Production and Treatment of Waste Solid in Industrial Enterprises by Region

计量单位:万吨　　　　(2017 年)　　　　(10 000 ton)

指　标	Item	固体废物产生量 Solid Waste Production	固体废物综合利用量 Comprehensive Utilization of Solid Waste	固体废物贮存量 Solid Waste Storage	固体废物处置量 Disposal of Solid Waste	固体废物倾倒丢弃量 Dumping and Dumping of Solid Waste
总　计	**Total**	**969.94**	**758.73**	**131.53**	**89.74**	**2.47**
煤炭开采和洗选业	Coal Mining and Washing Industry	25.66	25.66			
钢铁行业	Iron and Steel Industry	30.60	8.67		21.92	
有色金属矿采选业	Mining and Mining of Non—ferrous metals	28.49	…	28.49		
农副产品加工业	Agricultural and Sideline Products Processing Industry	6.12	5.50	0.37	0.59	0.30
食品制造业	Food Manufacturing Industry	17.29	16.14	0.11	1.02	0.03
纺织业	Textile Industry	0.26	0.05		0.21	0.01
化学原料及化学制品制造业	Chemical Raw Materials and Chemical Products Manufacturing Industry	301.77	285.45	0.03	15.74	0.60
非金属矿物制品业	Nonmetallic mineral products industry	4.15	3.38		0.72	0.05
黑色金属冶炼及压延加工业	Ferrous Metal Smelting and Calendering Industry	30.60	8.67		21.92	
电力、热力的生产和供应业	Production and Supply of Electricity and Heat	524.91	405.12	102.53	27.62	1.48
其他行业	Others	0.09	0.09	…		

5－12 环境污染治理投资

Investment in the Treatment of Environment Pollution

计量单位:万元　　　　(10 000 yuan)

指　标	Item	2016	2017
环境污染治理投资总额	**Total Investment in The Treatment of Environmental Pollution**	**4 561 329**	**4 092 549**
城镇环境基础设施建设投资	Investment in Urban Environmental Infrastructure Construction	50 345	11 349
# 污水处理	Waste Water Dispose	39 852	1 833
垃圾处理	Volume of Garbage Dispose	10 190	5 735
工业污染源治理投资	Investment in Industrial Pollution Sources	3 862	22 454
# 工业废水治理项目	Industrial Wastewater Treatment Project	2 512	874
工业废气脱硫治理项目	Industrial Waste Gas Desulphurization Project	810	8 638
工业废气脱硝治理项目	Control Project of Industrial Waste Gas Denitrification	260	5 247
污染物自动在线监测仪器安装项目	Installation Project of Automatic on—line Monitoring Instrument for Pollutants		110
当年完成环保验收项目环保投资	Completion of Environmental Protection Investment in Environmental Protection Acceptance Project	54 182	96 927
# 废水治理环保投资	Investment of in Waste Water Treatment	4 839	4 926
废气治理环保投资	Investment of in Waste Gas Treatment	28 279	64 315
固体废物治理环保投资	Investment of in Solid Wastes Treatment	3 236	3 932
噪声治理环保投资	Investment of in Noise Treatment	2 129	611
绿化及生态环保投资	Investment of Eco—environment Protection and Greening	6 672	976

5—13 工业污染治理投资完成情况

Investment Completed in the Treatment of Industrial Pollution

年 份 Year	汇总工业企业数（个） Number of Industrial Enterprises (unit)	污染治理项目本年完成投资（万元） Investment in the Treatment of Industrial Pollution (10 000 yuan)	治理废水 Waste Water Treatment	治理废气 Waste Gas Treatment	治理固体废物 Solid Waste Treatment	治理噪声 Noise Treatment	治理其他 other	本年施工项目数（个） Projects Under Construction (unit)	本年竣工项目数（个） Projects Completed (unit)
2011	28	13 423.40	10 449.40	2 359.00		75.00		22	12
2012	14	5 446.25	4 416.25	1 000.00				9	10
2013	21	8 400.20	3 414.00	4 964.20				14	14
2014	31	48 740.17	2 073.90	46 370.79	42.48			39	30
2015	13	14 170.00	1 200.00	12 970.00				10	8
2016	23	3 862.43	2 512.00	1 350.43				18	12
2017	46	22 453.87	874.05	16 497.72	119.35		4852.75	54	29

5—13 工业污染治理投资来源

Source of Investment in the Treatment of Industrial Pollution

计量单位：万元　　(10 000 yuan)

指　标	Item	2016	2017
施工项目本年投资来源	**Source of Funds for Investment of Projects Under Construction**	**3 862.43**	**22 453.87**
排污费补助	Pollution Charges Subsidies	38.00	50.00
政府其他补助	Other Government Subsidies	1 180.00	30.00
企业自筹	Self—raising Funds	2 644.43	22 373.87
# 银行贷款	Bank loans	80.00	

2018

BING TUAN

第六篇

财政和财务

Chapter 6 Government Finance

简要说明

一、本篇资料主要内容

本篇资料反映兵团公共财政预算收支情况及兵团国有及国有控股企业资产、主营业务收入、营业税金及附加、企业管理费用支出、营业外收入和支出及利润总额。

二、本篇资料来源

本篇资料由兵团财政局提供。

Brief Introduction

1. Main Contents

Data in this chapter present the conditions of public budget revenue and expenditure and assets of State-owned and State-holding enterprises, main business income, payable business tax and surcharges, management expenses, extra business revenue and expenditure.

2. Sources of Data

Data in this chapter are provided by the Financial Bureau of XPCC.

6－1 一般公共预算收支及增长速度

General Public Budget Revenue and Expenditure and Their Increase Rates

计量单位：万元 (10 000 yuan)

年 份 Year	一般公共预算收入 General Public Budget Revenue	一般公共预算支出 General Public Budget Expenditure	收支差额 Balance	增长速度(%)Increase Rate(%)	
				一般公共预算收入 General Public Budget Revenue	一般公共预算支出 General Public Budget Expenditure
2006	344 549	1 741 020	－1 396 471		
2007	398 789	1 795 424	－1 396 635	15.7	3.1
2008	424 551	2 382 468	－1 957 917	6.5	32.7
2009	472 955	2 986 947	－2 513 992	11.4	25.4
2010	576 935	3 430 328	－2 853 393	22.0	14.8
2011	476 726	4 392 252	－3 915 526	－17.4	28.0
2012	1 007 484	6 032 404	－5 024 920	111.3	37.3
2013	675 374	7 005 141	－6 329 767	－33.0	16.1
2014	797 564	7 814 788	－7 017 224	18.1	11.6
2015	833 079	10 484 476	－9 651 397	4.5	34.2
2016	1 064 829	9 350 070	－8 285 241	27.8	－10.8
2017	1 296 019	8 803 684	－7 507 665	21.7	－5.8

6—2 一般公共预算收入占兵团生产总值的比重

Proportion of General Public Budgetary Revenue to GDP of XPCC

计量单位:万元 (10 000 yuan)

年 份 Year	一般公共预算收入 General Public Budget Revenue	兵团生产总值 GDP of XPCC	一般公共预算收入相当于兵团生产总值的比重(%) Proportion of General Public Budgetary Revenue to GDP of XPCC(%)
2006	344 549	3 760 294	9.2
2007	398 789	4 412 150	9.0
2008	424 551	5 232 964	8.1
2009	472 955	6 106 945	7.7
2010	576 935	7 706 152	7.5
2011	476 726	9 656 558	4.9
2012	1 007 484	11 972 109	8.4
2013	675 374	14 998 657	4.5
2014	797 564	17 386 812	4.6
2015	833 079	19 349 122	4.3
2016	1 064 829	21 343 307	5.0
2017	1 296 019	23 390 728	5.5

6—3　各项税收收入与非税收入

Taxes and Non Taxes

计量单位:万元　　　　(10 000 yuan)

单　位 Unit	年　份 Year	税收收入 Taxes	# 国内增值税 VAT	# 营业税 Sales Tax	# 企业所得税 Corporate Income Tax	# 个人所得税 Individual Income Tax
	2006					
	2007					
	2008					
	2009					
	2010					
	2011					
	2012	299 924	31 365	126 967	45 135	16 912
	2013	392 194	47 102	165 155	48 110	28 190
	2014	445 015	53 585	177 066	45 455	38 238
	2015	512 276	53 165	195 632	56 195	60 603
	2016	607 312	160 817	113 573	70 559	63 172
	2017	677 645	279 789	3 346	124 653	67 839
一　师	Division 1					
二　师	Division 2					
三　师	Division 3					
四　师	Division 4					
五　师	Division 5					
六　师	Division 6					
七　师	Division 7					
八　师	Division 8					
九　师	Division 9					
十　师	Division 10					
十一师	Division 11					
十二师	Division 12					
十三师	Division 13					
十四师	Division 14					
兵团本级	XPCC					
阿拉尔市	Alar City	52 651	22 990	1 860	4 773	4 533
铁门关市	Tiemenguan City	11 747	3 200	1	757	1 538
图木舒克市	Tumxuk	26 128	12 440	82	3 792	3 566
可克达拉市	Kekedala City	10 008	5 577	21	638	379
双河市	Shuanghe City	3 253	2 122		138	340
五家渠市	Wujiaqu	183 507	84 309	653	38 396	5 528
石河子市	Shihezi City	369 856	140 984	517	74 409	50 157
北屯市	Beitun City	20 495	8 167	212	1 750	1 798
昆玉市市	Kunyu City					

6—3 续表 Continued

单位 Unit	年份 Year	非税收入 Special Income	# 专项收入 Special Income	# 行政事业性收费收入 Administrative Fees and Charges Income	# 国有资源(资产)有偿使用收入 Paid Use Income of State—owned Resources (assets)	# 其他收入 Other Income
	2006	34 498	2 435	5 039		24 197
	2007	41 062	1 418	8 047	16 742	12 418
	2008	64 051	889	8 258	39 019	14 301
	2009	79 791	1 635	7 145	46 439	21 494
	2010	125 173	918	21 594	54 238	45 508
	2011	164 947	1 664	35 579	49 326	71 965
	2012	198 113	13 188	48 874	58 226	63 271
	2013	283 180	28 547	59 920	61 485	117 270
	2014	352 549	75 541	101 930	76 807	72 941
	2015	320 803	102 275	69 533	82 754	31 222
	2016	457 517	150 140	61 334	92 038	113 580
	2017	618 374	115 292	85 353	167 407	87 019
一　师	Division 1	85 369	1 790	1 133	75 623	2 802
二　师	Division 2	34 932	11 848	4 637	4 235	1 083
三　师	Division 3	41 368	711	4 365	27 324	21
四　师	Division 4	42 374	2 525	5 751	1 210	30 422
五　师	Division 5	7 286	329	1 212	1 554	1 684
六　师	Division 6	23 268	3 361	2 702	4 579	7 059
七　师	Division 7	35 129	173	6 311	12 869	11 162
八　师	Division 8	16 172	4 554	3 672	1 687	59
九　师	Division 9	5 865	179	1 586	2 480	38
十　师	Division 10	28 228	2 122	11 232	3 480	6 727
十一师	Division 11	3 655	152	51	707	1 000
十二师	Division 12	55 112	28 592	4 317	3 433	11 987
十三师	Division 13	21 317	1 507	2 080	965	10 277
十四师	Division 14	9 357	80	1 037	1 345	682
兵团本级	XPCC	90 200	13 788	9 961	8 436	357
阿拉尔市	Alar City	19 632	2 720	1 259	434	
铁门关市	Tiemenguan City	3 406	326	91	188	1 000
图木舒克市	Tumxuk	7 864	1 361	4 828	435	
可克达拉市	Kekedala City	568	562		5	
双河市	Shuanghe City	220	214		3	
五家渠市	Wujiaqu	11 200	9 586	919	203	36
石河子市	Shihezi City	70 217	27 765	14 209	16 200	623
北屯市	Beitun City	5 635	1 047	4 000	12	
昆玉市市	Kunyu City					

6—4 公共财政预算收支情况

Public Budget Revenue and Expenditure

计量单位:万元 (10 000 yuan)

项　目	Item	2016	2017
收入总计	**Total Income**	**10 979 893**	**10 659 642**
一般公共预算收入	General Public Budget Revenue	1 064 829	1 296 019
税收收入	Tax Revenue	607 312	677 645
# 增值税	VAT	160 818	279 789
营业税	Sales Tax	113 572	3 346
企业所得税	Corporate Income Tax	70 559	124 653
个人所得税	Individual Income Tax	63 172	67 839
非税收入	Non Tax Income	457 517	618 374
# 专项收入	Special Income	150 140	115 292
行政事业性收费收入	Administrative Fees and Charges Income	61 334	85 353
国有资源(资产)有偿使用收入	Paid Use Income of State—owned Resources (assets)	92 038	167 407
其他收入	Other Income	84 379	87 019
上级补助收入	Grant from the Higher Authority	8 026 594	6 891 645
# 兵　团	Corps	7 849 790	6 739 157
接收其他地区援助收入	Receiving aid Income from Other Regions	206 039	179 740
债务转贷收入	Debt Lending Income	152 800	34 800
上年结余	Previous Balance	844 763	1 463 756
# 上年净结余	Net Balance of the Previous Year	—91 745	—70 523
调入预算稳定调节基金	Budget Adjustment Stabilization Fund	18 215	68 297
调入资金	Call in Funds	666 653	725 385
支出总计	**Total Expenditure**	**10 979 893**	**10 659 642**
一般公共预算支出	General Public Budget Expenditure	9 350 070	8 803 684
# 一般公共服务支出	General Public Service Expenditure	342 151	357 539
公共安全支出	Public Security Expenditure	520 587	762 406
教育支出	Educational Expenditure	905 574	888 984
社会保障和就业支出	Social Security and Employment Expenditure	2 118 655	2 194 238
农林水支出	Agriculture Forestry and Water Expenditure"	2 320 808	1 392 940
城乡社区支出	Urban and Rural Community Expenditure	913 900	1 041 703
交通运输支出	Transportation Expenditure	472 650	462 544
住房保障支出	Housing Expenditure	469 764	186 104
医疗卫生与计划生育支出	Expenditure on Health Care and Family Planning	376 307	417 237
文化体育与传媒支出	Cultural Sports and Media Expenditures	120 681	182 703
上解上级支出	Upper Level Expenditure	18 474	20 995
援助其他地区支出	Aid Spending in Other Regions		
债务还本支出	Debt Service	128 000	34 800
安排预算稳定调节基金	Budget Stabilization Fund	58 630	164 317
年终滚存结余	Accumulated Balance	1 424 719	1 635 846

6—5 各师公共预算收支情况

Public Budget Revenue and Expenditure by Division

计量单位：万元　　(10 000 yuan)

单　位	Unit	2016		2017	
		一般公共预算收入 General Public Budget Revenue	一般公共预算支出 General Public Budget Expenditure	一般公共预算收入 General Public Budget Revenue	一般公共预算支出 General Public Budget Expenditure
总　计	**Total**	**372 286**	**8 501 330**	**499 632**	**7 817 306**
一　师	Division 1	72 513	972 093	85 369	814 909
二　师	Division 2	26 333	766 215	34 932	663 284
三　师	Division 3	6 138	890 329	41 368	767 566
四　师	Division 4	47 538	658 068	42 374	685 721
五　师	Division 5	4 788	347 613	7 286	310 490
六　师	Division 6	19 415	813 602	23 268	742 880
七　师	Division 7	24 914	599 508	35 129	538 997
八　师	Division 8	6 978	1 163 454	16 172	1 025 566
九　师	Division 9	8 947	279 647	5 865	293 681
十　师	Division 10	21 070	384 263	28 228	372 081
十一师	Division 11	5 657	97 184	3 655	104 783
十二师	Division 12	34 469	265 768	55 112	254 665
十三师	Division 13	12 527	394 843	21 317	315 008
十四师	Division 14	6 218	114 399	9 357	187 065
兵团直属	Directly under XPCC	74 781	754 344	90 200	740 610

6—6 城市公共预算收支情况

Public Budget Revenue and Expenditure by City

计量单位：万元　　(10 000 yuan)

单　位	Unit	2016		2017	
		一般公共预算收入 General Public Budget Revenue	一般公共预算支出 General Public Budget Expenditure	一般公共预算收入 General Public Budget Revenue	一般公共预算支出 General Public Budget Expenditure
总　计	**Total**	**692 543**	**848 740**	**796 387**	**986 378**
阿拉尔市	Alar City	62 997	88 160	72 283	107 615
铁门关市	Tiemenguan City	13 151	14 175	15 153	14 527
图木舒克市	Tumxuk City	28 959	53 452	33 992	55 790
可克达拉市	Kekedala Ctiy			10 576	2 207
双河市	Shuanghe City	1 615	1 633	3 473	3 504
五家渠市	Wujiaqu City	174 298	157 840	194 707	251 296
石河子市	Shihezi City	388 815	498 628	440 073	511 568
北屯市	Beitun City	22 708	34 852	26 130	39 871

6—7 历年国有及国有控股企业年末固定资产

Year-end Fixed Assets of State-owned and State-holding Enterprises over the Years

计量单位:万元 (10 000 yuan)

年 份 Year	年末固定资产 Year-end Fixed Assets		年 份 Year	年末固定资产 Year-end Fixed Assets	
	原 值 Original Value	净 值 Net Value		原 值 Original Value	净 值 Net Value
1951	1 824	1 824	1985	210 326	127 114
1952	3 369	3 369	1986	251 174	153 479
1953	6 071	5 485	1987	278 465	174 624
1954	8 642	7 474	1988	285 797	187 176
1955	11 419	9 502	1989	325 862	216 598
1956	15 079	12 211	1990	377 860	253 976
1957	20 382	16 424	1991	440 031	309 211
1958	31 933	27 088	1992	518 094	362 604
1959	47 685	41 084	1993	666 525	480 289
1960	51 991	45 774	1994	848 349	619 784
1961	71 098	58 895	1995	1 198 480	851 377
1962	91 905	76 867	1996	1 538 539	1 112 888
1963	85 201	70 223	1997	1 834 230	1 340 750
1964	99 055	77 824	1998	2 224 568	1 626 352
1965	100 492	76 945	1999	2 397 769	1 709 282
1966	68 500	53 156	2000	2 385 124	1 676 272
1967	78 300	56 853	2001	2 549 525	1 792 884
1968	90 200	57 889	2002	2 846 283	2 002 413
1969	96 000	59 097	2003	3 063 855	2 153 063
1970	99 232	62 059	2004	3 448 049	2 421 280
1971	102 400	64 125	2005	4 100 982	2 667 261
1972	105 156	65 728	2006	4 501 324	2 931 719
1973	112 295	66 882	2007	5 060 407	3 277 708
1974	141 404	92 385	2008	5 853 140	3 639 694
1975	85 222	46 554	2009	6 869 041	4 283 575
1976	91 392	48 836	2010	8 058 931	4 993 187
1977	94 494	52 677	2011	9 619 392	6 059 886
1978	106 621	58 708	2012	11 259 544	7 070 653
1979	119 817	66 230	2013	13 676 775	8 491 593
1980	132 295	77 133	2014	15 539 986	9 666 803
1981	146 718	87 631	2015	18 496 802	11 543 421
1982	165 703	99 891	2016	21 322 953	13 197 689
1983	176 135	104 141	2017	25 661 827	15 473 602
1984	205 176	121 190			

6—8 按行业分历年国有及国有控股企业年末固定资产原值

Original Value of Year-end Fixed Assets of State-owned and State-holding Enterprises by Sector over the Years

计量单位:万元 (10 000 yuan)

年份 Year	合计 Total	农业 Agriculture	工业 Industry	建筑业 Construction and Installation	交通运输业 Transportation	商品流通企业 Commodity Circulation
1980	132 295	84 355	35 543	3 351	6 987	2 059
1981	146 718	91 426	39 282	5 818	7 649	2 544
1982	165 703	103 228	44 193	6 582	8 315	3 385
1983	176 135	108 071	46 949	7 080	9 159	4 876
1984	205 176	115 252	57 704	13 223	10 624	8 374
1985	210 326	122 079	60 283	8 348	10 885	8 731
1986	251 174	127 623	82 389	14 674	12 792	13 697
1987	278 465	133 923	100 429	15 777	14 722	13 614
1988	285 797	127 461	107 266	17 612	15 209	18 250
1989	325 862	137 945	130 526	20 063	17 161	20 168
1990	377 860	154 493	154 150	23 986	19 698	25 533
1991	440 031	176 441	182 156	27 516	25 703	28 216
1992	518 094	213 634	206 884	33 516	30 088	33 973
1993	666 525	284 488	262 878	41 217	35 134	42 808
1994	848 349	360 295	334 765	52 313	38 910	62 066
1995	1 198 480	524 775	451 348	68 747	52 447	101 163
1996	1 538 539	673 053	551 027	92 772	62 989	158 695
1997	1 834 230	852 675	604 035	103 467	68 231	205 822
1998	2 224 568	1 027 912	799 619	109 702	65 638	221 697
1999	2 397 769	1 125 450	827 609	111 734	69 311	263 665
2000	2 385 124	1 198 322	762 842	113 774	57 539	252 647
2001	2 549 525	1 383 590	733 891	122 718	46 540	262 786
2002	2 846 283	1 520 347	861 152	132 288	48 293	284 203
2003	3 063 855	1 645 733	866 215	135 397	27 884	388 626
2004	3 448 049	1 810 322	1 000 895	137 553	29 162	470 117
2005	4 100 982	2 119 150	1 255 836	147 698	21 600	556 698
2006	4 501 324	2 350 620	1 334 933	159 442	20 873	635 456
2007	5 060 407	2 626 552	1 612 408	189 607	27 174	604 666
2008	5 853 140	2 967 283	1 886 592	301 655	25 794	671 816
2009	6 869 041	3 242 464	2 640 312	317 285	24 850	644 130
2010	8 058 931	3 515 157	3 649 944	351 421	29 671	512 738
2011	9 619 392	3 933 135	4 539 788	426 254	22 726	697 489
2012	11 259 544	4 719 758	5 325 673	438 944	29 628	745 541
2013	13 676 775	5 759 083	6 432 968	512 666	53 761	918 297
2014	15 539 986	6 681 915	6 945 667	619 268	68 618	1 224 518
2015	18 496 802	7 835 515	8 249 141	780 113	100 997	1 531 037
2016	21 322 953	9 019 509	9 764 442	662 550	136 788	1 739 665
2017	25 661 827	11 199 779	11 306 803	790 469	143 944	2 220 832

6—9 各师国有及国有控股企业年末固定资产原值

Original Value of Year-end Fixed Assets of State-owned and State-holding Enterprises by Division

计量单位：万元 (2017 年) (10 000 yuan)

单 位 Unit	合 计 Total	农 业 Agriculture	工 业 Industry	建筑业 Construction and Installation	交通运输业 Transportation
总 计 Total	**25 661 827**	**11 199 779**	**11 306 803**	**790 469**	**143 944**
一 师 Division 1	3 468 454	1 494 357	1 930 288	13 216	3 784
二 师 Division 2	1 511 209	836 669	299 019	7 562	26 882
三 师 Division 3	1 662 929	1 017 422	531 434	13 360	13 861
四 师 Division 4	1 530 154	718 719	568 922	74 555	1 711
五 师 Division 5	686 417	562 168	80 824	7 553	12 196
六 师 Division 6	2 278 432	1 233 947	487 340	626	9 918
七 师 Division 7	2 215 319	907 814	1 148 671	73 956	7 530
八 师 Division 8	7 408 244	1 722 382	5 329 956	30 917	15 684
九 师 Division 9	569 607	468 772	89 611	2 116	3 415
十 师 Division 10	877 991	662 840	197 511		7 279
十一师 Division 11	804 039	130 456	102 410	544 757	542
十二师 Division 12	1 016 964	607 210	160 719	14 064	1 340
十三师 Division 13	621 494	531 316	41 420	2 505	4 424
十四师 Division 14	220 936	170 194	44 169	3 525	744
兵团直属 Directly under XPCC	789 639	135 514	294 508	1 759	34 633

单 位 Unit	商品流通业 Commodity Circulation	商 业 Commerce	外 贸 Foreign Trade	物 资 Materials	供 销 Supply and Marketing
总 计 Total	**2 220 832**	**1 945 011**	**13 168**	**4 320**	**258 333**
一 师 Division 1	26 809	26 809			
二 师 Division 2	341 077	341 073		4	
三 师 Division 3	86 852	74 424	4 540		7 889
四 师 Division 4	166 247	136 247	8 228		21 772
五 师 Division 5	23 675	19 692		295	3 688
六 师 Division 6	546 603	426 595			120 007
七 师 Division 7	77 347	77 347			
八 师 Division 8	309 306	296 546			12 759
九 师 Division 9	5 693	4 487			1 206
十 师 Division 10	10 361	10 361			
十一师 Division 11	25 874	25 718		66	89
十二师 Division 12	233 631	233 560	71		
十三师 Division 13	41 828	41 828			
十四师 Division 14	2 305	2 273	32		
兵团直属 Directly under XPCC	323 225	228 051	298	3 955	90 922

6—10 各师国有及国有控股企业年末固定资产净额

Net Value of Year-end Fixed Assets of State-owned and State-holding Enterprises by Division

计量单位:万元 (2017年) (10 000 yuan)

单位 Unit	合计 Total	农业 Agriculture	工业 Industry	建筑业 Construction and Installation	交通运输业 Transportation
总计 Total	**15 473 602**	**5 307 838**	**7 837 547**	**524 117**	**96 522**
一师 Division 1	2 159 004	761 789	1 371 769	7 468	1 362
二师 Division 2	985 387	494 859	183 286	2 576	24 190
三师 Division 3	982 370	462 186	443 721	5 613	9 717
四师 Division 4	770 463	151 852	413 249	66 275	1 064
五师 Division 5	374 899	316 866	29 260	4 013	7 985
六师 Division 6	1 386 998	607 450	277 203	311	6 562
七师 Division 7	1 122 097	237 902	796 352	47 026	3 975
八师 Division 8	4 823 241	876 861	3 704 781	10 558	6 390
九师 Division 9	312 848	271 557	35 619	765	1 889
十师 Division 10	514 817	337 788	165 411		4 691
十一师 Division 11	491 564	48 432	60 271	370 000	327
十二师 Division 12	698 261	369 554	119 601	5 941	656
十三师 Division 13	288 159	223 920	24 732	1 199	3 743
十四师 Division 14	73 683	41 319	27 856	2 257	552
兵团直属 Directly under XPCC	489 811	105 501	184 438	116	23 418

单位 Unit	商品流通业 Commodity Circulation	商业 Commerce	外贸 Foreign Trade	物资 Materials	供销 Supply and Marketing
总计 Total	**1 707 578**	**1 502 187**	**8 573**	**3 302**	**193 516**
一师 Division 1	16 616	16 616			
二师 Division 2	280 476	280 473		3	
三师 Division 3	61 133	52 167	3 765		5 201
四师 Division 4	138 023	121 433	4 662		11 929
五师 Division 5	16 776	14 673		179	1 924
六师 Division 6	495 472	377 684			117 787
七师 Division 7	36 841	36 841			
八师 Division 8	224 652	219 273			5 379
九师 Division 9	3 017	2 400			617
十师 Division 10	6 927	6 927			
十一师 Division 11	12 534	12 474		33	27
十二师 Division 12	202 510	202 449	61		
十三师 Division 13	34 566	34 566			
十四师 Division 14	1 698	1 678	21		
兵团直属 Directly under XPCC	176 338	122 534	65	3 087	50 652

6—11 各师国有及国有控股企业年末流动资产

Year-end Current Assets of State-owned and State-holding Enterprises by Division

计量单位:万元　　(2017 年)　　(10 000 yuan)

单位 Unit	合计 Total	农业 Agriculture	工业 Industry	建筑业 Construction and Installation	交通运输业 Transportation
总计 Total	**33 669 110**	**8 531 545**	**5 674 430**	**6 735 447**	**96 974**
一师 Division 1	2 746 214	830 920	889 359	262 306	5 458
二师 Division 2	1 937 989	768 058	377 388	290 536	3 486
三师 Division 3	2 277 929	966 370	457 706	233 746	27 980
四师 Division 4	2 308 528	655 977	405 676	366 581	4 080
五师 Division 5	744 501	466 027	33 991	52 173	1 548
六师 Division 6	3 009 123	1 002 763	211 677	134 379	3 402
七师 Division 7	2 136 166	659 926	505 991	422 967	1 193
八师 Division 8	5 151 226	1 564 660	1 560 630	785 691	19 806
九师 Division 9	445 542	170 406	111 443	32 804	1 361
十师 Division 10	694 152	280 130	59 913		751
十一师 Division 11	3 966 089	26 845	229 992	3 261 966	4 923
十二师 Division 12	2 673 621	655 379	152 363	512 677	2 327
十三师 Division 13	1 367 831	325 231	214 584	258 948	2 903
十四师 Division 14	245 838	86 850	29 593	59 781	65
兵团直属 Directly under XPCC	3 964 361	72 001	434 126	60 892	17 691

单位 Unit	商品流通业 Commodity Circulation	商业 Commerce	外贸 Foreign Trade	物资 Materials	供销 Suply and Marketing
总计 Total	**12 630 714**	**10 479 738**	**33 809**	**33 230**	**2 083 936**
一师 Division 1	758 170	758 170			
二师 Division 2	498 521	495 685		2 837	
三师 Division 3	592 128	519 855	1 201		71 073
四师 Division 4	876 215	683 493	5 287		187 435
五师 Division 5	190 763	14 663		3 496	172 604
六师 Division 6	1 656 902	1 652 806			4 096
七师 Division 7	546 089	546 089			
八师 Division 8	1 220 439	662 940			557 499
九师 Division 9	129 527	113 263			16 264
十师 Division 10	353 358	353 358			
十一师 Division 11	442 363	438 262		694	3 406
十二师 Division 12	1 350 875	1 347 671	3 203		
十三师 Division 13	566 164	566 164			
十四师 Division 14	69 549	67 290	2 258		
兵团直属 Directly under XPCC	3 379 651	2 260 029	21 860	26 203	1 071 559

6—12 各师国有及国有控股企业年末总资产

Year-end Total Assets of State-owned and State-holding Enterprises by Division

计量单位：万元　　　　(2017 年)　　　　(10 000 yuan)

单　位　Unit	合　计 Total	农　业 Agriculture	工　业 Industry	建筑业 Construction and Installation	交通运输业 Transportation
总　计 Total	**68 338 250**	**20 654 570**	**17 322 504**	**8 673 368**	**298 623**
一　师 Division 1	6 692 522	2 211 993	3 378 020	282 821	6 934
二　师 Division 2	4 463 565	2 249 431	760 841	509 892	33 410
三　师 Division 3	4 516 823	2 418 119	970 356	265 845	83 611
四　师 Division 4	4 120 810	1 181 287	1 060 157	446 670	5 407
五　师 Division 5	1 431 730	1 047 822	101 408	58 857	11 307
六　师 Division 6	5 992 790	2 008 749	581 146	144 035	12 735
七　师 Division 7	4 002 436	1 155 041	1 656 484	531 741	12 550
八　师 Division 8	12 816 158	3 263 935	6 086 253	889 967	29 095
九　师 Division 9	1 030 417	647 258	158 947	33 580	4 291
十　师 Division 10	1 718 300	843 404	284 824		7 141
十一师 Division 11	6 010 344	117 331	478 773	4 444 434	5 671
十二师 Division 12	5 196 638	1 792 129	411 251	549 201	4 404
十三师 Division 13	2 326 126	934 423	340 211	260 855	14 992
十四师 Division 14	990 225	572 212	68 188	63 106	674
兵团直属 Directly under XPCC	7 029 367	211 437	985 645	192 363	66 401

单　位　Unit	商品流通业 Commodity Circulation	商　业 Commerce	外　贸 Foreign Trade	物　资 Materials	供　销 Supply and Marketing
总　计 Total	**21 389 185**	**18 870 634**	**50 928**	**53 798**	**2 413 825**
一　师 Division 1	812 754	812 754			
二　师 Division 2	909 991	907 152		2 840	
三　师 Division 3	778 891	682 500	6 451		89 940
四　师 Division 4	1 427 288	1 188 035	12 025		227 229
五　师 Division 5	212 335	32 712		3 675	175 948
六　师 Division 6	3 246 126	3 102 243			143 883
七　师 Division 7	646 620	646 620			
八　师 Division 8	2 546 907	1 980 312			566 595
九　师 Division 9	186 341	168 563			17 778
十　师 Division 10	582 932	582 932			
十一师 Division 11	964 135	959 952		751	3 433
十二师 Division 12	2 439 653	2 435 731	3 922		
十三师 Division 13	775 645	775 645			
十四师 Division 14	286 045	283 766	2 279		
兵团直属 Directly under XPCC	5 573 522	4 311 718	26 252	46 533	1 189 019

6—13　各师国有及国有控股企业负债总额

Total Liabilities of Stater-holding Enterprises by Division

计量单位:万元　　　　(2017 年)　　　　(10 000 yuan)

单　位　Unit	合　计 Total	农　业 Agriculture	工　业 Industry	建筑业 Construction and Installation	交通运输业 Transportation
总　计　Total	**52 554 088**	**16 657 050**	**12 244 407**	**7 179 721**	**171 672**
一　师　Division 1	5 424 405	1 996 358	2 387 168	252 610	4 047
二　师　Division 2	3 066 739	1 752 055	347 112	414 154	20 241
三　师　Division 3	3 712 437	1 937 610	759 178	231 294	65 010
四　师　Division 4	3 091 256	965 529	792 311	372 149	4 105
五　师　Division 5	1 129 303	790 518	92 629	50 553	10 932
六　师　Division 6	4 804 417	1 666 855	543 412	132 935	10 031
七　师　Division 7	3 342 279	1 036 467	1 256 815	476 420	8 011
八　师　Division 8	9 825 404	2 673 403	4 481 738	708 104	13 092
九　师　Division 9	737 140	473 745	130 040	23 866	2 323
十　师　Division 10	1 348 562	631 251	228 046		8 228
十一师　Division 11	4 626 167	88 999	237 129	3 716 603	7 238
十二师　Division 12	4 064 192	1 310 878	248 707	415 893	2 936
十三师　Division 13	1 695 406	697 398	132 414	236 546	9 387
十四师　Division 14	731 063	469 264	39 377	55 236	637
兵团直属　Directly under XPCC	4 955 317	166 721	568 330	93 358	5 453

单　位　Unit	商品流通业 Commodity Circulation	商　业 Commerce	外　贸 Foreign Trade	物　资 Materials	供　销 Supply and Marketing
总　计　Total	**16 301 238**	**14 076 176**	**38 688**	**39 720**	**2 146 653**
一　师　Division 1	784 223	784 223			
二　师　Division 2	533 177	531 390		1 787	
三　师　Division 3	719 344	636 805	6 646		75 893
四　师　Division 4	957 162	753 488	4 319		199 356
五　师　Division 5	184 672	18 309		3 078	163 285
六　师　Division 6	2 451 185	2 413 324			37 861
七　师　Division 7	564 566	564 566			
八　师　Division 8	1 949 068	1 395 485			553 583
九　师　Division 9	107 166	93 460			13 706
十　师　Division 10	481 035	481 035			
十一师　Division 11	576 198	571 185		1 509	3 504
十二师　Division 12	2 085 777	2 082 225	3 551		
十三师　Division 13	619 662	619 662			
十四师　Division 14	166 548	165 002	1 546		
兵团直属　Directly under XPCC	4 121 455	2 966 017	22 627	33 345	1 099 466

6—14 各师国有及国有控股企业所有者权益总额

Owners' Equity of Stater-holding Enterprises by Division

计量单位:万元　　　　(2017年)　　　　(10 000 yuan)

单位 Unit		合计 Total	农业 Agriculture	工业 Industry	建筑业 Construction and Installation	交通运输业 Transportation
总计	**Total**	**15 784 162**	**3 997 520**	**5 078 097**	**1 493 647**	**126 950**
一师	Division 1	1 268 117	215 636	990 853	30 211	2 886
二师	Division 2	1 396 826	497 376	413 729	95 739	13 169
三师	Division 3	804 386	480 510	211 178	34 551	18 601
四师	Division 4	1 029 553	215 758	267 846	74 522	1 302
五师	Division 5	302 427	257 305	8 780	8 304	375
六师	Division 6	1 188 373	341 894	37 734	11 100	2 703
七师	Division 7	660 157	118 573	399 669	55 321	4 539
八师	Division 8	2 990 754	590 533	1 604 515	181 864	16 003
九师	Division 9	293 277	173 513	28 907	9 714	1 968
十师	Division 10	369 739	212 152	56 777		−1 087
十一师	Division 11	1 384 176	28 332	241 644	727 831	−1 568
十二师	Division 12	1 132 445	481 250	162 544	133 308	1 468
十三师	Division 13	630 719	237 026	207 797	24 308	5 605
十四师	Division 14	259 162	102 948	28 811	7 869	37
兵团直属	Directly under XPCC	2 074 050	44 715	417 314	99 005	60 948

单位 Unit		商品流通业 Commodity Circulation	商业 Commerce	外贸 Foreign Trade	物资 Materials	供销 Supply and Marketing
总计	**Total**	**5 087 948**	**4 794 458**	**12 240**	**14 078**	**267 172**
一师	Division 1	28 531	28 531			
二师	Division 2	376 814	375 762		1 052	
三师	Division 3	59 547	45 695	−195		14 047
四师	Division 4	470 126	434 546	7 706		27 874
五师	Division 5	27 663	14 404		597	12 663
六师	Division 6	794 942	688 920			106 022
七师	Division 7	82 054	82 054			
八师	Division 8	597 840	584 827			13 012
九师	Division 9	79 175	75 103			4 072
十师	Division 10	101 897	101 897			
十一师	Division 11	387 937	388 767		−758	−71
十二师	Division 12	353 876	353 505	370		
十三师	Division 13	155 983	155 983			
十四师	Division 14	119 497	118 764	733		
兵团直属	Directly under XPCC	1 452 067	1 345 701	3 625	13 187	89 553

6－15 历年国有及国有控股企业主营业务收入

Main Business Revenue of State-owned and State-holding Enterprises over the Years

计量单位：万元 (10 000 yuan)

年 份 Year	合 计 Total	农 业 Agriculture	工 业 Industry	建筑业 Construction and Installation	交通运输业 Transportation	商品流通业 Commodity Circulation
1979	171 816	90 388	29 475	5 962	6 744	39 247
1980	200 547	109 296	34 204	4 128	7 059	45 860
1981	218 198	121 538	35 709	6 169	6 414	48 341
1982	257 817	140 783	38 153	8 009	7 410	63 462
1983	305 120	166 004	46 752	14 016	8 185	70 163
1984	355 300	160 637	55 127	27 729	9 476	102 331
1985	306 995	123 211	57 700	19 331	9 107	97 646
1986	396 858	142 933	73 392	34 386	10 640	135 507
1987	557 759	247 556	90 064	44 956	13 087	162 096
1988	722 603	315 754	117 925	53 683	14 566	220 675
1989	792 980	359 030	127 402	56 751	16 786	233 191
1990	991 592	498 526	142 788	58 576	18 841	272 861
1991	1 398 548	666 837	168 097	68 467	26 961	468 186
1992	1 622 073	688 691	196 919	90 296	28 933	617 234
1993	2 167 075	920 930	286 103	137 341	30 560	792 141
1994	2 083 751	966 299	313 336	148 476	32 565	623 145
1995	2 978 017	1 354 316	363 080	172 991	31 875	1 055 755
1996	3 486 683	1 388 985	392 145	186 225	30 258	1 489 040
1997	3 611 481	1 565 781	389 380	202 006	34 438	1 419 876
1998	3 744 763	1 587 475	432 385	268 733	32 047	1 424 123
1999	3 458 441	1 351 546	443 893	284 729	25 869	1 352 404
2000	3 791 107	1 514 993	484 737	350 986	21 388	1 419 003
2001	3 337 440	1 223 521	434 814	376 807	16 241	1 286 057
2002	3 758 252	1 422 510	475 300	446 961	16 111	1 397 370
2003	4 441 033	1 671 487	524 604	490 699	14 691	1 739 552
2004	5 198 307	1 619 767	649 885	522 813	10 739	2 395 103
2005	6 718 567	2 005 357	722 023	493 342	10 914	3 486 931
2006	7 390 183	2 254 430	777 327	565 145	12 521	3 780 760
2007	9 069 015	2 609 118	1 171 507	775 284	12 228	4 500 878
2008	9 616 740	2 711 233	1 245 247	930 883	14 867	4 714 510
2009	10 625 814	2 664 132	1 726 262	1 176 041	13 927	5 045 452
2010	10 456 802	3 188 776	2 403 822	1 512 417	19 472	3 332 315
2011	13 182 558	3 676 385	3 000 298	2 355 278	16 727	4 133 870
2012	17 041 793	4 810 707	3 411 773	3 259 931	23 535	5 535 848
2013	23 195 846	5 276 235	3 890 076	4 477 247	38 005	9 514 282
2014	20 917 450	5 180 956	4 014 632	5 400 722	45 279	6 275 861
2015	21 650 968	5 203 141	4 146 194	5 488 807	69 912	6 742 915
2016	22 645 918	5 142 339	4 217 387	5 383 701	78 545	7 823 945
2017	24 457 513	4 847 159	4 706 745	5 793 024	106 363	9 004 221

6—16 各师国有及国有控股企业主营业务收入

Main Business Net Income of State-owned and State-holding Enterprises by Division

计量单位:万元 (2017年) (10 000 yuan)

单位 Unit	合计 Total	农业 Agriculture	工业 Industry	建筑业 Construction and Installation	交通运输业 Transportation
总计 Total	**24 457 513**	**4 847 159**	**4 706 745**	**5 793 024**	**106 363**
一师 Division 1	1 673 129	387 218	503 946	264 623	6 806
二师 Division 2	992 615	348 459	209 022	106 298	4 726
三师 Division 3	1 400 932	389 313	234 239	297 542	7 376
四师 Division 4	1 422 218	274 763	409 533	438 678	5 942
五师 Division 5	674 875	338 935	35 930	82 802	2 382
六师 Division 6	840 937	235 455	142 175	88 688	1 488
七师 Division 7	1 667 569	543 901	448 267	346 809	3 010
八师 Division 8	4 609 724	1 373 298	1 607 249	352 831	61 672
九师 Division 9	311 857	175 652	57 576	53 694	2 543
十师 Division 10	284 984	212 690	46 453		1 560
十一师 Division 11	3 945 367	120 849	207 362	3 168 565	1 332
十二师 Division 12	1 322 029	250 824	212 396	338 559	206
十三师 Division 13	487 157	135 487	46 353	138 573	2 080
十四师 Division 14	150 234	16 177	16 339	103 675	241
兵团直属 Directly under XPCC	4 673 885	44 139	529 905	11 686	5 000

单位 Unit	商品流通业 Commodity Circulation	商业 Commerce	外贸 Foreign Trade	物资 Materials	供销 Supply and Marketing
总计 Total	**9 004 221**	**5 404 579**	**44 140**	**16 966**	**3 538 537**
一师 Division 1	510 536	510 536			
二师 Division 2	324 110	321 452		2 659	
三师 Division 3	472 462	363 950	418		108 094
四师 Division 4	293 302	106 275	2 166		184 861
五师 Division 5	214 826	19 846		8 077	186 904
六师 Division 6	373 131	364 249			8 881
七师 Division 7	325 582	325 582			
八师 Division 8	1 214 673	726 816			487 857
九师 Division 9	22 392	6 674			15 718
十师 Division 10	24 281	24 281			
十一师 Division 11	447 259	446 839			421
十二师 Division 12	520 044	518 767	1 277		
十三师 Division 13	164 664	164 664			
十四师 Division 14	13 802	7 158	6 644		
兵团直属 Directly under XPCC	4 083 154	1 497 489	33 634	6 230	2 545 801

6—17 历年国有及国有控股企业应缴税金

Payable Taxes of State-owned and State-holding Enterprises over the Years

计量单位:万元 (10 000 yuan)

年份 Year	合计 Total	农业 Agriculture	工业 Industry	建筑业 Construction and Installation	交通运输业 Transportation	商品流通企业 Commodity Circulation
1979	4 971	1 966	2 724		186	95
1980	5 405	1 848	3 153	96	199	109
1981	5 444	1 793	3 341		182	128
1982	6 154	2 400	3 401		211	142
1983	7 608	3 183	3 860	118	241	206
1984	8 120	2 796	4 536	158	282	348
1985	8 756	2 874	4 990	105	294	493
1986	10 954	2 636	6 429	122	333	1 434
1987	13 971	4 489	7 151	197	419	1 715
1988	19 467	6 589	9 115	828	497	2 438
1989	26 780	8 453	13 869	1 137	561	2 760
1990	35 089	10 541	18 865	1 484	781	3 418
1991	42 036	11 996	21 571	2 012	1 113	5 344
1992	50 865	14 280	25 774	2 737	1 174	6 900
1993	54 347	16 670	20 975	3 762	1 268	11 672
1994	54 164	22 478	26 725	4 345	1 254	—638
1995	80 977	24 338	30 293	6 278	1 209	18 859
1996	93 801	25 818	29 645	6 071	1 402	30 865
1997	93 719	29 887	33 812	6 132	1 319	22 569
1998	103 827	28 847	36 745	7 576	1 085	29 574
1999	117 382	27 849	40 663	8 501	1 164	39 205
2000	90 695	25 730	39 957	11 076	1 010	12 922
2001	86 890	25 959	33 757	10 966	728	15 480
2002	101 002	27 462	36 193	14 011	606	22 730
2003	104 083	22 220	36 387	15 485	540	29 451
2004	148 227	19 212	46 475	16 378	740	65 422
2005	241 672	14 961	64 583	16 962	879	144 287
2006	215 054	19 168	70 391	20 861	686	103 948
2007	281 330	17 200	97 847	29 511	570	136 202
2008	336 312	21 784	123 859	34 106	982	155 581
2009	431 143	31 418	147 954	51 092	1 353	199 326
2010	349 777	32 158	218 946	66 463	1 634	30 576
2011	595 329	41 529	379 457	100 983	1 755	71 605
2012	643 394	61 354	290 557	144 214	2 391	144 878
2013	739 115	63 125	329 115	189 960	2 561	154 354
2014	787 607	78 556	319 586	212 740	4 268	172 457
2015	794 924	74 552	279 689	220 611	6 666	213 405
2016	910 083	90 528	381 758	260 597	4 600	172 599
2017	887 791	93 113	345 740	282 117	4 117	162 704

6—18 各师国有及国有控股企业营业税金及附加

Business Tax and Extra Charges of State-owned and State-holding Enterprises by Division

计量单位:万元　　(2017 年)　　(10 000 yuan)

单 位 Unit	合 计 Total	农 业 Agriculture	工 业 Industry	建筑业 Construction and Installation	交通运输业 Transportation
总 计 Total	**161 286**	**12 240**	**80 041**	**39 271**	**749**
一 师 Division 1	10 581	1 013	7 485	1 489	33
二 师 Division 2	5 221	633	2 872	530	46
三 师 Division 3	3 521	119	546	2 049	288
四 师 Division 4	32 517	520	29 435	2 143	15
五 师 Division 5	1 089	130	78	800	49
六 师 Division 6	7 499	296	2 652	1 103	7
七 师 Division 7	3 436	116	1 543	1 187	9
八 师 Division 8	35 140	1 313	29 975	2 310	166
九 师 Division 9	400	2	119	175	74
十 师 Division 10	3 002	2 705	166		8
十一师 Division 11	18 861		963	17 220	
十二师 Division 12	22 538	5 023	1 728	8 484	1
十三师 Division 13	1 445	196	423	583	10
十四师 Division 14	746	3	86	630	1
兵团直属 Directly under XPCC	15 289	171	1 970	567	40

单 位 Unit	商品流通业 Commodity Circulation	商 业 Commerce	外 贸 Foreign Trade	物 资 Materials	供 销 Supply and Marketing
总 计 Total	**28 985**	**28 204**	**56**	**22**	**704**
一 师 Division 1	560	560			
二 师 Division 2	1 140	1 135		5	
三 师 Division 3	519	455			64
四 师 Division 4	403	384	9		10
五 师 Division 5	33	1		6	26
六 师 Division 6	3 441	3 273			168
七 师 Division 7	581	581			
八 师 Division 8	1 377	1 377			
九 师 Division 9	31	29			2
十 师 Division 10	122	122			
十一师 Division 11	677	676			1
十二师 Division 12	7 302	7 301	1		
十三师 Division 13	233	233			
十四师 Division 14	26	15	12		
兵团直属 Directly under XPCC	12 541	12 063	34	11	433

6—19 各师国有及国有控股企业应缴税金

Payable Taxes of State-owned and State-holding Enterprises by Division

计量单位:万元 (2017 年) (10 000 yuan)

指标	Item	合计 Total	一师 Division 1	二师 Division 2	三师 Division 3	四师 Division 4	五师 Division 5	六师 Division 6	七师 Division 7
本年应缴税金总计	**Total Payable Taxes in This Year**	**887 791**	**102 129**	**29 677**	**10 374**	**96 888**	**9 126**	**46 723**	**26 546**
增值税	Value Added Tax	460 225	62 832	16 389	—6 470	39 071	5 538	23 236	14 759
消费税	Consumption Tax	35 377	542	22	1	25 633	4	53	15
资源税	Resource Tax	8 521	2 344	1 746		140		1 881	597
城市维护建设税	Urban Maintenance and Development Tax	28 650	2 232	811	803	1 846	241	940	687
关税	Tariff	8 221				6		1 277	
# 本年已交进口关税	Import Tariff	7 568				3		1 277	
本年已交出口关税	Export Tariff	653				3			
企业所得税	Enterprise Income Tax	188 652	16 970	3 856	8 783	17 960	1 801	9 717	5 655
教育费附加	Additional Education fee	24 396	1 946	745	600	3 079	143	1 248	696
其他各税	Others	133 749	15 262	6 109	6 656	9 153	1 399	8 372	4 136

指标	Item	八师 Division 8	九师 Division 9	十师 Division 10	十一师 Division 11	十二师 Division 12	十三师 Division 13	十四师 Division 14	兵团直属 Directly under XPCC
本年应缴税金总计	**Total Payable Taxes in This Year**	**225 064**	**6 693**	**17 427**	**142 661**	**80 626**	**13 703**	**5 875**	**74 279**
增值税	Value Added Tax	123 490	2 891	11 367	100 662	32 317	8 140	3 205	22 797
消费税	Consumption Tax	6		886	5	40			8 170
资源税	Resource Tax	1 171			200	94	329	19	1
城市维护建设税	Urban Maintenance and Development Tax	10 270	155	615	5 254	2 193	450	142	2 009
关税	Tariff		1 262		317			128	5 232
# 本年已交进口关税	Import Tariff		631		298			128	5 232
本年已交出口关税	Export Tariff		631		19				
企业所得税	Enterprise Income Tax	58 398	690	2 525	11 645	22 055	3 703	1 251	23 643
教育费附加	Additional Education fee	7 531	152	479	4 227	1 536	375	109	1 530
其他各税	Others	24 198	1 543	1 555	20 351	22 391	705	1 021	10 898

6—20 各师国有及国有控股企业管理费用支出

计量单位:万元 (2017年)

指标	Item	合计 Total	一师 Division 1	二师 Division 2	三师 Division 3	四师 Division 4	五师 Division 5
管理费用	**Administration Expenses**	**993 248**	**102 966**	**68 321**	**74 541**	**89 643**	**29 392**
职工薪酬	Wages	462 405	44 982	30 118	30 543	49 090	9 555
离退休人员医疗费补助	Medical Treatment Fee Subsidy for Retirees	16 157	2 103	2 925	139	637	541
业务招待费	Business Reception Fee	11 660	1 003	953	611	942	413
印花税	Stamp Taxes	3 056	486	214	370	142	85
土地使用税	Land Use Taxes	4 200	99	544	552	546	55
房产税	House Property Taxes	2 639	23	118	386	248	49
车船使用税	Car and Ship Use Taxes	1 580	19	1 499	5	7	3
坏账损失	Bad Loan Loss	4 044	76	221	42	4	3 100
# 提取的坏帐准备	Bad Loan Preparation Withdrawn	1 250	28	149		30	
技术开发费	Technique Development Fee	3 643	637	153	309	23	
技术转让费	Techigue Transfer Fee	98	3	0			
土地使用费	Land Use Fee	2 242	506	470	158	7	39
排污费	Pollution Discharge Fee	1 456	129	273	22	422	3
绿化费	Greening Fee	5 115	40	1 052	396	314	17
折旧费	Depreciation	163 064	33 173	10 826	16 347	10 766	5 055
修理费	Repairing	7 364	490	857	495	767	257
物料消耗	Material Depletion	5 740	480	430	461	836	136
低值易耗品摊销	Low Value Easy Consumables Apportion	1 350	234	20	226	35	7
住房公积金	Housing Provident Fund	17 232	813	1 172	1 792	2 382	921
递延资产摊销	Deferred Assets Apportion	19 434	1 748	1 350	8 477	543	2 331
无形资产摊销	Intangible Assets Apportion	12 071	3 812	536	428	479	295
差旅费	Public Errand Fee	17 161	1 501	1 201	1 746	1 279	462
办公费	Administrative Expenses	16 359	998	925	1 708	766	335
存货盘亏、毁废(减盘盈)	Inventory, Defacement (InventoryOverage Reduction)	−233	120	394	355	3	
其他	Others	214 868	9 489	12 071	8 975	19 404	5 733

Expenditures on Administration Expenses of State-owned and State-holding Enterprises by Division

(10 000 yuan)

六 师 Division 6	七 师 Division 7	八 师 Division 8	九 师 Division 9	十 师 Division 10	十一师 Division 11	十二师 Division 12	十三师 Division 13	十四师 Division 14	兵团直属 Directly under XPCC
95 531	**50 135**	**75 144**	**25 947**	**32 058**	**106 270**	**90 055**	**35 777**	**6 560**	**110 910**
44 572	23 449	25 274	11 774	15 152	61 220	41 557	20 961	3 027	51 130
85	1 467	6 946	821	75	166	83	98	65	5
1 109	484	373	387	218	2 393	857	180	68	1 667
178	167	31	75	70	215	251	30	30	712
72	287	231	330	177	235	564	99	30	378
10	417	79	172	212	138	502	74	8	203
6	2	3	4	3	4	9	7	0	8
341			18		121	34	82	5	
		543	16		155	317	8	4	
20	127	82	1		736	468			1 086
		41			10	1			43
	57	827	27	25	129		−3		
44	149	50	181	2	26	93	33		29
450	547	1 728	121	85	163	95	51	49	8
17 374	5 655	12 384	2 737	7 670	7 039	16 720	6 373	526	10 418
744	242	459	470	63	604	702	125	41	1 049
356	195	1 678	171	108	392	201	228	49	20
140	62	148	37	7	283	71	20	9	50
807	1 090	337	834	1 056	3 030	1 331	529	180	960
1 703	1	1 935		40	96	506	637	30	38
995	610	17	65	60	521	2 061	161	143	1 887
1 393	774	531	561	382	3 936	723	335	167	2 170
889	489	810	508	321	3 573	1 597	978	119	2 343
2 182	−108	1 139	0	1	20	65	80		−4 485
22 061	13 970	19 497	6 653	6 331	21 220	21 563	4 699	2 014	41 189

6—21 各师国有及国有控股企业营业外收入及营业外支出

计量单位:万元　　(2017 年)

指　　标	Item	合　计 Total	一　师 Division 1	二　师 Division 2	三　师 Division 3	四　师 Division 4	五　师 Division 5
营业外收入	**Extra-Business Revenue**	**1 147 696**	**90 920**	**69 381**	**246 858**	**118 434**	**37 189**
处理固定资产净收益	Net Gains of Fixed Assets Disposal	31 771	22 526	202	11	98	
固定资产盘盈	Inventory Losses of Fixed Assets	750	67		15		
教育费附加返还款	Repyament of Enucation Surtax	1 558	1 090	5		4	
罚款收入	Penalty Income	5 314	611	569	398	168	338
物资现金溢余收入	Surplus Income of Materials and Cash	2 685	990	127		69	7
其他社会性收入	Other Social Income	707 828	21 954	56 646	169 905	77 372	25 529
其　他	Others	397 790	43 682	11 832	76 529	40 723	11 314
营业外支出	**Extra-Business Expenditures**	**1 091 778**	**63 069**	**68 350**	**215 719**	**125 239**	**42 742**
处理固定资产净损失	Net Losses of Fixed Assets Disposal	17 548	2 115	270	475	40	
固定资产盘亏	Inventory Losses of Fixed Assets	43		26		0	
非常损失	Abnormal Losses	2 274	8	14		261	8
赔偿金、违约金	Solatium and Penalty	7 649	614	164	318	695	25
公益性捐赠支出	Public Welfare Donation Expenditure	2 098	114	106		79	1
中小学校经费	Fund for Primary and Secondary Schools	189 866	4 942	11 559	26 675	30 259	14 194
技工学校经费	Fund for Technical Schools						
安置老残干部	Settlement Allowance of Veteran and Disabled Cadres	320	87	7			8
专职政法人员经费	Fund for Full-Time Political-Legal Functionaries	4 802	897	112	471	1 476	88
边防民兵值勤经费	Fund on Duty for Frontier Defence Militia	30 633	2 785	2 963	2 566	7 218	2 547
防汛抢险支出	Expenditure For Flood and Emergency Control	458			6	58	
政府行政经费	Governmental Administration Fund	58 173	1 536	5 711	6 521	4 955	3 279
其他社会性支出	Other Social Expenditure	644 350	29 441	45 708	139 662	48 236	16 505
其　他	Others	133 563	20 530	1 708	39 027	31 962	6 087

Extra-Business Revenue and Extra-Business Expenditures of State-holding Enterprises by Division

(10 000 yuan)

六　师 Division 6	七　师 Division 7	八　师 Division 8	九　师 Division 9	十　师 Division 10	十一师 Division 11	十二师 Division 12	十三师 Division 13	十四师 Division 14	兵团直属 Directly under XPCC
162 350	**78 159**	**16 174**	**42 239**	**87 963**	**25 737**	**78 582**	**60 521**	**17 185**	**16 005**
719	1 201	444	35	1 180	1 008	2 529	202	1 376	241
237	4		2			38	6	381	
14	147	4			257	38			
287	689	313	42	261	710	463	393	33	39
	239		16		20	1 218			
89 443	53 219	9 030	25 044	57 767	10 742	51 396	47 482	12 129	169
71 650	22 660	6 383	17 101	28 755	13 001	22 900	12 437	3 266	15 556
117 249	**117 582**	**73 286**	**30 102**	**70 685**	**19 471**	**73 657**	**56 121**	**14 961**	**3 546**
1 499	1 671	2 625	293	524	441	6 155	518		923
17									
380	1 090	1	37	92	212	3	43		125
728	643	762	18	539	2 644	285	138	2	76
195	17	6	18	56	24	11	1 259	12	200
33 766	11 607	27 156	5 320	2 212		13 031	5 797	3 348	
	3	210	6						
324	45	1 293	15			48	34		
4 646	1 495	1 183	743	1 607	12	2 057	355	457	
271		9	114						
8 578	1 180	9 242	536	3 997		6 155	6 256	227	
60 995	86 383	30 799	21 045	60 105	12 743	42 796	40 601	9 291	41
5 852	13 449		1 958	1 553	3 395	3 115	1 122	1 624	2 182

6—22 各师国有及国有控股企业利润总额

Profit Amount of State-owned and State-holding Enterprises by Division

计量单位：万元 (2017 年) (10 000 yuan)

单位 Unit	合计 Total	农业 Agriculture	工业 Industry	建筑业 Construction and Installation	交通运输业 Transportation
总计 Total	**585 320**	**39 673**	**250 252**	**143 995**	**−1 126**
一师 Division 1	−28 404	−23 322	−21 549	9 381	−213
二师 Division 2	33 250	7 137	13 626	1 088	256
三师 Division 3	38 389	17 056	−4 593	20 682	535
四师 Division 4	56 852	−1 821	43 006	7 729	67
五师 Division 5	12 832	9 076	−800	2 506	−821
六师 Division 6	−17 423	−22 968	−14 324	1 691	271
七师 Division 7	41 206	29 822	1 552	6 190	160
八师 Division 8	195 914	15 855	180 100	19 387	−5
九师 Division 9	2 545	−601	−1 350	1 503	281
十师 Division 10	3 356	6 587	−4 385		−281
十一师 Division 11	57 893	684	3 433	45 643	42
十二师 Division 12	14 836	9 680	10 218	11 704	73
十三师 Division 13	19 145	2 061	652	5 929	115
十四师 Division 14	1 857	−2 397	1 318	2 167	−32
兵团直属 Directly under XPCC	153 072	−7 176	43 348	8 395	−1 573

单位 Unit	商品流通业 Commodity Circulation	商业 Commerce	外贸 Foreign Trade	物资 Materials	供销 Supply and Marketing
总计 Total	**152 526**	**138 905**	**−1 129**	**529**	**14 222**
一师 Division 1	7 299	7 299			
二师 Division 2	11 143	11 071		72	
三师 Division 3	4 710	4 074	−200		837
四师 Division 4	7 871	5 944	603		1 324
五师 Division 5	2 870	710		267	1 893
六师 Division 6	17 907	17 168			739
七师 Division 7	3 482	3 482			
八师 Division 8	−19 422	−20 403			981
九师 Division 9	2 711	2 603			108
十师 Division 10	1 435	1 435			
十一师 Division 11	8 091	8 090			1
十二师 Division 12	−16 840	−14 971	−1 868		
十三师 Division 13	10 389	10 389			
十四师 Division 14	802	686	115		
兵团直属 Directly under XPCC	110 077	101 327	222	190	8 339

2018
BING TUAN

第七篇
价格指数
Chapter 7 Price Indices

简要说明

一、本篇资料主要内容

本篇资料反映生产、流通、消费与投资、建设施工环节的价格变动趋势和变动幅度，主要包括1978年以来各种价格指数、居民消费价格指数、商品零售价格指数、农业生产资料价格指数、工业品出厂价格指数、原材料、燃料、动力购进价格指数、固定资产投资价格指数等。

二、本篇资料来源

本篇资料由国家统计局新疆调查总队、国家统计局兵团调查总队产业调查处、农业调查处整理提供。

Brief Introduction

1. Main Contents

Data in this chapter show the changing trends and the change rates in the prices of production, circulation, consumption, investment, construction, including mainly general price indices, consumer price indices, retail price indices, price indices of means for agricultural production, products, producer price indices for industrial products, purchasing price indices for raw materials, fuel, and power, price indices for investment in fixed assets since 1978.

2. Sources of Data

Data in this chapter are provided and compiled by the Survey Office of Xinjiang and by Industrial Survey Section and Agriculture Survey Section of the Survey Office of XPCC of National Bureau of Statistics of China.

7－1 历年各种价格指数

General Price Indices over the Years

年份 Year	居民消费价格指数 Consumers Price Index	城市 Urban Areas	农村 Rural Areas	商品零售价格指数 Retail Price Index for Commodities
上年＝100 **Preceding year＝100**				
1978	101.2	101.4	100.3	101.4
1980	102.8	104.1	102.0	104.2
1985	107.8	109.5	106.4	108.1
1990	105.0	104.5	105.9	104.1
1995	119.7	118.4	122.5	116.7
1996	110.5	110.4	110.6	108.8
1997	103.7	103.5	103.9	101.8
1998	100.2	99.9	100.8	99.7
1999	97.4	97.7	96.8	96.2
2000	99.4	100.1	97.6	98.3
2001	104.0	104.0	103.8	102.5
2002	99.4	98.9	100.9	97.9
2003	100.4	100.5	100.2	99.2
2004	102.7	102.1	104.5	100.7
2005	100.7	100.6	101.2	99.4
2006	101.3	101.0	102.0	101.8
2007	105.5	104.6	107.2	105.1
2008	108.1	107.3	109.5	108.5
2009	100.7	100.2	102.0	100.4
2010	104.3	103.6	105.8	104.6
2011	105.9	105.5	106.8	105.1
2012	103.8	103.4	104.7	103.3
2013	103.9	103.8	104.1	103.3
2014	102.1	102.3	101.7	101.7
2015	100.6	100.5	100.6	99.6
2016	101.4	101.4	101.3	100.5
2017	102.3	102.3	102.4	100.5
1978 年＝100				
1978	100.0	100.0	100.0	100.0
1980	105.1	106.6	103.8	107.8
1985	120.9	125.6	117.9	124.2
1990	194.3	206.0	184.0	197.6
1995	392.7	422.7	364.2	381.0
1996	433.9	466.7	402.9	414.6
1997	450.0	483.0	418.6	422.0
1998	450.9	482.5	421.9	420.8
1999	439.2	471.4	408.4	404.8
2000	436.5	471.9	398.6	397.9
2001	454.0	490.8	413.8	407.8
2002	451.3	485.4	417.5	399.3
2003	453.1	487.8	418.3	396.1
2004	465.3	498.1	437.1	398.9
2005	468.6	501.1	442.3	396.5
2006	474.7	506.1	451.1	403.6
2007	500.8	529.4	483.6	424.2
2008	541.4	568.0	529.5	460.3
2009	545.2	569.1	540.1	462.1
2010	568.6	589.6	571.4	483.4
2011	602.1	622.0	610.3	508.1
2012	625.0	643.1	639.0	524.9
2013	649.7	667.7	665.6	541.9
2014	663.4	683.0	677.2	551.1
2015	667.4	686.4	681.3	548.9
2016	676.7	696.0	690.2	551.6
2017	692.4	711.9	706.6	554.4

7—2 居民消费价格分类指数

Consumer Price Indices by Category

（上年＝100） （2017 年） (preceding year＝100)

指　　标	Item	全　区 Province	城　市 Urban Areas	农　村 Rural Areas
居民消费价格指数	**General Consumer Price Index**	**102.2**	**102.4**	**101.8**
服务价格指数	**Service Price Index**	**103.5**	**103.7**	**103.0**
食品烟酒	**Food、Alcohol and Tobacco**	**102.1**	**102.7**	**100.9**
食　品	Food	100.8	100.8	100.7
粮　食	Grain	100.7	101.6	99.9
大　米	Rice	99.9	100.9	98.7
面　粉	Flour	100.9	102.3	99.9
其他粮食	Others Grain	101.3	101.5	101.2
粮食制品	Grain Products	101.5	101.8	101.2
薯　类	Tubers	93.9	94.2	93.2
豆　类	Bean	102.2	102.7	101.2
食用油	Oil	99.5	100.0	99.0
菜	Vegetables	96.0	96.4	95.2
鲜　菜	Fresh Vegetables	95.2	95.7	94.2
畜肉类	Livestock Meat	103.4	104.1	102.4
猪　肉	Pork	87.6	88.5	86.2
牛　肉	Beef	108.7	109.3	107.8
羊　肉	Mutton	111.5	113.0	109.5
禽肉类	Meat Poultry and Their Products	100.1	99.5	101.1
鸡	Chicken	100.1	99.5	101.1
水产品	Aquatic Products	103.4	103.1	104.2
蛋　类	Eggs	100.0	100.2	99.7
鸡　蛋	Egg	100.0	100.2	99.6
奶　类	Dairy	99.4	99.4	99.3
鲜　奶	Milk	99.3	99.3	99.2
干鲜瓜果	Dried and Fresh Melons and Fruits	102.2	100.3	106.7
鲜瓜果	Fresh Fruits	103.7	101.2	109.6
糖果糕点类	Carbohydrate Products and Cakes	101.3	100.9	102.3
食　糖	Sugar	105.9	103.8	109.8
糖　果	Candy	100.0	100.0	99.9
糕　点	Cakes	101.6	101.2	102.5
其他糖果糕点	Others	99.9	99.9	100.0
调味品	Flavoring	101.4	102.0	100.3
食用盐	Edible Salt	100.4	100.6	100.0
酱　油	Soy Sauce	102.5	103.1	101.3
食　醋	Vinega	101.5	102.4	99.9
其他食品类	Other Food	100.0	100.0	99.9
方便食品	Instant Food	98.4	98.0	99.5
茶及饮料	Tea and Beverages	100.8	101.3	100.2
茶　叶	Tea	100.3	101.1	99.3

7—2 续表 1　Continued

（上年=100）　　（2017 年）　　（preceding year=100）

指　　标	Item	全　区 Province	城　市 Urban Areas	农　村 Rural Areas
烟　酒	Tobacco	101.4	101.7	101.0
烟　草	Liquor	100.1	100.0	100.1
酒　类	Articles	103.1	103.6	102.1
白　酒	Spirit	103.8	104.2	103.1
葡萄酒	Wine	102.7	103.2	101.8
啤　酒	Beer	100.2	100.8	99.1
在外餐饮	Catering Trade	106.6	107.6	101.9
正　餐	Dinner	100.9	100.9	100.3
快　餐	Fast Food	105.0	105.9	101.7
地方小吃	Local Snack	103.9	103.8	104.2
衣　着	**Clothing**	**101.3**	**100.9**	**102.2**
服　装	Garments	100.8	100.4	101.7
男式服装	Men's Wear	100.3	100.0	101.2
女式服装	Women's Wear	100.8	100.4	101.6
儿童服装	Childern's Wear	102.1	101.5	103.3
服装材料	Clothing Material	103.0	102.2	104.0
其他衣着及配件	Others	100.3	99.1	103.3
衣着加工服务费	Clothing Processing	105.4	105.7	104.7
鞋　类	Footwear	102.9	102.7	103.3
鞋	Shoes	101.7	101.2	102.7
鞋类加工服务	Footwear Processing Service	110.8	112.6	106.9
居　住	**Residence**	**100.4**	**100.2**	**100.8**
租赁房房租	Rental Housing Rent	102.4	102.3	103.3
公房房租	Public	107.1	108.1	99.9
私房房租	Private	101.0	100.6	104.3
住房保养维修及管理	Housing Maintenance and Management	100.8	100.7	101.2
住房装潢材料	Housing Decoration Material	100.3	99.8	101.4
物业管理费	Property Fee	103.1	102.8	103.8
住房装潢维修	Decoration Maintenance	101.1	101.6	99.9
水、电、燃料	Water, Electricity and Fuels	99.8	99.8	99.8
水	Water	103.2	103.8	102.0
电	Electricity	97.8	97.3	98.8
燃　气	Gas	100.1	100.2	99.9
取暖费	Heating Fee	100.1	100.1	100.0
其他燃料	Others	101.3	102.4	99.8
自有住房	Own Housing	100.4	100.0	101.3
生活用品及服务	**Daily Necessities and Service**	**101.5**	**101.7**	**100.9**
家具及室内装饰品	Furniture and Interior Decorations	101.0	100.8	101.5
家　具	Furniture	101.3	100.9	102.0
室内装饰品	Interior Decorations	99.5	100.2	97.7
家用器具	Household Appliances	100.9	101.7	99.4
大型家用器具	Large Household Appliance	100.9	101.9	99.0
小家电	Small Home Appliance	101.0	100.9	101.0

7—2 续表 2　Continued

（上年=100）　　（2017 年）　　（preceding year=100）

指　　标	Item	全　区 Province	城　市 Urban Areas	农　村 Rural Areas
家用纺织品	Home Textiles	100.7	100.4	101.3
床上用品	Bed Articles	98.2	97.0	100.7
窗帘门帘	Window and Door Curtain	107.2	108.6	103.9
其他家用纺织品	Others	100.6	101.0	99.8
家庭日用杂品	Daily Use Household Articles	100.3	100.2	100.5
洗涤卫生用品	Washing Sanitary Articles	100.7	101.3	99.8
厨具餐具茶具	Kitchenware、Tableware、Tea Set	100.4	100.3	100.7
家用手工工具	Hand Tools for Household Use	100.9	101.4	99.8
其他家庭日用杂品	Others	100.0	99.5	100.9
个人护理用品	Personal Care Articles	100.6	100.6	100.8
化妆品	Cosmetics	100.4	100.2	100.9
其他护理用品类	Others	100.9	101.0	100.6
家庭服务	Domestic Service	110.7	112.2	105.8
交通和通信	**Transportation and Communication**	**100.8**	**100.5**	**101.5**
交　通	Transportation	101.3	100.8	102.4
交通工具	Vehicle	98.4	97.9	99.4
小型汽车	Compact Car	98.0	97.7	99.0
电动自行车	Electric Bicycle	100.3	99.4	101.0
自行车	Bicycle	101.0	101.6	100.1
交通工具用燃料	Fuel for Vehicles	110.4	110.0	111.1
汽　油	Gasoline	112.0	111.9	112.2
柴　油	Diesel Oil	113.0	112.9	113.0
交通工具使用和维修	Vehicle Use and Maintenance	100.6	100.6	100.8
交通费	Traffic Expense	98.7	97.7	100.9
通　信	Communication	99.7	99.8	99.6
通信工具	Communication Tools	97.9	98.0	97.6
通信服务	Communication Service	100.3	100.2	100.5
邮递服务	Postal Service	100.7	101.3	99.8
教育文化和娱乐	**Education, Culture and Recreation**	**102.7**	**103.5**	**100.8**
教　育	Education	103.1	104.3	100.3
教育用品	Educational Supplies	100.6	99.7	102.6
教育服务	Educational Service	103.3	104.6	100.2
文化娱乐	Cultural and Recreational	101.9	101.9	101.9
文娱耐用消费品	Durable Consumer Goods for Recreationl Use	99.0	98.8	99.7
其他文娱用品	Others	100.8	100.7	101.0
文化娱乐服务	Cultural and Recreational services	100.7	101.0	99.9
电影票	Cinema Ticket	100.0	100.0	99.8
景点门票	Scenic Spot Ticket	100.7	101.0	100.0
有线电视	Cable TV	101.1	101.6	99.8
健身活动	Fitness Activities	102.5	102.8	101.5
旅　游	Touristry	107.9	107.7	108.4
旅行社收费	Travel Service Charges	104.1	106.0	99.3
其他旅游	Others	111.8	109.6	116.0

7—2 续表 3　Continued

（上年=100）　　（2017 年）　　（preceding year=100）

指　　标	Item	全　区 Province	城　市 Urban Areas	农　村 Rural Areas
医疗保健	**Medicine**	**109.6**	**111.1**	**107.3**
药品及医疗器具	Medicine and Medical Appliances	103.3	104.0	102.3
中　药	Chinese Medicine	103.6	104.6	102.2
西　药	Western Medicine	104.0	105.1	102.5
滋补保健品	Nourishing Health Products	100.4	99.7	101.4
医疗卫生器具	Medical Appliance	100.8	100.2	102.0
保健器具	Constitutional Appliances	100.5	100.2	100.8
医疗服务	Medical Service	112.5	114.4	109.6
综合医疗类	General Medical	127.9	131.5	121.9
一般医疗服务	Medical and Health Service	128.6	133.2	121.0
一般治疗操作	General Medical Procedure	121.7	125.0	115.9
护　理	Nursing	161.4	168.4	150.5
其他综合医疗服务	Other comprehensive medical services	100.1	100.2	100.0
诊断类	Diagnostic	101.7	102.8	100.0
病理学诊断	Pathological Diagnosis	120.9	125.0	114.3
实验室诊断	Laboratory Diagnosis	100.8	98.1	105.4
影像学诊断	Imaging Diagnosis	98.6	98.2	99.0
临床诊断	Clinical Diagnosis	98.8	101.0	95.9
治疗类	Therapeutic Category	113.7	116.1	110.1
临床手术治疗	Clinical Surgical Treatment	115.8	117.8	112.9
临床非手术治疗	Clinical Non—urgical Treatment	110.5	113.7	105.8
康复类	Rehabilitation	107.4	107.5	107.3
中医医疗服务类	Chinese Medicine Medical Service	108.9	108.8	109.0
其他医疗服务	Other Medical Services	104.1	104.4	103.4
其他用品和服务	**Other Supplies and Services**	**101.0**	**100.4**	**102.8**
其他用品类	Other Supplies	99.9	99.4	101.3
首饰手表	Jewelry Watch	101.6	101.3	102.3
其他杂项用品	Other Miscellaneous Goods	97.6	96.8	99.8
其他服务类	Other Services	102.0	101.3	104.2
旅馆住宿	Hotel Accommodation	104.4	101.6	111.7
宾馆住宿	Hotel Accommodation	104.8	104.1	107.3
其他住宿	Others	103.9	98.3	115.6
美容美发洗浴	Hairdressing Bath	104.1	104.8	102.1
美　容	Cosmetology	101.6	100.9	104.0
美　发	Salon	101.9	101.7	102.7
洗　浴	Bath	110.0	114.1	99.7
养老服务	Pension Service	100.6	100.0	102.4
金融保险	Financial Insurance	100.4	100.2	101.0
金融服务	financial Service	100.0	100.0	100.1
车辆保险	Vehicle Insurance	100.0	100.0	100.0
旅行保险	Travel Insurance	101.7	102.2	100.0
其他保险	Other Insurance	100.9	100.0	104.1
其他服务类	Other Service	101.2	101.0	101.9
中介服务	Intermediary Services	101.0	101.0	101.0
其他服务	Other Services	101.7	101.0	102.9

7—3 各市县居民消费价格分类指数

(上年=100)　　(2017年)

指　　标	Item	乌鲁木齐市 Urumqi City	克拉玛依市 Karamay City	高昌市 Gaochang Area	哈密市 Hami [Kumul] City	昌吉市 Changji City
居民消费价格指数	**General Consumer Price Index**	**102.8**	**100.6**	**102.3**	**102.8**	**102.6**
服务价格指数	**Service Price Index**	**103.9**	**100.7**	**101.9**	**104.9**	**104.1**
食品烟酒	**Food、Alcohol and Tobacco**	**104.7**	**99.9**	**103.2**	**101.3**	**101.4**
食　品	Food	101.4	99.4	104.3	101.2	102.1
粮　食	Grain	102.3	99.0	100.8	103.2	100.6
大　米	Rice	101.9	96.3	100.0	100.4	100.0
面　粉	Flour	104.4	100.4	100.0	99.6	100.1
其他粮食	The Others	96.0	96.4	103.4	99.4	99.0
粮食制品	Grain Products	101.2	101.1	100.0	112.1	102.2
薯　类	Tubers	98.6	89.4	108.6	95.1	88.7
豆　类	Bean	104.0	97.1	99.5	103.6	103.2
食用油	Oil	99.1	100.7	96.0	100.2	103.9
菜	Vegetables	97.4	95.5	98.9	95.4	95.8
鲜　菜	Fresh Vegetables	97.0	95.2	98.4	94.1	94.2
畜肉类	Livestock Meat	105.3	102.9	106.3	103.4	104.7
猪　肉	Pork	86.7	89.2	88.9	89.7	87.1
牛　肉	Beef	111.7	109.0	107.0	106.8	110.2
羊　肉	Mutton	115.6	111.8	113.5	111.6	111.4
禽肉类	Meat Poultry and Their Products	99.4	95.3	102.9	99.1	109.3
鸡	Chicken	97.9	94.4	103.8	99.7	111.3
水产品	Aquatic Products	104.2	102.7	100.0	104.7	99.2
蛋　类	Eggs	96.9	92.9	101.0	94.6	92.8
鸡　蛋	Egg	96.7	93.0	101.1	94.0	92.2
奶　类	Dairy	99.1	97.6	98.2	100.3	100.0
鲜　奶	Milk	100.1	94.4	100.0	100.1	98.3
干鲜瓜果	Dried and Fresh Melons and Fruits	100.1	98.4	121.3	104.4	107.8
鲜瓜果	Fresh Fruits	100.2	99.5	133.4	106.3	112.3
糖果糕点类	Carbohydrate Products and Cakes	100.2	101.5	105.0	102.5	99.7
食　糖	Sugar	102.0	93.7	115.9	105.6	115.3
糖　果	Candy	99.7	108.4	100.0	99.8	92.3
糕　点	Cakes	100.5	102.0	92.7	104.4	101.1
其他糖果糕点	Others	99.2	101.2	98.7	100.2	100.0
调味品	Flavoring	100.8	104.8	101.4	101.8	105.1
食用盐	Edible Salt	102.5	100.0	100.0	100.0	102.4
酱　油	Soy Sauce	101.3	109.8	104.2	104.2	107.2
食　醋	Vinega	101.2	108.8	101.3	101.1	104.9
其他食品类	Other Food	102.6	100.5	97.5	98.3	102.0
方便食品	Instant Food	102.6	99.5	97.0	97.6	99.5
茶及饮料	Tea and Beverages	102.3	100.5	99.2	104.5	103.8
茶　叶	Tea	100.1	100.0	95.7	100.0	111.4

Consumer Price Indices by Category in Cities and Counties

(preceding year=100)

博乐市 Bole [Bortala] City	库尔勒市 Korla City	焉耆回族自治县 Yanqi Hui Autonomous County	阿克苏市 Aksu City	库车县 Kuqa County	阿图什市 Artux City	喀什市 Kashgar [Kaxgar] City	莎车县 Shache [Yarkant] County	和田市 Hotan City	伊宁市 Yining [Gulja] City	塔城市 Tacheng [Qoqek] City	沙湾县 Shawan City	阿勒泰市 Altay City
102.3	**101.3**	**101.1**	**100.6**	**101.1**	**102.2**	**102.6**	**101.0**	**103.0**	**102.0**	**103.2**	**101.6**	**102.3**
103.4	**102.5**	**101.5**	**101.6**	**103.3**	**104.5**	**105.1**	**100.7**	**104.9**	**104.7**	**105.6**	**103.7**	**102.2**
101.4	**101.1**	**101.4**	**98.0**	**99.1**	**103.0**	**102.2**	**100.8**	**102.3**	**100.0**	**101.1**	**99.4**	**102.0**
101.4	101.2	101.4	97.1	98.7	103.5	102.9	100.6	102.5	98.3	101.0	99.0	101.7
100.7	103.8	99.9	100.1	100.1	102.8	100.0	98.1	99.9	99.4	100.0	100.6	99.5
99.2	102.4	97.5	97.3	99.1	98.1	101.6	96.8	101.1	99.0	100.0	101.6	100.0
102.2	104.5	99.3	99.5	100.0	104.0	99.4	96.6	100.0	99.4	100.0	98.5	100.0
97.0	116.3	88.6	115.4	103.7	110.6	92.8	104.8	98.2	95.2	100.0	96.1	96.5
101.6	100.0	108.3	100.0	100.0	100.0	100.4	100.7	98.8	100.2	100.0	104.4	99.0
103.7	94.0	90.5	94.0	82.3	94.2	96.7	87.0	90.0	88.1	87.2	90.3	100.1
99.9	99.4	99.1	108.5	99.1	107.4	93.0	99.6	96.2	103.5	101.9	104.5	95.3
98.7	102.7	98.8	99.7	101.4	103.4	100.3	98.9	101.7	99.1	100.0	94.8	100.1
97.0	99.4	100.1	87.0	90.2	95.8	103.1	97.2	97.7	94.7	94.4	89.1	100.6
96.1	99.1	99.1	85.6	89.3	95.5	103.2	96.9	97.4	92.8	94.0	86.7	100.6
102.9	101.8	105.5	102.7	101.1	106.8	106.6	101.2	106.2	99.3	100.8	101.7	102.1
81.1	89.5	90.2	89.8	87.0	91.1	96.8	82.5	92.2	84.0	85.7	94.4	85.9
110.1	105.0	116.5	108.5	108.1	106.2	110.5	107.0	102.8	104.4	106.7	103.7	110.3
111.2	113.3	108.6	110.2	105.6	112.9	110.4	109.5	116.6	102.7	106.5	103.8	109.4
101.1	101.9	98.0	95.9	101.3	102.0	101.5	100.6	103.0	100.3	106.2	100.1	102.3
100.2	102.8	97.9	94.9	101.1	99.4	101.7	101.6	103.9	99.7	109.3	98.1	102.9
105.3	107.1	102.7	103.0	101.0	102.6	101.5	115.3	105.3	101.0	101.5	103.2	101.8
99.3	108.7	96.8	105.3	97.7	98.6	99.7	105.8	112.7	105.8	100.7	98.0	98.5
99.5	108.5	97.9	105.9	97.0	98.6	99.9	105.9	114.2	106.4	100.7	97.7	98.6
98.6	101.7	99.8	94.8	103.0	99.8	98.8	99.9	102.0	99.1	99.9	100.1	100.0
96.9	100.0	99.7	90.8	103.2	100.0	99.5	100.0	104.0	98.1	101.2	100.0	100.0
107.1	97.7	102.5	89.5	94.0	107.9	106.1	109.7	104.8	94.8	111.9	101.2	111.9
108.9	96.8	101.3	86.7	92.3	117.0	112.6	113.4	106.8	94.2	115.4	102.9	114.8
107.2	104.3	103.4	102.2	102.2	100.5	101.2	100.8	101.6	100.0	100.6	98.0	102.2
113.4	102.3	135.5	115.6	100.1	104.1	107.3	110.4	113.0	96.4	107.0	100.0	109.5
103.6	101.9	101.6	100.0	102.6	100.0	99.9	100.0	99.1	100.1	100.0	94.1	100.0
108.7	105.9	100.4	100.0	103.2	100.0	98.4	100.7	101.6	100.7	100.0	99.8	100.2
103.6	104.2	92.3	100.4	99.0	100.3	101.6	97.7	99.4	100.0	100.0	100.0	99.8
99.6	108.6	90.4	100.0	100.4	105.6	104.4	100.5	101.2	100.4	101.4	100.2	99.7
100.0	97.1	100.0	100.0	100.0	100.0	103.4	100.0	100.0	100.0	100.0	100.0	100.0
99.6	104.6	80.4	100.0	101.5	117.9	116.9	102.0	100.4	100.4	100.0	100.0	100.0
98.6	109.1	90.5	100.0	99.6	98.6	101.0	100.0	102.8	100.0	105.0	100.0	99.3
98.7	92.0	94.4	100.4	102.2	102.0	99.4	100.8	96.7	99.5	100.0	103.9	99.6
96.9	81.8	92.9	100.0	102.0	100.0	97.7	101.8	90.9	100.1	99.8	107.0	99.1
101.1	104.8	98.1	100.6	100.4	100.6	99.8	100.0	99.4	100.0	101.6	100.0	99.8
101.2	100.0	94.7	101.7	101.1	100.0	101.1	100.0	100.2	100.0	100.0	100.0	100.0

7—3 续表 1

（上年＝100）　　（2017 年）

指　　标	Item	乌鲁木齐市 Urumqi City	克拉玛依市 Karamay City	高昌市 Gaochang Area	哈密市 Hami [Kumul] City	昌吉市 Changji City
烟　酒	Tobacco	102.1	99.8	100.7	100.8	100.6
烟　草	Liquor	100.0	100.7	101.1	100.0	100.0
酒　类	Articles	104.7	99.1	100.1	101.7	101.3
白　酒	Spirit	106.8	99.1	102.3	101.5	101.7
葡萄酒	Wine	102.2	100.4	100.0	100.0	102.6
啤　酒	Beer	96.5	96.5	96.9	103.1	99.7
在外餐饮	Catering Trade	112.9	101.0	100.1	101.7	99.6
正　餐	Dinner	100.7	102.9	100.0	100.1	99.0
快　餐	Fast Food	109.3	101.3	100.0	105.4	101.0
地方小吃	Local Snack	108.3	100.0	100.0	105.9	99.4
衣　着	**Clothing**	**99.8**	**99.1**	**100.4**	**101.8**	**102.8**
服　装	Garments	99.5	98.5	98.8	101.7	103.2
男式服装	Men's Wear	99.2	96.3	96.6	101.4	103.4
女式服装	Women's Wear	99.4	99.2	98.8	101.1	103.1
儿童服装	Childern's Wear	101.0	99.9	102.7	104.4	102.9
服装材料	Clothing Material	100.6	103.8	107.7	100.1	102.4
其他衣着及配件	Others	96.7	100.2	106.2	99.7	103.5
衣着加工服务费	Clothing Processing	110.3	110.1	104.6	102.7	100.0
鞋　类	Footwear	100.8	99.6	103.7	102.6	101.5
鞋	Shoes	101.0	99.5	104.1	101.7	101.6
鞋类加工服务	Footwear Processing Service	100.0	100.0	100.0	109.5	100.0
居　住	**Residence**	**100.1**	**100.2**	**101.4**	**101.3**	**101.9**
租赁房房租	Rental Housing Rent	100.0	98.2	100.0	104.9	101.9
公房房租	Public	100.0	100.0	100.0	100.0	100.0
私房房租	Private	100.0	97.9	100.0	106.2	102.3
住房保养维修及管理	Housing Maintenance and Management	99.6	100.7	101.4	100.8	103.0
住房装潢材料	Housing Decoration Material	97.4	100.0	101.6	101.3	105.2
物业管理费	Property Fee	106.1	100.0	100.0	100.0	100.0
住房装潢维修	Decoration Maintenance	100.0	102.9	101.8	100.0	100.3
水、电、燃料	Water, Electricity and Fuels	100.5	104.5	103.2	99.0	95.3
水	Water	101.9	133.3	112.5	100.0	100.0
电	Electricity	100.0	100.0	100.0	97.3	85.5
燃　气	Gas	101.1	100.0	100.0	98.9	100.0
取暖费	Heating Fee	100.0	100.0	100.0	100.0	100.0
其他燃料	Others	100.0	100.0	107.3	97.0	102.8
自有住房	Own Housing	100.0	96.8	100.0	102.5	106.4
生活用品及服务	**Daily Necessities and Service**	**101.8**	**100.5**	**101.4**	**101.8**	**102.8**
家具及室内装饰品	Furniture and Interior Decorations	100.1	100.9	101.5	102.6	103.0
家　具	Furniture	100.5	101.4	102.1	104.4	103.3
室内装饰品	Interior Decorations	98.5	98.9	99.1	96.0	101.5
家用器具	Household Appliances	99.6	102.3	98.2	100.1	105.9
大型家用器具	Large Household Appliance	99.3	102.6	97.7	99.3	106.3
小家电	Small Home Appliance	101.1	100.6	99.9	103.5	104.4

Continued

(preceding year=100)

博乐市 Bole [Bortala] City	库尔勒市 Korla City	焉耆回族自治县 Yanqi Hui Autonomous County	阿克苏市 Aksu City	库车县 Kuqa County	阿图什市 Artux City	喀什市 Kashgar [Kaxgar] City	莎车县 Shache [Yarkant] County	和田市 Hotan City	伊宁市 Yining [Gulja] City	塔城市 Tacheng [Qoqek] City	沙湾县 Shawan City	阿勒泰市 Altay City
101.5	101.2	101.6	100.0	100.0	101.4	101.5	99.8	101.2	104.4	102.7	100.3	102.3
100.0	100.0	100.0	100.0	100.0	100.0	99.9	100.0	100.0	100.0	100.0	100.0	100.0
103.2	102.5	103.4	100.0	100.0	103.8	103.4	99.6	104.4	110.1	105.9	100.8	105.1
105.7	100.1	104.2	100.0	99.6	102.4	104.8	99.7	105.3	110.4	108.8	100.3	108.5
99.7	108.4	104.0	100.0	107.3	100.0	100.0	100.0	98.4	111.9	99.5	105.8	100.6
98.9	105.6	102.3	100.0	98.8	105.4	102.5	100.0	106.0	102.9	91.8	100.0	100.0
101.4	100.6	102.3	99.9	101.0	101.2	100.7	103.3	102.3	102.4	100.0	101.6	104.6
100.7	104.1	100.3	100.0	101.6	100.0	100.2	100.0	102.3	100.0	100.0	104.5	100.2
100.0	107.8	116.8	101.0	103.3	100.0	100.0	106.8	101.0	100.0	100.0	100.0	108.6
104.2	98.3	100.0	96.9	100.0	99.8	102.8	104.5	100.0	100.0	100.0	102.6	111.3
104.4	**104.4**	**99.5**	**102.8**	**100.5**	**95.1**	**99.4**	**104.2**	**100.6**	**101.9**	**104.7**	**101.4**	**105.0**
103.9	100.4	99.2	102.7	100.0	92.9	100.5	103.8	100.3	101.4	102.9	101.7	105.3
102.7	100.0	99.4	101.3	99.5	93.4	98.9	105.4	100.1	99.5	103.5	101.5	104.7
104.6	103.0	99.4	102.8	100.1	91.8	101.1	102.4	100.2	99.6	102.8	102.1	106.0
104.0	93.7	97.9	104.4	100.4	97.1	102.9	104.8	100.8	107.3	101.9	100.6	104.6
105.6	87.6	100.0	109.3	100.6	100.0	111.0	100.0	100.0	93.7	103.3	104.2	110.8
110.1	99.7	100.0	101.7	104.8	102.2	99.8	100.5	100.0	99.5	102.2	102.3	100.0
113.4	120.4	100.5	103.0	100.0	100.0	92.2	125.9	102.7	102.6	101.3	100.0	100.0
104.6	117.7	100.4	102.9	101.4	100.1	94.5	104.9	101.3	104.5	110.2	100.4	105.0
103.4	101.0	100.2	103.0	101.5	99.7	94.7	103.7	100.3	104.9	106.6	100.5	105.7
112.2	195.8	101.8	100.0	100.0	103.9	91.6	113.1	107.7	100.0	130.6	100.0	100.0
101.3	**97.0**	**100.2**	**100.8**	**99.7**	**98.4**	**101.3**	**100.4**	**102.6**	**101.1**	**99.9**	**100.5**	**100.7**
100.1	98.7	100.0	100.0	100.7	99.7	108.4	100.0	120.1	100.8	100.0	102.8	99.1
100.0	101.1	100.0	100.0	100.0	98.2	100.0	100.0	147.3	100.0	100.0	100.0	100.0
100.1	98.1	100.0	100.0	100.9	100.0	112.0	100.0	100.0	101.0	100.0	103.6	98.8
101.4	100.4	100.9	101.0	102.8	96.7	100.6	102.5	99.7	104.6	99.5	102.8	101.6
102.6	101.6	100.6	102.1	99.9	99.6	101.3	101.9	99.5	101.5	99.2	104.1	102.7
100.0	100.0	100.0	100.0	120.4	100.0	100.0	122.2	100.0	100.0	100.0	100.0	100.0
99.9	98.6	101.6	100.0	100.6	89.1	100.0	100.0	100.0	112.8	100.0	101.2	100.0
100.0	94.3	100.2	101.8	99.7	96.5	101.0	100.0	100.7	99.5	99.9	99.5	98.1
100.0	100.0	100.0	114.2	100.0	100.0	100.0	100.0	100.0	100.0	100.0	100.0	100.0
100.0	84.8	100.0	100.0	100.0	95.1	100.0	100.0	97.4	100.0	96.8	100.0	94.9
100.0	100.0	100.0	100.0	100.0	100.4	101.6	100.0	101.9	98.0	100.0	100.0	98.4
100.0	100.0	100.0	100.0	100.0	100.0	100.0	100.0	103.9	100.0	100.0	100.0	100.0
99.6	100.0	102.6	106.9	96.9	93.1	106.1	100.0	120.3	100.0	108.7	95.5	102.0
102.0	97.5	100.0	100.0	98.5	100.0	99.4	100.0	100.0	100.6	100.0	100.2	102.2
102.4	**104.2**	**100.0**	**101.6**	**100.7**	**100.0**	**100.5**	**99.3**	**100.9**	**98.7**	**101.3**	**101.4**	**102.5**
102.0	99.9	100.0	103.2	97.6	99.0	99.7	98.2	98.1	101.6	103.0	104.0	104.5
102.4	100.1	100.0	101.9	97.6	100.0	100.5	98.0	97.4	102.2	103.3	104.7	105.1
100.0	99.0	100.0	104.6	97.5	92.8	95.3	100.0	100.5	100.0	100.0	100.0	100.5
103.1	114.1	96.9	102.5	101.3	97.5	102.3	95.9	100.6	93.2	100.0	100.4	104.9
103.0	114.4	95.1	102.8	101.1	96.6	102.7	94.8	101.1	95.7	100.0	100.5	105.9
103.7	113.2	104.0	101.8	102.1	100.6	99.6	100.1	96.6	89.2	100.0	100.1	100.8

7—3 续表 2

（上年=100）　　　　（2017 年）

指　　标	Item	乌鲁木齐市 Urumqi City	克拉玛依市 Karamay City	高昌市 Gaochang Area	哈密市 Hami [Kumul] City	昌吉市 Changji City
家用纺织品	Home Textiles	99.6	100.1	104.9	102.2	102.5
床上用品	Bed Articles	93.3	100.1	101.1	98.2	102.2
窗帘门帘	Window and Door Curtain	117.0	100.0	108.5	113.0	105.0
其他家用纺织品	Others	100.7	100.8	110.7	97.9	100.0
家庭日用杂品	Daily Use Household Articles	100.7	100.2	98.9	102.5	101.2
洗涤卫生用品	Washing Sanitary Articles	103.2	101.5	96.2	100.3	100.5
厨具餐具茶具	Kitchenware、Tableware、Tea Set	99.5	99.5	103.1	101.4	102.3
家用手工工具	Hand Tools for Household Use	99.7	100.0	97.8	100.0	102.0
其他家庭日用杂品	Others	99.4	99.0	96.6	105.2	101.3
个人护理用品	Personal Care Articles	99.9	99.5	101.7	100.4	101.8
化妆品	Cosmetics	99.5	99.7	101.8	100.2	102.1
其他护理用品类	Others	100.4	99.2	101.6	100.7	101.5
家庭服务	Domestic Service	119.3	100.0	111.0	103.7	101.8
交通和通信	**Transportation and Communication**	**99.7**	**101.4**	**101.4**	**100.2**	**102.3**
交　通	Transportation	99.8	101.9	102.2	101.2	102.5
交通工具	Vehicle	97.4	99.9	101.1	94.5	100.8
小型汽车	Compact Car	96.9	99.9	98.5	90.8	100.9
电动自行车	Electric Bicycle	102.3	100.0	103.2	96.2	100.7
自行车	Bicycle	100.0	100.0	98.5	107.1	101.0
交通工具用燃料	Fuel for Vehicles	110.8	108.0	107.5	111.7	109.3
汽　油	Gasoline	112.2	112.1	112.4	113.1	112.6
柴　油	Diesel Oil	113.4	112.1	113.9	114.6	113.5
交通工具使用和维修	Vehicle Use and Maintenance	101.6	101.2	104.1	100.1	99.6
交通费	Traffic Expense	94.5	99.2	99.6	101.2	102.1
通　信	Communication	99.4	99.8	99.3	97.9	101.7
通信工具	Communication Tools	97.7	97.4	97.9	92.9	107.4
通信服务	Communication Service	100.0	100.0	101.7	99.7	100.0
邮递服务	Postal Service	100.0	106.8	96.6	100.0	100.0
教育文化和娱乐	**Education, Culture and Recreation**	**105.4**	**101.7**	**103.1**	**100.2**	**99.6**
教　育	Education	107.2	100.7	101.3	100.8	99.8
教育用品	Educational Supplies	96.6	100.0	103.6	101.6	100.0
教育服务	Educational Service	107.9	100.8	100.9	100.8	99.8
文化娱乐	Cultural and Recreational	102.3	103.7	106.4	99.0	99.2
文娱耐用消费品	Durable Consumer Goods for Recreationl Use	95.9	99.9	96.8	99.0	103.7
其他文娱用品	Others	100.5	99.5	101.1	100.1	101.3
文化娱乐服务	Cultural and Recreational services	101.0	106.5	97.8	100.9	99.5
电影票	Cinema Ticket	100.0	100.4	93.8	100.0	100.0
景点门票	Scenic Spot Ticket	100.0	100.0	100.0	110.3	96.2
有线电视	Cable TV	100.0	117.2	100.0	100.0	100.0
健身活动	Fitness Activities	103.8	100.0	103.4	97.4	100.0
旅　游	Touristry	109.8	102.5	130.0	93.4	93.0
旅行社收费	Travel Service Charges	109.9	103.7	99.8	90.8	87.8
其他旅游	Others	100.0	100.0	173.2	100.0	100.0

Continued

(preceding year=100)

博乐市 Bole [Bortala] City	库尔勒市 Korla City	焉耆回族自治县 Yanqi Hui Autonomous County	阿克苏市 Aksu City	库车县 Kuqa County	阿图什市 Artux City	喀什市 Kashgar [Kaxgar] City	莎车县 Shache [Yarkant] County	和田市 Hotan City	伊宁市 Yining [Gulja] City	塔城市 Tacheng [Qoqek] City	沙湾县 Shawan City	阿勒泰市 Altay City
105.2	98.5	100.0	102.2	100.7	102.6	97.6	100.0	100.0	97.7	100.0	100.6	103.2
105.7	97.5	100.0	100.7	102.0	101.1	98.0	100.0	100.0	95.3	100.0	100.0	102.8
109.8	100.0	100.0	100.8	98.7	107.1	100.0	100.0	100.0	100.0	100.0	102.7	107.2
99.6	99.1	100.0	111.6	99.6	100.0	95.4	100.0	100.0	100.0	100.0	100.0	100.0
102.1	99.6	100.4	100.0	101.5	100.4	99.8	100.0	100.5	99.6	100.5	100.1	100.2
101.6	98.1	99.7	100.0	100.1	100.8	100.5	100.0	100.9	97.0	101.6	100.0	98.1
101.6	101.5	99.4	100.0	101.2	100.0	97.8	100.0	100.5	101.7	99.9	100.1	100.0
100.5	106.7	100.0	100.0	101.6	100.0	109.5	100.0	103.3	100.0	100.0	100.9	100.0
102.7	99.4	101.4	100.0	102.7	100.1	96.9	100.0	100.0	100.4	100.0	100.2	101.9
100.0	103.9	102.5	100.4	102.7	100.4	101.2	100.0	101.1	100.1	99.2	100.1	100.1
99.6	103.2	103.0	100.6	103.9	100.0	101.0	100.0	100.0	100.2	100.2	100.1	100.2
100.5	104.6	102.0	100.0	101.3	100.8	101.6	100.0	102.0	100.0	98.2	100.0	100.0
104.9	115.7	100.0	101.8	100.2	105.2	100.1	109.4	111.1	99.7	108.5	106.1	102.3
101.7	**101.8**	**98.9**	**100.3**	**101.7**	**101.8**	**99.9**	**100.1**	**102.4**	**100.4**	**102.1**	**105.5**	**101.4**
102.9	101.7	99.4	101.1	102.6	103.4	100.4	100.6	103.5	99.7	103.3	107.1	101.9
99.7	100.8	93.5	100.0	100.3	101.2	97.2	100.0	101.4	97.7	104.5	100.0	100.8
99.4	100.0	92.2	100.0	100.0	100.0	98.0	100.0	101.8	100.0	104.2	100.0	100.0
102.0	102.3	100.0	100.0	102.5	105.1	96.8	100.0	101.4	90.7	106.9	100.0	104.8
99.4	103.3	100.0	100.0	98.5	100.0	100.0	100.0	100.0	101.8	109.0	100.0	104.5
111.0	108.6	110.0	106.7	111.7	110.9	107.6	110.6	107.7	111.1	110.5	111.0	110.5
112.1	112.2	112.0	109.8	113.0	111.0	108.8	111.3	111.8	111.9	111.5	112.2	112.0
113.1	113.2	112.6	111.7	114.0	112.7	109.7	113.0	113.2	113.0	112.7	113.3	112.9
101.2	98.0	101.2	100.0	100.0	101.6	113.9	100.0	103.9	100.0	97.6	101.6	100.0
102.3	98.3	98.7	97.2	99.6	100.6	97.2	91.6	101.1	94.0	98.7	120.3	96.4
99.2	102.1	97.9	98.4	99.7	98.0	99.0	98.9	99.6	102.2	99.2	101.9	100.4
92.4	103.8	99.4	93.3	98.7	88.0	93.2	95.1	96.0	103.6	100.0	100.0	101.3
101.8	101.9	98.5	99.7	100.0	100.0	100.0	100.0	101.0	100.0	100.2	101.4	100.0
100.4	100.7	91.2	100.0	100.0	100.8	100.0	100.0	94.1	105.1	91.0	108.5	100.0
100.5	**101.7**	**100.4**	**102.4**	**100.0**	**103.7**	**103.4**	**101.0**	**100.2**	**102.7**	**102.0**	**100.4**	**100.7**
101.0	101.8	100.5	103.7	100.1	100.4	103.6	100.4	100.2	102.1	100.0	100.0	100.3
106.5	103.3	104.2	100.0	101.9	106.8	103.8	101.0	100.0	106.5	100.0	101.0	100.5
100.6	101.7	100.2	105.9	100.0	100.2	103.5	100.3	100.2	101.8	100.0	100.0	100.3
99.3	101.6	100.2	99.8	99.9	109.5	103.0	102.5	100.3	103.7	105.4	101.2	101.4
97.8	104.4	99.1	99.1	99.3	101.3	100.4	99.2	100.1	98.4	100.0	100.0	106.5
104.0	102.9	99.7	101.0	99.2	101.5	99.2	100.2	101.0	100.1	105.8	100.0	102.1
97.5	99.9	100.4	100.6	100.0	97.5	98.9	104.6	103.2	100.0	100.0	101.7	100.0
93.8	100.0	100.0	100.0	100.0	100.0	100.0	107.6	100.0	100.0	100.0	100.0	100.0
100.0	98.1	100.0	100.0	100.0	100.0	100.0	100.0	118.4	100.0	100.0	100.0	100.0
100.0	100.0	100.0	100.0	100.0	95.3	97.8	100.0	100.0	100.0	100.0	100.0	100.0
98.4	101.8	100.0	104.2	100.0	100.0	100.0	117.7	91.0	100.0	100.0	110.4	100.0
101.1	104.1	100.7	99.1	100.5	116.0	131.7	100.0	93.0	115.7	118.5	102.0	100.0
97.8	106.8	101.4	97.8	101.1	104.3	128.4	100.0	94.7	98.7	98.8	103.8	100.0
104.6	100.0	100.0	100.0	100.0	118.8	154.8	100.0	73.2	139.8	132.3	100.0	100.0

7—3 续表 3

（上年＝100）　　　　（2017 年）

指　　标	Item	乌鲁木齐市 Urumqi City	克拉玛依市 Karamay City	高昌市 Gaochang Area	哈密市 Hami [Kumul] City	昌吉市 Changji City
医疗保健	**Medicine**	**108.2**	**104.2**	**104.1**	**122.3**	**113.7**
药品及医疗器具	Medicine and Medical Appliances	102.4	101.5	104.1	116.6	106.6
中　药	Chinese Medicine	102.8	102.5	102.6	103.0	121.6
西　药	Western Medicine	103.4	100.9	104.2	126.2	101.7
滋补保健品	Nourishing Health Products	97.6	102.0	112.4	103.7	100.0
医疗卫生器具	Medical Appliance	100.8	103.4	101.6	106.9	101.2
保健器具	Constitutional Appliances	100.0	100.7	100.0	98.1	96.8
医疗服务	Medical Service	111.7	105.7	104.0	124.9	117.1
综合医疗类	General Medical	127.9	114.3	113.3	154.6	146.3
一般医疗服务	Medical and Health Service	117.8	117.8	113.6	156.9	146.7
一般治疗操作	General Medical Procedure	124.8	106.2	109.2	136.7	149.6
护　理	Nursing	160.8	126.3	119.8	198.7	161.6
其他综合医疗服务	Other comprehensive medical services	100.0	100.0	100.0	100.0	100.0
诊断类	Diagnostic	105.7	98.1	98.1	102.6	104.9
病理学诊断	Pathological Diagnosis	132.4	100.0	107.4	116.8	128.2
实验室诊断	Laboratory Diagnosis	93.9	96.1	93.2	93.4	113.6
影像学诊断	Imaging Diagnosis	97.6	95.9	99.2	97.1	92.7
临床诊断	Clinical Diagnosis	101.2	100.0	95.5	104.0	92.9
治疗类	Therapeutic Category	113.2	105.3	103.7	128.3	117.1
临床手术治疗	Clinical Surgical Treatment	114.3	107.1	106.7	128.3	116.4
临床非手术治疗	Clinical Non—urgical Treatment	111.6	103.8	101.8	128.2	118.1
康复类	Rehabilitation	110.7	107.5	106.1	104.4	99.4
中医医疗服务类	Chinese Medicine Medical Service	103.3	107.5	100.0	126.6	116.9
其他医疗服务	Other Medical Services	100.0	104.1	104.1	114.8	100.0
其他用品和服务	**Other Supplies and Services**	**99.6**	**101.6**	**100.3**	**99.6**	**101.4**
其他用品类	Other Supplies	97.6	101.8	102.4	99.7	99.9
首饰手表	Jewelry Watch	100.5	103.0	103.6	103.3	101.9
其他杂项用品	Other Miscellaneous Goods	93.8	99.8	100.4	94.7	97.0
其他服务类	Other Services	101.2	101.4	98.4	99.4	102.7
旅馆住宿	Hotel Accommodation	101.5	103.5	94.0	95.9	109.1
宾馆住宿	Hotel Accommodation	106.4	107.3	95.7	93.4	109.1
其他住宿	Others	94.1	90.8	88.9	100.0	109.1
美容美发洗浴	Hairdressing Bath	103.5	103.0	100.9	103.2	101.9
美　容	Cosmetology	98.6	100.0	100.0	100.0	101.3
美　发	Salon	100.0	105.7	102.0	104.9	102.9
洗　浴	Bath	121.8	100.0	100.0	106.2	98.3
养老服务	Pension Service	100.0	100.0	100.0	100.0	100.0
金融保险	Financial Insurance	100.6	100.0	100.0	100.0	100.0
金融服务	financial Service	100.0	100.0	100.0	100.0	100.0
车辆保险	Vehicle Insurance	100.0	100.0	100.0	100.0	100.0
旅行保险	Travel Insurance	104.2	100.0	100.0	100.0	100.0
其他保险	Other Insurance	100.0	100.0	100.0	100.0	100.0
其他服务类	Other Service	100.0	100.0	100.0	100.0	110.7
中介服务	Intermediary Services	100.0	100.0	100.0	100.0	115.4
其他服务	Other Services	100.0	100.0	100.0	100.0	100.0

Continued

(preceding year=100)

博乐市 Bole [Bortala] City	库尔勒市 Korla City	焉耆回族自治县 Yanqi Hui Autonomous County	阿克苏市 Aksu City	库车县 Kuqa County	阿图什市 Artux City	喀什市 Kashgar [Kaxgar] City	莎车县 Shache [Yarkant] County	和田市 Hotan City	伊宁市 Yining [Gulja] City	塔城市 Tacheng [Qoqek] City	沙湾县 Shawan City	阿勒泰市 Altay City
107.1	**107.8**	**108.8**	**107.8**	**110.1**	**111.9**	**117.2**	**101.8**	**116.9**	**114.5**	**116.9**	**104.2**	**106.7**
100.2	99.0	107.4	102.9	100.0	99.1	102.4	101.6	107.3	102.8	107.6	101.4	103.2
100.9	99.7	100.9	101.0	101.8	97.7	101.6	99.0	107.5	103.8	102.7	104.7	109.2
99.8	99.3	110.8	105.1	99.6	98.9	103.5	102.8	109.5	103.5	110.5	100.5	101.2
99.8	100.0	106.2	100.0	97.3	100.0	100.0	100.0	118.1	97.7	100.0	100.0	100.0
100.0	95.2	100.0	102.1	100.0	102.3	100.0	100.0	81.9	102.6	100.0	100.0	109.3
105.8	100.0	94.8	100.0	100.2	100.0	101.4	100.0	100.0	99.6	100.0	100.0	102.7
110.5	110.7	109.4	110.3	115.1	118.4	125.8	101.9	121.3	120.4	121.8	105.5	108.2
122.7	137.7	121.5	124.0	126.6	125.5	133.3	107.3	142.1	141.4	140.5	105.0	141.3
130.0	155.4	124.8	124.7	130.1	102.6	136.4	110.7	131.7	153.6	149.3	97.1	167.1
113.0	118.7	118.2	118.5	108.7	124.4	115.4	109.2	129.1	133.6	126.3	113.7	125.3
152.7	168.0	144.6	150.0	171.4	176.7	175.2	110.3	172.4	177.3	195.4	103.6	170.2
100.0	86.7	100.0	112.5	100.0	100.0	115.6	100.0	106.7	87.9	100.0	100.0	100.0
100.7	105.7	101.9	103.6	93.1	103.2	107.6	98.2	111.2	101.7	107.0	98.8	102.5
103.2	114.8	112.0	120.6	94.4	120.9	102.9	99.2	150.5	98.1	122.2	124.2	128.7
120.0	119.3	121.8	99.2	94.5	97.8	120.5	97.5	99.7	91.6	144.2	100.0	111.1
100.3	100.6	107.3	96.3	91.5	98.5	102.9	93.9	101.2	97.2	103.5	95.4	97.8
94.6	89.9	90.4	97.8	92.9	100.0	91.9	99.4	104.7	113.2	93.9	93.7	95.6
111.4	108.3	109.5	110.3	113.8	118.9	130.1	102.3	122.2	123.2	125.4	108.6	106.4
113.6	108.4	113.7	112.8	120.4	125.7	131.4	103.4	124.6	130.4	129.5	110.0	106.9
108.1	108.2	103.5	103.5	102.9	107.5	126.0	100.2	118.5	112.5	119.6	106.2	105.9
107.2	97.9	107.4	107.5	122.1	113.7	116.8	100.2	114.7	113.7	114.8	100.0	100.0
107.4	105.6	107.3	105.2	123.0	147.5	116.8	99.4	117.5	117.0	116.9	100.0	109.8
107.5	100.0	105.6	106.7	122.7	125.5	115.6	100.1	119.4	104.7	96.2	102.9	87.3
101.7	**101.9**	**100.5**	**99.9**	**101.7**	**102.2**	**102.2**	**103.8**	**101.7**	**101.4**	**106.2**	**113.2**	**99.5**
99.2	103.6	100.9	99.2	102.2	100.8	101.5	102.3	103.2	99.2	101.8	100.5	99.8
97.4	106.5	101.7	98.5	101.4	101.3	101.6	104.3	104.9	98.1	103.0	100.8	99.6
102.0	100.1	99.9	100.7	103.4	100.1	100.6	100.0	100.2	101.0	100.3	100.0	100.0
104.1	100.1	100.0	100.6	101.2	103.8	103.5	105.2	100.3	103.8	109.7	123.5	99.2
104.6	100.3	100.0	101.5	104.8	113.7	100.1	102.3	100.8	110.1	121.9	164.0	96.8
102.1	99.6	100.0	101.2	106.8	114.7	99.3	104.1	101.4	113.7	123.6	116.5	97.7
106.8	100.9	100.0	102.0	102.5	111.6	100.9	100.0	100.0	104.9	120.0	186.2	95.8
100.2	100.3	100.0	100.0	100.2	100.0	111.4	123.4	100.6	104.4	100.0	100.0	100.0
102.7	100.0	100.0	100.0	100.7	100.0	116.3	137.8	100.0	100.0	100.0	100.0	100.0
101.0	100.5	100.0	100.0	100.0	100.0	109.1	125.1	101.0	101.3	100.0	100.0	100.0
97.2	100.0	100.0	100.0	100.0	100.0	100.0	100.0	100.0	114.8	100.0	100.0	100.0
118.3	100.0	100.0	100.0	100.0	100.0	100.0	100.0	100.0	100.0	100.0	100.0	100.0
100.0	100.0	100.0	100.0	100.0	100.0	100.0	103.0	100.0	100.0	106.8	100.0	100.0
100.0	100.0	100.0	99.5	100.0	100.0	100.0	100.7	100.0	100.0	100.0	100.0	100.0
100.0	100.0	100.0	100.0	100.0	100.0	100.0	100.0	100.0	100.0	100.0	100.0	100.0
100.0	100.0	100.0	100.0	100.0	100.0	100.0	100.0	100.0	100.0	100.0	100.0	100.0
100.0	100.0	100.0	100.0	100.0	100.0	100.0	114.4	100.0	100.0	126.1	100.0	100.0
102.3	100.0	100.0	105.2	100.0	101.3	100.0	107.1	100.0	100.0	100.0	111.9	100.0
100.0	100.0	100.0	100.0	100.0	100.0	100.0	112.5	100.0	100.0	100.0	100.0	100.0
104.9	100.0	100.0	114.3	100.0	104.3	100.0	100.0	100.0	100.0	100.0	123.1	100.0

7—4 商品零售价格分类指数

Retail Price Indices by Category of Commodities

（上年＝100） （2017 年） （preceding year＝100）

指 标	Item	全 区 Province	城 市 Urban Areas	农 村 Rural Areas
商品零售价格指数	**Retail Price Index**	**100.9**	**100.9**	**101.3**
食 品	**Food**	**101.5**	**101.5**	**101.1**
粮 食	Grain	101.6	101.9	100.0
薯 类	Potato	95.7	95.9	94.9
豆 类	Beans	103.1	103.4	100.8
食用油	Cooking Oil	100.1	100.3	99.2
菜	Dishes	96.8	96.8	96.4
畜肉类	Livestock Meat	104.8	105.0	103.3
禽肉类	Poultry	100.4	100.3	101.4
水产品	Seafood	103.8	103.8	104.4
蛋 类	Eggs	99.0	98.9	99.4
奶 类	Milk	99.1	99.1	99.1
干鲜瓜果类	Fresh and Dried Fruits and Melons	100.8	100.2	107.7
糖果糕点类	Confectionery	100.8	100.7	102.9
调味品	Spices	101.5	101.5	100.3
其他食品类	Other food Categories	100.4	100.5	99.6
在外餐饮	Outside Catering	104.4	104.7	101.4
饮料、烟酒	**Drinks, Tobacco and Alcohol**	**101.8**	**101.9**	**100.8**
茶及饮料	Tea and Drinks	101.9	102.2	100.3
烟 草	Tobacco	100.0	100.0	100.3
酒 类	Alcohol	103.9	104.0	101.8
服装、鞋帽	**Clothing, Shoes and Hats**	**100.1**	**99.9**	**102.1**
服 装	Dresses	99.9	99.8	101.6
鞋帽袜	Shoes Socks	101.1	100.9	103.2
其他衣着配件	Other Clothing Accessories	97.7	97.5	102.7
纺织品	**Textiles**	**97.5**	**97.1**	**103.0**
服装材料	Clothing Materials	101.6	101.2	104.9
床上用品	Bedding	95.6	95.2	101.7
家用电器及音像器材	**Household Appliances and Audio—visual Equipment**	**100.0**	**100.0**	**99.9**
家庭设备	Home Appliances	101.1	101.2	100.1
文娱用耐用消费品	Durable Consumer Goods for Recreation	98.6	98.5	99.6
专业音像器材	Professional Audio and Video Equipment	100.2	100.3	100.0
文化办公用品	**Stationery Office Supplies**	**98.3**	**98.1**	**100.1**
纸张文具	Paper Stationery	100.4	100.2	101.7
台式计算机	Desktop Computer	96.9	96.6	99.5
笔记本平板	Laptop Tablet	96.4	96.3	98.8
电脑附件	Computer Accessories	100.0	100.0	99.7
打印复印机	Printer Copier	101.2	101.4	99.7
教学设备	Teaching Equipment	100.0	99.8	101.6

7—4 续表 Continued

（上年＝100） （2017 年） (preceding year＝100)

指 标	Item	全 区 Province	城 市 Urban Areas	农 村 Rural Areas
日用品	**Daily Necessities**	**100.7**	**100.8**	**100.3**
日用百货	Daily Necessities	99.4	99.2	101.1
厨具餐具茶具	Kitchenware，Tableware，Tea Set	99.9	99.8	100.8
清洗用品	Cleaning Supplies	103.1	103.4	99.3
其他日用品	Other Daily Necessities	98.7	98.6	100.0
体育娱乐用品	**Sports and Entertainment Supplies**	**99.7**	**99.5**	**102.0**
体育户外用品	Sports Outdoor Products	100.1	99.9	103.2
娱乐用品	Entertainment Supplies	99.3	99.2	101.0
交通、通信用品	**Traffic and Communication Supplies**	**98.5**	**98.5**	**98.4**
交通运输机械	Transportation Machinery	98.9	98.8	99.3
通信器材	Communication Equipment	98.1	98.1	97.3
家 具	**Furniture**	**101.0**	**100.9**	**102.4**
柜	Cabinet	103.9	103.8	104.5
床	Bed	100.9	100.8	101.3
桌	Table	99.3	98.9	103.8
椅	Chair	101.4	101.2	104.6
沙 发	Sofa	99.6	99.5	100.5
其他家具	Other Furniture	100.2	100.1	101.9
化妆品	**Cosmetics**	**100.4**	**100.4**	**100.8**
清洁化妆品	Cleaning Cosmetics	100.8	100.6	102.2
护肤化妆品	Skin Care Cosmetics	99.8	99.8	99.5
彩妆化妆品	Cosmetics	101.5	101.5	101.2
清洁类护理用品	Cleaning Supplies	100.1	100.0	100.6
护发美发用品	Hair Care Products	100.9	100.9	100.6
金银饰品	**Gold and Silver Jewelry**	**101.5**	**101.4**	**102.8**
金饰品	Gold Jewelry	102.4	102.3	104.5
银饰品	Silver Jewelry	99.2	99.2	98.4
铂金饰品	Platinum Jewelry	100.2	100.1	101.8
中西药品及医疗保健用品	**Chinese and Western Medicines and Health Care Products**	**102.8**	**102.8**	**102.8**
医疗卫生器具	Medical and Sanitary Appliances	100.9	100.8	102.4
中 药	Traditional Chinese Medicine	103.1	103.1	102.7
西 药	Western Medicine	103.8	103.9	102.9
保健器具及用品	Health Care Equipment and Supplies	99.1	98.9	102.7
书报杂志及电子出版物	**Books, Magazines and Electronic Publications**	**101.1**	**101.1**	**101.7**
教材及参考书	Teaching Materials and Reference Books	98.4	97.8	103.3
书报杂志	Books and Magazines	104.4	104.6	100.6
计算机办公软件	Computer Office Software	98.1	98.0	99.4
燃 料	**Fuel**	**105.9**	**105.9**	**106.0**
煤炭及制品	Coal and Products	101.1	100.4	103.9
石油及制品	Oil and Products	106.6	106.6	107.0
建筑材料及五金电料	**Building Materials and Hardware**	**99.9**	**99.8**	**101.2**
建筑装璜材料	Building Decoration Materials	99.2	99.0	101.5
五金水暖	Hardware Plumbing	101.9	102.1	100.5

7—5 各市县商品零售价格分类指数

（上年＝100） （2017 年）

指　　标	Item	乌鲁木齐市 Urumqi City	克拉玛依市 Karamay City	高昌区 Gaochang Area	哈密市 Hami [Kumul] City	昌吉市 Changji City
商品零售价格指数	**Retail Price Index**	**100.7**	**100.3**	**101.6**	**101.1**	**102.9**
食　品	**Food**	**102.0**	**99.5**	**103.6**	**101.2**	**101.5**
粮　食	Grain	102.4	99.0	100.8	103.3	100.6
薯　类	Potato	98.6	89.4	108.6	95.1	88.7
豆　类	Beans	104.0	97.1	99.5	103.6	103.2
食用油	Cooking Oil	100.0	100.8	96.0	100.2	104.2
菜	Dishes	97.2	95.4	98.9	94.6	95.1
畜肉类	Livestock Meat	105.6	102.6	106.3	103.3	104.9
禽肉类	Poultry	99.4	95.3	102.9	99.6	109.9
水产品	Seafood	104.2	102.7	100.0	104.5	99.2
蛋　类	Eggs	96.9	92.9	101.0	94.6	92.8
奶　类	Milk	98.7	97.6	98.2	100.4	100.4
干鲜瓜果类	Fresh and Dried Fruits and Melons	100.3	98.4	121.3	104.4	107.4
糖果糕点类	Confectionery	100.2	101.5	105.0	102.8	99.8
调味品	Spices	100.5	104.8	101.4	103.3	104.7
其他食品类	Other food Categories	102.6	99.9	97.5	98.2	101.2
在外餐饮	Outside Catering	106.4	101.2	100.1	102.4	99.8
饮料、烟酒	**Drinks, Tobacco and Alcohol**	**102.5**	**100.0**	**100.4**	**101.2**	**101.0**
茶及饮料	Tea and Drinks	102.3	100.5	99.2	104.5	103.1
烟　草	Tobacco	100.0	100.7	101.1	100.0	100.0
酒　类	Alcohol	104.8	99.1	100.1	101.6	101.4
服装、鞋帽	**Clothing, Shoes and Hats**	**99.5**	**98.9**	**100.6**	**101.3**	**102.9**
服　装	Dresses	99.2	98.5	98.9	101.4	103.2
鞋帽袜	Shoes Socks	100.9	99.6	105.7	101.4	101.7
其他衣着配件	Other Clothing Accessories	96.2	100.0	98.9	99.4	105.0
纺织品	**Textiles**	**95.6**	**100.9**	**103.2**	**98.8**	**102.6**
服装材料	Clothing Materials	100.6	103.8	107.7	100.1	102.4
床上用品	Bedding	93.3	100.1	101.0	98.2	102.6
家用电器及音像器材	**Household Appliances and Audio—visual Equipment**	**98.3**	**102.2**	**97.2**	**99.1**	**105.1**
家庭设备	Home Appliances	99.7	102.5	97.9	99.9	105.9
文娱用耐用消费品	Durable Consumer Goods for Recreation	96.4	101.4	96.2	98.1	104.2
专业音像器材	Professional Audio and Video Equipment	100.0	103.8	98.6	99.5	100.0
文化办公用品	**Stationery Office Supplies**	**97.4**	**99.2**	**99.3**	**100.0**	**102.0**
纸张文具	Paper Stationery	100.0	100.3	99.8	100.0	102.2
台式计算机	Desktop Computer	95.5	100.0	99.1	100.0	102.3
笔记本平板	Laptop Tablet	95.4	97.3	98.5	100.0	102.8
电脑附件	Computer Accessories	100.4	100.2	100.0	100.0	100.0
打印复印机	Printer Copier	102.4	100.0	95.2	100.0	100.0
教学设备	Teaching Equipment	100.0	100.0	100.2	100.0	102.3

Retail Price Indices by Category of Commoditles in Cities and Counties

(preceding year=100)

博乐市 Bole [Bortala] City	库尔勒市 Korla City	焉耆回族自治县 Yanqi Hui Autonomous County	阿克苏市 Aksu City	库车县 Kuqa County	阿图什市 Artux City	喀什市 Kashgar [Kaxgar] City	莎车县 Shache [Yarkant] County	和田市 Hotan City	伊宁市 Yining [Gulja] City	塔城市 Tacheng [Qoqek] City	沙湾县 Shawan City	阿勒泰市 Altay City
101.4	**101.9**	**100.8**	**100.2**	**100.4**	**100.2**	**101.0**	**100.6**	**102.3**	**100.5**	**102.1**	**100.8**	**102.5**
101.2	**102.0**	**101.1**	**98.1**	**98.7**	**101.9**	**102.5**	**100.9**	**102.8**	**99.1**	**100.7**	**98.9**	**102.0**
100.2	103.8	99.8	100.1	100.3	101.5	100.0	98.4	100.4	99.4	100.0	100.1	99.4
103.7	94.0	90.5	94.0	82.3	94.2	96.7	87.0	90.0	88.1	87.2	90.3	100.1
99.9	99.4	99.8	108.7	98.9	107.5	93.5	99.7	96.4	103.5	101.9	104.5	96.1
98.6	102.8	98.8	96.5	101.8	103.6	100.3	96.6	101.7	99.5	99.7	95.1	100.1
97.2	99.3	100.1	90.9	90.4	95.7	103.1	97.2	97.7	96.3	94.6	89.3	100.6
102.9	102.0	105.1	103.5	101.7	106.1	106.6	101.5	108.3	99.8	101.1	101.7	102.3
100.9	101.7	98.0	98.1	101.2	100.8	101.7	100.9	102.5	100.5	107.0	99.5	102.4
106.1	107.1	103.3	103.1	101.1	104.3	101.7	118.8	105.9	101.0	101.4	104.5	101.8
99.1	108.7	97.2	104.6	98.4	98.7	99.8	105.6	112.7	105.3	100.8	98.2	98.3
98.9	102.5	99.8	97.5	103.0	99.6	98.6	99.8	102.7	99.2	99.5	100.2	100.0
106.4	98.0	102.9	89.0	94.5	106.0	105.3	108.2	104.5	94.8	110.9	101.2	111.9
107.6	104.3	103.2	102.9	101.6	100.8	101.1	101.7	103.7	100.1	101.3	98.0	102.2
99.9	108.6	91.3	100.0	100.5	103.4	104.4	100.4	101.3	100.7	101.4	101.9	99.6
98.6	88.9	94.4	100.3	102.1	101.7	99.4	100.8	94.8	99.7	100.0	104.0	99.5
101.1	104.0	102.6	99.9	101.5	100.3	100.7	102.5	101.9	100.5	100.0	102.5	104.4
101.1	**101.7**	**100.4**	**100.1**	**100.3**	**101.5**	**100.6**	**99.9**	**101.7**	**103.9**	**101.3**	**100.4**	**101.3**
101.6	104.8	96.8	100.6	100.4	101.4	99.8	100.0	99.4	100.1	101.0	100.0	100.4
100.0	100.0	100.0	100.0	100.0	100.0	99.9	100.0	100.0	100.0	100.0	100.0	100.0
102.1	102.5	103.3	100.0	100.8	103.8	103.4	99.7	104.2	109.6	103.4	101.2	103.6
104.5	**101.3**	**99.5**	**102.6**	**101.3**	**95.8**	**99.0**	**104.1**	**100.2**	**101.7**	**103.6**	**101.2**	**104.3**
104.4	101.5	99.2	102.5	100.4	91.7	100.5	104.5	100.3	101.1	102.7	101.4	104.8
103.9	100.8	100.1	102.5	102.9	100.4	95.7	103.3	100.2	104.0	106.0	100.6	103.8
114.5	100.0	100.0	103.1	105.2	100.0	100.0	100.0	100.0	100.0	100.0	104.1	100.0
107.0	**95.0**	**100.0**	**103.5**	**101.8**	**100.4**	**104.7**	**100.0**	**100.0**	**94.8**	**101.3**	**101.7**	**106.9**
105.6	87.6	100.0	109.3	100.6	100.0	111.0	100.0	100.0	93.7	103.3	104.2	110.8
108.0	97.8	100.0	100.7	102.6	100.8	98.7	100.0	100.0	95.3	100.0	100.0	103.9
101.4	**111.3**	**97.9**	**101.6**	**100.3**	**99.5**	**101.8**	**96.4**	**100.0**	**96.9**	**100.0**	**100.1**	**106.0**
102.9	114.4	96.7	102.5	101.5	97.8	102.4	95.7	100.3	94.9	100.0	100.2	105.2
99.4	108.0	99.5	100.9	98.6	102.2	101.3	96.8	99.6	99.5	100.0	100.0	107.9
100.8	100.8	98.2	99.1	100.0	100.0	100.3	100.0	99.6	100.0	100.0	100.0	100.0
99.7	**99.9**	**99.5**	**97.4**	**100.0**	**102.0**	**99.5**	**100.1**	**101.7**	**98.1**	**100.0**	**100.0**	**101.2**
107.2	100.0	100.0	100.0	99.8	106.5	100.7	100.9	100.0	99.5	100.0	100.0	100.0
96.7	100.0	99.7	96.9	98.5	100.0	100.2	100.0	100.0	96.9	100.0	100.0	103.8
93.2	99.9	97.7	95.2	101.1	100.0	99.3	100.0	102.6	95.9	100.0	100.0	100.0
97.6	100.0	100.0	98.4	100.0	100.0	93.2	99.6	100.0	100.7	100.0	100.0	100.0
99.4	100.0	100.0	91.7	99.6	100.0	99.2	100.0	106.9	99.5	100.0	100.0	100.0
105.1	99.6	100.4	100.2	102.6	100.0	96.6	100.0	100.0	100.2	100.0	100.0	103.2

7—5 续表

（上年=100）　　　　　　　　　　　　　　　　　　　　　　　　　　　　　　（2017 年）

指　　标	Item	乌鲁木齐市 Urumqi City	克拉玛依市 Karamay City	高昌区 Gaochang Area	哈密市 Hami [Kumul] City	昌吉市 Changji City
日用品	**Daily Necessities**	**101.3**	**100.8**	**100.4**	**100.2**	**100.7**
日用百货	Daily Necessities	99.0	100.1	101.4	100.6	100.0
厨具餐具茶具	Kitchenware, Tableware, Tea Set	99.0	99.5	103.1	102.2	102.3
清洗用品	Cleaning Supplies	105.2	102.2	98.2	100.7	101.5
其他日用品	Other Daily Necessities	97.8	99.9	100.6	97.7	98.8
体育娱乐用品	**Sports and Entertainment Supplies**	**99.0**	**99.4**	**103.3**	**100.5**	**100.7**
体育户外用品	Sports Outdoor Products	99.8	100.0	107.4	100.0	100.0
娱乐用品	Entertainment Supplies	98.3	98.8	99.9	100.9	101.3
交通、通信用品	**Traffic and Communication Supplies**	**98.3**	**98.0**	**97.5**	**94.1**	**103.3**
交通运输机械	Transportation Machinery	98.8	98.6	99.9	95.2	100.4
通信器材	Communication Equipment	97.7	97.4	94.6	92.6	107.4
家　具	**Furniture**	**100.4**	**101.7**	**102.2**	**104.4**	**103.3**
柜	Cabinet	103.8	104.4	101.5	108.6	103.0
床	Bed	100.0	102.5	97.7	106.9	103.0
桌	Table	96.7	100.0	102.7	103.4	104.3
椅	Chair	101.1	102.3	117.9	99.0	103.3
沙　发	Sofa	99.1	100.0	100.2	101.9	102.7
其他家具	Other Furniture	100.0	100.0	102.8	100.8	105.4
化妆品	**Cosmetics**	**100.2**	**99.4**	**100.7**	**100.2**	**101.5**
清洁化妆品	Cleaning Cosmetics	100.6	100.0	106.7	99.9	100.7
护肤化妆品	Skin Care Cosmetics	99.5	99.2	97.3	100.0	99.9
彩妆化妆品	Cosmetics	101.5	100.0	100.0	100.0	105.6
清洁类护理用品	Cleaning Supplies	99.1	98.7	100.0	101.7	105.0
护发美发用品	Hair Care Products	101.3	99.4	103.6	100.0	95.8
金银饰品	**Gold and Silver Jewelry**	**101.2**	**103.2**	**103.6**	**103.9**	**101.9**
金饰品	Gold Jewelry	102.7	103.2	104.0	104.5	102.6
银饰品	Silver Jewelry	95.6	105.4	100.0	103.9	101.3
铂金饰品	Platinum Jewelry	100.0	102.6	105.6	102.1	100.0
中西药品及医疗保健用品	**Chinese and Western Medicines and Health Care Products**	**102.3**	**101.6**	**104.2**	**111.3**	**105.8**
医疗卫生器具	Medical and Sanitary Appliances	100.8	103.4	101.6	106.9	101.2
中　药	Traditional Chinese Medicine	102.8	102.5	102.6	103.0	115.6
西　药	Western Medicine	103.4	100.9	104.2	118.4	102.7
保健器具及用品	Health Care Equipment and Supplies	98.3	101.5	109.7	102.4	99.3
书报杂志及电子出版物	**Books, Magazines and Electronic Publications**	**99.9**	**99.6**	**101.6**	**101.2**	**100.9**
教材及参考书	Teaching Materials and Reference Books	95.2	100.0	103.6	102.4	100.0
书报杂志	Books and Magazines	106.6	99.1	100.0	100.0	101.1
计算机办公软件	Computer Office Software	96.7	100.0	100.0	102.0	101.9
燃　料	**Fuel**	**105.3**	**104.8**	**105.4**	**105.6**	**106.2**
煤炭及制品	Coal and Products	100.0	98.6	107.0	105.1	105.0
石油及制品	Oil and Products	106.8	107.9	104.8	105.7	106.4
建筑材料及五金电料	**Building Materials and Hardware**	**98.5**	**100.5**	**100.5**	**102.0**	**105.3**
建筑装璜材料	Building Decoration Materials	97.5	100.0	101.6	101.2	105.2
五金水暖	Hardware Plumbing	101.6	101.2	97.5	104.6	105.7

Continued

(preceding year=100)

博乐市 Bole [Bortala] City	库尔勒市 Korla City	焉耆回族自治县 Yanqi Hui Autonomous County	阿克苏市 Aksu City	库车县 Kuqa County	阿图什市 Artux City	喀什市 Kashgar [Kaxgar] City	莎车县 Shache [Yarkant] County	和田市 Hotan City	伊宁市 Yining [Gulja] City	塔城市 Tacheng [Qoqek] City	沙湾县 Shawan City	阿勒泰市 Altay City
100.9	**99.0**	**100.7**	**100.2**	**100.7**	**101.0**	**99.2**	**100.0**	**100.6**	**99.9**	**101.8**	**100.0**	**99.5**
102.4	100.8	102.2	100.0	100.7	102.3	99.2	100.0	100.9	95.7	103.0	100.0	101.9
101.0	101.5	99.2	100.0	101.1	100.0	98.0	100.0	100.5	101.7	99.9	100.2	100.0
99.0	96.3	99.9	100.0	100.0	100.5	99.9	100.0	100.5	100.0	103.2	100.0	95.6
101.5	100.0	100.7	100.9	101.6	99.3	98.4	100.0	100.7	101.8	100.1	100.0	100.0
102.6	**103.1**	**99.6**	**100.0**	**102.5**	**98.5**	**98.6**	**100.0**	**100.3**	**100.1**	**104.2**	**100.0**	**103.2**
103.1	100.0	100.0	100.0	104.0	100.0	100.6	100.0	100.0	100.0	100.0	100.0	104.0
102.2	105.5	99.3	100.0	101.2	96.6	96.5	100.1	100.6	100.2	107.5	100.0	102.5
97.3	**100.5**	**97.7**	**97.1**	**99.7**	**95.8**	**96.2**	**95.7**	**99.3**	**100.6**	**100.5**	**99.5**	**100.5**
99.8	99.0	96.2	100.0	100.0	100.0	99.0	100.0	100.8	100.0	100.8	99.1	100.0
94.3	102.7	99.5	93.5	99.3	89.9	92.2	90.4	97.2	101.2	100.0	100.0	100.9
102.1	**100.1**	**100.0**	**101.9**	**97.8**	**100.0**	**100.4**	**98.4**	**97.2**	**102.2**	**103.2**	**104.3**	**105.3**
100.2	100.3	100.0	102.0	99.9	100.0	102.3	96.3	101.0	105.4	104.7	100.0	107.9
102.8	100.0	100.0	104.7	97.4	100.0	101.1	98.3	104.0	98.0	103.5	107.7	106.5
100.3	100.0	100.0	102.1	99.4	100.0	100.4	107.6	101.5	103.9	105.6	104.8	108.8
103.3	100.0	100.0	101.6	98.2	100.0	94.9	102.8	100.0	106.4	101.3	105.1	100.0
102.4	100.0	100.0	100.0	96.0	100.0	100.2	93.9	102.6	99.8	100.6	102.6	103.4
105.1	100.0	100.0	100.6	95.8	100.0	100.0	94.2	87.9	102.1	105.1	107.4	102.6
99.5	**104.5**	**101.9**	**100.4**	**103.9**	**100.6**	**102.4**	**100.0**	**100.7**	**99.1**	**100.0**	**100.2**	**100.3**
100.3	103.2	104.5	100.0	104.0	100.0	100.0	100.0	100.0	99.9	100.0	100.0	100.0
99.5	105.3	103.4	100.0	103.7	100.0	104.0	100.0	100.0	100.4	100.0	100.0	100.0
97.3	101.3	100.0	102.1	107.8	100.0	100.5	100.0	100.0	100.0	105.8	101.3	101.9
99.8	105.9	100.4	100.0	102.8	102.0	104.8	100.1	102.6	94.6	100.0	100.0	100.0
100.1	109.1	100.7	100.0	100.7	100.0	96.8	100.0	102.0	99.9	94.8	100.0	100.1
98.8	**104.5**	**101.7**	**98.5**	**101.1**	**101.0**	**102.0**	**103.9**	**111.3**	**97.0**	**104.5**	**101.3**	**99.7**
102.9	101.8	102.1	101.9	101.3	97.1	102.9	105.1	103.7	98.4	106.3	102.2	101.8
84.8	114.4	103.0	100.0	97.2	96.0	96.7	114.3	144.3	100.0	100.0	100.0	92.8
98.7	106.7	100.0	90.9	103.1	113.2	100.1	96.7	100.0	93.9	103.3	100.0	100.0
100.6	**99.3**	**106.4**	**103.0**	**100.0**	**98.9**	**103.2**	**101.4**	**108.3**	**102.5**	**106.7**	**101.8**	**104.0**
100.0	95.2	100.0	102.1	100.0	102.3	100.0	100.0	81.9	102.6	100.0	100.0	109.3
101.5	99.7	100.9	101.3	101.3	97.7	101.6	98.9	107.5	103.8	102.5	104.9	109.2
99.8	99.4	110.8	104.7	99.6	98.9	104.5	103.3	109.5	103.3	110.8	100.6	101.5
101.8	100.0	103.1	100.0	98.2	100.0	100.6	100.0	116.4	98.3	100.0	100.0	100.8
102.9	**102.7**	**101.3**	**102.3**	**101.0**	**106.3**	**101.7**	**101.6**	**100.9**	**103.2**	**100.0**	**101.0**	**100.6**
106.7	102.9	104.2	100.0	102.0	107.8	103.8	103.1	100.0	108.0	100.0	101.9	100.5
100.0	101.4	100.0	105.2	100.0	105.5	100.0	100.0	101.9	100.0	100.0	100.0	101.1
97.2	105.9	96.0	100.0	100.3	100.0	100.0	100.0	100.0	100.0	100.0	100.0	100.0
105.3	**105.5**	**105.0**	**105.8**	**105.8**	**103.0**	**102.2**	**106.1**	**109.1**	**104.9**	**107.3**	**106.9**	**104.1**
100.9	100.4	102.3	106.1	102.2	94.5	97.5	104.1	120.3	100.0	108.3	106.4	101.6
107.4	106.2	106.2	105.8	107.7	105.0	104.4	107.4	107.6	105.5	106.8	107.2	105.8
103.2	**101.7**	**100.4**	**101.4**	**100.3**	**99.7**	**101.6**	**102.8**	**100.1**	**100.9**	**100.0**	**103.1**	**102.5**
103.0	101.6	100.5	101.9	100.1	99.6	101.3	101.7	99.5	101.8	99.8	104.1	102.8
103.6	102.2	100.0	100.0	100.8	100.0	103.0	105.2	102.1	98.6	100.6	100.4	101.7

7—6 农业生产资料价格分类指数

Price Indices for Means of Agricultural Production by Category

（上年＝100） (preceding year＝100)

指 标	Item	2010	2015	2016	2017
农业生产资料价格指数	**General Index**	**103.1**	**98.6**	**98.2**	**103.2**
农用手工工具	Farm-oriented Handwork Implemen	101.0	102.2	100.5	102.5
饲料类	Forage	114.0	99.3	95.0	102.5
产品畜	Animal for Products	127.1	95.5	109.8	93.1
半机械化农具	Semi-mechanized Farm Tools	101.7	99.8	99.5	100.8
机械化农具	Mechanized Farm Machinery	100.1	99.9	99.7	100.1
化学肥料	Chemical Fertilizer	95.3	96.4	92.2	109.6
农药及农药械	Pesticide and Its Appliances	101.7	100.0	101.6	101.1
农用机油	Oil for Farm Machinery	110.1	92.2	95.4	108.2
其他农业生产资料	Others General Index	100.7	100.0	99.4	99.9
农业生产服务	The Agriculture Produces Service	102.0	103.8	100.8	104.0

7—7 各市县农业生产资料价格指数

Price Indices for Means of Agricultural Production by Category in Cities and Counties

（上年＝100） （2017 年） (preceding year＝100)

指 标	Item	高昌区 Gaochang Area	博乐市 Bole [Bortala] City	焉耆回族自治县 Yanqi Hui Autonomous County	库车县 Kuqa County	阿图什市 Artux City	莎车县 Shache [Yarkant] County	塔城市 Kashgar [Kaxgar] City	沙湾县 Shawan City	阿勒泰市 Altay City
农业生产资料价格指数	**General Index**	**103.5**	**100.5**	**102.1**	**99.6**	**99.5**	**101.1**	**99.7**	**102.0**	**100.1**
农用手工工具	Farm-oriented Handwork Implemen	99.8	107.3	102.8	100.0	100.0	101.5	106.7	100.0	105.3
饲料类	Forage	101.7	100.3	103.0	95.7	108.9	100.8	100.5	99.6	102.7
产品畜	Animal for Products	98.2	93.4	102.0	101.4	79.3	111.3	81.5	93.5	103.7
半机械化农具	Semi-mechanized Farm Tools	103.9	98.2	99.9	100.0	86.6	101.2	101.6	100.0	95.6
机械化农具	Mechanized Farm Machinery	98.8	99.2	100.0	101.8	100.0	99.2	100.9	100.0	97.5
化学肥料	Chemical Fertilizer	109.2	104.3	103.6	97.5	98.2	99.6	94.5	104.5	94.0
农药及农药械	Pesticide and Its Appliances	107.0	100.9	100.9	105.7	100.0	100.0	105.5	100.2	100.0
农用机油	Oil for Farm Machinery	110.5	110.9	109.4	110.1	112.1	113.9	109.4	109.9	112.7
其他农业生产资料	Others General Index	106.7	98.6	101.7	98.8	100.1	97.2	96.2	102.4	95.4
农业生产服务	The Agriculture Produces Service	100.0	98.6	100.0	100.0	102.6	99.2	107.2	104.2	102.1

7—8 兵团农产品生产者价格分类指数

Producer Price Indices for Farm Products of XPCC by Category

（上年=100） (preceding year=100)

指　标	Item	2016	2017
农产品生产者价格指数	**General Farm Products Price Index**	**103.0**	**100.8**
农业产品	**Farm Products**	**103.8**	**100.6**
谷　物	Cereal	99.2	102.7
小　麦	Tubers	98.1	98.7
玉　米	Corn	99.7	105.0
棉花(籽棉)	Cotton(seed)	118.7	101.7
甜　菜	Beetroots	98.5	100.7
蔬　菜	Vegetable	106.2	104.1
水果、坚果	Fruit and Nut	97.2	94.8
园林水果	Horticulture Fruit	97.9	94.8
苹　果	Apple	95.2	110.4
香　梨	Snow Flake Peras	92.4	90.5
葡　萄	Grapes	100.4	101.6
瓜果类	Melon and Fruit	101.5	102.3
西　瓜	Melon	98.1	107.4
甜　瓜	Muskmelon	103.2	99.5
饲养动物及其产品	**Animal Husbandry and Products**	**100.0**	**100.3**
活牲畜	Livestock	100.3	99.6
活牛(毛重)	Cattle and Buffaloes	100.2	106.1
活羊(毛重)	Sheep and Goats	95.2	105.9
活猪(毛重)	Pig	107.7	89.4
活家禽	Poultry	101.2	104.0
活　鸡	Chicken	101.2	99.3
畜禽产品	Livestock and Poultry Products	97.3	100.9
牛　奶	Milk	97.0	102.1
绵羊毛	Sheep Wool	95.8	94.6
禽　蛋	Poultries Eggs	99.0	100.2
鸡　蛋	Egg	99.0	100.2
渔业产品	**Fishery Products**	**99.8**	**101.5**
淡水鱼类	Classified by Kind	99.8	101.0
鲤　鱼	Carp	97.2	101.0

7—9 各师农产品生产者价格分类指数

Producer Price Indices for Farm Products by Category and Division

（上年=100）　　　　（2017 年）　　　　(preceding year=100)

单　位	Unit	农产品生产者价格指数 Ceneral Farm Products Price	农业产品 Farm Products	谷物 Cereal	棉花（籽棉） Cotton (seed)	蔬菜 Vegetable and Horticulture	水果、坚果 Fruit and Nut	饲养动物及其产品 Animal Husbandry and
兵　团	**XPCC**	**100.8**	**100.6**	**102.7**	**101.7**	**100.0**	**94.8**	**100.3**
一　师	Division 1	100.9	100.7	105.9	102.4	100.8	99.7	104.6
二　师	Division 2	100.2	100.3	105.5	101.9	105.1	95.0	99.4
三　师	Division 3	100.2	99.6	103.7	100.7	98.1	99.4	103.3
四　师	Division 4	102.0	102.0	103.0	100.7	98.4	102.0	101.3
五　师	Division 5	102.5	102.7	103.5	103.5	101.1	100.7	101.3
六　师	Division 6	99.6	99.6	97.2	100.7	99.4	95.5	97.9
七　师	Division 7	101.0	101.1	103.9	102.0	118.7	116.2	99.4
八　师	Division 8	100.2	100.3	99.5	101.6	104.5	96.0	96.9
九　师	Division 9	100.5	100.2	100.0		99.8	111.1	100.1
十　师	Division 10	102.0	101.4	101.7	100.0	98.9	100.0	103.6
十二师	Division 12	99.5	97.6	100.0	100.0	101.3	94.6	102.5
十三师	Division 13	102.8	102.4	103.2	101.8	105.3	92.2	103.4
十四师	Division 14	102.1	101.5	102.1		100.8	106.2	108.5

单　位	Unit	活牲畜 Livestock	活猪（毛重） Pig	活牛（毛重） Cattle and Buffaloes	活羊（毛重） Sheep and Goats	畜禽产品 Livestock and Poultry Product	牛奶 Milk	禽蛋 Poultry Eggs	渔业 Fishery
兵　团	**XPCC**	**99.6**	**89.4**	**106.1**	**105.9**	**100.9**	**102.1**	**100.2**	**101.5**
一　师	Division 1	102.3	96.8	110.1	102.9	112.0	112.2	109.0	102.0
二　师	Division 2	98.5	91.5	102.8	110.5	104.5	105.7	102.7	93.7
三　师	Division 3	104.7	95.3	107.9	108.1	101.5	100.5	102.9	102.6
四　师	Division 4	100.2	93.6	103.5	103.1	101.5	99.9	105.5	105.3
五　师	Division 5	95.0	89.1	85.1	105.1		98.5	97.3	104.7
六　师	Division 6	97.7	89.9	102.7	101.6	97.4	106.9	90.8	106.7
七　师	Division 7	102.9	94.9	105.3	111.0	105.5	104.7	109.2	101.3
八　师	Division 8	92.9	88.6	106.8	107.7	100.1	99.8	101.7	100.4
九　师	Division 9	99.1	93.6	100.1	99.4	100.2	100.0	101.0	99.8
十　师	Division 10	102.9	90.8	106.2	107.0	100.7	106.6	93.5	101.5
十二师	Division 12	100.8	98.5	104.1	103.8	93.7	93.2	101.2	100.3
十三师	Division 13	104.5	94.1	108.9	106.9	95.6	96.8	95.0	115.7
十四师	Division 14	108.6	94.6	108.5	112.3	101.7	108.0	101.6	

7—10 固定资产投资价格指数

Price Indices for Investment in Fixed Assets

指　　标	Item	2005	2010	2015	2016	2017
固定资产投资	**Investment in Fixed Assets**	**102.8**	**104.6**	**98.3**	**99.9**	**103.5**
建筑安装工程	**Construction and Installation**	**102.7**	**105.9**	**97.6**	**99.9**	**104.5**
# 人工费	Manpower Expenses	103.8	110.6	102.7	101.8	102.9
材料费	Material Expenses	102.3	104.8	95.0	99.1	105.8
# 钢　材	Rolled Steel	101.7	104.4	90.8	97.1	111.2
木　材	Timber	102.5	104.8	100.1	100.4	101.5
水　泥	Cement	100.1	104.7	96.1	99.5	102.4
地方材料	Local Materials	102.0	104.6	98.6	99.5	102.5
化工材料	Chemical Materials	109.1	104.9	96.0	98.6	102.4
电　料	Electrical Wire	104.0	105.1	97.4	100.2	103.4
其他材料	Other Materials	99.9	101.7	100.0	99.8	100.4
机械使用费	Expenses of Machine Use	102.3	103.3	100.8	100.4	101.3
设备工器具	**Purchase of Equipment, Tools and Instruments**	**104.8**	**100.4**	**99.1**	**99.3**	**100.8**
其他费用	**Others**	**100.0**	**105.2**	**102.6**	**101.7**	**100.3**

7—11　工业生产者出厂价格分类指数

Producer Price Indices for Industrial Products by Category

（上年＝100）　　　　　　(preceding year＝100)

指　　标	Item	2005	2010	2015	2016	2017
全部工业品	**Total Industrial Products**	**116.6**	**125.3**	**82.4**	**94.5**	**113.7**
按轻重工业分	**Grouped by Light Inudustry and Heary Industry**					
轻工业	Light Industry	99.6	108.9	98.7	101.8	102.5
以农产品为原料	Using Farm Produces as Raw Materials	98.4	111.2	98.0	101.2	101.6
以非农产品为原料	Using Non-farm Produces as Raw Materials	101.9	104.6	102.1	105.3	106.8
重工业	Heavy Industry	122.5	128.7	79.7	93.4	115.4
采　掘	Mining and Quarrying	136.2	153.1	65.2	84.9	130.4
原　料	Raw Materials	114.2	114.0	83.2	94.3	110.3
加　工	Manufacturing	104.1	105.6	93.0	100.7	112.4
按生产生活分	**Grouped by Production and Consumer**					
生产资料	Means of Production	118.4	127.1	80.9	94.0	115.1
采　掘	Mining and Quarrying	136.0	151.9	65.2	84.9	130.4
原　料	Raw Materials	114.3	115.1	83.9	94.8	110.3
加　工	Manufacturing	100.4	107.3	93.8	100.7	111.6
生活资料	Consumer Goods	101.3	104.1	98.6	100.5	99.9
食　品	Food	101.7	104.4	98.4	101.1	99.4
衣　着	Clothing	96.4	101.5	99.5	101.6	100.1
一般日用品	Articles for Daily Use	101.1	101.4	99.3	97.1	102.3
耐用消费品	Durable Consumer Goods	99.2	102.3	100.0	100.1	99.7
按工业行业分	**Grouped by Setors**					
冶金工业	Metallurgical Industry	101.9	114.4	84.5	100.4	121.8
电力工业	Power Industry	100.9	100.7	99.9	97.3	98.8
煤炭及炼焦工业	Coal and coking Industry	109.4	104.0	94.2	96.0	118.3
石油工业	Petroleum Industry	130.5	141.6	67.3	85.4	123.3
化学工业	Chemical Industry	106.1	112.1	93.1	98.6	107.9
机械工业	Machine Buiding Industry	112.4	97.4	99.3	100.2	101.0
建筑材料工业	Buiding Materials Industry	99.4	101.1	97.2	102.1	101.5
森林工业	Timber Industry	99.9	101.7	97.1	90.6	102.2
食品工业	Food Industry	101.1	104.9	97.8	100.5	99.9
纺织工业	Textile Industry	92.1	122.8	97.4	102.8	107.9
缝纫工业	Tailoring Industry	96.3	101.5	99.4	101.6	100.1
皮革工业	Leather Industry	100.0	101.1	98.9	96.4	99.1
造纸工业	Paper Industry	102.6	127.8	100.2	99.9	103.0
文教艺术用品工业	Cultural,Educational and Handicraft Articles	99.7	101.1	100.2	97.0	98.5
其他工业	Other Industry	104.0	107.7	101.2	97.6	111.3

7—12 兵团工业生产者出厂价格分类指数

Producer Price Indices for Industrial Products of XPCC by Category

（上年=100） (preceding year=100)

指标	Item	2013	2014	2015	2016	2017
全部工业品	**Total Industrial Products**	**100.5**	**99.9**	**96.4**	**100.0**	**108.3**
按轻重工业分	**Grouped by Light Inudustry and Heary Industry**					
轻工业	Light Industry	102.2	101.5	97.3	98.1	102.5
以农产品为原料	Using Farm Produces as Raw Materials	102.1	101.5	97.3	98.1	102.5
以非农产品为原料	Using Non-farm Produces as Raw Materials	105.8	99.9	101.3	99.3	100.0
重工业	Heavy Industry	99.0	98.4	95.5	100.9	111.1
采　掘	Mining and Quarrying	93.0	94.2	95.0	91.3	108.4
原　料	Raw Materials	101.0	99.4	94.5	101.0	111.9
加　工	Manufacturing	96.3	97.1	97.2	101.9	109.3
按生产生活分	**Grouped by Production and Consumer**					
生产资料	Means of Production	98.8	98.3	96.2	100.4	110.5
采　掘	Mining and Quarrying	93.0	94.2	95.0	91.3	108.4
原　料	Raw Materials	100.3	98.6	94.8	101.1	111.9
加　工	Manufacturing	97.9	98.3	97.5	99.9	108.1
生活资料	Consumer Goods	105.0	104.0	96.9	98.7	100.8
食　品	Food	105.1	104.1	96.8	98.4	100.5
衣　着	Clothing	100.3	100.6	100.0	102.5	101.9
一般日用品	Articles for Daily Use	101.2	99.7	100.0	105.1	104.5
按工业行业分	**Grouped by Setors**					
冶金工业	Metallurgical Industry	92.6	96.0	90.3	110.1	115.0
电力工业	Power Industry	100.3	97.6	103.8	84.2	99.2
煤炭及炼焦工业	Coal and coking Industry	94.1	92.3	95.3	88.4	133.5
石油工业	Petroleum Industry	101.1	100.0	103.8	92.2	99.5
化学工业	Chemical Industry	100.8	100.3	93.5	100.9	106.4
机械工业	Machine Buiding Industry	100.0	99.9	95.2	95.7	116.7
建筑材料工业	Buiding Materials Industry	91.6	94.0	96.9	103.2	106.9
森林业	Timber Industry	100.0	100.0	100.0	99.0	100.0
食品工业	Food Industry	104.4	103.9	98.9	98.4	101.5
纺织工业	Textile Industry	98.2	97.3	90.9	95.2	105.0
缝纫工业	Tailoring Industry	100.3	100.6	100.0	102.5	101.9
皮革工业	Leather Industry					
造纸工业	Paper Industry	98.2	99.5	99.6	98.8	105.7
文教艺术用品工业	Cultural,Educational and Handicraft Articles	100.3	100.0	100.0		
其他工业	Other Industry	108.2	100.0	100.0	102.2	112.7

7—13 工业生产者购进价格分类指数

Purchasing Price Indices for Industrial Producers by Category

（上年＝100） (preceding year＝100)

指　　标	Iterm	2005	2010	2015	2016	2017
总指数	**Total of Raw Material**	**110.7**	**123.9**	**84.3**	**95.5**	**112.8**
燃料、动力类	Fuels and Power	132.0	137.6	69.9	92.5	118.1
黑色金属材料类	Materials of Ferrous Metals	113.8	105.0	88.7	99.5	117.8
# 钢　材	Rolled Steel	112.9	102.5	93.2	104.4	119.9
其　他	Other	114.9	112.3	80.4	92.5	114.5
有色金属材料和电线类	Materials of Non-Ferrous Metal and wires	108.5	139.6	91.5	95.4	107.9
化工原料类	Chemical Raw Materials	113.0	106.8	96.4	99.5	105.4
木材及纸浆类	Wood and Paper Pulp	102.0	104.0	99.7	97.4	107.9
建筑材料及非金属矿类	Building Materials and Non-metal Ore	103.9	103.0	98.1	98.6	102.7
其他工业原材料及半成品类	Other Industrial Raw Materials and Semi-finished Category	105.5	101.1	97.1	98.5	103.2
农副产品类	Agricultural and Side-line Produces	91.9	118.7	94.1	98.7	102.3
纺织原料类	Textile Raw Materials	93.0	144.2	95.3	101.4	108.5

7—14 兵团工业生产者购进价格分类指数

Purchasing Price Indices for Industrial Producers by Category

（上年＝100） (preceding year＝100)

指　　标	Item	2013	2014	2015	2016	2017
总指数	**Total of Raw Material**	**99.3**	**99.8**	**96.6**	**100.7**	**109.0**
燃料、动力类	Fuels and Power	101.0	100.6	99.6	96.2	108.9
黑色金属材料类	Materials of Ferrous Metals	94.7	95.6	95.0	102.8	106.1
# 钢　材	Rolled Steel	92.2	88.4	90.0	109.4	115.4
其　他	Other	95.9	99.2	97.4	99.7	101.4
有色金属材料和电线类	Materials of Non-Ferrous Metal and wires	84.1	100.0	100.0	103.7	119.9
化工原料类	Chemical Raw Materials	97.6	99.3	100.0	100.7	106.2
木材及纸浆类	Wood and Paper Pulp	98.0	99.4	100.0	99.5	110.6
建筑材料及非金属矿类	Building Materials and Non-metal Ore	99.4	99.1	89.2	102.2	104.4
其他工业原材料及半成品类	Other Industrial Raw Materials and Semi-finished Category	98.7	100.6	102.0	100.6	94.7
农副产品类	Agricultural and Side-line Produces	102.0	100.9	94.3	99.9	102.2
纺织原料类	Textile Raw Materials	99.0	98.4	96.9	102.1	115.4

2018
BING TUAN

第八篇

人民生活

Chapter 8 People's Living Conditions

简要说明

一、本篇资料主要内容

本篇资料反映兵团居民生活现状及发展变化情况，分为城镇常住居民家庭生活和连队常住居民家庭生活两部分。

二、本篇资料来源

本篇资料中城镇常住居民家庭生活状况数据和连队常住居民家庭生活状况数据均来源于国家统计局兵团调查总队住户调查处城乡一体化住户调查。调查内容主要包括家庭人口及其构成、家庭可支配收入构成及消费支出类型、主要商品购买数量及支出金额、劳动就业状况、居住状况和耐用消费品拥有量等。

三、本篇资料调查方法

统计调查方法为抽样调查。

Brief Introduction

1. Main Contens

Data in this chapter show the people's living conditions and their changes in XPCC,consisting of two parts on the life of urban and brigade permanent households respectively.

2. Sources of Data

Data of urban and brigade permanent households family life situation in this chapter are provided by the Urban and Rural Household Survey Section of National Statistics Bureau of XPCC on the integrated urban and rural household survey, including mainly family population and its composition, the composition of households disposable income and the type of consumption expenditure,the number of major commodities purchased and amount of expenditure,employment status,living conditions and possession of durable consumer goods.

3. Methodology of Survey

Survey method is sampled one.

8－1　历年居民收入情况

Income over the Years

计量单位:元　　　　(yuan)

年　份 Year	全体居民人均可支配收入 Per Capita Disposable Income of Households	城镇常住居民人均可支配收入 Per Capita Disposable Income of Urban Permanent Households	连队常住居民人均可支配收入 Per Capita Disposable Income of Brigade Permanent Households
2005		8 353	4 105
2006		8 966	4 827
2007		10 521	6 193
2008		11 836	6 771
2009		12 929	7 668
2010		14 559	8 782
2011		16 625	10 233
2012		19 641	12 106
2013	20 669	25 000	12 498
2014	22 806	27 558	13 930
2015	25 287	31 432	15 053
2016	27 215	34 089	16 401
2017	29 430	36 730	17 786

注:本表住户调查数据2013年起将城镇居民人均可支配收入和农工家庭人均纯收入数据改按新口径统计。
Note:Per Capita Annual Disposable Income of Urban Households and Per Capita Net Income of Rural Residents change as Per Capita Disposable Income of Urban and Brigade Permanent Households because of the reform of method system form 2013 .

8－2　兵团居民家庭平均每百户年底耐用消费品拥有量

Durable Consumer Goods Owned Per－100 Households at Year－end

（抽样调查 Sampled Survey）

指　标		Item		2016	2017
家用汽车	（辆）	Automobile	(unit)	34	35
摩托车	（辆）	Motorcycle	(unit)	54	53
电冰箱	（台）	Refrigerator	(set)	98	98
洗衣机	（台）	Washing Machine	(set)	98	99
热水器	（台）	Water-heater	(set)	85	85
# 太阳能热水器		Solar Water-heater		50	51
空　调	（台）	Air Conditioner	(unit)	17	18
彩色电视机	（台）	Color TV	(set)	104	105
照相机	（架）	Camera	(set)	21	20
计算机	（台）	Household-use Computer	(set)	62	62
# 接入互联网的计算机		Connect into the Internet		52	51
中高档乐器	（件）	Medium and High Grade Musical Instrument	(piece)	3	4
固定电话	（部）	Telephone	(set)	53	55
移动电话	（部）	Mobile Telephone	(unit)	212	214
# 接入互联网的移动电话		Mobile Telephone Access to the Internet		124	136

8—3 全体居民家庭基本情况

Basic Living Conditions of Urban Households

（抽样调查 Sampled Survey）

指　　标	Item	2016	2017
调查户数（户）	**Number of Households Surveyed (household)**	**1 680**	**1 680**
平均每户家庭人口（人）	**Average Household Size (person)**	**2.77**	**2.80**
平均每人可支配收入（元）	**Average Per Person Disposable Income (yuan)**	**27 478.79**	**29 430.36**
工资性收入	Income of Wages and Salaries	16 346.23	16 870.46
经营净收入	Net Income of Management	5 445.16	6 409.10
财产净收入	Net Income of Property	1 303.96	1 051.42
转移净收入	Net Income of Transfer	4 383.44	5 099.36
平均每人消费性支出（元）	**Per Capita Annual Living Expenditures forConsumption (yuan)**	**19 157.05**	**18 908.13**
食品烟酒	Food, Tobacco, Wine	5 048.19	5 145.39
衣　着	Clothing	1 898.39	1 695.96
居　住	Residence	3 126.92	3 107.11
生活用品及服务	Daily Necessities and Service	1 457.73	1 563.47
交通通信	Transport, Post and Communication Services	3 409.76	3 040.04
教育文化娱乐	Education, Cultural and Recreation Services	2 255.76	2 333.35
医疗保健	Medicine and Medical Service	1 575.56	1 607.47
其它商品和服务	Other Goods and Services	384.74	415.35
平均每人消费性支出构成（人均消费支出＝100）	**Composition of Per Capita Annual Living Expenditures for Consumption (Per Capita Annual Living=100)**	**100.00**	**100.00**
食品烟酒	Food, Tobacco, Wine	26.35	27.21
衣　着	Clothing	9.91	8.97
居　住	Residence	16.32	16.43
生活用品及服务	Daily Necessities and Service	7.61	8.27
交通通信	Transport, Post and Communication Services	17.80	16.08
教育文化娱乐	Education, Cultural and Recreation Services	11.78	12.34
医疗保健	Medicine and Medical Service	8.22	8.50
其它商品和服务	Other Goods and Services	2.01	2.20

8—4 城镇常住居民家庭基本情况

Basic Living Conditions of Urban Permanent Households

(抽样调查 Sampled Survey)

指 标		Item		2016	2017
调查户数	**(户)**	**Number of Households Surveyed**	**(household)**	**900**	**900**
平均每户家庭人口	**(人)**	**Average Household Size**	**(person)**	**2.63**	**2.65**
平均每人可支配收入	**(元)**	**Average Per Person Disposable Income**	**(yuan)**	**34 089.32**	**36 730.04**
工资性收入		Income of Wages and Salaries		23 764.28	24 988.19
经营净收入		Net Income of Management		4 232.60	4 599.86
财产净收入		Net Income of Property		1 694.18	1 464.56
转移净收入		Net Income of Transfer		4 398.26	5 677.43
平均每人消费性支出	**(元)**	**Per Capita Annual Living Expenditures forConsumption**	**(yuan)**	**22 355.29**	**21 826.99**
食品烟酒		Food, Tobacco, Wine		5 882.39	5 994.72
衣 着		Clothing		2 502.40	2 113.95
居 住		Residence		3 435.73	3 419.71
生活用品及服务		Daily Necessities and Service		1 681.59	1 838.08
交通通信		Transport, Post and Communication Services		3 910.29	3 460.70
教育文化娱乐		Education, Cultural and Recreation Services		2 488.46	2 587.48
医疗保健		Medicine and Medical Service		1 957.21	1 937.81
其它商品和服务		Other Goods and Services		497.22	474.54
平均每人消费性支出构成(人均消费支出=100)		**Composition of Per Capita Annual Living Expenditures for Consumption (Per Capita Annual Living=100)**		**100.00**	**100.00**
食品烟酒		Food, Tobacco, Wine		26.31	27.46
衣 着		Clothing		11.19	9.69
居 住		Residence		15.37	15.67
生活用品及服务		Daily Necessities and Service		7.52	8.42
交通通信		Transport, Post and Communication Services		17.49	15.86
教育文化娱乐		Education, Cultural and Recreation Services		11.13	11.85
医疗保健		Medicine and Medical Service		8.76	8.88
其它商品和服务		Other Goods and Services		2.22	2.17

8—5 城镇常住居民家庭年人均购买主要商品数量

Annual Per Capita Major Commodities Purchased by Urban Permanent Households

（抽样调查 Sampled Survey）

指　　标		Item		2016	2017
大　米	（千克）	Rice	(kg)	24.97	27.74
面　粉	（千克）	Flour	(kg)	26.32	25.21
食用植物油	（千克）	Edible Vegetable Oil	(kg)	12.03	12.1
猪　肉	（千克）	Pork	(kg)	11.74	12.16
牛　肉	（千克）	Beef	(kg)	4.53	4.38
羊　肉	（千克）	Mutton	(kg)	4.94	4.35
鸡	（千克）	Chicken	(kg)	5.85	6.21
鸭	（千克）	Duck	(kg)	0.60	0.54
鲜　蛋	（千克）	Fresh Eggs	(kg)	8.89	9.17
鱼	（千克）	Fish	(kg)	5.95	6.08
虾	（千克）	Shrimp	(kg)	0.79	0.90
鲜　菜	（千克）	Fresh Vegetables	(kg)	98.31	96.12
白　酒	（千克）	Liquor	(kg)	1.49	1.91
果　酒	（千克）	Fruit Wine	(kg)	0.51	0.38
啤　酒	（千克）	Beer	(kg)	3.18	2.91
饮　料	（元）	Aerated beverages	(yuan)	108.27	113.81
鲜瓜果	（千克）	Fresh Melons and Fruits	(kg)	64.38	63.01
糕　点	（千克）	Cake	(kg)	3.95	4.21
鲜　奶	（千克）	Milk	(kg)	12.44	13.42
奶　粉	（千克）	Milk Powder	(kg)	0.22	0.36
酸　奶	（千克）	Yogurt	(kg)	6.51	7.66
服　装	（元）	Clothing	(yuan)	1623	1565
鞋	（双）	Shoes	(pair)	2.95	2.53
水	（吨）	Water	(ton)	46.52	44.00
电	（千瓦时）	Electricity	(kwh)	377.72	395.12
煤　炭	（千克）	Coal	(kg)	58.30	58.86
罐装液化石油气	（千克）	Bottle Packs Liquefied Petrolum Gas	(kg)	6.38	3.66
管道天然气	（立方米）	Pipe Natural Gas	(stere)	73.41	75.87

8—6 城镇常住居民家庭平均每百户年底耐用消费品拥有量

Durable Consumer Goods Owned Per-100 Urban Permanent Households at Year-end

（抽样调查 Sampled Survey）

指 标		Item		2016	2017
家用汽车	（辆）	Automobile	(unit)	36	37
摩托车	（辆）	Motorcycle	(unit)	29	28
电冰箱	（台）	Refrigerator	(set)	98	98
洗衣机	（台）	Washing Machine	(set)	98	99
热水器	（台）	Water-heater	(set)	90	91
# 太阳能热水器		Solar Water-heater		51	52
空 调	（台）	Air Conditioner	(unit)	23	23
彩色电视机	（台）	Color TV	(set)	101	102
照相机	（架）	Camera	(set)	29	28
计算机	（台）	Household-use Computer	(set)	71	70
# 接入互联网的计算机		Connect into the Internet		62	61
中高档乐器	（件）	Medium and High Grade Musical Instrument	(piece)	5	5
固定电话	（部）	Telephone	(set)	62	65
移动电话	（部）	Mobile Telephone	(unit)	202	204
# 接入互联网的移动电话		Mobile Telephone Access to the Internet		131	140

8—7 各师城镇常住居民家庭年人均收支情况

Annual Per Capita Income and Expendture of Urban Permanent Households by Division

计量单位：元　　（2017 年）　　(yuan)

单 位	Unit	可支配收入 Disposable Income	消费性支出 Expenditure for Consumption
兵 团	**XPCC**	**36 730**	**21 827**
一 师	Division 1	36 485	17 780
二 师	Division 2	36 671	18 654
三 师	Division 3	36 412	17 029
四 师	Division 4	36 048	22 047
五 师	Division 5	36 140	17 611
六 师	Division 6	36 402	19 282
七 师	Division 7	36 601	17 303
八 师	Division 8	37 200	26 921
九 师	Division 9	35 954	23 758
十 师	Division 10	36 006	17 032
十 一 师	Division 11	38 178	30 153
十 二 师	Division 12	36 886	25 255
十 三 师	Division 13	38 115	28 254
十 四 师	Division 14	36 919	21 160

注：一师数据包含阿拉尔市，三师数据包含图木舒克市，六师数据包含五家渠市，八师数据包含石河子市，十师数据包含北屯市。
Note: Data of Division 1 included Alaer City, data of division 3 included Tumushuke City, data of Division 6 included Wujiaqu City, data of Division 8 included Shihezi City, data of Division 10 included Beitun City.

8—8 连队常住居民家庭基本情况

Basic Living Conditions of Brigade Permanent Households

（抽样调查 Sampled Survey）

指　　标		Item		2016	2017
调查户数	**（户）**	**Number of Households Surveyed**	**(household)**	**780**	**780**
平均每户家庭人口	**（人）**	**Average Household Size**	**(person)**	**3.03**	**3.10**
平均每人可支配收入	**（元）**	**Average Per Person Disposable Income**	**(yuan)**	**16 400.70**	**17 785.81**
工资性收入		Income of Wages and Salaries		3 997.87	3 920.95
经营净收入		Net Income of Management		7 352.58	9 295.24
财产净收入		Net Income of Property		690.13	392.26
转移净收入		Net Income of Transfer		4 360.12	4 177.36
平均每人消费性支出	**（元）**	**Per Capita Annual Living Expenditures forConsumption**	**(yuan)**	**14 126.00**	**14 251.93**
食品烟酒		Food, Tobacco, Wine		3 735.93	3 790.53
衣　着		Clothing		948.23	1029.18
居　住		Residence		2 641.15	2 608.45
生活用品及服务		Daily Necessities and Service		1 105.57	1 125.40
交通通信		Transport, Post and Communication Services		2 622.38	2 368.99
教育文化娱乐		Education, Cultural and Recreation Services		1 889.73	1 927.96
医疗保健		Medicine and Medical Service		975.20	1080.52
其它商品和服务		Other Goods and Services		207.81	320.90
平均每人消费性支出构成（人均消费支出＝100）		**Composition of Per Capita Annual Living Expenditures for Consumption (Per Capita Annual Living=100)**		**100.00**	**100.00**
食品烟酒		Food, Tobacco, Wine		26.45	26.60
衣　着		Clothing		6.71	7.22
居　住		Residence		18.70	18.30
生活用品及服务		Daily Necessities and Service		7.83	7.90
交通通信		Transport, Post and Communication Services		18.56	16.62
教育文化娱乐		Education, Cultural and Recreation Services		13.38	13.53
医疗保健		Medicine and Medical Service		6.90	7.58
其它商品和服务		Other Goods and Services		1.47	2.25

8—9 连队常住居民家庭年人均购买主要商品数量

Annual Per Capita Major Commodities Purchased by Brigade Permanent Households

(抽样调查 Sampled Survey)

指标		Item		2016	2017
大米	(千克)	Rice	(kg)	33.73	36.49
面粉	(千克)	Flour	(kg)	49.49	48.93
食用植物油	(千克)	Edible Vegetable Oil	(kg)	13.41	12.78
猪肉	(千克)	Pork	(kg)	11.13	11.28
牛肉	(千克)	Beef	(kg)	2.58	2.64
羊肉	(千克)	Mutton	(kg)	4.40	4.58
鸡	(千克)	Chicken	(kg)	4.49	4.62
鸭	(千克)	Duck	(kg)	0.35	0.38
鲜蛋	(千克)	Fresh Eggs	(kg)	6.52	7.27
鱼	(千克)	Fish	(kg)	4.70	4.46
虾	(千克)	Shrimp	(kg)	0.27	0.31
鲜菜	(千克)	Fresh Vegetables	(kg)	67.81	73.14
白酒	(千克)	Liquor	(kg)	2.43	2.18
果酒	(千克)	Fruit Wine	(kg)	0.24	0.31
啤酒	(千克)	Beer	(kg)	6.57	6.53
饮料	(元)	Aerated beverages	(yuan)	107.89	101.92
鲜瓜果	(千克)	Fresh Melons and Fruits	(kg)	48.94	48.33
糕点	(千克)	Cake	(kg)	1.92	1.62
鲜奶	(千克)	Milk	(kg)	5.90	5.82
奶粉	(千克)	Milk Powder	(kg)	0.20	0.13
酸奶	(千克)	Yogurt	(kg)	1.93	2.15
服装	(元)	Clothing	(yuan)	649	729
鞋	(双)	Shoes	(pair)	2.31	2.26
水	(吨)	Water	(ton)	39.39	38.24
电	(千瓦时)	Electricity	(kwh)	352.48	371.10
煤炭	(千克)	Coal	(kg)	378.06	348.57
罐装液化石油气	(千克)	Bottle Packs Liquefied Petrolum Gas	(kg)	12.82	17.60
管道天然气	(立方米)	Pipe Natural Gas	(stere)	29.09	36.53

8—10 连队常住居民家庭平均每百户年底耐用消费品拥有量

Durable Consumer Goods Owned by Per-100 Brigade Permanent Households at Year-end

(抽样调查 Sampled Survey)

指　　标		Item		2016	2017
家用汽车	(辆)	Automobile	(unit)	30	31
摩托车	(辆)	Motorcycle	(unit)	98	99
电冰箱	(台)	Refrigerator	(set)	99	98
洗衣机	(台)	Washing Machine	(set)	99	99
热水器	(台)	Water-heater	(set)	76	75
# 太阳能热水器		Solar Water-heater		48	48
空　调	(台)	Air Conditioner	(unit)	7	9
彩色电视机	(台)	Color TV	(set)	110	110
照相机	(架)	Camera	(set)	6	6
计算机	(台)	Household-use Computer	(set)	46	46
# 接入互联网的计算机		Connect into the Internet		34	33
中高档乐器	(件)	Medium and High Grade Musical Instrument	(piece)	1	2
固定电话	(部)	Telephone	(set)	38	37
移动电话	(部)	Mobile Telephone	(unit)	230	232
# 接入互联网的移动电话		Mobile Telephone Access to the Internet		112	128

8—11 各师连队常住居民家庭年人均收支情况

Per Capita Income and Expenditure of Brigade Permanent Households by Division

计量单位:元　　(2017 年)　　(yuan)

单　　位	Unit	可支配收入 Disposable Income	消费性支出 Expenditure for Consumption
兵　团	**XPCC**	**17 786**	**14 252**
一　师	Division 1	19 130	15 139
二　师	Division 2	18 105	12 949
三　师	Division 3	17 053	10 189
四　师	Division 4	16 242	11 870
五　师	Division 5	17 663	15 245
六　师	Division 6	17 798	14 723
七　师	Division 7	17 995	11 829
八　师	Division 8	19 020	18 366
九　师	Division 9	16 173	15 068
十　师	Division 10	16 898	12 437
十 二 师	Division 12	18 206	22 024
十 三 师	Division 13	17 808	15 343
十 四 师	Division 14	13 730	7 929

2018

BING TUAN

第九篇

农　业

Chapter 9 Agriculture

简要说明

一、本篇资料主要内容

本篇资料反映兵团农业生产和团场经济基本情况。主要内容包括团场劳动力、耕地资源、农业机械拥有量、农林牧渔业总产值、主要农产品产量和团场基本情况等统计资料。

二、本篇资料统计范围

包括全社会除农业科研机构进行的农业生产以外的所有农业生产内容。如各种专业性农、林、牧、渔场的农业生产活动；兵团各级机关、团体、学校进行的农业生产活动；集体所有制农场农业生产活动；工矿企业经营的农、林、牧、渔业生产活动；以及团场各种经济组织、农户经营的农、林、牧、渔业生产活动等。

1.农业:指对各种农作物的种植活动。包括谷物、豆类、薯类、棉花、油料、糖料、麻类、烟叶、蔬菜、园艺作物、水果、坚果、饮料和香料作物、中草药及其他作物的种植。

2.林业:包括林木的栽培(不包括茶园、桑园和果园的栽培、管理和收获等活动)、木材和竹材的采运、林产品的采集。

3.牧业：包括牲畜饲养和放牧、家禽饲养。

4.渔业：包括水生动物的养殖和捕捞。

5.农、林、牧、渔服务业:指对农、林、牧、渔业生产活动进行的各种支持性服务，但不包括各种科学技术和专业性技术服务活动。

三、本篇资料来源

本篇资料由国家统计局兵团调查总队农业调查处根据《兵团农林牧渔业统计报表制度》收集、汇总、整理、提供。

四、本篇资料调查方法

统计调查方法为全面统计。

Brief Introduction

1. Main Contents

Data in this chapter show the basic conditions of agricultural production and farm economy of XPCC. Contents mainly include farm labor force, resources of cultivated land, farming machinery possession, total output value of farming, forestry, animal husbandry and fishery, output of major farming products and farms.

2. Scope of Statistics

The statistical scope includes all agricultural production contents except for agricultural production of agricultural scientific research institutions, such as production activities of farms specializing in farming, forestry, animal husbandry and fishery; production activities of administrative agencies, institutions and schools, production activities of collective farms run by townships and villages; production activities of farming, forestry, animal husbandry and fishery run by industrial and mining enterprises; and production activities of farming, forestry, animal husbandry, and fishery undertaken by rural economic units of various types and by households .

2.1. Agriculture: refers to cultivation of farm crops, including cereals, beans, tuber crops, cotton, oil-bearing crops, sugar crops, hemp, tobacco leaves, vegetables, gardening plants, fruits, nuts, crops for beverages and spices, medicinal herbs and other farm crops.

2.2. Forestry: includes the planting of trees (excluding the operations of planting, management and harvesting on tea plantations, mulberry fields and orchards), cutting and transport of timber and bamboo and collection of forest products.

2.3. Animal husbandry: includes the raising and grazing of domestic animals and poultry.

2.4. Fishery: includes cultivation and catching of aquatic animals.

2.5. Services in support of agriculture, forestry, animal husbandry and fishery: include supporting services to production activities in agriculture, forestry, animal husbandry and fishery but do not include activities of science and technology and professional services.

3. Sources of Data

Data in this chapter are collected and prepared by the Agriculture Survey Section of Survey Office of XPCC of National Bureau of Statistics China according to *the Comprehensive Statistical Reporting Form System on Farming, Forestry, Animal Husbandry and Fishery of XPCC*.

4. Methodology of Survey

Survey method is comprehensive statistics.

9—1 各师国有农林牧渔场基本情况

Basic Statistics of State-owned Farms of Farming、Forestry、Animal Husbandry and Fishery by Division

(2017 年)

指 标 Item	合 计 Total	一 师 Division 1	二 师 Division 2	三 师 Division 3	四 师 Division 4	五 师 Division 5	六 师 Division 6
团场总数 (个) Total Regnient Farms (unit)	**178**	**16**	**19**	**18**	**21**	**11**	**19**
农 场 Number of Farms	166	16	19	16	19	11	18
牧 场 Number of Ranch	12	2	2	1			
团场户数 (户) Number of households on Farms (household)	**726 936**	**84 044**	**58 742**	**63 727**	**77 216**	**36 729**	**93 841**
# 牧业户数 (人) Number of Stock Raising Household (Person)	35 869	1 421	1 834	3 780	5 154	1 000	6 494
团场人口 (人) Population (Person)	**2 020 662**	**244 278**	**162 533**	**219 081**	**206 506**	**98 631**	**249 176**
# 牧业人口 (人) Stock-breeding Population (Person)	99 224	3 812	4 088	14 414	14 212	3 758	17 457
团场劳动力总计 (人) Total Labour on a Farm (Person)	**1 024 216**	**125 605**	**89 748**	**92 421**	**106 957**	**44 970**	**118 322**
# 男 Male	550 607	68 144	47 735	51 162	58 554	24 742	63 611
女 Female	473 609	57 461	42 013	41 259	48 403	20 228	54 711
场内实有就业人员 (人) Persons Actually Engaged on Farms (Person)	**908 850**	**120 864**	**76 675**	**84 822**	**91 796**	**44 658**	**116 275**
农业就业人员 Persons Engaged in Agriculture	386 235	45 555	31 726	41 944	42 349	21 175	50 578
工业就业人员 Persons Engaged in Industry	115 403	25 692	14 317	7 595	12 571	3 638	8 834
建筑业就业人员 Persons Engaged in Construction	45 875	6 686	1 115	5 962	1 967	2 451	8 356
交通运输业、仓储及邮电通迅业就业人员 Persons Engaged in Transportation,Storage and Postal Service and Telecommunications	54 901	3 927	3 672	1 748	5 803	1 962	9 577
信息传输、计算机服务和软件业就业人员 Persons Engaged in Information Deliver,Computer Service and Software	965	80	168	15	32	110	
批发和零售业就业人员 Persons Engaged in Wholesale and Retail Trade	117 307	15 607	11 766	9 820	8 058	5 222	14 815
住宿和餐饮业就业人员 Persons Engaged in Accommodation and Catering Services Industry	51 167	5 069	3 627	4 127	5 300	2 331	6 385
其他就业人员 Employed Persons in Other Trades	141 938	18 248	10 284	13 611	15 748	7 847	17 620

9—1续表 Continued

(2017年)

指 标 Item		七 师 Division 7	八 师 Division 8	九 师 Division 9	十 师 Division 10	十二师 Division 12	十三师 Division 13	十四师 Division 14
团场总数 Total Regiment Farms	**(个) (unit)**	**10**	**18**	**11**	**11**	**8**	**11**	**5**
农 场 Number of Farms		10	17	10	10	6	10	4
牧 场 Number of Ranch			1	1	1	2	1	1
团场户数 Number of households on Farms	**(户) (household)**	**62 470**	**117 601**	**21 387**	**21 608**	**40 056**	**34 320**	**15 195**
# 牧业户数 Number of Stock Raising Household	(人) (Person)	1 302	6 491	2 874	2 211	1 005	1 639	664
团场人口 Population	**(人) (Person)**	**166 979**	**305 457**	**57 464**	**57 390**	**110 298**	**89 589**	**53 280**
# 牧业人口 Stock-breeding Population	(人) (Person)	3 221	15 463	6 845	5 355	3 484	5 182	1 933
团场劳动力总计 Total Labour on a Farm	**(人) (Person)**	**81 875**	**183 374**	**31 165**	**26 219**	**45 628**	**45 861**	**32 071**
# 男 Male		42 376	96 837	16 598	14 634	24 248	24 812	17 154
女 Female		39 499	86 537	14 567	11 585	21 380	21 049	14 917
场内实有就业人员 Persons Actually Engaged on Farms	**(人) (Person)**	**77 298**	**130 841**	**28 822**	**28 845**	**37 616**	**51 386**	**23 689**
农业就业人员 Persons Engaged in Agriculture		26 958	56 303	17 633	12 613	9 148	13 862	16 391
工业就业人员 Persons Engaged in Industry		7 683	13 349	1 430	5 084	3 251	10 675	1 284
建筑业就业人员 Persons Engaged in Construction		5 650	8 350	993	1 133	994	2 103	25
交通运输业、仓储及邮电通迅业就业人员 Persons Engaged in Transportation,Storage and Postal Service and Telecommunications		10 116	5 488	1 133	1 770	3 710	5 491	504
信息传输、计算机服务和软件业就业人员 Persons Engaged in Information Deliver,Computer Service and Software		109	136	36	1	52	124	2
批发和零售业就业人员 Persons Engaged in Wholesale and Retail Trade		12 772	19 605	2 379	2 728	6 616	6 648	1 271
住宿和餐饮业就业人员 Persons Engaged in Accommodation and Catering Services Industry		4 633	9 153	1 385	1 614	3 420	3 418	705
其他就业人员 Employed Persons in Other Trades		9 377	18 457	3 833	3 902	10 425	9 065	3 521

9—2 农林牧渔业总产值

Total Output Value of Farming, Forestry, Animal Husbandry and Fishery

年 份 Year	单 位 Unit	农林牧渔业总产值（万元） Total (10 000 yuan)	农 业 Farming	林 业 Forestry	牧 业 Animal Husbandry	渔 业 Fishery	农林牧渔服务业 Services	构成% Composition% # 农 业 Farming	# 牧 业 Animal Husbandry
	1950	1 105	1 105					100.0	
	1952	4 494	3 854		640			85.8	14.2
	1954	3 153	2 521		632			80.0	20.0
	1957	8 233	6 668		1 565			81.0	19.0
	1962	21 809	15 224	224	3 488	126		69.8	16.0
	1965	34 818	26 714	533	5 121	122		76.7	14.7
	1970	44 521	34 112	583	5 623	160		76.6	12.6
	1975	37 313	28 131	384	6 325	119		75.4	17.0
	1978	62 305	46 629	498	9 664	131		74.8	15.5
	1980	75 351	59 751	900	8 386	179		79.3	11.1
	1985	149 853	113 893	6 116	19 981	599		76.0	13.3
	1990	383 188	320 256	5 776	45 352	2 645		83.6	11.8
	1995	1 055 545	925 635	7 260	116 540	6 110		87.7	11.0
	2000	1 414 310	1 253 291	12 949	141 028	7 042		88.6	10.0
	2001	1 267 685	1 081 188	16 944	161 583	7 970		85.3	12.7
	2002	1 590 270	1 367 883	29 778	182 708	9 901		86.0	11.5
	2003	2 187 989	1 775 231	43 331	207 217	10 305	151 905	81.1	9.5
	2004	2 315 994	1 831 921	33 233	245 737	11 861	193 242	79.1	10.6
	2005	2 645 643	2 142 398	32 343	255 228	14 136	201 538	81.0	9.6
	2006	2 982 673	2 431 520	30 798	272 286	15 493	232 576	81.5	9.1
	2007	3 415 178	2 748 722	33 475	367 703	18 238	247 040	80.5	10.8
	2008	3 854 118	2 981 537	35 718	525 293	22 626	288 944	77.4	13.6
	2009	4 326 567	3 353 245	43 031	618 642	24 232	287 417	77.5	14.3
	2010	5 692 849	4 504 030	54 456	768 463	30 387	335 513	79.3	13.5
	2011	6 688 632	5 103 113	67 275	1 026 339	39 283	452 622	76.3	15.3
	2012	8 020 942	6 194 701	92 688	1 145 271	47 578	540 704	77.2	14.3
	2013	9 080 395	7 011 738	124 392	1 320 766	54 961	568 538	77.2	14.5
	2014	9 385 456	7 104 792	133 103	1 475 882	67 922	603 757	75.7	15.7
	2015	9 712 236	7 413 143	155 861	1 448 661	74 028	620 543	76.3	14.9
	2016	10 592 637	8 124 702	186 290	1 535 314	83 882	662 449	76.7	14.5
	2017	11 458 643	8 729 494	203 408	1 691 184	92 833	741 724	76.2	14.8
一 师	Division 1	2 582 667	2 316 996	27 283	140 718	9 896	87 774	89.7	5.4
二 师	Division 2	900 822	705 982	7 734	133 433	10 025	43 648	78.4	14.8
三 师	Division 3	981 856	834 215	9 097	80 446	2 532	55 566	85.0	8.2
四 师	Division 4	915 652	591 120	11 907	254 544	16 940	41 141	64.6	27.8
五 师	Division 5	449 115	333 847	4 661	70 973	1 990	37 644	74.3	15.8
六 师	Division 6	1 174 358	794 774	8 830	249 202	4 605	116 947	67.7	21.2
七 师	Division 7	1 004 932	782 949	11 210	152 827	6 561	51 385	77.9	15.2
八 师	Division 8	1 945 970	1 362 531	86 635	286 761	8 780	201 263	70.0	14.7
九 师	Division 9	327 181	193 380	5 185	108 461	164	19 991	59.1	33.2
十 师	Division 10	369 902	224 218	5 641	79 963	27 657	32 423	60.6	21.6
十一师	Division 11	1 686	1 686					100.0	0.0
十二师	Division 12	230 093	144 773	18 926	43 460	3 280	19 654	62.9	18.9
十三师	Division 13	369 874	261 937	2 098	73 003	403	32 433	70.8	19.7
十四师	Division 14	204 535	181 086	4 201	17 393		1 855	88.5	8.5

9—3　农林牧渔业总产值及指数

Total Output Value of Farming, Forestry, Animal Husbandry and Fishery and Related Indices

年份 Year	单位 Unit	绝对数(万元) Gross Output Value of Farming, Forestry, Animal Husbandry and Fishery(10 000 yuan)					
		农林牧渔业总产值 Total	农业 Farming	林业 Forestry	牧业 Animal Husbandry	渔业 Fishery	农林牧渔服务业 Services
1950		2 788	2 788				
1952		11 856	9 721		2 135		
1954		8 465	6 358		2 107		
1957		22 037	16 822		5 215		
1962		47 359	35 740	1 232	9 678	709	
1965		90 593	70 870	2 793	15 965	965	
1970		112 053	88 401	3 228	19 476	948	
1975		87 107	65 013	1 764	19 745	585	
1978		126 393	96 902	2 232	26 648	611	
1980		147 898	118 924	3 317	25 057	600	
1985		241 561	190 289	10 038	40 036	1 198	
1990		388 892	332 603	6 274	46 989	3 026	
1995		548 982	483 787	6 180	55 150	3 865	
2000		850 899	761 350	8 050	76 146	5 353	
2001		835 151	740 405	9 346	79 682	5 718	
2002		991 718	882 968	15 149	86 875	6 726	
2003		1 139 699	910 682	20 053	97 892	7 020	104 052
2004		1 265 396	1 006 406	16 407	109 597	7 587	125 399
2005		1 378 114	1 107 445	15 233	119 731	8 520	127 185
2006		2 952 458	2 413 419	30 804	267 998	15 482	224 755
2007		3 214 280	2 616 086	33 279	303 085	17 719	244 111
2008		3 759 743	2 987 512	31 735	436 073	20 309	284 114
2009		4 125 448	3 161 755	42 183	613 245	23 129	285 136
2010		4 638 925	3 513 010	59 095	707 674	28 591	330 555
2011		6 064 383	4 711 400	58 280	830 360	34 910	429 433
2012		7 287 519	5 619 286	82 433	1 045 146	44 595	496 059
2013		8 693 346	6 792 286	100 381	1 192 771	55 393	552 515
2014		9 829 015	7 536 642	131 785	1 503 088	65 581	591 919
2015		9 989 678	7 692 376	137 322	1 482 158	70 637	607 185
2016		10 279 908	7 821 764	185 943	1 535 690	84 045	652 466
2017		11 371 809	8 676 194	203 850	1 686 674	91 423	713 668
一师	Division 1	2 558 656	2 299 976	28 069	134 517	9 702	86 392
二师	Division 2	899 354	704 151	7 734	134 184	10 702	42 583
三师	Division 3	980 091	837 818	9 097	77 838	2 468	52 870
四师	Division 4	898 045	579 529	11 907	251 228	16 087	39 294
五师	Division 5	437 974	324 944	4 661	70 062	1 901	36 406
六师	Division 6	1 178 536	798 286	8 830	254 547	4 316	112 557
七师	Division 7	995 389	774 813	11 210	153 811	6 477	49 078
八师	Division 8	1 942 237	1 358 320	87 070	295 874	8 745	192 228
九师	Division 9	325 633	193 033	5 185	108 320	164	18 931
十师	Division 10	362 755	221 057	5 519	77 214	27 240	31 725
十一师	Division 11	1 673	1 673				
十二师	Division 12	231 333	148 394	18 330	42 421	3 272	18 916
十三师	Division 13	359 788	255 873	2 012	70 637	348	30 918
十四师	Division 14	200 353	178 340	4 220	16 025		1 768

注：本表2005年(含2005年)以前数据按1990年可比价格计算，2006年以后数据按价格缩减指数计算。分师数据相加不等于合计。

Note: Data in this table are calculated at 1990 comparable prices before 2005(including 2005), and data after 2006 are calculated at price indices cut.

9—3 续表 Continued

年 份 单 位 Year Unit	指数(%)(上年=100) Indices of Gross Output Value of Farming, Forestry, Animal Husbandry and Fishery(%)(preceding year=100))					
	农林牧渔业总产值 Total	农 业 Farming	林 业 Forestry	牧 业 Animal Husbandry	渔 业 Fishery	农林牧渔服务业 Services
1950	100.0	100.0				
1952	276.3	236.6		1173.1		
1954	103.2	106.1		95.2		
1957	129.9	125.2		148.0		
1962	103.9	101.4	96.0	112.5	87.7	
1965	115.1	114.4	101.3	127.2	115.0	
1970	113.7	113.0	144.8	113.6	82.0	
1975	99.5	107.7	70.5	85.0	106.4	
1978	140.4	141.9	104.9	141.7	265.7	
1980	112.0	114.2	106.6	101.9	86.1	
1985	106.0	102.2	184.6	110.6	116.5	
1990	124.1	131.0	94.5	98.5	113.7	
1995	115.6	116.8	102.0	108.0	117.1	
2000	110.6	111.5	106.8	102.5	107.9	
2001	98.1	97.2	116.1	104.6	106.8	
2002	118.7	119.3	162.1	109.0	117.6	
2003	114.9	103.1	132.4	112.7	104.4	111.1
2004	111.0	110.5	81.8	112.0	108.1	120.5
2005	109.1	109.6	92.8	114.0	112.3	101.4
2006	113.4	114.2	96.5	112.3	109.8	110.6
2007	107.6	107.5	108.7	111.8	110.3	103.8
2008	110.1	108.7	94.8	118.6	111.4	115.0
2009	107.0	106.0	118.1	116.7	102.2	98.7
2010	107.2	104.8	137.3	114.4	118.0	115.0
2011	109.4	107.2	125.8	113.8	114.4	125.2
2012	109.0	110.1	122.5	101.8	113.5	109.6
2013	108.4	109.6	108.3	105.8	116.4	104.6
2014	108.2	107.5	105.9	113.8	119.3	104.1
2015	106.4	108.3	103.2	100.4	104.0	100.6
2016	105.9	105.5	119.3	106.0	113.5	105.1
2017	107.4	106.8	109.4	109.9	109.0	107.7
一 师 Division 1	106.0	105.7	104.0	110.8	103.2	108.5
二 师 Division 2	108.5	108.2	92.6	109.6	132.6	108.1
三 师 Division 3	107.9	108.2	122.4	104.7	79.4	107.3
四 师 Division 4	108.0	107.8	135.0	107.6	105.1	108.1
五 师 Division 5	109.3	109.9	99.0	108.5	110.5	106.3
六 师 Division 6	107.1	106.8	121.6	108.0	88.2	107.3
七 师 Division 7	107.3	105.5	113.2	116.3	124.3	106.5
八 师 Division 8	107.2	105.8	104.9	114.2	104.9	108.9
九 师 Division 9	107.1	108.2	107.6	105.5	71.0	106.0
十 师 Division 10	109.4	109.3	114.4	109.8	111.7	107.0
十一师 Division 11	91.6	91.6				
十二师 Division 12	103.9	98.2	150.1	111.0	109.0	104.5
十三师 Division 13	109.8	110.9	117.0	106.8	151.3	107.1
十四师 Division 14	110.7	112.5	67.9	109.9	100.0	107.3

9—4 各师按行业分列的农林牧渔业总产值

计量单位：万元 （2017年）

指　标	Item	合计 Total	一师 Division 1	二师 Division 2	三师 Division 3	四师 Division 4
农林牧渔业总产值总计	**Total Gross Output Value of Farming, Forestry, Animal Husbandry and Fishery**	**11 458 643**	**2 582 667**	**900 822**	**981 856**	**915 652**
农业产值合计	**Output Value of Farming**	**8 729 494**	**2 316 996**	**705 982**	**834 215**	**591 120**
谷物及其他作物	Cereal and Others	4 283 915	707 217	228 972	334 387	319 163
谷　物	Cereal	643 332	64 346	18 661	44 794	180 595
豆　类	Soybeans	16 076	212		984	8 348
薯　类	Tubers	38 070	2 391	20	1 671	16 085
油料作物	Oil-bearing Crops	122 973	1 336	775	4 260	38 731
棉　花	Cotton(lint)	2 938 560	608 958	180 645	249 980	27 616
# 棉　籽	Cotton Seed	477 750	111 460	31 629	40 236	3 950
麻　类	Fiber Crops	858				858
甜　菜	Beetroots	94 819	225	6 440		21 431
烟　叶	Tobacco					
其他作物	Others	429 227	29 749	22 431	32 698	25 499
蔬菜园艺作物	Vegetable and Horticultural Crops	1 020 275	61 594	170 246	75 658	54 226
# 工业用番茄	Tomato for Industry	154 971		26 181		345
工业用辣椒	Hot Pepper for Industry	203 818	22 190	94 939	28 672	50
水果、饮料和香料作物	Fruit, Beverage and Spice Crops	3 164 847	1 529 047	251 054	381 545	201 689
# 水　果	Fruit	2 753 064	1 410 807	245 966	293 105	153 199
瓜　类	Melon	203 779	4 932	4 481	39 406	11 339
药　材(种植)	Medical Materials(Planting)	260 457	19 138	55 710	42 625	16 042
林业产值合计	**Output Value of Forestry**	**203 408**	**27 283**	**7 734**	**9 097**	**11 907**
林木的培育和种植	Nurturing and Planting of Wood	190 465	25 582	4 959	8 684	9 737
林产品	Wood Products	2 700	853			165
木材采运	Timber Conveyance	10 243	848	2 775	413	2 005
牧业产值合计	**Output Value of Animal Husbandry**	**1 691 184**	**140 718**	**133 433**	**80 446**	**254 544**
牲畜饲养	Livestock Feeding	1 417 694	122 842	112 555	71 204	202 701
牛	Cattle and Buffaloes	210 098	18 281	12 763	4 961	47 558
羊	Sheep and Goats	458 867	38 705	33 903	44 906	54 122
猪	Hogs	433 987	30 058	56 006	15 844	46 181
其他牲畜饲养	Others	17 939	270	77	159	9 669
奶产品	Milk Products	260 205	32 375	8 472	4 103	38 409
毛绒产品	Hair and Cashere Products	30 118	3 153	1 334	1 231	6 762
其他牲畜产品	Other Livestock Products	6 480				
家禽的饲养	Poultry Feeding	223 009	12 454	13 374	6 057	31 112
# 禽　蛋	Poultry Eggs	94 044	4 895	4 948	3 032	17 226
其他动物及产品	Other Animal and Products	50 481	5 422	7 504	3 185	20 731
渔业产值合计	**Output Value of Fishery**	**92 833**	**9 896**	**10 025**	**2 532**	**16 940**
农林牧渔服务业产值合计	**Output Value of Farming, Forestry, Animal Husbandry and Fishery Services**	**741 724**	**87 774**	**43 648**	**55 566**	**41 141**

注：本表按当年价格计算。

Total Output Value of Agriculture Farming, Forestry Animal Husbandry and Fishery by Sector and Division

(10 000 yuan)

五 师 Division 5	六 师 Division 6	七 师 Division 7	八 师 Division 8	九 师 Division 9	十 师 Division 10	十一师 Division 11	十二师 Division 12	十三师 Division 13	十四师 Division 14
449 115	**1 174 358**	**1 004 932**	**1 945 970**	**327 181**	**369 902**	**1 686**	**230 093**	**369 874**	**204 535**
333 847	**794 774**	**782 949**	**1 362 531**	**193 380**	**224 218**	**1 686**	**144 773**	**261 937**	**181 086**
245 234	550 267	484 660	1 013 503	152 336	144 108	1 466	14 665	81 887	6 050
38 936	110 595	28 385	37 131	75 678	26 792	214	5 863	9 237	2 105
110	153		1 363	12	4 891		3		
406	11 871	1	951	79	3 918			352	325
4 057	13 888	11 900	572	22 545	21 541	113	2 989	236	30
186 940	361 059	389 109	854 821		9 313	1 003	292	68 824	
29 906	64 148	69 504	115 974		1 277	113	8	9 545	
6 804	6 229	11 871	3 153	33 666	5 000				
7 981	46 472	43 394	115 512	20 356	72 653	136	5 518	3 238	3 590
17 619	151 665	136 584	146 303	30 757	44 734	151	84 220	43 925	2 593
1 068	56 391	31 931	30 860	4 732			3 463		
	1 373	11 600	8 741	585	35 668				
68 734	69 738	87 181	202 254	5 360	17 977	69	45 311	133 805	171 083
63 067	27 857	81 548	145 932	4 890	4 102	69	42 584	114 476	165 462
3 387	41 881	5 633	56 322	470	13 875		2 727	16 277	3 049
2 260	23 104	74 521	471	4 927	17 399		577	2 320	1 360
4 661	**8 830**	**11 210**	**86 635**	**5 185**	**5 641**		**18 926**	**2 098**	**4 201**
4 353	6 616	11 138	86 292	3 873	4 828		18 926	1 730	3 747
		4		1 200	478				
308	2 214	68	343	112	335			368	454
70 973	**249 202**	**152 827**	**286 761**	**108 461**	**79 963**		**43 460**	**73 003**	**17 393**
56 090	202 774	120 154	244 458	100 901	66 828		40 515	62 963	13 709
4 805	39 034	13 786	20 900	16 376	15 363		4 370	10 739	1 162
18 956	76 979	26 291	15 271	68 479	29 949		8 331	33 562	9 413
22 931	68 590	28 255	115 237	6 738	14 984		14 022	13 118	2 023
49	759	240	2 080	450	850		280	2 161	895
1 227	11 654	48 313	89 568	6 287	4 667		13 396	1 688	46
1 642	5 758	3 269	1 402	2 571	1 015		116	1 695	170
6 480									
14 371	44 612	28 337	39 101	6 975	11 898		2 907	8 283	3 528
8 945	16 316	10 190	15 246	2 094	3 951		899	3 733	2 569
512	1 816	4 336	3 202	585	1 237		38	1 757	156
1 990	**4 605**	**6 561**	**8 780**	**164**	**27 657**		**3 280**	**403**	
37 644	**116 947**	**51 385**	**201 263**	**19 991**	**32 423**		**19 654**	**32 433**	**1 855**

Note: Data in this table are calculated at current prices.

9—5　各师农林牧渔业生产中间消耗

计量单位：万元　　　　（2017年）

指　标	Item	合计 Total	一师 Division 1	二师 Division 2	三师 Division 3	四师 Division 4
农林牧渔业生产中间消耗总计	**Total Indermediate Production Consumption**	**6 073 545**	**1 340 580**	**474 353**	**539 215**	**474 729**
农　业	**Farming**	**4 554 746**	**1 184 680**	**362 695**	**454 313**	**305 037**
中间物质消耗	Intermediate Material Consumption	2 924 021	824 873	287 858	237 043	166 556
用种量	Quantity of Seed	301 743	25 189	36 160	17 542	29 641
役畜用饲料、饲草	Animal Feed and Grass	19 390		150	6 953	189
# 饲料用粮	Grain for Animal Feed	2 982			1 906	14
农作物秸秆	Farm Crop Strain	2 111		34	536	162
肥　料	Fertilizers	929 465	280 445	118 816	85 809	54 443
# 化学肥料	Chemical Fertilizers	551 698	113 742	50 789	55 735	35 809
燃　料	Fuel	222 727	36 352	12 489	25 058	18 885
农　药	Pesticide	90 208	9 365	8 744	3 860	10 803
农用塑料簿膜	Farm Plastic Film	111 399	24 075	7 601	7 778	4 062
用电量	Electricity Consumed	140 515	9 539	11 118	11 871	3 897
小农具购置费	Purchases of Small Farm Implements	37 263	8 139	1 264	5 391	4 093
办公用品购置	Purchases of Office Equipment	26 806	10 529	994	3 475	2 092
其他物质消耗	Other Material Consumption	1 044 505	421 240	90 522	69 306	38 451
生产服务支出	Expenditures of Production Service	1 630 725	359 807	74 837	217 270	138 481
林　业	**Forestry**	**113 271**	**15 268**	**5 333**	**5 894**	**6 769**
# 中间物质消耗	Indermediate Material Consumption	72 217	11 476	3 026	2 431	2 287
牧　业	**Animal Husbandry**	**931 696**	**79 689**	**73 348**	**45 307**	**131 879**
中间物质消耗	Indermediate Material Consumption	821 372	72 290	67 647	40 807	112 445
用种量	Quantity of Seed	12 831	2 034	388	14	2 668
饲料、饲草	Animal Feed and Grass	710 555	55 877	59 689	38 494	94 783
# 饲料用粮	Grain for Animal Feed	214 488	17 890	22 377	9 264	35 654
饲料作物	Animal Feed Crop	51 744	2 305	4 735	4 568	3 063
农作物秸秆	Farm Crop Straw	45 011	5 512	1 137	2 748	5 234
饲　草	Forage	132 363	5 482	5 803	5 519	23 390
燃　料	Fuel	15 889	576	1 309	170	2 184
用电量	Electricity Consumed	6 654	366	730	172	433
畜牧用药品	Medicine for Animal Husbandry	18 246	1 532	2 185	662	4 311
其他物质消耗	Other Material Consumption	57 197	11 905	3 346	1 295	8 066
生产服务支出	Expenditures of Production Service	110 324	7 399	5 701	4 500	19 434
渔　业	**Fishery**	**53 916**	**4 943**	**6 758**	**1 473**	**8 556**
# 中间物质消耗	Intermediate Material Consumption	43 865	4 154	6 020	1 332	6 693
农林牧渔服务业合计	**Farming, Forestry, Animal Husbandry and Fishery Services**	**419 916**	**56 000**	**26 219**	**32 228**	**22 488**

Intermediate Production Consumption of Farming, Forestry, Animal, Husbandry and Fishery by Division

(10 000 yuan)

五 师 Division 5	六 师 Division 6	七 师 Division 7	八 师 Division 8	九 师 Division 9	十 师 Division 10	十一师 Division 11	十二师 Division 12	十三师 Division 13	十四师 Division 14
232 478	**622 654**	**521 641**	**1 030 043**	**170 930**	**228 956**	**902**	**132 652**	**191 663**	**112749**
169 861	**415 031**	**403 297**	**707 971**	**104 757**	**129 957**	**902**	**82 955**	**133 457**	**99833**
129 311	262 017	224 685	420 968	72 166	93 709	606	55 899	94 315	54015
12 260	46 771	23 897	30 743	18 809	30 711	99	19 757	8 428	1736
746	4		6 874						4474
350			198						514
68	3		129						1179
38 089	79 385	67 032	104 332	17 069	26 666	172	12 837	25 449	18921
28 489	67 489	43 022	86 746	10 349	20 916	172	5 672	14 253	18515
15 411	24 772	25 818	34 656	8 618	11 891	21	3 231	3 444	2081
6 094	12 092	5 257	19 077	866	8 274	17	1 052	1 527	3180
9 360	14 657	12 702	21 568	2 541	3 897	23	1 110	1 806	219
11 201	24 648	12 832	36 318	3 589	2 520	42	2 973	6 565	3402
364	3 722	4 498	5 291	1 229	1 459		188	1 334	291
1 568		3 847	2 314	360	835		95	608	89
34 218	55 966	68 802	159 795	19 085	7 456	232	14 656	45 154	19622
40 550	153 014	178 612	287 003	32 591	36 248	296	27 056	39 142	45818
2 660	**4 945**	**5 907**	**46 956**	**2 595**	**4 040**		**8 990**	**1 394**	**2520**
2 066	3 839	3 982	32 307	1 867	1 877		5 895	633	531
39 205	**138 307**	**82 817**	**157 977**	**53 497**	**53 687**		**27 362**	**39 232**	**9389**
35 404	123 829	73 048	131 257	49 268	47 348		24 179	35 036	8814
2 397	24	313	1 786	437	1 354		1 258	104	54
28 800	114 292	64 543	116 189	45 294	39 090		17 600	28 209	7695
16 764	41 913	14 772	28 672	8 272	8 411		4 359	4 011	2129
525	5 025	9 969	12 099	2 035	1 056		3 357	2 807	200
667	7 932	4 330	8 392	2 838	2 226		913	2 845	237
2 737	14 654	10 672	21 740	22 387	11 969		2 122	4 451	1437
1 597	1 803	1 948	1 403	968	2 523		515	328	565
446	186	1 447	1 494	131	427		159	542	121
1 032	1 203	1 578	2 420	672	1 588		600	206	257
1 132	6 321	3 219	7 965	1 766	2 366		4 047	5 647	122
3 801	14 478	9 769	26 720	4 229	6 339		3 183	4 196	575
1 023	**2 529**	**3 460**	**4 069**	**84**	**19 036**		**1 724**	**261**	
858	2 217	2 795	3 661	55	14 205		1 662	213	
19 729	**61 842**	**26 160**	**113 070**	**9 997**	**22 236**		**11 621**	**17 319**	**1007**

9—6　各师农业生产条件

（2017年）

指　标	Item	合　计 Total	一　师 Division 1	二　师 Division 2	三　师 Division 3	四　师 Division 4
耕地总资源　（千公顷）	**Cultivated Resource　(1 000 hectares)**					
年初耕地总资源	Cultivated Recource in Beginning of the Year	1 253.73	174.61	82.59	95.44	118.93
年内增加的耕地总资源	Increased Cultivated Recource in the Current Year	22.87		1.00	2.22	
年内减少的耕地总资源	Decreased Cultivated Resource in the Current Year	4.20	0.30	0.03	0.71	0.11
# 退耕还林还草占地	Land Converted to Forestry and Grass Land					
耕地改园地	Land Converted to Garden Area					
年末实有耕地总资源	Cultivated Resoure at the Year-end	1 272.40	174.31	83.56	96.95	118.82
水　田	Paddy Fields	7.68	0.16			7.13
旱　地	Dry Fields	54.54				30.89
水浇地	Irrigated Land	1 210.18	174.15	83.56	96.95	80.80
农业主要能源及物资消耗	**Main Engery and Material Consumption in Farm**					
农村用电量　（万千瓦小时）	Electricity Consumed in Rural Areas　(10 000 kwh)	373 688	29 183	26 282	23 841	15 298
农用化肥施用量	Consumption of Farm Chemical Fertilizers					
按实物量计算　（吨）	Compution Based on Material Objects　(ton)	1 629 149	321 569	168 597	153 849	129 488
氮　肥	Nitrogenous Fertilizers	698 436	88 004	77 713	73 492	50 012
磷　肥	Phosphate Fertilizers	315 293	48 481	24 107	47 460	33 407
钾　肥	Potash Fertilizers	156 089	24 133	20 501	11 367	12 302
复合肥	Compound Fertilizers	459 331	160 951	46 276	21 530	33 767
按折纯法计算　（吨）	Compution Based on Purity Deduction　(ton)	754 743	152 275	80 570	71 185	60 350
氮　肥	Nitrogenous Fertilizers	328 449	42 570	36 893	34 286	22 613
磷　肥	Phosphate Fertilizers	132 121	18 550	9 908	21 785	15 100
钾　肥	Potash Fertilizers	69 709	9 880	10 148	5 287	5 433
复合肥	Compound Fertilizers	224 450	81 275	23 621	9 827	17 204
农用塑料薄膜使用量　（吨）	Consumption of Farm Plastic Film　(ton)	71 135	10 749	5 869	5 702	3 032
# 地膜使用量	Consumption of Ground Plastic Film	66 733	10 435	5 521	5 483	2 607
地膜覆盖面积　（千公顷）	Areas Covered by Ground Plastic Pellicle　(1 000 hectares)	915	136	63	57	39
农用柴油使用量　（吨）	Consumption of Diesel　(ton)	252 125	51 123	22 635	21 204	17 192
农药使用量(实物量)　（公斤）	Consumption of Pesticide (Material Objects)　(kg)	12 102	1 268	852	622	1 173
农田水利建设情况	**Farmland Irrigation Development**					
有效灌溉面积　（千公顷）	Irrigated Area　(1 000 hectares)	1258.22	177.87	78.82	99.76	103.37
# 高新节水灌溉面积	Pelaxe and New Water-Saving Irrigated Area	1041.99	142.22	69.64	68.81	63.24
旱涝保收面积　（千公顷）	Area with Stable Yields Despite Drought or Flood　(1 000 hectares)	1164.39	155.73	78.15	85.99	83.97
机电排灌面积　（千公顷）	Electrical Irrigation and Drainage Area　(1 000 hectares)	891.39	118.58	64.43	66.12	44.16
机电井　（眼）	Machine Well　(unit)	21441	1859	986	4129	1028

注：本表耕地总资源数据来源于兵团国土资源局，为2015年数据。

Agriculture Production Conditions by Division

五 师 Division 5	六 师 Division 6	七 师 Division 7	八 师 Division 8	九 师 Division 9	十 师 Division 10	十一师 Division 11	十二师 Division 12	十三师 Division 13	十四师 Division 14
61.29	184.78	113.66	238.19	67.20	61.76	0.28	18.94	26.36	9.70
0.98	0.05	8.40	6.07		1.39		0.02	0.07	2.67
0.01	0.09	2.36	0.07	0.06	0.08		0.32	0.06	
62.26	184.74	119.70	244.19	67.14	63.07	0.28	18.64	26.37	12.37
	0.27		0.10						0.02
	1.54			22.11					
62.26	182.93	119.70	244.09	45.03	63.07	0.28	18.64	26.37	12.35
36 365	70 488	22 310	101 169	12 016	7 274	176	7 263	17 489	4 534
94 380	138 401	122 562	266 624	35 535	76 436	441	20 134	48 952	52 181
41 127	62 898	65 470	138 261	17 995	37 272	234	7 413	21 915	16 630
11 749	33 572	22 027	35 956	8 651	17 136	119	4 291	10 161	18 176
9 403	10 588	9 975	26 591	2 206	7 551	88	3 548	10 329	7 507
32 101	31 343	25 090	65 816	6 683	14 477		4 882	6 547	9 868
42 353	62 500	58 008	123 923	15 907	33 571	204	8 920	21 796	23 181
19 046	28 555	31 313	66 230	8 338	17 090	107	3 219	10 262	7 927
5 016	14 348	9 201	15 674	3 380	6 504	57	1 817	4 259	6 522
3 793	4 447	4 779	12 582	941	3 036	40	1 566	4 146	3 631
14 484	15 150	12 715	29 437	3 248	6 941		2 318	3 129	5 101
4 018	9 294	8 422	17 403	1 565	2 484	17	661	1 752	167
3 739	9 102	7 401	16 600	1 282	2 364	17	378	1 640	164
56	143	110	220	21	40	0	8	18	2
16 204	23 348	20 719	43 095	7 016	19 170	17	2 227	3 534	4 641
910	1 509	661	2 212	132	1 258	6	159	516	825
65.49	191.88	128.80	245.59	45.74	67.59	0.42	17.36	27.94	7.59
62.10	139.27	112.68	238.92	40.48	57.71	0.42	16.07	24.56	5.87
65.49	175.29	128.47	243.44	34.62	61.80	0.42	17.19	26.24	7.59
54.44	124.42	115.17	192.02	25.12	52.70	0.42	7.00	22.92	3.88
1318	2539	961	3865	890	753	15	510	2241	347

Note: Data of Cultivated resource in 2015 come from the Land and Resources Bureau of XPCC.

9—7　各师农业机械年末拥有量

（2017 年）

指　标		Item		合 计 Total	一 师 Division 1	二 师 Division 2	三 师 Division 3	四 师 Division 4
农业机械总动力	**（千瓦）**	**Total Power of Agricultural Machinery**	**（kw）**	**5 276 979**	**843 688**	**376 457**	**332 030**	**435 690**
柴油机动力		Diesel Engine Power		4 056 119	627 182	294 550	255 723	360 192
汽油机动力		Gasoline Engine Power		47 002	4 055	1 868	3 859	4 842
电动机动力		Electric Motor Power		1 173 858	212 451	80 039	72 448	70 656
其它机械动力		Ether Power						
主要机械与设备	**（千瓦）**	**Farming Machinery**	**（kw）**	**4 839 273**	**794 791**	**353 154**	**332 672**	**398 849**
大中型拖拉机	（台）	Large and Medium Agricultural Tractors	（unit）	51 400	6 871	4 423	3 040	4 940
	（千瓦）		（kw）	2 557 285	381 271	222 820	182 123	244 517
小型拖拉机	（台）	Mini-Tractors	（unit）	28 526	8 134	1 670	2 541	1 045
	（千瓦）		（kw）	376 864	107 075	23 247	32 192	13 219
大中型机引农具	（部）	Large and Medium Tractor Towing Farm Machinery	（unit）	82 898	8 138	5 860	4 620	6 693
小型机引农具	（部）	Small Tractor Towing Farm Machinery	（unit）	25 913	5 740	2 259	1 734	1 377
农用排灌柴油机	（台）	Farming Irrigated Machinery	（unit）	2 658	269	96	656	125
	（千瓦）		（kw）	53 110	8 142	3 011	11 668	1 497
农用排灌电动机	（台）	Diesel Engines	（unit）	25 097	3 381	2 068	3 159	1 032
	（千瓦）		（kw）	956 941	160 497	62 854	69 604	47 694
农用水泵	（台）	Farm Pump	（unit）	19 442	2 312	1 189	3 057	1 329
节水灌溉机械	（套）	Water-saving Irrigated Machinery	（set）	15 605	1 279	1 418	1 065	1 215
联合收割机	（台）	Combine Harvesters	（set）	3 160	403	134	32	655
	（千瓦）		（kw）	514 048	81 389	26 560	3 817	70 160
自走式机动割晒机	（台）	Self-propelled Swather Motor	（set）	88				63
	（千瓦）		（kw）	3 731				3 135
机动脱粒机	（台）	Mechanical Sheller	（set）	1 238		2	10	215
	（千瓦）		（kw）	11 552		28	88	2 677
渔业机械	（台）	Fishery Machinery	（set）	163	40	15	15	
	（千瓦）		（kw）	2 544	938	372	315	
农用运输车	（辆）	Farm Heavy-Duty Truck	（set）	16 495	4 139	392	2 590	236
	（千瓦）		（kw）	306 192	55 370	7 767	32 302	10 622

Major Agriculture Machinery at Year-end by Division

五 师 Division 5	六 师 Division 6	七 师 Division 7	八 师 Division 8	九 师 Division 9	十 师 Division 10	十一师 Division 11	十二师 Division 12	十三师 Division 13	十四师 Division 14
343 096	**702 403**	**427 633**	**995 133**	**182 639**	**303 416**	**1 321**	**77 782**	**175 103**	**80 588**
218 437	558 360	367 147	750 844	129 250	263 441	640	47 968	107 640	74 745
	2 591	3 502	6 660	5 139	331		12 143	1 443	569
124 659	141 452	56 984	237 629	48 250	39 644	681	17 671	66 020	5 274
312 845	**665 913**	**421 514**	**787 849**	**179 156**	**281 992**	**1 321**	**61 858**	**167 031**	**80 328**
3 269	6 294	3 698	7 772	1 462	5 108	6	538	1 152	2 827
144 396	328 800	235 272	410 618	82 042	194 642	262	26 136	47 475	56 911
675	7 590	998	2 035	1 145	433	6	468	1 410	376
8 952	100 939	13 388	27 304	15 177	5 106	72	6 115	18 650	5 428
2 298	15 057	9 545	16 858	2 257	5 110		1 114	2 435	2 913
814	7 815	1 141	1 015	1 409	420		319	1 153	717
7	148	32	20	30	1 205		37	5	28
308	3 366	3 465	382	896	18 916		450	230	779
1 333	3 093	1 271	4 980	1 112	779	15	422	2 324	128
81 959	138 098	48 896	193 092	44 685	32 729	681	14 568	56 900	4 684
458	2 510	875	2 346	1 003	956	15	352	2 493	547
1 107	1 477	853	3 208	277	2 309		218	494	685
189	374	339	671	146	160		6	42	9
37 414	40 496	82 635	125 004	21 463	18 639		669	5 127	675
	11	1	8	4					1
	253	50	120	158					15
50	354	11	88	281	82		11	66	68
1 458	2 378	190	812	288	946		77	690	1 920
	6		13		73		1		
	69		256		590		4		
399	2 810	2 240	366	406	370	1	515	1 539	492
11 464	51 451	37 364	13 253	14 447	10 424	300	13 632	37 880	9 916

9—8 主要农业机械化作业项目水平
Level of Major Agricultural Mechanization

计量单位:千公顷 (1 000 hectares)

指 标	Item	2016	2017
当年实际机耕面积(按耕地面积计算)	**Machine-Cultivated Area in the Current Year (Computed Based on Cultivated Area)**	**1 280.14**	**1 281.50**
当年机械播种面积(按播种面积计算)	**Machine-Sown Area in the Current Year (Computed Based on Sown Area)**	**1 370.38**	**1 362.76**
地膜覆盖栽培面积	**Cultivated Area with Plastic Film**	**782.73**	**759.31**
# 机械覆膜面积	Area of Plastic Film Layed with Machine	782.73	759.31
化学除草面积	**Area of Chemical Weeding**	**1 280.14**	**1 281.50**
# 机械化除面积	Area of Mechanized Weeding	1 280.14	1 281.50
中耕作业面积	**Cultivation Area**	**723.44**	**753.12**
# 机械中耕面积	Area of Mechanical Cultivation	723.44	753.12
机械施肥作业面积	**Area of Mechanical Fertilization**	**887.57**	**862.67**
# 液氨施肥面积	Area of Liquid Ammonia Application	34.75	39.63
化肥深施面积	Area of Deep Fertilizer Application	742.79	701.61
病虫害防治面积	**Area of Pest Control**	**1 004.64**	**1 062.58**
# 机力防治面积	Area of Mechanic Control	1 004.64	1 062.58
机电灌溉面积	**Machine-Irrigated Area**	**918.51**	**922.18**
# 喷灌面积	Spay-Irrigated Area	32.77	33.56
当年机械收割面积	**Machine-Harvested Area**	**1 059.95**	**1 090.20**
# 机收小麦面积	Wheat Area Harvested by Machine	184.10	144.41
机收水稻面积	Rice Area Harvested by Machine	19.02	20.61
机收玉米面积	Corn Area Havested by Machine	110.65	101.33
机收棉花面积	Cotton Area Havested by Machine	433.37	549.50
机收油料面积	Oil-Bearing Crops Area Harvested by Machine	15.07	21.52
机收甜菜面积	Beetroots Area Harvested by Machine	24.05	26.28
机收饲料面积	Animal Feed Area Harvested by Machine	113.96	93.34
机械秸秆还田面积	**Area of Straw Turning to Fields by Machine**	**817.57**	**842.79**
# 切粉碎还田	Area of Straw Shredding to Fields	795.57	842.79
机械植树面积	**Machine-Planting Trees Area**		
收获牧草数量(吨)	**Quantity of Haveast Animal Grass(ton)**	**449.70**	**485.22**
# 机械收割牧草	Machine-Havested Forage	440.20	477.94
机械收割农作物茎杆(吨)	**Crop Stalk Harvested by Machine(ton)**		
# 青黄储数量	Silage Quantity	358.92	308.10
机械剪毛羊只数(万只)	**Sheep Shearing with Machine(10 000 heads)**	**81.04**	**81.90**
飞机作业面积	**Area of Airplane Operation**		
# 飞机播种水稻	Rice Area Sown by Airplane		
飞机化除面积	**Area of Weed Control by Airplane**		
飞机防治病虫害面积	**Area of Pest Control by Airplane**		
飞机施肥面积	**Area of Fertilization by Airplane**		
附:农机管理标准化农场(个)	Attached:Farm of Agricultural Machinery Management Standardization(Unit)	86	89
农机管理标准化连队(个)	Brigade of Agricultural Machinery Management Standardization(Unit)	999	957
农机管理标准化机组(个)	Groups of Agricultural Machinery Management Standardization(Unit)	10 451	11 015

9—9 农作物播种面积、产量

Sown Areas and Output of Farm Crops

(2017年)

指 标	Item	正复播播种面积（千公顷） Total Sown Area (1 000 hectares)	正复播总产量（吨） Total Yield of Major Farm Crops (ton)	每公顷产量（公斤） Yield of Major Farm Crops Per Hectare (kg)	复播面积（千公顷） Multiple Sown Area (1 000 hectares)
农作物总播种面积	**Total Sown Area**	**1 362.77**			**49.93**
粮食作物合计	**Sown Area of Grain Crops**	**284.24**	**2 485 515**	**8 744**	**8.75**
谷 物	Cereal	270.69	2 393 451	8 842	7.38
水 稻	Rice	20.61	232 042	11 258	
小 麦	Wheat	144.41	1 011 372	7 003	0.30
# 冬小麦	Winter Wheat	77.38	562 632	7 271	0.02
春小麦	Spring Wheat	67.04	448 740	6 694	0.28
玉 米	Corn	101.33	1 116 588	11 019	6.60
谷 子	Millet	0.47	4 893	10 446	
高 粱	Sorghum	2.28	21 434	9 419	0.11
大 麦	Barley	0.89	5 139	5 750	
其他谷物	Other Cereal	0.70	1 983	2 816	0.37
豆 类	Beans	7.88	30 065	3 816	1.34
# 大豆(黄豆、黑豆等)	Soja	5.30	21 805	4 114	1.34
绿 豆	Green Bean	0.05	182	3 430	
薯 类	Tubers	5.67	61 999	10 939	0.03
油料作物	**Oil Bearing Crops**	**56.82**	**209 199**	**3 681**	**8.34**
花 生	Peanuts	1.00	6 594	6 620	
油菜籽	Rapeseeds	21.35	75 932	3 557	0.64
芝 麻	Sesame				
胡 麻	Flax	0.47	1 588	3 401	
向日葵籽	Sunflower	31.80	121 341	3 816	7.61
其他油料	Other	2.22	3 744	1 689	0.09
棉 花	**Cotton**	**686.93**	**1 678 827**	**2 444**	
# 长绒棉	Long Staple Cotton	0.44	977	2 222	
麻 类	**Hemp Crops**	**0.29**	**2 893**	**9 863**	
# 亚 麻	Flax	0.29	2 893	9 863	
甜 菜	**Beetroots**	**23.73**	**1 984 563**	**83 617**	**0.05**
烟 叶	**Tobacco**				
药 材	**Medicial Materials**	**23.46**	**188 655**	**8 043**	
# 枸 杞	Chinese Wolf Berry	11.78	39 640	3 365	
蔬菜(含菜用瓜)	**Vegetables**	**87.42**	**6 705 374**	**76 700**	**5.03**
香料原料	**Spice**	**9.26**	**35 732**	**3 857**	**3.62**
瓜果类	**Melons**	**24.57**	**1 522 662**	**61 971**	**0.10**
# 西 瓜	Muskmelon	11.31	885 365	78 252	0.05
甜 瓜	Strawbery	12.82	625 715	48 817	0.04
其他作物	**Other Farm Crops**	**166.03**			**24.05**
打瓜籽	Melon Seed	20.47	59 987	2 931	0.05
啤酒花	Hops	0.87	3 216	3 709	
苜蓿(包括当年新播)	Lucerne	53.02	771 186	14 545	1.32
其他饲料	Other Animal Feed	40.32	3 081 033	76 412	17.46
# 青贮玉米	Silage Corn	33.22	2 622 981	78 955	13.30
绿 肥(包括翻掉播种面积)	Green Manure	3.17			3.05
其他作物(包括安息茴香)	Others	48.18	136 893	2 841	2.18

9—10　农作物总播种面积

计量单位:千公顷

年份　单位 Year　Unit	农作物总播种面积 Total Sown Area	粮食作物播种面积 Sown Area of Grain Crops	谷物 Cereal	#水稻 Rice	#小麦 Wheat	#冬麦 Winter Wheat	#玉米 Corn	#大麦 Barley	豆类 Beans	薯类 Tubers
1950	55.68	41.83	41.33	6.56	18.96		6.61		0.50	
1952	108.14	80.71	80.08	13.21	45.15	13.73	14.54	0.67	0.63	
1954	59.11	44.71	43.44	4.82	28.09	15.50	6.69	1.11	1.27	
1957	147.58	92.36	88.57	6.59	42.03	21.65	25.33	2.67	3.79	
1962	430.59	284.53	279.69	8.05	129.30	72.66	90.99	3.94	4.84	
1965	514.75	321.58	314.29	19.50	197.82	113.23	79.08	3.10	7.29	
1970	656.59	432.07	424.54	36.80	247.11	130.65	116.69	4.61	7.53	
1975	675.75	446.98	438.22	32.09	253.49	168.77	105.34	0.10	4.49	4.27
1978	740.19	469.23	445.24	35.93	277.15	148.01	100.89	8.70	16.38	7.61
1980	740.28	441.08	420.82	33.43	288.21	160.29	80.41	7.36	14.81	5.45
1985	727.51	362.03	354.81	29.17	278.09	144.02	42.65	2.26	5.55	1.67
1990	780.80	369.07	359.80	32.00	244.13	132.67	54.40	23.93	8.00	1.27
1995	813.00	299.02	287.41	27.91	190.09	97.66	49.34	15.80	10.65	0.96
2000	909.80	221.03	207.38	26.33	142.67	63.68	28.82	9.18	11.69	1.96
2001	919.71	209.22	190.84	20.22	123.71	50.91	35.34	10.47	16.58	1.80
2002	931.80	207.69	193.08	19.01	118.53	52.78	41.96	10.90	12.57	2.04
2003	932.40	162.33	143.58	15.30	76.38	38.23	37.77	11.87	16.10	2.65
2004	983.65	179.11	157.84	14.89	84.15	24.66	50.56	6.52	17.92	3.35
2005	1 023.77	192.06	173.17	13.61	103.54	44.80	46.88	7.23	16.62	2.27
2006	1 032.81	191.47	178.40	23.24	97.95	49.07	44.59	11.46	10.48	2.59
2007	1 040.94	173.18	159.51	25.45	73.01	34.33	43.02	15.26	7.46	6.21
2008	1 068.90	235.40	215.30	23.93	119.68	41.58	59.60	10.53	10.66	9.44
2009	1 107.70	313.99	292.46	21.77	197.06	82.74	63.35	7.26	14.62	6.91
2010	1 119.20	284.69	269.59	18.19	156.18	99.05	85.61	6.60	9.06	6.04
2011	1 114.08	252.34	235.21	20.68	128.07	83.80	79.18	5.64	9.24	7.89
2012	1 130.15	274.61	261.33	22.17	131.16	66.00	101.52	4.49	7.74	5.54
2013	1 174.12	271.36	256.87	21.82	133.61	58.50	95.08	3.40	8.40	6.09
2014	1 327.85	279.15	266.45	19.40	153.89	78.16	88.72	1.08	7.82	4.88
2015	1 352.90	322.47	308.99	17.24	174.53	79.66	112.60	2.02	7.85	5.63
2016	1 372.21	331.71	319.17	19.07	184.04	84.30	110.49	1.74	6.73	5.81
2017	1 362.77	284.24	270.69	20.61	144.41	77.38	101.33	0.89	7.88	5.67
一　师　Division 1	174.18	19.94	19.63	10.05	3.05	2.60	6.54		0.05	0.26
二　师　Division 2	88.53	9.25	9.23	0.93	4.93		3.12			0.02
三　师　Division 3	128.32	26.47	25.93	0.02	10.54	7.89	15.38		0.28	0.26
四　师　Division 4	129.46	71.44	64.05	9.09	23.57	7.12	29.37		4.84	2.55
五　师　Division 5	68.92	15.09	14.96		8.18	6.77	6.77		0.06	0.07
六　师　Division 6	175.91	48.49	47.23	0.19	31.63	19.22	14.77	0.01	0.05	1.20
七　师　Division 7	135.14	13.00	12.99		9.93	9.93	3.06			0.01
八　师　Division 8	270.40	16.99	16.28	0.23	9.07	7.87	6.98		0.45	0.27
九　师　Division 9	81.22	36.19	36.17		23.14	6.61	12.27	0.70	0.01	0.02
十　师　Division 10	65.60	16.67	13.72	0.03	10.88	6.19	2.47		2.15	0.79
十一师　Division 11	0.42	0.10	0.10		0.10	0.09				
十二师　Division 12	12.81	3.08	3.07	0.09	2.80	2.80	0.04		0.01	
十三师　Division 13	26.54	4.74	4.58		4.15		0.25	0.18		0.16
十四师　Division 14	5.32	2.81	2.75		2.45	0.28	0.30			0.06

Total Sown Areas of Farm Crops

(1 000 hectares)

油料 Oil-bearing Crops	# 油菜籽 Rapeseeds	# 向日葵籽 Helianthus	棉花 Cotton	# 长绒棉 Long-staple Cotton	甜菜 Beetroots	烟叶 Tobacco	药材 Medicinal Materials	蔬菜 Vegetables	瓜果类 Melons	# 甜瓜 Muskmelon	打瓜籽 Melon Seed	苜蓿 Lucerne	绿肥 Green Manure
7.64	3.14		2.46									0.17	
9.54	3.93		13.98									0.11	
4.35	2.15	0.49	4.62									1.47	
4.54	2.44	1.10	27.57		0.19							12.93	0.93
23.00	17.18	1.60	19.86	3.40	8.47	4.59		23.84				41.93	0.15
32.27	26.71	3.18	43.56	6.77	10.02	1.27		15.53				67.54	4.82
32.06	22.00		45.59	3.95	11.92	0.51		17.99				85.11	
41.11	27.59	5.37	36.58		8.55	0.54	1.84	22.26				53.33	11.27
57.41	35.14	9.83	41.67	13.49	13.00	0.93	1.86	23.68	15.15			93.31	12.00
69.89	36.31	21.17	65.09	20.86	18.11	0.12	2.47	19.94	14.34			86.60	10.47
89.01	43.74	40.51	110.03	18.78	8.25	0.01	0.39	13.88	17.59	5.53	67.09	35.69	17.05
79.73	44.20	30.20	170.00	36.53	29.13	0.07	0.60	13.67	9.00	2.67	6.73	35.73	57.47
104.91	50.17	51.99	266.03	4.21	32.07	0.11	1.88	16.14	8.33	3.85	8.89	26.13	35.29
83.81	32.05	47.92	410.72	31.08	18.55	0.03	1.73	32.81	13.39	8.10	25.79	28.39	45.55
55.94	22.00	29.96	470.94	37.88	25.91	0.03	3.40	32.84	13.48	7.45	14.97	38.09	34.01
58.58	22.00	32.46	463.30	23.60	21.78	0.07	7.06	47.02	13.44	6.96	14.65	46.24	23.32
71.61	31.60	34.62	494.06	35.58	17.04	0.07	5.89	46.11	11.59	5.58	27.91	41.65	17.78
58.64	25.77	30.29	533.59	35.20	17.18	0.01	4.33	56.61	11.08	6.05	22.61	57.80	10.43
48.63	21.10	24.37	551.08	39.06	18.87	0.02	3.42	48.28	11.21	6.46	37.96	61.30	10.31
38.25	19.82	14.06	588.11	52.48	26.34		1.30	40.49	10.40	6.99	46.10	47.35	13.01
39.93	15.58	19.33	613.06	54.75	27.55		1.78	47.00	9.59	6.85	43.45	46.18	11.30
72.00	20.21	49.46	563.16	13.06	24.44		3.26	56.28	8.39	4.70	26.99	41.67	8.59
68.72	21.18	43.91	487.86	13.88	20.29		4.11	73.84	11.56	7.34	47.49	40.47	5.11
67.78	21.95	41.01	497.98	19.78	25.52	0.01	4.96	79.68	10.78	6.89	49.73	39.97	4.35
63.33	21.44	36.78	534.62	13.20	27.27		5.19	84.43	9.44	5.58	40.64	39.22	5.92
53.57	20.77	27.12	557.97	9.35	29.91		7.60	68.25	12.53	7.35	30.63	38.19	1.98
50.45	17.36	26.46	590.81	3.76	26.58		10.75	69.90	17.44	11.23	15.65	46.77	5.21
53.52	22.27	26.36	700.57	1.41	23.89		10.90	81.21	22.24	11.72	18.09	48.95	1.20
57.46	17.10	35.81	629.49	12.56	20.99		18.51	87.65	27.96	16.06	22.62	54.09	1.03
64.45	13.53	46.18	621.00	7.34	24.40		21.99	90.07	28.41	15.46	22.97	51.07	0.27
56.82	21.35	31.80	686.93	0.44	23.73		23.46	87.42	24.57	12.82	20.47	53.02	3.17
0.83	0.32	0.29	138.14	0.23	0.05		0.82	3.85	0.68	0.26	0.40	1.09	0.12
0.99		0.94	39.48		1.68		4.53	18.54	1.14	0.57	3.92	0.91	0.95
1.38	0.07	0.75	59.65	0.21			4.55	6.90	4.53	2.28	1.44	3.84	
22.48	18.25	3.71	7.54		5.15		2.33	3.32	1.58	0.59	2.45	3.71	2.09
1.81		1.81	44.54		1.90		0.51	1.22	0.35	0.33	0.87	1.43	
5.98		5.94	89.79		1.34		2.54	11.20	4.64	3.55	2.20	1.68	
3.18		3.07	87.69		2.56		4.26	11.59	0.89	0.37	0.97	2.85	
0.28		0.23	201.19		0.80		0.17	14.20	6.83	2.03	1.22	8.63	
9.43	2.10	5.31			8.94		0.44	3.08	0.05	0.02	2.53	19.73	
8.98	0.61	8.34	2.94		1.32		2.73	5.58	1.11	1.11	3.91	6.77	
0.03			0.27				0.00	0.00					
1.34		1.32	0.11				0.24	5.82	0.56	0.01	0.40	0.09	
0.09		0.09	15.59				0.23	1.75	1.83	1.46		1.61	
0.02							0.12	0.37	0.36	0.24	0.18	0.69	

9—11　农作物总产量

计量单位:万吨

年　份 Year	单　位 Unit	粮食作物合计 Total Grain Crops	谷　物 Cereal	#水　稻 Rice	#小　麦 Wheat	#冬　麦 Winter Wheat	#玉　米 Corn	#大　麦 Barley	豆　类 Beans	薯　类 Tubers
1950		3.29	3.27	0.92	1.29		0.53		0.02	
1952		9.96	9.94	2.77	4.48	1.37	1.77	0.11	0.02	
1954		7.18	7.08	1.16	3.80	2.53	1.31	0.16	0.10	
1957		12.24	12.03	0.98	5.25	2.77	4.36	0.23	0.21	
1962		30.92	30.74	1.10	9.48	5.97	15.48	0.14	0.18	
1965		56.11	55.67	3.75	27.08	19.60	23.29	0.25	0.44	
1970		77.63	77.13	7.34	33.11	19.70	34.32	0.56	0.50	
1975		65.39	64.95	7.28	30.84	20.32	23.26	0.09	0.44	
1978		87.60	86.09	12.12	44.48	27.32	24.81	1.01	1.51	0.91
1980		93.09	91.91	11.17	55.79	33.30	21.11	0.85	1.18	0.83
1985		104.10	103.49	12.15	76.01	42.06	14.16	0.29	0.61	0.45
1990		157.18	155.91	21.89	90.38	52.07	33.44	6.86	1.27	0.55
1995		145.77	143.51	19.53	80.37	45.85	36.00	5.58	2.26	0.51
2000		118.71	115.71	19.28	70.13	33.06	21.74	3.24	3.00	1.14
2001		113.31	107.90	13.70	63.93	27.55	25.24	4.26	4.43	0.98
2002		120.88	116.31	14.52	64.82	30.65	30.07	4.84	3.28	1.29
2003		94.53	87.94	11.36	41.80	21.69	27.72	5.62	4.82	1.77
2004		105.25	97.86	10.21	45.84	13.63	37.33	3.24	5.42	1.97
2005		118.12	111.64	11.34	60.79	27.31	34.60	3.36	5.01	1.47
2006		130.17	125.12	21.43	61.53	31.84	34.25	6.92	3.17	1.88
2007		124.19	117.93	22.61	45.50	22.18	36.75	10.49	2.54	3.72
2008		148.01	139.18	22.86	57.90	23.20	53.76	3.13	3.15	5.68
2009		217.35	207.31	20.13	119.62	52.30	60.27	4.34	4.41	5.63
2010		213.64	206.42	18.16	96.33	61.99	85.72	3.48	2.89	4.33
2011		167.29	159.24	18.02	74.28	49.17	63.59	2.17	2.62	5.43
2012		187.13	180.45	20.43	68.84	32.58	88.40	1.45	2.51	4.17
2013		206.31	198.13	21.03	84.77	36.85	87.75	2.08	2.68	5.50
2014		222.89	215.70	21.99	102.40	53.78	87.33	0.63	2.68	4.51
2015		265.37	256.88	19.26	120.93	57.39	113.43	1.35	2.79	5.70
2016		271.30	263.09	21.79	127.53	62.02	109.75	0.97	2.51	5.70
2017		248.55	239.35	23.20	101.14	56.26	111.66	0.51	3.01	6.20
一　师	Division 1	21.43	21.15	12.03	2.39	2.07	6.74		0.03	0.25
二　师	Division 2	7.00	6.99	0.86	3.64		2.36			0.01
三　师	Division 3	18.44	18.04	0.01	6.74	5.08	11.28		0.17	0.23
四　师	Division 4	67.76	62.87	9.88	17.23	5.00	34.03		1.87	3.01
五　师	Division 5	13.41	13.33		5.50	4.79	7.84		0.02	0.05
六　师	Division 6	44.68	43.27	0.20	24.01	14.90	18.27	0.01	0.02	1.39
七　师	Division 7	11.73	11.73		8.17	8.17	3.56			…
八　师	Division 8	15.16	14.68	0.14	6.11	5.31	8.43		0.27	0.21
九　师	Division 9	31.06	31.04		14.24	4.75	16.38	0.39	0.00	0.02
十　师	Division 10	11.04	9.60	0.02	7.20	4.05	2.29		0.62	0.82
十一师	Division 11	0.09	0.09		0.09	0.08	…			
十二师	Division 12	2.11	2.11	0.07	1.94	1.94	0.04		…	
十三师	Division 13	3.78	3.64		3.27		0.25	0.11		0.14
十四师	Division 14	0.86	0.80		0.62	0.12	0.18			0.06

Total Output of Farm Crops

(10 000 tons)

油 料 Oil-bearing Crops	#油菜籽 Rapes-eeds	#向日葵籽 Helian-thus	棉 花 Cotton	#长绒棉 Long-staple Cotton	甜 菜 Beetroots	烟 叶 Tobacco	蔬 菜 Vegeta-bles	瓜果类 Melons	#甜 瓜 Musk-melon	打瓜籽 Melon Seed	苜 蓿 Lucerne
0.19	0.06		0.04								
0.49	0.24		0.33								
0.21	0.09	0.03	0.19								
0.21	0.09	0.08	1.09		0.34						
0.63	0.49	0.06	0.60	0.10	7.16	0.51	29.73				
1.18	0.90	0.20	2.81	0.21	15.13	0.18	33.33				
1.06	0.68		2.28	0.12	18.09	0.05	23.28				
1.51	0.92	0.27	1.03		9.87	0.06	8.49				
2.29	1.17	0.62	1.95	0.55	12.55	0.14	22.60	15.87			16.90
4.05	1.92	1.54	3.48	0.94	30.01	0.04	30.95	20.66			14.67
8.66	3.33	4.89	8.27	1.32	20.68	0.01	28.98	44.12	12.80	4.87	9.16
8.87	3.63	4.47	19.48	3.42	91.96	0.03	43.68	32.44	6.34	0.81	14.80
15.01	4.40	10.29	38.19	0.56	128.21	0.03	49.53	25.40	8.17	1.12	10.21
14.97	4.16	10.35	69.39	3.72	106.07		140.36	35.54	11.69	3.05	12.75
12.04	4.51	7.02	64.45	6.01	150.35	0.01	128.38	41.79	15.87	1.84	20.82
13.41	5.05	7.72	82.17	3.73	132.80	0.04	223.54	47.55	16.19	1.83	27.36
18.00	8.24	9.12	85.46	5.56	105.82	0.04	265.03	39.35	13.70	3.66	38.78
14.05	5.73	7.97	93.40	6.40	107.25		339.99	39.00	16.63	3.42	41.56
9.88	3.15	6.24	106.85	6.84	119.18	0.01	284.39	39.29	18.46	5.72	41.20
9.16	4.79	3.76	121.82	10.71	171.84		270.13	42.40	24.74	6.75	31.39
10.33	3.97	5.71	124.72	11.51	188.05		291.03	35.17	20.67	7.07	32.09
16.91	2.44	14.03	131.34	2.71	158.20		373.83	32.13	13.58	4.95	21.55
18.63	5.24	12.63	113.43	2.67	145.33		598.78	43.77	22.16	9.55	27.86
18.62	5.68	11.92	115.01	3.63	181.66	…	581.62	42.80	22.50	8.75	28.19
17.87	6.15	10.70	129.31	2.69	205.92		625.67	38.13	16.19	8.44	30.03
13.57	3.27	8.55	141.77	1.55	216.25		460.20	52.04	25.35	5.80	28.14
17.15	5.53	8.92	146.52	0.71	216.54		493.95	77.63	40.99	3.34	49.65
16.99	6.50	9.02	163.61	0.26	203.57		614.85	127.49	47.21	4.63	61.94
19.32	5.42	12.67	146.53	1.41	184.41		682.07	162.00	66.51	6.14	70.57
23.43	4.66	17.38	149.57	1.73	208.20		675.12	166.68	67.24	6.66	72.33
20.92	7.59	12.13	167.88	0.10	198.46		670.54	152.27	62.57	6.00	77.12
0.21	0.03	0.05	33.40	0.05	0.44		16.20	3.23	1.09	0.51	2.66
0.18		0.16	10.14		14.40		129.51	4.61	1.69	0.90	2.03
0.69	0.03	0.33	15.02	0.05			29.23	21.24	11.14	0.79	12.83
8.20	6.74	1.27	1.56		46.43		20.80	8.99	2.91	0.56	6.04
0.64		0.64	10.79		13.72		10.91	1.65	1.54	0.21	2.43
2.31		2.30	20.15		11.96		139.10	25.12	13.43	0.61	3.49
1.70		1.58	21.99		24.24		109.14	5.76	1.87	0.52	6.28
0.10		0.08	50.28		8.47		120.47	61.50	15.37	0.29	19.60
3.17	0.57	2.27			70.11		23.61	0.26	0.11	0.58	9.47
3.18	0.23	2.94	0.55		8.69		22.04	6.32	6.32	0.90	7.82
0.01			0.06				0.04				
0.49		0.49	0.02				34.33	3.10	0.06	0.09	0.03
0.04		0.04	3.93				13.44	8.73	5.86		1.01
0.01							1.71	1.75	1.18	0.03	3.44

9—12　农作物公顷产量

计量单位:公斤/公顷

年　份 Year	单　位 Unit	粮食作物合　计 Total Grain Crops	谷　物 Cereal	#水　稻 Rice	#小　麦 Wheat	#冬　麦 Winter Wheat	#玉　米 Corn	#大　麦 Barley	豆　类 Beans	薯　类 Tubers
	1950	787	791	1 403	683		803		450	
	1952	1 234	1 241	2 093	990	998	1 215	1 725	285	
	1954	1 606	1 630	2 408	1 350	1 635	1 965	1 439	818	
	1957	1 325	1 358	1 493	1 245	1 283	1 725	875	548	
	1962	1 087	1 099	1 373	735	825	1 703	689	375	
	1965	1 745	1 771	1 920	1 373	1 733	2 948	814	608	
	1970	1 797	1 817	1 995	1 343	1 508	2 940	1 223	660	
	1975	1 463	1 482	2 273	1 215	1 208	2 205	885	983	
	1978	1 867	1 913	3 373	1 605	1 845	2 459	1 161	922	1 200
	1980	2 110	2 164	3 341	1 936	2 077	2 625	1 148	800	1 518
	1985	2 875	2 904	4 165	2 733	2 920	3 320	1 283	1 099	2 676
	1990	4 259	4 318	6 841	3 702	3 925	6 147	2 867	1 588	4 381
	1995	4 875	4 976	6 997	4 228	4 695	7 296	3 532	2 120	5 271
	2000	5 371	5 525	7 321	4 916	5 192	7 544	3 530	2 573	5 806
	2001	5 416	5 654	6 775	5 168	5 412	7 141	4 069	2 672	5 456
	2002	5 820	6 024	7 637	5 469	5 807	7 166	4 444	2 614	6 343
	2003	5 824	6 125	7 425	5 473	5 673	7 340	4 736	2 992	6 694
	2004	5 877	6 200	6 860	5 447	5 528	7 383	4 977	3 023	5 893
	2005	6 150	6 447	8 333	5 871	6 097	7 381	4 646	3 012	6 485
	2006	6 798	7 013	9 222	6 282	6 488	7 680	6 038	3 027	7 259
	2007	7 171	7 393	8 884	6 233	6 461	8 542	6 873	3 407	5 997
	2008	6 288	6 465	9 551	4 838	5 580	9 021	2 971	2 953	6 019
	2009	6 922	7 088	9 247	6 070	6 321	9 514	5 981	3 020	8 146
	2010	7 504	7 657	9 981	6 168	6 259	10 013	5 268	3 184	7 168
	2011	6 630	6 770	8 715	5 800	5 867	8 030	3 843	2 836	6 883
	2012	6 814	6 905	9 217	5 248	4 936	8 707	3 232	3 243	7 522
	2013	7 603	7 714	9 641	6 345	6 300	9 230	6 122	3 193	9 038
	2014	7 984	8 095	11 331	6 654	6 881	9 843	5 820	3 424	9 262
	2015	8 229	8 313	11 170	6 929	7 205	10 074	6 658	3 557	10 128
	2016	8 179	8 243	11 423	6 929	7 358	9 933	5 582	3 736	9 804
	2017	8 744	8 842	11 258	7 003	7 271	11 019	5 750	3 816	10 939
一　师	Division 1	10 743	10 774	11 971	7 843	7 981	10 301		5 582	9 316
二　师	Division 2	7 567	7 575	9 281	7 387		7 574			3 598
三　师	Division 3	6 968	6 955	7 627	6 394	6 445	7 338		6 303	9 000
四　师	Division 4	9 486	9 816	10 868	7 309	7 025	11 586		3 871	11 837
五　师	Division 5	8 887	8 915		6 718	7 069	11 569		3 909	6 955
六　师	Division 6	9 214	9 161	10 661	7 590	7 752	12 371	6 293	3 466	11 533
七　师	Division 7	9 029	9 031		8 228	8 228	11 639			3 077
八　师	Division 8	8 925	9 019	6 083	6 739	6 749	12 076		5 989	8 034
九　师	Division 9	8 582	8 582		6 153	7 182	13 344	5 598	3 529	9 960
十　师	Division 10	6 622	6 991	6 000	6 616	6 544	9 284		2 898	10 317
十一师	Division 11	8 814	8 814		8 814	8 872				
十二师	Division 12	6 868	6 876	8 250	6 915	6 915	10 500		818	
十三师	Division 13	7 986	7 950		7 891		10 126	6 300		9 000
十四师	Division 14	3 077	2 912		2 530	4 131	5 982			10 763

Output of Farm Crops Per Hectare

(kg/hectare)

油料 Oil-bearing Crops	#油菜籽 Rapeseeds	#向日葵籽 Helianthus	棉花 Cotton	#长绒棉 Long-staple Cotton	甜菜 Beetroots	烟叶 Tobacco	蔬菜 Vegetables	瓜果类 Melons	#甜瓜 Muskmelon	打瓜籽 Melon Seed	苜蓿 Lucerne
249	188		163		1 000						
514	615		236								
483	435	675	411								
463	353	705	395		17 895						
274	285	405	302	295	8 453	1 104	12 549				
366	338	623	645	316	15 100	1 443	21 470				
331	308		500	313	15 176	907	12 936				
367	330	495	282		11 544	1 185	3 810				
399	332	631	468	408	9 654	753	9 544	10 478			1 811
579	527	725	535	448	16 571	142	15 519	14 404			1 693
973	761	1 207	752	703	25 067	259	20 879	25 078	23 160	726	2 567
1 113	820	1 482	1 146	936	31 569	437	31 959	36 040	23 786	1 205	4 142
1 430	877	1 979	1 435	1 330	39 979	160	30 688	30 492	21 221	1 260	3 907
1 787	1 298	2 160	1 690	1 197	57 178		42 780	26 542	14 432	1 183	4 491
2 152	2 050	2 342	1 369	1 588	58 027	4 800	39 091	31 004	21 302	1 228	5 466
2 289	2 296	2 378	1 773	1 579	60 972	5 114	47 542	35 381	23 260	1 251	5 918
2 514	2 607	2 635	1 730	1 561	62 098	6 143	57 477	33 951	24 556	1 312	9 312
2 397	2 224	2 630	1 750	1 819	62 425		60 058	35 198	27 488	1 511	7 191
2 031	1 493	2 559	1 939	1 752	63 160	6 050	58 903	35 046	28 576	1 507	6 721
2 395	2 415	2 677	2 071	2 041	65 241		66 715	40 772	35 391	1 465	6 630
2 587	2 550	2 953	2 034	2 102	68 258		61 922	36 673	30 176	1 627	6 948
2 349	1 206	2 836	2 332	2 079	64 732		66 423	38 297	28 883	1 833	5 171
2 711	2 476	2 875	2 325	1 926	71 628		81 092	37 866	30 189	2 010	6 884
2 748	2 586	2 907	2 310	1 833	71 184	4 500	72 995	39 703	32 660	1 760	7 092
2 822	2 867	2 908	2 419	2 039	75 525		74 106	40 391	29 029	2 076	7 656
2 534	1 576	3 155	2 541	1 659	72 291		67 425	41 522	34 478	1 894	7 369
3 399	3 185	3 368	2 480	1 881	81 477		70 664	44 537	36 454	2 131	10 616
3 174	2 920	3 423	2 335	1 872	85 181		75 715	57 338	40 327	2 561	12 653
3 363	3 169	3 538	2 328	1 671	87 856		77 817	57 942	41 413	2 715	13 047
3 635	3 446	3 764	2 409	2 358	85 323		74 956	58 673	43 482	2 900	14 163
3 681	3 557	3 816	2 444	2 222	83 617		76 700	61 971	48 817	2 931	14 545
2 508	891	1 727	2 418	2 241	90 000		42 083	47 333	41 444	12 974	24 431
1 811		1 690	2 569		85 978		69 852	40 569	29 419	2 307	22 152
5 004	3 573	4 368	2 518	2 203			42 336	46 845	48 896	5 479	33 445
3 647	3 694	3 426	2 073		90 126		62 690	56 759	49 167	2 289	16 287
3 522		3 522	2 422		72 144		89 156	47 105	47 168	2 418	16 975
3 865		3 873	2 244		89 222		124 227	54 147	37 855	2 765	20 769
5 351		5 135	2 508		94 681		94 199	64 766	51 100	5 401	21 994
3 673		3 295	2 499		106 306		84 812	90 000	75 665	2 380	22 725
3 357	2 721	4 281			78 423		76 696	47 618	49 909	2 310	4 797
3 540	3 717	3 523	1 862		65 856		39 527	56 939	56 928	2 303	11 551
3 000			2 287				111 923				
3 680		3 695	1 731				59 008	55 019	58 966	2 295	3 115
4 273		4 273	2 519				76 616	47 675	40 104		6 297
2 278							46 399	48 490	50 153	1 422	49 880

9—13　农作物种植面积构成

Composition of Farm Crops Area

计量单位:%　　　　(%)

指　标	Item	2000	2005	2010	2015	2016	2017
农作物总播种面积	**Total Sown Areas of Farm Crops**	**100.0**	**100.0**	**100.0**	**100.0**	**100.0**	**100.0**
粮食作物	Grain Crops	24.3	18.8	25.4	23.8	24.2	20.9
谷　物	Cereal	93.8	90.2	94.7	95.8	96.2	95.2
稻　谷	Rice	12.7	7.9	6.8	5.6	6.0	7.6
小　麦	Wheat	68.8	59.8	57.9	56.5	57.7	53.3
玉　米	Corn	13.9	27.1	31.8	36.4	34.6	37.4
大　麦	Barley	4.4	4.2	2.5	0.7	0.5	0.3
其它谷物	Other Cereal	0.2	1.1	1.0	0.8	1.2	1.3
豆　类	Beans	5.3	8.7	3.2	2.4	2.0	2.8
薯　类	Tubers	0.9	1.2	2.1	1.8	1.8	2.0
油料作物	Oil-bearing Crops	9.2	4.8	6.1	4.2	4.7	4.2
# 花　生	Peanuts	0.1	0.2	0.7	1.7	1.5	1.8
油菜籽	Rapeseeds	38.2	43.4	32.4	29.8	21.0	37.6
芝　麻	Sesame			0.1		…	
胡麻籽	Linseed	0.2	3.4	…	1.4	1.1	0.8
向日葵	Sunflower	57.2	50.1	60.5	62.3	71.6	56.0
棉　花	Cotton	45.1	53.8	44.5	46.5	45.3	50.4
# 长绒棉	Long-staple Cotton	7.5	7.1	4.0	2.0	1.2	0.1
麻　类	Hemp Crops	…	0.3	…	…	…	…
# 亚　麻	Flax	95.8	100.0	100.0	41.3	100.0	100.0
甜　菜	Beetsroots	2.1	1.8	2.3	1.6	1.8	1.7
烟　叶	Tobacco	…		…			
药　材	Medicinal Materials	0.2	0.3	0.4	1.4	1.6	1.7
蔬　菜	Vegetables	3.6	4.7	7.1	6.5	6.6	6.4
瓜果类	melons	1.5	1.1	1.0	2.1	2.1	1.8
其他农作物	Other Farm Crops	14.0	14.4	13.2	13.9	13.8	12.9
# 苜　蓿	Lucerne	3.1	41.5	27.1	28.8	26.9	30.2

9—14 各师农作物复播面积

Multiple Cropping Areas of Farm Crops by Division

计量单位:千公顷 (2017年) (1 000 hectares)

指 标	Item	合 计 Total	一 师 Division 1	二 师 Division 2	三 师 Division 3	四 师 Division 4	五 师 Division 5	六 师 Division 6	七 师 Division 7
农作物复播面积	**Total Multiple Cropping Area**	**49.93**	**6.21**	**3.60**	**8.04**	**8.26**	**1.70**	**2.26**	**6.72**
粮食作物	Grain Crops	8.75	0.30	0.17	5.71	1.96	0.06	0.05	
谷 物	Cereal	7.38	0.30	0.17	5.68	0.61	0.06	0.05	
水 稻	Rice								
小 麦	Wheat	0.30						0.02	
玉 米	Corn	6.60	0.30	0.17	5.68	0.26	0.06	0.01	
谷 子	Millet								
其他谷物	Other Cerea	0.48				0.36		0.02	
豆 类	Beans	1.34				1.34			
# 大豆(黄豆、黑豆等)	Soja	1.34				1.34			
薯 类	Tubers	0.03			0.03				
# 马铃薯	Phaoto	0.03			0.03				
油料作物	Oil-bearing Crops	8.34	0.25	0.68	0.45	1.89	1.60	0.96	2.01
# 向日葵籽	Sunflower	7.61		0.68	0.45	1.89	1.60	0.96	2.01
棉 花	Cotton								
蔬菜(含菜用瓜)	Vegetables	5.03	0.58	0.09	0.59	0.53	0.04	0.24	0.63
香料原料	Spice	3.62	3.62						
瓜果类	Melons	0.10			0.07	0.01			0.02
其他作物	Other Farm Crops	24.05	1.46	2.65	1.22	3.87		1.01	4.07
打瓜籽	Melon Seed	0.05							
苜蓿(包括当年新播)	Lucerne	1.32				0.19			
其他饲料	Other Animal Feed	17.46	1.46	1.01	1.22	1.59		1.01	4.07
# 青贮玉米	Silage Corn	13.30	0.82	0.08	1.22	0.96		0.01	4.07
绿 肥(包括翻掉播种面积)	Green Manure	3.05		0.95		2.09			
其它作物(包括安息茴香)	Others	2.18		0.69					

指 标	Item	八 师 Division 8	九 师 Division 9	十 师 Division 10	十一师 Division 11	十二师 Division 12	十三师 Division 13	十四师 Division 14
农作物复播面积	**Total Multiple Cropping Area**	**7.08**	**0.86**	**3.79**		**0.83**	**0.40**	**0.18**
粮食作物	Grain Crops			0.28		0.10	0.03	0.09
谷 物	Cereal			0.28		0.10	0.03	0.09
水 稻	Rice							
小 麦	Wheat			0.28				
玉 米	Corn						0.03	0.09
谷 子	Millet							
其他谷物	Other Cerea					0.10		
豆 类	Beans							
# 大豆(黄豆、黑豆等)	Soja							
薯 类	Tubers							
# 马铃薯	Phaoto							
油料作物	Oil-bearing Crops			0.47			0.03	
# 向日葵籽	Sunflower						0.03	
棉 花	Cotton							
蔬菜(含菜用瓜)	Vegetables	0.35	0.86			0.73	0.34	0.03
香料原料	Spice							
瓜果类	Melons							
其他作物	Other Farm Crops	6.73		3.00				0.06
打瓜籽	Melon Seed			0.05				
苜蓿(包括当年新播)	Lucerne	0.30		0.84				
其他饲料	Other Animal Feed	6.43		0.62				0.06
# 青贮玉米	Silage Corn	5.47		0.62				0.06
绿 肥(包括翻掉播种面积)	Green Manure							
其它作物(包括安息茴香)	Others			1.49				

9—15　各师特色农作物播种面积

Seeded Areas of Specialty Crops by Division

计量单位:千公顷　　　　(2017年)　　　　(1000 hectares)

指　　标	Item	合　计 Total	一　师 Division 1	二　师 Division 2	三　师 Division 3	四　师 Division 4	五　师 Division 5	六　师 Division 6	七　师 Division 7
番　茄	Tomato	32.18	0.25	5.14	0.38	0.34	0.33	9.10	6.53
# 工业用番茄	Tomato for Industry	27.37		4.79		0.07	0.23	8.76	5.95
辣　椒	Pepper	27.59	2.03	11.15	2.94	0.31	0.14	0.60	1.75
# 工业用辣椒	Hot Pepper for Industry	22.22	1.61	10.84	2.47	0.01		0.19	1.24
打瓜籽	Melon Seed	20.47	0.40	3.92	1.44	2.45	0.87	2.20	0.97
甘　草	Licorice	6.47	0.34	0.98	4.19			0.05	0.85
枸　杞	Chinese Wolf Berry	11.78	0.40	2.88	0.15	0.03	0.50	2.15	3.34

指　　标	Item	八　师 Division 8	九　师 Division 9	十　师 Division 10	十一师 Division 11	十二师 Division 12	十三师 Division 13	十四师 Division 14
番　茄	Tomato	6.78	1.62	0.05	…	1.19	0.40	0.06
# 工业用番茄	Tomato for Industry	5.83	1.00			0.74		…
辣　椒	Pepper	2.68	0.57	5.11	…	0.12	0.15	0.05
# 工业用辣椒	Hot Pepper for Industry	0.69	0.07	5.09				0.02
打瓜籽	Melon Seed	1.22	2.53	3.91		0.40		0.18
甘　草	Licorice			0.06				
枸　杞	Chinese Wolf Berry	0.14		1.84		0.24	0.03	0.07

9－16 各师特色农作物产量

Output of Specialty Crops by Division

计量单位:吨 (2017 年) (ton)

指标	Item	合计 Total	一师 Division 1	二师 Division 2	三师 Division 3	四师 Division 4	五师 Division 5	六师 Division 6	七师 Division 7
番茄	Tomato	3 854 628	16 752	660 623	18 321	28 011	34 986	1 240 430	747 664
# 工业用番茄	Tomato for Industry	3 428 481		634 972		6 940	25 516	1 192 954	688 789
辣椒	Pepper	1 194 823	61 694	510 305	104 856	16 398	7 769	25 534	86 732
# 工业用辣椒	Hot Pepper for Industry	911 270	48 641	486 775	89 363	239		5 650	57 000
打瓜籽	Melon Seed	59 987	5 149	9 047	7 892	5 603	2 095	6 069	5 218
甘草	Licorice	131 135	5 594	21 384	75 215			1 612	26 477
枸杞	Chinese Wolf Berry	39 640	1 454	12 918	685	66	900	5 228	14 375

指标	Item	八师 Division 8	九师 Division 9	十师 Division 10	十一师 Division 11	十二师 Division 12	十三师 Division 13	十四师 Division 14
番茄	Tomato	791 033	171 531	3 465	316	103 209	34 580	3 707
# 工业用番茄	Tomato for Industry	685 779	118 291			75 238		2
辣椒	Pepper	153 042	22 954	188 638	12	5 870	8 331	2 688
# 工业用辣椒	Hot Pepper for Industry	31 624	3 900	188 078				
打瓜籽	Melon Seed	2 895	5 836	9 012		914		257
甘草	Licorice			853				
枸杞	Chinese Wolf Berry	473		3 209		191	76	65

9－17　造林面积、水果及水产品生产情况

Forestation Area, Fruits and Aquatic Production

年　份 Year	当年人工造林面积(公顷) Afforestation Area in the Current Year (hectare)	年末实有果园面积(公顷) Orchard Area at the Year-end (hectare)	# 结果面积 Orchard Area In the Current Year	水果总产量(吨) Total Output of Fruits (ton)	养殖面积(公顷) Culture Area (hectare)	水产品产量(吨) Aquatic Products(ton)
1950	71					
1952	674					
1954	466					
1957	1 063					
1962	1 863	4 514	505	805	2 227	1 869
1965	3 457	6 403	1 715	4 374	5 729	2 974
1970	1 151	7 099	3 608	10 727	9 300	2 775
1975	1 173	9 823	4 918	14 506	18 200	1 813
1978	2 516	12 111	6 120	25 717	18 943	2 956
1980	4 103	12 871	6 591	26 607	20 514	2 715
1985	28 391	12 107	6 811	31 318	30 248	3 269
1990	7 085	22 637	9 256	84 213	29 611	8 184
1995	7 369	29 538	14 796	157 912	30 795	10 003
2000	13 399	36 948	20 697	284 584	28 368	12 894
2005	21 831	71 005	33 692	459 012	31 908	20 026
2010	14 409	176 445	90 664	1 225 376	32 853	26 701
2011	13 323	188 870	114 761	1 264 456	35 186	30 897
2012	17 705	194 860	140 290	1 723 494	36 331	35 369
2013	14 663	198 551	155 829	2 189 328	36 443	39 334
2014	13 116	198 701	164 676	2 767 430	37 462	44 238
2015	19 430	205 015	170 964	3 489 107	37 287	46 117
2016	26 721	209 356	174 872	3 650 013	38 129	51 472
2017	16 424	208 294	176 666	3 921 608	38 624	53 876

9－18　牲畜年末头数及主要畜产品产量

Year-end Number of Livestock and Output of Major Livestock Products

年　份 Year	大小牲畜年末头数(万头、万只) Year-end Number of Livestock(head)	大牲畜 Large Animals	猪 Hogs	羊 Sheep and Goats	肉类产量(吨) Output of Meat (ton)	羊毛产量(吨) Wool (ton)	牛奶产量(吨) Cow Milk (ton)	禽蛋产量(吨) Poultry Eggs (ton)
1950	18.15	4.45	1.21	12.48		21		
1952	49.11	4.69	1.77	42.65		98		
1954	52.99	5.44	2.18	45.38	3 178	438	455	
1957	74.25	7.55	6.88	59.83	5 502	1 159	1 945	
1962	144.61	17.97	13.95	112.68	9 727	2 057	7 624	709
1965	210.05	28.43	20.74	160.88	19 459	3 434	10 799	1 393
1970	234.46	28.32	28.13	178.02	12 851	5 240	12 974	1 599
1975	245.15	30.85	27.24	187.06	15 611	5 823	12 223	1 765
1978	269.12	29.22	51.92	187.98	20 704	5 705	16 307	2 291
1980	267.09	27.10	47.32	192.67	29 406	5 692	14 106	2 442
1985	289.79	25.29	30.60	233.90	30 289	6 987	24 908	13 054
1990	331.10	25.75	32.40	272.94	47 102	8 545	43 455	15 365
1995	327.84	22.55	42.46	262.83	67 000	7 587	62 300	20 837
2000	403.97	23.90	51.35	328.72	106 875	8 528	75 908	24 568
2005	502.66	32.13	57.20	413.33	150 238	10 181	164 817	28 121
2010	624.06	40.88	155.42	427.76	319 923	11 314	443 099	45 731
2011	611.27	44.87	126.27	440.13	316 499	11 399	496 553	54 123
2012	603.06	43.30	130.53	429.23	324 583	11 819	535 570	60 041
2013	628.86	43.55	135.21	450.10	337 025	13 413	541 481	65 038
2014	730.78	48.26	151.97	530.55	377 222	15 206	590 663	76 208
2015	771.28	51.2	147.39	572.69	390 043	17 691	629 008	81 403
2016	763.85	52.97	149.64	561.24	411 478	19 068	629 238	94 261
2017	772.58	56.62	167.47	548.49	443 787	19 898	681 395	109 222

9—19 各师林业生产情况

Forestry Production by Division

计量单位:公顷 (2017 年) (hectare)

单 位 Unit	人工造林面积 Afforestation Area	人工造林面积按造林方式分 Woodland Restored from Cultivated Land					
		# 人工造林面积 Afforestation Area	用材林 Timber Forest	经济林 Economic Forest	防护林 Wind break	薪炭林 Firewood Forest	特种用途林 Forest for Special Purpose
总 计 Total	**27 105**	**16 424**		**8 264**	**7 417**		**743**
一 师 Division 1	2 353	2 328		1 120	1 208		
二 师 Division 2	3 114	2 910		2 637	273		
三 师 Division 3	3 069	3 069		1 824	1 245		
四 师 Division 4	2 680	2 515		1 326	446		743
五 师 Division 5	653	517		133	384		
六 师 Division 6	1 023	690			690		
七 师 Division 7	1 224	1 191		53	1 138		
八 师 Division 8	3 119	1 114		48	1 066		
九 师 Division 9	5 219	551		50	501		
十 师 Division 10	2 586	502		333	169		
十二师 Division 12	183	163		33	130		
十三师 Division 13	91	50		28	22		
十四师 Division 14	1 791	824		679	145		

单 位 Unit	当年零星(四旁)植树(万株) Fragmentary Planting (10 000 stubs)	年末实有封山育林面积 Area of Planting Trees	中、幼龄林抚育面积 Tending Area of Small and young Growth	年末实有育苗面积 Actual Sapling Breeding Area	当年苗木产量(万株) Output of Breeding and Trees (10000 stubs)	木材采伐量(立方米) Timber Felling Output in (cu.m)
总 计 Total	**335.3**	**114581**	**194 943**	**4 632**	**7 436.08**	**137 814**
一 师 Division 1	123.22	740	26 749	171	429.57	14 442
二 师 Division 2	83.17	14 613	10 513	284	701.50	41 076
三 师 Division 3		2 667	15 936	661	1 300.00	4 593
四 师 Division 4	59.15		43 353	654	970.83	33 468
五 师 Division 5	3.43	1 333	7 825	42	66.60	4 050
六 师 Division 6	26.10	2 999	14 270	846	736.00	22 100
七 师 Division 7	6.26		6 331	116	165.15	1 015
八 师 Division 8	28.07	62 316	20 828	1 137	1 479.68	2 859
九 师 Division 9	2.86	15 000	27 812	230	20.00	1 830
十 师 Division 10	3.00	3 046	13 763	100	441.61	5 878
十二师 Division 12			4 391	109	22.44	
十三师 Division 13		11 867	2 625	143	62.70	3 631
十四师 Division 14	0.04		547	139	1 040.00	2 872

9—20　各师水果生产情况

Fruit Production by Division

（2017 年）

指　　标	Item	合　计 Total	一　师 Division 1	二　师 Division 2	三　师 Division 3	四　师 Division 4	五　师 Division 5	六　师 Division 6
年末实有面积（公顷）	**Actual Area at the Year-end(hectare)**	**208 294**	**63 455**	**30 921**	**34 098**	**14 753**	**5 852**	**4 790**
苹　果	Apples	23 762	7 557	897	4 940	4 892	191	104
# 红富士苹果	Hongfushi Apples	17 024	6 823	635	4 360	2 581	62	61
黄元帅苹果	Huangyuangshuai Apples	1 364	682	75	347	155	8	
梨	Pears	20 788	7 021	9 373	4 278	44		1
# 香　梨	Snow Flake Pears	17 378	5 911	8 315	3 150	1		1
砀山梨	Duck Pears	2 246	314	909	1 023			
葡　萄	Grapes	44 351	525	2 683	829	5 844	5 458	4 242
# 无核葡萄	Seedless Grapes	14 227	153	1 337	59	735	1 875	980
红提葡萄	Hongti Grapes	11 573	87	330	16	2 273	2 140	1 017
酿酒葡萄	Grapes of Make Wining	13 121	18	324	539	2 543		2 214
桃	Peachs	4 301	105	229	332	1 524	36	149
# 蟠　桃	Pan Peachs	2 489	6	44	9	913	1	12
杏	Apricots	5 030	2 414	88	321	1 736		273
红　枣	Jujubes	107 498	45 515	17 243	22 379	309	20	17
石　榴	Pomegranate	19			18			
其　他	Others	2 545	318	408	1 001	404	147	4
产　量（吨）	**Output(ton)**	**3 921 608**	**1 698 277**	**405 629**	**499 080**	**347 201**	**103 826**	**58 700**
苹　果	Apples	630 818	283 521	4 979	126 149	149 676	2 393	603
# 红富士苹果	Hongfushi Apples	458 103	241 330	2 745	108 619	73 464	2 007	123
黄元帅苹果	huanyuanshuai Apples	62 418	39 982	1 515	12 378	5 807	351	
梨	Pears	531 781	243 510	201 868	84 009	1 593		
# 香　梨	Snow Flake Pears	406 258	213 046	149 260	43 931	21		
砀山梨	Dangshan Pears	98 450	12 936	45 890	39 624			
葡　萄	Grapes	794 264	11 736	31 401	6 955	119 415	100 829	56 732
# 无核葡萄	Seedless Grapes	229 860	1 595	13 059	607	14 979	28 474	13 252
红提葡萄	Hongti Grapes	220 184	1 828	5 519	305	55 572	38 355	14 247
酿酒葡萄	Grapes of Make Wining	219 060	798	2 888	2 316	44 214		27 377
桃	Peachs	92 191	2 155	3 596	5 955	49 591	415	579
# 蟠　桃	Pan Peachs	44 112	180	910	304	18 568	24	23
杏	Apricots	45 929	12 208	398	9 299	21 304		440
红　枣	Jujubes	1 817 304	1 144 677	162 791	266 126	1 000	159	72
石　榴	Pomegranate	26			10			
其　他	Others	9 295	470	596	577	4 622	30	274

9－20 续表 Continued

(2017 年)

指 标	Item	七 师 Division 7	八 师 Division 8	九 师 Division 9	十 师 Division 10	十一师 Division 11	十二师 Division 12	十三师 Division 13	十四师 Division 14
年末实有面积(公顷)	**Actual Area at the Year-end(hectare)**	**5 288**	**14 056**	**1 334**	**259**	**7**	**4 972**	**9 800**	**18 709**
苹 果	Apples	1 199	1 376	973	168		60	4	1 401
# 红富士苹果	Hongfushi Apples	977	915		146		58		406
黄元帅苹果	Huangyuangshuai Apples	65	1		22				9
梨	Pears	2	5		40		4	1	19
# 香 梨	Snow Flake Pears								
砀山梨	Dangshan Pears								
葡 萄	Grapes	3 923	11 869	170	40	6	3 602	5 004	156
# 无核葡萄	Seedless Grapes	209	3 612	44	36	6	738	4 443	
红提葡萄	Hongti Grapes	1 384	1 780	63	5		2 043	402	33
酿酒葡萄	Grapes of Make Wining	413	6 129				822	119	
桃	Peachs	90	597	36	11	1	1 172	9	10
# 蟠 桃	Pam Peachs	70	385		10		1 039		
杏	Apricots	2	3	71			60	61	1
红 枣	Jujubes	70	110	26			69	4 684	17 056
石 榴	Pomegranate		1						
其 他	Others	2	95	58			5	37	66
产 量(吨)	**Output(ton)**	**128 119**	**231 900**	**7 454**	**6 295**	**85**	**73 656**	**155 414**	**205 972**
苹 果	Apples	30 206	11 329	4 236	5 820	4	417	68	11 417
# 红富士苹果	Hongfushi Apples	23 540	1 130		4 393		412		340
黄元帅苹果	huanyuanshuai Apples	1 585	50		582				168
梨	Pears	64		10				60	667
# 香 梨	Snow Flake Pears								
砀山梨	Dangshan Pears								
葡 萄	Grapes	95 864	202 717	2 236	225	70	59 883	104 207	1 994
# 无核葡萄	Seedless Grapes	7 333	56 766	612	118	70	13 985	79 010	
红提葡萄	Hongti Grapes	33 035	24 680	712	107		35 386	10 433	5
酿酒葡萄	Grapes of Make Wining	12 300	116 875				10 132	2 160	
桃	Peachs	827	15 321	280	250	4	12 734	209	275
# 蟠 桃	Pam Peachs	665	11 092	2	250		12 094		
杏	Apricots	30	33	260		3	345	1 590	19
红 枣	Jujubes	1 083	1 106	155			179	48 455	191 501
石 榴	Pomegranate		16						
其 他	Others	45	1 378	277		4	98	825	99

9—21　畜牧业生产情况

Animal Husbandry Production

计量单位:万头(只)　　　　(2017 年)　　　　(10 000 heads)

指　　标	Item	合　计 Total	牛 Cattle and Buffaloes	# 奶　牛 Cows	马 Horses	驴 Donkeys	骡 Mules	骆　驼 Camels
年初数	**Number at the Beginning of the Year**	**763.85**	**47.59**	**23.31**	**3.56**	**1.29**		**0.53**
年内增加	**Increase in the Year**	**999.70**	**47.49**	**14.47**	**2.55**	**0.76**		**0.25**
繁殖成活数	Number of Breeding Survival	785.41	26.75	11.44	1.70	0.41		0.17
买入数	Buy in	214.27	20.74	3.03	0.85	0.33		0.08
其　他	Others	0.02				0.02		
年内减少	**Decrease in the Year**	**990.97**	**44.31**	**12.81**	**2.18**	**0.64**		**0.27**
成、幼畜死亡数	Death of Adult and Infant Animals	7.53	0.34	0.14	0.01			
卖出数	Sold out	881.82	39.42	11.89	1.95	0.54		0.18
# 仔　畜	Infant Animals	100.73	4.62	1.90	0.01			0.01
自宰自食数	Slaughtered and Eaten by Peasants Themselves	101.62	4.55	0.78	0.22	0.10		0.09
其　他	Others							
年末实有数	**Number at the Year-end**	**772.58**	**50.77**	**24.97**	**3.93**	**1.41**		**0.51**
# 实际参加农事劳役的	Draught Animal	0.16	0.03		0.01	0.12		
# 能繁殖的母畜	Reproducable Female Animals	464.80	33.45	17.82	1.93	0.73		0.23
年内仔畜死亡	**Death of Infant Animals in the Year**	**4.40**	**0.09**	**0.07**				

指　　标	Item	猪 Hogs	羊 Goats	山　羊 Milk Goats	绵　羊 Sheep	# 细毛羊及改良羊 Fine Wool Sheep and Improved Sheep	家　禽 Poultry	兔 Rabbits
年初数	**Number at the Beginning of the Year**	**149.64**	**561.24**	**50.04**	**511.20**	**139.13**		**3.00**
年内增加	**Increasein the Year**	**368.02**	**580.63**	**52.75**	**527.88**	**134.38**		
繁殖成活数	Number of Breeding Survival	305.90	450.48	38.84	411.64	104.29		
买入数	Buy in	62.12	130.15	13.91	116.24	30.09		
其　他	Others							
年内减少	**Decreasein the Year**	**350.19**	**593.38**	**55.73**	**537.65**	**138.50**		**9.00**
成、幼畜死亡数	Death of Adult and Infant Animals	2.81	4.37	0.17	4.20	2.50		
卖出数	Sold out	323.10	516.63	44.36	472.27	123.78	2 699.45	170.20
# 仔　畜	Infant Animals	66.00	30.09	0.79	29.30	12.21		2.00
自宰自食数	Slaughtered and Eaten by Peasants Themselves	24.28	72.38	11.20	61.18	12.22	340.12	63.29
其　他	Others							
年末实有数	**Number at the Year-end**	**167.47**	**548.49**	**47.06**	**501.43**	**135.01**	**1 397.06**	**46.65**
# 实际参加农事劳役的	Draught Animal							
# 能繁殖的母畜	Reproducable Female Animals	21.54	406.92	32.19	374.73	94.33		
年内仔畜死亡	**Death of Infant Animals in the Year**	**2.70**	**1.61**	**0.13**	**1.48**	**0.30**		

9—22 各师畜牧业生产情况

Animal Husbandry Production by Division

计量单位:万头(只) (2017 年) (10 000 heads)

指标	Item	合计 Total	一师 Division 1	二师 Division 2	三师 Division 3	四师 Division 4	五师 Division 5	六师 Division 6
年初数	**Number at the Beginning of the Year**	**763.85**	**64.67**	**65.80**	**87.38**	**113.01**	**35.75**	**90.36**
年内增加	**Increase in the Year**	**999.70**	**70.68**	**82.51**	**64.31**	**121.49**	**35.52**	**134.26**
繁殖成活数	Number of Breeding Survival	785.41	64.25	79.16	58.26	98.99	29.10	92.79
买入数	Buy in	214.27	6.43	3.35	6.05	22.50	6.40	41.47
其 他	Others	0.02					0.02	
年内减少	**Decrease in the Year**	**990.97**	**68.47**	**83.83**	**73.27**	**118.34**	**38.26**	**139.53**
成、幼畜死亡数	Death of Adult and Infant Animals	7.53	0.52	0.51	0.38	0.50	0.37	0.46
卖出数	Sold out	881.82	54.46	74.57	56.21	108.52	34.78	130.66
# 仔 畜	Infant Animals	100.73	2.69	2.84	0.13	0.14	1.51	2.49
自宰自食数	Slaughtered and Eaten by Peasants Themselves	101.62	13.49	8.75	16.68	9.32	3.11	8.41
其 他	Others							
年末实有数	**Number at the Year-end**	**772.58**	**66.88**	**64.48**	**78.42**	**116.16**	**33.01**	**85.09**
# 实际参加农事劳役的	Draught Animal	0.16	0.02		0.07	0.01		
# 能繁殖的母畜	Reproducable Female Animals	464.80	44.15	28.37	59.77	75.29	19.03	52.10
年内仔畜死亡	**Death of Infant Animals in the Year**	**4.40**	**0.15**	**1.31**	**0.32**	**0.06**	**0.14**	**0.02**

指标	Item	七师 Division 7	八师 Division 8	九师 Division 9	十师 Division 10	十二师 Division 12	十三师 Division 13	十四师 Division 14
年初数	**Number at the Beginning of the Year**	**53.44**	**77.94**	**83.10**	**34.81**	**12.29**	**30.21**	**15.09**
年内增加	**Increase in the Year**	**56.66**	**203.71**	**102.82**	**46.69**	**14.62**	**49.32**	**17.11**
繁殖成活数	Number of Breeding Survival	45.01	149.07	84.92	37.27	6.21	27.23	13.15
买入数	Buy in	11.65	54.64	17.90	9.42	8.41	22.09	3.96
其 他	Others							
年内减少	**Decrease in the Year**	**52.79**	**191.88**	**98.08**	**44.28**	**16.99**	**48.85**	**16.4**
成、幼畜死亡数	Death of Adult and Infant Animals	0.80	3.36	0.34	0.11	0.13	0.05	
卖出数	Sold out	43.53	180.50	91.98	42.56	15.93	34.04	14.08
# 仔 畜	Infant Animals	1.06	89.26	0.37	0.07	0.04	0.13	
自宰自食数	Slaughtered and Eaten by Peasants Themselves	8.46	8.02	5.76	1.61	0.93	14.76	2.32
其 他	Others							
年末实有数	**Number at the Year-end**	**57.31**	**89.77**	**87.84**	**37.22**	**9.92**	**30.68**	**15.8**
# 实际参加农事劳役的	Draught Animal							0.06
# 能繁殖的母畜	Reproducable Female Animals	28.87	27.03	63.95	26.48	5.59	22.63	11.54
年内仔畜死亡	**Death of Infant Animals in the Year**	**0.20**	**1.51**	**0.52**	**0.10**	**0.06**	**0.01**	

9—23　各师牲畜年底头数

Year-end Number of Livestock by Division

计量单位:万头(只)　　　　(2017 年)　　　　(10 000 heads)

单　位	Unit	合　计 Total	牛 Cattle and Buffaloes	#奶　牛 Cattle	马 Horses	驴 Donkeys	骆　驼 Camels	猪 Hogs	羊 Goats
总　计	**Total**	**772.58**	**50.77**	**24.97**	**3.93**	**1.41**	**0.51**	**167.47**	**548.49**
一　师	Division 1	66.88	5.36	2.92		0.16		13.15	48.21
二　师	Division 2	64.48	2.10	0.84	0.02	0.03	0.01	23.54	38.78
三　师	Division 3	78.42	2.53	0.94	0.08	0.40		6.24	69.17
四　师	Division 4	116.16	9.22	4.92	1.76	0.02		15.72	89.44
五　师	Division 5	33.01	1.73	0.37	0.08	0.02	0.01	8.75	22.42
六　师	Division 6	85.09	4.38	1.39	0.43	0.19	0.13	25.60	54.36
七　师	Division 7	57.31	6.42	3.77	0.09	0.01	0.07	9.57	41.15
八　师	Division 8	89.77	9.08	7.29	0.18	0.04	0.01	52.01	28.45
九　师	Division 9	87.84	4.36	0.78	0.23			2.30	80.95
十　师	Division 10	37.22	2.68	0.73	0.09			3.20	31.25
十 二 师	Division 12	9.92	1.73	0.92	0.10	0.02	0.04	1.54	6.49
十 三 师	Division 13	30.68	0.95	0.10	0.83	0.13	0.12	4.92	23.73
十 四 师	Division 14	15.80	0.23		0.04	0.39	0.12	0.93	14.09

单　位	Unit	绵　羊 Sheep	家　禽 Poultry	兔 Rabbits	牲畜出栏头数 Slaughtered Fattened Animals Slaughteyed	牛 Cattle and Buffaloes	猪 Hogs	羊 Goats	家　禽 Poultry
总　计	**Total**	**501.43**	**1397.06**	**46.65**	**882.71**	**39.35**	**281.38**	**558.92**	**3039.57**
一　师	Division 1	43.74	81.08	3.79	65.26	3.52	20.70	40.92	177.02
二　师	Division 2	37.34	131.44	5.24	80.48	1.57	37.33	41.55	164.90
三　师	Division 3	56.69	66.64	2.60	72.76	1.60	10.37	60.70	88.45
四　师	Division 4	88.11	177.28	3.88	117.70	7.30	31.18	78.17	342.84
五　师	Division 5	20.26	82.33	2.12	36.38	1.20	13.76	21.40	138.43
六　师	Division 6	44.54	362.81	2.50	136.58	8.19	44.32	83.86	744.62
七　师	Division 7	36.07	113.58	11.01	50.93	2.83	18.50	29.57	393.65
八　师	Division 8	27.16	216.19	11.74	99.26	4.18	77.34	17.23	611.67
九　师	Division 9	78.05	27.52	0.74	97.37	3.18	3.98	90.12	95.48
十　师	Division 10	30.03	42.00	0.30	44.10	2.81	6.54	34.65	100.21
十 二 师	Division 12	5.67	14.89		16.82	0.71	8.22	7.84	42.46
十 三 师	Division 13	20.07	50.60	2.50	48.67	1.97	7.95	38.23	113.76
十 四 师	Division 14	13.70	30.70	0.23	16.40	0.29	1.19	14.68	26.08

9—24 各师大牲畜生产情况

Large Animals Production by Division

计量单位:万头(只) (2017年) (10 000 heads)

指 标	Item	合 计 Total	一 师 Division 1	二 师 Division 2	三 师 Division 3	四 师 Division 4	五 师 Division 5	六 师 Division 6
年初数	**Number at the Beginning of the Year**	**52.97**	**5.75**	**2.35**	**2.74**	**9.88**	**1.72**	**5.19**
年内增加	**Increase in the Year**	**51.05**	**3.57**	**1.52**	**1.96**	**9.57**	**1.36**	**8.39**
繁殖成活数	Number of Breeding Survival	29.03	3.35	1.25	1.55	5.94	0.76	2.33
买入数	Buy in	22.00	0.22	0.27	0.41	3.63	0.58	6.06
其 他	Others	0.02					0.02	
年内减少	**Decrease in the Year**	**47.40**	**3.80**	**1.71**	**1.69**	**8.45**	**1.24**	**8.45**
成、幼畜死亡数	Death of Adult and Infant Animals	0.35	0.04	0.02		0.04		0.02
卖出数	Sold out	42.09	3.27	1.31	1.30	7.78	1.08	8.02
# 仔 畜	Infant Animals	4.64	0.12	0.09		0.06	0.02	0.03
自宰自食数	Slaughtered and Eaten by Peasants Themselves	4.96	0.49	0.38	0.39	0.63	0.16	0.41
其 他	Others							
年末实有数	**Number at the Year-end**	**56.62**	**5.52**	**2.16**	**3.01**	**11.00**	**1.84**	**5.13**
# 实际参加农事劳役的	Draught Animal	0.16	0.02		0.07	0.01		
# 能繁殖的母畜	Reproducable Female Animals	36.34	4.47	1.85	2.20	7.22	1.07	2.77
年内仔畜死亡	**Death of Infant Animals in the Year**	**0.09**		**0.01**				

指 标	Item	七 师 Division 7	八 师 Division 8	九 师 Division 9	十 师 Division 10	十二师 Division 12	十三师 Division 13	十四师 Division 14
年初数	**Number at the Beginning of the Year**	**6.02**	**8.36**	**4.13**	**2.56**	**1.67**	**1.81**	**0.79**
年内增加	**Increase in the Year**	**3.86**	**9.73**	**3.74**	**3.12**	**0.99**	**2.72**	**0.52**
繁殖成活数	Number of Breeding Survival	2.58	5.34	2.38	1.82	0.55	1.01	0.17
买入数	Buy in	1.28	4.39	1.36	1.30	0.44	1.71	0.35
其 他	Others							
年内减少	**Decrease in the Year**	**3.29**	**8.78**	**3.28**	**2.91**	**0.77**	**2.50**	**0.53**
成、幼畜死亡数	Death of Adult and Infant Animals	0.02	0.20	0.01				
卖出数	Sold out	2.96	8.18	2.88	2.82	0.72	1.49	0.28
# 仔 畜	Infant Animals	0.41	3.89			0.01	0.01	
自宰自食数	Slaughtered and Eaten by Peasants Themselves	0.31	0.40	0.39	0.09	0.05	1.01	0.25
其 他	Others							
年末实有数	**Number at the Year-end**	**6.59**	**9.31**	**4.59**	**2.77**	**1.89**	**2.03**	**0.78**
# 实际参加农事劳役的	Draught Animal							0.06
# 能繁殖的母畜	Reproducable Female Animals	3.53	6.10	2.66	1.80	1.05	1.39	0.23
年内仔畜死亡	**Death of Infant Animals in the Year**		**0.08**					

9—25　各师牛生产情况

Cattle Production by Division

计量单位:万头　　　　(2017 年)　　　　(10 000 heads)

指　　标	Item	合　计 Total	一　师 Division 1	二　师 Division 2	三　师 Division 3	四　师 Division 4	五　师 Division 5	六　师 Division 6
年初数	**Number at the Beginning of the Year**	**47.59**	**5.54**	**2.29**	**2.33**	**8.27**	**1.65**	**4.57**
年内增加	**Increase in the Year**	**47.49**	**3.50**	**1.49**	**1.80**	**8.35**	**1.30**	**8.04**
繁殖成活数	Number of Breeding Survival	26.75	3.28	1.22	1.41	4.94	0.74	2.02
买入数	Buy in	20.74	0.22	0.27	0.39	3.41	0.56	6.02
其　他	Others							
年内减少	**Decrease in the Year**	**44.31**	**3.68**	**1.68**	**1.60**	**7.40**	**1.22**	**8.23**
成、幼畜死亡数	Death of Adult and Infant Animals	0.34	0.04	0.02		0.04		0.01
卖出数	Sold out	39.42	3.17	1.28	1.23	6.85	1.06	7.84
# 仔　畜	Infant Animals	4.62	0.12	0.09		0.06	0.02	0.03
自宰自食数	Slaughtered and Eaten by Peasants Themselves	4.55	0.47	0.38	0.37	0.51	0.16	0.38
其　他	Others							
年末实有数	**Number at the Year-end**	**50.77**	**5.36**	**2.10**	**2.53**	**9.22**	**1.73**	**4.38**
# 实际参加农事劳役的	Draught Animal	0.03			0.02			
# 能繁殖的母畜	Reproducable Female Animals	33.45	4.37	1.82	1.88	6.24	1.05	2.34
年内仔畜死亡	**Death of Infant Animals in the Year**	**0.09**		**0.01**				

指　　标	Item	七　师 Division 7	八　师 Division 8	九　师 Division 9	十　师 Division 10	十二师 Division 12	十三师 Division 13	十四师 Division 14
年初数	**Number at the Beginning of the Year**	**5.87**	**8.09**	**3.91**	**2.44**	**1.55**	**0.86**	**0.22**
年内增加	**Increase in the Year**	**3.80**	**9.25**	**3.64**	**3.05**	**0.90**	**2.07**	**0.3**
繁殖成活数	Number of Breeding Survival	2.52	5.27	2.29	1.77	0.52	0.71	0.06
买入数	Buy in	1.28	3.98	1.35	1.28	0.38	1.36	0.24
其　他	Others							
年内减少	**Decrease in the Year**	**3.25**	**8.26**	**3.19**	**2.81**	**0.72**	**1.98**	**0.29**
成、幼畜死亡数	Death of Adult and Infant Animals	0.02	0.20	0.01				
卖出数	Sold out	2.92	7.68	2.79	2.72	0.67	1.09	0.12
# 仔　畜	Infant Animals	0.40	3.88			0.01	0.01	
自宰自食数	Slaughtered and Eaten by Peasants Themselves	0.31	0.38	0.39	0.09	0.05	0.89	0.17
其　他	Others							
年末实有数	**Number at the Year-end**	**6.42**	**9.08**	**4.36**	**2.68**	**1.73**	**0.95**	**0.23**
# 实际参加农事劳役的	Draught Animal							0.01
# 能繁殖的母畜	Reproducable Female Animals	3.50	6.02	2.55	1.75	1.02	0.85	0.06
年内仔畜死亡	**Death of Infant Animals in the Year**		**0.08**					

9—26 各师奶牛生产情况

Cow Production by Division

计量单位:万头 (2017 年) (10 000 heads)

指　　标	Item	合　计 Total	一　师 Division 1	二　师 Division 2	三　师 Division 3	四　师 Division 4	五　师 Division 5	六　师 Division 6
年初数	**Number at the Beginning of the Year**	**23.31**	**2.67**	**0.89**	**0.87**	**4.56**	**0.32**	**1.44**
年内增加	**Increase in the Year**	**14.47**	**1.59**	**0.32**	**0.55**	**3.17**	**0.31**	**0.81**
繁殖成活数	Number of Breeding Survival	11.44	1.59	0.31	0.42	2.33	0.20	0.74
买入数	Buy in	3.03		0.01	0.13	0.84	0.11	0.07
其　他	Others							
年内减少	**Decrease in the Year**	**12.81**	**1.34**	**0.37**	**0.48**	**2.81**	**0.26**	**0.86**
成、幼畜死亡数	Death of Adult and Infant Animals	0.14	0.04	0.01				
卖出数	Sold out	11.89	1.25	0.34	0.37	2.73	0.25	0.85
# 仔　畜	Infant Animals	1.90	0.08	0.05			0.02	
自宰自食数	Slaughtered and Eaten by Peasants Themselves	0.78	0.05	0.02	0.11	0.08	0.01	0.01
其　他	Others							
年末实有数	**Number at the Year-end**	**24.97**	**2.92**	**0.84**	**0.94**	**4.92**	**0.37**	**1.39**
# 实际参加农事劳役的	Draught Animal							
# 能繁殖的母畜	Reproducable Female Animals	17.82	2.34	0.73	0.58	3.35	0.29	0.96
年内仔畜死亡	**Death of Infant Animals in the Year**	**0.07**						

指　　标	Item	七　师 Division 7	八　师 Division 8	九　师 Division 9	十　师 Division 10	十二师 Division 12	十三师 Division 13	十四师 Division 14
年初数	**Number at the Beginning of the Year**	**3.42**	**6.77**	**0.72**	**0.68**	**0.85**	**0.12**	
年内增加	**Increase in the Year**	**2.07**	**4.34**	**0.65**	**0.24**	**0.38**	**0.04**	
繁殖成活数	Number of Breeding Survival	1.81	3.15	0.51	0.17	0.17	0.04	
买入数	Buy in	0.26	1.19	0.14	0.07	0.21		
其　他	Others							
年内减少	**Decrease in the Year**	**1.72**	**3.82**	**0.59**	**0.19**	**0.31**	**0.06**	
成、幼畜死亡数	Death of Adult and Infant Animals		0.09					
卖出数	Sold out	1.57	3.56	0.41	0.19	0.31	0.06	
# 仔　畜	Infant Animals	0.34	1.40			0.01		
自宰自食数	Slaughtered and Eaten by Peasants Themselves	0.15	0.17	0.18				
其　他	Others							
年末实有数	**Number at the Year-end**	**3.77**	**7.29**	**0.78**	**0.73**	**0.92**	**0.10**	
# 实际参加农事劳役的	Draught Animal							
# 能繁殖的母畜	Reproducable Female Animals	2.66	5.15	0.62	0.39	0.68	0.07	
年内仔畜死亡	**Death of Infant Animals in the Year**		**0.07**					

9—27 各师马生产情况

Horse Production by Division

计量单位:万匹 （2017年） (10 000 heads)

指 标	Item	合计 Total	一 师 Division 1	二 师 Division 2	三 师 Division 3	四 师 Division 4	五 师 Division 5	六 师 Division 6
年初数	**Number at the Beginning of the Year**	**3.56**		**0.01**	**0.07**	**1.58**	**0.06**	**0.32**
年内增加	**Increase in the Year**	**2.55**		**0.01**	**0.01**	**1.22**	**0.03**	**0.22**
繁殖成活数	Number of Breeding Survival	1.70		0.01	0.01	1.00	0.01	0.21
买入数	Buy in	0.85				0.22	0.02	0.01
其 他	Others							
年内减少	**Decrease in the Year**	**2.18**				**1.04**	**0.01**	**0.11**
成、幼畜死亡数	Death of Adult and Infant Animals	0.01						0.01
卖出数	Sold out	1.95				0.92	0.01	0.09
# 仔 畜	Infant Animals	0.01						
自宰自食数	Slaughtered and Eaten by Peasants Themselves	0.22				0.12		0.01
其 他	Others							
年末实有数	**Number at the Year-end**	**3.93**		**0.02**	**0.08**	**1.76**	**0.08**	**0.43**
# 实际参加农事劳役的	Draught Animal	0.01				0.01		
# 能繁殖的母畜	Reproducable Female Animals	1.93		0.01	0.06	0.97		0.25
年内仔畜死亡	**Death of Infant Animals in the Year**							

指 标	Item	七 师 Division 7	八 师 Division 8	九 师 Division 9	十 师 Division 10	十二师 Division 12	十三师 Division 13	十四师 Division 14
年初数	**Number at the Beginning of the Year**	**0.07**	**0.23**	**0.22**	**0.12**	**0.07**	**0.76**	**0.05**
年内增加	**Increase in the Year**	**0.02**	**0.46**	**0.10**	**0.07**	**0.06**	**0.33**	**0.02**
繁殖成活数	Number of Breeding Survival	0.02	0.05	0.09	0.05	0.02	0.22	0.01
买入数	Buy in		0.41	0.01	0.02	0.04	0.11	0.01
其 他	Others							
年内减少	**Decrease in the Year**		**0.51**	**0.09**	**0.10**	**0.03**	**0.26**	**0.03**
成、幼畜死亡数	Death of Adult and Infant Animals							
卖出数	Sold out		0.49	0.09	0.10	0.03	0.19	0.03
# 仔 畜	Infant Animals		0.01					
自宰自食数	Slaughtered and Eaten by Peasants Themselves		0.02				0.07	
其 他	Others							
年末实有数	**Number at the Year-end**	**0.09**	**0.18**	**0.23**	**0.09**	**0.10**	**0.83**	**0.04**
# 实际参加农事劳役的	Draught Animal							
# 能繁殖的母畜	Reproducable Female Animals		0.06	0.11	0.05	0.02	0.40	
年内仔畜死亡	**Death of Infant Animals in the Year**							

9—28 各师猪生产情况

Hogs Production by Division

计量单位:万头　　　　(2017 年)　　　　(10 000 heads)

指　　标	Item	合　计 Total	一　师 Division 1	二　师 Division 2	三　师 Division 3	四　师 Division 4	五　师 Division 5	六　师 Division 6
年初数	**Number at the Beginning of the Year**	**149.64**	**11.07**	**19.69**	**6.58**	**15.92**	**7.31**	**23.70**
年内增加	**Increase in the Year**	**368.02**	**25.35**	**42.87**	**10.09**	**31.21**	**16.21**	**48.94**
繁殖成活数	Number of Breeding Survival	305.90	21.86	41.74	9.33	28.59	14.03	39.96
买入数	Buy in	62.12	3.49	1.13	0.76	2.62	2.18	8.98
其　他	Others							
年内减少	**Decrease in the Year**	**350.19**	**23.27**	**39.02**	**10.43**	**31.41**	**14.77**	**47.04**
成、幼畜死亡数	Death of Adult and Infant Animals	2.81	0.37	0.11	0.03	0.17	0.27	0.29
卖出数	Sold out	323.10	19.19	35.55	9.42	29.39	13.41	45.13
# 仔　畜	Infant Animals	66.00	2.20	1.58	0.03	0.06	0.74	2.43
自宰自食数	Slaughtered and Eaten by Peasants Themselves	24.28	3.71	3.36	0.98	1.85	1.09	1.62
其　他	Others							
年末实有数	**Number at the Year-end**	**167.47**	**13.15**	**23.54**	**6.24**	**15.72**	**8.75**	**25.60**
# 能繁殖的母畜	Reproducable Female Animals	21.54	1.68	2.98	0.87	2.15	1.11	3.36
年内仔畜死亡	**Death of Infant Animals in the Year**	**2.70**	**0.10**	**1.20**	**0.06**	**0.02**	**0.05**	**0.01**

指　　标	Item	七　师 Division 7	八　师 Division 8	九　师 Division 9	十　师 Division 10	十二师 Division 12	十三师 Division 13	十四师 Division 14
年初数	**Number at the Beginning of the Year**	**8.51**	**43.51**	**2.00**	**3.17**	**3.29**	**4.12**	**0.77**
年内增加	**Increase in the Year**	**20.40**	**145.20**	**4.31**	**6.64**	**6.57**	**8.88**	**1.35**
繁殖成活数	Number of Breeding Survival	17.62	113.33	4.18	5.34	2.05	6.60	1.27
买入数	Buy in	2.78	31.87	0.13	1.30	4.52	2.28	0.08
其　他	Others							
年内减少	**Decrease in the Year**	**19.34**	**136.70**	**4.01**	**6.61**	**8.32**	**8.08**	**1.19**
成、幼畜死亡数	Death of Adult and Infant Animals	0.36	1.09	0.01		0.07	0.04	
卖出数	Sold out	16.44	130.40	3.16	6.12	8.02	5.79	1.08
# 仔　畜	Infant Animals	0.48	58.27	0.02	0.07	0.03	0.09	
自宰自食数	Slaughtered and Eaten by Peasants Themselves	2.54	5.21	0.84	0.49	0.23	2.25	0.11
其　他	Others							
年末实有数	**Number at the Year-end**	**9.57**	**52.01**	**2.30**	**3.20**	**1.54**	**4.92**	**0.93**
# 能繁殖的母畜	Reproducable Female Animals	1.26	6.47	0.31	0.43	0.13	0.63	0.16
年内仔畜死亡	**Death of Infant Animals in the Year**	**0.05**	**1.14**	**0.03**		**0.04**		

9—29　各师羊生产情况

Sheep and Goat Production by Division

计量单位:万只　　　　(2017 年)　　　　(10 000 heads)

指　　标	Item	合　计 Total	一　师 Division 1	二　师 Division 2	三　师 Division 3	四　师 Division 4	五　师 Division 5	六　师 Division 6
年初数	**Number at the Beginning of the Year**	**561.24**	**47.85**	**43.76**	**78.06**	**87.21**	**26.72**	**61.47**
年内增加	**Increase in the Year**	**580.63**	**41.76**	**38.12**	**52.26**	**80.71**	**17.95**	**76.93**
繁殖成活数	Number of Breeding Survival	450.48	39.04	36.17	47.38	64.46	14.31	50.50
买入数	Buy in	130.15	2.72	1.95	4.88	16.25	3.64	26.43
其　他	Others							
年内减少	**Decrease in the Year**	**593.38**	**41.40**	**43.10**	**61.15**	**78.48**	**22.25**	**84.04**
成、幼畜死亡数	Death of Adult and Infant Animals	4.37	0.11	0.38	0.35	0.29	0.10	0.15
卖出数	Sold out	516.63	32.00	37.71	45.49	71.35	20.29	77.51
# 仔　畜	Infant Animals	30.09	0.37	1.17	0.10	0.02	0.75	0.03
自宰自食数	Slaughtered and Eaten by Peasants Themselves	72.38	9.29	5.01	15.31	6.84	1.86	6.38
其　他	Others							
年末实有数	**Number at the Year-end**	**548.49**	**48.21**	**38.78**	**69.17**	**89.44**	**22.42**	**54.36**
# 能繁殖的母畜	Reproducable Female Animals	406.92	38.00	23.54	56.70	65.92	16.85	45.97
年内仔畜死亡	**Death of Infant Animals in the Year**	**1.61**	**0.05**	**0.10**	**0.26**	**0.04**	**0.09**	**0.01**

指　　标	Item	七　师 Division 7	八　师 Division 8	九　师 Division 9	十　师 Division 10	十二师 Division 12	十三师 Division 13	十四师 Division 14
年初数	**Number at the Beginning of the Year**	**38.91**	**26.07**	**76.97**	**29.08**	**7.33**	**24.28**	**13.53**
年内增加	**Increase in the Year**	**32.40**	**48.78**	**94.77**	**36.93**	**7.06**	**37.72**	**15.24**
繁殖成活数	Number of Breeding Survival	24.81	30.40	78.36	30.11	3.61	19.62	11.71
买入数	Buy in	7.59	18.38	16.41	6.82	3.45	18.10	3.53
其　他	Others							
年内减少	**Decrease in the Year**	**30.16**	**46.40**	**90.79**	**34.76**	**7.90**	**38.27**	**14.68**
成、幼畜死亡数	Death of Adult and Infant Animals	0.42	2.07	0.32	0.11	0.06	0.01	
卖出数	Sold out	24.13	41.92	85.94	33.62	7.19	26.76	12.72
# 仔　畜	Infant Animals	0.17	27.10	0.35			0.03	
自宰自食数	Slaughtered and Eaten by Peasants Themselves	5.61	2.41	4.53	1.03	0.65	11.50	1.96
其　他	Others							
年末实有数	**Number at the Year-end**	**41.15**	**28.45**	**80.95**	**31.25**	**6.49**	**23.73**	**14.09**
# 能繁殖的母畜	Reproducable Female Animals	24.08	14.46	60.98	24.25	4.41	20.61	11.15
年内仔畜死亡	**Death of Infant Animals in the Year**	**0.15**	**0.29**	**0.49**	**0.10**	**0.02**	**0.01**	

9—30 各师绵羊生产情况

Sheep Production by Division

计量单位:万只 (2017年) (10 000 heads)

指 标	Item	合 计 Total	一 师 Division 1	二 师 Division 2	三 师 Division 3	四 师 Division 4	五 师 Division 5	六 师 Division 6
年初数	**Number at the Beginning of the Year**	**511.20**	**43.61**	**42.33**	**63.74**	**85.86**	**24.71**	**50.46**
年内增加	**Increase in the Year**	**527.88**	**38.54**	**36.05**	**38.18**	**79.63**	**16.39**	**65.35**
繁殖成活数	Number of Breeding Survival	411.64	35.88	34.14	35.46	63.55	13.02	43.54
买入数	Buy in	116.24	2.66	1.91	2.72	16.08	3.37	21.81
其 他	Others							
年内减少	**Decrease in the Year**	**537.65**	**38.41**	**41.04**	**45.23**	**77.38**	**20.84**	**71.27**
成、幼畜死亡数	Death of Adult and Infant Animals	4.20	0.10	0.36	0.31	0.29	0.09	0.11
卖出数	Sold out	472.27	29.47	36.37	34.14	70.29	19.16	65.79
# 仔 畜	Infant Animals	29.30	0.37	1.16	0.09	0.02	0.75	0.03
自宰自食数	Slaughtered and Eaten by Peasants Themselves	61.18	8.84	4.31	10.78	6.80	1.59	5.37
其 他	Others							
年末实有数	**Number at the Year-end**	**501.43**	**43.74**	**37.34**	**56.69**	**88.11**	**20.26**	**44.54**
# 能繁殖的母畜	Reproducable Female Animals	374.73	34.44	22.30	46.64	65.23	15.63	39.77
年内仔畜死亡	**Death of Infant Animals in the Year**	**1.48**	**0.05**	**0.08**	**0.20**	**0.04**	**0.08**	**0.01**

指 标	Item	七 师 Division 7	八 师 Division 8	九 师 Division 9	十 师 Division 10	十二师 Division 12	十三师 Division 13	十四师 Division 14
年初数	**Number at the Beginning of the Year**	**34.22**	**24.44**	**74.30**	**28.01**	**6.45**	**20.02**	**13.05**
年内增加	**Increase in the Year**	**26.90**	**47.08**	**91.60**	**35.26**	**6.35**	**32.23**	**14.32**
繁殖成活数	Number of Breeding Survival	20.86	29.51	75.70	28.75	3.22	16.71	11.3
买入数	Buy in	6.04	17.57	15.90	6.51	3.13	15.52	3.02
其 他	Others							
年内减少	**Decrease in the Year**	**25.05**	**44.36**	**87.85**	**33.24**	**7.13**	**32.18**	**13.67**
成、幼畜死亡数	Death of Adult and Infant Animals	0.37	2.07	0.32	0.11	0.06	0.01	
卖出数	Sold out	20.36	40.15	83.41	32.14	6.48	22.49	12.02
# 仔 畜	Infant Animals	0.10	26.41	0.35			0.02	
自宰自食数	Slaughtered and Eatenby Peasants Themselves	4.32	2.14	4.12	0.99	0.59	9.68	1.65
其 他	Others							
年末实有数	**Number at the Year-end**	**36.07**	**27.16**	**78.05**	**30.03**	**5.67**	**20.07**	**13.7**
# 能繁殖的母畜	Reproducable Female Animals	21.72	13.96	58.66	23.50	4.13	17.77	10.98
年内仔畜死亡	**Death of Infant Animals in the Year**	**0.13**	**0.28**	**0.48**	**0.10**	**0.02**	**0.01**	

9—31　各师肉类生产情况
Meat Production by Division
(2017年)

指　标	Item	合计 Total	一师 Division 1	二师 Division 2	三师 Division 3	四师 Division 4	五师 Division 5	六师 Division 6
总产肉量(吨)	**Output of Meat(ton)**	**443 787**	**33 289**	**42 479**	**23 648**	**57 530**	**18 870**	**76 526**
牛	Beef	59 585	5 330	2 377	2 423	11 054	1 817	12 402
马	Horse	2 782				1 569		151
驴	Donkey	672	141	26	68	9	10	38
骡	Mule							
骆　驼	Camel	242						116
肉　猪	Pork	202 053	14 864	26 806	7 446	22 390	9 881	31 825
羊	Goats and sheep	107 364	7 860	7 981	11 660	15 016	4 111	16 109
山　羊	Goat	10 637	447	283	3 115	212	270	2 282
绵　羊	Sheep	96 727	7 413	7 698	8 545	14 804	3 841	13 827
家　禽	Poultry	63 581	3 703	3 449	1 850	7 171	2 896	15 576
兔	Rabbit	5 210	1 391	276	201	321	150	189
其他肉产量	Others	2 298		1 564			5	120
平均产肉量(公斤/头、只)	**Average Yield of Meat (kg/head)**							
牛	Beef	151	151	151	151	151	151	151
马	Horse	129				151		151
驴	Donkey	105	118	87	85	90	100	76
骡	Mule							
骆　驼	Camel	93						193
肉　猪	Pork	72	72	72	72	72	72	72
绵　羊	Sheep	19	20	19	19	19	19	19
家　禽	Poultry	2	2	2	2	2	2	2
兔	Rabbit	2	2	2	2	2	2	3

指　标	Item	七师 Division 7	八师 Division 8	九师 Division 9	十师 Division 10	十二师 Division 12	十三师 Division 13	十四师 Division 14
总产肉量(吨)	**Output of Meat(ton)**	**32 407**	**79 885**	**27 188**	**17 745**	**9 401**	**20 018**	**4 801**
牛	Beef	4 285	6 330	4 815	4 255	1 075	2 983	439
马	Horse		624	126			312	
驴	Donkey		12				246	122
骡	Mule							
骆　驼	Camel	45				15	66	
肉　猪	Pork	13 284	55 536	2 858	4 696	5 903	5 709	855
羊	Goats and sheep	5 680	3 310	17 311	6 656	1 506	7 344	2 820
山　羊	Goat	1 393	188	444	287	196	1 225	295
绵　羊	Sheep	4 287	3 122	16 867	6 369	1 310	6 119	2 525
家　禽	Poultry	8 234	12 795	1 997	2 096	888	2 380	546
兔	Rabbit	875	1 249	33	4	14	488	19
其他肉产量	Others	4	29	48	38		490	
平均产肉量(公斤/头、只)	**Average Yield of Meat (kg/head)**							
牛	Beef	151	151	151	151	151	151	151
马	Horse		125	140			120	
驴	Donkey		120				112	111
骡	Mule							
骆　驼	Camel	150				75	165	
肉　猪	Pork	72	72	72	72	72	72	72
绵　羊	Sheep	17	20	19	19	19	19	18
家　禽	Poultry	2	2	2	2	2	2	2
兔	Rabbit	2	2	2	1	2	2	3

9—32 各师畜产品产量

Output of Livestock Products by Division

(2017 年)

指标	Item	合计 Total	一师 Division 1	二师 Division 2	三师 Division 3	四师 Division 4	五师 Division 5	六师 Division 6
羊毛（吨）	Wool (ton)	19 898	2 268	1 048	1 805	3 433	902	2 839
绵羊毛（吨）	Sheep Wool (ton)	19 493	2 254	1 039	1 608	3 433	876	2 785
#细羊毛	Fine Wool	9 187	1 270	449	931	1 886	363	1 374
半细羊毛	Semi-Fine Wool	5 068	453	548	128	791	79	1 382
山羊毛（吨）	Goat Wool (ton)	405	14	9	197		26	54
山羊绒（公斤）	Cashmere (kg)	65 369	1 115	4 950	1 595	3 791	310	30 261
牛奶（吨）	Cow Milk (ton)	681 395	88 425	19 188	7 959	89 330	2 957	29 268
羊奶（吨）	Sheep Milk (ton)	1 844			1 663			25
牛皮（张）	Oxhide (sheet)	37 490	3 623	3 100	3 135	4 907	1 600	4 400
绵羊皮（张）	Sheep Skin (sheet)	500 802	68 508	34 200	72 452	70 900	15 900	57 300
山羊皮（张）	Goat Skin (sheet)	101 924	5 136	9 600	40 185	400	2 700	8 800
驼毛（吨）	Camel Hair (ton)	21						17
蜂群数（箱）	Bee Cluster (box)	153 421	24 281	3 657	10 086	55 766	3 300	19 586
蜂蜜产量（吨）	Honey (ton)	8 978	973	390	627	4 020	98	746
禽蛋产量（吨）	Poultry Eggs (ton)	109 222	4 994	6 755	3 179	20 987	11 358	21 468
年末养鹿（头）	Deer (head)	20 714	414	17 092	365	257		381
年内产鹿茸（公斤）	Pilose Antler (kg)	32 485	761	25 382	1 050	652		327

指标	Item	七师 Division 7	八师 Division 8	九师 Division 9	十师 Division 10	十二师 Division 12	十三师 Division 13	十四师 Division 14
羊毛（吨）	Wool (ton)	2 555	920	1 836	859	97	1 115	221
绵羊毛（吨）	Sheep Wool (ton)	2 450	920	1 836	859	97	1 115	221
#细羊毛	Fine Wool	1 012	415	355	190	97	804	41
半细羊毛	Semi-Fine Wool		252	943	249		76	167
山羊毛（吨）	Goat Wool (ton)	105						
山羊绒（公斤）	Cashmere (kg)	3 086	914	4 404		1 060	13 383	500
牛奶（吨）	Cow Milk (ton)	120 032	260 484	13 762	10 163	35 407	4 289	131
羊奶（吨）	Sheep Milk (ton)		40				116	
牛皮（张）	Oxhide (sheet)	1 150	1 110	3 900	700	285	7 880	1 700
绵羊皮（张）	Sheep Skin (sheet)	11 500	17 730	41 200	6 200	6 086	82 326	16 500
山羊皮（张）	Goat Skin (sheet)	3 000	90	4 100	400	600	23 813	3 100
驼毛（吨）	Camel Hair (ton)	2					2	
蜂群数（箱）	Bee Cluster (box)	12 439	8 905	70	8 624		3 707	3 000
蜂蜜产量（吨）	Honey (ton)	669	412	2	754		243	44
禽蛋产量（吨）	Poultry Eggs (ton)	10 699	15 229	2 236	4 246	1 007	4 495	2 569
年末养鹿（头）	Deer (head)	1 086	155	963		1		
年内产鹿茸（公斤）	Pilose Antler (kg)	2 178	828	1 307				

9—33　各师渔业生产情况

Fishery Production by Division

(2017 年)

单　位	Unit	水产品产量（吨） Catching Output(ton)	捕捞产量 Catching Output	养殖产量 Cultureed Output	按品种分 Classified by Type		
					鱼　类 Grass carp	虾蟹类 Carp	其　他 Others
总　计	**Total**	**53 876**	**898**	**52 978**	**51 434**	**1 490**	**54**
一　师	Division 1	5 127		5 127	4 967	160	
二　师	Division 2	7 137	660	6 477	6 407	70	
三　师	Division 3	1 759		1 759	1 746	13	
四　师	Division 4	10 400	238	10 162	10 104	56	2
五　师	Division 5	1 201		1 201	1 110	91	
六　师	Division 6	3 384		3 384	3 363	16	5
七　师	Division 7	4 527		4 527	4 379	148	
八　师	Division 8	7 457		7 457	7 221	236	
九　师	Division 9	30		30	28	2	
十　师	Division 10	10 668		10 668	9 970	698	
十二师	Division 12						
十三师	Division 13	1 924		1 924	1 877		47
十四师	Division 14	262		262	262		

单　位	Unit	按养殖方式分 Classified by mode			养殖面积（公顷） Culture Area (hectare)	池塘养殖 Puddle and Pond	水库养殖 Reservoirs	其他养殖 Other
		池塘养殖 Puddle and Pond	水库养殖 Reservoirs	其他养殖 Other				
总　计	**Total**	**34 127**	**11 943**	**6 908**	**38 624**	**3 079**	**28 204**	**7 341**
一　师	Division 1	3 742	1 385		8 531	397	8 134	
二　师	Division 2	5 780	667	30	1 521	398	577	546
三　师	Division 3	1 432	327		6 538	132	6 406	
四　师	Division 4	9 017	981	164	1 110	726	371	13
五　师	Division 5	1 138	50	13	267	251	13	3
六　师	Division 6	1 562	1 612	210	3 359	200	3 158	1
七　师	Division 7	1 907	2 260	360	2 960	194	2 720	46
八　师	Division 8	6 735	707	15	2 930	496	2 432	2
九　师	Division 9	22	8		248	8	240	
十　师	Division 10	878	3 674	6 116	10 439	90	3 619	6 730
十二师	Division 12							
十三师	Division 13	1 803	121		606	170	436	
十四师	Division 14	111	151		115	17	98	

9—34 按不同类型分团场基本情况

Basic Conditions of Farms by Different Types

(2017 年)

指标 Item	团场合计 Total	# 中心团场 Center Farm	# 小城镇团场 Small Town Farms	# 植棉团场 Cotton-planting Farm	# 边境团场 Border Farms	# 少数民族聚居团场 Minority Farms	# 贫困团场 Needy Farms	# 南疆困难和边境团场 Needy and Border Farms of South XJ
团场总数(个) Total Regient Farms(unit)	**178**	**33**	**38**	**84**	**58**	**37**	**61**	**77**
农场 Number of Farms	166	33	38	82	52	31	51	71
牧场 Number of Ranch	12			2	6	6	10	7
团场户数(户) Number of households on Farms(houshold)	**726 936**	**223 313**	**274 493**	**501 468**	**172 149**	**129 819**	**154 715**	**240 237**
# 牧业户数 Number of Stock-Raising Household	35 869	10 944	11 170	18 946	14 045	10 055	11 893	18 049
团场人口(人) Population(person)	**2 020 662**	**610 804**	**754 175**	**1 406 127**	**473 022**	**417 043**	**432 177**	**711 395**
# 牧业人口 Number of Persons in Stock-Raisung	99 224	29 012	26 904	53 638	38 274	32 412	33 229	52 987
团场劳动力总计(人) Total Labour on Farms(person)	**1 024 216**	**314 599**	**392 058**	**722 402**	**236 517**	**186 396**	**231 724**	**340 252**
男 Male	550 607	167 005	209 430	386 553	130 115	101 287	125 497	187 273
女 Female	473 609	147 594	182 628	335 849	106 402	85 109	106 227	152 979
场内实有就业人员(人) Persons Actually Engaged on Farms(person)	**908 850**	**267 888**	**342 959**	**641 553**	**216 543**	**166 803**	**196 220**	**313 300**
农业就业人员 Persons Engaged in Agriculture	386 235	96 474	113 464	224 069	96 177	74 831	82 972	143 691
工业就业人员 Persons Engaged in Industry	115 403	36 765	47 824	89 252	24 645	17 716	26 365	33 261
建筑业就业人员 Persons Engaged in Construction	45 875	17 501	20 013	36 865	7 674	4 542	6 897	13 636
交通运输业、仓储及邮电通迅业就业人员 Persons Engaged in Transportation,Storage and Postal Service and Telecommunications	54 901	15 711	24 250	37 712	12 907	8 387	12 720	14 740
信息传输、计算机服务和软件业就业人员 Persons Engaged in Information Deliver,Computer Service and software	965	216	422	728	83	81	122	100
批发和零售业就业人员 Persons Engaged in Wholesale and Retail Trade	117 307	33 023	44 279	89 595	19 196	17 121	16 936	29 637
住宿和餐饮业就业人员 Persons Engaged in Accomodation and catering Services Industry	51 167	14 786	21 175	36 923	11 646	9 046	10 383	16 127
其他就业人员 Employed Persons in Other Trades	141 938	53 412	71 532	126 409	44 215	35 079	39 825	62 108

注:本篇资料只包括纳入团场序列的 178 个团场资料(下同)。

Note:Data in this table only include 178 farms(the same as follow).

9－35　按不同类型分团场农林牧渔业总产值

Gross Output Value of Farming、Forestry、Animal Husbandry and Fishery for Farms by Different Types

计量单位：万元　　(2017 年)　　(10 000 yuan)

指　标	Item	团场合计 Total	# 中心团场 Center Farm	# 小城镇团场 Small Town Farms	# 植棉团场 Cotton-planting Farm	# 边境团场 Border Farms	# 少数民族聚居团场 Minority Farms	# 贫困团场 Needy Farms	# 南疆困难和边境团场 Needy and Border Farms of South XJ
农林牧渔业总产值总计	**Total Gross Output Value of Farming, Forestry, Animal Husbandry and Fishery**	**10 987 404**	**3 093 392**	**3 797 880**	**8 496 921**	**2 251 405**	**1 560 388**	**1 937 794**	**3 360 783**
农业产值合计	**Output Value of Farming**	**8 383 967**	**2 417 801**	**2 838 088**	**6 777 337**	**1 506 490**	**1 148 706**	**1 268 701**	**2 471 136**
谷物及其他作物	Cereal and Others	4 134 772	1 206 199	1 592 995	3 413 844	885 197	516 124	697 009	1 218 838
谷　物	Cereal	626 150	165 889	191 002	277 377	360 831	139 386	261 495	407 213
薯　类	Tubers	37 766	3 877	15 724	14 064	25 180	10 566	8 109	26 382
油料作物	Oil-bearing Crops	119 394	23 595	39 806	26 730	92 899	32 807	58 947	96 633
豆　类	Soybeans	15 176	7 050	1 920	2 702	10 608	1 628	6 437	11 592
棉花(皮棉)	Cotton(lint)	2 812 095	847 889	1 146 895	2 809 889	185 060	254 187	162 886	434 117
# 棉　籽	Cotton Seed	456 516	132 425	185 684	456 177	29 429	40 532	24 916	69 487
麻类(熟麻皮)	Fiber Crops	858				847			847
甜　菜	Beetroots	93 602	28 997	33 040	24 125	62 641	13 094	59 608	62 641
烟　叶	Tobacco								
其他作物	Others	429 731	128 902	164 608	258 957	147 131	64 456	139 527	179 413
蔬菜园艺作物	Vegetable and Horticultural Crops	977 093	305 663	339 453	621 032	176 266	151 155	173 424	248 541
# 工业用番茄	Tomato for Industry	148 920	43 591	48 842	103 264	8 076	9 282	15 643	8 076
工业用辣椒	Hot Pepper for Industry	201 425	84 703	66 292	90 192	44 016	20 246	30 066	72 688
水果、饮料和香料作物	Fruit, Beverage and Spice Crop	3 022 791	841 452	806 121	2 540 828	396 452	396 343	368 686	911 197
# 水　果	Fruit	2 615 592	732 544	723 053	2 209 051	303 195	311 115	300 705	724 777
瓜　类	Melon	202 512	74 024	30 864	167 301	37 386	40 619	42 275	79 039
药　材(种植)	Medical Materials(Planting)	249 311	64 487	99 519	201 633	48 575	85 084	29 582	92 560
林业产值合计	**Output Value of Forestry**	**169 049**	**32 680**	**59 762**	**117 450**	**35 333**	**33 008**	**34 755**	**46 584**
林木的培育和种植	Nurturing and Planting of Wood	157 113	29 491	54 458	112 011	30 172	31 231	30 476	40 558
林产品	Wood Procucts	1 847	180	306	4	1 843		1 843	1 843
木材采运	Timber Conveyance	10 089	3 009	4 998	5 435	3 318	1 777	2 436	4 183
牧业产值合计	**Output Value of Animal Husbandry**	**1 649 051**	**450 368**	**596 544**	**1 006 744**	**530 060**	**278 147**	**481 333**	**613 399**
牲畜饲养	Livestock Feeding	1 379 273	376 493	504 419	819 616	460 051	242 167	414 992	530 900
牛	Cattle and Buffaloes	203 165	43 915	60 463	96 687	75 303	64 283	68 417	80 169
羊	Sheep and Goats	445 686	133 683	147 377	218 484	204 266	102 082	204 209	247 414
猪	Pork Feeding	17 939	4 636	3 302	5 410	9 457	9 250	8 157	9 784
其他牲畜饲养	Others	249 551	50 745	99 433	176 315	55 671	36 091	53 037	59 285
奶产品	Milk Products	29 446	7 287	10 557	15 932	13 872	7 130	12 089	14 983
毛绒产品	Hair and Cashere Products	6 480			6 480	6 480			6 480
其他牲畜产品	Other Livestock Products	427 006	136 227	183 287	300 308	95 002	23 331	69 083	112 785
家禽的饲养	Poultry Feeding	220 344	60 701	80 141	161 311	55 585	24 439	54 017	64 800
# 禽　蛋	Poultry Eggs	93 341	26 489	34 094	71 270	26 610	11 627	21 378	32 010
其他动物及产品	Other Animal and Products	49 434	13 174	11 984	25 817	14 424	11 541	12 324	17 699
狩猎及捕捉动物	Hunting and Catching Animal	143	33	38	83	47	31	52	63
渔业产值合计	**Output Value of Fishery**	**78 436**	**38 637**	**17 773**	**31 420**	**39 081**	**7 011**	**39 680**	**40 736**
农林牧渔服务业产值合计	**Output Value of Farming, Forestry, Animal Husbandry and Fishery Services**	**706 901**	**153 906**	**285 713**	**563 970**	**140 441**	**93 516**	**113 325**	**188 928**

注：本表按当年价格计算。

Note: Data in this table are calculated at current prices.

9—36 按不同类型分团场农作物播种面积

Total Sown Areas of Farm Crops for Farms by Different Types

计量单位:千公顷 (2017 年) (1 000 hectares)

指标	Item	团场正复播播种面积 Total Sown Area	# 中心团场 Center Farm	# 小城镇团场 Small Town Farms	# 植棉团场 Cotton-planting Farm	# 边境团场 Border Farms	# 少数民族聚居团场 Minority Farms	# 贫困团场 Needy Farms	# 南疆困难和边境团场 Needy and Border Farms of South XJ
农作物总播种面积	**Total Sown Areas of Farm crops**	**1 312.05**	**382.08**	**480.03**	**970.98**	**361.94**	**203.69**	**289.28**	**491.86**
粮食作物合计	**Sown Area of Grain Crops**	**274.15**	**75.96**	**80.16**	**115.52**	**158.83**	**64.01**	**116.59**	**186.48**
谷 物	Cereal	260.99	71.95	77.32	113.03	149.17	61.61	111.99	176.35
水 稻	Rice	19.52	2.46	2.94	10.15	8.13	0.02	2.66	8.14
小 麦	Wheat	138.23	39.42	39.91	52.15	88.36	30.38	67.82	100.30
玉 米	Corn	98.94	29.55	32.61	49.73	51.27	30.55	39.98	66.49
谷 子	Millet	0.43	0.07	0.08	0.28	0.07	0.20	0.07	0.07
高 粱	Sorghum	2.27	0.21	1.45	0.53	0.10	0.37	0.21	0.10
大 麦	Barley	0.89	0.21	0.03	0.18	0.89		0.88	0.89
其他谷物	Other Cereal	0.70	0.03	0.31	0.01	0.35	0.08	0.38	0.35
豆 类	Beans	7.52	3.17	0.77	0.91	5.41	0.78	3.06	5.69
# 大 豆(黄豆、黑豆等)	Soja	4.94	1.08	0.76	0.84	2.89	0.38	0.90	3.16
绿 豆	Green Bean	0.05		0.01	0.05		0.04		
红小豆	Red Small Bean	0.02			0.01	0.02			0.02
薯 类	Tubers	5.64	0.84	2.06	1.58	4.25	1.62	1.54	4.45
油料作物	**Oil Bearing Crops**	**54.29**	**8.73**	**15.26**	**11.88**	**43.38**	**17.84**	**26.05**	**44.63**
# 化 生	Peanuts	1.00	0.14	0.15	0.73	0.24	0.37	0.30	0.75
油菜籽	Rapeseeds	21.18	0.53	1.22	0.62	20.71	14.75	4.63	20.71
芝 麻	Sesame								
胡 麻	Flax	0.47	0.07	0.07	0.18	0.37	0.14	0.19	0.44
向日葵籽	Sunflower	29.46	7.92	13.68	10.20	19.96	2.57	18.87	20.62
棉 花	**Cotton**	**656.07**	**196.44**	**273.03**	**655.36**	**44.73**	**61.13**	**39.58**	**104.19**
# 长绒棉	Long Staple Cotton	0.44	0.21	0.25	0.44				0.21
麻 类	**Hemp Crops**	**0.29**				**0.28**			**0.28**
# 亚 麻	Flax	0.29				0.28			0.28
甜 菜	**Beetroots**	**23.38**	**7.10**	**8.20**	**5.55**	**15.87**	**3.17**	**15.44**	**15.87**
烟 叶	**Tobacco**								
药 材	**Medicinal Materials**	**23.05**	**5.99**	**9.23**	**16.33**	**6.82**	**8.25**	**3.63**	**11.48**
蔬 菜	**Vegetables**	**83.54**	**26.65**	**28.47**	**50.40**	**14.96**	**11.83**	**14.58**	**21.92**
瓜果类(含菜用瓜)	**Melons**	**24.37**	**8.18**	**4.83**	**19.82**	**4.08**	**4.58**	**5.22**	**8.89**
其他作物	**Other Farm Crops**	**164.13**	**51.97**	**59.80**	**91.69**	**68.61**	**32.44**	**66.68**	**93.72**
# 苜蓿(包括当年新播)	Lucerne	52.85	11.84	19.97	23.63	32.12	6.52	30.79	35.97

9—37　按不同类型分团场农作物总产量

Total Output of Farm Crops for Farms by Different Types

计量单位:吨　　(2017 年)　　(ton)

指　标	Item	团场合计 Total	# 中心团场 Center Farm	# 小城镇团场 Small Town Farms	# 植棉团场 Cotton-planting Farm	# 边境团场 Border Farms	# 少数民族聚居团场 Minority Farms	# 贫困团场 Needy Farms	# 南疆困难和边境团场 Needy and Border Farms of South XJ
粮食作物	**Grain Crops**	**2 417 394**	**701 674**	**751 115**	**1 005 687**	**1 402 302**	**513 644**	**990 430**	**1 592 362**
谷　物	Cereal	2 327 441	683 319	725 688	984 132	1 336 548	490 728	965 568	1 522 973
水　稻	Rice	222 310	26 696	32 618	121 300	89 427	122	28 124	89 547
小　麦	Wheat	974 508	297 791	291 730	374 376	620 757	213 983	458 163	693 100
玉　米	Corn	1 097 309	355 841	387 583	478 421	618 998	269 002	471 462	732 960
高　粱	Sorghum	21 397	1 198	12 151	4 980	1 082	4 342	1 531	1 082
大　麦	Barley	5 139	1 311	177	1 134	5 139		5 053	5 139
其他谷物	Other Cereal	1 983	82	563	12	745	236	835	745
豆　类	Beans	28 305	10 733	3 661	4 944	18 883	3 068	9 640	20 623
# 大　豆（黄豆、黑豆等）	Soja	20 045	4 665	3 628	4 711	10 790	1 295	3 248	12 530
绿　豆	Green Bean	182		11	179	15	156	3	15
红小豆	Red Small Bean	58		4	54	58		4	58
薯　类	Tubers	61 648	7 622	21 766	16 611	46 871	19 848	15 222	48 766
油料作物	**Oil Bearing Crops**	**203 110**	**35 377**	**60 296**	**44 633**	**157 978**	**65 749**	**92 111**	**164 392**
# 花　生	Peanuts	6 594	741	948	4 562	2 019	2 164	2 064	5 256
油菜籽	Rapeseeds	75 932	1 397	3 857	2 282	74 518	54 408	14 487	74 518
芝　麻	Sesame								
胡　麻	Flax	1 588	229	229	674	1 307	507	658	1 531
向日葵籽	Sunflower	115 338	32 905	54 733	36 586	76 617	8 658	71 712	79 570
棉　花	**Cotton**	**1 607 641**	**488 845**	**656 058**	**1 606 395**	**107 173**	**149 066**	**95 071**	**256 859**
# 长绒棉	Long Staple Cotton	972	470	545	972				470
麻　类	**Hemp Crops**	**2 893**				**2 648**			**2 648**
# 亚　麻	Flax	2 893				2 648			2 648
甜　菜	**Beetroots**	**1 956 940**	**618 525**	**669 601**	**527 445**	**1 288 024**	**280 812**	**1 225 583**	**1 288 024**
烟　叶	**Tobacco**	**143**	**33**	**38**	**83**	**47**	**31**	**52**	**63**
药　材	**Medicinal Materials**	**184 679**	**51 886**	**33 585**	**158 736**	**17 415**	**91 664**	**28 439**	**95 460**
蔬　菜	**Vegetables**	**6 475 350**	**1 996 761**	**2 189 676**	**4 157 091**	**881 279**	**738 222**	**983 446**	**1 178 537**
瓜果类(含菜用瓜)	**Melons**	**1 512 760**	**572 434**	**236 653**	**1 299 203**	**212 729**	**217 680**	**226 953**	**438 202**
其他作物	**Other Farm Crops**	**3 460 762**	**665 937**	**1 560 633**	**2 920 679**	**665 372**	**573 089**	**654 832**	**936 176**
# 苜蓿(包括当年新播)	Lucerne	769 142	172 220	302 545	505 605	287 830	176 278	284 622	416 409

9—38 按不同类型分团场蔬菜及特种作物生产情况

Vegetable and Special Kind Crop Production for Farms by Different Types

计量单位:吨　　(2017 年)　　(ton)

指　标	Item	团场合计 Total	# 中心团场 Center Farm	# 小城镇团场 Small Town Farms	# 植棉团场 Cotton-planting Farm	# 边境团场 Border Farms	# 少数民族聚居团场 Minority Farms	# 贫困团场 Needy Farms	# 南疆困难和边境团场 Needy and Border Farms of South XJ
蔬菜合计	**Total**	**6 475 350**	**1 996 761**	**2 189 676**	**4 157 091**	**881 279**	**738 222**	**983 446**	**1 178 537**
叶菜类	Vegetable	240 562	89 551	65 369	181 352	32 967	43 083	32 550	65 204
白菜类	Chinese Cabbage	236 221	69 212	59 598	192 092	61 962	51 864	59 603	105 847
瓜菜类	Melon	225 250	69 199	107 092	140 015	47 068	53 592	44 466	61 244
# 黄　瓜	Cucumber	139 451	59 845	59 153	94 533	39 116	13 859	35 110	47 787
根茎类	Root Tuber	300 363	86 800	94 159	166 032	69 589	101 982	57 210	94 364
# 萝　卜	Radish	96 784	15 746	23 814	74 670	30 753	14 333	30 718	40 248
胡萝卜	Carrot	126 558	16 513	37 901	51 577	17 222	69 656	13 914	27 220
茄果菜类	Nightshade	4 996 164	1 580 572	1 731 548	3 162 382	596 368	355 092	695 043	730 231
# 番　茄	Tomato	3 699 312	1 112 562	1 239 380	2 514 013	299 956	234 828	482 735	318 595
# 工业用番茄	Tomato for Industry	3 285 885	999 118	1 062 787	2 231 164	191 598	193 735	367 439	191 600
辣　椒	Pepper	1 181 919	434 874	469 211	565 195	266 881	104 801	178 982	371 934
# 工业用辣椒	Hot Pepper for Industry	898 655	369 840	310 595	356 130	211 462	79 936	128 877	298 745
葱蒜类	Garlic	94 788	16 654	15 769	68 404	14 438	26 626	20 915	35 591
菜用豆类	Beans	94 516	25 950	30 437	74 163	13 659	19 121	12 270	26 109
# 四季豆	Legumina	46 649	9 811	11 671	34 760	6 135	9 507	4 752	12 529
# 豇　豆	Cownea	42 466	14 969	17 944	36 089	6 674	7 620	5 795	12 730
水生菜类	Aquatic Vegetable	1 881	500	950	1 168	38		183	171
其他蔬菜	Other Vegetable	140 860	20 545	30 734	73 584	13 175	59 578	28 828	19 264
食用菌(干鲜混合)	Edibte Mushroom (Dry, Fresh, Mix)	40 424	8 116	17 346	30 860	5 910	6 875	4 711	7 436
花卉种植面积(公顷)	**Edibte Mushroom (Dry, Fresh, Mix)**	**4 090**	**356**	**120**	**512**	**352**	**3 311**	**309**	**564**
鲜切花(万枝)	**Fresh Flower(10 000 sets)**	**1 279**	**298**	**252**	**532**	**186**	**430**	**324**	**391**
盆栽观赏植物(包括盆景)(盆)	**Potted Plant(set)**	**6 662 563**	**800 135**	**5 142 628**	**6 655 237**	**4 052 326**	**5 000**	**7 200**	**4 052 326**

9—39　按不同类型分团场水果生产情况

Fruit Production for Farms by Different Types

（2017 年）

指　　标	Item	团场合计 Total	#中心团场 Center Farm	#小城镇团场 Small Town Farms	#植棉团场 Cotton-planting Farm	#边境团场 Border Farms	#少数民族聚居团场 Minority Farms	#贫困团场 Needy Farms	#南疆困难和边境团场 Needy and Border Farms of South XJ
年末实有面积　（公顷）	**Actural Area at the Year-end　(hectare)**	**198 733**	**55 792**	**57 141**	**151 898**	**30 174**	**40 876**	**35 674**	**77 143**
苹　果	Apples	22 716	6 699	9 217	15 661	9 413	5 121	7 476	14 290
#红富士苹果	Hongfushi Apples	16 162	5 533	6 487	13 171	5 775	2 400	3 804	9 967
黄元帅苹果	Huangyuanshuai Apples	1 272	405	981	1 089	801	76	105	1 144
国光苹果	Guoguang Apples	73	42	15	59	14	3	48	53
梨	Pears	19 436	10 267	8 023	19 263	106	2 668	529	4 388
#香　梨	Fragrant Pear	16 253	8 659	6 864	16 248	10	1 994	343	3 160
砀山梨	Dangshan Pear	2 133	1 221	1 088	2 131	12	543	144	1 036
葡　萄	Grapes	42 463	9 603	17 428	31 499	8 595	9 401	8 662	9 475
#无核葡萄	Seedless Grapes	13 534	3 906	6 766	10 247	2 613	2 509	4 127	2 672
红提葡萄	Hongti Grapes	11 385	2 589	4 203	8 049	3 493	4 154	2 046	3 542
酿酒葡萄	Grapes of Make Wining	12 216	1 155	4 286	9 440	2 038	2 288	2 119	2 576
桃	Peachs	4 162	1 556	207	1 312	1 602	796	563	1 943
#蟠　桃	Pan peachs	2 445	958	43	445	931	560	104	940
杏	Apricots	4 965	619	530	882	3 983	704	2 950	4 226
红　枣	Jujubes	102 918	26 678	21 480	81 799	6 010	21 722	14 330	41 343
石　榴	Pomegranate	15	13		15		13		13
其　他	Other	2 059	357	255	1 467	465	450	1 163	1 465
产　量　（吨）	**Output　(ton)**	**3 735 887**	**1 061 265**	**1 178 269**	**3 073 128**	**590 203**	**526 314**	**499 044**	**1 248 342**
苹　果	Apples	622 884	158 695	306 576	478 290	292 301	88 756	169 462	420 126
#红富士苹果	Hongfushi Apples	453 321	133 632	229 995	391 340	202 538	30 582	106 954	309 709
黄元帅苹果	Huangyuanshuai Apples	60 277	13 415	49 197	53 765	44 474	3 546	3 763	56 320
国光苹果	Guoguang Apples	2 446	1 559	487	2 231	196	63	1 676	1 656
梨	Pears	502 064	247 014	210 574	495 230	3 124	32 400	14 199	87 593
#香　梨	Fragrant Pear	377 543	177 808	152 114	377 426	611	16 255	4 473	44 542
砀山梨	Dangshan Pear	97 971	64 699	57 211	97 941	923	14 256	8 241	40 547
葡　萄	Grapes	773 964	173 148	309 442	573 923	156 915	177 510	162 885	164 423
#无核葡萄	Seedless Grapes	224 540	58 370	115 350	171 377	43 074	45 366	68 137	43 681
红提葡萄	Hongti Grapes	216 821	58 581	79 843	158 669	72 775	84 501	45 284	73 085
酿酒葡萄	Grapes of make wining	208 325	14 496	68 472	157 660	34 114	27 391	33 807	36 430
桃	Peachs	89 543	27 550	2 299	23 712	50 219	11 013	7 009	56 449
#蟠　桃	Pan Peachs	44 046	18 654	724	12 264	18 868	7 898	1 235	19 172
杏	Apricots	45 691	5 421	4 587	15 406	24 741	17 877	23 292	32 835
红　枣	Jujubes	1 693 197	447 377	341 516	1 481 735	57 640	196 738	120 372	481 255
石　榴	Pomegranate	26	10		26		10		10
其　他	Other	8 518	2 050	3 275	4 806	5 263	2 010	1 825	5 651

9—40 按不同类型分团场牲畜年底头数

Year-end Number of Livestock for Farms by Different Types

计量单位:万头(只) (2017 年) (10 000 heads)

指标	Item	合计 Total	牛 Cattle and Buffaloes	#良种及改良种乳牛 Fine Breeds and Improved Dairy Cattle	马 Horses	驴 Donkeys	骡 Mules	骆驼 Camels
团场总计	**Total**	**749.10**	**46.72**	**23.89**	**3.90**	**1.34**		**0.51**
# 中心团场	Center Farms	204.06	9.88	5.28	1.19	0.41		0.22
# 小城镇团场	Small Town Farms	224.90	14.59	8.81	0.46	0.40		0.15
# 植棉团场	Cotton-Planting Farms	391.74	24.34	15.43	1.37	0.72		0.21
# 边境团场	Border Farms	306.59	18.80	7.09	2.54	0.40		0.34
# 少数民族聚居团场	Minority Farms	156.52	10.18	4.36	1.63	0.93		0.19
# 贫困团场	Needy Farms	308.08	17.37	6.32	2.46	0.71		0.36
# 南疆困难团场和边境团场	Needy and Border Farmsof South XJ	384.09	21.09	7.99	2.63	0.94		0.34

指标	Item	猪 Hogs	羊 Goats	山羊 Milk Goats	绵羊 Sheep	#细毛羊及改良羊 Fine Wool Sheep and Improved Sheep	家禽 Poultry	兔 Rabbits
团场总计	**Total**	**164.12**	**532.51**	**44.35**	**488.16**	**134.81**	**1373.16**	**45.19**
# 中心团场	Center Farms	52.20	140.16	15.93	124.23	27.71	481.31	15.35
# 小城镇团场	Small Town Farms	68.68	140.62	12.91	127.71	44.54	491.37	20.66
# 植棉团场	Cotton-Planting Farms	118.10	247.00	33.33	213.67	62.18	1059.02	35.87
# 边境团场	Border Farms	30.70	253.81	12.98	240.83	73.07	284.97	8.83
# 少数民族聚居团场	Minority Farms	5.99	137.60	18.52	119.08	36.42	158.07	3.39
# 贫困团场	Needy Farms	22.94	264.24	14.90	249.34	54.54	292.87	8.06
# 南疆困难团场和边境团场	Needy and Border Farms of South XJ	37.83	321.26	25.47	295.79	74.51	378.86	11.64

9—41　按不同类型分团场肉类生产情况

Meat Production for Farms by Different Types

计量单位:吨　　　　（2017 年）　　　　（ton）

指　标	Item	团场合计 Total	# 中心团场 Center Farm	# 小城镇团场 Small Town Farms	# 植棉团场 Cotton-planting Farm	# 边境团场 Border Farms	# 少数民族聚居团场 Minority Farms	# 贫困团场 Needy Farms	# 南疆困难和边境团场 Needy and Border Farms of South XJ
肉类总产量	**Output of Meat**	**434 080**	**125 690**	**160 753**	**273 807**	**126 528**	**64 814**	**115 188**	**151 161**
牛	Beef	57 947	12 184	17 645	28 289	21 134	18 788	18 814	23 372
马	Horse	2 782	946	187	1 056	1 365	1 342	1 206	1 365
驴	Donkey	672	324	307	447	114	179	256	264
骡	Mule								
骆　驼	Camel	242	101	16	111	134	96	166	134
肉　猪	Pork	198 641	62 795	84 325	141 669	41 245	10 890	29 396	49 503
羊	Goat	104 431	30 218	33 388	49 731	49 110	26 111	49 243	60 580
# 绵　羊	Sheep	94 149	26 581	30 433	41 466	46 757	21 258	46 155	55 075
家　禽	Poultry	62 438	15 986	22 445	46 361	12 618	6 689	15 332	14 917
兔	Rabbit	4 627	1 803	1 898	4 117	586	357	526	804
其他肉产量	Others	2 298	1 332	541	2 026	221	360	246	221

9—42　按不同类型分团场畜产品产量

Output of Livestock Products for Farms by Different Types

（2017 年）

指　标		Item		团场合计 Total	# 中心团场 Center Farm	# 小城镇团场 Small Town Farms	# 植棉团场 Cotton-planting Farm	# 边境团场 Border Farms	# 少数民族聚居团场 Minority Farms	# 贫困团场 Needy Farms	# 南疆困难和边境团场 Needy and Border Farms of South XJ
绵羊毛	（吨）	Sheep Wool	（ton）	19 081	4 875	6 830	10 516	8 665	4 657	7 885	10 073
# 细羊毛		Fine Wool		8 960	1 858	3 577	5 409	3 393	2 924	2 611	4 199
半细羊毛		Semi-Fine Wool		4 924	1 569	1 632	2 431	2 236	986	2 569	2 461
山羊毛	（吨）	Goat Wool	（ton）	402	174	78	369	25	244	77	222
山羊绒	（公斤）	Cashmere	（kg）	60 009	11 389	31 567	42 642	18 099	19 134	25 296	20 079
奶类产量	（吨）	Milk	（ton）	653 151	133 615	267 912	480 970	137 267	90 181	133 217	145 560
# 牛　奶		Cow Milk		650 849	133 463	267 872	479 931	136 367	88 495	131 375	143 793
羊　奶		Sheep Milk		1 844	152	40	1 039	893	1 235	1 384	1 760
牛　皮	（张）	Oxhide	（sheet）	35 990	5 245	14 540	22 276	11 802	14 329	11 943	15 037
羊　皮	（张）	Sheepskin	（sheet）	581 415	146 757	166 620	408 644	169 185	239 171	209 985	285 522
# 绵羊皮		Sheep Skin		485 391	112 794	147 220	331 045	152 160	184 086	166 072	228 212
驼　毛	（吨）	Camel Hair	（ton）	21	17		4	19	2	19	19
蜂群数	（箱）	Bee Cluster	（box）	144 601	33 716	45 720	64 823	53 871	36 039	41 470	66 792
蜂蜜产量	（吨）	Honey	（ton）	8 856	2 026	2 038	3 808	3 906	2 401	2 608	4 567
禽蛋产量	（吨）	Poultry Eggs	（ton）	108 333	31 168	37 583	81 923	30 973	13 186	23 853	36 520
年末养鹿	（头）	Deer	（head）	20 698	14 405	6 699	18 774	1 221	451	1 307	1 586
年内产鹿茸	（公斤）	Pilose Antler	（kg）	32 440	16 992	9 810	29 765	1 904	1 176	1 981	2 954

2018 BING TUAN

第十篇

工 业

Chapter 10 Industry

简要说明

一、本篇资料主要内容

本篇资料反映兵团工业经济主要发展情况；包括工业按师和主要指标分组的工业单位数、工业总产值和工业总产值指数及构成，规模以上工业企业按师和主要指标分组的主要经济指标和经济效益指标，包括企业单位数、工业总产值、工业销售产值、工业增加值、财务指标、效益指标和主要工业产品生产能力等；大中型工业企业主要指标；主要工业产品产量。

二、本篇资料统计范围

工业统计调查范围为隶属于兵团管理和在兵团辖区的工业企业和个体工业，包括工业法人企业、工业产业活动单位及个体工业。规模以上工业企业统计范围：2006年及以前为全部国有及年主营业务收入在500万元及以上的非国有工业法人企业，2007年起调整为年主营业务收入500万元及以上的全部工业法人企业，2011年起调整为年主营业务收入2000万元及以上的全部工业法人企业。

三、本篇资料来源

本篇资料由兵团统计局工业投资统计处根据《兵团工业统计报表制度》收集、汇总、整理、提供。

四、本篇资料调查方法

统计调查方法为全面调查。

Brief Introduction

1. Main Contents

Data in this chapter show industrial economic development of XPCC, including the number of industrial units by division and by main indicators, gross industrial output value, indices of gross industrial output value and composition. Main economic indicators and efficiency indicators of industrial enterprises above designated size by division and main indicators, including number of enterprises, gross industrial output value, industrial sales value, industrial value-added, main economic indicators, efficiency indicators and production capacity of main products. Main indicators of large and medium scale enterprises. Output of main industrial products.

2. Scope of Statistics

Industrial statistics cover all industrial enterprises and individual enterprises within XPCC, including industrial corporative enterprises, industrial active units and individual enterprises. The scopes of industrial enterprises above designated size cover all State-owned and non State-owned industrial corporative enterprises with annual main income above 5 million yuan in 2006 and before 2006, From 2007 on, it was adjusted as all industrial corporative enterprises with annual main income above 5 million yuan.From 2011 on, it was adjusted as all industrial corporation enterprises with annual main income above 20 million yuan.

3. Sources of Data

The industrial enterprises statistics in this chapter are collected according to *the Comprehensive Statistical reporting on Industry of XPCC*, which are provided by Industry and Assets Statistical Section of Statistics Bureau of XPCC.

4. Methodology of Survey

Survey method is comprehensive statistics.

10—1 工业单位数

Number of Industrial Units

计量单位:个 (unit)

年份 单位 Year Unit	工业单位数 Number of Industrial Enterprises	国有 State-owned	集体 Collective-owned	股份制 Share Holding	其他 Others	个体 Individuals	#法人企业 Corporative Enterprise	#大中型企业 Large Scale and Medium Scale
1952	42	42					29	
1954	87	87					40	
1957	115	115					32	
1962	319	319					108	
1965	268	268					108	
1970	352	352					119	
1975	351	351					5	
1978	507	498	9				75	
1980	647	626	21				102	6
1985	2 220	1 060	104			1 056	168	16
1990	2 182	1 224	153			805	291	22
1995	2 859	1 278	232		24	1 325	388	48
2000	4 053	952	113	25	49	2 914	270	50
2001	4 691	895	97	86	58	3 555	273	47
2002	4 796	877	68	71	61	3 719	240	42
2003	4 390	710	62	92	26	3 500	220	37
2004	3 006	565	55	296	164	1 926	480	35
2005	3 064	607	47	294	149	1 967	447	39
2006	3 005	561	21	297	140	1 986	450	45
2007	2 909	484	12	340	120	1 953	433	63
2008	4 035	535	11	623	187	2 679	722	64
2009	4 099	512	9	673	174	2 731	691	68
2010	4 222	426	7	848	204	2 737	1 103	80
2011	4 454	399	10	920	221	2 904	1 164	93
2012	5 339	381	6	1 144	311	3 497	1 486	102
2013	5 267	419	4	1 421	280	3 143	1 811	108
2014	5 605	358	9	1 869	369	3 000	2 362	117
2015	5 986	310	4	1 904	360	3 408	2 395	112
2016	7 124	317	8	2 553	592	3 654	3 343	111
2017	6 577	311	8	2 701	3 557	2 900	3 549	111
一 师 Division 1	604	17		408	179	55	533	13
二 师 Division 2	376	16		204	156	125	249	9
三 师 Division 3	211	25		119	67	24	182	5
四 师 Division 4	904	16	1	214	673	611	293	9
五 师 Division 5	359	23		88	248	217	139	2
六 师 Division 6	816	27		275	514	479	337	12
七 师 Division 7	444	33	2	218	191	178	246	11
八 师 Division 8	1 126	48	3	476	599	408	695	33
九 师 Division 9	171	22		63	86	74	80	2
十 师 Division 10	417	13		154	250	230	187	3
十一师 Division 11	50	7		41	2		44	1
十二师 Division 12	302	27	1	132	142	123	169	4
十三师 Division 13	651	30		255	366	301	325	3
十四师 Division 14	133	4	1	44	84	75	57	
兵团直属 Directly under XPCC	13	3		10			13	4

注:1.1980 年以前大中型企业无资料记载。2.从 1999 年开始将股份制企业由其他企业中分列出来。

Note: a) Data on Large-scale and Medium-scale enterprises are not recorded before 1980.

b) Since 1999 share holding enterprises have been Listed separately from other enterprises.

10—2 工业总产值及构成

Total Output Value of Industry and Its Composition

年 份 Year	工业总产值 Gross Industrial Output Value	按登记注册类型分 Grouped by Status of Registration				
		国 有 State-owned	集 体 Collective-owned	股份制 Share Holding	其 他 Others	个 体 Individuals
绝对数(万元) Value(10 000 yuan)						
1952	3 221	3 221				
1954	5 703	5 703				
1957	14 638	14 638				
1962	37 186	37 186				
1965	53 113	53 113				
1970	64 289	64 289				
1975	16 547	16 547				
1978	54 511	54 190	321			
1980	90 241	89 273	968			
1985	181 801	175 319	4 355			2 127
1990	444 490	430 738	11 285			2 467
1995	1 324 568	1 223 435	55 531		32 808	12 794
(1995)	709 290	626 295	46 612		25 937	10 446
2000	976 926	707 326	48 681	143 456	38 000	39 463
2005	1 756 428	562 559	8 537	1 019 391	61 861	104 080
2006	2 175 070	642 417	3 337	1 199 136	197 694	132 486
2007	2 887 118	700 813	3 388	1 713 611	256 348	212 958
2008	3 802 504	809 698	5 021	2 525 149	207 314	255 322
2009	4 972 441	811 616	1 433	3 592 201	252 071	315 120
2010	6 565 904	822 694	1 705	4 919 366	434 125	388 014
2011	9 062 832	1 093 780	7 995	6 826 247	583 962	550 848
2012	12 119 528	1 232 732	2 216	8 910 780	1 214 461	759 339
2013	15 020 036	1 517 226	12 047	11 643 999	1 048 381	798 383
2014	18 669 178	970 951	4 879	16 024 281	716 362	952 705
2015	20 467 613	865 434	3 316	17 734 189	830 863	1 033 811
2016	22 742 083	736 210	606	19 838 582	1 047 611	1 119 073
2017	23 978 669	556 858	507	21 506 427	1 183 761	731 116
构成(%) Composition(%)						
1952		100.0				
1954		100.0				
1957		100.0				
1962		100.0				
1965		100.0				
1970		100.0				
1975		100.0				
1978		99.4	0.6			
1980		98.9	1.1			
1985		96.4	2.4			1.2
1990		96.9	2.5			0.6
1995		92.4	4.2		2.5	0.9
(1995)		88.3	6.6		3.6	1.5
2000		72.4	5.0	14.7	3.9	4.0
2005		32.0	0.5	58.0	3.5	6.0
2006		29.5	0.2	55.1	9.1	6.1
2007		24.3	0.1	59.3	8.9	7.4
2008		21.3	0.1	66.4	5.5	6.7
2009		16.3	…	72.3	5.1	6.3
2010		12.6	…	74.9	6.6	5.9
2011		12.1	0.1	75.3	6.4	6.1
2012		10.2	…	73.5	10.0	6.3
2013		10.1	0.1	77.5	7.0	5.3
2014		5.2	…	85.8	3.8	5.1
2015		4.2	…	86.6	4.1	5.1
2016		3.2	0.1	87.2	4.6	4.9
2017		2.3	…	89.7	4.9	3.0

注：1.本表绝对数按当年价计算。2.1995年以后棉花加工按加工费计算总产值。3.本表2003年以后数据按照新口径统计，剔除了纤维原料初加工业；2002年前为老口径。(下表同)

Note：a)Data in value terms in this table are calculated at current prices.b)Gross output Value of cotton processing are calculated at processing expenses after 1995.c)Data in 2003 are calculated at new caliber，removing the initial processing on the fiber raw materials. Data prior to 2002 are at old caliber(the same as follows).

10—3 工业总产值及指数

Total Output Value of Industry and Its Indices

年 份 Year	工业总产值 Gross Industrial Output Value	按登记注册类型分 Grouped by Status of Registration				
		国 有 State-owned	集 体 Collective-owned	股份制 Share Holding	其 他 Others	个 体 Individuals
绝对数(万元) Value(10 000 yuan)						
1952	5 176	5 176				
1954	9 257	9 257				
1957	23 516	23 516				
1962	53 529	53 529				
1965	87 337	87 337				
1970	121 201	121 201				
1975	31 346	31 346				
1978	107 490	106 964	526			
1980	150 486	148 827	1 659			
1985	307 673	296 220	7 676			3 777
1990	474 344	458 596	13 011			2 737
1995	763 589	696 893	33 547		24 415	8 734
(1995)	476 580	419 996	31 603		17 284	7 697
2000	682 724	490 948	35 783	95 834	30 075	30 084
2005	1 253 271	364 282	6 928	722 647	79 044	80 370
2006	2 080 206	614 459	3 192	1 146 950	189 090	126 515
2007	2 795 428	678 556	3 280	1 659 190	248 207	206 195
2008	3 494 627	744 140	4 615	2 320 695	190 528	234 649
2009	5 022 973	819 898	1 448	3 628 851	254 441	318 335
2010	6 071 109	760 697	1 577	4 548 651	401 410	358 774
2011	8 337 472	1 006 237	7 355	6 279 896	537 224	506 760
2012	12 495 647	1 312 824	2 285	9 494 924	902 710	782 904
2013	15 173 286	1 532 706	12 170	11 762 803	1 059 078	806 529
2014	18 992 043	987 743	4 964	16 301 405	728 751	969 181
2015	21 393 972	904 603	3 466	18 536 834	868 468	1 080 601
2016	22 998 641	744 516	613	20 062 386	1 059 430	1 131 697
2017	23 038 691	535 029	487	20 663 362	1 137 357	702 456
环比指数(%) Indices(Preceding=100)						
1952	100.0	100.0				
1954	135.3	135.3				
1957	135.3	135.3				
1962	86.3	86.3				
1965	126.4	126.4				
1970	130.5	130.5				
1975	24.7	24.7				
1978	247.2	246.0				
1980	119.0	119.1	108.7			
1985	121.7	119.3	172.9			
1990	110.9	112.9	77.8			55.7
1995	113.2	111.1	120.0		195.6	128.5
(1995)						
2000	105.3	96.5	90.3	179.6	117.9	147.4
2005	121.6	113.6	98.1	128.5	119.7	120.6
2006	118.4	109.2	37.4	118.2	170.2	121.6
2007	128.5	105.6	98.3	138.4	125.6	155.6
2008	121.0	106.2	136.2	135.4	74.3	110.2
2009	132.1	101.3	28.8	143.7	122.8	124.7
2010	122.1	93.7	110.0	126.6	159.2	113.9
2011	127.0	122.3	431.4	127.7	123.7	130.6
2012	137.9	120.0	28.6	139.1	154.6	142.1
2013	132.1	120.4	549.2	137.2	121.0	106.2
2014	126.4	65.1	41.2	140.0	69.5	121.4
2015	114.6	93.2	71.0	115.7	121.2	113.4
2016	112.4	86.0	18.5	113.1	127.5	109.5
2017	101.3	72.7	80.4	104.2	108.6	62.8

注:(1)本表2005年以前绝对数为可比价数据,环比指数按可比价计算。(2)2006年绝对数为价格指数缩减数据,环比指数按价格指数缩减法计算。

Note: a) Data in this table before 2005 are value data and indices are calulated at comparable prices. b) Data of Value in 2006 and indices are calculated at price indices cut.

10－4　工业单位数及工业总产值

Number of Industrial Units and Output Value of Industry

计量单位:万元　　(2017 年)　　(10 000 yuan)

指　　标	Item	单位数(个) Number of Enterprises (unit)	工业总产值当年价格 At Current Prices
总　　计	**Total**	**3 677**	**23 247 553**
# 国有控股企业	State-controlled Shareholding Enterprises	413	7 291 396
按登记注册类型分	**Grouped by Status of Registration**		
内资企业	Domestic Enterprises	3 643	22 774 738
国有企业	State-owned Enterprises	311	556 858
集体企业	Collective-owned Enterprises	8	507
股份合作企业	Share Cooperative Enterprises	14	18 347
联营企业	Joint Ownership Enterprises	4	4 016
有限责任公司	Limited Liability Corporations	929	10 445 070
国有独资公司	State-owned Corporations with Private-Funds	68	837 260
其他有限责任公司	Other Limited Liability Corporations	861	9 607 810
股份有限公司	Share-holding Corporations Ltd.	62	1 433 161
私营企业	Private Enterprises	2 145	9 947 624
私营独资企业	Private-funded Enterprises	374	280 152
私营合伙企业	Private Partnership Enterprises	61	39 275
私营有限责任公司	Private Limited Liability Corporations	1 645	9 266 719
私营股份有限公司	Private Share-holding Corporations Ltd.	65	361 477
其他企业	Other Enterprises	170	369 155
港、澳、台商投资企业	Enterprises with Funds from Hong Kong Macao and Taiwan	11	63 759
合资经营企业(港或澳、台)	Joint-Venture Enterprises(with funds from Hong Kong Macao and Taiwan)	5	15 012
港、澳、台商独资经营企业	Enterprises with Funds from Hong Kong Macao and Taiwan	4	40 089
港澳台商投资股份有限公司	Share-holding Corporations Ltd. with Funds from Hong Kong Macao and Taiwan	1	3 747
其他港澳台商投资企业	Others	1	4 911
外商投资企业	Foreign Funded Enterprises	23	409 055
中外合资经营企业	Joint-Venture Enterprises	17	345 794
中外合作经营企业	Cooperative Enterprises	1	33 744
外资企业	Foreign Funded Enterprises	4	27 719
其他外商投资企业	Others	1	1 798
按轻重工业分	**Grouped by Light & Heavy Industry**		
轻工业	Light Industry	1 471	8 348 786
重工业	Heavy Industry	2 206	14 898 767
按企业规模分	**Grouped by Size of Enterprises**		
大型企业	Large-Scale Enterprises	21	7 250 268
中型企业	Medium-Scale Enterprises	90	4 435 581
小、微型企业	Small-Scale and Mini Enterprises	3 566	11 561 704
按工业行业分	**Grouped by Sector**		
采矿业	**Mining**	**153**	**534 887**
煤炭开采和洗选业	Coal Mining and Dressing	29	189 503

注:本表按当年价格计算,不含连队办工业(村办)及个体工业。(下表同)
Note:This table is not including county-run and individual industry(the same as follows).

10—4 续表 1 Continued

计量单位:万元 (2017 年) (10 000 yuan)

指 标	Item	单位数(个) Number of Enterprises (unit)	工业总产值 当年价格 At Current Prices
烟煤和无烟煤的开采洗选	Soft Coal and Hard Coal Mining and Dressing	29	189 503
黑色金属矿采选业	Ferrous Metals Mining and Dressing	26	190 600
铁矿采选	Prdding Mining and Dressing	26	190 600
有色金属矿采选业	Nonferrous Metals Mining and Dressing	6	12 293
常用有色金属矿采选	Common Nonferrous Metals Mining and Dressing	4	8 707
贵金属矿采选	Precious Metals Mining and Dressing	1	2 006
稀有稀土金属矿采选	Rare Tombarthite Metals Mining and Dressing	1	1 579
非金属矿采选业	Nonmetal Mineral Mining and Dressing	87	140 760
土砂石开采	Gravel and Sand Mining	60	73 279
化学矿采选	Chemical Mineral Mining and Dressing	3	1 015
采盐	Salt Mining	1	
石棉及其他非金属矿采选	Asbestos and Other Nonmetal Minerals Mining and Dressing	23	66 465
开采辅助活动	Mining Auxiliary Activity	5	1 731
煤炭开采和洗选助活动	Coal Mining and Washing Auxiliary Activity	4	1 731
石油和天然气开采辅助活动	Oil and Gas Extraction Assistance Activities	1	
制造业	**Manufacturing**	**3 217**	**20 209 605**
农副食品加工业	Farm and Sideline Food Processing	705	3 931 156
谷物磨制	Cereal Grain Grinding	80	337 596
饲料加工	Forage Processing	66	802 965
植物油加工	Plant Oil Processing	103	608 943
制糖业	Sugar Making	6	119 545
屠宰及肉类加工	Slaughtering and Meat Processing	77	232 942
水产品加工	Aquatic Production Processing	3	5 265
蔬菜、水果和坚果加工	Vegetable Fruit and Nuts Processing	280	1 338 555
其他农副食品加工	Other Farm and Sideline Food Processing	90	485 346
食品制造业	Food Manufacturing	128	1 371 154
焙烤食品制造	Bakery Products Manufacturing	8	9 471
糖果、巧克力及蜜饯制造	Candy,Chocolate and Candied Fruit Manufacturing	1	
方便食品制造	Convenient Food Manufacturing	15	52 987
乳制品制造	Liquid Milk and Dairy Products Manufacturing	20	377 051
罐头食品制造	Canned Food Manufacturing	43	325 245
调味品、发酵制品制造	Condiment and Fermented Products Manufacturing	16	451 346
其他食品制造	Other Food Manufacturing	25	155 054
酒、饮料和精制茶制造业	Liquor Brewing Beverage and Refined Tea Processing	125	695 211
酒的制造	Liquor Brewing	74	566 466
饮料制造	Beverage Manufacturing	47	127 027
精制茶加工	Refined Tea Processing	4	1 718

10—4 续表 2　Continued

计量单位:万元　　(2017 年)　　(10 000 yuan)

指　　标	Item	单位数(个) Number of Enterprises (unit)	工业总产值当年价格 At Current Prices
纺织业	Textile Industry	130	1 532 909
棉纺织及印染精加工	Cotton Textile Dying and Finishing Fine Processing	93	1 377 700
毛纺织和染整精加工	Woolen Textile Dying and Finishing Fine Processing	5	28 310
麻纺织及染整精加工	Homp Crops Textile Dying and Finishing Fine Processing	4	22 633
化纤织造及印染精加工	Chemical Fiber Weaving and Dyeing Fine Finishing	2	
针织或钩针编织物及其制品制造	Knitted Fabrics and Products Manufacturing	3	61 455
家用纺织制成品制造	Textile Products Manufacturing for Home	13	20 770
非家用纺织制成品制造	Other Textile Products Manufacturing	10	22 041
纺织服装、服饰业	Textile Clothing and Habilatory Manufacturing	20	38 039
机织服装制造	Textile Clothing Manufacturing	10	24 908
针织或钩针编织服装制造	Knit Clothing Manufacturing	4	7 641
服饰制造	Apparel Manufacturing	6	5 490
皮革、毛皮、羽毛及其制品和制鞋业	Leather Furriery Fecather and Its Manufacturing	4	17 394
毛皮鞣制及制品加工	Fur Tanning and Product Processing	3	8 351
羽毛(绒)加工及制品制造	Feather and Its Processing and Manufacturing	1	9 043
木材加工及木、竹、藤、棕、草制品业	Timber Processing Wood Bamboo Rattan Palm Fibre and Straw Products	78	109 432
木材加工	Timber Processing	42	50 718
人造板制造	Artificial Board Manufacturing	17	42 832
木制品制造	Wooden Products Manufacturing	16	12 293
竹、藤、棕、草等制品制造	Bamboo Rattan Palm Fibre and Straw Products Manufacturing	3	3 588
家具制造业	Furniture Manufacturing	21	22 978
木质家具制造	Wooden Furniture Manufacturing	17	20 055
金属家具制造	Metal Furniture Manufacturing	4	2 922
造纸及纸制品业	Paper Making and Paper Products	70	107 295
纸浆制造	Pulp Manufacturing	1	
造纸	Paper Making	17	32 604
纸制品制造	Paper Products Manufacturing	52	74 692
印刷和记录媒介复制业	Printing Industry and Recording Media	48	23 141
印刷	Printing	46	22 967
装订及印刷相关服务	Binding and Printing Related Services	2	174
文教、工美、体育和娱乐用品制造业	Culture and Education Handicraft Athletics and Amusement Things Manufacturing	18	30 014
工艺美术品制造	Handicraft Manufacturing	17	28 692
体育用品制造	Sporting Goods Manufacturing	1	1 322
石油加工、炼焦及核燃料加工业	Petroleum Processing Coking and Nuclear Material Processing	46	693 761
精炼石油产品制造	Refine Petroleum Processing	25	164 930
炼焦	Coking	21	528 832
化学原料及化学制品制造业	Chemical Materials and Chemical Products Manufacturing	249	2 558 210
基础化学原料制造	Basic Chemical Materials Manufacturing	26	110 592

10—4 续表 3 Continued

计量单位:万元 (2017 年) (10 000 yuan)

指 标	Item	单位数(个) Number of Enterprises (unit)	工业总产值当年价格 At Current Prices
肥料制造	Fertilizer Manufacturing	152	607 943
农药制造	Pesticide Manufacturing	5	3 598
涂料、油墨、颜料及类似产品制造	Paint Printing Ink Dyestuff and Similar Products Manufacturing	15	9 188
合成材料制造	Synthesize Material Manufacturing	11	1 473 723
专用化学产品制造	Special Chemical Products Manufacturing	26	326 637
炸药、火工及焰火产品制造	Detonator and Skyrocket Manufacturing	2	
日用化学产品制造	Daily Chemical Products Manufacturing	12	26 530
医药制造业	Pharmaceuticals Manufacturing	21	161 362
化学药品原料药制造	Chemical Pharmaceutical Material Medicine Manufacturing	2	976
化学药品制剂制造	Chemical Pharmaceutical Original Medicine Manufacturing	3	23 067
中药饮片加工	Chemical Pharmaceutical Manufacturing	7	10 553
中成药制造	Chinese Patent Drugs Troche Processing	6	41 625
兽用药品制造	Animal Pharmaceuticals Manufacturing	1	13 594
生物药品制造	Biopharmaceutical Manufacturing	1	65 980
卫生材料及医药用品制造	Chinese Patent Drugs Manufacturing	1	5 569
化学纤维制造业	Chemical Fibre Manufacturing	9	193 380
纤维素纤维原料及纤维制造	Cellulose Material and Fibre Manufacturing	7	189 764
合成纤维制造	Synthetic Fiber Manufacturing	2	3 616
橡胶和塑料制品业	Rubber and Plastic Products Manufacturing	389	856 967
橡胶制品业	Rubber Products Manufacturing	16	9 598
塑料制品业	Plastic Products Manufacturing	373	847 369
非金属矿物制品业	Nonmetal Mineral Products Manufacturing	587	2 217 385
水泥、石灰和石膏的制造	Cement Lime and Gypsum Manufacturing	52	474 443
石膏、水泥制品及类似制品制造	Gypsum Cement Producs Similar Producs Manufacturing	233	850 834
砖瓦、石材及其他建筑材料制造	Brick Tile Stone and Other Building Material Manufacturing	240	293 133
玻璃制造	Glass and Glass Producs Manufacturing	7	35 891
玻璃制品制造	Glass Producs Manufacturing	12	21 211
玻璃纤维和玻璃纤维增强塑料制品制造	Glass Fibre and Glass Fibre Plastic Producs Manufacturing	16	71 525
陶瓷制品制造	Ceramic Manufacturing	1	2 149
耐火材料制品制造	Fire-Resistant Material Producs Manufacturing	10	3 732
石墨及其他非金属矿物制品制造	Craphite and Other Nonmetal Mineral Products Manuracturing	16	464 467
黑色金属冶炼及压延加工业	Ferrous Metals Smelting and Rolling	40	469 887
炼 铁	Prdding	6	1 443
炼 钢	Steel Making	1	
黑色金属铸造	Noble Metal	10	9 668
钢压延加工	Steel Rolling Process	18	427 581
铁合金冶炼	Prdding Alloy Smelting	5	31 196
有色金属冶炼及压延加工业	Nonferrous Metals Smelting and Rolling	32	4 275 769
常用有色金属冶炼	Common Nonferrous Metals Smelting	10	3 531 927
稀有稀土金属冶炼	Rare Metals and Rare Soil Smelting	9	644 652

10－4 续表 4　Continued

计量单位:万元　　(2017 年)　　(10 000 yuan)

指　　标	Item	单位数（个） Number of Enterprises (unit)	工业总产值 当年价格 At Current Prices
有色金属合金制造	Nonferrous Metals Foundry	6	31 225
有色金属铸造	Nonferrous Metal Casting	1	
有色金属压延加工	Nonferrous Metals Rolling	6	67 965
金属制品业	Metal Product Manufacturing	161	288 958
结构性金属制品制造	Structural Metal Product Manufacturing	111	236 845
金属工具制造	Metal Tools Manufacturing	12	15 563
集装箱及金属包装容器制造	Container and Metal Packing Vessel Manufacturing	6	13 645
金属丝绳及其制品的制造	Metal Rope and Product Manufacturing	9	4 290
建筑、安全用金属制品制造	Construction and Safety Use Metal Product Manufacturing	11	9 169
金属表面处理及热处理加工	Metal Surface Treatment and Heat Treatment	2	1 963
搪瓷制品制造	Enamel Ware Product Manufacturing	1	
金属制日用品制造	Metal Daily Prodrct Manufacturing	2	1 232
其他金属制品品制造	Other Metal Product Manufacturing	7	6 249
通用设备制造业	General Equipment Manufacturing	68	58 412
锅炉及原动设备制造	Boiler and Motivity Equipment Manufacturing	13	18 247
金属加工机械制造	Metal Fabrication Machinery Manufacturing	4	20
物料搬运设备制造	Handbarrow Equipment Manufacturing	5	6 328
泵、阀门、压缩机及类似机械制造	Pump Valve Compressor and Allied Machine Manufacturing	5	2 046
轴承、齿轮和传动部件制造	Bearing Gear Transmission and Driving Component Manufacturing	2	1 040
烘炉、风机、衡器、包装等设备制造	Baker Blower Weighing Apparatus and Packing Manufacturing	10	17 548
文化、办公用机械制造	Culture Office Machinery Manufacturing	1	43
通用零部件制造	General Parts Manufacturing	21	8 328
其他通用设备制造业	Other General Equipment Manufacturing	7	4 811
专用设备制造业	Special Equipment Manufacturing	146	173 353
采矿、冶金、建筑专用设备制造	Mining Bmetallurgy and Architecture Special Equipment Manufacturing	19	9 680
化工、木材、非金属加工专用设备制造	Chemical Industry, Timber, Non－metallic Processing Special Equipment Manufacturing	1	
食品、饮料、烟草及饲料生产专用设备制造	Food Beverage Tobacco and Forage Special Equipment Manufacturing	2	1 777
印刷、制药、日化及日用品生产专用设备制造	Printing, Pharmacy, Daily Chemicals Special Equipment Manufacturing	2	271
纺织、服装和皮革加工专用设备制造	Textile Clothing and Leather Industry Special Equipment Manufacturing	3	42
电子和电工机械专用设备制造	Electrical and Electrical Machinery Special Equipment Manufacturing	3	
农、林、牧、渔专用机械制造	Special Machine Manufacturing for Farming Forestry Livestock and Fishing	99	147 357
医疗仪器设备及器械制造	Special Equipment Manufacturing for Medical Apparatus	4	2 659
环保、社会公共服务及其他专用设备制造	Environmental Protection Society Public Safety and Other Special Equipment Manufacturing	13	11 567
汽车制造业	Automobile Manufacturing	9	12 877
改装汽车制造	Refit Automobile Manufacturing	4	9 633
汽车车身、挂车制造	Autobody Trailer Manufacturing	2	1 501
汽车零部件及配件制造	Automobile Parts and Fitting Manufacturing	3	1 743
铁路、船舶、航空航天和其他运输设备制造业	Transportation and other Equipment Manufacturing	3	
摩托车制造	Motorcycle Manufacturing	1	
自行车制造	Bicycle Manufacturing	1	

10—4 续表 5 Continued

计量单位:万元 (2017 年) (10 000 yuan)

指 标	Item	单位数（个） Number of Enterprises (unit)	工业总产值 当年价格 At Current Prices
潜水救捞及其他未列明运输设备制造	Dive for and Other Unlist Equipment Manufacturing	1	
电气机械和器材制造业	Electric Machine and Equipment Manufacturing	71	303 739
电机制造	Motor Manufacturing	3	206 550
输配电及控制设备制造	Electricity Transmission and Distribution and Control Equipment Manufacturing	40	49 104
电线、电缆、光缆及电工器材制造	Wire Cable Optical Fibre and Electric Equipment Manufacturing	11	9 806
电池制造	Battery Manufacturing	1	
家用电力器具制造	Household Electricity Equipment Manufacturing	4	24 865
非电力家用器具制造	Non-Electricity Household Equipment Manufacturing	2	
照明器具制造	Illuminate Equipment Manufacturing	8	12 695
其他电气机械及器材制造	Other Electric Machine and Equipment Manufacturing	2	718
计算机、通信和其他电子设备制造业	Computer Communication and Other Electron Equipment Manufacturing	3	31 544
电子器件制造	Electron Component Manufacturing	2	26 657
电子元件制造	Electronic Component Manufacturing	1	4 887
仪器仪表制造业	Apparatus and Meter Manufacturing	4	5 859
通用仪器仪表制造	General Apparatus and Meter Manufacturing	2	5 115
专用仪器仪表制造	Special Apparatus and Metre Manufacturing	2	744
其他制造业	Other Manufacturing	4	1 787
煤制品制造	Coal Production Manufacturing	2	
废弃资源综合利用业	Abandon Resources and Discard Material Recovery Processing	11	19 497
金属废料和碎屑加工处理	Metal Waste Handle and Broken Bits Processing	4	10 377
非金属废料和碎屑加工处理	Nonmetal Waste Handle and Broken Bits Processing	7	9 120
金属制品、机械和设备修理业	Metal Product Machine and Equipment Repairing	17	8 136
金属制品修理	Metal Repairing	1	782
通用设备修理	General Equipment Maintenance	4	1 728
专用设备修理	Special Equipment Maintenance	8	4 339
电气设备修理	Electrical Equipment Maintenance	1	
其他机械和设备修理业	Other Machine and Equipment Repairing	3	1 286
电力、热力、燃气及水生产和供应业	**Electricity Heat Gass and Water Production and Supply**	**307**	**2 503 061**
电力、热力生产和供应业	Electricity and Heat Production and Supply	240	2 273 224
电力生产	Electricity Production	164	1 833 358
电力供应	Electricity Supply	18	347 473
热力生产和供应	Heat Production and Supply	58	92 394
燃气生产和供应业	Gass Production and Supply	30	177 205
水的生产和供应业	Water Production and Supply	37	52 631
自来水生产和供应	Tap Water Production and Supply	31	46 596
污水处理及其再生利用	Sewage Dispose and Regeneration Use	5	5 807
其他水的处理、利用与分配	Other Water Treatment Vtilization and Distribution	1	228

10—5 工业总产值行业构成

Composition of Gross Output Value of Industry by Sector

(2017 年)

指 标	Item	构 成（%）Composition（%）
总 计	**Total**	**100.0**
# 国有控股企业	State-controlled Shareholding Enterprises	31.4
按登记注册类型分	**Grouped by Status of Registration**	
内资企业	Domestic Enterprises	98.0
国有企业	State-owned Enterprises	2.4
集体企业	Collective-owned Enterprises	0.0
股份合作企业	Share Cooperative Enterprises	0.1
联营企业	Joint Ownership Enterprises	0.0
有限责任公司	Limited Liability Corporations	44.9
国有独资公司	State-owned Corporations with Private-Funds	3.6
其他有限责任公司	Other Limited Liability Corporations	41.3
股份有限公司	Share-holding Corporations Ltd.	6.2
私营企业	Private Enterprises	42.8
私营独资企业	Private-funded Enterprises	1.2
私营合伙企业	Private Partnership Enterprises	0.2
私营有限责任公司	Private Limited Liability Corporations	39.9
私营股份有限公司	Private Share-holding Corporations Ltd.	1.6
其他企业	Other Enterprises	1.6
港、澳、台商投资企业	Enterprises with Funds from Hong Kong Macao and Taiwan	0.3
合资经营企业(港或澳、台)	Joint-Venture Enterprises(with funds from Hong Kong Macao and Taiwan)	0.1
港、澳、台商独资经营企业	Enterprises with Funds from Hong Kong Macao and Taiwan	0.2
港澳台商投资股份有限公司	Share-holding Corporations Ltd. with Funds from Hong Kong Macao and Taiwan	0.0
其他港澳台商投资企业	Others	0.0
外商投资企业	Foreign Funded Enterprises	1.8
中外合资经营企业	Joint-Venture Enterprises	1.5
中外合作经营企业	Cooperative Enterprises	0.1
外资企业	Foreign Funded Enterprises	0.1
其他外商投资企业	Others	0.0
按轻重工业分	**Grouped by Light & Heavy Industry**	
轻工业	Light Industry	35.9
重工业	Heavy Industry	64.1
按企业规模分	**Grouped by Size of Enterprises**	
大型企业	Large-Scale Enterprises	31.2
中型企业	Medium-Scale Enterprises	19.1
小、微型企业	Small-Scale and Mini Enterprises	49.7
按工业行业分	**Grouped by Sector**	
采矿业	**Mining**	**2.3**
煤炭开采和洗选业	Coal Mining and Dressing	0.8

注:本表按当年价格计算,不含连队办工业(村办)及个体工业。(下表同)
Note:This table is not including county-run and individual industry(the same as follows).

10—5 续表 Continued

(2017 年)

指 标	Item	构 成 (%) Composition (%)
黑色金属矿采选业	Ferrous Metals Mining and Dressing	0.8
有色金属矿采选业	Nonferrous Metals Mining and Dressing	0.1
非金属矿采选业	Nonmetal Mineral Mining and Dressing	0.6
开采辅助活动	Mining Auxiliarv Activitv	
制造业	**Manufacturing**	**86.9**
农副食品加工业	Farm and Sideline Food Processing	16.9
食品制造业	Food Manufacturing	5.9
酒、饮料和精制茶制造业	Liquor Brewing Beverage and Refined Tea Processing	3.0
纺织业	Textile Industry	6.6
纺织服装、服饰业	Textile Clothing and Habilatory Manufacturing	0.2
皮革、毛皮、羽毛及其制品和制鞋业	Leather Furriery Fecather and Its Manufacturing	0.1
木材加工及木、竹、藤、棕、草制品业	Timber Processing Wood Bamboo Rattan Palm Fibre and Straw Products	0.5
家具制造业	Furniture Manufacturing	0.1
造纸及纸制品业	Paper Making and Paper Products	0.5
印刷和记录媒介复制业	Printing Industry and Recording Media	0.1
文教、工美、体育和娱乐用品制造业	Culture and Education HandicraftAthletics and Amusement Things Manufacturing	0.1
石油加工、炼焦及核燃料加工业	Petroleum Processing Coking and Nuclear Material Processing	3.0
化学原料及化学制品制造业	Chemical Materials and Chemical Products Manufacturing	11.0
医药制造业	Pharmaceuticals Manufacturing	0.7
化学纤维制造业	Chemical Fibre Manufacturing	0.8
橡胶和塑料制品业	Rubber and Plastic Products Manufacturing	3.7
非金属矿物制品业	Nonmetal Mineral Products Manufacturing	9.5
黑色金属冶炼及压延加工业	Ferrous Metals Smelting and Rolling	2.0
有色金属冶炼及压延加工业	Nonferrous Metals Smelting and Rolling	18.4
金属制品业	Metal Product Manufacturing	1.2
通用设备制造业	General Equipment Manufacturing	0.3
专用设备制造业	Special Equipment Manufacturing	0.7
汽车制造业	Automobile Manufacturing	0.1
铁路、船舶、航空航天和其他运输设备制造业	Transportation and other Equipment Manufacturing	
电气机械及器材制造业	Electric Machine and Equipment Manufacturing	1.3
计算机、通信和其他电子设备制造业	Computer Communicatin and Other Electron Epuipment Manufacturing	0.1
仪器仪表制造业	Apparatus and Meter Manufacturing	
其他制造业	Other Manufacturing	
废弃资源和废旧材料回收加工业	Abandon Resources and Discard Material Recovery Processing	0.1
金属制品、机械和设备修理业	Metal Product Machine and Equipment Repairing	
电力、热力、燃气及水生产和供应业	**Electricity Heat Gass and Water Production and Supply**	**10.8**
电力、热力的生产和供应业	Electricity and Heat Production and Supply	9.8
燃气生产和供应业	Gass Production and Supply	0.8
水的生产和供应业	Water Production and Supply	0.2

10－6　各师工业总产值

计量单位：万元　　　　(2017 年)

指　　标	Item	合　计 Total	一　师 Division 1	二　师 Division 2
总　　计	**Total**	**23 247 553**	**2 711 618**	**1 581 274**
# 国有控股企业	State-controlled Shareholding Enterprises	7 291 396	915 619	338 203
按登记注册类型分	**Grouped by Status of Registration**			
内资企业	Domestic Enterprises	22 774 738	2 680 677	1 581 274
国有企业	State-owned Enterprises	556 858	11 851	29 171
集体企业	Collective-owned Enterprises	507		
股份合作企业	Share Cooperative Enterprises	18 347		3 835
联营企业	Joint Ownership Enterprises	4 016		2 083
有限责任公司	Limited Liability Corporations	10 445 070	1 068 246	503 777
国有独资公司	State-owned Corporations with Private-Funds	837 260	57 053	26 332
其他有限责任公司	Other Limited Liability Corporations	9 607 810	1 011 194	477 446
股份有限公司	Share-holding Corporations Ltd.	1 433 161	36 954	22 601
私营企业	Private Enterprises	9 947 624	1 351 125	1 013 499
私营独资企业	Private-funded Enterprises	280 152	80 569	17 107
私营合伙企业	Private Partnership Enterprises	39 275	4 124	
私营有限责任公司	Private Limited Liability Corporations	9 266 719	1 266 433	935 228
私营股份有限公司	Private Share-holding Corporations Ltd.	361 477		61 164
其他企业	Other Enterprises	369 155	212 500	6 309
港、澳、台商投资企业	Enterprises with Funds from Hong Kong Macao and Taiwan	63 759	18 030	
合资经营企业(港或澳、台)	Joint-Venture Enterprises(with funds from Hong Kong Macao and Taiwan)	15 012		
港、澳、台商独资经营企业	Enterprises with Funds from Hong Kong Macao and Taiwan	40 089	18 030	
港澳台商投资股份有限公司	Share-holding Corporations Ltd. with Funds from Hong Kong Macao and Taiwan	3 747		
其他港澳台商投资企业	Others	4 911		
外商投资企业	Foreign Funded Enterprises	409 055	12 911	
中外合资经营企业	Joint-Venture Enterprises	345 794	12 911	
中外合作经营企业	Cooperative Enterprises	33 744		
外资企业	Foreign Funded Enterprises	27 719		
其他外商投资企业	Others	1 798		
按轻重工业分	**Grouped by Light & Heavy Industry**			
轻工业	Light Industry	8 348 786	1 818 325	1 040 006
重工业	Heavy Industry	14 898 767	893 294	541 268
按企业规模分	**Grouped by Size of Enterprises**			
大型企业	Large-Scale Enterprises	7 250 268	228 141	
中型企业	Medium-Scale Enterprises	4 435 581	299 022	411 716
小、微型企业	Small-Scale and Mini Enterprises	11 561 704	2 184 455	1 169 559
按工业行业分	**Grouped by Sector**			
采矿业	**Mining**	**534 887**	**38 458**	**63 695**
煤炭开采和洗选业	Coal Mining and Dressing	189 503	33 248	29 127

注：本表按当年价格计算，不含连队办工业(村办)及个体工业。(下表同)

Total Output Value of Industry by Division

(10 000 yuan)

三 师 Division 3	四 师 Division 4	五 师 Division 5	六 师 Division 6	七 师 Division 7	八 师 Division 8	九 师 Division 9	十 师 Division 10	十一师 Division 11	十二师 Division 12
1 273 968	**1 772 689**	**335 917**	**4 167 099**	**1 181 530**	**6 193 265**	**169 026**	**531 298**	**280 816**	**503 348**
554 199	649 332	106 879	280 051	474 070	2 637 738	83 820	102 892	192 123	335 148
1 268 371	1 756 936	335 917	4 142 645	1 167 022	5 857 418	169 026	524 374	280 816	464 560
59 260	15 291	38 074	37 783	65 697	156 843	14 220	14 213	14 747	24 056
	664	5 472	1 392	375	2 053	1 548	1 751		
					1 449				485
360 976	475 209	131 087	3 802 138	512 736	2 347 493	100 256	240 863	180 997	134 357
90 171	97 584	12 943	59 280	99 952	208 618	71 915	45 391	14 831	
270 805	377 625	118 144	3 742 858	412 785	2 138 875	28 341	195 472	166 166	134 357
209 333	217 061	9 848	22 151		594 405		10 536		236 173
606 518	1 033 697	131 949	277 090	588 214	2 749 693	49 796	251 673	85 072	68 985
42 971	52 978	7 392	3 487	10 429	34 862	10 546	7 645	1 155	390
3 791	6 944	2 858	1 234		5 261		2 088		258
559 756	778 350	120 917	257 351	575 601	2 642 086	38 316	238 206	83 917	68 336
	195 425	782	15 018	2 184	67 484	934	3 734		
32 283	15 014	19 488	2 090		5 484	3 206	5 336		506
			4 790	14 509	17 366		4 911		4 153
				14 509					503
			1 042		17 366				3 651
			3 747						
							4 911		
5 597	15 753		19 665		318 481		2 014		34 635
5 597	13 955		14 404		296 023		2 014		890
									33 744
			5 261		22 457				
	1 798								
762 343	894 830	124 426	724 556	404 177	1 218 155	106 542	254 404	719	368 079
511 625	877 859	211 491	3 442 543	777 353	4 975 110	62 484	276 894	280 098	135 270
149 148	328 716		2 537 414	58 514	3 948 335				
115 162	217 601	35 546	1 079 619	398 121	980 496	47 180	54 927	28 989	173 785
1 009 658	1 226 372	300 372	550 066	724 895	1 264 435	121 846	476 371	251 827	329 563
10 093	**36 717**	**29 919**	**34 360**	**12 397**	**21 560**	**146**	**23 811**	**1 454**	**6 048**
	28 037		34 007	12 397	19 829		13 332		5 615

Note: This table is not including county-run and individual industry(the same as follows).

10—6 续表1 Continued

计量单位:万元　　(2017年)　　(10 000 yuan)

指　标	Item	十三师 Division 13	十四师 Division 14	兵团直属 Directly under XPCC
总　计	**Total**	**2 089 523**	**59 496**	**396 685**
# 国有控股企业	State-controlled Shareholding Enterprises	195 875	29 349	396 102
按登记注册类型分	**Grouped by Status of Registration**			
内资企业	Domestic Enterprises	2 089 523	59 496	396 685
国有企业	State-owned Enterprises	70 763	1 693	3 196
集体企业	Collective-owned Enterprises		507	
股份合作企业	Share Cooperative Enterprises	1 257		
联营企业	Joint Ownership Enterprises			
有限责任公司	Limited Liability Corporations	304 765	37 024	245 146
国有独资公司	State-owned Corporations with Private-Funds	53 191		
其他有限责任公司	Other Limited Liability Corporations	251 574	37 024	245 146
股份有限公司	Share-holding Corporations Ltd.	1 744	6 375	65 980
私营企业	Private Enterprises	1 644 206	13 744	82 363
私营独资企业	Private-funded Enterprises	10 382	238	
私营合伙企业	Private Partnership Enterprises	12 718		
私营有限责任公司	Private Limited Liability Corporations	1 606 354	13 506	82 363
私营股份有限公司	Private Share-holding Corporations Ltd.	14 753		
其他企业	Other Enterprises	66 787	152	
港、澳、台商投资企业	Enterprises with Funds from Hong Kong Macao and Taiwan			
合资经营企业(港或澳、台)	Joint-Venture Enterprises(with funds from Hong Kong Macao and Taiwan)			
港、澳、台商独资经营企业	Enterprises with Funds from Hong Kong Macao and Taiwan			
港澳台商投资股份有限公司	Share-holding Corporations Ltd. with Funds from Hong Kong Macao and Taiwan			
其他港澳台商投资企业	Others			
外商投资企业	Foreign Funded Enterprises			
中外合资经营企业	Joint-Venture Enterprises			
中外合作经营企业	Cooperative Enterprises			
外资企业	Foreign Funded Enterprises			
其他外商投资企业	Others			
按轻重工业分	**Grouped by Light & Heavy Industry**			
轻工业	Light Industry	211 118	25 005	396 102
重工业	Heavy Industry	1 878 405	34 491	583
按企业规模分	**Grouped by Size of Enterprises**			
大型企业	Large-Scale Enterprises			
中型企业	Medium-Scale Enterprises	304 424		288 994
小、微型企业	Small-Scale and Mini Enterprises	1 785 099	59 496	107 691
按工业行业分	**Grouped by Sector**			
采矿业	**Mining**	**256 229**		
煤炭开采和洗选业	Coal Mining and Dressing	13 912		

10—6 续表 2 Continued

计量单位:万元　　(2017 年)　　(10 000 yuan)

指　　标	Item	合　计 Total	一　师 Division 1	二　师 Division 2
黑色金属矿采选业	Ferrous Metals Mining and Dressing	190 600		
有色金属矿采选业	Nonferrous Metals Mining and Dressing	12 293		
非金属矿采选业	Nonmetal Mineral Mining and Dressing	140 760	5 211	34 568
开采辅助活动	Mining Auxiliary Activity	1 731		
制造业	**Manufacturing**	**20 209 605**	**2 472 835**	**1 424 283**
农副食品加工业	Farm and Sideline Food Processing	3 931 156	1 154 055	507 254
食品制造业	Food Manufacturing	1 371 154	56 887	225 615
酒、饮料和精制茶制造业	Liquor Brewing Beverage and Refined Tea Processing	695 211	15 684	41 041
纺织业	Textile Industry	1 532 909	346 706	163 389
纺织服装、服饰业	Textile Clothing and Habilatory Manufacturing	38 039	4 764	
皮革、毛皮、羽毛及其制品和制鞋业	Leather Furriery Fecather and Its Manufacturing	17 394		9 043
木材加工及木、竹、藤、棕、草制品业	Timber Processing Wood Bamboo Rattan Palm Fibre and Straw Products	109 432	20 309	11 225
家具制造业	Furniture Manufacturing	22 978	2 922	1 778
造纸及纸制品业	Paper Making and Paper Products	107 295	36 555	41 547
印刷和记录媒介复制业	Printing Industry and Recording Media	23 141	2 980	216
文教、工美、体育和娱乐用品制造业	Culture and Education Handicraft Athletics and Amusement Things Manufacturing	30 014	2 527	9 989
石油加工、炼焦及核燃料加工业	Petroleum Processing Coking and Nuclear Material Processing	693 761		11 054
化学原料及化学制品制造业	Chemical Materials and Chemical Products Manufacturing	2 558 210	190 289	137 023
医药制造业	Pharmaceuticals Manufacturing	161 362	7 360	36 906
化学纤维制造业	Chemical Fibre Manufacturing	193 380	133 956	
橡胶和塑料制品业	Rubber and Plastic Products Manufacturing	856 967	169 956	97 503
非金属矿物制品业	Nonmetal Mineral Products Manufacturing	2 217 385	226 721	64 916
黑色金属冶炼及压延加工业	Ferrous Metals Smelting and Rolling	469 887	2 252	1 888
有色金属冶炼及压延加工业	Nonferrous Metals Smelting and Rolling	4 275 769	14 892	
金属制品业	Metal Product Manufacturing	288 958	12 100	13 466
通用设备制造业	General Equipment Manufacturing	58 412	3 525	1 902
专用设备制造业	Special Equipment Manufacturing	173 353	28 018	42 196
汽车制造业	Automobile Manufacturing	12 877		
铁路、船舶、航空航天和其他运输设备制造业	Transportation and other Equipment Manufacturing			
电气机械及器材制造业	Electric Machine and Equipment Manufacturing	303 739	35 698	6 332
计算机、通信和其他电子设备制造业	Computer Communic Apparatus and meter	31 544		
仪器仪表制造业	Apparatus and Meter Manufactring	5 859		
其他制造业	Other Manufacturing	1 787	1 718	
废弃资源和废旧材料回收加工业	Abandon Resources and Discard Material Recovery Processing	19 497		
金属制品、机械和设备修理业	Metal Product Machine and Equipment Repairing	8 136	2 964	
电力、热力、燃气及水生产和供应业	**Electricity Heat Gass and Water Production and Supply**	**2 503 061**	**200 325**	**93 296**
电力、热力的生产和供应业	Electricity and Heat Production and Supply	2 274 508	129 609	53 612
燃气生产和供应业	Gass Production and Supply	175 921	63 538	38 654
水的生产和供应业	Water Production and Supply	52 631	7 178	1 030

10—6 续表 3

计量单位:万元 (2017 年)

指 标	Item	三 师 Division 3	四 师 Division 4	五 师 Division 5	六 师 Division 6
黑色金属矿采选业	Ferrous Metals Mining and Dressing		1 707	28 550	
有色金属矿采选业	Nonferrous Metals Mining and Dressing				
非金属矿采选业	Nonmetal Mineral Mining and Dressing	10 093	6 972	1 368	353
开采辅助活动	Mining Auxiliary Activity				
制造业	**Manufacturing**	**1 123 839**	**1 579 066**	**246 442**	**3 627 058**
农副食品加工业	Farm and Sideline Food Processing	401 743	376 617	87 793	78 052
食品制造业	Food Manufacturing	576	28 120	3 023	533 283
酒、饮料和精制茶制造业	Liquor Brewing Beverage and Refined Tea Processing	75 876	397 311	319	7 693
纺织业	Textile Industry	169 162	22 075	11 995	75 623
纺织服装、服饰业	Textile Clothing and Habilatory Manufacturing	20 029	2 080		
皮革、毛皮、羽毛及其制品和制鞋业	Leather Furriery Fecather and Its Manufacturing			6 859	
木材加工及木、竹、藤、棕、草制品业	Timber Processing Wood Bamboo Rattan Palm Fibre and Straw Products		37 817	2 426	5 940
家具制造业	Furniture Manufacturing			4	707
造纸及纸制品业	Paper Making and Paper Products	8 187	5 111	969	5 369
印刷和记录媒介复制业	Printing Industry and Recording Media		9 267	142	303
文教、工美、体育和娱乐用品制造业	Culture and Education Handicraft Athletics and Amusement Things Manufacturing		1 074	1 983	12 103
石油加工、炼焦及核燃料加工业	Petroleum Processing Coking and Nuclear Material Processing			1 702	130 941
化学原料及化学制品制造业	Chemical Materials and Chemical Products Manufacturing	40 541	173 066	12 595	33 382
医药制造业	Pharmaceuticals Manufacturing	21 198	1 950		
化学纤维制造业	Chemical Fibre Manufacturing	57 678			
橡胶和塑料制品业	Rubber and Plastic Products Manufacturing	98 579	53 344	47 703	61 730
非金属矿物制品业	Nonmetal Mineral Products Manufacturing	193 035	197 958	51 711	339 055
黑色金属冶炼及压延加工业	Ferrous Metals Smelting and Rolling		1 572		212 430
有色金属冶炼及压延加工业	Nonferrous Metals Smelting and Rolling		240 906		2 107 048
金属制品业	Metal Product Manufacturing	11 890	14 655	3 431	3 249
通用设备制造业	General Equipment Manufacturing		2 371		2 593
专用设备制造业	Special Equipment Manufacturing		4 739	3 041	12 354
汽车制造业	Automobile Manufacturing			9 633	1 501
铁路、船舶、航空航天和其他运输设备制造业	Transportation and other Equipment Manufacturing				
电气机械及器材制造业	Electric Machine and Equipment Manufacturing	277	6 191	331	444
计算机、通信和其他电子设备制造业	Computer Communic Apparatus and meter	25 066			
仪器仪表制造业	Apparatus and Meter Manufactring				744
其他制造业	Other Manufacturing				
废弃资源和废旧材料回收加工业	Abandon Resources and Discard Material Recovery Processing		2 843		2 514
金属制品、机械和设备修理业	Metal Product Machine and Equipment Repairing			782	
电力、热力、燃气及水生产和供应业	**Electricity Heat Gass and Water Production and Supply**	**140 036**	**156 906**	**59 556**	**505 681**
电力、热力的生产和供应业	Electricity and Heat Production and Supply	125 009	155 167	59 556	476 494
燃气生产和供应业	Gass Production and Supply	7 416			25 392
水的生产和供应业	Water Production and Supply	7 611	1 739		3 795

Continued

(10 000 yuan)

七　师 Division 7	八　师 Division 8	九　师 Division 9	十　师 Division 10	十一师 Division 11	十二师 Division 12	十三师 Division 13	十四师 Division 14	兵团直属 Directly under XPCC
						160 343		
						12 293		
		146	10 480	1 454	433	69 681		
	1 731							
1 025 981	**5 375 761**	**143 149**	**450 042**	**279 340**	**467 477**	**1 548 926**	**48 720**	**396 685**
130 696	314 115	83 355	214 070		85 394	149 433	21 655	326 926
65 361	170 465	18 316	5 754		257 863	5 891		
13 660	111 663	1 143	17 961		6 045	6 772	45	
159 656	551 283		2 681			30 025	313	
	1 840				4 755	3 297	1 275	
	3		1 489					
3 330	16 919	750	1 773	2 127	2 086	1 732	2 999	
1 719	5 593				9	10 245		
4 682	4 482		31		361			
996	2 624		1 294		763		1 360	3 196
			2 009				329	
72 229	1 535				8 100	468 200		
213 152	1 702 943	1 006	17 781	6 448	3 640	24 751	1 011	583
1 510	19 163	976			6 292		28	65 980
	1 746							
64 621	106 082	9 125	76 072	4 174	6 064	61 552	464	
176 086	414 214	25 755	63 914	171 148	26 224	250 646	16 002	
31 092	28 679		2 314		849	188 812		
17 899	1 829 413					65 611		
25 327	34 151	2 474	18 071	90 820	16 838	41 300	1 187	
6 821	8 512	251	2 347		15 664	13 306	1 120	
19 142	40 668		12 733		7 342	2 848	271	
	1 743							
13 478			7 900	4 625	6 759	221 044	661	
	4 887					1 590		
					5 115			
					69			
4 525	1 752				5 993	1 870		
	1 286		1 850		1 253			
143 152	**795 944**	**25 731**	**57 445**	**22**	**29 823**	**284 368**	**10 776**	
133 267	754 255	22 978	50 267		26 848	276 670	10 776	
3 717	30 230		876		57	6 042		
6 167	11 460	2 753	6 303	22	2 917	1 656		

10—7　各师工业总产值指数

Indices of Gross Output Value of Industry by Division

计量单位:%　　（2017 年,上年=100）（2017,preceding year=100）　　（%）

单　位 Unit	工　业 总产值 Gross Industrial Output Value	国有企业 State-owned	集体企业 Collective-owned	股份制企业 Share Holding	其他企业 Others	个　体 Individuals
总　计 Total	**101.3**	**72.7**	**80.4**	**104.2**	**108.6**	**62.8**
一　师 Division 1	104.1	31.0		106.4	109.2	47.6
二　师 Division 2	101.7	91.9		102.3	84.1	100.8
三　师 Division 3	114.6	105.6		111.5	145.6	
四　师 Division 4	101.9	78.6		110.6	95.1	39.6
五　师 Division 5	80.2	82.1		90.1	83.6	37.5
六　师 Division 6	98.6	58.3		105.3	84.4	15.8
七　师 Division 7	110.0	101.9		116.1	50.0	87.2
八　师 Division 8	94.0	75.3		94.3	120.0	51.1
九　师 Division 9	101.1	117.1		109.8	175.7	40.8
十　师 Division 10	109.6	31.2		115.4	140.4	119.0
十一师 Division 11	80.8	13.8		110.8	94.6	
十二师 Division 12	132.4	141.2		134.9	463.4	47.1
十三师 Division 13	106.6	133.1		106.3	142.2	80.5
十四师 Division 14	102.7	133.8	86.4	113.5	18.9	61.8
兵团直属 Directly under XPCC	90.7	109.4		100.0		

注:本表按价格指数缩减法计算。
Note:Data in this table are calculated at price index.

10—8 规模以上工业企业数、总产值、销售产值及产销率

Number, Gross Output Value, Sale Value and Production-sale Ratio of Industrial Enterprises above Designated Size

计量单位:万元 (2017 年) (10 000 yuan)

指标	Item	企业单位数(个) Number of Enterprises (unit)	# 亏损企业 Losses	工业总产值(当年价格) Gross Industrial Output Value (At Current Prices)
总计	**Total**	**886**	**155**	**20 620 581**
# 国有控股企业	State-controlled Shareholding Enterprises	289	86	6 875 743
按登记注册类型分	**Grouped by Status of Registration**			
内资企业	Domestic Enterprises	866	151	20 155 651
国有企业	State-owned Enterprises	20	3	194 533
股份合作企业	Share Cooperative Enterprises	1		3 507
有限责任公司	Limited Liability Corporations	341	98	9 954 258
国有独资公司	State-owned Corporations with Private-Funds	53	19	825 067
其他有限责任公司	Other Limited Liability Corporations	288	79	9 129 191
股份有限公司	Share-holding Corporations Ltd.	25	7	1 285 152
私营企业	Private Enterprises	452	43	8 456 296
私营独资企业	Private-funded Enterprises	1	1	3 226
私营有限责任公司	Private Limited Liability Corporations	430	39	8 122 074
私营股份有限公司	Private Share-holding Corporations Ltd.	21	3	330 995
其他企业	Other Enterprises	27		261 905
港、澳、台商投资企业	Enterprises with Funds from Hong Kong, Macao and Taiwan	5	1	58 564
合资经营企业(港或澳、台)	Joint-Venture Enterprises(with funds from Hong Kong, Macao and Taiwan)	1		14 509
港、澳、台商独资经营企业	Enterprises with Funds from Hong Kong, Macao and Taiwan	2		35 397
港澳台商投资股份有限公司	Share-holding Corporations Ltd. with Funds from Hong Kong, Macao and Taiwan	1		3 747
其他港澳台商投资企业	Others	1	1	4 911
外商投资企业	Foreign Funded Enterprises	15	3	406 367
中外合资经营企业	Joint-Venture Enterprises	11	2	344 904
中外合作经营企业	Cooperative Enterprises	1		33 744
外资企业	Foreign Funded Enterprises	3	1	27 719
按轻重工业分	**Grouped by Light & Heavy Industry**			
轻工业	Light Industry	462	78	7 704 503
重工业	Heavy Industry	424	77	12 916 078
按企业规模分	**Grouped by Size of Enterprises**			
大型企业	Large-Scale Enterprises	21	3	7 250 268
中型企业	Medium-Scale Enterprises	90	32	4 435 581
小型企业	Small-Scale Enterprises	662	102	8 235 495
微型企业	Mini Enterprises	113	18	699 237
按工业行业分	**Grouped by Sector**			
采矿业	**Mining**	**30**	**7**	**414 513**
煤炭开采和洗选业	Coal Mining and Dressing	17	6	187 127
烟煤和无烟煤的开采洗选	Soft Coal and Hard Coal Mining and Dressing	17	6	187 127
黑色金属矿采选业	Ferrous Metals Mining and Dressing	6		163 877
铁矿采选	Prdding Mining and Dressing	6		163 877
有色金属矿采选业	Nonferrous Metals Mining and Dressing	2	1	8 707
常用有色金属矿采选	Common Nonferrous Metals Mining and Dressing	2	1	8 707
非金属矿采选业	Nonmetal Mineral Mining and Dressing	5		54 802
土砂石开采	Soil Sand Mining	2		7 031
石棉及其他非金属矿采选	Asbestos and Other Nonmetal Minerals Mining and Dressing	3		47 771
制造业	**Manufacturing**	**746**	**123**	**17 889 456**
农副食品加工业	Farm and Sideline Food Processing	227	28	3 382 946
谷物磨制	Cereal Grain Grinding	25	3	278 687
饲料加工	Forage Processing	32	3	737 258
植物油加工	Plant Oil Processing	39	9	509 936
制糖	Sugar Making	4		117 554
屠宰及肉类加工	Slaughtering and Meat Processing	11	4	168 437
蔬菜、水果和坚果加工	Vegetable, Fruit and Nuts Processing	88	4	1 139 511
其他农副食品加工	Other Farm and Sideline Food Processing	28	5	431 563

10—8 续表 1　Continued

计量单位：万元　　(2017 年)　　(10 000 yuan)

指　　标	Item	工业销售产值（当年价格） Sale Value of Industry (At Current Prices)	# 出口交货值 Export Commodities	产销率（%） Ratio of Production & Marketing (%)
总　计	**Total**	**20 144 283**	**136 916**	**97.7**
# 国有控股企业	State-controlled Shareholding Enterprises	6 650 953	91 434	96.7
按登记注册类型分	**Grouped by Status of Registration**			
内资企业	Domestic Enterprises	19 700 101	112 396	97.7
国有企业	State-owned Enterprises	194 407		99.9
股份合作企业	Share Cooperative Enterprises	3 507		100.0
有限责任公司	Limited Liability Corporations	9 732 830	82 595	97.8
国有独资公司	State-owned Corporations with Private-Funds	758 758	11 180	92.0
其他有限责任公司	Other Limited Liability Corporations	8 974 072	71 415	98.3
股份有限公司	Share-holding Corporations Ltd.	1 237 850	3 066	96.3
私营企业	Private Enterprises	8 276 608	26 735	97.9
私营独资企业	Private-funded Enterprises	3 312		102.7
私营有限责任公司	Private Limited Liability Corporations	7 954 264	26 735	97.9
私营股份有限公司	Private Share-holding Corporations Ltd.	319 032		96.4
其他企业	Other Enterprises	254 900		97.3
港、澳、台商投资企业	Enterprises with Funds from Hong Kong, Macao and Taiwan	49 986		85.4
合资经营企业(港或澳、台)	Joint-Venture Enterprises(with funds from Hong Kong, Macao and Taiwan)	14 509		100.0
港、澳、台商独资经营企业	Enterprises with Funds from Hong Kong, Macao and Taiwan	29 436		83.2
港澳台商投资股份有限公司	Share-holding Corporations Ltd. with Funds from Hong Kong, Macao and Taiwan	3 637		97.1
其他港澳台商投资企业	Others	2 404		49.0
外商投资企业	Foreign Funded Enterprises	394 196	24 520	97.0
中外合资经营企业	Joint-Venture Enterprises	333 158	24 520	96.6
中外合作经营企业	Cooperative Enterprises	33 744		100.0
外资企业	Foreign Funded Enterprises	27 294		98.5
按轻重工业分	**Grouped by Light & Heavy Industry**			
轻工业	Light Industry	7 330 908	124 178	95.2
重工业	Heavy Industry	12 813 376	12 738	99.2
按企业规模分	**Grouped by Size of Enterprises**			
大型企业	Large-Scale Enterprises	7 151 091	13 012	98.6
中型企业	Medium-Scale Enterprises	4 312 278	18 265	97.2
小型企业	Small-Scale Enterprises	7 981 145	97 668	96.9
微型企业	Mini Enterprises	699 769	7 971	100.1
按工业行业分	**Grouped by Sector**			
采矿业	**Mining**	**424 938**		**102.5**
煤炭开采和洗选业	Coal Mining and Dressing	195 547		104.5
烟煤和无烟煤的开采洗选	Soft Coal and Hard Coal Mining and Dressing	195 547		104.5
黑色金属矿采选业	Ferrous Metals Mining and Dressing	163 877		100.0
铁矿采选	Prdding Mining and Dressing	163 877		100.0
有色金属矿采选业	Nonferrous Metals Mining and Dressing	9 512		109.2
常用有色金属矿采选	Common Nonferrous Metals Mining and Dressing	9 512		109.2
非金属矿采选业	Nonmetal Mineral Mining and Dressing	56 003		102.2
土砂石开采	Soil Sand Mining	6 839		97.3
石棉及其他非金属矿采选	Asbestos and Other Nonmetal Minerals Mining and Dressing	49 164		102.9
制造业	**Manufacturing**	**17 422 409**	**136 916**	**97.4**
农副食品加工业	Farm and Sideline Food Processing	3 240 878	1 004	95.8
谷物磨制	Cereal Grain Grinding	267 692		96.1
饲料加工	Forage Processing	692 865		94.0
植物油加工	Plant Oil Processing	528 486		103.6
制糖	Sugar Making	90 078		76.6
屠宰及肉类加工	Slaughtering and Meat Processing	165 694		98.4
蔬菜、水果和坚果加工	Vegetable, Fruit and Nuts Processing	1 094 442		96.0
其他农副食品加工	Other Farm and Sideline Food Processing	401 622	1 004	93.1

10—8 续表 2 Continued

计量单位:万元 (2017 年) (10 000 yuan)

指标	Item	企业单位数（个） Number of Enterprises (unit)	# 亏损企业 Losses	工业总产值（当年价格） Gross Industrial Output Value (At Current Prices)
食品制造业	Food Manufacturing	53	18	1 188 439
焙烤食品制造	Bakery Products Manufacturing	1	1	3 371
方便食品制造	Convenient Food Manufacturing	4	1	40 634
乳制品制造	Milk and Dairy Products Manufacturing	8	3	246 271
罐头食品制造	Canned Food Manufacturing	24	9	313 119
调味品、发酵制品制造	Condiment and Fermented Products Manufacturing	8	3	446 873
其他食品制造	Other Food Manufacturing	8	1	138 172
酒、饮料和精制茶制造业	Liquor Brewing, Beverage and Refined Tea Processing	32	3	630 042
酒的制造	Liquor Brewing	24	2	525 485
软饮料制造	Soft Beverage Manufacturing	8	1	104 557
纺织业	Textile Industry	53	20	1 457 724
棉纺织及印染精加工	Cotton Textile, Dying and Finishing Fine Processing	46	19	1 321 428
毛纺织和染整精加工	Woolen Textile, Dying and Finishing Fine Processing	2		27 371
麻纺织及染整精加工	Homp Crops Textile, Dying and Finishing Fine Processing	1		20 166
针织或钩针编织物及其制品制造	Knitting or Crochet and Related Goods Manufacturing	1		60 486
家用纺织制成品制造	Textile Products Manufacturing for Home	2	1	12 530
非家用纺织制成品制造	Non-Textile Products Manufacturing for Home	1		15 744
纺织服装、服饰业	Textile Clothing and Habilatory Manufacturing	2		22 537
机织服装制造	Woven Garment Manufacturing	1		17 966
针织或钩针编织服装制造	Knitting or Crochet Clothing Manufacturing	1		4 570
皮革、毛皮、羽毛及其制品和制鞋业	Leather, Fur, Feather and Related Goods Manufacturing	2		15 902
毛皮鞣制及制品加工	Fur Tanning and Product Processing	1		6 859
羽毛(绒)加工及制品制造	Feather(eiderdown)Processing and Related Goods Manufacturing	1		9 043
木材加工和木、竹、藤、棕、草制品业	Wood Processing and Wood, Bamboo, Cane, Grass Products	7	2	52 326
木材加工	Wood Processing	3	2	19 770
人造板制造	Artificial Board Manufacturing	4		32 556
家具制造业	Furniture Manufacturing	2	1	12 624
木质家具制造	Woodiness Furniture Manufacturing	2	1	12 624
造纸及纸制品业	Paper Making and Paper Products	7	1	58 036
造纸	Paper Making	4	1	24 942
纸制品制造	Paper Products Manufacturing	3		33 094
印刷业和记录媒介的复制	Printing Industry and Recording Media	5		13 532
印刷	Printing	5		13 532
文教、工美、体育和娱乐用品制造业	Culture and Education, Handicraft, Athletics and Amusement Things Manufacturing	3		17 717
工艺美术品制造	Handicraft Manufacturing	3		17 717
石油加工、炼焦及核燃料加工业	Petroleum Processing, Coking and Nuclear Material Processing	16	3	671 487
精炼石油产品制造	Refined Petroleum Products Manufacturing	7	2	150 423
炼焦	Coking	9	1	521 064
化学原料及化学制品制造业	Chemical Materials and Chemical Products Manufacturing	54	7	2 393 599
基础化学原料制造	Basic Chemical Materials Manufacturing	5	3	94 246
肥料制造	Fertilizer Manufacturing	33	2	497 078
合成材料制造	Synthesize Material Manufacturing	6	1	1 468 820
专用化学产品制造	Special Chemical Products Manufacturing	8	1	314 775
日用化学产品制造	Daily Chemical Products Manufacturing	2		18 680
医药制造业	Pharmaceuticals Manufacturing	8	1	147 508
化学药品制剂制造	Chemical Pharmaceutical Original Medicine Manufacturing	1		22 601
中药饮片加工	Chemical Pharmaceutical Manufacturing	1		6 292
中成药生产	Chinese Medicine Production	3	1	33 473
兽用药品制造	Chinese Patent Drugs Troche Processing	1		13 594
生物药品制造	Biopharmacautical manufacturing	1		65 980
卫生材料及医药用品制造	Chinese Patent Drugs Manufacturing	1		5 569
化学纤维制造业	Chemical Fibre Manufacturing	4	1	188 017
纤维素纤维原料及纤维制造	Cellulose Material and Fibre Manufacturing	4	1	188 017
橡胶和塑料制品业	Rubber and Plastic Products Manufacturing	59	4	532 795
塑料制品业	Plastic Products Manufacturing	59	4	532 795

10—8 续表 3　Continued

计量单位:万元　　(2017 年)　　(10 000 yuan)

指　标	Item	工业销售产值（当年价格） Sale Value of Industry (At Current Prices)	#出口交货值 Export Commodities	产销率（%） Ratio of Production & Marketing (%)
食品制造业	Food Manufacturing	1 106 116	97 117	93.1
焙烤食品制造	Bakery Products Manufacturing	3 329		98.8
方便食品制造	Convenient Food Manufacturing	43 651		107.4
乳制品制造	Milk and Dairy Products Manufacturing	220 208		89.4
罐头食品制造	Canned Food Manufacturing	259 288	84 605	82.8
调味品、发酵制品制造	Condiment and Fermented Products Manufacturing	447 039	12 512	100.0
其他食品制造	Other Food Manufacturing	132 600		96.0
酒、饮料和精制茶制造业	Liquor Brewing,Beverage and Refined Tea Processing	605 007		96.0
酒的制造	Liquor Brewing	515 479		98.1
软饮料制造	Soft Beverage Manufacturing	89 528		85.6
纺织业	Textile Industry	1 373 235	6 282	94.2
棉纺织及印染精加工	Cotton Textile,Dying and Finishing Fine Processing	1 247 405	4 668	94.4
毛纺织和染整精加工	Woolen Textile,Dying and Finishing Fine Processing	24 331	896	88.9
麻纺织及染整精加工	Homp Crops Textile,Dying and Finishing Fine Processing	19 162		95.0
针织或钩针编织物及其制品制造	Knitting or Crochet and Related Goods Manufacturing	56 564	717	93.5
家用纺织制成品制造	Textile Products Manufacturing for Home	11 759		93.8
非家用纺织制成品制造	Non-Textile Products Manufacturing for Home	14 015		89.0
纺织服装、服饰业	Textile Clothing and Habilatory Manufacturing	19 341	3 094	85.8
机织服装制造	Woven Garment Manufacturing	14 604		81.3
针织或钩针编织服装制造	Knitting or Crochet Clothing Manufacturing	4 737	3 094	103.6
皮革、毛皮、羽毛及其制品和制鞋业	Leather,Fur,Feather and Related Goods Manufacturing	15 902	6 859	100.0
毛皮鞣制及制品加工	Fur Tanning and Product Processing	6 859	6 859	100.0
羽毛(绒)加工及制品制造	Feather(eiderdown)Processing and Related Goods Manufacturing	9 043		100.0
木材加工和木、竹、藤、棕、草制品业	Wood Processing and Wood、Bamboo、Cane、Grass Products	51 755		98.9
木材加工	Wood Processing	19 297		97.6
人造板制造	Artificial Board Manufacturing	32 458		99.7
家具制造业	Furniture Manufacturing	12 624	4 129	100.0
木质家具制造	Woodiness Furniture Manufacturing	12 624	4 129	100.0
造纸及纸制品业	Paper Making and Paper Products	53 546		92.3
造纸	Paper Making	23 916		95.9
纸制品制造	Paper Products Manufacturing	29 630		89.5
印刷业和记录媒介的复制	Printing Industry and Recording Media	13 111		96.9
印刷	Printing	13 111		96.9
文教、工美、体育和娱乐用品制造业	Culture and Education, Handicraft,Athletics and Amusement Things Manufacturing	17 704	5 694	99.9
工艺美术品制造	Handicraft Manufacturing	17 704	5 694	99.9
石油加工、炼焦及核燃料加工业	Petroleum Processing, Coking and Nuclear Material Processing	669 742		99.7
精炼石油产品制造	Refined Petroleum Products Manufacturing	149 911		99.7
炼焦	Coking	519 831		99.8
化学原料及化学制品制造业	Chemical Materials and Chemical Products Manufacturing	2 389 952	12 563	99.8
基础化学原料制造	Basic Chemical Materials Manufacturing	93 775	4 890	99.5
肥料制造	Fertilizer Manufacturing	487 017		98.0
合成材料制造	Synthesize Material Manufacturing	1 483 072	7 673	101.0
专用化学产品制造	Special Chemical Products Manufacturing	307 409		97.7
日用化学产品制造	Daily Chemical Products Manufacturing	18 680		100.0
医药制造业	Pharmaceuticals Manufacturing	130 717		88.6
化学药品制剂制造	Chemical Pharmaceutical Original Medicine Manufacturing	20 994		92.9
中药饮片加工	Chemical Pharmaceutical Manufacturing	6 243		99.2
中成药生产	Chinese Medicine Production	14 051		42.0
兽用药品制造	Chinese Patent Drugs Troche Processing	11 454		84.3
生物药品制造	Biopharmacautical manufacturing	73 354		111.2
卫生材料及医药用品制造	Chinese Patent Drugs Manufacturing	4 620		83.0
化学纤维制造业	Chemical Fibre Manufacturing	179 184		95.3
纤维素纤维原料及纤维制造	Cellulose Material and Fibre Manufacturing	179 184		95.3
橡胶和塑料制品业	Rubber and Plastic Products Manufacturing	528 390		99.2
塑料制品业	Plastic Products Manufacturing	528 390		99.2

10－8 续表 4 Continued

计量单位:万元 （2017 年） (10 000 yuan)

指 标	Item	企业单位数（个） Number of Enterprises (unit)	# 亏损企业 Losses	工业总产值（当年价格） Gross Industrial Output Value (At Current Prices)
非金属矿物制品业	Nonmetal Mineral Products Manufacturing	135	24	1 783 552
水泥、石灰和石膏的制造	Cement, Lime and Gypsum Manufacturing	31	15	461 307
水泥及石膏制品制造	Lime and Gypsum Manufacturing	71	6	655 916
砖瓦、石材及其他建筑材料制造	Brick, Tile, Stone and Other Building Material Manufacturing	15		94 982
玻璃制造	Glass a Manufacturing	3		35 839
玻璃制品制造	Glass Producs Manufacturing	2	1	14 591
玻璃纤维和玻璃纤维增强塑料制品制造	Glass Fibre and Glass Fibre Plastic Producs Manufacturing	5	1	62 162
石墨及其他非金属矿物制品制造	Craphite and Other Nonmetal Mineral Products Manuracturing	8	1	458 754
黑色金属冶炼及压延加工业	Ferrous Metals Smelting and Rolling	10	2	454 011
黑色金属铸造	Ferrous Metals casting	1	1	2 902
钢压延加工	Steel Rolling	7	1	421 798
铁合金冶炼	Ferroalloy Smelting	2		29 312
有色金属冶炼及压延加工业	Nonferrous Metals Smelting and Rolling	20	2	4 261 028
常用有色金属冶炼	Common Nonferrous Metals Smelting	4	1	1 446 164
稀有稀土金属冶炼	Rare Metals and Rare Soil Smelting	9		644 652
有色金属合金制造	Nonferrous Metals Alloy Manuracturing	2	1	21 192
有色金属压延加工	Nonferrous Metals Rolling	5		2 149 020
金属制品业	Metal Product Manufacturing	18	4	180 095
结构性金属制品制造	Structural Metal Product Manufacturing	14	2	160 596
集装箱及金属包装容器制造	Container and Metal Packing Vessel Manufacturing	2	1	12 400
建筑、安全用金属制品制造	Construction and Safety Metal Manufacturing	1		3 413
其他金属制品制造	Other Metal Product Manufacturing	1	1	3 686
通用设备制造业	General Equipment Manufacturing	4		20 388
锅炉及原动设备制造	Boiler and Motivity Equipment Manufacturing	1		4 050
物料搬运设备制造	Handbarrow Equipment Manufacturing	1		3 186
烘炉、风机、衡器、包装等设备制造	Oven, Fan, Weighing Apparatus, Paking Equipment Manufacturing	2		13 152
专用设备制造业	Special Equipment Manufacturing	10		88 201
农、林、牧、渔专用机械制造	Special Machine Manufacturing for Farming, Forestry, Livestock and Fishing	9		82 806
环保、社会公共服务及其他专用设备制造	Environmental Protection, Social Public Service and Other Special Equipment Manufacturing	1		5 396
汽车制造业	Automobile Manufacturing	1		9 633
改装汽车制造	Modified Car Manufacturing	1		9 633
电气机械和器材制造业	Electric Machine and Equipment Manufacturing	7		259 216
电机制造	Motor Manufacturing	2		206 550
输配电及控制设备制造	Transmission Electric and Control Equipment Manufacturing	3		21 214
家用电力器具制造	Household Electric Appliances Manufacturing	1		24 228
照明器具制造	Lighting Apparatus Manufacturing	1		7 225
计算机、通信和其他电子设备制造业	Computer, Communicationn and other Electronic Equipment Manufacturing	2	1	29 953
电子器件制造	Electronic Device Manufacturing	1		25 066
电子元件制造	Electronic Component Manufacturing	1	1	4 887
仪器仪表制造业	Apparatus and Meter Manufacturing	1	1	5 115
通用仪器仪表制造	General Apparatus and Meter Manufacturing	1	1	5 115
废弃资源和废旧材料回收加工业	Abandon Resources and Discard Material Recovery Processing	4		13 032
金属废料和碎屑的加工处理	metal Waste Handle and Broken Bits Processing	2		8 507
非金属废料和碎屑的加工处理	Nonmetal Waste Handle and Broken Bits Processing	2		4 525
电力、热力、燃气及水生产和供应业	**Electricity, Heat, Gass and Water Production and Supply**	**110**	**25**	**2 316 611**
电力、热力生产和供应业	Electricity and Heat Production and Supply	95	21	2 130 598
电力生产	Electricity Production	79	17	1 752 349.6
电力供应	Electricity Supply	11	3	345 173.3
热力生产和供应	Heat Production and Supply	5	1	33 075
燃气生产和供应业	Gass Production and Supply	8	2	158 381.8
水的生产和供应业	Water Production and Supply	7	2	27 631.7
自来水生产和供应	Tap Water Production and Supply	6	2	23 435.6
污水处理及其再生利用	Wastewater Treatment and its Reuse	1		4 196.1

10—8续表5 Continued

计量单位:万元 (2017年) (10 000 yuan)

指 标	Item	工业销售产值(当年价格) Sale Value of Industry (At Current Prices)	# 出口交货值 Export Commodities	产销率(%) Ratio of Production & Marketing (%)
非金属矿物制品业	Nonmetal Mineral Products Manufacturing	1 728 810		96.9
水泥、石灰和石膏的制造	Cement, Lime and Gypsum Manufacturing	438 485		95.1
水泥及石膏制品制造	Lime and Gypsum Manufacturing	647 028		98.6
砖瓦、石材及其他建筑材料制造	Brick, Tile, Stone and Other Building Material Manufacturing	94 599		99.6
玻璃制造	Glass a Manufacturing	32 314		90.2
玻璃制品制造	Glass Producs Manufacturing	16 113		110.4
玻璃纤维和玻璃纤维增强塑料制品制造	Glass Fibre and Glass Fibre Plastic Producs Manufacturing	60 105		96.7
石墨及其他非金属矿物制品制造	Craphite and Other Nonmetal Mineral Products Manuracturing	440 168		95.9
黑色金属冶炼及压延加工业	Ferrous Metals Smelting and Rolling	470 103		103.5
黑色金属铸造	Ferrous Metals casting	3 100		106.8
钢压延加工	Steel Rolling	438 527		104.0
铁合金冶炼	Ferroalloy Smelting	28 477		97.2
有色金属冶炼及压延加工业	Nonferrous Metals Smelting and Rolling	4 238 126	176	99.5
常用有色金属冶炼	Common Nonferrous Metals Smelting	1 404 352		97.1
稀有稀土金属冶炼	Rare Metals and Rare Soil Smelting	642 396		99.6
有色金属合金制造	Nonferrous Metals Alloy Manuracturing	21 394		101.0
有色金属压延加工	Nonferrous Metals Rolling	2 169 984	176	101.0
金属制品业	Metal Product Manufacturing	170 131		94.5
结构性金属制品制造	Structural Metal Product Manufacturing	156 325		97.3
集装箱及金属包装容器制造	Container and Metal Packing Vessel Manufacturing	9 860		79.5
建筑、安全用金属制品制造	Construction and Safety Metal Manufacturing	361		10.6
其他金属制品制造	Other Metal Product Manufacturing	3 585		97.2
通用设备制造业	General Equipment Manufacturing	20 388		100.0
锅炉及原动设备制造	Boiler and Motivity Equipment Manufacturing	3 915		96.7
物料搬运设备制造	Handbarrow Equipment Manufacturing	3 321		104.2
烘炉、风机、衡器、包装等设备制造	Oven, Fan, Weighing Apparatus, Paking Equipment Manufacturing	13 152		100.0
专用设备制造业	Special Equipment Manufacturing	85 440		96.9
农、林、牧、渔专用机械制造	Special Machine Manufacturing for Farming, Forestry, Livestock and Fishing	80 517		97.2
环保、社会公共服务及其他专用设备制造	Environmental Protection, Social Public Service and Other Special Equipment Manufacturing	4 923		91.2
汽车制造业	Automobile Manufacturing	3 300		34.3
改装汽车制造	Modified Car Manufacturing	3 300		34.3
电气机械和器材制造业	Electric Machine and Equipment Manufacturing	252 805		97.5
电机制造	Motor Manufacturing	202 130		97.9
输配电及控制设备制造	Transmission Electric and Control Equipment Manufacturing	21 234		100.1
家用电力器具制造	Household Electric Appliances Manufacturing	22 353		92.3
照明器具制造	Lighting Apparatus Manufacturing	7 088		98.1
计算机、通信和其他电子设备制造业	Computer, Communicationn and other Electronic Equipment Manufacturing	27 026		90.2
电子器件制造	Electronic Device Manufacturing	23 629		94.3
电子元件制造	Electronic Component Manufacturing	3 397		69.5
仪器仪表制造业	Apparatus and Meter Manufacturing	5 307		103.8
通用仪器仪表制造	General Apparatus and Meter Manufacturing	5 307		103.8
废弃资源和废旧材料回收加工业	Abandon Resources and Discard Material Recovery Processing	13 772		105.7
金属废料和碎屑的加工处理	metal Waste Handle and Broken Bits Processing	9 289		109.2
非金属废料和碎屑的加工处理	Nonmetal Waste Handle and Broken Bits Processing	4 483		99.1
电力、热力、燃气及水生产和供应业	**Electricity, Heat, Gass and Water Production and Supply**	**2 296 936**		**99.2**
电力、热力生产和供应业	Electricity and Heat Production and Supply	2 104 446		98.8
电力生产	Electricity Production	1 734 793.4		99.0
电力供应	Electricity Supply	341 017.3		98.8
热力生产和供应	Heat Production and Supply	28 634.9		86.6
燃气生产和供应业	Gass Production and Supply	164 806.2		104.1
水的生产和供应业	Water Production and Supply	27 684.6		100.2
自来水生产和供应	Tap Water Production and Supply	23 488.5		100.2
污水处理及其再生利用	Wastewater Treatment and its Reuse	4 196.1		100.0

10－9 各师规模以上工业企业单位数

Number of Industrial Enterprises above Designated Size by Division

计量单位:个 （2017 年） （unit）

指 标	Item	合 计 Total	一 师 Division 1	二 师 Division 2
总 计	**Total**	**886**	**167**	**82**
# 国有控股企业	State-controlled Shareholding Enterprises	289	45	24
按登记注册类型分	**Grouped by Status of Registration**			
内资企业	Domestic Enterprises	866	165	82
国有企业	State-owned Enterprises	20		1
股份合作企业	Share Cooperative Enterprises	1		
有限责任公司	Limited Liability Corporations	341	53	31
国有独资公司	State-owned Corporations with Private-Funds	53	4	2
其他有限责任公司	Other Limited Liability Corporations	288	49	29
股份有限公司	Share-holding Corporations Ltd.	25	2	1
私营企业	Private Enterprises	452	90	49
私营独资企业	Private-funded Enterprises	1		
私营有限责任公司	Private Limited Liability Corporations	430	90	48
私营股份有限公司	Private Share-holding Corporations Ltd.	21		1
其他企业	Other Enterprises	27	20	
港、澳、台商投资企业	Enterprises with Funds from Hong Kong,Macao and Taiwan	5	1	
合资经营企业(港或澳、台)	Joint-Venture Enterprises(with funds from Hong Kong,Macao and Taiwan)	1		
港、澳、台商独资经营企业	Enterprises with Funds from Hong Kong,Macao and Taiwan	2	1	
港澳台商投资股份有限公司	Share-holding Corporations Ltd. with Funds from Hong Kong,Macao and Taiwan	1		
其他港澳台商投资企业	Others	1		
外商投资企业	Foreign Funded Enterprises	15	1	
中外合资经营企业	Joint-Venture Enterprises	11	1	
中外合作经营企业	Cooperative Enterprises	1		
外资企业	Foreign Funded Enterprises	3		
按轻重工业分	**Grouped by Light & Heavy Industry**			
轻工业	Light Industry	462	120	52
重工业	Heavy Industry	424	47	30
按企业规模分	**Grouped by Size of Enterprises**			
大型企业	Large-Scale Enterprises	21	3	
中型企业	Medium-Scale Enterprises	90	10	9
小型企业	Small-Scale Enterprises	662	140	67
微型企业	Mini Enterprises	113	14	6
按工业行业分	**Grouped by Sector**			
采矿业	**Mining**	**30**	**1**	**4**
煤炭开采和洗选业	Coal Mining and Dressing	17	1	1
烟煤和无烟煤的开采洗选	Soft Coal and Hard Coal Mining and Dressing	17	1	1
黑色金属矿采选业	Ferrous Metals Mining and Dressing	6		
铁矿采选	Prdding Mining and Dressing	6		
有色金属矿采选业	Nonferrous Metals Mining and Dressing	2		
常用有色金属矿采选	Common Nonferrous Metals Mining and Dressing	2		
非金属矿采选业	Nonmetal Mineral Mining and Dressing	5		3
土砂石开采	Soil Sand Mining	2		1
石棉及其他非金属矿采选	Asbestos and Other Nonmetal Minerals Mining and Dressing	3		2
制造业	**Manufacturing**	**746**	**159**	**70**
农副食品加工业	Farm and Sideline Food Processing	227	90	19
谷物磨制	Cereal Grain Grinding	25	5	1
饲料加工	Forage Processing	32	3	2
植物油加工	Plant Oil Processing	39	14	1
制糖	Sugar Making	4		1
屠宰及肉类加工	Slaughtering and Meat Processing	11		1
蔬菜、水果和坚果加工	Vegetable,Fruit and Nuts Processing	88	67	6
其他农副食品加工	Other Farm and Sideline Food Processing	28	1	7

10—9 续表 1

计量单位:个　　　　　　　　　　　　　　　　　　　　　　　　　　　　　　(2017 年)

指　　标	Item	三　师 Division 3	四　师 Division 4	五　师 Division 5
总　　计	**Total**	**69**	**81**	**28**
# 国有控股企业	State-controlled Shareholding Enterprises	21	32	13
按登记注册类型分	**Grouped by Status of Registration**			
内资企业	Domestic Enterprises	68	80	28
国有企业	State-owned Enterprises	3	2	1
股份合作企业	Share Cooperative Enterprises			1
有限责任公司	Limited Liability Corporations	18	25	16
国有独资公司	State-owned Corporations with Private-Funds	5	3	2
其他有限责任公司	Other Limited Liability Corporations	13	22	14
股份有限公司	Share-holding Corporations Ltd.	4	5	1
私营企业	Private Enterprises	41	47	8
私营独资企业	Private-funded Enterprises			
私营有限责任公司	Private Limited Liability Corporations	41	38	8
私营股份有限公司	Private Share-holding Corporations Ltd.		9	
其他企业	Other Enterprises	2	1	1
港、澳、台商投资企业	Enterprises with Funds from Hong Kong,Macao and Taiwan			
合资经营企业(港或澳、台)	Joint-Venture Enterprises(with funds from Hong Kong,Macao and Taiwan)			
港、澳、台商独资经营企业	Enterprises with Funds from Hong Kong,Macao and Taiwan			
港澳台商投资股份有限公司	Share-holding Corporations Ltd. with Funds from Hong Kong,Macao and Taiwan			
其他港澳台商投资企业	Others			
外商投资企业	Foreign Funded Enterprises	1	1	
中外合资经营企业	Joint-Venture Enterprises	1	1	
中外合作经营企业	Cooperative Enterprises			
外资企业	Foreign Funded Enterprises			
按轻重工业分	**Grouped by Light & Heavy Industry**			
轻工业	Light Industry	37	40	17
重工业	Heavy Industry	32	41	11
按企业规模分	**Grouped by Size of Enterprises**			
大型企业	Large-Scale Enterprises	2	3	
中型企业	Medium-Scale Enterprises	3	6	2
小型企业	Small-Scale Enterprises	54	66	21
微型企业	Mini Enterprises	10	6	5
按工业行业分	**Grouped by Sector**			
采矿业	**Mining**		**3**	**1**
煤炭开采和洗选业	Coal Mining and Dressing		3	
烟煤和无烟煤的开采洗选	Soft Coal and Hard Coal Mining and Dressing		3	
黑色金属矿采选业	Ferrous Metals Mining and Dressing			1
铁矿采选	Prdding Mining and Dressing			1
有色金属矿采选业	Nonferrous Metals Mining and Dressing			
常用有色金属矿采选	Common Nonferrous Metals Mining and Dressing			
非金属矿采选业	Nonmetal Mineral Mining and Dressing			
土砂石开采	Soil Sand Mining			
石棉及其他非金属矿采选	Asbestos and Other Nonmetal Minerals Mining and Dressing			
制造业	**Manufacturing**	**54**	**69**	**24**
农副食品加工业	Farm and Sideline Food Processing	16	18	9
谷物磨制	Cereal Grain Grinding	6	7	
饲料加工	Forage Processing	6	1	4
植物油加工	Plant Oil Processing		3	3
制糖	Sugar Making		1	
屠宰及肉类加工	Slaughtering and Meat Processing			
蔬菜、水果和坚果加工	Vegetable,Fruit and Nuts Processing	4		1
其他农副食品加工	Other Farm and Sideline Food Processing		6	1

Continued

(unit)

六　师 Division 6	七　师 Division 7	八　师 Division 8	九　师 Division 9	十　师 Division 10	十一师 Division 11	十二师 Division 12	十三师 Division 13	十四师 Division 14	兵团直属 Directly under XPCC
78	**64**	**131**	**10**	**37**	**13**	**23**	**86**	**7**	**10**
20	23	45	4	9	8	15	16	4	10
75	63	122	10	35	13	22	86	7	10
4	2	3		1		1	1		1
38	26	57	8	14	8	16	20	4	7
4	7	12	4	3	1		6		
34	19	45	4	11	7	16	14	4	7
2		6		1		1		1	1
31	35	56	2	19	5	4	62	2	1
		1							
29	35	48	2	18	5	4	61	2	1
2		7		1			1		
							3		
1	1	1		1					
	1								
		1							
1									
				1					
2		8		1		1			
1		6		1					
						1			
1		2							
37	24	68	6	24		9	15	3	10
41	40	63	4	13	13	14	71	4	
3	1	9							
9	10	24	2	3	1	4	3		4
54	46	78	7	31	12	14	59	7	6
12	7	20	1	3		5	24		
3	**2**	**3**		**2**		**1**	**10**		
3	2	3		1		1	2		
3	2	3		1		1	2		
							5		
							5		
							2		
							2		
				1			1		
				1					
							1		
62	**54**	**117**	**7**	**32**	**13**	**19**	**50**	**6**	**10**
8	7	16	4	17		5	8	2	8
1		2	1	1		1			
1	3	4		1		1			6
2	3	7	1	2			2		1
	1		1						
1		3	1	1		1	2		1
1				1		2	4	2	
2				11					

10—9 续表 2

计量单位:个 (2017 年)

指 标	Item	合 计 Total	一 师 Division 1	二 师 Division 2	三 师 Division 3	四 师 Division 4
食品制造业	Food Manufacturing	53	3	12		1
焙烤食品制造	Bakery Products Manufacturing	1				
方便食品制造	Convenient Food Manufacturing	4				
乳制品制造	Milk and Dairy Products Manufacturing	8	1			
罐头食品制造	Canned Food Manufacturing	24		7		
调味品、发酵制品制造	Condiment and Fermented Products Manufacturing	8				1
其他食品制造	Other Food Manufacturing	8	2	5		
酒、饮料和精制茶制造业	Liquor Brewing,Beverage and Refined Tea Processing	32	2	2	2	12
酒的制造	Liquor Brewing	24	2	2	1	10
软饮料制造	Soft Beverage Manufacturing	8			1	2
纺织业	Textile Industry	53	9	4	6	1
棉纺织及印染精加工	Cotton Textile,Dying and Finishing Fine Processing	46	8	3	5	
毛纺织和染整精加工	Woolen Textile,Dying and Finishing Fine Processing	2				
麻纺织及染整精加工	Homp Crops Textile,Dying and Finishing Fine Processing	1				1
针织或钩针编织物及其制品制造	Knitting or Crochet and Related Goods Manufacturing	1	1			
家用纺织制成品制造	Textile Products Manufacturing for Home	2		1		
非家用纺织制成品制造	Non-Textile Products Manufacturing for Home	1			1	
纺织服装、服饰业	Textile Clothing and Habilatory Manufacturing	2			1	
机织服装制造	Woven Garment Manufacturing	1			1	
针织或钩针编织服装制造	Knitting or Crochet Clothing Manufacturing	1				
皮革、毛皮、羽毛及其制品和制鞋业	Leather,Fur,Feather and Related Goods Manufacturing]]	2		1		
毛皮鞣制及制品加工	Fur Tanning and Product Processing	1				
羽毛(绒)加工及制品制造	Feather(eiderdown)Processing and Related Goods Manufacturing	1		1		
木材加工和木、竹、藤、棕、草制品业	Wood Processing and Wood、Bamboo、Cane、Grass Products	7	2	1		2
木材加工	Wood Processing	3				1
人造板制造	Artificial Board Manufacturing	4	2	1		1
家具制造业	Furniture Manufacturing	2				
木质家具制造	Woodiness Furniture Manufacturing	2				
造纸及纸制品业	Paper Making and Paper Products	7	2	3		
造 纸	Paper Making	4	1	1		
纸制品制造	Paper Products Manufacturing	3	1	2		
印刷业和记录媒介的复制	Printing Industry and Recording Media	5				2
印 刷	Printing	5				2
文教、工美、体育和娱乐用品制造业	Culture and Education, Handicraft,Athletics and Amusement Things Manufacturing	3		1		
工艺美术品制造	Handicraft Manufacturing	3		1		
石油加工、炼焦及核燃料加工业	Petroleum Processing, Coking and Nuclear Material Processing	16		1		
精炼石油产品制造	Refined Petroleum Products Manufacturing	7		1		
炼 焦	Coking	9				
化学原料及化学制品制造业	Chemical Materials and Chemical Products Manufacturing	54	14	6	2	6
基础化学原料制造	Basic Chemical Materials Manufacturing	5				
肥料制造	Fertilizer Manufacturing	33	14	5	2	2
合成材料制造	Synthesize Material Manufacturing	6				1
专用化学产品制造	Special Chemical Products Manufacturing	8		1		1
日用化学产品制造	Daily Chemical Products Manufacturing	2				2
医药制造业	Pharmaceuticals Manufacturing	8	1	2	1	
化学药品制剂制造	Chemical Pharmaceutical Original Medicine Manufacturing	1		1		
中药饮片加工	Chemical Pharmaceutical Manufacturing	1				
中成药生产	Chinese Medicine Production	3	1	1	1	
兽用药品制造	Chinese Patent Drugs Troche Processing	1				
生物药品制造	Biopharmaceutical Manufacturing	1				
卫生材料及医药用品制造	Chinese Patent Drugs Manufacturing	1				
化学纤维制造业	Chemical Fibre Manufacturing	4	3		1	
纤维素纤维原料及纤维制造	Cellulose Material and Fibre Manufacturing	4	3		1	
橡胶和塑料制品业	Rubber and Plastic Products Manufacturing	59	10	8	10	2
塑料制品业	Plastic Products Manufacturing	59	10	8	10	2

Continued

(unit)

五　师 Division 5	六　师 Division 6	七　师 Division 7	八　师 Division 8	九　师 Division 9	十　师 Division 10	十一师 Division 11	十二师 Division 12	十三师 Division 13	十四师 Division 14	兵团直属 Directly under XPCC
1	11	7	14	2			2			
			1							
		1	3							
		1	4				2			
1	6	4	5	1						
	4	1	1	1						
	1									
	2	1	10		1					
	1	1	6		1					
	1		4							
1	6	4	18		1			3		
1	6	4	16					3		
			1		1					
			1							
							1			
							1			
1										
1										
			2							
			2							
			1					1		
			1					1		
	2									
	2									
			1						1	1
			1						1	1
	2									
	2									
	3	3					1	8		
	2	3					1			
	1							8		
1	3	7	12		1	1		1		
		2	1			1		1		
1	2	2	4		1					
			5							
	1	3	2							
			2				1			1
							1			
			1							
										1
			1							
5	6	5	5		5			3		
5	6	5	5		5			3		

10—9 续表 3

计量单位:个　　　　　　　　　　　　　　　　　　　　　　　　　　　　(2017 年)

指　　标	Item	合　计 Total	一　师 Division 1	二　师 Division 2	三　师 Division 3	四　师 Division 4
非金属矿物制品业	Nonmetal Mineral Products Manufacturing	135	15	6	14	16
水泥、石灰和石膏的制造	Cement, Lime and Gypsum Manufacturing	31	7	1	1	6
水泥及石膏制品制造	Lime and Gypsum Manufacturing	71	5	5	13	7
砖瓦、石材及其他建筑材料制造	Brick, Tile, Stone and Other Building Material Manufacturing	15	1			2
玻璃制造	Glass a Manufacturing	3				
玻璃制品制造	Glass Producs Manufacturing	2				1
玻璃纤维和玻璃纤维增强塑料制品制造	Glass Fibre and Glass Fibre Plastic Producs Manufacturing	5	1			
石墨及其他非金属矿物制品制造	Craphite and Other Nonmetal Mineral Products Manuracturing	8	1			
黑色金属冶炼及压延加工业	Ferrous Metals Smelting and Rolling	10	1			
黑色金属铸造	Ferrous Metals casting	1				
钢压延加工	Steel Rolling	7	1			
铁合金冶炼	Ferroalloy Smelting	2				
有色金属冶炼及压延加工业	Nonferrous Metals Smelting and Rolling	20	1			7
常用有色金属冶炼	Common Nonferrous Metals Smelting	4	1			
稀有稀土金属冶炼	Rare Metals and Rare Soil Smelting	9				7
有色金属合金制造	Nonferrous Metals Alloy Manuracturing	2				
有色金属压延加工	Nonferrous Metals Rolling	5				
金属制品业	Metal Product Manufacturing	18	1	2		2
结构性金属制品制造	Structural Metal Product Manufacturing	14	1	2		
集装箱及金属包装容器制造	Container and Metal Packing Vessel Manufacturing	2				1
建筑、安全用金属制品制造	Construction and Safety Metal Manufacturing	1				1
其他金属制品制造	Other Metal Product Manufacturing	1				
通用设备制造业	General Equipment Manufacturing	4				
锅炉及原动设备制造	Boiler and Motivity Equipment Manufacturing	1				
物料搬运设备制造	Handbarrow Equipment Manufacturing	1				
烘炉、风机、衡器、包装等设备制造	Oven, Fan, Weighing Apparatus, Paking Equipment Manufacturing	2				
专用设备制造业	Special Equipment Manufacturing	10	3	1		
农、林、牧、渔专用机械制造	Special Machine Manufacturing for Farming, Forestry, Livestock and Fishing	9	3	1		
环保、社会公共服务及其他专用设备制造	Environmental Protection, Social Public Service and Other Special Equipment Manufacturing	1				
汽车制造业	Automobile Manufacturing	1				
改装汽车制造	Modified Car Manufacturing	1				
电气机械和器材制造业	Electric Machine and Equipment Manufacturing	7	2	1		
电机制造	Motor Manufacturing	2				
输配电及控制设备制造	Transmission Electric and Control Equipment Manufacturing	3		1		
家用电力器具制造	Household Electric Appliances Manufacturing	1	1			
照明器具制造	Lighting Apparatus Manufacturing	1	1			
计算机、通信和其他电子设备制造业	Computer, Communicationn and other Electronic Equipment Manufacturing	2			1	
电子器件制造	Biopharmaceutical Manufacturing	1			1	
电子元件制造	Electronic Component Manufacturing	1				
仪器仪表制造业	Apparatus and Meter Manufacturing	1				
通用仪器仪表制造	General Apparatus and Meter Manufacturing	1				
废弃资源和废旧材料回收加工业	Abandon Resources and Discard Material Recovery Processing	4				
金属废料和碎屑的加工处理	metal Waste Handle and Broken Bits Processing	2				
非金属废料和碎屑的加工处理	Nonmetal Waste Handle and Broken Bits Processing	2				
电力、热力、燃气及水生产和供应业	**Electricity, Heat, Gass and Water Production and Supply**	**110**	**7**	**8**	**15**	**9**
电力、热力生产和供应业	Electricity and Heat Production and Supply	95	4	6	13	9
电力生产	Electricity Production	79	3	5	12	8
电力供应	Electricity Supply	11	1	1	1	1
热力生产和供应	Heat Production and Supply	5				
燃气生产和供应业	Gass Production and Supply	8	1	2	1	
水的生产和供应业	Water Production and Supply	7	2		1	
自来水生产和供应	Tap Water Production and Supply	6	1		1	
污水处理及其再生利用	Wastewater Treatment and its Reuse	1	1			

Continued

(unit)

五 师 Division 5	六 师 Division 6	七 师 Division 7	八 师 Division 8	九 师 Division 9	十 师 Division 10	十一师 Division 11	十二师 Division 12	十三师 Division 13	十四师 Division 14	兵团直属 Directly under XPCC
5	12	8	25	1	5	8	1	16	3	
1	1	1	10		1	1		1		
2	6	5	7		3	6	1	10	1	
1	3	1	3					3	1	
1					1	1				
			1							
				1				2	1	
	2	1	4							
	1	3	2		1		1	1		
		1								
	1	1	1		1		1	1		
		1	1							
	3	2	4					3		
			1					2		
			2							
	1							1		
	2	2	1							
		2	3		1	4	1	2		
		2	1		1	4	1	2		
			1							
			1							
							3	1		
							1			
							1			
							1	1		
	2	3	1							
	1	3	1							
	1									
1										
1										
							1	3		
								2		
							1	1		
			1							
			1							
							1			
							1			
	1	2					1			
	1						1			
		2								
3	**13**	**8**	**11**	**3**	**3**		**3**	**26**	**1**	
3	12	7	8	3	2		2	25	1	
2	6	7	7	2	2		1	24		
1	3		1	1					1	
	3						1	1		
	1		2					1		
		1	1		1		1			
		1	1		1		1			

10—10 各师规模以上工业企业总产值

计量单位:万元 (2017 年)

指 标	Item	合 计 Total	一 师 Division 1	二 师 Division 2	三 师 Division 3	四 师 Division 4
总 计	**Total**	**20 620 581**	**2 306 634**	**1 434 184**	**1 141 326**	**1 545 502**
# 国有控股企业	State-controlled Shareholding Enterprises	6 875 743	904 525	337 137	547 706	649 332
按登记注册类型分	**Grouped by Status of Registration**					
内资企业	Domestic Enterprises	20 155 651	2 275 693	1 434 184	1 135 729	1 531 548
国有企业	State-owned Enterprises	194 533		16 865	42 054	8 954
股份合作企业	Share Cooperative Enterprises	3 507				
有限责任公司	Limited Liability Corporations	9 954 258	1 023 502	470 394	343 113	431 240
国有独资公司	State-owned Corporations with Private-Funds	825 067	56 535	24 795	83 474	97 584
其他有限责任公司	Other Limited Liability Corporations	9 129 191	966 967	445 599	259 639	333 656
股份有限公司	Share-holding Corporations Ltd.	1 285 152	34 395	22 601	208 540	209 138
私营企业	Private Enterprises	8 456 296	1 042 499	924 324	511 191	875 278
私营独资企业	Private-funded Enterprises	3 226				
私营有限责任公司	Private Limited Liability Corporations	8 122 074	1 042 499	872 682	511 191	690 004
私营股份有限公司	Private Share-holding Corporations Ltd.	330 995		51 642		185 274
其他企业	Other Enterprises	261 905	175 298		30 831	6 938
港、澳、台商投资企业	Enterprises with Funds from Hong Kong,Macao and Taiwan	58 564	18 030			
合资经营企业(港或澳、台)	Joint-Venture Enterprises(with funds from Hong Kong,Macao and Taiwan)	14 509				
港、澳、台商独资经营企业	Enterprises with Funds from Hong Kong,Macao and Taiwan	35 397	18 030			
港澳台商投资股份有限公司	Share-holding Corporations Ltd. with Funds from Hong Kong,Macao and Taiwan	3 747				
其他港澳台商投资企业	Others	4 911				
外商投资企业	Foreign Funded Enterprises	406 367	12 911		5 597	13 955
中外合资经营企业	Joint-Venture Enterprises	344 904	12 911		5 597	13 955
中外合作经营企业	Cooperative Enterprises	33 744				
外资企业	Foreign Funded Enterprises	27 719				
按轻重工业分	**Grouped by Light & Heavy Industry**					
轻工业	Light Industry	7 704 503	1 639 401	1 039 900	807 988	805 559
重工业	Heavy Industry	12 916 078	667 233	394 284	333 338	739 944
按企业规模分	**Grouped by Size of Enterprises**					
大型企业	Large-Scale Enterprises	7 250 268	228 141		149 148	328 716
中型企业	Medium-Scale Enterprises	4 435 581	299 022	411 716	115 162	217 601
小型企业	Small-Scale Enterprises	8 235 495	1 654 910	933 900	842 231	945 205
微型企业	Mini Enterprises	699 237	124 561	88 569	34 784	53 981
按工业行业分	**Grouped by Sector**					
采矿业	**Mining**	**414 513**	**33 248**	**53 412**		**28 037**
煤炭开采和洗选业	Coal Mining and Dressing	187 127	33 248	29 127		28 037
烟煤和无烟煤的开采洗选	Soft Coal and Hard Coal Mining and Dressing	187 127	33 248	29 127		28 037
黑色金属矿采选业	Ferrous Metals Mining and Dressing	163 877				
铁矿采选	Prdding Mining and Dressing	163 877				
有色金属矿采选业	Nonferrous Metals Mining and Dressing	8 707				
常用有色金属矿采选	Common Nonferrous Metals Mining and Dressing	8 707				
非金属矿采选业	Nonmetal Mineral Mining and Dressing	54 802		24 285		
土砂石开采	Soil Sand Mining	7 031		2 357		
石棉及其他非金属矿采选	Asbestos and Other Nonmetal Minerals Mining and Dressing	47 771		21 929		
制造业	**Manufacturing**	**17 889 456**	**2 077 827**	**1 297 956**	**1 014 894**	**1 367 544**
农副食品加工业	Farm and Sideline Food Processing	3 382 946	967 042	476 388	385 589	331 215
谷物磨制	Cereal Grain Grinding	278 687	56 189	7 329	86 656	71 955
饲料加工	Forage Processing	737 258	13 788	119 509	134 296	20 275
植物油加工	Plant Oil Processing	509 936	184 839	17 145		75 892
制糖	Sugar Making	117 554		35 360		27 152
屠宰及肉类加工	Slaughtering and Meat Processing	168 437		15 964		
蔬菜、水果和坚果加工	Vegetable,Fruit and Nuts Processing	1 139 511	708 026	159 482	164 637	
其他农副食品加工	Other Farm and Sideline Food Processing	431 563	4 200	121 600		135 941

Total Output Value of Industrial Enterprise above Designated Size by Division

(10 000 yuan)

五 师 Division 5	六 师 Division 6	七 师 Division 7	八 师 Division 8	九 师 Division 9	十 师 Division 10	十一师 Division 11	十二师 Division 12	十三师 Division 13	十四师 Division 14	兵团直属 Directly under XPCC
252 187	**4 036 177**	**909 309**	**5 814 300**	**112 373**	**327 198**	**227 083**	**314 509**	**1 762 254**	**41 443**	**396 102**
104 315	280 051	433 945	2 497 973	71 870	102 892	153 907	212 631	154 338	29 020	396 102
252 187	4 012 765	894 800	5 478 453	112 373	320 274	227 083	280 764	1 762 254	41 443	396 102
23 551	28 572	17 005	11 932		2 032		14 529	25 843		3 196
3 507										
120 316	3 740 665	499 120	2 323 025	102 872	176 688	153 907	118 508	181 593	24 752	244 563
12 836	59 280	99 952	207 311	71 870	43 431	14 810		53 191		
107 480	3 681 385	399 169	2 115 714	31 002	133 258	139 097	118 508	128 402	24 752	244 563
6 075	17 904		592 720		4 234		117 192		6 375	65 980
82 658	225 625	378 675	2 550 775	9 501	137 320	73 177	30 535	1 522 061	10 315	82 363
			3 226							
82 658	212 857	378 675	2 483 671	9 501	134 639	73 177	30 535	1 507 308	10 315	82 363
	12 767		63 878		2 681			14 753		
16 081								32 758		
	3 747	14 509	17 366		4 911					
		14 509								
			17 366							
	3 747									
					4 911					
	19 665		318 481		2 014		33 744			
	14 404		296 023		2 014					
							33 744			
	5 261		22 457							
130 073	728 794	332 792	1 074 908	89 483	236 962		218 327	181 570	22 644	396 102
122 115	3 307 383	576 517	4 739 392	22 890	90 237	227 083	96 182	1 580 684	18 799	
	2 537 414	58 514	3 948 335							
35 546	1 079 619	398 121	980 496	47 180	54 927	28 989	173 785	304 424		288 994
200 104	360 877	431 491	826 329	62 697	263 172	198 094	83 644	1 284 291	41 443	107 108
16 538	58 267	21 183	59 141	2 496	9 099		57 079	173 539		
26 898	**34 007**	**12 397**	**19 829**		**18 006**		**5 615**	**183 065**		
	34 007	12 397	19 829		13 332		5 615	11 536		
	34 007	12 397	19 829		13 332		5 615	11 536		
26 898								136 979		
26 898								136 979		
								8 707		
								8 707		
					4 674			25 843		
					4 674					
								25 843		
178 249	**3 518 941**	**776 804**	**5 000 159**	**96 487**	**273 175**	**227 083**	**284 227**	**1 344 943**	**35 067**	**396 102**
72 464	67 432	95 661	209 469	71 212	183 435		75 744	99 085	21 284	326 926
	2 120		27 630	13 459	2 785		10 564			
41 095	10 412	35 695	82 512		10 358		33 744			235 574
16 691	17 686	44 523	83 918	10 573	8 890			12 809		36 971
		15 444		39 600						
	13 414		15 409	7 580	11 232		25 551	24 905		54 382
3 253	13 560				2 014		5 885	61 371	21 284	
11 426	10 240				148 156					

10—10 续表 1

计量单位:个　　　　　　　　　　　　　　　　　　　　　　　　　　　　(2017 年)

指　　标	Item	合　计 Total	一　师 Division 1	二　师 Division 2	三　师 Division 3	四　师 Division 4
食品制造业	Food Manufacturing	1 188 439	55 933	217 873		13 955
焙烤食品制造	Bakery Products Manufacturing	3 371				
方便食品制造	Convenient Food Manufacturing	40 634				
乳制品制造	Milk and Dairy Products Manufacturing	246 271	26 643			
罐头食品制造	Canned Food Manufacturing	313 119		111 633		
调味品、发酵制品制造	Condiment and Fermented Products Manufacturing	446 873				13 955
其他食品制造	Other Food Manufacturing	138 172	29 291	106 240		
酒、饮料和精制茶制造业	Liquor Brewing,Beverage and Refined Tea Processing	630 042	13 985	30 255	75 185	385 525
酒的制造	Liquor Brewing	525 485	13 985	30 255	20 635	380 453
软饮料制造	Soft Beverage Manufacturing	104 557			54 550	5 072
纺织业	Textile Industry	1 457 724	327 914	157 866	169 162	20 166
棉纺织及印染精加工	Cotton Textile,Dying and Finishing Fine Processing	1 321 428	267 428	151 233	153 419	
毛纺织和染整精加工	Woolen Textile,Dying and Finishing Fine Processing	27 371				
麻纺织及染整精加工	Homp Crops Textile,Dying and Finishing Fine Processing	20 166				20 166
针织或钩针编织物及其制品制造	Knitting or Crochet and Related Goods Manufacturing	60 486	60 486			
家用纺织制成品制造	Textile Products Manufacturing for Home	12 530		6 633		
非家用纺织制成品制造	Non-Textile Products Manufacturing for Home	15 744			15 744	
纺织服装、服饰业	Textile Clothing and Habilatory Manufacturing	22 537			17 966	
机织服装制造	Woven Garment Manufacturing	17 966			17 966	
针织或钩针编织服装制造	Knitting or Crochet Clothing Manufacturing	4 570				
皮革、毛皮、羽毛及其制品和制鞋业	Leather,Fur,Feather and Related Goods Manufacturing]]	15 902		9 043		
毛皮鞣制及制品加工	Fur Tanning and Product Processing	6 859				
羽毛(绒)加工及制品制造	Feather(eiderdown)Processing and Related Goods Manufacturing	9 043		9 043		
木材加工和木、竹、藤、棕、草制品业	Wood Processing and Wood,Bamboo,Cane,Grass Products	52 326	11 506	7 820		27 588
木材加工	Wood Processing	19 770				14 358
人造板制造	Artificial Board Manufacturing	32 556	11 506	7 820		13 230
家具制造业	Furniture Manufacturing	12 624				
木质家具制造	Woodiness Furniture Manufacturing	12 624				
造纸及纸制品业	Paper Making and Paper Products	58 036	14 692	38 723		
造　纸	Paper Making	24 942	11 692	8 629		
纸制品制造	Paper Products Manufacturing	33 094	3 000	30 094		
印刷业和记录媒介的复制	Printing Industry and Recording Media	13 532				7 081
印　刷	Printing	13 532				7 081
文教、工美、体育和娱乐用品制造业	Culture and Education, Handicraft,Athletics and Amusement Things Manufacturing	17 717		7 152		
工艺美术品制造	Handicraft Manufacturing	17 717		7 152		
石油加工、炼焦及核燃料加工业	Petroleum Processing, Coking and Nuclear Material Processing	671 487		9 075		
精炼石油产品制造	Refined Petroleum Products Manufacturing	150 423		9 075		
炼　焦	Coking	521 064				
化学原料及化学制品制造业	Chemical Materials and Chemical Products Manufacturing	2 393 599	171 533	128 096	30 298	158 073
基础化学原料制造	Basic Chemical Materials Manufacturing	94 246				
肥料制造	Fertilizer Manufacturing	497 078	171 533	118 975	30 298	26 500
合成材料制造	Synthesize Material Manufacturing	1 468 820				70 020
专用化学产品制造	Special Chemical Products Manufacturing	314 775		9 122		42 873
日用化学产品制造	Daily Chemical Products Manufacturing	18 680				18 680
医药制造业	Pharmaceuticals Manufacturing	147 508	7 360	28 289	20 425	
化学药品制剂制造	Chemical Pharmaceutical Original Medicine Manufacturing	22 601		22 601		
中药饮片加工	Chemical Pharmaceutical Manufacturing	6 292				
中成药生产	Chinese Medicine Production	33 473	7 360	5 688	20 425	
兽用药品制造	Chinese Patent Drugs Troche Processing	13 594				
生物药品制造	Biopharmaceutical Manufacturing	65 980				
卫生材料及医药用品制造	Chinese Patent Drugs Manufacturing	5 569				
化学纤维制造业	Chemical Fibre Manufacturing	188 017	130 339		57 678	
纤维素纤维原料及纤维制造	Cellulose Material and Fibre Manufacturing	188 017	130 339		57 678	
橡胶和塑料制品业	Rubber and Plastic Products Manufacturing	532 795	122 135	74 311	81 983	20 575
塑料制品业	Plastic Products Manufacturing	532 795	122 135	74 311	81 983	20 575

Continued

(unit)

五 师 Division 5	六 师 Division 6	七 师 Division 7	八 师 Division 8	九 师 Division 9	十 师 Division 10	十一师 Division 11	十二师 Division 12	十三师 Division 13	十四师 Division 14	兵团直属 Directly under XPCC
276	531 040	58 215	161 155	18 271			131 721			
			3 371							
		2 436	38 198							
		1 490	86 417				131 721			
276	108 720	52 157	26 463	13 871						
	419 679	2 133	6 706	4 400						
	2 641									
	4 254	7 429	97 806		15 603					
	1 548	7 429	55 576		15 603					
	2 706		42 229							
11 995	73 516	159 368	508 562		2 681			26 495		
11 995	73 516	159 368	477 975					26 495		
			24 690		2 681					
			5 897							
							4 570			
							4 570			
6 859										
6 859										
			5 412							
			5 412							
			4 287					8 337		
			4 287					8 337		
	4 622									
	4 622									
			1 895						1 360	3 196
			1 895						1 360	3 196
	10 565									
	10 565									
	127 301	67 568					7 311	460 232		
	66 469	67 568					7 311			
	60 832							460 232		
6 736	17 397	188 762	1 675 821		4 368	6 402		6 113		
		49 466	32 266			6 402		6 113		
6 736	13 089	111 225	14 354		4 368					
			1 398 800							
	4 308	28 070	230 402							
			19 163				6 292			65 980
							6 292			
			13 594							
										65 980
			5 569							
38 479	37 366	12 119	62 931		35 242			47 653		
38 479	37 366	12 119	62 931		35 242			47 653		

10—10 续表 2

计量单位:个　　　　　　　　　　　　　　　　　　　　　　　　　　　　　　　　　　　　　(2017 年)

指　标	Item	合　计 Total	一　师 Division 1	二　师 Division 2	三　师 Division 3	四　师 Division 4
非金属矿物制品业	Nonmetal Mineral Products Manufacturing	1 783 552	186 381	53 280	151 542	155 698
水泥、石灰和石膏的制造	Cement, Lime and Gypsum Manufacturing	461 307	126 322	11 092	11 806	54 769
水泥及石膏制品制造	Lime and Gypsum Manufacturing	655 916	46 948	42 188	139 736	64 733
砖瓦、石材及其他建筑材料制造	Brick, Tile, Stone and Other Building Material Manufacturing	94 982	6 496			31 245
玻璃制造	Glass a Manufacturing	35 839				
玻璃制品制造	Glass Producs Manufacturing	14 591				4 950
玻璃纤维和玻璃纤维增强塑料制品制造	Glass Fibre and Glass Fibre Plastic Producs Manufacturing	62 162	2 936			
石墨及其他非金属矿物制品制造	Craphite and Other Nonmetal Mineral Products Manuracturing	458 754	3 680			
黑色金属冶炼及压延加工业	Ferrous Metals Smelting and Rolling	454 011				
黑色金属铸造	Ferrous Metals casting	2 902				
钢压延加工	Steel Rolling	421 798				
铁合金冶炼	Ferroalloy Smelting	29 312				
有色金属冶炼及压延加工业	Nonferrous Metals Smelting and Rolling	4 261 028	14 892			240 906
常用有色金属冶炼	Common Nonferrous Metals Smelting	1 446 164	14 892			
稀有稀土金属冶炼	Rare Metals and Rare Soil Smelting	644 652				240 906
有色金属合金制造	Nonferrous Metals Alloy Manuracturing	21 192				
有色金属压延加工	Nonferrous Metals Rolling	2 149 020				
金属制品业	Metal Product Manufacturing	180 095	4 006	11 255		6 762
结构性金属制品制造	Structural Metal Product Manufacturing	160 596	4 006	11 255		
集装箱及金属包装容器制造	Container and Metal Packing Vessel Manufacturing	12 400				3 350
建筑、安全用金属制品制造	Construction and Safety Metal Manufacturing	3 413				3 413
其他金属制品制造	Other Metal Product Manufacturing	3 686				
通用设备制造业	General Equipment Manufacturing	20 388				
锅炉及原动设备制造	Boiler and Motivity Equipment Manufacturing	4 050				
物料搬运设备制造	Handbarrow Equipment Manufacturing	3 186				
烘炉、风机、衡器、包装等设备制造	Oven, Fan, Weighing Apparatus, Paking Equipment Manufacturing	13 152				
专用设备制造业	Special Equipment Manufacturing	88 201	18 655	42 196		
农、林、牧、渔专用机械制造	Special Machine Manufacturing for Farming, Forestry, Livestock and Fishing	82 806	18 655	42 196		
环保、社会公共服务及其他专用设备制造	Environmental Protection, Social Public Service and Other Special Equipment Manufacturing	5 396				
汽车制造业	Automobile Manufacturing	9 633				
改装汽车制造	Modified Car Manufacturing	9 633				
电气机械和器材制造业	Electric Machine and Equipment Manufacturing	259 216	31 453	6 332		
电机制造	Motor Manufacturing	206 550				
输配电及控制设备制造	Transmission Electric and Control Equipment Manufacturing	21 214		6 332		
家用电力器具制造	Household Electric Appliances Manufacturing	24 228	24 228			
照明器具制造	Lighting Apparatus Manufacturing	7 225	7 225			
计算机、通信和其他电子设备制造业	Computer, Communicationn and other Electronic Equipment Manufacturing	29 953			25 066	
电子器件制造	Electronic Device Manufacturing	25 066			25 066	
电子元件制造	Electronic Component Manufacturing	4 887				
仪器仪表制造业	Apparatus and Meter Manufacturing	5 115				
通用仪器仪表制造	General Apparatus and Meter Manufacturing	5 115				
废弃资源和废旧材料回收加工业	Abandon Resources and Discard Material Recovery Processing	13 032				
金属废料和碎屑的加工处理	metal Waste Handle and Broken Bits Processing	8 507				
非金属废料和碎屑的加工处理	Nonmetal Waste Handle and Broken Bits Processing	4 525				
电力、热力、燃气及水生产和供应业	**Electricity, Heat, Gass and Water Production and Supply**	**2 316 611**	**195 560**	**82 816**	**126 432**	**149 922**
电力、热力生产和供应业	Electricity and Heat Production and Supply	2 130 598	124 845	44 163	119 513	149 922
电力生产	Electricity Production	1 752 350	56 826	24 663	50 853	76 286
电力供应	Electricity Supply	345 173	68 018	19 500	68 660	73 636
热力生产和供应	Heat Production and Supply	33 075				
燃气生产和供应业	Gass Production and Supply	158 382	63 538	38 654	3 138	
水的生产和供应业	Water Production and Supply	27 632	7 178		3 781	
自来水生产和供应	Tap Water Production and Supply	23 436	2 982		3 781	
污水处理及其再生利用	Wastewater Treatment and its Reuse	4 196	4 196			

Continued

(unit)

五 师 Division 5	六 师 Division 6	七 师 Division 7	八 师 Division 8	九 师 Division 9	十 师 Division 10	十一师 Division 11	十二师 Division 12	十三师 Division 13	十四师 Division 14	兵团直属 Directly under XPCC
31 807	317 053	124 741	367 508	7 004	26 112	132 961	15 103	201 939	12 423	
3 197	28 249	23 561	166 272		3 012	21 126		11 902		
6 074	32 088	24 454	46 353		11 165	104 829	15 103	116 881	5 365	
5 638	8 105	2 985	12 520					25 884	2 108	
16 898					11 935	7 006				
			9 641							
				7 004				47 272	4 950	
	248 612	73 741	132 722							
	209 977	29 562	26 933		2 314		827	184 399		
		2 902								
	209 977	2 577	21 705		2 314		827	184 399		
		24 084	5 228							
	2 107 048	14 463	1 829 413					54 306		
			1 392 408					38 864		
			403 746							
	5 751							15 442		
	2 101 298	14 463	33 259							
		6 077	14 738		3 420	87 721	15 242	30 874		
		6 077	2 002		3 420	87 721	15 242	30 874		
			9 050							
			3 686							
							12 188	8 200		
							4 050			
							3 186			
							4 952	8 200		
	8 856	8 314	10 180							
	3 460	8 314	10 180							
	5 396									
9 633										
9 633										
							4 122	217 310		
								206 550		
							4 122	10 760		
			4 887							
			4 887							
							5 115			
							5 115			
	2 514	4 525					5 993			
	2 514						5 993			
		4 525								
47 041	**483 230**	**120 107**	**794 313**	**15 885**	**36 018**		**24 667**	**234 246**	**6 375**	
47 041	463 005	118 012	754 234	15 885	33 986		21 970	231 648	6 375	
23 490	439 529	118 012	689 992	5 066	33 986		4 736	228 911		
23 551	10 372		64 242	10 819					6 375	
	13 104						17 234	2 737		
	20 225		30 230					2 598		
		2 095	9 849		2 032		2 697			
		2 095	9 849		2 032		2 697			

10—11 各师规模以上工业企业销售产值

计量单位：万元 (2017 年)

指　　标	Item	合 计 Total	一 师 Division 1	二 师 Division 2	三 师 Division 3	四 师 Division 4
总　　计	**Total**	**20 144 283**	**2 252 002**	**1 404 683**	**996 235**	**1 519 480**
# 国有控股企业	State-controlled Shareholding Enterprises	6 650 953	891 190	347 149	449 128	640 078
按登记注册类型分	**Grouped by Status of Registration**					
内资企业	Domestic Enterprises	19 700 101	2 232 302	1 404 683	990 638	1 505 452
国有企业	State-owned Enterprises	194 407		18 258	41 087	8 954
股份合作企业	Share Cooperative Enterprises	3 507				
有限责任公司	Limited Liability Corporations	9 732 830	1 002 674	456 098	300 733	422 503
国有独资公司	State-owned Corporations with Private-Funds	758 758	55 985	21 344	78 322	97 877
其他有限责任公司	Other Limited Liability Corporations	8 974 072	946 689	434 754	222 411	324 626
股份有限公司	Share-holding Corporations Ltd.	1 237 850	34 764	20 994	152 087	208 621
私营企业	Private Enterprises	8 276 608	1 022 443	909 333	468 642	859 824
私营独资企业	Private-funded Enterprises	3 312				
私营有限责任公司	Private Limited Liability Corporations	7 954 264	1 022 443	861 530	468 642	677 582
私营股份有限公司	Private Share-holding Corporations Ltd.	319 032		47 803		182 242
其他企业	Other Enterprises	254 900	172 422		28 089	5 550
港、澳、台商投资企业	Enterprises with Funds from Hong Kong, Macao and Taiwan	49 986	11 819			
合资经营企业(港或澳、台)	Joint-Venture Enterprises(with funds from Hong Kong, Macao and Taiwan)	14 509				
港、澳、台商独资经营企业	Enterprises with Funds from Hong Kong, Macao and Taiwan	29 436	11 819			
港澳台商投资股份有限公司	Share-holding Corporations Ltd. with Funds from Hong Kong, Macao and Taiwan	3 637				
其他港澳台商投资企业	Others	2 404				
外商投资企业	Foreign Funded Enterprises	394 196	7 881		5 597	14 029
中外合资经营企业	Joint-Venture Enterprises	333 158	7 881		5 597	14 029
中外合作经营企业	Cooperative Enterprises	33 744				
外资企业	Foreign Funded Enterprises	27 294				
按轻重工业分	**Grouped by Light & Heavy Industry**					
轻工业	Light Industry	7 330 907	1 592 648	1 004 564	679 090	789 472
重工业	Heavy Industry	12 813 376	659 354	400 120	317 145	730 009
按企业规模分	**Grouped by Size of Enterprises**					
大型企业	Large-Scale Enterprises	7 151 091	208 412		100 578	323 821
中型企业	Medium-Scale Enterprises	4 312 278	288 941	414 660	106 990	214 311
小型企业	Small-Scale Enterprises	7 981 145	1 632 702	923 182	754 445	927 645
微型企业	Mini Enterprises	699 769	121 947	66 841	34 223	53 704
按工业行业分	**Grouped by Sector**					
采矿业	**Mining**	**424 938**	**33 248**	**59 376**		**28 218**
煤炭开采和洗选业	Coal Mining and Dressing	195 547	33 248	33 698		28 218
烟煤和无烟煤的开采洗选	Soft Coal and Hard Coal Mining and Dressing	195 547	33 248	33 698		28 218
黑色金属矿采选业	Ferrous Metals Mining and Dressing	163 877				
铁矿采选	Prdding Mining and Dressing	163 877				
有色金属矿采选业	Nonferrous Metals Mining and Dressing	9 512				
常用有色金属矿采选	Common Nonferrous Metals Mining and Dressing	9 512				
非金属矿采选业	Nonmetal Mineral Mining and Dressing	56 003		25 678		
土砂石开采	Soil Sand Mining	6 839		2 357		
石棉及其他非金属矿采选	Asbestos and Other Nonmetal Minerals Mining and Dressing	49 164		23 322		
制造业	**Manufacturing**	**17 422 409**	**2 022 847**	**1 262 491**	**873 478**	**1 342 107**
农副食品加工业	Farm and Sideline Food Processing	3 240 878	963 303	455 120	317 219	321 499
谷物磨制	Cereal Grain Grinding	267 692	55 815	7 329	80 582	67 608
饲料加工	Forage Processing	692 865	13 135	119 740	96 752	20 388
植物油加工	Plant Oil Processing	528 486	194 457	17 135		74 472
制糖	Sugar Making	90 078		22 237		27 064
屠宰及肉类加工	Slaughtering and Meat Processing	165 694		15 964		
蔬菜、水果和坚果加工	Vegetable, Fruit and Nuts Processing	1 094 442	695 696	159 331	139 885	
其他农副食品加工	Other Farm and Sideline Food Processing	401 622	4 200	113 384		131 967

Sale Value of Industrial Enterprises above Designated Size by Division

(10 000 yuan)

五 师 Division 5	六 师 Division 6	七 师 Division 7	八 师 Division 8	九 师 Division 9	十 师 Division 10	十一师 Division 11	十二师 Division 12	十三师 Division 13	十四师 Division 14	兵团直属 Directly under XPCC
243 208	**4 014 371**	**880 736**	**5 711 861**	**93 781**	**301 490**	**220 595**	**312 787**	**1 757 493**	**34 500**	**401 059**
98 708	232 467	420 081	2 492 649	52 647	82 363	152 792	213 778	154 867	21 997	401 059
243 208	3 993 426	866 227	5 380 620	93 781	297 073	220 595	279 043	1 757 493	34 500	401 059
23 551	28 572	16 716	11 683		1 406		15 142	25 843		3 196
3 507										
111 396	3 710 095	481 472	2 286 806	84 381	158 451	152 792	126 525	180 741	17 820	240 344
12 836	55 642	90 444	184 785	52 647	40 711	14 810		53 358		
98 561	3 654 453	391 028	2 102 022	31 734	117 740	137 983	126 525	127 383	17 820	240 344
6 015	26 512		596 912		4 234		107 982		6 375	73 354
82 658	228 247	368 040	2 485 219	9 401	132 982	67 803	29 394	1 518 152	10 305	84 165
			3 312							
82 658	215 305	368 040	2 420 229	9 401	131 105	67 803	29 394	1 505 662	10 305	84 165
	12 942		61 678		1 877			12 491		
16 081								32 758		
	3 637	14 509	17 617		2 404					
		14 509								
			17 617							
	3 637									
					2 404					
	17 308		313 625		2 014		33 744			
	12 046		291 592		2 014					
							33 744			
	5 261		22 032							
130 197	696 033	318 108	1 030 208	71 573	210 737		209 795	181 803	15 622	401 059
113 011	3 318 339	562 628	4 681 653	22 208	90 754	220 595	102 992	1 575 690	18 879	
	2 551 824	58 493	3 907 965							
38 039	1 035 966	384 695	962 271	34 231	40 228	28 989	164 391	303 500		295 066
185 566	367 012	416 934	760 047	57 155	252 968	191 606	92 432	1 278 958	34 500	105 993
19 603	59 570	20 614	81 579	2 396	8 295		55 964	175 035		
26 898	**34 007**	**12 339**	**19 829**		**21 724**		**5 431**	**183 869**		
	34 007	12 339	19 829		17 242		5 431	11 536		
	34 007	12 339	19 829		17 242		5 431	11 536		
26 898								136 979		
26 898								136 979		
								9 512		
								9 512		
					4 482			25 843		
					4 482					
								25 843		
169 470	**3 495 485**	**750 227**	**4 909 479**	**78 577**	**245 993**	**220 595**	**282 011**	**1 340 463**	**28 125**	**401 059**
70 128	77 345	90 497	213 487	58 914	160 624		75 692	98 105	14 437	324 509
	2 325		27 396	13 339	2 785		10 514			
41 035	10 727	37 226	79 037		10 257		33 744			230 824
14 414	26 731	39 598	91 597	11 344	7 034			12 690		39 015
		13 674		27 104						
	13 414		15 458	7 127	10 332		23 823	24 905		54 670
3 253	11 706				2 014		7 610	60 509	14 437	
11 426	12 443				128 203					

10—11 续表 1

计量单位:万元 （2017 年）

指 标	Item	合 计 Total	一 师 Division 1	二 师 Division 2	三 师 Division 3	四 师 Division 4
食品制造业	Food Manufacturing	1 106 116	54 176	215 298		14 029
焙烤食品制造	Bakery Products Manufacturing	3 329				
方便食品制造	Convenient Food Manufacturing	43 651				
乳制品制造	Milk and Dairy Products Manufacturing	220 208	24 886			
罐头食品制造	Canned Food Manufacturing	259 288		114 308		
调味品、发酵制品制造	Condiment and Fermented Products Manufacturing	447 039				14 029
其他食品制造	Other Food Manufacturing	132 600	29 291	100 990		
酒、饮料和精制茶制造业	Liquor Brewing,Beverage and Refined Tea Processing	605 007	13 402	27 332	65 285	383 536
酒的制造	Liquor Brewing	515 479	13 402	27 332	20 635	378 172
软饮料制造	Soft Beverage Manufacturing	89 528			44 650	5 364
纺织业	Textile Industry	1 373 235	296 404	155 730	144 891	19 162
棉纺织及印染精加工	Cotton Textile,Dying and Finishing Fine Processing	1 247 405	239 840	149 097	130 876	
毛纺织和染整精加工	Woolen Textile,Dying and Finishing Fine Processing	24 331				
麻纺织及染整精加工	Homp Crops Textile,Dying and Finishing Fine Processing	19 162				19 162
针织或钩针编织物及其制品制造	Knitting or Crochet and Related Goods Manufacturing	56 564	56 564			
家用纺织制成品制造	Textile Products Manufacturing for Home	11 759		6 633		
非家用纺织制成品制造	Non-Textile Products Manufacturing for Home	14 015			14 015	
纺织服装、服饰业	Textile Clothing and Habilatory Manufacturing	19 341			14 604	
机织服装制造	Woven Garment Manufacturing	14 604			14 604	
针织或钩针编织服装制造	Knitting or Crochet Clothing Manufacturing	4 737				
皮革、毛皮、羽毛及其制品和制鞋业	Leather,Fur,Feather and Related Goods Manufacturing]	15 902		9 043		
毛皮鞣制及制品加工	Fur Tanning and Product Processing	6 859				
羽毛(绒)加工及制品制造	Feather(eiderdown)Processing and Related Goods Manufacturing	9 043		9 043		
木材加工和木、竹、藤、棕、草制品业	Wood Processing and Wood,Bamboo,Cane,Grass Products	51 755	11 408	7 820		27 588
木材加工	Wood Processing	19 297				14 358
人造板制造	Artificial Board Manufacturing	32 458	11 408	7 820		13 230
家具制造业	Furniture Manufacturing	12 624				
木质家具制造	Woodiness Furniture Manufacturing	12 624				
造纸及纸制品业	Paper Making and Paper Products	53 546	14 692	34 941		
造 纸	Paper Making	23 916	11 692	8 312		
纸制品制造	Paper Products Manufacturing	29 630	3 000	26 630		
印刷业和记录媒介的复制	Printing Industry and Recording Media	13 111				6 573
印 刷	Printing	13 111				6 573
文教、工美、体育和娱乐用品制造业	Culture and Education, Handicraft, Athletics and Amusement Things Manufacturing	17 704		7 142		
工艺美术品制造	Handicraft Manufacturing	17 704		7 142		
石油加工、炼焦及核燃料加工业	Petroleum Processing, Coking and Nuclear Material Processing	669 742		8 742		
精炼石油产品制造	Refined Petroleum Products Manufacturing	149 911		8 742		
炼 焦	Coking	519 831				
化学原料及化学制品制造业	Chemical Materials and Chemical Products Manufacturing	2 389 952	165 240	127 927	27 191	152 457
基础化学原料制造	Basic Chemical Materials Manufacturing	93 775				
肥料制造	Fertilizer Manufacturing	487 017	165 240	118 806	27 191	25 700
合成材料制造	Synthesize Material Manufacturing	1 483 072				65 205
专用化学产品制造	Special Chemical Products Manufacturing	307 409		9 122		42 873
日用化学产品制造	Daily Chemical Products Manufacturing	18 680				18 680
医药制造业	Pharmaceuticals Manufacturing	130 717	3 846	25 481	5 718	
化学药品制剂制造	Chemical Pharmaceutical Original Medicine Manufacturing	20 994		20 994		
中药饮片加工	Chemical Pharmaceutical Manufacturing	6 243				
中成药生产	Chinese Medicine Production	14 051	3 846	4 487	5 718	
兽用药品制造	Chinese Patent Drugs Troche Processing	11 454				
卫生材料及医药用品制造	Chinese Patent Drugs Manufacturing	73 354				
化学纤维制造业	Chemical Fibre Manufacturing	4 620				
纤维素纤维原料及纤维制造	Cellulose Material and Fibre Manufacturing	179 184	125 400		53 784	
橡胶和塑料制品业	Rubber and Plastic Products Manufacturing	179 184	125 400		53 784	
橡胶制品业	Rubber Products Manufacturing	528 390	121 425	74 477	77 589	20 575
塑料制品业	Plastic Products Manufacturing	528 390	121 425	74 477	77 589	20 575

Continued

(10 000 yuan)

五　师 Division 5	六　师 Division 6	七　师 Division 7	八　师 Division 8	九　师 Division 9	十　师 Division 10	十一师 Division 11	十二师 Division 12	十三师 Division 13	十四师 Division 14	兵团直属 Directly under XPCC
2 513	487 152	49 366	147 799	12 659			123 124			
			3 329							
		2 436	41 216							
		1 450	70 749				123 124			
2 513	64 565	43 348	26 475	8 079						
	420 267	2 133	6 030	4 581						
	2 320									
	5 582	7 198	87 270		15 402					
	2 891	7 198	50 447		15 402					
	2 690		36 823							
14 488	73 291	158 437	481 978		1 877			26 978		
14 488	73 291	158 437	454 398					26 978		
			22 454		1 877					
			5 126							
							4 737			
							4 737			
6 859										
6 859										
			4 939							
			4 939							
			4 287					8 337		
			4 287					8 337		
	3 912									
	3 912									
			2 157						1 185	3 196
			2 157						1 185	3 196
	10 562									
	10 562									
	126 330	67 568					7 311	459 791		
	66 289	67 568					7 311			
	60 040							459 791		
7 264	15 765	186 635	1 693 252		3 411	4 593		6 217		
		49 466	33 498			4 593		6 217		
7 264	12 172	111 213	16 022		3 411					
			1 417 867							
	3 594	25 957	225 864							
			16 074				6 243			73 354
							6 243			
			11 454							
										73 354
			4 620							
36 209	38 188	12 610	66 102		32 833			48 382		
36 209	38 188	12 610	66 102		32 833			48 382		

10—11 续表 2

计量单位:万元 (2017 年)

指 标	Item	合 计 Total	一 师 Division 1	二 师 Division 2	三 师 Division 3	四 师 Division 4
非金属矿物制品业	Nonmetal Mineral Products Manufacturing	1 728 810	186 113	53 863	143 567	156 188
水泥、石灰和石膏的制造	Cement, Lime and Gypsum Manufacturing	438 485	126 790	11 674	11 693	55 152
水泥及石膏制品制造	Lime and Gypsum Manufacturing	647 028	46 948	42 189	131 875	64 733
砖瓦、石材及其他建筑材料制造	Brick, Tile, Stone and Other Building Material Manufacturing	94 599	6 496			31 245
玻璃制造	Glass a Manufacturing	32 314				
玻璃制品制造	Glass Producs Manufacturing	16 113				5 058
玻璃纤维和玻璃纤维增强塑料制品制造	Glass Fibre and Glass Fibre Plastic Producs Manufacturing	60 105	2 936			
石墨及其他非金属矿物制品制造	Craphite and Other Nonmetal Mineral Products Manuracturing	440 168	2 944			
黑色金属冶炼及压延加工业	Ferrous Metals Smelting and Rolling	470 103	300			
黑色金属铸造	Ferrous Metals casting	3 100				
钢压延加工	Steel Rolling	438 527	300			
铁合金冶炼	Ferroalloy Smelting	28 477				
有色金属冶炼及压延加工业	Nonferrous Metals Smelting and Rolling	4 238 126	14 892			237 165
常用有色金属冶炼	Common Nonferrous Metals Smelting	1 404 352	14 892			
稀有稀土金属冶炼	Rare Metals and Rare Soil Smelting	642 396				237 165
有色金属合金制造	Nonferrous Metals Alloy Manuracturing	21 394				
有色金属压延加工	Nonferrous Metals Rolling	2 169 984				
金属制品业	Metal Product Manufacturing	170 131	4 172	11 255		3 337
结构性金属制品制造	Structural Metal Product Manufacturing	156 325	4 172	11 255		
集装箱及金属包装容器制造	Container and Metal Packing Vessel Manufacturing	9 860				2 976
建筑、安全用金属制品制造		361				361
其他金属制品制造	Other Metal Product Manufacturing	3 585				
通用设备制造业	General Equipment Manufacturing	20 388				
锅炉及原动设备制造	Boiler and Motivity Equipment Manufacturing	3 915				
物料搬运设备制造	Handbarrow Equipment Manufacturing	3 321				
烘炉、风机、衡器、包装等设备制造	Oven, Fan, Weighing Apparatus, Paking Equipment Manufacturing	13 152				
专用设备制造业	Special Equipment Manufacturing	85 440	18 634	42 023		
农、林、牧、渔专用机械制造	Special Machine Manufacturing for Farming, Forestry, Livestock and Fishing	80 517	18 634	42 023		
环保、社会公共服务及其他专用设备制造	Environmental Protection, Social Public Service and Other Special Equipment Manufacturing	4 923				
汽车制造业	Automobile Manufacturing	3 300				
改装汽车制造	Modified Car Manufacturing	3 300				
电气机械和器材制造业	Electric Machine and Equipment Manufacturing	252 805	29 441	6 297		
电机制造	Motor Manufacturing	202 130				
输配电及控制设备制造	Transmission Electric and Control Equipment Manufacturing	21 234		6 297		
家用电力器具制造	Household Electric Appliances Manufacturing	22 353	22 353			
照明器具制造	Lighting Apparatus Manufacturing	7 088	7 088			
计算机、通信和其他电子设备制造业	Computer, Communicationn and other Electronic Equipment Manufacturing	27 026			23 629	
电子器件制造		23 629			23 629	
电子元件制造	Electronic Component Manufacturing	3 397				
仪器仪表制造业	Apparatus and Meter Manufacturing	5 307				
通用仪器仪表制造	General Apparatus and Meter Manufacturing	5 307				
废弃资源和废旧材料回收加工业	Abandon Resources and Discard Material Recovery Processing	13 772				
金属废料和碎屑的加工处理	metal Waste Handle and Broken Bits Processing	9 289				
非金属废料和碎屑的加工处理	Nonmetal Waste Handle and Broken Bits Processing	4 483				
电力、热力、燃气及水生产和供应业	**Electricity, Heat, Gass and Water Production and Supply**	**2 296 936**	**195 907**	**82 816**	**122 757**	**149 156**
电力、热力生产和供应业	Electricity and Heat Production and Supply	2 104 446	124 856	44 163	115 838	149 156
电力生产	Electricity Production	1 734 793	56 838	24 663	50 853	75 519
电力供应	Electricity Supply	341 017	68 018	19 500	64 985	73 636
热力生产和供应	Heat Production and Supply	28 635				
燃气生产和供应业	Gass Production and Supply	164 806	63 872	38 654	3 138	
水的生产和供应业	Water Production and Supply	27 685	7 178		3 781	
自来水生产和供应	Tap Water Production and Supply	23 489	2 982		3 781	
污水处理及其再生利用	Wastewater Treatment and its Reuse	4 196	4 196			

Continued

(10 000 yuan)

五　师 Division 5	六　师 Division 6	七　师 Division 7	八　师 Division 8	九　师 Division 9	十　师 Division 10	十一师 Division 11	十二师 Division 12	十三师 Division 13	十四师 Division 14	兵团直属 Directly under XPCC
28 710	310 321	112 541	346 316	7 004	26 112	131 846	15 103	198 622	12 503	
3 197	28 249	22 592	143 873		3 012	20 350		11 904		
6 502	32 088	23 898	46 894		11 165	104 491	15 103	115 778	5 365	
5 638	8 556	2 985	11 764					25 716	2 198	
13 373					11 935	7 006				
			11 055							
				7 004				45 225	4 940	
	241 429	63 066	132 730							
	214 443	29 523	26 098		2 314		7 688	189 738		
		3 100								
	214 443	2 339	21 705		2 314		7 688	189 738		
		24 084	4 393							
	2 121 660	17 360	1 795 007					52 043		
			1 352 859					36 601		
			405 231							
	5 953							15 442		
	2 115 707	17 360	36 917							
		5 877	12 471		3 420	84 156	14 284	31 160		
		5 877	2 002		3 420	84 156	14 284	31 160		
			6 884							
			3 585							
							12 188	8 200		
							3 915			
							3 321			
							4 952	8 200		
	7 804	8 132	8 848							
	2 881	8 132	8 848							
	4 923									
3 300										
3 300										
							4 177	212 890		
								202 130		
							4 177	10 760		
			3 397							
			3 397							
							5 307			
							5 307			
	3 130	4 483					6 158			
	3 130						6 158			
		4 483								
46 840	**484 879**	**118 170**	**782 553**	**15 204**	**33 773**		**25 345**	**233 160**	**6 375**	
46 840	458 564	116 075	742 475	15 204	32 367		21 970	230 563	6 375	
23 289	439 529	116 075	678 233	4 866	32 367		4 736	227 825		
23 551	10 372		64 242	10 338					6 375	
	8 664						17 234	2 737		
	26 315		30 230					2 598		
		2 095	9 849		1 406		3 375			
		2 095	9 849		1 406		3 375			

10—12　规模以上工业企业主要经济指标

计量单位:万元　　　　(2017年)

指　　标	Item	工业增加值(当年价) Added Value of Industry (At current Prices)	资产合计 Total Assets	流动资产合计 Circulating Assets
总　　计	**Total**	**5 474 291**	**37 882 365**	**13 787 060**
# 国有控股企业	State-controlled Shareholding Enterprises	2 033 313	19 445 916	6 468 586
按登记注册类型分	**Grouped by Status of Registration**			
内资企业	Domestic Enterprises	5 304 134	37 062 054	13 557 295
国有企业	State-owned Enterprises	68 596	247 682	81 232
股份合作企业	Share Cooperative Enterprises	1 432	5 124	3 052
有限责任公司	Limited Liability Corporations	2 588 052	22 015 608	7 902 784
国有独资公司	State-owned Corporations with Private-Funds	206 946	3 014 370	725 456
其他有限责任公司	Other Limited Liability Corporations	2 381 106	19 001 239	7 177 328
股份有限公司	Share-holding Corporations Ltd.	422 031	4 822 255	1 864 815
私营企业	Private Enterprises	2 146 226	9 842 448	3 644 569
私营独资企业	Private-funded Enterprises	471	3 370	2 503
私营有限责任公司	Private Limited Liability Corporations	2 055 968	9 634 472	3 543 286
私营股份有限公司	Private Share-holding Corporations Ltd.	89 788	204 607	98 779
其他企业	Other Enterprises	77 797	128 937	60 843
港、澳、台商投资企业	Enterprises with Funds from Hong Kong, Macao and Taiwan	10 317	84 264	54 456
合资经营企业(港或澳、台)	Joint-Venture Enterprises(with funds from Hong Kong, Macao and Taiwan)	5 693	35 427	25 163
港、澳、台商独资经营企业	Enterprises with Funds from Hong Kong, Macao and Taiwan	2 873	29 416	23 303
港澳台商投资股份有限公司	Share-holding Corporations Ltd. with Funds from Hong Kong, Macao and Taiwan	1 135	3 350	1 891
其他港澳台商投资企业	Others	617	16 072	4 100
外商投资企业	Foreign Funded Enterprises	159 840	736 046	175 309
中外合资经营企业	Joint-Venture Enterprises	147 159	642 281	141 357
中外合作经营企业	Cooperative Enterprises	4 962	18 944	8 246
外资企业	Foreign-Funded Enterprises	7 720	74 821	25 706
按轻重工业分	**Grouped by Light & Heavy Industry**			
轻工业	Light Industry	1 706 379	9 183 380	4 696 962
重工业	Heavy Industry	3 767 912	28 698 984	9 090 098
按企业规模分	**Grouped by Size of Enterprises**			
大型企业	Large-Scale Enterprises	1 881 472	13 953 750	4 886 790
中型企业	Medium-Scale Enterprises	1 204 152	11 658 605	4 171 248
小型企业	Small-Scale Enterprises	2 136 265	9 782 575	4 031 861
微型企业	Mini Enterprises	252 403	2 487 435	697 162

Main Economic Indicators of Industrial Enterprises above Designated Size

(10 000 yuan)

# 应收账款净额 Net Amunt of Accounts Receivable	# 产成品 Finished Product	固定资产合计 Fixed Assets	累计折旧 Accumulated Depreciation	负债合计 Total Liabilities	流动负债合计 Liquid Liabilities	非流动负债合计 Non-Liquid Liabilities	所有者权益合计 Creditors Equity	主营业务收入 Main Business Income
2 050 350	**1 386 197**	**17 941 550**	**6 325 226**	**24 900 392**	**16 205 724**	**8 083 101**	**12 991 255**	**20 071 605**
739 875	635 165	8 799 221	3 578 350	13 232 110	8 029 539	4 815 866	6 224 246	6 656 146
1 999 388	1 360 337	17 369 023	6 066 452	24 456 109	15 950 326	7 937 013	12 615 228	19 627 622
21 578	6 324	119 637	97 728	191 748	120 079	68 404	55 933	208 204
1 999		2 015	4 131	5 884	5 143	741	−760	3 404
1 268 249	804 845	11 024 706	4 227 759	15 578 979	10 484 110	4 663 681	6 432 258	9 764 961
89 251	80 637	1 640 754	450 547	2 331 078	1 365 746	897 037	685 064	777 580
1 178 998	724 207	9 383 952	3 777 212	13 247 901	9 118 364	3 766 644	5 747 194	8 987 381
113 087	128 659	1 265 895	529 953	2 694 626	1 493 778	1 179 409	2 141 970	1 244 226
581 076	413 913	4 911 987	1 196 726	5 924 244	3 809 590	2 010 692	3 917 517	8 150 697
1 526	505	444	389	2 468	2 468		902	3 320
556 977	387 853	4 831 030	1 147 068	5 811 191	3 699 384	2 008 904	3 822 594	7 832 305
22 574	25 555	80 513	49 268	110 586	107 739	1 788	94 021	315 072
13 399	6 597	44 784	10 157	60 628	37 626	14 087	68 310	256 130
8 999	7 929	28 060	23 470	58 819	47 618	11 201	25 445	51 278
5 736	876	10 264	5 492	28 531	28 531		6 895	14 509
2 888	4 694	6 092	14 829	24 236	13 035	11 201	5 180	30 499
336	253	1 458	1 447	101	101		3 249	3 637
40	2 106	10 246	1 702	5 951	5 951		10 121	2 634
41 963	17 931	544 467	235 304	385 465	207 779	134 888	350 582	392 704
30 968	16 411	496 086	215 976	340 208	183 422	113 988	302 073	332 031
2 100	402	2 781	6 563	10 644	10 644		8 300	33 379
8 895	1 118	45 600	12 765	34 613	13 713	20 900	40 208	27 294
623 728	858 512	3 318 268	1 470 870	5 480 603	4 214 784	949 713	3 722 382	7 414 434
1 426 622	527 685	14 623 282	4 854 356	19 419 789	11 990 940	7 133 388	9 268 873	12 657 171
177 969	372 388	7 172 250	2 100 772	9 459 378	5 282 917	4 133 661	4 494 372	6 954 583
728 244	387 029	4 753 917	2 222 908	7 587 068	5 550 338	2 011 141	4 071 536	4 447 609
932 915	580 668	4 520 274	1 696 050	6 101 472	4 538 832	1 279 425	3 674 654	7 975 293
211 222	46 112	1 495 110	305 496	1 752 474	833 636	658 874	750 693	694 121

10—12 续表 1

计量单位:万元　　　　(2017 年)

指　　标	Item	主营业务成　本 Main Business Cost	主营业务税金及附加 Main Business Tax and Affixture	其他业务利　润 Profits of Other Business	销　售费　用 Sale Expenses
总　　计	**Total**	**16 172 782**	**180 318**	**69 649**	**611 768**
# 国有控股企业	State-controlled Shareholding Enterprises	5 329 648	77 658	40 432	262 883
按登记注册类型分	**Grouped by Status of Registration**				
内资企业	Domestic Enterprises	15 862 113	175 668	69 488	595 853
国有企业	State-owned Enterprises	174 377	2 636	39	3 335
股份合作企业	Share Cooperative Enterprises	2 552	13		28
有限责任公司	Limited Liability Corporations	8 127 259	72 729	66 291	318 225
国有独资公司	State-owned Corporations with Private-Funds	668 281	5 303	3 968	39 117
其他有限责任公司	Other Limited Liability Corporations	7 458 978	67 426	62 324	279 107
股份有限公司	Share-holding Corporations Ltd.	901 506	31 748	1 627	64 667
私营企业	Private Enterprises	6 459 779	68 418	1 531	205 443
私营独资企业	Private-funded Enterprises	3 076	5		30
私营有限责任公司	Private Limited Liability Corporations	6 214 700	67 436	1 531	198 480
私营股份有限公司	Private Share-holding Corporations Ltd.	242 003	977		6 933
其他企业	Other Enterprises	196 642	124		4 156
港、澳、台商投资企业	Enterprises with Funds from Hong Kong,Macao and Taiwan	46 382	104		1 372
合资经营企业(港或澳、台)	Joint-Venture Enterprises(with funds from Hong Kong,Macao and Taiwan)	11 810			123
港、澳、台商独资经营企业	Enterprises with Funds from Hong Kong,Macao and Taiwan	28 935	15		884
港澳台商投资股份有限公司	Share-holding Corporations Ltd. with Funds from Hong Kong,Macao and Taiwan	2 886	21		97
其他港澳台商投资企业	Others	2 752	68		268
外商投资企业	Foreign Funded Enterprises	264 287	4 546	161	14 543
中外合资经营企业	Joint-Venture Enterprises	215 850	4 277	160	11 307
中外合作经营企业	Cooperative Enterprises	26 626	54		2 633
外资企业	Foreign-Funded Enterprises	21 811	215	1	603
按轻重工业分	**Grouped by Light & Heavy Industry**				
轻工业	Light Industry	6 036 591	74 347	15 168	240 590
重工业	Heavy Industry	10 136 191	105 971	54 481	371 178
按企业规模分	**Grouped by Size of Enterprises**				
大型企业	Large-Scale Enterprises	5 574 777	86 085	47 928	242 974
中型企业	Medium-Scale Enterprises	3 677 007	41 653	13 004	165 204
小型企业	Small-Scale Enterprises	6 414 406	46 946	7 964	192 247
微型企业	Mini Enterprises	506 593	5 634	753	11 344

Continued

(10 000 yuan)

管理费用 Administ-rative Expenses	财务费用 Financial Expenses	# 利息支出 Intrest Exjpend-iture	营业利润 Business Profits	利润总额 Total Profits	亏损企业亏损额 Total Loss	利税总额 Total Profits and Taxes	本年应交增值税 Value Added Taxes Payable	全部职工就业人员年平均人数(人) Average Number of Employees (person)
595 510	**508 688**	**539 439**	**2 047 743**	**2 237 352**	**279 964**	**2 971 321**	**542 362**	**158 727**
322 515	299 131	333 454	395 507	484 813	222 963	785 103	216 208	72 861
583 930	494 335	524 060	1 961 654	2 123 326	276 833	2 826 818	516 535	155 086
9 198	3 410	3 438	14 682	17 827	1 822	29 897	9 431	2 977
267	0		573	574		689	102	
341 662	333 732	334 294	601 063	724 512	243 277	1 110 240	306 616	86 426
36 794	43 430	43 745	−10 707	−2 282	58 699	17 830	14 251	10 122
304 869	290 302	290 550	611 770	726 794	184 578	1 092 410	292 365	76 304
66 087	44 327	75 049	158 674	164 333	8 476	237 139	40 645	11 525
161 883	112 282	110 698	1 136 680	1 166 097	23 258	1 397 650	158 645	52 229
145	57	57	7	−1	1	83	80	90
153 662	110 117	108 604	1 081 701	1 110 893	20 244	1 334 430	151 644	49 951
8 076	2 108	2 037	54 972	55 205	3 013	63 136	6 922	2 188
4 833	585	582	49 983	49 983		51 203	1 096	1 929
1 731	338	344	1 360	2 066	1 203	3 378	1 208	692
241	186	177	2 150	2 150		2 859	710	301
582	−16		98	788		1 129	326	266
303	−1		331	331		525	173	48
605	168	167	−1 218	−1 203	1 203	−1 136		77
9 850	14 015	15 035	84 728	111 960	1 928	141 126	24 619	2 949
7 290	13 348	13 672	79 078	106 187	1 802	134 530	24 067	2 325
1 111	−48	−8	3 147	3 201		3 273	18	335
1 449	714	1 371	2 503	2 572	126	3 322	535	289
224 072	80 835	82 135	759 593	865 244	94 604	1 089 627	148 387	75 228
371 438	427 853	457 303	1 288 149	1 372 108	185 360	1 881 694	393 975	83 499
148 356	215 056	215 824	723 138	778 858	1 964	1 098 133	231 288	46 409
196 681	130 495	159 309	256 557	333 933	151 317	518 596	139 127	49 671
229 533	118 983	120 132	956 916	1 012 466	116 273	1 220 523	155 766	60 590
20 939	44 153	44 173	111 131	112 095	10 410	134 069	16 181	2 057

10—12 续表 2

计量单位:万元 (2017 年)

指 标	Item	工业增加值（当年价） Added Value of Industry (At current Prices)	资产合计 Total Assets	流动资产合计 Circulating Assets
按工业行业分	**Grouped by Sector**			
采矿业	**Mining**	**129 103**	**1 166 429**	**273 314**
煤炭开采和洗选业	Coal Mining and Dressing	92 439	1 047 706	218 850
黑色金属矿采选业	Ferrous Metals Mining and Dressing	13 791	37 300	30 155
有色金属矿采选业	Nonferrous Metals Mining and Dressing	4 473	50 003	7 803
非金属矿采选业	Nonmetal Mineral Mining and Dressing	18 400	31 421	16 507
制造业	**Manufacturing**	**4 336 698**	**26 371 255**	**11 051 178**
农副食品加工业	Farm and Sideline Food Processing	739 991	2 563 949	1 484 186
食品制造业	Food Manufacturing	238 423	1 733 611	632 772
酒、饮料和精制茶制造业	Liquor Brewing, Beverage and Refined Tea Processing	282 858	755 281	400 472
纺织业	Textile Industry	272 016	2 388 235	1 260 973
纺织服装、服饰业	Textile Clothing and Habilatory Manufacturing	4 536	12 006	6 424
皮革、毛皮、羽毛及其制品和制鞋业	Leather, Fur, Feather and Related Goods Manufacturing	3 282	5 502	3 461
木材加工和木、竹、藤、棕、草制品业	Wood Processing and Wood、Bamboo、Cane、Grass Products	17 776	21 131	7 681
家具制造业	Furniture Manufacturing	2 898	4 474	2 088
造纸及纸制品业	Paper Making and Paper Products	16 442	87 482	26 224
印刷业和记录媒介的复制	Printing Industry and Recording Media	5 483	34 929	18 615
文教、工美、体育和娱乐用品制造业	Culture and Education, Handicraft, Athletics and Amusement Things Manufacturing	3 314	17 888	9 980
石油加工、炼焦及核燃料加工业	Oil Processing, Coking Plant and Nuclear Elding Processing	143 282	1 412 119	221 864
化学原料及化学制品制造业	Chemical Materials and Chemical Products Manufacturing	916 758	5 141 635	1 584 530
医药制造业	Pharmaceuticals Manufacturing	69 375	652 914	340 462
化学纤维制造业	Chemical Fibre Manufacturing	26 370	439 412	187 136
橡胶和塑料制品业	Rubber and Plastic Products Manufacturing	146 977	439 089	303 646
非金属矿物制品业	Nonmetal Mineral Products Manufacturing	485 940	3 983 209	1 730 785
黑色金属冶炼及压延加工业	Ferrous Metals Smelting and Rolling	54 757	612 926	360 148
有色金属冶炼及压延加工业	Nonferrous Metals Smelting and Rolling	774 883	5 546 160	2 205 702
金属制品业	Metal Product Manufacturing	44 519	153 060	97 020
通用设备制造业	General Equipment Manufacturing	8 873	41 495	23 091
专用设备制造业	Special Equipment Manufacturing	21 114	80 201	41 660
汽车制造业	Automobile Manufacturing	2 061	38 521	25 800
电气机械和器材制造业	Electric Machine and Equipment Manufacturing	48 049	100 283	46 390
计算机、通信和其他电子设备制造业	Computer, Communicationn and other Electronic Equipment Manufacturing	1 448	31 292	8 579
仪器仪表制造业	Apparatus and Meter Manufacturing	577	26 618	13 168
废弃资源和废旧材料回收加工业	Abandon Resources and Discard Material Recovery Processing	4 695	47 832	8 321
电力、热力、燃气及水生产和供应业	**Electricity, Heat, Gass and Water Production and Supply**	**1 008 490**	**10 344 681**	**2 462 568**
电力、热力的生产和供应业	Electricity and Heat Production and Supply	937 768	9 873 234	2 371 362
燃气生产和供应业	Gass Production and Supply	54 805	223 959	43 595
水的生产和供应业	Water Production and Supply	15 917	247 487	47 612

Continued

(10 000 yuan)

# 应收账款净额 Net Amunt of Accounts Receivable	# 产成品 Finished Product	固定资产合计 Fixed Assets	累计折旧 Accumulated Depreciation	负债合计 Total Liabilities	流动负债合计 Liquid Liabilities	非流动负债合计 Non-Liquid Liabilities	所有者权益合计 Creditors Equity	主营业务收入 Main Business Income
24 691	**16 734**	**472 056**	**227 085**	**942 125**	**753 025**	**186 235**	**224 304**	**420 958**
20 108	11 326	438 096	194 654	881 953	702 300	179 483	165 753	190 272
2 050	124	6 871	2 297	30 894	26 672	4 223	6 406	164 998
1	2 074	14 765	16 780	16 302	14 223	2 078	33 702	9 464
2 532	3 210	12 324	13 355	12 977	9 830	451	18 444	56 224
1 393 370	**1 368 548**	**11 351 463**	**4 326 408**	**17 067 221**	**12 428 398**	**4 176 864**	**9 313 318**	**17 501 244**
187 974	294 049	738 302	403 999	1 577 503	1 335 071	175 591	993 581	3 265 506
118 439	179 735	972 034	485 522	1 189 934	784 396	352 220	549 817	1 099 425
36 336	51 709	207 856	136 341	178 345	158 268	9 681	576 936	598 008
139 880	172 545	923 313	263 913	1 489 689	1 195 159	268 753	898 735	1 413 883
1 304	2 460	2 677	1 873	8 273	5 871	789	3 733	19 553
340	372	1 109	785	1 821	1 690		3 681	16 188
1 416	1 981	11 812	2 780	5 054	5 054		16 077	51 624
419	235	2 386	207	3 471	799		1 003	12 624
3 685	11 692	41 782	12 064	38 479	33 183	5 296	49 003	56 960
4 939	1 730	7 283	9 068	18 580	18 578	1	16 349	15 357
983	1 301	2 267	220	3 026	3 026		14 862	17 714
15 668	34 427	932 877	162 288	868 936	665 683	198 302	542 713	653 494
84 786	86 576	2 818 011	1 157 764	3 219 456	1 858 538	1 313 258	1 921 305	2 393 377
38 564	55 452	124 621	58 336	357 701	233 765	123 936	295 213	146 374
6 600	22 698	157 921	5 947	371 511	229 156	6 092	74 042	177 259
79 291	59 804	112 672	79 493	219 496	193 575	6 942	219 593	539 290
478 634	101 066	1 319 671	707 296	2 551 920	2 281 133	220 528	1 422 313	1 726 924
15 268	29 334	160 371	49 966	517 480	500 768	16 405	95 447	495 898
73 804	230 768	2 671 963	724 143	4 129 265	2 681 018	1 441 199	1 416 895	4 175 129
42 642	7 809	36 542	14 186	97 063	88 434	2 225	55 996	167 118
9 345	568	13 844	1 414	22 902	19 534	658	18 593	19 461
8 201	7 680	29 632	23 458	53 033	39 887	5 141	27 168	88 783
20 000	800	5 207	600	36 524	19 165	6 000	1 997	4 521
10 345	11 370	23 015	7 517	46 577	24 570	14 744	53 706	252 805
5 269	1 646	17 824	6 274	23 485	20 471	3 015	7 807	23 463
8 105	642	268	432	18 043	12 389	5 655	8 575	57 748
1 136	101	16 205	10 524	19 654	19 219	435	28 179	12 760
632 289	**915**	**6 118 030**	**1 771 734**	**6 891 047**	**3 024 300**	**3 720 003**	**3 453 633**	**2 149 403**
611 689	650	5 827 102	1 668 274	6 614 539	2 844 218	3 631 516	3 258 694	1 952 575
15 301	172	138 248	61 913	145 735	124 585	19 785	78 224	168 755
5 299	94	152 680	41 548	130 773	55 497	68 702	116 714	28 073

10—12 续表 3

计量单位:万元 (2017 年)

指 标	Item	主营业务成本 Main Business Cost	主营业务税金及附加 Main Business Tax and Affixture	其他业务利润 Profits of Other Business	销售费用 Sale Expenses
按工业行业分	**Grouped by Sector**				
采矿业	**Mining**	**344 495**	**11 118**	**170**	**6 757**
煤炭开采和洗选业	Coal Mining and Dressing	134 752	9 646	138	2 871
黑色金属矿采选业	Ferrous Metals Mining and Dressing	155 602	896		1 224
有色金属矿采选业	Nonferrous Metals Mining and Dressing	7 859	356	32	788
非金属矿采选业	Nonmetal Mineral Mining and Dressing	46 282	220		1 874
制造业	**Manufacturing**	**14 280 462**	**144 617**	**63 548**	**575 218**
农副食品加工业	Farm and Sideline Food Processing	2 675 622	9 482	7 357	76 853
食品制造业	Food Manufacturing	925 931	9 241	696	58 278
酒、饮料和精制茶制造业	Liquor Brewing,Beverage and Refined Tea Processing	368 430	44 902	—1 100	36 998
纺织业	Textile Industry	1 261 899	5 973	7 562	32 899
纺织服装、服饰业	Textile Clothing and Habilatory Manufacturing	16 572	75	35	702
皮革、毛皮、羽毛及其制品和制鞋业	Leather,Fur,Feather and Related Goods Manufacturing	12 663	2		810
木材加工和木、竹、藤、棕、草制品业	Wood Processing and Wood、Bamboo、Cane、Grass Products	36 296	214		1 116
家具制造业	Furniture Manufacturing	10 483	50		122
造纸及纸制品业	Paper Making and Paper Products	45 192	434		1 482
印刷业和记录媒介的复制	Printing Industry and Recording Media	12 749	136	47	149
文教、工美、体育和娱乐用品制造业	Culture and Education, Handicraft,Athletics and Amusement Things Manufacturing	16 518	103		76
石油加工、炼焦及核燃料加工业	Oil Processing,Coking Plant and Nuclear Elding Processing	556 683	1 410	—191	3 712
化学原料及化学制品制造业	Chemical Materials and Chemical Products Manufacturing	1 711 177	21 592	22 854	97 832
医药制造业	Pharmaceuticals Manufacturing	78 936	1 064	90	15 950
化学纤维制造业	Chemical Fibre Manufacturing	156 582	243		3 653
橡胶和塑料制品业	Rubber and Plastic Products Manufacturing	427 678	2 447	366	11 766
非金属矿物制品业	Nonmetal Mineral Products Manufacturing	1 457 385	11 253	6 480	45 149
黑色金属冶炼及压延加工业	Ferrous Metals Smelting and Rolling	422 524	1 455	294	13 240
有色金属冶炼及压延加工业	Nonferrous Metals Smelting and Rolling	3 543 893	32 572	18 817	166 271
金属制品业	Metal Product Manufacturing	145 638	731	242	2 543
通用设备制造业	General Equipment Manufacturing	16 090	114		425
专用设备制造业	Special Equipment Manufacturing	73 595	267		2 337
汽车制造业	Automobile Manufacturing	4 100			50
电气机械和器材制造业	Electric Machine and Equipment Manufacturing	212 623	347		1 905
计算机、通信和其他电子设备制造业	Computer,Communicationn and other Electronic Equipment Manufacturing	24 054	42		293
仪器仪表制造业	Apparatus and Meter Manufacturing	56 964	244		450
废弃资源和废旧材料回收加工业	Abandon Resources and Discard Material Recovery Processing	10 186	225		159
电力、热力、燃气及水生产和供应业	**Electricity,Heat,Gass and Water Production and Supply**	**1 547 825**	**24 584**	**5 931**	**29 794**
电力、热力的生产和供应业	Electricity and Heat Production and Supply	1 402 078	24 014	5 849	16 814
燃气生产和供应业	Gass Production and Supply	123 690	420		12 310
水的生产和供应业	Water Production and Supply	22 057	150	82	669

Continued

(10 000 yuan)

管理费用 Administrative Expenses	财务费用 Financial Expenses	# 利息支出 Intrest Exjpenditure	营业利润 Business Profits	利润总额 Total Profits	亏损企业亏损总额 Total Loss	利税总额 Total Profits and Taxes	本年应交增值税 Value Added Taxes Payable	全部就业人员年平均人数(人) Average Number of Employees (person)
39 902	**17 629**	**17 915**	**−3 580**	**5 307**	**27 271**	**38 344**	**21 766**	**7 107**
35 690	17 082	17 269	−14 189	−5 798	26 727	20 864	16 863	5 381
1 695	19	25	5 562	5 532		8 697	2 269	652
756	444	443	−737	−496	544	1 036	1 175	257
1 761	84	178	5 785	6 069		7 747	1 458	817
472 708	**308 620**	**337 569**	**1 772 492**	**1 920 626**	**163 147**	**2 493 693**	**418 532**	**134 240**
72 533	24 550	25 017	409 468	417 215	27 446	465 742	38 467	21 858
38 687	27 497	24 451	30 198	62 759	46 664	97 056	24 841	10 456
24 593	−304	1 673	121 616	130 926	7 934	214 158	38 258	5 252
37 501	23 198	24 433	62 922	112 403	8 875	143 900	25 107	25 595
907	72	36	578	1 699		2 440	666	597
817	311		1 986	1 986		1 987		84
667	191	269	13 141	13 141	26	14 170	815	362
274	24	17	1 671	1 716	142	1 803	37	93
1 291	635	233	7 925	7 922	53	10 006	1 649	537
1 510	6	15	1 048	2 306		2 903	461	427
311	106	101	601	1 118		2 310	1 089	284
14 267	14 350	13 865	62 541	63 446	9 991	51 610	−13 698	3 237
95 742	94 777	102 223	395 259	401 837	9 937	542 210	115 948	17 490
21 502	1 718	2 766	25 204	26 736	1 645	32 770	4 970	2 224
5 998	911	1 091	11 164	12 478	367	16 184	3 463	1 696
16 178	2 087	2 274	79 620	80 374	433	91 870	8 808	5 386
71 154	39 880	59 446	126 636	144 892	43 807	226 026	65 024	16 487
17 917	7 950	8 101	21 371	23 483	746	26 562	1 624	2 285
31 989	66 229	67 408	348 128	360 347	1 160	486 682	93 594	14 906
6 420	1 424	1 377	10 753	10 735	1 077	13 430	1 946	2 060
1 545	290	295	997	1 970		2 366	282	344
3 323	580	439	8 804	9 258		11 204	1 631	1 019
200	1	0	406	406		766	360	95
4 865	503	480	32 562	32 568		35 421	2 506	847
605	885	885	−2 240	−2 200	2 522	−2 158		182
902	396	330	−1 024	−322	322	134	211	211
1 013	356	348	1 160	1 429		2 143	473	226
82 901	**182 440**	**183 954**	**278 831**	**311 419**	**89 545**	**439 283**	**102 065**	**17 380**
74 240	177 201	178 732	254 222	281 957	87 280	405 742	99 653	15 254
6 166	3 296	3 309	23 803	26 618	647	29 383	1 285	1 312
2 495	1 943	1 914	806	2 844	1 618	4 159	1 127	814

10—13　规模以上工业企业主要经济效益指标

(2017 年)

指　　标	Item	工业经济效益综合指数 Comprehensive Index of industry Economic Results	总资产贡献率(%) Ratio of Total Assets to Industrial Output Value (%)
总　计	**Total**	**324.3**	**9.1**
# 国有控股企业	State-controlled Shareholding Enterprises	255.9	5.5
按登记注册类型分	**Grouped by Status of Registration**		
内资企业	Domestic Enterprises	320.5	8.9
国有企业	State-owned Enterprises	253.6	13.4
股份合作企业	Share Cooperative Enterprises		13.5
有限责任公司	Limited Liability Corporations	272.7	6.5
国有独资公司	State-owned Corporations with Private-Funds	171.0	2.0
其他有限责任公司	Other Limited Liability Corporations	285.2	7.2
股份有限公司	Share-holding Corporations Ltd.	335.0	5.8
私营企业	Private Enterprises	398.8	15.3
私营独资企业	Private-funded Enterprises	79.2	4.2
私营有限责任公司	Private Limited Liability Corporations	397.7	14.9
私营股份有限公司	Private Share-holding Corporations Ltd.	453.8	31.8
其他企业	Other Enterprises	490.3	40.1
港、澳、台商投资企业	Enterprises with Funds from Hong Kong, Macao and Taiwan	155.9	4.4
合资经营企业(港或澳、台)	Joint-Venture Enterprises(with funds from Hong Kong, Macao and Taiwan)	229.0	8.6
港、澳、台商独资经营企业	Enterprises with Funds from Hong Kong, Macao and Taiwan	146.2	3.8
港澳台商投资股份有限公司	Share-holding Corporations Ltd. with Funds from Hong Kong, Macao and Taiwan	256.2	15.6
其他港澳台商投资企业	Others	−48.6	−6.0
外商投资企业	Foreign Funded Enterprises	570.8	21.1
中外合资经营企业	Joint-Venture Enterprises	653.4	23.0
中外合作经营企业	Cooperative Enterprises	239.4	17.2
外资企业	Foreign-Funded Enterprises	258.6	5.4
按轻重工业分	**Grouped by Light & Heavy Industry**		
轻工业	Light Industry	265.0	12.7
重工业	Heavy Industry	383.9	8.0
按企业规模分	**Grouped by Size of Enterprises**		
大型企业	Large-Scale Enterprises	359.2	9.3
中型企业	Medium-Scale Enterprises	238.9	5.5
小型企业	Small-Scale Enterprises	350.5	13.6
微型企业	Mini Enterprises	874.6	7.2

Main Indicators on Economic Benefit of Industrial Enterprises above Designated Size

资本保值增值率 (%) Ratio of Capital Hold and Rise (%)	资产负债率 (%) Assets Liability Ratio (%)	流动资产周转次数(次/年) Number of Times of Annual Turnover Circulating Assets (times/year)	全员劳动生产率 (元/人·年) Over Labor Productivity (yuan/person-year)	工业成本费用利润率(%) Ratio of Profits to Industrial Cost (%)	工业销售率 (%) Ratio of Industrial Products Sold (%)	工业增加值率 (%) Ratio of Value Added to GrossIndustrial Output Value (%)
112.3	**65.7**	**1.5**	**344 887**	**11.8**	**97.7**	**26.5**
107.8	68.1	1.1	279 067	7.7	96.7	29.6
111.8	66.0	1.5	342 012	11.4	97.7	26.3
60.2	77.4	2.6	230 421	9.3	99.9	35.3
−11.3	114.8	1.1		20.2	100.0	40.8
113.1	70.8	1.3	299 453	7.8	97.8	26.0
105.6	77.3	1.1	204 451	−0.3	92.0	25.1
114.1	69.7	1.3	312 055	8.6	98.3	26.1
107.5	55.9	0.7	366 187	15.1	96.3	32.8
113.7	60.2	2.5	410 926	14.9	97.9	25.4
35.1	73.2	1.3	52 323	0.0	102.7	14.6
115.3	60.3	2.5	411 597	14.7	97.9	25.3
73.8	54.1	3.2	410 364	21.3	96.4	27.1
118.8	47.0	4.2	403 301	24.0	97.3	29.7
88.5	69.8	0.9	149 091	4.1	85.4	17.6
57.4	80.5	0.6	189 120	17.4	100.0	39.2
257.3	82.4	1.3	107 995	2.6	83.2	8.1
96.7	3.0	1.9	236 479	10.1	97.1	30.3
89.2	37.0	0.7	80 103	−31.4	49.0	12.6
137.3	52.4	2.3	542 015	36.7	97.0	39.3
144.6	53.0	2.4	632 940	42.5	96.6	42.7
96.3	56.2	4.1	148 122	10.6	100.0	14.7
106.3	46.3	1.1	267 116	10.4	98.5	27.9
107.5	59.7	1.6	226 828	13.0	95.2	22.1
114.4	67.7	1.5	451 252	11.2	99.2	29.2
114.7	67.8	1.6	405 411	11.1	98.6	26.0
133.9	65.1	1.1	242 425	7.8	97.2	27.1
95.6	62.4	2.0	352 577	14.4	96.9	25.9
98.1	70.5	1.0	1 227 044	19.1	100.1	36.1

10—13 续表

(2017 年)

指　　标	Item	工业经济效益综合指数 Comprehensive Index of industry Economic Results	总资产贡献率(%) Ratio of Total Assets to Industrial Output Value (%)
按工业行业分	**Grouped by Sector**		
采矿业	**Mining**	**170.5**	**4.7**
煤炭开采和洗选业	Coal Mining and Dressing	138.6	3.5
黑色金属矿采选业	Ferrous Metals Mining and Dressing	269.8	23.4
有色金属矿采选业	Nonferrous Metals Mining and Dressing	147.6	2.9
非金属矿采选业	Nonmetal Mineral Mining and Dressing	298.3	25.0
制造业	**Manufacturing**	**314.0**	**10.6**
农副食品加工业	Farm and Sideline Food Processing	352.7	19.0
食品制造业	Food Manufacturing	225.0	7.0
酒、饮料和精制茶制造业	Liquor Brewing,Beverage and Refined Tea Processing	540.0	28.3
纺织业	Textile Industry	164.3	7.0
纺织服装、服饰业	Textile Clothing and Habilatory Manufacturing	170.7	20.5
皮革、毛皮、羽毛及其制品和制鞋业	Leather,Fur,Feather and Related Goods Manufacturing	443.7	36.1
木材加工和木、竹、藤、棕、草制品业	Wood Processing and Wood、Bamboo、Cane、Grass Products		68.0
家具制造业	Furniture Manufacturing	422.1	40.6
造纸及纸制品业	Paper Making and Paper Products	322.6	11.7
印刷业和记录媒介的复制	Printing Industry and Recording Media	197.9	8.3
文教、工美、体育和娱乐用品制造业	Culture and Education, Handicraft,Athletics and Amusement Things Manufacturing	177.2	13.5
石油加工、炼焦及核燃料加工业	Oil Processing,Coking Plant and Nuclear Elding Processing	385.4	4.6
化学原料及化学制品制造业	Chemical Materials and Chemical Products Manufacturing	470.6	12.3
医药制造业	Pharmaceuticals Manufacturing	385.2	5.5
化学纤维制造业	Chemical Fibre Manufacturing	193.0	3.9
橡胶和塑料制品业	Rubber and Plastic Products Manufacturing	325.0	21.4
非金属矿物制品业	Nonmetal Mineral Products Manufacturing	273.7	6.6
黑色金属冶炼及压延加工业	Ferrous Metals Smelting and Rolling	223.6	5.6
有色金属冶炼及压延加工业	Nonferrous Metals Smelting and Rolling	422.6	9.9
金属制品业	Metal Product Manufacturing	231.2	9.6
通用设备制造业	General Equipment Manufacturing	256.4	6.4
专用设备制造业	Special Equipment Manufacturing	248.9	14.5
汽车制造业	Automobile Manufacturing	186.1	2.0
电气机械和器材制造业	Electric Machine and Equipment Manufacturing	559.7	35.8
计算机、通信和其他电子设备制造业	Computer,Communicationn and other Electronic Equipment Manufacturing	65.7	−4.1
仪器仪表制造业	Apparatus and Meter Manufacturing		1.7
废弃资源和废旧材料回收加工业	Abandon Resources and Discard Material Recovery Processing	231.5	5.2
电力、热力、燃气及水生产和供应业	**Electricity,Heat,Gass and Water Production and Supply**	**474.4**	**6.0**
电力、热力的生产和供应业	Electricity and Heat Production and Supply	494.4	5.9
燃气生产和供应业	Gass Production and Supply	426.1	14.6
水的生产和供应业	Water Production and Supply	212.2	2.4

Continued

资本保值增值率(%) Ratio of Capital Hold and Rise (%)	资产负债率(%) Assets Liability Ratio (%)	流动资产周转次数(次/年) Number of Times of Annual Turnover Circulating Assets (times/year)	全员劳动生产率(元/人·年) Over Labor Productivity (yuan/person-year)	工业成本费用利润率(%) Ratio of Profits to Industrial Cost (%)	工业销售率(%) Ratio of Industrial Products Sold (%)	工业增加值率(%) Ratio of Value Added to GrossIndustrial Output Value (%)
89.1	**80.8**	**1.6**	**181 656**	**1.3**	**102.5**	**31.1**
86.3	84.2	0.9	171 787	−2.9	104.5	49.4
90.4	82.8	5.5	211 523	3.5	100.0	8.4
97.7	32.6	1.7	174 049	−3.7	109.2	51.4
102.2	41.3	3.4	225 215	12.1	102.2	33.6
108.8	**64.7**	**1.7**	**323 056**	**11.6**	**97.4**	**24.2**
79.9	61.5	2.2	338 545	14.6	95.8	21.9
90.9	68.6	1.8	228 025	5.9	93.1	20.1
110.2	23.6	1.5	538 572	30.1	96.0	44.9
158.7	62.4	1.2	106 277	7.9	94.2	18.7
1.5	68.9	3.1	75 986	9.2	85.8	20.1
162.7	33.1	4.7	390 699	13.6	100.0	20.6
	23.9	6.7		34.3	98.9	
134.4	77.6	6.1	311 600	15.7	100.0	23.0
81.7	44.0	2.2	306 191	16.3	92.3	28.3
103.0	53.2	0.8	128 419	15.6	96.9	40.5
165.3	16.9	1.8	116 674	6.6	99.9	18.7
104.7	61.5	3.0	442 638	10.6	99.7	21.3
107.7	62.6	1.5	524 161	20.1	99.9	38.3
551.6	54.8	0.4	311 939	22.6	88.6	47.0
273.3	84.6	1.0	155 484	7.4	95.3	14.0
94.6	50.0	1.8	272 888	17.5	99.2	27.6
116.0	64.1	1.0	294 741	8.8	96.9	27.2
127.2	84.4	1.4	239 637	4.8	103.5	12.1
121.3	74.5	2.3	519 846	7.8	99.5	18.2
116.3	63.4	1.7	216 111	6.8	94.5	24.7
110.7	55.2	0.8	257 939	10.7	100.0	43.5
60.9	66.1	2.1	207 207	11.6	96.9	23.9
62.9	94.8	0.2	216 942	9.1	34.3	21.4
126.1	46.5	5.5	567 288	14.8	97.5	18.5
77.1	75.1	2.8	79 539	−8.5	90.2	4.8
	67.8	4.5		−0.5	103.8	11.3
120.6	41.1	1.6	207 762	11.0	105.7	36.0
125.3	**66.6**	**0.9**	**580 259**	**16.6**	**99.2**	**43.5**
124.9	67.0	0.8	614 769	16.6	98.8	44.0
104.2	65.1	4.0	417 720	17.9	104.1	34.6
161.6	52.8	0.6	195 539	9.9	100.2	57.6

10—14 规模以上国有及国有控股工业企业数、总产值、销售产值及产销率
Number, Gross Output Value, Sale Value and Production-Sale Ratio of State-owned and State-holding Industrial Enterprises above Designated Size

计量单位：万元 (2017 年) (10 000 yuan)

指 标	Item	企业单位数（个） Number of Enterprises (unit)	# 亏损企业 Losses	工业总产值（当年价格） Gross Industrial Output Value (At Current Prices)
总 计	**Total**	**289**	**86**	**6 875 743**
按轻重工业分	**Grouped by Light & Heavy Industry**			
轻工业	Light Industry	133	35	2 775 345
重工业	Heavy Industry	156	51	4 100 398
按企业规模分	**Grouped by Size of Enterprises**			
大型企业	Large-Scale Enterprises	13	3	2 445 963
中型企业	Medium-Scale Enterprises	50	22	1 910 149
小型企业	Small-Scale Enterprises	195	54	2 342 425
微型企业	Mini Enterprises	31	7	177 207
按工业行业分	**Grouped by Sector**			
采矿业	**Mining**	**16**	**5**	**190 711**
煤炭开采和洗选业	Coal Mining and Dressing	10	4	129 558
有色金属矿采选业	Nonferrous Metals Mining and Dressing	2	1	8 707
非金属矿采选业	Nonmetal Mineral Mining and Dressing	4		52 446
制造业	**Manufacturing**	**214**	**61**	**5 301 918**
农副食品加工业	Farm and Sideline Food Processing	62	13	1 237 897
食品制造业	Food Manufacturing	24	10	464 633
酒、饮料和精制茶制造业	Liquor Brewing, Beverage and Refined Tea Processing	11	3	279 929
纺织业	Textile Industry	8	4	302 988
纺织服装、服饰业	Textile Clothing and Habilatory Manufacturing	1		4 570
木材加工和木、竹、藤、棕、草制品业	Wood Processing and Wood, Bamboo, Cane, Grass Products	1		3 861
造纸及纸制品业	Paper Making and Paper Products	1		19 731
印刷业和记录媒介的复制	Printing Industry and Recording Media	4		11 637
石油加工、炼焦及核燃料加工业	Oil Processing, Coking Plant and Nuclear Elding Processing	3	1	150 829
化学原料及化学制品制造业	Chemical Materials and Chemical Products Manufacturing	18	4	1 704 335
医药制造业	Pharmaceuticals Manufacturing	4	1	99 453
化学纤维制造业	Chemical Fibre Manufacturing	3	1	176 557
橡胶和塑料制品业	Rubber and Plastic Products Manufacturing	13	2	162 581
非金属矿物制品业	Nonmetal Mineral Products Manufacturing	51	19	605 764
黑色金属冶炼及压延加工业	Ferrous Metals Smelting and Rolling	2	1	3 403
金属制品业	Metal Product Manufacturing	2	1	41 694
通用设备制造业	General Equipment Manufacturing	1		3 186
专用设备制造业	Special Equipment Manufacturing	2		13 640
电气机械和器材制造业	Electric Machine and Equipment Manufacturing	1		4 122
仪器仪表制造业	Apparatus and Meter Manufacturing	1	1	5 115
废弃资源和废旧材料回收加工业	Abandon Resources and Discard Material Recovery Processing	1		5 993
电力、热力、燃气及水生产和供应业	**Electricity, Heat, Gass and Water Production and Supply**	**59**	**20**	**1 383 115**
电力、热力的生产和供应业	Electricity and Heat Production and Supply	50	17	1 304 396
燃气生产和供应业	Gass Production and Supply	3	1	55 283
水的生产和供应业	Water Production and Supply	6	2	23 436

10—14 续表 Continued

计量单位:万元 (2017 年) (10 000 yuan)

指　　标	Item	工业销售产值(当年价格) Sale Value of Industry (At Current Prices)	# 出口交货值 Export Commodities	产销率(%) Ratio of Production & Marketing (%)
总　计	**Total**	**6 650 953**	**91 434**	**96.7**
按轻重工业分	**Grouped by Light & Heavy Industry**			
轻工业	Light Industry	2 567 860	83 762	92.5
重工业	Heavy Industry	4 083 094	7 673	99.6
按企业规模分	**Grouped by Size of Enterprises**			
大型企业	Large-Scale Enterprises	2 394 231	7 673	97.9
中型企业	Medium-Scale Enterprises	1 825 991	17 288	95.6
小型企业	Small-Scale Enterprises	2 244 331	63 408	95.8
微型企业	Mini Enterprises	186 401	3 066	105.2
按工业行业分	**Grouped by Sector**			
采矿业	**Mining**	**197 269**		**103.4**
煤炭开采和洗选业	Coal Mining and Dressing	134 111		103.5
有色金属矿采选业	Nonferrous Metals Mining and Dressing	9 512		109.2
非金属矿采选业	Nonmetal Mineral Mining and Dressing	53 646		102.3
制造业	**Manufacturing**	**5 084 221**	**91 434**	**95.9**
农副食品加工业	Farm and Sideline Food Processing	1 129 865	969	91.3
食品制造业	Food Manufacturing	417 638	79 700	89.9
酒、饮料和精制茶制造业	Liquor Brewing, Beverage and Refined Tea Processing	277 113		99.0
纺织业	Textile Industry	276 713		91.3
纺织服装、服饰业	Textile Clothing and Habilatory Manufacturing	4 737	3 094	103.6
木材加工和木、竹、藤、棕、草制品业	Wood Processing and Wood、Bamboo、Cane、Grass Products	3 861		100.0
造纸及纸制品业	Paper Making and Paper Products	16 280		82.5
印刷业和记录媒介的复制	Printing Industry and Recording Media	10 954		94.1
石油加工、炼焦及核燃料加工业	Oil Processing, Coking Plant and Nuclear Elding Processing	150 037		99.5
化学原料及化学制品制造业	Chemical Materials and Chemical Products Manufacturing	1 716 561	7 673	100.7
医药制造业	Pharmaceuticals Manufacturing	87 405		87.9
化学纤维制造业	Chemical Fibre Manufacturing	167 851		95.1
橡胶和塑料制品业	Rubber and Plastic Products Manufacturing	163 829		100.8
非金属矿物制品业	Nonmetal Mineral Products Manufacturing	578 967		95.6
黑色金属冶炼及压延加工业	Ferrous Metals Smelting and Rolling	10 027		294.6
金属制品业	Metal Product Manufacturing	41 694		100.0
通用设备制造业	General Equipment Manufacturing	3 321		104.2
专用设备制造业	Special Equipment Manufacturing	11 728		86.0
电气机械和器材制造业	Electric Machine and Equipment Manufacturing	4 177		101.3
仪器仪表制造业	Apparatus and Meter Manufacturing	5 307		103.8
废弃资源和废旧材料回收加工业	Abandon Resources and Discard Material Recovery Processing	6 158		102.8
电力、热力、燃气及水生产和供应业	**Electricity, Heat, Gass and Water Production and Supply**	**1 369 463**		**99.0**
电力、热力的生产和供应业	Electricity and Heat Production and Supply	1 290 691		98.9
燃气生产和供应业	Gass Production and Supply	55 283		100.0
水的生产和供应业	Water Production and Supply	23 489		100.2

10－15 规模以上国有及国有控股工业企业主要经济指标

计量单位:万元 (2017 年)

指 标	Item	工业增加值(当年价) Added Value of Industry (At current Prices)	资产合计 Total Assets	流动资产合 计 Circulating Assets	# 应收账款净额 Net Amunt of Accounts Receivable
总 计	**Total**	**2 033 313**	**19 445 916**	**6 468 586**	**739 875**
按轻重工业分	**Grouped by Light & Heavy Industry**				
轻工业	Light Industry	596 042	4 028 486	2 353 030	233 437
重工业	Heavy Industry	1 437 270	15 417 430	4 115 556	506 438
按企业规模分	**Grouped by Size of Enterprises**				
大型企业	Large-Scale Enterprises	930 689	6 394 176	1 925 744	52 775
中型企业	Medium-Scale Enterprises	478 082	7 739 744	2 480 065	221 966
小型企业	Small-Scale Enterprises	566 756	4 395 530	1 793 322	403 955
微型企业	Mini Enterprises	57 786	916 466	269 455	61 179
按工业行业分	**Grouped by Sector**				
采矿业	**Mining**	**93 944**	**934 404**	**202 063**	**15 149**
煤炭开采和洗选业	Coal Mining and Dressing	72 169	854 361	178 255	12 852
有色金属矿采选业	Nonferrous Metals Mining and Dressing	4 473	50 003	7 803	1
非金属矿采选业	Nonmetal Mineral Mining and Dressing	17 302	30 040	16 006	2 296
制造业	**Manufacturing**	**1 516 406**	**11 987 468**	**4 885 830**	**516 297**
农副食品加工业	Farm and Sideline Food Processing	192 580	1 180 266	810 679	66 638
食品制造业	Food Manufacturing	66 519	640 691	353 528	76 315
酒、饮料和精制茶制造业	Liquor Brewing, Beverage and Refined Tea Processing	164 899	446 640	260 793	6 336
纺织业	Textile Industry	65 358	503 170	262 662	15 443
纺织服装、服饰业	Textile Clothing and Habilatory Manufacturing	1 228	7 287	4 891	1 153
木材加工和木、竹、藤、棕、草制品业	Wood Processing and Wood、Bamboo、Cane、Grass Products	1 638	4 349	85	
造纸及纸制品业	Paper Making and Paper Products	4 373	14 157	7 322	375
印刷业和记录媒介的复制	Printing Industry and Recording Media	4 988	33 568	17 532	4 172
石油加工、炼焦及核燃料加工业	Oil Processing, Coking Plant and Nuclear Elding Processing	16 309	868 571	109 604	6 650
化学原料及化学制品制造业	Chemical Materials and Chemical Products Manufacturing	669 544	4 407 014	1 377 061	41 696
医药制造业	Pharmaceuticals Manufacturing	54 569	571 242	296 234	16 832
化学纤维制造业	Chemical Fibre Manufacturing	22 217	415 230	174 249	6 511
橡胶和塑料制品业	Rubber and Plastic Products Manufacturing	43 709	194 041	153 684	37 942
非金属矿物制品业	Nonmetal Mineral Products Manufacturing	185 559	2 461 814	945 721	193 825
黑色金属冶炼及压延加工业	Ferrous Metals Smelting and Rolling	1 137	40 827	16 391	206
金属制品业	Metal Product Manufacturing	12 174	59 054	38 532	21 692
通用设备制造业	General Equipment Manufacturing	2 392	26 094	12 652	5 592
专用设备制造业	Special Equipment Manufacturing	3 222	38 522	21 229	5 382
电气机械和器材制造业	Electric Machine and Equipment Manufacturing	912	6 487	5 098	1 380
仪器仪表制造业	Apparatus and Meter Manufacturing	577	26 618	13 168	8 105
废弃资源和废旧材料回收加工业	Abandon Resources and Discard Material Recovery Processing	2 505	41 827	4 716	53
电力、热力、燃气及水生产和供应业	**Electricity, Heat, Gass and Water Production and Supply**	**422 963**	**6 524 044**	**1 380 693**	**208 429**
电力、热力的生产和供应业	Electricity and Heat Production and Supply	392 601	6 181 496	1 321 485	199 691
燃气生产和供应业	Gass Production and Supply	17 172	113 050	13 879	3 557
水的生产和供应业	Water Production and Supply	13 190	229 498	45 329	5 181

Main Economic Indicators of State-owned and State-holding Industrial Enterprises above Designated Size

(10 000 yuan)

# 产成品 Finished Product	固定资产合计 Fixed Assets	累计折旧 Accumulated Depreciation	负债合计 Total Liabilities	流动负债合计 Liquid Liabilities	非流动负债合计 Non-Liquid Liabilities	所有者权益合计 Creditors Equity	主营业务收入 Main Business Income
635 165	**8 799 221**	**3 578 350**	**13 232 110**	**8 029 539**	**4 815 866**	**6 224 246**	**6 656 146**
492 338	1 056 818	621 316	2 565 013	2 080 330	261 784	1 482 890	2 658 959
142 827	7 742 403	2 957 034	10 667 098	5 949 209	4 554 082	4 741 356	3 997 187
86 866	3 268 682	1 124 628	4 018 585	1 960 876	2 057 707	2 375 590	2 215 264
257 444	2 979 471	1 438 124	5 260 091	3 466 673	1 785 080	2 479 653	1 946 721
273 891	2 071 083	893 242	3 173 637	2 388 109	638 384	1 215 445	2 317 900
16 964	479 985	122 354	779 797	213 882	334 696	153 558	176 261
14 196	**330 115**	**145 624**	**738 516**	**600 004**	**135 647**	**195 887**	**192 203**
8 913	303 906	115 530	710 065	576 778	133 118	144 296	128 872
2 074	14 765	16 780	16 302	14 223	2 078	33 702	9 464
3 210	11 444	13 315	12 149	9 003	451	17 890	53 867
620 074	**4 905 941**	**2 214 299**	**7 694 169**	**5 622 190**	**1 813 524**	**4 303 740**	**5 234 144**
183 684	249 822	210 828	865 306	732 439	104 636	322 095	1 165 590
133 744	198 207	150 384	544 400	488 138	8 763	102 431	416 106
6 367	79 995	60 547	87 810	76 609	2 933	358 830	284 931
45 022	225 746	81 488	285 529	251 553	31 454	217 641	299 018
1 856	2 291	1 786	6 455	5 667	789	832	5 052
85	4 264	779	81	81		4 268	3 861
5 874	6 835	3 413	4 012	4 012		10 145	16 280
1 677	7 006	8 690	17 926	17 924	1	15 642	13 201
23 630	646 261	75 641	670 541	498 192	172 349	198 029	130 928
59 360	2 332 616	1 039 887	2 799 450	1 625 499	1 173 951	1 607 564	1 737 465
43 078	87 964	46 938	288 056	176 202	111 853	283 186	102 430
22 698	153 590	4 090	361 165	224 434	467	60 207	165 917
46 491	35 479	48 928	92 947	92 059	887	101 094	174 940
38 362	825 107	461 851	1 500 413	1 269 354	195 387	952 426	573 611
583	7 650	619	37 475	37 475		3 352	10 270
134	7 688	2 956	50 043	50 043		9 011	48 247
219	10 824	958	14 290	13 632	658	11 805	3 321
5 169	9 676	3 680	28 644	25 338	3 306	9 878	14 896
1 400	67	106	3 227	3 227		3 260	4 177
642	268	432	18 043	12 389	5 655	8 575	57 748
	14 587	10 300	18 357	17 922	435	23 470	6 158
896	**3 563 166**	**1 218 427**	**4 799 425**	**1 807 345**	**2 866 695**	**1 724 618**	**1 229 799**
650	3 344 629	1 147 248	4 606 247	1 704 603	2 782 833	1 575 248	1 149 790
152	66 029	29 729	72 039	52 780	19 260	41 010	56 132
94	152 508	41 450	121 138	49 962	64 602	108 360	23 877

10—15 续表

计量单位:万元 （2017 年）

指　标	Item	主营业务成本 Main Business Cost	主营业务税金及附加 Main Business Tax and Affixture	其他业务利润 Profits of Other Business	销售费用 Sale Expenses
总　计	**Total**	**5 329 648**	**77 658**	**40 432**	**262 883**
按轻重工业分	**Grouped by Light & Heavy Industry**				
轻工业	Light Industry	2 188 638	40 231	11 564	115 484
重工业	Heavy Industry	3 141 010	37 427	28 868	147 399
按企业规模分	**Grouped by Size of Enterprises**				
大型企业	Large-Scale Enterprises	1 589 050	44 136	27 216	75 099
中型企业	Medium-Scale Enterprises	1 654 955	16 373	5 952	116 689
小型企业	Small-Scale Enterprises	1 954 812	15 948	7 124	67 634
微型企业	Mini Enterprises	130 832	1 200	140	3 462
按工业行业分	**Grouped by Sector**				
采矿业	**Mining**	**138 947**	**7 453**	**99**	**3 865**
煤炭开采和洗选业	Coal Mining and Dressing	86 676	6 876	67	1 203
有色金属矿采选业	Nonferrous Metals Mining and Dressing	7 859	356	32	788
非金属矿采选业	Nonmetal Mineral Mining and Dressing	44 413	220		1 874
制造业	**Manufacturing**	**4 179 510**	**63 362**	**35 565**	**230 118**
农副食品加工业	Farm and Sideline Food Processing	1 014 232	2 726	6 172	33 971
食品制造业	Food Manufacturing	348 890	2 628	545	36 056
酒、饮料和精制茶制造业	Liquor Brewing,Beverage and Refined Tea Processing	162 248	31 588	−1 122	18 624
纺织业	Textile Industry	276 921	1 330	5 433	7 806
纺织服装、服饰业	Textile Clothing and Habilatory Manufacturing	4 293	75	35	388
木材加工和木、竹、藤、棕、草制品业	Wood Processing and Wood、Bamboo、Cane、Grass Products	3 089	15		47
造纸及纸制品业	Paper Making and Paper Products	13 632	182		380
印刷业和记录媒介的复制	Printing Industry and Recording Media	10 869	129	39	149
石油加工、炼焦及核燃料加工业	Oil Processing,Coking Plant and Nuclear Elding Processing	117 556	695		1 732
化学原料及化学制品制造业	Chemical Materials and Chemical Products Manufacturing	1 258 664	16 874	22 854	85 766
医药制造业	Pharmaceuticals Manufacturing	49 739	655	98	9 896
化学纤维制造业	Chemical Fibre Manufacturing	148 809	233		3 340
橡胶和塑料制品业	Rubber and Plastic Products Manufacturing	146 881	592	366	4 732
非金属矿物制品业	Nonmetal Mineral Products Manufacturing	490 580	4 769	1 120	24 606
黑色金属冶炼及压延加工业	Ferrous Metals Smelting and Rolling	9 816	106	26	162
金属制品业	Metal Product Manufacturing	44 464	150		492
通用设备制造业	General Equipment Manufacturing	2 230	87		124
专用设备制造业	Special Equipment Manufacturing	11 206	88		1 129
电气机械和器材制造业	Electric Machine and Equipment Manufacturing	3 415	24		196
仪器仪表制造业	Apparatus and Meter Manufacturing	56 964	244		450
废弃资源和废旧材料回收加工业	Abandon Resources and Discard Material Recovery Processing	5 013	173		72
电力、热力、燃气及水生产和供应业	**Electricity,Heat,Gass and Water Production and Supply**	**1 011 191**	**6 843**	**4 768**	**28 900**
电力、热力的生产和供应业	Electricity and Heat Production and Supply	953 294	6 561	4 686	16 612
燃气生产和供应业	Gass Production and Supply	37 937	225		11 619
水的生产和供应业	Water Production and Supply	19 960	57	82	669

Continued

(10 000 yuan)

管理费用 Administ-rative Expenses	财务费用 Financial Expenses	#利息支出 Interest Expenditure	营业利润 Operation Business Profits	利润总额（亏损为负） Total Profits as Negative	亏损企业亏损总额 Total Loss	利税总额 Total Profits and Taxes	本年应交增值税 Value Added Taxes Payable	全部就业人员年平均人数(人) Average Number of Employees (person)
322 515	**299 131**	**333 454**	**395 507**	**484 813**	**222 963**	**785 103**	**216 208**	**72 861**
95 788	27 770	31 442	185 874	235 074	55 404	330 797	54 937	29 520
226 727	271 361	302 012	209 633	249 739	167 559	454 306	161 271	43 341
100 116	110 036	109 896	317 784	329 342	1 964	485 048	109 934	21 896
124 783	89 520	122 666	−32 268	2 221	121 206	70 756	48 647	28 359
90 475	77 191	78 461	96 282	140 273	90 381	211 902	54 490	22 221
7 140	22 384	22 431	13 709	12 977	9 412	17 397	3 138	385
26 237	**13 499**	**13 886**	**−2 724**	**3 213**	**20 561**	**25 167**	**14 352**	**4 503**
23 782	12 987	13 283	−7 362	−1 951	20 017	16 935	11 859	3 481
756	444	443	−737	−496	544	1 036	1 175	257
1 699	68	160	5 375	5 659		7 196	1 317	765
230 319	**154 739**	**187 030**	**416 859**	**486 019**	**113 562**	**717 131**	**161 596**	**53 731**
32 588	16 502	16 950	68 040	74 006	13 379	89 072	11 931	9 169
12 369	9 527	7 814	−2 842	21 888	28 097	31 266	6 694	4 300
9 730	−1 820	164	61 904	69 213	7 934	122 476	21 603	3 759
8 831	1 182	3 038	8 053	13 713	2 517	19 446	4 403	5 812
633	73	36	−1 056	64		195	56	346
51	0	0	658	658		674		81
675	393		1 019	1 019		2 296	1 096	80
1 484	6	15	797	2 055		2 583	399	411
7 438	12 630	12 174	−8 700	−8 412	9 851	−22 416	−15 151	1 866
81 345	78 869	86 324	239 078	242 313	8 716	352 434	90 569	12 995
17 263	392	1 471	22 484	23 792	1 645	27 463	3 015	1 209
5 868	814	1 091	8 145	9 439	367	13 043	3 371	1 578
5 688	703	861	16 837	17 386	422	20 466	2 470	2 481
39 994	32 984	54 764	2 678	17 185	40 255	55 856	31 434	8 488
266	−24	3	−30	−16	36	54	−36	77
1 867	980	927	458	473	22	−455	−1 078	163
830	289	291	−239	599		713	27	228
1 883	515	430	53	408		545	49	349
163	−18		397	403		517	91	36
902	396	330	−1 024	−322	322	134	211	211
450	347	348	151	154		768	442	92
65 959	**130 893**	**132 538**	**−18 628**	**−4 420**	**88 840**	**42 805**	**40 260**	**14 627**
60 212	128 390	130 052	−20 482	−10 055	86 600	35 075	38 485	12 974
3 568	877	888	2 752	4 845	622	6 189	1 119	874
2 178	1 627	1 598	−898	790	1 618	1 541	656	779

10－16　规模以上国有及国有控股工业企业主要经济效益指标

(2017年)

指　标	Item	工业经济效益综合指数 Comprehensive Index of industry Economic Benefit	总资产贡献率(%) Ratio of Total Assets to Industrial Output Value (%)
总　计	**Total**	**255.9**	**5.5**
按轻重工业分	**Grouped by Light & Heavy Industry**		
轻工业	Light Industry	223.8	8.9
重工业	Heavy Industry	281.1	4.7
按企业规模分	**Grouped by Size of Enterprises**		
大型企业	Large-Scale Enterprises	391.5	9.3
中型企业	Medium-Scale Enterprises	156.8	2.0
小型企业	Small-Scale Enterprises	234.5	6.5
微型企业	Mini Enterprises	979.1	4.3
按工业行业分	**Grouped by Sector**		
采矿业	**Mining**	**182.1**	**4.0**
煤炭开采和洗选业	Coal Mining and Dressing	164.3	3.3
有色金属矿采选业	Nonferrous Metals Mining and Dressing	147.6	2.9
非金属矿采选业	Nonmetal Mineral Mining and Dressing	295.2	24.2
制造业	**Manufacturing**	**270.8**	**7.2**
农副食品加工业	Farm and Sideline Food Processing	210.8	8.8
食品制造业	Food Manufacturing	162.6	6.1
酒、饮料和精制茶制造业	Liquor Brewing, Beverage and Refined Tea Processing	495.0	27.0
纺织业	Textile Industry	144.9	4.5
纺织服装、服饰业	Textile Clothing and Habilatory Manufacturing	73.6	3.0
木材加工和木、竹、藤、棕、草制品业	Wood Processing and Wood、Bamboo、Cane、Grass Products	704.2	15.5
造纸及纸制品业	Paper Making and Paper Products	435.7	16.2
印刷业和记录媒介的复制	Printing Industry and Recording Media	192.3	7.7
石油加工、炼焦及核燃料加工业	Oil Processing, Coking Plant and Nuclear Elding Processing	72.6	−1.2
化学原料及化学制品制造业	Chemical Materials and Chemical Products Manufacturing	442.2	9.7
医药制造业	Pharmaceuticals Manufacturing	521.2	5.1
化学纤维制造业	Chemical Fibre Manufacturing	201.1	3.4
橡胶和塑料制品业	Rubber and Plastic Products Manufacturing	215.3	11.0
非金属矿物制品业	Nonmetal Mineral Products Manufacturing	195.4	3.6
黑色金属冶炼及压延加工业	Ferrous Metals Smelting and Rolling	156.4	0.0
金属制品业	Metal Product Manufacturing	500.7	0.8
通用设备制造业	General Equipment Manufacturing	182.0	3.8
专用设备制造业	Special Equipment Manufacturing	109.0	2.5
电气机械和器材制造业	Electric Machine and Equipment Manufacturing	244.6	7.7
仪器仪表制造业	Apparatus and Meter Manufacturing	97.3	1.7
废弃资源和废旧材料回收加工业	Abandon Resources and Discard Material Recovery Processing	227.5	2.7
电力、热力、燃气及水生产和供应业	**Electricity, Heat, Gass and Water Production and Supply**	**225.3**	**2.6**
电力、热力的生产和供应业	Electricity and Heat Production and Supply	230.8	2.6
燃气生产和供应业	Gass Production and Supply	243.9	6.3
水的生产和供应业	Water Production and Supply	168.1	1.4

Main Indicators on Enconomic Benefit of State-owned and State-holding Industrial Enterprises above Designated Size

资本保值增值率(%) Ratio of Capital Hold and Rise (%)	资产负债率(%) Assets Liability Ratio (%)	流动资产周转次数(次/年) Number of Times of Annual Turnover Circulating Assets (times/year)	全员劳动生产率(元/人、年) Over Labor Productivity (yuan/person.year)	工业成本费用利润率(%) Ratio of Profits to Industrial Cost (%)	工业销售率(%) Ratio of Industrial Products Sold (%)	工业增加值率(%) Ratio of Value Added to Gross industrial Output Value(%)
107.8	**68.1**	**1.1**	**279 067.4**	**7.7**	**96.7**	**29.6**
105.2	63.7	1.1	201 911.4	9.6	92.5	21.5
108.6	69.2	1.0	331 619.1	6.5	99.6	35.1
110.6	62.9	1.2	425 049.9	17.5	97.9	38.1
149.6	68.0	0.8	168 582.0	0.1	95.6	25.0
73.3	72.2	1.3	255 054.2	6.3	95.8	24.2
49.1	85.1	0.7	1 500 930.6	7.8	105.2	32.6
90.1	**79.0**	**1.0**	**208 625.4**	**1.7**	**103.4**	**49.3**
87.6	83.1	0.7	207 322.0	−1.5	103.5	55.7
97.7	32.6	1.7	174 049.0	−3.7	109.2	51.4
99.1	40.4	3.4	226 172.3	11.8	102.3	33.0
104.2	**64.2**	**1.1**	**282 221.8**	**10.0**	**95.9**	**28.6**
53.5	73.3	1.5	210 033.6	6.7	91.3	15.6
66.7	85.0	1.2	154 694.5	5.3	89.9	14.3
118.8	19.7	1.1	438 677.3	35.7	99.0	58.9
117.8	56.8	1.2	112 453.7	4.6	91.3	21.6
105.3	88.6	1.1	35 479.8	1.2	103.6	26.9
98.0	1.9	45.4	202 185.2	20.7	100.0	42.4
74.1	28.3	2.2	546 596.3	6.8	82.5	22.2
98.6	53.4	0.8	121 358.6	16.0	94.1	42.9
93.3	77.2	1.2	87 402.2	−6.0	99.5	10.8
105.2	63.5	1.3	515 232.1	16.1	100.7	39.3
726.9	50.4	0.4	451 354.4	30.7	87.9	54.9
456.1	87.0	1.0	140 789.2	5.9	95.1	12.6
93.3	47.9	1.2	176 173.0	10.8	100.8	26.9
109.0	61.0	0.6	218 613.5	2.9	95.6	30.6
97.2	91.8	1.2	147 597.4	−0.1	294.6	33.4
90.9	84.7	1.3	746 889.0	1.0	100.0	29.2
138.7	54.8	0.3	104 907.5	17.3	104.2	75.1
87.3	74.4	0.7	92 315.5	2.8	86.0	23.6
32.7	49.8	0.8	253 394.4	10.7	101.3	22.1
83.6	67.8	4.5	27 323.2	−0.5	103.8	11.3
100.5	43.9	1.3	272 297.8	2.2	102.8	41.8
120.6	**73.6**	**0.9**	**289 165.8**	**−0.4**	**99.0**	**30.6**
119.0	74.5	0.9	302 606.1	−0.9	99.0	30.1
102.0	63.7	4.2	196 473.8	8.8	100.0	31.1
164.2	52.8	0.6	169 317.3	3.0	100.2	56.3

10—17 各师规模以上工业企业主要经济指标

Main Economic Indicators of Industrial Enterprises above Designated Size by Division

计量单位:万元 (2017年) (10 000 yuan)

单位	Unit	工业总产值(当年价格) Gross Industrial Output Value (at current prices)	工业增加值(当年价格) Added Value of Industry (atcurrent prices)	资产合计 Total Assets	流动资产合计 Circulation Assets	固定资产合计 Fixed Assets	负债合计 Total Liabilities	# 流动负债合计 Liquid Liabilities	所有者权益合计 Creditors Equity	# 国家资本 National Capital
总计	**Total**	**20 620 581**	**5 474 291**	**37 882 365**	**13 787 060**	**17 941 550**	**24 900 392**	**16 205 724**	**12 991 255**	**2 096 461**
一师	Division 1	2 306 634	658 152	4 408 704	1 638 312	1 708 854	2 707 392	1 807 654	1 696 414	212 026
二师	Division 2	1 434 184	338 690	1 471 179	631 868	437 440	798 567	535 069	671 738	152 117
三师	Division 3	1 141 326	272 717	1 826 934	760 378	941 282	1 079 345	695 878	742 224	245 082
四师	Division 4	1 545 502	608 106	1 956 979	653 299	1 011 139	1 211 675	952 101	745 304	137 180
五师	Division 5	252 187	43 141	483 952	160 448	258 279	424 565	221 107	59 386	73 331
六师	Division 6	4 036 177	882 296	6 944 405	2 868 599	3 354 949	4 846 723	3 996 226	2 097 680	250 535
七师	Division 7	909 309	243 502	2 167 381	704 896	882 565	1 569 710	970 317	597 671	277 038
八师	Division 8	5 814 300	1 598 588	13 531 598	4 418 169	6 977 481	8 896 707	4 886 609	4 659 393	343 701
九师	Division 9	112 373	17 097	252 947	147 723	84 052	201 828	137 047	51 119	48 551
十师	Division 10	327 198	121 250	555 663	193 059	291 406	382 823	236 744	172 839	52 475
十一师	Division 11	227 083	50 531	287 602	195 978	50 383	221 584	203 785	62 409	18 778
十二师	Division 12	314 509	66 910	708 673	256 013	272 549	498 360	383 181	209 842	94 439
十三师	Division 13	1 762 254	487 501	2 506 272	722 601	1 532 592	1 685 934	926 879	820 338	119 340
十四师	Division 14	41 443	11 897	105 164	57 559	40 746	61 149	43 295	44 015	12 122
兵团直属	Directly under XPCC	396 102	73 914	674 914	378 159	97 833	314 032	209 834	360 883	59 749

单位	Unit	主营业务收入 Main Business Income	主营业务成本 Main Business Cost	主营业务税金及附加 Main Business Tax and Affixture	销售费用 Sale Expenses	管理费用 Administrative Expenses	营业利润 Business Profits	利润总额 Total Profits	利税总额 Total Profits and Taxes	就业人员年平均人数(人) Average Annual Exployees (Person)
总计	**Total**	**20 071 605**	**16 172 782**	**180 318**	**611 768**	**595 510**	**508 688**	**2 237 352**	**2 971 321**	**158 727**
一师	Division 1	2 256 967	1 787 240	11 068	42 776	60 536	46 925	352 600	399 328	22 000
二师	Division 2	1 389 241	1 139 968	9 766	39 602	36 646	15 999	154 994	198 431	12 516
三师	Division 3	1 005 799	832 799	1 007	21 111	27 387	14 913	113 552	152 697	9 551
四师	Division 4	1 506 634	1 059 952	36 631	51 102	51 691	31 480	281 380	372 094	12 606
五师	Division 5	251 561	220 933	704	2 506	10 100	11 046	1 689	7 466	2 669
六师	Division 6	4 079 921	3 505 724	25 096	110 816	77 293	78 368	352 707	488 199	18 890
七师	Division 7	876 959	748 728	4 514	38 498	24 808	31 093	42 787	70 466	10 026
八师	Division 8	5 536 435	4 312 682	77 292	228 005	194 444	215 590	578 751	863 591	48 219
九师	Division 9	96 620	87 946	157	2 844	3 860	4 819	—59	496	1 387
十师	Division 10	303 509	210 784	5 021	11 484	21 090	8 842	52 435	64 608	3 788
十一师	Division 11	210 766	190 436	795	2 108	10 338	4 368	3 246	6 905	3 148
十二师	Division 12	367 928	311 787	2 017	20 407	20 292	9 637	14 759	22 997	3 935
十三师	Division 13	1 756 300	1 416 147	5 130	17 805	30 956	33 921	252 801	285 786	6 589
十四师	Division 14	34 840	29 779	93	287	2 026	648	3 304	5 324	766
兵团直属	Directly under XPCC	398 127	317 878	1 028	22 419	24 044	1 038	32 406	32 933	2 637

10－18 各师规模以上工业企业主要经济效益指标

Main Indicators on Economic Benefit of Industrial Enterprises above Designated Size by Division

(2017 年)

单 位 Unit	工业经济效益综合指数 Comprehensive Index of industry Economic Results	总资产贡献率(%) Ratio of Total Assets to Industrial Output Value (%)	资本保值增值率(%) Ratio of Capital Hold and Rise (%)	资产负债率(%) Assets Liability Ratio (%)	流动资产周转次数(次/年) Number of Times of Annual Turnover Circulating Assets (rimes-/year)	全员劳动生产率(元/人、年) Over Labor Productivity (yuan/person-year)	工业成本费用利润率(%) Ratio of Profits to Industrial Cost (%)	工业销售率(%) Ratio of Industrial Products Sold (%)	工业增加值率(%) Ratio of Value Added to Gross Industrial Output Value (%)
总 计 Total	**324.3**	**9.1**	**112.3**	**65.7**	**1.5**	**344 887**	**11.8**	**97.7**	**26.5**
一 师 Division 1	321.5	10.1	110.6	61.4	1.4	299 160	18.1	97.6	28.5
二 师 Division 2	296.8	14.4	96.7	54.3	2.2	270 605	12.5	97.9	23.6
三 师 Division 3	290.7	9.3	118.8	59.1	1.3	285 538	12.6	87.3	23.9
四 师 Division 4	482.1	20.6	112.1	61.9	2.3	482 395	23.5	98.3	39.3
五 师 Division 5	150.9	3.8	79.9	87.7	1.6	161 636	0.7	96.4	17.1
六 师 Division 6	385.4	8.0	118.2	69.8	1.5	467 070	9.2	99.5	21.9
七 师 Division 7	223.9	4.6	114.4	72.4	1.3	242 870	5.0	96.9	26.8
八 师 Division 8	306.3	7.9	114.5	65.8	1.5	331 527	9.9	98.2	27.5
九 师 Division 9	114.4	2.0	91.4	79.8	0.7	123 269	−0.1	83.5	15.2
十 师 Division 10	353.9	13.3	145.8	68.9	1.6	320 089	20.7	92.1	37.1
十一师 Division 11	151.8	3.8	81.6	77.1	1.1	160 519	1.6	97.1	22.3
十二师 Division 12	173.3	4.6	72.8	70.3	1.5	170 039	4.0	99.5	21.3
十三师 Division 13	598.9	12.7	120.3	67.3	2.4	739 871	16.8	99.7	27.7
十四师 Division 14	186.4	5.7	111.2	58.2	0.6	155 318	10.0	83.3	28.7
兵团直属 Directly under XPCC	259.9	5.0	103.8	46.5	1.1	280 294	8.9	101.3	18.7

10—19 各师规模以上国有及国有控股工业企业主要经济指标
Main Economic Indicators of State-owned and State-holding Industrial Enterprises above Designated Division

计量单位：万元 (2017 年) (10 000 yuan)

单 位	Unit	工业总产值（当年价格） Gross Industrial Output Value (atcurrent)	工业增加值（当年价格） Added Value of Industry (At current Prices)	资产合计 Total Assets	流动资产合计 Circulating Assets	固定资产合计 Fixed Assets	负债合计 Total Liabilities	# 流动负债合计 Liquid Liabilities	所有者权益合计 Creditors Equity	# 国家资本 National Capital
总 计	**Total**	**6 875 743**	**2 033 313**	**19 445 916**	**6 468 586**	**8 799 221**	**13 232 110**	**8 029 539**	**6 224 246**	**1 895 449**
一 师	Division 1	904 525	237 007	3 121 068	1 099 877	1 134 553	1 935 454	1 204 021	1 180 717	208 891
二 师	Division 2	337 137	81 328	716 070	289 886	148 921	456 368	244 886	259 702	150 554
三 师	Division 3	547 706	118 375	885 867	474 768	346 766	596 508	388 322	283 994	185 082
四 师	Division 4	649 332	297 644	1 454 657	505 764	714 936	1 047 516	813 155	407 140	130 935
五 师	Division 5	104 315	13 116	348 030	69 268	227 320	333 295	161 817	14 735	71 247
六 师	Division 6	280 051	32 825	1 408 489	391 901	861 079	1 168 029	856 308	240 460	226 332
七 师	Division 7	433 945	125 513	1 753 350	500 957	703 781	1 310 377	723 494	442 972	266 862
八 师	Division 8	2 497 973	849 884	7 171 968	2 014 921	3 758 063	4 670 463	2 498 067	2 525 818	315 931
九 师	Division 9	71 870	10 094	158 437	110 895	34 139	129 527	104 344	28 910	41 271
十 师	Division 10	102 892	34 140	310 123	86 453	181 968	245 371	126 217	64 752	50 917
十一师	Division 11	153 907	35 543	227 846	153 283	40 451	175 400	178 886	48 837	18 178
十二师	Division 12	212 631	52 696	590 360	225 606	219 971	411 355	331 913	179 005	93 685
十三师	Division 13	154 338	64 719	546 821	125 122	297 364	392 640	159 687	154 181	64 045
十四师	Division 14	29 020	6 515	77 917	41 725	32 077	45 775	28 590	32 142	11 772
兵团直属	Directly under XPCC	396 102	73 914	674 914	378 159	97 833	314 032	209 834	360 883	59 749

单 位	Unit	主营业务收入 Main Business Income	主营业务成本 Main Business Cost	主营业务税金及附加 Main Business Tax and Affixture	销售费用 Sale Expenses	管理费用 Administrative Expenses	营业利润 Business Profits	利润总额 Total Profits	利税总额 Total Profits and Taxes	就业人员年平均人数（人） Average Annual Exployees (Person)
总 计	**Total**	**6 656 146**	**5 329 648**	**77 658**	**262 883**	**322 515**	**299 131**	**484 813**	**785 103**	**72 861**
一 师	Division 1	908 537	772 112	8 185	20 923	36 322	35 730	67 594	99 918	10 137
二 师	Division 2	336 917	282 068	3 253	14 450	14 733	10 550	16 587	30 121	4 394
三 师	Division 3	470 544	407 360	700	12 998	16 102	10 068	28 306	45 565	5 449
四 师	Division 4	637 757	456 301	26 523	15 721	26 838	27 637	90 885	147 220	7 959
五 师	Division 5	110 756	101 271	547	322	6 049	10 439	−15 242	−10 203	1 679
六 师	Division 6	241 294	211 107	3 232	8 112	14 524	24 259	−5 419	−13 644	4 326
七 师	Division 7	423 658	355 592	2 918	26 765	15 508	26 826	5 172	21 338	5 664
八 师	Division 8	2 394 833	1 821 297	25 713	112 283	125 705	121 795	222 094	366 221	21 880
九 师	Division 9	54 793	51 510	119	1 925	3 113	2 191	−1 347	−1 102	1 105
十 师	Division 10	80 141	58 547	1 985	4 194	9 094	6 130	5 266	9 853	1 284
十一师	Division 11	152 908	137 198	719	1 778	6 583	2 918	4 259	6 675	1 495
十二师	Division 12	269 501	227 121	1 893	16 949	17 028	7 662	9 589	17 360	3 361
十三师	Division 13	153 778	110 164	779	3 842	5 226	11 241	23 477	30 032	997
十四师	Division 14	22 603	20 122	66	201	1 645	648	1 188	2 816	494
兵团直属	Directly under XPCC	398 127	317 878	1 028	22 419	24 044	1 038	32 406	32 933	2 637

10－20　各师规模以上国有及国有控股工业企业主要经济效益指标

Main Indicators on Economic Benefit of State-owned and State-holding Industrial Enterprises above Designated Size by Division

(2017 年)

单　位 Unit		工业经济效益综合指数 Comprehensive Index of industry Economic Results	总资产贡献率(%) Ratio of Total Assets to Industrial Output Value(%)	资本保值增值率(%) Ratio of Capital Hold and Rise(%)	资产负债率(%) Assets Liability Ratio(%)	流动资产周转次数(次/年) Number of Times of Annual Turnover Circulating Assets (times/year)	全员劳动生产率(元/人·年) Over Labor Productivity (yuan/person-year)	工业成本费用利润率(%) Ratio of Profits to Industrial Cost(%)	工业销售率(%) Ratio of Industrial Products Sold(%)	工业增加值率(%) Ratio of Value Added to Gross Industrial Output Value(%)
总　计	**Total**	**255.9**	**5.5**	**107.8**	**68.1**	**1.1**	**279 067**	**7.7**	**96.7**	**29.6**
一　师	Division 1	226.1	4.3	106.8	62.0	0.8	233 804	7.7	98.5	26.2
二　师	Division 2	189.7	5.5	86.8	63.7	1.2	185 088	5.1	103.0	24.1
三　师	Division 3	212.6	6.5	106.2	67.3	1.0	217 241	6.3	82.0	21.6
四　师	Division 4	364.5	12.0	121.7	72.0	1.3	373 971	17.2	98.6	45.8
五　师	Division 5	34.8	0.1	46.1	95.8	1.6	78 119	−12.9	94.6	12.6
六　师	Division 6	74.9	0.7	95.6	82.9	0.6	75 877	−2.0	83.0	11.7
七　师	Division 7	187.2	2.7	105.6	74.7	0.9	221 598	1.2	96.8	28.9
八　师	Division 8	337.7	6.8	118.0	65.1	1.2	388 430	10.1	99.8	34.0
九　师	Division 9	80.0	0.5	87.0	81.8	0.5	91 351	−2.2	73.3	14.0
十　师	Division 10	249.0	5.2	199.1	79.1	1.0	265 885	6.7	80.1	33.2
十一师	Division 11	202.9	4.2	74.4	77.0	1.0	237 747	2.9	99.3	23.1
十二师	Division 12	159.9	4.2	67.5	69.7	1.2	156 788	3.5	100.5	24.8
十三师	Division 13	520.9	7.5	96.8	71.8	1.3	649 142	17.5	100.3	41.9
十四师	Division 14	149.3	4.4	104.5	58.8	0.5	131 886	5.3	75.8	22.5
兵团直属	Directly under XPCC	260.2	5.0	106.4	46.5	1.1	280 294	8.9	101.3	18.7

10－21　个体工业主要指标

Main Indicators of Individual Industry

计量单位：万元　　(2017 年)　　(10 000 yuan)

指　标	Item	户数 Household (户) (household)	工业总产值 Gross Industrial (当年价格) (At Current Prices)
总　计	**Total**	**2 900**	**731 116**
一　师	Division 1	55	31 199
二　师	Division 2	125	44 887
三　师	Division 3	24	18 393
四　师	Division 4	611	76 124
五　师	Division 5	217	27 457
六　师	Division 6	479	43 561
七　师	Division 7	178	85 373
八　师	Division 8	408	76 352
九　师	Division 9	74	13 182
十　师	Division 10	230	69 044
十一师	Division 11		
十二师	Division 12	123	21 217
十三师	Division 13	301	96 658
十四师	Division 14	75	5 996

10—22　大中型工业企业主要指标

Main Indicators of Large and Medium-sized Industrial Enterprises

计量单位:万元　　(10 000 yuan)

指　　标	Item	2016	2017
企业单位数(个)	Number of Enterprises(unit)	111	111
# 亏损企业(个)	Loss(unit)	35	35
工业总产值(按当年价格计算)	Gross Industrial Output Value(atCurrantPrices)	10 443 961	11 685 849
工业销售产值(按当年价格计算生产法)	Sales Value of Industry Products(at Current Prices Produce Approach)	10 289 399	11 463 369
# 出口交货值	Delivery Value of Industry Export	148 744	31 277
工业增加值(按当年价格计算)	Added Value of Industry(At current Prices)	2 993 758	
流动资产小计	Circulating Assets	7 003 138	9 058 038
# 应收账款净额	Net Accounts Receivable	594 783	906 213
存　货	Stock	1 579 229	1 893 792
# 产成品	Finished Product	603 450	759 417
固定资产小计	Fixed Assets	11 731 323	11 926 166
固定资产原价	Original Fixed Assets	14 733 138	16 320 671
累计折旧	Accumulated Depreciation	3 527 817	4 323 681
资产合计	Total Assets	22 631 868	25 612 355
流动负债合计	Liquid Liabilities	9 308 843	10 833 255
非流动负债合计	Long-term Liabilities	6 271 764	6 144 801
负债合计	Total Liabilities	15 673 929	17 046 447
所有者权益合计	Creditors'Equity	6 957 758	8 565 908
主营业务收入	Main Business Income	10 145 967	11 402 192
主营业务成本	Main Business Cost	8 107 628	9 251 784
主营业务税金及附加	Main Business Tax and Affixture	63 311	127 738
其他业务利润	Profits of Other Business	44 021	60 932
销售费用	Sale Expenses	359 498	408 178
管理费用	Adiministrative Expenses	322 890	345 037
财务费用	Financial Expenses	384 082	345 551
# 利息支出	Intrest Exjpenditure	406 219	375 133
营业利润	Business Profits	912 001	979 696
补贴收入	Subsidy Income9	70 408	
利润总额(亏损为负)	Total Profits(Negative as Loss)	1 044 045	1 112 791
# 所得税费用	Income Tax Payable	101 713	162 162
利税总额	Total Profits and Tax	1 494 677	1 616 729
本年应付职工薪酬	Total Wages Payable	687 722	698 409
本年应交增值税	Value Added Taxes Payable	381 879	370 415
本年进项税额	Receipt Tax	858 877	1 068 427
本年销项税额	Sale Tax	1 225 176	1 321 208
全部职工(就业人员)年平均人数(人)	Average Number of Staff and Workers(person)	100 446	96 080

注:大中型企业划分标准按2011年新标准执行。所得税费用由两部分组成:当期所得税和延递所得税。当期所得税即应交所得税。

Note: Large scale and medium scale enterprises were classified by the standard of 2011. The income tax expense is made up of current income tax(income tax payable) and deferred income tax.

10—23 主要年份工业主要产品产量
Output of Major Industrial Products in Major Years

年 份 Year	原 煤(吨) Coal (ton)	大 米(吨) Rice (ton)	小麦粉(吨) Wheat Flour (ton)	精制食用植物油(吨) Refined Edible Vegetable Oil(ton)	成品糖(吨) Refinde Sugar (ton)	乳制品(吨) Dairy Products (ton)	罐 头(吨) Canned Food (ton)
1952	114 988	624	2 249	73			
1954	172 498	5 440	19 695	834			
1957	437 310	7 689	55 020	4 115			
1962	1 400 893	6 104	71 637	2 878	3 754	180	
1965	2 109 957	11 310	128 506	7 298	21 095	79	
1970	3 358 500	25 520	277 448	7 263	19 391	186	
1975	1 221 653	21 704	76 124	2 010	410	88	
1978	2 231 556	48 660	188 020	6 438	18 965	119	
1980	2 487 251	45 898	260 252	13 930	38 734	247	
1985	3 470 200	101 219	300 037	36 659	51 455	1 442	2 802
1990	3 430 868	101 488	308 284	46 922	57 764	6 566	22 519
1995	3 045 604	83 893	298 271	94 443	108 931	3 606	33 674
2000	3 359 203	89 859	200 000	188 294	106 382	1 828	118 115
2001	3 369 597	96 004	219 700	160 783	133 361	3 264	81 253
2002	3 712 242	68 027	291 000	157 100	135 424	4 422	209 296
2003	3 827 877	78 615	257 800	170 243	141 312	22 394	246 229
2004	4 022 989	83 856	220 754	195 112	132 153	18 000	349 193
2005	3 678 606	62 556	228 301	183 453	153 181	28 270	244 885
2006	3 802 198	70 995	221 239	193 055	163 530	36 806	368 127
2007	3 680 162	92 225	224 882	206 789	215 862	54 555	462 234
2008	6 118 672	83 365	173 797	231 440	183 140	63 441	413 255
2009	6 785 468	88 010	200 273	321 172	138 751	72 774	694 945
2010	9 258 299	78 849	224 662	307 264	172 356	96 244	675 695
2011	11 413 450	96 584	215 325	398 827	167 738	122 403	843 412
2012	10 521 288	155 655	296 641	571 496	194 362	127 444	446 833
2013	11 274 888	167 833	268 261	612 553	178 437	125 909	335 041
2014	9 400 367	213 055	341 049	758 938	153 725	133 616	516 502
2015	8 519 347	194 632	399 356	803 095	140 792	156 478	641 272
2016	10 851 974	211 536	372 938	871 701	146 507	199 404	609 553
2017	9 006 932	238 233	402 653	716 729	181 734	240 782	621 806

年 份 Year	味 精(吨) Monosodium Glutamate (ton)	饮料酒(千升) Beverage Wine (1000 liter)	#白 酒 White Spirit	饲 料(吨) Forage (ton)	纱(吨) Yarn (ton)	布(万米) Cloth (10 000 m)	服 装(万件) Garments (10 000 pieces)
1952					458	330	
1954							
1957							
1962		1 639	1 082		4 704	2 935	136
1965		1 103	1 103		9 180	4 644	127
1970		1 729	1 729		14 365	7 235	
1975		1 369	1 186		8 737	104	
1978		2 965	2 682		8 164	4 237	35
1980	62	6 048	5 130		9 434	4 179	36
1985	328	23 564	11 570	32 485	15 473	6 326	42
1990	1 229	28 022	19 201	95 021	38 481	9 676	97
1995	3 138	35 496	24 243	177 178	77 636	11 389	450
2000	3 901	56 041	45 870	230 703	121 422	12 690	337
2001	2 781	53 683	43 805	281 683	108 206	12 080	347
2002	2 132	53 304	43 308	273 454	106 380	8 913	396
2003	2 615	51 352	27 139	285 113	113 048	8 237	441
2004	2 300	41 709	27 905	322 014	111 769	9 073	367
2005	1 702	40 618	26 176	359 075	129 765	8 371	393
2006	2 417	43 613	28 426	404 414	137 192	7 865	363
2007	25	85 647	35 040	475 142	169 995	7 346	230
2008	1 900	102 124	30 625	567 810	171 880	6 896	199
2009	15 913	85 185	36 164	1 019 585	197 163	8 577	359
2010	20 910	149 712	42 969	1 083 029	225 210	8 974	384
2011	20 852	187 980	45 222	1 197 001	192 990	5 389	588
2012	16 547	232 635	58 764	1 515 141	257 200	5 300	538
2013	1 214	246 095	55 397	2 122 755	243 198	5 600	490
2014	93	241 994	54 710	2 655 331	210 102	5 975	414
2015	283	229 747	59 909	2 739 234	272 438	6 398	510
2016	173 238	220 975	60 689	3 196 717	407 423	11 537	674
2017	153 682	202 136	63 783	3 309 797	488 760	14 977	756

注:从 2003 年起,饮料酒与白酒执行新的计量单位:千升。
Note:Since 2003 beverage wine and white spirit are carried out new calculation Unit:1000 Liter.

10—23 续表 Continued

年 份 Year	机制纸及纸板(吨) Machine-made Paper and Paper-boards(ton)	发电量(万千瓦时) Electricity (10 000 kwh)	#水 电 Hydro-power	焦 炭(吨) Coke (ton)	硫 酸(吨) Sulfuric Acid (ton)	烧 碱(吨) Caustic Soda (ton)	农用化肥(吨) Farm Chemical Ferrilizer (ton)
1952		152		8 808			
1954		134					
1957		374					
1962	2 500	5 289	1 458	96 534	1 722	147	1 643
1965	6 739	8 804	4 018	78 200	4 382	563	4 099
1970	8 387	19 712	14 081	140 236	7 151	901	12 842
1975	880	10 785	8 024	16 714	7 889	454	3 026
1978	7 250	25 425	16 283	135 991	2 516	1 352	16 593
1980	14 797	24 244	14 743	65 895	6 907	1 121	1 249
1985	25 122	34 516	22 456	85 400	9 328	1 972	6 036
1990	43 248	70 384	38 189	105 775	13 945	7 479	7 449
1995	61 507	116 385	48 757	158 828	24 911	10 087	2 708
2000	49 893	178 745	58 050	130 414	34 852	20 257	12 295
2001	45 796	179 445	62 055	150 505	37 293	26 064	25 838
2002	56 600	191 905	63 060	174 121	34 705	33 965	19 187
2003	65 929	211 594	64 887	212 500	40 285	47 503	13 585
2004	66 854	256 317	65 148	265 016	47 855	56 192	9 612
2005	63 310	360 926	68 229	329 425	69 419	158 231	16 313
2006	86 993	478 980	71 501	423 818	65 988	215 416	13 485
2007	53 813	548 057	92 387	654 022	66 026	231 955	7 707
2008	60 380	756 605	93 887	644 057	80 288	302 270	31 068
2009	134 531	1 140 950	94 034	625 903	112 739	451 851	17 416
2010	127 026	1 348 687	102 408	1 676 530	90 539	505 264	11 528
2011	135 218	1 975 873	112 462	1 654 600	73 602	690 314	133 873
2012	144 868	3 319 617	178 759	3 197 978	59 312	790 782	478 163
2013	168 831	4 545 744	132 944	4 581 262	13 850	832 825	943 834
2014	149 032	5 720 536	115 849	8 879 192	11 902	949 178	527 921
2015	113 948	6 645 356	140 707	6 428 066	1 545	944 563	558 062
2016	130 302	7 517 859	169 602	7 296 901		947 463	503 816
2017	73 173	8 021 421	159 829	6 200 340		922 056	495 129

年 份 Year	酒 精(千升) Alcohol (1000 liter)	塑料制品(吨) Plastic Products (ton)	水 泥(吨) Cement (ton)	砖(万块) Brick (10 000 piece)	粗 钢(吨) Steel (ton)	钢 材(吨) Steel Products (ton)
1952				2 994	705	618
1954				7 538		
1957				14 911		
1962	243		4 421	5 676	1 974	2 199
1965	2 154		87 530	27 714	2 647	2 009
1970	1 729		104 963	18 741	10 298	5 152
1975	1 503		2 800	3 854	13 090	5 466
1978	1 287		76 620	29 134	10 425	9 009
1980	3 188		150 015	58 489	10 465	7 701
1985	3 364	3 126	549 700	117 797	18 620	13 547
1990	4 442	9 216	787 995	117 247	25 034	20 880
1995	16 814	28 281	1 133 672	143 609	21 121	16 577
2000	10 355	67 712	1 690 000	188 493		
2001	11 744	108 657	1 944 600	181 088		
2002	11 224	84 742	2 282 300	161 291		
2003	15 070	116 694	2 535 600	148 229		
2004	12 957	148 549	2 710 637	148 661		
2005	11 064	148 197	2 936 374	146 527		
2006	7 917	175 474	3 895 625	163 241		
2007	7 587	230 318	4 426 243	149 723		
2008	8 592	233 440	5 336 441	139 128		
2009	7 000	259 075	7 057 155	179 967	26 255	52 858
2010	5 193	314 388	9 668 886	205 101	17 219	69 901
2011	6 277	405 577	12 069 605	294 131	33 600	85 972
2012	53 731	510 511	15 345 449	693 309	120 191	150 292
2013	56 660	665 022	18 443 576	677 633	560 306	574 600
2014	52 725	808 378	18 066 409	771 181	1 241 236	1 024 928
2015	49 175	1 156 129	13 684 866	815 848	233 875	714 676
2016	43 374	833 749	12 352 657	828 164	674 262	802 660
2017		883 202	12 699 853	488 026	1 395 759	1 559 006

10—24 工业主要产品产量
Output of Major Industrial Products

指 标		Item		2017
原 煤	(万吨)	Coal	(10 000 tons)	900.69
小麦粉	(吨)	Wheate Flour	(ton)	402 653
大 米	(吨)	Rice	(ton)	238 233
配混合饲料	(吨)	Forage	(ton)	3 309 797
精制食用植物油	(吨)	Refined Edible Vegetable Oil	(ton)	716 729
成品糖	(吨)	Refined Sugar	(ton)	181 734
鲜冷藏冻肉	(吨)	Fresh Refuigerates Meet	(ton)	1 173
方便面	(吨)	Convenient Noodles	(ton)	21 230
乳制品	(吨)	Dairy Products	(ton)	240 782
# 液体乳		Liquid Milk		221 750
罐 头	(吨)	Canned Food	(ton)	621 806
# 番茄酱罐头		Canned Ketchup		608 128
味 精	(吨)	Monosodium Glutamate	(ton)	153 682
酱 油	(吨)	Soy	(ton)	330
发酵酒精(折96度,商品量)	(千升)	YmolyticAlcohol	(1 000 liter)	
饮料酒	(千升)	AlcoholBeverage	(1 000 liter)	202 136
# 白酒(折65度,商品量)		WhiteSpirit		63 783
啤酒		Beer		87 019
葡萄酒		Wine		47 280
软饮料	(吨)	Soft Drink	(ton)	524 910
# 碳酸饮料		Carbonated Beverag		41 476
果汁及果汁饮料		Fruit Juice and Berverage		126 376
纱	(吨)	Yarn	(ton)	488 760
布	(万米)	Cloth	(10 000 m)	14 977
# 棉 布		Cotton Cloth		14 260
呢 绒	(万米)	Woolen Goods	(10 000 m)	240
服 装	(万件)	Garments	(10 000 pieces)	756
# 梭织服装		Loom Clothing		142
人造板	(立方米)	Artificial Board	(cu.meter)	212 564
家 具	(件)	Funiture	(unit)	349 157
纸 浆	(吨)	Paper Pulp	(ton)	
机制纸及纸板	(吨)	Machine-made Paper and Paper Boards	(ton)	73 173
纸制品	(吨)	Paper Products	(ton)	149 939
焦 炭	(吨)	Coke	(ton)	6 200 340
# 机械化焦炉生产的焦炭		Coke Turnedout by Mechanized Coke Oven		6 200 340
盐酸(含量31%以上)	(吨)	Hydrochloric Acid(with Content of 31%)	(ton)	225 405
氢氧化钠(烧碱)(折100%)	(吨)	Caustic Soda	(ton)	922 056

10—24 续表　Continued

指　　标		Item		2017
电　石	(吨)	Calcium Carhide	(ton)	2 244 302
合成氨(无水氨)	(吨)	Synthetic Ammonia(Anhydrous Ammonia)	(ton)	459 430
农用氮、磷、钾化学肥料总计(折纯)	(吨)	Chemical Fertilizer	(ton)	495 129
化学农药	(吨)	Chemical Pesticides	(ton)	2 323
涂　料	(吨)	Paint	(ton)	26 072
塑料树脂及共聚物	(吨)	Plastics resin and	(ton)	1 352 104
# 聚氯乙烯树脂		Corvic		1 352 104
中成药	(吨)	Traditional Chinese Medicine	(ton)	315
化学纤维用浆粕	(吨)	Chemical Fibre Pulp	(ton)	59 152
# 化学纤维		Chemical Fibre		108 529
塑料制品	(吨)	Plastic Produces	(ton)	883 202
# 塑料薄膜		Plastic Pellicle		103 124
塑料管及其附件		Plastic PipeandIts Enclosure		554 448
硅酸盐水泥熟料	(万吨)	Cement Chamotte	(10 000 tons)	836.45
# 窑外分解窑水泥热料		Predecomposing Kiln Chamotle		836.45
水　泥	(万吨)	Cement	(10 000 tons)	1 269.99
商品混凝土	(万立方米)	Merchandise concrete	(10 000 cu.meters)	2 082.21
水泥排水管	(吨)	Cement Sewage Duct	(ton)	1 316
水泥电杆	(根)	Cement Electric Pole Piece	(unit)	86 288
砖(折标准砖)	(万块)	Brick(standardBrick)	(10 000 pieces)	488 026
瓦	(万片)	Tile	(10 000 pieces)	186
平板玻璃	(重量箱)	Plate Glass	(weight cases)	2 730 000
耐火材料制品	(吨)	Fire-Resistant Material Producs	(ton)	12 552
生　铁	(吨)	PigIron	(ton)	1 313 688
粗　钢	(吨)	CrudeSteel	(ton)	1 395 759
钢　材	(吨)	RolledSteel	(ton)	1 559 006
铁合金	(吨)	IronAlloys	(ton)	32 471
电解铝	(吨)	Electrolyzed Aluminum	(ton)	2 835 953
镁	(吨)	Magnesium	(ton)	26 084
铝　材	(吨)	Aluminum	(ton)	997 820
泵	(台)	Pump	(unit)	7 360
发电机组(发电设备)	(千瓦)	Generator Set	(kw)	192 600
# 风力发电机组		Wind Generator Set		192 600
发电量	(万千瓦时)	Electricity	(10 000 kwh)	8 021 421
# 火　电		Thermalpower		7 266 158
水　电		Hydropower		159 829
供热量	(万百万千焦)	Volume of Heat Supply	(10 billion kj)	10 547
自来水生产量	(万立方米)	Tap Water Production	(10 000 cu.meter)	24 704

10—25 各师工业主要产品产量

Output of Major Industrial Products by Division

(2017 年)

指 标		Item		合 计 Total	一 师 Division 1	二 师 Division 2	三 师 Division 3
原 煤	(万吨)	Coal	(10 000 ton)	900.69	101.23	211.21	
小麦粉	(吨)	Wheate Flour	(ton)	402 653	62 060	1 646	67 227
大 米	(吨)	Rice	(ton)	238 233	66 819	1 887	
配混合饲料	(吨)	Forage	(ton)	3 309 797	87 670	450 133	673 306
精制食用植物油	(吨)	Refined Edible Vegetable Oil	(ton)	716 729	139 898	59 429	103 679
成品糖	(吨)	Refined Sugar	(ton)	181 734	46 091		
乳制品	(吨)	Dairy Products	(ton)	240 782	35 793		
# 液体乳		Liquid Milk		221 750	32 821		
罐 头	(吨)	Canned Food	(ton)	621 806		212 479	
# 番茄酱罐头		Canned Ketchup		608 128		210 511	
饮料酒	(千升)	Alcohol Beverage	(1 000 liter)	202 136	32 695	11 015	6 476
白酒(折 65 度,商品量)		White Spirit		63 783	1 631	10 890	
啤 酒		Beer		87 019	29 741		
葡萄酒		Wine		47 280		122	5 680
软饮料	(吨)	Soft Drink	(ton)	524 910	47 137	3 622	70 258
纱	(吨)	Yarn	(ton)	488 760	116 908	67 700	48 520
布	(万米)	Cloth	(10 000 m)	14 977	3 165		6 284
呢 绒	(万米)	Woolen Piece Goods	(10 000 m)	240			
服 装	(万件)	Garments	(10 000 pieces)	756.18			144.57
家 具	(件)	Funiture	(unit)	349 157		41 594	450
机制纸及纸板	(吨)	Machine-made Paper and Paper Boards	(ton)	73 173	8 575	42 092	
焦 炭	(吨)	Coke	(ton)	6 200 340			
# 机械化焦炉生产的焦炭		Coke Turned out by Mechanized Coke Oven		6 200 340			
盐 酸(含量 31%以上)	(吨)	Hydrochloric Acid(with Content of 31%)	(ton)	225 405	17 500		
氢氧化钠(烧碱)(折 100%)	(吨)	Caustic Soda	(ton)	922 056			
电 石	(吨)	Calcium Carhide	(ton)	2 244 302			
合成氨(无水氨)	(吨)	Synthetic Ammonia(Anhydrous Ammonia)	(ton)	459 430			
塑料树脂及共聚物	(吨)	Plastics resin and	(ton)	1 352 104			
# 聚氯乙烯树脂		Corvic		1 352 104			
塑料制品	(吨)	Plastic Produces	(ton)	883 202	118 735	87 964	77 104
# 塑料薄膜		Plastic Pellicle		103 124	18 209	14 116	2 875
塑料制管子及其附件		Plastic Stick and Pipe Section		554 448	74 380	34 443	58 433
硅酸盐水泥熟料	(万吨)	Cement Familiar Material	(10 000 tons)	836.45	285.13	30.01	25.92
# 窑外分解窑熟料		Beforehand Resolve Kiln Familiar Material		836.45	285.13	30.01	25.92
水 泥	(万吨)	Cement	(10 000 tons)	1269.99	399.29	39.50	31.21
砖(折标准砖)	(万块)	Brick (standard Brick)	(10 000 pieces)	488 026	9 362	7 415	52 856
发电量	(万千瓦时)	Electricity	(10 000 kwh)	8 021 421	240 534	81 902	150 817
火 电		Coal-Fired Generation		7 266 158	211 514	58 413	104 979
水 电		Hydropower Generation		159 829	14 754	2 365	
供热量	(万百万千焦)	Volume of Heat Supply	(10 billion KJ)	10 547	1 629	226	351
自来水生产量	(万立方米)	Top Water Production	(10 000 cu.meter)	24 704	2 596	799	2 940

10－25 续表

（2017 年）

指　　标	Item	四　师 Division 4	五　师 Division 5	六　师 Division 6	七　师 Division 7
原　煤　（万吨）	Coal　(10 000 ton)	54.53		248.12	78.05
小麦粉　（吨）	Wheate Flour　(ton)	42 672	12 080	27 378	16 917
大　米　（吨）	Rice　(ton)	169 527			
配混合饲料　（吨）	Forage　(ton)	163 260	169 005	52 934	177 175
精制食用植物油　（吨）	Refined Edible Vegetable Oil　(ton)	58 522	19 209	72 061	98 251
成品糖　（吨）	Refined Sugar　(ton)	47 349			26 734
乳制品　（吨）	Dairy Products　(ton)	4 752			629
# 液体乳	Liquid Milk	4 147			27
罐　头　（吨）	Canned Food　(ton)		3 247	204 605	89 915
# 番茄酱罐头	Canned Ketchup		3 247	202 381	89 915
饮料酒　（千升）	Alcohol Beverage　(1 000 liter)	44 802	6	11 928	8 091
白酒(折 65 度,商品量)	White Spirit	30 253	6	2 482	7 614
啤　酒	Beer				
葡萄酒	Wine	12 568		9 446	477
软饮料　（吨）	Soft Drink　(ton)	40 848	8 851	29 670	246
纱　（吨）	Yarn　(ton)		5 601	26 652	56 614
布　（万米）	Cloth　(10 000 m)				530
呢　绒　（万米）	Woolen Piece Goods　(10 000 m)				
服　装　（万件）	Garments　(10 000 pieces)	21.21	0.04	5.97	
家　具　（件）	Funiture　(unit)	24 184		3 196	54 746
机制纸及纸板　（吨）	Machine-made Paper and Paper Boards　(ton)	6 700	1 421	9 057	3 032
焦　炭　（吨）	Coke　(ton)			476 235	
# 机械化焦炉生产的焦炭	Coke Turned out by Mechanized Coke Oven			476 235	
盐　酸(含量 31%以上)　（吨）	Hydrochloric Acid(with Content of 31%)　(ton)	3 410			
氢氧化钠(烧碱)(折 100%)　（吨）	Caustic Soda　(ton)	64 102			
电　石　（吨）	Calcium Carhide　(ton)	117 094			
合成氨(无水氨)　（吨）	Synthetic Ammonia(Anhydrous Ammonia)　(ton)			54 203	405 227
塑料树脂及共聚物　（吨）	Plastics resin and　(ton)	93 827			
# 聚氯乙烯树脂	Corvic	93 827			
塑料制品　（吨）	Plastic Produces　(ton)	49 567	76 112	86 293	73 261
# 塑料薄膜	Plastic Pellicle	4 633	14 638	8 692	12 214
塑料制管子及其附件	Plastic Stick and Pipe Section	35 049	48 957	75 855	39 621
硅酸盐水泥熟料　（万吨）	Cement Familiar Material　(10 000 tons)	93.91		25.43	
# 窑外分解窑熟料	Beforehand Resolve Kiln Familiar Material	93.91		25.43	
水　泥　（万吨）	Cement　(10 000 tons)	179.88	20.00	99.32	91.98
砖(折标准砖)　（万块）	Brick (standard Brick)　(10 000 pieces)	74 770	21 996	46 045	27 055
发电量　（万千瓦时）	Electricity　(10 000 kwh)	358 072	145 722	2 259 338	248 161
火　电	Coal-Fired Generation	323 713	100 344	2 203 370	185 128
水　电	Hydropower Generation	16 366	25 132		45 838
供热量　（万百万千焦）	Volume of Heat Supply　(10 billion KJ)	201	349	1 049	674
自来水生产量　（万立方米）	Top Water Production　(10 000 cu.meter)	1 315		2 630	3 229

Continued

八 师 Division 8	九 师 Division 9	十 师 Division 10	十一师 Division 11	十二师 Division 12	十三师 Division 13	十四师 Division 14	兵 团 直 属 Directly under XPCC
54.14		143.88		9.53			
77 463	41 956	14 750		32 134	6 097	273	
471 477	41 177	34 528		182 070	24 992		782 070
120 989	845	7 245		1 262	13 455		21 884
	61 561						
63 810		117		133 443	2 237		
49 075				133 443	2 237		
58 490	30 825	5 345		8 314	8 586		
58 490	30 825	4 825		7 934			
72 864	1 989	7 012		4 699	558	1	
1 279	2 051	7 012		6	558		
57 278							
14 294				4 693			
213 651	18 740	69 360		9 000	12 324	1 205	
154 518					11 919	329	
4 993					5		
240							
39.00			0.53	497.54	20.35	26.97	
80 308	3 605			30 855	110 217	2	
2 296							
					5 724 106		
					5 724 106		
204 495							
857 954							
2 127 208							
1 258 277							
1 258 277							
134 821	24 144	49 611	4 237	25 410	74 936	1 007	
20 386	515	4 132		634	2 080		
88 763	12 483	50 451		18 907	16 099	1 007	
335.15					40.90		
335.15					40.90		
302.25		7.31	56.85		42.41		
78 373	40 923	24 533		321	92 464	11 914	
4 063 001	15 567	72 456		27 864	348 907	9 080	
4 003 853	4 440	66 217		846	3 340		
50 116	2 284	2 139		614	220		
4 278	380	262		457	692		
4 920	534	3 306		1 130	1 305		

10—26　规模以上工业企业主要工业产品生产能力
Production Capacity of Major Industrial Products above Designated Size

主要产品名称		Item		2017
原煤(按核定能力填报)	(万吨)	Coal	(10 000 tons)	1 489
棉纺锭(环锭纺)	(万锭)	Cotton Hasp	(10 000 ingot)	442
气流纺锭(转杯纺)	(万头)	Air Current Hasp	(10 000 head)	9
棉布织机	(台)	Cotton Cloth Machine	(set)	2 089
焦　炭	(万吨)	Coke	(10 000 tons)	970
烧碱(折 100%)	(万吨)	Caustic Soda	(10 000 tons)	107
碳化钙(电石)(折 300 升/千克)	(万吨)	Carbonization Calcium	(10 000 tons)	269
初级形态的塑料	(万吨)	Plasticof Elementary Configuration	(10 000 tons)	146
硅酸盐水泥熟料	(万吨)	Cement Chamotte	(10 000 tons)	1 661
水　泥	(万吨)	Cement	(10 000 tons)	2 627
平板玻璃	(万重量箱)	Plate Glass	(10 000 weight cases)	350
生　铁	(万吨)	Pig Iron	(10 000 tons)	230
粗　钢	(万吨)	Crude Steel	(10 000 tons)	210
钢　材	(万吨)	Rolled Steel	(10 000 tons)	235
原铝(电解铝)	(万吨)	Electrolyzed Aluminum	(10 000 tons)	330
发电设备容量总计	(万千瓦)	Generate Electricity Equipment Capacity	(10 000 kw)	1 781
# 火　电	(万千瓦)	Thermal power	(10 000 kw)	1 409
水　电	(万千瓦)	Hydropower	(10 000 kw)	36
风　电	(万千瓦)	Windpower	(10 000 kw)	124

2018

BING TUAN

第十一篇

建筑业

Chapter 11 Construction

简要说明

一、本篇资料主要内容

本篇资料反映兵团建筑业概况和发展情况，主要包括建筑业企业规模、生产经营和效益情况，主要指标有企业个数、从业人员数、建筑业总产值、房屋建筑面积、机械设备、资产负债、企业总收入、利润税金、劳动生产率、技术装备率等。

二、本篇资料统计范围

建筑业统计范围2013年以前为有资质的建筑业法人企业和产业活动单位，2014年起为有资质的建筑业法人企业。

三、本篇资料来源

本篇资料由兵团统计局工业投资统计处根据《兵团建筑业统计报表制度》收集、汇总、整理、提供。

四、本篇资料调查方法

统计调查方法为全面调查。

Brief Introduction

1. Main Contents

Data in this chapter show the general situation and development of construction in XPCC, including scale, production and management, efficiency of construction enterprises, main indicators including number of enterprises, employed persons, gross output value of construction, floor space of buildings, machinery and equipment, assets and liabilities, total revenue of enterprises, profits and taxes, labor productivity, per capita machinery, etc.

2. Scope of Statistics

The statistical scope of construction in this chapter is qualified construction corporative enterprises and industrial activity units before 2013, from 2014 the statistical scope of construction is qualified construction corporative enterprises.

3. Sources of Data

The data in this chapter are collected, prepared and provided by Industry and Assets Statistical Section of Statistics Bureau of XPCC according to *the Comprehensive Statistical Reporting Form System on Construction of XPCC.*

4. Methodology of Survey

Survey method is comprehensive statistics.

11－1 建筑业单位基本情况
Basic Conditions of Construction Units

年份 单位 Year Unit	单位个数(个) Number of Construction Enterprises (unit)				从业人员年平均人数(万人) Average Annual Number of Employees(10 000 persons)			
	合计 Total	国有单位 State-owned Units	集体单位 Collective-owned Units	其他 Others	合计 Total	国有单位 State-owned Units	集体单位 Collective-owned Units	其他 Others
1951	57	57			0.83	0.83		
1952	172	172			2.55	2.55		
1954	207	207			3.59	3.59		
1957	142	142			4.62	4.62		
1962	185	185			7.84	7.84		
1965	201	201			12.49	12.49		
1970	171	171			10.24	10.24		
1975	170	170			3.25	3.25		
1978	106	106			3.22	3.22		
1980	264	264			7.28	7.28		
1985	317	317			11.69	11.69		
1990	238	233	5		11.28	11.05	0.23	
1995	269	261	7	1	10.48	10.38	0.10	…
2000	253	246	5	2	10.53	10.41	0.11	0.01
2001	253	242	3	8	11.94	10.53	0.09	1.32
2002	236	200	3	33	11.47	7.90	0.03	3.54
2003	250	179	7	64	10.83	5.87	0.05	4.91
2004	282	173	6	103	10.62	4.82	0.02	5.78
2005	303	162	2	139	10.98	4.99	0.02	5.97
2006	296	141	2	153	10.96	5.14	0.02	5.80
2007	275	143	1	131	12.49	6.12	0.02	6.35
2008	258	134	2	122	13.47	6.12	0.01	7.34
2009	250	115	2	133	14.94	4.93	0.01	10.00
2010	243	112	2	129	20.02	6.78	0.01	13.23
2011	242	106	2	134	25.20	7.23	0.01	17.95
2012	264	117	2	145	30.97	8.73	0.01	22.23
2013	218	101		117	35.51	6.97		28.54
2013(新)	121	10		111	32.60	4.21		28.39
2014	147	10		137	36.79	2.92		33.87
2015	178	10		168	42.22	2.90		39.32
2016	194	9		185	38.43	2.45		35.98
2017	224	8		216	37.45	0.88		36.57
一师 Division 1	28			28	3.88			3.88
二师 Division 2	5	1		4	2.29	0.02		2.27
三师 Division 3	13			13	1.90			1.90
四师 Division 4	8	1		7	1.24	0.04		1.20
五师 Division 5	7			7	1.12			1.12
六师 Division 6	32			32	4.58			4.58
七师 Division 7	17	1		16	2.88	0.02		2.86
八师 Division 8	39			39	6.08			6.08
九师 Division 9	10			10	0.49			0.49
十师 Division 10	20	1		19	0.55	0.05		0.50
十一师 Division 11	31	4		27	10.45	0.75		9.70
十二师 Division 12	7			7	0.67			0.67
十三师 Division 13	6			6	0.99			0.99
十四师 Division 14	1			1	0.33			0.33
兵团直属 Directly under XPCC								

注：2013(新)后统计口径为资质以上建筑业企业(下同)。
Data since 2013(new) are the figures of qualified construction enterprises(the same as follows).

11—2 按经济类型分建筑业总产值

Total Output Value of Construction by Economic Type

计量单位:万元 (10 000 yuan)

年 份 Year	单 位 Unit	合 计 Total	国有单位 State-owned Units	集体单位 Collective-owned Units	其 他 Others
	1950	2 061	2 061		
	1952	13 267	13 267		
	1954	10 740	10 740		
	1957	19 821	19 821		
	1962	9 978	9 978		
	1965	21 437	21 437		
	1970	11 676	11 676		
	1975	3 899	3 899		
	1978	9 631	9 631		
	1980	23 431	23 431		
	1985	64 608	64 524		84
	1990	96 386	88 298	1 298	6 790
	1995	291 989	274 991	2 663	14 335
	2000	582 768	567 042	4 685	11 041
	2001	676 917	584 312	3 701	88 904
	2002	747 247	508 803	1 778	236 666
	2003	848 001	450 195	3 599	394 207
	2004	942 376	387 958	2 200	552 218
	2005	1 002 400	423 107	819	578 474
	2006	1 116 687	497 224	982	618 481
	2007	1 359 304	697 029	197	662 078
	2008	1 757 883	821 465	980	935 438
	2009	2 225 015	659 113	980	1 564 922
	2010	2 984 683	957 905	980	2 025 798
	2011	4 612 095	1 351 874	980	3 259 241
	2012	6 570 392	1 697 386	980	4 872 026
	2013	8 740 771	1 546 342		7 194 429
	2013(新)	8 031 449	884 288		7 147 161
	2014	10 999 914	594 927		10 404 987
	2015	12 502 878	626 924		11 875 954
	2016	12 473 962	622 653		11 851 309
	2017	12 500 713	521 276		11 979 437
一 师	Division 1	1 803 096			1 803 096
二 师	Division 2	816 037			816 037
三 师	Division 3	657 267			657 267
四 师	Division 4	520 339	14 409		505 930
五 师	Division 5	211 333			211 333
六 师	Division 6	1 316 891			1 316 891
七 师	Division 7	1 318 938	5 400		1 313 538
八 师	Division 8	1 464 222			1 464 222
九 师	Division 9	146 923			146 923
十 师	Division 10	536 729	43 048		493 681
十一师	Division 11	3 028 693	458 419		2 570 274
十二师	Division 12	160 703			160 703
十三师	Division 13	296 291			296 291
十四师	Division 14	223 252			223 252
兵团直属	Directly under XPCC				

11—3 建筑业总产值、全员劳动生产率

Total Output Value and Labour Productivity of Construction

年份 单位 Year Unit	建筑业总产值（万元） Total value of construction (10 000 yuan)	#国有法人单位 State-owned Corporative Units	#国有产业活动单位 State-owned Number of Basic Units	#集体单位 Collective -owned Units	全员劳动生产率（元/人） Labour Productivity (Yuan/Person)	#国有法人单位 State-owned Corporative Units	#国有产业活动单位 State-owned Number of Basic Units	#集体单位 Collective -owned Units
1950	2 061	174	1 887					
1952	13 267	2 302	10 965					
1954	10 740	6 154	4 586					
1957	19 821	5 844	13 977					
1962	9 978	3 235	6 743					
1965	21 437	13 142	8 295					
1970	11 676	8 119	3 557					
1975	3 899	3 022	877					
1978	9 631	2 746	6 885		2 991	1 760	4 148	
1980	23 431	5 589	15 574		2 907	1 583	4 758	
1985	64 608	43 956	13 691		4 931	5 460	5 651	
1990	96 386	54 589	30 596	1 298	7 667	8 271	7 409	5 643
1995	291 989	177 922	97 069	2 663	26 495	33 194	19 336	26 630
2000	582 768	328 140	238 902	4 685	54 320	60 542	47 876	42 591
2001	676 917	310 954	273 358	3 701	55 826	59 684	51 374	41 122
2002	747 247	303 757	205 046	1 778	63 906	65 944	62 299	59 267
2003	848 001	252 620	197 575	3 599	76 510	80 603	72 105	70 431
2004	942 376	161 164	207 781	1 852	88 251	81 586	78 349	72 062
2005	1 002 400	206 623	216 484	819	89 748	93 920	77 316	40 935
2006	1 116 687	289 223	208 001	982	96 530	109 554	83 200	49 100
2007	1 359 304	479 840	217 189	197	106 696	124 848	95 447	
2008	1 757 883	554 869	266 596	980	130 504	130 383	142 565	70 000
2009	2 225 015	353 224	305 889	980	148 925	124 515	145 953	69 979
2010	2 984 683	577 052	380 853	980	149 112	134 555	153 101	70 000
2011	4 612 095	837 786	514 088	980	183 034	176 756	206 279	69 979
2012	6 570 392	930 387	766 998	980	212 134	187 608	203 200	69 979
2013	8 740 771	884 288	662 055		246 132	210 139	239 953	
2013(新)	8 031 449	884 288			246 363	210 044		
2014	10 999 914	594 927			290 701	193 422		
2015	12 502 878	626 924			296 158	216 561		
2016	12 473 962	622 653			324 574	253 647		
2017	12 500 713	521 276			333 808	1 675 187		
一师 Division 1	1 803 096				464 979			
二师 Division 2	816 037				356 177	54 626		
三师 Division 3	657 267				345 766			
四师 Division 4	520 339	14 409			421 293	208 769		
五师 Division 5	211 333				188 287			
六师 Division 6	1 316 891				287 550			
七师 Division 7	1 318 938	5 400			458 060	229 896		
八师 Division 8	1 464 222				240 747			
九师 Division 9	146 923				297 234			
十师 Division 10	536 729	43 048			971 806	932 943		
十一师 Division 11	3 028 693	458 419			289 935	248 953		
十二师 Division 12	160 703				238 893			
十三师 Division 13	296 291				300 650			
十四师 Division 14	223 252				677 548			
兵团直属 Directly under XPCC								

11—4 资质以上建筑业单位生产情况

Production of Construction Units above Qualification

(2017 年)

指　　标 Item	合　计 Total	国有法人单位 State-owned Corporative Units	有限责任公司 Limited Liability Corporations	股份有限公司 Stock Ltd.co.	私营企业 Private Enterprises
建筑业总产值(万元) Construction Output Value(10 000 yuan)	12 500 713	52 128	8 056 163	974 703	3 417 720
# 建筑工程产值 Construction	12 019 037	475 800	7 773 551	974 703	2 794 983
安装工程产值 Installation	371 338	59 718	217 484		94 135
其他产值 Others	110 339		65 128		45 211
竣工产值(万元) Completion Output Value(10 000 yuan)	6 144 685	355 719	3 976 100	65 000	1 747 865
房屋建筑施工面积(万平方米) Floor Space of Building Under Construction(10 000 sq.m)	5 085.66	673.6	3 382.66	30.24	999.16
# 本年新开工面积 Newly-opened Areas	2 433.20	375.82	1 414.16	26.23	616.99
房屋建筑竣工面积(万平方米) Floor Space of Building Construction Completed (10 000 sq.m)	1 761.67	134.76	1 153.49	17.94	455.49
# 住宅面积 Floor Space of Residence	1 031.89	89.67	653.13	13.02	276.08

11—5 各师按构成分资质以上建筑业总产值

Total Output Value of Qualification Construction by Composition and Division

计量单位:万元　　(2017 年)　　(10 000 yuan)

单　位	Unit	总产值 Output Value of Construction	建筑工程 Construction Engineering	安装工程 Installation Engineering	其　他 Others
总　计	**Total**	**12 500 713**	**12 019 037**	**371 338**	**110 339**
一　师	Division 1	1 803 096	1 759 238	19 414	24 443
二　师	Division 2	816 037	742 803	73 234	
三　师	Division 3	657 267	611 453	37 775	8 040
四　师	Division 4	520 339	519 609	730	
五　师	Division 5	211 333	155 270	21 897	34 166
六　师	Division 6	1 316 891	1 277 155	30 176	9 561
七　师	Division 7	1 318 938	1 307 840	7 682	3 416
八　师	Division 8	1 464 222	1 384 197	64 053	15 971
九　师	Division 9	146 923	142 459	1 109	3 355
十　师	Division 10	536 729	480 268	55 141	1 319
十一师	Division 11	3 028 693	2 971 428	57 266	
十二师	Division 12	160 703	152 684	771	7 248
十三师	Division 13	296 291	291 382	2 089	2 820
十四师	Division 14	223 252	223 252		
兵团直属	Directly under XPCC				

11—6 按登记注册类型、行业和资质等级分资质以上建筑业总产值

Total Output Value of Qualification Construction above Qualification by Registration Status, Sector and Qualification Grade

计量单位：万元 （2017 年） (10 000 yuan)

指　标 Item	建筑业总产值 Total Value of Construction	# 装修装饰产值 Output Value of Decoration	# 在外省完成的产值 Output Value Realized in Other Provinces	按构成分建筑业总产值 Total Output Value of Construction Sectors		
				建筑工程 Construction Works	安装工程 Installation Works	其　他 Others
总　计 Total	**12 500 713**	**228 786**	**1 140 954**	**12 019 037**	**371 338**	**110 339**
按登记注册类型分 Grouped by Types of Reyistration						
# 国有企业 State-owned Enterprises	521 276	484	48 845	475 800	59 718	
有限责任公司 Limited Liability Company	8 056 163	84 285	597 159	7 773 551	217 484	65 128
股份有限公司 Stock Ltd. co.	974 703		494 950	974 703		
私营企业 Private Enterprises	3 417 720	144 017		2 794 983	94 135	45 211
按国民经济行业分 Grouped by Sector						
房屋建筑业 Housing industry	9 039 734	218 661	392 895	8 692 895	251 579	95 260
土木工程建筑业 Civil engineering construction	3 357 064	1 090	748 059	3 303 591	41 037	12 436
建筑安装业 Installation of Wire, Tube and Equipments	17 307				17 307	
建筑装饰业和其他建筑业 Repair and Decoration or Others	86 610	9 035		22 551	61 416	2 643
按资质等级分 Grouped by Enterprise Qualification Grade						
# 施工总承包 Contruction Contract	12 374 269	219 751	1 139 341	11 929 090	337 483	107 696
特　级 Special Class	35 575	1 324		24 170	7 149	4 256
一　级 First Class	5 841 680	7 212	1 130 695	5 821 747	19 933	
二　级 Second Class	4 447 569	118 919	8 646	4 185 500	206 206	55 863
三　级 Third Class	2 049 446	92 296		1 897 674	104 195	47 577
# 专业承包 Professional Contract	126 445	9 035	1 613	89 947	33 855	2 643
特　级 Special Class						
一　级 First Glass	19 715	7 653	1 613	18 166		1 549
二　级 Second Glass	37 092			34 859	1 139	1 094
三　级 Third Glass	69 638	1 383		36 922	32 716	

11－7 建筑业施工单位房屋施工面积

Floor Space of Buildings under Construction of Construction Units

计量单位：万平方米 (10 000 sq.m)

年份 单位 Year Unit		房屋施工面积合计 Total Floor Space of Buildings under Construction	#国有法人单位 State-owned Corporative Units	#国有产业活动单位 State-owned Number of Basic Units	#集体单位 Collective-owned Units	#本年新开工面积 New-opened Area in this yesr
	1950	6.99	1.70	5.29		6.99
	1952	21.52	9.10	12.42		19.37
	1954	28.50	24.74	3.76		25.65
	1957	75.11	68.58	6.53		59.39
	1962	71.56	18.21	53.35		59.98
	1965	140.22	63.73	76.49		111.63
	1970	164.55	56.88	107.67		129.60
	1975	77.97	52.33	25.64		54.58
	1978	123.16	37.87	85.29		100.86
	1980	189.93	43.90	146.03		151.94
	1985	313.29	217.39	95.90		170.94
	1990	289.00	147.00	137.00	5.00	164.70
	1995	453.88	276.63	174.01	3.24	300.31
	2000	703.50	389.19	308.47	5.83	546.10
	2001	776.99	356.71	340.02	5.42	584.30
	2002	671.64	247.45	189.67	2.59	477.00
	2003	774.00	216.99	215.80	5.77	590.16
	2004	873.66	152.17	208.57	3.73	648.75
	2005	900.52	142.36	253.32		617.92
	2006	831.79	161.74	166.39	0.10	576.73
	2007	964.81	223.95	157.98	0.10	697.12
	2008	1 128.17	318.98	156.79		791.88
	2009	1 507.41	265.92	182.06		1 096.40
	2010	2 059.97	332.22	279.80		1 496.29
	2011	3 251.41	520.11	375.05		2 501.69
	2012	4 307.73	697.85	425.36		2 913.02
	2013	5 450.08	609.74	324.77		3 227.15
	2013(新)	5 099.62	609.74			2 929.29
	2014	6 597.95	615.25			3 671.15
	2015	5 967.73	513.69			2 828.62
	2016	5 355.54	504.08			2 545.98
	2017	5 085.66	660.94			2 433.20
一 师	Division 1	736.42				519.20
二 师	Division 2	312.54				166.90
三 师	Division 3	147.02				102.01
四 师	Division 4	211.62	11.68			125.97
五 师	Division 5	49.95				29.99
六 师	Division 6	310.03				223.99
七 师	Division 7	225.05				185.43
八 师	Division 8	689.48				334.18
九 师	Division 9	84.00				52.11
十 师	Division 10	110.56	6.94			70.99
十一师	Division 11	1 801.82	642.32			467.84
十二师	Division 12	113.52				50.43
十三师	Division 13	233.88				79.96
十四师	Division 14	59.75				24.20
兵团直属	Directly under XPCC					

11－8 建筑业施工单位房屋竣工面积

Floor Space of Buildings Completed of Construction Units

计量单位:万平方米 (10 000 sq.m)

年份 Year	单位 Unit	房屋竣工面积合计 Total Floor Space of Buildings under Construction	# 国有法人单位 State-owned Corporative Units	# 国有产业活动单位 State-owned Number of Basic Units	# 集体单位 Collective-owned Units	# 住宅竣工面积 Completed Floor Space of Residence
	1950	6.43	0.54	5.89		2.65
	1952	19.80	9.10	10.70		8.87
	1954	26.22	15.02	11.20		15.84
	1957	69.10	20.37	48.73		32.72
	1962	68.64	11.82	56.82		32.68
	1965	132.06	47.25	84.81		79.22
	1970	152.55	31.87	120.68		95.61
	1975	72.14	38.98	33.16		42.67
	1978	108.71	18.21	90.50		56.78
	1980	153.08	17.79	135.29		88.77
	1985	205.11	129.96	75.15		96.68
	1990	193.00	79.00	110.00	4.00	82.00
	1995	267.81	130.47	134.94	2.40	134.60
	2000	500.96	233.35	263.33	4.27	341.49
	2001	558.63	211.81	301.83	4.73	398.40
	2002	461.86	157.06	177.62	1.68	309.54
	2003	512.97	114.58	193.67	3.36	300.94
	2004	567.18	68.00	189.81	3.73	343.72
	2005	590.32	72.50	220.59		391.71
	2006	538.48	99.00	128.80		277.66
	2007	567.17	112.63	131.15		348.93
	2008	648.53	135.94	108.63		438.91
	2009	753.91	91.14	142.13		523.49
	2010	1 115.28	145.91	206.43		708.56
	2011	1 435.22	194.69	233.14		1 064.59
	2012	1 982.57	314.58	318.99		1 479.48
	2013	2 473.36	253.77	256.67		1 845.50
	2013(新)	2 216.69	253.77			1 676.51
	2014	3 009.59	279.88			1 970.87
	2015	2 555.62	185.04			1 701.28
	2016	2 327.46	174.30			1 378.42
	2017	1 761.67	128.71			1 031.89
一　师	Division 1	394.86				192.26
二　师	Division 2	124.05	0.73			102.92
三　师	Division 3	85.66				44.27
四　师	Division 4	31.32	2.96			30.81
五　师	Division 5	25.86				3.81
六　师	Division 6	163.90				77.89
七　师	Division 7	147.92	2.68			91.46
八　师	Division 8	301.51				205.32
九　师	Division 9	21.40				6.31
十　师	Division 10	49.91	18.67			21.32
十一师	Division 11	254.35	103.67			184.20
十二师	Division 12	35.97				1.10
十三师	Division 13	88.36				35.66
十四师	Division 14	36.61				34.55
兵团直属	Directly under XPCC					

11—9 资质建筑法人企业合同签订额

Contracts of Qualification Corporative Enterprises

计量单位:万元　　(2017 年)　　(10 000 yuan)

单　位	Unit	合　计 Total	按登记注册类型分 Grouped by Types of Registration			
			国有企业 State-owned Enterprises	有限责任公司 Limited Liability Corporations	股份有限公司 Stock Co.,Ltd.	私营企业 Private Enterprises
总　计	**Total**	**19 011 754**	**1 430 128**	**11 820 784**	**2 015 406**	**3 745 436**
一　师	Division 1	2 391 623		1 937 698		453 925
二　师	Division 2	926 442		538 138		388 304
三　师	Division 3	891 846		761 889		129 957
四　师	Division 4	1 010 558	15 433	96 850		898 275
五　师	Division 5	300 486		265 210		35 276
六　师	Division 6	1 523 225		825 335		697 890
七　师	Division 7	1 488 766	5 400	1 332 092		151 275
八　师	Division 8	1 787 364		1 638 081	94 049	55 234
九　师	Division 9	217 493		127 212		90 281
十　师	Division 1	967 118	54 903	188 110		724 105
十一师	Division 11	6 558 138	1 354 392	3 180 183	1 921 357	102 206
十二师	Division 12	273 469		273 469		
十三师	Division 13	433 898		415 191		18 707
十四师	Division 14	241 328		241 328		
兵团直属	Directly under XPCC					

单　位	Unit	按国民经济行业分 Grouped by Sector			
		房屋建筑业 Housing industry	土木工程建筑业 Civil engineering construction	建筑安装业 Construction and Installation	建筑装饰和其他建筑业 Repair and Decoration or Other
总　计	**Total**	**13 458 978**	**5 405 732**	**19 921**	**127 124**
一　师	Division 1	2 020 438	367 907	3 279	
二　师	Division 2	744 877	181 565		
三　师	Division 3	642 310	249 536		
四　师	Division 4	1 008 996		1 563	
五　师	Division 5	285 368	15 118		
六　师	Division 6	1 294 221	228 130	875	
七　师	Division 7	574 451	914 316		
八　师	Division 8	1 692 386	73 252	10 485	11 241
九　师	Division 9	203 659	13 835		
十　师	Division 10	880 137	86 981		
十一师	Division 11	3 180 131	3 262 493	3 074	112 439
十二师	Division 12	256 779	12 600	646	3 443
十三师	Division 13	433 898			
十四师	Division 14	241 328			
兵团直属	Directly under XPCC				

11—10 资质建筑法人企业主要财务指标

Major Financial Indicators of Qualification Construction Corporative Enterprises

计量单位:万元 （2017 年） (10 000 yuan)

指标 Item	合计 Total	按登记注册类型分 Grouped by Types of Registration			
		国有企业 State-owned Enterprises	有限责任公司 Limited Liability Corporations	股份有限公司 Stock Co., Ltd.	私营企业 Private Enterprises
流动资产小计 Circulating Assets	7 552 873	433 303	3 827 687	984 430	2 307 452
# 存　货 Stock	786 181	73 706	438 609	156 689	117 178
固定资产小计 Fixed Assets	844 825	163 877	473 588	17 102	190 258
固定资产原价 Original Value of Fixed Assets	859 500	169 734	427 612	55 595	206 560
累计折旧 Accumulated Depreciation	312 038	10 578	184 323	38 767	78 370
# 本年折旧 Depreciationin the Current Year	58 322	744	34 326	5 149	18 103
# 在建工程 Under Construction	152 408	4 721	112 243	35 444	
资产合计 Total Assets	**9 386 580**	**689 147**	**4 681 725**	**1 411 939**	**2 603 769**
流动负债小计 Liquid Liabilities	6 650 507	408 340	3 240 767	986 330	2 015 070
负债合计 Total Liabilities	**7 782 546**	**410 018**	**3 948 570**	**1 264 832**	**2 159 127**
所有者权益合计 Creditors' Equity	**1 604 034**	**279 129**	**733 155**	**147 107**	**444 643**
主营业务收入 Main Business Income	10 298 993	460 923	5 273 792	840 293	3 723 986
主营业务成本 Main Business Cost	9 758 211	460 557	4 994 287	796 310	3 507 056
主营业务税金及附加 Taxes and Extra Charges on Main Business	114 101	2 379	46 045	1 952	63 725
其他业务利润 Other Business Profit	6 158	42	4 099		2 017
管理费用 Management Expenses	196 353	7 897	98 306	16 327	73 822
利润总额 Total Profits	184 162	−13 727	125 377	2 374	70 138

11—10 续表 Continued

计量单位:万元 (2017 年) (10 000 yuan)

指 标 Item	按国民经济行业分 Grouped by Sector			
	房屋建筑业 Housing industry	土木工程建筑业 Civil engineering construction	建筑安装业 Construction and Installation	建筑装饰业和其他建筑业 Repair and Decoration or other
流动资产小计 Circulating Assets	5 311 041	2 159 267	66 419	16 145
# 存 货 Stock	536 124	242 325	7 240	491
固定资产小计 Fixed Assets	524 258	312 862	6 118	1 586
固定资产原价 Original Value of Fixed Assets	552 566	294 699	10 013	2 223
累计折旧 Accumulated Depreciation	193 827	112 265	5 155	791
# 本年折旧 Depreciationin the Current Year	32 854	24 742	335	391
# 在建工程 Under Construction	23 455	127 722	1 156	75
资产合计 Total Assets	**6 373 064**	**2 920 743**	**73 043**	**19 731**
流动负债小计 Liquid Liabilities	4 429 214	2 159 926	49 027	12 339
负债合计 Total Liabilities	**5 236 223**	**2 484 942**	**49 042**	**12 339**
所有者权益合计 Creditors' Equity	**1 136 841**	**435 801**	**24 000**	**7 391**
主营业务收入 Main Business Income	7 215 017	2 980 190	74 191	29 595
主营业务成本 Main Business Cost	6 841 481	2 819 558	69 831	27 341
主营业务税金及附加 Taxes and Extra Charges on Main Business	101 973	11 672	291	166
其他业务利润 Other Business Profit	5 818	93	247	
管理费用 Management Expenses	133 485	57 873	3 056	1 939
利润总额 Total Profits	130 298	52 060	1 107	699

11—11 各师资质建筑法人企业主要财务指标

Main Financial Indicators of Qualification Construction Corporative Enterprises by Division

计量单位:万元　　(2017 年)　　(10 000 yuan)

指标 Item	合计 Total	一师 Division 1	二师 Division 2	三师 Division 3	四师 Division 4	五师 Division 5	六师 Division 6	七师 Division 7
流动资产小计 Circulating Assets	7 552 873	438 888	211 039	288 057	335 234	74 480	709 177	412 498
# 存货 Stock	786 181	77 391	20 130	14 372	24 883	16 193	13 492	29 217
固定资产小计 Fixed Assets	844 825	43 762	5 945	20 191	64 730	13 892	27 991	96 649
固定资产原价 Original Value of Fixed Assets	859 500	75 757	12 977	16 588	65 887	19 968	27 332	62 776
累计折旧 Accumulated Depreciation	312 038	39 678	7 421	8 018	6 542	7 806	14 402	26 964
# 本年折旧 Depreciationin the Current Year	58 322	8 498	809	879	1 059	1 115	1 210	9 040
# 在建工程 Under Construction	152 408	6 489	26	11 600	272	992	1 126	57 225
资产合计 Total Assets	**9 386 580**	**520 881**	**224 840**	**326 043**	**425 323**	**91 219**	**780 121**	**520 459**
流动负债小计 Liquid Liabilities	6 650 507	379 374	194 805	260 663	346 583	51 234	636 962	456 475
负债合计 Total Liabilities	**7 782 546**	**434 398**	**197 114**	**265 962**	**354 218**	**71 315**	**669 557**	**475 188**
所有者权益合计 Creditors' Equity	**1 604 034**	**86 483**	**27 726**	**60 081**	**71 105**	**19 904**	**110 564**	**45 270**
主营业务收入 Main Business Income	10 378 573	1 178 107	509 413	436 537	465 011	212 880	1 281 687	1 314 517
主营业务成本 Main Business Cost	9 814 688	1 076 086	496 580	408 530	456 593	201 784	1 222 200	1 241 495
主营业务税金及附加 Taxes and Extra Charges on Main Business	118 414	27 049	6 908	4 982	2 284	2 122	26 814	12 617
其他业务利润 Other Business Profit	6 158	564	703		3			
管理费用 Management Expenses	196 353	17 568	3 980	13 771	6 015	3 769	13 746	24 691
利润总额 Total Profits	184 162	38 577	1 451	21 745	7 640	5 043	18 368	13 201

11—11 续表 Continued

计量单位:万元 (2017 年) (10 000 yuan)

指标 Item	八师 Division 8	九师 Division 9	十师 Division 10	十一师 Division 11	十二师 Division 12	十三师 Division 13	十四师 Division 14	兵团直属 Directly under XPCC
流动资产小计 Circulating Assets	1 019 725	82 051	259 263	3 217 252	133 583	315 709	55 918	
# 存货 Stock	211 211	7 514	9 361	332 926	11 415	18 078		
固定资产小计 Fixed Assets	93 014	2 731	38 397	430 164	1 947	3 020	2 391	
固定资产原价 Original Value of Fixed Assets	51 446	5 257	15 106	498 491	2 453	3 373	2 092	
累计折旧 Accumulated Depreciation	31 763	2 608	8 049	155 828	1 309	997	653	
# 本年折旧 Depreciationin the Current Year	8 201	202	1 557	25 354	52	243	104	
# 在建工程 Under Construction	2 430	83	29 832	40 566	769	47	952	
资产合计 Total Assets	**1 156 829**	**87 320**	**300 194**	**4 434 799**	**138 267**	**321 969**	**58 317**	
流动负债小计 Liquid Liabilities	926 251	63 768	174 072	2 718 885	101 820	286 844	52 771	
负债合计 Total Liabilities	**989 838**	**63 811**	**234 122**	**3 566 446**	**113 895**	**293 544**	**53 140**	
所有者权益合计 Creditors' Equity	**166 992**	**23 508**	**66 072**	**868 354**	**24 372**	**28 426**	**5 177**	
主营业务收入 Main Business Income	826 086	154 361	458 859	3 014 379	213 520	211 373	101 845	
主营业务成本 Main Business Cost	787 400	143 505	404 084	2 880 380	202 372	195 437	98 242	
主营业务税金及附加 Taxes and Extra Charges on Main Business	5 249	2 794	12 360	12 179	807	1 627	623	
其他业务利润 Other Business Profit	2 831	292	2	42	17	1 702		
管理费用 Management Expenses	20 169	4 352	13 741	63 709	3 029	6 761	1 054	
利润总额 Total Profits	1 673	3 795	27 175	29 393	6 709	7 287	2 107	

2018 BING TUAN

第十二篇 交通运输业

Chapter 12 Transportation Industry

简要说明

一、本篇资料主要内容

本篇资料反映兵团系统内公路里程、道路运输企业生产及历年发展基本状况，包括兵团现有公路里程、道路运输业基本情况及按经济类型分列的民用车辆年末保有量、客(货)运量、 周转量和法人企业财务状况等。

二、本篇资料统计范围

统计范围为兵团管辖道路及所属道路运输法人企业、产业活动单位和个体运输户。

三、本篇资料来源

公路里程由兵团交通运输局整理提供，道路运输业生产及财务状况由兵团统计局工业投资统计处根据《兵团交通运输业统计报表制度》收集、汇总、整理、提供。

四、本篇资料调查方法

统计调查方法为全面调查。

Brief Introduction

1. Main Contents

Data in this chapter show comprehensively length of highways, the basic conditions of road and transportation development, including the basic situations of road transportation in XPCC, year-end possession of civil vehicle, freight traffic and passenger traffic, and financial conditions of enterprises with independent accounting system.

2. Scope of Statistics

The statistical scope covers road of XPCC road and transportation enterprises with independent accounting system, industrial active units and individual transportation units.

3. Sources of Data

Data on length of highways are provided by the Traffic and Transportation Bureau of XPCC. Data on production of road and transportation enterprise and individual transportation are collected, prepared and provided by Industry and Assets Statistical Section of Statistics Bureau of XPCC according to the *Comprehensive Statistical Reporting Form System on Transportation Industry of XPCC*.

4. Methodology of Survey

Survey method is comprehensive statistics.

12—1 按登记注册类型分道路运输业单位数

Number of Road Transportation Units by Registration Status

计量单位:个 (unit)

年份 Year	单位 Unit	合计 Total	法人单位 Corporative Units	国有单位 State-owned Units	集体单位 Collective-owned Units	股份制单位 Share Holding System Units	产业活动单位 Number of Basic Units
	1980	207	15	14	1		192
	1985	236	19	18	1		217
	1986	239	17	16	1		222
	1987	258	24	20	4		234
	1988	260	25	21	4		235
	1989	270	24	20	4		246
	1990	269	23	20	3		246
	1991	264	23	19	4		241
	1992	286	25	21	4		261
	1993	278	24	21	3		251
	1994	250	30	25	5		220
	1995	227	30	24	6		197
	1996	190	32	28	4		158
	1997	171	29	23	6		142
	1998	116	25	22	1	2	91
	1999	90	24	20	1	3	66
	2000	90	25	21	1	3	65
	2001	50	22	17	1	4	28
	2002	44	19	14		5	25
	2003	36	21	15		6	15
	2004	37	28	12		16	9
	2005	38	29	12		17	9
	2006	36	29	12		17	7
	2007	33	28	13		15	5
	2008	30	26	10		16	4
	2009	36	33	4		29	3
	2010	35	32	9		23	3
	2011	36	33	7		26	3
	2012	37	34	7		27	3
	2013	48	45	10		35	3
	2014	61	58	6		52	3
	2015	64	62	7		55	3
	2016	66	66			66	
	2017	85	85			85	
一　师	Division 1	21	21			21	
二　师	Division 2	2	2			2	
三　师	Division 3	3	3			3	
四　师	Division 4	5	5			5	
五　师	Division 5	1	1			1	
六　师	Division 6	34	34			34	
七　师	Division 7	2	2			2	
八　师	Division 8	6	6			6	
九　师	Division 9	1	1			1	
十　师	Division 10	3	3			3	
十一师	Division 11	2	2			2	
十二师	Division 12	2	2			2	
十三师	Division 13	2	2			2	
十四师	Division 14	1	1			1	
兵团直属	Directly under XPCC						

12—2 道路运输业基本情况

Basic Coditions of Road Transportation

年份 Year	单位 Unit	民用汽车年末保有量(辆) Year-end Number of Civil Motor Vehicles (unit)	运量 Traffic 客运量(万人) Passenger Traffic (10 000 persons)	运量 Traffic 货运量(万吨) Freight Traffic (10 000 tons)	周转量 Kilometers 旅客周转量(万人公里) Passenger-Kilometers (10 000 passenger-km)	周转量 Kilometers 货物周转量(万吨公里) Freight Ton-Kilometers (10 000 ton-km)
	1950	1 277	13	15	16 512	2 866
	1952	1 761	11	143	17 272	14 946
	1954	2 194	9	176	12 557	19 058
	1957	2 530	17	260	9 672	27 890
	1962	3 277	54	269	9 065	30 433
	1965	3 964	44	677	22 057	64 620
	1970	5 824	28	563	10 765	68 000
	1975	1 760		142		29 910
	1978	4 882	40	394	6 250	50 085
	1980	6 941	57	560	7 304	66 461
	1985	12 913	388	1 197	31 821	103 233
	1990	17 135	1 246	2 007	95 259	186 613
	1995	25 818	2 400	2 854	148 470	272 375
	2000	31 925	5 206	4 637	237 061	312 763
	2001	35 010	5 936	4 717	272 149	319 858
	2002	37 186	6 303	7 229	281 738	332 954
	2003	38 896	6 623	6 128	285 844	384 837
	2004	36 442	7 082	5 494	293 678	416 363
	2005	62 689	7 458	6 552	335 394	443 260
	2006	66 306	7 882	7 158	374 164	517 592
	2007	72 106	8 197	8 329	401 687	620 291
	2008	98 780	9 139	8 765	511 314	714 652
	2009	106 906	9 860	9 766	579 487	864 163
	2010	125 197	11 019	11 853	665 999	1 067 475
	2011	138 017	11 750	15 280	627 542	1 389 782
	2012	169 563	13 352	22 879	713 271	2 037 772
	2013	195 227	15 116	30 216	826 366	2 895 089
	2014	226 644	18 191	41 050	989 916	4 015 144
	2015	260 881	21 172	49 431	1 166 603	5 467 514
	2016	288 074	22 724	58 216	1 299 168	6 942 946
	2017	309 579	25 013	68 105	1 427 411	8 668 945
一师	Division 1	39 486	2 927	11 929	243 374	1 396 716
二师	Division 2	12 133	1 805	3 826	75 571	221 594
三师	Division 3	11 674	894	898	62 464	107 284
四师	Division 4	17 817	1 968	3 512	126 332	528 671
五师	Division 5	9 511	924	762	60 482	136 378
六师	Division 6	29 768	3 081	15 669	162 838	1 684 417
七师	Division 7	18 563	3 505	5 282	326 475	957 669
八师	Division 8	118 666	1 519	11 895	178 158	2 654 595
九师	Division 9	6 569	679	906	31 513	151 668
十师	Division 10	9 202	3 246	1 070	67 655	232 743
十一师	Division 11	5 123	450	185	12 867	12 586
十二师	Division 12	8 049	2 158	6 298	36 692	195 559
十三师	Division 13	12 108	1 569	5 850	38 113	378 378
十四师	Division 14	6 133	285	12	4 857	3 309
兵团直属	Directly under XPCC	4 777	2	12	19	7 378

注:2005 年起,民用汽车保有量包括农用运输车(下同)。

Note: Year-end number of civil motor vehicles is includes trucks for agriculture use from 2005(the same as follows).

12—3 全部车辆年末保有量

Year-end Number of All Motor Vehicles

计量单位:辆 (2017 年) (unit)

指 标	Item	合 计 Total	国 有 法人单位 State-owned Corporative Units	股份制 法人单位 Share Holding System Corporative Units	其他单位 Other Units	个 人 Private
总 计	**Total**	**675 943**		**68 724**		**607 219**
民用汽车	Civil Motor Vehicles	309 579		43 181		266 398
载客汽车	Buses and Cars	219 217		21 810		197 407
# 大 型	Large Scale	2 908		1 891		1 017
中 型	Medium Scale	4 465		1 398		3 067
小 型	Small Scale	193 184		16 488		176 696
微 型	Miniature Scale	18 198		1 854		16 344
# 轿 车	Car	181 125		14 913		166 212
载货汽车	Trucks	59 795		16 942		42 853
# 重 型	Large Scale	20 537		8 951		11 586
中 型	Medium Scale	12 082		2 365		9 717
轻 型	Small Scale	22 259		4 448		17 811
微 型	Miniature Scale	4 631		892		3 739
# 普通载货	Ordinary Trucks	41 191		13 131		28 060
其他汽车	Others	30 567		4 429		26 138
# 三轮汽车	Three-wheeled	12 542		981		11 561
低速货车	Low Speed Truck	10 785		1 716		9 069
# 农用运输车	Tucks for Agriculture Use	19 714		2 143		17 571
摩托车	Motorcycles	270 271		16 744		253 527
普 通	Ordinary	221 044		14 476		206 568
轻 便	Easy and Convenient	49 227		2 176		47 051
拖拉机	Tractor	79 066		4 094		74 972
挂 车	Trailer Trucks	5 351		3 234		2 117
其他类型车	Others	11 676		1 471		10 205

12—4 各师按登记注册类型分民用汽车年末保有量

Year-end Number of Civil Motor Vehicles by Registration Status and Division

计量单位:辆 (2017 年) (unit)

单 位	Unit	合 计 Total	国 有 法人单位 State-owned Corporative Units	股份制 法人单位 Share Holding System Corporative Units	其他单位 Other Units	个 人 Private
总 计	**Total**	**309 579**		**43 181**		**266 398**
一 师	Division 1	39 486		3 617		35 869
二 师	Division 2	12 133		726		11 407
三 师	Division 3	11 674		2 685		8 989
四 师	Division 4	17 817		1 713		16 104
五 师	Division 5	9 511		769		8 742
六 师	Division 6	29 768		6 141		23 627
七 师	Division 7	18 563		1 428		17 135
八 师	Division 8	118 666		18 209		100 457
九 师	Division 9	6 569		699		5 870
十 师	Division 10	9 202		1 182		8 020
十一师	Division 11	5 123		2 089		3 034
十二师	Division 12	8 049		861		7 188
十三师	Division 13	12 108		548		11 560
十四师	Division 14	6 133		509		5 624
兵团直属	Directly under XPCC	4 777		2 005		2 772

12—5 各师全部车辆年末保有量

Year-end Number of All Motor Vehicles by Division

计量单位:辆 (2017 年) (unit)

指 标	Item	合 计 Total	一 师 Division 1	二 师 Division 2	三 师 Division 3	四 师 Division 4	五 师 Division 5	六 师 Division 6	七 师 Division 7
总 计	**Total**	**675 943**	**98 255**	**50 778**	**49 947**	**56 276**	**25 051**	**74 507**	**61 062**
民用汽车	Civil Motor Vehicles	309 579	39 486	12 133	11 674	17 817	9 511	29 768	18 563
载客汽车	Buses and Cars	219 217	26 734	8 854	7 114	13 009	5 332	16 619	9 237
# 大 型	Large Scale	2 908	409	115	124	142	59	510	140
中 型	Medium Scale	4 465	1 121	185	402	250	206	541	303
小 型	Small Scale	193 184	23 249	7 988	6 504	8 451	4 190	13 437	8 441
微 型	Miniature Scale	18 198	1 955	566	84	4 166	877	2 131	353
# 轿 车	Car	181 125	21 222	6 134	4 807	10 003	2 734	9 656	5 499
载货汽车	Trucks	59 795	4 811	2 546	1 379	3 961	2 328	8 527	4 921
# 重 型	Large Scale	20 537	2 593	676	490	1 565	243	4 200	1 216
中 型	Medium Scale	12 082	1 034	787	556	1 316	399	2 347	2 169
轻 型	Small Scale	22 259	772	736	281	747	1 211	1 358	1 154
微 型	Miniature Scale	4 631	412	347	52	333	475	622	382
# 普通载货	Ordinary Trucks	41 191	1 703	1 586	1 078	2 256	1 934	3 799	2 767
其他汽车	Others	30 567	7 941	733	3 181	847	1 851	4 622	4 405
# 三轮汽车	Three-wheeled	12 542	3 257	428	1 713	493	1 025	2 078	1 230
低速货车	Low Speed Truck	10 785	3 628	202	1 359	191	382	1 423	940
# 农用运输车	Tucks for Agriculture Use	19 714	5 049	297	2 230	293	964	2 841	3 450
摩托车	Motorcycles	270 271	44 217	31 974	30 090	35 506	10 133	29 176	36 630
普 通	Ordinary	221 044	33 992	26 026	22 903	30 318	8 553	25 087	26 742
轻 便	Easy and Convenient	49 227	10 225	5 948	7 187	5 188	1 580	4 089	9 888
拖拉机	Tractor	79 066	12 884	4 827	5 158	2 642	5 287	13 570	5 449
挂 车	Trailer Trucks	5 351	689	118		93	9	1 090	221
其他类型车	Others	11 676	979	1 726	3 025	218	111	903	199

指 标	Item	八 师 Division 8	九 师 Division 9	十 师 Division 10	十一师 Division 11	十二师 Division 12	十三师 Division 13	十四师 Division 14	兵团直属 Directly under XPCC
总 计	**Total**	**157 567**	**16 558**	**22 016**	**5 361**	**11 731**	**24 471**	**17 455**	**4 908**
民用汽车	Civil Motor Vehicles	118 666	6 569	9 202	5 123	8 049	12 108	6 133	4 777
载客汽车	Buses and Cars	94 566	4 461	6 940	4 356	5 847	7 010	4 817	4 321
# 大 型	Large Scale	1 057	44	118	15	35	72	27	41
中 型	Medium Scale	853	102	206	35	56	132	26	47
小 型	Small Scale	92 389	4 126	4 298	4 184	4 863	3 419	4 503	3 142
微 型	Miniature Scale	267	189	2 318	122	893	3 387	261	629
# 轿 车	Car	92 389	3 263	4 808	4 091	4 362	5 500	4 014	2 643
载货汽车	Trucks	21 556	1 414	1 677	684	1 742	3 035	769	445
# 重 型	Large Scale	6 918	290	427	488	123	1 221	60	27
中 型	Medium Scale	1 125	489	572	72	272	755	120	69
轻 型	Small Scale	13 510	524	485	115	235	722	376	33
微 型	Miniature Scale	3	111	193	9	1 112	337	213	30
# 普通载货	Ordinary Trucks	21 388	1 003	991	136	1 181	679	670	20
其他汽车	Others	2 544	694	585	83	460	2 063	547	11
# 三轮汽车	Three-wheeled	37	324	24	15	208	1 651	58	1
低速货车	Low Speed Truck	1 429	211	371		191	412	46	
# 农用运输车	Tucks for Agriculture Use	1 466	382	493		209	1 545	495	
摩托车	Motorcycles	22 042	7 232	6 975	13	3 150	9 484	3 594	55
普 通	Ordinary	21 993	6 376	6 437	13	1 987	7 623	2 940	54
轻 便	Easy and Convenient	49	856	538		1 163	1 861	654	1
拖拉机	Tractor	14 508	2 608	5 583	46	395	2 614	3 480	15
挂 车	Trailer Trucks	2 289	63	99	65		177	389	49
其他类型车	Others	62	86	157	114	137	88	3 859	12

12—6 各师按用途分民用汽车年末保有量

Year-end Number of Civil Motor Vehicles by Purpose and Division

计量单位:辆 (2017 年) (unit)

单 位	Unit	合 计 Total	载客汽车 Buses and Cars	# 轿 车 Car	载货汽车 Trucks	# 普通载货 Ordinary Trucks	其他汽车 Others Motor Vehicles	# 农用运输车 Tucks for Agriculture Use
总 计	**Total**	**309 579**	**219 217**	**181 125**	**59 795**	**41 191**	**30 567**	**19 714**
一 师	Division 1	39 486	26 734	21 222	4 811	1 703	7 941	5 049
二 师	Division 2	12 133	8 854	6 134	2 546	1 586	733	297
三 师	Division 3	11 674	7 114	4 807	1 379	1 078	3 181	2 230
四 师	Division 4	17 817	13 009	10 003	3 961	2 256	847	293
五 师	Division 5	9 511	5 332	2 734	2 328	1 934	1 851	964
六 师	Division 6	29 768	16 619	9 656	8 527	3 799	4 622	2 841
七 师	Division 7	18 563	9 237	5 499	4 921	2 767	4 405	3 450
八 师	Division 8	118 666	94 566	92 389	21 556	21 388	2 544	1 466
九 师	Division 9	6 569	4 461	3 263	1 414	1 003	694	382
十 师	Division 10	9 202	6 940	4 808	1 677	991	585	493
十 一 师	Division 11	5 123	4 356	4 091	684	136	83	
十 二 师	Division 12	8 049	5 847	4 362	1 742	1 181	460	209
十 三 师	Division 13	12 108	7 010	5 500	3 035	679	2 063	1 545
十 四 师	Division 14	6 133	4 817	4 014	769	670	547	495
兵团直属	Directly under XPCC	4 777	4 321	2 643	445	20	11	

12—7 各师按营运性质分民用汽车年末保有量

Year-end Number of Civil Motor Vehicles by Operation Property and Division

计量单位:辆 (2017 年) (unit)

单 位	Unit	合 计 Total	营运 Operation	非营运 Not Operation	# 进口 Import	# 新注册 Newly registered	# 校车 School bus	报废汽车 Discard Motor Vehicles
总 计	**Total**	**309 579**	**66 810**	**242 769**	**6 022**	**9 098**	**1 498**	**1 407**
一 师	Division 1	39 486	6 396	33 090	198	1 349	12	299
二 师	Division 2	12 133	2 599	9 534	48	529		48
三 师	Division 3	11 674	2 296	9 378	58	469	1 387	290
四 师	Division 4	17 817	5 440	12 377	62	916	23	65
五 师	Division 5	9 511	2 611	6 900	42	839	3	79
六 师	Division 6	29 768	10 825	18 943	101	445	2	162
七 师	Division 7	18 563	11 043	7 520	77	1 708	8	60
八 师	Division 8	118 666	14 982	103 684	5 226	1 088	10	8
九 师	Division 9	6 569	1 435	5 134	52	627	19	96
十 师	Division 10	9 202	2 965	6 237	13	292	10	18
十 一 师	Division 11	5 123	190	4 933	71	162	5	152
十 二 师	Division 12	8 049	1 535	6 514	55	348	9	10
十 三 师	Division 13	12 108	3 769	8 339	8	86	6	78
十 四 师	Division 14	6 133	411	5 722	1	228	1	13
兵团直属	Directly under XPCC	4 777	313	4 464	10	12	3	29

12—8 各师道路运输客运量

Passenger Traffic of Road Transportation by Division

计量单位:万人 (2017 年) (10 000 persons)

单位	Unit	合计 Total	国有法人单位 State-owned Corporative Units	股份制法人单位 Share Holding System Corporative Units	其他单位 Other Units	个体 Individuals
总计	**Total**	**25 013**		**5 919**		**19 094**
一师	Division 1	2 927		1 408		1 520
二师	Division 2	1 805		114		1 691
三师	Division 3	894				894
四师	Division 4	1 968				1 968
五师	Division 5	924				924
六师	Division 6	3 081		1 853		1 228
七师	Division 7	3 505		338		3 167
八师	Division 8	1 519				1 519
九师	Division 9	679		64		616
十师	Division 10	3 246		876		2 370
十一师	Division 11	450		280		169
十二师	Division 12	2 158		820		1 338
十三师	Division 13	1 569		155		1 414
十四师	Division 14	285		9		276
兵团直属	Directly under XPCC	2		2		

12—9 各师道路运输货运量

Freight Traffic of Road Transportation by Division

计量单位:万吨 (2017 年) (10 000 tons)

单位	Unit	合计 Total	国有法人单位 State-owned Corporative Units	股份制法人单位 Share Holding System Corporative Units	其他单位 Other Units	个体 Individuals
总计	**Total**	**68 105**		**18 238**		**49 867**
一师	Division 1	11 929		4 380		7 549
二师	Division 2	3 826		74		3 752
三师	Division 3	898		41		857
四师	Division 4	3 512				3 512
五师	Division 5	762				762
六师	Division 6	15 669		7 747		7 921
七师	Division 7	5 282		187		5 095
八师	Division 8	11 895				11 895
九师	Division 9	906		160		746
十师	Division 10	1 070		130		940
十一师	Division 11	185		137		48
十二师	Division 12	6 298		5 139		1 159
十三师	Division 13	5 850		231		5 619
十四师	Division 14	12				12
兵团直属	Directly under XPCC	12		12		

12—10 按登记注册类型分旅客周转量

Passenger-kilometers by Registration Status

计量单位:万人公里 (10 000 passenger-km)

年份 Year	单位 Unit	合计 Total	国有法人单位 State-owned Corporative Units	股份制法人单位 Share Holding System Corporative Units	产业活动单位 Number of Basic Units	集体单位 Collective-owned Units	其他单位 Other Units	个体 Individuals
	1980	7 304	7 183		121			
	1985	31 821	24 079		2 683		1 844	3 214
	1990	95 259	54 542		21 615		8 111	10 991
	1991	112 043	63 953		29 976		6 079	12 035
	1992	112 794	66 852		25 655		6 913	13 374
	1993	123 806	61 055		29 744		6 727	26 280
	1994	138 724	55 495		23 778		9 106	50 345
	1995	148 470	50 857		21 731	770	10 300	64 812
	1996	163 677	55 330		15 137	420	12 816	79 974
	1997	168 478	59 630		12 056	119	10 931	85 742
	1998	198 387	62 109		12 407		22 808	101 064
	1999	204 099	53 385		10 477	860	21 432	117 944
	2000	237 061	55 483		8 784	7 616	25 242	139 936
	2001	272 149	35 150	39 584	7 904		33 520	155 992
	2002	281 738	38 801	47 660	4 446		17 267	173 564
	2003	285 844	55 575	54 278	3 847		6 733	165 411
	2004	293 678	60 841	48 726	4 942		5 827	173 342
	2005	335 394	63 827	53 085	5 088		11 187	202 207
	2006	374 164	57 772	62 446	4 750		4 865	244 330
	2007	401 687	57 155	83 538	4 850		5 637	250 507
	2008	511 314	54 091	86 915	4 404		80 658	285 247
	2009	579 487	52 663	105 740	1 350		101 525	318 209
	2010	665 999	54 296	103 467	1 552		126 224	380 460
	2011	627 542	59 938	105 371	1 863		27 896	432 473
	2012	713 271	66 399	94 525	7 528		29 124	515 695
	2013	826 366	94 488	136 564	6 166		27 020	562 128
	2014	989 916	32 597	214 530	72 117		28 530	642 142
	2015	1 166 603	89 419	222 994	8 812		29 046	816 332
	2016	1 299 168		341 205				957 964
	2017	1 427 411		313 946				1 113 465
一 师	Division 1	243 374		105 250				138 124
二 师	Division 2	75 571		2 729				72 842
三 师	Division 3	62 464						62 464
四 师	Division 4	126 332						126 332
五 师	Division 5	60 482						60 482
六 师	Division 6	162 838		83 063				79 775
七 师	Division 7	326 475		68 413				258 062
八 师	Division 8	178 158						178 158
九 师	Division 9	31 513		9 350				22 163
十 师	Division 10	67 655		18 270				49 385
十一师	Division 11	12 867		10 132				2 735
十二师	Division 12	36 692		16 024				20 668
十三师	Division 13	38 113		644				37 469
十四师	Division 14	4 857		51				4 806
兵团直属	Directly under XPCC	19		19				

12—11 按登记注册类型分货物周转量

Freight Ton-kilometers by Registration Status

计量单位:万吨公里　　　　(10 000 ton-km)

年　份 Year	单　位 Unit	合　计 Total	国　有 法人单位 State-owned Corporative Units	股份制 法人单位 Share Holding System Corporative Units	产　业 活动单位 Number of Basic Units	集　体 单　位 Collective-owned Units	其他单位 Other Units	个　体 Individuals
	1980	66 461	31 248		34 522			691
	1985	102 923	32 775		44 940	128		25 080
	1986	104 746	33 952		46 276	113		24 405
	1987	135 573	41 624		57 606	787	11 552	24 003
	1988	162 176	48 735		62 624	968	20 352	29 496
	1989	177 825	52 168		71 247	1 026	20 408	32 976
	1990	186 613	60 412		79 530	948	17 303	28 420
	1991	210 988	72 649		87 676	1 332	18 194	31 137
	1992	226 582	73 031		95 551	1 372	21 879	34 749
	1993	233 909	75 099		95 167	128	28 201	35 314
	1994	263 911	75 549		87 755	1 429	42 117	57 061
	1995	272 375	69 199		75 972	1 843	43 755	81 606
	2000	312 763	38 040		20 664	2 933	21 638	229 489
	2001	319 858	20 711	6 026	26 205	343	13 282	253 292
	2002	332 954	4 078	11 812	14 116		15 837	287 112
	2003	384 837	44 410	19 865	6 370		4 648	309 544
	2004	416 363	37 474	29 150	8 067		5 073	336 598
	2005	443 260	39 937	33 880	7 777		1 327	360 339
	2006	517 592	7 893	38 720	12 745		1 502	456 732
	2007	620 291	16 380	54 078	14 226		840	534 768
	2008	714 652	15 350	46 067	15 110		427	637 698
	2009	864 163	2 350	76 236	22 088		535	762 954
	2010	1 067 475	17 105	47 591	49 858		1 702	951 219
	2011	1 389 782	10 239	63 422	55 871		2 077	1 258 173
	2012	2 037 772	13 806	32 676	68 809		5 968	1 916 513
	2013	2 895 089	68 174	186 089	70 509		7 827	2 562 490
	2014	4 015 144	60 443	690 505	30 947		57 825	3 175 424
	2015	5 467 514	47 903	931 241	75 551		61 208	4 351 611
	2016	6 942 946		1 351 890				5 591 056
	2017	8 668 945		1 737 767				6 931 178
一　师	Division 1	1 396 716		367 759				1 028 957
二　师	Division 2	221 594		4 411				217 183
三　师	Division 3	107 284		17 923				89 361
四　师	Division 4	528 671						528 671
五　师	Division 5	136 378						136 378
六　师	Division 6	1 684 417		1 070 337				614 080
七　师	Division 7	957 669		23 723				933 946
八　师	Division 8	2 654 595						2 654 595
九　师	Division 9	151 668		32 700				118 968
十　师	Division 10	232 743		14 087				218 656
十一师	Division 11	12 586		10 411				2 175
十二师	Division 12	195 559		173 036				22 523
十三师	Division 13	378 378		16 002				362 376
十四师	Division 14	3 309						3 309
兵团直属	Directly under XPCC	7 378		7 378				

12—12 各师公路里程

Total Length of Highways by Division

计量单位:公里 (2017 年) (km)

单 位	Unit	按行政等级分 by Administrative level						
		合计 Total	国道 National	省道 Provinces	县道 Country	乡道 Townships	专用公路 Special	村道 Village
总 计	**Total**	**34 727**	**867**	**3 724**	**6 422**	**12 087**	**3 760**	**7 867**
一 师	Division 1	3 128	117	436	417	1 140	159	860
二 师	Division 2	3 230		269	616	528	769	1 047
三 师	Division 3	2 905	115	525	487	848	357	572
四 师	Division 4	2 784	130	104	277	1 439	363	471
五 师	Division 5	2 269	53	190	266	1 032	157	571
六 师	Division 6	4 689	164	735	1 005	2 142	14	628
七 师	Division 7	2 773		259	1 022	672	19	801
八 师	Division 8	3 340	134	491	386	924	110	1 297
九 师	Division 9	1 516	72	97	310	286	395	356
十 师	Division 10	2 896	82	369	193	560	1 113	580
十 一 师	Division 11	126			7	119		
十 二 师	Division 12	966			405	509		52
十 三 师	Division 13	2 756		135	740	1 661	208	12
十 四 师	Division 14	1 350		113	291	229	94	622

单 位	Unit	按技术等级分 by Technique level					
		合计 Total	一级 Level 1	二级 Level 2	三级 Level 3	四级 Level 4	等外 Below Level 4
总 计	**Total**	**34 727**	**73**	**3 879**	**5 278**	**12 850**	**12 647**
一 师	Division 1	3 128		553	717	992	865
二 师	Division 2	3 230		308	532	1 155	1 235
三 师	Division 3	2 905	4	619	687	1 186	408
四 师	Division 4	2 784	6	174	433	1 283	887
五 师	Division 5	2 269		193	215	791	1 069
六 师	Division 6	4 689		639	391	1 522	2 137
七 师	Division 7	2 773		350	394	914	1 115
八 师	Division 8	3 340	2	404	410	1 413	1 111
九 师	Division 9	1 516		146	119	672	579
十 师	Division 10	2 896	2	36	322	1 145	1 391
十 一 师	Division 11	126		16		110	
十 二 师	Division 12	966		84	278	340	263
十 三 师	Division 13	2 756	58	202	504	921	1 071
十 四 师	Division 14	1 350		157	276	403	515

12—13 道路运输法人企业财务状况

Financial Indicators of Road Transportation Corporative Enterprises

计量单位:万元 (10 000 yuan)

指　　标	Item	2016	2017
企业单位数(个)	Number of Enterprises(unit)	66	85
# 亏损企业	Loss	5	5
年初存货	Stock at the Beginning of the Year	694	605
资产总计	Total Assets	237 146	233 801
流动资产合计	Working Capitals	91 161	87 088
# 存　货	Stock at the Year-end	633	2 667
固定资产原价	Original Fixed Assets	152 863	149 510
累计折旧	Accumulation Depreciation	55 995	56 706
# 本年折旧	Current Year Depreciation	19 367	12 729
负债合计	Total Liabilities	142 587	123 916
所有者权益合计	Creditors Equity	94 559	109 886
# 实收资本	Paid-up Capital	53 510	49 202
# 国家资本	National Capital	13 778	14 758
个人资本	Individual Capital	9 306	4 445
主营业务收入	Revenue from Principal Business	608 334	594 270
主营业务成本	Cost of Principal Business	527 550	511 109
主营业务税金及附加	Taxes and Other Charges on Principal Business	18 487	16 865
其他业务利润	Profits from Other Business	534	431
管理费用	Administrative Expenses	37 015	48 810
# 税　金	Taxes	533	288
差旅费	Travel Allowance	132	86
财务费用	Financial Expenses	2 853	2 601
# 利息净支出	Intrest Expenditure	861	418
营业利润	Operating Profits	16 883	9 082
利润总额	Total Profits	21 167	13 489
应交所得税	Income Tax Payable	1 151	1 029

2018

BING TUAN

第十三篇

国内贸易

Chapter 13 Domestic Trade

简要说明

一、本篇资料主要内容

本篇资料反映兵团国内贸易基本情况、批发和零售市场的发展和批发和零售业商品流转情况、住宿和餐饮业经营情况以及主要财务状况。主要内容包括：批发和零售业、住宿和餐饮业基本情况、商品流转和经营情况及财务状况；社会消费品零售总额；连锁批发和零售业及餐饮业经营情况；亿元以上商品交易市场概况及交易情况等。

二、本篇资料统计范围

（一）批发和零售业商品流转情况统计范围为批发和零售业的法人企业、产业活动单位和个体经营户。

（二）住宿和餐饮业基本情况统计范围为住宿和餐饮业的法人企业、产业活动单位和个体经营户。

（三）社会消费品零售总额统计范围为批发和零售业、住宿和餐饮业以及其他行业有零售业务的法人企业、产业活动单位对城乡居民和社会集团的消费品零售额总和。

（四）连锁店（公司）基本情况统计范围为批发和零售、餐饮业的连锁集团、法人企业和产业活动单位。

（五）限额以上批发和零售、住宿和餐饮业企业及个体经营户统计限额标准：批发业，年主营业务收入2000万元及以上；零售业为年主营业务收入500万元及以上；住宿和餐饮业为年主营业务收入200万元及以上。

三、本篇资料来源

本篇资料由兵团统计局社会科技贸易统计处根据《兵团批发和零售业统计报表制度》《住宿和餐饮业统计报表制度》整理提供。

四、本篇资料调查方法

调查方法为全面调查。

Brief Introduction

1. Main Contents

Data in this chapter reflect the development of XPCC's domestic market, development of wholesale and retail trade, and circulation of commodities through wholesale and retail trades, and the operation of hotels and catering services. Main contents include the basic conditions of the wholesale and retail trades, hotels and catering services; circulation of commodities (in operation and financial terms); total retail sales of consumer goods; development of chain stores of wholesale and retail trades and catering services; basic statistics on commodity exchange markets of transaction value above 100 million yuan.

2. Scope of Statistics

(1) The statistics of circulation of commodities through wholesale and retail trades cover corporation enterprises, economic active establishments and self-employed individuals of wholesale and retail trades.

(2) The statistics of hotels and catering services cover corporation enterprises, economic active establishments and self-employed individuals of hotels and catering services.

(3) The statistics of total retail sales of consumer goods cover corporation enterprises, economic active establishments of wholesale and retail trades, hotels and catering services, and other sectors with retail business

(4) The statistics of chain stores cover chain groups, corporation enterprises, economic active establishments of wholesale and retail trades and catering services.

(5) Criteria for wholesale and retail sale trades, hotels and catering services above designated size are as follows: wholesale trade, main business income over 20 million yuan; retail trade, main business income above 5 million yuan; hotels and catering services, main business income over 2 million yuan.

3. Sources of Data

Data in this chapter are compiled and provided by the Society, Science and Trade Statistics Section of the Statistics Bureau of XPCC in accordance with the Statistical Reporting Form System on Wholesale and retail Trades, hotels and Catering Services.

4. Methods of Survey

It is comprehensive statistics.

13—1 国内贸易基本情况

Basic Conditions of Domestic Trade

指 标	Item	1995	2000	2005	2010	2015	2016	2017
法人单位数 （个）	**Number of Corporation Unit （unit）**	**277**	**178**	**718**	**967**	**2 893**	**3 357**	**4 283**
批发和零售业	Wholesale and Retail Trades	244	170	634	869	2 784	3 244	4 154
住宿和餐饮业	Accommodation and Catering Trade	33	8	84	98	109	113	129
产业活动单位 （个）	**Number of Economic Active Unit （unit）**	**790**	**300**	**1 099**	**532**	**1 326**	**1 464**	**722**
批发和零售业	Wholesale and Retail Trades	727	256	944	488	987	1 028	712
住宿和餐饮业	Accommodation and Catering Trade	63	44	155	44	339	436	10
批发和零售业	**Wholesale and Retail Trades**							
商品销售总额 （亿元）	Total Sales （100 million yuan）	146.00	185.43	369.31	649.36	2 926.35	3 341.37	3 826.13
批发额	Wholesale Value				477.65	2 466.81	2 825.16	3 252.61
零售额	Retail Value				171.71	459.54	516.21	573.52
住宿和餐饮业	**Accommodation and Catering Trade**							
营业额 （亿元）	Turnover （100 million yuan）				36.73	113.04	141.41	171.35
住宿业	Accommodation Trade				4.71	22.14	26.71	29.88
餐饮业	Catering Trade				32.02	90.90	114.70	141.47
社会消费品零售总额 （亿元）	**Total Retail Sales of Consumer Goods （100 million yuan）**	**35.71**	**54.00**	**93.38**	**202.87**	**552.34**	**632.29**	**708.37**
按销售单位所在地分	Grouped by Location of Establishments							
城 镇	Urban				178.20	493.21	564.00	630.08
# 城 区	Urban Areas				114.57	338.03	373.94	447.54
乡 村	Rural				24.67	59.13	68.29	78.29
按消费形态分	Grouped by Sector							
商品零售	Wholesale and Retail Trade	17.42	31.18	73.03	171.71	459.54	523.30	574.62
餐饮收入	Accommodation and Catering Trade	1.42	5.12	12.42	31.16	92.80	108.99	133.75

注：1950—2015 年社会消费品零售总额执行按行业（批发和零售业、住宿和餐饮业）分组，从 2016 年起，执行按消费形态分组，取消行业分组。

Note: Total Retail Sales of Consumer Goods grouped by industries in 1950—2015, Grouped by Sector(Wholesale and Retail Trade、Accommodation and Catering Trade)is effective from 2016.

13—2 各师批发和零售业基本情况

Basic Conditions of Wholesale And Retail Trades by Division

计量单位：万元　　（2017 年）　　(10 000 yuan)

单 位	Unit	法人单位数（个） Number of Corporation Units (unit)	商品销售总额 Total Sales	批发额 Wholesale Value	零售额 Retail Value
总 计	**Total**	**4 154**	**38 261 340**	**32 526 111**	**5 735 229**
一 师	Division 1	548	3 087 012	2 477 175	609 837
二 师	Division 2	208	1 715 598	1 104 881	610 717
三 师	Division 3	181	1 596 148	1 219 380	376 767
四 师	Division 4	212	1 402 675	1 172 538	230 137
五 师	Division 5	187	1 028 813	851 130	177 683
六 师	Division 6	441	2 392 627	1 456 675	935 952
七 师	Division 7	69	2 338 016	1 900 556	437 460
八 师	Division 8	1 312	6 522 785	5 613 701	909 084
九 师	Division 9	81	303 246	190 492	112 754
十 师	Division 10	505	1 712 606	1 450 578	262 028
十 一 师	Division 11	53	566 553	554 955	11 598
十 二 师	Division 12	263	9 881 471	9 310 458	571 013
十 三 师	Division 13	20	1 328 532	1 224 613	103 919
十 四 师	Division 14	17	40 813	29 309	11 505
兵团直属	Direct under XPCC	57	4 344 446	3 969 671	374 775

13—3 限额以上批发和零售业法人单位基本情况和商品购销存情况

(2017年)

指 标	Item	法人单位数（个）Number of Corporation Units (unit)	年末从业人员（人）Number of Engaged Persons at the Year-end (person)
总 计	**Total**	**463**	**21 892**
批发业	**Wholesale Trade**	**334**	**16 475**
按批发行业分	**Group by Wholesale Trade Sector**		
农、林、牧产品批发	Wholesale of Farm, Forestry and Animal Husbandry Products	100	5 093
食品、饮料及烟草制品批发	Wholesale of Food, Beverages and Tobaccos	70	4 566
纺织、服装及日用品批发	Wholesale of Textiles, Garments and Daily Consumer Articles	12	233
医药及医疗器材批发	Wholesale of Medicines and Mdedical Appliances	13	1 116
矿产品、建材及化工产品批发	Wholesale of Mineral Products, Building Materials and Chemical Products	98	3 412
机械设备、五金交电及电子产品批发	Wholesale of Machinery, Hardware and Electronic Equipment	36	1 928
贸易经纪与代理	Trade Broker and Agency	3	11
其他批发业	Others Wholesale Trade	1	113
按登记注册类型分	**Grouped by Status of Registration**		
内资企业	Domestic Enterprises	331	15 922
国有企业	State-owned Enterprises	25	2 131
有限责任公司	Limited Liability Corporations	134	6 778
股份有限公司	State-controlled Corporations Ltd.	11	750
私营企业	Private Enterprises	126	4 306
其他企业	Other Enterprises	35	1 957
外商投资企业	Foreign-invested Enterprises	3	553
按控股情况分	**Grouped by Share-holding Controlled**		
国有控股	Share-holding Controlled of State-owned	162	9 953
集体控股	Share-holding Controlled of Collective-owned	7	205
私人控股	Share-holding Controlled of Private	143	5 377
其 他	Others	22	940
按经营形式分	**Grouped by Operate Form**		
独立门店	Store of Independent	165	7 698
连锁总店	Total Store of Catena	1	278
其 他	Others	168	8 499
按单位规模分	**Grouped by Size**		
大 型	Large	8	2 820
中 型	Medium-sized	120	9 863
小 型	Small	171	3 677
微 型	Micro	35	115
零售业	**Retail Trade**	**129**	**5 417**
按零售行业分	**Group by Retail Trade Sector**		

Basic Conditions and Total Purchases, Sales and Stock of Corporation Units above Designated Size of Wholesale and Retail Trades

商品购进总额 (万元) Total Purchases Value (10 000 yuan)	商品销售总额 (万元) Total Sales Value (10 000 yuan)	批 发 Wholesale Value	零 售 Retail Value	年末库存总额 (万元) Stock at the Year-end (10 000 yuan)
13 253 434	**13 575 012**	**12 233 209**	**1 341 803**	**1 998 318**
12 041 659	**12 259 154**	**12 071 647**	**187 507**	**1 942 213**
6 503 749	6 106 649	6 096 196	10 453	1 573 167
1 049 752	1 203 972	1 188 461	15 511	46 192
262 891	326 557	326 318	239	37 249
181 942	215 770	202 405	13 365	21 937
3 183 445	3 404 882	3 281 884	122 998	213 097
854 271	990 405	965 633	24 773	48 236
5 039	5 107	5 107	664	
403	5 643	5 643	1 626	
12 017 620	12 227 590	12 040 083	187 507	1 940 406
3 116 240	3 274 781	3 258 814	15 967	396 064
6 591 026	6 314 247	6 231 239	83 008	1 267 769
492 889	541 920	541 579	342	118 285
1 585 682	1 800 339	1 713 263	87 076	144 353
231 784	296 303	295 189	1 114	13 035
24 039	31 564	31 564	1 807	
10 105 554	10 044 289	9 945 013	99 275	1 769 956
71 565	88 702	87 651	1 050	9 915
1 735 597	1 963 162	1 876 045	87 117	157 227
128 944	163 001	162 937	64	5 115
4 347 776	4 630 137	4 564 609	65 528	753 723
46 596	45 027	36 268	8 758	9 248
7 647 288	7 583 990	7 470 770	113 220	1 179 242
3 462 095	3 530 694	3 509 193	21 502	333 863
6 330 796	6 279 067	6 174 685	104 382	1 430 510
2 066 936	2 259 407	2 198 877	60 530	152 486
181 832	189 985	188 892	1 093	25 354
1 211 775	**1 315 859**	**161 563**	**1 154 296**	**56 105**

13－3 续表

(2017 年)

指　　标	Item	法人单位数（个）Number of Corporation Units (unit)	年末从业人员（人）Number of Engaged Persons at the Year-end (person)
综合零售	Integrated Retail	15	1 193
食品、饮料及烟草制品专门零售	Retail of Food,Beverage and Tobaccos	5	222
纺织、服装及日用品专门零售	Special Retail of Textiles,Garments and Daily Consumer Articles	3	161
文化、体育用品及器材专门零售	Retail of Culture,Sports Appliances and Equipments	3	111
医药及医疗器材专门零售	Retail of Medicines and Mdedical Appliances	9	493
汽车、摩托车、燃料及零配件专门零售	Retail of Motor Vehicles,Motorcycles Fuel and Parts	71	2 912
家用电器及电子产品专门零售	Special Retail of Household Electric Appliances and Electronic Products	13	165
五金、家具及室内装饰材料专门零售	Special Retail of Hardware,Furniture and Interior	6	61
货摊、无店铺及其他零售业	Stall、Non-shop and others	4	99
按登记注册类型分	**Grouped by Status of Registration**		
内资企业	Domestic Enterprises	129	5 417
国有企业	State-owned Enterprises	2	78
有限责任公司	Limited Liability Corporations	33	2 503
股份有限公司	State-controlled Corporations Ltd.	2	207
私营企业	Private Enterprises	91	2 579
其他企业	Other Enterprises	1	50
按控股情况分	**Grouped by Share-holding Controlled**		
国有控股	Share-holding Controlled of State-owned	26	1 920
集体控股	Share-holding Controlled of Collective-owned	1	10
私人控股	Share-holding Controlled of Collective-owned	98	3 148
其　他	Others	4	339
按经营形式分	**Grouped by Operate Form**		
独立门店	Store of Independent	114	4 550
连锁总店	Total Store of Catena	5	320
连锁门店	Store of Catena	2	40
其　他	Others	8	507
按单位规模分	**Grouped by Size**		
大　型	Large	1	314
中　型	Medium-sized	34	3 557
小　型	Small	59	1 361
微　型	Micro	35	185
按零售业态分	**Group by Retail Trade Form**		
有店铺零售	Retail Trade Form with Store	118	5 169
食杂店	Grocery Store	1	13
折扣店	Discount Store	1	22
超　市	Supermarket	10	411
大型超市	Large Supermarket	5	760
百货店	General Store	1	30
专业店	Profession Store	63	2 830
专卖店	Monopoly Store	30	836
家居建材商店	Home Building Materials Store	2	16
购物中心	Shopping Mall	4	149
厂家直销中心	Factory Outlets Center	1	102
无店铺零售	Retail Trade Form without Store	11	248

Continued

商品购进总额（万元） Total Purchases Value (10 000 yuan)	商品销售总额（万元） Total Sales Value (10 000 yuan)	批 发 Wholesale Value	零 售 Retail Value	年末库存总额（万元） Stock at the Year-end (10 000 yuan)
270 488	301 173		301 173	8 130
13 346	15 642	6 623	9 019	1 017
44 348	51 326		51 326	939
12 409	11 713		11 713	3 632
18 264	27 388	1 169	26 219	7 409
815 563	869 005	145 676	723 329	27 254
16 809	19 077	3 742	15 335	3 868
5 174	5 994	387	5 607	392
15 374	14 541	3 965	10 576	3 465
1 211 775	1 315 859	161 563	1 154 296	56 105
8 962	8 904		8 904	2 362
624 473	664 217	145 781	518 436	15 600
24 875	24 007		24 007	2 218
549 817	615 046	12 101	602 946	35 762
3 648	3 685	3 681	4	163
571 472	597 778	138 503	459 274	16 552
489	533		533	43
610 945	678 886	15 781	663 105	38 920
28 870	38 661	7 278	31 384	590
1 128 648	1 209 035	145 657	1 063 378	45 856
10 710	19 058		19 058	3 506
1 941	1 614		1 614	1 996
70 476	86 151	15 906	70 245	4 747
201 436	226 332		226 332	1 730
639 634	689 891	150 444	539 447	28 332
320 350	345 911	9 574	336 337	23 237
50 355	53 725	1 545	52 180	2 807
1 150 760	1 251 332	153 917	1 097 415	51 683
5 504	6 640	982	5 657	400
899	925		925	26
20 396	23 163		23 163	3 219
234 042	261 874		261 874	4 634
16 593	16 874		16 874	423
637 735	685 548	151 752	533 797	28 804
222 486	239 664	1 183	238 482	12 935
2 280	2 956		2 956	122
9 390	12 055		12 055	1 052
1 435	1 634		1 634	70
61 015	64 527	7 646	56 881	4 422

13—4 限额以上住宿和餐饮业法人单位经营情况

Basic Conditions of Corporative Units above Designated Size of Hotels and Catering Services

(2017 年)

指　标	Item	法人单位数（个）Number of Corporation Units (unit)	年末从业人员（人）Number of Engaged Persons at the Year-end (person)	营业额（万元）Turnover (10 000 yuan)
总　计	**Total**	**47**	**3 309**	**53 664**
住宿业	**Hotels**	**33**	**2 634**	**41 516**
按住宿行业分	**Group by Hotels Sector**			
旅游饭店	Travel Hotel	25	2 381	37 331
一般旅馆	General Hotel	8	253	4 185
按登记注册类型分	**Grouped by Types of Registration**			
内资企业	Domestic Enterprises	32	2 549	40 475
国有企业	State-owned Enterprises	11	1 076	19 093
有限责任公司	Limited Liability Corporations	7	339	7 753
股份有限公司	Share-holding Corporations Ltd	1	126	820
私营企业	Private Enterprises	13	1 008	12 809
外商投资企业	Foreign-invested Enterprises	1	85	1 042
按控股情况分	**Grouped by Share-holding Controlled**			
国有控股	Share-holding Controlled of State-owned	17	1 481	25 689
私人控股	Share-holding Controlled of Private	15	1 068	14 786
外商控股	Share-holding Controlled of Foreign	1	85	1 042
按经营形式分	**Grouped by Management**			
独立门店	Independent Store	30	2 441	37 239
其　他	Others	3	193	4 277
按单位规模分	**Grouped by Size**			
中　型	Medium-sized	5	845	15 420
小　型	Small	26	1 772	25 623
微　型	Micro	2	17	473
按星级分	**Group by Hotels Star**			
四　星	4 Stars	6	862	11 993
三　星	3 Stars	17	1 099	20 400
二　星	2 Stars	1	11	242
一　星	1 Stars	1	85	893
其　他	Others	8	577	7 988
餐饮业	**Catering Services**	**14**	**675**	**12 148**
按餐饮行业小类分	**Grouped by Catering Trade**			
正餐服务	Restaurant	13	637	9 867
快餐服务	Snack Counter	1	38	2 281
按登记注册类型分	**Grouped by Types of Registration**			
内资企业	Domestic Enterprises	14	675	12 148
有限责任公司	Limited Liability Corporations	3	134	3 511
股份有限公司	Share-holding Corporations Ltd	1	88	784
私营企业	Private Enterprises	10	453	7 852
按控股情况分	**Grouped by Share-holding Controlled**			
国有控股	Share-holding Controlled of State-owned	1	54	741
私人控股	Share-holding Controlled of Private	12	583	9 126
其　他	Others	1	38	2 281
按经营形式分	**Grouped by Management**			
独立门店	Independent Store	13	637	9 867
其　他	Others	1	38	2 281
按单位规模分	**Grouped by Size**			
小　型	Small	14	675	12 148

13—4 续表 1 Continued

(2017 年)

指　标	Item	客房收入 Rooms Income	餐费收入 Catering Services Income	商品销售收　入 Total Sales Income	其他收入 Others
总　计	**Total**	**27 330**	**21 775**	**866**	**3 693**
住宿业	**Hotels**	**24 610**	**13 445**	**320**	**3 141**
按住宿行业分	**Group by Hotels Sector**				
旅游饭店	Travel Hotel	21 599	12 663	192	2 876
一般旅馆	General Hotel	3 011	781	128	265
按登记注册类型分	**Grouped by Types of Registration**				
内资企业	Domestic Enterprises	24 142	13 445	320	2 568
国有企业	State-owned Enterprises	10 806	6 656	73	1 558
有限责任公司	Limited Liability Corporations	5 296	2 054	1	402
股份有限公司	Share-holding Corporations Ltd	453	320		47
私营企业	Private Enterprises	7 587	4 415	246	561
外商投资企业	Foreign-invested Enterprises	468			574
按控股情况分	**Grouped by Share-holding Controlled**				
国有控股	Share-holding Controlled of State-owned	15 480	8 139	74	1 996
私人控股	Share-holding Controlled of Private	8 662	5 305	246	572
外商控股	Share-holding Controlled of Foreign	468			574
按经营形式分	**Grouped by Management**				
独立门店	Independent Store	22 797	11 162	320	2 959
其　他	Others	1 813	2 283		182
按单位规模分	**Grouped by Size**				
中　型	Medium-sized	8 484	5 990	47	899
小　型	Small	15 690	7 431	261	2 243
微　型	Micro	436	25	12	
按星级分	**Group by Hotels Star**				
四　星	4 Stars	6 466	5 037	158	333
三　星	3 Stars	12 889	5 574	41	1 896
二　星	2 Stars	81	161		
一　星	1 Stars	893			
其　他	Others	4 281	2 672	121	913
餐饮业	**Catering Services**	**2 721**	**8 330**	**545**	**552**
按餐饮行业小类分	**Grouped by Catering Trade**				
正餐服务	Restaurant	2 721	6 395	200	552
快餐服务	Snack Counter		1 935	346	
按登记注册类型分	**Grouped by Types of Registration**				
内资企业	Domestic Enterprises	2 721	8 330	545	552
有限责任公司	Limited Liability Corporations	462	2 538	364	147
股份有限公司	Share-holding Corporations Ltd	285	256	23	220
私营企业	Private Enterprises	1 974	5 536	158	185
按控股情况分	**Grouped by Share-holding Controlled**				
国有控股	Share-holding Controlled of State-owned	184	410		147
私人控股	Share-holding Controlled of Private	2 537	5 984	200	405
其　他	Others		1 935	346	
按经营形式分	**Grouped by Management**				
独立门店	Independent Store	2 721	6 395	200	552
其　他	Others		1 935	346	
按单位规模分	**Grouped by Size**				
小　型	Small	2 721	8 330	545	552

13—4 续表 2 Continued

(2017 年)

指　标	Item	客房间数（间）Rooms (unit)	床位数（个）Beds (unit)	餐位数（位）Dinner Seat (unit)
总　计	**Total**	**5 510**	**9 531**	**16 165**
住宿业	**Hotels**	**4 710**	**8 157**	**10 285**
按住宿行业分	**Group by Hotels Sector**			
旅游饭店	Travel Hotel	3 865	6 560	9 608
一般旅馆	General Hotel	845	1 597	677
按登记注册类型分	**Grouped by Types of Registration**			
内资企业	Domestic Enterprises	4 543	7 910	10 285
国有企业	State-owned Enterprises	1 699	3 045	3 700
有限责任公司	Limited Liability Corporations	906	1 712	2 060
股份有限公司	Share-holding Corporations Ltd	55	89	868
私营企业	Private Enterprises	1 883	3 064	3 657
外商投资企业	Foreign-invested Enterprises	167	247	
按控股情况分	**Grouped by Share-holding Controlled**			
国有控股	Share-holding Controlled of State-owned	2 463	4 502	5 668
私人控股	Share-holding Controlled of Private	2 080	3 408	4 617
外商控股	Share-holding Controlled of Foreign	167	247	
按经营形式分	**Grouped by Management**			
独立门店	Independent Store	4 235	7 498	8 685
其　他	Others	475	659	1 600
按单位规模分	**Grouped by Size**			
中　型	Medium-sized	1 073	1 814	3 100
小　型	Small	3 553	6 165	7 148
微　型	Micro	84	178	37
按星级分	**Group by Hotels Star**			
四　星	4 Stars	1 216	1 975	3 520
三　星	3 Stars	2 286	4 156	4 165
二　星	2 Stars	36	72	160
一　星	1 Stars	110	170	
其　他	Others	1 062	1 784	2 440
餐饮业	**Catering Services**	**800**	**1 374**	**5 880**
按餐饮行业小类分	**Grouped by Catering Trade**			
正餐服务	Restaurant	800	1 374	5 625
快餐服务	Snack Counter			255
按登记注册类型分	**Grouped by Types of Registration**			
内资企业	Domestic Enterprises	800	1 374	5 880
有限责任公司	Limited Liability Corporations	161	272	628
股份有限公司	Share-holding Corporations Ltd	68	118	320
私营企业	Private Enterprises	571	984	4 932
按控股情况分	**Grouped by Share-holding Controlled**			
国有控股	Share-holding Controlled of State-owned	67	119	213
私人控股	Share-holding Controlled of Private	733	1 255	5 412
其　他	Others			255
按经营形式分	**Grouped by Management**			
独立门店	Independent Store	800	1 374	5 625
其　他	Others			255
按单位规模分	**Grouped by Size**			
小　型	Small	800	1 374	5 880

13—5 各师住宿和餐饮业基本情况

Basic Conditions of Hotels and Catering Services by Division

计量单位:万元 (2017 年) (10 000 yuan)

单 位	Unit	法人单位数(个) Number of Corporation Units (unit)	营业额 Turnover		
				住宿业 Accommodation Trade	餐饮业 Catering Trade
总 计	**Total**	**129**	**1 713 451**	**298 758**	**1 414 693**
一 师	Division 1	23	189 499	23 139	166 359
二 师	Division 2	6	95 230	19 974	75 257
三 师	Division 3	5	107 679	30 640	77 039
四 师	Division 4	9	90 627	27 105	63 522
五 师	Division 5	2	56 143	10 727	45 416
六 师	Division 6	13	231 500	38 730	192 770
七 师	Division 7	4	119 187	14 142	105 045
八 师	Division 8	31	432 302	92 421	339 881
九 师	Division 9	1	36 620	2 811	33 809
十 师	Division 10	21	124 301	9 867	114 434
十一师	Division 11	1	3 392	76	3 316
十二师	Division 12	4	104 939	6 172	98 767
十三师	Division 13	5	94 842	10 268	84 573
十四师	Division 14	1	9 069	1 885	7 185
兵团直属	Direct under XPCC	3	18 123	10 802	7 321

13—6 按销售单位所在地分社会消费品零售总额

Total Retail Sales of Consumer Goods by Location of Sales Units

计量单位:万元 （2017年） (10 000 yuan)

年份 Year	单位 Unit	社会消费品零售总额 Total Retail Sales of Consumer Goods	城镇 Urban	#城区 Urban Areas	乡村 Rural
1950		2 446			
1952		5 883			
1954		4 113			
1957		8 696			
1962		28 383			
1965		30 601			
1970		40 069			
1975		42 846			
1978		57 076			
1980		78 701			
1985		106 667			
1990		197 041			
1995		357 082			
2000		540 004			
2005		933 828			
2006		1 113 810			
2007		1 301 564			
2008		1 601 327			
2009		1 797 787			
2010		2 028 683	1 782 012	1 145 699	246 671
2011		2 427 057	2 185 493	1 374 565	241 564
2012		2 962 303	2 660 200	1 570 965	302 103
2013		3 856 430	3 471 285	2 345 849	385 145
2014		4 588 184	4 141 568	2 814 085	446 616
2015		5 523 395	4 932 108	3 380 290	591 287
2016		6 322 942	5 639 980	3 739 440	682 963
2017		7 083 724	6 300 821	4 475 378	782 903
一　师	Division 1	769 203	672 641	348 668	96 562
二　师	Division 2	692 372	675 766	624 233	16 606
三　师	Division 3	463 970	458 674	280 856	5 296
四　师	Division 4	299 877	288 177	66 020	11 700
五　师	Division 5	222 772	210 441	190 876	12 331
六　师	Division 6	1 102 411	851 444	695 398	250 966
七　师	Division 7	541 609	521 413	10 607	20 196
八　师	Division 8	1 193 705	1 003 743	901 966	189 963
九　师	Division 9	146 979	132 970	129 985	14 009
十　师	Division 10	373 363	325 602	226 174	47 761
十一师	Division 11	14 989	14 989	14 989	
十二师	Division 12	669 780	665 155	580 072	4 625
十三师	Division 13	189 480	144 819	107 542	44 661
十四师	Division 14	18 665	18 148	2 984	517
兵团直属	Direct under XPCC	384 549	316 837	295 007	67 711

注:2010年起社会消费品零售总额按销售单位所在地分组执行。

Note:From 2010,total retail sales of consumer goods are grouped by new caliber.

13—7 各师按消费形态分社会消费品零售总额

Total Retail Sales of Consumer Goods by Sector and Division

计量单位:万元 (2017) (10 000 yuan)

单　位	Unit	社会消费品零售总额 Total Retail Sales of Consumer Goods	商品零售 Goods Retail	餐饮收入 Catering Income
总　计	**Total**	**7 083 724**	**5 746 153**	**1 337 571**
一　师	Division 1	769 203	613 914	155 289
二　师	Division 2	692 372	612 016	80 356
三　师	Division 3	463 970	377 403	86 568
四　师	Division 4	299 877	230 181	69 696
五　师	Division 5	222 772	177 683	45 089
六　师	Division 6	1 102 411	937 408	165 003
七　师	Division 7	541 609	438 752	102 858
八　师	Division 8	1 193 705	910 988	282 717
九　师	Division 9	146 979	112 754	34 225
十　师	Division 10	373 363	262 028	111 335
十一师	Division 11	14 989	11 598	3 392
十二师	Division 12	669 780	571 038	98 742
十三师	Division 13	189 480	103 919	85 560
十四师	Division 14	18 665	11 677	6 988
兵团直属	Direct under XPCC	384 549	374 795	9 754

13—8 连锁批发和零售企业基本情况

Basic Conditions of Wholesale and Retail Enterprises

(2017 年)

指　标	Item	合　计 Total	直营店 Under Direct Management	加盟店 Through License Arrangement
总店数 (个)	Number of Head Stores (unit)	12		
门店总数 (个)	Number of Stores (unit)	1 309	940	369
年末从业人员 (人)	Number of Stores (person)	2 103	1 669	434
年末零售营业面积 (平方米)	Operating Area of Catering Enterprises at Year-end (sq.m)	80 374	58 174	22 200
连锁门店商品购进额 (万元)	Total Purchases Value (10 000 yuan)	257 475	223 338	34 137
# 统一配送商品购进额	Centralized Purchase and Delivery	173 056	140 203	32 853
连锁门店商品销售额 (万元)	Total Sales of Commodities Value (10 000 yuan)	236 798	228 638	8 160
# 零售额	Total Retail Value	23 672	19 112	4 560

13—9 限额以上批发和零售业法人单位主要财务指标

计量单位：万元 (2017年)

指　　标	Item	固定资产合　　计 Total Value of Fixed Assets	固定资产原　　价 Original Value of Fixed Assets	累计折旧 Accumulation Depreciation
总　计	**Total**	**520 759**	**837 234**	**348 332**
批发业	**Wholesale Trade**	**436 297**	**695 886**	**287 556**
按批发行业分	**Group by Wholesale Trade Sector**			
农、林、牧产品批发	Wholesale of Farm, Forestry and Animal Husbandry Products	197 330	357 456	169 912
食品、饮料及烟草制品批发	Wholesale of Food, Beverages and Tobaccos	103 340	140 705	42 080
纺织、服装及日用品批发	Wholesale of Textiles, Garments and Daily Consumer Articles	4 876	10 130	5 256
医药及医疗器材批发	Wholesale of Medicines and Mdedical Appliances	16 086	22 253	7 642
矿产品、建材及化工产品批发	Wholesale of Mineral Products, Building Materials and Chemical Products	93 619	141 927	59 913
机械设备、五金交电及电子产品批发	Wholesale of Machinery, Hardware and Electronic Equipment	20 565	22 141	1 960
贸易经纪与代理	Trade Agent and Agency	3	44	42
其他批发业	Other Wholesale Trade	477	1 226	749
按登记注册类型分	**Grouped by Status of Registration**			
内资企业	Domestic Enterprises	435 452	693 905	286 420
国有企业	State-owned Enterprises	70 919	150 918	83 583
有限责任公司	Limited Liability Corporations	215 892	345 227	137 926
股份有限公司	State-controlled Corporations Ltd.	33 624	60 261	27 826
私营企业	Private Enterprises	85 256	99 633	24 636
其他企业	Other Enterprises	29 762	37 866	12 449
外商投资企业	Foreign-invested Enterprises	845	1 981	1 136
按控股情况分	**Grouped by Share-holding Controlled**			
国有控股	Share-holding Controlled of State-owned	298 557	529 739	243 811
集体控股	Share-holding Controlled of Collective-owned	4 902	6 865	1 963
私人控股	Share-holding Controlled of Private	107 635	128 418	32 549
其　他	Others	25 203	30 864	9 234
按经营形式分	**Grouped by Operate Form**			
独立门店	Store of Independent	222 528	363 871	159 389
连锁总店	Total Store of Catena	4 141	4 548	407
其　他	Others	209 627	327 468	127 760
按单位规模分	**Grouped by Size**			
大　型	Large	69 847	146 241	79 046
中　型	Medium-sized	222 890	356 820	144 555
小　型	Small	112 013	160 428	58 619
微　型	Micro	31 546	32 398	5 336

Main Financial Indicators of Corporative Units above Designated Size of Wholesale and Retail Trade

(10 000 yuan)

# 本年折旧 Current Year Depreciation	在建工程 Construction in Progress	资产总计 Total Assets	流动负债合计 Working Liability	# 应付帐款 Account Payable	非流动负债合计 Non-Current Liability
55 609	**201 504**	**9 410 603**	**7 165 473**	**1 216 408**	**619 545**
43 196	**167 396**	**8 822 346**	**6 836 690**	**1 160 314**	**601 975**
18 612	40 541	5 202 528	4 481 193	552 890	239 875
13 338	49 277	1 026 421	370 131	76 883	256 840
478	19 967	278 545	188 264	67 812	25 530
1 265	798	147 863	113 398	52 510	3 210
9 072	54 291	1 873 550	1 471 166	307 233	63 983
387	2 523	285 316	210 990	102 147	12 538
4		851	160	146	
40		6 313	1 038	642	
43 044	167 396	8 806 611	6 818 552	1 143 636	601 975
6 761	17 188	1 654 683	1 451 669	117 016	39 647
22 834	106 280	5 638 873	4 260 315	698 533	505 619
3 197	32 326	632 899	504 022	83 430	18 143
6 154	11 603	778 097	564 179	238 515	27 389
4 099		102 060	38 367	6 141	11 178
152		15 735	18 139	16 678	
31 678	152 795	7 847 709	6 174 922	891 429	558 996
691	1	36 088	14 602	3 791	5 035
8 254	12 258	879 878	617 592	255 219	33 483
2 573	2 342	58 671	29 574	9 875	4 462
22 135	54 097	3 602 106	2 705 172	360 085	264 979
255	913	36 138	24 447	5 303	3 373
20 807	112 386	5 184 103	4 107 071	794 926	333 624
6 134	22 167	1 960 601	1 765 301	382 458	18 653
20 258	83 021	5 041 289	3 854 668	511 378	369 736
15 091	59 567	1 706 053	1 156 133	249 419	208 890
1 713	2 641	114 403	60 589	17 059	4 696

13—9 续表 1

计量单位:万元 (2017 年)

指　　标	Item	负　债 合　计 Total Liabilities	所有者权益 合　计 Total Owners' Equities	实收资本 Paicl-up Capitals
总　计	**Total**	**7 785 758**	**1 624 845**	**940 466**
批发业	**Wholesale Trade**	**7 439 405**	**1 382 941**	**800 600**
按批发行业分	**Group by Wholesale Trade Sector**			
农、林、牧产品批发	Wholesale of Farm, Forestry and Animal Husbandry Products	4 721 279	481 249	325 148
食品、饮料及烟草制品批发	Wholesale of Food, Beverages and Tobaccos	627 500	398 922	136 684
纺织、服装及日用品批发	Wholesale of Textiles, Garments and Daily Consumer Articles	213 794	64 751	49 570
医药及医疗器材批发	Wholesale of Medicines and Mdedical Appliances	116 607	31 256	19 586
矿产品、建材及化工产品批发	Wholesale of Mineral Products, Building Materials and Chemical Products	1 535 149	338 402	243 101
机械设备、五金交电及电子产品批发	Wholesale of Machinery, Hardware and Electronic Equipment	223 528	61 788	22 350
贸易经纪与代理	Trade Agent and Agency	160	690	560
其他批发业	Other Wholesale Trade	1 038	5 275	3 000
按登记注册类型分	**Grouped by Status of Registration**			
内资企业	Domestic Enterprises	7 421 267	1 385 344	784 580
国有企业	State-owned Enterprises	1 491 316	163 367	87 075
有限责任公司	Limited Liability Corporations	4 766 462	872 410	475 299
股份有限公司	State-controlled Corporations Ltd.	522 165	110 734	108 864
私营企业	Private Enterprises	591 568	186 529	98 148
其他企业	Other Enterprises	49 756	52 304	15 194
外商投资企业	Foreign-invested Enterprises	18 139	—2 404	16 020
按控股情况分	**Grouped by Share-holding Controlled**			
国有控股	Share-holding Controlled of State-owned	6 734 447	1 113 263	643 417
集体控股	Share-holding Controlled of Collective-owned	19 637	16 451	7 021
私人控股	Share-holding Controlled of Private	651 075	228 803	141 938
其　他	Others	34 247	24 424	8 225
按经营形式分	**Grouped by Operate Form**			
独立门店	Store of Independent	2 970 151	631 955	367 954
连锁总店	Total Store of Catena	27 820	8 317	2 000
其　他	Others	4 441 435	742 668	430 646
按单位规模分	**Grouped by Size**			
大　型	Large	1 783 954	176 647	73 718
中　型	Medium-sized	4 224 404	816 886	484 284
小　型	Small	1 365 763	340 290	216 022
微　型	Micro	65 285	49 118	26 576

Continued

(10 000 yuan)

营业收入 Revenue Business	主营业务收入 Revenue from Principal Business	营业成本 Cost of Business	主营业务成本 Cost of Principal Business	营业税金及附加 Taxes and Other Changes on Business	主营业务税金及附加 Taxes and Other Changes on Principal Business
12 357 665	**12 272 415**	**11 557 427**	**11 480 596**	**36 139**	**35 687**
11 137 794	**11 085 792**	**10 465 988**	**10 433 210**	**31 718**	**31 320**
5 523 581	5 494 024	5 307 619	5 301 520	2 536	2 524
1 150 448	1 142 491	957 287	955 444	23 409	23 192
280 996	280 722	245 094	245 094	502	502
187 450	187 313	166 989	166 985	555	555
3 121 725	3 107 791	2 973 753	2 948 927	3 086	2 916
863 616	863 473	807 637	807 630	1 621	1 621
4 987	4 987	4 061	4 061	11	11
4 823	4 823	3 410	3 410		
11 107 050	11 055 048	10 437 604	10 404 826	31 707	31 308
2 943 268	2 929 175	2 867 723	2 866 389	928	928
5 741 081	5 713 128	5 406 769	5 376 669	24 214	23 907
493 607	484 653	451 553	451 347	644	644
1 651 493	1 650 786	1 489 679	1 488 778	5 573	5 573
277 601	277 307	221 880	221 643	348	257
30 744	30 744	28 384	28 384	12	12
9 103 268	9 054 930	8 650 963	8 620 874	25 553	25 246
85 117	85 117	70 672	70 672	149	149
1 805 093	1 801 428	1 630 119	1 627 502	5 877	5 786
144 317	144 317	114 234	114 163	139	139
4 241 226	4 233 244	3 897 288	3 891 441	17 183	17 096
40 787	40 787	39 734	39 734	62	62
6 855 782	6 811 762	6 528 966	6 502 036	14 474	14 162
3 183 400	3 173 049	3 096 314	3 096 314	5 513	5 513
5 720 008	5 688 737	5 290 503	5 262 730	22 737	22 560
2 064 962	2 056 029	1 924 645	1 921 015	3 057	2 835
169 426	167 979	154 525	153 151	411	411

13－9 续表 2

计量单位:万元 (2017 年)

指 标	Item	其他业务利润 Profits from Other Business	销售费用 Sales Expenses	管理费用 Administrative Expenses
总 计	**Total**	**－4 281**	**255 571**	**156 505**
批发业	**Wholesale Trade**	**－7 712**	**190 914**	**128 361**
按批发行业分	**Group by Wholesale Trade Sector**			
农、林、牧产品批发	Wholesale of Farm,Forestry and Animal Husbandry Products	6 516	68 077	42 535
食品、饮料及烟草制品批发	Wholesale of Food,Beverages and Tobaccos	－1 136	39 716	31 101
纺织、服装及日用品批发	Wholesale of Textiles,Garments and Daily Consumer Articles		11 712	8 584
医药及医疗器材批发	Wholesale of Medicines and Mdedical Appliances		6 795	7 384
矿产品、建材及化工产品批发	Wholesale of Mineral Products,Building Materials and Chemical Products	－13 164	40 274	33 722
机械设备、五金交电及电子产品批发	Wholesale of Machinery,Hardware and Electronic Equipment	72	23 632	4 157
贸易经纪与代理	Trade Agent and Agency		462	209
其他批发业	Other Wholesale Trade		241	654
按登记注册类型分	**Grouped by Status of Registration**			
内资企业	Domestic Enterprises	－6 419	189 740	125 283
国有企业	State-owned Enterprises	419	32 904	16 838
有限责任公司	Limited Liability Corporations	－13 022	88 307	69 051
股份有限公司	State-controlled Corporations Ltd.	6 378	14 295	11 317
私营企业	Private Enterprises	－194	40 725	23 673
其他企业	Other Enterprises		13 510	4 404
外商投资企业	Foreign-invested Enterprises	－1 293	1 174	3 078
按控股情况分	**Grouped by Share-holding Controlled**			
国有控股	Share-holding Controlled of State-owned	－6 225	135 261	95 448
集体控股	Share-holding Controlled of Collective-owned		3 805	1 490
私人控股	Share-holding Controlled of Private	－1 488	42 676	29 086
其 他	Others		9 173	2 337
按经营形式分	**Grouped by Operate Form**			
独立门店	Store of Independent	766	91 732	62 872
连锁总店	Total Store of Catena		977	1 125
其 他	Others	－8 479	98 205	64 364
按单位规模分	**Grouped by Size**			
大 型	Large		31 864	21 642
中 型	Medium-sized	－8 006	118 643	75 465
小 型	Small	294	35 157	29 366
微 型	Micro		5 251	1 888

Continued

(10 000 yuan)

财务费用 Financial Expenses	营业利润 Operating Profits	利润总额 Total Profits	应交所得税 Income Tax Payable	应付职工薪酬(本年贷方累计发生额) Unemployment Insurance	本年应交增值税 Current Year VAT Payable
78 553	**285 830**	**299 407**	**33 287**	**520 494**	**110 364**
73 130	**259 900**	**273 537**	**28 755**	**475 487**	**67 779**
37 752	70 799	84 485	9 347	394 758	2 572
9 328	93 659	87 383	1 788	31 592	14 823
3 211	12 126	12 458	183	1 780	3 808
1 320	4 865	5 392	523	7 682	18 475
18 824	54 399	58 316	12 319	33 917	20 267
2 636	23 324	24 775	4 532	5 061	7 834
33	226	226	1	62	
	518	518	63	624	
73 124	261 810	277 071	28 693	471 400	67 779
16 686	21 076	28 095	5 927	18 033	2 024
40 900	119 064	130 555	17 247	417 603	40 414
8 457	−499	1 241	473	6 655	627
6 121	85 669	87 724	4 949	15 990	24 688
959	36 500	29 457	96	13 118	26
6	−1 910	−3 535	63	4 087	
65 679	142 794	163 104	23 154	444 026	41 909
236	8 763	5 264	20	1 041	117
6 842	90 283	89 351	5 267	22 092	25 476
373	18 060	15 818	315	8 327	278
32 535	135 652	144 962	18 866	54 449	33 034
426	−1 546	214	168	1 682	168
40 169	125 794	128 361	9 722	419 356	34 577
10 822	29 047	38 204	6 116	19 685	1 748
42 239	165 823	175 143	18 664	429 574	49 211
19 624	58 131	53 082	3 240	25 350	13 428
446	6 900	7 108	735	878	3 392

13—9 续表 3

计量单位:万元　　　　　　　　　　　　　　　　　　　　　　　　　　　　(2017 年)

指　　标	Item	固定资产合　计 Total Value of Fixed Assets	固定资产原　价 Original Value of Fixed Assets	累计折旧 Accumulation Depreciation
零售业	**Retail Trade**	**84 463**	**141 347**	**60 776**
按零售行业分	**Group by Retail Trade Sector**			
综合零售	Integrated Retail	5 823	9 208	3 438
食品、饮料及烟草制品专门零售	Retail of Food, Beverage and Tobaccos	7 227	7 650	1 648
纺织、服装及日用品专门零售	Special Retail of Textiles, Garments and Daily Consumer Articles	1 060	1 319	288
文化、体育用品及器材专门零售	Retail of Culture, Sports Appliances and Equipments	732	2 152	1 420
医药及医疗器材专门零售	Retail of Medicines and Mdedical Appliances	321	719	558
汽车、摩托车、燃料及零配件专门零售	Retail of Motor Vehicles, Motorcycles Fuel and Parts	61 278	111 095	52 167
家用电器及电子产品专门零售	Special Retail of Household Electric Appliances and Electronic Products	471	666	195
五金、家具及室内装饰材料专门零售	Special Retail of Hardware, Furniture and Interior	525	543	93
货摊、无店铺及其他零售业	Stall、Non—shop and Others	7 026	7 995	969
按登记注册类型分	**Grouped by Status of Registration**			
内资企业	Domestic Enterprises	84 463	141 347	60 776
国有企业	State-owned Enterprises	805	2 138	1 334
有限责任公司	Limited Liability Corporations	54 175	93 717	41 452
股份有限公司	State-owned Corporations Ltd.	502	949	452
私营企业	Private Enterprises	28 897	44 459	17 538
其他企业	Others	84	84	
按控股情况分	**Grouped by Share-holding Controlled**			
国有控股	Share-holding Controlled of State-owned	33 022	61 035	29 923
集体控股	Share-holding Controlled of Collective-owned			
私人控股	Share-holding Controlled of Collective-owned	31 803	50 991	21 169
其　他	Others	19 638	29 322	9 684
按经营形式分	**Grouped by Operate Form**			
独立门店	Store of Independent	75 308	124 371	52 892
连锁总店	Total Store of Catena	186	482	358
连锁门店	Store of Catena	454	633	179
其　他	Others	8 515	15 862	7 347
按单位规模分	**Grouped by Size**			
大　型	Large	726	1 264	548
中　型	Medium-sized	60 426	98 925	41 541
小　型	Small	21 209	38 419	17 933
微　型	Micro	2 102	2 739	754
按零售业态分	**Group by Retail Trade Form**			
有店铺零售	Retail Trade Form with Store	75 762	131 511	59 641
食杂店	Grocery Store	260	350	90
折扣店	Discount Store	6	7	1
超　市	Supermarket	3 435	4 675	1 316
大型超市	Large Supermarket	1 808	3 602	1 804
百货店	General Store	544	841	297
专业店	Profession Store	45 410	78 954	35 711
专卖店	Monopoly Store	17 219	35 724	18 816
家居建材商店	Home Building Materials Store	216	217	76
购物中心	Shopping Mall	170	446	305
厂家直销中心	Factory Outlets Center	6 696	6 696	1 226
无店铺零售	Retail Trade Form without Store	8 701	9 837	1 136

Continued

(10 000 yuan)

# 本年折旧 Current Year Depreciation	在建工程 Construction in Progress	资产总计 Total Assets	流动负债合计 Working Liability	# 应付帐款 Account Payable	非流动负债合计 Non-Current Liability
12 413	**34 109**	**588 257**	**328 783**	**56 094**	**17 569**
608	53	45 657	26 572	6 625	4 570
326	1 596	20 095	7 794	1 236	
109		95 817	95 238	7 836	
83	3 809	11 853	4 213	839	2 220
68		16 050	12 015	2 630	843
10 783	28 651	370 413	170 445	29 470	4 365
67		7 988	3 765	317	342
33		2 279	679	368	
336		18 106	8 062	6 775	5 230
12 413	34 109	588 257	328 783	56 094	17 569
62	3 812	9 639	2 236	509	2 220
6 613	5 737	292 803	153 135	22 046	5 069
94		9 379	7 381	1 442	
5 644	24 559	274 657	165 442	31 909	10 280
		1 779	591	188	
3 618	6 990	240 503	126 675	11 481	2 969
		155	79	24	40
6 889	24 818	300 394	177 805	36 172	10 560
1 905	2 301	47 206	24 224	8 418	4 000
11 352	33 275	457 504	209 118	44 010	17 335
36		13 063	8 999	1 093	742
11		2 303	1 547	1 125	
1 014	834	115 387	109 119	9 866	—508
48		18 014	7 762	658	3 624
5 951	10 005	308 230	186 489	32 496	11 229
6 243	22 744	237 783	117 183	17 182	2 055
172	1 360	24 230	17 350	5 759	661
12 021	34 109	473 802	227 903	41 331	12 299
27		1 782	574	574	
1		675	11	1	
378	53	9 585	7 544	2 875	946
148		33 264	18 698	3 714	3 624
28		2 146	292		
4 223	24 339	231 903	124 282	18 072	7 730
6 804	8 121	176 240	67 388	15 238	
29		1 178	160	120	
114		5 622	4 933	338	
268	1 596	11 410	4 019	399	
393		114 455	100 881	14 763	5 270

13—9 续表 4

计量单位:万元　　　　(2017 年)

指　标	Item	负债合计 Total Liabilities	所有者权益合计 Total Owners' Equities	实收资本 Paicl-up Capitals
零售业	**Retail Trade**	**346 352**	**241 905**	**139 866**
按零售行业分	**Group by Retail Trade Sector**			
综合零售	Integrated Retail	31 141	14 515	4 207
食品、饮料及烟草制品专门零售	Retail of Food,Beverage and Tobaccos	7 794	12 302	6 969
纺织、服装及日用品专门零售	Special Retail of Textiles,Garments and Daily Consumer Articles	95 238	579	1 055
文化、体育用品及器材专门零售	Retail of Culture,Sports Appliances and Equipments	6 433	5 420	1 780
医药及医疗器材专门零售	Retail of Medicines and Mdedical Appliances	12 859	3 191	1 814
汽车、摩托车、燃料及零配件专门零售	Retail of Motor Vehicles,Motorcycles Fuel and Parts	174 810	195 603	116 941
家用电器及电子产品专门零售	Special Retail of Household Electric Appliances and Electronic Products	4 107	3 880	2 682
五金、家具及室内装饰材料专门零售	Special Retail of Hardware,Furniture and Interior	679	1 600	799
货摊、无店铺及其他零售业	Stall、Non—shop and Others	13 292	4 814	3 620
按登记注册类型分	**Grouped by Status of Registration**			
内资企业	Domestic Enterprises	346 352	241 905	139 866
国有企业	State-owned Enterprises	4 455	5 183	1 250
有限责任公司	Limited Liability Corporations	158 204	134 600	89 890
股份有限公司	State-owned Corporations Ltd.	7 381	1 998	800
私营企业	Private Enterprises	175 722	98 935	47 746
其他企业	Others	591	1 188	180
按控股情况分	**Grouped by Share-holding Controlled**			
国有控股	Share-holding Controlled of State-owned	129 644	110 858	77 138
集体控股	Share-holding Controlled of Collective-owned	119	36	5
私人控股	Share-holding Controlled of Collective-owned	188 366	112 028	53 574
其　他	Others	28 224	18 982	9 149
按经营形式分	**Grouped by Operate Form**			
独立门店	Store of Independent	226 452	231 051	131 815
连锁总店	Total Store of Catena	9 741	3 322	2 070
连锁门店	Store of Catena	1 547	756	602
其　他	Others	108 612	6 775	5 379
按单位规模分	**Grouped by Size**			
大　型	Large	11 386	6 628	500
中　型	Medium-sized	197 718	110 512	93 512
小　型	Small	119 238	118 546	40 307
微　型	Micro	18 011	6 219	5 547
按零售业态分	**Group by Retail Trade Form**			
有店铺零售	Retail Trade Form with Store	240 202	233 600	134 793
食杂店	Grocery Store	574	1 208	500
折扣店	Discount Store	11	663	1 000
超　市	Supermarket	8 490	1 095	1 772
大型超市	Large Supermarket	22 322	10 942	1 550
百货店	General Store	292	1 854	80
专业店	Profession Store	132 012	99 891	87 237
专卖店	Monopoly Store	67 388	108 852	35 606
家居建材商店	Home Building Materials Store	160	1 019	600
购物中心	Shopping Mall	4 933	689	1 447
厂家直销中心	Factory Outlets Center	4 019	7 390	5 000
无店铺零售	Retail Trade Form without Store	106 151	8 304	5 073

Continued

(10 000 yuan)

营业收入 Revenue Business	主营业务收入 Revenue from Principal Business	营业成本 Cost of Business	主营业务成本 Cost of Principal Business	营业税金及附加 Taxes and Other Changes on Business	主营业务税金及附加 Taxes and Other Changes on Principal Business
1 219 871	**1 186 622**	**1 091 439**	**1 047 386**	**4 421**	**4 368**
293 346	285 796	263 518	234 733	724	691
15 139	14 914	11 693	11 639	80	80
46 495	46 485	43 629	43 629	130	130
10 569	10 522	7 849	7 843	32	32
23 463	23 463	19 295	19 295	55	55
793 553	768 696	713 965	698 913	2 972	2 952
17 314	16 756	14 925	14 769	46	46
5 730	5 730	4 618	4 618	63	63
14 261	14 261	11 947	11 947	319	319
1 219 871	1 186 622	1 091 439	1 047 386	4 421	4 368
8 309	8 261	5 936	5 930	3	3
602 435	581 324	540 613	525 578	1 938	1 918
20 379	18 568	18 100	16 833	123	123
585 063	574 785	524 641	496 896	2 333	2 300
3 685	3 685	2 150	2 150	25	25
530 452	516 772	485 715	474 228	1 411	1 391
532	532	419	419	2	2
646 190	631 686	574 580	545 478	2 721	2 688
42 697	37 633	30 726	27 261	287	287
1 122 075	1 088 827	1 010 163	966 109	4 111	4 082
16 196	16 196	13 070	13 070	34	34
1 456	1 456	1 071	1 071	23	23
80 144	80 143	67 135	67 135	253	229
225 972	221 539	208 591	181 164	413	413
620 075	598 497	561 209	544 998	1 898	1 855
326 110	319 030	276 518	276 215	2 013	2 013
47 714	47 556	45 122	45 007	97	88
1 159 281	1 126 032	1 038 089	994 067	3 913	3 860
6 321	6 321	4 993	4 993	19	19
1 060	925	929	925	1	1
21 545	21 483	17 876	17 876	147	114
258 014	250 526	235 679	206 894	575	575
14 422	14 422	10 438	10 438	4	4
602 413	584 321	551 993	536 972	1 344	1 324
240 822	233 361	202 674	202 462	1 763	1 763
2 734	2 734	2 135	2 135	5	5
10 316	10 306	9 777	9 777	55	55
1 634	1 634	1 595	1 595		
60 590	60 590	53 351	53 318	508	508

13—9 续表 5

计量单位:万元 (2017 年)

指　　标	Item	其他业务利润 Profits from Other Business	销售费用 Sales Expenses	管理费用 Administrative Expenses
零售业	**Retail Trade**	**3 431**	**64 657**	**28 144**
按零售行业分	**Group by Retail Trade Sector**			
综合零售	Integrated Retail	1 212	15 748	11 567
食品、饮料及烟草制品专门零售	Retail of Food,Beverage and Tobaccos	171	753	1 098
纺织、服装及日用品专门零售	Special Retail of Textiles,Garments and Daily Consumer Articles	10	2 412	716
文化、体育用品及器材专门零售	Retail of Culture,Sports Appliances and Equipments	41	1 436	741
医药及医疗器材专门零售	Retail of Medicines and Mdedical Appliances		2 853	572
汽车、摩托车、燃料及零配件专门零售	Retail of Motor Vehicles,Motorcycles Fuel and Parts	1 561	39 575	11 920
家用电器及电子产品专门零售	Special Retail of Household Electric Appliances and Electronic Products	435	1 446	851
五金、家具及室内装饰材料专门零售	Special Retail of Hardware,Furniture and Interior		126	281
货摊、无店铺及其他零售业	Stall、Non－shop and Others		309	398
按登记注册类型分	**Grouped by Status of Registration**			
内资企业	Domestic Enterprises	3 431	64 657	28 144
国有企业	State-owned Enterprises	41	1 109	707
有限责任公司	Limited Liability Corporations	2 431	42 125	3 168
股份有限公司	State-owned Corporations Ltd.		1 188	725
私营企业	Private Enterprises	959	20 235	23 058
其他企业	Others			485
按控股情况分	**Grouped by Share-holding Controlled**			
国有控股	Share-holding Controlled of State-owned	716	36 972	－1 010
集体控股	Share-holding Controlled of Collective-owned		31	5
私人控股	Share-holding Controlled of Collective-owned	1 710	22 792	27 161
其　他	Others	1 004	4 862	1 988
按经营形式分	**Grouped by Operate Form**			
独立门店	Store of Independent	3 431	55 931	26 028
连锁总店	Total Store of Catena		2 470	281
连锁门店	Store of Catena		215	75
其　他	Others		6 042	1 761
按单位规模分	**Grouped by Size**			
大　型	Large		8 146	8 269
中　型	Medium-sized	2 777	43 215	3 821
小　型	Small	635	12 588	14 979
微　型	Micro	19	709	1 074
按零售业态分	**Group by Retail Trade Form**			
有店铺零售	Retail Trade Form with Store	3 431	62 289	26 624
食杂店	Grocery Store		379	32
折扣店	Discount Store		1	346
超　市	Supermarket	60	1 488	1 611
大型超市	Large Supermarket	1 152	11 293	9 445
百货店	General Store		2 859	453
专业店	Profession Store	2 005	39 556	633
专卖店	Monopoly Store	203	5 739	13 364
家居建材商店	Home Building Materials Store		25	88
购物中心	Shopping Mall	10	948	321
厂家直销中心	Factory Outlets Center		1	330
无店铺零售	Retail Trade Form without Store		2 369	1 520

Continued

(10 000 yuan)

财务费用 Financial Expenses	营业利润 Operating Profits	利润总额 Total Profits	应交所得税 Income Tax Payable	应付职工薪酬(本年贷方累计发生额) Unemployment Insurance	本年应交增值税 Current Year VAT Payable
5 423	**25 930**	**25 871**	**4 531**	**45 008**	**42 585**
647	1 152	1 395	192	6 618	1 788
314	1 202	1 203	5	1 464	135
-267	-48	-48	247	1 110	600
13	532	531	1	837	109
152	536	290	58	1 434	286
4 044	21 104	21 125	3 880	31 838	39 201
26	20	-141	16	824	182
32	610	594		335	26
464	824	923	133	549	257
5 423	25 930	25 871	4 531	45 008	42 585
-1	587	581		723	39
1 663	13 029	12 625	1 908	25 487	19 406
46	198	292	63	1 065	271
3 712	11 094	11 350	2 561	17 432	22 870
3	1 023	1 023		301	
921	6 562	6 245	1 316	21 280	11 947
3	74	7	2	33	6
4 060	14 885	15 242	3 021	20 234	27 439
439	4 409	4 376	193	3 462	3 194
5 378	20 517	20 630	4 229	39 730	41 723
79	263	7	48	1 020	205
6	66	77	8	152	28
-40	5 084	5 157	247	4 106	629
431	123	122	31	1 242	329
1 735	8 348	8 703	973	27 462	12 134
2 990	17 015	16 846	3 470	8 929	28 753
268	444	199	58	7 374	1 370
5 199	23 235	23 242	4 150	43 301	41 895
190	708	708		92	44
-2	-216	-176		192	166
129	285	432	9	1 456	650
513	527	626	163	3 324	729
-2	670	670	26	1 852	431
1 513	7 432	6 987	588	30 522	9 360
2 719	14 564	14 750	3 363	4 599	30 244
1	480	464		105	16
14	-798	-801		579	256
125	-417	-417		580	
224	2 695	2 629	382	1 707	690

13—10 各师限额以上批发和零售业法人单位主要财务指标

Main Financial Indicators of Corporative Units above Designated Size of Wholesale and Retail Trade

计量单位:万元 (2017年) (10 000 yuan)

单位	Unit	固定资产合计 Total Value of Fixed Assets	固定资产原价 Original Value of Fixed Assets	累计折旧 Accumulation Depreciation	#本年折旧 Current Year Depreciation	在建工程 Construction in Progress	资产总计 Total Assets	流动负债合计 Working Liability
总计	**Total**	**520 759**	**837 234**	**348 332**	**55 609**	**201 504**	**9 410 603**	**7 165 473**
一师	Division 1	54 216	80 783	27 007	4 502	23 568	954 490	853 783
二师	Division 2	60 953	90 029	36 640	7 253	2 381	576 712	383 786
三师	Division 3	27 510	35 643	10 856	2 287	8 136	1 266 932	997 720
四师	Division 4	24 597	37 527	14 234	2 647	6 878	371 142	304 060
五师	Division 5	56 079	84 905	29 186	4 224	1 769	370 090	289 753
六师	Division 6	16 744	21 149	7 368	2 282	18 397	382 027	265 008
七师	Division 7	29 799	76 962	47 331	2 922	2 015	402 286	331 957
八师	Division 8	46 615	89 856	45 217	5 514	9 284	1 309 736	1 161 294
九师	Division 9	9 434	11 797	2 365	582	65	58 906	39 739
十师	Division 10	34 087	32 046	2 995	858	7 533	111 630	64 965
十一师	Division 11	11 452	9 179	4 743	390	222	284 996	200 287
十二师	Division 12	37 912	60 593	22 737	8 328	71 226	1 043 310	395 418
十三师	Division 13	18 983	30 757	11 774	3 167	10 468	246 637	203 992
十四师	Division 14	158	304	146	22		5 505	3 817
兵团直属	Directly under XPCC	92 220	175 702	85 732	10 630	39 563	2 026 205	1 669 896

单位	Unit	#应付帐款 Account Payable	非流动负债合计 Non-Current Liability	负债合计 Total Liabilities	所有者权益合计 Total Owners' Equities	实收资本 Paicl-up Capitals	营业收入 Revenue Business	主营业务收入 Revenue from Principal Business
总计	**Total**	**1 216 408**	**619 545**	**7 785 758**	**1 624 845**	**940 466**	**12 357 665**	**12 272 415**
一师	Division 1	345 540	18 492	872 275	82 216	58 905	931 316	925 938
二师	Division 2	51 580	17 668	401 665	175 047	87 310	1 120 867	1 111 789
三师	Division 3	57 646	191 976	1 189 695	77 237	32 158	938 961	938 961
四师	Division 4	53 136	2 517	306 576	64 566	42 233	428 389	428 389
五师	Division 5	33 146	2 795	293 077	77 012	60 526	490 674	486 414
六师	Division 6	41 115	37 185	302 193	79 833	70 918	401 365	396 504
七师	Division 7	36 570	7 991	339 948	62 338	30 582	529 559	529 461
八师	Division 8	258 634	42 824	1 204 117	105 619	82 618	1 613 475	1 604 561
九师	Division 9	10 940	1 851	41 590	17 316	20 194	57 405	57 378
十师	Division 10	23 495	5 100	70 065	41 565	18 478	103 970	103 651
十一师	Division 11	33 528	17 675	217 961	67 035	63 472	460 493	460 259
十二师	Division 12	46 253	238 008	633 426	409 884	120 744	877 130	857 177
十三师	Division 13	14 141	3 517	207 508	39 129	20 048	449 004	448 738
十四师	Division 14	721	9	3 826	1 679	2 341	12 719	12 667
兵团直属	Directly under XPCC	209 962	31 939	1 701 834	324 370	229 941	3 942 340	3 910 530

13—10 续表 Continued

计量单位:万元 (2017 年) (10 000 yuan)

单 位	Unit	营业成本 Cost of Business	主营业务成本 Cost of Principal Business	营业税金及附加 Taxes and Other Changes on Business	主营业务税金及附加 Taxes and Other Changes on Principal Business	其他业务利润 Profits from Other Business	销售费用 Sales Expenses	管理费用 Administrative Expenses
总 计	**Total**	**11 557 427**	**11 480 596**	**36 139**	**35 687**	**−4 281**	**255 571**	**156 505**
一 师	Division 1	875 792	875 623	1 312	1 288	3 110	11 077	10 476
二 师	Division 2	1 022 846	991 163	1 227	1 227		29 767	18 736
三 师	Division 3	853 507	853 507	1 708	1 708		29 410	13 457
四 师	Division 4	374 155	374 155	527	527		19 721	14 736
五 师	Division 5	450 417	448 015	680	464		11 673	4 702
六 师	Division 6	375 595	372 611	685	680	−1 293	7 446	8 837
七 师	Division 7	507 833	507 831	1 057	1 057	95	7 898	4 771
八 师	Division 8	1 529 945	1 509 533	10 025	9 855	−11 668	31 761	19 280
九 师	Division 9	52 322	52 296	32	32		3 631	1 572
十 师	Division 10	91 533	91 198	1 054	1 045	304	2 955	3 459
十一师	Division 11	446 424	446 186	395	395	10	4 871	4 951
十二师	Division 12	765 991	759 570	12 690	12 690	786	13 569	27 909
十三师	Division 13	400 525	400 525	2 289	2 289		2 771	4 638
十四师	Division 14	11 584	11 584	12	12		518	402
兵团直属	Directly under XPCC	3 798 959	3 786 801	2 446	2 419	4 375	78 504	18 579

单 位	Unit	财务费用 Financial Expenses	营业利润 Operating Profits	利润总额 Total Profits	应交所得税 Income Tax Payable	应付职工薪酬(本年贷方累计发生额) Unemployment Insurance	本年应交增值税 Current Year VAT Payable
总 计	**Total**	**78 553**	**285 830**	**299 407**	**33 287**	**520 494**	**110 364**
一 师	Division 1	1 507	29 600	32 500	2 843	6 716	2 633
二 师	Division 2	3 231	45 735	40 564	473	22 826	9 211
三 师	Division 3	10 838	31 352	36 936	6 477	8 619	12 480
四 师	Division 4	1 800	18 552	19 767	863	8 657	5 313
五 师	Division 5	4 113	18 861	18 152	424	5 032	783
六 师	Division 6	4 786	4 355	1 462	1 849	374 402	2 366
七 师	Division 7	3 020	5 002	9 696	1 890	6 942	9 514
八 师	Division 8	6 749	13 869	14 107	3 081	26 748	8 937
九 师	Division 9	765	−960	−977	5	1 145	74
十 师	Division 10	1 116	3 910	3 800	187	2 564	1 044
十一师	Division 11	2 179	2 461	2 453	551	3 437	4 088
十二师	Division 12	12 224	49 257	49 312	5 292	13 176	40 592
十三师	Division 13	2 159	35 969	38 220	1 021	3 278	1 772
十四师	Division 14	97	101	208	51	244	27
兵团直属	Directly under XPCC	23 970	27 768	33 209	8 280	36 708	11 532

13—11 限额以上住宿和餐饮业法人单位主要财务指标

计量单位:万元 （2017 年）

指　　标	Item	固定资产合计 Total Value of Fixed Assets	固定资产原价 Original Value of Fixed Assets	累计折旧 Accumulation Depreciation
总　计	**Total**	**95 070**	**137 335**	**47 060**
住宿业	**Hotels**	**69 009**	**107 578**	**41 844**
按住宿行业分	**Group by Hotels Sector**			
旅游饭店	Travel Hotel	60 959	98 038	40 271
一般旅馆	General Hotel	8 050	9 540	1 574
按登记注册类型分	**Grouped by Types of Registration**			
内资企业	Domestic Enterprises	68 972	107 502	41 805
国有企业	State-owned Enterprises	19 994	39 398	19 604
有限责任公司	Limited Liability Corporations	8 912	16 770	7 861
股份有限公司	Share-holding Corporations Ltd	11 868	16 783	7 723
私营企业	Private Enterprises	28 199	34 552	6 617
外商投资企业	Foreign-invested Enterprises	37	76	39
按控股情况分	**Grouped by Share-holding Controlled**			
国有控股	Share-holding Controlled of State-owned	37 881	67 761	32 889
私人控股	Share-holding Controlled of Private	31 091	39 740	8 916
外商控股	Share-holding Controlled of Foreign	37	76	39
按经营形式分	**Grouped by Management**			
独立门店	Independent Store	45 295	77 949	35 716
其　他	Others	23 714	29 629	6 128
按单位规模分	**Grouped by Size**			
中　型	Medium-sized	32 042	49 425	17 496
小　型	Small	36 495	57 613	24 281
微　型	Micro	472	539	67
按星级分	**Group by Hotels Star**			
四　星	4 Stars	7 274	15 706	8 435
三　星	3 Stars	33 522	57 533	27 020
二　星	2 Stars			
一　星	1 Stars	3 017	3 197	180
其　他	Others	25 196	31 141	6 209
餐饮业	**Catering Services**	**26 061**	**29 757**	**5 215**
按餐饮行业小类分	**Grouped by Catering Trade**			
正餐服务	Restaurant	26 036	29 644	5 128
快餐服务	Snack Counter	25	113	88
按登记注册类型分	**Grouped by Types of Registration**			
内资企业	Domestic Enterprises	26 061	29 757	5 215
有限责任公司	Limited Liability Corporations	5 472	6 706	1 282
股份有限公司	Share-holding Corporations Ltd	3 563	3 563	1 456
私营企业	Private Enterprises	17 027	19 489	2 478
按控股情况分	**Grouped by Share-holding Controlled**			
国有控股	Share-holding Controlled of State-owned	3 782	4 562	828
私人控股	Share-holding Controlled of Private	22 254	25 083	4 300
其　他	Others	25	113	88
按经营形式分	**Grouped by Management**			
独立门店	Independent Store	26 036	29 644	5 128
其　他	Other	25	113	88
按单位规模分	**Grouped by Size**			
小　型	Small	26 061	29 757	5 215

Main Financial Indicators of Corporative Units above Designated Size of Accommodation and Catering Services Industry

(10 000 yuan)

# 本年折旧 Current Year Depreciation	在建工程 Construction in Progress	资产总计 Total Assets	流动负债合计 Working Liability	# 应付帐款 Account Payable	非流动负债合计 Non-Current Liability
4 391	**14 345**	**299 631**	**138 523**	**9 098**	**30 570**
2 534	**13 486**	**224 139**	**111 506**	**8 511**	**20 824**
2 355	13 224	211 864	106 552	7 639	19 985
179	262	12 275	4 954	872	839
2 529	13 478	161 278	55 231	5 313	20 824
1 222	16	34 952	12 501	1 801	641
455	78	34 306	20 051	449	43
569	2 411	26 856	4 740	317	648
283	10 973	65 165	17 939	2 746	19 492
5	8	62 861	56 275	3 198	
2 020	2 505	72 611	26 004	2 308	1 332
509	10 973	88 667	29 228	3 005	19 492
5	8	62 861	56 275	3 198	
2 464	13 486	191 093	108 091	7 267	20 763
70		33 046	3 415	1 244	61
647		50 192	15 510	1 988	580
1 885	13 486	173 385	95 817	6 518	20 044
3		562	179	5	200
603	10 932	54 089	19 720	2 146	18 454
1 594	2 505	65 107	22 216	1 784	1 332
		44	44		
166	38	4 487	4 659	49	
172	11	100 413	64 867	4 532	1 039
1 857	**859**	**75 492**	**27 017**	**587**	**9 747**
1 844	859	75 233	26 415	430	9 747
14		260	602	157	
1 857	859	75 492	27 017	587	9 747
403	12	6 258	2 645	206	154
106		40 980	15 548		8 743
1 349	847	28 255	8 824	381	851
281		3 960	96	49	154
1 563	859	71 273	26 319	381	9 593
14		260	602	157	
1 844	859	75 233	26 415	430	9 747
14		260	602	157	
1 857	859	75 492	27 017	587	9 747

13－11 续表 1

计量单位:万元 (2017 年)

指　　标	Item	负债合计 Total Liabilities	所有者权益合计 Total Owners' Equities	实收资本 Paicl-up Capitals
总　计	**Total**	**169 094**	**130 538**	**148 353**
住宿业	**Hotels**	**132 330**	**91 809**	**129 258**
按住宿行业分	**Group by Hotels Sector**			
旅游饭店	Travel Hotel	126 537	85 327	128 080
一般旅馆	General Hotel	5 793	6 482	1 179
按登记注册类型分	**Grouped by Types of Registration**			
内资企业	Domestic Enterprises	76 055	85 223	119 550
国有企业	State-owned Enterprises	13 142	21 810	23 136
有限责任公司	Limited Liability Corporations	20 094	14 212	26 399
股份有限公司	Share-holding Corporations Ltd	5 388	21 468	26 767
私营企业	Private Enterprises	37 431	27 734	43 248
外商投资企业	Foreign-invested Enterprises	56 275	6 586	9 709
按控股情况分	**Grouped by Share-holding Controlled**			
国有控股	Share-holding Controlled of State-owned	27 335	45 276	64 088
私人控股	Share-holding Controlled of Private	48 720	39 947	55 462
外商控股	Share-holding Controlled of Foreign	56 275	6 586	9 709
按经营形式分	**Grouped by Management**			
独立门店	Independent Store	128 854	62 239	90 465
其　他	Others	3 476	29 570	38 793
按单位规模分	**Grouped by Size**			
中　型	Medium-sized	16 091	34 101	53 287
小　型	Small	115 861	57 524	75 781
微　型	Micro	379	184	190
按星级分	**Group by Hotels Star**			
四　星	4 Stars	38 174	15 915	18 118
三　星	3 Stars	23 547	41 560	61 841
二　星	2 Stars	44		1
一　星	1 Stars	4 659	－173	100
其　他	Others	65 905	34 507	49 199
餐饮业	**Catering Services**	**36 764**	**38 729**	**19 094**
按餐饮行业小类分	**Grouped by Catering Trade**			
正餐服务	Restaurant	36 162	39 071	18 694
快餐服务	Snack Counter	602	－343	400
按登记注册类型分	**Grouped by Types of Registration**			
内资企业	Domestic Enterprises	36 764	38 729	19 094
有限责任公司	Limited Liability Corporations	2 799	3 459	1 254
股份有限公司	Share-holding Corporations Ltd	24 291	16 689	12 800
私营企业	Private Enterprises	9 675	18 580	5 041
按控股情况分	**Grouped by Share-holding Controlled**			
国有控股	Share-holding Controlled of State-owned	250	3 710	54
私人控股	Share-holding Controlled of Private	35 912	35 361	18 641
其　他	Others	602	－343	400
按经营形式分	**Grouped by Management**			
独立门店	Independent Store	36 162	39 071	18 694
其　他	Other	602	－343	400
按单位规模分	**Grouped by Size**			
小　型	Small	36 764	38 729	19 094

Continued

(10 000 yuan)

营业收入 Revenue Business	主营业务收入 Revenue from Principal Business	营业成本 Cost of Business	主营业务成本 Cost of Principal Business	营业税金及附加 Taxes and Other Changes on Business	主营业务税金及附加 Taxes and Other Changes on Principal Business
51 457	**50 190**	**23 609**	**22 399**	**838**	**732**
40 379	**39 137**	**16 159**	**15 618**	**718**	**617**
36 380	35 314	14 698	14 299	606	506
4 000	3 823	1 461	1 320	111	111
39 397	38 197	15 948	15 412	672	571
18 936	18 081	7 635	7 242	258	258
7 545	7 319	2 618	2 593	179	179
820	820	1 879	1 879	101	
12 096	11 978	3 815	3 698	134	134
983	939	211	206	46	46
25 375	24 293	10 577	10 158	527	426
14 022	13 904	5 371	5 254	145	145
983	939	211	206	46	46
36 317	35 143	14 579	14 038	701	600
4 063	3 994	1 580	1 580	17	17
15 446	14 805	4 801	4 587	96	96
24 464	23 865	11 207	10 881	620	520
469	467	152	150	2	2
11 860	11 710	5 573	5 423	77	77
19 848	18 914	7 763	7 493	524	424
231	231	230	230		
860	860	162	162	6	6
7 580	7 422	2 431	2 310	110	110
11 077	**11 054**	**7 450**	**6 781**	**120**	**115**
9 570	9 547	6 150	6 131	116	111
1 507	1 507	1 300	650	4	4
11 077	11 054	7 450	6 781	120	115
2 568	2 568	1 978	1 328	10	10
774	774	455	455	1	1
7 735	7 711	5 017	4 998	109	104
699	699	447	447	4	4
8 872	8 848	5 703	5 684	112	106
1 507	1 507	1 300	650	4	4
9 570	9 547	6 150	6 131	116	111
1 507	1 507	1 300	650	4	4
11 077	11 054	7 450	6 781	120	115

13—11 续表 2

计量单位:万元 (2017 年)

指 标	Item	其他业务利润 Profits from Other Business	营业费用 Business Expenses	管理费用 Administrative Expenses
总 计	**Total**	**405**	**13 346**	**19 445**
住宿业	**Hotels**	**405**	**12 573**	**15 406**
按住宿行业分	**Group by Hotels Sector**			
旅游饭店	Travel Hotel	371	11 930	14 468
一般旅馆	General Hotel	34	643	938
按登记注册类型分	**Grouped by Types of Registration**			
内资企业	Domestic Enterprises	367	12 301	14 834
国有企业	State-owned Enterprises		6 765	4 037
有限责任公司	Limited Liability Corporations	367	1 801	2 954
股份有限公司	Share-holding Corporations Ltd		43	343
私营企业	Private Enterprises		3 692	7 500
外商投资企业	Foreign-invested Enterprises	38	272	571
按控股情况分	**Grouped by Share-holding Controlled**			
国有控股	Share-holding Controlled of State-owned	367	8 480	7 141
私人控股	Share-holding Controlled of Private		3 821	7 693
外商控股	Share-holding Controlled of Foreign	38	272	571
按经营形式分	**Grouped by Management**			
独立门店	Independent Store	405	11 494	11 529
其 他	Others		1 080	3 877
按单位规模分	**Grouped by Size**			
中 型	Medium-sized		5 544	7 226
小 型	Small	405	6 949	8 024
微 型	Micro		81	156
按星级分	**Group by Hotels Star**			
四 星	4 Stars		3 986	2 295
三 星	3 Stars	367	6 666	6 883
二 星	2 Stars			1
一 星	1 Stars		12	690
其 他	Others	38	1 909	5 539
餐饮业	**Catering Services**		**773**	**4 040**
按餐饮行业小类分	**Grouped by Catering Trade**			
正餐服务	Restaurant		603	3 978
快餐服务	Snack Counter		170	62
按登记注册类型分	**Grouped by Types of Registration**			
内资企业	Domestic Enterprises		773	4 040
有限责任公司	Limited Liability Corporations		178	820
股份有限公司	Share-holding Corporations Ltd		3	523
私营企业	Private Enterprises		592	2 697
按控股情况分	**Grouped by Share-holding Controlled**			
国有控股	Share-holding Controlled of State-owned		8	588
私人控股	Share-holding Controlled of Private		595	3 390
其 他	Others		170	62
按经营形式分	**Grouped by Management**			
独立门店	Independent Store		603	3 978
其 他	Other		170	62
按单位规模分	**Grouped by Size**			
小 型	Small		773	4 040

Continued

(10 000 yuan)

财务费用 Financial Expenses	营业利润 Operating Profits	营业外收入 Revenue Outside Business	利润总额 Total Profits	应交所得税 Income Tax Payable	应付职工薪酬(本年贷方累计发生额) Unemployment Insurance	应交增值税 Value Added Tax Payable
1 168	**−7 035**	**489**	**−5 667**	**299**	**16 308**	**1 049**
822	**−5 382**	**348**	**−4 144**	**298**	**13 298**	**940**
503	−5 910	320	−4 674	251	11 912	873
318	528	28	530	46	1 386	67
819	−5 261	347	−4 023	298	12 810	866
−91	248	131	1 035	261	6 053	557
52	−59	184	110	32	1 711	171
63	−1 609	1	−1 638		680	
795	−3 841	31	−3 529	5	4 365	138
3	−121	1	−121		489	74
19	−1 453	316	−524	292	8 042	669
800	−3 808	31	−3 499	5	4 768	198
3	−121	1	−121		489	74
821	−2 890	257	−1 743	298	12 318	921
1	−2 492	91	−2 401		981	19
−70	−2 162	184	−1 993	111	4 708	357
876	−3 285	164	−2 215	181	8 533	582
15	64		64	5	57	2
690	−772	42	−764	99	3 930	435
102	−2 161	304	−1 098	170	5 823	308
					28	
4	−13	1	−12		312	33
27	−2 436	1	−2 270	29	3 206	164
346	**−1 653**	**141**	**−1 523**	**2**	**3 010**	**108**
343	−1 621	139	−1 492	2	2 838	108
3	−32	1	−30		172	
346	−1 653	141	−1 523	2	3 010	108
5	−421	7	−415		621	55
3	−211	31	−186		311	9
339	−1 021	103	−921	2	2 077	44
1	−348	5	−344		270	31
343	−1 273	134	−1 148	2	2 568	77
3	−32	1	−30		172	
343	−1 621	139	−1 492	2	2 838	108
3	−32	1	−30		172	
346	−1 653	141	−1 523	2	3 010	108

13－12 各师限额以上住宿和餐饮业法人单位主要财务指标

Main Financial Indicators of Units above Designated Size of Hotel and Catering Services by Division

计量单位:万元 (2017年) (10 000 yuan)

单位	Unit	固定资产合计 Total Value of Fixed Assets	固定资产原价 Original Value of Fixed Assets	累计折旧 Accumulation Depreciation	#本年折旧 Current Year Depreciation	在建工程 Construction in Progress
总计	**Total**	**95 070**	**137 335**	**47 060**	**4 391**	**14 345**
一师	Division 1	4 202	5 750	1 548	422	
二师	Division 2	6 964	8 984	2 020	211	16
三师	Division 3	5 201	7 918	2 901	310	
四师	Division 4	7 794	20 084	12 290	710	
五师	Division 5	3 372	5 809	2 440	226	
六师	Division 6	31 463	37 939	8 093	508	12
七师	Division 7	98	98	4	4	
八师	Division 8	15 240	23 493	11 060	611	13 105
九师	Division 9	1 302	2 332	1 029	92	78
十师	Division 10	15 043	16 719	1 788	1 047	847
十二师	Division 12	52	379	327		
十三师	Division 13	152	157	72	41	249
十四师	Division 14	3 017	3 197	180	166	38
兵团直属	Directly under XPCC	1 170	4 479	3 308	45	

单位	Unit	资产总计 Total Assets	流动负债合计 Working Liability	#应付帐款 Account Payable	非流动负债合计 Non-Current Liability	负债合计 Total Liabilities
总计	**Total**	**299 631**	**138 523**	**9 098**	**30 570**	**169 094**
一师	Division 1	6 080	1 414	17	1 750	3 164
二师	Division 2	9 479	3 929	887		3 929
三师	Division 3	8 512	4 266	143		4 266
四师	Division 4	16 275	6 223	849	580	6 803
五师	Division 5	25 859	12 445	258		12 445
六师	Division 6	78 569	21 294	1 450	8 896	30 190
七师	Division 7	1 784	810			810
八师	Division 8	115 235	69 002	4 373	19 101	88 103
九师	Division 9	1 556	76		43	118
十师	Division 10	23 464	6 898	302	200	7 098
十二师	Division 12	410	34	23		34
十三师	Division 13	1 368	1 918	200		1 918
十四师	Division 14	4 487	4 659	49		4 659
兵团直属	Directly under XPCC	6 554	5 555	547		5 555

13－12 续表 1 Continued

计量单位:万元 (2017 年) (10 000 yuan)

单 位	Unit	所有者权益合计 Total Owners' Equities	实收资本 Paicl-up Capitals	营业收入 Revenue Business	主营业务收入 Revenue from Principal Business	营业成本 Cost of Business
总 计	**Total**	**130 538**	**148 353**	**51 457**	**50 190**	**23 609**
一 师	Division 1	2 916	880	3 777	3 708	2 661
二 师	Division 2	5 549	1 361	4 645	4 642	2 723
三 师	Division 3	4 246	4 543	5 419	5 303	2 044
四 师	Division 4	9 472	15 626	8 707	7 920	2 798
五 师	Division 5	13 414	12 914	3 021	3 021	1 620
六 师	Division 6	48 379	52 054	6 794	6 794	3 412
七 师	Division 7	975	21	763	763	669
八 师	Division 8	27 132	50 333	7 068	7 025	3 621
九 师	Division 9	1 438	1 438	457	290	123
十 师	Division 10	16 366	5 044	4 155	4 132	2 530
十 二 师	Division 12	376	500	564	564	189
十 三 师	Division 13	－551	1 098	1 732	1 732	285
十 四 师	Division 14	－173	100	860	860	162
兵团直属	Directly under XPCC	998	2 442	3 496	3 437	774

单 位	Unit	主营业务成本 Cost of Principal Business	营业税金及附加 Taxes and Other Changes on Business	主营业务税金及附加 Taxes and Other Changes on Principal Business	其他业务利润 Profits from Other Business	营业费用 Business Expenses
总 计	**Total**	**22 399**	**838**	**732**	**405**	**13 346**
一 师	Division 1	2 661	63	63		2
二 师	Division 2	2 722	20	20		396
三 师	Division 3	1 929	178	178		1 078
四 师	Division 4	2 404	41	41		4 617
五 师	Division 5	1 620	76	76		775
六 师	Division 6	2 762	18	18		1 261
七 师	Division 7	669	2	2		15
八 师	Division 8	3 615	248	147	38	2 141
九 师	Division 9	122	2	2	333	259
十 师	Division 10	2 511	56	50		540
十 二 师	Division 12	189	2	2		30
十 三 师	Division 13	285	36	36		274
十 四 师	Division 14	162	6	6		12
兵团直属	Directly under XPCC	749	91	91	34	1 949

13—12 续表 2 Continued

计量单位:万元　　(2017 年)　　(10 000 yuan)

单　位	Unit	管理费用 Administrative Expenses	财务费用 Financial Expenses	营业利润 Operating Profits	营业外收入 Revenue Outside Business
总　计	**Total**	**19 445**	**1 168**	**−7 035**	**489**
一　师	Division 1	156	11	884	
二　师	Division 2	1 232	10	253	12
三　师	Division 3	1 319	14	713	26
四　师	Division 4	1 170	−93	174	2
五　师	Division 5	648	10	−107	
六　师	Division 6	5 101	8	−3 004	38
七　师	Division 7	340		−263	3
八　师	Division 8	3 876	465	−3 284	174
九　师	Division 9	106	1	−34	12
十　师	Division 10	2 253	341	−1 565	191
十二师	Division 12	329	2	13	
十三师	Division 13	797	278	63	26
十四师	Division 14	690	4	−13	1
兵团直属	Directly under XPCC	1 429	118	−865	4

单　位	Unit	利润总额 Total Profits	应交所得税 Income Tax Payable	应付职工薪酬(本年贷方累计发生额) Unemployment Insurance	应交增值税 Value Added Tax Payable
总　计	**Total**	**−5 667**	**299**	**16 308**	**1 049**
一　师	Division 1	884		713	22
二　师	Division 2	260	48	1 071	251
三　师	Division 3	904	151	2 089	127
四　师	Division 4	173	95	3 001	216
五　师	Division 5	30		653	59
六　师	Division 6	−2 974		1 547	64
七　师	Division 7	−260		358	
八　师	Division 8	−3 155	1	2 605	133
九　师	Division 9	−22		114	20
十　师	Division 10	−1 372		1 463	31
十二师	Division 12	12		63	1
十三师	Division 13	63		690	33
十四师	Division 14	−12		312	33
兵团直属	Directly under XPCC	−197	3	1 629	59

13—13 亿元以上商品交易市场基本情况

Basic Statistics on Commodity Exchange Markets of Transaction Value over 100 Million Yuan

（2017 年）

指 标	Item	市场数（个） Number of Market (unit)	摊位总数（个） Number of Booths (unit)	年末出租摊位数(个) Number of Rented Booths at the Yearend (unit)	年末营业面积（平方米） Operating Area (sq.m)	成交额（万元） Turnover (10 000 yuan)
总 计	**Total**	**24**	**12 812**	**11 622**	**1 252 497**	**11 350 335**
按市场类别分	**Group by Type of Markets**					
综合市场	Integrated Markets	5	3 695	3 246	172 516	1 055 211
综合贸易市场	Integrated Trade Markets	5	3 695	3 246	172 516	1 055 211
工业消费品综合市场	Industrial Products Integrated Markets	1	1 275	1 146	69 005	387 815
农产品综合市场	Farm Produce Integrated Markets	1	649	649	60 000	554 141
其他综合市场	Other Integrated Markets	3	1 771	1 451	43 511	113 255
专业市场	Special Markets	19	9 117	8 376	1 079 981	10 295 124
生产资料市场	Productions Markets	3	348	276	181 623	5 809 832
农用生产资料市场	Agricultural Productions Markets	1	81	81	8 835	46 820
建材市场	Building Materials Markets	1	127	55	82 000	15 839
金属材料市场	Metal Material Markets	1	140	140	90 788	5 747 173
农产品市场	Agricultural Products Markets	7	4 802	4 390	337 872	3 500 517
肉食禽蛋市场	Meat, Poultry and Eggs Markets	1	230	230	30 001	305 742
蔬菜市场	Vegetables Markets	3	2 780	2 549	233 795	1 502 633
干鲜果品市场	Dry and Fresh Fruit Markets	2	1 518	1 337	66 676	1 658 427
其他农产品市场	Other Agricultural Products Markets	1	274	274	7 400	33 715
纺织、服装、鞋帽市场	Textile, Garments, Footwear and Hat Wear Markets	2	712	662	118 471	65 632
服装市场	Garments Markets	2	712	662	118 471	65 632
电器、通讯器材、电子设备市场	Electric Appliances, Communication Equipment, Electronics Equipments Markets	2	1 152	988	27 000	182 550
通讯器材市场	Communication Equipment Markets	1	780	735	18 000	110 450
计算机及辅助设备市场	Computer and Auxiliary Equipment Markets	1	372	253	9 000	72 100
家具、五金及装饰材料市场	Furniture, Hardware and Decorative Material Markets	2	668	668	160 931	84 865
厨具、盥洗设备市场	Kitchenware, Toilet Equipment Markets	1	200	200	53 300	11 820
其他装修市场	Other Renovation Markets	1	468	468	107 631	73 045
汽车、摩托车及零配件市场	Automobile, Motorcycle and Parts Markets	3	1 435	1 392	254 084	651 728
汽车市场	Automobil Markets	2	414	371	139 790	434 716
机动车零配件市场	Motor Vehicle Parts Markets	1	1 021	1 021	114 294	217 012
按营业状态分	**Group by Business Appearance**					
常年营业	Throughout the Year	24	12 812	11 622	1 252 497	11 350 335
按经营方式分	**Group by Management Way**					
以批发为主	Wholesale	16	8 570	8 038	871 129	10 515 536
以零售为主	Retail	8	4 242	3 584	381 368	834 799
按经营环境分	**Group by Operate Environment Way**					
露天式	Open-air Type	1	230	230	30 001	305 742
封闭式	Closed Type	16	7 764	7 056	900 905	2 055 144
其 他	Other	7	4 818	4 336	321 591	8 989 449

13－14 亿元以上商品交易市场商品销售类值

Commodity Exchange Markets by Category of Commodities of Transaction Value over 100 Million Yuan

(2017 年)

指　标	Item	年末出租摊位数（个）Number of Rented Booths at the Yearend (unit)	成交额（万元）Turnover (10 000yuan)
总　计	**Total**	**11 622**	**11 350 335**
粮油、食品类	Grain and Oil,Food	5 450	4 050 825
# 粮油类	GrainandOil	161	72 205
肉禽蛋类	Meat,Poultry and Eggs	379	343 232
水产品类	Aquatic Products	373	365 611
蔬菜类	Vegetables	2 369	1 338 046
干鲜果品类	Dried and Fresh Melons and Fruits	2 167	1 931 731
饮料类	Beverages	84	21 713
烟酒类	Tobacco and Liquor	94	13 344
服装、鞋帽、针纺织品类	Clothing,Shoes,Hats and Textiles	1 534	177 304
# 服装类	Clothing	1 284	140 850
鞋帽类	Footwear and Hats	150	23 536
针纺织品类	Knitwear and Textiles	100	12 918
化妆品类	Cosmetics	92	11 141
金银珠宝类	Gold,Silver and Jeweller	61	11 617
日用品类	Articles for DailyUse	179	36 866
# 儿童玩具类	Children Toys	24	1 010
五金、电料类	Hardware & Electrical Materials	143	12 520
体育、娱乐用品类	Sports & Recreational Articles	9	1 040
书报杂志类	Newspapers and Magazines	10	840
电子出版物及音像制品类	E-ournal and Video Products	9	620
家用电器和音像器材类	Household Appliances and Vide Equipments	66	41 752
中西药品类	Traditional Chinese and Western Medicine	33	9 882
# 西药类	Western Medicine	22	9 635
文化办公用品类	Cultural and official Goods	275	79 064
# 计算机及其配套产品	Computer and Related Products	255	72 389
家具类	Furniture	38	23 657
通讯器材类	Communication Appliances	844	140 245
木材及制品类	Wood and Wooden Products	112	11 290
石油及制品类	Oil and Oil Products	25	26 700
化工材料及制品类	Chemical Materials and Products	44	76 828
# 化肥类	Chemical Fertilizer	44	76 828
金属材料类	Metal Material Markets	143	5 747 355
建筑及装潢材料类	Building and Decoration Materials	461	51 410
机电产品及设备类	Mechanical & Electrical Products	4	312
汽车类	Automobile	1 396	665 676
种子饲料类	Seed and Feedstuff	229	88 517
其他类	Others	287	49 817

2018

BING TUAN

第十四篇

能源生产与消费

Chapter 14 Energy Production and Consumption

简要说明

一、本篇资料主要内容

本篇资料反映兵团规模以上工业法人企业分行业主要能源品种消费、库存量及能源加工转换量，分行业能源消费量；兵团道路运输企业主要能源品种的消费量。

二、本篇资料统计范围

统计范围为兵团规模以上工业法人企业和道路交通运输法人企业。

三、本篇资料来源

本篇资料由兵团统计局工业投资统计处根据《兵团能源统计报表制度》整理提供。

四、本篇资料调查方法

统计调查方法为全面调查。

Brief Introduction

1. Main Contents

Data in this chapter show energy consumption and inventory of industrial enterprises and output of energy processing conversion of industrial enterprises by category of energy above designated size, consumption by industrial branch; consumption of main energy varieties of road transportation enterprises.

2. Scope of Statistics

The statistical scope covers industrial corporate enterprises above designated size, road transportation corporate enterprises of XPCC.

3. Sources of Data

The data in this chapter are prepared and provided by Industry and Assets Statistical Section of Statistics Bureau of XPCC according to *the Comprehensive Statistical Reporting Form System on Energy of XPCC*.

4. Methodology of Survey

Survey method is comprehensive statistics.

14－1 规模以上工业企业能源消费与库存量

Energy Consumption and Inventory of Industrial Enterprises above Designated Size

（2017 年）

指 标	Item	年初库存量 Inventory at the Beginning of the year	本年消费量 Consumption in the Year	工业生产消费 Industry Consumption	非工业生产消费 Non-industry Consumption	# 车辆用油 Vehicle Oil	年末库存量 Inventory at the Year-end
能源总计（吨标准煤）	**Total Energy Production (tons of SCE)**		**53 414 976**	**53 379 276**	**35 700**		
原 煤 （吨）	Coal (ton)	2 952 006	55 292 235	55 271 650	20 585		3 824 112
洗精煤(用于炼焦)(吨)	Dressing Coal(Used for Coking) (ton)	24 990	797 855	797 855			23 615
其他洗煤 （吨）	Other Dressing Coal (ton)	29 159	716 455	716 455			12 909
焦 炭 （吨）	Coke (ton)	77 499	1 909 856	1 909 856			226 952
焦炉煤气（万立方米）	Coke Oven Coal Gas (10 000 cu.m)		17 183	17 183			
天然气 （万立方米）	Natural Gas (10000 cu.m)	29	21 668	21 457	211	8	3 825
汽 油 （吨）	Gasoline (ton)	32	4 120	2 597	1 524	3 345	10
柴 油 （吨）	Diesel Oil (ton)	1 712	58 092	54 740	3 351	23 653	1 702
液化石油气 （吨）	Liquefied Petroleum Gas (ton)	20	71	70	1		20
石油焦 （吨）	Petroleum Coke (ton)	14 561	244 887	244 887			20 912
热 力 （百万千焦）	Heat (million KJ)		48 018 148	47 902 033	116 116		
电 力 （万千瓦时）	Electricity (10 000 kwh)		7 425 110	7 419 277	5 833	508	
煤矸石(用于燃料)(吨)	Coal Gangue(Used for Fuel) (ton)	38 216	65 900	65 844	57		2 397
余热余压 （百万千焦）	Remaining Hot and Pressure (million KJ)		326 044	326 044			

注：由于规模以上工业统计口径变化，本表 2016 年数据与《2017 年兵团统计年鉴》相同指标数据不可比，下同。
Note: Due to changes of statistical caliber, same item in 2016 in this table are not same as statistical yearbook－2017 of XPCC.(the same as follows).

14－2 规模以上工业加工转换企业按能源品种分能源加工转换量

Output of Energy Processing Conversion of Industrial Processing Conversion Enterprises above Designated Size by Category of Energy

（2017 年）

指 标	Item	工业生产消费 Industry Consumption	加工转换投入合计 Total Processing Conversion Devoted	# 火电投入 Thermal Power Consumption	# 供热投入 Heating Consumption	# 原煤入洗 Coal Dressing	# 炼焦投入 Coking Consumption	# 制气 Making Gas	能源转换产出量 Energy Output Conversion	回收利用 Recycling
能源总计（吨标准煤）	**Total Energy Production (tons of SCE)**	**44 315 610**	**35 552 597**	**21 770 925**	**3 540 062**	**814 291**	**9 285 599**	**141 719**	**19 781 139**	**11 118**
原 煤 （吨）	Coal (ton)	52 481 906	49 511 247	31 674 899	4 998 839	1 092 776	11 553 968	190 765		
洗精煤(用于炼焦)（吨）	Dressing Coal(Used for Coking) (ton)	797 855	797 855				797 855		756 734	
其他洗煤 （吨）	Other Dressing Coal (ton)								31 691	
焦 炭 （吨）	Coke (ton)	1 095 784							6 200 340	
其他焦化产品 （吨）	Other Coking Product (ton)								998 847	
焦炉煤气 （万立方米）	Coke Oven Coal Gas (10 000 cu.m)	17 183							26 891	
天然气 （万立方米）	Natural Gas (10 000 cu.m)	5 717	5 390		5 390				2 162	
汽 油 （吨）	Gasoline (ton)	121	17		17					
柴 油 （吨）	Diesel Oil (ton)	7 867	693	671	22					
燃料油 （吨）	Fuel Oil (ton)	272	272	272						
热 力 （百万千焦）	Heat (million KJ)	38 078 753							86 273 379	
电 力 （万千瓦时）	Electricity (10 000 kwh)	3 393 820							7 132 313	
煤矸石(用于燃料)（吨）	Coal Gangue(Used for Fuel) (ton)	65 844	64 439	31 877	32 562				10 050	
余热余压 （百万千焦）	Remaining Hot and Pressure (million KJ)	326 044	326 044	326 044						326 044
其他燃料 （吨标准煤）	Ofher Fuel (tons of SCE)	29 030	29 030		29 030					

14—3 规模以上工业企业按行业分产值能耗

Output Value Energy Consumption of Industrial Enterprises above Designated Size by Industrial Branch

指 标	Item	2016	
		综合能源消费量（吨标准煤）Comsuption of Comprehensive Energy (ton standard coal)	产值能耗（吨标准煤/万元）Energy Comsuption of Output Value (ton standard coal /10 000 yuan)
总 计	**Total**	**31 504 922**	**1.6 683**
按工业行业大类分列	**Grouped by Sector**		
采矿业	**Mining**	**232 953**	**0.6 855**
煤炭开采和洗选业	Coal Mining and Dressing	191 004	1.0 925
黑色金属矿采选业	Ferrous Metals Mining and Dressing	31 861	0.3 089
有色金属矿采选业	Nonferrous Metals Mining and Dressing	2 432	0.2 007
非金属矿采选业	Nonmetal Minerals Mining and Dressing	7 656	0.1 539
制造业	**Manufacturing**	**22 342 314**	**1.3 618**
农副食品加工业	Food Processing	410 611	0.1 269
食品制造业	Food Manufacturing	1 254 635	1.1 024
酒、饮料和精制茶制造业	Beverage Production	86 363	0.1 214
纺织业	Textile Industry	189 333	0.1 484
纺织服装、服饰业	Textile Wearing and Finery Manufacturing	117 566	4.8 757
皮革、毛皮、羽毛及其制品和制鞋业	Leather, Fur, Feather and Related Goods Manufacturing	157	0.0 155
木材加工和木、竹、藤、棕、草制品业	Wood Processing and wood、Bamboo、Rattan、Coir、Grass Products	5 739	0.1 422
家具制造业	Furniture Manufacturing	46	0.0 046
造纸和纸制品业	Paper making and Paper Products	25 074	0.2 130
印刷和记录媒介复制业	Printing Industry and Recording Media	541	0.0 352
文教、工美、体育和娱乐用品制造业	Culture and Education, Handicraft, Athletics and Amusement Things Manufacturing	194	0.0 090
石油加工、炼焦和核燃料加工业	Petroleum, Processing Coking and Nucler Fuel	2 607 395	4.5 111
化学原料和化学制品制造业	Raw Chemical Materials and Chemical Products	7 774 853	3.4 410
医药制造业	Medical and Pharmaceutical Products	31 558	0.2 042
化学纤维制造业	Chemical Fiber	143 527	0.7 189
橡胶和塑料制品业	Rubber and Plastics Products Manufacturing	35 027	0.0 669
非金属矿物制品业	Nonmetal Mineral Products	1 337 972	0.8 550
黑色金属冶炼和压延加工业	Ferrous Metals Smelting and Rolling	461 192	2.4 443
有色金属冶炼和压延加工业	Non-Ferrous Metals Smelting and Rolling	7 832 506	2.1 019
金属制品业	Metal Products	6 507	0.0 425
通用设备制造业	Ordinary Machinery	437	0.0 302
专用设备制造业	Special Purpose Equipment	4 278	0.0 372
汽车制造业	Automobile Manufacturing	19	0.0 020
电气机械和器材制造业	Electric Machine and Equipment Manufacturing	3 273	0.0 112
计算机、通信和其他电子设备制造业	Computer, Communicationn and other Electronic Equipment Manufacturing	4 307	0.2 928
仪器仪表制造业	Measuring Instruments Manufacturing	189	0.0 251
废弃资源综合利用业	Worn-out Resource Synthetical Using	9 014	1.8 251
电力、热力、燃气及水的生产和供应业	**Electricity, Heat Power, Gas and Water Production and Supply**	**8 929 655**	**4.1 766**
电力、热力生产和供应业	Electricity and Heat Production and Supply	8 918 856	4.5 377
燃气生产和供应业	Gas Production and Supply	4 147	0.0 281
水的生产和供应业	Water Production and Supply	6 651	0.2 670
按轻重工业分	**Grouped by Light & Heavy Industry**		
轻工业	Light Industry	2 294 335	0.3 245
重工业	Heavy Industry	29 210 588	2.4 724

14—3 续表 Continued

指 标	Item	2017 综合能源消费量(吨标准煤) Comsuption of Comprehensive Energy (ton standard coal)	2017 产值能耗(吨标准煤/万元) Energy Comsuption of Output Value (ton standard coal /10 000 yuan)
总 计	**Total**	**33 587 019**	**1.6 252**
按工业行业大类分列	**Grouped by Sector**		
采矿业	**Mining**	**172 757**	**0.4 256**
煤炭开采和洗选业	Coal Mining and Dressing	127 501	0.7 476
黑色金属矿采选业	Ferrous Metals Mining and Dressing	35 623	0.2 159
有色金属矿采选业	Nonferrous Metals Mining and Dressing	2 489	0.2 859
非金属矿采选业	Nonmetal Minerals Mining and Dressing	7 145	0.1 158
制造业	**Manufacturing**	**24 601 104**	**1.3 751**
农副食品加工业	Food Processing	383 738	0.1 160
食品制造业	Food Manufacturing	1 354 346	1.1 703
酒、饮料和精制茶制造业	Beverage Production	65 429	0.0 993
纺织业	Textile Industry	187 981	0.1 294
纺织服装、服饰业	Textile Wearing and Finery Manufacturing	68 945	2.1 442
皮革、毛皮、羽毛及其制品和制鞋业	Leather,Fur,Feather and Related Goods Manufacturing	224	0.0 139
木材加工和木、竹、藤、棕、草制品业	Wood Processing and wood,Bamboo,Rattan,Coir,Grass Products	1 580	0.0 302
家具制造业	Furniture Manufacturing	87	0.0 069
造纸和纸制品业	Paper making and Paper Products	18 057	0.2 884
印刷和记录媒介复制业	Printing Industry and Recording Media	512	0.0 376
文教、工美、体育和娱乐用品制造业	Culture and Education, Handicraft,Athletics and Amusement Things Manufacturing	271	0.0 150
石油加工、炼焦和核燃料加工业	Petroleum,Processing Coking and Nucler Fuel	3 371 374	4.7 972
化学原料和化学制品制造业	Raw Chemical Materials and Chemical Products	7 483 898	3.0 571
医药制造业	Medical and Pharmaceutical Products	25 516	0.1 757
化学纤维制造业	Chemical Fiber	149 993	0.7 620
橡胶和塑料制品业	Rubber and Plastics Products Manufacturing	21 768	0.0 377
非金属矿物制品业	Nonmetal Mineral Products	1 397 727	0.8 157
黑色金属冶炼和压延加工业	Ferrous Metals Smelting and Rolling	858 046	1.9 053
有色金属冶炼和压延加工业	Non-Ferrous Metals Smelting and Rolling	9 176 262	2.1 541
金属制品业	Metal Products	4 918	0.0 264
通用设备制造业	Ordinary Machinery	367	0.0 179
专用设备制造业	Special Purpose Equipment	4 642	0.0 476
汽车制造业	Automobile Manufacturing	19	0.0 021
电气机械和器材制造业	Electric Machine and Equipment Manufacturing	3 393	0.0 146
计算机、通信和其他电子设备制造业	Computer,Communicationn and other Electronic Equipment Manufacturing	4 361	0.0 814
仪器仪表制造业	Measuring Instruments Manufacturing	488	0.9 749
废弃资源综合利用业	Worn-out Resource Synthetical Using	17 160	1.4 300
电力、热力、燃气及水的生产和供应业	**Electricity,Heat Power,Gas and Water Production and Supply**	**8 813 157**	**3.7 187**
电力、热力生产和供应业	Electricity and Heat Production and Supply	8 800 030	4.0 569
燃气生产和供应业	Gas Production and Supply	3 850	0.0 227
水的生产和供应业	Water Production and Supply	9 277	0.2 998
按轻重工业分	**Grouped by Light & Heavy Industry**		
轻工业	Light Industry	2 283 651	0.3 159
重工业	Heavy Industry	31 303 368	2.3 295

14—4 规模以上工业企业按行业分主要能源消费

(2017 年)

指 标	Item	原 煤 (吨) Coal (ton)	洗精煤(用于炼焦)(吨) Dressing Coal (Used for Coking) (ton)	其他洗煤 (吨) Other Dressing Coal (ton)	焦 炭 (吨) Coke (ton)
总 计	**Total**	**55 292 235**	**797 855**	**716 455**	**1 909 856**
按工业行业大类分列	**Grouped by Sector**				
采矿业	**Mining**	**980 620**			
煤炭开采和洗选业	Coal Mining and Dressing	977 900			
黑色金属矿采选业	Ferrous Metals Mining and Dressing				
有色金属矿采选业	Nonferrous Metals Mining and Dressing	737			
非金属矿采选业	Nonmetal Minerals Mining and Dressing	1 983			
制造业	**Manufacturing**	**31 461 802**	**797 855**	**716 455**	**1 909 856**
农副食品加工业	Food Processing	448 847		2 810	11 117
食品制造业	Food Manufacturing	1 218 271			
酒、饮料和精制茶制造业	Beverage Production	58 771		6 357	
纺织业	Textile Industry	18 518			
纺织服装、服饰业	Textile Wearing and Finery Manufacturing	3 779			
皮革、毛皮、羽毛及其制品和制鞋业	Leather, Fur, Feather and Related Goods Manufacturing				
木材加工和木、竹、藤、棕、草制品业	Wood Processing and wood, Bamboo, Rattan, Coir, Grass Products	1 125			
家具制造业	Furniture Manufacturing	16			
造纸和纸制品业	Paper making and Paper Products	12 205			
印刷和记录媒介复制业	Printing Industry and Recording Media				
文教、工美、体育和娱乐用品制造业	Culture and Education, Handicraft, Athletics and Amusement Things Manufacturing	275			
石油加工、炼焦和核燃料加工业	Petroleum, Processing Coking and Nucler Fuel	13 403 344	797 855		
化学原料和化学制品制造业	Raw Chemical Materials and Chemical Products	8 308 577		13 933	1 166 218
医药制造业	Medical and Pharmaceutical Products	8 539			
化学纤维制造业	Chemical Fiber	186 655			
橡胶和塑料制品业	Rubber and Plastics Products Manufacturing	2 080			
非金属矿物制品业	Nonmetal Mineral Products	1 366 209			
黑色金属冶炼和压延加工业	Ferrous Metals Smelting and Rolling	90 587			732 041
有色金属冶炼和压延加工业	Non-Ferrous Metals Smelting and Rolling	6 315 880		693 355	
金属制品业	Metal Products	393			
通用设备制造业	Ordinary Machinery	107			
专用设备制造业	Special Purpose Equipment	148			
汽车制造业	Automobile Manufacturing				
电气机械和器材制造业	Electric Machine and Equipment Manufacturing	10			480
计算机、通信和其他电子设备制造业	Computer, Communicationn and other Electronic Equipment Manufacturing				
仪器仪表制造业	Measuring Instruments Manufacturing				
废弃资源综合利用业	Worn-out Resource Synthetical Using	17 466			
电力、热力、燃气及水的生产和供应业	**Electricity, Heat Power, Gas and Water Production and Supply**	**22 849 813**			
电力、热力生产和供应业	Electricity and Heat Production and Supply	22 849 364			
燃气生产和供应业	Gas Production and Supply				
水的生产和供应业	Water Production and Supply	449			
按轻重工业分	**Grouped by Light & Heavy Industry**				
轻工业	Light Industry	1 968 017		9 167	11 117
重工业	Heavy Industry	53 324 218	797 855	707 288	1 898 739

Main Energy Consumption of Industrial Enterprises above Designated Size by Industrial Branch

焦炉煤气（万立方米）Coke Oven Coal Gas (10000 cu.m)	天然气（万立方米）Natural Gas (10000 cu.m)	汽油（吨）Gasoline (ton)	柴油（吨）Diesel Oil (ton)	液化石油气（吨）Liquefied Petroleum Gas (ton)	石油焦（吨）Petroleum Coke (ton)	热力（百万千焦）Heat (million kj)	电力（万千瓦时）Electricity (10 000 kwh)	煤矸石（用于燃料）（吨）Coal Gangue (Used for Fuel) (ton)	余热余压（百万千焦）Residual Heat and Pressure (million kj)
17 183	**21 668**	**4 120**	**58 092**	**71**	**244 887**	**48 018 148**	**7 425 110**	**65 900**	**326 044**
		205	**21 888**				**23 480**		
		186	532				13 461		
			18 949				6 515		
		16	34				1 555		
		2	2 372				1 949		
17 183	**16 275**	**3 329**	**34 454**	**71**	**244 887**	**47 985 568**	**6 924 014**	**32 817**	**326 044**
	1 159	772	1 589	1		1 564 208	60 549	1 405	
	267	350	1 217			21 875 550	118 759		
	212	73	102			739 403	10 606		
	91	178	158			567 397	130 152		
		3				1 311 432	18 390		
							192		
			84				543		
	3	26					43		
	327	5					4 078		
	13	7	10			2 523	203		
							61		
17 183	519	5	1 757				62 522	31 413	
	11 105	225	4 497	70	1 137	21 457 134	1 512 499		
	245	204	54			236 586	6 297		
		37	49			42 940	10 041		
	12	227	191			16 085	15 813		
	2 190	852	23 149		109 371	121 555	194 417		326 044
	32	32	28			13 230	65 895		
	35	66	1 433		134 379		4 696 912		
	53	168	111				3 082		
	10	45	1			104	130		
	2	31	23			15 988	3 248		
							16		
		5	2			430	2 372		
						7 122	3 372		
		16				13 880	12		
							3 811		
	5 393	**586**	**1 750**			**32 581**	**477 616**	**33 083**	
	5 390	552	1 725			27 946	467 193	33 083	
		13				4 635	3 082		
	3	22	26				7 342		
	3 058	1 683	3 289	1		26 340 040	367 722	1 405	
17 183	18 610	2 437	54 803	70	244 887	21 678 109	7 057 387	64 496	326 044

14—5 各师规模以上工业企业主要能源消费

Main Energy Consumption of Industrial Entrprises above Designated Size by Division

(2017 年)

指 标	Item	合 计 Total	一 师 Division 1	二 师 Division 2	三 师 Division 3	四 师 Division 4	五 师 Division 5	六 师 Division 6	七 师 Division 7
能源合计(吨标准煤)	**Total Energy Production (tons of SCE)**	**53 414 976**	**1 531 285**	**435 659**	**405 278**	**2 683 742**	**552 943**	**13 406 084**	**1 681 424**
原 煤 (吨)	Coal (ton)	55 292 235	1 605 113	535 410	420 539	2 969 994	804 535	11 900 086	1 954 778
洗精煤(用于炼焦)(吨)	Dressing Coal (Used for Coking) (ton)	797 855						797 855	
其他洗煤 (吨)	Other Dressing Coal (ton)	716 455				106 514			13 933
焦炭 (吨)	Coke (ton)	1 909 856		1 942		84 239		312 052	1 281
焦炉煤气(万立方米)	Coke Oven Coal Gas (10 000 cu.m)	17 183						17 183	
天然气(万立方米)	Natural Gas (10 000 cu.m)	21 668	10 656	694	15			574	298
汽油 (吨)	Gasoline (ton)	4 120	534	645	125	224	378	199	57
柴油 (吨)	Diesel Oil (ton)	58 092	2 161	3 423	705	2 716	439	3 946	514
液化石油气(吨)	Liquefied Petroleum Gas (ton)	71	1						70
石油焦 (吨)	Petroleum Coke (ton)	244 887				65 710			56 795
热力(百万千焦)	Heat (million KJ)	48 018 148	82 005	564 403		1 353 099	112 304	20 780 310	
电力(万千瓦时)	Electricity (10 000 kwh)	7 425 110	131 861	46 840	55 875	342 717	20 091	2 732 150	153 484
煤矸石(用于燃料)(吨)	Coal Gangue(Used for Fuel) (ton)	65 900				33 083		31 413	
余热余压(百万千焦)	Remaining Hot and Pressure (million KJ)	326 044	286 758	32 945		6 340			

指 标	Item	八 师 Division 8	九 师 Division 9	十 师 Division 10	十一师 Division 11	十二师 Division 12	十三师 Division 13	十四师 Division 14	兵团直属 Directly under XPCC
能源合计(吨标准煤)	**Total Energy Production (tons of SCE)**	**22 513 223**	**175 426**	**266 228**	**22 059**	**232 920**	**9 491 833**	**1 624**	**15 247**
原 煤 (吨)	Coal (ton)	22 223 389	158 756	398 672	4 032	200 667	12 111 703	210	4 351
洗精煤(用于炼焦)(吨)	Dressing Coal (Used for Coking) (ton)								
其他洗煤 (吨)	Other Dressing Coal (ton)	596 008							
焦炭 (吨)	Coke (ton)	1 086 609	3 264				420 470		
焦炉煤气(万立方米)	Coke Oven Coal Gas (10 000 cu.m)								
天然气(万立方米)	Natural Gas (10 000 cu.m)	3 410			19	5 492		13	497
汽油 (吨)	Gasoline (ton)	566	95	623	213	276	119	24	43
柴油 (吨)	Diesel Oil (ton)	11 661	94	1 608	7 565	1 205	21 619	315	122
液化石油气(吨)	Liquefied Petroleum Gas (ton)								
石油焦 (吨)	Petroleum Coke (ton)	122 382							
热力(百万千焦)	Heat (million KJ)	23 649 242	1 453 579	300		14 674			8 232
电力(万千瓦时)	Electricity (10 000 kwh)	3 837 910	5 498	12 437	4 872	10 920	66 099	663	3 694
煤矸石(用于燃料)(吨)	Coal Gangue(Used for Fuel) (ton)					1 405			
余热余压(百万千焦)	Remaining Hot and Pressure (million KJ)								

14—6 规模以上工业企业主要能源按工业行业分年末库存量
Year-end Main Energy Inventory of Industrial Enterprises above Designated Size by Industrial Branch

(2017 年)

计量单位：吨 (ton)

指标	Item	原煤 Coal	洗精煤(用于炼焦) Dressing Coal (Used for Coking)	焦炭 Coke	柴油 Diesel Oil	石油焦 Petroleum Coke
总计	**Total**	**3 824 112**	**23 615**	**226 952**	**1 702**	**20 912**
按工业行业大类分列	**Grouped by Sector**					
采矿业	**Mining**	**3 793**			**21**	
煤炭开采和洗选业	Coal Mining and Dressing	3 513				
黑色金属矿采选业	Ferrous Metals Mining and Dressing					
有色金属矿采选业	Nonferrous Metals Mining and Dressing	145			9	
非金属矿采选业	Nonmetal Minerals Mining and Dressing	135			11	
制造业	**Manufacturing**	**2 132 083**	**23 615**	**226 952**	**1 112**	**20 912**
农副食品加工业	Food Processing	106 948		7 492	23	
食品制造业	Food Manufacturing	37 342			1	
酒、饮料和精制茶制造业	Wine，Beverage and Tea Production	5 502			8	
纺织业	Textile Industry	4 866				
纺织服装、服饰业	Textile Clothing, Shoes and Hats Manufacturing					
皮革、毛皮、羽毛及其制品和制鞋业	Leather，Fur，Feather and Related Goods Manufacturing					
木材加工和木、竹、藤、棕、草制品业	Wood Processing and Wood、Bamboo、Cane、Grass Products					
家具制造业	Furniture Manufacturing	10				
造纸和纸制品业	Papermaking and Paper Products	365				
印刷和记录媒介复制业	Printing Industry and Recording Media					
文教、工美、体育和娱乐用品制造业	Culture and Education, Handicraft, Athletics and Amusement Things Manufacturing					
石油加工、炼焦和核燃料加工业	Petroleum Processing，Coking and Nuclear Fuel Processing	242 349	23 615			
化学原料和化学制品制造业	Raw Chemical Materials and Chemical Products	403 150		133 664	273	434
医药制造业	Medical and Pharmaceutical Products	14 806				
化学纤维制造业	Chemical Fiber	50 956				
橡胶和塑料制品业	Rubber and Plastics Products Manufacturing	90			5	
非金属矿物制品业	Nonmetal Mineral Products	129 297			685	11 606
黑色金属冶炼和压延加工业	Ferrous Metals Smelting and Rolling	3 398		85 796		
有色金属冶炼和压延加工业	Non-Ferrous Metals Smelting and Rolling	1 132 651			105	8 872
金属制品业	Metal Products	10				
通用设备制造业	General Equipment Manufacturing	14				
专用设备制造业	Special Purpose Equipment				13	
汽车制造业	Automobile Manufacturing					
电气机械和器材制造业	Electric Machine and Equipment Manufacturing	29				
计算机、通信和其他电子设备制造业	Computer，Communicationn and other Electronic Equipment Manufacturing					
仪器仪表制造业	Instrument Manufacturing					
废弃资源综合利用业	Abandon Resources Comprehensive Use	300				
电力、热力、燃气及水的生产和供应业	**Electricity，Heat Power，Gas and Water Production and Supply**	**1 688 236**			**569**	
电力、热力生产和供应业	Electricity and Heat Production and Supply	1 688 236			569	
燃气生产和供应业	Gas Production and Supply					
水的生产和供应业	Water Production and Supply					
按轻重工业分	**Grouped by Light & Heavy Industry**					
轻工业	Light Industry	220 795		7 492	32	
重工业	Heavy Industry	3 603 317	23 615	219 460	1 670	20 912

14—7 各师规模以上工业企业总产值能耗

Output Value Energy Consumption of Industrial Enterprises above Designated Size by Division

单 位	Unit	2016		2017	
		综合能源消费量（吨标准煤） Comsuption of Comprehensive Energy(ton standard coal)	产值能耗（吨标准煤/万元） Energy Comsuption of Output Value (ton standard coal /10 000 yuan)	综合能源消费量（吨标准煤） Comsuption of Comprehensive Energy(ton standard coal)	产值能耗（吨标准煤/万元） Energy Comsuption of Output Value (ton standard coal /10 000 yuan)
总 计	**Total**	**31 504 922**	**1.6 683**	**33 587 019**	**1.6 252**
一 师	Division 1	1 022 570	0.4 697	1 111 483	0.4 796
二 师	Division 2	261 424	0.1 890	320 853	0.2 248
三 师	Division 3	339 668	0.3 471	294 222	0.2 554
四 师	Division 4	1 592 886	1.1 461	1 872 122	1.2 100
五 师	Division 5	103 811	0.3 748	334 457	1.2 861
六 师	Division 6	8 250 047	2.2 631	9 428 036	2.3 112
七 师	Division 7	1 656 511	2.1 621	1 464 661	1.6 225
八 师	Division 8	14 985 337	2.7 318	15 881 682	2.7 376
九 师	Division 9	82 509	0.7 994	100 391	0.8 950
十 师	Division 10	58 006	0.2 089	136 418	0.4 158
十一师	Division 11	29 903	0.1 354	21 208	0.0 912
十二师	Division 12	143 674	0.4 765	105 440	0.3 442
十三师	Division 13	2 959 686	2.0 448	2 499 757	1.4 185
十四师	Division 14	1 780	0.0 442	1 513	0.0 363
兵团直属	Directly under XPCC	17 110	0.0 437	14 776	0.0 373

14—8 各师规模以上工业企业主要能源年末库存量

Year-end Main Energy Inventory of Industrial Enterprises above Designated Size by Division

计量单位:吨　　　　(2017 年)　　　　(ton)

单 位	Unit	原 煤 Coal	洗精煤（用于炼焦） Dressing Coal (Used for Coking)	焦 炭 Coke	柴 油 Diesel Oil	石油焦 Petroleum Coke
总 计	**Total**	**3 824 112**	**23 615**	**226 952**	**1 702**	**20 912**
一 师	Division 1	262 395			132	
二 师	Division 2	47 835		58	17	
三 师	Division 3	92 283			66	
四 师	Division 4	250 225		20 311	103	1 042
五 师	Division 5	62 998			135	
六 师	Division 6	698 380	23 615	26 846	3	
七 师	Division 7	133 097		1 377	58	1 001
八 师	Division 8	2 100 608		117 964	618	18 869
九 师	Division 9	28 794		1 446		
十 师	Division 10	66 874			55	
十一师	Division 11	154			24	
十二师	Division 12	56 142				
十三师	Division 13	23 839		58 950	491	
十四师	Division 14	92				
兵团直属	Directly under XPCC	396			1	

14—9 规模以上工业企业按行业分水消费

Water Consumption of Industrial Enterprises above Designated Size by Industrial Branch

计量单位:万立方米 (2017 年) (10 000 cu.m)

指 标	Item	工业取水总量合计 Water Used by Industry	# 地表水 Surface Water	# 地下水 Ground Water	# 自来水 Tap Water	重复用水 Recycling Water
总 计	**Total**	**28 483.01**	**12 738.60**	**11 656.29**	**3 847.17**	**127 526.69**
按工业行业大类分列	**Grouped by Sector**					
采矿业	**Mining**	248.04	78.06	125.13	18.81	76.70
煤炭开采和洗选业	Coal Mining and Dressing	134.26	72.00	18.10	18.12	35.07
黑色金属矿采选业	Ferrous Metals Mining and Dressing	59.86	6.05	53.13	0.69	17.33
有色金属矿采选业	Nonferrous Metals Mining and Dressing	51.34		51.34		24.30
非金属矿采选业	Nonmetal Minerals Mining and Dressing	2.57	0.01	2.56		
制造业	**Manufacturing**	**11 766.79**	**3 610.45**	**4 785.06**	**3 156.73**	**57 015.25**
农副食品加工业	Food Processing	845.58	209.13	352.58	262.95	308.03
食品制造业	Food Manufacturing	2 778.86	1 218.19	985.94	553.72	2 153.68
酒、饮料和精制茶制造业	Beverage Production	459.59	6.00	107.10	279.45	68.10
纺织业	Textile Industry	746.95	0.16	103.57	632.10	62.03
纺织服装、服饰业	Textile Wearing and Finery Manufacturing	140.76		140.70	0.06	46.27
皮革、毛皮、羽毛及其制品和制鞋业	Leather,Fur,Feather and Related Goods Manufacturing	0.24			0.24	
木材加工和木、竹、藤、棕、草制品业	Wood Processing and Wood,Bamboo,Cane,Grass Products	0.18		0.06	0.12	0.02
家具制造业	Furniture Manufacturing	0.37			0.37	
造纸和纸制品业	Paper making and Paper Products	53.19	0.02	1.22	51.95	
印刷和记录媒介复制业	Printing Industry and Recording Media	2.38			2.38	
文教、工美、体育和娱乐用品制造业	Culture and Education, Handicraft,Athletics and Amusement Things Manufacturing	0.06		0.05	0.01	
石油加工、炼焦和核燃料加工业	Petroleum,Processing Coking and Nucler Fuel	711.68	309.72	228.00	103.96	456.20
化学原料和化学制品制造业	Raw Chemical Materials and Chemical Products	3 617.49	1 416.89	1 712.33	488.26	49 141.44
医药制造业	Medical and Pharmaceutical Products	144.80		19.88	124.92	79.87
化学纤维制造业	Chemical Fiber	740.39		739.46	0.87	443.97
橡胶和塑料制品业	Rubber and Plastics Products Manufacturing	135.95	0.41	74.83	60.62	45.48
非金属矿物制品业	Nonmetal Mineral Products	615.28	143.77	242.95	204.44	234.57
黑色金属冶炼和压延加工业	Ferrous Metals Smelting and Rolling	278.55	93.23		185.32	2 413.70
有色金属冶炼和压延加工业	Non-Ferrous Metals Smelting and Rolling	460.75	212.19	66.83	181.62	1 556.76
金属制品业	Metal Products	11.05		4.83	6.16	0.58
通用设备制造业	Ordinary Machinery	2.05	0.75		1.30	
专用设备制造业	Special Purpose Equipment	6.86		0.11	6.75	
汽车制造业	Automobile Manufacturing	4.20		4.20		
电气机械和器材制造业	Electric Machine and Equipment Manufacturing	1.86		0.42	1.44	
计算机、通信和其他电子设备制造业	Computer,Communicationn and other Electronic Equipment Manufacturing	7.71			7.71	4.55
电力、热力、燃气及水的生产和供应业	**Electricity,Heat Power,Gas and Water Production and Supply**	**16 468.17**	**9 050.09**	**6 746.10**	**671.63**	**70 434.73**
电力、热力生产和供应业	Electricity and Heat Production and Supply	5 016.18	3 163.76	1 189.85	662.23	70 434.73
燃气生产和供应业	Gas Production and Supply	5.95		0.79	5.16	
水的生产和供应业	Water Production and Supply	11 446.04	5 886.33	5 555.46	4.25	
按轻重工业分	**Grouped by Light & Heavy Industry**					
轻工业	Light Industry	17 368.89	7 319.83	8 008.40	1 920.50	3 167.11
重工业	Heavy Industry	11 114.12	5 418.78	3 647.90	1 926.66	124 359.57

14—10 各师规模以上工业企业水消费

Water Consumption of Industrial Enterprises above Designated Size by Division

计量单位:万立方米　　(2017 年)　　(10 000 cu.m)

单　位	Unit	工业取水总量合计 Water used by Industry	# 地表水 Surface Water	# 地下水 Ground Water	# 自来水 Tap water	重复用水 Recycling water
总　计	**Total**	**28 483.01**	**12 738.60**	**11 656.29**	**3 847.17**	**127 526.69**
一　师	Division 1	4 768.42	2 947.67	855.99	964.42	620.62
二　师	Division 2	595.89	191.61	195.64	182.95	131.01
三　师	Division 3	481.34	1.30	309.22	170.82	64.39
四　师	Division 4	1 555.16	823.05	565.11	89.22	1 344.76
五　师	Division 5	145.62	70.67	67.51	7.44	2 315.52
六　师	Division 6	4 822.47	3 710.03	767.22	272.78	43 240.01
七　师	Division 7	1 301.59	678.19	309.22	314.08	170.09
八　师	Division 8	12 722.33	3 059.28	8 106.16	1 545.45	77 114.49
九　师	Division 9	230.67		225.59	5.07	147.04
十　师	Division 10	107.28	57.94	14.77	34.48	39.71
十一师	Division 11	60.14		2.34	49.60	0.13
十二师	Division 12	1 277.70	1 096.06	100.42	37.03	10.04
十三师	Division 13	359.22	102.81	129.19	126.55	2 328.87
十四师	Division 14	8.47			8.47	
兵团直属	Directly under XPCC	46.69		7.90	38.79	

14—11 各师交通运输法人企业主要能源消费

Main Energy Consumption of Transportation Corporative Enterprises by Division

(2017 年)

单　位	Unit	原　煤(吨) Coal (ton)	汽　油(吨) Gasoline (liter)	煤　油(吨) Kerosene (ton)	柴　油(吨) Diesel Oil (liter)	液化石油气(吨) Liquefied Petroleum Gase(ton)	天然气(立方米) Natrual Gas (cu.m)
总　计	**Total**	**550**	**9 478**	**383**	**72 231**	**320**	**4 122**
一　师	Division 1	4	2 649		7 816	278	759
二　师	Division 2		655		147		6
三　师	Division 3	40	2 002		5 436	18	30
四　师	Division 4	405	143		1 821	24	
五　师	Division 5	40	35		184		30
六　师	Division 6	18	88		31 696		861
七　师	Division 7				230		112
八　师	Division 8	1	159		10 961		363
九　师	Division 9		14		1 920		34
十　师	Division 10		1		3 193		1 899
十一师	Division 11		2 157		2 928		
十二师	Division 12	42	2		35		21
十三师	Division 13		3		1 981		4
十四师	Division 14		6		21		3
兵团直属	Directly under XPCC		1 564	383	3 862		

2018

BING TUAN

第十五篇

对外贸易、经济技术协作、旅游业和规模以上服务业

Chapter 15 Foreign Trade、Technological Cooperation、Tourism and Sevices aboveDesignated Size

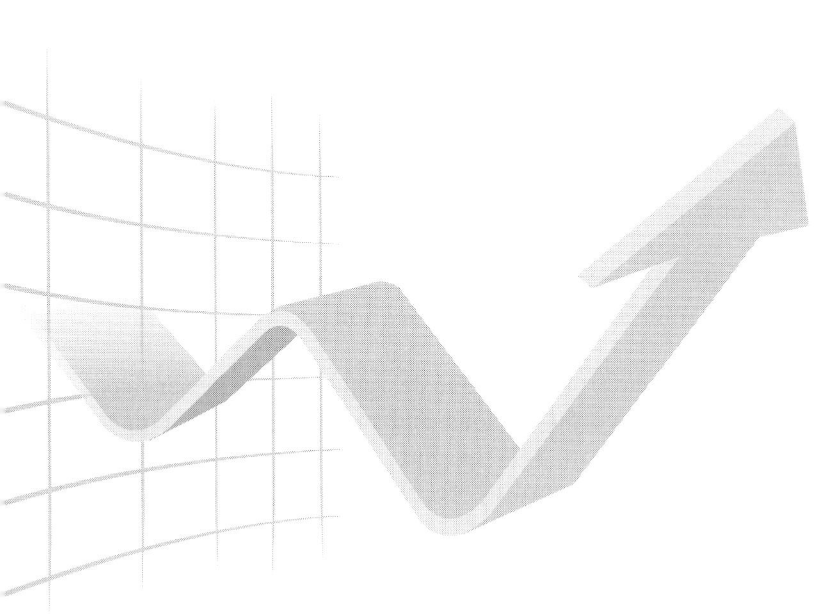

简要说明

本篇资料综合反映兵团主要年份对外贸易、经济技术协作、利用外资及旅游业概况。

一、对外贸易主要内容包括主要年份按国别（地区）分列的兵团、各师进出口总额及主要进出口商品量、金额和出口商品供货情况。兵团利用外资、外商投资及对外经济技术合作总体状况，统计范围为兵团范围内所有利用外资单位和部门，以及经批准在兵团范围内设立的中外合资经营企业、合作经营企业、外资企业、外商投资股份制企业、合作开发项目等法人企业(包括港澳台地区投资企业）外资利用情况；对外承包工程、对外劳务合作及对外经济合作情况。资料由兵团商务局整理提供。

二、经济技术协作主要内容包括主要年份兵团与区外、区内签定的经济技术协作项目、人才协作及效益完成情况。资料由兵团经济协作办公室整理提供。

三、旅游业部分主要内容兵团旅游业基本情况 、兵团星级旅游饭店情况以及兵团A级旅游景区基本情况。统计范围包括国际旅游和国内旅游。资料由兵团旅游局和兵团统计局社会科技贸易统计处整理提供。

四、规模以上服务企业主要财务指标统计范围是指年末从业人员50人及以上，或年营业收入1000万元及以上服务业法人企业。由兵团统计局国民经济核算设计管理处根据《规模以上服务业企业统报表制业度》整理提供。

Brief Introduction

Data in this chapter show the general situations of foreign trade, economic and technological cooperation，utilization of foreign capital and tourism.

1. The part of foreign trade in XPCC include total value of exports and imports by country(region) by division, and imports and exports of major commodities, value, and supply of exporting commodities; the conditions of economic and technological cooperation, utilization of foreign capital; The statistical scope of the general situations of foreign capital utilization, foreign investment and economic cooperation refers to units and department of foreign capital utilization, Sino-foreign joint ventures, cooperative enterprises, ventures exclusively with foreign own investment, shareholding enterprises with foreign investment, projects of cooperative development, and utilization of foreign capital of enterprises with corporate (including enterprises invested from Hong Kong, Macao and Taiwan), conditions of contracted projects and labor cooperation in foreign countries or regions and foreign economic cooperation. The data come from the Bureau of Commercial Affairs of XPCC.

2. The part of economic and technological cooperation in XPCC include mainly projects of economic and technological cooperation of XPCC signed with outside Xinjiang and inside Xinjiang, cooperation of talented persons and efficiency completion. The data are compiled and provided by the Office of Economic and Technological Cooperation.

3. The part of tourism in XPCC include mainly the basic conditions of tourism in XPCC, tourism hotels with stars, A-grade scenic (spot) Area in XPCC. The statistical scope includes international tourism and domestic tourism. The data come from the Tourism Bureau of XPCC and the Society,Science and Trade Statistics Section of the Statistics Bureau of XPCC .

4.The Statistics of nain financial indicators enterprises above designated size in service cover corporative enterprises with employment above 50 persons and main business income above 10 million yuan. The data are provided by the Service Survey Section of Survey Office of National Bureau of Statistics of XPCC according to *the Statistical Reporting Form System on Service Enterprises above the Designated Size.*

15－1 进出口贸易总额

Total Imports and Exports

计量单位:万美元 (USD 10 000)

单位 Unit	年份 Year	进出口总额 Total Imports and Exports	出口总额 Total Exports	#一般贸易 General Trade	#边境贸易 Border Trade	进口总额 Total Imports	#一般贸易 General Trade	#边境贸易 Border Trade
	1985	240	27			213		
	1990	2 022	1 299			723		
	1991	3 853	3 025			828		
	1992	7 132	4 179			2 953		
	1993	13 572	7 553	2 788	4 765	6 019	15	6 004
	1994	14 141	8 138	4 218	3 920	6 003	1 294	4 709
	1995	18 225	8 040	4 934	3 106	10 185	2 028	8 157
	1996	20 079	5 359	3 682	1 677	14 720	1 656	13 064
	1997	24 561	7 046	5 227	1 819	17 515	2 848	14 667
	1998	28 546	10 246	7 372	2 874	18 300	5 602	12 698
	1999	40 909	24 251	12 471	11 780	16 658	3 581	13 077
	2000	75 280	44 990	18 908	26 082	30 290	7 417	22 873
	2001	65 380	30 014	8 865	21 149	35 366	6 233	29 133
	2002	124 900	55 300	36 100	19 200	69 600	10 600	59 000
	2003	161 838	86 557	31 531	55 026	75 281	32 861	42 420
	2004	197 235	83 523	22 456	61 067	113 712	54 660	59 052
	2005	310 586	189 249	35 046	154 203	121 337	74 874	46 463
	2006	350 529	295 697	51 654	237 221	54 832	24 714	28 139
	2007	556 042	519 256	130 484	388 700	36 786	16 775	14 747
	2008	881 951	842 376	121 608	720 493	39 575	14 735	18 316
	2009	466 030	426 005	50 365	343 783	40 025	25 385	7 233
	2010	558 874	498 008	58 311	386 253	60 866	44 194	10 036
	2011	763 697	649 556	182 756	426 151	114 141	55 294	56 081
	2012	964 981	834 324	353 558	436 279	130 657	53 954	62 170
	2013	1 159 111	1 036 969	528 604	477 535	122 142	33 618	64 423
	2014	1 198 773	1 095 455	522 599	557 466	103 318	75 459	14 655
	2015	1 024 806	962 075	445 625	493 496	62 731	45 967	9 271
	2016	707 619	658 531	142 552	484 911	49 088	35 272	10 820
	2017	759 018	663 270	94 381	547 924	95 748	78 757	12 166
一　师 Division 1		1 123	791	340	279	332	46	132
二　师 Division 2		8 088	8 020	7 957	63	68	68	
三　师 Division 3		75 532	69 408	3 224	63 805	6 125	4 162	1 962
四　师 Division 4		248 555	246 462	3 095	241 670	2 093	1 444	661
五　师 Division 5		59 089	52 575	1 137	39 111	6 513	1 858	5 532
六　师 Division 6		22 341	21 737	21 104	3 315	604	117	
七　师 Division 7		10 029	9 290	71	7 413	739		
八　师 Division 8		45 553	40 473	35 344	4 279	5 081	1 523	164
九　师 Division 9		18 668	17 928	1 002	16 926	740	88	652
十　师 Division 10		94 539	92 894	678	91 582	1 645	1 291	354
十一师 Division 11		28 593	27 097	3 076	23 537	1 497	1 497	
十二师 Division 12		11 351	11 336	1 146	10 190	14	14	
十三师 Division 13		5 855	4 740	47	4 693	1 115	1 115	
十四师 Division 14		623	7	7		616	391	225
兵团直属 Directly under XPCC		129 080	60 512	16 154	41 062	68 568	65 143	2 483

注:2001年以前为业务统计数据,2002年以后为海关统计数据。
Note:The data prior to 2001 is offered by the bureau of foreign economic and trade,data after 2002 is offered by Customs House。

15—2 主要进出口商品数量和金额

Main Imports and Exports in Volume and Value

计量单位:万美元 (USD 10 000)

指 标		Item		2017		2017年比2016年增减% Increase Rate in 2017 over 2016(%)	
				数 量 Volume	金 额 Value	数 量 Volume	金 额 Value
主要出口商品		**Main Export Commodities**					
纺织纱线、织物及制品	(吨)	Cotton Yarm	(ton)	309	47 822	49.3	33.9
服 装		Garments			183 916		10.6
番茄酱	(吨)	Tomato Jam	(ton)	250	18 302	31.6	33.1
机电产品		Machine and Electricity Product			133 489		−15.8
纸及纸板(未切成型的)	(吨)	Paper and Paperboard in Rolls	(ton)	1	291	−17.9	−7.3
塑料制品	(吨)	Plastic Products	(ton)	14	7 829	9.8	−10.2
鲜、干水果及坚果	(吨)	Fresh,Dry Fruit and Nut	(ton)	58	6 933	75.7	138.6
蔬 菜	(吨)	Vegetable	(ton)	25	2 155	28.9	16.2
鞋 类	(千双)	Leather Shoes	(1 000 pairs)		111 879		−2.5
主要进口商品		**Main Import Commodities**					
棉花(原棉)	(吨)	Cotton (Raw Cotton)	(ton)	50	9 158	198.4	224.5
钢 材	(吨)	Rolled Steel	(ton)	196	828	−58.9	−40.7
原 木	(立方米)	Logs	(cu.m)	7	173	58.2	20.3
锯 材	(立方米)	Logs	(cu.m)	196	5 209	44.4	61.6
机电产品		Machine Electricity Product			20 075		58.9
成品油	(吨)	Finished Product Oil	(ton)	1	76	144.4	79.3
肥 料	(吨)	Fertilizers	(ton)	46	1 011	526.8	448.0
铁矿砂及其精矿	(吨)	Iron ore and concentrates	(ton)	648	2 746	−0.6	22.8
羊 毛	(吨)	Wool	(ton)	18	2 041	15.8	10.0
高新技术产品		High and New Technical Product		4 004	3 967	62.7	−23.5

15—3 出口商品分类金额

Value of Exports by Category of Commodities

计量单位:万美元 (USD 10 000)

指　标	Item	2005	2010	2015	2016	2017
总　计	**Total**	**189 249**	**498 008**	**962 075**	**658 531**	**663 270**
初级产品	Primary Goods	12 914	89 634	76 732	54 169	43 992
食品及活动物	Food and Live Animals Used Chiefly for Food	11 128	7 353	36 328	22 540	23 065
饮料及烟草	Beverges and Tobacco	19	16 922	120	91	269
非食用原料	Non-edible Raw Materials	744	12 942	36 166	26 995	19 909
矿物燃料润滑油及有关原料	Mineral Fuels Lubricants and Related Materials	1 023	52 417	4 119	4 543	749
动、植物油脂及蜡	Animal and Vegetable Oils Fats and Wax					
工业制成品	Manufactured Goods	176 335	408 374	885 343	604 362	619 278
化学品及有关产品	Chemicals and Related Products	6 456	3 592	22 907	22 199	19 515
轻纺产品、橡胶制品、矿冶产品及其制品	Light and Textile Industrial Products Rubber Products Minerals Metal-lurgical Products	40 329	262 422	493 396	345 964	401 449
机械及运输设备	Machinery and Transport Equipment	6 596	97 794	39 013	150 439	43 641
杂项制品	Miscellaneous Products	122 954	44 566	330 027	85 760	154 673

15—4 进口商品分类金额

Value of Imports by Category of Commodities

计量单位:万美元 (USD 10 000)

指　标	Item	2005	2010	2015	2016	2017
总　计	**Total**	**121 337**	**60 866**	**62 731**	**49 088**	**95 748**
初级产品	Primary Goods	28 306	25 825	35 495	25 100	33 914
食品及活动物	Food and Live Animals Used Chiefly for Food	505	2 735	2 991	13 570	28 737
饮料及烟草	Beverges and Tobacco			102	602	949
非食用原料	Non-edible Raw Materials	27 701	22 175	14 195	2 822	1 249
矿物燃料润滑油及有关原料	Mineral Fuels Lubricants and Related Materials	100	915	18 207	8 106	2 978
动、植物油脂及蜡	Animal and Vegetable Oils Fats and Wax					
工业制成品	Manufactured Goods	93 031	35 041	27 236	23 988	61 834
化学品及有关产品	Chemicals and Related Products	3 237	6 483	900	754	2 481
轻纺产品、橡胶制品、矿冶产品及其制品	Light and Textile Industrial Products Rubber Products Minerals Metal-lurgical Products	69 050	14 238	12 520	8 425	10 341
机械及运输设备	Machinery and Transport Equipment	5 139	7 050	7 509	12 510	7 850
杂项制品	Miscellaneous Products	15 605	7 270	6 307	2 299	41 162

15—5 兵团同各国(地区)进出口总额

XPCC's Total Value of Imports and Exports by Country (Region) of Origin / Destination

计量单位:万美元 (USD 10 000)

国别(地区)	Country(Territory)	2016 进出口 Total Imports and Exports	2016 出口 Total Exports	2016 进口 Total Imports	2017 进出口 Total Imports and Exports	2017 出口 Total Exports	2017 进口 Total Imports
总　额	**Total**	**707 619**	**658 531**	**49 088**	**759 018**	**663 270**	**95 748**
亚　洲	**Asia**	**51 756**	**41 679**	**10 077**	**66 621**	**41 880**	**24 741**
阿富汗	Afghanistan	5	1	4	47	47	
巴　林	Bahrain	36	36		61	61	
孟加拉国	Banglagdesh	404	404		743	743	
缅　甸	Myanmar	669	669		82	82	
柬埔寨	Cambodia	20	20		55	55	
塞浦路斯	Cyprus	4	4				
中国香港	Hong Kong,China	378	369	9	745	740	5
印　度	India	14 654	13 970	684	16 217	8 820	7 397
印度尼西亚	Indonesia	3 809	1 507	2 302	7 955	1 633	6 322
伊　朗	Iran	1 358	1 039	319	1 674	442	1 233
伊拉克	Iraq	171	171		20	20	
以色列	Israel	229	161	68	441	352	89
日　本	Japan	1 819	520	1 299	4 719	859	3 860
约　旦	Jordan	129	129		195	195	
科威特	Kuwait	45	45		67	67	
黎巴嫩	Lebanon	265	265		273	273	
马来西亚	Malaysia	1 631	1 504	127	528	494	34
蒙　古	Mongolia	2 405	99	2 306	2 473	25	2 448
阿　曼	Aman	229	229		453	453	
巴基斯坦	Pakistan	10 480	9 131	1 349	17 167	15 501	1 666
菲律宾	The Philippines	1 279	1 279		1 318	1 318	
卡塔尔	Qatar	113	113		2	2	
沙特阿拉伯	Saudi Arbia	1 465	859	606	1 283	1 283	
新加坡	Singapore	1 317	987	330	851	433	417
韩　国	Republic of Korea	1 629	1 488	141	1 510	1 278	232
斯里兰卡	Sri Lanka	255	255		74	74	
叙利亚	Syria	43	43		11	11	
泰　国	Thailand	979	976	3	1 037	1 036	1
土耳其	Turkey	611	580	32	1 073	417	656
阿联酋	United Arab Emirates	1 594	1 577	17	1 136	1 126	10
也门共和国	Arab Republic of Yemen	811	811		919	919	
越　南	Viet Nam	2 151	1 928	223	2 791	2 459	332
老　挝	Laos						
中国台湾	China Taiwan	490	470	19	175	173	2
文　莱	Brunei	40	40		9	9	
澳　门	Macao				10	10	
其他国家	Others	238	…	238	507	469	38
非　洲	**Africa**	**8 771**	**8 439**	**332**	**14 576**	**13 337**	**1 238**
阿尔及利亚	Algeria	512	512		720	720	
安哥拉	Angola	250	124	126	617	584	33
贝　宁	Beining	129	129		470	470	
喀麦隆	Cameroon	296	296		754	719	35
刚　果	Congo	98	98		443	443	
吉布提	Jiebuti	44	44		101	101	
埃　及	Egypt	621	563	58	1 015	153	862
埃塞俄比亚	Ethiopian	1	1		15	15	

15—5 续表 1 Continued

计量单位:万美元 (USD 10 000)

国别(地区)	Country(Territory)	2016 进出口 Total Imports and Exports	2016 出口 Total Exports	2016 进口 Total Imports	2017 进出口 Total Imports and Exports	2017 出口 Total Exports	2017 进口 Total Imports
冈比亚	Gambia	57	57		128	128	
加　纳	Ghana	1 213	1 213		2 538	2 538	
科特迪瓦共和国	Guinea	634	634		987	987	
肯尼亚	Kenya	148	148		254	254	
毛里求斯	Mauritius	78	78		95	95	
摩洛哥	Morocco	61	61				
尼日利亚	Nigeria	1 961	1 961		3 031	3 031	
塞内加尔	Senegal	729	729		559	559	
塞拉利昂	Sierra Leone	77	77		240	240	
南　非	South Arfica	822	695	127	1 021	773	248
苏　丹	Sudan	265	265		622	622	
坦桑尼亚	Tanzania	266	266		269	269	
莫桑比克	Mozambique	40	40		46	46	
多　哥	Togo	186	186		240	240	
乌干达	Uganda	10	10		87	87	
突尼斯	Tunisia	7	7				
马达加斯加	Madagascar	46	46		63	63	
赞比亚	Zambia	18	1	17	19	19	
其他国家	Others	199	196	3	240	180	60
欧　洲	**Europe**	**587 063**	**553 527**	**33 536**	**651 322**	**593 758**	**57 565**
比利时	Belgium	1 169	1 168	1	584	584	0
丹　麦	Denmark	163	114	50	44	12	32
英　国	United Kingdom	5 011	4 792	219	1 632	1 295	337
德　国	Federal Repulic of Germany	6 555	2 987	3 568	9 369	1 050	8 319
法　国	France	2 826	790	2 036	1 271	398	873
爱尔兰	Ireland	338	102	236	630	30	600
意大利	Italy	3 479	2 360	1 119	3 565	2 599	966
荷　兰	Netherlands	5 827	5 518	309	3 358	3 178	179
希　腊	Greece	216	216		76	74	2
葡萄牙	Portugal	191	176	15	79	79	
西班牙	Spain	2 807	2 743	64	1 824	1 817	8
奥地利	Austria	163		163	170		170
保加利亚	Bulgaria	50	50		83	83	
芬　兰	Finland	61	6	55	63		62
匈牙利	Hungary	36	10	25	374	325	49
马耳他	Malta	378	378		45	45	
挪　威	Norway	181	86	95	215	156	58
波　兰	Poland	782	782		783	705	78
罗马尼亚	Romania	213	175	39	201	55	145
瑞　典	Sweden	190	25	165	64	3	61
瑞　士	Switzerland	211	50	161	318		318
爱沙尼亚	Estonian				3		3
拉脱维亚	Latvia	5	5		3	3	
立陶宛	Lithuania	873	830	44	1 177	1 134	43
格鲁吉亚	Venezuela	90	51	39	836	382	454
亚美尼亚	Armenia				1		
阿塞拜疆	North America	3 002	2 947	55	120	60	60

15—5 续表 2　Continued

计量单位:万美元　　　　(USD 10 000)

国别(地区)	Country(Territory)	2016			2017		
		进出口 Total Imports and Exports	出口 Total Exports	进口 Total Imports	进出口 Total Imports and Exports	出口 Total Exports	进口 Total Imports
白俄罗斯	Canada	89	4	86	34	14	20
俄罗斯联邦	United States	74 582	71 128	3 454	60 536	55 253	5 283
哈萨克斯坦	Kazakhstan	329 208	315 841	13 366	393 575	366 682	26 893
吉尔吉斯斯坦	Kirgizistan	83 782	82 978	804	102 698	101 688	1 010
塔吉克斯坦	Tajikistan	47 733	47 708	25	44 210	44 170	41
土库曼斯坦	Turkmenistan	827	758	69	583	579	4
乌兹别克斯坦	Uzbekistan	14 905	7 757	7 148	22 020	10 777	11 244
乌克兰	Ukraine	288	288		255	255	
克罗地亚	Croatia	98	98		87	87	
斯洛文尼亚	Slovenia	87	87	1	16	16	
捷克共和国	Czecho	428	304	124	123	117	6
其他国家	Other	216	216		297	49	248
拉丁美洲	**Latin America**	**5 185**	**4 040**	**1 145**	**10 801**	**3 752**	**7 049**
阿根廷	Argentina	503	501	2	314	314	
巴　西	Brazil	907	863	44	1 765	1 765	
智　利	Chile	495	447	48	204	198	5
哥伦比亚	Colombia	321	321		155	155	
多米尼加	Dominican Republic				34	34	
哥斯达黎加	Costarica	13	13		57	28	29
古　巴	Cuba	14	14		27	27	
多米尼加共和国	Dominican Republic	6	6		34	34	
厄瓜多尔	Ecuador	253	46	207	433	63	370
格林纳达	Grenada	21	21		5	5	
危地马拉	Guatemala	28	28		22	22	
几内亚	Guinea	168	168		87	87	
海　地	Haiti	160	160		116	116	
洪都拉斯	Honduras	15	15		13	13	
牙买加	Jamaica	28	28		13	13	
墨西哥	Mexico	653	640	13	397	389	8
尼加拉瓜	Nicaragua	56	56		7	7	
巴拿马	Panama	108	108		98	98	
巴拉圭	Paraguay	33	33		60	60	
秘　鲁	Peru	1 153	321	832	6 888	250	6 637
波多黎各	Puerto Rico	20	20		29	29	
萨尔瓦多	El Salvador				11	11	
特立尼达和多巴哥	Trinidad				2	2	
乌拉圭	Uruguay	88	88		32	32	
委内瑞拉	Venezuela	142	142		451	451	
马拉维	Malawi						
北美洲	**North America**	**53 757**	**49 802**	**3 955**	**13 198**	**8 076**	**5 122**
加拿大	Canada	2 101	2 007	94	419	378	41
美　国	The United States	51 656	47 795	3 861	12 779	7 698	5 081
大洋洲	**Oceania**	**1 088**	**1 044**	**44**	**2 034**	**1 914**	**120**
澳大利亚	Australia	792	750	42	1 893	1 784	109
斐　济	Fiji	12	12		16	16	
新西兰	New Zealand	266	266		106	95	11
巴布亚新几内亚	Papua New Guinea	18	16	2	19	19	
其他国家	Other						125

15—6 出口商品供货情况

Supply of Export Commodities

(2017 年)

指　标		Item		数　量 Volume	金　额 Value
出口商品供货总额	**(万元)**	**Supply Value Of Export Commodities**	**(10 000 yuan)**		**663 270**
主要出口商品		**Major Export Commodities**			
农产品类总额	(万元)	Total Value of Agriculture Products	(10 000 yuan)	361	30 460
鲜、干水果及坚果	(吨)	Edible Dried Fruit	(ton)	58	6 933
甘　草	(吨)	Lipuorice	(ton)		67
蔬　菜	(吨)	Vegetable	(ton)	25	2 155
其　他		Others		278	21 305
工业产品类总额	(万元)	Total Value of Industry Products	(10 000 yuan)		
大　米	(吨)	Rice	(ton)		
罐　头	(吨)	Can	(ton)		17 986
# 番茄罐头		Tomato Can			17 768
棉纱、布、呢绒、丝制品	(万米)	Cotton Cloth, Woolen Goods, Silk	(10000 m)		15 022
各种服装	(万件)	Garments	(10000 units)	64 485	18 392
鞋　类	(万双)	Leather Shoes	(10000 pair)		111 879
焦　炭	(吨)	Coke	(ton)	42	739
工作车	(台)	Work Vehicle	(set)		38
其　他		Others			450 987

15—7 按贸易方式和经济类型分进出口额

Total Imports and Exports by Trade Mode and Economic Type

单位:万美元 (USD 10 000)

指　标	Item	2016			2017		
		进出口总额 Total Imports and Exports	出口总额 Total Exports	进口总额 Total Imports	进出口总额 Total Imports	出口总额 Total Exports	进口总额 Total Imports
总　计	**Total**	**707 619**	**658 531**	**49 088**	**759 018**	**663 270**	**95 748**
按贸易方式分	**Grouped by Trade Mode**						
一般贸易	General Trade	177 824	142 552	35 272	173 138	94 381	78 757
加工贸易	Processing Trade	360	96	264	215	31	184
边境贸易	Border Trade	495 731	484 911	10 820	560 089	547 924	12 166
其　他	Others	33 704	30 972	2 732	25 576	20 935	4 641
按经济类型分	**Grouped by Economic**						
国有企业	State-owned Enterprises	120 459	96 806	23 653	159 060	94 470	64 589
民营企业	Private-owned Enterprises	586 444	561 308	25 136	599 255	568 342	30 912
三资企业	Three Kinds of Ventures	716	417	299	688	457	231
集体企业	Collective-owned Enterprises				17	1	15

15—8 招商引资情况

Conditions of Attraction Investment

计量单位:万元 (2017年) (10 000 yuan)

指 标	Item	项目个数(个) Number of Item(unit)	总投资 Total Investment	投资方当年已到位资金 Funds Arrived Outside XPCC in this Year	投资方累计到位资金 Investment Side Accumulated Funds	投产后预计提供就业岗位 PostProduction Forecast to Provide Jobs
总 计	**Total**	**3 095**	**6 863.31**	**1 757.09**	**3 770.56**	**330 528**
按产业分	**Grouped by Industry**					
第一产业	Primary Industry	519	241.70	117.75	142.90	20 322
第二产业	Secondary Industry	1 514	4 304.57	971.33	2 326.83	163 838
第三产业	Tertiary Industry	1 062	2 317.04	668.01	1 300.84	146 368
按所有制分	**Grouped by Ownership**					
国 有	State-owned	203	1 104.10	209.35	574.35	20 898
非国有	Non-state-owned	2 892	5 759.21	1 547.75	3 196.22	309 630
按新增或续建分	**Grouped by Newly Increased or Continue to Construction**					
新 增	Newly Increased	2 284	2 760.65	1 098.09	1 151.35	109 317
续 建	Continue to Construction	811	4 102.66	659.00	2 619.21	221 211
按引资区域分	**Grouped by Attraction Investment District**					
新 疆	Xin jiang	2 324	3 379.79	950.84	1 923.80	160 074
#上市公司	Listed Companies of XPCC					
外 省	Other Province	760	3 442.61	798.80	1 832.27	168 124
外 资	Foreign Investment	11	40.91	7.45	14.49	2 330
按单位分	**Grouped by Unit**					
一 师	Division 1	418	493.01	186.84	273.57	44 296
二 师	Division 2	227	328.13	73.85	98.88	11 925
三 师	Division 3	156	195.20	80.91	133.59	16 746
四 师	Division 4	287	616.13	145.38	210.34	13 678
五 师	Division 5	169	75.42	52.87	58.12	2 896
六 师	Division 6	281	1 031.63	189.42	647.48	97 416
七 师	Division 7	218	485.09	171.25	293.87	24 509
八 师	Division 8	533	1 910.50	438.15	1 165.91	66 242
九 师	Division 9	152	40.17	22.39	26.25	2 389
十 师	Division 10	186	200.07	54.16	77.55	5 061
十一师	Division 11	113	52.71	18.89	27.94	3 843
十二师	Division 12	146	725.05	135.44	458.07	38 867
十三师	Division 13	171	687.04	180.54	285.12	
十四师	Division 14	38	23.15	7.01	13.88	2 660
兵团直属	Directly under XPCC					

15—9 人民币汇率(中间价)

Reference Exchange Rate of Renminbi(Middle Rate)

计量单位:人民币元 (RMB yuan)

年 份 Year	100 美元 100 US Dollars	100 日元 100 Japanese Yen	100 港元 100 Hong Kong Dollars	100 欧元 100 Euros
1985	293.66	1.25	37.57	
1990	478.32	3.32	61.39	
1995	835.10	8.92	107.96	
2000	827.84	7.69	106.18	
2001	827.70	6.81	106.08	
2002	827.70	6.62	106.07	800.58
2003	827.70	7.15	106.24	936.13
2004	827.68	7.66	106.23	1 029.00
2005	819.17	7.45	105.30	1 019.53
2006	797.18	6.86	102.62	1 001.90
2007	760.40	6.46	97.46	1 041.75
2008	694.51	6.74	89.19	1 022.27
2009	683.10	7.30	88.12	952.70
2010	676.95	7.73	87.13	897.25
2011	645.88	8.11	82.97	900.11
2012	631.25	7.90	81.38	810.67
2013	619.32	6.33	79.85	822.19
2014	614.28	5.82	79.22	816.51
2015	622.84	5.15	80.34	691.41
2016	664.23	6.12	85.58	734.26
2017	675.18	6.02	86.64	763.03

15—10 利用外资概况

Utilization of Foreign Capital

计量单位:个,万美元 (unit, USD 10 000)

年 份 Year	总 计 Total 项 目 Number of Projects	金 额 Value	对外借款 Foreign Loans 项 目 Number of Projects	金 额 Value	外商直接投资 Foreign Investments 项 目 Number of Projects	金 额 Value
签订利用外资(合同)金额 Total Amount of Foreign Capital to Be Utilized through the Signed Agreements and Contracts						
2000	17	352	1	270	16	82
2005	17	4 791	9	3 494	8	1 297
2006	16	14 428	7	9 145	9	5 283
2007	15	13 552	3	7 122	12	6 430
2008	14	28 979	1	11 000	13	17 979
2009	6	8 739			6	5 706
2010	10	6 348			10	3 610
2011	11	37 161			11	37 161
2012	6	12 704	1	7 898	5	4 806
2013	7	4 128			7	4 128
2014	5	11 951			5	11 951
2015	5	2 544			5	2 544
2016	7	6 698			7	6 698
2017	24	41 340			24	41 340
实际利用外资金额 Total Amount of Foreign Capital Actually Used						
2000		363		270		93
2005		3 136		2 503		634
2006	16	6 100	7	2 721	9	3 379
2007	15	7 007	3	4 160	12	2 847
2008	14	6 139	1	3 657	13	2 482
2009	6	4 170		2 946	6	1 224
2010	10	3 845			10	3 845
2011	11	7 905		850	11	7 054
2012	6	12 864	1	7 898	5	4 966
2013	7	11 635			7	11 635
2014	5	6 232			5	6 232
2015	7	26 785			5	4 789
2016	9	33 242			7	1 998
2017	14	41 054			5	1 038

15—11 按方式分利用外资情况

Foreign Capital by Utilization Mode

计量单位:个,万美元 (unit,USD 10 000)

指　标	Item	2016 项　目 Number of Projects	2016 合　同 外资金额 Contract Value	2016 实　际 使用金额 Used Value	2017 项　目 Number of Projects	2017 合　同 外资金额 Contract Foreign Investment Value	2017 实　际 使用金额 Used Value
总　计	**Total**	**7**	**6 698**	**1 998**	**24**	**41 340**	**1 038**
对外借款	**Foreign Loans**						
外国政府贷款	Government Loans						
国际金融组织贷款	Loans from International Financial Organizations						
外国商业银行贷款	Commercial Loans						
出口信贷	Export Loans						
对外发行债券	External Bonds						
外商直接投资	**Foreign Direct Investments**	**7**	**6 698**	**1 998**	**24**	**41 340**	**1 038**
外资企业	Foreign Investment Enterprises	2	3 030	176	22	41 235	
合资经营企业	Joint Ventures Enterprises	4	1 350	396	2	105	
合作经营企业	Cooperative Operation Enterprises	1	2 318				
股份制企业	Foreign Investment Share Enterprises						
其他:(历年外资到位)	Other:(Foreign Capital Arrived Former Year)			1 426			1 038

15—12 外国和港澳台地区在兵团直接投资情况

Overseas Direct Investment in XPCC by Foreign Countries and Regions from Hongkong,Macao and Taiwan

(2017 年)

计量单位:个、万美元 (unit,USD 10 000)

指　标	Item	签订协议情况 Signed Agreements 合同数 Number of Contracts	签订协议情况 Signed Agreements 客商投资额 Used Amount of Foreign Investment	客商实际投资额 Actually Used Amount offoreign Investment	年末实有企业个数 Number of Enterprises
总　计	**Total**	**24**	**41 340**	**41 054**	**77**
按投资方式分	**Grouped by Investment Mode**	**24**	**41 340**	**41 054**	**77**
外资企业	Foreign Investment Enterprises	22	41 235	8 470	45
合资经营企业	Joint Ventures Enterprises	2	105	32 584	28
合作经营企业	Cooperative Enterprises				2
股份制企业	Corporate Enterprises				2
其他:历年外资到位	Other:(Foreign Capital Arrived in Former Year)				
按国民经济行业分	**Grouped by Economic Sector**	**24**	**41 340**	**41 054**	**77**
制造业	Manufacturing	3	34 385	37 323	34
批发零售贸易、餐饮业	Wholesale and Retail Trade and Catering Services				10
农　业	Agriculture	1	135		12
服务业	Services	20	6 820	3 731	21
其他:历年外资到位	Other:(Foreign Capital Arrived in Former Year)				
按国别、地区分	**Grouped by country or Territory**	**24**	**41 340**	**41 054**	**77**
香港特别行政区	Hong Kong SAR	4	41 045	17 523	27
比利时	Belgium				3
美国	U.S.A				4
马来西亚	Malaysia				1
其他:历年外资到位	Other:(Foreign Capital Arrived in Former Year)	20	295	23 531	42

15－13 各师利用外商直接投资情况

Foreign Direct Investment Used by Division

计量单位:个、万美元 (unit, USD 10 000)

单位	Unit	2016			2017		
		签订合同数 Number of Contracts	合同金额 Contract Value	实际利用投资 Amount of Foreign Capital Acturally Used	签订合同数 Number of Contracts	合同金额 Contract Value	实际利用投资 Amount of Foreign Capital Acturally Used
总计	**Total**	**7**	**6 698**	**1 998**	**24**	**41 340**	**41 054**
一师	Division 1	1	727	396			1 428
二师	Division 2						
三师	Division 3						
四师	Division 4	1	450		9	1 973	
五师	Division 5				1	41	
六师	Division 6	1	152		1	76	10 308
七师	Division 7						1 325
八师	Division 8	2	2 960	176	12	5 650	24 207
十师	Division 10						
十二师	Division 12				1	33 600	
十三师	Division 13						
兵团直属	Directly under XPCC	2	2 409				3 786
其他:历年外资到位	Other:(Foreign Capital Arrived in Former Year)			1 426			

15－14 外商投资企业年底注册登记情况

Registration Status of Foreign Enterprises at Year-end

指标	Item	2016	2017
企业数(个)	**Number of Enterprises(unit)**	**7**	**24**
合资企业	Joint-Venture Enterprises	4	2
合作企业	Cooperative Enterprises	1	
独资企业	Private-Funds Enterprises	2	22
投资总额(万美元)	**Total Investment (USD 10 000)**	**24 500**	**112 761**
合资企业	Joint-Venture Enterprises	2 184	104
合作企业	Cooperative Enterprises	13 636	
独资企业	Private-Funds Enterprises	8 680	112 657
注册资本(万美元)	**Registered Capital (USD 10 000)**	**9 635**	**40 774**
合资企业	Joint-Venture Enterprises	2 050	104
合作企业	Cooperative Enterprises	4 545	
独资企业	Private-Funds Enterprises	3 040	40 670
外方出资(万美元)	**Foreign Investment (USD 10 000)**	**6 698**	**41 340**
合资企业	Joint-Venture Enterprises	1 340	105
合作企业	Cooperative Enterprises	2 318	
独资企业	Private-Funds Enterprises	3 040	41 235

15—15 对外经济合作主要指标

Main Indicators of Foreign Economic Cooperation

年 份 Year	境外投资 Foreign Investment				对外工程承包 Foreign Contracted Projects			劳务合作 Labor Cooperation		外派劳务人员（人） Labor Force (person)
	项目数（个） Number of Projects (unit)	合同金额（万美元） Contracted Value (USD 10 000)	# 中方合同金额 Contract Value of China	# 中方实际投资额 Actually Investment of China	新签合同数（个） Newly Signed Number of Contract(units)	新签合同金额（万美元） Newly Signed Contrcted Value (USD 10000)	完成营业额（万美元） Completed Value (USD 10000)	项目数（个） Number of Projects (unit)	合同金额（万美元） Contracted Value (USD 10 000)	
1995	5	79	50	16	2	296		2	55	262
1996	4	134	121	13						
1997	3	40	40	20				2	20	100
1998	6	3 386	3 385	313				2	150	80
1999	2	2 401	1 201	1 201						
2000	4	1 456	533	533						
2001	3	20	13	13						
2002	5	179	157	157	1	3 100	65			
2003	6	150	150	281	1	434				221
2004	13	1 972	1 216	1 216	5	6 739	2 030			740
2005	12	1 530	1 530	1 083	4	858	2 729			603
2006	12	1 692	1 354	1 354	6	35 227	4 492	4	338	1 386
2007	12	57 000	57 000	57 000	1	2 260	9 980	4	331	2 697
2008	8	3 000	3 000	3 000	10	54 719	16 409	1	257	3 422
2009	17	3 900	3 900	3 900	2	27 226	24 028			3 126
2010	7	10 281	9 684	9 684	10	18 253	30 769			3 813
2011	6	2 582	1 979	837	6	38 268	34 184			2 712
2012	5	5 159	5 159	5 159	15	63 638	45 642			2 544
2013	5	733	733	733	25	31 210	54 244			2 656
2014	11	15 117	10 157	8 604	21	29 420	58 232			2 663
2015	24	7 160			25	115 325	60 297			2 064
2016	23	7 952			20	57 779	66 921	1	2	3 140
2017	17	8 797			10	23 490	68 051			491

15—16 对外承包工程和劳务合作

Contracted Projects and Labor Cooperation with Foreign Countries or Regions

指 标	Item	2016	2017
承包工程	**Contracted Projects**		
新签合同数 （个）	Newly SignedNumber of Contract (unit)	20	10
新签合同金额 （万美元）	Newly Signed Contrcted Value (USD 10 000)	57 779	23 490
劳务合作	**Labor Cooperation**		
新签合同数 （个）	Newly Signed Number of Contract (unit)	1	
新签合同金额 （万美元）	Newly Signed Contrcted Value (USD 10 000)	2	

15—17 旅游业发展情况

Development of Tourism

指 标		Item		2005	2010	2015	2016	2017
旅行社总数	**(个)**	**Total Numberof Travel Agencies**	**(unit)**	**79**	**98**	**134**	**131**	**141**
# 出境组团社		Outbound Travel Agencies		3	6	22	23	22
旅行社职工人数	**(人)**	**Number of staff and Workers of Travel Agencies**	**(person)**	**743**	**562**	**1 709**	**1 817**	**1 980**
# 出境组团社		Outbound Travel Agencies		295	134	1 239	1 316	1 285
星级饭店	**(个)**	**Star-rating Tourist Hotal**	**(unit)**	**30**	**50**	**62**	**62**	**62**
旅游人数	**(万人次)**	**Number of Tourist**	**(10 000 person-time)**	**227.54**	**401.00**	**1054.22**	**1 422.40**	**1 896.12**
入境旅游人数		Total Number of International Tourists Inbound		8.09	13.00	15.70	19.00	20.90
国内旅游人数		Total Number of Domestic Tourist		218.85	387.50	1 029.30	1 403.40	1 871.10
出境旅游人数		Total Number of Domestic Outbound		0.60	0.51	9.22		4.12
旅游总收入	**(万元)**	**Income of Tourism**	**(10 000 yuan)**	**58 735**	**169 000**	**528 000**	**740 000**	**1 018 000**
旅游景区及其它旅游单位	**(个)**	**Scenic Spots and other Tourism Units**	**(unit)**	**12**	**35**	**109**	**136**	**178**
年末就业人数	(人)	Year-end Employed Persons	(person)	596	1 062	4 323	5 198	23 000
景区年接待人数	(万人次)	Tourists of Scinic Area	(10 000 person-time)	93	429	403	538	717
营业收入	(万元)	Business Income	(10 000 yuan)	1 653	18 037	28 129	36 255	48 317
年门票收入	(万元)	Tickets Income	(10 000 yuan)	385	3 226	2 521	3 352	3 048
利润总额	(万元)	Total Profits	(10 000 yuan)	309	1 443	2 263	2 917	3 785

15—18 旅游业情况

Tourism

指 标	Item	旅游总收入(万元) Tourism Receipts (10 000 yuan)		入境旅游者(人次) International Tourists (person-time)		国内旅游者(人次) Domestic Tourists (person-time)	
		2016	2017	2016	2017	2016	2017
总 计	**Total**	**740 000**	**1 018 000**	**190 000**	**209 000**	**14 034 000**	**18 711 000**
饭 店	Hotel	85 322	93 546	109 516	124 680	3 414 472	3 356 810
旅 行 社	Travel Agencies	329 226	215 838	58 900	43 200	4 328 086	4 748 850
旅游景区	Scenic Area	36 255	41 365		31 426	5 380 000	7 170 000
其 他	Others	289 197	667 251	21 584	9 694	911 442	3 435 340

15—19 规模以上服务业企业主要财务指标

Main Financial Indicators of Enterprises above Designated Size of Services

计量单位:万元 (2017年)

指标	Item	单位数(个) Number of Units(unit)	固定资产原价 Original Value of Fixed Assets	本年折旧 Depreciation in this Year
总计	**Total**	**346**	**1 785 092**	**130 138**
按登记注册类型分	**Grouped by Status of Registration**	**346**	**1 785 092**	**130 139**
内资企业	Domestic Enterprises	343	1 682 596	105 556
国有企业	State-owned Enterprises	19	150 925	4 767
集体企业	Collective Enterprises	1	1 526	38
有限责任公司	Limited Liability Corporations	160	1 134 601	73 299
国有独资公司	State-owned Corporations with Private-Funds	49	384 786	9 161
其他有限责任公司	Other Limited Liability Corporations	111	749 816	64 138
股份有限公司	Share-holding Corporations Ltd.	12	211 865	15 499
私营企业	Private Enterprises	148	182 454	11 824
私营独资企业	Private-funded Enterprises	7	8 333	769
私营有限责任公司	Private Limited Liability Corporations	140	174 077	11 053
私营股份有限	Private Limited by Share Ltd	1	44	1
其他企业	Others	3	1 225	129
港、澳、台商投资企业	Enterprises with Funds from Hong Kong,Macao and Taiwan	2	66 793	5 016
合资经营企业(港或澳、台资)	Joint Venture Enterptise(Hongkong、Macao、Taiwan)	1		
港、澳、台商投资股份有限公司	Share-holding Corporations Ltd. with Funds from Hong Kong,Macao and Taiwan	1	66 793	5 016
外商投资股份有限公司	Share-holding Corporations Ltd. With Foreign Investment	1	35 703	19 567
外商投资股份有限公司	Share-holding Corporations Ltd. With Foreign Investment	1	35 703	19 567
按控股情况分	**Grouped by Shareholding-Controlled**	**346**	**1 785 092**	**130 138**
国有控股	State-controlled Shareholding-Controlled	161	1 411 860	88 960
集体控股	Collective-owned Shareholding-Controlled	4	6 193	394
私人控股	Private Shareholding-Controlled	171	227 208	15 459
港澳台商控股	Hong Kong,Macao and Taiwan Shareholding-Controlled	1	66 793	5 016
其他	Others	9	73 038	20 309
按行业分	**Grouped by Sector**	**346**	**1 785 092**	**130 138**
交通运输、仓储和邮政业	Transport,Storage,and Postal Service Industry	64	301 135	22 514
道路运输业	Road Transport	45	178 590	15 888
航空运输业	Air Transport	2	34 464	1 594
装卸搬运和运输代理业	Pack,Unload Porterage and Other Transport	3	9 473	1 001
仓储业	Storage	13	70 768	3 610
邮政业	Postal Service	1	7 840	421
信息传输、软件和信息技术服务业	Information Deliver,Software and Information Technology Service	18	365 999	68 687
电信、广播电视和卫星传输服务	Telecommunications,Broadcast,Television and Satellite Service	7	362 046	68 294
互联网和相关服务	Internet and Related Services	1	269	16
软件和信息技术服务业	Software and Information Technology Service	10	3 684	377
房地产业	Real Estate Trade	65	77 731	4 359
租赁和商务服务业	Leasing and Business Service	86	663 960	21 041
租赁业	Leasing	6	169 209	10 373
商务服务业	Business Service	80	494 751	10 668
科学研究和技术服务业	Scientific Research and Technical Service	42	56 238	3 714
研究和试验发展	Research and Development	2	1 519	130
专业技术服务业	Professional Technique Service	34	38 103	2 564
科技推广和应用服务业	Science and Technology Promotion and Application Service Industry	6	16 616	1 020
水利、环境和公共设施管理业	Water Conservancy,Environment and Public Facilities Management	36	265 348	5 983
水利管理业	Water Conservancy Management	5	215 683	3 891
公共设施管理业	Public Facilities Management	31	49 665	2 092
居民服务、修理和其他服务业	Resident and Other Services	13	19 621	796
居民服务业	Resident Services	7	18 989	688
机动车、电子产品和日用产品修理业	Repair of Motor Vehicle,Electronic Products and Daily Use Products	5	309	16
其他服务业	Other Services	1	323	92
教育	Education	4	13 888	838
教育	Primary Education	4	13 888	838
卫生和社会工作	Health Care and Social Security	3	2 878	189
卫生	Health Care	2	2 774	165
社会工作	Social Work	1	104	24
文化、体育和娱乐业	Culture、Sport and Entertainment	15	18 294	2 017
广播、电视、电影和影视录音制作业	Radio、TV、Movie and Video Recording Industry	6	10 171	1 261
文化艺术业	Culture and Art	4	2 274	97
娱乐业	Entertainment	5	5 849	659

Main Financial Indicators of Enterprises above Designated Size of Services

(10 000 yuan)

资产总计 Total Assets	负债合计 Total Liabilities	所有者权益合计 Total Owners' Equity	营业收入 Revenue Business	营业成本 Cost of Business	营业税金及附加 Taxes and Other Changes on Business	销售费用 Sales Expenses
13 110 502	**8 689 250**	**4 421 252**	**1 797 488**	**1 300 157**	**16 676**	**59 507**
13 110 503	**8 689 250**	**4 421 252**	**1 797 488**	**1 300 157**	**16 676**	**59 507**
13 055 521	8 629 450	4 426 071	1 739 497	1 264 388	16 501	54 305
346 541	249 038	97 502	140 565	113 579	598	9 211
4 853	3 676	1 177	4 728	2 625	49	
11 116 380	7 763 074	3 353 306	931 444	710 685	10 003	33 226
6 986 087	5 033 192	1 952 894	302 628	214 477	3 492	4 376
4 130 293	2 729 881	1 400 412	628 816	496 208	6 511	28 850
1 133 292	354 123	779 169	79 779	50 174	669	4 756
452 558	258 451	194 107	580 979	386 065	5 159	7 110
8 118	2 055	6 063	6 105	3 747	180	31
444 209	256 272	187 937	571 894	379 859	4 972	6 999
231	124	107	2 980	2 459	7	80
1 897	1 088	810	2 002	1 260	23	2
35 408	20 952	14 456	15 275	13 075	62	1 551
			1 324	1 090	1	11
35 408	20 952	14 456	13 951	11 985	60	1 540
19 574	38 848	−19 275	42 716	22 694	113	3 651
19 574	38 848	−19 275	42 716	22 694	113	3 651
13 110 502	**8 689 250**	**4 421 252**	**1 797 488**	**1 300 157**	**16 676**	**59 507**
12 385 458	8 242 258	4 143 201	929 025	693 875	10 177	36 770
22 458	10 947	11 511	23 039	9 473	169	4 151
531 992	301 711	230 281	661 935	450 279	5 626	11 851
35 408	20 952	14 456	13 951	11 985	60	1 540
135 186	113 382	21 803	169 538	134 545	644	5 195
12 890 049	**8 689 250**	**4 421 252**	**1 797 488**	**1 300 157**	**16 676**	**59 507**
597 971	370 435	227 535	332 798	304 212	2 045	10 409
267 284	162 870	104 414	202 729	184 980	1 783	3 920
68 398	8 037	60 361	5 151	10 549	40	0
16 611	14 765	1 845	12 238	10 986	62	774
239 034	179 947	59 087	101 211	87 224	67	5 715
6 644	4 816	1 828	11 469	10 473	93	0
350 144	304 871	45 273	348 985	178 539	1 941	15 425
193 961	189 150	4 810	123 901	81 459	418	14 827
413	183	230	1 011	848		1
155 770	115 538	40 233	224 073	96 232	1 523	597
91 230	57 414	33 816	68 623	48 983	1 185	3 648
10 860 246	7 311 442	3 548 805	635 282	486 902	7 587	7 622
372 755	241 265	131 490	66 665	47 277	305	382
10 487 491	7 070 177	3 417 315	568 617	439 625	7 282	7 240
305 325	194 156	111 168	229 078	148 538	1 771	12 466
7 637	2 620	5 018	6 406	3 982	38	1
260 205	162 580	97 624	193 682	120 864	1 603	12 102
37 483	28 956	8 526	28 990	23 692	130	363
554 815	401 182	374 088	116 345	94 489	1 302	862
276 873	114 778	162 095	33 783	26 171	201	
277 942	286 404	211 993	82 562	68 318	1 101	862
28 237	11 743	16 494	24 111	12 428	88	3 341
26 507	10 390	16 117	20 791	9 521	35	3 148
1 562	1 193	369	3 110	2 644	53	99
168	160	8	210	263		94
20 955	11 433	9 522	13 287	8 489	208	
20 955	11 433	9 522	13 287	8 489	208	
1 039	880	160	1 478	510		369
870	697	173	996	298		369
169	183	−13	482	212		
80 087	25 694	54 391	27 501	17 067	549	5 365
20 823	10 925	9 898	11 892	9 184	124	541
52 068	12 708	39 360	8 566	2 753	132	4 817
7 196	2 061	5 133	7 043	5 130	293	7

15—19续表

计量单位:万元　　(2017年)

指　标	Item	管理费用 Administrative Expenses	#税　金 Taxe	财务费用 Financial Expenses
总　计	**Total**	**187 640**		**47 709**
按登记注册类型分	**Grouped by Status of Registration**	**187 641**		**47 709**
内资企业	Domestic Enterprises	185 533		46 433
国有企业	State-owned Enterprises	15 248		282
集体企业	Collective Enterprises	1 643		−2
有限责任公司	Limited Liability Corporations	124 406		38 886
国有独资公司	State-owned Corporations with Private-Funds	37 786		27 917
其他有限责任公司	Other Limited Liability Corporations	86 620		10 969
股份有限公司	Share-holding Corporations Ltd.	14 309		5 564
私营企业	Private Enterprises	29 478		1 696
私营独资企业	Private-funded Enterprises	541		84
私营有限责任公司	Private Limited Liability Corporations	28 524		1 608
私营股份有限	Private Limited by Share Ltd	413		4
其他企业	Others	449		7
港、澳、台商投资企业	Enterprises with Funds from Hong Kong,Macao and Taiwan	998		1 275
合资经营企业(港或澳、台资)	Joint Venture Enterptise(Hongkong、Macao、Taiwan)	143		−1
港、澳、台商投资股份有限公司	Share-holding Corporations Ltd. with Funds from Hong Kong,Macao and Taiwan	854		1 276
外商投资股份有限公司	Share-holding Corporations Ltd. With Foreign Investment	1 110		1
外商投资股份有限公司	Share-holding Corporations Ltd. With Foreign Investment	1 110		1
按控股情况分	**Grouped by Shareholding-Controlled**	**187 640**		**47 709**
国有控股	State-controlled Shareholding-Controlled	140 572		44 639
集体控股	Collective-owned Shareholding-Controlled	5 807		50
私人控股	Private Shareholding-Controlled	36 845		1 790
港澳台商控股	Hong Kong,Macao and Taiwan Shareholding-Controlled	854		1 276
其　他	Others	3 562		−46
按行业分	**Grouped by Sector**	**187 640**		**47 709**
交通运输、仓储和邮政业	Transport,Storage,and Postal Service Industry	22 425		2 057
道路运输业	Road Transport	13 216		784
航空运输业	Air Transport	1 628		54
装卸搬运和运输代理业	Pack,Unload Porterage and Other Transport	804		103
仓储业	Storage	6 071		1 094
邮政业	Postal Service	706		22
信息传输、软件和信息技术服务业	Information Deliver,Software and Information Technology Service	14 599		4 091
电信、广播电视和卫星传输服务	Telecommunications,Broadcast,Television and Satellite Service	7 479		4 037
互联网和相关服务	Internet and Related Services	32		
软件和信息技术服务业	Software and Information Technology Service	7 088		54
房地产业	Real Estate Trade	11 139		505
租赁和商务服务业	Leasing and Business Service	80 825		39 777
租赁业	Leasing	3 829		5 629
商务服务业	Business Service	76 996		34 148
科学研究和技术服务业	Scientific Research and Technical Service	38 658		−105
研究和试验发展	Research and Development	1 257		−8
专业技术服务业	Professional Technique Service	35 546		−763
科技推广和应用服务业	Science and Technology Promotion and Application Service Industry	1 855		666
水利、环境和公共设施管理业	Water Conservancy,Environment and Public Facilities Management	11 148		890
水利管理业	Water Conservancy Management	5 907		488
公共设施管理业	Public Facilities Management	5 241		402
居民服务、修理和其他服务业	Resident and Other Services	4 050		130
居民服务业	Resident Services	3 893		101
机动车、电子产品和日用产品修理业	Repair of Motor Vehicle,Electronic Products and Daily Use Products	150		28
其他服务业	Other Services	7		1
教　育	Education	1 656		227
教　育	Primary Education	1 656		227
卫生和社会工作	Health Care and Social Security	600		1
卫　生	Health Care	228		1
社会工作	Social Work	372		
文化、体育和娱乐业	Culture、Sport and Entertainment	2 540		136
广播、电视、电影和影视录音制作业	Radio、TV、Movie and Video Recording Industry	818		−33
文化艺术业	Culture and Art	1 443		154
娱乐业	Entertainment	279		15

Continued

(10 000 yuan)

#利息支出 Interest Expenditure	投资收益 Investment Income	营业利润 Operating Profits	利润总额 Total Profits	应交所得税 Income Tax Payable	应付职工薪酬 Unemployment Insurance	应交增值税 Appreciation Tax Payable	从业人员平均人数(人) Average Number of Staff and Workers(person)
104 738	**112 736**	**207 778**	**225 938**	**33 422**	**288 420**	**56 942**	**40 257**
104 737	**112 736**	**207 778**	**225 939**	**33 422**	**288 420**	**56 942**	**40 257**
104 737	113 259	194 802	212 894	31 114	281 200	53 888	39 424
1 820	587	4 400	5 161	751	26 488	1 012	4 114
	1	414	340		2 125	14	144
93 373	89 513	129 884	147 695	25 623	173 313	31 413	20 952
70 026	73 587	113 672	123 650	17 182	75 630	14 456	8 111
23 347	15 927	16 212	24 045	8 441	97 683	16 956	12 841
8 187	22 451	−421	−933	1 324	18 356	1 475	1 509
1 357	707	60 264	60 313	3 415	60 497	19 972	12 517
80	17	1 541	1 541	259	1 044	182	237
1 278	690	58 706	58 754	3 155	59 429	19 781	12 275
		17	19	1	24	9	5
		261	318	1	421	2	188
		−1 645	−1 552		2 942	1 148	516
		79	79		1 090	11	410
		−1 725	−1 632		1 851	1 137	106
	−523	14 621	14 597	2 308	4 278	1 906	317
	−523	14 621	14 597	2 308	4 278	1 906	317
104 738	**112 736**	**207 778**	**225 938**	**33 422**	**288 420**	**56 942**	**40 257**
103 191	112 358	117 527	134 986	24 486	199 131	31 367	23 888
84	1	3 386	3 327	448	8 485	1 097	617
1 450	900	64 529	64 721	4 642	70 623	20 596	14 834
		−1 725	−1 632		1 851	1 137	106
13	−523	24 061	24 536	3 846	8 330	2 745	812
104 738	**112 736**	**207 778**	**225 938**	**33 422**	**288 420**	**56 942**	**40 257**
4 306	−61	−977	4 021	1 537	46 208	841	6 849
791	26	−1 675	1 918	1 306	28 902	3 890	5 083
63	−168	−3 341	−2 057		6 654	−3 636	444
70		−489	−337		1 424	228	323
3 382	81	4 353	4 321		4 521	285	584
		175	176		4 707	74	415
2 836	−167	42 005	42 221	2 363	18 720	14 729	1 501
2 759	−523	15 078	15 124	2 311	15 429	3 123	1 089
		130	130	1	71	2	11
77	356	26 797	26 967	51	3 220	11 604	401
382	116	3 297	4 849	751	28 106	1 510	6 936
94 662	111 242	117 536	124 822	21 832	67 267	22 907	11 612
6 034	92	8 159	7 951	807	6 944	2 167	644
88 628	111 150	109 377	116 871	21 025	60 323	20 740	10 968
1 086	1 130	28 498	30 506	4 995	83 409	10 887	6 838
		1 100	1 131	64	3 041	207	229
375	1 167	25 014	26 959	4 860	78 246	10 139	6 406
711	−37	2 384	2 416	71	2 122	541	203
926	267	8 950	10 155	601	27 368	4 806	4 182
9	1	1 542	1 402	202	9 289	166	1 326
917	266	7 408	8 753	399	18 079	4 640	2 856
136		4 075	4 088	726	4 849	279	653
107		4 094	4 107	714	4 102	178	513
29		136	138	10	565	95	65
		−155	−157	2	182	6	75
248		2 343	2 406	178	3 282	81	340
248		2 343	2 406	178	3 282	81	340
1		−1	56		765		215
1		101	101		545		125
		−102	−45		220		90
155	209	2 052	2 814	439	8 446	902	1 131
31	175	1 435	1 624	113	4 503	448	449
114	33	−700	−123	165	3 315	163	501
10	1	1 317	1 313	161	628	291	181

15—20 星级旅游饭店情况

Conditions of Tourism Star-rated Hotels

（2017 年）

指　标		Item		合　计 Total
星级饭店	（个）	Star-rated Hotels	(unit)	62
接待住宿人数	（人次）	Persons Received	(person-time)	3 481 490
海外旅游者	（人次）	Internationa Tourists	(person-time)	124 680
客房间数	（间）	Rooms	(unit)	8 239
床位张数	（张）	Beds	(unit)	16 480
从业人数	（人）	Employed Persons	(person)	4 115
固定资产	（万元）	Fixed Assets	(10 000 yuan)	123 432
营业收入	（万元）	Business Income	(10 000 yuan)	40 583
经营利润	（万元）	Business Profits	(10 000 yuan)	−1 622
营业税金及附加	（万元）	Business Taxes and Extra Charges	(10 000 yuan)	1 580
利润总额	（万元）	Total Profits	(10 000 yuan)	−914
客房收入	（万元）	Rooms Income	(10 000 yuan)	24 548
餐饮收入	（万元）	Catering Services Income	(10 000 yuan)	12 254

15—21 A 级旅游景区(景点)主要情况

Conditions of A-grade Scenic Area(Spot)

（2017 年）

指　标		Item		合　计 Total
A 级景区(景点)总数	（家）	A-grade Scenic Area	(Spot)	55
# 5A 级		5A Grade		1
4A 级		4A Grade		17
3A 级		3A Grade		31
2A 级		2A Grade		6
营业收入	（万元）	Revenue Business	(10 000 yuan)	36 414
# 门票收入	（万元）	Tickets Income		3 048
营业税金及附加	（万元）	Taxes and Other Changes on Business	(10 000 yuan)	
利润总额	（万元）	Total Profits	(10 000 yuan)	2 785
固定资产原值	（万元）	Original Value of Fixed Assets	(10 000 yuan)	
固定资产净值	（万元）	Net Value of Fixed Assets	(10 000 yuan)	
年末就业人数	（人）	Year-end Employed Persons	(person)	3 798
# 转移农村劳动力		Transfer Village Labor Force		
接待人数	（万人次）	Persons Received	(10 000 person-time)	717
# 境外人数		Internationa Tourists		31 426
本年实际完成投资额	（万元）	Reality Accomplish Investment	(10 000 yuan)	35 588
# 基础设施建设		Infrastructure Construction		30 693
设备购置		Purchase of Equipment		
其　他		Others		

第十六篇

金融业和上市公司

Chapter 16 Financial Intermediation and Listed Company

简要说明

一、本篇资料主要内容

本篇主要反映中国农业银行兵团分行本外币资产负债情况和兵团上市公司基本情况。

二、本篇资料来源

金融资料由中国农业银行兵团分行提供，兵团统计局国民经济综合统计处整理。上市公司资料由兵团金融工作办公室提供。

Brief Introduction

1. Main Contents

Data in this chapter show mainly the basic conditions of total assets and liabilities in XPCC Branch of the Agricultural Bank of China, and listed corporations of XPCC.

2. Sources of Data

Data on Banking are provided by XPCC Branch of the Agricultural Bank of China, and are prepared by the Comprehensive Office of Statistics Bureau of XPCC. Data of listed companies are provided by the Financial Work Office of XPCC.

16—1 兵团农业银行本外币资产负债情况

Total Assets and Liabilities of the Agricultural Bank of China of XPCC

计量单位:万元 (10 000 yuan)

指　　标	Item	2017
资产合计	**Total Assets**	**12 981 323.87**
现金及银行存款	Cash and Bank Deposit	80 097.40
存放中央银行款项	Deposit the National Central Bank Amount of Money	8.67
存放同业款项	Due from Bank Amount of Money	371.11
存放系统内款项	Funds Deposited in the System	6 246 130.88
应收利息	Receivable Interest	15 652.56
贸易融资	Trade Margin	440 197.66
贷　款	Loan	6 143 818.07
贴现及买断式转贴现	Discount and Discounted Discount	1 131.99
拆放同业款项	Borrows the Same Profession Amount of Money	10 689.33
其他应收款	Other Receivable Loan	2 460.08
投　资	Investment	
长期待摊费用	Long—term Prepaid Expenses	880.14
固定资产净值	Net Worth of Fixed Assets	101 320.83
固定资产原价	Original Value of Fixed Assets	202 303.57
减:累计折旧	Reduce:Accumulated Ddepreciation	100 982.74
在建工程	Under Construction	5 574.37
无形资产	Immaterial Assets	13 510.42
抵债资产	The Assets Wait For to Handle	
递延所得税资产	Deferred Tax Assets	18 715.13
其他资产	Other Assets	26 966.96
资产减值准备	The Preparation of Assets Reduced	126 201.72
负债及所有者权益总计	**Total Liabilities and Creditord Equity**	**12 981 323.87**
负债合计	**Total Liabilities**	**12 841 351.15**
单位存款	Unit Deposits	6 619 286.92
储蓄存款	Individual Deposits	5 958 032.68
应解汇款	Should Solve the Remittance	350.93
保证金存款	Security Deposit	49 684.00
汇出汇款	Remit Remittance	
同业存放款项	Same Profession Deposits	35 397.30
境内商业银行	Domestic Commercial Banks	786.40
境内其他银行业金融机构	Other Banking Financial Institutions within the Territory	31 433.12
境内证券业金融机构	Domestic Securities Industry Financial Institution	3 167.20
境内其他金融机构	Other Financial Institutions within the Territory	
境外金融机构	Offshore Financial Institution	10.58
系统内存放款项	System Memory Loan Entries	49 291.43
同业拆借款项	Same Profession Borrow	
应付利息	Payable Interest	79 128.86
应交税费	Payable Taxes	7 307.94
应付职工薪酬	Payable Wages	22 625.17
其他应付款	Other Payable	15 275.18
递延收益	Deferred Income	1 217.42
预计负债	Anticipate Liabilities	137.81
其他负债	Other Liabilities	3 615.51
所有者权益合计	**Total Creditord Equity**	**139 972.72**
实收资本	Paid—up Capital	15 588.46
未分配利润	Did not Assign Profits	124 384.26
# 本年利润	Profits	124 384.26
附注项目	**Notes**	
各项存款	Deposits	12 627 354.52
各项贷款	Loans	6 581 582.41
生息资产	Interest—earning Assets	12 838 782.39
付息负债	Interest—earning Liabilties	12 712 043.26

注:本资料未包括七师、十三师、十四师。

Note:Data in this table is not including Division 7,Division 13 and Division 14.

16—2 上市公司基本情况

Basic Conditions of Listed Companies

计量单位:万元 (2017 年) (10 000 yuan)

指 标	Item	新疆百花村股份有限公司 XJ Bai huacun Ltd.,Co.	新疆天业股份有限公司 XJ Tianye Ltd.,Co.	新疆塔里木农业综合开发股份有限公司 XJ Tarimu Agi-cultural Compr-ehensive Develo-pment Ltd.,Co.	新疆伊力特实业股份有限公司 XJ Yilite Industry Ltd.,Co.
股票简称	Stock Brief Name	百花村 Bai Huacun	新疆天业 Xinjiang Tiangye	新农开发 Xinnong Development	伊力特 Yilite
股票代码	Stock Code	600721	600075	600359	600197
股票上市时间	Listed Time	1996-6-26	1997-6-17	1999-4-29	1999-9-16
股票上市交易所	Listing Stock Exchange	上交所 SHSE	上交所 SHSE	上交所 SHSE	上交所 SHSE
董事长	President	郑彩红	宋晓玲	白宏本	陈 智
总经理	General Manager	张孝清	关 刚	王 青	陈双英
公司地址	Company Address	新疆乌鲁木齐市中山路141号 141 Zhongshan Road Urumqi, XJ	新疆石河子市经济开发区北三东路36号 36 East Road Beisan Economic Development Zone Shihezi XJ	新疆阿拉尔南口镇迎宾路1号 The army reclamation avenue autonomous region is 12 floors ahead of commercial office building Uygur,XJ	新疆新源县肖尔布拉克 XJ Xinyuan County
邮政编码	Post Code	830002	832000	843000	835811
发行时总股本 (万股)	Total Capital Stock (10 000 share)	6 127.50	6 300.00	29 400.00	22 050.00
国有股	National Stock	2 672.50	3 600.00	20 400.00	13 450.00
法人股	Corporative Stock	455.00			1 100.00
流通股	Circulating Stock	3 000.00	2 430.00	9 000.00	7 500.00
其 他	Other		270.00		
发行募集资金 (万元)	Floated Raised Funds (10 000 yuan)	12 600.00	16 896.00	34 740.00	46 950.00
年末总股本 (万股)	Stock Capital at the Year-end (10 000 share)	40 038.64	97 252.24	38 151.28	44 100.00
国有股	National Stock	1 628.66	18 622.32		
法人股	Corporative Stock				
其 他	Other	8 154.71	17 227.04		
流通股	Circulating Stock	30 255.26	61 402.88	38 151.28	44 100.00
年末累计募集资金 (万元)	Capital Raised Year-end (10 000 yuan)	299 239.65	366 698.96	144 790.00	46 950.00
流动资产合计 (万元)	Circulating Funds (10 000 yuan)	52 743.24	251 847.31	167 401.74	249 142.01
# 存 货	Stock	27 299.94	92 577.37	28 134.84	77 937.97
非流动资产合计 (万元)	Non-Circulating Funds (10 000 yuan)	150 533.26	637 804.53	88 108.43	57 754.77
资产总计 (万元)	Total Assets (10 000 yuan)	203 276.50	889 651.83	255 510.18	306 896.78
流动负债合计 (万元)	Liquid Liabilities (10 000 yuan)	25 511.41	325 485.95	138 818.05	81 425.19
非流动负债合计 (万元)	Non-Liquid Liabilities (10 000 yuan)	4 462.14	87 475.71	49 059.77	1 832.57
股东权益合计 (万元)	Share-holders Equity (10 000 yuan)	173 302.95	476 690.17	67 632.37	223 639.02
营业总收入 (万元)	Total Revenue of Business (10 000 yuan)	41 950.25	497 716.26	108 470.14	191 881.27
营业总成本 (万元)	Total Cost of Business (10 000 yuan)	97 934.47	432 622.10	134 889.06	143 064.33
管理费用 (万元)	Administrative Expenses (10 000 yuan)	4 781.21	30 981.11	11 049.61	7 284.12
财务费用 (万元)	Financial Expenses (10 000 yuan)	227.25	10 849.36	5 047.41	−1 648.43
营业利润 (万元)	Business Profits (10 000 yuan)	−55 449.53	65 549.49	2 061.67	48 740.62
投资收益 (万元)	Investment Income (10 000 yuan)	−81.77	−294.34	−128.60	−607.55
营业外收入 (万元)	Extra-business Revenue (10 000 yuan)	68.54	372.34	43.01	950.12
营业外支出 (万元)	Extra-business Expenditures (10 000 yuan)	26.86	88.06	438.71	154.78
利润总额 (万元)	Total Profits (10 000 yuan)	−55 407.84	65 833.77	1 665.97	49 535.96
净利润 (万元)	Net Profits (10 000 yuan)	−56 509.44	53 665.64	1 526.73	35 685.90
每股收益 (元)	Net Income per Share (yuan)	−1.41	0.55	0.09	0.80
每股净资产 (元)	Net Assets per Share (yuan)	4.30	4.46	1.82	4.92
净资产收益率 (%)	Net Assets of Yield (%)	−28.2	12.4	5.0	17.4

16—2 续表 1 Continued

计量单位：万元　　　　(2017 年)　　　　(10 000 yuan)

指　　标	Item	中　　基实业股份有限公司 Zhongji Health Industry Stock Ltd., Co.	新疆天润乳业股份有限公司 XJ Tianrun Milk Industry Stock Ltd., Co.	新疆天富能源股份有限公司 XJ Tianfu Energy Stock Ltd., Co.	新疆冠农果茸股份有限公司 XJ Guannong guorong Group Stock Ltd., Co.	新疆青松建材化工(集团)股份有限公司 XJ Qinsong Building Material and Chemical Industry Ltd., Co.
股票简称	Stock Brief Name	* ST 中基 * STzhongji	天润乳业 Xinjiang Tianrun	天富能源 Tianfu Thermoelectricity	冠农股份 Guannong Shares	* ST 青松 * STQinsong
股票代码	Stock Code	000972	600419	600509	600251	600425
股票上市时间	Listed Time	2000-9-26	2001-6-28	2002-2-28	2003-6-9	2003-7-24
股票上市交易所	Listing Stock Exchange	深交所 SZSE	上交所 SHSE	上交所 SHSE	上交所 SHSE	上交所 SHSE
董事长	President	李　豫	刘　让	赵　磊	郭　良	郑术建
总经理	General Manager	李　润	胡　刚		章　睿	杨万川
公司地址	Company Address	新疆乌鲁木齐市青年路17号 8 North First Lane Youth RD. Urumqi, XJ	新疆乌鲁木齐市经济技术开发区(头屯河区)乌昌公路2702号 2702 Road Wuchang Economic Development Zone Urumqi, XJ	新疆石河子市北一东路2号 2 Beiyidong RD. Shihezi, XJ	新疆库尔勒市团结南路48号 48 Tuanjie South RD. korla, XJ	新疆阿克苏市林园 Linyuan RD. Aksu, XJ
邮政编码	Post Code	830002	830088	832002	841000	843005
发行时总股本(万股)	Total Capital Stock (10 000 share)	12 458.92	8 016.00	16 908.50	12 000.00	18 492.75
国有股	National Stock	6 559.27	4 752.00	10 672.50	8 000.00	12 426.08
法人股	Corporative Stock	1 399.65	264.00	236.00		
流通股	Circulating Stock	4 500.00	3 000.00	6 000.00	4 000.00	6 000.00
其　他	Other					66.67
发行募集资金(万元)	Floated Raised Funds (10 000 yuan)	22 500.00	16 633.00	39 990.00	21 609.00	24 265.00
年末总股本(万股)	Stock Capital at the year-end (10 000 share)	77 128.36	10 355.72	115 141.50	78 484.20	137 879.01
国有股	National Stock		1 405.83	6 531.20		
法人股	Corporative Stock					
其　他	Other			18 040.64		
流通股	Circulating Stock	77 128.36	8 949.90	90 569.66	78 484.20	137 879.01
年末累计募集资金(万元)	Capital Raised Year-end (10 000 yuan)	210 585.00	62 832.81	587 621.00	107 929.00	670 408.00
流动资产合计(万元)	Circulating Funds (10 000 yuan)	127 372.10	45 300.98	357 669.81	291 712.38	199 963.00
# 存　货	Stock	90 093.96	12 959.92	63 087.76	138 586.77	47 135.00
非流动资产合计(万元)	Non-Circulating Funds (10 000 yuan)	117 160.88	12 959.92	1 587 745.94	212 853.63	778 625.00
资产总计(万元)	Total Assets (10 000 yuan)	244 532.99	142 946.10	1 945 415.75	504 566.01	978 588.00
流动负债合计(万元)	Liquid Liabilities (10 000 yuan)	150 619.80	36 092.78	447 085.87	227 509.80	323 814.00
非流动负债合计(万元)	Non-Liquid Liabilities (10 000 yuan)	5 408.06	13 446.07	836 319.82	46 453.69	246 992.00
股东权益合计(万元)	Share-holders Equity (10 000 yuan)	88 505.12	93 407.25	662 010.06	230 602.52	407 781.00
营业总收入(万元)	Total Revenue of Business (10 000 yuan)	51 771.06	124 019.72	423 783.54	160 232.75	210 112.00
营业总成本(万元)	Total Cost of Business (10 000 yuan)	66 457.59	111 531.18	403 632.77	168 169.40	243 379.00
管理费用(万元)	Administrative Expenses (10 000 yuan)	5 496.21	4 921.85	27 150.60	11 054.71	28 179.00
财务费用(万元)	Financial Expenses (10 000 yuan)	4 371.18	—39.56	40 217.49	6 148.69	27 684.00
营业利润(万元)	Business Profits (10 000 yuan)	—12 754.42	13 656.75	24 699.65	8 359.36	—325.00
投资收益(万元)	Investment Income (10 000 yuan)	1 440.82		—853.61	14 935.47	24 781.00
营业外收入(万元)	Extra-business Revenue (10 000 yuan)	23 878.46	269.68	545.13	609.80	430.00
营业外支出(万元)	Extra-business Expenditures (10 000 yuan)	307.55	1 820.97	3 589.17	145.97	119.00
利润总额(万元)	Total Profits (10 000 yuan)	10 816.49	12 105.46	21 655.62	8 823.20	—14.00
净利润(万元)	Net Profits (10 000 yuan)	10 023.29	10 525.79	16 725.23	8 419.50	—6 076.00
每股收益(元)	Net Income per Share (yuan)	0.05	0.96	0.19	0.11	0.04
每股净资产(元)	Net Assets per Share (yuan)	1.14	8.08	5.65	2.50	2.94
净资产收益率(%)	Net Assets of Yield (%)	4.3	12.6	3.6	4.4	1.3

16—2 续表 2 Continued

计量单位:万元　　(2017 年)　　(10 000 yuan)

指标	Item	新疆赛里木现代农业股份有限公司 XJ Sarimu Modern Agricultural Stock Ltd.,Co	新疆天业节水灌溉股份有限公司 Xj Tianye Water-Saving Irrigated Stock Ltd.,Co.	天康生物技术股份有限公司 Xj Tianye Water—Saving Irrigated Stock Ltd.,Co.	新疆北新路桥集团股份有限公司 Xj Beixin Roadway and Bridge Group Stock Ltd.,Co.	新疆西部牧业股份有限公司 Xi West Animal Husbandry Stock Ltd.,Co.
股票简称	Stock Brief Name	新赛股份 Xinsai Shares	天业节水 Tianye Jieshui	天康生物 Tiankang Shengwu	北新路桥 beixin luqiao	西部牧业 Xibumuye
股票代码	Stock Code	600540	8280	002100	002307	300106
股票上市时间	Listed Time	2004-1-7	2006-2-28	2006-12-26	2009-11-11	2010-8-20
股票上市交易所	Listing Stock Exchange	上交所 SHSE	香港联交所	深交所 SZSE	深交所 SZSE	深交所 SZSE
董事长	President	马晓宏	陈　林	杨　焰	汪　伟	秦　江
总经理	General Manager	刘　江	张　强	成　辉	熊保恒	陈光谱
公司地址	Company Address	新疆博乐市红星路 158 号 158 HongXin RD.Bole,XJ	新疆石河子市经济开发区北三东路 36 号 36 East Road Beisan Economic Development Zone Shihezhi XJ	新疆乌鲁木齐市高新区长春南路 528 号 528 Changchun South RD.Hightnew Zone Urumqi,XJ	新疆乌鲁木齐市高新区高新街 217 号 217 Hight-tech Rd.High-tech Zone,Urumqi,XJ	新疆石河子市开发区北三东路 29—2 号 5—2 Xisi RD. Shihezi,XJ
邮政编码	Post Code	833400	832000	830011	830011	832000
发行时总股本　(万股)	Total Capital Stock　(10 000 share)	15 000.00	51 952.16	6 400.00	18 495.00	11 700.00
国有股	National Stock	10 000.00	20 216.50	3 462.00	11 184.94	5 485.61
法人股	Corporative Stock		9 722.95	698.40	3 010.06	2 604.30
流通股	Circulating Stock	5 000.00	20 240.00	1 600.00	4 750.00	3 000.00
其　他	Other		1 772.71	639.60		610.09
发行募集资金　(万元)	Floated Raised Funds　(10 000 yuan)	31 441.00	24 838.00	17 376.00	37 635.00	35 700.00
年末总股本　(万股)	Stock Capital at the year-end　(10 000 share)	47 092.33	51 952.20	96 338.46	56 137.90	21 133.23
国有股	National Stock	780.00	31 388.59	25 393.85	405.19	
法人股	Corporative Stock					
流通股	Circulating Stock		323.46		0.79	103.35
其　他	Other	46 312.33	20 240.00	70 944.61	55 731.93	21 029.88
年末累计募集资金　(万元)	Capital Raised Year-end　(10 000 yuan)	114 107.00	24 838.00	275 679.53	130 635.00	75 341.95
流动资产合计　(万元)	Circulating Funds　(10 000 yuan)	125 487.00	81 148.00	357 539.00	1 159 735.00	106 551.00
# 存　货	Stock	62 178.00	43 512.00	90 105.00	380 391.00	52 993.00
非流动资产合计　(万元)	Non-Circulating Funds　(10 000 yuan)	100 238.00	19 186.00	229 746.00	792 313.00	135 739.00
资产总计　(万元)	Total Assets　(10 000 yuan)	225 725.00	100 333.00	587 285.00	1 952 048.00	242 290.00
流动负债合计　(万元)	Liquid Liabilities　(10 000 yuan)	161 298.00	32 823.00	176 292.00	1 084 423.00	159 569.00
非流动负债合计　(万元)	Non-Liquid Liabilities　(10 000 yuan)	8 628.00	887.00	105 474.00	543 959.00	11 135.00
股东权益合计　(万元)	Share-holders Equity　(10 000 yuan)	55 798.00	66 623.00	305 518.00	323 666.00	71 585.00
营业总收入　(万元)	Total Revenue of Business　(10 000 yuan)	110 260.00	73 812.00	463 003.00	980 644.00	69 256.00
营业总成本　(万元)	Total Cost of Business　(10 000 yuan)	109 409.00	73 799.00	420 756.00	969 137.00	94 706.00
管理费用　(万元)	Administrative Expenses　(10 000 yuan)	5 379.00	3 151.00	33 970.00	34 719.00	7 807.00
财务费用　(万元)	Financial Expenses　(10 000 yuan)	2 269.00	—162.00	27 382.00	18 353.00	5 181.00
营业利润　(万元)	Business Profits　(10 000 yuan)	2 463.00	219.00	42 575.00	12 639.00	—34 902.00
投资收益　(万元)	Investment Income　(10 000 yuan)	—586.00	—9.00	—532.00	159.00	—8 976.00
营业外收入　(万元)	Extra-business Revenue　(10 000 yuan)	272.00	30.00	358.00	2 177.00	352.00
营业外支出　(万元)	Extra-business Expenditures　(10 000 yuan)	58.00	10.00	72.00	2 622.00	2 405.00
利润总额　(万元)	Total Profits　(10 000 yuan)	2 676.00	239.00	42 861.00	12 193.00	—36 955.00
净利润　(万元)	Net Profits　(10 000 yuan)	2 433.00	188.00	40 378.00	5 045.00	—37 600.00
每股收益　(元)	Net Income per Share　(yuan)	0.02	0.00	0.42	0.09	—1.74
每股净资产　(元)	Net Assets per Share　(yuan)	1.33	1.28	3.10	3.26	2.92
净资产收益率　(%)	Net Assets of Yield　(%)	1.8	0.3	14.7	2.8	—45.8

2018

BING TUAN

第十七篇

科技、教育、文化和卫生

Chapter 17 Science and Technology,Education,
Culture and Public Health

简要说明

本篇资料主要反映兵团科学技术事业、教育文化事业、卫生事业以及兵团9个城市发展基本情况。

一、科技部分主要内容和资料来源：事业单位、公有制企业专业技术人员情况由兵团人力资源和社会保障局提供；兵团、各师科技活动规模、科技人员构成以及科技经费收支情况由兵团科技局提供；兵团规模以上工业企业科技开发基本情况由兵团统计局社会科技贸易统计处提供。

二、教育部分主要包括兵团高等教育、普通中等教育、初等教育以及各级各类成人教育基本情况，主要指标有学校数、在校学生数、招生数、毕业生数、教职工人数及构成情况、各类学校基本状况等，由兵团教育局提供。

三、文化部分主要包括兵团艺术团体、新闻出版以及广播电台、电视台基本情况，由兵团宣传部提供。

四、卫生部分主要反映兵团卫生事业发展情况，包括卫生机构、人员、床位数等，由兵团卫生和计划生育委员会提供。

Brief Introduction

The data in this chapter show the basic conditions of causes and development of XPCC′ s science and technology, health, education, culture and nine cities of XPCC.

1. Main content and sources of data on science and technology.

The data in conditions of scientific and technical personnel in Public Institutions and Public-Owned Enterprises are provided by the Organizational Department of XPCC. Number of institutions of XPCC and division, the situation on scales of scientific and technological activities, composition of scientific and technological personnel, and revenue and expenditure of scientific and technological funds are provided by the Science and Technology Bureau of XPCC. The data on technical development of above designated size industrial enterprise are collected from the Comprehensive Statistical Reporting on Technical Activities of Industrial Enterprise of XPCC, which are provided by the Society Science Trade Statistical Section of the Statistics Bureau of XPCC.

2.The data on education cover mainly the situation on higher Education, regular secondary education, primary education and adult education of various types and at various levels. The main indicators cover number of schools, number of student enrollment, number of new student enrollment, number of graduates, number of staff and workers, number and composition of teachers, basic conditions on schools by level and type, which are provided by the Education Bureau of XPCC.

3. The data on culture cover mainly the basic conditions on arts group, news and publication, and radio and TV broadcasting stations, which are provided by the Propaganda Department of XPCC.

4.The data on public health cover mainly the basic conditions on development of XPCC′ s public health, including number of health institutions, beds, persons and etc, which are provided by the Health and Family Planning Commission of XPCC.

17—1 科技活动基本情况

Basic Statistics on Scientific and Technological Activities

指　　标	Item	2016	2017
从事科技活动人员情况　（人）	**Personnel Engaged in Scientific and Technological Activities　(person)**		
从业人员总数	Number of Employed Persons	1 166	1 135
科技活动人员	Persons Engaged in Scientific and Technological Activities	948	919
# 大学本科及以上学历	University Graguate or above	721	747
按工作性质分	By employment character		
科技管理人员	Scientific and manage	190	136
课题活动人员	Subject Activities	621	607
科技服务人员	Scientific and Technological Service	137	76
按学历分	By Records		
博　士	Doctor's Degree	30	28
硕　士	Master's Degree	285	280
本　科	Regular College Course	406	439
其　他	Others	227	144
按职称分	By Records and the Title of a Technical Post		
高　级	Senior	345	372
中　级	Intermediate	357	357
其　他	Other	246	140
科技活动课题情况	**Subjects of Scientific and Technological Activities**		
课题个数　（个）	Subject　(pcs)	487	487
# R&D 课题	Subject of R&D	315	333
课题经费内部支出　（万元）	Inner Expenditure for Subject　(10 000 yuan)	12 532	16 107
# 政府资金	Government Funds	10 934	15 042
# R&D 课题	Subject of R&D	6 924	12 681
课题投入人员　（人年）	Personnel for Subjects　(Person-Year)	775	731
# R&D	R&D	490	696
# 外聘流动研究人员	Hired Transient Personnel		3
# 在读研究生	Graduate Student Enrollment	52	36
经费收入总额　（万元）	Total Fund revenue for S&T Subject　(10 000 yuan)	35 739	33 773
经费支出总额　（万元）	Total Expenditure　(10 000 yuan)	35 817	34 612
科技产出及成果情况	**Statistics on S&T Outputs and Results**		
发表科技论文　（篇）	Scientific Papers Issued　(piece)	434	389
出版科技著作　（种）	Publication on Science and Technology　(kind)	2	9
专利申请受理数　（件）	Number of Patents Application Accepted　(piece)	200	132
# 发明专利	Inventions	82	80
专利申请授权数　（件）	Number of Patents Application Granted　(piece)	130	79
# 发明专利	Inventions	37	33

注：科技活动情况仅包括兵、师两级独立科研机构情况。
Note: Scientific and technological activities only include independnet science research institutions at the levels of XPCC and divisions and exclude datd at farm level.

17—2 国有科学研究与开发机构基本情况

Basic Statistics on State-owned Scientific Research and Development Institutions

指　标		Item		2016	2017
机构基本情况		**Basic Statistics on Institutions**			
机构数	（个）	Number of R&D Institutions	（unit）	18	18
# 中央属		Subordinated to Central Level			
地方属		Subordinated to Local Level		18	18
研究与试验发展（R&D）投入情况		**Statistics on R&D Input**			
R&D 人员	（人）	R&D Personnel	（person）	781	746
R&D 人员全时当量	（人年）	Full-time Equivalent of R&D Personnel	（Person-year）	717	646
# 基础研究		Basic Research		73	
应用研究		Applied Research		109	
试验发展		Experimental Development		307	
R&D 经费内部支出	（万元）	Intramural Expenditure on R&D	（10 000 yuan）	21 001	20 543
# 基础研究		Basic Research		3 172	1 891
应用研究		Applied Research		9 018	8 541
试验发展		Experimental Development		6 517	8 244
# 政府资金		Government Appropriation Funds		15 060	13 631
企业资金		Self-raised Funds by Enterprises		122	62
R&D 项目（课题）情况		**Statistics on R&D Topics**			
R&D 项目（课题）数	（项）	Projects of R&D	（item）	315	333
R&D 项目（课题）人员全时当量	（人年）	Participants	（Person-year）	490	696
R&D 项目（课题）经费内部支出	（万元）	Intramural Expenditure	（10 000 yuan）	6 924	12 681
科技产出及成果情况		**Statistics on S&T Outputs and Results**			
发表科技论文	（篇）	Scientific Papers Issued	（piece）	434	389
# 国外发表		Published in Foreign Periodicals		2	
出版科技著作	（种）	Publication on Science and Technology	（kind）	2	9
专利申请受理数	（件）	Number of Patents Applications Accepted	（piece）	200	132
# 发明专利		Inventions		82	80
专利申请授权数	（件）	Number of Patents Applications Granted	（piece）	130	79
# 发明专利		Inventions		37	33

17—3　国有科学研究与开发机构经费及固定资产情况

Statistics on Fund of State-owned Scientific Research and Development Institutions

计量单位:万元　　　　(2017 年)　　　　(10 000 yuan)

指　　标	Item	合　计 Total
科技活动收入	**S&T Activities Revenue**	**24 167**
政府资金	Government Funds	18 491
财政拨款	Finance Appropriate Fouds	10 165
承担政府科研项目收入	Income form Government A&T Item	8 000
其　他	Other	326
非政府资金	Non—Government Funds	1 708
技术性收入	Technique Income	1 479
生产经营收入	**Production and Operation Revenue**	**4 123**
其他收入	**Other Revenue**	**9 856**
科技经费内部支出	**Total Inner Expenditure for S&T Activities**	**31 053**
科技经费日常支出	Total Daily Expenditure for S&T Activities	27 642
人员劳务费	Personnel Work fee	13 111
设备购置费	Equipment Purchase Fee	3 868
其他日常支出	Other Daily Expenditure for S&T Activities	10 285
科研基本建设	S&T Infrastructure	3 411
生产经营支出	**Production and Operation Expenditure**	**3 306**
其他支出	**Other**	**6 007**
年末固定资产原价	**Fixed Assets**	**39 196**
科研仪器设备	Apparatus of Scientific Research	11 067
# 进　口	Import	2 094

17—4　事业单位、公有制企业专业技术人员及构成

Number of Scientific and Technical Personnel and its Composition in Public Institutions and Public Owned Enterprise

计量单位:万人　　　　(2017 年)　　　　(10 000 persons)

指　　标	Item	事业单位 年末人数(人) Personnel at the Year—end(person)	事业单位 构成(%) Composition(%)	公有制企业 年末人数(人) Personnel at the Year—end(person)	公有制企业 构成(%) Composition(%)
专业技术人员合计	**Total**	**51 666**	**100.0**	**58 878**	**100.0**
工程技术人员	Engineering	1 516	2.9	20 322	34.5
农业技术人员	Agriculture	973	1.9	11 935	20.3
卫生技术人员	Health Care	16 614	32.2	397	0.7
教学人员	Teaching	28 490	55.1	372	0.6
其他人员	The Others	4 073	7.9	25 852	43.9

17—5 各师事业单位专业技术人员及构成

Number of Scientific and Technical Personnel and its Composition in Public Institutions

计量单位:人 (2017 年) (person)

单　位	Unit	年末专业技术人员合计 Total Professional and Technical Personnel at the Year-end	#工　程 Engineering	#农　业 Agriculture	#卫　生 Health Care	#教　学 Teaching
总　计	**Total**	**51 666**	**1 516**	**973**	**16 614**	**28 490**
一　师	Division 1	3 436	202	72	1 178	2 609
二　师	Division 2	2 390	116	34	1 374	2 145
三　师	Division 3	2 646	121	64	1 052	2 733
四　师	Division 4	2 617	42	40	1 416	2 310
五　师	Division 5	2 162	64	64	893	1 811
六　师	Division 6	3 702	156	141	1 930	2 895
七　师	Division 7	2 376	62	102	1 195	1 967
八　师	Division 8	6 172	383	146	2 606	5 672
九　师	Division 9	1 242	48	50	702	945
十　师	Division 10	1 628	72	83	766	1 216
十一师	Division 11	847	52		238	793
十二师	Division 12	583	78	30	245	444
十三师	Division 13	1 441	44	125	713	1 083
十四师	Division 14	470	23	16	171	579
兵团直属	Directly under XPCC	19 954	53	6	2 135	1 288

17—6 各师公有制企业专业技术人员数

Number of Professional and Technical Personnel in Public Owned Enterprise by Division

计量单位:人 (2017 年) (person)

单　位	Unit	年末专业技术人员合计 Total Professional and Technical Personnel at the Year-end	#工　程 Engineering	#农　业 Agriculture	#卫　生 Health Care	#教　学 Teaching
总　计	**Total**	**58 878**	**20 322**	**11 935**	**397**	**372**
一　师	Division 1	5 892	1 365	1 749	38	51
二　师	Division 2	4 588	1 317	1 326	112	50
三　师	Division 3	1 927	559	672	18	
四　师	Division 4	5 296	1 033	911	3	46
五　师	Division 5	2 734	528	770	5	19
六　师	Division 6	4 814	463	1 826	14	17
七　师	Division 7	4 785	1 730	1 093	6	25
八　师	Division 8	11 865	4 592	1 941	137	136
九　师	Division 9	1 742	261	434	1	
十　师	Division 10	2 226	410	535	33	12
十一师	Division 11	7 600	5 807	7	2	
十二师	Division 12	2 261	561	327	4	9
十三师	Division 13	1 334	464	272	6	5
十四师	Division 14	381	219	55	1	
兵团直属	Directly under XPCC	1 433	1 013	17	17	2

17—7 规模以上工业企业研发活动基本情况

Basic Statistics on R&D Activities of Industrial Enterprise above Designated Size

（2017 年）

指标		Item		规模以上工业企业 Industrial Enterprise above Designated Size	#大中型工业企业 Large-Scale and Medium-Scale Industrial Enterprise
企业基本情况		**Statistics on Industrial Enterprises**			
企业数	（个）	Number of Enterprises	（unit）	841	110
# 有 R&D 活动企业数		Number of Enterprises Having R&D Activities		92	34
# 有研发机构企业数		Number of Enterprises Having R&D Institutions		40	17
研究与试验发展(R&D)活动情况		**Statitstics on R&D Activities**			
R&D 人员	（人）	R&D Personnel	（Person）	3 178	2 482
R&D 人员全时当量	（人年）	Full—time Equivalent of R&D Personnel	（man—years）	1 530	1 317
R&D 经费内部支出	（万元）	Expenditure on R&D	（10 000 yuan）	132 633	121 728
R&D 项目数	（项）	R&D Projects	（item）	375	274
企业办 R&D 机构情况		**Statistics on R&D Institutions**			
机构数	（个）	Number of R&D Institutions	（unit）	48	23
机构人员数	（人）	R&D Personnel	（person）	1 695	1 381
机构经费支出	（万元）	Expenditure on R&D	（10 000 yuan）	29 290	26 212
新产品开发及生产情况		**Statitstics on New Products Development and Production**			
新产品开发项目数	（项）	Number of New Products	（unit）	354	235
新产品开发经费支出	（万元）	Expenditure on New Products Development	（10 000 yuan）	123 924	110 398
新产品销售收入	（万元）	Sales Revenue of New Products	（10 000 yuan）	536 319	480 454
# 新产品出口		Export		6 256	4 856
专利情况		**Statistics on Patents**			
专利申请数	（件）	Patent Applications	（piece）	504	286
# 发明专利		Inventions		178	119
有效发明专利数	（件）	Inventions In Force	（piece）	421	273
技术获取和技术改造情况		**Statistics on Technology Acquisition and Technology Reconstruction**			
引进境外技术经费支出	（万元）	Expenditure for Acquisition of Foreign Technology	（10 000 yuan）		
引进技术消化吸收经费支出	（万元）	Expenditure for Assimilation of Technology	（10 000 yuan）		
购买境内技术经费支出	（万元）	Expenditure for Purchase of Domestic Technology	（10 000 yuan）	810	
技术改造经费支出	（万元）	Expenditure for Technical Renovation	（10 000 yuan）	17 674	17 221

17—8 各师规模以上工业企业研发活动基本情况

Basic Statistics on R&D Activities of Industrial Enterprise above Designated Size by Division

(2017 年)

单 位	Unit	有R&D活动企业数（个）Number of Enterprises Having R&D Activities (unit)	# 大中型工业企业 Large-Scale and Medium-Scale Industrial Enterprise	有研发机构企业数（个）Number of Enterprises Having R&D Institutions (unit)	# 大中型工业企业 Large-Scale and Medium-Scale Industrial Enterprise
总 计	**Total**	**92**	**34**	**40**	**17**
一 师	Division 1	16	4	3	1
二 师	Division 2	8	3	3	1
三 师	Division 3	2	1	2	1
四 师	Division 4	10	5	3	2
五 师	Division 5	2	1		
六 师	Division 6	6	2		
七 师	Division 7	3		3	2
八 师	Division 8	20	12	13	8
九 师	Division 9	2	1		
十 师	Division 10	6			
十一师	Division 11				
十二师	Division 12	6	3	4	2
十三师	Division 13	10	1	9	
十四师	Division 14				
兵团直属	Directly under XPCC	1	1		

单 位	Unit	R&D人员全时当量（人年）Full—time Equivalent of R&D Personnel (man—years)	# 大中型工业企业 Large-Scale and Medium-Scale Industrial Enterprise	R&D经费内部支出（万元）Expenditure on R&D(10 000 yuan)	# 大中型工业企业 Large-Scale and Medium-Scale Industrial Enterprise
总 计	**Total**	**1 530**	**1 317**	**132 633**	**121 728**
一 师	Division 1	39	14	2 457	1 786
二 师	Division 2	82	46	2 555	1 535
三 师	Division 3	3	2	81	21
四 师	Division 4	80	70	2 921	1 976
五 师	Division 5	5	4	90	75
六 师	Division 6	71	60	18 890	16 906
七 师	Division 7	5		449	
八 师	Division 8	908	843	78 216	76 565
九 师	Division 9	1	1	46	18
十 师	Division 10	8		667	
十一师	Division 11				
十二师	Division 12	93	58	3 160	2 195
十三师	Division 13	16	1	2 850	400
十四师	Division 14				
兵团直属	Directly under XPCC	219	219	20 252	20 252

17－8 续表 Continued

(2017 年)

单 位	Unit	R&D项目数（项）R&D Projects (Item)	# 大中型工业企业 Large-Scale and Medium-Scale Industrial Enterprise	机构经费支出（万元）Expenditure on R&D (10 000 yuan)	# 大中型工业企业 Large-Scale and Medium-Scale Industrial Enterprise
总 计	**Total**	**375**	**274**	**29 290**	**26 212**
一 师	Division 1	28	7	631	220
二 师	Division 2	27	10	367	99
三 师	Division 3	2	1	89	46
四 师	Division 4	14	9	6 328	6 261
五 师	Division 5	2	1		
六 师	Division 6	11	5		
七 师	Division 7	3		427	301
八 师	Division 8	129	109	17 326	16 146
九 师	Division 9	2	1		
十 师	Division 10	12			
十一师	Division 11				
十二师	Division 12	25	20	3 528	3 140
十三师	Division 13	10	1	594	
十四师	Division 14				
兵团直属	Directly under XPCC	110	110		

单 位	Unit	新产品开发经费支出（万元）Expenditure on New Products Development (10 000 yuan)	# 大中型工业企业 Large-Scale and Medium-Scale Industrial Enterprise	专利申请数（件）Patent Applications (Piece)	# 大中型工业企业 Large-Scale and Medium-Scale Industrial Enterprise
总 计	**Total**	**123 924**	**110 398**	**504**	**286**
一 师	Division 1	8 197	7 276	16	2
二 师	Division 2	2 461	847	49	2
三 师	Division 3	429	116		
四 师	Division 4	2 800	1 772	10	6
五 师	Division 5	15			
六 师	Division 6	16 001	14 922	84	12
七 师	Division 7	4 916	4 754	5	
八 师	Division 8	56 289	53 449	307	238
九 师	Division 9	112	24		
十 师	Division 10	2 789	12	2	
十一师	Division 11				
十二师	Division 12	6 715	5 295	6	1
十三师	Division 13	1 270			
十四师	Division 14				
兵团直属	Directly under XPCC	21 931	21 931	25	25

17—9 教育事业基本情况

Basic Statistics on Education

指标	Item	1990	1995	2000	2005
学校数 (所)	**Number of Schools (unit)**				
普通高等学校	Regular Institutions of Higher Education	5	5	2	4
成人高等学校	Adult Education Schools	7	7	3	2
中等职业学校	Secondary Vocational Schools	45	57	42	34
普通中等专业学校	Specialized Secondary Schools	6	7	8	20
成人中等专业学校	Secondary Schools for Adults	33	38	23	3
技工学校	Technical Schools	6	12	11	11
普通中学	Regular Secondary Schools	477	330	293	277
高　中	Senior Secondary Schools	214	127	95	77
初　中	Junior Secondary Schools	263	203	198	200
职业中学	Vocational Secondary Schools	52	42	25	6
小　学	Primary Schools	801	541	463	317
盲聋哑学校	Special Schools	1	1		
幼儿园	Kindergartens	510	223	255	177
毕业生数 (人)	**Graduates (person)**				
普通高等学校	Regular Institutions of Higher Education	1 584	2 186	2 101	6 136
成人高等学校	Adult Education Schools	1 290	1 427	934	6 681
中等职业学校	Secondary Vocational Schools	7 783	7 058	9 828	6 057
普通中等专业学校	Specialized Secondary Schools	629	931	2 178	3 910
成人中等专业学校	Secondary Schools for Adults	5 774	3 513	5 484	450
技工学校	Technical Schools	1 380	2 614	2 166	1 697
普通中学	Regular Secondary Schools	77 066	34 889	30 380	60 152
高　中	Senior Secondary Schools	25 621	10 419	9 322	16 420
初　中	Junior Secondary Schools	51 445	24 470	21 068	43 732
职业中学	Vocational Secondary Schools	7 641	4 064	3 156	262
小　学	Primary Schools	40 263	23 840	41 124	49 187
盲聋哑学校	Special Schools	10	15		
幼儿园	Kindergartens	10 914	33 665	28 330	24 933
招生数 (人)	**New Student Enrollment (person)**				
普通高等学校	Regular Institutions of Higher Education	1 750	2 646	3 700	9 428
成人高等学校	Adult Education Schools	2 072	2 843	3 190	5 351
中等职业学校	Secondary Vocational Schools	8 140	13 208	6 288	11 604
普通中等专业学校	Specialized Secondary Schools	917	1 751	2 458	7 824
成人中等专业学校	Secondary Schools for Adults	5 995	8 872	1 114	300
技工学校	Technical Schools	1 228	2 585	2 716	3 480
普通中学	Regular Secondary Schools	61 354	35 709	52 218	70 952
高　中	Senior Secondary Schools	22 617	11 618	10 814	21 748
初　中	Junior Secondary Schools	38 737	24 091	41 404	49 204
职业中学	Vocational Secondary Schools	10 435	4 063	2 386	103
小　学	Primary Schools	26 665	45 741	45 671	39 655
盲聋哑学校	Special Schools	16	10		
幼儿园	Kindergartens	16 288	22 100	35 070	28 221
在校学生 (人)	**Student Enrollment (person)**				
普通高等学校	Regular Institutions of Higher Education	5 827	8 568	11 735	30 663
成人高等学校	Adult Education Schools	5 723	8 282	7 652	12 286
中等职业学校	Secondary Vocational Schools	18 853	25 632	18 181	27 117
普通中等专业学校	Specialized Secondary Schools	2 621	4 327	7 820	19 563
成人中等专业学校	Secondary Schools for Adults	12 725	16 940	5 708	468
技工学校	Technical Schools	3 507	4 365	4 653	7 086
普通中学	Regular Secondary Schools	200 822	107 491	129 812	206 440
高　中	Senior Secondary Schools	77 550	34 204	29 298	59 816
初　中	Junior Secondary Schools	123 272	73 287	100 514	146 624
职业中学	Vocational Secondary Schools	24 337	9 565	6 897	381
小　学	Primary Schools	199 624	209 351	288 707	269 811
盲聋哑学校	Special Schools	107	80		
幼儿园	Kindergartens	30 681	56 210	57 603	49 676
教职工数 (人)	**Number of Teachers and Staff (person)**				
普通高等学校	Regular Institutions of Higher Education	4 473	4 479	3 138	4 023
成人高等学校	Adult Education Schools	664	563	901	938
中等职业学校	Secondary Vocational Schools	933	1 615	1 401	2 417
普通中等专业学校	Specialized Secondary Schools	436	522	550	1 662
成人中等专业学校	Secondary Schools for Adults	1 380	1 242	1 624	201
技工学校	Technical Schools	497	1 093	851	755
普通中学	Regular Secondary Schools	22 126	15 953	13 952	17 548
高　中	Senior Secondary Schools	5 253	3 164	2 506	
初　中	Junior Secondary Schools	9 040	6 650	6 841	
职业中学	Vocational Secondary Schools	1 750	1 324	695	79
小　学	Primary Schools	14 245	14 122	16 791	17 545
盲聋哑学校	Special Schools	43	21		
幼儿园	Kindergartens	2 180	3 401	3 762	2 882

17－9 续表 Continued

指 标	Item	2010	2015	2016	2017
学校数 (所)	**Number of Schools (unit)**				
普通高等学校	Regular Institutions of Higher Education	4	6	6	6
成人高等学校	Adult Education Schools	2	2	2	2
中等职业学校	Secondary Vocational Schools	32	31	31	30
普通中等专业学校	Specialized Secondary Schools	21	20	20	19
成人中等专业学校	Secondary Schools for Adults	1	1	1	1
技工学校	Technical Schools	10	10	10	10
普通中学	Regular Secondary Schools	251	247	249	237
高 中	Senior Secondary Schools	51	47	46	47
初 中	Junior Secondary Schools	200	200	203	190
职业中学	Vocational Secondary Schools	1			
小 学	Primary Schools	85	50	54	55
盲聋哑学校	Special Schools				
幼儿园	Kindergartens	189	257	274	281
毕业生数 (人)	**Graduates (person)**				
普通高等学校	Regular Institutions of Higher Education	10 243	12 449	13 604	13 662
成人高等学校	Adult Education Schools	3 463	6 813	6 545	7 543
中等职业学校	Secondary Vocational Schools	18 787	15 088	11 257	16 460
普通中等专业学校	Specialized Secondary Schools	10 374	9 299	8 478	7 145
成人中等专业学校	Secondary Schools for Adults	3 226	2 258		1 331
技工学校	Technical Schools	5 187	3 531	2 779	7 984
普通中学	Regular Secondary Schools	62 410	49 629	47 483	45 689
高 中	Senior Secondary Schools	20 368	18 927	18 320	17 899
初 中	Junior Secondary Schools	42 042	30 702	29 163	27 790
职业中学	Vocational Secondary Schools	81			
小 学	Primary Schools	40 186	27 596	27 106	26 902
盲聋哑学校	Special Schools				
幼儿园	Kindergartens	21 329	22 796	24 566	25 604
招生数 (人)	**New Student Enrollment (person)**				
普通高等学校	Regular Institutions of Higher Education	13 370	14 873	14 959	15 014
成人高等学校	Adult Education Schools	3 909	6 208	8 196	7 944
中等职业学校	Secondary Vocational Schools	20 878	12 895	12 935	9 913
普通中等专业学校	Specialized Secondary Schools	12 110	8 899	7 678	7 576
成人中等专业学校	Secondary Schools for Adults	3 000	2 413	2 288	1 736
技工学校	Technical Schools	5 768	1 583	2 969	601
普通中学	Regular Secondary Schools	63 429	47 296	47 171	47 631
高 中	Senior Secondary Schools	20 921	18 843	18 898	18 275
初 中	Junior Secondary Schools	42 508	28 453	28 273	29 356
职业中学	Vocational Secondary Schools				
小 学	Primary Schools	33 255	25 647	26 398	27 476
盲聋哑学校	Special Schools				
幼儿园	Kindergartens	28 130	28 423	31 234	35 323
在校学生 (人)	**Student Enrollment (person)**				
普通高等学校	Regular Institutions of Higher Education	46 776	51 595	52 843	53 758
成人高等学校	Adult Education Schools	10 857	22 206	23 303	21 237
中等职业学校	Secondary Vocational Schools	51 373	36 744	36 828	28 183
普通中等专业学校	Specialized Secondary Schools	30 120	24 946	21 879	20 926
成人中等专业学校	Secondary Schools for Adults	5 500	4 569	6 552	6 243
技工学校	Technical Schools	15 753	7 229	8 397	1 014
普通中学	Regular Secondary Schools	190 362	141 730	138 672	138 890
高 中	Senior Secondary Schools	59 956	55 166	55 014	54 910
初 中	Junior Secondary Schools	130 406	86 564	83 658	83 980
职业中学	Vocational Secondary Schools	178			
小 学	Primary Schools	217 600	160 032	160 350	162 228
盲聋哑学校	Special Schools				
幼儿园	Kindergartens	51 313	61 642	67 505	78 161
教职工数 (人)	**Number of Teachers and Staff (person)**				
普通高等学校	Regular Institutions of Higher Education	4 201	4 605	4 654	4 627
成人高等学校	Adult Education Schools	948	924	916	924
中等职业学校	Secondary Vocational Schools	3 158	2 629	2 589	2 370
普通中等专业学校	Specialized Secondary Schools	1 968	1 554	1 491	1 321
成人中等专业学校	Secondary Schools for Adults	84	84	84	151
技工学校	Technical Schools	1 190	1 075	1 098	1 049
普通中学	Regular Secondary Schools	17 589	16 267	16 196	15 979
高 中	Senior Secondary Schools		4 897	4 923	5 072
初 中	Junior Secondary Schools		11 370	11 273	10 907
职业中学	Vocational Secondary Schools	23			
小 学	Primary Schools	15 568	13 187	13 179	13 252
盲聋哑学校	Special Schools				
幼儿园	Kindergartens	3 253	5 542	6 013	6 784

17—10 各级各类学校基本情况

Basic Statistics on Schools by Level and Type

计量单位:人　　(2017 年)　　(person)

指　标	Item	校数(所) Number of Schools (unit)	毕业生数 Graduates	招生数 New Student Enrollment	在校学生数 Student Erollment	教职工数 Staff and Teachers	#专任教师 Full-Time Teachers
普通高等学校	Regular Institutions of Higher Education	6	13 662	15 014	53 758	4 627	3 295
成人高等学校	Adult Institutions of Higher Education	2	7 543	7 944	21 237	924	651
# 普通高校成教院	Adult Colleges of Institutions of Higher Education	2	6 495	7 039	19 103		
普通中等专业学校	Regular Specialized Secondary Schools	19	7 145	7 576	20 926	1 321	959
成人中等专业学校	Specialized Secondary Schools for Adults	1	1 331	1 736	6 243	151	70
技工学校	Technical Schools	10	7 984	601	1 014	1 049	693
普通中学	Regular Secondary Schools	237	45 689	47 631	138 890	15 979	13 274
高　中	Senior Secondary Schools	47	17 899	18 275	54 910	5 072	4 271
初中(含九年一贯制)	Junior Secondary Schools	190	27 790	29 356	83 980	10 907	9 003
小　学	Primary Schools	55	26 902	27 476	162 228	13 252	11 458
幼儿园	Kindergartens	281	25 604	35 323	78 161	6 784	3 970

注:本表普通高等学校毕业生数、招生数、在校学生数包括研究生数。
Note: Data in this table on regular institutions of higher education include postgraduates and other tables.

17—11 普通高等学校研究生情况

Postgraduates of Regular Institutions of Higher Education

计量单位:人　　(2017 年)　　(person)

指　标	Item	毕业生数 Graduates	授硕士学位的 With Master's Degree	招生数 New Student Enrollment	在校生数 Student Enrollment
总　计	**Total**	**1 134**	**1 195**	**1 638**	**4 306**
# 女	Female	613	632	930	2331
博　士	Doctor's Degree	10	24	85	334
# 女	Female	5	13	41	158
硕　士	Master's Degree	1 124	1 171	1 553	3 972
# 女	Female	608	619	889	2173

17—12 普通本科、专科分专业学生数

Number of Students in Undergraduate and Junior Colleges by Field of Study

计量单位:人 (2017 年) (person)

指 标	Item	毕业生数 Graduates	#授予学位数 Degrees Conferred	招生数 New Student Enrollment	在校学生数 Student Enrollment	一年级 Grade One	二年级 Grade Two	三年级 Grade Three	四年级 Grade Four	五年级及以上 Grade Five and above
总 计	**Tota**	**12 528**	**7 841**	**13 376**	**49 452**	**13 693**	**13 707**	**13 252**	**8 311**	**489**
# 女	Female	6 063	4 013	6 160	24 202	6 365	6 728	6 481	4 330	298
本 科	Undergraduate Courses	8 666	7 841	9 153	35 836	9 470	8 766	8 800	8 311	489
# 女	Female	4 242	4 013	4 494	18 237	4 699	4 500	4 410	4 330	298
专科(含五年制高职)	Specialized Courses	3 862		4 223	13 616	4 223	4 941	4 452		
# 女	Female	1 821		1 666	5 965	1 666	2 228	2 071		

17—13 普通高等学校现有校舍面积

Floor Space of Present Buildings of Regular Institutions of Higher Education

计量单位:平方米 (2017 年) (sq.m)

单 位	unit	校舍建筑面积 Floor Space of Buildings	教学用房 Teaching Buildings	#教 室 Classrooms	#图书馆 Library	#实验室及实习场所 Laboratories and Fieldwork Buildings	生活用房 Life and Welfare Building	#学生宿舍 Dormitories	#教工宿舍 Teachers' Quarters	#教工住宅 Teachers' House
总 计	**Total**	**2 002 048**	**815 328**	**279 695**	**106 996**	**340 009**	**672 644**	**486 990**	**25 778**	**390 181**
石河子大学	Shihezi University	1 169 795	452 488	155 703	55 132	181 993	383 972	280 095	22 098	258 978
塔里木大学	Tarim University	526 821	200 145	51 314	36 000	88 308	186 045	120 224	3 600	113 716
石河子大学科技学院	The Technological College of Shihezi University	32 414	19 488	10 077	6 718	2 693	9 914	7 413	80	
兵团警官高等专科学校	XPCC Police Officer Junior College	58 539	16 815	5 394	2 100	8 040	15 409	13 231		12 205
石河子职业技术学院	Shihezi Worker's University	128 320	82 685	46 265	2 048	34 373	44 293	42 918		
兵团兴新职业技术学院	XPCC Xingxin Workers' University	86 160	43 706	10 941	4 998	24 603	33 010	23 110		5 283

17—14 普通、成人高等学校教师专业职务情况

Teacher Professional Titles of Regular and Adult Institutions of Higher Education

计量单位：人 （2017 年） (person)

单 位	Unit	合 计 Total	# 女 性 Female	教 授 Professors	副教授 Associate Professors	讲 师 Lecturers	助 教 Assistants	教 员 Instructors
普通高等学校	**Regular Institutions of Higher Education**	**3 295**	**1 647**	**352**	**1 213**	**1 403**	**201**	**126**
石河子大学	Shihezi University	1 749	877	247	628	761	58	55
塔里木大学	Tarim University	885	422	98	421	314	34	18
石河子大学科技学院	The Technological College of	25	6	3	14	5	3	
兵团警官高等专科学校	XPCC Police Junior College	98	49	1	28	42	5	22
石河子职业技术学院	Shihezi Vocational and Technical University	355	197	3	72	204	61	15
兵团兴新职业技术学院	XPCC Xingxin Workers' University	183	96		50	77	40	16
成人高等学校	**Adult Institutions of Higher Education**	**651**	**342**	**26**	**173**	**204**	**203**	**45**
兵团教育学院	XPCC Educational College	248	116	13	110	68	57	
兵团电视大学	XPCC TV University	403	226	13	63	136	146	45

17—15 普通中等专业学校教师专业职务情况

Teacher Professional Titles of Regular Specialized Secondary Schools

计量单位：人 （2017 年） (person)

单 位	Unit	合 计 Total	# 女 性 Female	高级教师 Senior Lecturers	讲 师 Lecturers	助理讲师 Assistants Lecturers	教员（含无职称） Instructors (Without Professional Titles)
总 计	**total**	**959**	**550**	**163**	**311**	**256**	**229**
一师阿拉尔职业技术学校	Alaer Vocational and Technical School of Division1	86	52	11	45	19	11
二师华山职业技术学校	Huashan vocational and Technical School of Division 2	78	45	11	30	23	14
三师图木舒克职业技术学校	The Vocational and Technical School of Tumushuke of Division 3	48	19		7	17	24
四师伊犁职业技术学校	Yili Vocational and Technical School of Division4	38	26	7	6	15	10
五师博乐职业技术学校	Bole Vocational and Technical School of Division5	38	22	11	15	12	
六师五家渠职业技术学校	Wujiaqu Vocational Middle School of Division 6	79	50	3	27	30	19
七师奎屯职业技术学校	Kuytun Vocational and Technical School of Division 7	46	26	7	8	11	20
石河子文化艺术学校	Shihezi Culture and Art School	26	17	8	13	2	3
石河子卫生学校	Shihezi Health School	58	47	13	14	12	19
九师中等职业技术学校	The Vocational and Technical School of Division 9	31	22	10	10	5	6
十师北屯职业技术学校	Beitun Vocational and Technical School ofDivision 10	38	18	7	5	12	14
十一师职业技术学校	The Vocational and Technical School of Construction Division 11	71	50	12	37	12	10
十二师职业技术学校	The Vocational and Technical School of Division 12	23	19	5	12	6	
十三师职业技术学校	The Vocational and Technical School of Division 13	32	17	4	11	2	15
十四师职业技术学校	The Vocational and Technical School of Division 14	32	10		5	7	20
石河子工程技术学校	Shihezi Engineering Technique School	119	49	23	25	41	30
石河子大学护士学校	The Nurse School of Shihezi University	39	27	8	9	11	11
兵团竞技体育运动学校	XPCC Athletics school	9	1	1	2	4	2
兵团民族师范学校	The Nationality Teachers' School	68	33	22	30	15	1

17—16 按专业职务、年龄分中小学教师数

Teachers of Primary and Secondary Schools by Professional Title and Age

计量单位：人 （2017 年） (person)

指 标	Item	合 计 Total	24 岁以下 Under 24	25—29 岁 Between 25—29	30—34 岁 Between 30—34	35—39 岁 Between 35—39	40—44 岁 Between 40—44	45—49 岁 Between 45—49	50—54 岁 Between 50—54	55—59 岁 Between 55—59	60 岁以上 above 60
高中教师	**Teachers of Secondary Schools**	**4 271**	**283**	**743**	**908**	**845**	**491**	**413**	**468**	**120**	
# 女	Female	2 417	173	463	559	448	278	254	236	6	
# 少数民族	Minority Nationality	406	12	77	105	71	65	43	27	6	
高 级	Senior	1 046			9	85	192	286	374	100	
一 级	Level 1	1 323		23	329	523	242	101	86	19	
二 级	Level 2	1 307	52	410	524	231	55	26	8	1	
三 级	Level 3	15	9	5	1						
未评级	Not Evaluated	580	222	305	45	6	2				
初中教师	**Teachers of Junior Secondary Schools**	**9 003**	**453**	**1 445**	**1 352**	**1 589**	**1 424**	**1 251**	**1 205**	**283**	**1**
# 女	Female	5 769	320	959	897	1 038	920	868	762	5	
# 少数民族	Minority Nationality	955	33	179	172	178	156	140	78	19	
高 级	Senior	1 608				46	269	450	691	151	1
一 级	Level 1	3 303		20	293	840	928	644	463	115	
二 级	Level 2	2 460	16	530	817	656	220	154	50	17	
三 级	Level 3	38		16	15	1	5	1			
未评级	Not Evaluated	1 594	437	879	227	46	2	2	1		
小学教师	**Teachers of Primary Schools**	**11 458**	**637**	**1 634**	**1 396**	**1 781**	**2 181**	**1 955**	**1 590**	**281**	**3**
# 女	Female	8 836	485	1 239	1 114	1 413	1 719	1 603	1 257	6	
# 少数民族	Minority Nationality	1 980	84	249	262	406	434	301	203	41	
中教高级	Senior for Secondary Education	297			1	6	27	46	177	40	
小学高级	Senior	5 232		15	208	746	1 429	1 445	1 197	189	3
一 级	Level 1	3 516	22	466	811	850	675	439	204	49	
二 级	Level 2	287	5	87	94	52	22	13	11	3	
三 级	Level 3	14		5	2	2	5				
未评级	Not Evaluated	2 112	610	1 061	280	125	23	12	1		

17－17 普通中小学及幼儿园专任教师学历情况

Teacher Records of Formal Schooling of Regular and Secondary Schools and Vocational Middel Schools and Kindergartens

（2017 年）

指　　标	Item	专任教师人数（人） Full-time Teachers (person)	#少数民族 Minority Nationality	专任教师学历合格率（%） Qualified Rate of Schooling Records of Full-time Teacher (%)	#少数民族 Minority Nationality
高　中	**Senior Secondary Schools**	**4 271**	**404**		
大学本科毕业及以上	Graduation from Universities and above	4 237	392	99.20	97.03
大学专科毕业	Graduation from Junior College	33	12	0.77	2.97
高中阶段毕业	Graducation from Senior Secondary Schools	1		0.02	
高中毕业阶段以下	Graduation from Senior Secondary Schools and below				
初　中	**Junior Secondary Schools**	**9 003**	**956**		
大学本科毕业及以上	Graduation from Universities and above	8 162	717	90.66	75.00
大学专科毕业	Graduation from Junior College	840	238	9.33	24.90
高中阶段毕业	Graducation from Senior Secondary Schools	1	1	0.01	0.10
高中毕业阶段以下	Graduation from Senior Secondary Schools and below				
小　学	**Primary Schools**	**11 458**	**1 981**		
大学本科毕业及以上	Graduation from Universities and above	7 494	865	65.40	43.66
大学专科毕业	Graduation from Junior College	3 914	1 090	34.16	55.02
高中阶段毕业	Graduation from Senior Secondary Schools	50	26	0.44	1.31
高中毕业阶段以下	Graduation from Senior Secondary Schools and below				
幼儿园	**Kindergartens**	**3 970**	**759**		
大学本科毕业及以上	Graduation from Senior Secondary Schools and above	1 010	134	25.44	17.65
大学专科毕业	Graduation from Secondary Teachers' Schools	2674	529	67.36	69.70
高中阶段毕业	Graduation from Senior Secondary Schools	281	96	7.08	12.65
高中毕业阶段以下	Graduation from Senior Secondary Schools and below	5		0.13	

17—18 各师普通中学校数、学生数

Regular Secondary Schools and Student Enrollment by Division

计量单位:人 (2017 年) (person)

单位	Unit	校数(所) School (Unit)	初中 Junior Secondary Schools	高中 Senior Secondary Schools	毕业生数 Graduates 初中 Junior Secondary Schools	毕业生数 Graduates 高中 Senior Secondary Schools	招生数 New Student Enrollment 初中 Junior Secondary Schools	招生数 New Student Enrollment 高中 Senior Secondary Schools	在校学生数 StudentEnrollment 初中 Junior Secondary Schools	在校学生数 StudentEnrollment 高中 Senior Secondary Schools
总计	**Total**	**237**	**190**	**47**	**27 790**	**17 899**	**29 356**	**18 275**	**83 980**	**54 910**
一师	Division 1	22	19	3	3 235	1 933	3 515	2 125	9 951	6 137
二师	Division 2	25	22	3	2 132	1903	2 378	1 723	6 935	5 228
三师	Division 3	21	17	4	3 443	2 327	3 960	2 371	10 936	7 387
四师	Division 4	23	16	7	2 432	1 631	2 466	1 625	7 320	5 037
五师	Division 5	14	11	3	1 556	1 123	1 376	1 093	4 192	3 462
六师	Division 6	25	18	7	2 747	2 133	2 963	2 026	8 159	5 989
七师	Division 7	13	11	2	1 625	860	1 364	879	4 254	2 823
八师	Division 8	34	27	7	3 986	1 878	4 399	2 475	12 432	6 696
九师	Division 9	13	12	1	653	495	592	292	1 838	1 094
十师	Division 10	12	11	1	1 068	966	1 108	1 013	3 207	3 014
十一师	Division 11	5	3	2	582	689	580	653	1 681	2 044
十二师	Division 12	9	7	2	1 116	564	1 263	539	3 506	1 663
十三师	Division 13	13	10	3	1 069	655	1 028	655	2 973	1 972
十四师	Division 14	5	4	1	683	123	823	187	2 445	456
兵团直属	Directly under XPCC	3	2	1	1 463	619	1 541	619	4 151	1 908

17—19 各师普通中学教职工人数

Staff and Teachers in Regular Secondary Schools by Division

计量单位:人 (2017 年) (person)

单位	Unit	教职工合计 Total Staff and Teachers	专任教师 Full-Time Teachers	行政人员 Adminis-trative Staff	教辅人员 Teaching Auxiliaries	工勤人员 Logistic Staff	校办厂人员 Personnel of Factories Run by Schools	代课教师 Supply Teachers	兼任教师 Part-Time Teachers
总计	**Total**	**25 390**	**21 491**	**815**	**1 011**	**2 069**	**4**	**289**	**11**
一师	Division 1	3 095	2 702	109	61	223		12	
二师	Division 2	2 641	2 137	67	82	355		1	
三师	Division 3	2 535	2 236	77	39	183		38	
四师	Division 4	2 601	2 021	111	96	373		8	
五师	Division 5	1 519	1 312	39	52	116			
六师	Division 6	2 583	2 279	56	93	155			
七师	Division 7	1 946	1 577	44	127	198			
八师	Division 8	2 757	2 292	92	240	129	4	77	4
九师	Division 9	949	814	43	32	60			
十师	Division 10	1 231	1 122	44	35	30		5	
十一师	Division 11	650	531	27	22	70		5	
十二师	Division 12	863	738	35	36	54		11	
十三师	Division 13	1 027	890	39	25	73		56	7
十四师	Division 14	382	327	10	9	36		11	
兵团直属	Directly under XPCC	611	513	22	62	14		65	

注:本表数据包含一贯制学校小学部职工情况。
Note data in this table includes staff and teachers in primary schools.

17—20 各师普通中学现有校舍面积

Floor Space of Present Buildings of Regular Secondary Schools by Division

计量单位:平方米 (2017 年) (sq.m)

单 位	Unit	学校占地面积 Areas of Schools	校舍建筑面积 Floor Space of Buildings	教学用房合计 Total Teaching Buildings	#教室 Classrooms	#实验室 Laboratories	#图书馆 Libraries	行政用房 Administrative Buildings	生活用房 Life Buildings	其他用房 Others
总 计	**Total**	**16 127 517**	**4 060 040**	**2 017 831**	**1 228 165**	**309 500**	**113 116**	**361 152**	**1 484 372**	**196 685**
一 师	Division 1	1 804 304	542 642	270 863	167 860	54 682	16 699	51 116	208 320	12 342
二 师	Division 2	1 612 015	426 283	207 829	115 064	32 847	11 873	45 569	152 747	20 138
三 师	Division 3	1 726 177	459 033	229 128	142 030	32 117	18 074	33 963	192 018	3 923
四 师	Division 4	1 499 441	354 243	195 534	120 699	24 408	8 299	33 591	125 119	
五 师	Division 5	806 509	192 546	102 196	68 484	12 070	3 598	14 926	67 205	8 219
六 师	Division 6	1 695 271	390 728	185 465	121 733	25 690	10 627	33 899	171 365	
七 师	Division 7	1 213 503	260 979	134 301	94 845	16 826	3 781	19 391	90 091	17 196
八 师	Division 8	1 798 107	501 918	232 064	136 786	41 971	16 901	46 850	179 864	43 140
九 师	Division 9	691 581	157 615	79 093	36 016	11 940	4 445	11 754	47 527	19 241
十 师	Division 10	1 294 750	247 264	107 704	64 634	11 239	5 555	15 754	87 592	36 214
十一师	Division 11	180 527	75 064	48 388	36 366	4 544	2 157	4 967	19 136	2 572
十二师	Division 12	616 104	126 586	64 965	41 714	9 138	2 883	11 630	37 967	12 024
十三师	Division 13	831 607	161 612	90 637	44 998	23 512	4 830	15 574	42 652	12 749
十四师	Division 14	263 770	85 037	29 843	20 280	3 935	743	4 155	46 365	4 674
兵团直属	Directly under XPCC	93 851	78 491	39 820	16 654	4 582	2 650	18 013	16 405	4 252

17—21 各师中等专业学校基本情况

Basic Statistics on Secondary Vocational Schools by Division

计量单位:人 (2017 年) (person)

单 位	Unit	校数(所) Schools (unit)	毕业生数 Graduates	招生数 New Student Enrollment	在校学生数 Student Enrollment	教职工数 Staff and Teachers	#专任教师 Full-Time Teachers
总 计	**Total**	**20**	**8 476**	**9 312**	**27 169**	**1 472**	**1 029**
一 师	Division 1	1	489	776	1 746	100	86
二 师	Division 2	1	561	450	1 391	90	78
三 师	Division 3	1	79	456	677	75	48
四 师	Division 4	1	47	122	341	49	38
五 师	Division 5	1	25	72	72	68	38
六 师	Division 6	1	460	200	1 044	108	79
七 师	Division 7	1	201	302	704	75	46
八 师	Division 8	2	580	666	2 120	134	84
九 师	Division 9	1	22	83	134	48	31
十 师	Division 10	1	79	295	610	46	38
十一师	Division 11	1	211	316	664	124	71
十二师	Division 12	1	73	87	272	34	23
十三师	Division 13	1	214	318	918	40	32
十四师	Division 14	1	173	105	382	48	32
兵团直属	Directly under XPCC	5	5 262	5 064	16 094	433	305

17—22 各师小学校数、学生数

Primary Schools and Pupil Enrollment by Division

(2017 年)

单 位	Unit	学 校 (所) Schools (unit)	毕业生数 (人) Graduates (person)	招生数 (人) New Student Enrollment(person)	在校学生数 (人) Student Enrollment (person)
总 计	**Total**	**55**	**26 902**	**27 476**	**162 228**
一 师	Division 1	4	3 319	3 503	20 914
二 师	Division 2		1 716	1 675	10 828
三 师	Division 3	14	3 750	5 592	28 035
四 师	Division 4	3	2 561	2 469	14 911
五 师	Division 5	2	1 495	1 184	7 937
六 师	Division 6	10	2 959	2 830	16 976
七 师	Division 7		1 428	936	6 813
八 师	Division 8	16	3 937	3 317	20 499
九 师	Division 9		635	585	3 683
十 师	Division 10		1 033	1 010	6 325
十一师	Division 11		652	531	3 721
十二师	Division 12	1	1 147	1 364	7 557
十三师	Division 13		1 116	1 248	6 978
十四师	Division 14	5	889	968	5 431
兵团直属	Directly under XPCC		265	264	1 620

17—23 各师小学教职工人数

Staff and Teachers of Primary Schools by Division

计量单位:人　　(2017 年)　　(person)

单 位	Unit	教职工合计 Total Staff and Teachers	专任教师 Full-Time Teachers	行政人员 Adminis-trative Staff	教辅人员 Teaching Auxiliaries	工勤人员 Logistic Staff	校办厂人员 Personnel of Factories Run by Schools	代课教师 Supply Teachers	兼任教师 Part-Time Teachers
总 计	**Total**	**3 841**	**3 241**	**110**	**140**	**349**	**1**	**23**	**4**
一 师	Division 1	236	168	11		57		3	
二 师	Division 2								
三 师	Division 3	977	828	23	29	97		14	
四 师	Division 4	361	276	9	2	74			
五 师	Division 5	233	215	6	6	6			
六 师	Division 6	645	601	15	13	16			
七 师	Division 7								
八 师	Division 8	1 053	878	42	85	47	1		4
九 师	Division 9								
十 师	Division 10								
十一师	Division 11								
十二师	Division 12	147	138	4	3	2			
十三师	Division 13	34	29			5		5	
十四师	Division 14	155	108		2	45		1	
兵团直属	Directly under XPCC								

注:本表为独立小学教职工情况。
Note:Data in this table are staff and teachers of independence primary scholls.

17—24 各师学龄儿童入学率及小学毕业升学率

Percentage of School-age Enrolled and Percentage of Primary School Pupils Graduated by Division

(2017 年)

单位	Unit	学龄儿童入学率 Percentage of School-Age Children Enrolled			小学毕业升学率 Percentage of Graduates of Primary Schools Entering Junior Secondary Schools		
		学龄儿童数（人） School-Age Children (person)	已入学数（人） School-Age Children Enrolled in Schools(person)	入学率（%） Erollment Rate (%)	小学毕业生数（人） Graduates from Primary Schools (person)	初中招生数（人） Students Entering Junior Secondary Schools(person)	升学率（%） Enrollment Rate (%)
总 计	**Total**	**151 581**	**151 581**	**100.00**	**26 902**	**29 356**	**109.12**
一 师	Division 1	18 869	18 869	100.00	3 319	3 515	105.91
二 师	Division 2	9 686	9 686	100.00	1 716	2 378	138.58
三 师	Division 3	26 917	26 917	100.00	3 750	3 960	105.60
四 师	Division 4	13 223	13 223	100.00	2 561	2 466	96.29
五 师	Division 5	7 136	7 136	100.00	1 495	1 376	92.04
六 师	Division 6	16 968	16 968	100.00	2 959	2 963	100.14
七 师	Division 7	6 024	6 024	100.00	1 428	1 364	95.52
八 师	Division 8	20 268	20 268	100.00	3 937	4 399	111.73
九 师	Division 9	3 239	3 239	100.00	635	592	93.23
十 师	Division 10	5 716	5 716	100.00	1 033	1 108	107.26
十一师	Division 11	3 454	3 454	100.00	652	580	88.96
十二师	Division 12	7 444	7 444	100.00	1 147	1 263	110.11
十三师	Division 13	5 899	5 899	100.00	1 116	1 028	92.11
十四师	Division 14	5 225	5 225	100.00	889	823	92.58
兵团直属	Directly under XPCC	1 513	1 513	100.00	265	1 541	581.51

17—25 各师小学现有校舍面积

Floor Space of Present Buildings of Primary Schools by Division

计量单位：平方米　　(2017 年)　　(sq.m)

单位	Unit	学校占地面积 Areas of Schools	校舍建筑面积 Floor Space of Buildings	教学用房合计 Total Teaching Buildings	#教室 Classrooms	#实验室 Laboratories	#图书馆 Libraries	行政用房 Administrative Buildings	生活用房 Life Buildings	其他用房 Others
总 计	**Total**	**2 248 938**	**503 700**	**266 200**	**204 780**	**15 648**	**8 640**	**38 013**	**170 095**	**29 391**
一 师	Division 1	118 156	31 081	15 462	13 224	710	648	1 667	13 715	236
二 师	Division 2	1 810	789	477	201	141	55	70	41	200
三 师	Division 3	717 762	159 101	83 416	62 676	4 653	1 884	8 899	64 348	2 438
四 师	Division 4	171 193	42 317	21 179	15 471	2 281	559	4 007	17 132	
五 师	Division 5	83 254	22 363	16 245	14 449	682	472	3 039	1 297	1 782
六 师	Division 6	260 785	72 539	50 692	40 406	1 775	2 106	5 546	16 301	
七 师	Division 7									
八 师	Division 8	679 567	138 027	62 966	47 029	4 609	2 371	12 199	45 332	17 531
九 师	Division 9									
十 师	Division 10									
十一师	Division 11									
十二师	Division 12	33 000	10 682	3 218	2 743	97	117	973	3 742	2 749
十三师	Division 13	83 437	5 829	3 059	2 526	221	114	716	1 171	883
十四师	Division 14	99 974	20 972	9 486	6 057	480	314	898	7 016	3 572
兵团直属	Directly under XPCC									

17—26 各师中小学平均每班学生数、教师数及每一教师负担学生数

Students and Teachers of Primary and Secondary Schools Per Class and Student-Teacher Ratio by Division

计量单位:人　　(2017 年)　　(person)

单位	Unit	平均每班学生数 Per Class Students			平均每班教师数 Per Class Teachers			平均每一教师负担学生数 Students-Teacher Ratio		
		高中 Senior Secondary Schools	初中 Junior Secondary Schools	小学 Primary Schools	高中 Senior Secondary Schools	初中 Junior Secondary Schools	小学 Primary Schools	高中 Senior Secondary Schools	初中 Junior Secondary Schools	小学 Primary Schools
总　计	**Total**	**37.23**	**37.00**	**47.54**	**2.63**	**3.97**	**3.70**	**14.16**	**9.33**	**12.86**
一　师	Division 1	39.46	37.41	49.10	2.49	3.94	4.03	15.86	9.50	12.18
二　师	Division 2	33.21	33.67	46.68	2.65	4.16	3.71	12.52	8.10	12.57
三　师	Division 3	38.62	42.89	48.60	2.36	3.37	3.23	16.36	12.73	15.04
四　师	Division 4	35.76	35.19	48.90	2.56	3.94	3.98	13.96	8.94	12.29
五　师	Division 5	33.49	29.94	46.78	2.78	4.26	3.69	12.06	7.03	12.68
六　师	Division 6	36.27	35.63	41.59	2.90	4.36	3.65	12.51	8.18	11.41
七　师	Division 7	31.84	30.60	43.43	3.24	4.63	3.69	9.82	6.62	11.76
八　师	Division 8	38.68	39.34	49.60	2.82	3.79	3.53	13.69	10.39	14.07
九　师	Division 9	29.70	27.43	36.47	2.88	5.09	3.87	10.32	5.39	9.43
十　师	Division 10	37.21	36.03	51.08	2.81	4.51	4.12	13.23	8.00	12.40
十一师	Division 11	42.28	40.02	53.79	2.58	3.74	3.87	16.39	10.71	13.90
十二师	Division 12	44.72	39.84	61.59	2.68	3.52	4.19	16.68	11.31	14.72
十三师	Division 13	35.42	34.17	46.95	2.35	3.71	3.19	15.10	9.20	14.72
十四师	Division 14	43.45	42.16	35.08	1.77	3.03	2.92	24.57	13.89	12.00
兵团直属	Directly under XPCC	45.00	51.89	53.00	2.44	3.50	4.03	18.41	14.83	13.16

17—27 各师幼儿园基本情况

Basic Statistics on Kindergartens by Division

(2017 年)

单位	Unit	园数(所) Kindergartens (unit)	班数(个) Classes (unit)	幼儿数(人) Children (person)	教职工数(人) Staff and Teachers (person)	#教师 Teachers
总　计	**Total**	**281**	**2 115**	**78 161**	**6 784**	**3 970**
一　师	Division 1	25	252	9 788	1007	518
二　师	Division 2	22	151	3 997	429	234
三　师	Division 3	36	437	19 829	971	716
四　师	Division 4	29	158	6 020	572	292
五　师	Division 5	12	90	3 187	345	190
六　师	Division 6	42	266	8 909	932	554
七　师	Division 7	12	86	2 905	311	208
八　师	Division 8	32	165	5 526	481	315
九　师	Division 9	12	52	1 550	134	108
十　师	Division 10	12	84	3 128	364	187
十一师	Division 11	1	8	362	38	16
十二师	Division 12	18	120	3 914	494	231
十三师	Division 13	13	107	3 151	279	198
十四师	Division 14	13	105	4 643	271	132
兵团直属	Directly under XPCC	2	34	1 252	156	71

17—28 技工学校基本情况

Basic Statistics on Technical Schools

计量单位：人　　(2017 年)　　(person)

单　位	Unit	学 生 数 Students			教职工数					
		毕业生数 Graduates	招生数 New Student Enrollment	在校学生数 Student Enrollment	Staff and Teachers	专任教师 Full-Time Teachers	教辅人员 Auxiliary Teaching Staff	行政人员 Administrative Personnel	工勤人员 Logistic Personnel	兼任教师数 Part-time Teachers
总　计	**Total**	**7 984**	**601**	**1 014**	**1 049**	**693**	**102**	**89**	**45**	**120**
兵团高级技校	XPCC Senior Technical School	3 707	112	95	257	114	44	39	10	50
一师技工学校	The Technical School of Division 1	250			113	83	4	5	7	14
二师技工学校	The Technical School of Division 2	1 457			98	78	3	5	4	8
四师技工学校	The Technical School of Division 4	19			53	35	11	4	3	
五师技工学校	The Technical School of Division 5	136			73	32	11	8	6	16
六师技工学校	The Technical School of Division 6	923			94	68	3	8	5	10
七师技工学校	The Technical School of Division 7				9	1	7		1	
八师技工学校	The Technical School of Division 8	479	489	919	228	202		6		20
十师技工学校	The Technical School of Division 10				2		2			
十一师技工学校	The Technical School of Division 11	1 013			122	80	17	14	9	2

17—29 文化艺术事业基本情况

Basic Statistics on Culture and Art

(2017 年)

单　位	Unit	主管机关 Department in Charge	剧　种 Type of Drama	职工人数（人） Staff and Workers (person)	#演　员 Actors	演出场次数（场次） Number of Performances (time)	观众人次数（人次） Number of Spectators (person-time)
三师文工团	The Art Troupe of Division 3	三　师 Division 3	歌　舞 Song and Dance	23	15	147	120 000
石河子艺术剧院	Shihezi College of Art	八　师 Dvision 8	歌舞、话剧、豫剧 Song, Dance, Drama and Yu Opera	136	130	120	100 000
九师豫剧团	The Yuju Opera Troupe of Division 9	九　师 Division 9	豫　剧 Yu Opera	27	20	23	7 513
兵团秦剧团	Qin Opera Troupe of XPCC	兵团宣传部 Propaganda Department of XPCC	秦　腔 Qin Opera	59	31	102	30 000
兵团豫剧团	Yu Opera Troupe of XPCC	兵团宣传部 Propaganda Department of XPCC	豫　剧 Yu Opera	77	33	119	79 000
兵团杂技团	The Acrobatic Troupe of XPCC	兵团宣传部 Propaganda Department of XPCC	杂　技 Acrobatics	59 24	47 16	508	700 000
兵团歌舞团	The Song, Dance and Drama Troupe of XPCC	兵团宣传部 Propaganda Department of XPCC	歌舞、话剧 Song, Dance and Drama	153	128	177	12 960

17—30 报刊、杂志出版发行情况

Publication and Distribution of Newspaper and Magazines

(2017 年)

报刊、杂志名称 Name of Newspaper and Magazines	出版单位 Publishers	创办时间 The Initial Issue Time	出版期数（期） Publishing Issues (issue)	出版版数（版） Publishing Pages (Pages)	平均每期发行份数（份） Average Distribution Copiesper Issue(copy)	全年发行总份数（万份） Total Distribution Copies (10 000 copy)
兵团日报(汉) XPCC Daily(Han)	兵团党委 The Party Committee of XPCC	1953 年	355	对开 8 版	104 800	3 720.40
兵团日报(维) XPCC Daily(Uygur)	兵团党委 The Party Committee of XPCC	1953 年	100	四开 4 版	3 800	38.00
生活晚报 Life Evening Paper	兵团日报社 XPCC Daily Office	2001 年	99	四开 12 版	65 262	646.09
塔里木报 Tarim Paper	一师党委 The Party Committee of Division 1	1938 年	240	四开 8 版	13 050	313.20
绿原报 Luyuan Paper	二师党委 The Party Committee of Division 2	1948 年	153	对开 4 版	12 000	183.60
叶尔羌报 Yerqiang Paper	三师党委 The Party Committee of Division 3	1984 年	149	对开 4 版	9 501	141.56
叶尔羌报(维) Yerqiang Paper(Uygur)	三师党委 The Party Committee of Division 3	2003 年	99	对开 4 版	6 094	60.33
伊犁垦区报 Yili Reclamation Region Paper	四师党委 The Party Committee of Division 4	1988 年	152	对开 4 版	13 000	197.60
北疆开发报 Northern Part of XJ Development Paper	五师党委 The Party Committee of Division 5	1944 年	156	对开 4 版	7 350	114.66
准噶尔时报 Zhunger Times	六师党委 The Party Committee of Division 6	1983 年	150	对开 4 版	12 700	190.50
奎屯日报 Kutun Daily	七师党委 The Party Committee of Division 7	1950 年	245	对开 4 版	9 300	227.85
石河子日报 Shihezi Daily	八师党委 The Party Committee of Division 8	1950 年	248	对开 4 版	19 105	473.80
北疆时报 Western Frontier Times	九师党委 The Party Committee of Division 9	1984 年	144	对开 4 版	6 000	86.40
新疆北屯报 Xinjiang Beitun Paper	十师党委 The Party Committee of Division 10	1989 年	108	对开 4 版	5 500	59.40
天山建设报 Tianshan Construction Paper	十一师党委 The Party Committee of Division 11	1993 年	99	对开 4 版	7 000	69.30
哈密开发报 Hami Development Paper	十三师党委 The Party Committee of Division	1993 年	154	对开 4 版	8 000	123.20
石河子广播电视报 Shihezi Broadcasting and TV Paper	石河子广播电视局 Shihezi Broadcasting and TV Bureau	1986 年	52	四开 16 版	20 000	104.00
石河子大学报 Shihezi University	石河子大学 Shihezi University	1996 年	16	对开 4 版	8 000	12.80
塔里木大学报 Tarim University	塔里木大学 Tarim University	1958 年	8	四开 4 版	3 000	2.40
当代兵团 Contemporary XPCC	兵团党委 The Party Committee of XPCC	1999 年	22	16 开 56 页	32 600	71.72
新疆农垦经济 Xinjiang Nongken Economics	石河子大学 Shihezi University	1981 年	12	16 开 92 页	1 500	1.80
新疆农垦科技 Xinjiang Nongken Science and Technology	兵团科技局 The Science and Technology Bureau of XPCC	1978 年	12	大 16 开 64 页	14 000	16.80
兵团医学 XPCC Medicine	兵团卫生局 XPCC Health Bureau	1984 年	4	16 开 72 页	3 000	1.20
兵团工运 XPCC Worker's Movement	兵团工会 XPCC Trade Union	1984 年	12	大 16 开 56 页	11 005	13.21
绿　洲 Oasis	兵团文联 XPCC Literary and Art Federation	1957 年	6	16 开 144 页	5 080	3.05
兵团党校学报 The Academic Journal ofXPCC Party School	兵团党校 XPCC Party School	1989 年	6	16 开 112 页	1 000	0.60
石河子大学学报(自然科学版) The Academic Journal of Shihezi University(Natural Science Edition)	石河子大学 Shihezi University	1997 年	6	大 16 开 132 页	1 000	0.60

17—30 续表 Continued

（2017 年）

报刊、杂志名称 Name of Newspaper and Magazines	出版单位 Publishers	创办时间 The Initial Issue Time	出版期数（期）Publishing Issues (issue)	出版版数（版）Publishing Pages (Pages)	平均每期发行份数（份）Average Distribution Copiesper Issue(copy)	全年发行总份数（万份）Total Distribution Copies (10 000 copy)
石河子大学学报（哲学社会科学版）The Academic Journal of Shihezi University(Philosophy and SocialScience Edition)	石河子大学 Shihezi University	1983 年	6	大16开128页	1 050	0.63
兵团教育学院学报 The Academic Journal of XPCC Educational College	兵团教育学院 XPCC Educational College	1991 年	6	16 开 84 页	600	0.36
农垦医学 Nongken Medicine	石河子大学医学院 The Medical College of Shihezi University	1979 年	4	16 开 72 页	3 000	1.20
塔里木大学学报 The Academic Journal of Tarim University	塔里木大学 Tarim University	1978 年	4	大16开112页	250	0.10
石河子科技 Shihezi Science and Technology	石河子市科技局 The Science and Technology Bureau of Shiheze City	1976 年	6	大16开66页	1 300	0.78
绿　风 Green Wind	石河子市文联 The Literary and Art Federation of Shiheze City	1978 年	6	大32开128页	2 500	1.50
兵团画报 XPCC Pictorial	当代兵团杂志社 Contemporary XPCC Magazine	2015 年	6	大16开32页	33 000	19.80
绿洲农业科学与工程 Oasis Agriculture Science and Engineering	新疆农垦科学院 XJ Academy of Agricultural Reclamation	2015 年	4	大16开64页	2 000	0.80
兵团年鉴 XPCC yearbook	兵团史志编纂委员会 XPCC Chorography Editorial Board	1986 年	1	大16开700页	2 000	0.20
和田屯垦报（汉）Hetiantunkenbao(Han)	十四师党委 The Party Committee of Division 14	2010 年	100	四开 4 版	1 500	15.00
和田屯垦报（维）Hetiantunkenbao(Uygur)	十四师党委 The Party Committee of Division 14	2011 年	100	四开 4 版	1 500	15.00
天山时报 Tianshan Tines	十二师党委 The Party Committee of Division 12	2017 年	107	四开 4 版	6 750	72.23

17—31 广播电视基本情况

Basic Statistics on Radio and Television

（2017 年）

单　位	Unit	广播节目综合人口覆盖率（%）Radio Coverage Rate of the Population (%)	电视节目综合人口覆盖率（%）TV Coverage Rate of Population (%)	有线广播电视用户数（万户）Number of Users of Cable Radio and TV (10 000 households)	广播电视总收入（万元）Revenue of Radio and TV (10000 yuan)	广播电视从业人员数（人）Staff and Workers of Radio and TV (person)	调频转播发射台（座）Relaying Stations of Frequency Modulation roadcasting (unit)	电视转播发射台（座）TV Transmission and Relaying Stations (unit)
总　计	**Total**	**97.7**	**98.4**	**373 856**	**19 961.16**	**1 930**	**184**	**113**
兵团广播电视台	Broadcast and TV Station of XPCC			2 3000	346.00	345	1	
一　师	Division 1	97.5	99.3	23 000	1 557.34	186	18	9
二　师	Division 2	99.6	99.4	40 151	787.25	47	16	8
三　师	Division 3	98.7	97.5	3 800	786.00	4	17	13
四　师	Division 4	96.5	96.3	28 000	226.00	226	22	14
五　师	Division 5	98.0	98.0	18 000	587.00	33	12	6
六　师	Division 6	98.0	96.0	38 000	1 328.60	260	19	11
七　师	Division 7	98.1	99.8	21 426	927.89	150	10	9
八　师	Division 8	96.5	99.0	67 000	3 586.90	384	19	19
九　师	Division 9	100.0	100.0	10 670	555.90	14	12	6
十　师	Division 10	94.0	99.0	15 892	483.13	107	13	10
十 二 师	Division 12	100.0	100.0	4 3143	1 616.95	5	9	1
十 三 师	Division 13	98.0	98.0	21 774	2 225.26	169	12	4
十 四 师	Division 14	95.0	97.0	20 000	51.00		4	3

备注：本次统计有线广播电视用户数为正在交纳有线电视费的户数，有线电视可通达用户约 75 万户。
Note：The number of users of cable radio and TV is the number of pay cable TV.

17—32 主要年份卫生机构、人员数

Number of Health Institutions and Persons Engaged in Health Institutons in Major Years

年 份 Year	机构数（个） Institutions (unit)	#医 院 Hospitals	人员总数（人） Total Personnel (person)	#卫生技术人员 Medical Technical Personnel	#医生(士) Doctors	#护 士 Nurses	床位数（张） Beds (pcs)
1954	68	15	3 937	3 150	675	866	3 981
1957	247	11	3 629	2 885	933	835	4 606
1962	511	25	8 741	7 396	1 754	2 394	9 672
1965	537	29	14 047	11 334	3 223	2 427	14 752
1970	506	34	13 893	11 184	2 954	5 222	18 101
1975	189	7	12 977	9 733	2 765	2 466	12 801
1980	475	26	27 016	20 280	4 639	5 562	20 258
1985	595	213	28 015	22 361	7 869	5 238	19 873
1990	680	217	28 666	22 763	9 824	6 302	20 058
1995	622	222	29 952	23 781	10 090	6 720	19 872
2000	665	221	27 636	22 664	10 331	9 641	17 253
2005	673	225	24 332	20 617	9 023	7 186	16 537
2006	648	222	24 576	20 780	8 886	7 083	16 518
2007	1506	225	24 553	20 470	8 751	7 195	17 045
2008	1555	216	23 779	20 052	8 112	7 249	17 084
2009	1327	212	23 997	20 278	8 063	7 647	17 561
2010	1339	209	24 186	20 559	8 058	7 967	18 193
2011	1356	210	25 387	21 775	8 172	8 696	18 575
2012	1356	210	26 776	23 045	8 316	9 493	20 051
2013	1348	211	28 569	24 602	8 514	10 407	20 396
2014	1303	211	29 216	24 940	8 650	10 599	20 624
2015	1305	211	30 182	25 941	9 174	11 113	21 165
2016	1226	209	30 083	25 850	9 106	11 295	21 390
2017	1212	211	31 072	26 610	9 717	11 847	22 194

注：自 2002 年度开始，有关指标发生变动，本表中 2002 年的医生和护士人数反映的是执业医师、执业助理医师和注册护士的人数。2007 年起机构数包含营利性机构。2013 年起机构数含计划生育服务机构。2016 年卫生监督机构脱离卫生部门，表中不在再反映卫生监督机构数及人员数。

Note: Number of doctors and nurses in this table have reflected the number of doctors with license and nurses registered since 2002. Number of health institutions included mercantil institutions since 2007. Health supervision authorities sepatated from Ministry of Health in 2016, number of health supervision institutions and staff in table.

17—33 卫生机构、床位、人员数

Number of Health Institutions, Beds and Persons

(2017 年)

类 别	Category	机构数（个） Instituti-ons(unit)	床位数(张)Beds(pcs) 编制床位 Planned beds	 实有床位 Real Beds	人员总数（人） Total Personnel (person)	卫生技术人员 Medical Technical Personnel	其他技术人员 Other Technical Personnel	管理人员 Manag-erial Personnel	工勤人员 Logisgic Personnel
总 计	**Total**	**1 212**	**18 839**	**22 194**	**31 072**	**26 610**	**1 439**	**1 375**	**1 648**
医院合计	Total Hospitals	211	18 431	21 729	26 894	22 741	1 333	1 278	1 542
综合医院	Comprehensive Hospitals	200	17 103	19 808	25 855	21 911	1 233	1 242	1 469
中医医院	Traditional Chinese Medicine Hospitals	4	278	671	290	220	40	17	13
专科医院	Specialty Hospitals	7	1 050	1 250	749	610	60	19	60
妇幼保健所、站	Maternity and Child Care Centers	1	30	30	94	84	7		3
门诊部	Clinics	14		41	229	207	8	4	10
卫生院	Health Centers	1	20		23	20		3	
社区卫生服务中心(站)	Community Health Service Centers	117	358	394	1 062	983	40	21	18
卫生所、医务室、社区医疗服务站	Health Offices, Health Centers, Community Health Service Stations	752			1 536	1491	8	3	34
紧急救援中心	Urgent Rescue Center	1			22	14	2	1	5
疾病预防控制中心(防疫站)	Disease Prevention and Control Hospitals or Stations	99			1 072	970	28	51	23
卫生监督所	Health Direct Offices								
采供血机构	Blood Collection and Supply Units	7			110	81	9	8	12
计划生育服务机构	Family Planning Serve Organization	9			30	19	4	6	1

17－34 各师卫生机构、床位、人员数

Number of Health Institutions, Beds and Persons by Division

(2017 年)

指　标	Item	合　计 Total	一　师 Division 1	二　师 Division 2	三　师 Division 3	四　师 Division 4	五　师 Division 5	六　师 Division 6	七　师 Division 7
卫生机构　(个)	**Health Institutions　(unit)**	**1212**	**102**	**76**	**45**	**46**	**64**	**176**	**115**
# 医　院	Hospitals	211	21	21	15	21	13	22	14
编制床位　(张)	**Planned Beds　(unit)**	**18 839**	**1 879**	**1 544**	**1 048**	**1 632**	**656**	**1 817**	**1 139**
实有床位数　(张)	Real Beds　(unit)	22 194	2 462	1 866	1 399	1 643	962	2 100	2 233
人员总数　(人)	**Total Personnel　(person)**	**31 072**	**3 262**	**2 731**	**1 846**	**2 257**	**1 193**	**3 243**	**2 342**
卫生技术人员	Medical Technical Personel	26 610	2 818	2 423	1 573	1 916	1 024	2 866	2 055
执业医师	Doctors with Licence	7 896	757	637	307	534	308	819	583
执业助理医师	Asistan Doctors with Licence	1 821	224	177	155	143	96	179	204
注册护士	Nurses Registered	11 847	1 325	1 081	659	855	357	1 292	857
药剂人员	Pharmaceutical Personnel	1 083	93	100	59	98	67	118	80
检验人员	Laborotory Technical Personnel	1 021	118	87	51	78	42	107	83
影像人员	Shadow Personnel	462	50	41	31	36	21	42	34
其他卫生技术人员	Other Health Technical Personnel	2 480	251	300	311	172	133	309	214
其他技术人员	Other Technical Personnel	1 439	71	134	69	66	32	164	60
管理人员	Managerial Personnel	1 375	206	48	79	120	51	72	141
工勤人员	Logistic Personnel	1 648	167	126	125	155	86	141	86
平均每千人口拥有卫生技术人员　(人)	**Number of Health Technical Personnel per 1 000 Population　(person)**	**9**	**8**	**11**	**6**	**8**	**8**	**8**	**9**

指　标	Item	八　师 Division 8	九　师 Division 9	十　师 Division 10	十一师 Division 11	十二师 Division 12	十三师 Division 13	十四师 Division 14	兵团直属 Directly under XPCC
卫生机构　(个)	**Health Institutions　(unit)**	**381**	**40**	**43**	**14**	**31**	**66**	**9**	**4**
# 医　院	Hospitals	30	13	13	2	7	14	4	1
编制床位　(张)	**Planned Beds　(unit)**	**5 081**	**682**	**872**	**135**	**349**	**1 000**	**205**	**800**
实有床位数　(张)	Real Beds　(unit)	4 971	891	985	98	380	1 100	182	922
人员总数　(人)	**Total Personnel　(person)**	**7 830**	**1 127**	**1 359**	**142**	**440**	**1 705**	**299**	**1 296**
卫生技术人员	Medical Technical Personel	6 540	943	1 113	119	383	1 441	264	1 132
执业医师	Doctors with Licence	2 402	240	280	62	129	422	38	378
执业助理医师	Asistan Doctors with Licence	352	92	66	4	36	63	29	1
注册护士	Nurses Registered	2 981	415	522	41	146	666	106	544
药剂人员	Pharmaceutical Personnel	223	47	46	5	16	66	16	49
检验人员	Laborotory Technical Personnel	227	31	50	5	14	47	10	71
影像人员	Shadow Personnel	108	17	23	2	10	14	7	26
其他卫生技术人员	Other Health Technical Personnel	247	101	126		32	163	58	63
其他技术人员	Other Technical Personnel	508	75	102	9	14	114	9	12
管理人员	Managerial Personnel	360	52	53	9	18	34	5	127
工勤人员	Logistic Personnel	422	57	91	5	25	116	21	25
平均每千人口拥有卫生技术人员　(人)	**Number of Health Technical Personnel per 1 000 Population　(person)**	**10**	**12**	**11**	**2**	**3**	**13**	**5**	**28**

2018

BING TUAN

第十八篇

公共管理、社会保障和其他

Chapter 18 Data on Public Mangement、Social Security and Others

简要说明

一、本篇资料主要内容

本篇资料主要综合反映兵团人力资源和社会保障基本情况及检察机关办理各类案件、律师工作及法院收案、结案、开发区发展、社会救济及社会团体的基本情况。

二、本篇资料来源

本篇资料分别由兵团人力资源和社会保障局、检察院司法局、法院、八师统计局和兵团民政局提供，兵团统计局国民经济综合统计处整理。

Brief Introduction

1.Main Contents

The data in this chapter cover the basic conditions of social security and cases dealt by procurator'soffices, lawyer's work, case acceptance, settlement of courts, Human Resources and social security, development zone, social relief and public organizations.

2.Sources of Data

The data in this chapter are provided by XPCC's Procurate, Court, the Bureau of justice, the Bureau of Human Resources and Social Security, the Bureau of Water Conservancy, the Statistics Bureau of Shihezi and the Bureau of Civil Affairs of XPCC, and prepared by the Comprehensive office of the statistics Bureau of XPCC.

18－1 检察机关直接立案侦查案件情况

Cases under Direct Investigation by Procurator's Offices

(2017 年)

案件分类	Case Item	受案（件）Cases Accepted (case)	立案件数（件）Number of Cases Registered (case)	立案人数（人）Person of case Registered (person)	#要案 Key Case	结案件数（件）Number of Cases Settled (cases)	结案人数（人）Person of cases Settled(person)
总　计	**Total**	**190**	**103**	**111**	**10**	**92**	**95**
贪污贿赂案件小计	**Sub-total of Cases on Corruption and Bribery**	**180**	**102**	**110**	**9**	**91**	**94**
贪　污	Corruption	45	15	21	1	23	26
贿　赂	Bribery	96	60	60	8	44	44
挪用公款	Misappropriation of Public Funds	39	27	29		24	24
集体私分	Collective Illegal Possession of Public Funds						
巨额财产来源不明	Unstated Source of Large Properties						
其　他	Others						
渎职侵权案件小计	**Sub-total of Cases on Abuse and Dereliction of Duty**	**10**	**1**	**1**	**1**	**1**	**1**
滥用职权	Abuse of Power	6	1	1	1	1	1
玩忽职守	Dereliction o fDuty						
徇私舞弊	Fraudulent Practice	2					
其　他	Others	2					

18－2 检察机关处理申诉案件情况

Appeals Handled by Procurator's Offices

计量单位.件　　(2017 年)　　(case)

案件分类	Case Item	受理 Cases Accepted	立案复查 Cases Registered for Reinvestigation	结案 Cases Settled	改变原决定 Original Decision Changed
总　计	**Total**	**10**	**7**	**6**	
不服检察机关处理决定小计	**Appealsagainst Decision of Procurator's Offices**	**2**	**2**	**1**	
不服不批捕	Appeals against Rejection of Arrest				
不服不起诉	Appeals against Rejection of Prosecuting	2	2	1	
不服撤案	Appeals against With drawal of the Case				
不服原免予起诉	Appeals against Original Exemption of Lawsuit				
其　他	Others				
不服法院刑事判决裁定小计	**Appealsagainst Judgment of Criminal Case**	**8**	**5**	**5**	
刑罚执行中被害人申诉	Appeals of the Victimat the Punishment	1			
刑罚执行中被告人申诉	Appeals of the Defendant at the Punishment				
刑罚执行完毕后被害人申诉	Appeals of the Victim after the Punishment	2			
刑罚执行完毕后被告人申诉	Appeals of the Defendant after the Punishment	5	5	5	

18—3 检察机关审查批准、决定逮捕犯罪嫌疑人和提起公诉被告人情况

Arrests of criminal suspects and Defendants under Public Prosecution Approved by Procurator's Offices

(2017 年)

指　　标	Item	批捕、决定逮捕合计 Total of Arrests		起诉合计 Total of Public Prosecution	
		件 (Case)	人 (Person)	件 (Case)	人 (Person)
总　计	**Total**	**777**	**1 379**	**1 256**	**1 948**
公安、安全、监狱机关侦查案件小计	Sub-total of Requests by Departments of State and Public	737	1 339	1 171	1 855
危害国家安全案	Offences Against State Security	3	3	2	2
危害公共安全案	Offences Against Public Security	83	360	316	549
破坏社会主义市场经济秩序案	Offences Against Socialist Economic Order	37	47	46	74
侵犯公民人身、民主权利案	Offences Against Citizens'personal and Democratic Rights	159	211	232	306
侵犯财产案	Offences Against Properties	283	417	362	551
妨害社会管理秩序案	Offences Against Social Management of Order	172	301	213	373
其他案件	Other Offences				
检察机关立案侦查案件小计	Sub-total of Cases Handled by Procuratorates	40	40	85	93
贪污贿赂案	Offences on Corruption and Bribery	38	38	83	91
渎职侵权案	Offences on Abuse and Dereliction of Duty	2	2	2	2

18—4 律师、公证、基层法律服务、人民调解工作基本情况

Basic Statistics on Lawyers, Notarization, Grassroots Legal Service and Mediation Work

指　　标		Item		2015	2016	2017
律师工作		**Lawyers**				
律师事务所	(所)	Law Offices	(unit)	46	50	53
执业律师	(人)	Lawyers	(person)	459	475	484
担任法律顾问	(家)	Units with Permanent Legal Advisers	(unit)	640	660	1419
刑事诉讼辩护及代理	(件)	Agent of Criminal Defense	(case)	564	650	975
民事案件诉讼代理	(件)	Agent of Civil Case	(case)	4 310	4 540	6 856
经济案件诉讼代理	(件)	Agent of Economic Case	(case)	1 300	1 315	1 271
行政案件诉讼代理	(件)	Agent of Administration Action	(case)	23	56	84
非诉讼法律事务	(件)	Off-court Case	(case)	54	216	392
解答法律咨询	(人次)	Agent of Legal Advisory Services	(person)	9 129	13 800	15 690
索回赔欠款	(万元)	Claim for Compensation	(10 000 yuan)	14 600	15 100	17 050
公证工作		**Notarization**				
公证处	(个)	Notary Offices	(unit)	25	23	23
执业公证员	(人)	Notarial Personnel	(person)	59	46	48
办理公证文书	(件)	Notarized Document	(case)	35 442	14 701	19 119
基层法律服务工作		**Basic Law Servings**				
基层法律服务所	(所)	Basic Law Offices	(unit)	194	194	193
基层法律工作者	(人)	Basic Law Operator	(person)	653	631	589
担任法律顾问	(家)	Unitswith Permanent Legal Advisers	(unit)	2 530	2 997	2 317
代理民事经济诉讼事务	(件)	Agent of Civil Case	(case)	575	756	2 004
代理非诉讼事务	(件)	Agent of Off-court Case	(case)	832	983	3 412
审查办理合同和涉农事务	(件)	Censor and Transact Contract and Come Down to Agricultural Business	(case)	132 700	135 600	126 700
调解纠纷	(件)	Disputes Mediated	(case)	8 560	16 258	5 976
挽回经济损失	(万元)	Redeem Economic losing	(10 000 yuan)	16 800	15 873	11 093
人民调解工作		**People's Mediation**				
人民调解委员会	(个)	People's Mediation Committees	(unit)	3 629	3 681	3 687
调解人员	(人)	Mediators	(person)	22 041	22 121	21 818
调解民间纠纷	(件)	Civil Disputes Mediated	(case)	16 829	17 143	15 656
法律援助		**LawHelp**				
法律援助工作站	(个)	Law Help Station	(unit)	330	349	383
受理申请	(件)	Accepted	(unit)	3 965	3 581	3 863
获得批准	(件)	Approvaled	(unit)	3 940	3 562	3 683
办　结	(件)	Settled	(unit)	3 940	3 562	3 683

18－5　法院民商事案件收案和结案情况

Civil and Commercial Cases Accepted and Settled by People's Court

计量单位：件　　(2017 年)　　(case)

指　　标	Item	收　案 Cases Accepted	结　案 Cases Settled	判　决 Judgement	裁　定 Adjudication	调　解 Mediation	移　送 Handover
民商事案件	Civil and commercial cases	36 828	32 338	15 139	8 412	8 500	287
人格权纠纷	Dissension of personality right	652	574	331	102	140	1
婚姻家庭、继承纠纷	Marriage and family, inheritance disputes	4 021	3 695	945	965	1 760	25
物权纠纷	Real right dispute	15	15	4	7	4	
不动产登记纠纷	Real estate registration dispute	4	3	2	1		
物权保护纠纷	Disputes over the protection of real right	826	717	353	232	122	10
所有权纠纷	Dispute of ownership	199	181	78	48	52	3
用益物权纠纷	Usufructuary right dispute	79	72	34	22	12	4
担保物权纠纷	Dispute of real right of security	4	4	1		3	
占有保护纠纷	Possession of protection disputes	13	13	8	4	1	
缔约过失责任纠纷	Liability for negligence in contracting	5	4	3		1	
确认合同效力纠纷	Confirm the dispute of contract validity	213	178	107	44	26	1
债权人代位权纠纷	Dissension of the creditor's subrogation	4	4	3	1		
债权人撤销权纠纷	Dissension of creditor's right of revocation	5	4	3	1		
债权转让合同纠纷	Dispute on contract of transfer of creditor's rights	45	33	11	11	10	1
债务转移合同纠纷	Debt transfer contract dispute	16	13	11		2	
债权债务概括转移合同纠纷	Creditor's debt and debt summary transfer contract dispute	3	3	2	1		
悬赏广告纠纷	Offer a reward for advertising disputes	4	4	1			3
买卖合同纠纷	Contract dispute	6 315	5 684	2 587	1 675	1 399	23
招标投标买卖合同纠纷	Dispute on contract of bid and bid	2	1	1			
建设用地使用权合同纠纷	Contract disputes of the right to use the construction land	18	8	6	1	1	
采矿权转让合同纠纷	Disputes on the transfer of mining rights	1	1		1		
房地产开发经营合同纠纷	Dispute of real estate development and management contract	28	19	12	4	3	
房屋买卖合同纠纷	Housing contract dispute	2 062	1 743	689	324	725	5
房屋拆迁安置补偿合同纠纷	Disputes on compensation contract for housing relocation and resettlement	114	98	60	22	15	1
供用电合同纠纷	Power supply contract dispute	8	6	3	1	2	
供用水合同纠纷	Water supply contract dispute	4	4	1	2	1	
供用气合同纠纷	Contract dispute of supply and use of gas	1	1	1			
供用热力合同纠纷	Supply and use of thermal contract disputes	363	344	108	184	52	
赠与合同纠纷	Contract disputes	6	6	2	4		
借款合同纠纷	Loan contract dispute	8 066	7 184	3 728	1 744	1 678	34
保证合同纠纷	Guarantee the contract dispute	19	17	13	4		
抵押合同纠纷	Mortgage contract dispute	11	10	4	4	2	
定金合同纠纷	Deposit contract dispute	14	13	7	5	1	
储蓄存款合同纠纷	Dispute of savings deposit contract	5	4	3	1		
银行卡纠纷	Bank card dispute	10	10	6	4		
租赁合同纠纷	Leasehold contract dispute	945	809	371	252	178	8
融资租赁合同纠纷	Dispute of financing lease contract	23	17	11	5	1	

18—5 续表 Continued

计量单位:件 (2017 年) (case)

指 标	Item	收 案 Cases Accepted	结 案 Cases Settled	判 决 Judgement	裁 定 Adjudication	调 解 Mediation	移 送 Handover
承揽合同纠纷	Contract disputes	999	870	375	276	215	4
建设工程合同纠纷	Contract disputes in Construction Engineering	1 680	1 349	741	403	192	13
运输合同纠纷	Dispute of transportation contract	207	181	94	40	47	
保管合同纠纷	Custody of contract disputes	2	2	1		1	
仓储合同纠纷	Warehousing contract dispute	3	3	3			
委托合同纠纷	Dispute of entrustment contract	43	43	21	12	10	
委托理财合同纠纷	Dispute of entrustment of financial contract	7	7	4	1	2	
居间合同纠纷	Inter contract disputes	42	37	18	16	3	
借用合同纠纷	Borrowing contract disputes	2	1		1		
典当纠纷	Pawnpawn dispute	23	18	11	2	5	
合伙协议纠纷	Partnership agreement dispute	207	173	92	45	35	1
种植、养殖回收合同纠纷	Dispute over the contract of cultivation and Cultivation	213	164	76	47	41	
农业承包合同纠纷	Disputes on agricultural contract	206	181	123	41	16	1
林业承包合同纠纷	Disputes on the contract of forestry	6	3	2	1		
渔业承包合同纠纷	Dispute on contract of fishery	4	4	4			
牧业承包合同纠纷	Dispute of contract for animal husbandry	7	7	3	1	3	
农村土地承包合同纠纷	Rural land contract disputes	342	290	145	97	45	3
服务合同纠纷	Service contract dispute	473	446	134	263	49	
劳务合同纠纷	dispute over a labor contract	2 100	1 944	942	446	535	21
广告合同纠纷	Advertising contract dispute	4	4	3			1
追偿权纠纷	Dispute of recourse	446	384	217	71	96	
不当得利纠纷	Unjust enrichment dispute	554	487	259	121	102	5
无因管理纠纷	No dispute over management	11	8	5	2		1
知识产权合同纠纷	Intellectual property contract disputes	16	15	4	3	8	
知识产权权属、侵权纠纷	Intellectual property rights, tort disputes	19	19	7	7	5	
劳动争议、人事争议	Labor dispute and personnel dispute	971	823	495	172	130	26
与公司、证券、保险、票据等有关的民事纠纷	Civil disputes related to company, securities, insurance, negotiable instruments, etc.	8	8		7	1	
与企业有关的纠纷	Business related disputes	17	13	10	1	2	
与公司有关的纠纷	A company related dispute	170	141	89	35	10	7
合伙企业纠纷	Partnership disputes	11	10	4	4	2	
与破产有关的纠纷	An insolvency related dispute	75	64	52	5	4	3
证券纠纷	Securities disputes	25	24	22	2		
保险纠纷	Insurance dispute	151	132	89	24	17	2
票据纠纷	dispute over commercial instrument	13	12	8	1	3	
侵权责任纠纷	Tort liability dispute	2 683	2 327	1245	374	684	24
适用特殊程序案件	Application of special procedure cases	111	84	57	22	1	4
其 他	Other	854	564	274	193	45	52

18—6 法院各类申诉、申请再审案件收案和结案情况

Various Litigation, Application and Re-appeal Cases Accepted and Settled by People's Court

计量单位:件 (2017 年) (case)

指 标	Item	收 案 Cases Accepted	结 案 Cases Settled	驳 回 Reject	撤 诉 Withdrawal	裁定或决定 Adjudication	终 结 Termination	其 他 Other
各类申诉、申请再审案件	**Various Litigation Application and Re-appeal Cases**	**862**	**803**	**586**	**51**	**165**		**1**
刑事案件	Criminal Cases	32	28	25	1	2		
民事案件	Civil Cases	778	730	522	50	157		1
# 婚姻家庭、继承案件	Marriages Family and Inheritance Cases	25	23	19	1	3		
合同案件	Contract Cases	545	511	358	31	121		1
权属、侵权案件	Right Infringement Cases							
行政案件	Administrative Cases	52	45	39		6		
其 他	Others							

18—7 法院执行案件收案和结案情况

Execution Cases Accepted and Settled by People's Court

计量单位:件 (2017 年) (case)

指 标	Item	收 案 Cases Accepted	结 案 Cases Settled	不予执行 Rejection of Prosecuting	自动履行 Automatically Implement	和 解 Reconciliation	强制执行 Compulsory Execution	终 结 Termination	其 他 Other
执行案件	**Executive Cases**	**21 256**	**15 503**	**1 092**	**2 869**	**291**	**4 281**	**1 822**	**5 148**
刑事案件	Criminal Cases	716	578	9	90		85	122	272
民事案件	Civil Cases	17 084	12 125	993	2 488		2 627	1 434	4 583
婚姻家庭、继承	Marriages Family and Inheritance	617	483	64	190		113	35	81
合 同	Contract	14 607	10 232	742	1 877		2 178	1 278	4 157
权属、侵权	Authorityed and Infringement	3	2		2				
其 他	Others	1 857	1 408	187	419		336	121	345
行政案件	Administrativc Ca3c3	31	9	3	5		1		
行政非诉审查与执行	Administrative Examination and Exection	14	4		1		3		
仲 裁	Arbitration	58	43		18		13	3	9
公证债权文书	Notary Creditor Document	548	361	11	35		76	149	90
其 他	Others	2 805	2 383	76	232	291	1 476	114	194

18—8 法院行政案件收案和结案情况

Administrative Cases Accepted and Settled by People's Court

计量单位:件 (2017 年) (case)

指 标	Item	收 案 Cases Accepted	结 案 Cases Settled	判 决 Judgement	裁 定 Adjudication	行政赔偿 Mediation
行政案件	**Adminstrative Case**	**380**	**335**	**114**	**220**	**1**
处罚类	Punishment class	48	42	19	23	
强制措施类	Coercive measures	8	8	1	7	
侵犯经营自主权类	Infringement of business autonomy	1	1		1	
许可类	License class	1	1	1		
保护人身、财产权类	Protection of personal and property rights	3	3		3	
抚恤金类	Pensions	5	3	2	1	
违法要求履行义务类	Violation of the law requires the performance of the obligation category	1	1		1	
侵权类	Tort	31	29	10	19	
确权类	Definite right class	9	9	3	6	
赔偿类	Compensation category	42	40	11	29	
其 他	Others	231	198	67	130	1

18—9 基本养老保险情况

Conditions of Basic Pension Insurance

（2017 年）

指 标	Item	参保职工期末人数（人） Active Contributors at the Initial Stage (person)	实际缴费人员期末数（人） Active Contributors at the Final Stage (person)	离退休（职）人员期末数（人） Retirees and Retirees with Honours at the Final Stage(person)	#退休人员 Retirees	本期办理退休人员（人） Retirement in the Year (person)	应发养老金额（万元） Payable Persion (10 000 yuan)	#退休金 Retiement Pension	实发养老金额（万元） Actually Payed Persion (10 000 yuan)	#退休金 Retirement Pension
总 计	**Total**	**1 022 963**	**936 405**	**659 079**	**654 698**	**37 872**	**2 438 233**	**2 400 183**	**2 438 233**	**2 400 183**
企业养老保险制度	**Enterprise Endowment Insurance**	**929 424**	**843 831**	**594 179**	**589 798**	**37 465**	**2 063 267**	**2 025 217**	**2 063 267**	**2 025 217**
企 业	Enterprises	643 642	591 718	467 783	463 660	26 768	1 739 503	1 703 833	1 739 503	1 703 833
国有企业	State-owned Enterprises	553 631	512 177	456 519	452 412	25 537	1 698 207	1 662 659	1 698 207	1 662 659
集体企业	Collective-owned Enterprises	149	149	548	548	5	1 745	1 745	1 745	1 745
其他企业	Others	89 862	79 392	10 716	10 700	1 226	39 551	39 429	39 551	39 429
港澳台及外资企业	Enterprises with Funds from Hong Kong, Macao, Taiwan and Foreign									
机关、事业	Govermental Organs and Institutions			258			2 380		2 380	
其 他	Others	285 782	252 113	126 138	126 138	10 697	321 384	321 384	321 384	321 384
机关事业养老保险制度	**Govermental Organs and Institutions Units Endowment Insurance**	**93 539**	**92 574**	**64 900**	**64 900**	**407**	**374 966**	**374 966**	**374 966**	**374 966**
机 关	Govermental Organs	26 626	26 215	11 877	11 877	149	73 480	73 480	73 480	73 480
事 业	Institutions Units	66 913	66 359	53 023	53 023	258	301 486	301 486	301 486	301 486
其 他	Others									

指 标	Item	社会化发放人数（人） Retirees Payed by Social Institutions (person)	社会化发放养老金金额（万元） Pension Payed by Social Institutions (10 000 yuan)	缴费基数总额（万元） Payment Base Amount(10 000yuan)		全额缴拨（万元） Full Payment (10 000 yuan)			
				单 位 Unit	个 人 Individual	单位应缴金额 Payable Amount by Units	单位实缴金额 Actual Payment Amount by Units	个人应缴金额 Payable Amount by Individuals	个人实缴金额 Actual Payment Amount by Individuals
总 计	**Total**	**659 079**	**2 438 233**	**3 069 758**	**3 897 105**	**590 209**	**587 222**	**411 055**	**400 398**
企业养老保险制度	**Enterprise Endowment Insurance**	**594 179**	**2 063 267**	**2 376 534**	**3 203 881**	**451 566**	**448 579**	**355 595**	**344 938**
企 业	Enterprises	467 783	1 739 503	2 376 534	2 376 534	451 566	448 579	190 125	188 868
国有企业	State-owned Enterprises	456 519	1 698 207	2 040 081	2 040 081	387 639	386 641	163 208	162 788
集体企业	Collective-owned Enterprises	548	1 745	610	610	116	116	49	49
其他企业	Others	10 716	39 551	335 843	335 843	63 811	61 822	26 868	26 031
港澳台及外资企业	Enterprises with Funds from Hong Kong, Macao, Taiwan and Foreign								
机关、事业	Govermental Organs and Institutions	258	2 380						
其 他	Others	126 138	321 384		827 347			165 470	156 070
机关事业养老保险制度	**Govermental Organs and Institutions Units Endowment Insurance**	**64 900**	**374 966**	**693 224**	**693 224**	**138 643**	**138 643**	**55 460**	**55 460**
机 关	Govermental Organs	11 877	73 480	209 366	209 366	41 872	41 872	16 751	16 751
事 业	Institutions Units	53 023	301 486	483 858	483 858	96 771	96 771	38 709	38 709
其 他	Others								

18－10 各师职工基本养老保险情况

Conditions of Basic Pension Insurance for Staff by Division

(2017 年)

单 位	Unit	参保职工期末人数(人) Active Contributors at the Initial Stage (person)	实际缴费人员期末人数(人) Active Contributors at the Final Stage (person)	离退休(职)人员期末人数(人) Retirees and Retirees with Honours at the Final Stage(person)	# 退休人员 Retirees	本期办理退休人员(人) Retirement in the Year (person)	应发养老金额(万元) Payable Persion (10 000 yuan)	# 退休金 Retiement Pension	实发养老金额(万元) Actually Payed Persion (10 000 yuan)	# 退休金 Retirement Pension
总 计	**Total**	**1 022 963**	**936 405**	**659 079**	**654 698**	**37 872**	**2 438 233**	**2 400 183**	**2 438 233**	**2 400 183**
一 师	Division 1	116 642	107 841	67 034	66 554	6 841	244 490	240 178	244 490	240 178
二 师	Division 2	83 076	70 085	64 057	63 471	4 976	242 846	237 172	242 846	237 172
三 师	Division 3	42 581	42 381	29 837	29 512	1 163	103 930	101 326	103 930	101 326
四 师	Division 4	86 124	80 327	61 253	60 798	2 945	229 504	225 709	229 504	225 709
五 师	Division 5	46 042	42 363	24 962	24 829	2 073	85 735	84 583	85 735	84 583
六 师	Division 6	111 890	107 898	78 571	78 258	4 227	280 937	278 447	280 937	278 447
七 师	Division 7	72 130	62 173	58 935	58 618	2 718	216 464	214 040	216 464	214 040
八 师	Division 8	265 658	248 589	162434	161 449	7 199	612 634	604 270	612 634	604 270
九 师	Division 9	32 390	29 153	21 890	21 693	1 392	82 317	80 438	82 317	80 438
十 师	Division 10	34 617	31 060	23 005	22 799	1 119	83 958	81 947	83 958	81 947
十 一 师	Division 11	15 862	13 445	10 757	10 667	423	41 643	40 740	41 643	40 740
十 二 师	Division 12	30 868	28 372	20 175	20 062	1 206	71 269	70 320	71 269	70 320
十 三 师	Division 13	37 898	35 696	18 471	18 386	873	64 661	64 035	64 661	64 035
十 四 师	Division 14	17 540	15 794	4 647	4 624	197	18 031	17 772	18 031	17 772
兵团直属	Directly under XPCC	29 645	21 228	13 051	12 978	520	59 814	59 206	59 814	59 206

单 位	Unit	社会化发放人数(人) Retirees Payed by Social Institutions (person)	社会化发放养老金额(万元) Pension Payed by Social Institutions (10 000 yuan)	缴费基数总额(万元) Payment Base Amount(10 000 yuan)		全额缴拨(万元) Full Payment (10 000 yuan)			
				单 位 Unit	个 人 Individual	单位应缴金额 Payable Amount by Units	单位实缴金额 Actual Payment Amount by Units	个人应缴金额 Payable Amount by Individuals	个人实缴金额 Actual Payment Amount by Individuals
总 计	**Total**	**659 079**	**2 438 233**	**3 069 758**	**3 897 105**	**590 209**	**587 222**	**411 055**	**400 398**
一 师	Division 1	67 034	244 490	345 519	425 764	66 530	66 530	43 690	43 690
二 师	Division 2	64 057	242 846	235 162	281 662	45 191	45 191	28 113	28 113
三 师	Division 3	29 837	103 930	163 737	182 962	31 666	31 666	16 944	16 944
四 师	Division 4	61 253	229 504	231 652	306 518	44 464	44 464	33 507	33 507
五 师	Division 5	24 962	85 735	140 128	168 128	26 922	26 922	16 810	16 810
六 师	Division 6	78 571	280 937	325 714	444 716	62 560	62 560	49 857	49 857
七 师	Division 7	58 935	216 464	200 595	249 895	38 486	38 486	25 907	25 907
八 师	Division 8	162 434	612 634	789 477	1 080 652	151 659	148 672	121 394	110 737
九 师	Division 9	21 890	82 317	104 465	116 940	20 058	20 058	10 853	10 853
十 师	Division 10	23 005	83 958	101 751	124 476	19 587	19 587	12 685	12 685
十 一 师	Division 11	10 757	41 643	64 759	71 304	12 387	12 387	6 490	6 490
十 二 师	Division 12	20 175	71 269	86 296	112 366	16 578	16 578	12 118	12 118
十 三 师	Division 13	18 471	64 661	107 655	143 119	20 671	20 671	15 708	15 708
十 四 师	Division 14	4 647	18 031	61 310	61 915	11 766	11 766	5 026	5 026
兵团直属	Directly under XPCC	13 051	59 814	111 538	126 688	21 684	21 684	11 953	11 953

18—11 参加职工基本医疗保险人员及缴费基数情况

Statistics on Medical Care Insurance and Fund Collection for Staff and Workers

(2017 年)

指　标	Item	基本医疗参保人数（人） Active Contributors of Basic Medical Insurance (person)	年末在岗职工 Staff and Workers on the Job at the Final Stage	年末退休人员 Retirees at the Final Stage	统帐结合缴费基数总额（万元） Payment Base Amount (10 000 yuan)		单建统筹缴费基数总额（万元） Signal Payment Base Amount (10 000 yuan)	特殊人员人数（人） Number of Special People (person)		
					单　位 Unit	个　人 Individual		医疗照顾人员 Persons Cared by Medical Treament	离休及老红军 Retirees with Honours and Veteran Red Army	1—6级革命伤残军人 Disabled Army with Level 1 — Level 6
总　计	**Total**	**1 353 566**	**807 803**	**545 763**	**3 422 692**	**3 187 640**	**569 228**	**171**	**4 386**	**27**
企　业	Enterprises	1 029 964	574 869	455 095	2 579 710	2 365 999		5	4 009	25
事　业	Institutions	124 260	73 730	50 530	566 190	547 960		38	238	2
机　关	Governmental Organs	41 027	29 409	11 618	249 147	246 036		128	139	
其　他	Others	158 315	129 795	28 520	27 645	27 645	569 228			

18—12 各师参加职工基本医疗保险人员及缴费基数情况

Statistics on Medical Care Insurance and Funds Collection for Staff and Workers by Division

(2017 年)

单　位	Unit	基本医疗参保人数（人） Active Contributors of Basic Medical Insurance (person)	年末在岗职工 Staff and Workers on the Job at the Final Stage	年末退休人员 Retirees at the Final Stage	统帐结合缴费基数总额（万元） Payment Base Amount (10 000 yuan)		单建统筹缴费基数总额（万元） Signal Payment Base Amount (10 000 yuan)	特殊人员人数（人） Number of Special People (person)		
					单　位 Unit	个　人 Individual		医疗照顾人员 Persons Cared by Medical Treament	离休及老红军 Retirees with Honours and Veteran Red Army	1—6级革命伤残军人 Disabled Army with Level 1 — Level 6
总　计	**Total**	**1 353 566**	**807 803**	**545 763**	**3 422 692**	**3 187 640**	**569 228**	**171**	**4 386**	**27**
一　师	Division 1	151 097	91 059	60 038	351 040	351 040	42 017		480	
二　师	Division 2	126 003	70 176	55 827	235 600	235 600	31 071		586	
三　师	Division 3	59 338	37 432	21 906	179 364	179 364	2 342		325	
四　师	Division 4	111 630	59 260	52 370	231 769	231 769	7 029		455	19
五　师	Division 5	58 609	38 575	20 034	142 911	142 911	13 107		133	
六　师	Division 6	161 634	95 983	65 651	340 460	340 460	94 636		313	
七　师	Division 7	100 833	50 443	50 390	357 445	205 265	28 045	32	317	
八　师	Division 8	330 955	206 308	124 647	867 636	784 764	283 686	109	985	8
九　师	Division 9	48 070	28 439	19 631	115 290	115 290			197	
十　师	Division 10	48 009	29 260	18 749	105 600	105 600	19 800		206	
十一师	Division 11	24 106	14 816	9 290	65 139	65 139	9 980		90	
十二师	Division 12	39 531	22 555	16 976	138 819	138 819			118	
十三师	Division 13	39 970	26 313	13 657	108 834	108 834	9 827	30	85	
十四师	Division 14	19 850	15 594	4 256	61 700	61 700			23	
兵团直属	Directly under XPCC	33 931	21 590	12 341	121 085	121 085	27 688		73	

18－13 职工基本医疗保险费征缴情况

Conditions of Funds Collection of Basic Medical Care Insurance Premium for Staff and Workers

计量单位：万元　　(2017年)　　(10 000 yuan)

指标	Item	统帐结合缴费基数总额(万元) Payment Base Amount(10 000 yuan)							单建统筹缴费基数总额(万元) Signal Payment Base Amount (10 000 yuan)	
		期初欠费 Arreas at the Initial Stage	应缴基本医疗保险费 Payable Basic Medical Insurance Premium			实缴基本医疗保险费 Actual Payment of Basic Medical Insurance Premium			应缴基本医疗保险费 Payable Basic Medical Insurance Premium	实缴基本医疗保险费 Actual Payment of Basic Medical Insurance Premium
			合计 Total	单位 Unit	个人 Individual	合计 Total	单位 Unit	个人 Individual		
总计	**Total**		**344 501**	**280 752**	**63 749**	**343 596**	**279 998**	**63 598**	**35 489**	**34 908**
企业	Enterprises		257 583	210 269	47 314	256 678	209 515	47 163		
事业	Institutions		58 564	47 604	10 960	58 564	47 604	10 960		
机关	Governmental Organs		25 745	20 824	4 921	25 745	20 824	4 921		
其他	Others		2 609	2 055	554	2 609	2 055	554	35 489	34 908

18－14 各师职工基本医疗保险费征缴情况

Conditions of Funds Collection of Basic Medical Insurance Premium for Staff and Workers by Division

计量单位：万元　　(2017年)　　(10 000 yuan)

单位	Unit	统帐结合缴费基数总额(万元) Payment Base Amount(10 000 yuan)							单建统筹缴费基数总额(万元) Signal Payment Base Amount (10 000 yuan)	
		期初欠费 Arreas at the Initial Stage	应缴基本医疗保险费 Payable Basic Medical Insurance Premium			实缴基本医疗保险费 Actual Payment of Basic Medical Insurance Premium			应缴基本医疗保险费 Payable Basic Medical Insurance Premium	实缴基本医疗保险费 Actual Payment of Basic Medical Insurance Premium
			合计 Total	单位 Unit	个人 Individual	合计 Total	单位 Unit	个人 Individual		
总计	**Total**		**344 501**	**280 752**	**63 749**	**343 596**	**279 998**	**63 598**	**35 489**	**34 908**
一师	Division 1		35 104	28 084	7 020	35 104	28 084	7 020	2 521	2 521
二师	Division 2		25 920	21 210	4 710	25 920	21 210	4 710	2 175	2 175
三师	Division 3		19 729	16 142	3 587	19 729	16 142	3 587	164	164
四师	Division 4		23 176	18 541	4 635	23 176	18 541	4 635	492	492
五师	Division 5		14 292	11 433	2 859	14 292	11 433	2 859	852	852
六师	Division 6		34 046	27 237	6 809	34 046	27 237	6 809	6 151	6 151
七师	Division 7		27 339	23 234	4 105	27 339	23 234	4 105	1 402	1 402
八师	Division 8		91 545	75 850	15 695	90 640	75 096	15 544	17 872	17 291
九师	Division 9		11 529	9 223	2 306	11 529	9 223	2 306		
十师	Division 10		10 560	8 448	2 112	10 560	8 448	2 112	1 386	1 386
十一师	Division 11		7 166	5 863	1 303	7 166	5 863	1 303	499	499
十二师	Division 12		13 724	10 948	2 776	13 724	10 948	2 776		
十三师	Division 13		10 882	8 706	2 176	10 882	8 706	2 176	590	590
十四师	Division 14		6 170	4 936	1 234	6 170	4 936	1 234		
兵团直属	Directly under XPCC		13 319	10 897	2 422	13 319	10 897	2 422	1 385	1 385

18－15 职工基本医疗保险基金支出情况

Expenses of Basic Medical Care Insurance for Staff and Workers

（2017 年）

指　标	Item	在岗职工 Staff and Workers on the Job			退休人员 Retirees		
		费用支出（万元）Expenditure (10 000 yuan)	住院人次（人次）Inpatients (person)	累计院床日（床日）Accumulated Hospitalization Bed Days(day)	费用支出（万元）Expenditure (10 000 yuan)	住院人次（人次）Inpatients (person)	累计院床日（床日）Accumulated Hospitalization Bed Days(day)
总　计	**Total**	**104 704**	**136 050**	**1 343 199**	**265 889**	**310 357**	**3 128 791**
三级医疗机构	Medical Organs with Level 3	59 201	42 639	501 688	143 788	92 506	981 142
二级医疗机构	Medical Organs with Level 2	34 502	45 746	433 504	94 774	102 779	1 092 032
一级医疗机构	Medical Organs with Level 1	11 001	47 665	408 007	27 327	115 072	1 055 617
未定级医疗机构	Not Evaluated Medical Organs						

18－16 各师职工基本医疗保险住院费用支出情况

Hospitalization Expenses Medical Care Insurance for Staff and Workers by Division

（2017 年）

单　位	Unit	在岗职工 Staff and Workers on the Job			退休人员 Retirees		
		费用支出（万元）Expenditure (10 000 yuan)	住院人次（人次）Inpatients (person)	累计院床日（床日）Accumulated Hospitalization Bed Days(day)	费用支出（万元）Expenditure (10 000 yuan)	住院人次（人次）Inpatients (person)	累计院床日（床日）Accumulated Hospitalization Bed Days(day)
总　计	**Total**	**104 704**	**136 050**	**1 343 199**	**265 889**	**310 357**	**3 128 791**
一　师	Division 1	10 037	16 617	137 268	26 938	34 829	337 275
二　师	Division 2	7 761	10 837	93 601	24 357	29 759	279 164
三　师	Division 3	5 143	8 017	74 434	11 360	14 283	149 184
四　师	Division 4	5 321	7 548	77 663	17 003	27 777	290 049
五　师	Division 5	5 015	7 533	70 334	10 200	12 156	124 430
六　师	Division 6	10 070	13 175	121 105	28 990	37 580	351 606
七　师	Division 7	5 453	8 221	154 948	21 130	26 535	277 364
八　师	Division 8	34 320	38 704	366 557	75 533	73 739	743 345
九　师	Division 9	3 769	4 898	44 660	7 782	9 617	93 243
十　师	Division 10	3 181	4 695	46 065	8 197	10 715	110 145
十一师	Division 11	2 386	1 987	18 909	6 541	5 130	56 470
十二师	Division 12	3 742	3 634	40 466	10 799	10 081	128 759
十三师	Division 13	4 132	5 558	53 471	6 843	8 713	91 060
十四师	Division 14	793	1 344	12 153	1 390	2 681	25 087
兵团直属	Directly under XPCC	3 581	3 282	31 565	8 826	6 762	71 610

18—17 参加工伤保险人员及基金征缴情况

Statistics on Work Injury Insurance and Fund Collection

（2017 年）

指 标	Item	参保职工人数（人）Active Con-tributors (person)	缴费基数总额（万元）Total Payment Base A mount (10 000 yuan)	应缴工伤保险费（万元）Payable Industrial Injury Insurance Premium(10 000 yuan)	实缴工伤保险费（万元）Actual Payment of Industrial Injury Insurance Premium(10 000 yuan)	本期补缴（万元）Overdue Payment at the Current Stage (10 000 yuan)	期末累计欠费（万元）Accumulated Arrears at the Final Stage (10 000 yuan)	享受待遇的受伤或致残人数（人）Number of Enjoying Industrial Injury and Disabled Treatment(person)			
								合 计 Total	# 职业病 Occupational Disease	一至四级 Level 1—Level 4	# 职业病 Occupational Disease
总 计	**Total**	**799 754**	**3 271 311**	**27 437**	**27 429**			**3 618**	**85**	**1 113**	**53**
企 业	Enterprises	656 252	2 490 060	24 564	24 556			3 382	85	1 097	53
事 业	Institutions	74 683	532 455	2 025	2 025			165		11	
其 他	Other	68 819	248 796	848	848			71		5	

指 标	Item	享受待遇的受伤或致残人数（人）Number of Enjoying Industrial Injury and Disabled Treatment(person)						因工死亡人数（人）Number of Death from In-dustrial Injury (person)	供养直系亲属（人）Number of Supporting Lineal Relative (person)
		五至六级 Level 5—Level 6	# 职业病 Occupational Disease	七至十级 Level 7—Level 10	# 职业病 Occupational Disease	其 他 Other	# 职业病 Occupational Disease		
总 计	**Total**	**145**	**5**	**1 398**	**8**	**962**	**19**	**149**	**913**
企 业	Enterprises	140	5	1 255	8	890	19	142	891
事 业	Institutions	3		113		38		4	12
其 他	Other	2		30		34		3	10

18－18 各师参加工伤保险人员及基金征缴情况

Statistics on Work Injury Insurance and Fund Collection by Division

(2017 年)

单 位	Unit	参保职工人数（人）Active Contributors (person)	缴费基数总额（万元）Total Payment Base A mount (10 000 yuan)	应缴工伤保险费（万元）Payable Industrial Injury Insurance Premium(10 000 yuan)	实缴工伤保险费（万元）Actual Payment of Industrial Injury Insurance Premium(10 000 yuan)	本期补缴（万元）Overdue Payment at the Current Stage (10 000 yuan)	期末累计欠费（万元）Accumulated Arrears at the Final Stage (10 000 yuan)	享受待遇的受伤或致残人数(人) Number of Enjoying Industrial Injury and Disabled Treatment(person)			
								合 计 Total	# 职业病 Occupational Disease	一至四级 Level 1—Level 4	# 职业病 Occupational Disease
总 计	**Total**	**799 754**	**3 271 311**	**27 437**	**27 429**			**3 618**	**85**	**1 113**	**53**
一 师	Division 1	106 258	350 975	3 529	3 529			443	12	184	10
二 师	Division 2	59 328	236 800	1 328	1 328			798		188	
三 师	Division 3	39 521	179 108	2 005	2 005			161	1	49	1
四 师	Division 4	67 566	254 785	1 347	1 347			187		35	
五 师	Division 5	41 701	143 506	1 188	1 188			120		31	
六 师	Division 6	77 817	429 902	4 083	4 083			334		101	
七 师	Division 7	56 219	205 265	1 587	1 587			186	6	65	6
八 师	Division 8	159 606	811 406	5 927	5 919			791	21	208	10
九 师	Division 9	25 427	106 557	952	952			74		5	
十 师	Division 10	23 856	106 070	915	915			88		40	
十一师	Division 11	64 382	64 759	1 034	1 034			79	4	34	3
十二师	Division 12	19 306	87 041	1 130	1 130			157	24	74	20
十三师	Division 13	23 754	112 352	1 257	1 257			114		73	
十四师	Division 14	19 730	61 700	739	739			9		2	
兵团直属	Directly under XPCC	15 283	121 085	416	416			77	17	24	3

单 位	Unit	享受待遇的受伤或致残人数(人) Number of Enjoying Industrial Injury and Disabled Treatment(person)						因工死亡人数（人）Number of Death from Industrial Injury (person)	供养直系亲属（人）Number of Supporting Lineal Relative (person)
		五至六级 Level 5—Level 6	# 职业病 Occupational Disease	七至十级 Level 7—Level 10	# 职业病 Occupational Disease	其 他 Other	# 职业病 Occupational Disease		
总 计	**Total**	**145**	**5**	**1 398**	**8**	**962**	**19**	**149**	**913**
一 师	Division 1	48		174	1	37	1	8	141
二 师	Division 2	11		107		492		7	115
三 师	Division 3	2		18		92		15	94
四 师	Division 4	11		24		117		5	22
五 师	Division 5	6		58		25		6	54
六 师	Division 6	9		212		12		29	134
七 师	Division 7	2		99		20		5	44
八 师	Division 8	29	4	501	5	53	2	45	152
九 师	Division 9			20		49		1	1
十 师	Division 10	7		25		16		5	33
十一师	Division 11	3	1	40		2		13	20
十二师	Division 12	3		57	2	23	2	2	46
十三师	Division 13	12		28		1		3	28
十四师	Division 14	1		5		1		2	23
兵团直属	Directly under XPCC	1		30		22	14	3	6

18—19 参加生育保险人员及基金征缴情况

Statistics on Maternity Insurance and Fund Collection

（2017 年）

指 标 Item	参保职工人数（人）Active Contributors (person)	#女性 Female	缴费基数总额（万元）Payment Base Total Amount (10 000 yuan)	应缴生育保险费（万元）Payable Birth Insurance Premium (10 000 yuan)	实缴生育保险费（万元）Actual Payment of Birth Insurance Premium (10 000 yuan)	本期享受生育保险待遇人数（人）Persons Enjoying Birth Insurance Treatment (person)	#本期生育人数 Birth Number	#顺产人数 Birth Number	#计划生育手术人次 Family Planning Operations	#流产人数 Abortion Number
总 计 Total	**679 556**	**281 932**	**3 115 213**	**12 655**	**12 571**	**17 086**	**6 514**	**2 683**	**6 394**	**881**
企 业 Enterprises	576 375	230 117	2 334 484	9 372	9 288	11 747	4 276	1 789	5 880	589
事 业 Institutions	73 884	43 091	536 366	2 249	2 249	4 531	1 917	752	465	249
机 关 Governmental Organs	29 297	8 724	244 363	1 034	1 034	808	321	142	49	43
其 他 Others										

18—20 各师参加生育保险人员及基金征缴情况

Statistics on Maternity Insurance and Fund Collection by Division

（2017 年）

单 位 Unit	参保职工人数（人）Active Contributors (person)	#女性 Female	缴费基数总额（万元）Payment Base Total Amount (10 000 yuan)	应缴生育保险费（万元）Payable Birth Insurance Premium (10 000 yuan)	实缴生育保险费（万元）Actual Payment of Birth Insurance Premium (10 000 yuan)	本期享受生育保险待遇人数（人）Persons Enjoying Birth Insurance Treatment (person)	#本期生育人数 Birth Number	#顺产人数 Birth Number	#计划生育手术人次 Family Planning Operations	#流产人数 Abortion Number
总 计 Total	**679 556**	**281 932**	**3 115 213**	**12 655**	**12 571**	**17 086**	**6 514**	**2 683**	**6 394**	**881**
一 师 Division 1	80 460	30 818	349 600	1 748	1 748	2 230	721	387	447	164
二 师 Division 2	53 806	21 478	235 000	235	235	1 257	481	239	181	79
三 师 Division 3	36 971	16 890	179 108	716	716	1 022	399	164	136	119
四 师 Division 4	58 475	27 776	231 657	463	463	908	352	201	102	22
五 师 Division 5	34 793	16 782	140 128	448	448	883	308	58	187	58
六 师 Division 6	73 536	25 977	311 845	1 247	1 247	1 900	695	150	224	132
七 师 Division 7	47 103	17 881	205 265	478	478	634	288	117	54	29
八 师 Division 8	159 173	67 694	807 313	4 037	3 953	4 032	1 610	717	579	78
九 师 Division 9	25 427	10 542	106 557	532	532	509	231	112	12	12
十 师 Division 10	23 834	10 030	106 000	530	530	551	232	94	56	17
十一师 Division 11	11 464	3 570	64 759	329	329	529	196	29	41	35
十二师 Division 12	19 264	7 611	86 798	435	435	698	269	90	80	51
十三师 Division 13	22 848	10 510	108 398	542	542	793	328	140	55	25
十四师 Division 14	17 142	7 767	61 700	309	309	426	125	51	4178	2
兵团直属 Directly under XPCC	15 260	6 606	121 085	606	606	714	279	134	62	58

18—21 参加失业保险人员及基金征缴情况

Statistics on Unemployment Insurance and Fund Collection

(2017 年)

指 标	Item	参保职工人数（人）Active Contributors (person)	单位缴费基数总额（万元）Total Payment Fund (10 000 yuan)	个人缴费基数总额（万元）Total Payment Fund (10 000 yuan)	应缴失业保险费（万元）Payable Unemployment Insurance Premium (10 000 yuan)	#个人 Individual	实缴失业保险费（万元）Actual Payment of Umenployment Insurance Premium (10 000 yuan)	#个人 Individual
总 计	**Total**	**665 621**	**2 885 787**	**2 885 787**	**28 857**	**14 430**	**28 734**	**14 368**
企 业	Enterprises	596 021	2 421 405	2 421 405	24 214	12 108	24 091	12 046
事 业	Institutions	69 600	464 382	464 382	4 643	2 322	4 643	2 322
其 他	Other							

18—22 各师参加失业保险人员及基金征缴情况

Statistics on Unemployment Insurance and Fund Collection by Division

(2017 年)

单 位	Unit	参保职工人数（人）Active Contributors (person)	单位缴费基数总额（万元）Total Payment Fund (10 000 yuan)	个人缴费基数总额（万元）Total Payment Fund (10 000 yuan)	应缴失业保险费（万元）Payable Unemployment Insurance Premium (10 000 yuan)	#个人 Individual	实缴失业保险费（万元）Actual Payment of Umenployment Insurance Premium (10 000 yuan)	#个人 Individual
总 计	**Total**	**665 621**	**2 885 787**	**2 885 787**	**28 857**	**14 430**	**28 734**	**14 368**
一 师	Division 1	78 439	317400	317 400	3 174	1 587	3 174	1 587
二 师	Division 2	52 917	220 000	220 000	2 200	1 100	2 200	1 100
三 师	Division 3	34 267	149 400	149 400	1 494	747	1 494	747
四 师	Division 4	56 413	221 537	221 537	2 216	1 108	2 216	1 108
五 师	Division 5	34 151	133 400	133 400	1 334	667	1 334	667
六 师	Division 6	69 896	308 271	308 271	3 082	1 542	3 082	1 542
七 师	Division 7	45 329	188 105	188 105	1 881	941	1 881	941
八 师	Division 8	162 822	758 619	758 619	7 587	3 794	7 464	3 732
九 师	Division 9	24 764	100 223	100 223	1 002	501	1 002	501
十 师	Division 10	23 443	98 700	98 700	987	493	987	493
十一师	Division 11	12 482	63 684	63 684	637	318	637	318
十二师	Division 12	19 623	78 232	78 232	782	391	782	391
十三师	Division 13	22 756	101 402	101 402	1 014	507	1 014	507
十四师	Division 14	15 398	56 100	56 100	561	281	561	281
兵团直属	Directly under XPCC	12 921	90 714	90 714	906	453	906	453

18—23 各师参加居民基本医疗保险人员情况

Statistics on Basic Medical Care Insurance for Residents by Division

计量单位：人 (2017 年) (person)

单位	Unit	合计 Total	成年人 Adult	# 困难人员 Poor Personnel	享受最低生活保障 Receiving Minimum Living	重残 Disabled	低收入老年人 Low Income Aged	其他 Others
总计	**Total**	**1 096 628**	**625 448**	**68 951**	**48 711**	**7 228**	**12 979**	**33**
一师	Division 1	135 449	82 516	8 366	8 366			
二师	Division 2	76 508	46 137	3 577	3 033	197	347	
三师	Division 3	148 076	85 702	8 137	7 722	415		
四师	Division 4	94 330	52 795	4 212	3 182	785	222	23
五师	Division 5	47 716	25 397	2 608	1 645	212	751	
六师	Division 6	118 540	67 550	11 621	6 266	2 308	3 047	
七师	Division 7	70 304	50 257	5 578	4 634	86	858	
八师	Division 8	236 577	129 336	17 856	8 562	1 922	7 372	
九师	Division 9	18 353	9 024	983	792	140	51	
十师	Division 10	33 820	16 643	1 190	777	389	24	
十一师	Division 11	7 797	2 563	189	114	74	1	
十二师	Division 12	35 804	18 440	683	435	248		
十三师	Division 13	49 023	28 596	2 682	2 227	325	120	10
十四师	Division 14	22 535	9 255	1 230	939	106	185	
兵团直属	Directly under XPCC	1 796	1 237	39	17	21	1	

单位	Unit	中小学生 Students of Regular Secondary Schools and Primary Schools	# 困难人员 Poor Personnel	享受最低生活保障 Receiving Minimum Living	重残 Disabled	其他 Others	大学生 Students of University	# 困难人员 Poor Personnel
总计	**Total**	**450 251**	**10 498**	**8 548**	**595**	**1 355**	**20 929**	**568**
一师	Division 1	50 700					2 233	
二师	Division 2	30 371	194	179	10	5		
三师	Division 3	62 374	1 076	1 025	51			
四师	Division 4	41 535	1 526	1 412	102	12		
五师	Division 5	22 319	191	168	23			
六师	Division 6	48 216	610	345	146	119	2 774	
七师	Division 7	20 047	501	483	18			
八师	Division 8	91 484	2 366	1 037	112	1 217	15 757	551
九师	Division 9	9 329	528	504	24			
十师	Division 10	17 155	311	276	35		22	5
十一师	Division 11	5 234	17	15	2			
十二师	Division 12	17 364	130	115	15			
十三师	Division 13	20 403	1 009	984	23	2	24	
十四师	Division 14	13 262	2 039	2 005	34		18	12
兵团直属	Directly under XPCC	458					101	

18—24 各师社会救济情况

Social Relief by Division

(2017 年)

单 位	Unit	城镇居民最低生活保障人数(人) Bottommost Living Security of Urban Households (person)	城镇居民最低生活保障家庭数(户) Number of Bottommost Living Security of Urban Households (household)	城镇临时救济人次数(人次) Temporarily Relief of Urban Households (person-time)
总 计	**Total**	**75 198**	**49 525**	**181 436**
一 师	Division 1	5 112	3 385	22 874
二 师	Division 2	6 511	3 778	20 044
三 师	Division 3	13 271	9 428	16 397
四 师	Division 4	7 821	4 225	12 779
五 师	Division 5	3 516	2 947	6 294
六 师	Division 6	5 712	5 340	17 947
七 师	Division 7	7 481	5 462	10 328
八 师	Division 8	13 010	8 538	19 547
九 师	Division 9	1 993	1 113	6 904
十 师	Division 10	2 330	1 260	16 322
十一师	Division 11	822	614	4 287
十二师	Division 12	1 066	718	9 995
十三师	Division 13	2 890	1 480	11 355
十四师	Division 14	3 338	1 029	5 082
兵团直属	Directly under XPCC	325	208	1 281

18—25 民办非企业单位

Private Non-enterprises Units

计量单位:个 (2017 年) (unit)

单 位	Unit	年末实有民办非企业单位 Actual Number of Non-enterprises Units of Civil-Run at the Year-end	按性质分 Grouped by Kindby Sector: 法 人 Corporation	合 伙 Partnership	个 体 Individual	职工人数(人) Staff and Workers (person)	# 女 性 Female
总 计	**Total**	**339**	**336**		**3**	**3 011**	**1 793**
兵团本级	XPCC	17	17			672	210
一 师	Division 1	1	1			12	8
二 师	Division 2	19	19			50	20
三 师	Division 3	5	5			20	15
四 师	Division 4	2			2	11	9
五 师	Division 5						
六 师	Division 6	46	46			495	339
七 师	Division 7						
八 师	Division 8	233	233			1 476	995
九 师	Division 9						
十 师	Division 10	4	4			102	78
十一师	Division 11	1	1			3	2
十二师	Division 12	9	9			145	93
十三师	Division 13	2	1		1	25	24
十四师	Division 14						
兵团直属	Directly under XPCC						

18－26 社会团体机构情况

Basic Statistics on Public Organization

计量单位:个 (2017 年) (unit)

单 位	Unit	年末实有社团 Actual Number of Public Organizations at the Year-end	按活动区域分 Grouped by Active District 省级社团 Public Organizations at the Provincial Level	地级社团 Public Organizations at the Prefectural Level	县级社团 Public Organizations at the County Level	职工人数(人) Staff and Workers (person)	#女 性 Female
总 计	**Total**	**591**	**122**	**220**	**249**	**3 006**	**1 039**
兵团本级	XPCC	122	122			565	123
一 师	Division 1	39		39		482	217
二 师	Division 2	30		16	14	126	37
三 师	Division 3	32		32		50	12
四 师	Division 4	29		17	12	52	27
五 师	Division 5	13		11	2	51	1
六 师	Division 6	40			40	130	6
七 师	Division 7	42		41	1	207	128
八 师	Division 8	105			105	554	254
九 师	Division 9	23		23		368	79
十 师	Division 10	52			52	232	101
十一师	Division 11	9		4	5	12	3
十二师	Division 12	10		7	3	30	14
十三师	Division 13	33		19	14	105	23
十四师	Division 14	12		11	1	42	14
兵团直属	Directly under XPCC						

18－27 兵团级社会团体名录

Directory of Public Organizations at the Level of XPCC

(2017 年)

名 称	Name	主管单位	Department in Charge
兵团工会	The Trade Union of XPCC	中华全国总工会	Annula Check and Only on Record National Labor Union of China
兵团工商业联合会	The Industry and Commerce Association of XPCC	兵团党委统战部	The United Front Department of XPCC Party Committee
兵团保安协会	The Ensure Public Security Association of XPCC	兵团公安局	The Public Security Bureau of XPCC
石河子大学对外文化交流协会	The Foreign Culture Communion Association of Shihezi University	兵团文化广播电视局	The culture,Broadcast and Television Bureau of XPCC
兵团有机产品协会	The Organic Product Association of XPCC	兵团环保局	The Environmental Protection Bureau of XPCC
兵团民营经济研究会	The Private Economy Research Society of XPCC	兵团工商联	The Industry and Commerce Association of XPCC
兵团煤炭工业协会	The Coal Industry Association of XPCC	兵团工业和信息化委员会	The Industry and Informatization Commission of XPCC
兵团福建商会	Fujian Commerce of XPCC	兵团经济技术协作办公室	The Economic and Technological Co-operation Office of XPCC
兵团建材行业商会	The Building Material Commerce of XPCC	兵团工商联	The Industry and Commerce Association of XPCC
兵团老年大学协会	The Association of Agedness University	兵团老龄协会办公室	The Aged Association Office of XPCC
兵团安徽商会	Anhui Commerce of XPCC	兵团经济技术协作办公室	The Economic and Technological Co-operation Office of XPCC
兵团职业技术教育学会	Vocational Technical Education Institute of XPCC	兵团教育局	Education Bureau of XPCC
兵团温岭商会	Wenling Commerce of XPCC	兵团经济技术协作办公室	Economic and Technical Cooperation Office of XPCC
兵团江苏商会	Jiangsu Commerce of XPCC	兵团经济技术协作办公室	Economic and Technical Cooperation Office of XPCC

18－27 续表 1　Continued

（2017 年）

名　称	Name	主管单位	Department in Charge
兵团导游协会	Tour Guide Association of XPCC	兵团旅游局	Tourism Bureau of XPCC
兵团浙江商会	Zhejiang Commerce of XPCC	兵团经济技术协作办公室	Economic and Technical Cooperation Office of XPCC
兵团水土保持学会	Soil Conservation Association of XPCC	兵团水利局	Water Conservancy Bureau of XPCC
兵团河南商会	Henan Commerce of XPCC	兵团经济技术协作办公室	Economic and Technical Cooperation Office of XPCC
兵团川渝商会	The chamber of Commerce in Sichuan and Chong of XPCC	兵团经济技术协作办公室	Economic and Technical Cooperation Office of XPCC
兵团旅游产业发展商会	Tourism Industry Development Association of XPCC	兵团旅游局	The Tour Bureau of XPCC
兵团养老行业协会	Pension Industry Association of XPCC	兵团民政局	The Civil Affairs Bureau of XPCC
兵团果业协会	Fruit Association of XPCC	兵团供销合作社	Supply and Marketing Corporation General
兵团辽宁商会	The chamber of Commerce in Liaoning of XPCC	兵团经济技术协作办公室	Economic and Technical Cooperation Office of XPCC
兵团公安文学艺术联合会	The Public Security Literature and Art Association of XPCC	兵团公安局	The Public Security Bureau of XPCC
兵团检察官文学艺术联合会	The Procurator Literature and Art Association of XPCC	兵团检察院	XPCC Procuratorate
兵团旗袍协会	Chiese Dress Association of XPCC	兵团妇女联合会	National Women Federation of XPCC
兵团党外知识分子联谊会	The Intellectual Outside of Party Sodality of XPCC	兵团党委统战部	The United Front Deparment of XPCC Party Committee
兵团宝玉石行业协会	Gem Industry Association of XPCC	兵团工商联	Industrial and Commercial Association of XPCC
兵团国际人才交流协会	Xinjiang Association for International Expertise Exchange	兵团人力资源和社会保障局	The Manpower Resource and Social Security Bureau of XPCC
兵团计划生育协会	The Family Planning Association of XPCC	兵团计生委	The Family Planning Commission
兵团土地学会	The Land Society of XPCC	兵团科协	The Technology Association of XPCC
兵团毛泽东屯垦思想研究会	The Garrison and Reclamation Research Society of Mao Zhedong Thought of XPCC	兵团党委宣传部	The Propaganda Department of XPCC Party Committee
兵团青年志愿者协会	The Youth Volunteer Association of XPCC	兵团团委	The Communist Youth League Commission of XPCC
兵团审计学会	The Auditing Society of XPCC	兵团审计局	The Auditing Bureau of XPCC
兵团质量协会	The Quality Control Association of XPCC	兵团质量技术监督局	The Quality Control Bureau of XPCC
兵团职工思想政治研究会	The Workers' Thought Politics Research Society of XPCC	兵团党委宣传部	The Propaganda Department of XPCC Party Committee
兵团药学会	The Pharmaceutics Society of XPCC	兵团药监局	The Drugs Management Bureau of XPCC
兵团医学会	The Medicine Society of XPCC	兵团卫生局	The Health Bureau of XPCC
兵团党建研究会	The Party Building Theory Reaearch Society of XPCC	兵团党委组织部	The Organizational Department of XPCC Party Committee
兵团农产品加工业协会	The Farm Produce Process Association of XPCC	兵团农业局	The Agricultural Bureau of XPCC
兵团慈善总会	The Charity Federation of XPCC	兵团民政局	The Civil Affairs Bureau of XPCC
兵团宏观经济学会	The Planning Society of XPCC	兵团发展与改革委员会	The Development and Reform Commission of XPCC
兵团检察官协会	The Procurator Association of XPCC	兵团检察院	XPCC Procuratorate
兵团工程咨询协会	The Engineering Consultancy Association of XPCC	兵团发展与改革委员会	The Development and Reform Commission of XPCC
兵团机关事务工作协会	The Authority Affairs Association of XPCC	兵团机关事务管理局	The Authority Affairs Management Bureau of XPCC
兵团社区卫生协会	The Community Health Association of XPCC	兵团卫生局	The Health Bureau of XPCC
兵团西域文化研究会	The Western Regions Culture Research Society of XPCC	兵团党委宣传部	The Propaganda Department of XPCC Party Committee
兵团植物营养与肥料学会	The Plant Nourishment and Fertilizer Society of XPCC	兵团科协	The Technology Association of XPCC
兵团慈善交流协会	The Charitable Communion Association of XPCC	兵团民政局	The Civil Affairs Bureau of XPCC
兵团国际商会	International Commerce of XPCC	兵团贸促会	The Trade Promotes Commission of XPCC
兵团如皋商会	Rugao Commerce of XPCC	兵团经济技术协作办公室	The Economic and Technological Cooperation Office of XPCC
兵团妇女联合会	The Woman Union of XPCC	中华全国妇女联合会	National Women Federation of China
兵团财政学会	The Finance Society of XPCC	兵团财政局	The Financial Bureau of XPCC
兵团东方智慧企业家联合会	The Eastern Intelligence Enterpriser Association of XPCC	兵团工商联	The Industry and Commerce Association of XPCC
兵团监狱工作协会	The Prison Working Society of XPCC	兵团监狱管理局	The Prison Management Bureau of XPCC
兵团社区工作者协会	The Community Worker Association of XPCC	兵团民政局	The Civil Affairs Bureau of XPCC
兵团第八师温州商会	Division 8 Wenzhou Commerce of XPCC	第八师经济技术协作办公室	The Division 8 Ecoomic Cooperation office of XPCC
兵团海外联谊会	The Foreign Sodality of XPCC	兵团党委统战部	The United Front Deparment of XPCC Party Committee
兵团医疗保险研究会	The Medical Insurance Research Society of XPCC	兵团人力资源和社会保障局	The Manpower Resource and Social Security Bureau of XPCC
兵团软件行业协会	The Software Conveyance of XPCC	兵团工业和信息化委员会	The Industry and Informatization Commission of XPCC
兵团继续教育协会	The Continue Education Association of XPCC	兵团人力资源和社会保障局	The Manpower Resource and Social Security Bureau of XPCC
兵团女法官协会	The Woman Judge Association of XPCC	兵团法院	The People's Count of XPCC
兵团法官协会	The Judge Association of XPCC	兵团法院	The People's Count of XPCC
兵团棉花协会	The Cotton Association of XPCC	兵团供销合作社	The Supply and Marketing Cooperation of XPCC
兵团张家港商会	Zhangjiagang Commerce of XPCC	兵团经济技术协作办公室	The Economic and Technological Cooperation Office of XPCC
兵团国际货运代理物流协会	The Goods Circulation and International Freight Transportation Agency of XPCC	兵团商务局	The Commerce Bureau of XPCC
兵团老教授协会	The Old Professor of XPCC	兵团科协	The Technology Association of XPCC
兵团农业生产资料协会	The Agriculture Supplies Association of XPCC	兵团供销合作社	The Supply and Marketing Cooperation of XPCC
兵团老军垦文艺协会	The Old Garrison and Reclamation Literature Association of XPCC	兵团党委老干部局	The Senile Cadres Bureau of XPCC Party Committee

18－27 续表 2 Continued

（2017 年）

名 称	Name	主管单位	Department in Charge
兵团社会组织促进会	The Society Organizes Promote Association of XPCC	兵团民政局	The Civil Affairs Bureau of XPCC
兵团医院协会	The Hospital Association of XPCC	兵团卫生局	The Health Bureau of XPCC
石河子大学纪检监察学会	The Disciplinary Supervision Society of Shihezi University	石河子大学	The Discipline Inspection Commission of XPCC
兵团农垦经济研究会	Nongken Economics Research Society of XPCC	兵团党委政策研究室	The System Restructuring Commission of XPCC Party Committee
兵团监狱纪检监察学会	The Disciplinary Supervision Society of XPCC Prison	兵团监狱管理局	The Prison Management Bureau of XPCC
兵团总商会	The Commerce Chamber of XPCC	兵团党委统战部	The United Front Deparment of XPCC Party Committee
兵团社会治安见义勇为协会	The XPCC Association of XPCC	兵团社会治安综合治理委员会	The Public Security Comprehensive Management Commission of XPCC
兵团统一战线理论研究会	United Front Theories Research Society of XPCC	兵团党委统战部	The United Front Deparment of XPCC Party Committee
兵团律师协会	The Lawyer Association of XPCC	兵团司法局	The Judicial Bureau of XPCC
兵团女检察官协会	The Female Procurator Association of XPCC	兵团检察院	XPCC Procuratorate
兵团技术市场协会	The Market Technology Association of XPCC	兵团科技局	The Technology Bureau of XPCC
兵团红十字会	The Red Cross Association of XPCC	中国红十字会总会	The Red Cross Federation of China
兵团棉花学会	The Cotton Society of XPCC	兵团科协	The Technology Association of XPCC
石河子大学校友会	The Schoolfellow Society of Shihezi University	兵团教育局	The Education Bureau of XPCC
兵团进出口商会	The Imports and Exports Chamber of XPCC	兵团工商联	The Industry and Commerce Association of XPCC
兵团企业联合会	The Enterprise Association of XPCC	兵团工商联	The Industry and Commerce Association of XPCC
兵团旅游协会	The Tour Association of XPCC	兵团旅游局	The Tour Bureau of XPCC
兵团纪检监察学会	The Disciplinary Supervision Society of XPCC	兵团纪检监察局	The Discipline Inspection Commission of XPCC
兵团人口理论研究会	The Population Theory Research Society of XPCC	兵团计生委	The Family Planning Commission
兵团光彩事业促进会	The Gloss Career Promote Association of XPCC	兵团党委统战部	The United Front Deparment of XPCC Party Committee
兵团人力资源管理协会	The Association Resource Control Association of XPCC	兵团人力资源和社会保障局	The Manpower Resource and Social Security Bureau of XPCC
兵团外语教育学会	The Foreign Language Education Society of XPCC	兵团教育局	The Education Bureau of XPCC
兵团乒乓球协会	The Ping－pong Association of XPCC	兵团体育局	The Sports Bureau of XPCC
兵团烟花爆竹行业协会	The Smoke Flower Firecracker Association of XPCC	兵团供销合作社	The Supply and Marketing Cooperation of XPCC
兵团诗词楹联家协会	The Verse Association of XPCC	兵团文联	The literature and Art Federation of XPCC
兵团劳动模范协会	The Labor Model Association of XPCC	兵团工会	The Trade Union of XPCC
塔里木大学校友会	The Schoolfellow Society of Talimu University	兵团教育局	The Education Bureau of XPCC
兵团作物学会	Farm Crop Association of XPCC	兵团科协	The Technology Association of XPCC
兵团屯垦戍边理论研究会(中心)	United Guard Frontier Theories Research Society of XPCC	兵团党委宣传部	The Propaganda Department of XPCC Party Committee
兵团道路运输协会	The Road Conveyance of XPCC	兵团交通局	The Ransportation Bureau of XPCC
兵团交通运输协会	The Transportation Conveyance of XPCC	兵团交通局	The Ransportation Bureau of XPCC
兵团公路学会	Accounting Society of XPCC	兵团交通局	The Ransportation Bureau of XPCC
兵团教育学会	The Education Society of XPCC	兵团教育局	The Education Bureau of XPCC
兵团青少年科技辅导员协会	The Juvenile Scientific and Technological Instructors Association of XPCC	兵团教育局	The Education Bureau of XPCC
兵团新闻工作者协会	The Jounalist Association of XPCC	兵团党委宣传部	The Propaganda Department of XPCC Party Committee
兵团老年书画协会	The Senile Painting and Caligraphy Association of XPCC	兵团党委老干部局	The Senile Cadres Bureau of XPCC Party Committee
兵团工人运动研究会	Labour Movement Reaearch Society of XPCC	兵团工会	The Trade Union of XPCC
兵团老年人体育协会	The Senile Sports Association of XPCC	兵团党委老干部局	The Senile Cadres Bureau of XPCC Party Committee
兵团珠算心算协会	Abacus Society of XPCC	兵团财务局	The Financial Bureau of XPCC
兵团统计学会	The Statistic Society of XPCC	兵团统计局	The Statistics Bureau of XPCC
兵团机关离退休妇女干部联谊会	The Woman Cadre Sodality of XPCC Organ	兵团党委老干部局	The Senile Cadres Bureau of XPCC Party Commitee
兵团会计学会	Accounting Society of XPCC	兵团财务局	The Financial Bureau of XPCC
兵团青少年工作研究会	The Juvenile Work Research Society of XPCC	兵团团委	The Communist Youth League Commission of XPCC
兵团学生联合会	The Student Union of XPCC	兵团团委	The Communist Youth League Commission of XPCC
兵团青年企业家协会	The Youth Entrepreneur Association of XPCC	兵团团委	The Communist Youth League Commission of XPCC
兵团卫生思想政治工作促进会	The Thought Political Work Research Society of XPCC Health System	兵团卫生局	The Health Bureau of XPCC
兵团预防医学会	The Preventive Medicine Society of XPCC	兵团卫生局	The Health Bureau of XPCC
兵团护理学会	The Nursing Society of XPCC	兵团卫生局	The Health Bureau of XPCC
兵团风景园林学会	Society of Landscape Architecture of XPCC	兵团林业局	Forestry Bureau of XPCC
兵团国学文化交流协会	Association for Cultural and Cultural Exchanges of XPCC	兵团文化广播电视局	Culture、Radio and TV Bureau of XPCC
兵团食品行业协会	Food Industry Association of XPCC	兵团工商联	Federation of Industry and Commerce of XPCC
兵团湖南商会	Hunan Commerce Chamber of XPCC	兵团经济技术协作办公室	Economic and Technical Cooperation Office of XPCC
兵团欧美同学会(兵团留学人员联谊会)	Eurpean and American Classmate Association of XPCC	兵团党委统战部	The United Front Deparment of XPCC Party Committee

18—28 石河子市开发(合作)区主要情况

Basic Statistics on Development (Cooperation) Zones of Shihezi City

指 标		Item		2016	2017
规划土地面积	(公顷)	Planned Land Area	(Hectare)	8 620	8 620
#本年开发面积		Developed Area in the Year			
土地出让面积	(公顷)	Land Transfer Area	(Hectare)	137	100
吸取土地出让金	(万元)	Attracted Land Transfer Fund	(10 000 yuan)	7 753	25 885
就业人员平均人数(人)		Average Number of Employment Personnel	(Person)	73 795	74 320
生产总值(当年价)	(万元)	Gross Domestic Product(at Current Prices)	(10000 yuan)	2 156 091	2 020 190
第一产业		Primary Industry			
第二产业		Secondary Industry		1 541 296	1 440 202
第三产业		Tertiary Industry		614 795	579 988
固定资产投资完成额	(万元)	Completion Value of Fixed Assets Investment	(10 000 yuan)	1 115 463	1 080 214
#基础设施投资		Infrastructure Investment		38 874	43 210
水		Water		500	
电		Electricity			
路		Road		15 030	
其 他		Other		23 344	
#房屋建设投资额		Investment Value of Building Construction		35 019	
农业总产值	(当年价,万元)	Total Output Value of Agriculture	(at Current Prices,10 000 yuan)		
工业总产值	(当年价,万元)	Total Output Value of Industry	(at Current Prices,10000 yuan)	4 835 112	4 970 097
三资企业		Foreign—funded Enterprises		198 897	296 862
内资企业		Domestic—funded Enterprises		4 636 215	4 673 235
建筑业总产值	(万元)	Total Output Value of Construction	(10 000 yuan)	745 744	539 769
实现税收	(万元)	Realized Taxes Revenue	(10 000 yuan)	445 700	520 195
进出口总额	(万美元)	Total Value of Imports and Exports	(USD 10 000)	36 067	38 790
进 口		Imports		1 538	1 566
出 口		Exports		34 529	37 224
当年注册登记企业数	(个)	Number of Registered Enterprised in the Year	(unit)	439	431
#三资企业		Foreign—funded Enterprises		1	
内资企业		Domestic—funded Enterprises		438	431
当年注册登记企业资本		Capital of Registered Enterprises in the Year		880 581	1 280 490
#三资企业	(万美元)	Foreign—funded Enterprises	(USD 10 000)	2 794	
内资企业	(万元)	Domestic—funded Enterprises	(10 000 yuan)	880 581	1 280 490
利用外资合同总额	(万美元)	Total Contractual Value of Utilizing Foreign Capital	(USD 10 000)		
内联合同金额	(万元)	Contractual Value of Domestic Co—operation	(10 000 yuan)	1 659 000	1 685 100
外引内联实际利用外资总额	(万美元)	Actually Utilized Foreign Capital Value of Foreign Attraction and Domestic Cooperation	(USD 10 000)	170	
期末全部投产(开业)企业数	(个)	Number of Complete Operation(Starting Business)at Final Period	(unit)	2 298	2 729
#三资企业		Foreign—funded Enterprises		19	19
内资企业		Domestic—funded Enterprises		2 279	2 710
工业企业实现利税总额	(万元)	Realized Profit and Tax Value of Industrial Enterprises	(10000 yuan)	810 859	759 796

2018
BING TUAN

第十九篇
城市、乡（镇）和团场基本情况

Chapter 19 Basic Conditions of Cities、Townships (towns) and Farms

简要说明

一、本篇资料主要内容

本篇资料主要反映兵团各城市、乡（镇）和团场基本概况、主要经济和社会指标完成情况。

二、本篇资料来源

本篇资料由兵团统计局农业统计处根据专业统计数据整理提供。

Brief Introduction

1. Main Contents

The data in this chapter mainly show the basic conditions of cities、townships (towns) and Farms and main indicators completed of economic and social.

2. Sources of Data

The data in this chapter are prepared and provided by Agricultural Statistics Section of the Statistics Bureau of XPCC in accordance with professional statistical data.

19—1 城市主要经济与社会指标

Main Economic and Social Indicators by City

(2017 年)

指 标		Item		阿拉尔市 Alaer City
基本情况		**Basic Situation**		
行政区域面积	(平方公里)	Administrative Area	(10 000 square kilometre)	6 937
乡个数	(个)	Number of Wownships	(unit)	1
镇个数	(个)	Number of Towns	(unit)	3
街道办事处个数	(个)	Number of Street Offices	(unit)	4
人口与就业		**Population and Employment**		
常住户数	(户)	Number of Permanent Accounts	(household)	114 413
常住人口	(万人)	Permanent Population	(10 000 person)	33.23
户籍人口	(万人)	Census Register Population	(10 000 person)	26.40
从业人员	(人)	Practitioners	(person)	163 883
第一产业		Primary Industry		39 801
第二产业		Secondary Industry		51 553
第三产业		Tertiary industry		72 529
综合经济		**Comprehensive Economy**		
地区生产总值	(万元)	Gross Regional Product	(10 000 yuan)	2 957 036
# 第一产业		Primary Industry		1 189 630
第二产业		Secondary Industry		1 159 654
第三产业		Tertiary industry		607 752
# 工 业		Industry		753 957
财政、金融	(万元)	Finance	(10 000 yuan)	
一般公共预算收入		General Public Budget Revenue		72 283
# 税收收入		Taxes Revenue		52 651
一般公共预算支出		General Public Budget Expenditure		107 615
年末金融机构各项存款余额		Savings Balance of Financial Institutions at the end of the Year		2 239 856
# 居民储蓄存款余额		Resident Savings Deposit Balance		918 967
年末金融机构各项贷款余额		Loan Balances of Financial Institutions at the end of the year		1 880 361
农 业		**Agriculture**		
农作物播种面积	(公顷)	Crop Sown Area	(hectare)	169 102.33
粮 食		Grain		16 110.80
棉 花		Cotton		829.07
农产品产量	(吨)	Production of Agricultural Aroducts	(ton)	
粮 食		Grain		172 568
棉 花		Cotton		2 079
园林水果		Gardening Fruit		1 687 972
肉 类		Meat		31 921
年末生猪存栏	(头)	Pig Store	(head)	130 000
年末牛存栏	(头)	Cow Store	(head)	48 200
年末羊存栏	(只)	Sheep Store	(head)	433 100
禽 蛋		Eggs		4 829
蔬 菜		Vegetables		143 816
水产品		Aquatic Product		5 127
工业及建筑业		**Industry and Construction Industry**		
规模以上工业企业单位数	(个)	Number of Industrial Enterprises above scale	(unit)	165
规模以上工业总产值	(万元)	Total Industrial Output Value above scale	(10 000 yuan)	2 301 980
规模以上工业企业从业人员年平均人数	(人)	Annual Average Number of Employees in Industrial Enterprises above Designated Size	(person)	25 250
规模以上工业企业主营业务收入	(万元)	Main Business Income of Industrial Enterprises above Designated Size	(10 000 yuan)	2 255 051
建筑业企业单位数	(个)	Number of Enterprise Units in Construction Industry	(unit)	27
交通、通讯与能源		**Transportation, Communication and Energy**		
公路里程	(公里)	Road Mileage	(kilometer)	3 117
民用汽车拥有量	(辆)	Car Ownership	(unit)	38 852

19—1 续表 1

(2017 年)

指　　标	Item	铁门关市 Tiemenguan City
基本情况	**Basic Situation**	
行政区域面积　(平方公里)	Administrative Area　(10 000 square kilometre)	563
乡个数　(个)	Number of Wownships　(unit)	
镇个数　(个)	Number of Towns　(unit)	2
街道办事处个数　(个)	Number of Street Offices　(unit)	
人口与就业	**Population and Employment**	
常住户数　(户)	Number of Permanent Accounts　(household)	14 125
常住人口　(万人)	Permanent Population　(10 000 person)	3.98
户籍人口　(万人)	Census Register Population　(10 000 person)	2.40
从业人员　(人)	Practitioners　(person)	20 434
第一产业	Primary Industry	6 575
第二产业	Secondary Industry	5 405
第三产业	Tertiary industry	8 454
综合经济	**Comprehensive Economy**	
地区生产总值　(万元)	Gross Regional Product　(10 000 yuan)	180612
# 第一产业	Primary Industry	96 564
第二产业	Secondary Industry	59 777
第三产业	Tertiary industry	24 271
# 工　业	Industry	59 776
财政、金融　(万元)	Finance　(10 000 yuan)	
一般公共预算收入	General Public Budget Revenue	15 153
# 税收收入	Taxes Revenue	11 747
一般公共预算支出	General Public Budget Expenditure	14 527
年末金融机构各项存款余额	Savings Balance of Financial Institutions at the end of the Year	55 161
# 居民储蓄存款余额	Resident Savings Deposit Balance	38 783
年末金融机构各项贷款余额	Loan Balances of Financial Institutions at the end of the year	
农　业	**Agriculture**	
农作物播种面积　(公顷)	Crop Sown Area　(hectare)	20 596.20
粮　食	Grain	156.67
棉　花	Cotton	2.47
农产品产量　(吨)	Production of Agricultural Aroducts　(ton)	
粮　食	Grain	1 645
棉　花	Cotton	15
园林水果	Gardening Fruit	100 947
肉　类	Meat	15 085
年末生猪存栏　(头)	Pig Store　(head)	106 700
年末牛存栏　(头)	Cow Store　(head)	4 400
年末羊存栏　(只)	Sheep Store　(head)	21 800
禽　蛋	Eggs	4 042
蔬　菜	Vegetables	85 650
水产品	Aquatic Product	
工业及建筑业	**Industry and Construction Industry**	
规模以上工业企业单位数　(个)	Number of Industrial Enterprises above scale　(unit)	13
规模以上工业总产值　(万元)	Total Industrial Output Value above scale　(10 000 yuan)	129 013
规模以上工业企业从业人员年平均人数　(人)	Annual Average Number of Employees in Industrial Enterprises above Designated Size　(person)	1 594
规模以上工业企业主营业务收入　(万元)	Main Business Income of Industrial Enterprises above Designated Size　(10 000 yuan)	126 653
建筑业企业单位数　(个)	Number of Enterprise Units in Construction Industry　(unit)	1
交通、通讯与能源	**Transportation, Communication and Energy**	
公路里程　(公里)	Road Mileage　(kilometer)	308
民用汽车拥有量　(辆)	Car Ownership　(unit)	3 328

Continued

图木舒克市 Tumushuke City	克可达拉市 Kekedala City	双河市 Shuanghe City	五家渠市 Wujiaqu City	石河子市 Shihezi City	北屯市 Beitun City	昆玉市 Kunyu City
2 003	1 735	1 727	740	460	911	1 654
		5			3	
1			2	2		
3		3	3	5	3	
55 858	31 109	25 417	51 111	163 892	27 727	17 683
17.53	8.95	6.68	13.21	43.01	6.73	5.70
16.25	6.88	6.46	9.73	43.01	5.19	4.60
77 256	36 166	28 640	61 177	245 299	27 776	26 726
27 974	13 947	12 109	5 884	10 451	4 856	15 719
18 499	4 574	4 517	21 188	108 446	7 291	2 867
30 783	17 645	12 014	34 105	126 402	15 629	8 140
829 208	394 082	256 297	1 624 126	3 338 601	439 051	195 362
238 434	145 369	133 237	74 656	106 806	55 493	90 938
383 663	146 528	81 995	1 153 902	1 903 289	223 404	62 120
207 111	102 185	88 491	395 568	1 328 506	160 154	42 304
235 778	144 431	63 395	905 738	1 533 737	147 038	11 888
33 992	10 576	3 473	194 707	440 075	26 130	196 736
26 128	10 008	3 253	183 507	369 856	20 495	
55 790	2 207	3 504	251 296	511 568	39 871	176 405
967 855	248 440	225 485	1 518 624	405 834	1 203 864	
289 076	174 352	36 065	758 423	262 145	588 051	
420 013	67 159	51 300	1292 171	260 637	843 888	
82 098.00	44 762.13	43 381.10	20 255.93	25 107.00	23 978.33	5 322.00
18 009.00	24 847.73	8 485.03	3 318.53	4 153.00	6 627.00	2 810.00
985.00	1 102.67	1 713.70	2 376.50	207.00	1 826.67	23.00
130 926	249 396	78 717	23 010	40 309	39 665	8 647
4 915	3 631	6 098	8 526	888	5 433	53
207 485	109 212	64 400	16 002	60 702	1 545	205 972
12 854	17 078	14 063	17 208	22 983	10 330	4 801
20 500	50 500	75 100	75 000	197 400	27 100	9 300
9 900	15 900	11 600	2 300	25 700	13 600	2 300
399 300	246 400	110 300	48 400	36 700	140 600	140 900
1 649	4 120	10 103	1 420	6 708	3 653	2 569
220 396	111 257	29 266	282 984	101 855	29 252	17 149
977	5 057	238	2 049	5 347	8 460	
47	13	15	44	102	28	7
930 066	389 962	165 875	3 663 578	5 499 061	230 487	9 955
6 645		1 005	14 498	45 397	2 291	766
814 260		162 398	3 752 451	5 302 242	205 462	34 840
13	2	4	21	77	13	1
1 747	955	602	561	643	649	1 350
6 097	7 297	6 602	14 741	92 559	6 118	6 133

19—1 续表 2

(2017 年)

指　　标		Item		阿拉尔市 Alaer City
年末公交车路数	(路)	Number of Bus Routes	(unit)	4
年末实有公共汽(电)车营运车辆数	(辆)	Number of Public Vehicles (Electric) Operating Vehicles	(unit)	26
年末实有出租汽车数	(辆)	Number of taxi	(unit)	70
固定电话用户	(户)	Fixed Phone Users	(households)	43 400
移动电话用户	(户)	Mobile Phone Users	(households)	349 200
互联网宽带接入用户	(户)	Internet Broadband Access Users	(households)	73 000
全社会用电量	(万千瓦时)	Power Consumption in the Whole Society	(10 000 kilowatt hours)	203 744
贸易、外经		**Trade, Sutra**		
社会消费品零售总额	(万元)	Total Retail sales of Consumer Goods	(10 000 yuan)	747 616
出口总额	(万美元)	Total Export	(USD 10 000)	791
当年实际使用外资金额	(万美元)	The Actual Use of Foreign Capital in the Year—end	(USD 10 000)	520
星级饭店客房总数	(间)	Number of Guest Rooms in Star Rated Hotels	(unit)	373
固定资产投资	**(万元)**	**Investment in Fixed Assets**	**(10 000 yuan)**	
固定资产投资		Investment in Fixed Assets		1 790 666
新增固定资产		New Fixed Assets		1 110 307
房地产开发投资		Investment in Real Estate Development		48 868
教育、科技、文化、卫生		**Education, Science and Technology, Culture, Health**		
普通中学	(所)	Ordinary Middle School	(unit)	21
中等职业教育学校		Secondary Vocational Education School		1
小学数		Primary School		23
普通中学专任教师数	(人)	Number of Full—time Teachers in Ordinary Middle Schools	(person)	1 540
中等职业教育学校专任教师数		Number of Full—time Teachers in Secondary Vocational Education Schools		86
小学专任教师数		Number of Full—time Teachers in Primary Schools		1 298
普通中学在校学生数		Number of Students in Ordinary Middle Schools		23 843
中等职业教育学校在校学生数		Number of Students in Secondary Vocational Education Schools		1 746
小学在校学生数		Number of students in Primary School		20 492
专业技术人员		Professional and Technical Personnel		13 042
# 农业技术人员		Agriculture Technicians		1 843
全年专利授权数	(件)	Number of Patents Granted for a year	(unit)	88
公共图书馆图书总藏量	(千册)	The Total Amount of Books in the Library of the Public Library	(1 000 copies)	1 243
剧场、影剧院个数	(个)	number of Theaters and Heaters	(unit)	3
体育场馆个数	(个)	Number of Stadiums and Gymnasiums	(unit)	16
医疗卫生机构床位数	(床)	Number of Medical and Health Institutions	(unit)	2 296
医疗卫生机构技术人员	(人)	Technical Personnel of Medical and Health Institutions	(person)	2 363
# 执业(助理)医师		Practitioner(assistant)		1 294
社会保障	**(人)**	**Social Security**	**(person)**	
城镇基本养老保险参保人数		Number of Urban Basic Endowment Insurance		218 645
城镇基本医疗保险参保人数		Urban Basic Medical Insurance Participation		286 546
失业保险参保人数		Unemployment Insurance Participation		78 439
城镇居民最低生活保障人数		Number of Minimum Living Security for Urban Residents		3 062
农村居民最低生活保障人数		Number of Minimum Living Security for Rural Residents		
资源与环境		**Resources and Environment**		
森林面积	(公顷)	Forest Area	(hectare)	139 795
工业二氧化硫排放量	(吨)	Industrial Sulfur Dioxide Emissions	(ton)	1 950
氮氧化物排放量	(吨)	Nitrogen Oxide Emission	(ton)	5 055
烟(粉)尘排放量	(吨)	Smoke (powder) Dust Emission	(ton)	3 307
污水处理厂数	(座)	Sewage Treatment Plant Number	(unit)	2
污水处理厂集中处理率	(%)	Concentration of Wastewater Treatment Plant	(%)	95.0
垃圾处理站数	(个)	Number of Garbage Disposal Stations	(unit)	1
城区空气质量优良以上天数	(天)	Urban Air Quality Above the Number of Days	(day)	305

Continued

铁门关市 Tiemenguan City	图木舒克市 Tumushuke City	克可达拉市 Kekedala City	双河市 Shuanghe City	五家渠市 Wujiaqu City	石河子市 Shihezi City	北屯市 Beitun City
				18	36	5
31	81		170	145	503	83
	81	69		513	1 196	398
6 757	19 029	17 080	13 170	30 000	112 255	35 249
17 884	124 753	38 383	38 225	76 000	698 880	117 432
5 969	25 148		10 548	27 519	150 345	28 456
12 841	65 381	49 516	25 245	2 721 867	3 910 526	21 828
43 877	290 724	46 919	74 729	468 674	1 081 735	256 791
	26 189			21 737	50 800	92 894
	75			212	567	165
174 107	1 179 896	199 370	191 213	1 404 402	2 516 559	870 811
85 713	1 198 545	133 488	104 864	882 242	4 165 569	317 447
	3 575	4 676	3 996	607 051	268 300	25 675
2	9	7	6	6	29	6
	1			1	8	1
2	10	7	4	5	10	5
97	1 280	457	404	640	2 107	495
	48			79	314	38
110	713	387	310	413	1 316	319
1 177	10 500	4 335	2 798	7 154	28 901	5 333
	677			1 044	11 606	610
1 257	21 200	5 369	3 572	6 718	21 949	4 539
1 419	5 476		1 315	1 319	24 462	2 633
870	595		163	212	2 711	612
				49	609	5
6	66	40	67	344	268	160
2	1		3	3	6	4
	1	3	4	4	21	8
50	838	406	226	855	4016	825
64	851	442	318	1 134	5 092	619
30	313	166	183	441	2 028	216
7 297	56 751	46 799	25 116	68 696	268 124	19 513
7 297	133 292	64 166	33 245	95 517	346 329	54 273
7 297	14 826	15 796	18 545	28 641	111 814	13 444
584	11 058	3 146	1 500	1 107	3 896	1 314
584			511			
10 235				15 835	8 100	14 860
	550			20 154		1 164
	411			17 351		740
	130			7 654		803
	1		5	2	1	1
	97.0		306.0	93.0	100.0	85.3
1	2		3	3	1	1
	178			246	235	363

19—1 续表 3　Continued

(2017 年)

指　　标		Item		昆玉市 Kunyu City
年末公交车路数	(路)	Number of Bus Routes	(unit)	2
年末实有公共汽(电)车营运车辆数	(辆)	Number of Public Vehicles (Electric) Operating Vehicles	(unit)	4
年末实有出租汽车数	(辆)	Number of taxi	(unit)	65
固定电话用户	(户)	Fixed Phone Users	(households)	5 434
移动电话用户	(户)	Mobile Phone Users	(households)	29 637
互联网宽带接入用户	(户)	Internet Broadband Access Users	(households)	16 683
全社会用电量	(万千瓦时)	Power Consumption in the Whole Society	(10 000 kilowatt hours)	12 989
贸易、外经		**Trade, Sutra**		
社会消费品零售总额	(万元)	Total Retail sales of Consumer Goods	(10 000 yuan)	18 665
出口总额	(万美元)	Total Export	(USD 10 000)	7
当年实际使用外资金额	(万美元)	The Actual Use of Foreign Capital in the Year—end	(USD 10 000)	
星级饭店客房总数	(间)	Number of Guest Rooms in Star Rated Hotels	(unit)	
固定资产投资	**(万元)**	**Investment in Fixed Assets**	**(10 000 yuan)**	
固定资产投资		Investment in Fixed Assets		455 248
新增固定资产		New Fixed Assets		333 542
房地产开发投资		Investment in Real Estate Development		9 910
教育、科技、文化、卫生		**Education, Science and Technology, Culture, Health**		
普通中学	(所)	Ordinary Middle School	(unit)	4
中等职业教育学校		Secondary Vocational Education School		1
小学数		Primary School		4
普通中学专任教师数	(人)	Number of Full—time Teachers in Ordinary Middle Schools	(person)	214
中等职业教育学校专任教师数		Number of Full—time Teachers in Secondary Vocational Education Schools		32
小学专任教师数		Number of Full—time Teachers in Primary Schools		221
普通中学在校学生数		Number of Students in Ordinary Middle Schools		2 901
中等职业教育学校在校学生数		Number of Students in Secondary Vocational Education Schools		382
小学在校学生数		Number of students in Primary School		5 431
专业技术人员		Professional and Technical Personnel		
# 农业技术人员		Agriculture Technicians		
全年专利授权数	(件)	Number of Patents Granted for a year	(unit)	
公共图书馆图书总藏量	(千册)	The Total Amount of Books in the Library of the Public Library	(1 000 copies)	8
剧场、影剧院个数	(个)	number of Theaters and Heaters	(unit)	
体育场馆个数	(个)	Number of Stadiums and Gymnasiums	(unit)	1
医疗卫生机构床位数	(床)	Number of Medical and Health Institutions	(unit)	205
医疗卫生机构技术人员	(人)	Technical Personnel of Medical and Health Institutions	(person)	262
# 执业(助理)医师		Practitioner(assistant)		
社会保障	**(人)**	**Social Security**	**(person)**	
城镇基本养老保险参保人数		Number of Urban Basic Endowment Insurance		17 540
城镇基本医疗保险参保人数		Urban Basic Medical Insurance Participation		19 850
失业保险参保人数		Unemployment Insurance Participation		15 398
城镇居民最低生活保障人数		Number of Minimum Living Security for Urban Residents		3 338
农村居民最低生活保障人数		Number of Minimum Living Security for Rural Residents		
资源与环境		**Resources and Environment**		
森林面积	(公顷)	Forest Area	(hectare)	3 007
工业二氧化硫排放量	(吨)	Industrial Sulfur Dioxide Emissions	(ton)	735
氮氧化物排放量	(吨)	Nitrogen Oxide Emission	(ton)	1 176
烟(粉)尘排放量	(吨)	Smoke (powder) Dust Emission	(ton)	379
污水处理厂数	(座)	Sewage Treatment Plant Number	(unit)	5
污水处理厂集中处理率	(%)	Concentration of Wastewater Treatment Plant	(%)	82.0
垃圾处理站数	(个)	Number of Garbage Disposal Stations	(unit)	3
城区空气质量优良以上天数	(天)	Urban Air Quality Above the Number of Days	(day)	

19—2 乡(镇)社会经济基本情况

Main Economic Indicators of Farms Basic social and economic situation of township (town)

(2017 年)

指　　标		Item		一师阿拉尔市金银川镇(一团、二团、三团) Jinyinchuan Town Alaer City Division 1	一团 Farm 1	二团 Farm 2	三团 Farm 3
基本情况		**Basic Situation**					
行政区域面积	(公顷)	Administrative Area	(hectare)	127 200	37 878	40 100	49 222
居民委员会(社区)个数	(个)	Number of Residents' Committees	(unit)	10	6	2	2
人口与就业		**Population and Employment**					
户籍户数	(户)	Household Register Number(household registration statistics of police station)	(household)	20 013	9 371	4 825	5 817
户籍人口	(人)	Census Register Population(census register statistics of police station)	(person)	54 145	26 181	13 510	14 454
全家外出户数	(户)	Family Number	(household)	681	681		
全家外出人口	(人)	Family Outgoing Population	(person)	1 609	1 609		
常住户数	(户)	Number of Permanent Accounts	(household)	18 463	6 820	5 511	6 132
常住人口	(人)	Permanent Population	(person)	55 716	23 685	15 731	16 300
从业人员		Practitioners		25 916	9 979	7 503	8 434
第一产业		Primary Industry		7 899	2 002	3 343	2 554
第二产业		Secondary Industry		5 367	2 587	1 375	1 405
第三产业		Tertiary industry		12 650	5 390	2 785	4 475
农　业		**Agriculture**					
耕地面积	(公顷)	Arable Area	(hectare)	38 531	12 782	15 578	10 171
设施农业占地面积	(公顷)	Facility Agricultural Area	(hectare)	162	37	42	83
农作物播种面积	(公顷)	Crop Sown Area	(hectare)	39 037	12 782	15 578	10 677
# 粮　食		Grain		4 339	1 608	2 050	681
农民合作社个数	(个)	Number of Farmers' Cooperatives	(unit)	62	36	20	6
农民合作社成员数	(户)	Number of Farmers' Cooperatives Leaguer	(household)	362	211	120	31
耕地流转面积	(公顷)	Arable land transfer Area	(hectare)				
种植大户数	(户)	Number of Large Households	(household)	6 470	2 484	2 264	1 722
畜禽养殖大户数	(户)	Number of Large Livestock and Poultry Farmers	(household)	17	7	7	3
财政、经济		**Finance and Economy**					
一般公共预算收入	(万元)	General Public Budget Revenue	(10 000 yuan)	2 133	2 133		
一般公共预算支出	(万元)	General Public Budget Expenditure	(10 000 yuan)	76 826	25 862	26 200	24 764
资产总额	(万元)	Total Assets	(USD 10 000)	627 342	140 765	239 059	247 518
债务总额	(万元)	Total Debt	(USD 10 000)	433 924	118 555	213 619	101 750
企业个数	(个)	Number of Enterprises	(unit)	271	130	67	74
企业从业人员	(人)	Enterprise Practitioners	(person)	6 829	2 601	1 757	2 471
企业实交税金	(万元)	Tax payment for enterprises	(10 000 yuan)	1 400	732	635	33
工　业		**Industry**					
工业企业单位数	(个)	Unit Number of Industrial Enterprises	(unit)	81	31	21	29
# 规模以上工业		Above Scale Industry		29	10	9	10
工业总产值	(万元)	Total Industrial Output Value	(10 000 yuan)	480 958	212 966	131 886	136 106
# 规模以上工业		Above Scale Industry		406 288	173 680	107 020	125 588

19—2 续表 1

(2017 年)

指　　标		Item		一师阿拉尔市沙河镇(五团) Shahe Town (Farm 5) Alaer City Division 1	一师阿拉尔市双城镇(六团) Shuangchen Town (Farm 6) Alaer City Division 1	一师阿拉尔市托喀依乡 Tuokayi Town Alaer City Division 1
基本情况		**Basic Situation**				
行政区域面积	(公顷)	Administrative Area	(hectare)	79 073	14 101	12 205
居民委员会(社区)个数	(个)	Number of Residents' Committees	(unit)	5	3	1
人口与就业		**Population and Employment**				
户籍户数	(户)	Household Register Number(household registration statistics of police station)	(household)	7 353	4 184	994
户籍人口	(人)	Census Register Population(census register statistics of police station)	(person)	19 722	11 790	3 449
全家外出户数	(户)	Family Number	(household)	216	323	51
全家外出人口	(人)	Family Outgoing Population	(person)	630	991	211
常住户数	(户)	Number of Permanent Accounts	(household)	7 894	4 184	994
常住人口	(人)	Permanent Population	(person)	21 153	11 790	3 470
从业人员		Practitioners		9 651	6 266	1 258
第一产业		Primary Industry		4 449	1 935	1 047
第二产业		Secondary Industry		1 368	2 901	
第三产业		Tertiary industry		3 834	1 430	211
农　业		**Agriculture**				
耕地面积	(公顷)	Arable Area	(hectare)	6 408	4 972	6 786
设施农业占地面积	(公顷)	Facility Agricultural Area	(hectare)	10	36	
农作物播种面积	(公顷)	Crop Sown Area	(hectare)	8 037	4 079	6 786
# 粮　食		Grain		1 313	1 424	333
农民合作社个数	(个)	Number of Farmers' Cooperatives	(unit)	36	31	7
农民合作社成员数	(户)	Number of Farmers' Cooperatives Leaguer	(household)	509	253	56
耕地流转面积	(公顷)	Arable land transfer Area	(hectare)			
种植大户数	(户)	Number of Large Households	(household)	817		346
畜禽养殖大户数	(户)	Number of Large Livestock and Poultry Farmers	(household)	38	2	148
财政、经济		**Finance and Economy**				
一般公共预算收入	(万元)	General Public Budget Revenue	(10 000 yuan)	134		
一般公共预算支出	(万元)	General Public Budget Expenditure	(10 000 yuan)	19 255	23 388	
资产总额	(万元)	Total Assets	(USD 10 000)	113 183	67 969	861
债务总额	(万元)	Total Debt	(USD 10 000)	86 027	66 259	
企业个数	(个)	Number of Enterprises	(unit)	141	131	
企业从业人员	(人)	Enterprise Practitioners	(person)	9 651	4 395	
企业实交税金	(万元)	Tax payment for enterprises	(10 000 yuan)	941		
工　业		**Industry**				
工业企业单位数	(个)	Unit Number of Industrial Enterprises	(unit)	22	46	
# 规模以上工业		Above Scale Industry		9	9	
工业总产值	(万元)	Total Industrial Output Value	(10 000 yuan)	71 901	149 972	
# 规模以上工业		Above Scale Industry		50 131	92 580	

Continued

二师铁门关市 博古其镇 (二十九团) Boguqi Town (Farm 20) Tiemenguan City Division 2	二师铁门关市 双丰镇 (三〇团) Shuangfeng Town (Farm 30) Tiemenguan City Division 2	三师图木舒克市 草湖镇 (四十一团) Caohu Town (Farm 41) Tumushuke City Division 3	六师五家渠市 梧桐镇 (一〇二团) Wutong Town (Farm 102) Wujiaqu City Division 6	六师五家渠市 蔡家湖镇 (一〇三团) Caijiahu Town (Farm 103) Wujiaqu City Division 6	八师石河子市 北泉镇 (石河子总场) Beiquan Town (Shihezi Farm) Shihezi City Division 8	八师石河子市 石河子镇 Shihezi Town Shihezi City Division 8
16 640	27 711	7 766	34 549	54 600	47 500	3 957
2	2	1	6	4	12	
3 538	4 446	3 541	7 566	6 775	17 233	2 354
10 615	11 044	9 993	18 810	16 153	51 698	9 411
205	300	162	484	103		1 941
615	500	471	1 055	205		2 450
3 008	3 880	4 589	7 309	6 896	17 233	2 502
9 025	10 098	10 708	19 763	16 820	51 698	11 352
4 215	5 605	3 514	8 749	6 865	23 989	7 471
1 485	1 479	1 127	1 902	2 785	3 966	4 625
1 365	1 147	578	1 556	706	4 920	2 135
1 365	2 979	1 809	5 291	3 374	15 103	711
3 842	7 700	3 080	8 998	11 259	19 866	3 094
298	9	51	26	9	118	
3 842	6 615	2 064	6 351	11 296	17 008	3 094
		562	1 619	1 259	1 857	1 927
15	15	5	8	46	53	18
300	300	35	108	311	1 199	164
			1 000	870	360	1 080
	390	11	150	181	322	137
5	10	10	64	218	450	51
			26	42		
27 278	19 795	29 551	25 122	21 924		
12 999	164 200	265 029	133 198	127 041	406 606	3 957
9 998	141 500	218 717	123 408	123 070	314 252	268
45	28	14	55	27	803	68
1 650	2 550	605	1 422	1 081	20 023	2 100
	13	2 515	3 533	2 973	2 865	319
13	11	10	20	13	148	28
4	4	4	11	3	21	2
59 702	51 529	96 842	92 235	22 401	449 709	4 270
47 297	37 209	87 686	84 332	18 497	200 562	1 491

19—2 续表 2

（2017 年）

指　　标	Item	一师阿拉尔市金银川镇（一团、二团、三团） Jinyinchuan Town Alaer City Division 1	一团 Farm 1	二团 Farm 2	三团 Farm 3
建筑业	**Construction Business**	4	3	1	
建筑业企业单位数 （个）	Number of Enterprise Units in Construction Industry (unit)	157 700	51 893	105 807	
建筑业总产值 （万元）	Total Output Value of Construction Industry (10 000 yuan)				
贸易、市场	**Trade, market**	6	2	1	3
住宿餐饮业企业个数 （个）	Number of Enterprises for Accommodation and Catering Industry (unit)	3 490	1 640	170	1 680
住宿餐饮业企业营业总收入（万元）	Total Revenue of the Enterprise of Accommodation and Catering Industry (10 000 yuan)	91 350	50 028	17 984	23 338
社会消费品零售总额 （万元）	Total retail sales of consumer goods (10 000 yuan)	6 894	6 225	669	
# 限额以上	Limit the Total Retail Sales of Social Consumer Goods (10 000 yuan)	121	7	57	57
营业面积 50 平米以上的综合商店或超市个数（个）	Number of Comprehensive Stores or Supermarkets with a Business Area of 50 Square meters or more (unit)				
教育、文化、卫生	**Education, Culture, Health**	4	2	1	1
幼儿园、托儿所个数 （个）	Number of Kindergartens and Uursery Schools (unit)	4	2	1	1
小学校数 （所）	Primary School Number (unit)	228	123	39	66
小学专任教师数 （人）	Number of Full－time Teachers in Primary Schools (person)	1 489	687	854	422
小学在校学生数 （人）	Number of Students in Primary School (person)	3	1	1	
图书馆、文化站个数 （个）	Number of Libraries and Cultural Stations (unit)	1	1	1	
剧场、影剧院个数 （个）	Number of Theaters and Theaters (unit)	2	1	1	
体育场馆个数 （个）	Number of Stadiums and Gymnasiums (unit)	2	1	1	1
医疗卫生机构个数（个）	Number of Medical and Health Institutions (unit)	120	80	50	60
医疗卫生机构床位数	Bed Number of Medical and Health Institutions (unit)	32	36	25	17
执业(助理)医师数(人)	Practising (Assistant) Doctor Number (person)				
社会保障	**Social Security**	1			
本级政府创办的敬老院个数（个）	Number of Old Homes Established by the Government at the Same Level (unit)	8 995	6 389	6 958	2 525
城乡居民基本养老保险参保人数（人）	Number of Basic Old－age Insurance for Urban and Rural Residents (person)	6 433	8 883	10 233	1 972
城乡居民基本医疗保险参保人数（人）	Number of Basic Medical Insurance for Urban and Rural Residents (person)	305	148	79	351
城乡居民最低生活保障人数（人）	The number of Minimum Living Security for Urban and Rural Residents (person)				
公用事业	**Public Utility**	7 894	5 511	5 639	2 526
自来水用水户数 （户）	Number of Water Users (household)	4 420	3 094	4 235	1 250
管道燃气用气户数 （户）	Number of Gas Accounts for Pipeline Gas (household)	3	2	3	3
金融机构网点数 （个）	Number of Branches of Financial Institutions (unit)	4	2	4	2
公园及休闲健身广场个数 （个）	Number of Park and Leisure Fitness Square (unit)	250	230	735	24
生活垃圾月均处理量（吨/月）	Monthly Average Treatment of Domestic Waste (ton / month)				

Continued

一师阿拉尔市 沙河镇 (五团) Shahe Town (Farm 5) Alaer City Division 1	一师阿拉尔市 双城镇 (六团) Shuangchen Town (Farm 6) Alaer City Division 1	一师阿拉尔市 托喀依乡 Tuokayi Town Alaer City Division 1	二师铁门关市 博古其镇 (二十九团) Boguqi Town (Farm 29) Tiemenguan City Division 2	二师铁门关市 双丰镇 (三〇团) Shuangfeng Town (Farm 30) Tiemenguan City Division 2	三师图木舒克市 草湖镇 (四十一团) Caohu Town (Farm 41) Tumushuke City Division 3	六师五家渠市 梧桐镇 (一〇二团) Wutong Town (Farm 102) Wujiaqu City Division 6
2	1				1	1
185 736	11 713				35 135	2 359
6					1	1
3 922					430	510
34 565	24 782	133	9 798	21 866	40 035	107 947
3 473	2 319				12 855	1 337
506	12	1	15	5	290	38
2	4	4	1	1	1	3
1	1	5	1	1	1	1
96	56	75	65	83	44	83
825	1 870	866	744	365	398	712
1	1				1	1
	1					
	1					
1	1	1	1	1	1	1
45	100	43	50	55	25	65
21	40	40	30	24	7	37
	2			1	1	
5 020	6 862	650	3 266	2 566	1 634	5 151
8 031	8 788	3 855	3 266	2 566	1 644	4 582
202	3 547	271		379	118	169
3 905	6 432	3 008	3 880	4 230	1 265	6 896
2 804	4 000		2 500	3 067	960	1 860
2	3	1	5	3	2	4
3	4		1	1	1	1
180	527	210	325	285	30	47

19－2 续表 3 Continued

(2017 年)

指标	Item	六师五家渠市蔡家湖镇(一〇三团) Caijiahu Town (Farm 103) Wujiaqu City Division 6	八师石河子市北泉镇(石河子总场) Beiquan Town (Shihezi Farm) Shihezi City Division 8	八师石河子市石河子镇 Shihezi Town Shihezi City Division 8
建筑业	**Construction Business**			
建筑业企业单位数 (个)	Number of Enterprise Units in Construction Industry (unit)	3	1	
建筑业总产值 (万元)	Total Output Value of Construction Industry (10 000 yuan)	160 502	288 944	
贸易、市场	**Trade, market**			
住宿餐饮业企业个数 (个)	Number of Enterprises for Accommodation and Catering Industry (unit)		4	39
住宿餐饮业企业营业总收入 (万元)	Total Revenue of the Enterprise of Accommodation and Catering Industry (10 000 yuan)		630	1 011
社会消费品零售总额 (万元)	Total retail sales of consumer goods (10 000 yuan)	3 917	121 102	182
# 限额以上	Limit the Total Retail Sales of Social Consumer Goods (10 000 yuan)	1 634	59 499	
营业面积50平米以上的综合商店或超市个数(个)	Number of Comprehensive Stores or Supermarkets with a Business Area of 50 Square meters or more (unit)	2	8	
教育、文化、卫生	**Education, Culture, Health**			
幼儿园、托儿所个数 (个)	Number of Kindergartens and Uursery Schools (unit)	2	9	
小学校数 (所)	Primary School Number (unit)	1	2	1
小学专任教师数 (人)	Number of Full－time Teachers in Primary Schools (person)	70	232	26
小学在校学生数 (人)	Number of Students in Primary School (person)	937	227	1 505
图书馆、文化站个数 (个)	Number of Libraries and Cultural Stations (unit)		9	1
剧场、影剧院个数 (个)	Number of Theaters and Theaters (unit)			3
体育场馆个数 (个)	Number of Stadiums and Gymnasiums (unit)			1
医疗卫生机构个数(个)	Number of Medical and Health Institutions (unit)	2	7	2
医疗卫生机构床位数	Bed Number of Medical and Health Institutions (unit)	47		120
执业(助理)医师数(人)	Practising (Assistant) Doctor Number (person)	16	18	102
社会保障	**Social Security**			
本级政府创办的敬老院个数 (个)	Number of Old Homes Established by the Government at the Same Level (unit)			2
城乡居民基本养老保险参保人数 (人)	Number of Basic Old－age Insurance for Urban and Rural Residents (person)	8 160	1 005	11 369
城乡居民基本医疗保险参保人数 (人)	Number of Basic Medical Insurance for Urban and Rural Residents (person)	10 262	7 685	18 579
城乡居民最低生活保障人数 (人)	The number of Minimum Living Security for Urban and Rural Residents (person)	161	1 481	1 063
公用事业	**Public Utility**			
自来水用水户数 (户)	Number of Water Users (household)	4 389	2 354	13 566
管道燃气用气户数 (户)	Number of Gas Accounts for Pipeline Gas (household)	1 765		7 682
金融机构网点数 (个)	Number of Branches of Financial Institutions (unit)	4		6
公园及休闲健身广场个数 (个)	Number of Park and Leisure Fitness Square (unit)	1		3
生活垃圾月均处理量 (吨/月)	Monthly Average Treatment of Domestic Waste (ton / month)	900	1 300	852

19—3 团场主要经济指标

Main Economic Indicators of Farms

(2017 年)

指标	Item	一师一团(七师代管) Farm 1 Division 1 (Division 7)	一师二团 Farm 2 Division 1	一师三团 Farm 3 Division 1	一师四团 Farm 4 Division 1
基本情况	**Basic Situation**				
行政区域面积 (公顷)	Administrative Area (hectare)	37 878	40 100	49 222	41 000
居民委员会(社区)个数 (个)	Number of Residents' Committees (unit)	6	2	2	1
人口与就业	**Population and Employment**				
户籍户数 (户)	Household Register Number (household)	9 371	4 825	5 817	3 150
户籍人口 (人)	Census Register Population (person)	26 181	13 510	14 454	7 874
全家外出户数 (户)	Family Number (household)	681			60
全家外出人口 (人)	Family Outgoing Population (person)	1 609			148
常住户数 (户)	Number of Permanent Accounts (household)	6 820	5 511	6 132	2 526
常住人口 (人)	Permanent Population (person)	23 685	15 731	16 300	6 273
从业人员	Practitioners	9 979	7 503	8 434	3 715
第一产业	Primary Industry	2 002	3 343	2 554	2 085
第二产业	Secondary Industry	2 587	1 375	1 405	173
第三产业	Tertiary industry	5 390	2 785	4 475	1 457
生产总值 (万元)	**Gross Domestic Products (10 000 yuan)**	**206 222**	**181 629**	**151 920**	**36 315**
# 第一产业	Primary Industry	83 712	97 837	90 396	20 683
第二产业	Secondary Industry	89 359	63 412	36 580	6 196
第三产业	Tertiary Industry	33 151	20 380	24 944	9 436
# 工业	Industry	77 683	39 605	36 580	6 196
固定资产投资总额 (万元)	**Investment in Fixed Assets (10 000 yuan)**	**80 811**	**59 376**	**58 081**	**7 562**
农业	**Agriculture**				
耕地面积 (公顷)	Arable Area (hectare)	12 782	15 578	10 171	5 216
设施农业占地面积 (公顷)	Facility Agricultural Area (hectare)	37	42	83	5
农作物播种面积 (公顷)	Crop Sown Area (hectare)	12 782	15 578	10 677	5 080
# 粮食	Grain	1 608	2 050	681	3 833
农民合作社个数 (个)	Number of Farmers' Cooperatives (unit)	36	20	6	14
农民合作社成员数 (户)	Number of Farmers' Cooperatives Leaguer (household)	211	120	31	73
耕地流转面积 (公顷)	Arable land transfer Area (hectare)				
种植大户数 (户)	Number of Large Households (household)	2 484	2 264	1 722	3
畜禽养殖大户数 (户)	Number of Large Livestock and Poultry Farmers (household)	7	7	3	6
财政、经济	**Finance and Economy**				
一般公共预算收入 (万元)	General Public Budget Revenue (10 000 yuan)	2 133			
一般公共预算支出 (万元)	General Public Budget Expenditure (10 000 yuan)	25 862	26 200	24 764	21 940
资产总额 (万元)	Total Assets (10 000 yuan)	140 765	239 059	247 518	115 777
债务总额 (万元)	Total Debt (10 000 yuan)	118 555	213 619	101 750	104 857
企业个数 (个)	Number of Enterprises (unit)	130	67	74	4
企业从业人员 (人)	Enterprise Practitioners (person)	2 601	1 757	2 471	206
企业实交税金 (万元)	Tax payment for enterprises (10 000 yuan)	732	635	33	1 572

19—3 续表 1

(2017 年)

指　　标	Item	一师五团(十一师代管) Farm 5 Division 1 (Division 11)	一师六团 Farm 6 Division 1	一师七团 Farm 7 Division 1	一师八团 Farm 8 Division 1
基本情况	**Basic Situation**				
行政区域面积 (公顷)	Administrative Area (hectare)	79 073	14 101	22 720	20 851
居民委员会(社区)个数 (个)	Number of Residents' Committees (unit)	5	3	2	3
人口与就业	**Population and Employment**				
户籍户数 (户)	Household Register Number (household)	7 353	4 184	5 582	4 512
户籍人口 (人)	Census Register Population (person)	19 722	11 790	13 398	11 388
全家外出户数 (户)	Family Number (household)	216	323	120	
全家外出人口 (人)	Family Outgoing Population (person)	630	991	274	
常住户数 (户)	Number of Permanent Accounts (household)	7 894	4 184	5 971	4 200
常住人口 (人)	Permanent Population (person)	21 153	11790	14728	11640
从业人员	Practitioners	9 651	6 266	8 215	6 003
第一产业	Primary Industry	4 449	1 935	2 112	1 841
第二产业	Secondary Industry	1 368	2 901	2 594	1 480
第三产业	Tertiary industry	3 834	1 430	3 509	2 682
生产总值 (万元)	**Gross Domestic Products (10 000 yuan)**	**162 699**	**85 406**	**144 122**	**119 666**
# 第一产业	Primary Industry	68 667	42 379	70 551	61 226
第二产业	Secondary Industry	70 543	25 567	50 323	42 071
第三产业	Tertiary Industry	23 489	17 460	23 248	16 369
# 工　业	Industry	28 752	23 013	49 322	32 287
固定资产投资总额 (万元)	**Investment in Fixed Assets (10 000 yuan)**	**52 069**	**62 715**	**68 314**	**42 108**
农　业	**Agriculture**				
耕地面积 (公顷)	Arable Area (hectare)	6 408	4 972	10 026	9 132
设施农业占地面积 (公顷)	Facility Agricultural Area (hectare)	10	36	192	
农作物播种面积 (公顷)	Crop Sown Area (hectare)	8 037	4 079	9 326	9 644
# 粮　食	Grain	1 313	1 424	1 333	1 233
农民合作社个数 (个)	Number of Farmers' Cooperatives (unit)	36	31	35	9
农民合作社成员数 (户)	Number of Farmers' Cooperatives Leaguer (household)	509	253	170	45
耕地流转面积 (公顷)	Arable land transfer Area (hectare)				
种植大户数 (户)	Number of Large Households (household)	817		425	3
畜禽养殖大户数 (户)	Number of Large Livestock and Poultry Farmers (household)	38	2	10	3
财政、经济	**Finance and Economy**				
一般公共预算收入 (万元)	General Public Budget Revenue (10 000 yuan)	134			
一般公共预算支出 (万元)	General Public Budget Expenditure (10 000 yuan)	19 255	23 388	19 734	21 358
资产总额 (万元)	Total Assets (10 000 yuan)	113 183	67 969	150 207	147 902
债务总额 (万元)	Total Debt (10 000 yuan)	86 027	66 259	125 175	135 277
企业个数 (个)	Number of Enterprises (unit)	141	131	116	63
企业从业人员 (人)	Enterprise Practitioners (person)	9 651	4 395	3 238	1 634
企业实交税金 (万元)	Tax payment for enterprises (10 000 yuan)	941		263	29

Continued

一　师 十　团 Farm10 Division 1	一　师 十一团 Farm 11 Division 1	一　师 十二团 Farm 12 Division 1	一　师 十三团 Farm 13 Division 1	一　师 十四团 Farm 14 Division 1	一　师 十六团 Farm 16 Division 1	一　师 阿拉尔农场 Alaer Farm Division 1	一　师 幸福农场 Xingfu Farm Division 1	二　师 二十一团 Farm 21 Division 2
97 835	43 007	49 255	35 490	47 507	35 046	15 593	17 580	28 325
2		1	2	2	3	2	1	1
6 507	3 626	6 982	7 098	4 320	6 026	3 392	1 400	5 838
19 509	13 215	20 875	22 287	12 014	16 360	9 308	3 858	11 943
451		296	282	35			11	593
904		365	703	93			36	1 577
6 700	3 626	7 272	7 658	4 320	6 026	3 215	1 989	4 230
19 579	13 215	21 860	24 036	12 014	16 360	10 798	5 116	10 572
8 770	6 537	13 628	11 370	4 714	10 043	4 485	1 551	4 558
3 461	1 881	2 431	3 295	2 568	2 998	2 249	781	1 595
1 306	1 718	6 712	4 802	503	2 702	597	231	1 280
4 003	2 938	4 485	3 273	1 643	4 343	1 639	539	1 683
225 684	**119 248**	**259 886**	**193 180**	**114 979**	**218 778**			**53 199**
109 558	64 058	106 054	111 130	70 964	100 762			18 358
79 577	40 914	129 570	55 163	15 346	86 342			27 859
36 549	14 276	24 262	26 887	28 669	31 674			6 982
73 988	30 938	64 816	49 498	14 700	53 166			27 859
91 137	**46 095**	**59 398**	**65 001**	**51 840**	**45 682**			**27 166**
17 678	6 883	13 411	11 600	7 306	17 635	8 400	7 355	6 117
82	10	94	45	33	24	70	24	89
16 321	6 883	13 524	11 759	5 326	18 195	8 400	7 686	6 595
612	663	1 190	900	578	1 024	586	240	2 180
50	39	30	24	47	39	20	14	8
1 300		458	121	502	1 736	95	141	307
	212							
496	15		30	436		340	228	
50	3	3	6	10	25	1	5	16
	21 576	33 461	37 062	25 380	26 660	17 487	11 146	12 618
162 133	173 743	240 078	213 073	99 166	234 844	126 592	112 576	134 290
142 682	155 147	230 866	195 897	89 687	216 575	127 889	99 552	103 357
27	20	143	186	67	114	25	11	22
3 149	6 537	8 462	1 827	4 715	10 043	569	318	1 448
1 899	296	568	905	345	955		133	

19—3 续表 2

(2017 年)

指　　标	Item	二　师 二十二团 Farm 22 Division 2	二　师 二十四团 Farm 24 Division 2	二　师 二十五团 Farm 25 Division 2	二　师 二十七团 Farm 27 Division 2
基本情况	**Basic Situation**				
行政区域面积 (公顷)	Administrative Area (hectare)	16 931	21 319	5 389	27 539
居民委员会(社区)个数 (个)	Number of Residents' Committees (unit)	22		2	4
人口与就业	**Population and Employment**				
户籍户数 (户)	Household Register Number (household)	8 545	5 020		4 426
户籍人口 (人)	Census Register Population (person)	20 747	13 338		10 878
全家外出户数 (户)	Family Number (household)				1 521
全家外出人口 (人)	Family Outgoing Population (person)		176		3 522
常住户数 (户)	Number of Permanent Accounts (household)	7 507	5 020	1 832	4 023
常住人口 (人)	Permanent Population (person)	19 066	13 327	5 333	10 788
从业人员	Practitioners	9 078	5 050	1 455	4 707
第一产业	Primary Industry	3 959	2 092	575	1 320
第二产业	Secondary Industry	1 442	666	536	683
第三产业	Tertiary industry	3 677	2 292	344	2 704
生产总值 (万元)	**Gross Domestic Products (10 000 yuan)**	**113 780**	**62 250**	**16 909**	**50 790**
# 第一产业	Primary Industry	36 081	30 347	7 883	17 506
第二产业	Secondary Industry	63 482	18 214	2 633	23 700
第三产业	Tertiary Industry	14 217	13 689	6 393	9 584
# 工　业	Industry	63 482	18 214	2 633	23 700
固定资产投资总额 (万元)	**Investment in Fixed Assets (10 000 yuan)**	**70 842**	**71 582**	**25 359**	**65 019**
农　业	**Agriculture**				
耕地面积 (公顷)	Arable Area (hectare)	8 863	6 582	1 924	4 406
设施农业占地面积 (公顷)	Facility Agricultural Area (hectare)	180	256	213	80
农作物播种面积 (公顷)	Crop Sown Area (hectare)	9 976	5 493	1 570	4 023
# 粮　食	Grain	1 118	1 645	292	652
农民合作社个数 (个)	Number of Farmers' Cooperatives (unit)	28	10	11	12
农民合作社成员数 (户)	Number of Farmers' Cooperatives Leaguer (household)	421	440	574	332
耕地流转面积 (公顷)	Arable land transfer Area (hectare)				
种植大户数 (户)	Number of Large Households (household)		5		32
畜禽养殖大户数 (户)	Number of Large Livestock and Poultry Farmers (household)	97	13		51
财政、经济	**Finance and Economy**				
一般公共预算收入 (万元)	General Public Budget Revenue (10 000 yuan)				12
一般公共预算支出 (万元)	General Public Budget Expenditure (10 000 yuan)	32 593	19 355	14 661	16 322
资产总额 (万元)	Total Assets (10 000 yuan)	212 300	97 983	52 546	133 745
债务总额 (万元)	Total Debt (10 000 yuan)	173 500	68 907	44 949	110 389
企业个数 (个)	Number of Enterprises (unit)	26	25		32
企业从业人员 (人)	Enterprise Practitioners (person)	1 442	1 001		678
企业实交税金 (万元)	Tax payment for enterprises (10 000 yuan)				49

Continued

二师 三十九团 Farm 29 Division 2	二师 三十团 Farm 30 Division 2	二师 三十一团 Farm 31 Division 2	二师 三十三团 Farm 33 Division 2	二师 三十四团 Farm 34 Division 2	二师 三十六团 (四师代管) Farm 36 Division 2 (Division 4)	二师 三十七团 Farm 37 Division 2	二师 三十八团 Farm 38 Division 2	二师 二二三团 Farm 223 Division 2
70 600	27 711	51 771	54 335	88 800	55 649	11 200	19 528	642
8	2	2	3	2	2	2	7	13
8 377	4 446	3 541	6 318	4 951	3 015	418	1 801	9 380
25 130	11 044	11 072	15 493	14 546	7 561	1 177	4 325	3 221
565	300	586	1 524	407	1 030	30		774
1 695	500	1 752	4 512	1 487	2 627	73		815
10 230	3 880	3 735	4 832	4 544	3 016	866	1 801	2 447
29 665	10 098	10 082	14 198	13 059	8 136	2 954	6 788	8 565
14 841	5 605	6 350	5 249	5 543	4 139	1 841	3 980	3 102
5 096	1 479	1 431	1 551	1 152	1 176	905	1 781	1 333
4 285	1 147	1 372	1 137	1 497	988	314	305	339
5 460	2 979	3 547	2 561	2 894	1 975	622	1 894	1 430
210 959	**60 001**	**69 938**	**111 948**	**82 047**	**59 320**	**8 854**	**7 560**	**25 924**
66 193	31 226	37 810	54 071	56 954	29 891	5 256	5 176	10 665
113 528	18 562	16 157	38 627	11 246	15 902	1 705	168	7 168
31 238	10 213	15 971	19 250	13 847	13 527	1 893	2 216	8 091
113 528	18 562	16 157	38 627	11 246	15 902	1 705	168	7 168
118 208	**66 499**	**90 795**	**100 880**	**91 280**	**68 051**	**63 737**	**37 896**	**22 395**
12 443	7 700	8 895	7 975	8 505	2 951		5 526	822
300	9	16	15				1	39
13 609	6 615	8 599	12 631	8 220	903		3 068	1 406
157		533	519	301			1529	1406
28	15	13	7	6	17		2	1
480	300	85	142	831	358		15	6
	390	68	202	5	33		25	
25	10	35	29		10	1	2	18
				752			164	
27 278	19 795	21 987	23 712	23 091	25 748	24 998	19 081	19 696
346 525	164 200	136 620	10 256	13 239	118 384	2 087	186 082	98 300
280 515	141 500	103 082	6 461	9 963	75 054	835	144 568	93 500
130	28	29	37	12	30	17	97	8
4 520	2 550	1 542	5 249	1 876	2 784	365	3 980	312
	13	6 945	236		183	6		6

19—3 续表 3

(2017 年)

指　　标	Item	三　师 四十一团 Farm 41 Division 3	三　师 四十二团 Farm 42 Division 3	三　师 四十四团 Farm 44 Division 3	三　师 四十五团 Farm 45 Division 3
基本情况	**Basic Situation**				
行政区域面积　(公顷)	Administrative Area　(hectare)	7 766	14 655	61 333	88 667
居民委员会(社区)个数　(个)	Number of Residents' Committees　(unit)	1	1		2
人口与就业	**Population and Employment**				
户籍户数　(户)	Household Register Number　(household)	3 423	1 044	7 765	9 212
户籍人口　(人)	Census Register Population　(person)	9 902	3 946	31 063	25 999
全家外出户数　(户)	Family Number　(household)	9	48		68
全家外出人口　(人)	Family Outgoing Population　(person)	29	163		212
常住户数　(户)	Number of Permanent Accounts　(household)	4 589	1 265	7 371	9 212
常住人口　(人)	Permanent Population　(person)	10 708	4 275	27 714	25 999
从业人员	Practitioners	3 514	1 942	9 986	10 979
第一产业	Primary Industry	1 127	779	2 249	3 865
第二产业	Secondary Industry	578	247	2 357	3 070
第三产业	Tertiary industry	1 809	916	5 380	4 044
生产总值　(万元)	**Gross Domestic Products　(10 000 yuan)**	**62 286**	**34 963**	**114 313**	**144 154**
# 第一产业	Primary Industry	14 619	12 960	54 876	69 585
第二产业	Secondary Industry	33 570	14 935	33 512	44 483
第三产业	Tertiary Industry	14 097	7 068	25 925	30 086
# 工　业	Industry	24 184	14 935	33 512	22 636
固定资产投资总额　(万元)	**Investment in Fixed Assets　(10 000 yuan)**	**106 706**	**9 084**	**33 010**	**54 289**
农　业	**Agriculture**				
耕地面积　(公顷)	Arable Area　(hectare)	3 080	3 863	13 087	15 528
设施农业占地面积　(公顷)	Facility Agricultural Area　(hectare)	51	3	16	28
农作物播种面积　(公顷)	Crop Sown Area　(hectare)	2 064	6 166	16 504	17 731
# 粮　食	Grain	562	683	3 067	1 529
农民合作社个数　(个)	Number of Farmers' Cooperatives　(unit)	5	9	19	14
农民合作社成员数　(户)	Number of Farmers' Cooperatives Leaguer　(household)	35	167	142	460
耕地流转面积　(公顷)	Arable land transfer Area　(hectare)				
种植大户数　(户)	Number of Large Households　(household)	11	148	69	442
畜禽养殖大户数　(户)	Number of Large Livestock and Poultry Farmers　(household)	10	52	19	17
财政、经济	**Finance and Economy**				
一般公共预算收入　(万元)	General Public Budget Revenue　(10 000 yuan)				
一般公共预算支出　(万元)	General Public Budget Expenditure　(10 000 yuan)	29 551	12 472	38 420	37 251
资产总额　(万元)	Total Assets　(10 000 yuan)	265 029	55 542	362 598	199 100
债务总额　(万元)	Total Debt　(10 000 yuan)	218 717	30 265	303 829	135 700
企业个数　(个)	Number of Enterprises　(unit)	14	8	26	33
企业从业人员　(人)	Enterprise Practitioners　(person)	605	1 942	9 986	10 979
企业实交税金　(万元)	Tax payment for enterprises　(10 000 yuan)	2 515	13	23	6 624

Continued

三　师 四十六团 Farm 46 Division 3	三　师 四十八团 Farm 48 Division 3	三　师 四十九团 Farm 49 Division 3	三　师 五 〇 团 (六师代管) Farm 50 Division 3 (Division 6)	三　师 五十一团 Farm 51 Division 3	三　师 五十三团 Farm 53 Division 3	三　师 伽师总场 Jiashi Farm Division 3	三　师 叶城牧场 Yechen Farm Division 3	三　师 东风农场 Dongfen Farm Division 3	三　师 红旗农场 Redflag Farm Division 3
19 733	17 000	30 800	55 300	141 117	126 590	50 533	64 933	7 487	9 247
9	1	1	2			1		1	
1 224	2 850	4 323	6 671	14 321	7 105	3 743	563	565	1 119
3 513	7 829	16 442	22 187	48 830	24 245	14 016	1 644	1 677	4 232
24			66		483		191	5	
48			154		498		341	20	
1 200	2 850	4 323	6 605	14 321	6 135	3 972	372	550	1 181
3 463	7 829	16 442	23 597	48 830	24 137	15 068	1 303	1 730	4 212
1 437	2 931	6 766	8 472	19 282	9 833	6 068	459	598	1 428
542	896	2 685	3 973	11 997	5 571	2 566	162	422	1 064
271	415	1 726	1 964	1 321	1 398	771	69	15	52
624	1 620	2 355	2 535	5 964	2 864	2 731	228	161	312
29 052	**66 640**	**97 811**	**76 752**	**82 846**	**79 002**	**60 800**	**5 977**	**4 377**	**7 140**
15 759	38 554	51 854	38 350	37 512	37 238	31 830	3 296	2 143	4 415
5 497	12 375	21 080	18 416	21 941	22 188	16 742	889	136	333
7 796	15 711	24 877	19 986	23 393	19 576	12 228	1 792	2 098	2 392
1 764	12 375	16 606	18 416	21 941	13 170	16 742	889	136	333
10 043	**15 228**	**24 884**	**30 085**	**54 317**	**40 281**	**47 895**	**7 053**	**12 115**	**15 788**
3 283	4 831	14 448	12 226	16 252	9 483	7 256	19	373	1 232
87		54	46	21	7	2			
1 091	2 380	18 001	13 926	17 731	11 773	13 044	606	1 208	2 308
87	570	3 280	2 553	5 673	2 873	1 993	180	901	1 407
2	4	5	16	16	20	5	1	1	
22	65	30	368	860	557	155	23	60	
			120	300	2712				
56	15		132	186	423	105		3	25
1	6	16	62	120	276	20	12	2	
12 835	18 280	28 765	30 416	51 597	30 001	37 870	6 808	12 330	10 149
63 308	136 303	176 147	184 829	360 388	266 230	264 764	35 088	32 266	42 451
45 302	95 565	140 041	154 903	344 480	178 263	218 183	26 316	25 426	29 788
2	8	16	21	18	22	7	5	1	1
1 437	596	901	583	1 321	1 505	225	62	15	22
		1 571	429		6 877	2 561	12	7	20

19—3 续表 4

(2017 年)

指　　标	Item	三　师 托云牧场 Rouyun Farm Division 3	三　师 五十四团 Farm 54 Division 3	四　师 六十一团 Farm 61 Division 4	四　师 六十二团 Farm 62 Division 4
基本情况	**Basic Situation**				
行政区域面积　(公顷)	Administrative Area　(hectare)	49 330	4 133	105 300	13 607
居民委员会(社区)个数　(个)	Number of Residents' Committees　(unit)	1	1	2	5
人口与就业	**Population and Employment**				
户籍户数　(户)	Household Register Number　(household)	378	381	6 060	8 028
户籍人口　(人)	Census Register Population　(person)	378	872	14 659	18 315
全家外出户数　(户)	Family Number　(household)			612	
全家外出人口　(人)	Family Outgoing Population　(person)			1 482	
常住户数　(户)	Number of Permanent Accounts　(household)	378	1 339	4 386	8 521
常住人口　(人)	Permanent Population　(person)	1 144	1 339	13 289	20 031
从业人员	Practitioners	598	904	5 907	8 378
第一产业	Primary Industry	251	247	2371	2 546
第二产业	Secondary Industry	69	58	802	1 565
第三产业	Tertiary industry	278	594	2 734	4 267
生产总值　(万元)	**Gross Domestic Products　(10 000 yuan)**	**2 720**	**1 093**	**96 259**	**126 593**
# 第一产业	Primary Industry	1 191	550	30 779	31 325
第二产业	Secondary Industry	477		53 269	59 762
第三产业	Tertiary Industry	1 052	543	12 211	35 506
# 工　业	Industry	477		51 055	56 320
固定资产投资总额　(万元)	**Investment in Fixed Assets　(10 000 yuan)**	**5 916**	**73 593**	**57 800**	**101 733**
农　业	**Agriculture**				
耕地面积　(公顷)	Arable Area　(hectare)		1 806	8 333	5 667
设施农业占地面积　(公顷)	Facility Agricultural Area　(hectare)		1 286	5	62
农作物播种面积　(公顷)	Crop Sown Area　(hectare)		1 806	5 602	3 878
# 粮　食	Grain		1 665	3 711	3 185
农民合作社个数　(个)	Number of Farmers' Cooperatives　(unit)			15	16
农民合作社成员数　(户)	Number of Farmers' Cooperatives Leaguer　(household)			122	356
耕地流转面积　(公顷)	Arable land transfer Area　(hectare)				
种植大户数　(户)	Number of Large Households　(household)			18	51
畜禽养殖大户数　(户)	Number of Large Livestock and Poultry Farmers　(household)	12		12	85
财政、经济	**Finance and Economy**				
一般公共预算收入　(万元)	General Public Budget Revenue　(10 000 yuan)			9	48
一般公共预算支出　(万元)	General Public Budget Expenditure　(10 000 yuan)	7 623	20 887	16 188	16 718
资产总额　(万元)	Total Assets　(10 000 yuan)	18 823	135 757	47 741	98 640
债务总额　(万元)	Total Debt　(10 000 yuan)	14 348	131 020	39 345	78 169
企业个数　(个)	Number of Enterprises　(unit)	3	1	21	185
企业从业人员　(人)	Enterprise Practitioners　(person)	69	529	634	4 903
企业实交税金　(万元)	Tax payment for enterprises　(10 000 yuan)		8		2 590

Continued

四　师 六十三团 Farm 63 Division 4	四　师 六十四团 Farm 64 Division 4	四　师 六十六团 Farm 66 Division 4	四　师 六十七团 Farm 67 Division 4	四　师 六十八团 Farm 68 Division 4	四　师 六十九团 Farm 69 Division 4	四　师 七 〇 团 Farm 70 Division 4	四　师 七十一团 Farm 71 Division 4	四　师 七十二团 Farm 72 Division 4
28 717	36 300	33 660	61 598	13 231	10 203	12 255	16 000	22 755
1	1	3	1	1	1	2	3	3
4 139	26 617	10 522	4 450	3 712	6 836	5 625	5 775	5 423
10 121	10 279	26 023	13 759	8 584	3 053	13 057	12 126	11 456
409			406			212	775	110
1 394			1126			586	2 016	246
3 297	9 005	10 144	4 458	3 689	3 050	4 815	5 325	4 598
9 054	25 899	29 494	13 927	9 650	7 063	11 796	11 483	11 375
4 499	9 992	11 532	5 614	3 322	2 526	5 213	5 998	5 056
2 169	4 552	3 689	2 313	1 224	752	1 760	2 618	2 037
340	903	1 680	501	335	731	1 414	1 167	638
1 990	4 537	6 163	2 800	1 763	1 043	2 039	2 213	2 381
64 970	**96 769**	**124 113**	**62 623**	**45 607**	**52 405**	**73 512**	**87 833**	**48 197**
22 075	34 985	35 260	34 952	18 097	15 733	23 051	24 856	15 782
27 436	43 842	48 018	12 549	14 683	28 229	35 659	41 513	12 363
15 459	17 942	40 835	15 122	12 827	8 443	14 802	21 464	20 052
27 436	43 842	48 018	12 369	12 766	21 749	32 065	39 987	10 562
27 768	**52 570**	**66 701**	**37 596**	**22 303**	**38 226**	**12 888**	**37 282**	**13 476**
5 947	8 477	5 185	10 664	6 178	5 037	5 493	6 753	6 441
28	9	177	2	30	39	62	17	1
6 997	8 247	6 800	16 593	6 125	5 145	4 450	7 280	6 833
1 872	7 809	4 779	7 457	5 929	2 582	2 283	6 725	4 435
7	4	9	5		3	8	14	14
72	432	651	260			366	406	704
1 544			5 266			899	21	2 278
54			4		10	97	6	283
36		24	2		5	135	32	412
21	45	3		27	10	30	7	5
9 074	21 430	23 380	16 071	14 823	10 086	10 834	18 082	15 320
49 156	84 056	93 595	48 291	47 897	105 671	49 484	140 000	50 510
35 289	73 416	64 561	38 196	38 203	87 523	38 997	120 000	48 554
6	11	22	23	37	11	22	37	15
281	239	1 044	186	1 752	286	5 213	1 732	2 732
127					236	930	4014	1 257

19—3 续表 5

(2017 年)

指标	Item	四师七十三团 Farm 73 Division 4	四师七十四团 Farm 74 Division 4	四师七十五团 Farm 75 Division 4	四师七十六团 Farm 76 Division 4
基本情况	**Basic Situation**				
行政区域面积 (公顷)	Administrative Area (hectare)	28 700	77 800	7 908	60 153
居民委员会(社区)个数 (个)	Number of Residents' Committees (unit)	4	2	2	
人口与就业	**Population and Employment**				
户籍户数 (户)	Household Register Number (household)	3 215	1 416	1 342	5 149
户籍人口 (人)	Census Register Population (person)	7 760	3 406	3 495	12 024
全家外出户数 (户)	Family Number (household)		126	28	50
全家外出人口 (人)	Family Outgoing Population (person)		378	63	147
常住户数 (户)	Number of Permanent Accounts (household)	3 074	1 428	1 235	3 816
常住人口 (人)	Permanent Population (person)	7 561	3 678	3 231	10 874
从业人员	Practitioners	4 678	2 225	1 789	6 451
第一产业	Primary Industry	743	809	937	3 492
第二产业	Secondary Industry	2 046	396	251	634
第三产业	Tertiary industry	1 889	1 020	601	2 325
生产总值 (万元)	**Gross Domestic Products (10 000 yuan)**	**108 233**	**32 999**	**40 111**	**67 598**
# 第一产业	Primary Industry	19 444	13 164	9 261	29 556
第二产业	Secondary Industry	70 974	8 662	20 734	24 783
第三产业	Tertiary Industry	17 815	11 173	10 116	13 259
# 工业	Industry	70 974	8 662	20 734	24 783
固定资产投资总额 (万元)	**Investment in Fixed Assets (10 000 yuan)**	**40 933**	**11 111**	**13 436**	**22 453**
农业	**Agriculture**				
耕地面积 (公顷)	Arable Area (hectare)	3 264	4 882	7 090	14 500
设施农业占地面积 (公顷)	Facility Agricultural Area (hectare)	100		8	5
农作物播种面积 (公顷)	Crop Sown Area (hectare)	4 956	4 882	6 927	14 990
# 粮食	Grain	3 188	2 144	3 775	6 108
农民合作社个数 (个)	Number of Farmers' Cooperatives (unit)	7	15	7	22
农民合作社成员数 (户)	Number of Farmers' Cooperatives Leaguer (household)	80	180	104	647
耕地流转面积 (公顷)	Arable land transfer Area (hectare)			1 568	613
种植大户数 (户)	Number of Large Households (household)	80	96	384	118
畜禽养殖大户数 (户)	Number of Large Livestock and Poultry Farmers (household)	180	21	38	131
财政、经济	**Finance and Economy**				
一般公共预算收入 (万元)	General Public Budget Revenue (10 000 yuan)	67		10	7
一般公共预算支出 (万元)	General Public Budget Expenditure (10 000 yuan)	14 718	9 421	5 267	20 726
资产总额 (万元)	Total Assets (10 000 yuan)	38 426	49 991	50 500	78 052
债务总额 (万元)	Total Debt (10 000 yuan)	26 223	40 553	47 300	66 251
企业个数 (个)	Number of Enterprises (unit)	67	7	10	6
企业从业人员 (人)	Enterprise Practitioners (person)	2 046	145	131	6 451
企业实交税金 (万元)	Tax payment for enterprises (10 000 yuan)	285	43	2 657	158

Continued

四　师 七十七团 Farm 77 Division 4	四　师 七十八团 Farm 78 Division 4	四　师 七十九团 Farm 79 Division 4	五　师 八十一团 Farm 81 Division 5	五　师 八十三团 Farm 83 Division 5	五　师 八十四团 Farm 84 Division 5	五　师 八十六团 Farm 86 Division 5	五　师 八十七团 Farm 87 Division 5	五　师 八十八团 Farm 88 Division 5	五　师 八十九团 Farm 89 Division 5
39 070	68 600	24 360	12 382	46 060	75 200	34 000	19 461	32 700	17 541
	3	1		2		2		1	3
2 842	2 061	2 372	3 925	7 140	3 312	6 263	1 963	1 820	5 604
8 696	5 381	5 417	11 735	21 294	8 737	17 219	5 035	4 377	16 807
	356	120		655	635	1 412	365	52	310
	641	380		2 044	1 620	3 899	994	146	940
2 479	1 744	1 749	3 894	7 140	3 378	8 888	1 719	1 272	5 906
7 611	5 021	5 005	11 188	21 294	7 815	22 315	4 190	3 045	16 446
3 843	2 457	2 312	4 388	10 886	3 246	8 028	1 915	1 843	7 935
1 781	846	959	2 311	3 123	1 083	3 180	1 071	823	3 307
662	284	456	457	1 783	1 073	757	149	288	1 523
1 400	1 327	897	1 620	5 980	1 090	4 091	695	732	3 105
78 837	**36 198**	**35 411**	**62 981**	**108 651**	**48 126**	**66 009**	**16 444**	**17 863**	**82 124**
27 933	18 726	15 462	31 945	39 304	19 678	33 276	8 440	7 598	23 079
34 751	8 379	13 389	14 722	20 042	15 445	11 512	1 792	3 291	37 985
16 153	9 093	6 560	16 314	49 305	13 003	21 221	6 212	6 974	21 060
34 751	8 379	13 389	13 366	10 099	15 445	11 060	1 792	3 291	23 105
18 407	**11 700**	**12 228**	**47 878**	**55 739**	**32 176**	**16 970**	**9 194**	**15 445**	**74 025**
13 855	2 134	3 126	6 766	14 253	10 340	10 250	3 375	6 122	8 607
2	1	4	20	24	30	35	6	17	1
14 566	826	3 826	6 761	14 253	10 340	9 653	3 107	4 133	8 301
6 085	480	1 875	82	467	7 033	1 270	2 917	2 873	67
14	12	6	1	32	29	3	7	17	56
212	233	260	5	712	1255	26	245	338	321
				186	1 237		499		230
83	12	10	101	692	655	322	212		
72	1	20	2	21	189	122	2	7	5
37	6		18	436	22	43	120	80	50
16 377	6 869	6 804	20 160	25 790	18 850	21 334	10 190	10 151	18 686
96 533	18 828	28 162	141 266	142 466	98 835	110 000	45 612	58 581	212 345
51 266	18 053	21 705	90 758	111 130	76 528	74 261	31 855	1 202	178 213
9	9	9	80	46	13	28	7	7	38
3 843	115	2 312	4 388	8 218	365	571	158	201	6 273
	61	9	62	248	56	222	60	80	1 449

19—3 续表 6

(2017 年)

指 标		Item		五 师 九 〇 团 Farm 90 Division 5	五 师 九十一团 Farm 91 Division 5	六 师 一〇一团 Farm 101 Division 6	六 师 一〇二团 Farm 102 Division 6
基本情况		**Basic Situation**					
行政区域面积	(公顷)	Administrative Area	(hectare)	33 543	15 744	9 104	34 549
居民委员会(社区)个数	(个)	Number of Residents' Committees	(unit)	1			6
人口与就业		**Population and Employment**					
户籍户数	(户)	Household Register Number	(household)	3 165	1 499	2 531	7 566
户籍人口	(人)	Census Register Population	(person)	10 085	4 178	5 882	18 810
全家外出户数	(户)	Family Number	(household)	64	13		484
全家外出人口	(人)	Family Outgoing Population	(person)	154	30		1 055
常住户数	(户)	Number of Permanent Accounts	(household)	3 164	1 368	10 200	7 309
常住人口	(人)	Permanent Population	(person)	8 462	3 876	23 701	19 763
从业人员		Practitioners		4 533	1 884	13 255	8 749
第一产业		Primary Industry		2 228	670	1 067	2 360
第二产业		Secondary Industry		448	283	3 521	1 556
第三产业		Tertiary industry		1 857	931	8 323	4 833
生产总值	**(万元)**	**Gross Domestic Products**	**(10 000 yuan)**	**45 183**	**14 457**	**222 248**	**171 208**
# 第一产业		Primary Industry		25 959	8 627	15 100	21 330
第二产业		Secondary Industry		2 331	2 508	113 752	96 761
第三产业		Tertiary Industry		16 893	3 322	93 396	53 117
# 工 业		Industry		585	2 508	3 518	96 195
固定资产投资总额	**(万元)**	**Investment in Fixed Assets**	**(10 000 yuan)**	**21 480**	**11 735**	**613 113**	**50 020**
农 业		**Agriculture**					
耕地面积	(公顷)	Arable Area	(hectare)	8 072	4 598	3 778	8 998
设施农业占地面积	(公顷)	Facility Agricultural Area	(hectare)	10		70	46
农作物播种面积	(公顷)	Crop Sown Area	(hectare)	8 072	3 553	2 609	6 333
# 粮 食		Grain		33	300	441	1619
农民合作社个数	(个)	Number of Farmers' Cooperatives	(unit)	26	11	29	8
农民合作社成员数	(户)	Number of Farmers' Cooperatives Leaguer	(household)	396	62	162	108
耕地流转面积	(公顷)	Arable land transfer Area	(hectare)		43	803	1 000
种植大户数	(户)	Number of Large Households	(household)	8	45	51	150
畜禽养殖大户数	(户)	Number of Large Livestock and Poultry Farmers	(household)	4	15		64
财政、经济		**Finance and Economy**					
一般公共预算收入	(万元)	General Public Budget Revenue	(10 000 yuan)	766	139	756	26
一般公共预算支出	(万元)	General Public Budget Expenditure	(10 000 yuan)	14 863	10 132	55 216	25 122
资产总额	(万元)	Total Assets	(10 000 yuan)	10 857	81 500	184 217	133 198
债务总额	(万元)	Total Debt	(10 000 yuan)	69 076	72 500	134 129	123 408
企业个数	(个)	Number of Enterprises	(unit)	8	6	119	55
企业从业人员	(人)	Enterprise Practitioners	(person)	3 855	85	7 809	1 422
企业实交税金	(万元)	Tax payment for enterprises	(10 000 yuan)	188	28	64 818	3 533

Continued

六　师 一〇三团 Farm 103 Division 6	六　师 一〇五团 Farm 105 Division 6	六　师 一〇六团 Farm 106 Division 6	六　师 芳草湖农场 Fang Caohu Farm Division 6	六　师 新湖农场 Xinhu Farm Division 6	六　师 军户农场 Junhu Farm Division 6	六　师 共青团农场 Communist League Farm Division 6	六　师 六运湖农场 Liu Yunhu Farm Division 6	六　师 土墩子农场 TudunZi Farm Division 6	六　师 红旗农场 Red Flag Farm Division 6
54 600	23 319	28 186	94 641	83 233	9 100	22 733	5 200	8 464	1 468
4	2		10	5		2	1	1	2
6 775	4 867	2 554	22 348	14 439	5 692	3 629	3 048	2 133	5 518
16 153	13 542	6 912	55 709	36 969	14 847	9 952	6 985	6 031	15 378
103	1 985	589		392		45	80	98	
205	2 382	1 429		1 163		125	212	294	
6 896	4 966	1 965	22 348	14 412	5 778	3 629	2 558	2 133	5 025
16 820	13 807	5 483	61 316	36 897	15 024	10 886	6 010	5 509	13 201
6 865	5 057	3 185	24 235	15 736	5 275	5 675	2 799	3 572	5 930
3 301	2 005	1 770	6 134	5 383	3 084	3 231	1 284	1 081	2 869
706	534	355	3 132	2 178	114	884	286	636	830
2 858	2 518	1 042	14 969	8 133	2 001	2 898	1 229	1 855	2 231
115 507	**69 331**	**33 443**	**261 249**	**205 035**	**51 220**	**94 996**	**20 091**	**27 644**	**59 240**
38 226	28 594	16 412	92 565	102 048	28 421	48 967	8 020	12 575	26 088
47 697	16 753	7 059	51 006	28 330	2 154	21 909	1 292	6 661	5 348
29 584	23 984	9 972	117 678	74 657	20 645	24 120	10 779	8 408	27 804
8 952	3 965	1 733	41 176	24 480	2 154	2 491	1 292	6 661	5 348
36 259	**23 540**	**6 870**	**91 896**	**93 383**	**13 114**	**37 475**	**5 554**	**35 400**	**18 663**
11 259	10 456	6 267	40 122	37 811	6 793	13 333	3 744	5 180	13 718
9	8	1	332	13	15	35	2	5	3
11 296	9 102	5 578	36 467	37 285	6 029	12 000	3 363	5 006	14 205
1 259	708	10	1 974	3 196	4 840	2 151	763	2 384	10 509
46	10	5	168	104	37	20	10	13	53
311	266	110	900	1 228	811	445	138	1 053	533
870	1 268			5 236		48	1 354	928	5 125
181	237		906	193	599	120	12	24	155
218	139	5	63	321	1 305	45	7	12	803
42	56	5	281	113	20	39	8	22	8
21 924	12 004	12 739	46 540	32 218	9 348	13 720	6 811	6 687	15 437
127 041	127 600	56 320	306 183	287 971	75 853	165 829	30 712	73 306	79 626
123 070	89 808	51 814	287 966	230 236	43 875	129 998	27 342	53 708	53 525
27	32	3	92	30	15	58	14	23	15
1 081	5 057	355	11 295	2 178	114	2 311	299	294	373
2 973	474		39	1 269	252	102		226	

19－3 续表 7

(2017 年)

指　　标	Item	六　师 奇台农场 Qitai Farm Division 6	六　师 北塔山牧场 Bei Tashan Farm Division 6	七　师 一二三团 Farm 123 Division 7	七　师 一二四团 Farm 124 Division 7
基本情况	**Basic Situation**				
行政区域面积　(公顷)	Administrative Area　(hectare)	76 400	225 300	23 150	92 898
居民委员会(社区)个数 (个)	Number of Residents' Committees　(unit)		1	5	4
人口与就业	**Population and Employment**				
户籍户数　(户)	Household Register Number　(household)	11 956	1 176	8 318	5 610
户籍人口　(人)	Census Register Population　(person)	33 332	4 060	20 220	16 568
全家外出户数　(户)	Family Number　(household)	1 213	40	72	300
全家外出人口　(人)	Family Outgoing Population　(person)	2 910	117	195	905
常住户数　(户)	Number of Permanent Accounts　(household)	10 887	1 116	8 503	6 017
常住人口　(人)	Permanent Population　(person)	28 613	3 864	22 957	17 029
从业人员	Practitioners	14 015	1 933	9 662	5 421
第一产业	Primary Industry	6 135	1 223	2 491	2 712
第二产业	Secondary Industry	3 135	68	1 673	438
第三产业	Tertiary industry	4 745	642	5 498	2 271
生产总值　(万元)	**Gross Domestic Products　(10 000 yuan)**	**190 091**	**22 548**	**105 134**	**91 067**
# 第一产业	Primary Industry	55 756	2 497	42 730	56 185
第二产业	Secondary Industry	62 108	12 132	22 185	7 481
第三产业	Tertiary Industry	72 227	7 919	40 219	27 401
# 工　业	Industry	45 430	12 132	13 045	7 481
固定资产投资总额　(万元)	**Investment in Fixed Assets　(10 000 yuan)**	**9 447**	**27 634**	**74 735**	**27 185**
农　业	**Agriculture**				
耕地面积　(公顷)	Arable Area　(hectare)	26 418	934	12 387	15 740
设施农业占地面积　(公顷)	Facility Agricultural Area　(hectare)	8	1	18	7
农作物播种面积　(公顷)	Crop Sown Area　(hectare)	24 609	934	12 223	16 660
# 粮　食	Grain	18 376	260		4 420
农民合作社个数　(个)	Number of Farmers' Cooperatives　(unit)	95	10	4	27
农民合作社成员数　(户)	Number of Farmers' Cooperatives Leaguer　(household)	2 150	415	63	240
耕地流转面积　(公顷)	Arable land transfer Area　(hectare)	14 767	620		
种植大户数　(户)	Number of Large Households　(household)	340	2	102	40
畜禽养殖大户数　(户)	Number of Large Livestock and Poultry Farmers　(household)	175	3	21	25
财政、经济	**Finance and Economy**				
一般公共预算收入　(万元)	General Public Budget Revenue　(10 000 yuan)	115		14	16
一般公共预算支出　(万元)	General Public Budget Expenditure　(10 000 yuan)	30 668	13 031	19 360	15 979
资产总额　(万元)	Total Assets　(10 000 yuan)	178 268	53 105	110 750	80 326
债务总额　(万元)	Total Debt　(10 000 yuan)	132 800	37 812	130 235	58 344
企业个数　(个)	Number of Enterprises　(unit)	61	2	14	40
企业从业人员　(人)	Enterprise Practitioners　(person)	3 019	68	3 568	990
企业实交税金　(万元)	Tax payment for enterprises　(10 000 yuan)	5 348		319	75

Continued

七　师 一二五团 Farm 125 Division 7	七　师 一二六团 Farm 126 Division 7	七　师 一二七团 Farm 127 Division 7	七　师 一二八团 Farm 128 Division 7	七　师 一二九团 Farm 129 Division 7	七　师 一三〇团 Farm 130 Division 7	七　师 一三一团 Farm 131 Division 7	七　师 一三七团 Farm 137 Division 7	八　师 一二一团 Farm 121 Division 8	八　师 一三三团 Farm 133 Division 8
43 051	20 004	18 548	28 600	30 456	63 070	36 600	59 791	58 500	57 594
5	3	3	3	3	5	3	2		6
6 863	4 092	5 290	5 446	6 430	7 221	7 236	3 309	14 526	8 816
18 484	12 379	13 390	14 185	16 400	18 923	16 317	8 582	35 795	22 984
572	609	367			260	32	94	1 250	465
1 715	1 705	883			490	89	283	2 634	1 163
7 079	4 059	5 136	4 885	7 191	7 861	8 371	3 668	15 390	8 711
18 893	11 760	14 647	14 655	18 039	21 435	18 835	8 980	37 969	22 108
9 881	4 444	5 186	7 872	10 770	11 567	7 723	4 772	16 729	7 842
3 345	1 423	1 807	2 292	2 789	3 597	2 097	1 539	6 838	3 209
2 024	252	1 153	1 281	2 687	2 339	1 385	659	2 943	957
4 512	2 769	2 226	4 299	5 294	5 631	4 241	2 574	6 948	3 676
111 113	**60 536**	**51 136**	**116 488**	**142 372**	**146 152**	**123 363**	**42 199**	**162 435**	**74 756**
64 987	28 920	24 980	51 921	49 225	57 877	54 659	16 398	84 745	51 514
18 618	4 248	8 731	37 802	46 144	46 848	21 584	5 709	16 308	1 739
27 508	27 368	17 425	26 765	47 003	41 427	47 120	20 092	61 382	21 503
10 697	4 248	4 368	37 802	36 086	45 358	14 624	5 709	5 715	902
36 596	**23 957**	**27 528**	**44 227**	**54 938**	**85 855**	**24 980**	**20 685**	**135 084**	**29 975**
16 273	7 876	9 652	15 856	14 087	17 980	13 067	1 883	40 873	23 436
247	1	9	100	78	28	11 650	521	57	72
21 320	9 920	8 944	13 688	14 807	18 195	14 373	1 593	36 948	23 068
1 213	120	93	36	1 000	2 118	3 466	160	1 347	333
16	7	4	5	13	4	6	15	40	32
207	41	36	496	67	39	32	82	792	346
				521				1063	
167	196	382	68	386	150	912	153	1 215	102
20	16	19	38	16	11	38	78	182	22
11	14	7	10	21	32		21		
23 473	14 815	15 368	14 918	23 715	27 558	12 660	14 162	49 062	36 770
161 157	85 822	52 327	120 549	48 347	199 740	87 437	52 978	301 797	210 000
119 243	86 267	66 472	103 726	27 615	192 573	55 085	52 978	292 645	160 000
10	27	8	14	32	54	17	63	9	44
9 881	255	968	965	3 936	5 725	1 214	4 772	3 820	7 842
1 696	…	…	278	8 306	1 530	52	594	620	59

19—3 续表 8

(2017 年)

指　　标	Item	八　师 一三四团 Farm 134 Division 8	八　师 一三六团 Farm 136 Division 8	八　师 一四一团 Farm 141 Division 8	八　师 一四二团 Farm 142 Division 8
基本情况	**Basic Situation**				
行政区域面积　(公顷)	Administrative Area　(hectare)	58 000	19 411	20 003	70 000
居民委员会(社区)个数 (个)	Number of Residents' Committees　(unit)	3	4	2	4
人口与就业	**Population and Employment**				
户籍户数　(户)	Household Register Number　(household)	7 311	4 087	4 489	10 049
户籍人口　(人)	Census Register Population　(person)	21 034	11 036	11 539	25 042
全家外出户数　(户)	Family Number　(household)		310	206	1 324
全家外出人口　(人)	Family Outgoing Population　(person)		781	605	3 294
常住户数　(户)	Number of Permanent Accounts　(household)	7 311	4 072	4 138	10 166
常住人口　(人)	Permanent Population　(person)	21 034	11 119	10 765	25 333
从业人员	Practitioners	8 584	4 455	4 060	11 012
第一产业	Primary Industry	5 306	1 923	2 029	3 475
第二产业	Secondary Industry	1 068	238	550	1 686
第三产业	Tertiary industry	2 210	2 294	1 481	5 851
生产总值　(万元)	**Gross Domestic Products　(10 000 yuan)**	**82 685**	**75 361**	**82 825**	**188 096**
# 第一产业	Primary Industry	51 441	35 591	46 886	108 126
第二产业	Secondary Industry	2 208	914	6 148	16 304
第三产业	Tertiary Industry	29 036	38 856	29 791	63 666
# 工　业	Industry	1 338	914	3 802	7 254
固定资产投资总额　(万元)	**Investment in Fixed Assets　(10 000 yuan)**	**92 605**	**32 598**	**51 752**	**109 083**
农　业	**Agriculture**				
耕地面积　(公顷)	Arable Area　(hectare)	19 509	14 107	12 642	32 335
设施农业占地面积　(公顷)	Facility Agricultural Area　(hectare)	141	65	70	49
农作物播种面积　(公顷)	Crop Sown Area　(hectare)	17 786	13 202	12 642	34 072
# 粮　食	Grain	467		333	4 044
农民合作社个数　(个)	Number of Farmers' Cooperatives　(unit)	36	18	30	67
农民合作社成员数　(户)	Number of Farmers' Cooperatives Leaguer (household)	282	841	273	451
耕地流转面积　(公顷)	Arable land transfer Area　(hectare)				
种植大户数　(户)	Number of Large Households　(household)	1 320	267	114	
畜禽养殖大户数　(户)	Number of Large Livestock and Poultry Farmers　(household)	36	37	7	27
财政、经济	**Finance and Economy**				
一般公共预算收入　(万元)	General Public Budget Revenue　(10 000 yuan)				
一般公共预算支出　(万元)	General Public Budget Expenditure　(10 000 yuan)	34 973	19 940	17 810	39 635
资产总额　(万元)	Total Assets　(10 000 yuan)	209 223	120 073	135 000	247 094
债务总额　(万元)	Total Debt　(10 000 yuan)	205 655	11 513	99 100	219 728
企业个数　(个)	Number of Enterprises　(unit)	6	10	14	104
企业从业人员　(人)	Enterprise Practitioners　(person)	584	628	288	11 012
企业实交税金　(万元)	Tax payment for enterprises　(10 000 yuan)	15	298	246	495

Continued

八　师 一四三团 Farm 143 Division 8	八　师 一四四团 Farm 144 Division 8	八　师 石河子总场 Shihezi Farm Division 8	八　师 一四七团 Farm 147 Division 8	八　师 一四八团 Farm 148 Division 8	八　师 一四九团 Farm 149 Division 8	八　师 一五〇团 Farm 150 Division 8	八　师 一五二团 Farm 152 Division 8	九　师 一六一团 Farm 161 Division 9	九　师 一六三团 Farm 163 Division 9
93 627	31 583	47 500	22 485	30 196	42 192	45 073	10 159	124 104	20 597
7	3	12	3	4		3	3		2
13 703	5 355	17 233	6 549	9 583	6 214	6 899		2 228	3 846
37 155	12 751	51 698	16 236	24 731	15 414	17 289		5 128	9 561
2 032			330	73		526		107	137
5 697			931	218		1 262		269	322
13 523	5 355	17 233	6 440	9 394	6 485	5 872	2 232	2 157	3 481
34 088	12 751	51 698	15 472	24 259	16 606	15 446	6 397	5 379	7 224
14 145	3 163	23 989	5 456	9 717	7 964	4 849	4 111	2 631	5 225
5 351	2 565	3 966	1 964	4 128	4 380	2 029	1 166	1 466	2 184
3 194	342	4 920	792	1 603	895	722	1 769	206	856
5 600	256	15 103	2 700	3 986	2 689	2 098	1 176	999	2 186
184 397	**132 272**	**567 102**	**87 328**	**102 640**	**80 112**	**107 694**	**107 512**	**29 269**	**51 414**
70 617	74 484	103 292	36 905	40 874	38 869	53 968	16 024	15 616	21 369
57 293	7 781	174 659	10 009	9 795	3 338	19 064	26 245	1 516	12 995
56 487	50 007	289 151	40 414	51 971	37 905	34 662	65 243	12 137	17 050
26 235	7 781	105 312	10 009	7 510	3 338	7 506	17 478	501	5 853
119 235	**45 689**	**142 521**	**105 076**	**80 300**	**91 618**	**91 850**	**54 245**	**34 983**	**35 454**
16 288	20 492	19 866	13 867	16 446	13 757	19 003	882	7 918	8 605
129	19	118	137	57	54	67	32	3	463
16 638	19 000	17 008	13 867	16 446	13 757	18 941	236	12 311	8 903
3 407	1 207	1 857	400	333	200	400	53	6 365	5 745
21	9	53	32	17		36		5	16
770	611	1 199	1 127	420		676		25	122
		360	64	824				821	
375	355	322	648	120	165	367		321	706
483	66	450	154	32	20	26	5	431	107
						4			
29 144	23 177	47 026	19 147	27 618	23 889	27 497	7 713	14 797	9 480
227 153	191 900	406 606	14 393	217 874		295 459	146 772	55 921	97 497
218 806	155 200	314 252	2 424	182 804		225 401	122 470	41 243	70 677
83	8	803	225	24	5	12	15	28	67
14 145	61	20 023	3 115	9 717	485	1 121	4 111	131	645
1 037	2 865	2 180	369		1 468	2 901	202	308	

19—3 续表 9

(2017 年)

指 标	Item	九 师 一六四团 Farm 164 Division 9	九 师 一六五团 Farm 165 Division 9	九 师 一六六团 Farm 166 Division 9	九 师 一六七团 Farm 167 Division 9
基本情况	**Basic Situation**				
行政区域面积 (公顷)	Administrative Area (hectare)	19 161	93 876	49 433	40 900
居民委员会(社区)个数 (个)	Number of Residents' Committees (unit)	1	1		2
人口与就业	**Population and Employment**				
户籍户数 (户)	Household Register Number (household)	2 578	2 055	2 513	2 415
户籍人口 (人)	Census Register Population (person)	6 361	5 283	8 150	6 173
全家外出户数 (户)	Family Number (household)	228	26	484	
全家外出人口 (人)	Family Outgoing Population (person)	664	80	1 029	
常住户数 (户)	Number of Permanent Accounts (household)	2 412	1 751	2 513	2 112
常住人口 (人)	Permanent Population (person)	5 981	5 940	8 150	5 708
从业人员	Practitioners	3 258	2 439	4 081	2 972
第一产业	Primary Industry	1 554	1 471	1 458	1 824
第二产业	Secondary Industry	141	245	286	134
第三产业	Tertiary industry	1 515	723	286	1 024
生产总值 (万元)	**Gross Domestic Products (10 000 yuan)**	**31 043**	**21 859**	**42 835**	**26 466**
# 第一产业	Primary Industry	18 979	13 298	25 894	15 533
第二产业	Secondary Industry	44 33	3 789	6 823	3 399
第三产业	Tertiary Industry	7 631	4 772	10 118	7 534
# 工 业	Industry	2 270	707	6 823	1 253
固定资产投资总额 (万元)	**Investment in Fixed Assets (10 000 yuan)**	**20 629**	**16 957**	**32 850**	**21 651**
农 业	**Agriculture**				
耕地面积 (公顷)	Arable Area (hectare)	10 027	3 941	13 694	10 639
设施农业占地面积 (公顷)	Facility Agricultural Area (hectare)	127	9	146	233
农作物播种面积 (公顷)	Crop Sown Area (hectare)	9 891	8 687	14 731	11 904
# 粮 食	Grain	6 281	2 218	6 533	5 115
农民合作社个数 (个)	Number of Farmers' Cooperatives (unit)	12	9	16	23
农民合作社成员数 (户)	Number of Farmers' Cooperatives Leaguer (household)	79	220	2 853	525
耕地流转面积 (公顷)	Arable land transfer Area (hectare)			475	
种植大户数 (户)	Number of Large Households (household)	450	92	378	5
畜禽养殖大户数 (户)	Number of Large Livestock and Poultry Farmers (household)	201	106	312	4
财政、经济	**Finance and Economy**				
一般公共预算收入 (万元)	General Public Budget Revenue (10 000 yuan)				
一般公共预算支出 (万元)	General Public Budget Expenditure (10 000 yuan)	13 301	14 218	20 376	19 884
资产总额 (万元)	Total Assets (10 000 yuan)	107 791	74 773	79 781	92 139
债务总额 (万元)	Total Debt (10 000 yuan)	79 631	54 254	53 544	69 915
企业个数 (个)	Number of Enterprises (unit)	27	13	29	16
企业从业人员 (人)	Enterprise Practitioners (person)	49	34	139	89
企业实交税金 (万元)	Tax payment for enterprises (10 000 yuan)	175	152	3	532

Continued

九　师 一六八团 Farm 168 Division 9	九　师 一七〇团 Farm 170 Division 9	九　师 团结农场 Tuanjie Farm Division 9	十　师 一八一团 Farm 181 Division 10	十　师 一八二团 Farm 182 Division 10	十　师 一八三团 Farm 183 Division 10	十　师 一八四团 Farm 184 Division 10	十　师 一八五团 Farm 185 Division 10	十　师 一八六团 Farm 186 Division 10	十　师 一八七团 Farm 187 Division 10
42 400	97 400	5 369	76 000	35 756	35 363	72 424	90 795	62 190	29 030
2	3	1	1	1	1	2		1	1
4 048	988	1 376	5 165	2 290	3 188	2 510	1 402	986	2 806
9 772	3 432	3 652	12 359	6 021	8 674	6 930	3 543	2 819	7 201
12	165	216	1 523				171	2	
27	364	513	1 946				509	6	
4 036	1 534	1 391	3 752	2 017	3 418	3 217	1 163	987	2 611
9 745	3 396	3 631	10 683	5 306	9 294	8 009	3 346	2 650	6 796
4 572	2 005	1 638	5 024	2 486	4 269	4 429	1 494	1 149	3 621
2 880	911	827	2 368	1 416	2 173	1 539	827	446	1 179
295	376	293	774	39	996	936	23	213	1 121
1 397	698	518	1 882	1 031	1 100	1 954	644	490	1 321
45 679	**18 466**	**17 625**	**82 838**	**42 705**	**96 197**	**117 311**	**21 431**	**16 773**	**62 267**
21 651	5 174	8 743	16 190	11 275	27 835	39 147	5 932	2 722	12 535
9 292	8 217	5 390	41 102	19 196	41 105	52 559	3 451	7 836	33 635
14 736	5 075	3 492	25 546	12 234	27 257	25 605	12 048	6 215	16 097
1 801	8 217	3 806	28 419	12 936	30 933	27 490	1 272	4 261	23 949
29 541	**13 879**	**12 466**	**52 569**	**37 889**	**38 997**	**38 024**	**38 110**	**21 770**	**40 809**
8 867	529	2 916	7 987	7 498	9 948	18 031	3 916	2 567	8 959
223	71	194		5	485	62	13	575	79
11 559	410	2 826	10 000	8 067	12 157	16 526	4 667	2 358	7 363
2 890	61	980	1 780	2 267	2 860	3 546	1 379	1 071	2 383
6	9	2	22	25	20	8	10		28
43	101	30	1 594	522	212	174	197		685
567			680	1 426	2 563		672		2 973
406	5	3	48		460	75			48
912	19	14	167	1	185	59	1	2	34
			396	100	195	574	105	465	113
23 080	10 212	10 162	20 577	24 736	17 645	20 600	17 000	11 972	16 741
77 003	28 602	34 760	139 324	72 508	117 055	167 680	65 559	63 209	77 431
61 662	18 522	24 296	84 378	59 495	93 614	112 264	51 925	48 351	55 376
31	28	19	23	37	16	16	4	10	26
207	187	260	5 024	2 486	318	936	205	220	592
675	364	519	202	113	2 966	1 324	97	35	

19—3 续表 10

(2017 年)

指　标	Item	十师 一八八团 Farm 188 Division 10	十二师 一〇四团 Farm 104 Division 12	十二师 三坪农场 Sanping Farm Division 12	十二师 五一农场 Wuyi Farm Division 12
基本情况	**Basic Situation**				
行政区域面积 (公顷)	Administrative Area (hectare)	39 000	233 840	7 849	6 124
居民委员会(社区)个数 (个)	Number of Residents' Committees (unit)	2	12	8	4
人口与就业	**Population and Employment**				
户籍户数 (户)	Household Register Number (household)	4 558	8 353	4 891	3 517
户籍人口 (人)	Census Register Population (person)	12 762	20 384	13 121	9 752
全家外出户数 (户)	Family Number (household)	1 214	650	41	25
全家外出人口 (人)	Family Outgoing Population (person)	3 672	1 690	143	74
常住户数 (户)	Number of Permanent Accounts (household)	4 443	8 288	8 310	5 887
常住人口 (人)	Permanent Population (person)	11 306	24 461	20 392	15 728
从业人员	Practitioners	6 373	9 383	5 932	6 788
第一产业	Primary Industry	1 408	2 194	1 224	1 055
第二产业	Secondary Industry	2 179	1 510	598	1 102
第三产业	Tertiary industry	2 786	7 244	4 110	4 518
生产总值 (万元)	**Gross Domestic Products (10 000 yuan)**	**119 907**	**144 241**	**70 115**	**70 687**
# 第一产业	Primary Industry	14 803	8 681	16 947	19 689
第二产业	Secondary Industry	66 091	24 837	12 985	9 892
第三产业	Tertiary Industry	39 013	110 723	40 183	41 106
# 工　业	Industry	54 047	24 685	12 311	9 757
固定资产投资总额 (万元)	**Investment in Fixed Assets (10 000 yuan)**	**81 722**	**215 145**	**11 628**	**102 836**
农　业	**Agriculture**				
耕地面积 (公顷)	Arable Area (hectare)	7 413	1 082	3 466	3 016
设施农业占地面积 (公顷)	Facility Agricultural Area (hectare)	83	255	97	64
农作物播种面积 (公顷)	Crop Sown Area (hectare)	4 459	706		1 038
# 粮　食	Grain	1 384			
农民合作社个数 (个)	Number of Farmers' Cooperatives (unit)	31	1		4
农民合作社成员数 (户)	Number of Farmers' Cooperatives Leaguer (household)	702	30		56
耕地流转面积 (公顷)	Arable land transfer Area (hectare)	487			1 711
种植大户数 (户)	Number of Large Households (household)	189			
畜禽养殖大户数 (户)	Number of Large Livestock and Poultry Farmers (household)	15	25		
财政、经济	**Finance and Economy**				
一般公共预算收入 (万元)	General Public Budget Revenue (10 000 yuan)	2 171	613		
一般公共预算支出 (万元)	General Public Budget Expenditure (10 000 yuan)	17 505	21 620	10 389	9 239
资产总额 (万元)	Total Assets (10 000 yuan)	140 636	448 700	133 636	146 819
债务总额 (万元)	Total Debt (10 000 yuan)	125 892	366 600	107 270	91 088
企业个数 (个)	Number of Enterprises (unit)	175	195	35	100
企业从业人员 (人)	Enterprise Practitioners (person)	2 100	4 193	5 932	6 657
企业实交税金 (万元)	Tax payment for enterprises (10 000 yuan)	3 513	24 250		1 845

Continued

十二师头屯河农场 Toutunhe Farm Division 12	十二师西山农场 Xishan Farm Division 12	十二师二二一团 Farm 221 Division 12	十二师二二二团 Farm 222 Division 12	十三师红星一场 Red Star No.1 Farm Division 13	十三师红星二场 Red Star No.2 Farm Division 13	十三师红星四场 Red Star No.4 Farm Division 13	十三师黄田农场 Huangtian Farm Division 13	十三师火箭农场 Huojian Farm Division 13	十三师柳树泉农场 Liushuquan Farm Division 13
4 147	9 121	9 687	17 756	15 000	20 300	125 500	100 085	18 150	142 345
6	4	1	9	1		1	2	3	2
3 122	2 480	1 886	4 533	3 383	2 732	2 712	3 241	6 055	3 554
9 082	6 356	5 118	10 801	9 875	7 271	8 346	11 057	20 402	11 301
	296	55	101		12	345			
	789	155	262		41	1 120			
5 985	4 220	1 886	3 909	3 728	3 124	2 768	3 540	6 658	3 774
15 955	12 252	5 393	10 713	15 510	8 378	8 732	12 214	22 432	11 521
6 324	2 761	2 690	3 738	7 021	4 017	4 832	8 644	11 921	5 550
1 557	748	1 022	1 279	1 248	791	1 118	1 741	1 887	2 979
18	400	265	1 339	1 990	1 164	1 355	3 352	2 686	605
4 682	1 613	1 403	1 130	3 783	2 062	2 359	3 551	7 348	1 966
66 535	**42 552**	**25 557**	**70 026**	**128 453**	**126 474**	**81 416**	**138 158**	**186 633**	**78 410**
12 450	5 154	7 118	17 570	31 156	19 220	18 797	32 107	23 075	18 364
978	9 553	7 312	23 639	66 294	88 391	38 015	83 287	101 046	46 584
53 107	27 845	11 127	28 817	31 003	18 863	24 604	22 764	62 512	13 462
978	8 975	7 312	19 963	65 969	88 391	38 015	83 287	75 143	46 584
41 300	**105 101**	**31 786**	**50 631**	**153 077**	**251 204**	**157 949**	**158 121**	**282 704**	**87 335**
412	2 315	724	7 655	3 774	3 407	3 600	2 536	3 319	328
33	63	20	6	74	24	106	82	85	23
1 652	1 015	636	7 087	3 798	3 407	3 600	5 217	2 634	328
			3493	27	2		160		260
4	3	6	19	9	13	10	21	19	15
20	25	35	95	662	782	218	105	378	50
			45		44	35		281	
	1		7	35	36	28	8	22	1
		305				1		42 081	11 071
17 358	14 518	9 273	18 835	18 708	10 910	16 613	19 055	42 081	11 071
109 554	161 234	77 191	292 600	129 713	102 020	110 699	231 607	142 856	47 296
88 268	122 321	62 647	189 133	85 504	77 834	71 121	178 378	112 658	46 286
9	15	12	67	50	66	27	50	374	26
248	627	2 690	2 391	1 506	1 550	1 355	8 644	6 217	900
1 177	2 320		645	270	448	1 661			150

19—3 续表 11 continued

(2017 年)

指　　标	Item	十三师红山农场 Hongshan Farm Division 13	十三师淖毛湖农场 Nao Maohu Farm Division 13	十四师四十七团(十二师代管) Farm 47 Division 14 (Division 12)	十四师皮山农场 Pishan Farm Division 14	十四师一牧场 Ranch 1 Division 14	十四师二二四团 Farm 224 Division 14
基本情况	**Basic Situation**						
行政区域面积　(公顷)	Administrative Area　(hectare)	326 100	3 553	15 399	44 528	84 493	32 020
居民委员会(社区)个数 (个)	Number of Residents' Committees　(unit)		1	4	1	1	1
人口与就业	**Population and Employment**						
户籍户数　(户)	Household Register Number　(household)	4 062	719	1 476	7 037	809	3 282
户籍人口　(人)	Census Register Population　(person)	12 463	2 266	4 376	26 852	2 237	11 439
全家外出户数　(户)	Family Number　(household)	24	25	6	75	6	20
全家外出人口　(人)	Family Outgoing Population　(person)	51	45	11	263	26	78
常住户数　(户)	Number of Permanent Accounts　(household)	4 606	1 197	2 094	8 160	1 014	4 121
常住人口　(人)	Permanent Population　(person)	13 586	2 851	5 874	30 189	2 854	14 349
从业人员	Practitioners	6 974	2 427	2 898	10 168	1 667	8 956
第一产业	Primary Industry	2 225	456	1 985	5 759	2 117	7 002
第二产业	Secondary Industry	431	954	40	947	97	160
第三产业	Tertiary industry	923	1 017	876	3 462	496	1 794
生产总值　(万元)	**Gross Domestic Products　(10 000 yuan)**	**135 153**	**126 848**	**14 612**	**33 103**	**7 972**	**64 057**
# 第一产业	Primary Industry	15 181	5 197	10 406	19 371	5 260	55 779
第二产业	Secondary Industry	106 088	103 744	333	2 203	507	593
第三产业	Tertiary Industry	13 884	17 907	3 873	11 529	2 205	7 685
# 工　业	Industry	106 088	103 744	333	2 203	507	593
固定资产投资总额　(万元)	**Investment in Fixed Assets　(10 000 yuan)**	**67 046**	**221 412**	**14 646**	**55 330**	**10 573**	**60 183**
农　业	**Agriculture**						
耕地面积　(公顷)	Arable Area　(hectare)	5 864	1 314	2 792	669	1 775	433
设施农业占地面积　(公顷)	Facility Agricultural Area　(hectare)	40	5	200	84	31	37
农作物播种面积　(公顷)	Crop Sown Area　(hectare)	5 864	1 314	970	1 322	1 775	1 254
# 粮　食	Grain	4 247	645	508	342	1 018	943
农民合作社个数　(个)	Number of Farmers' Cooperatives　(unit)	15	8	3	17	6	27
农民合作社成员数　(户)	Number of Farmers' Cooperatives Leaguer　(household)	686	265	80	595	32	280
耕地流转面积　(公顷)	Arable land transfer Area　(hectare)			33			
种植大户数　(户)	Number of Large Households　(household)	23	37	151	10		
畜禽养殖大户数　(户)	Number of Large Livestock and Poultry Farmers　(household)	163	2	14	75	60	3
财政、经济	**Finance and Economy**						
一般公共预算收入　(万元)	General Public Budget Revenue　(10 000 yuan)	17 854	9 340	25 826	34 568	16 031	61 872
一般公共预算支出　(万元)	General Public Budget Expenditure　(10 000 yuan)	17 854	8 801	20 209	32 571	16 031	61 872
资产总额　(万元)	Total Assets　(10 000 yuan)	108 024	48 402	81 691	276 161	78 500	44
债务总额　(万元)	Total Debt　(10 000 yuan)	77 175	35 645	572	254 332	53 900	61 872
企业个数　(个)	Number of Enterprises　(unit)	30	15	2	5	10	15
企业从业人员　(人)	Enterprise Practitioners　(person)	431	907	40	365	97	210
企业实交税金　(万元)	Tax payment for enterprises　(10 000 yuan)	2 814	559	55		10	

19—3 续表 12 continued

(2017 年)

指标	Item	一师一团（七师代管）Farm 1 Division 1 (Division 7)	一师二团 Farm 2 Division 1	一师三团 Farm 3 Division 1	一师四团 Farm 4 Division 1
工业	**Industry**				
工业企业单位数（个）	Unit Number of Industrial Enterprises (unit)	31	21	29	4
# 规模以上工业	Above Scale Industry	10	9	10	2
工业总产值（万元）	Total Industrial Output Value (10 000 yuan)	212 966	131 886	136 106	12 047
# 规模以上工业	Above Scale Industry	173 680	107 020	125 588	8 104
建筑业	**Construction Business**				
建筑业企业单位数（个）	Number of Enterprise Units in Construction Industry (unit)	3	1		
建筑业总产值（万元）	Total Output Value of Construction Industry (10 000 yuan)	51 893	105 807		
贸易、市场	**Trade, market**				
住宿餐饮业企业个数（个）	Number of Enterprises for Accommodation and Catering Industry (unit)	2	1	3	
住宿餐饮业企业营业总收入（万元）	Total Revenue of the Enterprise of Accommodation and Catering Industry (10 000 yuan)	1 640	170	1 680	
社会消费品零售总额（万元）	Total retail sales of consumer goods (10 000 yuan)	50 028	17 984	23 338	21 587
# 限额以上	Limit the Total Retail Sales of Social Consumer Goods	6 225	669		1 511
营业面积50平米以上的综合商店或超市（个）	Number of Comprehensive Stores or Supermarkets with a Business Area of 50 Square meters or more (unit)	7	57	57	3
教育、文化、卫生	**Education, Culture, Health**				
幼儿园、托儿所个数（个）	Number of Kindergartens and Uursery Schools (unit)	2	1	1	1
小学校数（所）	Primary School Number (unit)	2	1	1	1
小学专任教师数（人）	Number of Full—time Teachers in Primary Schools (person)	123	39	66	23
小学在校学生数（人）	Number of Students in Primary School (person)	687	854	422	1489
图书馆、文化站个数（个）	Number of Libraries and Cultural Stations (unit)	1	1		3
剧场、影剧院个数（个）	Number of Theaters and Theaters (unit)	1	1		1
体育场馆个数（个）	Number of Stadiums and Gymnasiums (unit)	1	1		2
医疗卫生机构个数（个）	Number of Medical and Health Institutions (unit)	1	1	1	2
医疗卫生机构床位数（个）	Bed Number of Medical and Health Institutions (unit)	80	50	60	120
执业（助理）医师数（人）	Practising (Assistant) Doctor Number (person)	36	25	17	32
社会保障	**Social Security**				
本级政府创办的敬老院个数（个）	Number of Old Homes Established by the Government at the Same Level (unit)				1
城乡居民基本养老保险参保人数（人）	Number of Basic Old—age Insurance for Urban and Rural Residents (person)	6 389	6 958	2 525	8 995
城乡居民基本医疗保险参保人数（人）	Number of Basic Medical Insurance for Urban and Rural Residents (person)	8 883	10 233	1 972	6 433
城乡居民最低生活保障人数（人）	The number of Minimum Living Security for Urban and Rural Residents (person)	148	79	351	305
公用事业	**Public Utility**				
自来水用水户数（户）	Number of Water Users (household)	5 511	5 639	2 526	7 894
管道燃气用气户数（户）	Number of Gas Accounts for Pipeline Gas (household)	3 094	4 235	1 250	4 420
金融机构网点数（个）	Number of Branches of Financial Institutions (unit)	2	3	3	3
公园及休闲健身广场个数（个）	Number of Park and Leisure Fitness Square (unit)	2	4	2	4
生活垃圾月均处理量（吨/月）	Monthly Average Treatment of Domestic Waste (ton / month)	230	735	24	250

19—3 续表 13

(2017 年)

指　　标	Item	一　师 五　团 (十一师代管) Farm 5 Division 1 (Division 11)	一　师 六　团 Farm 6 Division 1	一　师 七　团 Farm 7 Division 1	一　师 八　团 Farm 8 Division 1
工　业	**Industry**				
工业企业单位数　(个)	Unit Number of Industrial Enterprises　(unit)	22	46	53	24
# 规模以上工业	Above Scale Industry	9	9	14	8
工业总产值　(万元)	Total Industrial Output Value　(10 000 yuan)	71 901	149 972	196 562	113 045
# 规模以上工业	Above Scale Industry	50 131	92 580	145 112	86 347
建筑业	**Construction Business**				
建筑业企业单位数　(个)	Number of Enterprise Units in Construction Industry　(unit)	2	1	2	1
建筑业总产值　(万元)	Total Output Value of Construction Industry　(10 000 yuan)	185 736	11 713	4 447	43 486
贸易、市场	**Trade, market**				
住宿餐饮业企业个数　(个)	Number of Enterprises for Accommodation and Catering Industry　(unit)	6		4	
住宿餐饮业企业营业总收入(万元)	Total Revenue of the Enterprise of Accommodation and Catering Industry　(10 000 yuan)	3 922		468	
社会消费品零售总额 (万元)	Total retail sales of consumer goods　(10 000 yuan)	34 565	24 782	33 134	35 792
# 限额以上	Limit the Total Retail Sales of Social Consumer Goods	3 473	2 319	2 947	13 423
营业面积 50 平米以上的综合商店或超市　(个)	Number of Comprehensive Stores or Supermarkets with a Business Area of 50 Square meters or more　(unit)	506	12	3	2
教育、文化、卫生	**Education, Culture, Health**				
幼儿园、托儿所个数　(个)	Number of Kindergartens and Uursery Schools (unit)	2	4	1	1
小学校数　(所)	Primary School Number　(unit)	1	1	1	1
小学专任教师数　(人)	Number of Full－time Teachers in Primary Schools　(person)	96	56	53	48
小学在校学生数　(人)	Number of Students in Primary School　(person)	825	863	745	717
图书馆、文化站个数　(个)	Number of Libraries and Cultural Stations　(unit)	1	1	11	1
剧场、影剧院个数　(个)	Number of Theaters and Theaters　(unit)		1		1
体育场馆个数　(个)	Number of Stadiums and Gymnasiums　(unit)		2		1
医疗卫生机构个数　(个)	Number of Medical and Health Institutions (unit)	1	1	1	1
医疗卫生机构床位数　(个)	Bed Number of Medical and Health Institutions　(unit)	45	50	60	70
执业(助理)医师数　(人)	Practising (Assistant) Doctor Number　(person)	21	15	20	22
社会保障	**Social Security**				
本级政府创办的敬老院个数　(个)	Number of Old Homes Established by the Government at the Same Level　(unit)				1
城乡居民基本养老保险参保人数 (人)	Number of Basic Old－age Insurance for Urban and Rural Residents　(person)	5 020	4 060	7 923	5 162
城乡居民基本医疗保险参保人数 (人)	Number of Basic Medical Insurance for Urban and Rural Residents　(person)	8 031	5 820	8 145	4 265
城乡居民最低生活保障人数 (人)	The number of Minimum Living Security for Urban and Rural Residents　(person)	202	170	94	125
公用事业	**Public Utility**				
自来水用水户数　(户)	Number of Water Users　(household)	3 905	4 454	3 605	4 531
管道燃气用气户数　(户)	Number of Gas Accounts for Pipeline Gas　(household)	2 804	3 494	1 287	1 880
金融机构网点数　(个)	Number of Branches of Financial Institutions　(unit)	2	3	3	2
公园及休闲健身广场个数 (个)	Number of Park and Leisure Fitness Square　(unit)	3	2	1	1
生活垃圾月均处理量 (吨/月)	Monthly Average Treatment of Domestic Waste (ton / month)	180	490	125	550

Continued

一师 十团 Farm10 Division 1	一师 十一团 Farm 11 Division 1	一师 十二团 Farm 12 Division 1	一师 十三团 Farm 13 Division 1	一师 十四团 Farm 14 Division 1	一师 十六团 Farm 16 Division 1	一师 阿拉尔农场 Alaer Farm Division 1	一师 幸福农场 Xingfu Farm Division 1	二师 二十一团 Farm 21 Division 2
24	13	37	25	18	25	16	7	12
10	6	14	8	8	7	5	5	8
205 247	92 348	215 729	134 335	56 213	182 729	45 014	41 048	133 754
184 379	82 837	180 691	106 767	45 220	152 192	34 421	38 218	127 515
2	2	1	2	1	2	1	1	
24 840	44 336	287 796	25 181	2 871	147 447	32 704	7 097	
	3		1	1	7	1		1
	11 523		607	1 951	11 489	576		518
75 535	38 026	33 218	30 137	13 442	47 084	20 098	2 406	6 204
400	8 366	3 002	6 073	1 951	14 294			
1		2	18	50	6		6	13
1	1	1	2	1	1	1		1
1	1	1	2	1	2	1	2	1
40	48	103	82	41	64	123	39	34
824	1 713	1 222	653	725	2 192	370	279	392
	2			1			1	1
				1	1			
		1	1	1				
1	1	4	1	1	1	1	1	1
40	120	70	50	63	88		20	100
16	46	5	25	16	26	2	12	47
3 067	11 160	8 990	1 962	6 457	2 558	1 131	3 446	5 046
3 071	9 614	13 910	5 485	7 764	2 566	2 457	2 267	5 046
664	210	576	216	95	60	320	208	630
3 626	7 272	7 275	2 800	6 021	2 610	1 989	994	7 432
3 004	4 223	3 545	2 360	3 358	400			5 476
3	4	5	2	2				3
1	1	2	1	4				
55	30	200	240	589		25	279	

19—3 续表 14

(2017 年)

指标	Item	二师 二十二团 Farm 22 Division 2	二师 二十四团 Farm 24 Division 2	二师 二十五团 Farm 25 Division 2	二师 二十七团 Farm 27 Division 2
工　业	**Industry**				
工业企业单位数　(个)	Unit Number of Industrial Enterprises　(unit)	21	16	6	16
# 规模以上工业	Above Scale Industry	6	5	1	8
工业总产值　(万元)	Total Industrial Output Value　(10 000 yuan)	202 333	41 434	10 078	88 085
# 规模以上工业	Above Scale Industry	177 694	26 524	5 144	78 042
建筑业	**Construction Business**				
建筑业企业单位数　(个)	Number of Enterprise Units in Construction Industry　(unit)				
建筑业总产值　(万元)	Total Output Value of Construction Industry　(10 000 yuan)				
贸易、市场	**Trade, market**				
住宿餐饮业企业个数　(个)	Number of Enterprises for Accommodation and Catering Industry　(unit)		63	18	
住宿餐饮业企业营业总收入　(万元)	Total Revenue of the Enterprise of Accommodation and Catering Industry　(10 000 yuan)		3 454	4 196	
社会消费品零售总额　(万元)	Total retail sales of consumer goods　(10 000 yuan)	11 786	10 424	2 984	14 528
# 限额以上	Limit the Total Retail Sales of Social Consumer Goods	11 447	2 485		
营业面积 50 平米以上的综合商店或超市　(个)	Number of Comprehensive Stores or Supermarkets with a Business Area of 50 Square meters or more　(unit)	150	8	3	7
教育、文化、卫生	**Education, Culture, Health**				
幼儿园、托儿所个数　(个)	Number of Kindergartens and Uursery Schools　(unit)	2	1	1	1
小学校数　(所)	Primary School Number　(unit)	2	2	1	1
小学专任教师数　(人)	Number of Full−time Teachers in Primary Schools　(person)	76	94	18	33
小学在校学生数　(人)	Number of Students in Primary School　(person)	730	226	335	1 588
图书馆、文化站个数　(个)	Number of Libraries and Cultural Stations　(unit)	2	1	1	4
剧场、影剧院个数　(个)	Number of Theaters and Theaters　(unit)	1			1
体育场馆个数　(个)	Number of Stadiums and Gymnasiums　(unit)	3	1		
医疗卫生机构个数　(个)	Number of Medical and Health Institutions　(unit)	2	1	1	2
医疗卫生机构床位数　(个)	Bed Number of Medical and Health Institutions　(unit)	49	30	26	94
执业(助理)医师数　(人)	Practising (Assistant) Doctor Number　(person)	25	9	26	89
社会保障	**Social Security**				
本级政府创办的敬老院个数　(个)	Number of Old Homes Established by the Government at the Same Level　(unit)				
城乡居民基本养老保险参保人数　(人)	Number of Basic Old−age Insurance for Urban and Rural Residents　(person)	912	1 798	2 105	1 484
城乡居民基本医疗保险参保人数　(人)	Number of Basic Medical Insurance for Urban and Rural Residents　(person)	5 160	1 636	2 105	9 382
城乡居民最低生活保障人数　(人)	The number of Minimum Living Security for Urban and Rural Residents　(person)	377	124	756	657
公用事业	**Public Utility**				
自来水用水户数　(户)	Number of Water Users　(household)	3 538	2 335	3 931	10 230
管道燃气用气户数　(户)	Number of Gas Accounts for Pipeline Gas　(household)	3 218	1 288	2 776	3 965
金融机构网点数　(个)	Number of Branches of Financial Institutions　(unit)	4	3	5	6
公园及休闲健身广场个数　(个)	Number of Park and Leisure Fitness Square　(unit)	2	1		2
生活垃圾月均处理量　(吨/月)	Monthly Average Treatment of Domestic Waste　(ton / month)	496	285	161	450

Continued

二师 三十九团 Farm 29 Division 2	二师 三〇团 Farm 30 Division 2	二师 三十一团 Farm 31 Division 2	二师 三十三团 Farm 33 Division 2	二师 三十四团 Farm 34 Division 2	二师 三十六团 (四师代管) Farm 36 Division 2 (Division 4)	二师 三十七团 Farm 37 Division 2	二师 三十八团 Farm 38 Division 2	二师 二二三团 Farm 223 Division 2
36	11	14	13	8	14	7	2	8
16	4	5	7	6	1		2	3
451 965	51 529	101 986	105 946	74 669	49 516	9 150	4 525	21 582
425 671	37 209	97 312	96 513	69 214	33 969		4 525	18 343
			1				35	1
			135				1 204	263
37 688	21 866	11 051	18 723	16 082	11 779	1 895	2 286	6 076
			7194		3148		2012	2787
65	5	10	17		59		5	8
3	1	1	2	2	1	1	1	1
2	1	1	2	2	1	1	1	1
121	83	36	64	63	36	12	41	55
744	570	731	579	398	91	722	613	605
	1	3	14	2	1	2	1	2
				1			1	1
1	1	3	2	2	1	1	1	1
50	40	74	81	60		30	38	25
30	15	64	31	18	3	26	14	13
		1		1			1	1
3 266	2 258	3 592	4 248	5 675	730	3 169	1 950	3 112
3 266	2 258	3 590	4 248	7 339	730	5 720	1 950	7 067
	337	366	144	182	13		301	196
3 880	3 735	4 467	4 454	3 016	866	1 801	2 447	4 583
2 500	3 179	3 528	2 063	2 293	389	1 801	2 272	3 377
5	3	3	3	2		1	1	2
1	1	3	1	5	1	1	1	1
325	180	316	65	17		211	240	1 000

19－3 续表 15

（2017 年）

指　标	Item	三　师 四十一团 Farm 41 Division 3	三　师 四十二团 Farm 42 Division 3	三　师 四十四团 Farm 44 Division 3	三　师 四十五团 Farm 45 Division 3
工　业	**Industry**				
工业企业单位数　（个）	Unit Number of Industrial Enterprises　(unit)	10	7	21	15
# 规模以上工业	Above Scale Industry	4	4	6	6
工业总产值　（万元）	Total Industrial Output Value　(10 000 yuan)	96 842	46 720	114 501	76 682
# 规模以上工业	Above Scale Industry	87 686	40 826	93 208	68 857
建筑业	**Construction Business**				
建筑业企业单位数　（个）	Number of Enterprise Units in Construction Industry　(unit)	1			1
建筑业总产值　（万元）	Total Output Value of Construction Industry　(10 000 yuan)	35 135			86 210
贸易、市场	**Trade, market**				
住宿餐饮业企业个数　（个）	Number of Enterprises for Accommodation and Catering Industry (unit)	1	1	130	9
住宿餐饮业企业营业总收入（万元）	Total Revenue of the Enterprise of Accommodation and Catering Industry　(10 000 yuan)	430	2 415	5 520	10 901
社会消费品零售总额（万元）	Total retail sales of consumer goods (10 000 yuan)	40 035	3 829	34 640	42 941
# 限额以上	Limit the Total Retail Sales of Social Consumer Goods	12 855	428	14 615	26 109
营业面积 50 平米以上的综合商店或超市　（个）	Number of Comprehensive Stores or Supermarkets with a Business Area of 50 Square meters or more　(unit)	290	26	18	42
教育、文化、卫生	**Education, Culture, Health**				
幼儿园、托儿所个数　（个）	Number of Kindergartens and Uursery Schools (unit)	1	1	2	3
小学校数　（所）	Primary School Number　(unit)	1	1	3	3
小学专任教师数　（人）	Number of Full－time Teachers in Primary Schools　(person)	44	36	368	160
小学在校学生数　（人）	Number of Students in Primary School　(person)	398	4 406	2 132	256
图书馆、文化站个数　（个）	Number of Libraries and Cultural Stations　(unit)	1		1	1
剧场、影剧院个数　（个）	Number of Theaters and Theaters　(unit)			1	
体育场馆个数　（个）	Number of Stadiums and Gymnasiums　(unit)			3	
医疗卫生机构个数　（个）	Number of Medical and Health Institutions (unit)	1	1	2	1
医疗卫生机构床位数　（个）	Bed Number of Medical and Health Institutions　(unit)	25	90	128	20
执业(助理)医师数　（人）	Practising (Assistant) Doctor Number　(person)	7	39	63	3
社会保障	**Social Security**				
本级政府创办的敬老院个数　（个）	Number of Old Homes Established by the Government at the Same Level　(unit)	1		1	
城乡居民基本养老保险参保人数（人）	Number of Basic Old－age Insurance for Urban and Rural Residents　(person)	1 634		11 760	1 476
城乡居民基本医疗保险参保人数（人）	Number of Basic Medical Insurance for Urban and Rural Residents　(person)	1 644		11 004	2 536
城乡居民最低生活保障人数（人）	The number of Minimum Living Security for Urban and Rural Residents　(person)	118		433	77
公用事业	**Public Utility**				
自来水用水户数　（户）	Number of Water Users　(household)	1 265	7 371	9 212	1 200
管道燃气用气户数　（户）	Number of Gas Accounts for Pipeline Gas　(household)	960	6 857	7 514	830
金融机构网点数　（个）	Number of Branches of Financial Institutions　(unit)	2	3	6	3
公园及休闲健身广场个数（个）	Number of Park and Leisure Fitness Square　(unit)	1	5	3	1
生活垃圾月均处理量（吨/月）	Monthly Average Treatment of Domestic Waste (ton / month)	30		30	7

Continued

三　师 四十六团 Farm 46 Division 3	三　师 四十八团 Farm 48 Division 3	三　师 四十九团 Farm 49 Division 3	三　师 五 〇 团 (六师代管) Farm 50 Division 3 (Division 6)	三　师 五十一团 Farm 51 Division 3	三　师 五十三团 Farm 53 Division 3	三　师 伽师总场 Jiashi Farm Division 3	三　师 叶城牧场 Yechen Farm Division 3	三　师 东风农场 Dongfen Farm Division 3	三　师 红旗农场 Redflag Farm Division 3
1	6	11	11	18	11	7	4	1	1
1	4	3	5	5	3	6			
7 153	47 086	58 796	74 963	87 123	41 819	43 921	3 142	595	1 820
7 153	43 918	51 416	59 746	62 189	31 185	41 806			
1		1			1				
15 216		19 885			40 055				
	1	2	8			2	1		
	1 325	2 456	4 045						
7 199	14 356	38 714	32 099	61 854	59 060	19 294	170	108	881
	257	5 222	10 858		12 771	5 331			
87	18	563	12	50	13	35	1		2
1	1	1	2	3	1	1	1	1	1
1	1	3	3	4	4	1	1	1	1
20	57	126	152	587	190	79	17	28	47
585	1 563	2 528	9 748	2 020	192	278	190	553	123
1		23	1	2	1	1			1
		0				1			
1		2		1		1			1
1	1	2	1	1	1	1	1	1	1
35	50	150	150	70		10			12
19	21	29	28	26	1	2	2		3
	1								
2 899	5 500	4 532	26 895	1 158	199	344	516	712	58
5 222	11 476	3 272	44 234	1 449	538	344	459	524	527
249	642	477	2 804	1 850	202	126	158	278	148
2 850	4 323	6 671	14 321	6 135	481	272	550	1 181	378
1 348	3 138	4 680	1 600	800	329		550	89	378
1	1	2	3	3				1	
1	2	21	1	4		1	1		1
45	750	620	300	300		2	12	150	17

19—3 续表 16

(2017 年)

指　　标	Item	三　师 托云牧场 Tuoyun Farm Division 3	三　师 五十四团 Farm 54 Division 3	四　师 六十一团 Farm 61 Division 4	四　师 六十二团 Farm 62 Division 4
工　业	**Industry**				
工业企业单位数　(个)	Unit Number of Industrial Enterprises　(unit)	3		18	23
# 规模以上工业	Above Scale Industry			6	4
工业总产值　(万元)	Total Industrial Output Value　(10 000 yuan)			130 875	124 511
# 规模以上工业	Above Scale Industry			115 060	87 207
建筑业	**Construction Business**				
建筑业企业单位数　(个)	Number of Enterprise Units in Construction Industry　(unit)			1	1
建筑业总产值　(万元)	Total Output Value of Construction Industry　(10 000 yuan)			7 565	15 007
贸易、市场	**Trade, market**				
住宿餐饮业企业个数　(个)	Number of Enterprises for Accommodation and Catering Industry (unit)	11			
住宿餐饮业企业营业总收入(万元)	Total Revenue of the Enterprise of Accommodation and Catering Industry　(10 000 yuan)	120	60		
社会消费品零售总额(万元)	Total retail sales of consumer goods (10 000 yuan)		85	11 901	49 119
# 限额以上	Limit the Total Retail Sales of Social Consumer Goods				7 050
营业面积 50 平米以上的综合商店或超市　(个)	Number of Comprehensive Stores or Supermarkets with a Business Area of 50 Square meters or more　(unit)		2	1	110
教育、文化、卫生	**Education, Culture, Health**				
幼儿园、托儿所个数　(个)	Number of Kindergartens and Uursery Schools (unit)	1	1	1	1
小学校数　(所)	Primary School Number　(unit)	1	1	1	1
小学专任教师数　(人)	Number of Full-time Teachers in Primary Schools　(person)	18	11	73	87
小学在校学生数　(人)	Number of Students in Primary School　(person)	839	1 657	1 287	371
图书馆、文化站个数　(个)	Number of Libraries and Cultural Stations　(unit)			14	
剧场、影剧院个数　(个)	Number of Theaters and Theaters　(unit)				
体育场馆个数　(个)	Number of Stadiums and Gymnasiums　(unit)		1		
医疗卫生机构个数　(个)	Number of Medical and Health Institutions (unit)	1	1	1	1
医疗卫生机构床位数　(个)	Bed Number of Medical and Health Institutions　(unit)	60	72	65	40
执业(助理)医师数　(人)	Practising (Assistant) Doctor Number　(person)	25	15	40	16
社会保障	**Social Security**				
本级政府创办的敬老院个数　(个)	Number of Old Homes Established by the Government at the Same Level　(unit)	1		1	
城乡居民基本养老保险参保人数(人)	Number of Basic Old-age Insurance for Urban and Rural Residents　(person)	3 824	3 027	302	6 657
城乡居民基本医疗保险参保人数(人)	Number of Basic Medical Insurance for Urban and Rural Residents　(person)	3 824	4 501	8 230	8 692
城乡居民最低生活保障人数(人)	The number of Minimum Living Security for Urban and Rural Residents　(person)	402	512	469	271
公用事业	**Public Utility**				
自来水用水户数　(户)	Number of Water Users　(household)	4 386	3 972	7 797	2 295
管道燃气用气户数　(户)	Number of Gas Accounts for Pipeline Gas　(household)	2 500	2 500	2 116	360
金融机构网点数　(个)	Number of Branches of Financial Institutions　(unit)	3	1	4	3
公园及休闲健身广场个数(个)	Number of Park and Leisure Fitness Square　(unit)	4	1	2	1
生活垃圾月均处理量(吨/月)	Monthly Average Treatment of Domestic Waste (ton / month)	694	126	618	780

Continued

四　师 六十三团 Farm 63 Division 4	四　师 六十四团 Farm 64 Division 4	四　师 六十六团 Farm 66 Division 4	四　师 六十七团 Farm 67 Division 4	四　师 六十八团 Farm 68 Division 4	四　师 六十九团 Farm 69 Division 4	四　师 七 〇 团 Farm 70 Division 4	四　师 七十一团 Farm 71 Division 4	四　师 七十二团 Farm 72 Division 4
5	11	22	12	13	8	19	15	10
2	6	4		1	5	7	6	2
74 245	118 395	128 313	25 762	43 247	58 353	105 437	88 426	24 165
69 681	94 756	82 704		23 130	46 157	82 778	66 096	6 495
			1	1	1	1	1	1
			811	14 422	27 000	14 500	5 600	7 407
			7			1	2	
			522			1 095	1330	
9 680	17 680	27 077	12 248	7 311	3 535	9 547	16 569	18 952
1	10	6	2	29	3	3	20	5
1	1	2	1	1	1	2	2	3
1	1	3	1	1	1	2	1	1
36	132	116	66	37	33	62	36	57
1 886	1 423	1 277	112	451	662	281	517	641
	3	1		2		12		1
						1		1
	2	1		1		1		1
1	3	1	1	1	2	2	1	1
60	228	38	40	35	64	72	70	35
40	74	16	20	42	47	26	27	14
2						1	1	1
12 467	16 880	5 098	5 697	5 222	4 256	8 926	7 099	2 053
19 429	22 203	10 278	3 564	6 523	6 757	7 427	8 464	1 178
1 213	852	672	138	118	265	229	191	560
	9 502	4 430	3 540	3 050	4 815	5 325	4 598	3 074
4 538			1 635	860	1 262	3 223	2 296	1 280
4	6	2	3	3	3	3	4	3
6	3	3	3	11	1	5	2	8
667	1 100	180	4 579	7	305	165	1 500	2

19—3 续表 17

(2017 年)

指 标	Item	四 师 七十三团 Farm 73 Division 4	四 师 七十四团 Farm 74 Division 4	四 师 七十五团 Farm 75 Division 4	四 师 七十六团 Farm 76 Division 4
工 业	**Industry**				
工业企业单位数 (个)	Unit Number of Industrial Enterprises (unit)	30	4	5	5
# 规模以上工业	Above Scale Industry	11		2	2
工业总产值 (万元)	Total Industrial Output Value (10 000 yuan)	231 560	17 513	55 549	71 334
# 规模以上工业	Above Scale Industry	213 517		44 186	60 093
建筑业	**Construction Business**				
建筑业企业单位数 (个)	Number of Enterprise Units in Construction Industry (unit)				
建筑业总产值 (万元)	Total Output Value of Construction Industry (10 000 yuan)				
贸易、市场	**Trade, market**				
住宿餐饮业企业个数 (个)	Number of Enterprises for Accommodation and Catering Industry (unit)	1	1		1
住宿餐饮业企业营业总收入 (万元)	Total Revenue of the Enterprise of Accommodation and Catering Industry (10 000 yuan)	318	881		500
社会消费品零售总额 (万元)	Total retail sales of consumer goods (10 000 yuan)	11 696	7 807	3 213	11 085
# 限额以上	Limit the Total Retail Sales of Social Consumer Goods	2207			
营业面积 50 平米以上的综合商店或超市 (个)	Number of Comprehensive Stores or Supermarkets with a Business Area of 50 Square meters or more (unit)	56	15	2	6
教育、文化、卫生	**Education, Culture, Health**				
幼儿园、托儿所个数 (个)	Number of Kindergartens and Uursery Schools (unit)	1	1	1	1
小学校数 (所)	Primary School Number (unit)	1	1	1	1
小学专任教师数 (人)	Number of Full—time Teachers in Primary Schools (person)	31	16	23	48
小学在校学生数 (人)	Number of Students in Primary School (person)	181	293	804	516
图书馆、文化站个数 (个)	Number of Libraries and Cultural Stations (unit)	8		1	
剧场、影剧院个数 (个)	Number of Theaters and Theaters (unit)				
体育场馆个数 (个)	Number of Stadiums and Gymnasiums (unit)				
医疗卫生机构个数 (个)	Number of Medical and Health Institutions (unit)	1	1	1	1
医疗卫生机构床位数 (个)	Bed Number of Medical and Health Institutions (unit)	20	30	55	37
执业(助理)医师数 (人)	Practising (Assistant) Doctor Number (person)	7	7	17	14
社会保障	**Social Security**				
本级政府创办的敬老院个数 (个)	Number of Old Homes Established by the Government at the Same Level (unit)				
城乡居民基本养老保险参保人数 (人)	Number of Basic Old—age Insurance for Urban and Rural Residents (person)	2 416	98	6 348	3 440
城乡居民基本医疗保险参保人数 (人)	Number of Basic Medical Insurance for Urban and Rural Residents (person)	2 990	1 612	9 486	5 837
城乡居民最低生活保障人数 (人)	The number of Minimum Living Security for Urban and Rural Residents (person)	115	60	444	577
公用事业	**Public Utility**				
自来水用水户数 (户)	Number of Water Users (household)	1 428	1 235	3 743	2 125
管道燃气用气户数 (户)	Number of Gas Accounts for Pipeline Gas (household)				
金融机构网点数 (个)	Number of Branches of Financial Institutions (unit)	2	3	5	2
公园及休闲健身广场个数 (个)	Number of Park and Leisure Fitness Square (unit)	3	3	1	
生活垃圾月均处理量 (吨/月)	Monthly Average Treatment of Domestic Waste (ton / month)	75	19	945	310

Continued

四　师 七十七团 Farm 77 Division 4	四　师 七十八团 Farm 78 Division 4	四　师 七十九团 Farm 79 Division 4	五　师 八十一团 Farm 81 Division 5	五　师 八十三团 Farm 83 Division 5	五　师 八十四团 Farm 84 Division 5	五　师 八十六团 Farm 86 Division 5	五　师 八十七团 Farm 87 Division 5	五　师 八十八团 Farm 88 Division 5	五　师 八十九团 Farm 89 Division 5
8	4	8	12	8	11	12	5	6	22
2		1	5		3	1			4
94 841	17 854	29 532	42 634	38 359	53 688	39 884	4 462	6 853	79 032
69 023		8 322	28 480		43 360	9 810			51 054
			1	1		1			1
			6 026	46 245		2 010			81 332
	1		67	36	2	9			
	315		1 645	6 398	3 474	15 353			
11 874	2 625	3 794	42 613	34 223	10 994	29 203	4 406	10 223	14 673
			30 345						
12			5	15	12	6	7	1	36
1	4	1	1	2	1	2	1	1	1
1	1	1	1	2	1	2	1	1	1
40	29	39	66	119	46	78	34	28	81
364	498	570	1 238	520	1 029	225	432	1 075	378
1		1	1	1	21	8	1	1	2
		2						1	
1			1	1	1	1	1	1	2
1	1	1	2	1	2	1	1	1	1
22	23	52	114	23	55	30	23	64	32
9	16	49	151	27	32	19	21	47	28
				1	1			1	
4 062	3 299	3 197	10 148	2 250	8 980	3 322	1 375	5 912	4 777
4 062	3 480	5 243	18 160	2 250	12 569	4 193	1 375	5 912	7 271
975	452	125	545	386	575	141	112	367	172
1 955	1 700	3 894	7 140	3 150	8 888	1 648	1 272	5 906	3 164
151		2 100		2 650	2 512	863	820	886	2 154
1	2	4	6	3	5	2	1	4	4
1	3	2	2	1	3	7	2	2	3
205	240	380	795	240	212		90	750	196

19－3 续表 18

(2017 年)

指　　标	Item	五　师 九〇团 Farm 90 Division 5	五　师 九十一团 Farm 91 Division 5	六　师 一〇一团 Farm 101 Division 6	六　师 一〇二团 Farm 102 Division 6
工　业	**Industry**				
工业企业单位数　(个)	Unit Number of Industrial Enterprises　(unit)	7	6	10	20
# 规模以上工业	Above Scale Industry			3	11
工业总产值　(万元)	Total Industrial Output Value　(10 000 yuan)	2 485	10 015	12 931	92 235
# 规模以上工业	Above Scale Industry			11 080	84 332
建筑业	**Construction Business**				
建筑业企业单位数　(个)	Number of Enterprise Units in Construction Industry　(unit)	1		6	1
建筑业总产值　(万元)	Total Output Value of Construction Industry　(10 000 yuan)	8 119		459 248	2 359
贸易、市场	**Trade, market**				
住宿餐饮业企业个数　(个)	Number of Enterprises for Accommodation and Catering Industry　(unit)			1	1
住宿餐饮业企业营业总收入(万元)	Total Revenue of the Enterprise of Accommodation and Catering Industry　(10 000 yuan)			519	510
社会消费品零售总额(万元)	Total retail sales of consumer goods　(10 000 yuan)	7 591	843	172 831	107 947
# 限额以上	Limit the Total Retail Sales of Social Consumer Goods			58 842	1 337
营业面积 50 平米以上的综合商店或超市　(个)	Number of Comprehensive Stores or Supermarkets with a Business Area of 50 Square meters or more　(unit)	79	18	12	38
教育、文化、卫生	**Education, Culture, Health**				
幼儿园、托儿所个数　(个)	Number of Kindergartens and Uursery Schools　(unit)	1	1	1	3
小学校数　(所)	Primary School Number　(unit)	1	1	1	1
小学专任教师数　(人)	Number of Full-time Teachers in Primary Schools　(person)	39	25	76	83
小学在校学生数　(人)	Number of Students in Primary School　(person)	215	849	1 551	712
图书馆、文化站个数　(个)	Number of Libraries and Cultural Stations　(unit)			1	1
剧场、影剧院个数　(个)	Number of Theaters and Theaters　(unit)			1	
体育场馆个数　(个)	Number of Stadiums and Gymnasiums　(unit)		1		
医疗卫生机构个数　(个)	Number of Medical and Health Institutions　(unit)	1	1	1	1
医疗卫生机构床位数　(个)	Bed Number of Medical and Health Institutions　(unit)	25	100	60	65
执业(助理)医师数　(人)	Practising (Assistant) Doctor Number　(person)	13	48	30	37
社会保障	**Social Security**				
本级政府创办的敬老院个数　(个)	Number of Old Homes Established by the Government at the Same Level　(unit)			1	
城乡居民基本养老保险参保人数(人)	Number of Basic Old-age Insurance for Urban and Rural Residents　(person)	1 395	3 358	4 433	5 151
城乡居民基本医疗保险参保人数(人)	Number of Basic Medical Insurance for Urban and Rural Residents　(person)	1 399	2 994	4 433	4 582
城乡居民最低生活保障人数(人)	The number of Minimum Living Security for Urban and Rural Residents　(person)	198	197	213	169
公用事业	**Public Utility**				
自来水用水户数　(户)	Number of Water Users　(household)	1 368		7 180	6 896
管道燃气用气户数　(户)	Number of Gas Accounts for Pipeline Gas　(household)	954		4 933	1 860
金融机构网点数　(个)	Number of Branches of Financial Institutions　(unit)	2		4	4
公园及休闲健身广场个数(个)	Number of Park and Leisure Fitness Square　(unit)	1		2	1
生活垃圾月均处理量(吨/月)	Monthly Average Treatment of Domestic Waste　(ton / month)	50		900	47

Continued

六　师 一〇三团 Farm 103 Division 6	六　师 一〇五团 Farm 105 Division 6	六　师 一〇六团 Farm 106 Division 6	六　师 芳草湖农场 Fang Caohu Farm Division 6	六　师 新湖农场 Xinhu Farm Division 6	六　师 军户农场 Junhu Farm Division 6	六　师 共青团农场 Communist League Farm Division 6	六　师 六运湖农场 Liu Yunhu Farm Division 6	六　师 土墩子农场 TudunZi Farm Division 6	六　师 红旗农场 Red Flag Farm Division 6
13	7	2	27	29	6	9	4	13	10
3	3		9	8		2		1	
22 401	25 854	4 858	133 225	95 656	8 756	13 394	5 608	24 723	17 532
18 497	11 747		98 819	56 760		7 300		4 994	
3	1	2	2	1		2			
160 502	53 284	22 193	40 958	16 041		80 910			
3 917	30 203	9 246	168 016	77 936	15 611	25 953	9 626	8 332	20 506
1 634				15 630	674				
2	55	2	54	15	11	258	6	68	45
2	1	1	13	6	1	1	1	1	3
1	1	1	1	2	1	1	1	1	1
70	90	73	205	192	82	47	39	27	65
937	354	2 576	1 863	1 345	619	391	275	529	1 086
			1	1		1	1	1	
	1								
	1					1		1	
2	1	4	1	1	1	1	1	2	4
47	20	150	100	25	26	20	20	20	30
16	3	123	88	12	13	7	6	13	37
		1	1	1					1
8 160		17 075	12 860	2 655	3 309	3 143	1 328	1 072	9 661
10 262		13 981	9 353	2 655	2 466	4 425	1 685	1 073	6 663
161		886	1 346	248	121	293	125	456	401
4 389	1 965	16 700	14 439	5 778	3 629	2 506	2 096	5 025	10 887
1 765	895	15 621	6 895	3 841	1 715	800	2 016		2 300
4	2	4	4	2	4	3	4	3	3
1	2		8	1		1	2	1	4
900	120	2 000	150	60	300	113	123	58	687

19—3 续表 19

(2017 年)

指　　标	Item	六　师 奇台农场 Qitai Farm Division 6	六　师 北塔山牧场 Bei Tashan Farm Division 6	七　师 一二三团 Farm 123 Division 7	七　师 一二四团 Farm 124 Division 7
工　业	**Industry**				
工业企业单位数　(个)	Unit Number of Industrial Enterprises　(unit)	18	2	12	7
# 规模以上工业	Above Scale Industry	8	2	3	3
工业总产值　(万元)	Total Industrial Output Value　(10 000 yuan)	142 068	24 841	47 607	19 212
# 规模以上工业	Above Scale Industry	85 259	24 841	28 045	9 278
建筑业	**Construction Business**				
建筑业企业单位数　(个)	Number of Enterprise Units in Construction Industry　(unit)	2		1	
建筑业总产值　(万元)	Total Output Value of Construction Industry　(10 000 yuan)	69 492		38 084	
贸易、市场	**Trade, market**				
住宿餐饮业企业个数　(个)	Number of Enterprises for Accommodation and Catering Industry (unit)			1	
住宿餐饮业企业营业总收入(万元)	Total Revenue of the Enterprise of Accommodation and Catering Industry　(10 000 yuan)			281	
社会消费品零售总额(万元)	Total retail sales of consumer goods (10 000 yuan)	64 246	1 048	100 974	46 186
# 限额以上	Limit the Total Retail Sales of Social Consumer Goods			2 344	7392
营业面积 50 平米以上的综合商店或超市　(个)	Number of Comprehensive Stores or Supermarkets with a Business Area of 50 Square meters or more　(unit)			13	20
教育、文化、卫生	**Education, Culture, Health**				
幼儿园、托儿所个数　(个)	Number of Kindergartens and Uursery Schools (unit)	4	7	1	1
小学校数　(所)	Primary School Number　(unit)	1	1	1	1
小学专任教师数　(人)	Number of Full—time Teachers in Primary Schools　(person)	116	19	67	75
小学在校学生数　(人)	Number of Students in Primary School　(person)	300	838	891	540
图书馆、文化站个数　(个)	Number of Libraries and Cultural Stations　(unit)	7	25	1	1
剧场、影剧院个数　(个)	Number of Theaters and Theaters　(unit)		1		1
体育场馆个数　(个)	Number of Stadiums and Gymnasiums　(unit)		1	1	1
医疗卫生机构个数　(个)	Number of Medical and Health Institutions (unit)	1	1	1	1
医疗卫生机构床位数　(个)	Bed Number of Medical and Health Institutions　(unit)	25	100	45	50
执业(助理)医师数　(人)	Practising (Assistant) Doctor Number　(person)	8	20	40	41
社会保障	**Social Security**				
本级政府创办的敬老院个数　(个)	Number of Old Homes Established by the Government at the Same Level　(unit)		1	1	
城乡居民基本养老保险参保人数(人)	Number of Basic Old—age Insurance for Urban and Rural Residents　(person)	1 544	3 349	607	12 905
城乡居民基本医疗保险参保人数(人)	Number of Basic Medical Insurance for Urban and Rural Residents　(person)	2 771	10 593	7 816	14 870
城乡居民最低生活保障人数(人)	The number of Minimum Living Security for Urban and Rural Residents　(person)	394	657	751	857
公用事业	**Public Utility**				
自来水用水户数　(户)	Number of Water Users　(household)	1 116	8 054	5 620	6 738
管道燃气用气户数　(户)	Number of Gas Accounts for Pipeline Gas　(household)		6 074	3 900	4 917
金融机构网点数　(个)	Number of Branches of Financial Institutions　(unit)	1	4	3	4
公园及休闲健身广场个数(个)	Number of Park and Leisure Fitness Square　(unit)		3	1	1
生活垃圾月均处理量(吨/月)	Monthly Average Treatment of Domestic Waste (ton / month)	40	1 141	300	583

Continued

七师一二五团 Farm 125 Division 7	七师一二六团 Farm 126 Division 7	七师一二七团 Farm 127 Division 7	七师一二八团 Farm 128 Division 7	七师一二九团 Farm 129 Division 7	七师一三〇团 Farm 130 Division 7	七师一三一团 Farm 131 Division 7	七师一三七团 Farm 137 Division 7	八师一二一团 Farm 121 Division 8	八师一三三团 Farm 133 Division 8
3	3	6	14	19	17	15	6	8	6
1			4	4	6	1	1	1	1
32 171	6 662	20 291	112 288	80 547	153 087	54 481	12 135	16 972	6 236
12 770			85 654	55 056	142 742	3 089	4 906	5 000	1 590
1		1		1	1	1		1	1
33 267		18 179		41 910		29 000		44 136	3 486
							1		145
							171		4112
26 380	39 539	19 807	37 231	75 659	44 153	53 350	35 569	54 416	8 615
			373	8 931	6 467				
12	4	11	29	407	80	2	7	7	6
1	1	1	1	1	1	2	1	2	2
1	1	1	1	1	1	1	1	2	2
74	53	64	60	71	85	186	30	145	91
438	422	401	722	820	1657	399	3 445	895	901
	2	1	2	1	18	1	1		
		1	2				1		
		1	1	1		1			
1	1	1	1	1	1	1	1	2	2
30	80	85	150	60	220	30	140	80	141
16	49	35	56	49	140	44	116	64	46
	1	1		1		1	2	2	
3 724	6 409	3 506	12 741	10 571	3 195	1 135	38 458	5 045	5 832
4 878	10 545	3 506	13 573	15 041	3 195	3 821	47 675	5 052	9 907
560	350	544	448	448	1241	252	824	1116	460
3 780	5 136	4 492	7 191	7 006	8 371	3 291	16 371	8 711	6 896
1 558	1 903	2 373	5 565	4 956	6 354	2 465	16 888	5 600	4 262
4	5	4	4	4	4	1	9	5	5
1	2	3	1	1	2	1	2		2
600	296	852	759	960	110	15	3 200		30

19—3 续表 20

(2017 年)

指　　标	Item	八　　师 一三四团 Farm 134 Division 8	八　　师 一三六团 Farm 136 Division 8	八　　师 一四一团 Farm 141 Division 8	八　　师 一四二团 Farm 142 Division 8
工　业	**Industry**				
工业企业单位数　(个)	Unit Number of Industrial Enterprises　(unit)	3	3	8	10
# 规模以上工业	Above Scale Industry	2		2	3
工业总产值　(万元)	Total Industrial Output Value　(10 000 yuan)	7 425	3 964	20 528	26 907
# 规模以上工业	Above Scale Industry	4 600		12 200	21 349
建筑业	**Construction Business**				
建筑业企业单位数　(个)	Number of Enterprise Units in Construction Industry　(unit)	1		1	1
建筑业总产值　(万元)	Total Output Value of Construction Industry　(10 000 yuan)	1 264		9 775	37 268
贸易、市场	**Trade, market**				
住宿餐饮业企业个数　(个)	Number of Enterprises for Accommodation and Catering Industry (unit)			3	93
住宿餐饮业企业营业总收入(万元)	Total Revenue of the Enterprise of Accommodation and Catering Industry　(10 000 yuan)			1 242	4 898
社会消费品零售总额(万元)	Total retail sales of consumer goods (10 000 yuan)	7 881	68 271	32 225	69 080
# 限额以上	Limit the Total Retail Sales of Social Consumer Goods	2 430	43 124	1 242	11 516
营业面积50平米以上的综合商店或超市　(个)	Number of Comprehensive Stores or Supermarkets with a Business Area of 50 Square meters or more　(unit)	46	30	15	10
教育、文化、卫生	**Education, Culture, Health**				
幼儿园、托儿所个数　(个)	Number of Kindergartens and Uursery Schools (unit)	2	1	1	2
小学校数　(所)	Primary School Number　(unit)	2	1	1	1
小学专任教师数　(人)	Number of Full-time Teachers in Primary Schools　(person)	94	89	38	60
小学在校学生数　(人)	Number of Students in Primary School　(person)	669	418	785	1 287
图书馆、文化站个数　(个)	Number of Libraries and Cultural Stations　(unit)	1		3	1
剧场、影剧院个数　(个)	Number of Theaters and Theaters　(unit)				1
体育场馆个数　(个)	Number of Stadiums and Gymnasiums　(unit)	1		2	
医疗卫生机构个数　(个)	Number of Medical and Health Institutions (unit)	1	1	1	2
医疗卫生机构床位数　(个)	Bed Number of Medical and Health Institutions　(unit)	40	50	90	110
执业(助理)医师数　(人)	Practising (Assistant) Doctor Number　(person)	16	34	54	63
社会保障	**Social Security**				
本级政府创办的敬老院个数　(个)	Number of Old Homes Established by the Government at the Same Level　(unit)	1	1	1	
城乡居民基本养老保险参保人数(人)	Number of Basic Old-age Insurance for Urban and Rural Residents　(person)	4 315	2 748	1 114	589
城乡居民基本医疗保险参保人数(人)	Number of Basic Medical Insurance for Urban and Rural Residents　(person)	5 520	2 748	9 628	14 262
城乡居民最低生活保障人数(人)	The number of Minimum Living Security for Urban and Rural Residents　(person)	277	434	882	1037
公用事业	**Public Utility**				
自来水用水户数　(户)	Number of Water Users　(household)	4 072	4 138	8 484	12 112
管道燃气用气户数　(户)	Number of Gas Accounts for Pipeline Gas　(household)	3 463	2 986	6 730	9 040
金融机构网点数　(个)	Number of Branches of Financial Institutions　(unit)	5	4	4	4
公园及休闲健身广场个数(个)	Number of Park and Leisure Fitness Square　(unit)	2	3	2	4
生活垃圾月均处理量(吨/月)	Monthly Average Treatment of Domestic Waste (ton / month)	360	147	750	900

Continued

八　师 一四三团 Farm 143 Division 8	八　师 一四四团 Farm 144 Division 8	八　师 石河子总场 Shihezi Farm Division 8	八　师 一四七团 Farm 147 Division 8	八　师 一四八团 Farm 148 Division 8	八　师 一四九团 Farm 149 Division 8	八　师 一五〇团 Farm 150 Division 8	八　师 一五二团 Farm 152 Division 8	九　师 一六一团 Farm 161 Division 9	九　师 一六三团 Farm 163 Division 9
36	8	148	20	5	5	11	11	5	3
6	1	21	5	3	1	5	3		
165 306	27 600	449 709	48 978	7 510	20 648	40 781	40 662	1 567	14 717
116 202	16 628	200 562	41 306	3 280	17 148	35 048	33 136		
2		1		1		1	1	1	3
129 408		288 944		2 285		48 158	36 531	4 719	24 633
		4	205						
		630	21 860						
102 425	40 790	121 102	29 561	1 800		26 274	18 130	12 565	6 297
7 973		59 499							559
10		8	8	5		27	6	2	3
4	1	9	1	1	1	1		1	2
1	1	2	1	1	1	1	3		
146	55	232	53	96	58	76	76	19	49
1 301	3 445	531	1 120	610	745	949	143	389	256
	1	2		1	24			1	
	1			1					
				1	4				
1	1	1	1	1	1	1	1	2	1
108	140	60	80	60	100	30	34	50	32
44	116	57	145	38	19	8	19	18	14
1	2			1	1		1	2	
3 412	38 458	7 152	17 449	7 120	11 991	1 704	1 838	3 117	2 019
3 412	47 675	8 824	17 146	7 120	9 347	1 704	3 359	5 510	3 976
26	824	674	844	602	504	192	83	202	140
5 355	16 371	5 369	9 583	6 485	6 899	2 232	1 957	3 023	2 360
5 355	16 888	3 150	9 583	2 789	3 072	1 129	1 170	2 910	1 531
3	9	3	3	4	4		1	5	3
1	2	2	1	2	2		1	3	
73	3 200	50		1 500	656	185	161	300	179

19—3 续表 21

(2017 年)

指标	Item	九师一六四团 Farm 164 Division 9	九师一六五团 Farm 165 Division 9	九师一六六团 Farm 166 Division 9	九师一六七团 Farm 167 Division 9
工业	**Industry**				
工业企业单位数 (个)	Unit Number of Industrial Enterprises (unit)	2	5	7	2
# 规模以上工业	Above Scale Industry			1	
工业总产值 (万元)	Total Industrial Output Value (10 000 yuan)	8 029	2 407	19 099	3 906
# 规模以上工业	Above Scale Industry			7 004	
建筑业	**Construction Business**				
建筑业企业单位数 (个)	Number of Enterprise Units in Construction Industry (unit)	1	1		1
建筑业总产值 (万元)	Total Output Value of Construction Industry (10 000 yuan)	8 928	13 835		9 980
贸易、市场	**Trade, market**				
住宿餐饮业企业个数 (个)	Number of Enterprises for Accommodation and Catering Industry (unit)				
住宿餐饮业企业营业总收入 (万元)	Total Revenue of the Enterprise of Accommodation and Catering Industry (10 000 yuan)				
社会消费品零售总额 (万元)	Total retail sales of consumer goods (10 000 yuan)	4 746	2 745	8 155	3 414
# 限额以上	Limit the Total Retail Sales of Social Consumer Goods				
营业面积50平米以上的综合商店或超市 (个)	Number of Comprehensive Stores or Supermarkets with a Business Area of 50 Square meters or more (unit)		1	2	1
教育、文化、卫生	**Education, Culture, Health**				
幼儿园、托儿所个数 (个)	Number of Kindergartens and Uursery Schools (unit)	1	1	1	1
小学校数 (所)	Primary School Number (unit)				
小学专任教师数 (人)	Number of Full-time Teachers in Primary Schools (person)	31	41	31	32
小学在校学生数 (人)	Number of Students in Primary School (person)	210	225	252	347
图书馆、文化站个数 (个)	Number of Libraries and Cultural Stations (unit)				
剧场、影剧院个数 (个)	Number of Theaters and Theaters (unit)				
体育场馆个数 (个)	Number of Stadiums and Gymnasiums (unit)				1
医疗卫生机构个数 (个)	Number of Medical and Health Institutions (unit)	1	1	1	2
医疗卫生机构床位数 (个)	Bed Number of Medical and Health Institutions (unit)	30	40	35	60
执业(助理)医师数 (人)	Practising (Assistant) Doctor Number (person)	13	17	19	21
社会保障	**Social Security**				
本级政府创办的敬老院个数 (个)	Number of Old Homes Established by the Government at the Same Level (unit)		1	1	
城乡居民基本养老保险参保人数 (人)	Number of Basic Old-age Insurance for Urban and Rural Residents (person)	1 627	2 978	2 316	3 412
城乡居民基本医疗保险参保人数 (人)	Number of Basic Medical Insurance for Urban and Rural Residents (person)	3 092	5 285	4 255	6 179
城乡居民最低生活保障人数 (人)	The number of Minimum Living Security for Urban and Rural Residents (person)	369	235	184	378
公用事业	**Public Utility**				
自来水用户数 (户)	Number of Water Users (household)	1 506	2 386	1 980	3 860
管道燃气用气户数 (户)	Number of Gas Accounts for Pipeline Gas (household)		1 552	1 020	2 434
金融机构网点数 (个)	Number of Branches of Financial Institutions (unit)	2	3	2	4
公园及休闲健身广场个数 (个)	Number of Park and Leisure Fitness Square (unit)	1	4	1	2
生活垃圾月均处理量 (吨/月)	Monthly Average Treatment of Domestic Waste (ton / month)	165	245	171	292

Continued

九 师 一六八团 Farm 168 Division 9	九 师 一七〇团 Farm 170 Division 9	九 师 团结农场 Tuanjie Farm Division 9	十 师 一八一团 Farm 181 Division 10	十 师 一八二团 Farm 182 Division 10	十 师 一八三团 Farm 183 Division 10	十 师 一八四团 Farm 184 Division 10	十 师 一八五团 Farm 185 Division 10	十 师 一八六团 Farm 186 Division 10	十 师 一八七团 Farm 187 Division 10
4	8	7	20	14	15	12	2	5	19
	2		2	2	5	3			3
5 920	16 248	10 341	66 641	33 370	69 902	68 525	3 252	11 055	67 493
	4 866		21 627	10 405	48 191	46 529			36 805
1		1	1	2	1	2	1	1	1
31 211		6 600	46 584	26 936	45 615	91 160	9 270	23 521	43 048
			1					1	
			1 167					156	
10 556	10 503	2 206	34 465	17 426	28 290	32 308	22 034	7 202	24 537
			6 658	2 629	13 197	1 438	2 449		11 685
2	2	2	2	20	12	13	29	30	
2	1	1	1	1	1	2	1	1	1
			1	1	1	1	1	1	1
39	18	19	33	31	49	38	18	20	34
225	199	452	353	521	556	140	164	240	747
		1	1	1	1	1	1		
							1		
		1	1	2		1	1		
1	1	1	11	1	1	1	1	1	1
20	20	48	25	35	25	25	20	35	295
5	13	31	15	19	17	7	7	17	39
		1			1	1			
886	1 185	4 059	2 201	5 139	1 960	23	847	1 767	199
1 634	2 003	6 733	3 705	4 612	1 960	534	847	1 767	4 825
104	143	457	172	215	105	86	68	157	298
1 277	1 191	3 610	1 662	2 915	2 771	1 163	987	2 128	4 443
	1 010	1 046			1 107		565	768	2 175
3	2	3	4	3	3			1	
1	1	3	9	2	3	1	5	1	
102	109	480	300		900	610	10	150	750

19—3 续表 22

(2017 年)

指 标	Item	十 师 一八八团 Farm 188 Division 10	十二师 一〇四团 Farm 104 Division 12	十二师 三坪农场 Sanping Farm Division 12	十二师 五一农场 Wuyi Farm Division 12
工 业	**Industry**				
工业企业单位数 (个)	Unit Number of Industrial Enterprises (unit)	46	21	14	24
# 规模以上工业	Above Scale Industry	5	3		2
工业总产值 (万元)	Total Industrial Output Value (10 000 yuan)	126 773	869 211	13 869	58 046
# 规模以上工业	Above Scale Industry	34 252	471 061		41 515
建筑业	**Construction Business**				
建筑业企业单位数 (个)	Number of Enterprise Units in Construction Industry (unit)	1		1	1
建筑业总产值 (万元)	Total Output Value of Construction Industry (10 000 yuan)	51 249		2 867	576
贸易、市场	**Trade, market**				
住宿餐饮业企业个数 (个)	Number of Enterprises for Accommodation and Catering Industry (unit)	1	30		2
住宿餐饮业企业营业总收入 (万元)	Total Revenue of the Enterprise of Accommodation and Catering Industry (10 000 yuan)	1 250	25 720		
社会消费品零售总额 (万元)	Total retail sales of consumer goods (10 000 yuan)	26 064	122 891	40 443	34 131
# 限额以上	Limit the Total Retail Sales of Social Consumer Goods	6 464	52 382		
营业面积 50 平米以上的综合商店或超市 (个)	Number of Comprehensive Stores or Supermarkets with a Business Area of 50 Square meters or more (unit)	51	105	53	42
教育、文化、卫生	**Education, Culture, Health**				
幼儿园、托儿所个数 (个)	Number of Kindergartens and Uursery Schools (unit)	1	5	2	2
小学校数 (所)	Primary School Number (unit)	1	1	1	1
小学专任教师数 (人)	Number of Full－time Teachers in Primary Schools (person)	49	143	51	43
小学在校学生数 (人)	Number of Students in Primary School (person)	2 148	1 038	646	986
图书馆、文化站个数 (个)	Number of Libraries and Cultural Stations (unit)	15	2	3	1
剧场、影剧院个数 (个)	Number of Theaters and Theaters (unit)				1
体育场馆个数 (个)	Number of Stadiums and Gymnasiums (unit)		2	2	1
医疗卫生机构个数 (个)	Number of Medical and Health Institutions (unit)	1	1	1	1
医疗卫生机构床位数 (个)	Bed Number of Medical and Health Institutions (unit)	100	40	30	99
执业(助理)医师数 (人)	Practising (Assistant) Doctor Number (person)	29	27	17	14
社会保障	**Social Security**				
本级政府创办的敬老院个数 (个)	Number of Old Homes Established by the Government at the Same Level (unit)				
城乡居民基本养老保险参保人数 (人)	Number of Basic Old－age Insurance for Urban and Rural Residents (person)	2 986	2 076	4 993	1 106
城乡居民基本医疗保险参保人数 (人)	Number of Basic Medical Insurance for Urban and Rural Residents (person)	2 986	4 490	3 767	1 236
城乡居民最低生活保障人数 (人)	The number of Minimum Living Security for Urban and Rural Residents (person)	320	144	75	100
公用事业	**Public Utility**				
自来水用水户数 (户)	Number of Water Users (household)	7 500	8 210	5 887	5 985
管道燃气用气户数 (户)	Number of Gas Accounts for Pipeline Gas (household)	7 500	5 821	5 832	5 985
金融机构网点数 (个)	Number of Branches of Financial Institutions (unit)	15	3	3	4
公园及休闲健身广场个数 (个)	Number of Park and Leisure Fitness Square (unit)	1	3	3	1
生活垃圾月均处理量 (吨/月)	Monthly Average Treatment of Domestic Waste (ton / month)	1 850	787	1 800	768

Continued

十二师头屯河农场 Toutunhe Farm Division 12	十二师西山农场 Xishan Farm Division 12	十二师二二一团 Farm 221 Division 12	十二师二二二团 Farm 222 Division 12	十三师红星一场 Red Star No.1 Farm Division 13	十三师红星二场 Red Star No.2 Farm Division 13	十三师红星四场 Red Star No.4 Farm Division 13	十三师黄田农场 Huangtian Farm Division 13	十三师火箭农场 Huojian Farm Division 13	十三师柳树泉农场 Liushuquan Farm Division 13
6	7	7	14	45	38	23	50	40	14
	2	1	4	15	9	5	10	14	8
1 727	236 241	214 221	30 220	309 938	290 910	99 241	296 744	255 609	148 627
	18 834	3 366	22 251	236 084	229 995	36 785	217 878	155 843	106 198
	1		1	1				4	
	2 460		15 643	1 443				115 125	
14			2	1		2		1	1
6 541			511	4 108		886		903	1 330
75 043	29 415	14 343	9 661	24 159	18 892	21 786	28 551	57 030	14 890
6 825	863		828	4 008				37 155	2 510
58	45	6	5	38	5	320		297	24
2	1	1	1	1	1	2	1	5	1
1	1	1	1	1	1	2	1	2	3
53	44	22	32	63	28	69	53	102	56
787	342	405	1 101	429	832	830	1 666	730	378
2	2	1	1	1	10	1	1	9	1
		1	1				2	1	1
2	1	1	1	3			1	1	1
1	1	7	1	1	2	7	3	1	2
30	20	66	45	40	50	40	362	35	60
11	4	27	49	19	35	20	27	19	
	1	1	1						1
3 318	1 334	2 087	3 328	3 031	4 233	4 092	9 540	4 914	7 540
2 258	1 334	2 106	3 326	3 800	8 042	3 005	6 420	9 964	11 128
153	39	198	205	177	662	230	186	653	898
4 220	1 886	3 442	3 728	3 124	2 344	3 540	6 658	2 160	4 366
3 578	320	2 648	3 582	2 147	1 020	3 256	5 712	1 100	1 786
2	2	3	3	2	2	3	7	2	3
2	1	2	1	3	1	1	3	1	1
12	80	150	280	120	160		673	500	180

19—3 续表 23　continued

(2017 年)

指　　标	Item	十三师 红山农场 Hongshan Farm Division 13	十三师 淖毛湖农场 Nao Maohu Farm Division 13	十四师 四十七团 (十二师代管) Farm 47 Division 14 (Division 12)	十四师 皮山农场 Pishan Farm Division 14	十四师 一牧场 Ranch 1 Division 14	十四师 二二四团 Farm 224 Division 14
工　业	**Industry**						
工业企业单位数　(个)	Unit Number of Industrial Enterprises　(unit)	30	14	2	3	1	6
# 规模以上工业	Above Scale Industry	13	5				1
工业总产值　(万元)	Total Industrial Output Value　(10 000 yuan)	209 398	332 797	587	9 932	986	9 169
# 规模以上工业	Above Scale Industry	189 577	320 588				7 284
建筑业	**Construction Business**						
建筑业企业单位数　(个)	Number of Enterprise Units in Construction Industry　(unit)						
建筑业总产值　(万元)	Total Output Value of Construction Industry　(10 000 yuan)						
贸易、市场	**Trade, market**						
住宿餐饮业企业个数　(个)	Number of Enterprises for Accommodation and Catering Industry　(unit)		1				
住宿餐饮业企业营业总收入(万元)	Total Revenue of the Enterprise of Accommodation and Catering Industry　(10 000 yuan)		2 238			320	
社会消费品零售总额(万元)	Total retail sales of consumer goods　(10 000 yuan)	11 659	9 696	1 821	6 234	871	5 643
# 限额以上	Limit the Total Retail Sales of Social Consumer Goods		600				3191
营业面积50平米以上的综合商店或超市　(个)	Number of Comprehensive Stores or Supermarkets with a Business Area of 50 Square meters or more　(unit)			6	83	2	48
教育、文化、卫生	**Education, Culture, Health**						
幼儿园、托儿所个数　(个)	Number of Kindergartens and Uursery Schools　(unit)	2	1	3	5	1	3
小学校数　(所)	Primary School Number　(unit)	2	1	1	3	1	2
小学专任教师数　(人)	Number of Full-time Teachers in Primary Schools　(person)	50	16	29	108	26	64
小学在校学生数　(人)	Number of Students in Primary School　(person)	221	567	2 987	500	1 457	1 457
图书馆、文化站个数　(个)	Number of Libraries and Cultural Stations　(unit)	1	1		1		
剧场、影剧院个数　(个)	Number of Theaters and Theaters　(unit)						
体育场馆个数　(个)	Number of Stadiums and Gymnasiums　(unit)	1			1		
医疗卫生机构个数　(个)	Number of Medical and Health Institutions　(unit)	1	1	2	1	1	1
医疗卫生机构床位数　(个)	Bed Number of Medical and Health Institutions　(unit)	20	25	168	25	50	50
执业(助理)医师数　(人)	Practising (Assistant) Doctor Number　(person)	5	4	39	4	6	6
社会保障	**Social Security**						
本级政府创办的敬老院个数　(个)	Number of Old Homes Established by the Government at the Same Level　(unit)		1	1			
城乡居民基本养老保险参保人数(人)	Number of Basic Old-age Insurance for Urban and Rural Residents　(person)	1 667	1 881	8 622	695	6 544	6 544
城乡居民基本医疗保险参保人数(人)	Number of Basic Medical Insurance for Urban and Rural Residents　(person)	2 540	1 881	8 622	695	11 312	11 312
城乡居民最低生活保障人数(人)	The number of Minimum Living Security for Urban and Rural Residents　(person)	41	282	2245	200	606	691
公用事业	**Public Utility**						
自来水用水户数　(户)	Number of Water Users　(household)	1 197	1 530	7 985	884	4 121	4 121
管道燃气用气户数　(户)	Number of Gas Accounts for Pipeline Gas　(household)	939	1 047	3 801	661	1 526	1 526
金融机构网点数　(个)	Number of Branches of Financial Institutions　(unit)	5	1	2		4	4
公园及休闲健身广场个数(个)	Number of Park and Leisure Fitness Square　(unit)		1	2	1		
生活垃圾月均处理量(吨/月)	Monthly Average Treatment of Domestic Waste (ton / month)	80	35	540	6	708	708

2018
BING TUAN

第二十篇

各师、团场主要经济指标排序

Chapter 20 Ranking of Main Economic Indicators by Division、Farm

简要说明

一、本篇资料主要内容

本篇资料为兵团各师、团场各行业及企业主要指标排序资料，主要包括分师生产总值、工农业总产值、工农业增加值及人均指标排序，团场主要指标排序。

二、本篇资料来源

本篇资料由兵团统计局、国家统计局兵团调查总队有关处室根据统计年报资料加工整理。

Brief Introduction

1. Main Contents

The data in this chapter cover ranking data of main indicators by division and farm and by sector, including ranking data of Gross Domestic Product by division, Gross Output value of agriculture and industry, value-added of agriculture and industry, and per capita indicators; ranking of main indicators of farms.

2. Sources of Data

The data in this chapter are compiled by relevant Section of the Statistics Bureau of XPCC and Survey Office of the National Bureau of Statistics of XPCC in accordance with annual reports.

20—1 各师生产总值、人均生产总值排序

Ranking of Gross Domestic Product,Per Capita Gross Domestic Product by Division

(2017 年)

单 位	Unit	生产总值（万元） Gross Domestic Product (10 000 yuan)	排 序 Ranking	单 位	Unit	人均生产总值（元） Per Gross Domestic Product(yuan)	排 序 Ranking
一 师	Division 1	2 993 351	2	一 师	Division 1	87 422	5
二 师	Division 2	1 381 750	7	二 师	Division 2	66 965	11
三 师	Division 3	1 205 862	8	三 师	Division 3	49 336	12
四 师	Division 4	1 756 372	5	四 师	Division 4	73 353	9
五 师	Division 5	581 968	13	五 师	Division 5	46 856	14
六 师	Division 6	2 715 833	3	六 师	Division 6	77 334	7
七 师	Division 7	1 610 672	6	七 师	Division 7	69 810	10
八 师	Division 8	5 053 487	1	八 师	Division 8	80 859	6
九 师	Division 9	360 950	14	九 师	Division 9	47 565	13
十 师	Division 10	731 566	12	十 师	Division 10	74 938	8
十 一 师	Division 11	1 039 890	10	十 一 师	Division 11	151 254	3
十 二 师	Division 12	1 806 768	4	十 二 师	Division 12	159 324	2
十 三 师	Division 13	1 163 283	9	十 三 师	Division 13	110 068	4
十 四 师	Division 14	195 362	15	十 四 师	Division 14	36 155	15
兵团直属	Directly under XPCC	793 617	11	兵团直属	Directly under XPCC	195 311	1

注：本表数按当年价格计算。

Note：Data in value terms in this table are calculated at current prices.

20—2 各师工业增加值率、农业增加值率排序

Ranking of the Rates of Value-added of Industry and Farming、Forestry、Animal Husbandry、Fishery by Division

计量单位：% (2017 年) (%)

单 位	Unit	工业增加值率 Ratio of Value-added to Gross Industrial Output Value	排 序 Ranking	单 位	Unit	农业增加值率 Ratio of Value-added to Farming Output Value	排 序 Ranking
一 师	Division 1	28.5	4	一 师	Division 1	48.1	4
二 师	Division 2	23.6	9	二 师	Division 2	47.3	7
三 师	Division 3	23.9	8	三 师	Division 3	45.1	11
四 师	Division 4	39.4	1	四 师	Division 4	48.2	3
五 师	Division 5	17.1	14	五 师	Division 5	48.2	1
六 师	Division 6	21.9	11	六 师	Division 6	47.0	9
七 师	Division 7	26.8	7	七 师	Division 7	48.1	5
八 师	Division 8	27.5	6	八 师	Division 8	47.1	8
九 师	Division 9	15.2	15	九 师	Division 9	47.8	6
十 师	Division 10	37.1	2	十 师	Division 10	38.1	14
十 一 师	Division 11	22.3	10	十 一 师	Division 11	46.5	10
十 二 师	Division 12	21.3	12	十 二 师	Division 12	42.3	13
十 三 师	Division 13	27.7	5	十 三 师	Division 13	48.2	2
十 四 师	Division 14	28.7	3	十 四 师	Division 14	44.9	12
兵团直属	Directly under XPCC	18.7	13	兵团直属	Directly under XPCC		

注：增加值率＝增加值/总产出×100%。

Note：Ratio of Value-added＝Value-added÷Total Output×100%.

20—3 各师人均工业增加值、人均农林牧渔业增加值排序

Ranking of Per Capita Value-added of Industry and Farming、Forestry、Animal Husbandry、Fishery by Division

计量单位:元 (2017年) (yuan)

单位	Unit	人均工业增加值 Per Capita Value-added of Industry	排序 Ranking	单位	Unit	人均农林牧渔业增加值 Per Capita Value-added to Farming、Forestry、Animal Husbandry、Fishery Output Value	排序 Ranking
一师	Division 1	22 212	7	一师	Division 1	36 276	1
二师	Division 2	20 605	8	二师	Division 2	20 668	3
三师	Division 3	12 813	11	三师	Division 3	18 110	6
四师	Division 4	32 074	3	四师	Division 4	18 415	5
五师	Division 5	9 049	13	五师	Division 5	17 442	7
六师	Division 6	30 403	4	六师	Division 6	15 710	10
七师	Division 7	15 796	10	七师	Division 7	20 947	2
八师	Division 8	26 885	5	八师	Division 8	14 655	11
九师	Division 9	6 441	14	九师	Division 9	20 590	4
十师	Division 10	23 790	6	十师	Division 10	14 438	12
十一师	Division 11	11 243	12	十一师	Division 11	114	14
十二师	Division 12	58 542	2	十二师	Division 12	8 593	13
十三师	Division 13	61 534	1	十三师	Division 13	16 862	9
十四师	Division 14	2 200	15	十四师	Division 14	16 986	8
兵团直属	Directly under XPCC	20 566	9	兵团直属	Directly under XPCC		

注:本表按当年价格计算。

Note: Data in value terms in this table are calculated at current prices.

20—4 各师人均农林牧渔业总产值、人均工业总产值排序

Ranking of Per Capita Total Output Value of Agriculture、Forestry、Animal Husbandry、Fishery and Industry by Division

计量单位:元 (2017年) (yuan)

单位	Unit	人均农业总产值 Per Capita Gross Output Value Of Agriculture	排序 Ranking	单位	Unit	人均工业总产值 Per Capita Gross Output Value Of Industry	排序 Ranking
一师	Division 1	75 428	1	一师	Division 1	80 105	5
二师	Division 2	43 657	2	二师	Division 2	78 810	6
三师	Division 3	40 171	5	三师	Division 3	52 875	10
四师	Division 4	38 241	6	四师	Division 4	77 214	7
五师	Division 5	36 160	9	五师	Division 5	29 256	13
六师	Division 6	33 440	11	六师	Division 6	119 900	2
七师	Division 7	43 556	3	七师	Division 7	54 911	9
八师	Division 8	31 137	12	八师	Division 8	100 317	3
九师	Division 9	43 115	4	九师	Division 9	24 011	14
十师	Division 10	37 891	7	十师	Division 10	61 496	8
十一师	Division 11	245	14	十一师	Division 11	40 845	12
十二师	Division 12	20 290	13	十二师	Division 12	46 257	11
十三师	Division 13	34 997	10	十三师	Division 13	206 853	1
十四师	Division 14	37 852	8	十四师	Division 14	12 120	15
				兵团直属	Direcly under XPCC	97 625	4

20－5 各师常住人口、人口自然增长率排序

Ranking of Permanent Population、Natural Population Growth Rate By Division

(2017 年) (yuan)

单 位	Unit	常住人口(人) Permanent Population (person)	排 序 Ranking	单 位	Unit	人口自然增长率(%) Natural Population Growth Rate(%)	排 序 Ranking
一 师	Division 1	357 961	2	一 师	Division 1	4.7	5
二 师	Division 2	214 820	7	二 师	Division 2	－0.4	11
三 师	Division 3	253 704	4	三 师	Division 3	7.2	2
四 师	Division 4	245 195	5	四 师	Division 4	0.4	10
五 师	Division 5	127 214	8	五 师	Division 5	3.4	6
六 师	Division 6	355 279	3	六 师	Division 6	1.5	9
七 师	Division 7	233 479	6	七 师	Division 7	－1.3	13
八 师	Division 8	641 117	1	八 师	Division 8	1.9	7
九 师	Division 9	77 243	12	九 师	Division 9	－1.7	14
十 师	Division 10	101 229	11	十 师	Division 10	1.6	8
十 一 师	Division 11	69 107	13	十 一 师	Division 11	－1.2	12
十 二 师	Division 12	122 408	9	十 二 师	Division 12	6.4	4
十 三 师	Division 13	108 879	10	十 三 师	Division 13	6.9	3
十 四 师	Division 14	57 028	14	十 四 师	Division 14	8.0	1
兵团直属	Directly under XPCC	40 646	15				

20－6 各师在岗职工工资总额、平均工资排序

Ranking of Total Wages and Annual Average Wage of Staff and Workers By Division

计量单位:元 (2017 年) (yuan)

单 位	Unit	工资总额 Total Wages	排 序 Ranking	单 位	Unit	在岗职工平均工资 Annual Average Wage	排 序 Ranking
一 师	Division 1	498 480	3	一 师	Division 1	52 236	11
二 师	Division 2	328 582	8	二 师	Division 2	54 555	8
三 师	Division 3	360 247	7	三 师	Division 3	64 368	2
四 师	Division 4	377 542	6	四 师	Division 4	54 665	7
五 师	Division 5	216 195	9	五 师	Division 5	52 298	10
六 师	Division 6	442 980	4	六 师	Division 6	56 570	5
七 师	Division 7	378 627	5	七 师	Division 7	59 734	4
八 师	Division 8	986 115	1	八 师	Division 8	63 346	3
九 师	Division 9	90 398	15	九 师	Division 9	38 194	14
十 师	Division 10	100 162	14	十 师	Division 10	44 634	13
十 一 师	Division 11	627 149	2	十 一 师	Division 11	66 457	1
十 二 师	Division 12	139 401	11	十 二 师	Division 12	56 265	6
十 三 师	Division 13	111 463	12	十 三 师	Division 13	54 208	9
十 四 师	Division 14	111 429	13	十 四 师	Division 14	49 290	12
兵团直属	Directly under XPCC	166 606	10				

20—7 各师一般公共预算收入、一般公共预算支出排序

Ranking of General Public Budget Revenue and General Public Budget Expenditure By Division

计量单位:万元 (2017 年) (10 000 yuan)

单 位	Unit	一般公共预算收入 General Public Budget Revenue	排 序 Ranking	单 位	Unit	一般公共预算支出 General Public Budget Expenditure	排 序 Ranking
一 师	Division 1	85 369	2	一 师	Division 1	814 909	2
二 师	Division 2	34 932	7	二 师	Division 2	663 284	7
三 师	Division 3	41 368	5	三 师	Division 3	767 566	3
四 师	Division 4	42 374	4	四 师	Division 4	685 721	6
五 师	Division 5	7 286	13	五 师	Division 5	310 490	11
六 师	Division 6	23 268	9	六 师	Division 6	742 880	4
七 师	Division 7	35 129	6	七 师	Division 7	538 997	8
八 师	Division 8	16 172	11	八 师	Division 8	1 025 566	1
九 师	Division 9	5 865	14	九 师	Division 9	293 681	12
十 师	Division 10	28 228	8	十 师	Division 10	372 081	9
十一师	Division 11	3 655	15	十一师	Division 11	104 783	15
十二师	Division 12	55 112	3	十二师	Division 12	254 665	13
十三师	Division 13	21 317	10	十三师	Division 13	315 008	10
十四师	Division 14	9 357	12	十四师	Division 14	187 065	14
兵团直属	Directly under XPCC	90 200	1	兵团直属	Directly under XPCC	740 610	5

20—8 各师城镇常住居民人均可支配收入、连队常住居民人均可支配收入排序

Ranking of Per Capita Disposable Income of Urban Permanent Households and Brigade Permanent Households by Division

计量单位:元 (2017 年) (yuan)

单 位	Unit	城镇常住居民人均可支配收入 Per Capita Disposable Income of Urban Permanent Households	排 序 Ranking	单 位	Unit	连队常住居民人均可支配收入 Per Capita Disposable Income of Brigade Permanent Households	排 序 Ranking
一 师	Division 1	36 485	8	一 师	Division 1	19 130	1
二 师	Division 2	36 671	6	二 师	Division 2	18 105	4
三 师	Division 3	36 412	9	三 师	Division 3	17 053	9
四 师	Division 4	36 048	12	四 师	Division 4	16 242	11
五 师	Division 5	36 140	11	五 师	Division 5	17 663	8
六 师	Division 6	36 402	10	六 师	Division 6	17 798	7
七 师	Division 7	36 601	7	七 师	Division 7	17 995	5
八 师	Division 8	37 200	3	八 师	Division 8	19 020	2
九 师	Division 9	35 954	14	九 师	Division 9	16 173	12
十 师	Division 10	36 006	13	十 师	Division 10	16 898	10
十一师	Division 11	38 178	1	十一师	Division 11		
十二师	Division 12	36 886	5	十二师	Division 12	18 206	3
十三师	Division 13	38 115	2	十三师	Division 13	17 808	6
十四师	Division 14	36 919	4	十四师	Division 14	13 730	13

20—9　各师粮食、棉花总产量排序

Ranking of Grain and Cotton Output by Division

计量单位:吨　　(2017 年)　　(ton)

单　位	Unit	粮食产量 Total Output of Grain	排　序 Ranking	单　位	Unit	棉花产量 Total Output of Cotton	排　序 Ranking
一　师	Division 1	214 253	4	一　师	Division 1	333 958	2
二　师	Division 2	69 993	10	二　师	Division 2	101 420	7
三　师	Division 3	184 433	5	三　师	Division 3	150 164	5
四　师	Division 4	667 607	1	四　师	Division 4	15 631	9
五　师	Division 5	134 073	7	五　师	Division 5	107 881	6
六　师	Division 6	446 764	2	六　师	Division 6	201 456	4
七　师	Division 7	117 344	8	七　师	Division 7	219 920	3
八　师	Division 8	151 645	6	八　师	Division 8	502 826	1
九　师	Division 9	310 557	3	九　师	Division 9		
十　师	Division 10	110 383	9	十　师	Division 10	5 481	10
十一师	Division 11	852	14	十一师	Division 11	625	11
十二师	Division 12	21 125	12	十二师	Division 12	198	12
十三师	Division 13	37 839	11	十三师	Division 13	39 267	8
十四师	Division 14	8 647	13	十四师	Division 14		

20—10　各师人均粮食、人均棉花产量排序

Ranking of Per Capita Grain and Cotton Output by Division

计量单位:公斤　　(2017 年)　　(kg)

单　位	Unit	人均粮食产量 Per Capita Grain	排　序 Ranking	单　位	Unit	人均棉花产量 Per Capita Cotton	排　序 Ranking
一　师	Division 1	626	7	一　师	Division 1	975	1
二　师	Division 2	339	10	二　师	Division 2	492	7
三　师	Division 3	755	6	三　师	Division 3	614	5
四　师	Division 4	2 830	2	四　师	Division 4	65	9
五　师	Division 5	1 079	5	五　师	Division 5	869	3
六　师	Division 6	1 272	3	六　师	Division 6	574	6
七　师	Division 7	509	8	七　师	Division 7	953	2
八　师	Division 8	243	11	八　师	Division 8	805	4
九　师	Division 9	4 092	1	九　师	Division 9		
十　师	Division 10	1 131	4	十　师	Division 10	56	10
十一师	Division 11	12	14	十一师	Division 11	9	11
十二师	Division 12	186	12	十二师	Division 12	2	12
十三师	Division 13	358	9	十三师	Division 13	372	8
十四师	Division 14	160	13	十四师	Division 14		

20—11 各师粮食、棉花单产排序

Ranking of Average Unit Output of Grain and Cotton by Division

计量单位:公斤/公顷 （2017 年） (kg/hectare)

单 位	Unit	粮食单产 Average Unit Output of Grain	排 序 Ranking	单 位	Unit	棉花单产 Average Unit Output of Cotton	排 序 Ranking
一 师	Division 1	10 743	1	一 师	Division 1	2 418	7
二 师	Division 2	7 567	10	二 师	Division 2	2 569	1
三 师	Division 3	6 968	11	三 师	Division 3	2 518	3
四 师	Division 4	9 486	2	四 师	Division 4	2 073	10
五 师	Division 5	8 887	6	五 师	Division 5	2 422	6
六 师	Division 6	9 214	3	六 师	Division 6	2 244	9
七 师	Division 7	9 029	4	七 师	Division 7	2 508	4
八 师	Division 8	8 925	5	八 师	Division 8	2 499	5
九 师	Division 9	8 582	8	九 师	Division 9		
十 师	Division 10	6 622	13	十 师	Division 10	1 862	11
十一师	Division 11	8 814	7	十一师	Division 11	2 287	8
十二师	Division 12	6 868	12	十二师	Division 12	1 731	12
十三师	Division 13	7 986	9	十三师	Division 13	2 519	2
十四师	Division 14	3 077	14	十四师	Division 14		

20—12 各师油料、甜菜总产量排序

Ranking of Output of Oil-bearing and Beetroots by Division

计量单位:吨 （2017 年） (ton)

单 位	Unit	油料产量 Total Output of Oil-bearing	排 序 Ranking	单 位	Unit	甜菜产量 Total Output of Beetroots	排 序 Ranking
一 师	Division 1	2 079	9	一 师	Division 1	4 410	9
二 师	Division 2	1 796	10	二 师	Division 2	144 047	4
三 师	Division 3	6 927	6	三 师	Division 3		
四 师	Division 4	81 983	1	四 师	Division 4	464 267	2
五 师	Division 5	6 373	7	五 师	Division 5	137 214	5
六 师	Division 6	23 113	4	六 师	Division 6	119 557	6
七 师	Division 7	17 000	5	七 师	Division 7	242 395	3
八 师	Division 8	1 020	11	八 师	Division 8	84 655	8
九 师	Division 9	31 654	3	九 师	Division 9	701 088	1
十 师	Division 10	31 787	2	十 师	Division 10	86 930	7
十一师	Division 11	86	13	十一师	Division 11		
十二师	Division 12	4 940	8	十二师	Division 12		
十三师	Division 13	388	12	十三师	Division 13		
十四师	Division 14	53	14	十四师	Division 14		

20—13 各师人均油料、人均甜菜产量排序

Ranking of Per Capita Oil-bearing and Beetroots Output by Division

计量单位:公斤 (2017 年) (kg)

单位	Unit	人均油料产量 Per Capita Oil-bearing	排序 Ranking
一师	Division 1	6	10
二师	Division 2	9	9
三师	Division 3	28	8
四师	Division 4	342	2
五师	Division 5	51	6
六师	Division 6	66	5
七师	Division 7	74	4
八师	Division 8	2	12
九师	Division 9	417	1
十师	Division 10	326	3
十一师	Division 11	1	13
十二师	Division 12	44	7
十三师	Division 13	4	11
十四师	Division 14	1	14

单位	Unit	人均甜菜产量 Per Capita Beetroots Output	排序 Ranking
一师	Division 1	13	9
二师	Division 2	698	6
三师	Division 3		
四师	Division 4	1 939	2
五师	Division 5	1 105	3
六师	Division 6	340	7
七师	Division 7	1 051	4
八师	Division 8	135	8
九师	Division 9	9 239	1
十师	Division 10	890	5
十一师	Division 11		
十二师	Division 12		
十三师	Division 13		
十四师	Division 14		

20—14 各师油料、甜菜单产排序

Ranking of Average Unit Output of Oil-bearing and Beetroots by Division

计量单位:公斤/公顷 (2017 年) (kg/hectare)

单位	Unit	油料单产 Total Output of Oil-Bearing	排序 Ranking
一师	Division 1	2 508	12
二师	Division 2	1 811	14
三师	Division 3	5 004	2
四师	Division 4	3 647	7
五师	Division 5	3 522	9
六师	Division 6	3 865	4
七师	Division 7	5 351	1
八师	Division 8	3 673	6
九师	Division 9	3 357	10
十师	Division 10	3 540	8
十一师	Division 11	3 000	11
十二师	Division 12	3 680	5
十三师	Division 13	4 273	3
十四师	Division 14	2 278	13

单位	Unit	甜菜单产 Average Unit Yield of Beetroots	排序 Ranking
一师	Division 1	90 000	4
二师	Division 2	85 978	6
三师	Division 3		
四师	Division 4	90 126	3
五师	Division 5	72 144	8
六师	Division 6	89 222	5
七师	Division 7	94 681	2
八师	Division 8	106 306	1
九师	Division 9	78 423	7
十师	Division 10	65 856	9
十一师	Division 11		
十二师	Division 12		
十三师	Division 13		
十四师	Division 14		

20—15 各师牲畜年末头数、肉类产量排序

Ranking of Number of Livestock at Year-end and Output of Meat by Division

(2017 年)

单位	Unit	牲畜年末头数（万头/只）Number of Livestock (10 000heads)	排序 Ranking	单位	Unit	肉类产量（吨）Output of Meat (ton)	排序 Ranking
一师	Division 1	66.88	6	一师	Division 1	33 289	5
二师	Division 2	64.48	7	二师	Division 2	42 479	4
三师	Division 3	78.42	5	三师	Division 3	23 648	8
四师	Division 4	116.16	1	四师	Division 4	57 530	3
五师	Division 5	33.01	10	五师	Division 5	18 870	10
六师	Division 6	85.09	4	六师	Division 6	76 526	2
七师	Division 7	57.31	8	七师	Division 7	32 407	6
八师	Division 8	89.77	2	八师	Division 8	79 885	1
九师	Division 9	87.84	3	九师	Division 9	27 188	7
十师	Division 10	37.22	9	十师	Division 10	17 745	11
十二师	Division 12	9.92	13	十二师	Division 12	9 401	12
十三师	Division 13	30.68	11	十三师	Division 13	20 018	9
十四师	Division 14	15.80	12	十四师	Division 14	4 801	13

20—16 各师规模以上工业企业主营业务收入、利润总额排序

Ranking of Main Business Revenue and Total Profit Value of Industrial Enterprises above Designated Size by Division

计量单位：万元　　(2017 年)　　(10 000 yuan)

单位	Unit	主营业务收入 Main Business Revenue	排序 Ranking	单位	Unit	利润总额 Total Profit	排序 Ranking
一师	Division 1	2 256 967	3	一师	Division 1	352 600	3
二师	Division 2	1 389 241	6	二师	Division 2	154 994	6
三师	Division 3	1 005 799	7	三师	Division 3	113 552	7
四师	Division 4	1 506 634	5	四师	Division 4	281 380	4
五师	Division 5	251 561	12	五师	Division 5	1 689	14
六师	Division 6	4 079 921	2	六师	Division 6	352 707	2
七师	Division 7	876 959	8	七师	Division 7	42 787	9
八师	Division 8	5 536 435	1	八师	Division 8	578 751	1
九师	Division 9	96 620	14	九师	Division 9	−59	15
十师	Division 10	303 509	11	十师	Division 10	52 435	8
十一师	Division 11	210 766	13	十一师	Division 11	3 246	13
十二师	Division 12	367 928	10	十二师	Division 12	14 759	11
十三师	Division 13	1 756 300	4	十三师	Division 13	252 801	5
十四师	Division 14	34 840	15	十四师	Division 14	3 304	12
兵团直属	Directly under XPCC	398 127	9	兵团直属	Directly under XPCC	32 406	10

20—17 各师规模以上工业企业经济效益综合指数、全员劳动生产率排序
Ranking of Comprehensive Index of Industry Economic Results and Overall Labor Productivity of Industrial Enterprises above Designated Size by Division

（2017 年）

单　位	Unit	经济效益综合指数 Comprehensive Index of Industry Economic Results	排　序 Ranking	单　位	Unit	全员劳动生产率（元/人·年） Overall Labor Productivity (yuan/person.year)	排　序 Ranking
一　师	Division 1	321.49	5	一　师	Division 1	299 160	6
二　师	Division 2	296.85	7	二　师	Division 2	270 605	9
三　师	Division 3	290.70	8	三　师	Division 3	285 538	7
四　师	Division 4	482.11	2	四　师	Division 4	482 394	2
五　师	Division 5	150.93	14	五　师	Division 5	161 636	12
六　师	Division 6	385.43	3	六　师	Division 6	467 070	3
七　师	Division 7	223.87	10	七　师	Division 7	242 870	10
八　师	Division 8	306.32	6	八　师	Division 8	331 526	4
九　师	Division 9	114.43	15	九　师	Division 9	123 269	15
十　师	Division 10	353.87	4	十　师	Division 10	320 089	5
十一师	Division 11	151.85	13	十一师	Division 11	160 519	13
十二师	Division 12	173.29	12	十二师	Division 12	170 039	11
十三师	Division 13	598.94	1	十三师	Division 13	739 871	1
十四师	Division 14	186.38	11	十四师	Division 14	155 317	14
兵团直属	Directly under XPCC	259.89	9	兵团直属	Directly under XPCC	280 294	8

20—18 各师资质以上建筑业主营业务收入和全员劳动生产率排序
Ranking of Main Business Income and Equipment of Construction Units by Division

（2017 年）

单　位	Unit	主营业务收入（万元） Main Business Income	排　序 Ranking	单　位	Unit	全员劳动生产率（元/人） Labour Productivity (yuan/person)	排　序 Ranking
一　师	Division 1	1 177 379	4	一　师	Division 1	464 979	3
二　师	Division 2	506 488	6	二　师	Division 2	356 177	6
三　师	Division 3	436 119	8	三　师	Division 3	345 766	7
四　师	Division 4	463 605	7	四　师	Division 4	421 293	5
五　师	Division 5	209 190	12	五　师	Division 5	188 287	14
六　师	Division 6	1 280 884	3	六　师	Division 6	287 550	11
七　师	Division 7	1 314 517	2	七　师	Division 7	458 060	4
八　师	Division 8	817 998	5	八　师	Division 8	240 747	12
九　师	Division 9	147 188	13	九　师	Division 9	297 234	9
十　师	Division 10	428 484	9	十　师	Division 10	971 806	1
十一师	Division 11	2 994 362	1	十一师	Division 11	289 935	10
十二师	Division 12	210 633	10	十二师	Division 12	238 893	13
十三师	Division 13	209 622	11	十三师	Division 13	300 650	8
十四师	Division 14	101 845	14	十四师	Division 14	677 548	2

20—19 各师道路运输法人企业固定资产原值、主营业务收入排序

Ranking of Original Value of Fixed Assets and Main Business Income of Road Transportation Corporative Enterprises by Division

计量单位:万元　　(2017年)　　(10 000 yuan)

单　位	Unit	固定资产原值 Original Value of Fixed Assets	排　序 Ranking	单　位	Unit	主营业务收入 Main Business Income	排　序 Ranking
一　师	Division 1	14 076	5	一　师	Division 1	121 722	2
二　师	Division 2	27 161	1	二　师	Division 2	5 281	7
三　师	Division 3	13 879	6	三　师	Division 3	9 715	5
四　师	Division 4	14 654	4	四　师	Division 4	19 488	4
五　师	Division 5	12 196	7	五　师	Division 5	3 365	10
六　师	Division 6	19 613	3	六　师	Division 6	383 153	1
七　师	Division 7	7 572	8	七　师	Division 7	5 031	8
八　师	Division 8	22 629	2	八　师	Division 8	27 767	3
九　师	Division 9	3 129	11	九　师	Division 9	9 052	6
十　师	Division 10	7 279	9	十　师	Division 10	1 531	12
十一师	Division 11	813	13	十一师	Division 11	2 849	11
十二师	Division 12	1 340	12	十二师	Division 12	187	14
十三师	Division 13	4 424	10	十三师	Division 13	4 889	9
十四师	Division 14	744	14	十四师	Division 14	241	13

20—20 各师批发和零售业主营业务收入、商品销售总额排序

Ranking of Main Business Income and Total Sales Value of Commodities of Wholesale and Retail Enterprises by Division

计量单位:万元　　(2017年)　　(10 000 yuan)

单　位	Unit	主营业务收入 Main Business Income	排　序 Ranking	单　位	Unit	销售总额 Total Sales Value	排　序 Ranking
一　师	Division 1	925 938	5	一　师	Division 1	3 087 012	4
二　师	Division 2	1 111 789	3	二　师	Division 2	1 715 598	7
三　师	Division 3	938 961	4	三　师	Division 3	1 596 148	9
四　师	Division 4	428 389	11	四　师	Division 4	1 402 675	10
五　师	Division 5	486 414	8	五　师	Division 5	1 028 813	12
六　师	Division 6	396 504	12	六　师	Division 6	2 392 627	5
七　师	Division 7	529 461	7	七　师	Division 7	2 338 016	6
八　师	Division 8	1 604 561	2	八　师	Division 8	6 522 785	2
九　师	Division 9	57 378	14	九　师	Division 9	303 246	14
十　师	Division 10	103 651	13	十　师	Division 10	1 712 606	8
十一师	Division 11	460 259	9	十一师	Division 11	566 553	13
十二师	Division 12	857 177	6	十二师	Division 12	9 881 471	1
十三师	Division 13	448 738	10	十三师	Division 13	1 328 532	11
十四师	Division 14	12 667	15	十四师	Division 14	40 813	15
兵团直属	Directly under XPCC	3 910 530	1	兵团直属	Directly under XPCC	4 344 446	3

20—21 各师规模以上工业企业综合能源消费量、产值能耗排序

Ranking of Comprehensive Energy Consumption and Output Value Energy Consumption of Industrial Enterprises above Designated Size by Division

(2017 年)

单 位	Unit	综合能源消费量（吨标准煤）Comprehensive Energy Consumption (ton Standard Coal)	排 序 Ranking	单 位	Unit	产值能耗（吨标准煤/万元）Output Value Energy Consum-ption (ton Stan-dard Coal/ 10 000 yuan)	排 序 Ranking
一 师	Division 1	1 111 483	6	一 师	Division 1	0.4796	8
二 师	Division 2	320 853	8	二 师	Division 2	0.2248	12
三 师	Division 3	294 222	9	三 师	Division 3	0.2554	11
四 师	Division 4	1 872 122	4	四 师	Division 4	1.2100	6
五 师	Division 5	334 457	7	五 师	Division 5	1.2861	5
六 师	Division 6	9 428 036	2	六 师	Division 6	2.3112	2
七 师	Division 7	1 464 661	5	七 师	Division 7	1.6225	3
八 师	Division 8	15 881 682	1	八 师	Division 8	2.7376	1
九 师	Division 9	100 391	12	九 师	Division 9	0.8950	7
十 师	Division 10	136 418	10	十 师	Division 10	0.4158	9
十一师	Division 11	21 208	13	十一师	Division 11	0.0912	13
十二师	Division 12	105 440	11	十二师	Division 12	0.3442	10
十三师	Division 13	2 499 757	3	十三师	Division 13	1.4185	4
十四师	Division 14	1 513	15	十四师	Division 14	0.0363	15
兵团直属	Directly under XPCC	14 776	14	兵团直属	Directly under XPCC	0.0373	14

20—22 各师进出口总额、出口总额排序

Ranking Of Total Import and Export and Total Export By Division

计量单位:万美元 (2017 年) (USD 10 000)

单 位	Unit	进出口总额 Total Imports and Exports	排 序 Ranking	单 位	Unit	出口总额 Total Exports	排 序 Ranking
一 师	Division 1	1 123	14	一 师	Division 1	791	14
二 师	Division 2	8 088	12	二 师	Division 2	8 020	12
三 师	Division 3	75 532	4	三 师	Division 3	69 408	3
四 师	Division 4	248 555	1	四 师	Division 4	246 462	1
五 师	Division 5	59 089	5	五 师	Division 5	52 575	5
六 师	Division 6	22 341	8	六 师	Division 6	21 737	8
七 师	Division 7	10 029	11	七 师	Division 7	9 290	11
八 师	Division 8	45 553	6	八 师	Division 8	40 473	6
九 师	Division 9	18 668	9	九 师	Division 9	17 928	9
十 师	Division 10	94 539	3	十 师	Division 10	92 894	2
十一师	Division 11	28 593	7	十一师	Division 11	27 097	7
十二师	Division 12	11 351	10	十二师	Division 12	11 336	10
十三师	Division 13	5 855	13	十三师	Division 13	4 740	13
十四师	Division 14	623	15	十四师	Division 14	7	15
兵团直属	Directly under XPCC	129 080	2	兵团直属	Directly under XPCC	60 512	4

20—23 团场生产总值及常住人口前20名

Ranking of The Top 20 Farms by Gross Domestic Product And Permanent Population

(2017年)

单位	Unit	生产总值(万元) Gross Domestic Product (10 000 yuan)	排序 Ranking	单位	Unit	常住人口(人) Permanent Population (person)	排序 Ranking
石河子总场	Shihezi Farm	567 102	1	芳草湖农场	Fang Caohu Farm	61 316	1
芳草湖农场	Fang Caohu Farm	261 249	2	石河子总场	Shihezi Farm	51 698	2
十二团	Farm 12	259 886	3	五十一团	Farm 51	50 122	3
十团	Farm 10	225 684	4	一二一团	Farm 121	37 969	4
一〇一团	Farm 101	222 248	5	新湖农场	Xinhu Farm	36 939	5
十六团	Farm 16	218 778	6	一四三团	Farm 143	34 088	6
二十九团	Farm 29	210 959	7	皮山农场	Pishan Farm	30 189	7
一团	Farm 1	206 222	8	二十九团	Farm 29	29 665	8
新湖农场	Xinhu Farm	205 035	9	六十六团	Farm 66	29 494	9
十三团	Farm 13	193 180	10	奇台农场	Qitai Farm	28 613	10
奇台农场	Qitai Farm	190 091	11	四十四团	Farm 44	27 714	11
一四二团	Farm 142	188 096	12	四十五团	Farm 45	25 999	12
火箭农场	Huojian Farm	186 633	13	六十四团	Farm 64	25 899	13
一四三团	Farm 143	184 397	14	一四二团	Farm 142	25 333	14
二团	Farm 29	181 629	15	一四八团	Farm 148	24 761	15
一〇二团	Farm 102	171 208	16	一〇四团	Farm 104	24 461	16
五团	Farm 5	162 699	17	五十三团	Farm 53	24 137	17
一二一团	Farm 121	162 435	18	十三团	Farm 13	24 036	18
三团	Farm 3	151 920	19	一团	Farm 1	23 685	19
一三〇团	Farm 130	146 152	20	五十团	Farm 50	23 597	20

20—24 团场粮食、棉花产量前20名

Ranking of the Top 20 Farms by Output of Grain and Cotton

计量单位:吨 (2017年) (ton)

单位	Unit	粮食产量 Output of Grain	排序 Ranking	单位	Unit	棉花产量 Output of Cotton	排序 Ranking
奇台农场	Qitai Farm	194 456	1	新湖农场	Xinhu Farm	73 269	1
六师红旗农场	Hongqi Farm	92 217	2	一二一团	Farm 121	73 037	2
七十一团	Farm 71	84 878	3	芳草湖农场	Fangcaohu Farm	64 458	3
一六三团	Farm 163	75 592	4	一四二团	Farm 142	56 907	4
六十七团	Farm 67	67 137	5	一三三团	Farm 133	56 800	5
六十八团	Farm 68	66 307	6	一三四团	Farm 134	46 690	6
八十四团	Farm 84	64 640	7	一二五团	Farm 125	44 463	7
一六六团	Farm 166	64 086	8	十六团	Farm 16	38 975	8
一六四团	Farm 164	56 506	9	一五〇团	Farm 150	38 016	9
七十六团	Farm 76	52 018	10	十团	Farm 10	36 105	10
六十四团	Farm 64	51 101	11	一四四团	Farm 144	35 412	11
七十二团	Farm 72	45 764	12	一四八团	Farm 148	33 930	12
五十一团	Farm 51	44 210	13	二团	Farm 2	33 522	13
六十六团	Farm 66	44 118	14	一三六团	Farm 136	30 139	14
七十七团	Farm 77	43 651	15	一四九团	Farm 149	29 964	15
四团	Farm 4	41 685	16	一二八团	Farm 128	29 713	16
一四三团	Farm 143	38 982	17	一三〇团	Farm 130	28 200	17
一二四团	Farm 124	38 628	18	石河子总场	Shihezi Farm	27 800	18
一六七团	Farm 167	37 060	19	一二九团	Farm 129	27 710	19
一三一团	Farm 131	36 550	20	一二三团	Farm 123	26 965	20

20—25 团场粮食、棉花单产前20名

Ranking of the Top 20 Farms by Grain and Cotton Average Unit Yield

计量单位:公斤/公顷 (2017年) (kg/hectare)

单位	Unit	粮食单产 Grain Average Unit Output	排序 Ranking	单位	Unit	棉花单产 Cotton Average Unit Output	排序 Ranking
一三七团	Farm 137	15 343	1	红星四场	Hongxing No.4 Farm	2 822	1
红星二场	Hongxing No.2 Farm	14 000	2	七团	Farm 7	2 813	2
二团	Farm 2	13 970	3	幸福农场	Xingfu Farm	2 798	3
团结农场	Tuanjie Farm	13 624	4	三〇团	Farm 30	2 670	4
一团	Farm 1	13 286	5	一三三团	Farm 133	2 663	5
一六三团	Farm 163	13 158	6	火箭农场	Huojian Farm	2 657	6
八十九团	Farm 89	12 900	7	三十四团	Farm 34	2 640	7
七十一团	Farm 71	12 622	8	三十三团	Farm 33	2 631	8
二十七团	Farm 27	12 357	9	二团	Farm 2	2 625	9
石河子总场	Shihezi Farm	11 827	10	三十一团	Farm 31	2 625	10
一七〇团	Farm 170	11 511	11	一三四团	Farm 134	2 625	11
一四三团	Farm 143	11 442	12	一四四团	Farm 144	2 624	12
十三团	Farm 13	11 380	13	八十六团	Farm 86	2 623	13
七团	Farm 7	11 363	14	九〇团	Farm 90	2 619	14
六十八团	Farm 68	11 183	15	红星一场	Hongxing No.1 Farm	2 612	15
六十三团	Farm 63	11 071	16	一四八团	Farm 148	2 610	16
六团	Farm 6	10 933	17	伽师总场	Jiashi Farm	2 586	17
四团	Farm 4	10 875	18	四十九团	Farm 49	2 582	18
八团	Farm 8	10 784	19	五十一团	Farm 51	2 581	19
八十七团	Farm 87	10 714	20	一二五团	Farm 125	2 565	20

20—26 团场油料、甜菜产量前20名

Ranking of the Top 20 Farms by Output of Oil-bearing and Beetroots

计量单位:吨 (2017年) (ton)

单位	Unit	油料产量 Output of Oil-bearing	排序 Ranking	单位	Unit	甜菜产量 Output of Beetroots	排序 Ranking
七十六团	Farm 76	27 559	1	一六六团	Farm 166	190 030	1
七十七团	Farm 77	25 755	2	一六八团	Farm 168	170 907	2
一六八团	Farm 168	12 565	3	一三一团	Farm 131	147 200	3
奇台农场	Qitai Farm	9 300	4	一六七团	Farm 167	136 850	4
一八一团	Farm 181	9 223	5	一六四团	Farm 164	128 300	5
一八二团	Farm 182	7 000	6	八十八团	Farm 88	84 660	6
七十四团	Farm 74	6 986	7	一四三团	Farm 143	83 857	7
一三一团	Farm 131	6 600	8	七十九团	Farm 79	77 120	8
一〇三团	Farm 103	6 463	9	六十三团	Farm 63	75 508	9
一六七团	Farm 167	6 347	10	一八一团	Farm 181	74 700	10
八十四团	Farm 84	6 000	11	六十七团	Farm 67	74 392	11
七十五团	Farm 75	5 943	12	六十四团	Farm 64	74 300	12
一六五团	Farm 165	5 336	13	一六三团	Farm 163	73 500	13
一三〇团	Farm 130	4 860	14	奇台农场	Qitai Farm	63 733	14
二二二团	Farm 222	4 700	15	七十二团	Farm 72	55 463	15
一八六团	Farm 186	3 891	16	二十二团	Farm 22	51 421	16
一八四团	Farm 184	3 666	17	七〇团	Farm 70	44 309	17
七十三团	Farm 73	3 371	18	一二四团	Farm 124	39 000	18
一六一团	Farm 161	2 856	19	六师红旗农场	Hongqi Farm	36 312	19
四十九团	Farm 49	2 715	20	二十九团	Farm 29	29 202	20

20—27 团场油料、甜菜单产前20名

Ranking of the Top 20 Farms of Oil-bearing and Beetroots Average Unit Output

计量单位:公斤/公顷　　(2017年)　　(kg/hectare)

单位	Unit	油料单产 Oil-bearing Average Unit Output	排序 Ranking	单位	Unit	甜菜单产 Beetroots Average Unit Output	排序 Ranking
十一团	Farm 11	11 250	1	六十三团	Farm 63	112 833	1
一三七团	Farm 137	8 720	2	一二四团	Farm 124	112 500	2
四十八团	Farm 48	8 250	3	七〇团	Farm 70	108 000	3
一三一团	Farm 131	8 250	4	一四三团	Farm 143	107 785	4
二十九团	Farm 29	6 081	5	六十四团	Farm 64	104 953	5
二十四团	Farm 24	5 997	6	九〇团	Farm 90	102 570	6
一五二团	Farm 152	5 524	7	六十六团	Farm 66	101 899	7
四十九团	Farm 49	5 419	8	奇台农场	Qitai Farm	100 822	8
军户农场	Junhu Farm	5 217	9	二十七团	Farm 27	96 750	9
三十八团	Farm 38	5 175	10	一三一团	Farm 131	96 000	10
团结农场	Tuanjie Farm	4 721	11	一〇三团	Farm 103	93 074	11
一六八团	Farm 168	4 564	12	七十一团	Farm 71	93 000	12
四十一团	Farm 41	4 545	13	二十一团	Farm 21	91 499	13
五团	Farm 5	4 526	14	五团	Farm 5	90 000	14
六十九团	Farm 69	4 500	15	二十九团	Farm 29	90 000	15
黄田农场	Huangtian Farm	4 428	16	六师红旗农场	Hongqi Farm	90 000	16
一二五团	Farm 125	4 425	17	一二九团	Farm 129	87 375	17
奇台农场	Qitai Farm	4 403	18	二十五团	Farm 25	87 003	18
四十五团	Farm 45	4277	19	三十一团	Farm 31	87 000	19
一六三团	Farm 163	4 225	20	一六六团	Farm 166	86 377	20

20—28 团场牲畜存栏头数、肉类产量前20名

Ranking of the Top 20 Farms by Livestock and Output of Meat

(2017年)

单位	Unit	牲畜存栏头数（万头只） Number of Livestock (10 000 heads)	排序 Ranking	单位	Unit	肉类产量（吨） Out put of Meat (ton)	排序 Ranking
一三七团	Farm 22	19.09	1	石河子总场	Shihezi Farm	18 292	1
一六一团	Farm 137	16.9	2	一四二团	Farm 142	13 652	2
石河子总场	Shihezi Farm	16.58	3	二十九团	Farm 144	12 574	3
二十二团	Fangcaohu Farm	15.78	4	奇台农场	Qitai Farm	11 957	4
芳草湖农场	Farm 161	15.15	5	一四四团	Junhu Farm	11 368	5
一六五团	Farm 165	15.08	6	共青团农场	Gongqintuan Farm	9 303	6
新湖农场	Qitai Farm	13.17	7	军户农场	Xinhu Farm	9 184	7
奇台农场	Xinhu Farm	12.1	8	新湖农场	Farm 102	8 583	8
红山农场	Hongshan Farm	11.49	9	一四三团	Farm 105	8 419	9
二十九团	Farm 77	11.05	10	一〇三团	Farm 103	7 188	10
一四三团	Farm 29	10.7	11	一〇二团	Farm 143	7 052	11
一四二团	Farm 142	10.6	12	一〇五团	Fangcaohu Farm	7 045	12
七十七团	Farm 45	10.59	13	芳草湖农场	Farm 123	6 852	13
一六六团	Farm 53	10.16	14	一二三团	Farm 62	6 286	14
七十九团	Farm 166	9.63	15	六十六团	Farm 66	5 489	15
一八一团	Farm 79	9.49	16	二十四团	Farm 188	5 273	16
一六三团	Farm 181	9.46	17	二十二团	Farm 161	5 196	17
五十一团	Farm 44	9.4	18	一八八团	Farm 131	5 059	18
五十三团	Farm 51	9.39	19	七十三团	Farm 165	4 798	19
一四四团	Farm 78	9.33	20	一三一团	Farm 73	4 779	20

2018

BING TUAN

附录1

各省(区、市)主要经济指标排序

Appendix I Ranking of Main Economic Indicators by Province

简要说明

一、本篇资料主要内容

本篇资料主要反映各省（区、市）主要经济指标排序情况。

二、本篇资料来源

资料取自《2017年中国统计年鉴》，反映2016年及以前年度资料，由兵团统计局国民经济综合统计处整理。

Brief Introduction

1. Main Contents

The data in this chapter mainly show the conditions on ranking of main economic indicators by province and comparison of main indicators on the economic belt of the northern slope of the Tianshan Mountains, 16 prefectures and cities of the Eastern, Middle, Western and 3 Northeastern provinces to national total.

2. Sources of Data

The data are collected from *China Statistical Yearbook -2017*. Data in 2016 and before are prepared by the Comprehensive Office of the Statistics Bureau of XPCC.

附录 1－1　各省(区、市)生产总值及指数、人均指标排序

Ranking of Gross Domestic Product and its Indices, Per Capita GDP by Region

(2016 年)

地　区	Region	生产总值（亿元） Gross Domestic Product (100 million yuan)	排　序 Ranking	生产总值指数（上年＝100） Gross Domestic Product Indices (preceding year＝100)	排　序 Ranking	人均生产总值（元） Per Capita GDP (yuan)	排　序 Ranking
全　国	**China**	**741 140.40**		**106.7**		**53 980**	
北　京	Beijing	25 669.13	12	106.8	29	118 198	1
天　津	Tianjin	17 885.39	19	109.1	4	115 053	3
河　北	Hebei	32 070.45	8	106.8	28	43 062	20
山　西	Shanxi	13 050.41	24	104.5	31	35 532	28
内蒙古	Inner Mongolia	18 128.10	18	107.2	25	72 064	9
辽　宁	Liaoning	22 246.90	14	97.5	32	50 791	15
吉　林	Jilin	14 776.80	23	106.9	26	53 868	13
黑龙江	Heilongjiang	15 386.09	21	106.1	30	40 432	23
上　海	Shanghai	28 178.65	11	106.9	26	116 562	2
江　苏	Jiangsu	77 388.28	2	107.8	15	96 887	4
浙　江	Zhejiang	47 251.36	4	107.6	21	84 916	5
安　徽	Anhui	24 407.62	13	108.7	8	39 561	26
福　建	Fujian	28 810.58	10	108.4	9	74 707	7
江　西	Jiangxi	18 499.00	16	109.0	6	40 400	24
山　东	Shandong	68 024.49	3	107.6	17	68 733	10
河　南	Henan	40 471.79	5	108.1	10	42 575	21
湖　北	Hubei	32 665.38	7	108.1	11	55 665	12
湖　南	Hunan	31 551.37	9	108.0	13	46 382	17
广　东	Guangdong	80 854.91	1	107.5	22	74 016	8
广　西	Guangxi	18 317.64	17	107.3	24	38 027	27
海　南	Hainan	4 053.20	28	107.5	23	44 347	18
重　庆	Chongqing	17 740.59	20	110.7	1	58 502	11
四　川	Sichuan	32 934.54	6	107.8	15	40 003	25
贵　州	Guizhou	11 776.73	25	110.5	2	33 246	30
云　南	Yunnan	14 788.42	22	108.7	7	31 093	31
西　藏	Tibet	1 151.41	32	110.1	3	35 184	29
陕　西	Shanxi	19 399.59	15	107.6	17	51 015	14
甘　肃	Gansu	7 200.37	27	107.6	17	27 643	32
青　海	Qinghai	2 572.49	30	108.0	13	43 531	19
宁　夏	Ningxia	3 168.59	29	108.1	11	47 194	16
新　疆	Xinjiang	9 649.70	26	107.6	17	40 564	22
新疆建设兵团	XPCC	2 134.33	31	109.1	4	76 230	6

注:本表按当年价计算。
Note: Data in value in this table are calculated at current prices.

附录 1—2　各省(区、市)三次产业增加值排序

Ranking of Value-added of Three Industries by Region

计量单位:亿元　　(2016 年)　　(100 million yuan)

地　区	Region	第一产业 Primary Industry	排　序 Ranking	第二产业 Secondary Industry	排　序 Ranking	第三产业 Tertiary Industry	排　序 Ranking
全　国	**China**	**63 670.70**		**296 236.00**		**384 220.50**	
北　京	Beijing	129.79	30	4 944.44	23	20 594.90	5
天　津	Tianjin	220.22	29	7 571.35	19	10 093.82	14
河　北	Hebei	3 492.81	8	15 256.93	6	13 320.71	11
山　西	Shanxi	784.78	25	5 028.99	22	7 236.64	22
内 蒙 古	Inner Mongolia	1 637.39	20	8 553.63	15	7 937.08	19
辽　宁	Liaoning	2 173.06	14	8 606.54	14	11 467.30	13
吉　林	Jilin	1 498.52	21	7 004.95	20	6 273.33	24
黑 龙 江	Heilongjiang	2 670.46	10	4 400.69	25	8 314.94	17
上　海	Shanghai	109.47	32	8 406.28	16	19 662.90	6
江　苏	Jiangsu	4 077.18	3	34 619.50	2	38 691.60	2
浙　江	Zhejiang	1 965.18	15	21 194.61	4	24 091.57	4
安　徽	Anhui	2 567.72	11	11 821.58	11	10 018.32	15
福　建	Fujian	2 363.22	12	14 093.47	8	12 353.89	12
江　西	Jiangxi	1 904.53	16	8 829.54	13	7 764.93	20
山　东	Shandong	4 929.13	1	31 343.67	3	31 751.69	3
河　南	Henan	4 286.21	2	19 275.82	5	16 909.76	7
湖　北	Hubei	3 659.33	6	14 654.38	7	14 351.67	10
湖　南	Hunan	3 578.37	7	13 341.17	10	14 631.83	9
广　东	Guangdong	3 694.37	5	35 109.66	1	42 050.88	1
广　西	Guangxi	2 796.80	9	8 273.66	17	7 247.18	21
海　南	Hainan	948.35	24	905.95	31	2 198.90	28
重　庆	Chongqing	1 303.24	22	7 898.92	18	8 538.43	16
四　川	Sichuan	3 929.33	4	13 448.92	9	15 556.29	8
贵　州	Guizhou	1 846.19	17	4 669.53	24	5 261.01	25
云　南	Yunnan	2 195.11	13	5 690.16	21	6 903.15	23
西　藏	Tibet	115.78	31	429.17	32	606.46	32
陕　西	Shanxi	1 693.85	18	9 490.72	12	8 215.02	18
甘　肃	Gansu	983.39	23	2 515.56	27	3 701.42	27
青　海	Qinghai	221.19	28	1 249.98	29	1 101.32	30
宁　夏	Ningxia	241.60	27	1 488.44	28	1 438.55	29
新　疆	Xinjiang	1 648.97	19	3 647.01	26	4 353.72	26
新疆建设兵团	XPCC	467.87	26	965.58	30	700.88	31

注:本表按当年价计算。
Note:Data in value in this table are calculated at current prices.

附录 1－3　各省(区、市)三次产业增加值指数排序

Ranking of Compotision of Value-added of the Three Industries by Region

计量单位:%　　(2016 年)　　(preceding year=100)

地　区	Region	第一产业 Primary Industry	排　序 Ranking	第二产业 Secondary Industry	排　序 Ranking	第三产业 Tertiary Industry	排　序 Ranking
全　国	**China**	**103.3**		**106.1**		**107.8**	
北　京	Beijing	91.3	32	106.3	22	107.0	30
天　津	Tianjin	103.0	24	108.4	8	110.0	9
河　北	Hebei	103.5	20	104.9	27	109.9	10
山　西	Shanxi	102.8	26	101.5	30	106.9	31
内蒙古	Inner Mongolia	103.0	24	106.9	16	108.3	28
辽　宁	Liaoning	95.4	30	92.3	32	102.5	32
吉　林	Jilin	103.9	15	106.2	23	108.8	24
黑龙江	Heilongjiang	105.3	7	102.6	29	108.5	27
上　海	Shanghai	93.4	31	101.2	31	109.6	13
江　苏	Jiangsu	100.7	29	106.6	19	109.8	11
浙　江	Zhejiang	102.7	27	105.7	26	109.7	12
安　徽	Anhui	102.7	28	108.1	9	111.1	3
福　建	Fujian	103.6	19	106.8	17	111.4	2
江　西	Jiangxi	104.2	12	108.5	6	111.1	4
山　东	Shandong	103.9	15	106.6	19	109.3	19
河　南	Henan	104.2	11	107.3	15	110.3	7
湖　北	Hubei	103.9	15	107.8	11	109.5	16
湖　南	Hunan	103.3	22	106.5	21	110.6	6
广　东	Guangdong	103.1	23	106.1	25	109.2	20
广　西	Guangxi	103.4	21	107.4	13	108.6	26
海　南	Hainan	104.0	13	104.7	28	110.2	8
重　庆	Chongqing	104.6	8	111.3	2	111.0	5
四　川	Sichuan	103.8	18	107.6	12	109.2	21
贵　州	Guizhou	106.0	1	111.3	3	111.4	1
云　南	Yunnan	105.6	4	108.9	5	109.5	16
西　藏	Tibet	104.5	9	112.2	1	109.6	13
陕　西	Shanxi	104.0	13	107.3	14	108.8	24
甘　肃	Gansu	105.5	5	106.8	17	108.9	23
青　海	Qinghai	105.4	6	108.5	6	108.0	29
宁　夏	Ningxia	104.5	9	107.9	10	109.0	22
新　疆	Xinjiang	105.8	3	106.2	23	109.4	18
新疆建设兵团	XPCC	106.0	2	110.2	4	109.6	13

注:本表按当年价计算。
Note:Data in value terms in this table are calculated at current prices.

附录1－4　各省(区、市)总人口排序(2014－2016年)

Ranking of Total Population by Region(2014－2016)

计量单位:万人　　(10 000 persons)

地　区	Region	2014	排序 Ranking	2015	排序 Ranking	2016	排序 Ranking
全　国	**China**	**136 782**		**137 462**		**138 271**	
北　京	Beijing	2 152	26	2 171	26	2 173	26
天　津	Tianjin	1 517	27	1 547	27	1 562	27
河　北	Hebei	7 384	6	7 425	6	7 470	6
山　西	Shanxi	3 648	18	3 664	18	3 682	18
内蒙古	Inner Mongolia	2 505	23	2 511	23	2 520	23
辽　宁	Liaoning	4 391	14	4 382	14	4 378	14
吉　林	Jilin	2 752	21	2 753	21	2 733	21
黑龙江	Heilongjiang	3 833	15	3 812	16	3 799	17
上　海	Shanghai	2 426	24	2 415	24	2 420	24
江　苏	Jiangsu	7 960	5	7 976	5	7 999	5
浙　江	Zhejiang	5 508	10	5 539	10	5 590	10
安　徽	Anhui	6 083	8	6 144	8	6 196	8
福　建	Fujian	3 806	16	3839	15	3 874	15
江　西	Jiangxi	4 542	13	4 566	13	4 592	13
山　东	Shandong	9 789	2	9 847	2	9 947	2
河　南	Henan	9 436	3	9 480	3	9 532	3
湖　北	Hubei	5 816	9	5 852	9	5 885	9
湖　南	Hunan	6 737	7	6 783	7	6 822	7
广　东	Guangdong	10 724	1	10 849	1	10 999	1
广　西	Guangxi	4 754	11	4 796	11	4 838	11
海　南	Hainan	903	28	911	28	917	28
重　庆	Chongqing	2 991	20	3 017	20	3 048	20
四　川	Sichuan	8 140	4	8 204	4	8 262	4
贵　州	Guizhou	3 508	19	3 530	19	3 555	19
云　南	Yunnan	4 714	12	4 742	12	4 771	12
西　藏	Tibet	318	31	324	31	331	31
陕　西	Shanxi	3 775	17	3 793	17	3 813	16
甘　肃	Gansu	2 591	22	2 600	22	2 610	22
青　海	Qinghai	583	30	588	30	593	30
宁　夏	Ningxia	662	29	668	29	675	29
新　疆	Xinjiang	2 298	25	2 360	25	2 398	25
新疆建设兵团	XPCC	273	32	277	32	283	32

附录 1－5　各省(区、市)城镇居民人均可支配收入排序(2014－2016 年)

Ranking of Per Capita Disposable Income by Region(2014－2016)

计量单位:元　　(yuan)

地　　区	Region	2014	排　序 Ranking	2015	排　序 Ranking	2016	排　序 Ranking
全　　国	**China**	**28 844**		**31 195**		**33 616**	
北　　京	Beijing	48 532	2	52 859	2	57 275	2
天　　津	Tianjin	31 506	6	34 101	6	37 110	6
河　　北	Hebei	24 141	22	26 152	23	28 249	23
山　　西	Shanxi	24 069	23	25 828	24	27 352	25
内 蒙 古	Inner Mongolia	28 350	10	30 594	11	32 975	10
辽　　宁	Liaoning	29 082	9	31 126	10	32 876	11
吉　　林	Jilin	23 218	26	24 901	28	26 530	30
黑 龙 江	Heilongjiang	22 609	28	24 203	31	25 736	31
上　　海	Shanghai	48 841	1	52 962	1	57 692	1
江　　苏	Jiangsu	34 346	4	37 173	4	40 152	4
浙　　江	Zhejiang	40 393	3	43 714	3	47 237	3
安　　徽	Anhui	24 839	15	26 936	15	29 156	15
福　　建	Fujian	30 722	7	33 275	7	36 014	7
江　　西	Jiangxi	24 309	19	26 500	16	28 673	16
山　　东	Shandong	29 222	8	31 545	8	34 012	9
河　　南	Henan	23 672	24	25 576	25	27 233	26
湖　　北	Hubei	24 852	14	27 051	14	29 386	14
湖　　南	Hunan	26 570	12	28 838	12	31 284	12
广　　东	Guangdong	32 148	5	34 757	5	37 684	5
广　　西	Guangxi	24 669	16	26 416	18	28 324	22
海　　南	Hainan	24 487	17	26 356	20	28 453	19
重　　庆	Chongqing	25 147	13	27 239	13	29 610	13
四　　川	Sichuan	24 234	21	26 205	22	28 335	21
贵　　州	Guizhou	22 548	29	24 580	29	26 743	29
云　　南	Yunnan	24 299	20	26 373	19	28 611	17
西　　藏	Tibet	22 016	31	25 457	26	27 802	24
陕　　西	Shanxi	24 366	18	26 420	17	28 440	20
甘　　肃	Gansu	21 804	32	23 767	32	25 693	32
青　　海	Qinghai	22 307	30	24 542	30	26 757	28
宁　　夏	Ningxia	23 285	25	25 186	27	27 153	27
新　　疆	Xinjiang	23 214	27	26 275	21	28 463	18
新疆建设兵团	XPCC	27 558	11	31 432	9	34 089	8

附录 1—6　各省(区、市)农村居民人均可支配收入排序(2014—2016 年)

Ranking of Per Capita Disposable Income of Rural Households by Region(2014—2016)

计量单位:元　　(yuan)

地　区	Region	2014	排序 Ranking	2015	排序 Ranking	2016	排序 Ranking
全　国	**China**	**10 489**		**11 422**		**12 363**	
北　京	Beijing	18 867	3	20 569	3	22 310	3
天　津	Tianjin	17 014	4	18 482	4	20 076	4
河　北	Hebei	10 186	14	11 051	15	11 919	15
山　西	Shanxi	8 809	23	9 454	24	10 082	25
内蒙古	Inner Mongolia	9 976	17	10 776	20	11 609	20
辽　宁	Liaoning	11 191	10	12 057	10	12 881	10
吉　林	Jilin	10 780	12	11 326	12	12 123	13
黑龙江	Heilongjiang	10 453	13	11 095	14	11 832	17
上　海	Shanghai	21 192	1	23 205	1	25 520	1
江　苏	Jiangsu	14 958	5	16 257	5	17 606	5
浙　江	Zhejiang	19 373	2	21 125	2	22 866	2
安　徽	Anhui	9 916	19	10 821	19	11 720	18
福　建	Fujian	12 650	7	13 793	7	14 999	7
江　西	Jiangxi	10 117	15	11 139	13	12 138	12
山　东	Shandong	11 882	9	12 930	9	13 954	9
河　南	Henan	9 966	18	10 853	18	11 697	19
湖　北	Hubei	10 849	11	11 844	11	12 725	11
湖　南	Hunan	10 060	16	10 993	16	11 930	14
广　东	Guangdong	12 246	8	13 360	8	14 512	8
广　西	Guangxi	8 683	25	9 467	23	10 359	23
海　南	Hainan	9 913	20	10 858	17	11 843	16
重　庆	Chongqing	9 490	21	10 505	21	11 549	21
四　川	Sichuan	9 348	22	10 247	22	11 203	22
贵　州	Guizhou	6 671	31	7 387	31	8 090	31
云　南	Yunnan	7 456	28	8 242	29	9 020	29
西　藏	Tibet	7 359	29	8 244	28	9 094	28
陕　西	Shanxi	7 932	27	8 689	27	9 396	27
甘　肃	Gansu	6 277	32	6 936	32	7 457	32
青　海	Qinghai	7 283	30	7 933	30	8 664	30
宁　夏	Ningxia	8 410	26	9 119	26	9 852	26
新　疆	Xinjiang	8 724	24	9 425	25	10 183	24
新疆建设兵团	XPCC	13 930	6	15 053	6	16 401	6

附录 1—7 各省(区、市)粮食总产量排序(2014—2016 年)

Ranking of Grain Output by Region(2014—2016)

计量单位:万吨 (10 000 tons)

地区	Region	2014	排序 Ranking	2015	排序 Ranking	2016	排序 Ranking
全国	**China**	**60 702.6**		**62 143.9**		**61 625.0**	
北京	Beijing	63.9	32	62.6	32	53.7	32
天津	Tianjin	176.0	28	181.7	28	196.4	27
河北	Hebei	3 360.2	8	3 363.8	8	3 460.2	7
山西	Shanxi	1 330.8	18	1 259.6	18	1 318.5	18
内蒙古	Inner Mongolia	2753.0	10	2827.0	10	2 780.3	10
辽宁	Liaoning	1 753.9	14	2 002.5	13	2 100.6	13
吉林	Jilin	3 532.8	4	3 647.0	4	3 717.2	4
黑龙江	Heilongjiang	6 242.2	1	6 324.0	1	6 058.5	1
上海	Shanghai	112.5	29	112.1	29	99.2	31
江苏	Jiangsu	3 490.6	5	3 561.3	5	3 466.0	6
浙江	Zhejiang	757.4	23	752.2	23	752.2	23
安徽	Anhui	3 415.8	6	3 538.1	6	3 417.4	8
福建	Fujian	667.0	24	661.1	24	650.9	24
江西	Jiangxi	2 143.5	12	2 148.7	12	2 138.1	12
山东	Shandong	4 596.6	3	4 712.7	3	4 700.7	3
河南	Henan	5 772.3	2	6 067.1	2	5 946.6	2
湖北	Hubei	2 584.2	11	2 703.3	11	2 554.1	11
湖南	Hunan	3 001.3	9	3 002.9	9	2 953.2	9
广东	Guangdong	1 357.3	17	1 358.1	17	1 360.2	17
广西	Guangxi	1 534.4	15	1 524.8	15	1 521.3	15
海南	Hainan	186.6	27	184.0	27	177.9	28
重庆	Chongqing	1 144.5	21	1 154.9	22	1 166.0	21
四川	Sichuan	3 374.9	7	3 442.8	7	3 483.5	5
贵州	Guizhou	1 138.5	22	1 180.0	20	1 192.4	20
云南	Yunnan	1 860.7	13	1 876.4	14	1 902.9	14
西藏	Tibet	98.0	31	100.6	31	101.9	30
陕西	Shanxi	1 197.8	19	1 226.8	19	1 228.3	19
甘肃	Gansu	1 158.7	20	1 171.1	21	1 140.6	22
青海	Qinghai	104.8	30	102.7	30	103.5	29
宁夏	Ningxia	377.9	25	372.6	25	370.6	25
新疆	Xinjiang	1 414.5	16	1 521.3	16	1 512.3	16
新疆建设兵团	XPCC	222.9	26	265.4	26	271.3	26

附录1—8　各省(区、市)棉花总产量排序(2014—2016年)

Ranking of Cotton Output by Region(2014—2016)

计量单位:万吨　　(10 000 tons)

地　　区	Region	2014	排　序 Ranking	2015	排　序 Ranking	2016	排　序 Ranking
全　　国	**China**	**617.8**		**560.3**		**529.9**	
北　　京	Beijing	0.0	23			0.0	24
天　　津	Tianjin	3.8	13	2.6	13	2.3	12
河　　北	Hebei	43.1	4	37.3	4	30.0	4
山　　西	Shanxi	2.4	15	1.4	15	1.0	15
内 蒙 古	Inner Mongolia	0.2	18			0.0	20
辽　　宁	Liaoning	0.0	24			0.0	21
吉　　林	Jilin	0.1	21				
黑 龙 江	Heilongjiang						
上　　海	Shanghai	0.1	19			0.0	19
江　　苏	Jiangsu	16.0	7	11.7	9	7.4	9
浙　　江	Zhejiang	2.5	14	2.0	14	1.7	14
安　　徽	Anhui	26.3	6	23.4	6	18.5	6
福　　建	Fujian	…	25			…	23
江　　西	Jiangxi	13.4	9	11.5	10	7.3	10
山　　东	Shandong	66.5	3	53.7	3	54.8	3
河　　南	Henan	14.7	8	12.6	8	9.8	8
湖　　北	Hubei	36.0	5	29.8	5	18.8	5
湖　　南	Hunan	12.9	10	14.5	7	12.3	7
广　　东	Guangdong						
广　　西	Guangxi	0.3	17	0.3	17	0.3	17
海　　南	Hainan						
重　　庆	Chongqing						
四　　川	Sichuan	1.2	16	1.0	16	0.9	16
贵　　州	Guizhou	0.1	20	0.1	18	0.1	18
云　　南	Yunnan	0.0	22			0.0	22
西　　藏	Tibet						
陕　　西	Shanxi	4.2	12	3.9	12	3.4	11
甘　　肃	Gansu	6.4	11	4.3	11	2.0	13
青　　海	Qinghai						
宁　　夏	Ningxia						
新　　疆	Xinjiang	367.7	1	350.3	1	359.4	1
新疆建设兵团	XPCC	163.6	2	146.5	2	149.6	2

附录1—9　各省(区、市)油料总产量排序(2014—2016年)

Ranking of Oil-bearing Crop Output by Region(2014—2016)

计量单位:万吨　　(10 000 tons)

地区	Region	2014	排序 Ranking	2015	排序 Ranking	2016	排序 Ranking
全国	**China**	**3 507.4**		**3 537.0**		**3 629.5**	
北京	Beijing	0.7	31	0.6	31	0.6	32
天津	Tianjin	0.5	32	0.4	32	1.6	30
河北	Hebei	150.2	8	151.5	8	156.5	8
山西	Shanxi	17.3	24	15.3	26	15.4	26
内蒙古	Inner Mongolia	170.3	7	193.6	7	220.0	6
辽宁	Liaoning	63.7	16	46.1	20	81.3	14
吉林	Jilin	85.7	13	76.4	13	82.5	13
黑龙江	Heilongjiang	17.1	25	18.3	25	21.7	25
上海	Shanghai	1.3	30	1.2	30	0.9	31
江苏	Jiangsu	146.6	9	143.1	9	131.9	9
浙江	Zhejiang	30.7	22	31.3	21	29.1	23
安徽	Anhui	228.8	6	227.9	6	214.8	7
福建	Fujian	29.8	23	30.7	22	31.0	21
江西	Jiangxi	121.7	10	124.0	10	122.0	10
山东	Shandong	335.9	3	324.1	3	326.8	3
河南	Henan	584.3	1	599.7	1	619.1	1
湖北	Hubei	341.7	2	339.6	2	329.8	2
湖南	Hunan	233.8	5	242.9	5	242.9	5
广东	Guangdong	105.5	11	110.3	11	113.3	11
广西	Guangxi	61.3	18	64.7	16	68.9	17
海南	Hainan	11.6	28	11.3	28	11.2	28
重庆	Chongqing	56.9	20	59.9	19	62.7	20
四川	Sichuan	300.8	4	307.6	4	311.3	4
贵州	Guizhou	98.0	12	101.3	12	103.4	12
云南	Yunnan	64.7	15	65.9	15	68.5	18
西藏	Tibet	6.4	29	6.4	29	6.2	29
陕西	Shanxi	62.3	17	62.7	18	63.8	19
甘肃	Gansu	72.4	14	71.6	14	76.0	15
青海	Qinghai	31.5	21	30.5	23	30.0	22
宁夏	Ningxia	16.5	27	15.3	27	14.7	27
新疆	Xinjiang	59.3	19	62.9	17	71.4	16
新疆建设兵团	XPCC	17.0	26	19.3	24	23.4	24

附录1—10 各省(区、市)糖料总产量排序(2014—2016年)

Ranking of Sugar Crop Output by Region(2014—2016)

计量单位:万吨 (10 000 tons)

地区	Region	2014	排序 Ranking	2015	排序 Ranking	2016	排序 Ranking
全国	**China**	**13 361.2**		**12 500.0**		**12 339.1**	
北京	Beijing						
天津	Tianjin						
河北	Hebei	75.6	9	89.2	9	93.1	9
山西	Shanxi	8.0	23	5.5	22	3.3	23
内蒙古	Inner Mongolia	160.2	8	230.1	6	266.2	5
辽宁	Liaoning	10.1	21	5.2	23	9.4	21
吉林	Jilin	6.4	24	1.3	24	1.4	24
黑龙江	Heilongjiang	41.1	15	7.3	21	11.4	19
上海	Shanghai	0.6	25	0.6	25	0.6	25
江苏	Jiangsu	10.1	22	9.5	20	9.0	22
浙江	Zhejiang	62.7	12	62.2	12	62.1	12
安徽	Anhui	19.7	19	20.3	17	20.2	17
福建	Fujian	53.1	14	43.6	14	37.0	15
江西	Jiangxi	64.5	11	65.8	11	65.8	11
山东	Shandong					0.0	28
河南	Henan	27.3	17	24.3	16	23.5	16
湖北	Hubei	30.4	16	32.0	15	37.3	14
湖南	Hunan	65.9	10	66.0	10	66.2	10
广东	Guangdong	1 504.7	3	1 452.9	3	1 479.3	3
广西	Guangxi	7 952.6	1	7 504.9	1	7 461.3	1
海南	Hainan	424.9	5	264.8	5	204.6	7
重庆	Chongqing	10.3	20	9.8	19	9.7	20
四川	Sichuan	55.8	13	54.2	13	49.6	13
贵州	Guizhou	168.3	7	156.1	8	117.8	8
云南	Yunnan	2 110.4	2	1 930.1	2	1 738.4	2
西藏	Tibet						
陕西	Shanxi	0.1	26	0.2	26	0.2	26
甘肃	Gansu	26.4	18	16.0	18	16.6	18
青海	Qinghai	0.1				0.1	27
宁夏	Ningxia						
新疆	Xinjiang	471.9	4	448.3	4	555.0	4
新疆建设兵团	XPCC	203.6	6	184.4	7	208.2	6

附录1—11 各省(区、市)人均粮食产量排序(2014—2016年)

Ranking of Per Capita Grain Output by Region(2014—2016)

计量单位:公斤/人 (kg/person)

地区	Region	2014	排序 Ranking	2015	排序 Ranking	2016	排序 Ranking
全国	**China**	**445**		**453**		**447**	
北京	Beijing	30	32	29	32	25	32
天津	Tianjin	118	30	119	30	126	29
河北	Hebei	457	11	454	13	465	12
山西	Shanxi	366	20	345	20	359	20
内蒙古	Inner Mongolia	1 101	3	1 127	3	1 105	3
辽宁	Liaoning	399	17	456	12	480	9
吉林	Jilin	1 284	2	1 325	2	1 355	2
黑龙江	Heilongjiang	1 628	1	1 654	1	1 592	1
上海	Shanghai	46	31	46	31	41	31
江苏	Jiangsu	439	15	447	15	434	16
浙江	Zhejiang	138	28	136	28	135	28
安徽	Anhui	564	8	579	7	554	7
福建	Fujian	176	27	173	27	169	27
江西	Jiangxi	473	9	472	10	467	11
山东	Shandong	471	10	480	9	475	10
河南	Henan	612	6	641	6	626	6
湖北	Hubei	445	14	463	11	435	14
湖南	Hunan	447	13	444	16	434	15
广东	Guangdong	127	29	126	29	125	30
广西	Guangxi	324	22	319	23	316	23
海南	Hainan	207	25	203	25	195	25
重庆	Chongqing	384	19	384	19	385	19
四川	Sichuan	415	16	421	17	423	17
贵州	Guizhou	325	21	335	21	337	21
云南	Yunnan	396	18	397	18	400	18
西藏	Tibet	311	24	314	24	311	24
陕西	Shanxi	318	23	324	22	323	22
甘肃	Gansu	448	12	451	14	438	13
青海	Qinghai	181	26	175	26	175	26
宁夏	Ningxia	574	7	561	8	552	8
新疆	Xinjiang	620	5	653	5	636	5
新疆建设兵团	XPCC	820	4	965	4	969	4

附录1—12 各省(区、市)人均棉花产量排序(2014—2016年)

Ranking of Per Capita Cotton Output by Region(2014—2016)

计量单位:公斤/人 (kg/person)

地区	Region	2014	排序 Ranking	2015	排序 Ranking	2016	排序 Ranking
全国	**China**	**4.53**		**4.09**		**3.84**	
北京	Beijing	0.01	23			0.00	22
天津	Tianjin	2.55	8	1.67	9	1.50	9
河北	Hebei	5.86	5	5.04	5	4.02	4
山西	Shanxi	0.65	14	0.40	14	0.28	15
内蒙古	Inner Mongolia	0.06	17	0.01	20	0.01	20
辽宁	Liaoning	0.00	24			…	21
吉林	Jilin	0.03	21				
黑龙江	Heilongjiang						
上海	Shanghai	0.05	19	0.02	19	0.01	19
江苏	Jiangsu	2.01	10	1.47	11	0.92	11
浙江	Zhejiang	0.45	15	0.36	15	0.30	14
安徽	Anhui	4.35	6	3.82	6	2.99	6
福建	Fujian	…	25			…	24
江西	Jiangxi	2.95	7	2.53	7	1.60	8
山东	Shandong	6.81	3	5.47	3	5.54	3
河南	Henan	1.56	12	1.34	12	1.03	10
湖北	Hubei	6.19	4	5.10	4	3.21	5
湖南	Hunan	1.92	11	2.14	8	1.80	7
广东	Guangdong						
广西	Guangxi	0.05	18	0.05	17	0.05	17
海南	Hainan						
重庆	Chongqing						
四川	Sichuan	0.15	16	0.12	16	0.11	16
贵州	Guizhou	0.03	20	0.03	18	0.03	18
云南	Yunnan	0.01	22			…	23
西藏	Tibet						
陕西	Shanxi	1.12	13	1.02	13	0.89	12
甘肃	Gansu	2.49	9	1.64	10	0.76	13
青海	Qinghai						
宁夏	Ningxia						
新疆	Xinjiang	161.18	2	150.40	2	151.07	2
新疆建设兵团	XPCC	601.00	1	533.00	1	534.00	1

附录1－13　各省(区、市)人均油料产量排序(2014－2016年)

Ranking of Per Capita Oil-bearing Crop Output by Region(2014－2016)

计量单位:公斤/人　　(kg/person)

地　区	Region	2014	排　序 Ranking	2015	排　序 Ranking	2016	排　序 Ranking
全　国	**China**	**25.71**		**25.79**		**26.33**	
北　京	Beijing	0.32	32	0.26	32	0.26	32
天　津	Tianjin	0.35	31	0.28	31	1.03	30
河　北	Hebei	20.41	16	20.47	16	21.01	16
山　西	Shanxi	4.76	28	4.19	29	4.20	29
内蒙古	Inner Mongolia	68.09	1	77.19	1	87.46	1
辽　宁	Liaoning	14.51	21	10.51	24	18.57	19
吉　林	Jilin	31.14	10	27.76	11	30.09	10
黑龙江	Heilongjiang	4.47	29	4.80	28	5.71	27
上　海	Shanghai	0.53	30	0.49	30	0.37	31
江　苏	Jiangsu	18.44	19	17.96	19	16.52	21
浙　江	Zhejiang	5.57	27	5.68	27	5.23	28
安　徽	Anhui	37.78	6	37.27	7	34.82	8
福　建	Fujian	7.87	26	8.02	26	8.05	26
江　西	Jiangxi	26.85	13	27.22	13	26.65	14
山　东	Shandong	34.41	9	33.01	9	33.02	9
河　南	Henan	62.00	3	63.41	3	65.13	3
湖　北	Hubei	58.84	4	58.21	4	56.19	4
湖　南	Hunan	34.82	8	35.93	8	35.70	7
广　东	Guangdong	9.87	25	10.23	25	10.37	25
广　西	Guangxi	12.94	23	13.55	22	14.31	23
海　南	Hainan	12.87	24	12.41	23	12.23	24
重　庆	Chongqing	19.10	18	19.93	18	20.68	17
四　川	Sichuan	37.03	7	37.63	6	37.81	6
贵　州	Guizhou	27.97	12	28.80	10	29.20	12
云　南	Yunnan	13.76	22	13.94	21	14.40	22
西　藏	Tibet	20.26	17	19.97	17	18.99	18
陕　西	Shanxi	16.53	20	16.56	20	16.78	20
甘　肃	Gansu	28.00	11	27.58	12	29.18	13
青　海	Qinghai	54.27	5	52.02	5	50.83	5
宁　夏	Ningxia	25.11	15	22.95	15	21.83	15
新　疆	Xinjiang	26.00	14	27.00	14	30.01	11
新疆建设兵团	XPCC	63.00	2	70.00	2	84.00	2

附录1—14 各省(区、市)人均糖料产量排序(2014—2016年)

Ranking of Per Capita Sugar Crops Output by Region(2014—2016)

计量单位:公斤/人 (kg/person)

地区	Region	2014	排序 Ranking	2015	排序 Ranking	2016	排序 Ranking
全国	**China**	**97.94**		**91.16**		**89.50**	
北京	Beijing						
天津	Tianjin						
河北	Hebei	10.28	14	12.04	11	12.51	11
山西	Shanxi	2.21	24	1.50	22	0.91	24
内蒙古	Inner Mongolia	64.04	8	91.75	7	105.82	7
辽宁	Liaoning	2.31	22	1.19	24	2.15	22
吉林	Jilin	2.31	22	0.47	25	0.52	25
黑龙江	Heilongjiang	10.71	13	1.91	21	2.99	20
上海	Shanghai	0.25	26	0.24	26	0.23	26
江苏	Jiangsu	1.27	25	1.19	23	1.13	23
浙江	Zhejiang	11.39	12	11.25	13	11.16	12
安徽	Anhui	3.25	20	3.32	18	3.28	18
福建	Fujian	14.02	11	11.40	12	9.60	14
江西	Jiangxi	14.24	10	14.45	10	14.36	10
山东	Shandong					…	29
河南	Henan	2.89	21	2.57	20	2.47	21
湖北	Hubei	5.24	18	5.49	17	6.36	16
湖南	Hunan	9.81	16	9.76	14	9.73	13
广东	Guangdong	140.83	6	134.69	6	135.42	6
广西	Guangxi	1 679.00	1	1 571.71	1	1 548.96	1
海南	Hainan	472.41	3	291.87	4	223.87	5
重庆	Chongqing	3.45	19	3.25	19	3.20	19
四川	Sichuan	6.87	17	6.63	15	6.02	17
贵州	Guizhou	48.01	9	44.36	9	33.26	9
云南	Yunnan	449.00	4	408.23	3	365.49	3
西藏	Tibet						
陕西	Shanxi	0.04	28	0.04	27	0.04	28
甘肃	Gansu	10.21	15	6.18	16	6.38	15
青海	Qinghai	0.17				0.09	27
宁夏	Ningxia						
新疆	Xinjiang	206.86	5	192.48	5	233.30	4
新疆建设兵团	XPCC	749.80	2	670.58	2	743.57	2

2018

BING TUAN

附 录2

东、中、西部和东北地区主经济指标

Appendix II Main Economic Indicators Development of Eastern,Middle, Western and Northeastern Provinces

简要说明

一、本篇资料主要内容

本篇资料主要反映东、中、西部和东北地区主要经济指标及占全国比重情况。

二、本篇资料来源

资料取自《2017年中国统计年鉴》，反映2016年度资料，由兵团统计局国民经济综合统计处整理。

Brief Introduction

1. Main Contents

This article mainly reflects the main economic indicators and the proportion of the whole country in the East,middle,West and northeast Provinces.

2. Sources of Data

The data are collected from *China statistical Yearbook-2017,* which reflects the data of the year 2016, prepared by the Comprehensive Office of the statistics Bureau of XPCC .

附录 2－1 东、中、西部和东北地区主要经济指标

Main Economic Indicators of Eastern, Middle, Western and Northeastern Provinces

(2016 年)

指标	Item	东部 10 省(市)合计 Total of 10 Eastern Provinces	中部 6 省合计 Total of 6 Middle Provinces	西部 12 省(区、市)合计 Total of 12 Western Provinces	东北 3 省合计 Total of 3 North eastern Provinces
人口	**Population**				
年底总人口（万人）	Population at Year－end (10 000 persons)	52 951	36 709	37 414	10 910
国民经济核算	**National Accounting**				
国内(地区)生产总值（亿元）	Gross Domestic Product (100 million yuan)	410 186.4	160 645.6	156 828.2	52 409.8
第一产业	Primary Industry	21 929.7	16 780.9	18 612.8	6 342.0
第二产业	Secondary Industry	173 445.9	72 951.5	67 355.7	20 012.2
第三产业	Tertiary Industry	214 810.9	70 913.2	70 859.6	26 055.6
固定资产投资	**Investment in Fixed Assets**				
全社会固定资产投资总额（亿元）	Total Investment in Fixed Assets (100 million yuan)	252 922.8	159 705.6	157 195.4	31 263.8
# 房地产开发	Real Estate Development	54 138.6	21 404.4	23 061.2	3 976.4
国内贸易	**Domestic Trade**				
社会消费品零售总额（亿元）	Total Retail Sales of Consumer Goods (100 million yuan)	171 143.2	69 819.4	61 488.0	29 127.0
对外贸易	**Foreign Trade**				
货物进出口总额（亿美元）	Total Value of Imports and Exports (100 million USD)	202 659.3	15 728.6	16 975.2	8 023.3
出口额	Exports	114 716.6	10 223.0	10 031.5	3 448.2
进口额	Imports	87 942.8	5 505.6	6 943.7	4 575.1
财政	**Government Finance**				
地方一般公共预算收入（亿元）	General Public Budget Revenue (100 million yuan)	50 026.8	15 334.7	17 265.2	4 612.7
地方一般公共预算支出（亿元）	General Public Budget Expenditure (100 million yuan)	67 884.1	33 785.1	46 291.3	12 390.9
农业	**Agriculture**				
主要农产品产量（万吨）	Output of Major Farm Products (10 000 tons)				
粮食	Grain	14 917.3	18 327.9	16 503.4	11 876.3
棉花	Cotton	96.2	67.7	366.0	
油料	Oil－bearing Crops	802.9	1 544.0	1 097.0	185.6

附录 2—1 续表　Continued

（2016 年）

指　　标		Item		东部 10 省(市) 合　计 Total of 10 Eastern Provinces	中部 6 省 合　计 Total of 6 Middle Provinces	西部 12 省 (区、市) 合　计 Total of 12 Western Provinces	东北 3 省 合　计 Total of 3 North eastern Provinces
工　业		**Industry**					
主要工业产品产量		Output of Major Industrial Products					
原　油	（万吨）	Crude Oil	（10 000 tons）	7 872.7	373.8	6 437.9	5 284.0
发电量	（亿千瓦小时）	Electricity	（100 million kwh）	24 284.9	12 389.9	21 310.6	3 439.4
粗　钢	（万吨）	Crude Steel	（10 000 tons）	46 142.8	16 459.1	10 925.7	7 233.3
水　泥	（万吨）	Cement	（10 000 tons）	82 072.6	66 501.3	82 300.0	10 157.2
原　煤	（亿吨）			2.2	11.2	19.5	1.2
天然气	（亿立方米）	Natural Gas	（100 million cu. m）	137.3	51.4	1116.5	63.3
钢　材	（万吨）	Rolled Steel	（10 000 tons）	71 088.4	19 979.7	15 192.2	7 200.5
汽　车	（万辆）	Motor Vehicles	（10 000 sets）	1 272.4	543.0	627.0	369.5
交通运输业		**Transportation**					
铁路营业里程	（公里）	Length of Railways in Operation	（km）	28 935	27 975	50 236	16 845
公路里程	（公里）	Length of Highways	（km）	1 135 649	1 267 456	1 905 561	387 599
# 高速公路		Expressways		37 286	34 434	47 592	11 658
客运量	（万人）	Passenger Traffic	（10 000 persons）	642 980.3	515 633.6	544 856.9	147 927.5
货运量	（万吨）	Freight Traffic	（10 000 tons）	1 582 139.9	1 244 833.8	1 165 232.1	305 692.8
邮电通信业		**Postal and Telecommunication Services**					
邮电业务总量	（亿元）	Total Business Revenue	（100 million yuan）	5 653.4	900.8	626.8	216.2
电信业务总量	（亿元）	Total Business Telecommunications	（100 million yuan）	7 801.6	3 033.5	3 684.5	1 097.3
教　育		**Education**					
普通高等学校		Regular Institutions of Higher Education		1 000.0	677.0	661.0	258.0
本专科在校学生数	（万人）	Graduates of Undergraduates and College Students	（10 000 persons）	1 042	744	672	238
卫　生		**Health Care**					
医院数	（个）	Number of Hospitals	（unit）	10 031	6 807	9 419	2 883
执业(助理)医师	（万人）	Licensed (Assistant) Doctors	（10 000 persons）	133	79	80	26
医院床位数	（万张）	Number of Beds of Medical Institutions	（10 000 beds）	209.4	145.0	159.9	54.6
人民生活		**People's Living Conditions**					
居民人均可支配收入	（元）	Per Capita Disposable Income of Households	（yuan）	30 655	20 006	18 407	22 352
城镇居民人均可支配收入	（元）	Annual Per Capita Disposable Income of Urban Households	（yuan）	39 651	28 879	28 610	29 045
农村居民人均可支配收入	（元）	Annual Per Capita Disposable Income of Rural Households	（yuan）	15 498	11 794	9 918	12 275

附录 2－2　东、中、西部和东北地区主要经济指标占全国比重

Percentage of Main Economic Indicators of Eastern, Middle, Western and Northeast to National Total

计量单位：%　　　　(2016 年)　　　　(%)

指　　标	Item	东部 10 省(市) 合　计 Total of 10 Eastern Provinces	中部 6 省 合　计 Total of 6 Middle Provinces	西部 12 省 (区、市) 合　计 Total of 12 Western Provinces	东北 3 省 合　计 Total of 3 Northeastern Provinces
人　口	**Population**				
年底总人口	Population at Year－end	38.4	26.6	27.1	7.9
国民经济核算	**National Accounting**				
国内(地区)生产总值	Gross Domestic Product	52.6	20.6	20.1	6.7
# 第一产业	Primary Industry	34.4	26.4	29.2	10.0
第二产业	Secondary Industry	52.0	21.9	20.2	6.0
第三产业	Tertiary Industry	56.1	18.5	18.5	6.8
固定资产投资	**Investment in Fixed Assets**				
全社会固定资产投资总额	Total Investment in Fixed Assets	42.1	26.6	26.2	5.2
# 房地产开发	Real Estate Development	52.8	20.9	22.5	3.9
国内贸易	**Domestic Trade**				
社会消费品零售总额	Total Retail Sales of Consumer Goods	51.6	21.1	18.5	8.8
对外贸易	**Foreign Trade**				
货物进出口总额	Total Value of Imports and Exports	83.3	6.5	7.0	3.3
出口额	Exports	82.9	7.4	7.2	2.5
进口额	Imports	83.8	5.2	6.6	4.4
财　政	**Government Finance**				
地方一般公共预算收入	General Public Budget Revenue	57.3	17.6	19.8	5.3
地方一般公共预算支出	General Public Budget Expenditure	42.3	21.1	28.9	7.7
农　业	**Agriculture**				
主要农产品产量	Output of Major Farm Products				
粮　食	Grain	24.2	29.7	26.8	19.3
棉　花	Cotton	18.2	12.8	69.1	0.0
油　料	Oil－bearing Crops	22.1	42.5	30.2	5.1

附录 2—2 续表　Continued

计量单位：%　　(2016 年)　　(%)

指　　标	Item	东部 10 省(市)合　计 Total of 10 Eastern Provinces	中部 6 省 合　计 Total of 6 Middle Provinces	西部 12 省(区、市)合　计 Total of 12 Western Provinces	东北 3 省 合　计 Total of 3 North eastern Provinces
工　业	**Industry**				
主要工业产品产量	Output of Major Industrial Products				
原　油	Crude Oil	39.4	1.9	32.2	26.5
发电量	Electricity	39.5	20.2	34.7	5.6
粗　钢	Crude Steel	57.1	20.4	13.5	9.0
水　泥	Cement	34.1	27.6	34.1	4.2
原　煤	Crede Coal	6.6	32.9	57.1	3.4
天然气	Natural Gas	10.0	3.8	81.6	4.6
钢　材	Rolled Steel	62.7	17.6	13.4	6.3
汽　车	Motor Vehicles	45.3	19.3	22.3	13.1
交通运输业	**Transportation**				
铁路营业里程	Length of Railways in Operation	23.3	22.6	40.5	13.6
公路里程	Length of Highways	24.2	27.0	40.6	8.3
# 高速公路	Expressways	28.5	26.3	36.3	8.9
客运量	Passenger Traffic	34.7	27.9	29.4	8.0
货运量	Freight Traffic	36.8	29.0	27.1	7.1
邮电通信业	**Postal and Telecommunication Services**				
邮电业务总量	Total Business Revenue	76.4	12.2	8.5	2.9
电信业务总量　(亿元)	Total Business Telecommunications (100 million yuan)	50.0	19.4	23.6	7.0
教　育	**Education**				
普通高等学校	Regular Institutions of Higher Education	38.5	26.1	25.5	9.9
本专科在校学生数	Total Enrollment of Undergraduates and College Students	38.6	27.6	24.9	8.8
卫　生	**Health Care**				
医院数	Number of Hospitals	34.4	23.4	32.3	9.9
执业(助理)医师	Licensed (Assistant) Doctors	41.7	24.8	25.2	8.3
医院床位数	Number of Beds of Medical Institutions	36.8	25.5	28.1	9.6

2018

BING TUAN

附 录3

新疆各地州主要经济指标

Appendix III Main Economic Indicators of Xinjiang' s Prefectures, Autonomous Prefectures and Cities

简要说明

一、本篇资料主要内容

本篇资料主要反映新疆各地州市主要经济指标情况。

二、本篇资料来源

资料取自《2017年新疆统计年鉴》，反映2016年度资料，由兵团统计局国民经济综合统计处整理。

Brief Introduction

1. Main Contents

The data mainly reflects the main economic indicators of Xinjiang's prefectures, Autonomous Prefectures and cities.

2. Sources of Data

The data are collected from *Xinjiang Statistical Yearbook -2017,* which reflects the data of the year 2016, prepared by the Comprehensive Office of the statistics Bureau of XPCC .

附录 3－1 新疆各地州市主要经济指标

Main Economic Indicators of Xinjiang's Prefecture, Autonomous Prefecture and City

（2016 年）

指 标	Item	乌鲁木齐市 Urumqi-city	克拉玛依市 Karamay-city	吐鲁番市 Turpan-city
行政区划 （个）	**Administrative Divisions (units)**			
地级区划数	Prefecture Level Division Number	1	1	1
县级区划数	County Division Number	8	4	3
# 县	County	1		2
乡级区划数	The Number of Divisions	95	14	30
# 镇	Town	8	1	14
乡	Country	13	1	12
土地面积 （平方公里）	**Land area (sq.km)**	**14 876**	**8 654**	**67 563**
人 口 （万人）	**Population (10 000 persons)**			
年末总人口	Year-end Population	267.87	30.45	63.27
# 少数民族	Minority Population	69.34	7.70	52.06
# 维吾尔族	Uygur	33.56	4.73	48.07
生产总值 （亿元）	**Gross Domestic Product (100 million yuan)**	**2 458.98**	**621.00**	**221.57**
# 第一产业	Primary Industry	28.14	5.32	50.02
第二产业	Secondary Industry	704.08	431.92	92.10
第三产业	Tertiary Industry	1 726.76	183.75	79.44
# 工 业	Industry	535.26	466.12	67.25
建筑业	Construction	169.74	24.77	31.03
交通运输、仓储和邮政业	Transportation, Warehousing and Postal Services	347.36	11.91	10.93
批发和零售业	Wholesale and Retail Trade	200.86	8.88	6.69
人均生产总值 （元）	Per Capita Gross Domestic Product (yuan)	69 565	137 307	35 333
全社会固定资产投资（亿元）	**Total Investment in Fixed Assets (100 million yuan)**	**1 352.71**	**247.64**	**350.71**
农 业	**Agriculture**			
总播种面积 （千公顷）	Total Sown Area (1 000 hectares)	40.36	15.74	55.70
农林牧渔业总产值 （亿元）	Gross Output Value of Farming, Forestry, Animal Husbandry and Fishery (100 million yuan)	38.72	13.23	82.05
农 业	Farming	16.24	4.70	68.11
林 业	Forestry	0.56	2.82	0.95
牧 业	Animal Husbandry	20.57	4.74	11.90
渔 业	Fishery	0.70	0.13	0.07
服务业	Services	0.65	0.83	1.00
主要农产品产量 （万吨）	Output of Major Farm Products (10 000 tons)			
粮 食	Grain	8.80	2.73	2.32
棉 花	Cotton	0.04	1.05	1.59
油 料	Oil-bearing Crops	0.76	0.57	0.20

附录 3—1 续表 1

(2016 年)

指 标	Item	哈密地区 Hami [Kumul] Adminis-trative Offices	昌吉回族自治州 Changji Hui Auto-nomous Prefecture	伊犁哈萨克自治州 Ili Kazak Autonomous Prefecture	伊犁州直属县(市) Counties (Cities) Direct Under Ili Prefecture
行政区划 (个)	**Administrative Divisions (units)**				
地级区划数	Prefecture Level Division Number	1	1	3	1
县级区划数	County Division Number	3	7	25	11
# 县	County	1	4	17	7
乡级区划数	The Number of Divisions	42	79	247	114
# 镇	Town	14	43	93	35
乡	Country	20	16	109	52
土地面积 (平方公里)	**Land area (sq.km)**	**142 095**	**73 140**	**268 779**	**56 382**
人 口 (万人)	**Population (10 000 persons)**				
年末总人口	Year-end Population	56.16	140.10	466.21	297.32
# 少数民族	Minority Population	19.13	38.87	276.88	191.13
# 维吾尔族	Uygur	11.04	6.84	83.47	78.30
生产总值 (亿元)	**Gross Domestic Product (100 million yuan)**	**403.68**	**1 118.24**	**1 562.61**	**782.00**
# 第一产业	Primary Industry	38.84	223.24	452.61	186.16
第二产业	Secondary Industry	215.16	544.28	445.85	228.85
第三产业	Tertiary Industry	149.68	350.72	664.15	366.98
# 工 业	Industry	133.86	421.35	261.70	146.52
建筑业	Construction	81.30	122.93	184.60	82.75
交通运输、仓储和邮政业	Transportation, Warehousing and Postal Services	36.15	39.89	50.31	29.01
批发和零售业	Wholesale and Retail Trade	19.08	59.16	98.41	61.01
人均生产总值 (元)	Per Capita Gross Domestic Product (yuan)	65 298	70 162	33 120	27 847
全社会固定资产投资 (亿元)	**Total Investment in Fixed Assets (100 million yuan)**	**592.03**	**1 557.04**	**1 131.88**	**396.25**
农 业	**Agriculture**				
总播种面积 (千公顷)	Total Sown Area (1 000 hectares)	75.56	529.00	1368.54	511.38
农林牧渔业总产值 (亿元)	Gross Output Value of Farming, Forestry, Animal Husbandry and Fishery (100 million yuan)	55.43	324.71	641.84	279.49
农 业	Farming	30.18	140.98	342.76	114.55
林 业	Forestry	1.67	2.86	9.46	5.62
牧 业	Animal Husbandry	22.58	175.25	274.16	152.63
渔 业	Fishery	0.27	2.10	4.08	1.81
服务业	Services	0.73	3.51	11.38	4.88
主要农产品产量 (万吨)	Output of Major Farm Products (10 000 tons)				
粮 食	Grain	13.28	198.63	655.07	304.49
棉 花	Cotton	5.29	15.59	43.44	1.09
油 料	Oil-bearing Crops	0.20	14.45	27.12	7.01

Continued

塔城地区 Tacheng [Tarbagatai] Adminis -trative Offices	阿勒泰地区 Altay Admini -strative Offices	博尔塔拉蒙古自治州 Bortala Mongol Autonomous Prefecture	巴音郭楞蒙古自治州 Bayangol Mongol Autonomous Prefecture	阿克苏地区 Aksu Adminis -trative Prefecture	克孜勒苏克尔柯孜自治州 Kizilsu Kirgiz Autonomous Prefecture	喀什地区 Kashgar [Kaxgar] Adminis -trative Offices	和田地区 Hotan Adminis -trative Offices
1	1	1	1	1	1	1	1
7	7	4	9	9	4	12	8
4	6	2	7	8	3	10	7
75	58	21	90	96	39	176	95
34	24	9	32	36	6	38	20
28	29	8	52	47	30	128	69
94 698	**117 699**	**24 934**	**470 954**	**127 145**	**72 468**	**137 579**	**249 147**
101.69	67.20	47.76	122.95	250.83	60.29	451.47	244.98
45.36	40.39	17.33	57.32	204.79	56.14	422.85	237.76
4.23	0.94	6.90	44.50	201.42	39.41	416.27	237.26
563.32	**217.30**	**277.55**	**904.89**	**792.80**	**100.33**	**759.86**	**236.33**
217.13	49.32	61.61	199.28	233.38	15.02	260.03	64.69
149.02	67.97	79.55	440.25	253.76	33.73	191.34	36.52
197.16	100.01	136.39	265.36	305.66	51.58	308.49	135.13
77.54	37.64	46.44	359.45	172.09	18.51	70.76	10.44
71.49	30.36	33.11	92.00	81.68	15.22	120.58	26.08
11.83	9.46	18.10	30.03	24.34	2.67	19.27	2.72
28.81	8.59	28.69	28.02	40.29	2.45	68.06	11.68
44 296	33 874	57 987	64 142	28 289	16 736	16 860	9 901
468.12	**267.52**	**303.40**	**720.51**	**653.06**	**138.76**	**995.66**	**322.74**
611.26	245.90						
281.04	81.31	86.64	286.31	286.73	32.81	511.79	136.41
185.30	42.91	66.74	219.37	224.68	18.60	357.43	88.62
1.81	2.04	0.48	4.41	2.89	0.72	13.06	3.62
88.33	33.20	14.06	52.39	51.15	11.73	130.25	41.88
0.51	1.76	0.42	1.13	2.27	0.03	1.64	0.45
5.10	1.41	4.94	9.01	5.74	1.73	9.41	1.84
313.62	36.95	68.25	64.50	210.01	37.55	328.26	112.16
42.35		18.63	44.92	85.65	1.65	63.76	3.72
3.33	16.78	2.18	1.86	2.15	0.07	1.89	1.02

附录 3—1　续表 2

（2016 年）

指　　标	Item	乌鲁木齐市 Urumqi -city	克拉玛依市 Karamay -city	吐鲁番市 Turpan -city
甜　菜	Beetroots	0.02	0.12	
水　果	Fruits	0.67	0.02	102.69
牲畜存栏头数(万头只)	Number of Livestock (10 000 heads)	78.09	16.93	98.23
肉　类 (万吨)	Meat (10 000 tons)	6.08	1.11	4.30
工　业	**Industry**			
工业总产值(规模以上)(亿元)	Gross Industrial Output Value (100 million yuan)	1 976.48	1 004.54	210.95
主要工业产品产量	Output of Major Industrial Products			
纱 (吨)	Yarn (ton)	10 858		3 820
布 (万米)	Cloth (10 000 meter)	65		
成品糖 (万吨)	Machine—made Sugar (10000 tons)			
发电量 (亿千瓦小时)	Electricity (100 Million kwh)	272.26	68.57	82.90
水　泥 (万吨)	Cement (10 000 tons)	293.95		193.05
机制纸及纸板 (吨)	Machine-made Paper and Paperboard (ton)	76 398		
饮料酒 (千升)	Alcohol Beverage (1 000 liter)	147 094		6 730
建筑业总产值 (亿元)	**Total Output Value of Contruction (100 million yuan)**	**666.59**	**71.20**	**28.24**
国内贸易	**Domestic Trade**			
社会消费品零售总额(亿元)	Total Retail Sales of Consumer Goods (100 million yuan)	1 006.30	62.72	45.88
进出口总额 (万美元)	**Total Exports and Imports (USD 100 million)**	**490 258**	**13 179**	**2 147**
出口总额	Total Exports	420 620	6 330	1 909
进口总额	Total Imports	69 638	6 849	238
财　政 (万元)	**Finance (10 000 yuan)**			
一般公共预算收入	General Public Budget Revenue	3 696 734	791 422	327 874
一般公共预算支出	General Public Budget Expenditure	4 175 602	995 636	762 089
在校学生数 (人)	**Student Enrollment (person)**			
普通高等学校	Institution of Higher Education	185 908	5 562	310
中等专业学校	Specialized Secondary Schools	52 565	931	4 217
普通中学	Regular Secondary Schools	152 717	25 025	35 125
小　学	Primary Schools	208 581	24 279	60 943
人民生活 (元)	**People's Livelihood (yuan)**			
城镇常住居民人均可支配收入	Per Capita Disposable Income of Urban Permanent Households	34 190	35 770	28 201
农村常住居民人均可支配收入	Per Capita Disposable Income of Brigade Permanent Households	16 351		11 226
卫　生	**Health Care**			
机构数 (个)	Number of institutions (unit)	1 743	84	428
医院床位数 (张)	Hospital Beds (units)	29 405	1 894	3 511
卫生技术人员数 (人)	Medical Technical Personnel (person)	38 326	3 338	4 048

Continued

哈密地区 Hami [Kumul] Adminis -trative Offices	昌吉回族自治州 Changji Hui Auto -nomous Prefecture	伊犁哈萨克自治州 Ili Kazak Autonomous Prefecture	伊犁州直属县(市) Counties (Cities) Direct Under Ili Prefecture	塔城地区 Tacheng [Tarbagatai] Adminis -trative Offices	阿勒泰地区 Altay Admini -strative Offices	博尔塔拉蒙古自治州 Bortala Mongol Autonomous Prefecture	巴音郭楞蒙古自治州 Bayangol Mongol Autonomous Prefecture
	45.43	154.33	108.76	45.50	0.08	12.97	74.96
9.87	15.96	36.01	29.02	5.67	1.33	0.41	68.13
122.79	435.15	1 477.43	664.83	495.14	317.47	126.31	433.01
6.80	48.74	62.11	34.39	19.34	8.38	2.59	11.99
390.45	1 416.53	746.00	414.98	221.09	109.93	107.51	733.02
10 528	50 951	109 879	61 291	48 588		55 623	259 924
		5 745		5 745			254
	6.96	13.56	13.56			2.93	2.79
356.79	747.75	198.57	119.40	33.03	46.14	15.52	78.50
103.54	356.46	582.26	240.68	214.82	126.77	141.33	161.09
	184 843	4 253	4 253				8 691
3 281	84 176	130 951	39 156	91 399	396	1 020	27 517
61.73	**147.34**	**385.43**	**236.57**	**90.44**	**58.41**	**61.18**	**160.88**
85.96	243.93	353.44	206.12	79.01	68.31	40.46	104.29
54 593	**114 107**	**603 350**	**451 544**	**56 857**	**94 949**	**107 613**	**39 347**
51 284	101 541	581 374	440 512	53 925	86 937	53 021	14 621
3 309	12 566	21 976	11 032	2 932	8 012	54 592	24 726
567 109	1 214 010	1 483 653	731 819	438 264	313 570	200 671	750 847
1 120 440	2 749 708	5 732 121	2 744 664	1 564 463	1 422 994	869 417	2 129 360
1 121	27 444	18 840	18 840				5 510
2 929	11 284	22 037	14 855	4 317	2 865	1 646	10 484
32 251	71 568	242 753	154 758	54 180	33 815	20 575	72 660
34 140	81 641	362 751	242 858	69 348	50 545	28 838	114 581
30 456	27 955		26 144	26 628	25 707	27 019	28 804
14 240	16 439		14 145	15 280	10 632	6 001	7 918
445	1 225	3 411	1 512	1 206	693	501	1 035
3 073	8 980	23 663	14 914	5 369	3 380	2 440	7 965
4 626	11 332	25 883	15 268	6 249	4 366	3 393	9 091

附录 3—1　续表 3

（2016 年）

指　　标		Item		阿克苏地区 Aksu Adminis -trative Prefecture	克孜勒苏克尔柯孜自治州 Kizilsu Kirgiz Autonomous Prefecture	喀什地区 Kashgar [Kaxgar] Adminis -trative Offices	和田地区 Hotan Adminis -trative Offices
甜　菜		Beetroots		58.95			
水　果		Fruits		187.37	16.13	156.18	52.59
牲畜存栏头数(万头只)		Number of Livestock	(10 000 heads)	608.14	175.95	869.60	531.64
肉　类	(万吨)	Meat	(10 000 tons)	26.35	4.14	46.50	15.16
工　业		**Industry**					
工业总产值(规模以上)(亿元)		Gross Industrial Output Value	(100 million yuan)	374.15	44.64	153.75	27.98
主要工业产品产量		Output of Major Industrial Products					
纱	(吨)	Yarn	(ton)	126148	787	94077	7867
布	(万米)	Cloth	(10 000 meter)			16	
成品糖	(万吨)	Machine—made Sugar	(10000 tons)	2.99		0.03	0.03
发电量	(亿千瓦小时)	Electricity	(100 Million kwh)	65.04	23.56	40.12	21.43
水　泥	(万吨)	Cement	(10 000 tons)	300.41	151.11	567.18	245.93
机制纸及纸板	(吨)	Machine-made Paper and Paperboard	(ton)			630	
饮料酒	(千升)	Alcohol Beverage	(1 000 liter)	66820		885	78
建筑业总产值	**(亿元)**	**Total Output Value of Contruction**	**(100 million yuan)**	**135.30**	**20.01**	**72.92**	**51.30**
国内贸易		**Domestic Trade**					
社会消费品零售总额(亿元)		Total Retail Sales of Consumer Goods	(100 million yuan)	130.57	20.08	175.57	37.59
进出口总额	**(万美元)**	**Total Exports and Imports**	**(USD 100 million)**	**15 495**	**30 502**	**286 317**	**1 869**
出口总额		Total Exports		13 772	26 846	282 347	1 759
进口总额		Total Imports		1 723	3 656	3 970	110
财　政	**(万元)**	**Finance**	**(10 000 yuan)**				
一般公共预算收入		General Public Budget Revenue		848 378	115 945	637 550	210 873
一般公共预算支出		General Public Budget Expenditure		2 868 840	1 191 001	4 902 979	2 536 008
在校学生数	**(人)**	**Student Enrollment**	**(person)**				
普通高等学校		Institution of Higher Education		4 473		12 233	8 293
中等专业学校		Specialized Secondary Schools		21 001	2 661	48 367	26 365
普通中学		Regular Secondary Schools		156 178	39 775	294 771	132 699
小　学		Primary Schools		256 505	63 273	500 830	252 119
人民生活	**(元)**	**People's Livelihood**	**(yuan)**				
城镇常住居民人均可支配收入		Per Capita Disposable Income of Urban Permanent Households		26 098	24 487	22 732	24 466
农村常住居民人均可支配收入		Per Capita Disposable Income of Brigade Permanent Households		6 883	11 433	14 461	10 162
卫　生		**Health Care**					
机构数	(个)	Number of institutions	(unit)	1 524	358	3 184	1 783
医院床位数	(张)	Hospital Beds	(units)	12 985	4 016	25 397	21 206
卫生技术人员数	(人)	Medical Technical Personnel	(person)	11 203	3 819	19 701	9 676

中国统计出版社最新资料书简目

（仅供参考，以最后出书为准）

统计资料

中国统计年鉴

中国统计摘要

中国第三产业统计年鉴

中国第三次全国农业普查综合资料

国际统计年鉴

金砖国家联合统计手册

中国—东盟国家统计手册

中国农村统计年鉴

中国县域统计年鉴

中国农产品价格调查年鉴

中国城市统计年鉴

中国价格统计年鉴

中国贸易外经统计年鉴

中国零售和餐饮连锁企业统计年鉴

中国商品交易市场统计年鉴

大中型批发零售和住宿餐饮企业统计年鉴

中国住户调查年鉴

中国工业统计年鉴

中国环境统计年鉴

中国能源统计年鉴

中国建筑业统计年鉴

中国房地产统计年鉴

中国固定资产投资统计年鉴

中国对外直接投资统计公报

中国人口和就业统计年鉴

中国劳动统计年鉴

中国社会统计年鉴

中国科技统计年鉴

中国高技术产业统计年鉴

全国企业创新调查年鉴

中国文化及相关产业统计年鉴

2018年时间利用调查资料

中国妇女儿童状况统计资料

中国基本单位统计年鉴

中国教育统计年鉴

中国教育经费统计年鉴

中国民族统计年鉴

中国残疾人事业统计年鉴

省级综合统计年鉴系列

北京　天津　河北　山西　内蒙古　辽宁

吉林　黑龙江　上海　江苏　浙江　安徽

福建　江西　山东　河南　湖北　湖南

广东　广西　海南　重庆　四川　贵州

云南　西藏　陕西　甘肃　青海　宁夏

新疆　新疆生产建设兵团

市(县)级综合统计年鉴系列

滨海新区　石家庄　唐山　邯郸　保定

沧州　邢台　廊坊　承德　衡水　秦皇岛

张家口　太原　大同　阳泉　长治　晋城

朔州　晋中　运城　忻州　临汾　吕梁

呼和浩特　呼和浩特新城区　鄂尔多斯

包头　沈阳　大连　长春　吉林　延吉

四平　通化　松原　哈尔滨　齐齐哈尔

黑龙江垦区　上海浦东新区　南京　无锡

徐州　常州　苏州　南通　连云港　淮安

盐城　扬州　镇江　泰州　宿迁　江阴

丹阳　海门　杭州　宁波　温州　嘉兴

湖州　绍兴　金华　衢州　舟山　台州

丽水　合肥　安庆　马鞍山　福州　厦门

宁德　漳州　龙岩　南昌　九江　上饶

新余　抚州　萍乡　赣州　吉安　景德镇

济南　青岛　潍坊　枣庄　日照　滕州

郑州　洛阳　平顶山　三门峡　商丘　信阳

济源　汝州　武汉　十堰　荆州　宜昌

荆门　咸宁　长沙　广州　深圳　惠州

东莞　汕尾　南宁　柳州　桂林　梧州

来宾　河池　防城港　海口　三亚　成都

贵阳　黔南　毕节　昆明　西安　咸阳

延安　宝鸡　安康　铜川　汉中　榆林

兰州　庆阳　银川　乌鲁木齐　兵团一师

兵团十师

调查年鉴系列

天津　内蒙古　上海　浙江　福建　河南

湖北　湖南　广东　广西　重庆　四川

云南　甘肃　宁夏

统计方法应用/使用手册

实用 SAS 统计分析教程

Python 数据分析基础

统计公文知识问答

领导干部统计知识问答

乡镇统计人员岗位知识培训系列教材：

辅助调查员岗位基础知识

乡镇统计人员岗位基础知识

县级统计人员岗位知识培训系列教材：

Excel 在统计工作中的应用

简明统计分析

地市级统计人员岗位知识培训系列教材：

统计报告与演示

中国国民经济核算体系(2016)基础知识

全国统计专业技术资格考试系列考试用书：

统计业务知识(第四版)

统计业务知识学习指导与习题

全国统计专业技术资格考试系列考试用书：

统计相关知识(第四版)

统计相关知识学习指导与习题

统计通俗读物/统计科普图书

我国 20 个统计指标的历史变迁

联合国工业发展组织：2016 年工业发展报告

中国古代统计发展史

理解国民账户

重点图书

波澜壮阔四十年

砥砺奋进铸就辉煌—改革开放 40 年

与时俱进的中国统计

新编英汉汉英统计大词典

中国国民经济核算体系 2016

国民经济行业分类注释

挑大学选专业 2019—考研择校指南

挑大学选专业 2019—高考志愿填报指南

中华医学统计百科全书

中国统计出版社发行部电话：(010)63376907 63376908　同椑行书店电话：68783171 68783172
地址：北京市丰台区西三环南路甲 6 号　邮政编码：100073　网址：http://www.zgtjcbs.com

New Published Statistical Yearbook by China Statistics Press

China Statistical Yearbook

Chinese Statistical Summary

Statistical Yearbook of China's Third Industry

Comprehensive Data of the Third National Agricultural Census in China

International Statistical Yearbook

BRICs Joint Statistical Manual

China — ASEAN National Statistical Handbook

China's Rural Statistical Yearbook

County Statistical Yearbook in China

An Annals of China's Agricultural Product Price Survey

Chinese Urban Statistical Yearbook

China's Annual Price Statistics Yearbook

Statistical Yearbook of China's Trade in Foreign Trade

Statistical Yearbook of Retail and Catering Chain Enterprises in China

Statistical Yearbook of China's Commodity Trading Market

Statistical Yearbook of Large and Medium—Sized Wholesale, Retail and Accommodation Catering Enterprises

China Household Survey Yearbook

China Industrial Statistics Yearbook

China Environmental Statistics Yearbook

China Energy Statistics Yearbook

Statistical Yearbook of China's Construction Industry

China Real Estate Statistics Yearbook

Statistical Yearbook of Fixed Assets Investment in China

Statistical Bulletin of China's Foreign Direct Investment

Statistical Yearbook of Population and Employment in China

Annals of China's Labor Statistics

Chinese Social Statistics Yearbook

Chinese Science and Technology Statistics Yearbook

Statistical Yearbook of High Technology Industry in China

National Enterprise Innovation Survey Yearbook

Statistical Yearbook of Chinese Culture and Related Industries

Use of Survey Data in 2018

Statistics of the Status of Women and Children in China

Statistical Yearbook of Basic units in China

Educational Statistics Yearbook of China

China Educational Finance Statistical YearbookChi-nese National Statistical Yearbook

Statistical Yearbook for the Cause of Disabled Persons in China

Provinces Statisticses Yearbook Series

Beijing Tianjin Hebei Shanxi Neimenggu Liaoning
Jilin Heilongjiang Shanghai Jiangsu Zhejiang
Anhui Fujian Jiangxi Shandong Henan Hubei
Hunan Guangdong Guangxi Hainan Chongqing
Sichuan Guizhou Yunnan Tibet Shanxi Gansu
Qinghai Xinjiang XPCC

City(County) Statisticses Yearbook Series

Binhai New Area Shijiazhuang Tangshan Handan
Baoding Cangzhou Xingtai Langfang Chengde
Hengshui Qinhuangdao Zhangjiakou Taiyuan
Datong Yangquan Changzhi Jincheng Suzhou
Jinzhong Yuncheng Yizhou Linfen Lvliang Hohhot
Hohhot New Aera Erdos Baotou Shenyang Dalian
Changchun Jilin Yanji Siping Tonghua Songyuan
Harbin Qigihar Heilongjiang reclamation area
Shanghai Pudong New Area Nanjing Wuxi Xuzhou

2018

新疆生产建设兵团

统计年鉴

XINJIANG PRODUCTION & CONSTRUCTION CORPS

STATISTICAL YEARBOOK